"Uncle Sam" Poster

Drawing by Albert T. Reid

On the opposite page is a reproduction of a poster used in connection with the juvenile activities of the United States George Washington Bicentennial Commission. This poster was distributed to Boy Scout and Girl Scout units throughout the United States, and was also given wide general distribution. It is from a drawing by Albert T. Reid, the well known artist and cartoonist, and features the Houdon statue of George Washington in the Capitol at Richmond, Virginia.

Drawing by Albert T. Reid

REPRODUCTION OF POSTER USED IN CONNECTION WITH JUVENILE ACTIVITIES OF
THE UNITED STATES GEORGE WASHINGTON BICENTENNIAL COMMISSION.

HISTORY

OF THE

GEORGE WASHINGTON

BICENTENNIAL CELEBRATION

VOLUME II
Literature Series

1 9 3 2

UNITED STATES
GEORGE WASHINGTON BICENTENNIAL COMMISSION
WASHINGTON, D. C.

United States George Washington Bicentennial Commission

President of the United States
Chairman

Vice President of the United States

Speaker of the House of Representatives

United States Senate

Simeon D. Fess, *Vice Chairman*
Ohio

Arthur Capper
Kansas

Carter Glass
Virginia

Millard E. Tydings
Maryland

House of Representatives

Willis C. Hawley
Oregon

John Q. Tilson
Connecticut

Joseph W. Byrns
Tennessee

R. Walton Moore
Virginia

Presidential Commissioners

Mrs. Anthony Wayne Cook
Pennsylvania

Mrs. John Dickinson Sherman
Colorado

Henry Ford
Michigan

C. Bascom Slemp
Virginia

Wallace McCamant
Oregon

Albert Bushnell Hart
Historian
Massachusetts

Joseph Scott
California

Director
Representative Sol Bloom
New York

PREFACE

THIS is the second of a series of three volumes containing the literature prepared and issued by the United States George Washington Bicentennial Commission in connection with the Celebration of the Two Hundredth Anniversary of the birth of George Washington.

First in this volume is the address by President Calvin Coolidge at a joint session of Congress, February 22, 1927, on the significance of the George Washington Bicentennial in 1932. Following is the address by President Herbert Hoover at a joint session of Congress, February 22, 1932, officially opening the Bicentennial Celebration.

"The United States Congress on George Washington," compiled by Myrtis Jarrell, under the direction of H. H. B. Meyer of the Legislative Reference Service, Library of Congress, is a comprehensive and valuable reference work, listing addresses in honor of George Washington as recorded in the proceedings of the United States Congress from 1789 to 1932; Acts of Congress, Official Documents and other tributes in honor of Washington; and extracts from the official papers and writings of George Washington, which were read into the record during debates in Congress.

"Selected George Washington Bicentennial Addresses," delivered by the Director of the United States George Washington Bicentennial Commission, include the majority of the addresses broadcast to nation-wide audiences. Addresses were made from Independence Hall, Fort Necessity, the home of Mary Ball Washington, old Pohick Church, Arlington National Cemetery, from the home of Francis Scott Key, before the Tomb of George Washington at Mount Vernon, and at various other shrines. The purpose of these addresses was to make the true character of the Father of Our Country better known throughout the nation. A radio address entitled "The Mother of George Washington," by Mrs. John Dickinson Sherman, former President of the General Federation of Women's Clubs, and an address by Honorable R. Walton Moore, former President of the Virginia Bar Association and former Representative from the Mount Vernon district, are also included.

"Colonial Gardens," a manuscript prepared by the American Society of Landscape Architects, treats on the landscape architecture of George Washington's time and received wide distribution.

The musical section of the volume is especially interesting. The "Music of George Washington's Time," by John Tasker Howard, editor of the Commission's Music Division, provided authoritative and comprehensive information on the music of the Washington period. The collection of patriotic tunes, piano and dance music, songs and operatic airs under the title "Music from the Days of George Washington" was made by Dr. Carl Engel, Chief, Division of Music, Library of Congress, and the music was edited by W. Oliver Strunk, Dr. Engel's assistant. Following these is the song written for the American people by George M. Cohan, entitled, "Father of the Land We Love."

With one out of every four of the total population of our nation in school either as student or teacher, the scope of the school activities may be realized. Practically every school of the nation participated in the Bicentennial Celebration. In the colleges the George Washington Appreciation Course has touched the lives of thousands of young men and women about to become active in the duties and responsibilities of citizenship. The Bicentennial Contests held in schools and colleges were avenues through which lessons of patriotism and good citizenship were taught by the study of the life of George Washington. The section containing the pamphlets on the Oratorical, Essay and Declamatory Contests in schools and colleges, compiled by Hazel B. Nielson, in charge of Educational Activities, is preceded by an address of President Calvin Coolidge before the Department of Superintendence of the National Education Association in Washington, D. C., February 22, 1926. Samples of Braille printing for the blind demonstrate the type of material issued by the Commission for the sightless. "Sermons on George Washington," by ministers of various denominations are reprinted.

"Wakefield," A Folk-Masque of America, Being a Midwinter Night's Dream of the Birth of Washington, by Percy MacKaye, is also reprinted, as well as the many George Washington pageants which were made available for production all over the nation during 1932.

Sol Bloom,
Director,
United States George Washington
Bicentennial Commission

CONTENTS

THE UNITED STATES CONGRESS ON GEORGE WASHINGTON

Compiled by MYRTIS JARRELL

under the direction of

H. H. B. MEYER,

Legislative Reference Service, Library of Congress

Part I

Part II

Part III

SELECTED GEORGE WASHINGTON BICENTENNIAL ADDRESSES

Delivered by HON. SOL BLOOM

CONTENTS—*Continued*

GEORGE WASHINGTON AS A FRIEND AND PATRON OF MUSIC

Taken from "The Musical Side of Our First President," contained in "Essays in Music" by the late O. G. Sonneck, former Chief, Division of Music, Library of Congress.

MUSIC FROM THE DAYS OF GEORGE WASHINGTON

Collected and Provided With An Introduction by
CARL ENGEL
Chief, Division of Music, Library of Congress
The Music Edited by
W. OLIVER STRUNK
Assistant, Division of Music, Library of Congress

FATHER OF THE LAND WE LOVE

Written by GEORGE M. COHAN
for the American People

To commemorate the Two Hundredth Anniversary of the Birth of George Washington.

GEORGE WASHINGTON AND EDUCATION

By PRESIDENT CALVIN COOLIDGE

An address before the Department of Superintendence, National Education Association, Washington, D. C., February 22, 1926

ORATIONS AND ESSAYS OF THE GEORGE WASHINGTON BICENTEN-NIAL NATION-WIDE ORATORI-CAL, ESSAY, AND DECLAMA-TORY CONTESTS IN SCHOOLS AND COLLEGES

Compiled by

HAZEL B. NIELSON

Director of Educational Activities

CONTENTS—*Continued*

CONTENTS—*Continued*

ORGANIZATION AND REGULATIONS OF THE DECLAMATORY, ESSAY, AND ORATORICAL CONTESTS

Prepared by HAZEL B. NIELSON
Director of Educational Activities

SELECTIONS RELATING TO GEORGE WASHINGTON FOR DECLAMATORY CONTESTS IN THE ELEMENTARY SCHOOLS

Compiled by HAZEL B. NIELSON,
Director of Educational Activities

GROUP I—GRADES 1 AND 2

GROUP II—GRADES 3 AND 4

GROUP III—GRADES 5 AND 6

GROUP IV—GRADES 7 AND 8

CONTENTS—*Continued*

CHARACTERISTIC ACTIVITIES OF SCHOOLS

FLAGS OF AMERICAN LIBERTY

SAMPLES OF BRAILLE PRINTING FOR THE BLIND

As issued by the Braille Department of the United States George Washington Bicentennial Commission

In Charge of DOROTHEA E. JENNINGS

SERMONS ON GEORGE WASHINGTON

(Listed Alphabetically According to Names of Ministers)

A COLLECTION OF
GEORGE WASHINGTON POETRY

Compiled by BEATRIX REYNOLDS AND JAMES GABELLE

CONTENTS—*Continued*

GEORGE WASHINGTON ACTIVITIES FOR 4-H CLUBS

By BELVA CUZZORT

PROGRAM OF WAKEFIELD A FOLK-MASQUE OF AMERICA

WAKEFIELD, A FOLK-MASQUE OF AMERICA

Being a Midwinter Night's Dream of the Birth of
WASHINGTON

By PERCY MACKAYE

INTRODUCTORY

TEXT OF THE MASQUE

In Thirty-Three Actions and Five Tableaux

PROLOGUE—*BIRTH*

PART ONE—*GROWTH AND DRIFT*

INTERLUDE—*RE-BIRTH*

CONTENTS—Continued

GEORGE WASHINGTON PAGEANTS

HOW TO PRODUCE A PAGEANT IN HONOR OF GEORGE WASHINGTON
By ESTHER WILLARD BATES

List of Illustrations

LIST OF ILLUSTRATIONS—*Continued*

LIST OF ILLUSTRATIONS—*Continued*

Publications of the United States George Washington Bicentennial Commission

The commemorative volumes issued by the United States George Washington Bicentennial Commission contain the complete history of the George Washington Bicentennial Celebration.

LITERATURE SERIES

The literature series, of which this is the second volume, consists of volumes I, II and III, and contains the publications of the United States George Washington Bicentennial Commission, issued in connection with the Celebration of the Two Hundredth Anniversary of the Birth of George Washington. These volumes present authentic historical information concerning George Washington, which was obtained after the most painstaking research.

FOREIGN PARTICIPATION

The series on Foreign Participation contains the activities of the Celebration in 81 foreign countries, divided into sections as follows: Western Europe, Eastern Europe, Near East, Far East, Canada, Mexico, Central America, South America, West Indies, and Africa.

ACTIVITIES OF THE CELEBRATION

The series on the Activities of the Celebration contains the report of the National Organizations, States, cities, towns, and communities, including municipal activities and programs given by religious, fraternal, patriotic, educational and other groups.

UNITED STATES
GEORGE WASHINGTON BICENTENNIAL COMMISSION
WASHINGTON, D. C.

An Address

of

President Calvin Coolidge

AT A JOINT SESSION OF
THE CONGRESS OF THE UNITED STATES

FEBRUARY 22, 1927

ON THE SIGNIFICANCE

of the

GEORGE WASHINGTON BICENTENNIAL CELEBRATION IN 1932

President Calvin Coolidge Delivering an Address on the Significance of the George Washington Bicentennial Celebration, at a Joint Session of Congress, February 22, 1927

2

ADDRESS

OF

PRESIDENT CALVIN COOLIDGE

Delivered at a Joint Session of Congress
February 22, 1927

MY FELLOW AMERICANS: On the 22d day of February, 1932, America will celebrate the two hundredth anniversary of the birth of George Washington. Wherever there are those who love ordered liberty, they may well join in the observance of that event. Although he belongs to us, yet by being a great American he became a great world figure. It is but natural that here under the shadow of the stately monument rising to his memory, in the Capital City bearing his name, the country made independent by his military genius, and the Republic established by his statesmanship, should already begin preparations to proclaim the immortal honor in which we hold the Father of our Country.

In recognition of the importance of this coming anniversary, more than two years ago the Congress passed a joint resolution establishing a commission, which was directed to have this address made to the American people reminding them of the reason and purpose for holding the coming celebration. It was also considered that now would be an appropriate time to inform the public that this commission desires to receive suggestions concerning plans for the proposed celebration and to express the hope that the States and their political subdivisions under the direction of their governors and local authorities would soon arrange for appointing commissions and committees to formulate programs for cooperation with the Federal Government. When the plans begin to be matured they should embrace the active support of educational and religious institutions, of the many civic, social, and fraternal organizations, agricultural and trade associations, and of other numerous activities which characterize our national life.

It is greatly to be hoped that out of the studies pursued and the investigations made a more broad and comprehensive understanding and a more complete conception of Washington, the man, and his relation to all that is characteristic of American life may be secured. It was to be expected that he would be idealized by his countrymen. His living at a time when there were scanty reports in the public press, coupled with the inclination of early biographers, resulted in a rather imaginary character being created in response to the universal desire to worship his memory. The facts of his life were of record, but were not easily accessible. While many excellent books, often scholarly and eloquent, have been written about him, the temptation has been so strong to represent him as an heroic figure composed of superlatives that the real man among men, the human being subjected to the trials and temptations common to all mortals, has been too much obscured and forgotten. When we regard him in this character and have revealed to us the judgment with which he met his problems, we shall all the more understand and revere his true greatness. No great mystery surrounds him; he never relied on miracles. But he was a man endowed with what has been called uncommon common sense, with tireless industry, with a talent for taking infinite pains, and with a mind able to understand the universal and eternal problems of mankind.

Washington has come to be known to the public almost exclusively as the Virginia colonel who accompanied the unfortunate expedition of General Braddock, as the commander in chief of the Continental Army during the Revolutionary War, as the first President of the United States, and as the master of the beautiful estate at Mount Vernon. This general estimate is based to a large extent on the command he held in time of war and the public office he held in time of peace. A recital of his courage and patriotism, his loyalty and devotion, his self-sacrifice, his refusal to be king, will always arouse the imagination and inspire the soul of everyone who loves his country. Nothing can detract from the exalted place which this record entitles him to hold. But he has an appeal even broader than this, which today is equally valuable to the people of the United States. Not many of our citizens are to be called on to take high commands or to hold high public office. We are all necessarily engaged in the ordinary affairs of life. As a valuable example to youth and to maturity, the experience of Washington in these directions is worthy of much more attention than it has received.

We all share in the benefits which accrued from the independence he won and the free Republic he did so much to establish. We need a diligent comprehension and understanding of the great principles of government which he wrought out, but we shall also secure a wide practical advantage if we go beyond this record, already so eloquently expounded, and consider him also as a man of affairs. It was in this field that he developed that executive ability which he later displayed in the camp and in the council chamber.

It ought always to be an inspiration to the young people of the country to know that from earliest youth Washington showed a disposition to make the most of his opportunities. He was diligently industrious—a most admirable and desirable, if seemingly uninteresting, trait. His father, who had been educated in England, died when his son was 11 years old. His mother had but moderate educational advantages. There were no great incentives to learning in Virginia in 1732, and the facilities for acquiring knowledge were still meager. The boy might well have grown up with very little education, but his eager mind and indomitable will led him to acquire learning and information despite the handicaps surrounding him.

His formal schooling, which was of a rather primitive character, ended at the age of 13. His copy and exercise books, still in existence, contain forms of bills, receipts, and like documents, showing he had devoted considerable time to that branch of his studies. He was preparing himself to be a practical business man. When his regular instruction ended, his education was just beginning. It continued up to his death, December 14, 1799. If ever there was a self-made man, it was George Washington. Through all his later years he was constantly absorbing knowledge from contact with men, from reading whenever time and facilities permitted, and from a wide correspondence.

When 16 he became a surveyor and for four years earned a living and much experience in that calling. Although considerable has been written about it, not many people think of our first President as an agriculturist. Those who have studied this phase of his life tell us he was probably the most successful owner and director of an agricultural estate in his day. A visitor in 1785 declared "Washington's greatest pride was to be thought the first farmer in America." Toward the end of his life he wrote:

I am led to reflect how much more delightful to an undebauched mind is the task of making improvements on the earth than all the vain glory that can be acquired from ravaging it by the most uninterrupted career of conquests.

He always had a great affection for Mount Vernon. He increased his land holdings from 2,700 to over 8,000 acres, 3,200 of which he had under cultivation at one time.

His estate was managed in a thoroughly business-like fashion. He kept a very careful set of account books for it, as he did for his other enterprises. Overseers made weekly statements showing just how much each laborer had been employed, what crops had been planted or gathered. While he was absent reports were sent to him, and he replied in long letters of instruction, displaying wonderful familiarity with details. He was one of the first converts to the benefits of scientific fertilization and to the rotation of crops, for that purpose making elaborate tables covering five-year periods. He overlooked no detail in carrying on his farm according to the practice of those days, producing on the premises most of the things needed there, even to shoes and textiles. He began the daily round of his fields at sunrise, and often removed his coat and helped his men in the work of the day.

He also showed his business ability by the skillful way in which he managed the considerable estates left to his two step-children by their father. So successfully was this done that John Parke Custis became, at the age of 21, the richest young man in the Old Dominion. Prussing tells us that Martha Custis was advised to get the ablest man in the colony to manage her estate

and to pay him any salary within reason. And he adds: "That she chose wisely in marrying the young colonel, and got the best of a good bargain, is the opinion of many."

He was engaged in many business enterprises. That of the Dismal Swamp, comprising drainage and lumber operations south of Norfolk, was handled efficiently by Washington for five years subsequent to 1763. In addition to his landholdings, wisely chosen, the rise in value of which accounted in no small degree for his fortune, Washington participated in a number of real estate and transportation companies. As a private citizen he was constantly on the outlook for sound investments and for ways to increase his capital. In the purchase of frontier lands and in the promotion of plans for the building up and development of new parts of the country he was performing important public service.

Dr. Albert Bushnell Hart, distinguished historian and a member of our commission, says:

Washington has been criticized for buying up land warrants and holding on to his title in the face of squatters. Actually no American has ever done so much to open up vast tracts of land, first under the British, and then under the American flag, fitted to become the home of millions of American farmers.

After 13 years of effort Washington forced the British government to give to the Virginia veterans of the French and Indian wars the 200,000 acres of western lands promised by the governor of that colony. His management and distribution of these bounties were carried out in an eminently efficient and satisfactory manner. He acquired two large farms in Maryland. During a trip in New York State in 1783 he saw the possibilities of a waterway from the sea to the Great Lakes by way of the Hudson River and the Mohawk Valley—the present route of a great barge canal. Because of his business vision he joined with General Clinton in the purchase of 6,000 acres near Utica.

To Washington, the man of affairs, we owe our national banks, for had he followed the advice of other leaders, great but less enlightened on matters of finance, the plans of Alexander Hamilton would not have been realized. As a result of the war the country was deeply in debt and had no credit, but the solution of our financial difficulties suggested by the first Secretary of the Treasury was opposed by those from rural communities. They argued that the large commercial cities would dominate to the detriment of other parts of the country. Both Jefferson, Secretary of State, and Randolph, Attorney General, in writing opposed the incorporation by Congress of a national bank. They were joined by Madison and Monroe. All argued against the constitutionality of this proposition. Hamilton answered their arguments fully in his famous opinion. But had the President not been a man of affairs, had he not been for many years a holder of stock in the Bank of England, coming from the estate of Daniel Parke Custis, he might have yielded to the opposition. Because he knew something about bank accounts and bank credits the bill was signed and the foundation of our financial system laid.

Washington was also a stockholder in the Bank of Alexandria

and in the Bank of Columbia at Georgetown. In his last will and testament he directed that such moneys as should be derived from the sale of his estate during the lifetime of Mrs. Washington should be invested for her in good bank stocks.

After his retirement from the Presidency in March, 1797, Washington spent more than two and a half happy years at Mount Vernon. In his last summer he made a will, one of the most remarkable documents of its kind of which we have record. Again he showed his versatility in disposing of his many properties under a variety of bequests and conditions without legal advice. It has been called an autobiographic will—it shows in its manifold provisions his charitable thoughtfulness for his dependents and his solicitude for the future welfare of his country.

As President he was always an exponent of sound and honest public finance. He advocated the payment of our debts in full to holders of record, and the assumption by the Nation of the debts incurred by the various States to carry on the Revolution. His support of financial integrity, because it was morally right, strengthened the Union.

This practical business ability and interest in broad and general affairs made him one of the first to realize that the future of the American empire lay in the regions beyond the Alleghenies, in the territory of the Ohio and the Mississippi. Because of this belief, he is said to have been the moving spirit in the first plans for the organization of our public lands. His association with the West may have started in the period 1749-1751, when he assisted his brother, Lawrence, in his various business enterprises, among them the Ohio Co., which had a grant of 500,000 acres of land on the east side of the Ohio River. The French having begun to build forts in the upper Ohio Valley and to exclude the English traders, Washington, at the age of 21, was sent by the Governor of Virginia to bear a remonstrance. The comprehensive report of this young man was considered of enough importance to be printed in London and circulated widely in Europe, by way of justifying Great Britain in making war upon France. In 1763 he organized the Mississippi Co. to take the place of the Ohio Co., which was one of the casualties of the war. He applied for a grant of 1,000,000 acres of land, though he did not receive it. But he made his own investments, so that in the schedule of his property attached to his will we find western lands appraised at over $400,000—along the Ohio, the Great Kanawha, in western Pennsylvania, in Kentucky, and in the Northwest Territory.

Having a vision of what the West meant in the future prosperity of the new Republic, Washington in 1784 journeyed out into the wilds. His diary of the trip is filled with interest and enthusiasm over the possibilities of that region. Hulbert, who has made a study of it, calls him our first expansionist, the originator of the idea of possessing the West through commercial relations.

It was a pioneer idea, instinct with genius,

this author writes,

and Washington's advocacy of it marks him as the first commercial American, the first man typical of the America that was to be.

Due to his investments, he became the president of the James River Co. and of the Potomac River Co., organized in 1785 to look into the possibility of opening navigation through to the West. To the Potomac Co., which involved the first interstate commerce negotiations in this country, he devoted four years of service. It has been thought that these negotiations entered into by Washington led up almost directly to the calling of the Constitutional Convention. They revealed clearly the difficulty under the Articles of Confederation of accomplishing anything involving the welfare of all the States, and showed the need of a more strongly centralized national government. His ability as a business man was the strong support of his statesmanship. It made his political ideas intensely practical.

Washington's Atlantic-Mississippi waterway plan was never carried out. But his advocacy of it without doubt had much to do with preventing a break in the Union which threatened serious consequences. The people who lived in the upper Ohio Valley, shut off from the east by mountains, had no outlet to the sea other than the Mississippi, and Spain, controlling the mouth of this river, levied heavy tribute on all commerce passing through it. The settlers, in what is now eastern Tennessee, established a separate State and started negotiations for an association with Spain; but this action was rescinded with the development of economic unionism after Washington put forth his waterway plan.

That he should have been responsible in large measure for the opening of the West and for calling attention to the commercial advantages the country might derive therefrom is by no means the least of his benefactions to the Nation. He demonstrated that those who develop our resources, whether along agricultural, commercial, and industrial lines or in any other field of endeavor, are entitled to the approval, rather than the censure, of their countrymen.

Washington was a builder—a creator. He had a national mind. He was constantly warning his countrymen of the danger of settling problems in accordance with sectional interests. His ideas in regard to the opening of our western territory were thought out primarily for the benefit of the Nation. It has been said that he would have been "the greatest man in America had there been no Revolutionary War."

He was largely instrumental in selecting the site for our National Capital, influenced in no small degree by his vision of the commercial possibilities of this locality. It included his plan of the waterway to the West, through the Potomac, the Monongahela, and the Ohio Rivers, which he used to speak of as "the channel of commerce to the extensive and valuable trade of a rising empire." He, of course, could not foresee the development of railway transportation and the great ocean-going vessels, because of which the seat of our Government became separated from active contact with commerce and was left to develop as the cultural and intellectual center of the Nation. Due to the genius of L'Enfant, the great engineer, this city from the first has had a magnificent plan of development. Its adoption was due in no small degree to the engineering foresight and executive ability of Washington. By 1932 we shall have made much progress toward perfecting the ideal city planned by him in the closing days of the eighteenth century.

Washington had the ability to translate ideals into the practical affairs of life. He was interested in what he believed contributed to the betterment of everyday existence. Perhaps because he realized the deficiency of his own early education, he was solicitous to provide liberal facilities for the youth of the future. Because as a man of affairs he knew the everyday uses of learning, in an early message to the Congress and in his will he sought methods for the establishment of a national university. Even in his Farewell Address we find this exhortation:

> Promote, then, as an object of primary importance, institutions for the general diffusion of knowledge. In proportion as the structure of a government gives force to public opinion, it is essential that public opinion should be enlightened.

He desired his system of education to be thoroughly American and thoroughly national. It was to support the people in a knowledge of their rights, in the creation of a republican spirit, and in the maintenance of the Union.

It was with the same clear vision that he looked upon religion. For him there was little in it of emotionalism. He placed it on a firmer, more secure foundation, and stated the benefits which would accrue to his country as the results of faith in spiritual things. He recognized that religion was the main support of free institutions. In his Farewell Address he said:

> Of all the dispositions and habits which lead to political prosperity, religion and morality are indispensable supports. In vain would that man claim the tribute of patriotism who should labor to subvert these great pillars of human happiness—these firmest props of the duties of men and citizens. The mere politician, equally with the pious man, ought to respect and to cherish them. A volume could not trace all their connections with private and public felicity. Let it simply be asked, Where is the security for property, for reputation, for life, if the sense of religious obligation desert the oaths which are the instruments of investigation in courts of justice? And let us with caution indulge the supposition that morality can be maintained without religion. Whatever may be conceded to the influence of refined education on minds of peculiar structure, reason and experience both forbid us to expect that national morality can prevail in exclusion of religious principle. It is substantially true that virtue or morality is a necessary spring of popular government. The rule indeed extends with more or less force to every species of free government. Who that is a sincere friend to it can look with indifference upon attempts to shake the foundation of the fabric?

Without bigotry, without intolerance, he appeals to the highest spiritual nature of mankind. His genius has filled the earth. He has been recognized abroad as "the greatest man of our own or any age." He loved his fellow men. He loved his country. That he intrusted their keeping to a Divine Providence is revealed in the following prayer which he made in 1794:

> Let us unite in imploring the Supreme Ruler of Nations to spread His holy protection over these United States; to turn the machinations of the wicked to the confirming of our Constitution; to enable us at all times to root our internal sedition and put invasion to flight; to perpetuate to our country that prosperity which His goodness has already conferred; and to verify the anticipations of this Government being a safeguard to human rights.

He was an idealist in the sense that he had a very high standard of private and public honor. He was a prophet to the extent of being able to forecast with remarkable vision the growth of the Nation he founded and the changing conditions which it would meet. But essentially he was a very practical man. He analyzed the problems before him with a clear intellect. Having a thorough understanding, he attacked them with courage and energy, with patience and persistence. He brought things to pass. When Patrick Henry was asked in 1774 whom he thought was the greatest man in the Continental Congress he replied:

> If you speak of eloquence, Mr. Rutledge, of South Carolina, is by far the greatest orator; but if you speak of solid information and sound judgment Colonel Washington is unquestionably the greatest man on that floor.

His accomplishments were great because of an efficiency which marked his every act and a sublime, compelling faith in the ultimate triumph of the right. As we study his daily life, as we read his letters, his diaries, his state papers, we come to realize more and more his wisdom, his energy, and his efficiency. He had the moral efficiency of an abiding religious faith, emphasizing the importance of the spiritual side of man; the social efficiency shown by his interest in his fellow men, and in his realization of the inherent strength of a people united by a sense of equality and freedom; the business efficiency of a man of affairs, of the owner and manager of large properties; the governmental efficiency of the head of a new Nation, who, taking an untried political system, made it operate successfully, of a leader able to adapt the relations of the Government to the people. He understood how to translate political theory into a workable scheme of government. He knew that we can accomplish no permanent good by going to extremes. The law of reason must always be applied. He followed Milton, who declared—

> . . . law in a free nation hath ever been public reason,

and he agreed with Burke that—

> men have no right to what is not reasonable.

It is a mark of a great man that he surrounds himself by great men. Washington placed in the most important positions in his Cabinet Jefferson with his advocacy of the utmost degree of local self-government and of State rights, and Hamilton whose theories of a strong national government led him to advocate the appointment of State governors by the President. Either theory carried to the extreme soon would have brought disaster to what has proved the most successful experiment in liberty under proper governmental restraint in the history of the world.

It is due to his memory that we guard the sovereign rights of the individual States under our Constitution with the same solicitude that we maintain the authority of the Federal Government in all matters vital to our continued national existence.

Such is the background of a man performing the ordinary duties of life. As it was George Washington, of course he performed them extraordinarily well. The principles which he adopted in his early youth and maintained throughout his years are the source of all true greatness. Unless we understand this side of him we shall fail in our comprehension of this true character. It was because of this training that he was able to assume the leadership of an almost impossible cause, carry it on through a long period of discouragement and defeat, and bring it to a successful conclusion. In advance of all others, he saw that war was coming. With an Army that was never large and constantly shifting, poorly supported by a confederation inexperienced, inefficient, and lacking in almost all the essential elements of a government, he was victorious over the armies of seasoned troops commanded by Howe, Burgoyne, Clinton, and Cornwallis, supported by one of the most stable and solid of governments, possessed of enormous revenues and ample credit, representing the first military power of the world.

As an example of generalship, extending over a series of years from the siege of Boston to the fall of Yorktown, the Commander in Chief of the Continental Armies holds a position that is unrivaled in the history of warfare. He never wavered, he never faltered from the day he modestly undertook the tremendous task of leading a revolution to the day when with equal modesty he surrendered his commissions to the representatives of the independent Colonies. He triumphed over a people in the height of their glory who had acknowledged no victor for 700 years.

Washington has come to personify the American Republic. He presided over the convention that framed our Constitution. The weight of his great name was the deciding factor in securing its adoption by the States. These results could never have been secured had it not been recognized that he would be the first President. When we realize what it meant to take 13 distracted Colonies, impoverished, envious, and hostile, and weld them into an orderly federation under the authority of a central government, we can form some estimate of the influence of this great man. But when we go further and remember that the Government which he did so much to bring into being not only did not falter when he retired from its administration, but, withstanding every assault, has constantly grown stronger with the passage of time and been found adequate to meet the needs of nearly 120,000,000 people occupying half a continent and constituting the greatest power the world has ever known, we can judge something of the breadth and soundness of his statesmanship.

We have seen many soldiers who have left behind them little but the memory of their conflicts; but among all the victors the power to establish among a great people a form of self-government, which the test of experience has shown will endure, was bestowed upon Washington and Washington alone. Many others have been able to destroy. He was able to construct. That he had around him many great minds does not detract from his glory. His was the directing spirit without which there would have been no independence, no Union, no Constitution, and no Republic. His ways were the ways of truth. He built for eternity. His influence grows. His stature increases with the increasing years. In wisdom of action, in purity of character, he stands alone. We can not yet estimate him. We can only indicate our reverence for him and thank the Divine Providence which sent his to serve and inspire his fellow men.

The Capitol After Restoration, 1836 (East Front)

The Capitol, 1836, From Pennsylvania Avenue

An Address

OF

Herbert Hoover
President of the United States

AT A JOINT SESSION OF
THE CONGRESS OF THE UNITED STATES

FEBRUARY 22, 1932

AT THE
Opening of the Celebration
OF THE
Bicentennial of the Birth of George Washington

President Herbert Hoover Delivering an Address on the Opening of the George Washington Bicentennial Celebration at a Joint Session of Congress on February 22, 1932

ADDRESS

OF

HERBERT HOOVER

President of the United States

Delivered at a Joint Session of Congress February 22, 1932

Just one hundred years ago in this city Daniel Webster, in commemoration of the birth of George Washington, said:

"A hundred years hence, other disciples of Washington will celebrate his birth with no less of sincere admiration than we now commemorate it. When they shall meet, as we now meet, to do themselves and him that honor, so surely as they shall see the blue summits of his native mountains rise in the horizon, so surely as they shall behold the river on whose banks he lived, and on whose banks he rests, still flowing on toward the sea, so surely may they see, as we now see, the flag of the Union floating on top of the Capitol; and then, as now, may the sun in his course visit no land more free, more happy, more lovely, than this, our own country."

The time that Webster looked forward to is here. We "other disciples of Washington" whom he foresaw are gathered today. His prophecy is borne out, his hope fulfilled. That flag "still floats from the top of the Capitol." It has come unscathed through foreign war and the threat of internal division. Its only change is the symbol of growth. The thirteen stars that Washington saw, and the twenty-four that Webster looked upon, now are forty-eight. The number of those who pay loyalty to that flag has multiplied tenfold. The respect for it beyond our borders, already great when Webster spoke a hundred years ago, has increased—not only in proportion to the power it symbolizes, but even more by the measure in which other peoples have embraced the ideals for which it stands. To Webster's expression of hope we may reasonably answer, Yes—"The sun in his course visits no land more free, more happy, more lovely, than this, our own country." Proudly we report to our forefathers that the Republic is more secure, more constant, more powerful, more truly great than at any other time in its history.

Today the American people begin a period of tribute and gratitude to this man whom we revere above all other Americans. Continuing until Thanksgiving Day they will commemorate his birth in every home, every school, every church, and every community under our flag.

In all this multitude of shrines and forums they will recount the life history and accomplishments of Washington. It is a time in which we will pause to recall for our own guidance, and to summarize and emphasize for the benefit of our children, the experiences, the achievements, the dangers escaped, the errors redressed—all the lessons that constitute the record of our past.

The ceremonial of commemorating the founder of our country is one of the most solemn that either an individual or a nation ever performs; carried out in high spirit it can be made one of the most fruitful and enriching. It is a thing to be done in the mood of prayer, of communing with the spiritual springs of patriotism and of devotion to country. It is an occasion for looking back to our past, for taking stock of our present, and, in the light of both, setting the compass for our future. We look back that we may recall those qualities of Washington's character which made him great, those principles of national conduct which he laid down, and by which we have come thus far. We meet to reestablish our contact with them, renew our fidelity to them.

From this national revival of interest in the history of the American Revolution and of the independence of the United States will come a renewal of those inspirations which strengthened the patriots who brought to the world a new concept of human liberty and a new form of government.

So rich and vivid is the record of history, that Washington in our day lives again in the epic of the foundation of the Republic. He appears in the imagination of every succeeding generation as the embodiment of the wisdom, the courage, the patience, the endurance, the statesmanship, and the absence of all mean ambition, which transformed scattered communities of the forest and the frontiers into a unity of free and independent people.

It is not necessary for me to attempt a eulogy of George Washington. That has been done by masters of art and poetry during more than a hundred years. To what they have said I attempt to make no addition.

The true eulogy of Washington is this mighty Nation. He contributed more to its origins than any other man. The influence of his character and of his accomplishments has contributed to the building of human freedom and ordered liberty, not alone upon this continent but upon all continents. The part which he played in the creation of our institutions has brought daily harvest of happiness to hundreds of millions of humanity. The inspirations from his genius have lifted the vision of succeeding generations. The definitions of those policies in government whch he fathered have stood the test of 150 years of strain and stress.

From the inspiration and the ideals which gave birth to this

Nation, there has come the largest measure of liberty that man has yet devised. So securely were the foundations of this free Government laid that the structure has been able to adapt itself to the changing world relations, the revolutions of invention and the revelations of scientific discovery, the fabulous increase of population and of wealth, and yet to stand the kaleidoscopic complexities of life which these changes have brought upon it.

What other great, purely human institution, devised in the era of the stagecoach and the candle, has so marvelously grown and survived into this epoch of the steam engine, the airplane, the incandescent lamp, the wireless telephone, and the battleship?

If we are to get refreshment to our ideals from looking backward to Washington, we should strive to identify the qualities in him that made our revolution a success and our Nation great. Those were the qualities that marked Washington out for immortality.

We find they were not spectacular qualities. He never charged with a victorious army up the capital streets of a conquered enemy. Excepting only Yorktown and Trenton, he won no striking victories. His great military strength was in the strategy of attrition, the patient endurance of adversity, steadfast purpose unbent by defeat. The American shrine most associated with Washington is Valley Forge, and Valley Forge was not a place of victory—except the victory of Washington's fortitude triumphant above the weakness and discouragement of lesser men. Washington had courage without excitement, determination without passion.

The descriptions of George Washington by his contemporaries give us no clear picture of the inner man, the Washington whose spiritual force so palpably dominated his whole epoch. As a mirror, his own writings do him indifferent justice, whilst the writings of others are clouded by their awe or are obscured by their venom. We must deduce mainly from other records why he stood out head and shoulders above all the crowd around him. It was an extraordinary crowd, living at white heat, comprising men as varied, as brilliant, as versatile as the extraordinary demands which the times made upon them. They were men flexible in intellect, and versed in the ways of the world. Yet in every crisis, and for every role, they turned to Washington. They forced upon him the command of Indian fighters; they made him a general against trained British troops; they demanded that he be a constitutionalist and a national statesman; they insisted he must guide his country through the skillful ambushes of European kings; they summoned him to establish the nonexistent credit of an insolvent infant nation. Why did his brilliant fellow-patriots always thus turn to him?

The answer of history is unmistakable: They brought their problems to Washington because he had more character, a finer character, a purer character, than any other man of his time. In all the shifting pressures of his generation, all men acknowledged that the one irresistible force was the overwhelming impact of his moral power. Motives and men were measured by their stature when standing in his shadow. Slander fell harmless before him, sham hung its head in shame, folly did not risk to look him in the face, corruption slunk from his presence, cowardice dared not show its quaking knees.

In his integrity, all our men of genius in his day found their one sure center of agreement. In his wisdom and authority they found the one sure way to practical fulfillment of their dreams.

We need no attempt at canonization of George Washington. We know he was human, subject to the discouragements and perplexities that come to us all. We know that he had moments of deepest anxiety. We know of his sufferings, and the sacrifices and anguish that came to him. We know of his resentment of injustice and misrepresentation. And yet we know that he never lost faith in our people.

Nor have I much patience with those who undertake the irrational humanizing of Washington. He had, indeed, the fine qualities of friendliness, of sociableness, of humanness, of simple hospitality; but we have no need to lower our vision from his unique qualities of greatness, or to seek to depreciate the unparalleled accomplishments of the man who dominated and gave birth to the being of a great nation.

What we have need of today in this celebration is to renew in our people the inspiration that comes from George Washington as a founder of human liberty, as the father of a system of government, as the builder of a system of national life.

It is of primary importance that we of today shall renew that spark of immortal purpose which burned within him, shall know of the resolution and the steadfastness which carried him forward to the establishment of a Nation. That establishment was not a momentary flash of impulse in a people rebellious and passionate under oppression, destined to fade into a dictatorship or the chaos so often born of revolutions. On the contrary, it was builded upon foundations of principles and ideals which have given the power and strength that made this Nation and inspired the establishment of ordered liberty in a score of other nations.

We have need to refresh to the remembrance of the American people the great tests and trials of character of the men who founded our Republic. We have need to remember the fiber of those men who brought to successful conclusion the eight years of revolution. We have need again to bring forth the picture of the glories and the valor of Lexington and Concord, of Bunker Hill, the sufferings and fortitude of Valley Forge, the victory of Yorktown. We have need to revive the meaning and the sheer moral courage of the Declaration of Independence, the struggle of the Continental Congress, the forming of the Constitution. We have need at all times to review the early crises of the Republic, the consolidation of the Union, the establishment of national solidarity, the building of an administration of government, and the development of guarantees of freedom. No incident and no part in these great events, which have echoed and reechoed throughout the world for a century and a half, can be separated from the name and the dominant leadership of George Washington.

Upon these foundations of divine inspiration laid by our forefathers, and led by Washington, our Nation has builded up during this century and a half a new system of life, a system unique to the American people. It is hallowed by the sacrifice and glorious valor of men. It is assured by a glorious charter of human rights.

It comprises a political system of self-government by the majority, resting upon the duties of individual men to the community, and of the local communities to the Nation. It is a government designed in spirit to sustain a dual purpose; to protect our people among nations by great national power, and to preserve individual freedom by local self-government.

It comprises a social system free of inherited position, based upon the ideal of equality of all men before the law, the equal privilege of men to strive and to achieve, and the responsibilities of men to their neighbors.

It embraces an economic system based upon the largest degree of freedom and stimulation to initiative and enterprise which can be permitted and still maintain the ideal of equality of opportunity among men.

Finally, it embraces a system of relationships to other nations based upon no thought of imperialism, no desire to dominate; a determined national self-reliance in defense and independence in action; freedom from all commitment to the unknown future, and an aspiration to promote peace and good will among all men.

Perhaps no single part of this system is different from some instance in history or in some part of the world. But in its composite form it is distinctly unique and distinctly American, a system under which we have reached an assured position among the most powerful of the nations of the world.

This destiny of national greatness was clearly foreseen by George Washington. More fully than any man of his time was he gifted with vision of the future. He spoke habitually of the "American Empire," and predicted its expansion from ocean to ocean. He planned and wrought for the binding forces of transportation and peaceful commerce. He thought in terms of almost imperial grandeur, and he wrought in terms of republican solidity. His far-flung dreams have come true, and he lives today in his works, in the names of our towns or cities and our States, and in the affectionate reverence of us who so immeasurably benefit by his wisdom.

Our American system of national life is dependent upon a trust in the principles of government as established by George Washington; a trust in his example to our people; a trust in and a devotion to religious faith, which he himself so devoutly practised; a trust in that divine inspiration which he so sedulously invoked and which is expressed in the common mind of our people; and above all a trust in the Divine Providence which has always given guidance to our country.

From Washington's spirit there has grown an infusion of social ideals with the quality of magnanimity: upholding prosperity with generosity, dignity with forbearance, security without privilege, which has raised our institutions to a level of humanity and nobility nowhere else attained.

We have the faith that Webster expressed, that a hundred years hence our countrymen will again celebrate his birth, will review the memory of his services with no less sincere admiration and gratitude than we now commemorate it, and that they too will see, as we now see, "the flag of the Union floating on the top of the Capitol."

From the room where I conduct my high office I hourly see the monument which Washington's proud and grateful countrymen have raised to his memory. It stands foursquare to the world, its base rooted steadfast in the solid substance of American soil. Its peak rises towards the heavens with matchless serenity and calm. Massive in its proportions, as was the character of Washington himself, overwhelming in its symmetry, simplicity, and sincerity, it most fittingly, beautifully, and nobly proclaims the founder of our commonwealth and our acceptance of his faith. Around that monument have grown steadily and surely the benevolent and beneficent agencies of orderly government dedicated to the spirit of Washington.

Beyond any other monument built by the hand of man out of clay and stone, this shaft is a thing of the spirit. Whether seen in darkness or in light, in brightness or in gloom, there is about it a mantle of pure radiance which gives it the aspect of eternal truth. It is a pledge in the sight of all mankind, given by Washington's countrymen, to carry forward the continuing fulfillment of his vision of America.

Senate Chamber, 1830

House of Representatives Chamber, 1830

14

THE UNITED STATES CONGRESS

ON

GEORGE WASHINGTON

PART I

List of addresses in honor of *George Washington* as recorded in the proceedings of the United States Congress from 1789 to 1932

PART II

Acts of Congress, Official Documents and other tributes in honor of *George Washington* from 1789 to 1932

PART III

Extracts from the official papers and writings of *George Washington* read into the *Record* during debates in the United States Congress from 1789-1932

Compiled by
MYRTIS JARRELL
under the direction of
H. H. B. MEYER
Legislative Reference Service
Library of Congress

INTRODUCTION

T HE legends of other great men of the eighteenth century "slowly take shape round their memory," writes a distinguished biographer in France; "in the case of Washington it formed itself out of the man himself and in his lifetime. . . . The others were obliged to wait for the hand of Time; Washington, on the contrary, without having either to die or to wait for long years to pass, stepped with firm tread into immortality."

To one who has followed the course of General Washington's name, as it constantly recurs throughout the record of official proceedings in the United States Congress, these words make an instant appeal, because they seem to express so truly what the record reveals.

In the early weeks of April in 1789, Charles Thomson accompanied General Washington on his journey to New York where he was to take the oath of office as first President of the United States, and witnessed his triumphant progress, which, Thomson mentions in his report to the Senate, "was retarded by the tender and affectionate leave . . . his neighbors and friends took of him; by the congratulatory addresses . . . he was obliged to receive by the way; and by the testimonies of public esteem and joy, to which it was necessary for him to pay attention, in the several States through which he passed."

John Adams, in a message to Congress in 1799, spoke of him as "our excellent fellow-citizen, George Washington, by the purity of his character and a long series of services to his country, rendered illustrious throughout the world."

John Marshall—then a member of the House of Representatives—declared that "however the public confidence may change, and the public affections fluctuate with respect to others, yet with respect to him they have, in war and in peace, in public and in private life, been as steady as his own firm mind, and as constant as his own exalted virtues."

Benjamin Franklin—upon bequeathing to General Washington . . . *the friend of mankind* his "fine crab-tree walking-stick, with a gold head curiously wrought in the form of a cap of Liberty," recorded in his Will these lofty words:

"If it were a scepter, he has merited it and would become it."

And so it is revealed to those who turn to the record of the Congress how the fame of George Washington is ever-increasing; how from the earliest days of our nation's history even to the present hour, the most gifted among our statesmen and jurists delight to do him honor; the wisest seek his guidance; and famous men throughout the world extol his name.

The United States Congress
on
GEORGE WASHINGTON

PART ONE
List of Addresses in Honor of George Washington as Recorded in the
Official Proceedings of the United States Congress—1789-1932

FIRST SESSION OF THE FIRST CONGRESS: 1789

Text of an address by CHARLES THOMSON, Esq., April 14, 1789, at Mount Vernon, where, by order of the Senate, he delivered to GENERAL WASHINGTON a certificate of his election to the Office of President of the United States.
American State Papers, Misc., 1:5-6.

Address of the Senate to GEORGE WASHINGTON, President of the United States—reported, May 7, 1789, from the Select Committee appointed to prepare an answer to the President's Address to both Houses of Congress at the opening of the session.
Annals of Congress, V. 1: pp. 31-32.
[*Journal of the Senate*, pp. 22-23.]

Address of the House of Representatives to GEORGE WASHINGTON, President of the United States, reported, May 5, 1789, from the Select Committee appointed for the purpose, by the Hon. James Madison, Jr., a Representative from Virginia.
Annals of Congress, V. 1: pp. 247-248.
[*Journal of the House of Representatives*, pp. 27-28.]

SECOND SESSION OF THE FOURTH CONGRESS:
1796-1797

Address of the Senate to GEORGE WASHINGTON, President of the United States, adopted, December 10, 1796, as reported from the Select Committee appointed to prepare an answer to the President's Address to both Houses of Congress at the opening of the session.
Annals of Congress, V. 6: pp. 1520-1521.
[*Journal of the Senate*, pp. 300-301.]

Address of the House of Representatives to GEORGE WASHINGTON, President of the United States—pronounced, December 15, 1796, by the *Speaker*, the HON. JONATHAN DAYTON, of New Jersey, "when, attended by the House, in a body, he waited upon the President."
Annals of Congress, V. 6: pp. 1673-1674.
[*Journal of the House of Representatives*, pp. 618-619.]

FIRST SESSION OF THE SIXTH CONGRESS: 1799-1800

An address by the HON. JOHN MARSHALL, a Representative from Virginia, December 19, 1799, announcing in the House of Representatives the death of GEORGE WASHINGTON.
Annals of Congress, V. 10: pp. 203-204.

Address of the Senate to JOHN ADAMS, President of the United States, upon the death of GEORGE WASHINGTON—reported,

December 23, 1799, from the Select Committee appointed for the purpose by the HON. SAMUEL DEXTER, a Senator from Massachusetts.
Annals of Congress, V. 10: pp. 17-18.
[*Journal of the Senate*, p. 12]
[*American State Papers*, Misc., 1:190.]

Address by JOHN ADAMS, President of the United States, December 23, 1799, in reply to the Address of the Senate upon the death of GEORGE WASHINGTON.
Annals of Congress, V. 10: pp. 18-19.
[*Journal of the Senate*, pp. 12-13.]
[*American State Papers*, Misc., 1:190.]

Address of the House of Representatives to JOHN ADAMS, President of the United States, upon the death of GENERAL WASHINGTON—pronounced December 19, 1799, by the *Speaker*, the HON. THEODORE SEDGWICK, of Massachusetts, "when, attended by the House, in a body, he waited upon the *President*".
Annals of Congress, V. 10: p. 206.
[*Journal of the House of Representatives*, p. 541.]
[*American State Papers*, Misc., 1:190.]

An address by JOHN ADAMS, President of the United States, December 19, 1799, in reply to the address of the House of Representatives upon the death of GEORGE WASHINGTON.
Annals of Congress, V. 10: p. 206.
[*Journal of the House of Representatives*, p. 541.]
[*American State Papers*, Misc., 1:190.]

An oration by MAJOR-GENERAL HENRY LEE, a Representative from Virginia, delivered, December 26, 1799, before the two Houses of the United States Congress upon the occasion of the funeral of GENERAL WASHINGTON—and communicated to the House of Representatives, December 30, 1799, to be recorded in the official proceedings of Congress.
Annals of Congress, V. 10: Appendix, pp. 1305-1311.
[*American State Papers*, Misc., 1:192-194.]

FIRST SESSION OF THE FOURTEENTH CONGRESS:
1815-1816

Speech by the HON. BENJAMIN HUGER, a Representative from South Carolina, delivered in the House of Representatives, February 16th and February 17th, 1816, relative to *a monument* to GENERAL WASHINGTON.
Annals of Congress, V. 29: pp. 1007-1008, 1009-1010.
[*American State Papers*, Misc. 2:298.]

Speech by the Hon. ERASTUS ROOT, a Representative from New York, delivered in the House of Representatives, February 17, 1816, relative to *a monument to* GENERAL WASHINGTON.

Annals of Congress, V. 29: pp. 1009-1010.

FIRST SESSION OF THE SIXTEENTH CONGRESS:
1819-1820

Speech by the Hon. JAMES ERVIN, a Representative from South Carolina, delivered in the House of Representatives, April 6, 1820, relative to certain resolutions submitted by him providing for *a monument to* GENERAL WASHINGTON.

Annals of Congress, V. 36: pp. 1792-1799.

FIRST SESSION OF THE EIGHTEENTH CONGRESS:
1823-1824

Speech by the Hon. JAMES BUCHANAN, a Representative from Pennsylvania, delivered in the House of Representatives, January 15, 1824, upon presenting a resolution calling for the appointing of a committee to inquire in what manner the resolutions of Congress, passed on the 24th of December, 1799, relative to the *erection of a monument to* GENERAL WASHINGTON, may be best accomplished.

Annals of Congress, V. 41: pp. 1044-1046, 1047.

Speech by the Hon. GEORGE CARY, a Representative from Georgia, delivered in the House of Representatives, January 15, 1824, on the *Buchanan resolution* calling for the appointment of a committee to report on the propriety of erecting *a monument or mausoleum to the memory of* WASHINGTON.

Annals of Congress, V. 41: pp. 1046-1047.

Speech by the Hon. DAVID TRIMBLE, a Representative from Kentucky, delivered in the House of Representatives, January 15, 1824, relative to the erection of a *monument or mausoleum in the Capitol to the memory of* WASHINGTON.

Annals of Congress, V. 41: p. 1048.

FIRST SESSION OF THE NINETEENTH CONGRESS:
1825-1826

Debate in the House of Representatives, February 21, 1826, relative to a motion by the Hon. JOHN COCKE, a Representative from Tennessee, that the House adjourn on the morrow in honor of the anniversary of the birth of GEORGE WASHINGTON:

Debates in Congress, V. 2: Part 1, pp. 1419-1421:
Hon. John Cocke, of Tennessee.
Hon. John Forsyth, of Georgia.
Hon. Sam Houston, of Tennessee.
Hon. John W. Campbell, of Ohio.
Hon. John Barney, of Maryland.

FIRST SESSION OF THE TWENTY-SECOND CONGRESS:
1831-1832

Remarks during debate in the Senate, February 13, 1832, on the *Report*, submitted by the Hon. HENRY CLAY, of Kentucky, from the Joint Committee appointed to make arrangements for the *celebration of the centennial birthday of* GEORGE WASHINGTON.

Debates in Congress, V. 8: Part 1, pp. 367-377:
[Journal of the Senate, pp. 129-132.]
[S. Doc. No. 62 . . . . . Serial 213]
Hon. Henry Clay, of Kentucky.
Hon. John Forsyth, of Georgia.
Hon. Daniel Webster, of Massachusetts.
Hon. L. W. Tazewell, of Virginia.
Hon. George M. Bibb, of Kentucky.
Hon. John Tyler, of Virginia.

Speeches during debate in the House of Representatives, February 13th, 14th, and 16th, 1832—on the Report submitted by the Hon. PHILEMON THOMAS, of Louisiana, from the Joint Committee appointed to make arrangements for the *celebration of the centennial birthday of* GEORGE WASHINGTON.

Debates in Congress, V. 8: Part 2, pp. 1782-1809, 1810-1813, 1818-1820:
[S. Doc. No. 62 . . . . . Serial 213.]
Hon. William McCoy, of Virginia.
Hon. Charles F. Mercer, of Virginia.
Hon. William F. Gordon, of Virginia.
Hon. Richard Coke, Jr., of Virginia.
Hon. Edward Everett, of Massachusetts.
Hon. Wiley Thompson, of Georgia.
Hon. Charles A. Wickliffe, of Kentucky.
Hon. William Drayton, of South Carolina.
Hon. Mark Alexander, of Virginia.
Hon. Augustin S. Clayton, of Georgia.
Hon. Joel B. Sutherland, of Pennsylvania.
Hon. Charles C. Johnston, of Virginia.
Hon. Tristam Burges, of Rhode Island.
Hon. Samuel P. Carson, of North Carolina.
Hon. Churchill C. Cambreleng, of New York.
Hon. James M. Wayne, of Georgia.
Hon. John Q. Adams, of Massachusetts.
Hon. William S. Archer, of Virginia.
Hon. Benjamin C. Howard, of Maryland.

Remarks during debate in the House of Representatives, February 17, 1832, on the resolution reported from the Committee on Public Buildings by the Hon. LEONARD JARVIS, of Maine, authorizing the Clerk of the House to employ JOHN VANDERLYN, of New York, to paint a portrait of GEORGE WASHINGTON to be placed in the Hall of Representatives:

Debates in Congress, V. 8: Part 2, pp. 1824-1827:
[Journal of the House of Representatives, p. 342 and p. 376.]
Hon. Aaron Ward, of New York.
Hon. Churchill C. Cambreleng, of New York.
Hon. John G. Watmough, of Pennsylvania.
Hon. Charles F. Mercer, of Virginia.
Hon. Henry A. S. Dearborn, of Massachusetts.
Hon. William Drayton, of South Carolina.

Hon. *Leonard Jarvis*, of Maine.
Hon. *Edward Everett*, of Massachusetts.
Hon. *John W. Taylor*, of New York.
Hon. *Gulian C. Verplanck*, of New York.

Remarks during debate in the House of Representatives, February 18, 1832, on the resolution reported from the Committee on Public Buildings by the HON. LEONARD JARVIS, a Representative from Maine, authorizing the President of the United States to employ HORATIO GREENOUGH, of Massachusetts, *to execute a full-length pedestrian statute of* GEORGE WASHINGTON.

> *Debates in Congress*, V. 8: Part 2, pp. 1829-1830:
> [*H. Rept. No.* 459 . . . *Serial* 226.]
> [*H. Doc. No.* 45 . . . *Serial* 392.]
> [*H. Rept. No.* 21 . . . *Serial* 236.]
> > Hon. *Leonard Jarvis*, of Maine.
> > Hon. *Henry A. S. Dearborn*, of Massachusetts.

Remarks during debate in the Senate, June 25, 1832, on the joint resolution (S.J.Res. No. 4) reported from the Committee on the Library by the HON. ASHER ROBBINS, of Rhode Island, authorizing the President of the United States to contract for a *full-length pedestrian statue* of GEORGE WASHINGTON:

> *Debates in Congress*, V. 8: Part 1, pp. 1126-1127:
> [*See H. Rept. No.* 459 . . . *Serial* 226.]
> > Hon. *John Forsyth*, of Georgia.
> > Hon. *George Poindexter*, of Mississippi.
> > Hon. *Henry Clay*, of Kentucky.

FIRST SESSION OF THE TWENTY-THIRD CONGRESS: 1833-1834

Remarks during debate in the House of Representatives, June 26, 1834, on the bill (H. R. No. 446) reported from the Committee on Foreign Affairs by the HON. WILLIAM ARCHER, a Representative from Virginia, to enable the Secretary of State to purchase the *papers and books of* GENERAL WASHINGTON.

> *Debates in Congress*, V. 10: Part 4, pp. 4781-4782:
> [*H. Rept. No.* 381 . . . *Serial* 262.]
> > Hon. *Richard H. Wilde*, of Georgia.
> > Hon. *Leonard Jarvis*, of Maine.
> > Hon. *William S. Archer*, of Virginia.
> > Hon. *James Parker*, of New Jersey.
> > Hon. *M. T. Hawkins*, of North Carolina.
> > Hon. *James M. Wayne*, of Georgia.

SECOND SESSION OF THE TWENTY-FIFTH CONGRESS: 1837-1838

Speech by the HON. THOMAS MORRIS, a Senator from Ohio, delivered in the Senate, 19 June 1838, on the subject of granting a portion of public ground in the city of Washington for the erection of a *monument to* GEORGE WASHINGTON.

> *Congressional Globe*, V. 6: Part 1, pp. 460-461.

THIRD SESSION OF THE TWENTY-SEVENTH CONGRESS: 1842-1843

Address by the HON. GEORGE W. SUMMERS, a Representative from Virginia, delivered before the House of Representatives, February 7, 1843, upon presenting to the Nation, in the name and on the behalf of MR. SAMUEL T. WASHINGTON, of Kanawha County, Virginia, *a sword worn by* GENERAL WASHINGTON and *a staff which* BENJAMIN FRANKLIN *gave to* WASHINGTON.

> *Congressional Globe*, V. 12: Part 1, p. 254.
> [*Journal of the House of Representatives*, pp. 329-332.]
> [*H. Doc. No.* 144 . . . . *Serial* 421.]
> Reprinted in the *Record*, February 22, 1922, by request of the HON. R. WALTON MOORE, of Virginia, as part of his remarks.
> > *Congressional Record*, V. 62: Part 3, pp. 2906-2907.

Address by the HON. JOHN QUINCY ADAMS, a Representative from Massachusetts, delivered before the House of Representatives, February 7, 1843, upon submitting a resolution presenting the thanks of Congress to SAMUEL T. WASHINGTON, of Kanawha County, Virginia, for the *sword worn by* GENERAL WASHINGTON and *the staff bequeathed to him by* FRANKLIN.

> *Congressional Globe*, V. 12: Part 1, pp. 254-255.
> [*Journal of the House of Representatives*, pp. 332-333.]
> [*H. Doc. No.* 144 . . . . *Serial* 421.]

Address by the HON. WILLIAM S. ARCHER, a Senator from Virginia, delivered in the Senate, February 8, 1843, upon his motion that the Senate proceed to immediate consideration of the resolution (H. J. Res. No. 35) received from the House for the concurrence of the Senate in extending the thanks of Congress to SAMUEL T. WASHINGTON for his present to the Nation of GENERAL WASHINGTON's *sword and* FRANKLIN's *staff*.

> *Congressional Globe*, V. 12: Part 1, pp. 255-256.

FIRST SESSION OF THE TWENTY-EIGHTH CONGRESS: 1843-1844

Address by the HON. JOHN QUINCY ADAMS, a Representative from Massachusetts, delivered, April 18, 1844, upon presenting to the House of Representatives, in compliance with one of the clauses of the last will and testament of MR. WILLIAM SYDNEY WINDER, of Maryland, the *camp chest used by* GENERAL WASHINGTON *during the Revolutionary War*.

> *Congressional Globe*, V. 13: Part 1, pp. 533, 536.

Address by the HON. JAMES A. PEARCE, a Senator from Maryland, delivered, April 19, 1844, upon presenting to the Senate *the camp chest used by* GENERAL WASHINGTON *during the Revolutionary War*, and requesting the concurrence of the Senate in the resolution (H. J. Res. No. 27) received from the House accepting the gift in behalf of the Nation.

> *Congressional Globe*, V. 13, Part 1, p. 537.

SECOND SESSION OF THE TWENTY-EIGHTH CONGRESS: 1844-1845

Speech by the HON. JOHN J. CRITTENDEN, a Senator from Kentucky, delivered in the Senate, January 20, 1845, upon submitting a resolution that the Committee on the Library be instructed to inquire into the expediency of employing Luigi Persico to execute for the United States *an equestrian statue*, in bronze *of* George Washington.

Congressional Globe, V. 14: Part 1, p. 156.

FIRST SESSION OF THE TWENTY-NINTH CONGRESS:
1845-1846

Remarks by the Hon. Thomas H. Benton, a Senator from Missouri, during debate in the Senate, January 8th and January 13th, 1846, relative to the erection of a monument to George Washington *by the National Monument Association*.

Congressional Globe, V. 15: Part 1, pp. 161, 189-190.

FIRST SESSION OF THE THIRTIETH CONGRESS:
1847-1848

An oration by the Hon. Robert C. Winthrop, of Massachusetts, Speaker of the House of Representatives, July 4, 1848, on the occasion of laying the corner-stone of the *National Washington Monument*.

S. Doc. No. 224 . . . . Serial 4436.[1]

SECOND SESSION OF THE THIRTIETH CONGRESS:
1848-1849

Speech by the Hon. Richard K. Meade, a Representative from Virginia, delivered in the House of Representatives, February 5, 1849, upon his submitting a resolution that the Committee on Public Expenditures inquire into the expediency of having a copy of the *Washington Statue in the Capitol of Virginia* reproduced in American marble and placed in the Rotunda of the United States Capitol.

Congressional Record, V. 18: Part 1, p. 454.

FIRST SESSION OF THE THIRTY-FIRST CONGRESS:
1849-1850

Speech by the Hon. James Cooper, a Senator from Pennsylvania, delivered in the Senate, January 28, 1850, upon his presenting a memorial of Mr. Crawford, an American sculptor, proposing to execute for the United States Congress *an equestrian statue, in bronze,* of General Washington.

Congressional Globe, V. 19: Part 1, p. 232.

Speeches by the following Senators during debate in the Senate, January 24, 1850, on the resolution (S.J.Res. No. 3) submitted by the Hon. Henry Clay, of Kentucky, relative to the *purchase of the manuscript of* Washington's *Farewell Address*:

Congressional Globe, V. 19: Part 1, pp. 226-228:
    Hon. *Henry Clay*, of Kentucky.
    Hon. *Henry S. Foote*, of Mississippi.

---

[1] This oration by the Hon. Robert C. Winthrop was hardly accessible until, on motion by Mr. Gallinger, a Senator from New Hampshire, February 6, 1903, (57th Congress, 2nd Session) the History of the Washington Monument was ordered to be printed as a Senate document. This oration will be found on pages 113-130 of the document cited above.

    Hon. *Daniel Webster*, of Massachusetts.
    Hon. *Jefferson Davis*, of Mississippi.

Speeches by the following Members of the House of Representatives during debate in the House, January 29, 1850, and February 6, 1850, on the Clay resolution (S.J.Res. No. 3) authorizing the *purchase of the manuscript of* Washington's *Farewell Address*:

Congressional Globe, V. 19: p. 243, and pp. 296-298:

    Hon. *Andrew Johnson*, of Tennessee.
    Hon. *Alexander H. Stevens*, of Georgia
    Hon. *Joseph R. Chandler*, of Pennsylvania.
    Hon. *David K. Cartter*, of Ohio.
    Hon. *Samuel W. Inge*, of Alabama.

Remarks by the Hon. Henry Clay, a Senator from Kentucky, upon his presenting to the Senate, January 24, 1850, a petition from citizens in the State of Pennsylvania, requesting Congress *to purchase Mount Vernon*.

Congressional Globe, V. 19: Part 1, p. 225.

SECOND SESSION OF THE THIRTY-SECOND CONGRESS: 1852-1853

Debate in the House of Representatives, January 17, 1853, on the bill (H.R. No. 343) authorizing the President of the United States to employ Clark Mills, the American artist, to erect at the capital of the Nation *an equestrian statue of* George Washington:

Congressional Globe, V. 22: Part 1, pp. 323-325:

    Hon. *Gilbert Dean*, of New York.
    Hon. *George W. Jones*, of Tennessee.
    Hon. *Abraham W. Venable*, of North Carolina.
    Hon. *Richard H. Stanton*, of Kentucky.
    Hon. *Alexander H. Stephens*, of Georgia.
    Hon. *John C. Breckinridge*, of Kentucky.

Remarks by the Hon. James Shields, a Senator from Illinois, upon reporting from the Committee on the District of Columbia, January 18, 1853, the bill (H.R. No. 343) authorizing the President of the United States to employ Clark Mills, the American artist, to erect at the capital of the Nation *an equestrian statue of* George Washington.

Congressional Globe, V. 22: Part 1, p. 329.

SECOND SESSION OF THE THIRTY-THIRD CONGRESS:
1854-1855

Remarks by the Hon. Henry May, a Representative from Maryland, upon submitting to the House of Representatives, February 17, 1855, and February 22, 1855, a Report from the Select Committee appointed to consider the subject of *a National Monument to* George Washington.

Congressional Globe, V. 24: Part 1, pp. 795-796, 900.

FIRST SESSION OF THE THIRTY-FIFTH CONGRESS:
1857-1858

Remarks by the Hon. Albert Gallatin Brown, a Senator from Mississippi, during debate in the Senate, April 15, 1858, on the bill (S. No. 152), proposing to incorporate *the Washington National Monument Society*.

Congressional Globe, V. 27: Part 2, pp. 1597-1598.

Remarks in the House of Representatives, May 24, 1858, on the Senate bill (S. No. 152) to incorporate the *Washington National Monument Society*:

Congressional Globe, V. 27: Part 3, p. 2372:

> *Hon. Edward Dodd*, of New York.
> *Hon. Elihu B. Washburne*, of Illinois.
> *Hon. William Smith*, of Virginia.
> *Hon. Thomas B. Florence*, of Pennsylvania.
> *Hon. Warner L. Underwood*, of Kentucky.
> *Hon. William O. Goode*, of Virginia.

FIRST SESSION OF THE THIRTY-SIXTH CONGRESS:
1859-1860

Speeches in the Senate, February 16, 1860, during debate on the joint resolution, submitted by the Hon. ALBERT G. BROWN, a Senator from Mississippi, relative to the appointment of a committee to make arrangements "for the inauguration of the equestrian statue of GEORGE WASHINGTON":

Congressional Globe, V. 29: Part 1, pp. 797-800:

> *Hon. James A. Pearce*, of Maryland.
> *Hon. Albert G. Brown*, of Mississippi.
> *Hon. William P. Fessenden*, of Maine.
> *Hon. James H. Hammond*, of South Carolina.
> *Hon. Jefferson Davis*, of Mississippi.
> *Hon. John P. Hale*, of New Hampshire.
> *Hon. John C. Ten Eyck*, of New Jersey.

Remarks by the following Senators, February 20, 1860, during debate on the resolution (H.J.Res. No. 8) providing an appropriation "for the inauguration of the equestrian statue of GENERAL WASHINGTON":

Congressional Globe, V. 29: Part 1, pp. 836-837:

> *Hon. James H. Hammond*, of South Carolina.
> *Hon. Jefferson Davis*, of Mississippi.
> *Hon. William P. Fessenden*, of Maine.
> *Hon. Hannibal Hamlin*, of Maine.
> *Hon. John J. Crittenden*, of Kentucky.
> *Hon. George Ellis Pugh*, of Ohio.

SECOND SESSION OF THE THIRTY-SEVENTH CONGRESS: 1861-1862

Remarks by the Hon. ANDREW JOHNSON, a Senator from Tennessee, upon presenting, in the Senate, February 11, 1862, a memorial of the mayor and other citizens of Philadelphia, praying that GEORGE WASHINGTON's *Farewell Address to the People of the United States* may be read to both Houses of Congress and to the Army and Navy of the United States on the approaching 22nd day of February.

Congressional Globe, V. 32: Part 1, p. 738.
[*Journal of the Senate*, pp. 193-194.]

Remarks by the Hon. JOHN J. CRITTENDEN, a Representative from Kentucky, upon presenting, in the House of Representatives, February 10, 1862, a memorial of the mayor and other citizens of Philadelphia, praying that GEORGE WASHINGTON's *Farewell Address to the people of the United States* may be read to both Houses of Congress and to the Army and Navy of the United States on the approaching 22nd day of February.

Congressional Globe, V. 32: Part 1, pp. 726-727, 835.
[*Journal of the House of Representatives*, pp. 288, 311, 339, 372, 421.]

THIRD SESSION OF THE FORTIETH CONGRESS:
1868-1869

Speech by the Hon. THOMAS L. JONES, a Representative from Kentucky, delivered in the House of Representatives, March 3, 1869, on the resolution reported by MR. COVODE, of Pennsylvania, from the Committee on Public Buildings and Grounds, relative to certain articles—once the property of the WASHINGTON family—which were taken from Arlington House by the Federal authorities.

Congressional Globe, V. 4: Appendix, pp. 295-297.
[*H. Rept. No. 36 . . . . Serial 1437*.]

THIRD SESSION OF THE FORTY-SECOND CONGRESS:
1872-1873

Speech by the Hon. NORTON P. CHIPMAN, Delegate from the District of Columbia, delivered in the House of Representatives, February 18, 1873, on the bill (H.R. No. 1179) introduced by him in the preceding Session—providing for an appropriation to complete the *Washington Monument*.

Congressional Globe, V. 46; Appendix, pp. 96-99.
[*H. Rept. No. 48 . . . . Serial 1528*.]

Remarks by the Hon. NORTON P. CHIPMAN, Delegate from the District of Columbia, January 27, 1873, upon his submitting a resolution that a Select Committee of thirteen be appointed by the Speaker to confer with the officers and members of the Washington National Monument Society upon the practicability of completing the *Washington Monument* by the approaching centennial.

Congressional Globe, V. 46: Part 2, p. 891.

> Report from the Select Committee of Thirteen was submitted by MR. CHIPMAN, February 22, 1873.
> *Congressional Globe*, V. 46: Appendix, pp. 114-117.

FIRST SESSION OF THE FORTY-THIRD CONGRESS:
1873-1874

Speech by the Hon. RICHARD C. McCORMICK, Delegate from the Territory of Arizona, June 4, 1874—the House having under consideration the Report submitted from the Select Committee on the *Washington National Monument*.

Congressional Record, V. 2: Appendix, p. 504.
[*H. Rept. No. 485 . . . . Serial 1625*.]

FIRST SESSION OF THE FORTY-FOURTH CONGRESS:
1875-1876

Speech by the Hon. LEVI A. MACKEY, Representative from Pennsylvania, delivered in the House of Representatives, April 29, 1876, on the *Washington National Monument*.

Congressional Record, V. 4: Appendix, pp. 63-67.

Remarks during debate in the Senate, July 22, 1876, on the Sherman bill (S. No. 982) providing for the completion of the *Washington Monument*.

> *Congressional Record*, V. 4: Part 5, pp. 4811-4816:
> > Hon. *John Sherman*, of Ohio.
> > Hon. *Justin Morrill*, of Vermont.
> > Hon. *George F. Edmunds*, of Vermont.
> > Hon. *Thomas F. Bayard*, of Delaware.
> > Hon. *William P. Whyte*, of Maryland.

Remarks by the Hon. CHARLES FOSTER, a Representative from Ohio, July 27, 1876, upon submitting a Report from the Committee on Appropriations on the Senate bill (S. No. 982) providing for the completion of the *Washington Monument*.

> *Congressional Record*, V. 4: Part 5, pp. 4906-4907.

SECOND SESSION OF THE FORTY-FIFTH CONGRESS:
1877-1878

Remarks in the House of Representatives, April 2, 1878, during debate on the resolution (H.J.Res. No. 152) to enable the Joint Commission to carry into effect the Act of Congress providing for the completion of the *Washington Monument*.

> *Congressional Record*, V. 7: Part 3, pp. 2203-2206:
> > Hon. *Charles Foster*, of Ohio.
> > Hon. *Omar D. Conger*, of Michigan.
> > Hon. *Eugene Hale*, of Maine.
> > Hon. *Samuel S. Cox*, of New York.
> > Hon. *Benjamin F. Butler*, of Massachusetts.
> > Hon. *Hiester Clymer*, of Pennsylvania.

Speeches during debate in the Senate, May 10, 1878, on the resolution (H.J.Res. No. 152) to enable the Joint Commission to carry into effect the Act of Congress providing for the completion of the *Washington Monument*.

> *Congressional Record*, V. 7: Part 4, pp. 3350-3353.
> > Hon. *Henry L. Dawes*, of Massachusetts.
> > Hon. *Roscoe Conkling*, of New York.

Speech by the Hon. HENRY L. DAWES, a Senator from Massachusetts, during debate in the Senate, June 10, 1878, on the conference report on the resolution (H.J.Res. No. 152) to enable the Joint Commission to carry into effect the Act of Congress providing for the completion of the *Washington Monument*.

> *Congressional Record*, V. 7: Part 5, pp. 4351-4352.

THIRD SESSION OF THE FORTY-FIFTH CONGRESS:
1878-1879

Speeches during debate in the Senate, February 28, 1879, on that provision of the Sundry Civil Appropriation bill (H.R. 6471) authorizing necessary funds for the completion of the *Washington Monument*.

> *Congressional Record*, V. 8: Part 3, pp. 2094-2096:
> > Hon. *Henry L. Dawes*, of Massachusetts.
> > Hon. *Roscoe Conkling*, of New York.
> > Hon. *Eli Saulsbury*, of Delaware.
> > Hon. *Daniel W. Voorhees*, of Indiana.
> > Hon. *Allen G. Thurman*, of Ohio.

FIRST SESSION OF THE FORTY-SIXTH CONGRESS:
1879

Remarks by the Hon. JOHN T. HARRIS, a Representative from Virginia, June 10, 1879, requesting unanimous consent of the House to submit a resolution (H.J.Res. No. 94) authorizing an appropriation for a monument to mark *the birthplace of* GEORGE WASHINGTON.

> *Congressional Record*, V. 9: Part 2, p. 1890.

Remarks by the Hon. DANIEL W. VOORHEES, a Senator from Indiana, June 10, 1879, on the resolution (H.J.Res. No. 94) authorizing an appropriation for building a monument to mark *the birthplace of* GEORGE WASHINGTON.

> *Congressional Record*, V. 9: Part 2, p. 1888.

THIRD SESSION OF THE FORTY-SIXTH CONGRESS:
1880-1881

Remarks during debate in the Senate, February 22, 1881, on the resolution (H.J.Res. No. 315) amending and re-enacting a joint resolution, approved June 14, 1879, providing for a monument to mark *the birthplace of* GEORGE WASHINGTON.

> *Congressional Record*, V. 11: Part 3, pp. 1913-1918:
> > Hon. *Francis M. Cockrell*, of Missouri.
> > Hon. *Eli Saulsbury*, of Delaware.
> > Hon. *John J. Ingalls*, of Kansas.
> > Hon. *Roscoe Conkling*, of New York.
> > Hon. *George F. Hoar*, of Massachusetts.
> > Hon. *John W. Johnston*, of Virginia.
> > Hon. *John J. Morgan*, of Alabama.

FIRST SESSION OF THE FORTY-EIGHTH CONGRESS:
1883-1884

Remarks by the Hon. FETTER S. HOBLITZELL, of Maryland, December 14, 1883, relative to a resolution (H.J.Res. No. 65) submitted by him to the House of Representatives, requesting the President of the United States to issue a Proclamation urging all religious denominations throughout the country to commemorate *the one-hundredth anniversary of the surrender by* GEORGE WASHINGTON *of his commission as Commander-in-chief of the patriotic forces of America on the 23rd of December, 1783, at Annapolis, Maryland*.

> *Congressional Record*, V. 15: Part 1, pp. 145-146.

SECOND SESSION OF THE FORTY-EIGHTH
CONGRESS: 1884-1885

Remarks by the Hon. JOHN SHERMAN, a Senator from Ohio, upon reporting to the Senate, February 10, 1885, a bill (S. No. 2615) to authorize medals commemorating the completion and *dedication of the Washington Monument*.

> *Congressional Record*, V. 16: Part 2, pp. 1477-1478.

Remarks by the Hon. WILLIAM DORSHEIMER, of New York, January 29, 1885, upon submitting to the House of Representatives the *Report of the Joint Commission*, appointed under a Joint Resolution of Congress approved May 13, 1884, relative to ceremonies to be authorized *at the dedication of the Washington Monument*.

> *Congressional Record*, V. 16: Part 2, pp. 1052-1053.

An address by the HON. GEORGE F. EDMUNDS, of Vermont, President *pro-tempore* of the Senate, introductory to ceremonies held in the Hall of Representatives, United States Capitol, February 21, 1885, upon the completion and *dedication of the Washington Monument.*

> *Congressional Record*, V. 16: Part 3, p. 1992.
> [S. *Misc. Doc. No. 56* . . *Serial 2267.*]
> [S. *Doc. No. 224* . . . . *Serial 4436.*]

An oration by the HON. ROBERT C. WINTHROP, of Massachusetts, upon the *dedication of the Washington Monument*— read in the Hall of Representatives, United States Capitol, February 21, 1885, by the HON. JOHN D. LONG, a Representative from the State of Massachusetts.

> *Congressional Record*, V. 16: Part 3, pp. 1992-1998.
> [S. *Misc. Doc. No. 56* . . *Serial 2267.*]
> [S. *Doc. No. 224* . . . . *Serial 4436.*]

An oration by the HON. JOHN W. DANIEL, a Senator from Virginia, delivered in the Hall of Representatives, United States Capitol, February 21, 1885, upon the completion and *dedication of the Washington Monument.*

> *Congressional Record*, V. 16: Part 3, pp. 1998-2003.
> [S. *Misc. Doc. No. 56* . . *Serial 2267.*]
> [S. *Doc. No. 224* . . . . *Serial 4436.*]

Remarks during debate in the House of Representatives, February 26, 1885, on the resolution—accompanying the Report of the Joint Commission appointed to arrange appropriate ceremonies at the dedication of the Washington Monument— that Congress extend a vote of thanks to BRIGADIER-GENERAL THOMAS LINCOLN CASEY, Corps of Engineers, United States Army, *and to his assistants*, for their admirable work in the *completion of the monument to the name and fame* of GEORGE WASHINGTON.

> *Congressional Record*, V. 16: Part 3, pp. 2200-2203.

SECOND SESSION OF THE FORTY-NINTH CONGRESS: 1886-1887

Speeches by the following Senators, February 2, 1887, during debate on the bill (H.R. 5097) to regulate the use of the *grounds about the Washington Monument.*

> *Congressional Record*, V. 18: Part 2, pp. 1284-1287:
> Hon. John C. Spooner, of Wisconsin.
> Hon. John J. Ingalls, of Kansas.
> Hon. Justin S. Morrill, of Vermont.

FIRST SESSION OF THE FIFTIETH CONGRESS: 1887-1888

Remarks during debate in the Senate, April 11, 1888, on the bill (S. No. 2564) authorizing the *Secretary of War* to purchase from MISS VIRGINIA TAYLOR LEWIS a sword worn by GENERAL WASHINGTON when he resigned his commission at Annapolis, and at public receptions while President.

> *Congressional Record*, V. 19: Part 3, pp. 2892-2893:
> *Hon. William Evarts*, of New York.
> *Hon. Daniel W. Voorhees*, of Indiana.
> *Hon. George F. Hoar*, of Massachusetts.
> *Hon. George Graham Vest*, of Missouri.
> *Hon. John H. Reagan*, of Texas.

FIRST SESSION OF THE FIFTY-FIRST CONGRESS: 1889-1890

An oration by MELVILLE W. FULLER, Chief-Justice of the United States, delivered, December 11, 1889, in the Hall of the House of Representatives, in commemoration of the inauguration of GEORGE WASHINGTON, *the first President of the United States.*

> *Congressional Record*, V. 21: Part 1, pp. 147-153.
> [H. *Mis. Doc. No. 168* . . *Serial 2768.*]

SECOND SESSION OF THE FIFTY-SIXTH CONGRESS: 1900-1901

An address by the HON. GEORGE F. HOAR, a Senator from Massachusetts, delivered in the Hall of the House of Representatives, December 12, 1900, before the Senate and House in joint convention assembled to celebrate the one hundredth anniversary of the establishment of the permanent seat of Government in the District of Columbia.

> *Report of the Joint Committee*, pp. 126-129.
> [H. *Doc. No. 552* . . . . *Serial 4207.*]

Speech by the HON. GEORGE F. HOAR, a Senator from Massachusetts, February 15, 1901, in support of the McMillan bill (S. No. 4142) proposing an appropriation for the purchase of a replica of the bronze *equestrian statue of* GENERAL WASHINGTON by DANIEL CHESTER FRENCH and EDWARD C. POTTER.

> *Congressional Record*, V. 34: Part 3, pp. 2442-2443.

SECOND SESSION OF THE FIFTY-SEVENTH CONGRESS: 1902-1903

Remarks by the HON. JACOB H. GALLINGER, a Senator from New Hampshire, and the HON. GEORGE F. HOAR, a Senator from Massachusetts, February 6, 1903, relative to printing, as a Senate document, certain pages, then out of print, relating to the *history of the Washington Monument.*

> *Congressional Record*, V. 36: Part 2, p. 1776.
> [S. *Doc. No. 224* . . . . *Serial 4436.*]

SECOND SESSION OF THE FIFTY-EIGHTH CONGRESS: 1903-1904

Remarks by the HON. SHELBY M. CULLOM, a Senator from Illinois, upon reporting from the Committee on Foreign Relations, January 28, 1904, the resolution (S.J.Res. No. 36) accepting *a reproduction of the bust of* GENERAL WASHINGTON *by* DAVID D'ANGERS from certain citizens of the Republic of France.

> *Congressional Record*, V. 38: Part 2, p. 1299.
> [S. *Doc. No. 78* . . . . *Serial 4588.*]
> [S. *Doc. No. 78, Part 2* . . *Serial 4588.*]

THIRD SESSION OF THE FIFTY-EIGHTH CONGRESS: 1904-1905

Remarks by the HON. GEORGE PEABODY WETMORE, a Senator from Rhode Island, March 3, 1905, upon submitting from the Joint Committee on the Library the *Report of Proceed-*

ings in connection with the formal presentation, February 22, 1905, of *a reproduction of a bust of* WASHINGTON by certain citizens of the Republic of France.

> *Congressional Record*, V. 39: Part 4, p. 3929.
> [*S. Rept. No.* 4397 . . . *Serial* 4778.]
> [*S. Doc. No.* 505 . . . . *Serial* 4916.]

Text of the address by M. JUSSERAND, the French Ambassador, delivered, February 22, 1905—upon the formal presentation of *a reproduction of the bust of* WASHINGTON from certain citizens of the Republic of France—will be found in the *Report of Proceedings*, pp. 6-9.

> [*S. Rept. No.* 4397 . . . *Serial* 4778.]

Text of the address of the HON. GEORGE PEABODY WETMORE, a Senator from Rhode Island, delivered February 22, 1905—accepting, on the part of the Senate, *a reproduction of the bust of* WASHINGTON from certain citizens of the Republic of France—will be found in the *Report of Proceedings*, pp. 9-12.

> [*S. Rept. No.* 4397 . . . *Serial* 4778.]

Text of the address of the HON. JAMES T. McCLEARY, a Representative from Minnesota, delivered, February 22, 1905—accepting, on the part of the House of Representatives, *a reproduction of the bust of* WASHINGTON from certain citizens of the Republic of France—will be found in the *Report of Proceedings*, pp. 13-19.

> [*S. Rept. No.* 4397 . . . *Serial* 4778.]

Remarks by the HON. THEODORE E. BURTON, a Representative from Ohio, February 22, 1905, calling the attention of Members of the House to the example GEORGE WASHINGTON left us of unselfishness and patriotism, which was the delight and the wonder of his time.

> *Congressional Record*, V. 39: Part 3, p. 3079.

FIRST SESSION OF THE FIFTY-NINTH CONGRESS:
1905-1906

Remarks by MR. KEIFER, of Ohio, and MR. PAYNE, of New York, February 22, 1906, on non-observance in the House of Representatives on that day of WASHINGTON's birthday anniversary.

> *Congressional Record*, V. 40: Part 2, pp. 2874, 2878.

FIRST SESSION OF THE SIXTIETH CONGRESS:
1907-1908

Remarks by the HON. RICHARD WAYNE PARKER, a Representative from New Jersey, February 22, 1908, on the subject of WASHINGTON's *Farewell Address*.

> *Congressional Record*, V. 42: Part 3, p. 2354.

Remarks by the HON. JAMES R. MANN, a Representative from Illinois, March 17, 1908, on the resolution (H.J.Res. No. 124) authorizing the transfer of *the statue of* PRESIDENT WASHINGTON, now located in the Capitol grounds, to the Smithsonian Institution.

> *Congressional Record*, V. 42: Part 4, pp. 3461-3462.

. . . .

> Report submitted in House by MR. McCALL, of Massachusetts, February 14, 1908, Part 3, p. 2051.

> [*H. Rept. No.* 900 . . . . *Serial* 5225.]

. . . .

> Report submitted in Senate by MR. WETMORE, of Rhode Island, May 15, 1908, Part 7, p. 6307.

> [*S. Rept. No.* 543 . . . . *Serial* 5219.]

SECOND SESSION OF THE SIXTIETH CONGRESS:
1908-1909

Remarks by the HON. WILLIAM SULZER, a Representative from New York, February 22, 1909, requesting that an editorial in the *New York American* of the 21st of February, 1909, entitled *Washington's Inspiration* be read before the House, and printed in the *Record* as part of his remarks.

> *Congressional Record*, V. 43: Part 3, pp. 2912-2913.

FIRST SESSION OF THE SIXTY-FIRST CONGRESS:
1909

Speech by the HON. CHARLES C. CARLIN, a Representative from Virginia, April 22, 1909, relative to the celebration in Alexandria, Virginia, on the 30th of April, 1909, of the *one dred and twentieth anniversary* of PRESIDENT WASHINGTON's *first inauguration.*

> *Congressional Record*, V. 44: Part 2, pp. 1477-1478.

Remarks by the HON. MICHAEL E. DRISCOLL, a Representative from New York, April 22, 1909, accepting on behalf of the Speaker and Members of the House of Representatives an invitation to attend the celebration in Alexandria, Virginia, on the 30th of April, 1909, of the *one hundred and twentieth anniversary* of PRESIDENT WASHINGTON's *first inauguration.*

> *Congressional Record*, V. 44: Part 2, p. 1478.

SECOND SESSION OF THE SIXTY-FIRST CONGRESS:
1909-1910

An address by the HON. FRANK MELLEN NYE, a Representative from Minnesota, delivered in the House of Representatives, February 22, 1910, in which he pays homage to the life and character of GEORGE WASHINGTON, *the great Father of his Country.*

> *Congressional Record*, V. 45: Part 2, pp. 2228-2230.

THIRD SESSION OF THE SIXTY-FIRST CONGRESS
1910-1911

An address by the HON. MORRIS SHEPPARD, a Representative from Texas, delivered in the House of Representatives, February 22, 1911, in eulogy of GEORGE WASHINGTON, the *great statesman, pre-eminent among the illustrious founders and preservers of States, empires, and nations.*

> *Congressional Record*, V. 46: Part 4, pp. 3130-3131.

SECOND SESSION OF THE SIXTY-SECOND CONGRESS:
1911-1912

Remarks by the HON. JAMES R. MANN, a Representative from Illinois, February 29, 1912, with regard to the reading of GEORGE WASHINGTON's *Farewell Address to the people of the United States* before the House of Representatives on the anniversary of the birth of WASHINGTON.

Congressional Record, V. 48: Part 3, pp. 2640-2641.

An address by the HON. OSCAR W. UNDERWOOD, a Representative from Alabama, delivered, February 22, 1912, at the annual banquet of the Pennsylvania State Society of the Cincinnati, held in Philadelphia, *on* WASHINGTON'S *birthday*—printed in the *Record*, March 8, 1912, by request of the HON. WILLIAM SCHLEY HOWARD, of Georgia.

Congressional Record, V. 48: Part 3, pp. 3056-3059.

Remarks during debate in the Senate, April 15, 1912, on the bill (S. No. 5494) to provide a site for the erection of a building to be known as the *George Washington Memorial Building*.

Congressional Record, V. 48: Part 5, p. 4799:

[*S. Rept. No. 552 . . . . Serial 6121.*]

Hon. George Sutherland, of Utah.
Hon. Lee S. Overman, of North Carolina.
Hon. Augustus O. Bacon, of Georgia.

Remarks during debate in the House of Representatives, May 20, 1912, on the bill (S. No. 5494) to provide a site for the erection of a building to be known as the *George Washington Memorial Building*.

Congressional Record, V. 48: Part 7, pp. 6846-6847:

[*H. Rept. No. 1055 . . . Serial 6133.*]

Hon. James R. Mann, of Illinois.
Hon. Richard W. Austin, of Texas.

Hon. John E. Raker, of California.
Hon. Finis J. Garrett, of Tennessee.

FIRST SESSION OF THE SIXTY-THIRD CONGRESS: 1913

An address by EDWIN D. MEAD, entitled *The Principles of the Founders*, delivered, July 4, 1903, in Faneuil Hall, Boston—and printed in the *Record*, July 13, 1913, by request of the HON. RICHARD BARTOLDT, of Missouri, under the title *Washington, Jefferson, and Franklin on War*.

Congressional Record, V. 50: Appendix, pp. 200-202.

SECOND SESSION OF THE SIXTY-THIRD CONGRESS: 1913-1914

Remarks by the HON. THOMAS R. MARSHALL, Vice President of the United States, February 23, 1914, introductory to the reading, in the Senate, of WASHINGTON'S *Farewell Address to the People of the United States*.

Congressional Record, V. 51: Part 4, p. 3783.

Addresses delivered, October 1, 1914, at the *Washington Monument*, upon the dedication of a memorial stone placed in the Monument by the State of Washington—and printed in the *Record*, October 5, 1914, by request of the HON. MILES POINDEXTER, a Senator from Washington.

Congressional Record, V. 51: Part 16, pp. 16171-16178:

Hon. Franklin K. Lane, Secretary of the Interior.
Colonel William W. Harts, United States Army—Director of the Office of Public Buildings and Public Parks in the National Capital—accepting

ADOPTION OF THE CONSTITUTION BY THE FEDERAL CONVENTION, SEPTEMBER 15, 1787

the memorial stone from the State of Washington. *Hon. Wesley Jones,* a Senator from the State of Washington.

Hon. William E. Humphrey, a Representative from the State of Washington.

Brigadier-General John M. Wilson, United States Army, retired.

Hon. William L. LaFollette, a Representative from the State of Washington.

Hon. James W. Bryan, a Representative from the the State of Washington.

Hon. J. A. Falconer, a Representative from the State of Washington.

Hon. Albert Johnson, a Representative from the State of Washington.

Mr. Frederick L. Harvey, secretary of the Washington National Monument Society.

Hon. Miles Poindexter, a Senator from the State of Washington.

THIRD SESSION OF THE SIXTY-THIRD CONGRESS:
1914-1915

Remarks by the HON. THOMAS R. MARSHALL, Vice-President of the United States, February 22, 1915, introductory to the reading, in the Senate, of GEORGE WASHINGTON's *Farewell Address to the people of the United States on the 17th of September,* 1796.

Congressional Record, V. 52: Part 4, pp. 4260-4261.

Historical account of the authorship of GEORGE WASHINGTON's *Farewell Address to the people of the United States* by the HON. SIMEON D. FESS, a Representative from Ohio—printed in the *Record,* February 22, 1915, by request of the HON. CLARENCE E. MILLER, of Minnesota.

Congressional Record, V. 52: Appendix, pp. 441-443.

Speech by the HON. KENNETH D. MCKELLAR, a Representative from Tennessee, February 22, 1915, on military training schools, reminding Members of the House, on this especial day, that GENERAL WASHINGTON, in one of his addresses, urged the Congress to prepare a better system for training officers—and West Point was created.

Congressional Record, V. 52: Part 4, pp. 4334, 4335-4336.

FIRST SESSION OF THE SIXTY-FOURTH CONGRESS:
1915-1916

An address by the HON. HENRY CABOT LODGE, a Senator from Massachusetts, delivered, February 22, 1916, at Morristown, New Jersey, before the Washington Association of New Jersey, on WASHINGTON's *policies of neutrality and national defense.*

[S. *Doc. No.* 343 . . . . . *Serial* 6952.]

Remarks by the HON. THOMAS R. MARSHALL, Vice-President of the United States, February 22, 1916, introductory to the reading, in the Senate, of WASHINGTON's *Farewell Address to the people of the United States,* September 17, 1796.

Congressional Record, V. 53: Part 3, p. 2922.

Remarks by the HON. JAMES E. MARTINE, a Senator from New Jersey, on Saint Patrick's Day, March 17, 1916—requesting that three *letters written by* GEORGE WASHINGTON *to the Irish people* to be read before the Senate, and printed in the *Record.*

Congressional Record, V. 53: Part 5, pp. 4274-4275.

SECOND SESSION OF THE SIXTY-FOURTH CONGRESS:
1916-1917

Remarks by the HON. BLAIR LEE, a Senator from Maryland, February 22, 1917, calling the attention of Senators to the text of PRESIDENT WASHINGTON's *Farewell Address to the Senate and House, in joint session, December 7, 1796,* dealing exclusively with the question of national defense.

Congressional Record, V. 54: Part 4, p. 3892.

Remarks by the HON. CLAUDE KITCHEN, a Representative from North Carolina, February 17, 1917, requesting unanimous consent that immediately after the reading of the *Journal* on February the 22nd, WASHINGTON's *Farewell Address to the People of the United States, September 17, 1796,* be read before the House by MR. NEELY, a Representative from West Virginia.

Congressional Record, V. 54: Part 4, p. 3541.

An address by the HON. HORACE M. TOWNER, a Representative from Iowa, delivered in the House of Representatives February 22, 1917, on WASHINGTON *and American Neutrality.*

Congressional Record, V. 54: Part 4, pp. 3913-3916.

An address by the HON. WILLIAM H. COLEMAN, a Representative from Pennsylvania, February 22, 1917, entitled *Washington.*

Congressional Record, V. 54: Appendix, pp. 499-503.

FIRST SESSION OF THE SIXTY-FIFTH CONGRESS:
1917

Addresses delivered at the *tomb of* WASHINGTON, April 29, 1917, upon the visit to Mount Vernon of the British and the French War Missions to the United States—printed in the *Record,* March 30, 1917, from a current issue of the *Washington Post,* by request of the HON. W. FRANK JAMES, a Representative from Michigan.

Congressional Record, V. 55: Part 2, pp. 1567-1568:

M. René Viviani, Head of the French War Mission.
M. Joseph Joffre, Marshal of France.
Hon. Arthur James Balfour, Head of the British War Mission.

Hon. Henry Carter Stuart, Governor of Virginia.

An address by M. RENE VIVIANI, May 3, 1917, upon the visit of the French War Commission to the House of Representatives.

Congressional Record, V. 55: Part 2, p. 1755.

Text in French with accompanying translation in English printed in the *Record* by request of the *Secretary of State,* July 7, 1917, Part 4, p. 3274.

An address by M. JUSSERAND, ambassador from France to the United States, May 3, 1917, upon the visit of the French War Commission to the House of Representatives.

Congressional Record, V. 55: Part 2, p. 1755.

An address by the HON. JOSEPHUS DANIELS, Secretary of the Navy, August 26, 1917, delivered at the *tomb of WASHINGTON* upon the visit to Mount Vernon of the Imperial Japanese Mission to the United States.

[S. *Doc. No. 85 . . . . Serial 7265.*]

An address by VISCOUNT ISHII, ambassador extraordinary and plenipotentiary from Japan, 26 August 1917, upon the visit to the *tomb of WASHINGTON* of the Imperial Japanese Mission of the United States.

[S. *Doc. No. 85 . . . . Serial 7265.*]

Address by the HON. CHAMP CLARK, of Missouri, *Speaker* of the House of Representatives, delivered, June 19, 1917, at the dedication of the *Washington Memorial Arch at Valley Forge*, Pennsylvania—printed in the *Record*, June 30, 1917, by request of the HON. HENRY WATSON, of Pennsylvania.

Congressional Record, V. 55: Appendix, pp. 364-367.

Address by the HON. MARTIN G. BRUMBAUGH, Governor of Pennsylvania, delivered, June 19, 1917, at the dedication of the *Washington Memorial Arch at Valley Forge*, Pennsylvania—printed in the *Record*, June 30, 1917, by request of the HON. HENRY W. WATSON, of Pennsylvania.

Congressional Record, V. 55: Appendix, p. 367.

SECOND SESSION OF THE SIXTY-FIFTH CONGRESS:
1917-1918

An address by the HON. WARREN G. HARDING, a Senator from Ohio, delivered, February 22, 1918, at a celebration on WASHINGTON's *Birthday*, held in the city of Washington under the auspices of the Sons of the American Revolution—and printed in the *Record*, February 25, 1918, by request of SENATOR POMERENE, of Ohio; and ordered to be printed as a public document.

Congressional Record, V. 56: Part 3, p. 2586.

[S. *Doc. No. 180 . . . . Serial 7329.*]

An address by the HON. SIMEON D. FESS, a Representative from Ohio, delivered, February 22, 1918, before the House of Representatives on the *birthday anniversary of* GEORGE WASHINGTON.

Congressional Record, V. 56: Part 3, pp. 2524-2527.

An address by the HON. W. FRANK JAMES, a Representative from Michigan, delivered, February 22, 1918, before the Pittsburgh Commercial Club on the *birthday anniversary of* GEORGE WASHINGTON—and printed in the *Record*, March 6, 1918, by request of the HON. M. CLYDE KELLY, of Pennsylvania.

Congressional Record, V. 56: Appendix, pp. 194-199.

An address by the HON. LOUIS W. FAIRFIELD, a Representative from Indiana, delivered, February 22, 1918, at Gettysburg, Pennsylvania, on the *birthday anniversary of* GEORGE WASHINGTON—and printed in the *Record*, March 23, 1918, by request of the HON. WILLIAM R. WOOD, of Indiana.

Congressional Record, V. 56: Appendix, pp. 243-246.

An address by WOODROW WILSON, *President of the United States*, delivered before the Members of the Diplomatic Corps, July 4, 1918, at the *tomb of* GEORGE WASHINGTON *at Mount Vernon* in the State of Virginia.

Congressional Record, V. 56: Part 9, p. 8671.

[S. *Doc. No. 258 . . . . Serial 7330.*]

THIRD SESSION OF THE SIXTY-FIFTH CONGRESS:
1918-1919

An address by the HON. HENRY CABOT LODGE, a Senator from Massachusetts, delivered in the Senate, December 21, 1918, on *The Coming Treaty of Peace*, in which he reviews *the Messages of* PRESIDENT WASHINGTON with regard to the treaty-making power in the United States, the precedent established by him in this respect and followed by Presidents who succeeded him.

Congressional Record, V. 57: Part 1, pp. 728-734.

[S. *Doc. No. 104 . . . . Serial 4230.*]

An address by the HON. HENRY CABOT LODGE, a Senator from Massachusetts, delivered in the Senate, February 28, 1919, on the *Constitution of the League of Nations*, in which he pays homage to GEORGE WASHINGTON as not only a very great man but also very wise, and warns against abandoning the policy laid down by such a man in his *Farewell Address*—a political testament which has been of living force down to the present instant.

Congressional Record, V. 57: Part 5, pp. 4520-4524, 4525-4528.

SECOND SESSION OF THE SIXTY-SIXTH CONGRESS:
1919-1920

An address in the House of Representatives by the HON. JAMES G. MONAHAN, a Representative from Wisconsin, February 23, 1920, in memory of the late MR. LAWRENCE WASHINGTON, a great-great-grandnephew of GENERAL WASHINGTON.

Congressional Record, V. 59: Part 4, pp. 3355-3356.

An address in the House of Representatives by the HON. R. WALTON MOORE, a Representative from Virginia, February 23, 1920, in memory of the late MR. LAWRENCE WASHINGTON, a great-great-grandnephew of GENERAL WASHINGTON.

Congressional Record, V. 59: Part 4, pp. 3356-3357.

An address by the HON. ROSCOE C. McCULLOCH, a Representative from Ohio, February 12, 1920, at Defiance, Ohio—printed in the *Record*, March 4, 1920, by request of MR. KEARNS, a Representative from Ohio.

Congressional Record, V. 59: Appendix, pp. 8892-8893.

THIRD SESSION OF THE SIXTY-SIXTH CONGRESS:
1920-1921

An address by the HON. PHILIP P. CAMPBELL, a Representative from Kansas, delivered in the House of Representatives, February 22, 1921, on *Government under the Constitution of the United States*.

Congressional Record, V. 60: Part 4, pp. 3621-3623.

SECOND SESSION OF THE SIXTY-SEVENTH CONGRESS: 1921-1922

Remarks by the HON. HAMILTON FISH, JR., a Representative from New York, February 22, 1922, calling the attention of Members of the House to the views of GEORGE WASHINGTON on the subject of adjusted compensation for the officers and men of the Revolutionary Army.

Congressional Record, V. 62: Part 3, p. 2908.

An address by the HON. HENRY W. WATSON, a Representative from Pennsylvania, delivered, February 22, 1922, before the House of Representatives, on the *Battle of Trenton* and GENERAL WASHINGTON'S *conduct of the campaign leading to that engagement.*

Congressional Record, V. 62: Part 3, pp. 2900-2902.

Remarks by the HON. R. WALTON MOORE, a Representative from Virginia, February 22, 1922, relative to the resolution (S. J. Res. No. 137) transferring to the Smithsonian Institution *the sword of* WASHINGTON, *the staff which* FRANKLIN *gave to* WASHINGTON, *and the sword of* ANDREW JACKSON.

. . . .

Text of an address by the HON. GEORGE W. SUMMERS, a Representative from Virginia, delivered, February 7, 1843, in the House of Representatives, upon the presentation to the United States Government of WASHINGTON's *sword and* FRANKLIN's *staff*—reprinted in the Record, February 22, 1922, by request of the HON. R. WALTON MOORE, as part of his remarks.

. . . .

Text of an address by the HON. LEWIS CASS, a Senator from Michigan, delivered in the Senate, February 26, 1855, in which he pays tribute to GENERAL WASHINGTON "who in life was first in the affections of his countrymen and in death is now first in their memory"—reprinted in the *Record,* February 22, 1922, by request of the HON. R. WALTON MOORE as part of his remarks.

Congressional Record, V. 62: Part 3, pp. 2906-2908.

Speech by the HON. THOMAS E. WATSON, a Senator from Georgia, delivered, June 21, 1922, in the United States Senate, on the *Attitude of* GEORGE WASHINGTON *toward a bonus for soldiers.*

Congressional Record, V. 62: Part 9, p. 9100.

FOURTH SESSION OF THE SIXTY-SEVENTH CONGRESS: 1922-1923

Remarks in the House of Representatives by the HON. SCHUYLER O. BLAND, a Representative from Virginia, February 22, 1923, in the interest of the restoration of Kenmore, the home of BETTY LEWIS, *sister of* GEORGE WASHINGTON.

Congressional Record, V. 64: Part 4, pp. 4269-4270.

Speech by the HON. FREDERICK C. HICKS, a Representative from New York, delivered, February 24, 1923, in the House of Representatives, on behalf of the *George Washington Memorial Association.*

Congressional Record, V. 64, Part 5, pp. 4556-4559.

An address by the HON. ANDREW J. MONTAGUE, a Representative from Virginia, delivered, February 22, 1923, at the *Washington Day exercises* at the *University of Pennsylvania*—printed in the *Record,* March 3, 1923, by request of the HON. H. GARLAND DUPRE, of Louisiana.

Congressional Record, V. 64, Part 6, pp. 5524-5526.

FIRST SESSION OF THE SIXTY-EIGHTH CONGRESS: 1923-1924

An address by the HON. B. G. LOWREY, a Representative from Mississippi, delivered, February 22, 1924, at the Masonic Temple in Washington, District of Columbia, on the subject *George Washington the Citizen*—printed in the *Record,* February 23, 1924, by request of the HON. JAMES W. COLLIER, of Mississippi.

Congressional Record, V. 65, Part 3, pp. 2973-2974.

An address by the HON. ROYAL S. COPELAND, a Senator from New York, delivered, February 22, 1924, at Memorial Hall in Washington, District of Columbia, on the subject *George Washington, First in Peace*—printed in the *Record,* March 14, 1924, by request of SENATOR ROBINSON, of Arkansas.

Congressional Record, V. 65: Part 4, pp. 4122-4124.

Speech by the HON. SCHUYLER O. BLAND, a Representative from Virginia, delivered, March 28, 1924, during debate in the House on the War Department Appropriations bill (H.R. 7877), relative to the appropriation for repair and maintenance of *Wakefield, Virginia, the birthplace of* GEORGE WASHINGTON.

Congressional Record, V. 65: Part 5, p. 5185.

Addresses delivered, April 15, 1924, at the *Washington Monument* upon the dedication of a memorial stone placed in the Monument by the State of Arizona—and printed in the *Record,* April 23, 1924, by request of SENATOR CAMERON, of Arizona:

Congressional Record, V. 65: Part 7, pp. 6973-6975.

Hon. *Ralph H. Cameron,* a Senator from Arizona.

Mrs. *Hoval A. Smith,* State regent, Arizona, Daughters of the American Revolution—presenting the memorial stone on behalf of the State of Arizona.

Lieut.-Colonel *Clarence O. Sherrill,* United States Army—Director of the Office of Public Buildings and Public Parks in the National Capital.

Hon. *Henry F. Ashurst,* a Senator from Arizona.

Mrs. *Anthony Wayne Cook,* President-General of the National Society of the Daughters of the American Revolution.

Hon. *Carl Hayden,* a Representative from Arizona.

Calvin Coolidge, President of the United States.

SECOND SESSION OF THE SIXTY-EIGHTH CONGRESS: 1924-1925

An address by the HON. FREDERICK W. DALLINGER, a Representative from Massachusetts, delivered, February 21, 1925, in Pittsburgh, Pennsylvania, before the Pennsylvania State Society of the Sons of the American Revolution, *at a celebration of the birthday anniversary of* GEORGE WASHING-

TON—and printed in the *Record*, February 23, 1925, by request of the HON. M. CLYDE KELLY, of Pennsylvania.

Congressional Record, V. 66: Part 5, pp. 4443-4445.

An address by the HON. R. WALTON MOORE, a Representative from Virginia, delivered, February 21, 1925, in Pittsburgh, Pennsylvania, at the *annual Washington banquet of the Sons of the American Revolution*—and printed in the *Record*, February 23, 1925, by request of the HON. M. CLYDE KELLY, of Pennsylvania.

Congressional Record, V. 66: Part 5, pp. 4445-4447.

An address by the HON. JAMES M. BECK, Solicitor-General of the United States, delivered, February 23, 1925, in Carnegie Hall, New York City, *at the celebration of the birthday anniversary of* GEORGE WASHINGTON—and printed in the *Record*, February 24, 1925, by request of SENATOR MOSES, of New Hampshire.

Congressional Record, V. 66: Part 5, pp. 4544-4547.

Remarks by the HON. MAURICE THATCHER, a Representative from Kentucky, February 26, 1925, in the House of Representatives, requesting that a *letter written, May 5, 1789, by* GEORGE WASHINGTON *to* EDWARD RUTLEDGE, of South Carolina, on Presidential patronage be printed in the *Record*.

Congressional Record, V. 66: Part 5, pp. 4742-4743.

FIRST SESSION OF THE SIXTY-NINTH CONGRESS:
1925-1926

An address by CALVIN COOLIDGE, President of the United States, on the subject *George Washington: A Great Teacher*, delivered, February 22, 1926, in the city of Washington, before the Department of Superintendence of the National Education Association—printed in the *Record*, February 23, 1926, by request of SENATOR FESS, of Ohio; and ordered to be printed as a public document.

Congressional Record, V. 67: Part 4, pp. 4370-4373.
[*S. Doc. No.* 68 . . . . *Serial* 8557.]

Remarks in the Senate by the HON. COLE L. BLEASE, a Senator from South Carolina, February 22, 1926, requesting that an editorial from the *Washington Herald on* GEORGE WASHINGTON, be printed in the *Record*.

Congressional Record, V. 67: Part 4, p. 4330.

Remarks in the Senate by the HON. J. THOMAS HEFLIN, a Senator from Alabama, February 22, 1926, requesting that a poem by HORACE C. CARLISLE, entitled *Washington*, be printed in the *Record*.

Congressional Record, V. 67: Part 4, p. 4329.

Remarks in the House of Representatives by the HON. WILLIAM D. UPSHAW, of Georgia, February 22, 1926, requesting that a place be given in the *Record* for the printing of a *general order issued by* GENERAL GEORGE WASHINGTON, *in New York, July, 1776, against profanity in the Army*.

Congressional Record, V. 67: Part 4, p. 4367.

Remarks in the House of Representatives by the HON. EMANUEL CELLER, of New York, March 24, 1926, during which he refers to GEORGE WASHINGTON as represented by Paul Leicester Ford in his book "The True George Washington".

Congressional Record, V. 67: Part 6, pp. 6186-6187.

SECOND SESSION OF THE SIXTY-NINTH CONGRESS:
1926-1927

Remarks by the HON. WILLIS C. HAWLEY, a Representative from Oregon, January 29, 1927, upon submitting to the House of Representatives on behalf of the Bi-Centennial Commission a resolution (H.Con.Res. No. 49) providing that, on the following 22nd day of February, the *President of the United States* address the two Houses of Congress, in joint session, on the subject: GEORGE WASHINGTON.

Congressional Record, V. 68: Part 3, pp. 2550-2551.

An address by CALVIN COOLIDGE, President of the United States, on GEORGE WASHINGTON—delivered, February 22, 1927, in the Hall of Representatives, before the two Houses of Congress, the Supreme Court of the United States, Members of the Cabinet, the Chief Naval officer, the Chief-of-Staff, Commandant of Marines, the Diplomatic Corps, and descendants of the family of GEORGE WASHINGTON.

Congressional Record, V. 68: Part 4, pp. 4457-4459.
[*S. Doc. No.* 249 . . . . *Serial* 8709.]

An address by the HON. EMANUEL CELLER, a Representative from New York, delivered by radio, February 21, 1927, on the *True* GEORGE WASHINGTON—and printed in the *Record*, February 22, 1927, under extension of remarks.

Congressional Record, V. 68: Part 4, pp. 4492-4493.

Remarks by the HON. LUTHER A. JOHNSON, a Representative from Texas, February 22, 1927, in the House of Representatives—requesting that place be given in the *Record* for an editorial from the *London Times* of November 9, 1796, announcing the contemplated retirement of GEORGE WASHINGTON *as President of the United States of America*.

Congressional Record, V. 68: Part 4, p. 4466.

FIRST SESSION OF THE SEVENTIETH CONGRESS:
1927-1928

An address by the HON. SIMEON D. FESS, a Senator from Ohio, February 22, 1928, in Alexandria, Virginia, *at the celebration of the anniversary of the birth of* GEORGE WASHINGTON—printed in the *Record*, February 28, 1928, by request of SENATOR CAPPER, of Kansas.

Congressional Record, V. 69: Part 4, pp. 3668-3669.

Remarks by the HON. R. WALTON MOORE, a Representative from Virginia, February 10, 1928, in the House of Representatives, relative *to the celebration*, in *Alexandria, Virginia, on the anniversary of the birth of* GEORGE WASHINGTON.

Congressional Record, V. 69: Part 3, pp. 2847-2848.

An address by the HON. RICHARD YATES, a Representative from Illinois, February 22, 1928, before the Association of Oldest Inhabitants of the District of Columbia, on *the anniversary of the birth of* GEORGE WASHINGTON—printed in the *Record* under extension of remarks.

Congressional Record, V. 69: Part 3, pp. 3450-3454.

An address by the HON. WILLIAM TYLER PAGE, Clerk of the House of Representatives, delivered by radio, February 22, 1928, *on the celebration of the two hundredth anniversary of the birth of* GEORGE WASHINGTON—and printed in the *Record*, March 23, 1928, by request of the HON. WILLIS C. HAWLEY, of Oregon.

Congressional Record, V. 69: Part 5, pp. 5243-5244.

Remarks by the HON. BUTLER B. HARE, a Representative from South Carolina, March 29, 1928, in the House of Representatives, relative to the bequest made by GEORGE WASHINGTON for the founding of a national university in the District of Columbia.

Congressional Record, V. 69: Part 5, p. 5595.

SECOND SESSION OF THE SEVENTIETH CONGRESS: 1928-1929

An address by the HON. JAMES M. BECK, a Representative from Pennsylvania, February 22, 1929, before the House of Representatives, on the *Political Philosophy of* GEORGE WASHINGTON.

Congressional Record, V. 70: Part 4, pp. 4053-4057.

[H. Doc. No. 611 . . . . Serial 9021.]

An address by the HON. R. WALTON MOORE, a Representative from Virginia, October 14, 1928, in Alexandria, Virginia, at the unveiling of a monument to DR. JAMES CRAIK, *the physician and friend of* GEORGE WASHINGTON—printed in the *Record*, February 22, 1929, by request of the HON. JOHN W. SUMMERS, of the State of Washington.

Congressional Record, V. 70: Part 4, pp. 4062-4063.

An address by CALVIN COOLIDGE, *President of the United States*, delivered, February 22, 1929, at the Washington Auditorium, *on the Life of* GEORGE WASHINGTON—printed in the *Record*, February 25, 1929, by request of SENATOR FESS, of Ohio.

Congressional Record, V. 70: Part 4, pp. 4103-4105.

An address by the HON. NICHOLAS LONGWORTH, *Speaker of the House of Representatives*, delivered, February 22, 1929, at the University of Pennsylvania, on GEORGE WASHINGTON *and the Effect of his Example and Precepts upon the Government of the United States To-day*—printed in the *Record*, February 25, 1929, by request of the HON. JOHN Q. TILSON, of Connecticut.

Congressional Record, V. 70: Part 4, pp. 4253-4255.

An address by the HON. JAMES HAMILTON LEWIS, of Illinois, delivered, February 22, 1929, at Poli's Theater in the City of Washington, on *the Life and Achievements of* GEORGE WASHINGTON—printed in the *Record*, February 27, 1929, by request of SENATOR HARRISON, of Mississippi.

Congressional Record, V. 70: Part 5, pp. 4504-4505.

An address by MR. FRANKLIN FORD, of New York, delivered by radio, February 22, 1929, on *the Anniversary of the birth of* GEORGE WASHINGTON—printed in the *Record*, February 27, 1929, by request of SENATOR HEFLIN, of Alabama.

Congressional Record, V. 70: Part 5, pp. 4494-4496.

An address by the HON. CHARLES E. WINTER, a Representative from Wyoming, delivered, February 25, 1929, in the House of Representatives, on the subject *Washington, Lincoln, and our National Life*—printed in the *Record* under extension of remarks.

Congressional Record, V. 70: Part 4, pp. 4251-4253.

Article by the HON. JOHN E. RANKIN, a Representative from Mississippi, entitled *Foch at the Tomb of Washington*—printed in the *Record*, March 4, 1929, under extension of remarks.

Congressional Record, V. 70: Part 5, pp. 5233-5234.

FIRST SESSION OF THE SEVENTY-FIRST CONGRESS: 1929

An address by the HON. SIMEON D. FESS, a Senator from Ohio, delivered by radio, September 7, 1929, on the GEORGE WASHINGTON *Bi-Centennial Celebration*—and printed in the *Record*, September 9, 1929, by request of SENATOR CAPPER, of Kansas.

Congressional Record, V. 71: Part 3, pp. 3413-3418.

SECOND SESSION OF THE SEVENTY-FIRST CONGRESS: 1929-1930

Speech by the HON. CLAUDE A. SWANSON, a Senator from Virginia, during debate in the Senate, December 19, 1929, on the bill (S. No. 1784) appropriating money for improvements upon Government-owned land at *Wakefield, Westmoreland County, Virginia, the birthplace of* GEORGE WASHINGTON.

Congressional Record, V. 72: Part 1, p. 955.

Remarks by the HON. SIMEON D. FESS, a Senator from Ohio, during debate in the Senate, February 1, 1930, and February 8, 1930, on the bill (S. No. 3398) providing for the publication of the *Writings of George Washington* as a memorial in connection with the George Washington Bi-Centennial Commission.

Congressional Record, V. 72: Part 3, pp. 2812-2813; Part 3, pp. 3278-3279.

An address by the HON. GUY D. GOFF, a Senator from West Virginia, delivered at Clarksburg, West Virginia, February 22, 1930, before the State Society of the Sons of the Revolution on the subject *The Voice of Washington*—printed in the *Record*, February 24, 1930, by request of SENATOR HATFIELD, of West Virginia.

Congressional Record, V. 72: Part 4, pp. 4133-4135.

An address by the HON. SAMUEL M. SHORTRIDGE, a Senator from California, delivered in the city of Washington, February 22, 1930, before the Federal Bar Association—and printed in the *Record*, February 27, 1930, by request of SENATOR ASHURST, of Arizona.

Congressional Record, V. 72: Part 4, pp. 4340-4342.

. . . .

Remarks during debate in the House of Representatives, December 21, 1929, and January 20, 1930, on the bill (S. No. 1784) authorizing an appropriation for improvements upon the Government-owned land at *Wakefield, Westmoreland County, Virginia, the birthplace of* GEORGE WASHINGTON.

Congressional Record, V. 72: Part 1, pp. 1078-1081; Part 2, pp. 1991-1995:

Hon. Schuyler O. Bland, of Virginia.

Hon. *Louis Cramton*, of Michigan.
Hon. *J. Mayhew Wainwright*, of New York.
Hon. *William H. Stafford*, of Wisconsin.
Hon. *R. Walton Moore*, of Virginia.
Hon. *Arthur H. Greenwood*, of Indiana.
Hon. *Robert Luce*, of Massachusetts.

Remarks by the HON. JOHN Q. TILSON, a Representative from Connecticut, during debate in the House of Representatives, February 18, 1930, on the bill (S. No. 3398) providing for the publication of the *Writings of George Washington* as a memorial in connection with the George Washington Bi-Centennial Commission.

> *Congressional Record*, V. 72: Part 4, pp. 3898, 3899, 3900.

An address by the HON. JOHN J. McSWAIN, a Representative from South Carolina, delivered in the House of Representatives, February 13, 1930, on the subject *Washington on National Defense; as revealed in an unpublished manuscript submitted by* GENERAL WASHINGTON *to the Congress, May 2, 1783, before the demobilization of the Revolutionary Army.*

> *Congressional Record*, V. 72: Part 4, pp. 3630-3631.

An address by the HON. JOHN Q. TILSON, Representative from Connecticut, delivered in the House of Representatives, February 22, 1930, on the *George Washington Bi-Centennial Celebration.*

> *Congressional Record*, V. 72: Part 4, p. 4104.

Speech in the House of Representatives by the HON. WILLIAM TYLER PAGE, Clerk of the House, February 22, 1930, on the *plans approved and proposed for the George Washington Bi-Centennial Celebration.*

> *Congressional Record*, V. 72: Part 4, pp. 4104-4108.

An address by the HON. R. WALTON MOORE, Representative from Virginia, delivered in the House of Representatives, February 22, 1930, on *Some Work of* WASHINGTON *in his Home County.*

> *Congressional Record*, V. 72: Part 4, 4108-4111.

An address by the HON. C. ELLIS MOORE, Representative from Ohio, delivered in House of Representatives, February 22, 1930, on WASHINGTON *as a Pioneer.*

> *Congressional Record*, V. 72: Part 4, pp. 4111-4112.

An address by the HON. JOHN J. McSWAIN, Representative from South Carolina, delivered in the House of Representatives, February 22, 1930, on WASHINGTON *as a Soldier.*

> *Congressional Record*, V. 72: Part 4, pp. 4112-4114.

An address by the HON. ROBERT LUCE, Representative from Massachusetts, delivered in the House of Representatives, February 22, 1930, on WASHINGTON *and the Constitution.*

> *Congressional Record*, V. 72: Part 4, pp. 4114-4116.

An address by the HON. LOUIS CRAMTON, Representative from Michigan, delivered in the House of Representatives, February 22, 1930, on WASHINGTON *and the Potomac.*

> *Congressional Record*, V. 72: Part 4, pp. 4116-4119.

An address by the HON. CHARLES H. SLOAN, Representative from Nebraska, delivered in the House of Representatives, February 22, 1930, on WASHINGTON *the Business Farmer.*

> *Congressional Record*, V. 72: Part 4, pp. 4120-4121.

An address by the HON. HENRY W. TEMPLE, Representative from Pennsylvania, delivered in the House of Representatives, February 22, 1930, on WASHINGTON'S *Place among his Contemporaries.*

> *Congressional Record*, V. 72: Part 4, pp. 4121-4122.

An address by the HON. MANUEL ROXAS, *Speaker* of the Philippine House of Representatives, delivered by radio, February 22, 1930, as a tribute to the memory of GEORGE WASHINGTON, *the great American liberator*—printed in the *Record*, February 27, 1930, by request of the HON. CAMILO OSIAS, Resident Commissioner from the Philippine Islands.

> *Congressional Record*, V. 72: Part 4, pp. 4423-4424.

An address by the HON. ROSCOE POUND, dean of the Law School, Harvard University, February 22, 1930, delivered at the tenth anniversary dinner of the Federal Bar Association, in the city of Washington, on the subject of WASHINGTON'S *Birthday Memorial*—and printed in the *Record*, March 18, 1930, by request of the HON. GEORGE R. STOBBS, a Representative from Massachusetts.

> *Congressional Record*, V. 72: Part 5, pp. 5533-5535.

An address by the HON. THOMAS A. YON, Representative from Florida, delivered, February 28, 1930, at Seat Pleasant, Maryland, on the subject GEORGE WASHINGTON *as Soldier, Statesman, and Mason*—printed in the *Record*, March 7, 1930, by request of the HON. JAMES V. McCLINTIC, *of* Oklahoma.

> *Congressional Record*, V. 72: Part 5, pp. 4981-4982.

An address by the HON. SOL BLOOM, Representative from New York, delivered by radio, June 12, 1930, on the *George Washington Bi-Centennial Celebration in* 1932—and printed in the *Record*, June 16, under extension of remarks.

> *Congressional Record*, V. 72: Part 10, pp. 10934-10936.

An address by the HON. R. WALTON MOORE, of Virginia, delivered in the House of Representatives, June 20, 1930, on GEORGE WASHINGTON'S *Boyhood Home.*

> *Congressional Record*, V. 72: Part 10, pp. 11344-11345.

THIRD SESSION OF THE SEVENTY-FIRST CONGRESS: 1930-1931

An address by the HON. SCHUYLER O. BLAND, a Representative from Virginia, delivered at Richmond, Virginia, on the subject WASHINGTON *the Lover of Trees*—and printed in the *Record*, December 15, 1930, under extension of remarks.

> *Congressional Record*, V. 74: Part 1, pp. 732-734.

An address by the HON. FRANK M. RAMEY, a Representative from Illinois, delivered by radio, February 19, 1931, on the subject WASHINGTON AND LINCOLN—and printed in the *Record*, February 24, 1931, under extension of remarks.

> *Congressional Record*, V. 74: Part 6, pp. 5862-5864.

An address by the HON. JAMES M. BECK, a Representative from Pennsylvania, delivered in the House of Representatives, February 23, 1931, on the subject WASHINGTON's *Conception of the Union.*

> *Congressional Record,* V. 74: Part 6, pp. 5735-5741. [*H. Doc. No.* 792 . . . . *Serial* 9367.]

The address by the HON. ALBEN W. BARKLEY, a Senator from Kentucky, delivered in the Senate, February 23, 1931, on the subject WASHINGTON *and his Contemporaries.*

> *Congressional Record,* V. 74: Part 6, pp. 5693-5695.

An address by the HON. WILLIAM BORAH, a Senator from Idaho, delivered in the Senate, February 23, 1931, on the subject WASHINGTON's *Attitude toward the French Revolution.*

> *Congressional Record,* V. 74: Part 6, pp. 5695-5696.

An address by the HON. THOMAS CAMPBELL WASHINGTON, great-great-great-grandnephew of GENERAL WASHINGTON, delivered by radio, February 23, 1931, on the subject GEORGE WASHINGTON: *His Farewell Address, and its Applicability to Present-Day Conditions*—printed in the *Record,* February 28, 1931, by request of SENATOR MCKELLAR, of Tennessee.

> *Congressional Record,* V. 74: Part 7, pp. 6469-6470.

Remarks by the HON. CLAUDE A. SWANSON, a Senator from Virginia, February 23, 1931, requesting that a poem by Horace C. Carlisle, entitled *Wakefield* be printed in the *Record.*

> *Congressional Record,* V. 74: Part 6, p. 5697.

Speech by the HON. SCHUYLER O. BLAND, a Representative from Virginia, March 2, 1931, in the House of Representatives, on the work of the *Wakefield Memorial Association in the restoration of the birthplace of* GENERAL WASHINGTON.

> *Congressional Record,* V. 74: Part 7, pp. 6882-6883.

An address by HERBERT HOOVER, President of the United States, May 30, 1931, at *Valley Forge, Pennsylvania,* on the subject *The Moral Grandeur of* GENERAL WASHINGTON.

> [Printed separately, G. P. O. 1931.]

FIRST SESSION OF THE SEVENTY-SECOND CONGRESS: 1931-1932

An address by the HON. CHARLES CURTIS, *Vice-President of the United States,* delivered January 26, 1932, at a meeting in the city of Washington of the Washington Chamber of Commerce—printed in the *Record,* January 27, 1932, by request of the HON. SIMEON D. FESS, a Senator from Ohio.

> *Congressional Record,* V. 75: Part 3, p. 2770.

Speech by the HON. SIMEON D. FESS, a Senator from Ohio, January 16, 1932, upon submitting to the Senate a report on the progress of the *Washington Bicentennial celebration* to be held this year, beginning on the 22nd of February.

> *Congressional Record,* V. 75: Part 2, pp. 2100-2102, 2103-2104.

Remarks by the HON. JAMES E. WATSON, a Senator from Indiana, February 19, 1932, relative to arrangements for the joint session of the two Houses of Congress in commemoration of the *two hundredth anniversary of the birth of* GEORGE WASHINGTON.

> *Congressional Record,* V. 75: Part 4, p. 4335; February 22, 1932, Part 4, p. 4448.

Remarks during debate in the Senate, January 16, 1932, on that clause of the Deficiency Appropriations bill (H. R. 6660) which provides an additional amount for the *George Washington Bi-Centennial Commission* . . .

> *Congressional Record,* V. 75: Part 2, pp. 2117-2119:
>
> > Hon. *Royal S. Copeland,* a Senator from New York.
> > Hon. *Millard E. Tydings,* a Senator from Maryland.
> > Hon. *Wesley L. Jones,* a Senator from Washington.
> > Hon. *Ellison D. Smith,* a Senator from South Carolina.

. . . .

Remarks during debate in the House of Representatives, January 4th and January 5th, 1932, on that clause of the Deficiency Appropriations bill (H. R. No. 6660) which provides an additional amount for the *George Washington Bicentennial Commission.*

> *Congressional Record,* V. 75: Part 2, pp. 1227-1231; 1324-1332:
>
> > Hon. *Sol Bloom,* a Representative from New York.
> > Hon. *Joseph W. Byrns,* a Representative from Tennessee.
> > Hon. *George Huddleston,* a Representative from Alabama.
> > Hon. *F. H. LaGuardia,* a Representative from New York.
> > Hon. *L. C. Dyer,* a Representative from Missouri.
> > Hon. *William H. Stafford,* a Representative from Wisconsin.
> > Hon. *Earl C. Michener,* a Representative from Michigan.
> > Hon. *A. T. Treadway,* a Representative from Massachusetts.
> > Hon. *James M. Beck,* a Representative from Pennsylvania.
> > Hon. *Charles L. Abernethy,* a Representative from North Carolina.
> > Hon. *U. S. Guyer,* a Representative from Kansas.

An address by the HON. M. CLYDE KELLY, a Representative from Pennsylvania, delivered in Alexandria, Virginia, December 14, 1931, at ceremonies held under the auspices of the Washington Society of Alexandria in commemoration of the *two hundred and first birthday anniversary of* DR. JAMES CRAIK, *friend of* GEORGE WASHINGTON—printed in the *Record,* December 21, 1931, by request of the HON. WILLIAM R. COYLE, a Representative from Pennsylvania.

> *Congressional Record,* V. 75: Part 1, pp. 1018-1019.

Speech by the HON. DANIEL A. REED, a Representative from New York, delivered in the House of Representatives, December 17, 1931, on certain charges made against GEORGE

WASHINGTON in 1794 that may cause men in high places to reflect upon their responsibilities as representatives of the people.

Congressional Record, V. 75: Part 1, pp. 731-732.

An address by the HON. SOL BLOOM, *Associate Director of the United States George Washington Bi-centennial Commission,* delivered by radio, January 1, 1932, from the home of MARY BALL WASHINGTON, *the mother of* GEORGE WASHINGTON, at Fredericksburg, Virginia—printed in the *Record,* February 23, 1932, under extension of remarks.

Congressional Record, V. 75: Part 4, pp. 4523-4524.

An address by the HON. SOL BLOOM, *Associate Director of the United States George Washington Bi-centennial Commission,* delivered by radio, January 1, 1932, to the people of Somerville, Massachusetts, in connection with the *George Washington Bi-centennial Celebration*—printed in the *Record,* July 15, 1932, under extension of remarks.

Congressional Record, V. 75: Part 14, pp. 15547-15548.

Speech by the HON. JAMES M. BECK, a Representative from Pennsylvania, delivered in the House of Representatives, January 18, 1932, on *Benjamin Franklin, greatest con-*

temporary of GEORGE WASHINGTON, *and his contribution to the foundation of the American commonwealth.*

Congressional Record, V. 75: Part 2, pp. 2169-2172.

Statement by DR. GEORGE C. HAVENNER, *Executive Vice-Chairman of the District of Columbia Commission, George Washington Bi-centennial,* relative to the program for the observance, in the National Capital, of the *bi-centennial of* GEORGE WASHINGTON'S *birth*—printed in the *Record,* January 11, 1932, by request of the HON. GORDON BROWNING, a Representative from Tennessee.

Congressional Record, V. 75: Part 2, pp. 1720-1727.

Statement by the HON. CLIFTON A. WOODRUM, a Representative from Virginia, January 20, 1932, upon submitting to the House of Representatives, on behalf of the Joint Committee, the *Order of Arrangements* for ceremonies on the part of the United States Congress, February 22, 1932, in commemoration of the *two-hundredth anniversary of the birth of* GEORGE WASHINGTON—printed in the *Record,* January 20, 1932, under extension of remarks.

Congressional Record, V. 75: Part 3, pp. 2342-2343.

An address by the HON. SOL BLOOM, *Associate Director of the United States George Washington Bi-centennial Commission,* delivered by radio from *Pohick Church* in Virginia,

FINAL INAUGURAL ADDRESS OF GEORGE WASHINGTON, AT FEDERAL HALL, NEW YORK CITY, APRIL 30, 1789

February 21, 1932, on *Sunday Reflections at Old Pohick Church where* GEORGE WASHINGTON *and his Family Worshipped*—printed in the *Record*, February 23, 1932, under extension of remarks.

Congressional Record, V. 75: Part 4, pp. 4524-4525.

Addresses in Commemoration of the Two-Hundredth Anniversary of the Birth of George Washington, February 22, 1932, in Joint Session of the House and Senate:

Introductory address by the HON. SIMEON D. FESS, *Vice-Chairman of the United States George Washington Bi-centennial Commission,* upon presenting the *President of the United States.*

Congressional Record, V. 75: Part 4, p. 4449.

An address by HERBERT HOOVER, *President of the United States,* paying homage to GEORGE WASHINGTON, upon the bicentennial of his birthday, as one who contributed more to the origins of this mighty Nation than any other man, and the influence of whose character and achievements has contributed to the building of human freedom throughout the world.

Congressional Record, V. 75: Part 4, pp. 4449-4451.

Addresses in Commemoration of the Two-Hundredth Anniversary of the Birth of George Washington, February 22, 1932, at the East Front of the United States Capitol:

Address of welcome delivered by DR. LUTHER H. REICHELDERFER, *president of the Board of Commissioners of the District of Columbia,* before the throng attending the ceremonial in honor of WASHINGTON's *birthday.*

Congressional Record, V. 75: Part 4, pp. 4451-4552.

An address by the HON. JAMES M. BECK, a Representative from Pennsylvania, paying homage to GEORGE WASHINGTON, upon the bi-centennial of his birthday, as the founder of this great Republic, which is his noblest monument, and which will remain as long as his people are faithful to his ideals of government.

Congressional Record, V. 75: Part 4, pp. 4552-4553.

Other Tributes in Commemoration of the Two-Hundredth Anniversary of the Birth of George Washington:

An article by CALVIN COOLIDGE, *former President of the United States,* published in the *Philadelphia Inquirer,* February 21, 1932, on the genius of GEORGE WASHINGTON in business and practical affairs—printed in the *Record,* February 22, 1932, by request of the HON. BERTRAND H. SNELL, a Representative from New York.

Congressional Record, V. 75: Part 4, pp. 4453-4455.

A tribute to the character and the achievements of GEORGE WASHINGTON by LORD BROUGHAM—read into the *Record,* February 23, 1932, by request of the HON. WILLIAM E. BORAH, a Senator from Idaho.

Congressional Record, V. 75: Part 4, pp. 4479-4480.

An address by DANIEL WEBSTER, a Senator from Massachusetts, delivered at a public dinner in the city of Washington, February 22, 1832, in honor of the *one-hundredth birthday* of GEORGE WASHINGTON—printed in the *Record,*

February 23, 1932, by request of the HON. SIMEON D. FESS, a Senator from Ohio.

Congressional Record, V. 75: Part 4, pp. 4480-4482.

An address by the HON. DAVID I. WALSH, a Senator from Massachusetts, delivered at Wakefield and Somerville in Massachusetts, February 22, 1932, upon the occasion of the official opening of the *bi-centennial celebration of* GEORGE WASHINGTON's *birth*—printed in the *Record,* March 24, 1932, by request of the HON. SIMEON D. FESS, a Senator from Ohio.

Congressional Record, V. 75: Part 6, pp. 6784-6786.

. . . .

An address by the HON. SOL BLOOM, *Associate Director of the United States George Washington Bi-centennial Commission,* delivered by radio from Washington, February 23, 1932, upon the formal opening of the *George Washington* bi-centennial celebration—printed in the *Record,* under the extension of remarks.

Congressional Record, V. 75: Part 4, pp. 4525-4526; Part 14, p. 15543.

An address by the HON. ALLEN T. TREADWAY, a Representative from Massachusetts, February 22, 1932, at Alexandria-Washington Lodge No. 22, A. F. and A. M., at Alexandria, Virginia, on the *Opinions of great Men about* WASHINGTON *and his Life as a Mason*—printed in the *Record,* February 23, 1932, by request of the HON. CLIFTON A. WOODRUM, a Representative from Virginia, under extension of remarks.

Congressional Record, V. 75: Part 4, pp. 4517-4519.

An address by MR. JOHN H. NEWVAHNER, entitled *George Washington the Mason,* delivered, February 22, 1932, at the Masonic Banquet in Jackson, Ohio—printed in the *Record,* July 7, 1932, by request of the HON. THOMAS A. JENKINS, a Representative from Ohio.

Congressional Record, V. 75: Part 13, pp. 14828-14830.

An address by the HON. WILLIAM N. ROGERS, a Representative from New Hampshire, delivered before the New England Society, in the city of Washington, February 22, 1932, on GEORGE WASHINGTON *the Statesman*—printed in the *Record,* February 23, 1932, under extension of remarks.

Congressional Record, V. 75: Part 4, p. 4513.

An address by the HON. CAMILO OSIAS, Resident-Commissioner from the Philippine Islands, entitled *"If Washington were here,"* delivered before the Maryland State Society of the Sons of the American Revolution, February 22, 1932, at a dinner in Baltimore, in commemoration of the *two-hundredth anniversary of* WASHINGTON's *birthday*—printed in the *Record,* February 23, 1932, by request of the HON. J. CHARLES LINTHICUM, a Representative from Maryland.

Congressional Record, V. 75: Part 4, pp. 4513-4515.

An address in the House of Representatives by the HON. SOL BLOOM, *Associate Director of the United States George Washington Bi-centennial Commission,* February 23, 1932, in *Explanation of the Date and Day of* GEORGE WASHINGTON's *Birth,* February 11, 1731, *and how it corresponds with February 22, 1932, the Date we Celebrate*—printed in the *Record*, March 12, 1932, under extension of remarks.

> *Congressional Record*, V. 75: Part 4, p. 4526.

Tributes throughout the Union on dates other than the twenty-second of February recorded in the Official Proceedings of the United States Congress in Commemoration of the Bi-centennial of the Birth of George Washington:

An article by the HON. R. WALTON MOORE, a former Member of the House of Representatives from the State of Virginia, published in the March issue of the *Journal of the American Bar Association* under the title GEORGE WASHINGTON *as a Judge*—printed in the *Record*, March 4, 1932, by request of the HON. SIMEON D. FESS, a Senator from Ohio.

> *Congressional Record*, V. 75: Part 5, pp. 5236-5238.
> [*Journal of the American Bar Association*, V. XVIII:
> No. 3, pp. 151-155.]

Remarks in the Senate by the HON. SIMEON D. FESS, *Vice-Chairman of the United States George Washington Bi-centennial Commission*, March 8, 1932, on the subject of the *George Washington* bi-centennial historical loan exhibition of portraits of GEORGE WASHINGTON and his associates, at the Corcoran Gallery of Art, in the city of Washington, from the 5th of March through the 24th of November, 1932.

> *Congressional Record*, V. 75: Part 5, pp. 5433-5434.

An address on GEORGE WASHINGTON, written jointly by three high-school boys—printed in the *Record*, March 21, 1932, by request of the HON. ROYAL S. COPELAND, a Senator from New York.

> *Congressional Record*, V. 75: Part 6, pp. 6528-6529.

An address by the HON. SIMEON D. FESS, *Vice-Chairman of the United States George Washington Bi-centennial Commission*, May 2, 1932, in which he reviews, in connection with the one hundred and forty-third anniversary of the inauguration of the first President of the United States, the opinions of British statesmen as to GEORGE WASHINGTON'S *contribution to the civilization of the world.*

> *Congressional Record*, V. 75: Part 8, p. 9297; Part 9,
> pp. 9372-9373.

Remarks in the Senate, May 2, 1932, with reference to the proposed publication of an edition of SELECTED WORKS OF GEORGE WASHINGTON for general distribution throughout the United States.

> *Congressional Record*, V. 75: Part 9, pp. 9373-9374:
> Hon. *William E. Borah*, a Senator from Idaho.
> Hon. *Simeon D. Fess*, a Senator from Ohio.
> Hon. *Henrik Shipstead*, a Senator from Minnesota.

. . . .

An address by the HON. HARRY L. HAINES, a Representative from Pennsylvania, delivered at Whitehall, Maryland, February 27, 1932, on the *Life of* WASHINGTON *and the Bi-centennial Celebration*—printed in the *Record*, March 2, 1932, by request of the HON. WILLIAM P. COLE, a Representative from Maryland.

> *Congressional Record*, V. 75: Part 5, pp. 5126-5128.

An address by the HON. SOL BLOOM, *Associate Director of the United States George Washington Bi-centennial Commission*, delivered by radio, March 17, 1932, on the planting of flowers in memory of GEORGE WASHINGTON—printed in the *Record*, July 15, 1932, under extension of remarks.

> *Congressional Record*, V. 75: Part 14, p. 15544.

An address by the HON. SOL BLOOM, *Associate Director of the United States George Washington Bi-centennial Commission*, delivered in the House of Representatives, March 22, 1932, on the *centenary of the death of* JOHANN WOLFGANG VON GOETHE, asking that Americans extend to the German people a fitting return for the honors they have tendered the memory of GEORGE WASHINGTON *in this bi-centennial year of his birth.*

> *Congressional Record*, V. 75: Part 6, p. 6658.

An address by the HON. SOL BLOOM, *Associate Director of the United States George Washington Bi-centennial Commission*, delivered, April 6, 1932, before the Veterans of Foreign Wars, at York, Pennsylvania—printed in the *Record*, July 15, 1932, under extension of remarks.

> *Congressional Record*, V. 75: Part 14, pp. 15541-15542.

An address by the HON. SCOTT LEAVITT, a Representative from Montana, delivered in Carnegie Hall, New York City, April 12, 1932, on *Prosperity Preparedness*, in which he declares "that much of the steadiness of thought and conduct of the American people in these trying days is due to the turning of the Nation's thought in this bi-centennial year to the steadfast character of WASHINGTON"—printed in the *Record*, April 21, 1932, by request of the HON. ADDISON T. SMITH, a Representative from Idaho.

> *Congressional Record*, V. 75: Part 8, pp. 8607-8609.

An address by the HON. SOL BLOOM, *Associate Director of the United States George Washington Bi-centennial Commission*, delivered by radio before the National Security League, April 9, 1932, on GEORGE WASHINGTON *and National Security*—printed in the *Record*, July 15, 1932, under extension of remarks.

> *Congressional Record*, V. 75: Part 14, pp. 15546-15547.

An address by the HON. SOL BLOOM, *Associate Director of the United States George Washington Bi-centennial Commission*, delivered under the Japanese cherry trees—at the Tidal Basin, Washington, April 13, 1932, after having introduced His Excellency the Japanese Ambassador—printed in the *Record*, July 15, 1932, under extension of remarks.

> *Congressional Record*, V. 75: Part 14, p. 15539.

An address by the HON. ROBERT S. HALL, a Representative from Mississippi, April 18, 1932, on the proposed purchase of Mount Vernon by the Federal Government—printed in the *Record* under extension of remarks.

> *Congressional Record*, V. 75: Part 8, pp. 8444-8446.

An address by the HON. JOHN L. CABLE, a Representative from Ohio, delivered in the House of Representatives, April 19,

1932, on GEORGE WASHINGTON *to whom we owe American citizenship—our greatest heritage.*

Congressional Record, V. 75: Part 8, pp. 8525-8527.

An address by the HON. SOL BLOOM, *Associate Director of the United States George Washington Bi-centennial Commission,* delivered in Edenton, North Carolina, April 28, 1932, at the *Unveiling of a Monument to* JOSEPH HEWES, signer of the Declaration of Independence—printed in the *Record,* April 30, 1932, by request of the HON. LINDSAY WARREN, a Representative from North Carolina.

Congressional Record, V. 75: Part 8, pp. 9304-9305.

An address by the HON. C. O. CASE, superintendent of public instruction for the State of Arizona, delivered April 30, 1932, upon the presentation of the bust of GEORGE WASHINGTON presented to that State by the *United States Commission for the Celebration of the Two-Hundredth Anniversary of the Birth of* GEORGE WASHINGTON—printed in the *Record,* May 10, 1932, by request of the HON. HENRY F. ASHURST, a Senator from Arizona.

Congressional Record, V. 75: Part 9, p. 9880.

An address by *His Excellency,* GEORGE W. P. HUNT, Governor of Arizona, April 30, 1932, upon accepting on behalf of the State, the bust of GEORGE WASHINGTON presented by the *United States George Washington Bi-centennial Commission*—printed in the *Record,* May 10, 1932, by request of the HON. HENRY F. ASHURST, a Senator from Arizona.

Congressional Record, V. 75: Part 9, pp. 9880-9881.

An address by the HON. SOL BLOOM, *Associate Director of the United States George Washington Bi-centennial Commission,* delivered at the Tomb of GEORGE WASHINGTON, Mount Vernon, Virginia, May 2, 1932, under the auspices of the American Conference on Institutions for the Establishment of International Justice—printed in the *Record* under extension of remarks.

Congressional Record, V. 75: Part 9, pp. 9448-9449.

An address by the HON. WILLIAM L. TIERNEY, a Representative from Connecticut, delivered, May 3, 1932, before the Polish societies at Saint Michael's Church Hall in Bridgeport, Connecticut, upon the *joint anniversary of the first constitution of Poland and the bi-centennial of* GEORGE WASHINGTON— printed in the *Record,* June 3, 1932, under extension of remarks.

Congressional Record, V. 75: Part 11, pp. 11903-11904.

An address by the HON. SOL BLOOM, *Associate Director of the United States George Washington Bi-centennial Commission,* delivered at historic Fredericksburg, Virginia, May 6, 1931— printed in the *Record,* July 15, 1932, under extension of remarks.

Congressional Record, V. 75: Part 14, pp. 15554-15555.

An address by the HON. SOL BLOOM, *Associate Director of the United States George Washington Bi-centennial Commission,* delivered by radio from Washington, May 10, 1931, on the *Mother's Day Program in connection with the George Wash-ington Bi-centennial Celebration*—printed in the *Record,* February 23, 1932, under extension of remarks.

Congressional Record, V. 75: Part 4, p. 4519.

An address by the HON. SOL BLOOM, *Associate Director of the United States George Washington Bi-centennial Commission,* delivered by radio from Arlington Memorial Amphitheatre, on Memorial Day, May 30, 1931, in connection with the *George Washington Bi-centennial Celebration*—printed in the *Record,* July 15, 1932, under extension of remarks.

Congressional Record, V. 75: Part 14, p. 15553.

An address by the HON. SOL BLOOM, *Associate Director of the United States George Washington Bi-centennial Commission,* delivered by radio from Washington, June 5, 1931, on GEORGE WASHINGTON *and His Relationship to the South*— printed in the *Record,* July 15, 1932, under extension of remarks.

Congressional Record, V. 75: Part 14, pp. 15552-15553.

An address by the HON. SOL BLOOM, *Associate Director of the United States George Washington Bi-centennial Commission,* delivered by radio from the home of BETSY ROSS in Philadelphia, June 14, 1931, on the *Observance of Flag Day in connection with the George Washington Bi-centennial Celebration*—printed in the *Record,* February 23, 1932, under extension of remarks.

Congressional Record, V. 75: Part 4, pp. 4519-4520.

An address by the HON. SOL BLOOM, *Associate Director of the United States George Washington Bi-centennial Commission,* delivered by radio from *Independence Hall,* Philadelphia, July 4, 1931, on *Independence Day Observance in connection with the George Washington Bi-centennial Celebration*— printed in the *Record,* February 23, 1932, under extension of remarks.

Congressional Record, V. 75: Part 4, pp. 4520-4522.

An address by the HON. JOHN M. NELSON, a Representative from Wisconsin, delivered July 17, 1931, at Madison, Wisconsin, upon the presentation of the bust of GEORGE WASHINGTON presented to that State by the *United States George Washington Bi-centennial Commission*—printed in the *Record,* May 3, 1932, under extension of remarks.

Congressional Record, V. 75: Part 9, pp. 9485-9487.

An address by His Excellency, PHILIP F. LaFOLLETTE, Governor of the State of Wisconsin, July 17, 1931, upon accepting on behalf of the State the bust of GEORGE WASHINGTON— printed in the *Record,* May 3, 1932, by request of the HON. JOHN M. NELSON, a Representative from Wisconsin.

Congressional Record, V. 75: Part 9, p. 9487.

An address by the HON. SOL BLOOM, *Associate Director of the United States George Washington Bi-centennial Commission,* delivered by radio from Washington, August 15, 1931, for the *National Grange on George Washington the Planter*— printed in the *Record,* July 15, 1932, under extension of remarks.

Congressional Record, V. 75: Part 14, pp. 15550-15551.

An address by the HON. SOL BLOOM, *Associate Director of the United States George Washington Bi-centennial Commission,* delivered by radio from *Fort Necessity* in Pennsylvania,

September 29, 1931, at the *Fort Necessity ground-breaking ceremony*, commemorating GEORGE WASHINGTON's *first experience in battle*—printed in the *Record*, February 23, 1932, under extension of remarks.

Congressional Record, V. 75: Part 4, pp. 4522-4523.

An address by the HON. SOL BLOOM, of New York, *Associate Director of the United States George Washington Bi-centennial Commission*, delivered, December 8, 1931, before the National Rivers and Harbors Congress at the Willard Hotel in the city of Washington, under the title *George Washington the Builder*—printed in the *Record*, July 15, 1932, under extension of remarks.

Congressional Record, V. 75: Part 14, pp. 15565-15567.

.   .   .   .

An address by the HON. SOL BLOOM, *Associate Director of the George Washington Bi-centennial Commission*, delivered in the House of Representatives, May 11, 1932, under the title *Washington was the First President of the United States.*

Congressional Record, V. 75: Part 9, pp. 10040-10041.

An address by the HON. CLYDE KELLY, a Representative from Pennsylvania, May 21, 1932, on the WASHINGTON *Bi-centennial and Post Office Day, July 26, 1932*—printed in the *Record* under extension of remarks.

Congressional Record, V. 75: Part 10, pp. 10858-10864.

An address by the HON. SCOTT LEAVITT, a Representative from Montana, delivered May 25, 1932, upon the occasion of Memorial Services in the House of Representatives—paying tribute to departed colleagues in this bi-centennial year especially set apart and dedicated to the memory of the immortal WASHINGTON "as being still of his devoted company in the eternal service of our country."

Congressional Record, V. 75: Part 10, pp. 11155-11157.

An address by the HON. HAMILTON FISH, JR., a Representative from New York, delivered, May 28, 1932, at Temple Hill in the State of New York upon the occasion of the Statewide *George Washington Bi-centennial Celebration*—printed in the *Record*, June 3, 1932, under extension of remarks.

Congressional Record, V. 75: Part 11, pp. 11906-11907.

An address by the HON. JAMES A. REED, a former United States Senator from the State of Missouri, delivered on Memorial Day, May 30, 1932, at Arlington National Cemetery upon the occasion of *National Memorial Services in honor of the War-Dead*—printed in the *Record*, May 31, 1932, by request of the HON. CLEMENT C. DICKINSON, a Representative from Missouri.

Congressional Record, V. 75: Part 10, p. 11673.

An address by the HON. SOL BLOOM, *Associate Director of the United States George Washington Bi-centennial Commission*, delivered by radio on Memorial Day, May 30, 1932, from Arlington National Cemetery under the title *Remember the Soldiers of Long Ago*—printed in the *Record*, June 8, 1932, by request of the HON. EDWARD B. ALMON, a Representative from Alabama.

Congressional Record, V. 75: Part 11, p. 12362.

An address by COMMANDER WILLIAM SEAMAN BAINBRIDGE, delivered on Memorial Day, May 30, 1932, upon the dedication of the Revolutionary Cemetery at *Morristown, New Jersey*, headquarters of GENERAL WASHINGTON's *Army*—printed in the *Record*, July 9, 1932, by request of the HON. W. WARREN BARBOUR, a Senator from New Jersey.

Congressional Record, V. 75: Part 14, pp. 14943-14944.

An address by the HON. AUGUSTINE LONERGAN, a Representative from Connecticut, delivered in the House of Representatives, June 10, 1932, on JOHN HANSON, *President of the Continental Congress*—printed in the *Record* under extension of remarks.

Congressional Record, V. 75: Part 11, pp. 12584-12585.

An address by the HON. SOL BLOOM, of New York, *Associate Director of the United States George Washington Bi-centennial Commission*, delivered by radio, June 14, 1932, from the home of FRANCIS SCOTT KEY, in Georgetown, District of Columbia, *on the significance of Flag Day in this year in which we celebrate the two-hundredth anniversary of the birth of* GEORGE WASHINGTON—printed in the *Record*, June 18, 1932, under extension of remarks.

Congressional Record, V. 75: Part 12, pp. 13425-13426.

An address by MR. GEORGE SEIBEL, of Pittsburgh, Pennsylvania, entitled "GEORGE WASHINGTON *Among His Books*"—printed in the *Record*, June 24, 1932, by request of the HON. GERALD P. NYE, a Senator from North Dakota.

Congressional Record, V. 75: Part 13, pp. 13815-13816.

An address by the HON. SOL BLOOM, *Associate Director of the United States George Washington Bi-centennial Commission*, delivered, June 30, 1932, before the Kiwanis Club and other civic groups in Wilkes-Barre, Pennsylvania, on WASHINGTON *The Everyday Man*—printed in the *Record*, July 6, 1932, by request of the HON. C. MURRAY TURPIN, a Representative from Pennsylvania.

Congressional Record, V. 75: Part 13, pp. 14715-14717.

An address by the HON. SAMUEL B. PETTENGILL, a Representative from Indiana, delivered in the House of Representatives, July 1, 1932, on PULASKI *and* WASHINGTON—printed in the *Record* under extension of remarks.

Congressional Record, V. 75: Part 13, p. 14512.

An address by the HON. CHARLES A. EATON, a Representative from New Jersey, delivered, July 4, 1932, at the Centennial Celebration in Buffalo, New York, under the title GEORGE WASHINGTON's *Message to Modern America*—printed in the *Record*, July 5, 1932, under extension of remarks.

Congressional Record, V. 75: Part 13, pp. 14611-14612.

An address by the HON. ANTHONY J. GRIFFIN, a Representative from New York, delivered, July 4, 1932, at Saint Ann's Church in the Bronx, New York City, upon the *Unveiling of a Memorial to* GOUVERNEUR MORRIS, *friend and associate of* GEORGE WASHINGTON—printed in the *Record*, July 5, 1932, under extension of remarks.

Congressional Record, V. 75: Part 13, pp. 14610-14611.

An address by the HON. SOL BLOOM, of New York, *Associate Director of the United States George Washington Bi-centennial Commission*, delivered by radio, July 4, 1932, as part of the

Nation-wide Independence Day program of the American Farm Bureau Federation, *in commemoration of the two-hundredth anniversary of the birth of* GEORGE WASHINGTON—printed in the *Record*, July 15, 1932, under extension of remarks.

> *Congressional Record*, V. 75: Part 14, pp. 15532-15533.

An address by the HON. CHARLES A. WOLVERTON, a Representative from New Jersey, delivered in the House of Representatives, July 16, 1932, on GENERAL CASIMIR DE PULASKI —*A Polish Patriot in the Cause of American Independence*—printed in the *Record* under extension of remarks.

> *Congressional Record*, V. 75: Part 14, pp. 15766-15768.

PART TWO

Acts of Congress, Resolutions, Official Documents and Other Tributes in Honor of George Washington, 1789-1932

FIRST SESSION OF THE FIRST CONGRESS: 1789

Ordered by the Senate of the United States, 6 April 1789, that CHARLES THOMSON, Esq., wait upon GEORGE WASHINGTON, Esq., with a certificate of his election to the office of President of the United States, and that MR. SYLVANUS BOURN wait upon JOHN ADAMS, Esq., with a certificate of his election to the office of Vice-President of the United States.

> *Journal of the Senate*, pp. 8-9.
> [*Annals of Congress*, V. 1: p. 18.]

Report—submitted to the Senate by CHARLES THOMSON, Esq., 25 April 1789, upon his return from Mount Vernon where, by order of the Senate, he delivered to GENERAL WASHINGTON a certificate of his election to the office of President of the United States.

> *American State Papers*, Mis., V. 1: pp. 5-6.

FIRST SESSION OF THE SECOND CONGRESS: 1791-1792

Resolution—moved in the House of Representatives, 6 December 1791, and adopted:

> That MR. BENSON, MR. GERRY, and MR. SMITH, of South Carolina, be appointed a committee on the part of this House, jointly with such committee as shall be appointed on the part of the Senate, to consider and report to Congress the most eligible manner for carrying into effect the resolution of the United States in Congress assembled, of the 7th of August 1783, *directing that an equestrian statue of* GENERAL WASHINGTON *should be erected*.

> *Journal of the House of Representatives*, p. 468.
> *Journal of the Senate*, p. 349.
> [*Annals of Congress*, V. 3: pp. 41-228.]

FIRST SESSION OF THE SIXTH CONGRESS: 1799-1800

Message from JOHN ADAMS, *President of the United States*, 19 December 1799, transmitting to the Congress a letter from TOBIAS LEAR, announcing *the death of* GEORGE WASHINGTON.

> *Journal of the House of Representatives* (5th and 6th Congresses), pp. 540-541.
> *Journal of the Senate* (6th, 7th, and 8th Congresses), p. 11.

> [*Annals of Congress*, V. 10: pp. 16, 205-206.]
> [*American State Papers*, Mis. V. 1: pp. 189-190.]

From an Alexandria Paper of 21 December 1799:

> Statement signed by DR. JAMES CRAIK, attending physician and DR. ELISHA C. DICK, consulting physician, during the last illness and death of GENERAL WASHINGTON—printed, 23 December 1799, in the record of Proceedings in the House of Representatives.

> *Annals of Congress*, V. 10: pp. 205-206.

Resolutions upon receiving intelligence of the death of GEORGE WASHINGTON—submitted to the House of Representatives by the HON. JOHN MARSHALL, a Representative from Virginia, 19 December 1799, and unanimously adopted:

1. That this House will wait on the President of the United States in condolence of this national calamity.

2. That the Speaker's chair be shrouded with black, and that the members and officers of the House wear mourning during the session.

3. That a joint committee of both Houses be appointed to report measures suitable to the occasion. . . . .

> *Journal of the House of Representatives* (5th and 6th Congresses), p. 540.
> *Journal of the Senate* (6th, 7th, and 8th Congresses), p. 11.
> [*Annals of Congress*, V. 10: pp. 16-17, 204.]

Joint Resolutions—reported to the Senate by the HON. JONATHAN DAYTON, a Senator from New Jersey, 23 December 1799, from the Joint Select Committee appointed, on the part of the Senate, 19 December 1799, on the receipt of the intelligence of the *death of* GENERAL GEORGE WASHINGTON, to report measures suitable to the occasion.

> *Journal of the Senate*, p. 13.
> [*Annals of Congress*, V. 10: p. 19.]
> [*American State Papers*, Mis., V. 1: p. 191.]

Joint Resolutions—reported to the House of Representatives by the HON. JOHN MARSHALL, a Representative from Virginia, 23 December 1799, from the Joint Select Committee appointed, on the part of the House, 19 December 1799, to report measures suitable to the occasion, and expressive of the profound sorrow with which Congress is penetrated *on the loss of their highly valued fellow-citizen,* GEORGE WASHINGTON.

> *Journal of the House of Representatives* (5th and 6th Congresses), pp. 542-543.
> [*Annals of Congress*, V. 10: pp. 207-208.]

Resolution—unanimously adopted by the House of Representatives, on motion made and seconded, 27 December 1799:

That the *Speaker* present the thanks of this House to MAJOR-GENERAL LEE, a Member of the House from the State of Virginia, for the oration delivered by him to both Houses of Congress on Thursday, the twenty-sixth instant, conformably to the resolution of Congress, *in honor of the memory of* GEORGE WASHINGTON, *late General of the Armies of the United States;* and request that he will permit a copy thereof to be taken for publication.

> *Journal of the House of Representatives,* p. 545.
> [*Annals of Congress,* V. 10: pp. 211-212.]

Letter of the HON. THEODORE SEDGWICK, *Speaker of the House of Representatives,* in pursuance of the resolution unanimously adopted by the House, 27 December 1799, to make known to MAJOR-GENERAL HENRY LEE how highly they had been gratified with the manner in which he had performed the service assigned to him in preparing and delivering *an oration on the death of* GENERAL WASHINGTON; and to request a copy of the oration for publication.

> *Journal of the House of Representatives,* pp. 545-546.
> [*Annals of Congress,* V. 10: pp. 222-223.]
> [*American State Papers,* Mis., V. 1: p. 192.]

Resolution—reported to the House of Representatives by the HON. JOHN MARSHALL, a Representative from Virginia, 30 December 1799, from the Joint Select Committee appointed to *prepare and report measures in honor of the memory of* GEORGE WASHINGTON, proposing that it be recommended to the people of the United States to assemble on the 22nd day of February, next, *to testify publicly their grief for the death of* GENERAL GEORGE WASHINGTON by suitable eulogies, orations, and discourses, or by public prayers . . . And . . . that the *President of the United States* be requested to recommend the same by proclamation. . . . . .

> *Journal of the House of Representatives* (5th and 6th Congresses), p. 547.
> *Journal of the Senate* (6th, 7th, and 8th Congresses), p. 16.
> [*Annals of Congress,* V. 10: pp. 22, 223.]

Message from JOHN ADAMS, *President of the United States,* 8 January 1800, transmitting to the Congress a letter from MRS. WASHINGTON in answer to the entreaty of the President, in compliance with the resolution adopted by the Congress, 23 December 1799, that she assent to the *interment of* GENERAL WASHINGTON'S *remains in the United States Capitol.*

> *Journal of the Senate,* pp. 18-19.
> *Journal of the House of Representatives,* pp. 554-555.
> [*Annals of Congress,* V. 10: pp. 24, 284-285.]
> [*American State Papers,* Mis., V. 1: p. 195.]

Resolution—adopted by the Senate, on motion made and seconded, 21 February 1800:

Resolved, That the Senate will tomorrow, at half-past twelve o'clock, meet at the Senate chamber, and from thence walk in procession to the German Calvinist Church in Race street, to hear the *eulogium pronounced on the character of* GENERAL WASHINGTON.

> *Journal of the Senate,* p. 33.
> *Journal of the House of Representatives,* p. 600.
> [*Annals of Congress,* V. 10: pp. 50, 536.]

House bill (H.R. No. 230)—submitted to the House of Representatives by the HON. HENRY LEE, a Representative from Virginia, 28 March 1800, extending to MARTHA WASHINGTON the privilege of franking letters and packages for and during her life.—*Approved,* 3 April 1800.

> *Journal of the House of Representatives,* pp. 644, 646, 648, 650, 651, 652.
> [*Annals of Congress,* V. 10: pp. 147, 148, 647, 649.]

Resolutions—reported by the HON. HENRY LEE, a Representative from Virginia, 8 May 1800, from the Joint Select Committee appointed to prepare and report measures in honor of the memory of GEORGE WASHINGTON.

Resolved, That the resolution of Congress, passed in 1783, respecting an *equestrian statue of* GENERAL WASHINGTON, be carried into immediate execution, and that the statue be placed in the centre of an area to be formed in front of the Capitol.

Resolved, That a marble monument be erected by the United States in the Capitol at the city of Washington in honor of GENERAL WASHINGTON.

> *Journal of the House of Representatives,* pp. 703, 704.
> [*Annals of Congress,* V. 10: p. 708.]
> [*American State Papers,* Mis., V. 1: p. 214.]

House bill (H.R. No. 268)—submitted in the House of Representatives by the HON. THOMAS EVANS, a Representative from Virginia, 9 May 1800, authorizing the erection of a *mausoleum for* GEORGE WASHINGTON *in the City of Washington.*—*Postponed* in the Senate.

> *Journal of the House of Representatives,* pp. 705, 709, 714.
> [*Annals of Congress,* V. 10: pp. 178, 181, 711, 712.]

SECOND SESSION OF THE SIXTH CONGRESS: 1800-1801

House bill (H.R. No. 270)—reported to the House of Representatives by the HON. HENRY LEE, a Representative from Virginia, 2 December 1800, from the Joint Select Committee appointed to prepare and report measures in honor of the memory of GEORGE WASHINGTON, directing that a mausoleum be erected in his honor.[1]

> *Journal of the House of Representatives,* pp. 733, 738.
> [*Annals of Congress,* V. 10: pp. 796, 799, 817, 818.]

House bill (H.R. No. 274) reported by the HON. HENRY LEE, a Representative from Virginia, 19 December 1800, from the Joint Select Committee to whom was re-committed the bill (H.R. No. 270) for the erection of a *Mausoleum for* GEN-

---

[1] On motion by MR. CHAMPLIN, of Rhode Island, this bill was re-committed to the Joint Select Committee, 10 December 1800, with instructions to inquire into the expediency of adopting measures to carry into effect a resolution passed by Congress, 7 August 1783, directing that an *equestrian statue of* GENERAL WASHINGTON be erected at the place where the residence of Congress shall be established. Accordingly MAJOR-GENERAL HENRY LEE reported another bill (H. R. No. 274) as cited above.

ERAL WASHINGTON—recommending an adherence to the plan heretofore adopted by the House of Representatives for the erection of *a monument and an equestrian statue in honor of* GENERAL WASHINGTON.—*Postponed* in the Senate.

> *Journal of the House of Representatives,* pp. 743, 746, 749, 785, 839, 842.
> [*Annals of Congress,* V. 10: (House) pp. 837, 855, 874, 875, 1003, 1071-1072; (Senate), pp. 732, 733, 735, 736, 737, 738, 758.]
> [*American State Papers,* Mis., V. 1: pp. 215-216.]

FIRST SESSION OF THE FOURTEENTH CONGRESS:
1815-1816

Report—submitted in the House of Representatives by the HON. BENJAMIN HUGER, a Representative from South Carolina, 14 March 1816, from the Joint Committee appointed under a resolution of the 16th of February 1816 to examine into the proceedings of a former Congress, *upon the death of* GENERAL WASHINGTON, and to take into consideration what further measures it may be expedient to adopt at the present time in relation to that solemn and interesting subject.

> [*Annals of Congress,* V. 29: pp. 1212, 1458.]
> [*American State Papers,* Mis., V. 2: p. 298.]

SECOND SESSION OF THE FIFTEENTH CONGRESS:
1818-1819

Resolution—submitted in the Senate by the HON. ROBERT H. GOLDSBOROUGH, a Senator from Maryland, 25 November 1818, proposing to erect a *monument over the remains of* GENERAL WASHINGTON *where they now lie.*

> *Journal of the Senate,* pp. 32, 41, 44, 134, 160, 252-253.
> [*Annals of Congress,* V. 33: pp. 23, 26, 31, 33, 111-112, 162, 164, 228, 229.]
> [*S. Doc. No. 7 . . . . . Serial* 14.]

FIRST SESSION OF THE SIXTEENTH CONGRESS:
1819-1820

Resolutions—submitted in the House of Representatives by the HON. JAMES ERVIN, a Representative from South Carolina, 6 April 1820, requesting that the President of the United States take measures to have the remains of the late GENERAL WASHINGTON brought to the Capitol, that he cause to be erected over them a suitable mausoleum, and that he cause to be procured an equestrian statue of bronze, to be placed on the top of the said mausoleum.

> *Journal of the House of Representatives,* pp. 383-384.
> [*Annals of Congress,* V. 36: pp. 1792-1793.]

FIRST SESSION OF THE EIGHTEENTH CONGRESS:
1823-1824

Joint Resolution—submitted in the Senate by the HON. RICHARD M. JOHNSON, a Senator from Kentucky, 23 March 1824, authorizing the President of the United States to procure an *equestrian portrait of* WASHINGTON.

> *Journal of the Senate* pp. 243, 245.
> [*Annals of Congress,* V. 41: pp. 417-418.]

Resolution—submitted in the House of Representatives by the HON. JAMES BUCHANAN, a Representative from Pennsyl-

vania, 15 January 1824, proposing that a committee be appointed to inquire in what manner the resolution of Congress passed, 23 December 1799, relative to the erection of a marble *monument, in the Capitol, at the city of Washington, in honor of* GENERAL WASHINGTON may be best accomplished.

> *Journal of the House of Representatives,* p. 148.
> [*Annals of Congress,* V. 41: p. 1044.]

FIRST SESSION OF THE NINETEENTH CONGRESS:
1825-1826

Report—submitted to the House of Representatives by the HON. LOUIS MCLANE, a Representative from Delaware, 28 April 1826, from the Committee on Ways and Means, accompanied by a bill authorizing the *Washington Monument Association of Massachusetts* to import into Boston, free of duty, from the city of London, a *statue of* GEORGE WASHINGTON *by Chantrey.*

> *Journal of the House of Representatives,* pp. 379, 483, 558, 561, 618, 630, 632, 634.
> [*H. Rept. No.* 181 . . . . *Serial* 142]

FIRST SESSION OF THE TWENTY-FIRST CONGRESS:
1829-1830

Resolution—adopted in the House of Representatives, on motion by the HON. GEORGE EDWARD MITCHELL, a Representative from Maryland, 22 February 1830:
Resolved, That the resolutions of the Congress of the United States unanimously adopted on the 23rd of December, 1799, and the *Message of* PRESIDENT ADAMS on the 8th of January, 1800,[1] to the Congress, respecting the *entombment of the remains of* GENERAL GEORGE WASHINGTON *in this Capitol,* be referred to a select committee, and that the said committee be authorized to report by bill or otherwise.

> *Journal of the House of Representatives,* p. 327.

Report—submitted to the House of Representatives by the HON. GEORGE EDWARD MITCHELL, a Representative from Maryland, 15 March 1830, from the Select Committee upon the subject of a *national entombment of the remains of the late* GENERAL GEORGE WASHINGTON *in the United States Capitol, and the erection of a full-length pedestrian statue in his honor.*

> *Journal of the House of Representatives,* pp. 327, 441.
> [*H. Rept. No.* 318 . . . . *Serial* 201.]

FIRST SESSION OF THE TWENTY-SECOND CONGRESS:
1831-1832

Joint Resolution—submitted in the Senate by the HON. HENRY CLAY, a Senator from Kentucky, 13 February 1832, authorizing the President of the Senate and the Speaker of the House of Representatives to make application to MR. JOHN A. WASHINGTON, of Mount Vernon, for the body of GEORGE WASHINGTON to be removed and deposited in the

---

[1] These papers are embodied in the Report of the Select Committee; and, also, printed 22 February 1830 in the *House Journal.*

Capitol, at the city of Washington on the 22nd day of February 1832.

> *Journal of the Senate,* p. 131.
> *Debates in Congress,* V. 8: Part 1, pp. 369, 390-391, 414.

Report—submitted to the Senate by the HON. HENRY CLAY, a Senator from Kentucky, 13 February 1832, from the Joint Committee appointed to make arrangements for the purpose of *celebrating the centennial birthday of* GEORGE WASHINGTON.[2]

> *Journal of the Senate,* pp. 117, 129-131.
> [*Debates in Congress,* V. 8: Part 1, pp. 295-296, 367-369.]
> [*S. Doc. No. 62 . . . . Serial* 213.]

Joint Resolution—adopted in the Senate, 20 February 1832, on motion by MR. CLAY, of Kentucky, and by unanimous consent:

That, in respect to the *centennial birthday of* GEORGE WASHINGTON, the two Houses will adjourn from the 21st to the 23rd of the present month. . . .

> *Journal of the Senate,* p. 144.
> *Journal of the House of Representatives,* p. 392.

Joint Resolution—submitted in the House of Representatives by the HON. PHILEMON THOMAS, a Representative from Louisiana, 3 February 1832, that, if the Senate concur herein, a joint committee of the two Houses be appointed for the purpose of making arrangements for the *celebration of the centennial birthday of* GEORGE WASHINGTON.

> *Journal of the House of Representatives,* pp. 249, 283, 302.
> [*Debates in Congress,* V. 8: Part 2, pp. 1732-1733.]

Report—submitted to the House of Representatives by the HON. PHILEMON THOMAS, a Representative from Louisiana, 13 February 1832, from the Joint Committee appointed to make arrangements for the purpose of celebrating the *centennial birthday of* GEORGE WASHINGTON.

> *Journal of the House of Representatives,* pp. 339-340, 343, 350, 351, 366, 392, 393.
> [*Debates in Congress,* V. 8: Part 2, pp. 1782, 1808-1809.]
> [*See* S. Doc. No. 62 . . . . *Serial* 213.]

Joint Resolution—submitted in the House of Representatives by the HON. PHILEMON THOMAS, a Representative from Louisiana, 13 February 1832, authorizing the President of the Senate and the Speaker of the House of Representatives to make application to MR. JOHN A. WASHINGTON, of Mount Vernon, for the body of GEORGE WASHINGTON to be removed and deposited in the Capitol on the 22nd day of February 1832.

Journal of the House of Representatives, p. 340.
[*Debates in Congress,* V. 8: Part 2, p. 1782.]

Joint Resolution—submitted in the House of Representatives by the HON. JAMES BATES, a Representative from Maine, 14 February 1832, authorizing the President of the Senate and the Speaker of the House of Representatives to make application to MR. JOHN A. WASHINGTON, of Mount Vernon, and to MR. GEORGE WASHINGTON PARKE CUSTIS, grandson of MRS. WASHINGTON, for the remains of MRS. WASHINGTON to be removed to the Capitol at the same time with those of GENERAL WASHINGTON.

> *Journal of the House of Representatives,* pp. 343, 350.
> [*Debates in Congress,* V. 8: Part 1, pp. 390-391; Part 2, p. 1811.]

Letter from JOHN AUGUSTINE WASHINGTON, dated at Mount Vernon, 15 February 1832—written in response to the request on the part of the United States Congress, 14 February 1832, for his consent to the *removal of the remains of* GENERAL GEORGE WASHINGTON and of MARTHA WASHINGTON to the United States Capitol.

> *Journal of the Senate,* pp. 140-141.
> *Journal of the House of Representatives,* pp. 366-367.
> [*Debates,* V. 8: Part 1, pp. 414-415; Part 2, pp. 1818-1819.]

Letter from GEORGE WASHINGTON PARKE CUSTIS, dated at Arlington House, Tuesday night, 14 February 1832—written in response to the request on the part of the United States Congress, 14 February 1832, for his consent to the *removal of the remains of* MRS. MARTHA WASHINGTON to be deposited at the same time with those of her husband in the United States Capitol.

> *Journal of the Senate,* pp. 140-141.
> *Journal of the House of Representatives,* pp. 367-368.
> [*Debates,* V. 8: Part 1, p. 415; Part 2, p. 1819.]

Letter from FRANCIS T. BROOKE, 24 February 1832—transmitting to the United States Congress a letter from the *Governor of the State of Virginia,* and certain *resolutions adopted by the General Assembly of that State* with regard to the contemplated *removal of the remains of* GEORGE WASHINGTON *from Mount Vernon to the United States Capitol.*

> *Journal of the Senate,* pp. 150-151.
> *Journal of the House of Representatives,* pp. 404-405.
> [*Debates,* V. 8: Part 2, pp. 1857-1858.]
> [*H. Ex. Doc. No. 124 . . . . Serial* 219]

Joint Resolution (S.J.Res. No. 4)—submitted in the Senate by the HON. GEORGE POINDEXTER, a Senator from Mississippi, 25 April 1832, authorizing the President of the United States to contract for *a full-length pedestrian statue of* GEORGE WASHINGTON.—*Provided for in Appropriation bill* H.R. No. 601.[1]

---

[2] Embodied in the Report from the Select Committee appointed to make arrangements for the celebration of the *centennial of the birth of* GEORGE WASHINGTON will be found the letter, signed by HENRY CLAY, on the part of the Senate, inviting CHIEF-JUSTICE MARSHALL to make the principal address upon the occasion, and the reply of the Chief-Justice, declining the honor on account of his advanced age.

[1] A resolution, reported by MR. JARVIS, of Maine, 14 February 1832, from the Committee on Public Buildings for the same object, was passed by the House; but the Senate resolution (S.J.Res. No. 4) seems to have been provided for in the appropriation bill.

> *Journal of the House of Representatives,* p. 342.
> [*Debates,* V. 8: Part 2, pp. 1809-1810, 1830, 2175.]
> [*See* H. Rept. No. 459 . . . . *Serial* 226.]

Journal of the Senate, pp. 257, 258, 264, 355, 367, 369.
Journal of the House of Representatives, pp. 1025, 1152, 1153.
[*Debates*, V. 8: Part 1, pp. 867, 1126, 1127; Part 2, p. 2175.]

Resolution—submitted in the Senate by the Hon. Theodore Frelinghuysen, a Senator from New Jersey, 27 April 1832, proposing that the Committee on the Library, on the part of the Senate, inquire into the expediency of purchasing from Mr. Rembrandt Peale, of New York, his *original portrait of* George Washington.

Journal of the Senate, pp. 259, 365, 382.
[*Debates in Congress*, V. 8: Part 1, pp. 866-867.]

Joint Resolution—submitted in the Senate by the Hon. Asher Robbins, a Senator from Rhode Island, 24 May 1832, proposing that the Committee on the Library be instructed to inquire into the expediency of procuring *an equestrian statue of* General Washington to be erected in the square east of the Capitol, in the city of Washington.

Journal of the Senate, pp. 298, 480.
[*Debates in Congress*, V. 8: Part 1, p. 951.]

Resolution—reported to the House of Representatives by the Hon. Leonard Jarvis, a Representative from Maine, 27 February 1832, proposing that the Clerk of the House be directed to employ John Vanderlyn, of New York, to paint a *full-length portrait of* George Washington to be placed in the Hall of Representatives. . . . .

Journal of the House of Representatives, pp. 342, 376.
[*Debates in Congress*, V. 8: Part 2, p. 1809.]

Report—submitted to the House of Representatives by the Hon. Edward Everett, a Representative from Massachusetts, 30 April 1832, from the Joint Committee on the Library, who were instructed, by the Senate, to inquire into the expediency of procuring a *pedestrian statue of* Washington, to be placed in the rotunda of the Capitol.

Journal of the House of Representatives, p. 674.
[H. Rept. No. 459 . . . . Serial 226.]

SECOND SESSION OF THE TWENTY-SECOND CONGRESS: 1832-1833

Message from Andrew Jackson, *President of the United States*, 21 December 1832, transmitting to the Congress a communication from the Secretary of State, enclosing a correspondence between him and the artist employed to execute *the statue of* Washington that is to be placed in the rotunda of the Capitol.

Journal of the House of Representatives, p. 87.
[*Messages and Papers of the Presidents*, V. 3: pp. 1170-1171.]

Report—submitted in the House of Representatives by Hon. Leonard Jarvis, a Representative from Maine, 2 January 1833, from the Committee on Public Buildings, to whom was referred the *Message of the President of the United States*, transmitting a communication from the Secretary of State, enclosing a correspondence between him and the artist employed to execute *the statue of* Washington that is to be placed in the rotunda of the Capitol.

Journal of the House of Representatives, pp. 87, 121.
[H. Rept. No. 21 . . . . Serial 236.]

FIRST SESSION OF THE TWENTY-THIRD CONGRESS: 1833-1834

House bill (H.R. No. 446)—reported to the House of Representatives by the Hon. William S. Archer, a Representative from Virginia, 24 April 1834, from the Committee on Foreign Affairs, to enable the Secretary of State to purchase the *papers and books of* General Washington.—*Approved*, 30 June 1834.

Journal of the House of Representatives, pp. 560, 847, 867, 872, 889, 914, 915, 916.
[*Debates in Congress*, V. 10: Part 4, pp. 4781-4782, 4796.]

Report—submitted to the House of Representatives by the Hon. William S. Archer, a Representative from Virginia, 1 April 1834, from the Committee on Foreign Affairs, to whom was referred, 11 March 1834, a resolution instructing them to inquire into the expediency of purchasing the *library and the official and private manuscript papers of* General Washington, *to be deposited in the Department of State.*

Journal of the House of Representatives, pp. 397, 469, 560.
[H. Rept. No. 381 . . . . Serial 262.]

Resolution—reported to the House of Representatives by the Hon. Leonard Jarvis, a Representative from Maine, 14 June 1834, from the Committee on Public Buildings, directing the Clerk of the House to pay to John Vanderlyn fifteen hundred dollars as additional compensation for the *full length portrait of* Washington, executed by him, to be placed in the Hall of Representatives, in pursuance of a resolution of the House, 17 February 1832.

Journal of the House of Representatives, p. 855.
[*Debates in Congress*, V. 10: Part 4, p. 4787.]

SECOND SESSION OF THE TWENTY-THIRD CONGRESS: 1834-1835

Joint Resolution (H.J.Res. No. 14)—reported to the House of Representatives by the Hon. Edward Everett, a Representative from Massachusetts, 8 January 1835, from the Committee on the Library, permitting Jared Sparks to retain Washington's *papers* until otherwise ordered by Congress.—*Negatived* in the House.

Journal of the House of Representatives, pp. 183, 191.
[*Debates in Congress*, V. 11: Part 1, pp. 966, 976-978.]

House bill (H.R. No. 551)—reported to the House of Representatives (in the preceding session) by the Hon. Edward Everett, a Representative from Massachusetts, 25 June 1834, from the Committee on the Library, making provision for the purchase of the *fac simile of* George Washington's *accounts.*—Laid on table, 28 February 1835.

Journal of the House of Representatives, pp. 330, 351.
Journal of the Senate, pp. 151, 153, 162, 209.

Joint Resolution—submitted in the House of Representatives by the HON. HENRY A. WISE, a Representative from Virginia, 16 February 1835, authorizing the purchase of one thousand copies of the *works* of GENERAL GEORGE WASHINGTON from Russell Odiorne and Company.

> *Journal of the House of Representatives,* pp. 398-399.
> [*Debates in Congress,* V. 11: Part 2, pp. 1401-1402.]

FIRST SESSION OF THE TWENTY-FOURTH CONGRESS:
1835-1836

Report—submitted in the House of Representatives by the HON. AMOS LANE, a Representative from Indiana, 24 March 1836, from the Committee on the District of Columbia, accompanied by a bill (H.R. No. 487) authorizing the *Washington National Monument Society to erect a monument to the memory of* GEORGE WASHINGTON *on the public mall.*

> *Journal of the House of Representatives,* pp. 559, 1092, 1093.
> *Journal of the Senate,* pp. 477, 478, 491.
> [*Debates in Congress,* V. 12: Part 4, pp. 4490-4491.]
> [*H. Rept. No. 483 . . . . Serial 294.*]

SECOND SESSION OF THE TWENTY-FIFTH CONGRESS:
1837-1838

Petition of JOHN ELY, a soldier of the Revolution, imploring Congress to consider and decide on the propriety of erecting a *monument to* GEORGE WASHINGTON *at Mount Vernon, on the spot where his ashes are now at rest.*—Presented in the Senate, 3 January 1838, by JAMES BUCHANAN, a Senator from Pennsylvania; presented in the House of Representatives, 3 January 1838, by CHARLES NAYLOR, a Representative from Pennsylvania.

> *Journal of the Senate,* p. 102.
> *Journal of the House of Representatives,* p. 202.
> [*S. Doc. No. 67 . . . . Serial 314.*]

House bill (H.R. No. 473)—reported to the House of Representatives by the HON. DANIEL JENIFER, a Representative from Maryland, 25 January 1838, from the Committee on the District of Columbia, authorizing the officers and managers of the *Washington Monument Society to erect a monument to* GEORGE WASHINGTON *on the public mall.*[1]

> *Journal of the House of Representatives,* pp. 314-315, 375, 1109.
> *Journal of the Senate,* pp. 214, 222, 233, 473.
> [*Congressional Globe,* V. 6: Part 1, pp. 135, 172, 178, 454.]

FIRST SESSION OF THE TWENTY-SIXTH CONGRESS:
1839-1840

Joint Resolution (S.J.Res. No. 8)—submitted in the Senate by the HON. WILLIAM C. PRESTON, a Senator from South

---

[1] A memorial from the committee of the Board and Managers of the Washington National Monument Society was presented in the House of Representatives, 29 December 1837, by the HON. WILLIAM C. JOHNSON, of Maryland, requesting the United States Congress to grant one of the public squares in the city of Washington for the site of a contemplated *monument to the memory of* GEORGE WASHINGTON. The memorial was referred to the Committee on the District of Columbia; on the 25th of January 1838, the Committee reported a bill, as cited above; the bill, which passed the House, was postponed indefinitely in the Senate.

FIRST PRESIDENTIAL MANSION, FRANKLIN SQUARE, NEW YORK CITY, 1789

Carolina, 9 April 1840, authorizing the Committee on the Library to take measures for the importation of the *statue of* WASHINGTON *by Greenough.—Approved 27 May 1840.*

> *Journal of the Senate,* pp. 293, 303, 307, 387, 391, 392, 393, 394, 400.
>
> *Journal of the House of Representatives,* pp. 794, 795, 988-989, 1023, 1025, 1059.
>
> [*Congressional Globe,* V. 8: Part 1, pp. 310, 320, 325.]

Documents—submitted in the House of Representatives by the HON. LEVI LINCOLN, a Representative from Massachusetts, 5 March 1840, from the Committee on Public Buildings, giving estimates by ROBERT MILLS, architect of public buildings, relative to the cost of preparing suitable foundations for supporting the *statue of* WASHINGTON *in the centre of the rotunda of the Capitol.*

> [*H. Doc. No. 124 . . . . Serial* 365.]

FIRST SESSION OF THE TWENTY-SEVENTH CONGRESS: 1841

Message from JOHN TYLER, *President of the United States,* 2 August 1841, transmitting to the House of Representatives certain documents relative to the *statue of* GEORGE WASHINGTON, *by Greenough,* and asking an appropriation for the payment of transportation expenses.

> *Journal of the House of Representatives,* pp. 317-318.
>
> [*H. Doc. No.* 45 . . . . *Serial* 392.]

Letter from GEORGE E. BADGER, *Secretary of the Navy,* 13 August 1841, transmitting to MILLARD FILLMORE, chairman of the Committee on Ways and Means, the receipt of the officer in command at the Navy Yard, in the city of Washington, for the *statue of* GEORGE WASHINGTON *by Greenough.*

> *Journal of the House of Representatives,* p. 361.
>
> [*H. Doc. No.* 53 . . . . *Serial* 392.]

House bill (H.R. No. 29)—reported to the House of Representatives by the HON. THOMAS W. GILMER, a Representative from Virginia, 16 August 1841, to provide for placing *Greenough's statue of* WASHINGTON in the rotunda of the Capitol.—*Approved,* 9 September 1841.

> *Journal of the House of Representatives,* pp. 358, 421, 459, 464, 484.
>
> *Journal of the Senate,* pp. 217, 218, 232, 237, 239, 253.

SECOND SESSION OF THE TWENTY-SEVENTH CONGRESS: 1841-1842

Joint Resolution—submitted in the Senate by the HON. WILLIAM C. PRESTON, a Senator from South Carolina, 22 December 1841, proposing that a joint committee be appointed, to consist of three on the part of the Senate, to meet a committee on the part of the House, to arrange the placing of the *statue of* WASHINGTON in the rotunda, and to direct the details of the pedestal.

> *Journal of the Senate,* pp. 47, 54.
>
> *Journal of the House of Representatives,* pp. 92, 101.
>
> [*Congressional Globe,* V. 11: Part 1, p. 48.]

THIRD SESSION OF THE TWENTY-SEVENTH CONGRESS: 1842-1843

Memorial of HORATIO GREENOUGH, sculptor, requesting the removal of the *statue of* WASHINGTON from its present position in the rotunda to the grounds in front of the western facade of the Capitol—presented in the House of Representatives, 10 January 1843, by the HON. JOHN QUINCY ADAMS, a Representative from Massachusetts; presented in the Senate, 11 January 1843, by the HON. ISAAC C. BATES, a Senator from Massachusetts.

> *Journal of the House of Representatives,* pp. 167-168.
>
> *Journal of the Senate,* pp. 92, 100.
>
> [S. *Doc. No.* 57 . . . . *Serial* 414.]

Joint Resolution (H.J.Res. No. 43)—reported to the House of Representatives by the HON. JOSEPH L. TILLINGHAST, a Representative from Rhode Island, 22 February 1843, from the Joint Committee on the Library, to whom was referred the *memorial of* HORATIO GREENOUGH, sculptor, requesting the removal of the *statue of* WASHINGTON from the rotunda of the Capitol. . . . .

> *Journal of the House of Representatives,* pp. 429, 550.
>
> [*H. Rept. No.* 219 . . . . *Serial* 427.]

Joint Resolution (H.J.Res. No. 35)—moved in the House of Representatives by the HON. JOHN QUINCY ADAMS, a Representative from Massachusetts, 7 February 1843, presenting the thanks of Congress to SAMUEL T. WASHINGTON for the *service sword of* GENERAL WASHINGTON *and the staff of* BENJAMIN FRANKLIN.—

> *Journal of the House of Representatives,* pp. 333, 338, 419.
>
> *Journal of the Senate,* pp. 158, 194, 203.
>
> [*See H. Doc. No.* 11 (28th Congress, 1st Session) . . . . . . *Serial* 439.]

Ordered by the House of Representatives, 7 February 1843—on motion by MR. TALIAFERRO, a Representative from Virginia, that the addresses by MR. SUMMERS *and* MR. ADAMS, accepting the *sword of* WASHINGTON *and the staff of* FRANKLIN be entered on the *Journal.*

> *Journal of the House of Representatives,* p. 333.
>
> [*Congressional Globe,* V. 12: p. 255.]
>
> [*H. Doc. No.* 144 . . . . *Serial* 421.]

Resolution—moved in the House of Representatives by the HON. JOHN TALIAFERRO, a Representative from Virginia, 8 February 1843, that 20,000 copies be printed of the full journal of the proceedings of the House of Representatives upon the presentation to the Nation of WASHINGTON's *sword and* FRANKLIN's *staff.*

> *Journal of the House of Representatives,* p. 334.
>
> [*Congressional Globe,* V. 12: p. 256.]

FIRST SESSION OF THE TWENTY-EIGHTH CONGRESS: 1883-1884

Message from JOHN TYLER, *President of the United States,* 16 December 1843, relative to the presentation to the Nation of WASHINGTON's *sword and* FRANKLIN's *staff.*

Journal of the House of Representatives, p. 58.
[*Congressional Globe*, V. 13: Part 1, p. 40.]
[*H. Doc. No. 11 . . . . Serial* 439.]

Joint Resolution (H.J.Res. No. 9)—reported to the House of representatives by the Hon. EDMUND BURKE, a Representative from New Hampshire, 15 February 1844, from the Committee on the Library, accepting the *sword of WASHINGTON and the staff of FRANKLIN.*—Approved, 4 March 1844.

> *Journal of the House of Representatives*, pp. 404, 440, 518, 520.
> *Journal of the Senate*, pp. 124, 129, 135, 147, 152.

Joint Resolution (H.J.Res. No. 27)—submitted in the House of Representatives by the Hon. JOHN QUINCY ADAMS, a Representative from Massachusetts, 18 April 1844, accepting the *camp chest of GENERAL WASHINGTON.*—Approved, 30 April 1844.

> *Journal of the House of Representatives*, pp. 819, 829, 845, 863, 873.
> *Journal of the Senate*, pp. 247, 249, 259, 263.

Joint Resolution (H.J.Res. No. 28)—submitted in the House of Representatives by the Hon. JOHN QUINCY ADAMS, a Representative from Massachusetts, 18 April 1844, that the Senate and House of Representatives take pleasure in recognizing to the widow and family of the late WILLIAM SYDNEY WINDER their high sense of the value of the bequest contained in his will, and in expressing their respect for the memory of the donor.—Approved, 30 April 1844.

> *Journal of the House of Representatives*, pp. 819, 829, 845, 863, 873.
> *Journal of the Senate*, pp. 247, 249, 259, 263.
> [*Congressional Globe*, V. 13: Part 1, pp. 536, 537.]

Resolution—moved in the House of Representatives by the Hon. JOHN P. KENNEDY, a Representative from Maryland, 18 April 1844, that the letters and papers accompanying the *bequest of the camp chest of GENERAL WASHINGTON by the late WILLIAM SYDNEY WINDER*, of Maryland, be entered upon the *Journal.* . . . .

> *Journal of the House of Representatives*, pp. 817-819.
> [*Congressional Globe*, V. 13: Part 1, p. 536.]

Joint Resolution (H.J.Res. No. 23)—reported to the House of Representatives by the Hon. ZADOCK PRATT, a representative from New York, 12 April 1844, from the Committee on Public Buildings, relative to the erection of a *national monument on public grounds.* . . . .

> *Journal of the House of Representatives*, pp. 778, 813.
> [*H. Rept. No. 434 . . . . Serial* 446.]

Resolution—reported to the House of Representatives by the Hon. SAMUEL SIMONS, a Representative from Connecticut, 18 April 1844, from the Committee on Engraving, to whom was referred the joint resolution (H.J.Res. No. 23) relative to the erection of a *national monument on public grounds.* . . . .

> *Journal of the House of Representatives*, p. 813.
> [*Congressional Globe*, V. 13: Part 1, pp. 533-534.]

Report—submitted in the House of Representatives by the Hon. ZADOCK PRATT, a Representative from New York, 25 May 1844, from the Committee on Public Buildings and Grounds, to accompany the joint resolution (H.J.Res. No. 33) relative to *fencing and laying out Monument Square.*

> *Journal of the House of Representatives*, p. 969.
> [*Congressional Globe*, V. 13: Part 1, p. 623.]
> [*H. Rept. No. 514 . . . . Serial* 446.]

Joint Resolution—reported to the House of Representatives by the Hon. ZADOCK PRATT, a Representative from New York, 25 May 1844, from the Committee on Public Buildings and Grounds, proposing to remove and make sale of the building in which the *statue of WASHINGTON* has been placed; and, with the money arising from such sale, to enclose the statue with a suitable railing.

> *Journal of the House of Representatives*, p. 969.
> [*Congressional Globe*, V. 13: Part 1, pp. 623-624.]

Resolution—submitted in the Senate by the Hon. DANIEL E. HUGER, a Senator from South Carolina, 10 May 1844, proposing that the Committee on Public Buildings be instructed to inquire if it would not be more appropriate to remove the naval monument, on the west of the Capitol, to the navy yard, and substitute in its place the *statue of WASHINGTON by Greenough.*

> *Journal of the Senate*, p. 273.
> . . . .
> [*Congressional Globe*, V. 13: Part 1, p. 589.]

Report—submitted in the Senate by the Hon. ISAAC C. BATES, a Senator from Massachusetts, 15 June 1844, from the Committee on Pensions, to whom was referred the resolution, introduced on March the 6th by the Hon. WILLIAM S. ARCHER, of Virginia, instructing the Committee to inquire into the expediency of transferring a part of the WASHINGTON *Papers from the State Department to the Department of War.*

> *Journal of the Senate*, pp. 150, 154, 368.
> . . . .
> [*S. Doc. No. 398 . . . . Serial* 436.]

SECOND SESSION OF THE TWENTY-EIGHTH CONGRESS: 1844-1845

Resolution—submitted in the Senate by the Hon. JOHN J. CRITTENDEN, a Senator from Kentucky, 20 January 1845, proposing that the Committee on the Library be instructed to inquire into the expediency and propriety of employing LUIGI PERSICO to execute, for the United States, *an equestrian statue, in bronze, of GEORGE WASHINGTON.*

> *Journal of the Senate*, p. 96.
> . . . .
> [*Congressional Globe*, V. 14: Part 1, p. 156.]

Joint Resolution—reported to the House of Representatives by the Hon. ZADOCK PRATT, a Representative from New York, 31 December 1844, from the Committee on Public Buildings and Grounds, to provide for the selection of a site for the *national Washington monument.* . . . .

Journal of the House of Representatives, p. 153.

. . . .

[*Congressional Globe,* V. 14: Part 1, p. 77.]

Letter from JOHN C. CALHOUN, *Secretary of State,* 8 January 1845, in answer to a resolution of the House of Representatives of the 4th instant, requesting information as to the number of volumes of the *manuscript papers of the Confederation and of* WASHINGTON, to which indices are being prepared; the progress therein; when the work will be completed; and the probable additional expense—read before the House, 24 January 1845, and referred to the Committee on Ways and Means.

> *Journal of the House of Representatives,* p. 256.
> [*Congressional Globe,* V. 14: Part 1, p. 185.]
> [*H. Ex. Doc. No. 63* . . . . *Serial 464.*]

FIRST SESSION OF THE TWENTY-NINTH CONGRESS: 1845-1846

Joint Resolution (S.J.Res. No. 4)—reported to the Senate by the HON. SIMON CAMERON, a Senator from Pennsylvania, 6 January 1846, from the Committee on Public Buildings, authorizing the Washington National Monument Society to erect the contemplated *monument to the memory of* GEORGE WASHINGTON upon such portion of the public grounds or reservations in the city of Washington . . . as shall be selected by the President of the United States and the Board of Managers of said society.[1]

> *Journal of the Senate,* pp. 86, 88-89.
> [*Congressional Globe,* V. 15: Part 1, pp. 145, 154.]

Joint Resolution (S.J.Res. No. 22)—reported to the Senate by the HON. JAMES A. PEARCE, a Senator from Maryland, 27 April 1846, from the Committee on the Library, who were instructed by a resolution of the Senate to inquire into the expediency of employing HIRAM POWERS to execute an *equestrian statue of* GENERAL WASHINGTON.

> *Journal of the Senate,* pp. 165, 168, 263.
> [*Congressional Globe,* V. 15: Part 1, pp. 422, 429, 728.]
> [*S. Doc. No. 314* . . . . *Serial 476.*]

Joint Resolution (H.J.Res. No. 6)—submitted in the House of Representatives by the HON. ISAAC E. HOLMES, a Representative from South Carolina, 7 January 1846, authorizing the Washington National Monument Society to erect the proposed *monument to the memory of* GEORGE WASHINGTON upon such portion of the public grounds or reservations within the city of Washington . . . as shall be designated by the President of the United States and the Board of Managers of said society.

> *Journal of the House of Representatives,* p. 200.

Journal of the Senate, pp. 88-89, 92, 335, 375, 380, 455.

[*Congressional Globe,* V. 15: Part 1, pp. 155, 158, 160, 1038, 1040, 1162.]

Resolved in the House of Representatives, Saturday, 21 February 1846—on motion by the HON. WILLIAM L. YANCEY, a Representative from Alabama: That when this House adjourn, it stand adjourned until Tuesday next, in honor of the memory, and in respect to the anniversary of the *birthday of* GEORGE WASHINGTON, *the father of his country.*

> *Journal of the House of Representatives,* p. 445.
> [*Congressional Globe,* V. 15: Part 1, p. 413.]

Joint Resolution (H.J.Res. No. 30)—reported to the House of Representatives by the HON. RICHARD BRODHEAD, JR., a Representative from Pennsylvania, 11 May 1846, from the Committee on the Library, relative to an *equestrian statue of* WASHINGTON.

> *Journal of the House of Representatives,* p. 784.
> [*Congressional Globe,* V. 15: Part 1, p. 789.]

FIRST SESSION OF THE THIRTIETH CONGRESS: 1847-1848

Joint Resolution (S.J.Res. No. 2)—reported to the Senate by the HON. JACOB W. MILLER, a Senator from New Jersey, 6 January 1848, from the Committee on the District of Columbia, authorizing the erection on the public grounds, in the city of Washington, of a *monument to* GEORGE WASHINGTON.—*Approved,* 31 January 1848.

> *Journal of the Senate,* pp. 57, 97, 131, 136, 138, 144, 147.
> *Journal of the House of Representatives,* p. 298.
> [*Congressional Globe,* V. 17: Part 1, pp. 121, 230, 245.]

Resolution—submitted in the Senate by the HON. JOHN A. DIX, a Representative from New York, 15 February 1848, proposing that the Committee on the Library be instructed to inquire into the expediency of purchasing a *marble bust of* WASHINGTON *by Houdon,* in possession of MR. GEORGE GIBBS.

> *Journal of the Senate,* p. 174.
> [*Congressional Globe,* V. 17: Part 1, p. 361.]

Resolution—submitted in the Senate by the HON. JOHN H. CLARKE, a Senator from Rhode Island, 24 April 1848, directing the Joint Committee on the Library to ascertain, from the present owner of the *library of the late* GEORGE WASHINGTON, whether the same is now for sale, of what number and value are the books in said library, and at what price the same can be purchased by Congress.[1]

> *Journal of the Senate,* p. 294.
> [*Congressional Globe,* V. 17: Part 1, p. 665.]

---

[1] The Senate Joint Resolution (S. J. Res. No. 4) was ordered to be laid on the table, 7 January 1846, on motion by MR. CRITTENDEN, of Kentucky, and the House Joint Resolution (H. J. Res. No. 6) was considered in lieu thereof. On motion by MR. BENTON, of Missouri, 29 July 1846, the latter resolution, also, was ordered to be laid on the table.

[1] Purchase of the manuscript books and papers of GENERAL GEORGE WASHINGTON was provided for in the Civil and Diplomatic Appropriation bill (H. R. No. 692) which was approved in the Second Session of the Thirtieth Congress—3 March 1849.

Resolved in the Senate, 27 June 1848—on motion by the HON. JOHN M. CLAYTON, a Senator from Delaware, that the Senate attend the ceremony upon the *laying of the cornerstone of the Washington Monument* on the 4th of July next.

> *Journal of the Senate*, p. 422.
> [*Congressional Globe*, V. 17: Part 1, pp. 875, 893.]
> [See S. *Doc. No. 224.* (57th Congress, 2nd Session.) *Serial 4436.*]

SECOND SESSION OF THE THIRTIETH CONGRESS:
1848-1849

Resolution—submitted in the House of Representatives by the HON. HENRY C. MURPHY, a Representative from New York, 19 January 1849, proposing that the Committee on the Library be instructed to inquire into the expediency of purchasing the *diaries and other private papers of* GENERAL WASHINGTON.

> *Journal of the House of Representatives*, p. 276.

> . . . .

> [*Congressional Globe*, V. 18: Part 1, pp. 302, 662, 664.]

Resolution—submitted in the House of Representatives by the HON. RICHARD K. MEADE, a Representative from Virginia, 5 February 1849, proposing that the Committee on Public Expenditures inquire into the expediency of causing a copy of *Washington's statue,* in the capitol of Virginia, to be taken in American marble by an American artist, and placed in the rotunda of the Capitol in the city of Washington.

> *Journal of the House of Representatives*, p. 378.

> . . . .

> [*Congressional Globe*, V. 18: Part 1, p. 454.]

FIRST SESSION OF THE THIRTY-FIRST CONGRESS:
1849-1850

Joint Resolution—submitted in the Senate by the HON. HENRY CLAY, a Senator from Kentucky, 23 January 1850, authorizing the Joint Committee on the Library to purchase the *manuscript of* GEORGE WASHINGTON's *Farewell Address to people of the United States 17 September 1796.—Approved,* 12 February 1850.

> *Journal of the Senate*, pp. 102, 106, 136, 137, 138, 148
> *Journal of the House of Representatives*, pp. 419, 431, 481, 521, 535.
> [*Congressional Globe*, V. 19: Part 1, p. 220.]

FIRST SESSION OF THE THIRTY-SECOND CONGRESS:
1851-1852

Memorial of citizens of Washington, requesting an appropriation for the erection of an *equestrian statue of* GENERAL WASHINGTON, under the resolution of Congress of 1783—presented in the House of Representatives, 15 December 1851, by the HON. MEREDITH P. GENTRY, a Representative from Tennessee; presented in the Senate, 16 December 1851, by the HON. LEWIS CASS, a Senator from Michigan.

> *Journal of the House of Representatives*, p. 87.
> *Journal of the Senate*, p. 65.

Resolution—submitted in the Senate by the HON. JOHN P. HALE, a Senator from New Hampshire, 26 March 1852, proposing that the Committee on Public Buildings be instructed to inquire into the propriety of purchasing the great national painting of *Washington crossing the Delaware,* and causing the same to be placed in the mansion of the President of the United States.

> *Journal of the Senate*, pp. 308, 315.

> . . . .

> [*Congressional Globe*, V. 21: Part 2, p. 878.]

Resolution—submitted in the Senate by the HON. JAMES COOPER, a Senator from Pennsylvania, 8 April 1852, proposing that the Committee on the Library be . . . instructed to inquire into the expediency of employing MR. LEUTZE to re-paint for Congress his painting representing *Washington crossing the Delaware,* together with a fellow to it representing *Washington rallying the American troops at the battle of Monmouth;* also, of employing MR. HEALY to paint two pictures, one representing *The throwing overboard of the tea in Boston harbor;* the other, *The Battle of Bunker Hill.*

> *Journal of the Senate*, p. 339.

> . . . .

SECOND SESSION OF THE THIRTY-SECOND
CONGRESS: 1852-1853.

House bill (H. R. No. 343)—submitted in the House of Representatives by the HON. GILBERT DEAN, a Representative from New York, 17 January 1853, to carry into effect the resolution of Congress, passed August 7, 1783, to erect at the capital of the Nation an *equestrian statue of* WASHINGTON.—*Approved,* 25 January 1853.

> *Journal of the House of Representatives*, pp. 123-124, 135, 151, 180, 185, 202.
> *Journal of the Senate*, pp. 103, 105, 109, 110, 128, 132, 146.
> [*Congressional Globe*, V. 22: Part 1, pp. 321, 329, 323, 343, 389.]

FIRST SESSION OF THE THIRTY-THIRD CONGRESS:
1853-1854

Resolution—submitted in the House of Representatives by the HON. BERNHART HENN, a Representative from Iowa, 22 December 1853, proposing that the Committee on Public Buildings be requested to inquire into the expediency of setting apart an appropriate room in the Executive Mansion to be furnished exclusively with articles used by GEORGE WASHINGTON during his life-time.

> *Journal of the House of Representatives*, p. 135.
> [*Congressional Globe*, V. 23: Part 1, p. 88.]

Resolution—submitted in the House of Representatives by the HON. JOHN L. TAYLOR, a Representative from Ohio, 30 January 1854, that the Committee on Revolutionary Claims be instructed to inquire into the expediency of causing an *index to be made of the* WASHINGTON *papers* in the Department of State.

> *Journal of the House of Representatives*, p. 286.

Memorial of the Board of Managers of the *Washington National Monument Society*, requesting the aid of Congress in the erection of the *Washington Monument*—presented in the Senate, 1 July 1854, by the HON. LEWIS CASS, a Senator from Michigan; presented in the House of Representatives, 13 July 1854, by the HON. HENRY MAY, a Representative from Maryland.

> *Journal of the Senate*, p. 471.
> *Journal of the House of Representatives*, p. 1133.
> [*Congressional Globe*, V. 23: Part 3, p. 1710.]

SECOND SESSION OF THE THIRTY-THIRD CONGRESS:
1854-1855

Senate bill (S. No. 693)—reported to the Senate by the HON. WILLIAM C. DAWSON, a Senator from Georgia, 3 March 1855, from the Committee on the District of Columbia, proposing to incorporate the *Washington National Monument Society.*—

> *Journal of the Senate*, pp. 219, 361, 389.
> [*Congressional Globe*, V. 24: Part 1, pp. 1081, 1138.]

Report—submitted to the House of Representatives by the HON. HENRY MAY, a Representative from Maryland, 22 February 1855, from the Select Committee of Thirteen, to whom was referred the memorial of the Board of Managers of the *Washington National Monument Society.*

> *Journal of the House of Representatives*, pp. 390, 435.
> [*Congressional Globe*, V. 24: Part 1, p. 900.]
> [*H. Rept. No. 94 . . . . Serial 808.*]

Resolution—reported to the House of Representatives by the HON. RICHARD H. STANTON, a Representative from Kentucky, 23 February 1855, from the Committee on Printing, to whom was referred the motion by MR. MAY, a Representative from Maryland, relative to the printing of extra copies of the report of the Select Committee of Thirteen on the subject of the *Washington National Monument.*

> *Journal of the House of Representatives*, p. 446.
> [*Congressional Globe*, V. 24: Part 1, p. 908.]

Joint Resolution (H.J.Res. No. 62)—submitted in the House of Representatives by the HON. JOHN C. BRECKINRIDGE, a Representative from Kentucky, 2 March 1855, for the relief of CLARK MILLS.—*Approved, 3 March 1855.*

> *Journal of the House of Representatives*, pp. 508, 525, 526, 548, 559.
> [*Congressional Globe*, V. 24: Part 1, pp. 1031, 1073, 1079.]

FIRST SESSION OF THE THIRTY-FIFTH CONGRESS:
1857-1858

Senate bill (S. No. 152)—reported to the Senate by the HON. ALBERT G. BROWN, a Senator from Mississippi, 25 February 1858, from the Committee on the District of Columbia, proposing to incorporate the *Washington Monument Society. . . . .*

> *Journal of the Senate*, pp. 197, 215, 344.
> *Journal of the House of Representatives*, pp. 637, 765, 881, 894, 901.
> [*Congressional Globe*, V. 27: Part 1, pp. 735, 861;

Part 2, pp. 1541, 1597-1598; Part 3, pp. 2309, 2372, 2386.]

Resolution—submitted in the Senate by the HON. WILLIAM BIGLER, a Senator from Pennsylvania, 5 April 1858, that the Committee on the Library be instructed to inquire into the propriety of purchasing the *equestrian portrait of* WASHINGTON *by Rembrandt Peale.* . . . .

> *Journal of the Senate*, p. 315.

. . . .

> [*Congressional Globe*, V. 27: Part 2, p. 1459.]

Petition of CLARK MILLS, sculptor, requesting an amendment of the act of Congress of the 25th of January, 1853, authorizing the erection of an *equestrian statue of* WASHINGTON—presented in the Senate, 20 May 1858, by the HON. JAMES HENRY HAMMOND, a Senator from South Carolina.

> *Journal of the Senate*, p. 489.

. . . .

> [*Congressional Globe*, V. 27: Part 3, p. 2258.]

Joint Resolution (S.J.Res. No. 50)—submitted in the Senate by the HON. JAMES A. PEARCE, a Senator from Maryland, 2 June 1858, authorizing the President to designate a *site for the equestrian statue of* WASHINGTON.—

> *Journal of the Senate*, p. 583.
> *Journal of the House of Representatives*, p. 1010.
> [*Congressional Globe*, V. 27: Part 3, p. 2630, 2679.]

SECOND SESSION OF THE THIRTY-FIFTH CONGRESS:
1858-1859

Senate bill (S. No. 544)—reported to the Senate by the HON. JESSE D. BRIGHT, a Senator from Indiana, 29 January 1859, from the Committee on Public Buildings and Grounds, to whom the subject had been referred, to incorporate the *Washington National Monument Society.*—Approved, 26 February 1859.

> *Journal of the Senate*, pp. 232-233, 364, 370, 385, 386.
> *Journal of the House of Representatives*, pp. 296, 462, 467, 494, 501.
> [*Congressional Globe*, V. 28: Part 1, pp. 662, 665; Part 2, pp. 1240, 1289, 1385.]

FIRST SESSION OF THE THIRTY-SIXTH CONGRESS:
1859-1860

Joint Resolution—submitted in the Senate by the HON. JAMES A. PEARCE, a Senator from Maryland, 8 February 1860, in relation to the *dedication of the statue of* WASHINGTON.

> *Journal of the Senate*, p. 136.
> [*Congressional Globe*, V. 29: Part 1, p. 700.]

Joint Resolution—submitted in the Senate by the HON. ALBERT G. BROWN, a Senator from Mississippi, 15 February 1860, proposing that a committee of three be appointed on the part of the Senate, to act in concert with such committee as may be appointed on the part of the House of Representatives in making suitable arrangements for the inauguration of the *equestrian statue of* GENERAL WASHINGTON on the approaching 22nd day of February.

> *Journal of the Senate*, pp. 165, 167, 173.
> *Journal of the House of Representatives*, pp. 320, 331.
> [*Congressional Globe*, V. 29: Part 1. pp. 789, 797.]

Joint Resolution—submitted in the House of Representatives by the HON. LAURENCE M. KEITT, a Representative from South Carolina, 17 February 1860, from the Joint Committee, making an appropriation for the *inauguration of the equestrian statue* of WASHINGTON.

> *Journal of the House of Representatives,* pp. 332, 347, 348, 376.
> *Journal of the Senate,* pp. 173-174, 185, 186, 187, 279.
> [*Congressional Globe,* V. 29: Part 1, pp. 830, 857, 878.]

Memorial of the members and incorporators of the *Washington National Monument Society,* requesting the aid of Congress in the erection of a *monument to* GEORGE WASHINGTON at the seat of the Federal Government—presented in the Senate, 14 February 1860, by the HON. JESSE D. BRIGHT, a Senator from Indiana; presented in the House of Representatives, 15 February 1860, by the HON. HENRY C. BURNETT, a Representative from Kentucky.

> *Journal of the Senate,* p. 151.
> *Journal of the House of Representatives,* p. 281.
> [*Congressional Globe,* V. 29: Part 1, p. 758.]

House bill (H.R. No. 769)—reported to the House of Representatives by the HON. GEORGE W. HUGHES, a Representative from Maryland, 24 May 1860, from a minority of the Committee on the District of Columbia, to whom was referred the memorial of the *Washington National Monument Society,* requesting aid of Congress in the erection of a *monument to* GEORGE WASHINGTON at the seat of the Federal Government.

> *Journal of the House of Representatives,* p. 918.

> . . . .

> [*Congressional Globe,* V. 29: Part 3, p. 2326.]
> [*H. Rept. No. 567* . . . *Serial 1070.*]

Petition of THERON HAMILTON, requesting the Congress to have 5000 copies of the *Declaration of Independence and* WASHINGTON's *Farewell Address to the People of the United States* printed together and distributed—presented in the Senate, 9 March 1850, by the HON. KINGSLEY S. BINGHAM, a Senator from Michigan.

> *Journal of the Senate,* p. 235, 736.

> . . . .

> [*Congressional Globe,* V. 29: Part 2, p. 1075.]

FIRST SESSION OF THE THIRTY-SEVENTH CONGRESS: 1861

House bill (— —) submitted in the House of Representatives by the HON. FRANCIS P. BLAIR, a Representative from Missouri, 8 July 1861, proposing to repeal the act by which that portion of the District of Columbia originally ceded by the State of Virginia was retroceded to that State, and to *extend the boundaries of the District of Columbia,* with the consent of the said State of Virginia, *so as to include Mount Vernon.*

> *Journal of the House of Representatives,* p. 41.

SECOND SESSION OF THE THIRTY-SEVENTH CONGRESS: 1861-1862

Memorial of citizens of Philadelphia, praying that GEORGE WASHINGTON's *Farewell Address to the people of the United*

States may be read to both Houses of Congress and to the Army and Navy of the United States on the approaching 22nd day of February—presented in the House of Representatives, 10 February 1862, by the HON. JOHN J. CRITTENDEN, a Representative from Kentucky; presented in the Senate, 11 February 1862, by the HON. ANDREW JOHNSON, a Senator from Tennessee.

> *Journal of the House of Representatives,* pp. 288, 289, 290.
> *Journal of the Senate,* pp. 193, 194.

Concurrent Resolutions—submitted in the Senate by the HON. ANDREW JOHNSON, a Senator from Tennessee, 11 February 1862, proposing that the two Houses of Congress assemble in the chamber of the House of Representatives on Saturday, the 22nd day of February, instant, at twelve o'clock meridian; and that, in the presence of the two Houses of Congress, thus assembled, the *Farewell Address of* GEORGE WASHINGTON *to the people of the United States* shall be read. . . . That the President of the United States be requested to direct that orders be issued for the reading to the Army and Navy of the United States of the *Farewell Address of* GEORGE WASHINGTON on the 22nd day of February, instant . . . That 10,000 copies of the proceedings of the two Houses of Congress together with the *Farewell Address of* GEORGE WASHINGTON, be printed for distribution by the Members of the two Houses of Congress to the people of the United States.

> *Journal of the Senate,* pp. 193, 212, 231.
> *Journal of the House of Representatives,* pp. 294, 304, 310, 311, 324, 338-341.

Joint Resolution—submitted in the House of Representatives by the HON. CHARLES R. TRAIN, a Representative from Massachusetts, 18 February 1862, proposing that the Commissioner of Public Buildings cause the public buildings in the city of Washington to be illuminated on Saturday evening next, the 22nd of February, in honor of recent victories by the army and navy of the United States.

> *Journal of the House of Representatives,* pp. 321, 323, 325, 338.

Resolution—submitted in the House of Representatives by the HON. JAMES S. ROLLINS, a Representative from Missouri, 28 February 1862, providing that 10,000 additional copies of the *Farewell Address of* GEORGE WASHINGTON be printed for the use of the House; and that the trustees, professors, and teachers of the different colleges, academies, and common schools *in all the States,* be respectfully requested to have said address permanently placed in their respective institutions, where the same may be read, and where the lesson of wisdom, of patriotism, and of Union, which it teaches, may be indelibly impressed upon the youthful mind of the country.

> *Journal of the House of Representatives,* p. 372.

Resolution—reported to the House of Representatives by the HON. E. P. WALTON, a Representative from Vermont, 11 March 1862, from the Committee on Printing, providing that 50,000 extra copies of the *Farewell Address of* GEORGE

WASHINGTON, together with the *Proclamation of* PRESIDENT JACKSON, 10 December 1932, and the *Declaration of Independence,* be printed for the use of the House.

Journal of the House of Representatives, p. 426.

FIRST SESSION OF THE THIRTY-EIGHTH CONGRESS: 1863-1864

Resolution—submitted in the House of Representatives by the HON. THOMAS T. DAVIS, a Representative from New York, 30 May 1864, proposing that the Committee on the District of Columbia be instructed to inquire into the present condition of the *Washington National Monument Society,* to ascertain the amount of funds collected for the association since its last report; the amount expended for the construction of the monument, and the amount expended and paid for salaries, since said report, to the respective officers of the company; and also, in what manner the funds on hand are invested or kept; and that said Committee be authorized to make any other inquiries which they may think best, and also to send, if necessary, for books and papers and witnesses, and that they report to the House.

Journal of the House of Representatives, pp. 715-716.

Motion by the HON. LEWIS W. ROSS, a Representative from Illinois, 2 July 1864, that 10,000 copies of WASHINGTON's *Farewell Address* be printed for the use of the House.

Journal of the House of Representatives, p. 1032.

FIRST SESSION OF THE FORTIETH CONGRESS: 1867

Resolution—submitted in the House of Representatives by the HON. JOHN F. DRIGGS, a Representative from Michigan, 16 July 1867, proposing that the Secretary of the Interior be requested to inform this House, so far as may be in his power, what becomes of the money collected for an association known as the *Washington Monument Association*— which collections are continued in the United States Patent Office; and whether he has any knowledge of the present condition of the association, who its officers are, and what they propose to do with the funds.

Journal of the House of Representatives, pp. 216, 221.
[*Congressional Globe,* V. 38: Part 1, pp. 675, 698.]

Letter from ORVILLE H. BROWNING, *Secretary of the Interior,* 17 July 1867—in answer to a resolution of the House of Representatives of the 16th of July 1867, in regard to the *Washington Monument Association.*

Journal of the House of Representatives, pp. 216, 221.
[*H. Exc. Doc. No. 26 . . . Serial* 1311.]

SECOND SESSION OF THE FORTIETH CONGRESS: 1867-1868

Resolution—proposed, as a privileged question, in the House of Representatives by the HON. CHARLES A. ELDRIDGE, a Representative from Wisconsin, 22 February 1868, that in honor and commemoration of the *Father of his Country,* this being the anniversary of his birthday, his memorable *Farewell Address* be read by the Clerk of the House, and that upon the conclusion thereof this house adjourn. . . .

Journal of the House of Representatives, p. 386.
[*Congressional Globe,* V. 39: Part 2, p. 1355.]

THIRD SESSION OF THE FORTIETH CONGRESS: 1868-1869

Resolution—submitted in the House of Representatives by the HON. JOHN A. LOGAN, a Representative from Illinois, 1 March 1869, instructing the Committee on Public Buildings and Grounds to make investigations relative to a number of articles, once the property of GEORGE WASHINGTON, which were taken from Arlington House, when that place fell into possession of the Federal Army.[1]

Journal of the House of Representatives, pp. 480, 481
[*Congressional Globe,* V. 40: Part 3, pp. 1742-1743.]

Report—submitted to the House of Representatives by the HON. JOHN COVODE, a Representative from Pennsylvania, 3 March 1869, from the Committee on Public Buildings and Grounds, accompanied by the following resolution: "That the articles known as the effects of GEORGE WASHINGTON, *the Father of his country,* now in custody of the Department of the Interior, are of right the property of the United States; and any attempt on the part of the present administration, or any department thereof, to deliver the same to GENERAL ROBERT E. LEE is an insult to the loyal people of the United States; and they ought to be kept as relics in the Patent Office, and ought not to be delivered to any one without the consent of Congress."

Journal of the House of Representatives, p. 547.
[*Congressional Globe,* V. 40: Part 3, p. 1895.]

Report—submitted in the House of Representatives by the HON. THOMAS L. JONES, a Representative from Kentucky, 3 March 1869, from a minority of the Committee on Public Buildings and Grounds, accompanied by the following resolution, proposed as a substitute for that submitted by MR. COVODE of Pennsylvania:

That the articles in the Patent Office which have been identified as the property of MRS. MARY CUSTIS LEE, and which were taken without the authority of the Government from her home at Arlington, as they are of but little value except as heirlooms in her family bequeathed to her by her father, GEORGE WASHINGTON PARKE CUSTIS, be at her request restored to her possession.

Journal of the House of Representatives, p. 547.
[*Congressional Globe,* V. 40: Part 3, p. 1895.]

FIRST SESSION OF THE FORTY-FIRST CONGRESS: 1869

Senate bill (S. No. 209)—submitted in the Senate by the HON JAMES W. NYE, a Senator from Nevada, 26 March 1869, to resume the completion of the *Washington Monument.*

[1] See also the Resolution introduced in the House, 27 February 1869, by the HON. HAMILTON WARD, a Representative from New York. *Congressional Globe,* V. 40: Part 3, p. 1685.

Journal of the Senate, p. 89.
[*Congressional Globe*, V. 41: Part 1, p. 291.]

Senate bill (S. No. 245)—submitted in the Senate by the Hon. Thomas Ward Osborn, a Senator from Florida, 1 April 1869, to secure the completion of the *Washington and Lincoln monuments*. . . . .

Journal of the Senate, p. 114.

. . . .

House bill (H. R. No. 412)—submitted in the House of Representatives by the Hon. Thomas Boles, a Representative from Arkansas, 9 April 1869, to secure the completion of the Washington *and* Lincoln *Monuments*. . . . .

Journal of the House of Representatives, p. 206.
[*Congressional Globe*, V. 41: Part 1, p. 652.]

Resolution—submitted in the House of Representatives by the Hon. Thomas L. Jones, a Representative from Kentucky, 5 April 1869, proposing that the Committee on the Judiciary be instructed to inquire into the propriety of restoring to Mrs. Mary Custis Lee the articles now in the Patent Office known as the "Mount Vernon relics", and said to have been taken from her house at Arlington during the war.

Journal of the House of Representatives, p. 167.
[*Congressional Globe*, V. 41: Part 1, p. 506.]

SECOND SESSION OF THE FORTY-SECOND CONGRESS: 1871-1872

Report—submitted in the House of Representatives by the Hon. William Williams, a Representative from Indiana, 19 April 1872, from the Committee on the District of Columbia, to whom was referred the House bill (H. R. No. 1179), appropriating two hundred thousand dollars for the completion of the *Washington National Monument*.

Journal of the House of Representatives, pp. 198, 713.
[*H. Rept. No. 48* . . . . *Serial* 1528.]

House bill (H. R. No. 1600)—submitted in the House of Representatives by the Hon. John F. McKinney, a Representative from Louisiana, 19 February 1872, to amend an act entitled "An act to incorporate the *Washington National Monument Society*" approved 26 February 1859.

. . . .

Journal of the House of Representatives, pp. 364, 864.
Journal of the Senate, pp. 750, 754.

THIRD SESSION OF THE FORTY-SECOND CONGRESS: 1872-1873

Resolution—submitted in the House of Representatives by the Hon. John B. Storm, a Representative from Pennsylvania, 20 January 1873, proposing that the Committee on Public Buildings and Grounds be instructed to inquire what sum of money will be required to complete the *Washington Monument*, in the city of Washington, according to the original plan and design for the erection of the same, and to report the facts to this House; also to inquire and report whether any change in the proposed plan and design is expedient.

Journal of the House of Representatives, p. 212.

Resolution—submitted in the House of Representatives by the Hon. Norton P. Chipman, Delegate from the District of Columbia, 27 January 1873, proposing that a committee of thirteen be appointed by the *Speaker*, whose duty it shall be to confer with officers and members of the *Washington National Monument Society* upon the practicability of completing the *Washington Monument* by the approaching centennial.

Journal of the House of Representatives, pp. 259, 466.

House bill (H. R. 3674)—submitted in the House of Representatives by the Hon. Daniel W. Voorhees, a Representative from Indiana, 27 January 1873, for the completion of the *National Monument to the memory of* George Washington.

Journal of the House of Representatives, pp. 252, 442.

FIRST SESSION OF THE FORTY-THIRD CONGRESS: 1873-1874

Resolution—submitted in the Senate by the Hon. Justin S. Morrill, a Senator from Vermont, 11 May 1874, proposing that the Committee on Public Buildings and Grounds be instructed to ascertain whether or not the materials of the present unfinished *Washington Monument* would be sufficient for the erection of an arch, imposing as to size and artistic in form, to be called the *Arch of Washington*; the probable expense of such a change; and also to ascertain if the *Washington National Monument Society* will give their assent to such an arrangement provided Congress should agree to the same.

Journal of the Senate, p. 545.

Resolution—submitted in the House of Representatives by the Hon. Norton P. Chipman, Delegate from the District of Columbia, 12 January 1874, proposing that a committee of thirteen be appointed by the *Speaker*, whose duty it shall be to confer with the officers and members of the *Washington National Monument Association* upon the practicability of completing the *Washington Monument* by the approaching centennial.

Journal of the House of Representatives, pp. 224, 293.

Report—submitted in the House of Representatives by the Hon. Norton P. Chipman, Delegate from the District of Columbia, 1 May 1874, from the *Select Committee on the Washington National Monument*, to accompany the bill providing for the completion of the *Washington Monument*.

Journal of the House of Representatives, pp. 889-890, 908.
[*H. Rept. No. 485* . . . . *Serial* 1625.]

Resolution—submitted in the House of Representatives by the Hon. Charles A. Eldredge, a Representative from Wisconsin, 11 June 1874, that it shall be in order to move an amendment to the *Sundry Civil Appropriation* bill in Committee of the Whole providing for an appropriation of $75,-000 to aid in the completion of the *Washington National Monument* by the one-hundredth anniversary of Amercan Independence, with the proviso that the *Washington National Monument Association* be required to re-convey to the United States reservation No. 3, in the city of Washington, on which the unfinished monument now stands.

> *Journal of the House of Representatives,* p. 1159.

FIRST SESSION OF THE FORTY-FOURTH CONGRESS: 1875-1876

Memorial of the Washington Monument Society, requesting an appropriation for the completion of the *Washington Monument*—presented in the House of Representatives, 21 January 1876, by the *Speaker* of the House; presented in the Senate, 10 February 1876, by the HON. GEORGE F. EDMUNDS, a Senator from Vermont.

> *Journal of the House of Representatives,* p. 236.
> *Journal of the Senate,* p. 187.
> [*Congressional Record,* V. 4: Part 1, pp. 541, 992.]

Concurrent Resolution—submitted in the House of Representatives by the HON. THOMAS J. CASON, a Representative from Indiana, 18 February 1876, proposing that for the promotion of national feeling throughout the Union on the occasion of the centennial year of our independence, and believing this to be the proper time for the expression of our appreciation of the great services rendered to the people and the cause of liberty by *the father of our Country,* GEORGE WASHINGTON, the 22nd day of the present month shall be treated and deemed a national holiday throughout the United States.—

. . . .

> *Journal of the House of Representatives,* pp. 422, 430.
> *Journal of the Senate,* p. 218.
> [*Congressional Record,* V. 4; Part 2, pp. 1164, 1184.]

Resolution—submitted in the Senate by the HON. GEORGE F. EDMUNDS, a Senator from Vermont, 9 February 1876, instructing the Committee on Public Buildings and Grounds to inquire into the expediency of making an adequate provision for the speedy completion of the *Washington Monument,* in the city of Washington, and that it have leave to report by bill or otherwise.

> *Journal of the Senate,* p. 184.
> [*Congressional Record,* V. 4: Part 1, p. 957.]

Concurrent Resolution—submitted in the Senate by the HON. JOHN SHERMAN, a Senator from Ohio, 5 July 1876, for consideration:

. . . .

We, the Senate and House of Representatives in Congress assembled, in the name of the people of the United States, at this the beginning of the second century of national existence, do assume and direct the completion of the *Washington Monument* in the city of Washington, and instruct the Committees on Appropriation of the respective Houses to propose suitable provision of law to carry this resolution into effect.

> *Journal of the Senate,* pp. 677, 684.

> [*Congressional Record,* V. 4: Part 5, pp. 4375-4376.]
> [*S. Mis. Doc. No. 123 . . . Serial 1665.*]

Senate bill (S. No. 982)—submitted in the Senate by the HON. JOHN SHERMAN, a Senator from Ohio, 8 July 1876, providing for the completion of the *Washington Monument.*—Approved, 2 August 1876.[1]

> *Journal of the Senate,* pp. 688, 700, 743-744, 764, 765, 767, 772, 783.
> [*Congressional Record,* V. 4: Part 5, pp. 4469, 4514, 4861, 4919; Part 6, p. 5099.]

SECOND SESSION OF THE FORTY-FIFTH CONGRESS: 1877-1878

Report of the Joint Commission created to direct and supervise the completion of the *Washington Monument*—transmitted to the Congress, 3 December 1877, with the *Annual Message of the President of the United States.*

> *Journal of the Senate,* p. 23.
> *Journal of the House of Representatives,* p. 25.
> [*H. Ex. Doc. No. 1, Part 8 . . Serial 1802.*]

Memorial of the Washington Monument Society, remonstrating against the abandonment or any material modification of the original plan for the erection of the *Washington Monument*—presented in the Senate, 15 April 1878, by the HON. JOHN J. INGALLS, a Senator from Kansas.

> *Journal of the Senate,* p. 389.
> [*Congressional Record,* V. 7: Part 3, p. 2508.]

Joint Resolution (H.J.Res. No. 76)—submitted in the House of Representatives by the HON. CHARLES FOSTER, a Representative from Ohio, 14 January 1878, to enable the Joint Commission to carry into effect the act of Congress providing for the completion of the *Washington Monument.*

. . .

> *Journal of the House of Representatives,* pp. 182, 782.
> [*Congressional Record,* V. 7: Part 1, p. 314.]

Joint Resolution (H.J.Res. No. 152)—reported to the House of Representatives by the HON. CHARLES FOSTER, a Representative from Ohio, 2 April 1878, from the Committee on Appropriations, as substitute for the House Joint Resolution No. 76, to enable the Joint Commission to carry into effect the act of Congress providing for the completion of the *Washington Monument.*—Approved, 14 June 1878.

> *Journal of the House of Representatives,* pp. 782-783, 1053, 1101, 1146, 1149, 1256-1257, 1264, 1269, 1305, 1340.
> *Journal of the Senate,* pp. 496, 649, 793.
> [*Congressional Record,* V. 7: Part 3, p. 2203.]

THIRD SESSION OF THE FORTY-FIFTH CONGRESS: 1878-1879

Letter of W. W. CORCORAN, chairman of the Joint Commission for the completion of the Washington Monument, communicating a report of the engineer in charge of the con-

---

[1] Under the provisions of this Act a Joint Commission was appointed by the United States Congress to direct and supervise the completion of the *Washington Monument.*

struction of the monument, showing the extent and progress made in the work and the amount of money expended to the 30th of November, 1878—presented in the Senate, 13 December 1878, by the *Vice-President;* presented in the House of Representatives, 13 December 1878, by the *Speaker* of the House.

> *Journal of the Senate,* p. 51.
> *Journal of the House of Representatives,* p. 91.
> [*Congressional Record,* V. 8; Part 1, p. 180.]
> [*H. Mis. Doc. No. 7 . . . Serial* 1861.]

Letter of W. W. CORCORAN, *chairman of the Joint Commission for the completion of the Washington Monument,* submitting certain papers in relation to the proposed modification in the plan of the monument—presented in the Senate, 8 January 1879, by the *Vice-President;* presented in the House of Representatives, 15 January 1879, by the *Speaker* of the House.

> *Journal of the Senate,* p. 92.
> *Journal of the House of Representatives,* p. 181.
> [*Congressional Record,* V. 8: Part 1, pp. 367, 462.]

Letter of W. W. CORCORAN, *chairman of the Joint Commission for the completion of the Washington Monument,* communicating a resolution of the commission in relation to a further expenditure for the strengthening of the foundations thereof—presented in the Senate, 12 February 1879, by the *Vice-President;* presented in the House of Representatives, 15 February 1879, by the *Speaker* of the House.

> *Journal of the Senate,* p. 260.
> *Journal of the House of Representatives,* p. 449.
> [*Congressional Record,* V. 8: Part 2, p. 1427.]
> [*H. Mis. Doc. No. 7, Part 2 . . Serial* 1861.]

Joint Resolution (H.J.Res. No. 212)—submitted in the House of Representatives by the HON. BENJAMIN A. WILLIS, a Representative from New York, 20 January 1879, to facilitate, simplify, and economize the work on the *Washington National Monument* in the District of Columbia.

> *Journal of the House of Representatives,* p. 223.
> [*Congressional Record,* V. 8: Part 1, p. 574.]

FIRST SESSION OF THE FORTY-SIXTH CONGRESS:
1879

Joint Resolution (H.J.Res. No. 32)—submitted in the House of Representatives by the HON. THOMPSON H. MURCH, a Representative from Maine, 5 May 1879, authorizing the completion of the foundation of the *Washington Monument—Approved,* 27 June 1879.

> *Journal of the House of Representatives,* pp. 232, 493, 549, 560, 576, 583.
> *Journal of the Senate,* pp. 205, 206, 239, 249, 263, 264, 270, 285.
> [*Congressional Record,* V. 9: Part 1, p. 1050; Part 2, pp. 1983, 1985, 2195, 2271, 2307, 2369, 2423.]

Joint Resolution (H.J.Res. No. 94)—submitted in the House of Representatives by the HON. JOHN T. HARRIS, a Representative from Virginia, 10 June 1879, directing that a monument be erected to mark the *birthplace of* GEORGE WASHINGTON.—*Approved,* 14 June 1879.

Journal of the House of Representatives, pp. 472, 477, 481, 505, 532.
Journal of the Senate, pp. 196, 197, 200, 240.
[*Congressional Record,* V. 9: Part 2, pp. 1888, 1890, 1923, 1932, 2195.]

Resolution—submitted in the Senate by the HON. JAMES DONALD CAMERON, a Senator from Pennsylvania, 31 March 1879, proposing that the Committee on the Library be instructed to inquire into the expediency of purchasing the full-size portrait of GENERAL GEORGE WASHINGTON, painted from life by CHARLES WILLSON PEALE. . . .

> *Journal of the Senate,* p. 54.
> [*Congressional Record,* V. 9: Part 1, p. 129.]

SECOND SESSION OF THE FORTY-SIXTH CONGRESS:
1879-1880

Letter of W. W. CORCORAN, *chairman of the Joint Commission for the completion of the Washington Monument,* transmitting the annual report of LIEUT.-COLONEL THOMAS L. CASEY, U. S. A., engineer in charge of the monument, detailing the work done toward the completion of the same during the year ending November 30, 1879, together with statement of moneys expended upon the same, and two sheets of tracings—presented in the House of Representatives, 16 December 1879, by the *Speaker* of the House; presented in the Senate, 17 December 1879, by the *Vice-President.*

> [*Congressional Record,* V. 10: Part 1, p. 134.]
> [*S. Mis. Doc. No. 17 . . . Serial* 1890.]

Resolution—submitted in the Senate by the HON. DANIEL W. VOORHEES, a Senator from Indiana, 9 February 1880, proposing that the Committee on the Library be instructed to inquire into the expediency and propriety of purchasing the *full-length portrait of* MARTHA WASHINGTON by ANDREWS, for the East Room of the Executive Mansion.

> *Journal of the Senate,* p. 208.
> [*Congressional Record,* V. 10: Part 1, p. 753.]

Letter from the Norfolk and Portsmouth Mexican Veteran Association, extending to the United States Senate an invitation to attend the ceremonies in Norfolk, 23 February 1880, in honor of WASHINGTON's *birthday,* the anniversary of the battle of Buena Vista, and the occasion of the national convention of the survivors of the Mexican War—presented in the Senate, 16 February 1880, by the *Vice-President.*

> *Journal of the Senate,* p. 226.
> [*Congressional Record,* V. 10: Part 1, p. 909.]

Concurrent Resolution—reported to the Senate by the HON. CHARLES W. JONES, a Senator from Florida, 29 March, 1880, from the Committee on Public Buildings and Grounds that the Committee on Public Buildings and Grounds of the Senate and of the House of Representatives, acting jointly, be instructed to examine whether or not further legislation is required, and what additional appropriations will be necessary, in relation to the foundation and completion of the *Washington Monument;* what time it will take to finish the same; whether or not any contracts have been made for materials or otherwise, and, if any have been made, their character and amount; whether any changes of the original plan or design have been authorized, adopted, or are desirable, and to what extent; together with an estimate of the ultimate cost of the completed structure, and report thereon, by bill or otherwise, to the Senate and the House of Representatives, on the second Monday of December next.

> *Journal of the Senate*, pp. 378, 529.
> [*Congressional Record*, V. 10: Part 2, p. 1920.]
> [*S. Mis. Doc. No. 86 . . . Serial* 1891.]

Memorial of the Washington Monument Association, requesting an appropriation for the completion of the *Washington Monument*—presented in the Senate, 28 April 1880, by the *Vice-President*; presented in the House of Representatives, 29 April 1880, by the HON. EDWARD L. MARTIN, a Representative from Delaware.

> *Journal of the Senate*, pp. 485, 488, 592.
> *Journal of the House of Representatives*, p. 1142.
> [*Congressional Record*, V. 10: Part 3, pp. 2810-2811.]
> [*H. Mis. Doc. No. 37 . . . Serial* 1931.]

Report—submitted in the House of Representatives by the HON. EDWARD L. MARTIN, a Representative from Delaware, 9 April 1880, from the Committee on the District of Columbia, to accompany the bill (H.R. No. 5714), providing for the completion of the *Washington National Monument*.

> *Journal of the House of Representatives*, p. 993.
> [*H. Rept. No. 1107 . . . Serial* 1937.]

Communication from WILLIAM M. EVARTS, *Secretary of State*, in reference to a monument to mark the *birthplace of* GEORGE WASHINGTON—presented in the House of Representatives, 3 June 1880, by the HON. SAMUEL J. RANDALL, of Pennsylvania, *Speaker* of the House.

> [*Congressional Record*, V. 10: Part 5, pp. 4117-4118.]

Joint Resolution (H.J.Res. No. 315)—submitted in the House of Representatives by the HON. JOHN T. HARRIS, a Representative from Virginia, 3 June 1880, amending and re-enacting a joint resolution approved 14 June 1879, directing that a monument be erected to mark the *birthplace of* GEORGE WASHINGTON.—*Approved*, 26 February 1881.

> *Journal of the House of Representatives*, p. 1366.
> *Journal of the Senate*, pp. 651, 692.
> [*Congressional Record*, V. 10: Part 5, pp. 4118, 4101, 4308.]

THIRD SESSION OF THE FORTY-SIXTH CONGRESS: 1880-1881

Letter of W. W. CORCORAN, *chairman of the Joint Commission for the completion of the Washington Monument*, 8 December 1880, transmitting the annual report of said commission and the report of LIEUTENANT-COLONEL THOMAS L. CASEY, Corps of Engineers, U. S. A., in charge of the construction of the *Monument*.

> [*Congressional Record*, V. 11: Part 1, pp. 48, 49, 74.]
> [*S. Mis. Doc. No. 9 . . . Serial* 1944.]
> [*S. Mis. Doc. No. 9, Part 2 . . Serial* 1944.]

House bill (H.R. No. 5384)—reported to the House of Representatives by the HON. GEORGE W. GEDDES, a Representa-

tive from Ohio, 27 March 1880, from the Committee on the Library, granting permission to the Chamber of Commerce in New York to erect a statue on the Sub-Treasury building in the city of New York in commemoration of WASHINGTON's *first inauguration as President of the United States.—Approved*, 23 December 1880.

> *Journal of the House of Representatives*, pp. 46, 106, 110, 122, 125.
> [*Congressional Record*, V. 10: Part 2, p. 1903; V. 11: Part 1, pp. 60, 93, 206, 262, 294, 318, 355.]

Joint Resolution (S.J.Res. No. 139)—submitted in the Senate by the HON. WILLIAM P. WHYTE, a Senator from Maryland, 5 January 1881, for the purchase of a sword formerly belonging to GEORGE WASHINGTON.—

> *Journal of the Senate*, pp. 86, 192-193.
> [*Congressional Record*, V. 11: Part 1, p. 340; Part 2, p. 1128.]

Senate bill (S. No. 2147)—submitted in the Senate by the HON. JOHN W. JOHNSTON, a Senator from Virginia, 3 February 1881, to provide for the purchase from MRS. HUBBARD of a *bronze statue* of GENERAL WASHINGTON.

> *Journal of the Senate*, p. 197.
> [*Congressional Record*, V. 11: Part 2, p. 1160.]

Joint Resolution (S.J.Res. No. 158)—submitted in the Senate by the HON. WILLIAM A. WALLACE, a Senator from Pennsylvania, 12 February 1881, to allow the State Society of the Cincinnati of Pennsylvania to import free of duty a *Monument to* GENERAL WASHINGTON. . . .

> *Journal of the Senate*, pp. 244, 258.
> [*Congressional Record*, V. 11: Part 2, pp. 1489, 1582.]

FIRST SESSION OF THE FORTY-SEVENTH CONGRESS: 1881-1882

Resolution—submitted in the Senate, for consideration, by the HON. DANIEL W. VOORHEES, a Senator from Indiana, 7 December 1881, proposing that the Committee on the Library be instructed to inquire into the expediency of purchasing the full-size portrait of GENERAL GEORGE WASHINGTON, painted from life by CHARLES WILLSON PEALE.

> *Journal of the Senate*, pp. 82, 268.

Resolution—submitted in the Senate by the HON. DANIEL W. VOORHEES, a Senator from Indiana, 3 May 1882, proposing that the Committee on the Library be instructed to inquire into the expediency and propriety of purchasing 5,000 copies of the work entitled *Original Portraits of* WASHINTON by ELIZABETH BRYANT JOHNSON, for distribution to the public libraries throughout the United States.[1] . . . .

> *Journal of the Senate*, p. 661.
> [*Congressional Record*, V. 13: Part 4, p. 3536.]

---

[1] SENATOR VOORHEES introduced the resolution again, 10 December 1883, and it was agreed to in the Senate; whereupon, SENATOR VOORHEES offered an amendment providing for the purchase to the Sundry Civil Appropriations bill (H.R. 7380), which was adopted by the Senate. *Journal of the Senate* (48th Congress, 1st Session), p. 67 and p. 896. SENATOR VOORHEES re-introduced the resolution 20 Jan. 1885, and it was referred to the Committee on the Library. *Journal of the Senate* (48th Congress, 2d Session), p. 156.

Letter of W. W. CORCORAN, *chairman of the Joint Commission for the completion of the Washington Monument*, 19 December 1881, transmitting the annual report of said commission, in compliance with the law of its creation.

> [*Congressional Record*, V. 13: Part 1, pp. 184, 435.]
>
> [*S. Mis. Doc. No.* 19 . . . *Serial* 1993.]

Memorial of the State Society of the Cincinnati of Pennsylvania, requesting the passage of a law authorizing the importation free of duty of a *monument to* GEORGE WASHINGTON—presented in the Senate, 10 January 1882, by the HON. JAMES DONALD CAMERON, a Senator from Pennsylvania; presented in the House of Representatives, 10 January 1882, by the HON. CHARLES O'NEILL, a Representative from Pennsylvania.

> *Journal of the Senate*, p. 164.
>
> *Journal of the House of Representatives*, p. 252.

Memorial of the Mayor and Common Council of Fredericksburg, Virginia, requesting an appropriation for the completion of the *monument to the mother of* GEORGE WASHINGTON—presented in the Senate, 6 February 1882, by the HON. JOHN W. JOHNSTON, a Senator from Virginia; presented in the House of Representatives, 6 February 1882, by the HON. GEORGE GARRISON, a Representative from Virginia.

> *Journal of the Senate*, p. 263.
>
> *Journal of the House of Representatives*, p. 487.

Report—submitted to the House of Representatives by the HON. WILLIAM McKINLEY, JR., a Representative from Ohio, 8 February 1882, from the Committee on Ways and Means, to accompany the joint resolution (H. J. Res. No. 109), introduced, 23 January 1882, by MR. O'NEILL, a Representative from Pennsylvania, proposing to admit free of duty a *monument to* GENERAL WASHINGTON.[2]—

> *Journal of the House of Representatives*, pp. 367, 525.
>
> [*Congressional Record*, V. 13: Part 1, pp. 565, 989.]
>
> [*H. Rept. No.* 306 . . . . *Serial* 2065.]

Report—submitted in the House of Representatives by the HON. J. HYATT SMITH, a Representative from New York, 15 July 1882, from the Committee on Public Buildings and Grounds, to accompany the bill (H. R. No. 4135), introduced by MR. GARRISON, of Virginia, 6 February 1882, for the completion of the *monument to* MARY, *the mother of* WASHINGTON, at Fredericksburg, Virginia.

> *Journal of the House of Representatives*, pp. 503, 1649.
>
> [*Congressional Record*, V. 13: Part 1, p. 932; Part 6, p. 6103.]
>
> [*H. Rept. No.* 1659 . . . *Serial* 2070.]

House bill (H. R. No. 5573)—reported to the House of Representatives by the HON. FRANK HISCOCK, a Representative from New York, 1 April 1882, from the Committee on

---

[2] The House joint resolution (H.J.Res. No. 109), authorizing the State Society of the Cincinnati of Pennsylvania to bring in, free of duty a *monument to* GENERAL WASHINGTON, was passed in the second session of the Forty-Seventh Congress, and *approved*, 17 February 1883.

PRESIDENT JOHN ADAMS ON DECEMBER 23, 1799, MADE AN ADDRESS BEFORE THE SENATE UPON THE DEATH OF GEORGE WASHINGTON

Appropriations, making appropriations to supply a deficiency for dies, paper, and stamps for the fiscal year 1882, and to continue work on the *Washington Monument* for the fiscal year 1883.—*Approved*, 17 April 1882.

> *Journal of the House of Representatives*, pp. 955, 989-990, 1038, 1041, 1053, 1058.
>
> *Journal of the Senate*, pp. 547, 569, 585, 613.
>
> [*Congressional Record*, V. 13: Part 3, pp. 2488, 2654-2656, 2644, 2857, 2907, 2934, 2950.]

Joint Resolution (H. J. Res. No. 176)—reported to the House of Representatives by the HON. MARK L. DEMOTTE, a Representative from Indiana, 3 May 1882, from the Committee on Public Buildings and Grounds, authorizing the Secretary of War to erect at WASHINGTON'S *headquarters, in Newburgh, New York,* a memorial column, and to aid in defraying the expenses of the centennial celebration to be held at that city in the year 1883.—*Approved*, 1 July 1882.

> [*Congressional Record*, V. 13: Part 4, p. 3552; Part 5, pp. 4833, 4843, 5124, 5259; Part 6, pp. 5282, 5610.]
>
> [*H. Rept. No.* 1167 . . . *Serial* 2068.]

SECOND SESSION OF THE FORTY-SEVENTH CONGRESS: 1882-1883

Letter of W. W. CORCORAN, *chairman of the Joint Commission for the completion of the Washington Monument*, 23 December 1882, transmitting, in compliance with law, the report of the Joint Commission.

> *Congressional Record*, V. 14: Part 1, pp. 584, 664.
> [*S. Mis. Doc. No.* 13 . . . *Serial* 2083.]

Joint Resolution (S. J. Res. No. 113)—submitted in the Senate by the HON. ISHAM G. HARRIS, a Senator from Tennessee, 7 December 1882, authorizing the engineer in charge of the *Washington Monument* to pay to certain stone-cutters and laborers certain wages withheld from them.—

> *Journal of the Senate*, pp. 42, 307.
> [*Congressional Record*, V. 14: Part 1, p. 71; Part 3, p. 2333.]

Joint Resolution (S. J. Res. No. 138)—submitted in the Senate by the HON. WARNER MILLER, a Senator from New York, 16 February 1883, concerning the erection of a memorial column at WASHINGTON's *headquarters in Newburgh, New York.—Approved*, 3 March 1883.

> *Journal of the Senate*, pp. 350, 545, 550.
> *Journal of the House of Representatives*, pp. 459, 645.
> [*Congressional Record*, V. 14; Part 3, p. 2770; Part 4, pp. 3031, 3768, 3704, 3772.]

FIRST SESSION OF THE FORTY-EIGHTH CONGRESS: 1883-1884

Letter of W. W. CORCORAN, *chairman of the Joint Commission for the completion of the Washington Monument*, 13 December 1883; transmitting, in obedience to law, the annual report of the Commission.

> *Congressional Record*, V. 15: Part 1, pp. 137, 148.
> [*S. Mis. Doc. No.* 22 . . . *Serial* 2170.]

Resolution—submitted in the Senate by the HON. JAMES B. GROOME, a Senator from Maryland, 3 April 1884, that the Committee on the Library be directed to inquire into the expediency of purchasing from the Lewis family, for the United States, *a sword worn by* GENERAL GEORGE WASHINGTON upon the occasion of his resigning his commission at Annapolis, 23 December 1783.

> *Journal of the Senate*, p. 496.
> [*Congressional Record*, V. 15: Part 3, p. 2534.]

Joint Resolution (S. J. Res. No. 82)—reported to the Senate by the HON. JUSTIN S. MORRILL, a Senator from Vermont, 29 April 1884, from the Committee on Public Buildings and Grounds, in relation to ceremonies to be authorized upon the completion of the *Washington Monument.—Approved*, 13 May 1884.[1]

> *Journal of the Senate*, pp. 593, 600, 623, 637, 649, 667, 714.

---

[1] Under the provisions of the Senate joint resolution (S. J. Res. No. 82), a Joint Commission was appointed to make arrangements for the ceremonies to be authorized upon the completion of the *Washington Monument*.

Journal of the House of Representatives, pp. 1164, 1202, 1208, 1237, 1332.

> [*Congressional Record*, V. 15: Part 4, pp. 3516, 3568, 3976, 3997, 3999, 4147.]

Joint Resolution (H. J. Res. No. 65)—reported to the House of Representatives by the HON. FETTER S. HOBLITZELL, a Representative from Maryland, 20 December 1883, from the Select Committee appointed to consider the joint resolution relating to the *surrender by* GEORGE WASHINGTON *of his commission as Commander-in-Chief of the patriotic forces of America.—Approved*, 26 December 1883.

> *Journal of the House of Representatives*, pp. 140, 156, 162, 167, 181.
> [*Congressional Record*, V. 15: Part 1, pp. 220, 210, 223, 246.]

Joint Resolution (H. J. Res. No. 98)—submitted in the House of Representatives by the HON. JOHN TURNER WAIT, a Representative from Connecticut, 8 January 1884, in relation to the purchase of four historical paintings representing leading events in the life of GEORGE WASHINGTON.

> *Journal of the House of Representatives*, p. 244.
> [*Congressional Record*, V. 15: Part 1, p. 298.]

Petition of the common council of the city of Fredericksburg, asking for an appropriation for the completion of a monument to MARY, *the mother of* GEORGE WASHINGTON—presented in the House of Representatives, 23 February 1884, by the HON. JOHN S. WISE, a Representative from Virginia.

> *Journal of the House of Representatives*, pp. 648-649.
> [*Congressional Record*, V. 15: Part 2, p. 1336.]

Report—submitted to the House of Representatives by the HON. GILBERT M. WOODWARD, a Representative from Wisconsin, 7 May 1884, from the Committee on the Library, to accompany the House bill (H. R. 5410), introduced by the HON. GEORGE D. WISE, of Virginia, 25 February 1884, for the completion of the monument to MARY, *the mother of* WASHINGTON, at Fredericksburg in Virginia. . . . .

> *Journal of the House of Representatives*, pp. 667, 1197.
> [*Congressional Record*, V. 15: Part 2, pp. 1356-1357: Part 4, p. 3936.]
> [*H. Rept. No.* 1512 . . . *Serial* 2257.]

Message from CHESTER A. ARTHUR, *President of the United States*, 19 May 1884, transmitting to the Congress a communication from the Secretary of State, recommending an additional appropriation of $6,000 for the construction of a wharf and roadway as a means of approach to the monument to be erected at *Wakefield, Westmoreland County, Virginia*, to mark the birthplace of GEORGE WASHINGTON.

> *Journal of the House of Representatives*, p. 1270.
> [*Congressional Record*, V. 15: Part 5, p. 4311.]
> [*H. Ex. Doc. No.* 160 . . . *Serial* 2207.]

Report—submitted to the House of Representatives by the Hon. John Kean, Jr., a Representative from New Jersey, 5 July 1884, from the Committee on Public Buildings and Grounds, to whom was referred the joint resolution (H. J. Res. No. 197) authorizing the Secretary of War to assist in canceling the debt and enlarging and improving the grounds and collections of Washington's *Headquarters in Morristown, New Jersey,* and in securing suitable ground in which to gather the remains of Revolutionary soldiers there buried, and in erecting a monument over the same. . . . .

> *Journal of the House of Representatives,* pp. 785-786.
> [*Congressional Record,* V. 15: Part 2, p. 1756; Part 6, p. 6087.]
> [*H. Rept. No.* 2143 . . . Serial 2259.]

SECOND SESSION OF THE FORTY-EIGHTH CONGRESS: 1884-1885

Joint Resolution (S. J. Res. No. 101)—submitted in the Senate by the Hon. John Sherman, a Senator from Ohio, 11 December 1884, in relation to the ceremonies to be authorized upon the completion of the *Washington Monument.—Approved,* 18 December 1884.

> *Journal of the Senate,* pp. 48, 55, 59, 74, 76.
> [*Congressional Record,* V. 16: Part 1, pp. 187, 218, 296, 299, 328.]

Letter of W. W. Corcoran, *chairman of the Joint Commission for the completion of the Washington Monument,* transmitting, 19 December 1884, in obedience to law, the annual report of the Commission.—

> *Congressional Record,* V. 16: Part 1, pp. 347, 363.
> [*H. Mis. Doc.* No. 8 . . . Serial 2310.]

Letter from the Secretary of the Treasury, 14 January 1885, transmitting an estimate from the Commissioners of the District of Columbia of an appropriation of $10,000 to enable them to maintain public order during the ceremonies attending the *dedication of the Washington Monument.*

> *Congressional Record,* V. 16: Part 1, p. 723.
> [*H. Ex. Doc. No.* 81 . . . Serial 2302.]

Joint Resolution (S. J. Res. No. 108)—submitted in the Senate by the Hon. William J. Sewell, a Senator from New Jersey, 7 January 1885, authorizing the Secretary of War to assist in canceling the debt and in enlarging and improving the grounds and collections of Washington's *headquarters in Morristown, New Jersey,* and in securing suitable ground in which to gather the remains of Revolutionary soldiers there buried, and in erecting a monument over the same.

. . . .

> *Journal of the Senate,* pp. 105-106.
> [*Congressional Record,* V. 16: Part 1, p. 506.]

Resolution—reported to the Senate by the Hon. John Sherman, a Senator from Ohio, 29 January 1885, from the *Joint Committee on the Dedication of the Washington Monument,* that the order of proceedings adopted by the commission appointed under the joint resolution of Congress approved May 13, 1884, for the *dedication of the Washington Monument,* on the 21st day of February next, be approved.—

> *Journal of the Senate,* p. 195.
> [*Congressional Record,* V. 16: Part 2, pp. 1051, 1052-1053.]

Senate bill (S. No. 2615)—reported to the Senate by the Hon. John Sherman, a Senator from Ohio, 10 February 1885, from the Committee on Finance, authorizing *medals commemorating the completion and dedication of the Washington Monument.*—

> *Journal of the Senate,* pp. 232, 258.
> [*Congressional Record,* V. 16: Part 2, pp. 1450, 1477-1478.]

Ordered by the Senate, 25 February 1885—upon the submission of the Report by the Hon. John Sherman, a Senator from Ohio—that the *Report and Proceedings of the Joint Commission* appointed to provide suitable ceremonies for the *dedication of the Washington Monument* be printed as a public document.

> *Congressional Record,* V. 16: Part 3, p. 2117.
> [*S. Mis. Doc. No.* 56 . . . Serial 2267.]

Concurrent Resolution—submitted in the Senate by the Hon John Sherman, a Senator from Ohio, 25 February 1885, from the Committee appointed to provide suitable ceremonies for the *Dedication of the Washington Monument,* proposing that 10,000 extra copies of the report and proceedings of the commission to provide suitable ceremonies for the *dedication of the Washington Monument,* together with the engraved card thereto, be printed in memorial form, under the direction of the Committee on Printing.

> *Journal of the Senate,* p. 375, 394.
> *Journal of the House of Representatives,* p. 681.
> [*Congressional Record,* V. 16: Part 3, p. 2117.]

Concurrent Resolution—reported by the Hon. John Sherman, a Senator from Ohio, 25 February 1885, from the Committee appointed to provide suitable ceremonies for the *dedication of the Washington Monument,* proposing that the thanks of Congress are hereby tendered to Colonel Thomas Lincoln Casey, Corps of Engineers, United States Army, and to his assistants, and to the workmen, for the admirable manner in which he and they have performed their respective duties in the completion of the *Monument to the name and fame of* George Washington.

> *Journal of the Senate,* pp. 375-376.
> *Journal of the House of Representatives,* p. 681.
> [*Congressional Record,* V. 16: Part 3, p. 2117.]

Senate bill (S. No. 2666)—reported to the Senate by the Hon. Charles F. Manderson, a Senator from Nebraska, 27 February 1885, from the Committee on Printing, providing for the printing of the *Report and Proceedings of the Joint Commission,* appointed to arrange suitable ceremonies for the *dedication of the Washington Monument.—Approved,* 3 March 1885.

> *Journal of the Senate,* pp. 397, 440, 453, 488, 489.
> *Journal of the House of Representatives,* pp. 710, 759, 766, 822.
> [*Congressional Record,* V. 16: Part 3, pp. 2236-2237.]

Joint Resolution (H. J. Res. No. 326)—submitted in the House of Representatives by the HON. WILLIAM R. COX, a Representative from North Carolina, 2 February 1885, to provide more suitable accommodations for the public at the dedication ceremonies upon the completion of the *Washington Monument.*—

> *Journal of the House of Representatives*, pp. 415-416.
> [*Congressional Record*, V. 16: Part 3, p. 1164.]

FIRST SESSION OF THE FORTY-NINTH CONGRESS:
1885-1886

Letter of W. W. CORCORAN, *chairman of the Joint Commission for the completion of the Washington Monument*, 15 December 1885, transmitting, in obedience to law, the annual report of the Commission.

> *Congressional Record*, V. 17: Part 1, pp. 177, 225.
> [*S. Ex. Doc. No. 6 . . . Serial* 2333.]

Joint Resolution (H. J. Res. No. 45)—submitted in the House of Representatives by the HON. WILLIAM W. PHELPS, a Representative from New Jersey, 5 January 1886, to enlarge and improve WASHINGTON's *headquarters at Morristown, New Jersey.* . . .

> *Journal of the House of Representatives*, p. 216.
> [*Congressional Record*, V. 17: Part 1, p. 430.]

House bill (H. R. No. 4780)—submitted in the House of Representatives by the HON. THOMAS CROXTON, a Representative from Virginia, 26 January 1886, for the completion of the *monument to* MARY, *the mother of* WASHINGTON, at *Fredericksburg, Virginia.* . . .

> *Journal of the House of Representatives*, p. 474.
> [*Congressional Record*, V. 17: Part 1, p. 895.]

Report—submitted to the House of Representatives by the HON. SAMUEL DIBBLE, a Representative from South Carolina, 16 April 1886, from the Committee on Public Buildings and Grounds, to whom was referred the bill (H. R. No. 5097) to regulate the use of the grounds of the *Washington Monument*, known as public reservation No. 3, in the city of Washington, District of Columbia.

> *Journal of the House of Representatives*, pp. 1275-1276.
> [*Congressional Record*, V. 17: Part 4, pp. 3578, 3596-3597, 3600.]
> [*H. Rept. No.* 1758 . . . *Serial* 2440.]

SECOND SESSION OF THE FORTY-NINTH CONGRESS:
1886-1887

Senate bill (S. No. 2982)—reported to the Senate by the HON. ISHAM G. HARRIS, a Senator from Tennessee, 17 December 1886, from the Committee on the District of Columbia, authorizing the Commissioners of the District of Columbia to permit the temporary occupation of streets by a railway for the purpose of transporting material to fill about the base of the *Washington Monument.*—*Approved*, 28 February 1887.

> *Congressional Record*, V. 18: Part 1, pp. 242, 273, 315; Part 2, pp. 1301, 1748, 1873, 1884; Part 3, p. 2378.
> [*H. Rept. No.* 3915 . . . *Serial* 2501.]

Senate bill (S. No. 3182)—submitted in the Senate by the HON. WILLIAM MAHONE, a Senator from Virginia, 20 January 1887, for the completion of the *monument to* MARY, *the mother of* WASHINGTON.—

> *Journal of the Senate*, pp. 178, 209, 458.
> [*Congressional Record*, V. 18: Part 1, p. 825; Part 2, p. 1030; Part 3, pp. 2320, 2435.]

Communication from the Citizens' Committee of Alexandria, Virginia, inviting the United States Senate to unite with them in celebrating WASHINGTON's *birthday*—presented in the Senate, 19 February 1887, by the President *pro tempore.*

> *Congressional Record*, V. 18: Part 2, p. 1941.

Joint Resolution (S. J. Res. No. 115)—reported to the Senate by the HON. DANIEL W. VOORHEES, a Senator from Indiana, 28 February 1887, from the Committee on the Library, amending and re-enacting the joint resolution approved 14 June 1879, directing a monument to mark the *birthplace* of GEORGE WASHINGTON as amended and re-enacted 26 February 1881.

> *Journal of the Senate*, p. 467.
> [*Congressional Record*, V. 18: Part 3, p. 2373.]

Letter of W. W. CORCORAN, *chairman of the Joint Commission for the completion of the Washington Monument*, 11 January 1887, transmitting, in obedience to law, the annual report of the Commission.

> *Congressional Record*, V. 18: Part 1, pp. 512, 534.
> [*H. Mis. Doc. No.* 57 . . . *Serial* 2488.]

Resolution—submitted in the House of Representatives by the HON. ANDREW J. CALDWELL, a Representative from Tennessee, 10 January 1887, proposing that the Committee on the Library take into consideration the matter of protecting GREENOUGH's *statue of* WASHINGTON from damage by weather and desecration by vandals.

> *Journal of the House of Representatives*, p. 214.
> [*Congressional Record*, V. 18: Part 1, p. 501.]
> [*H. Mis. Doc. No.* 67 . . . *Serial* 2488.]

House bill (H. R. No. 4780)—reported to the House of Representatives by the HON. CHARLES O'NEILL, a Representative from Pennsylvania, 20 January 1887, from the Committee on the Library, for the Completion of the *monument to* MARY, *the mother of* WASHINGTON, *at Fredericksburg, Virginia.*—

> *Journal of the House of Representatives*, p. 328.
> [*Congressional Record*, V. 18: Part 1, p. 833.]
> [*H. Rept. No.* 3703 . . . *Serial* 2500.]

FIRST SESSION OF THE FIFTIETH CONGRESS:
1887-1888

Letter of W. W. CORCORAN, *chairman of the Joint Commission for the completion of the Washington Monument*, 4 January 1888, transmitting, in obedience to law, the annual report of the Commission.

> *Congressional Record*, V. 19: Part 1, pp. 183, 304.
> [*S. Mis. Doc. No.* 22 . . . *Serial* 2516.]

Senate bill (S. No. 1211)—submitted in the Senate by the Hon. John W. Daniel, a Senator from Virginia, 5 January 1888, for the completion of the *monument to* Mary, *the mother of* Washington, *at Fredericksburg, Virginia.*—

> *Journal of the Senate,* pp. 122, 362, 563.
> [*Congressional Record,* V. 19: Part 1, p. 258; Part 2, p. 1402; Part 3, pp. 2337, 2471, 2481, 2570.]

Report—submitted in the House of Representatives by the Hon. Charles O'Neill, a Representative from Pennsylvania, 28 July 1888, from the Committee on the Library, to whom was referred the Daniel bill (S. No. 1211) for the completion of the *monument to* Mary, *the mother of* Washington, *at Fredericksburg, Virginia.*

> *Journal of the House of Representatives,* Part 1, pp. 1378, 1386; Part 2, p. 2492.
> [*Congressional Record,* V. 19: Part 7, p. 6986.]
> [*H. Rept. No. 3102 . . . Serial 2605.*]

Senate bill (S. No. 1803)—submitted in the Senate by the Hon. M. S. Quay, a Senator from Pennsylvania, 31 January 1888, in aid of the *Centennial and Memorial Association of Valley Forge, and to secure the* Washington *headquarters mansion and grounds, occupied by the Continental Army of 1777-'78.*

> *Congressional Record,* V. 19: Part 1, p. 828; Part 2, p. 1402; Part 3, pp. 2480, 2570.

Resolution—submitted in the Senate by the Hon. George F. Hoar, a Senator from Massachusetts, 20 February 1888, proposing that, on Wednesday, the 22nd of February, next, the *Farewell Address of* Washington be read to the Senate by the presiding officer, after the conclusion of the morning business.

> *Journal of the Senate,* pp. 344, 356-357.
> [*Congressional Record,* V. 19: Part 2, p. 1331.]

Senate bill (S. No. 2309)—submitted in the Senate by the Hon. John C. Spooner, a Senator from Wisconsin, 12 March 1888, to regulate the use of the *grounds of the Washington Monument,* known as public reservation No. 3 in the city of Washington, District of Columbia.—

> *Journal of the Senate,* p. 454.
> [*Congressional Record,* V. 19: Part 2, p. 1941.]

Letter from the *Chairman of the Joint Commission for the completion of the Washington Monument,* transmitting resolutions adopted by the Commission, 18 April 1888, recommending that the custody, care, and protection of the *Washington Monument* be placed under the charge of the *Secretary of War*—presented in the Senate, 23 April 1888, by the President *pro tempore;* presented in the House of Representatives, 25 April 1888, by the *Speaker.*

> *Congressional Record,* V. 19: Part 4, pp. 3219, 3348.
> [*S. Mis. Doc. No. 98 . . . Serial 2516.*]

Letter from the Commissioners for the completion of the *Washington Monument* with relation to memorial blocks, recommending an appropriation of $1,500 for the inserting of memorial tablets in the walls of said monument—presented in the Senate, 25 June 1888, by the President *pro tempore.*

> *Journal of the Senate,* p. 1000.
> [*Congressional Record,* V. 19: Part 6, pp. 5523-5524.]
> [*S. Mis. Doc. No. 142 . . . Serial 2517.*]

Resolution—submitted in the Senate by the Hon. George Graham Vest, a Senator from Missouri, 7 May 1888, instructing the Committee on the Library to inquire as to the expediency of removing Greenough's *statue of* Washington and its pedestal from their present location east of the Capitol to some other place on the grounds, and the protection of said statue by a suitable canopy or otherwise.—

> *Journal of the Senate,* pp. 777-778, 823.
> [*Congressional Record,* V. 19: Part 4, p. 3770; Part 5, p. 4150.]

Concurrent Resolution—reported to the Senate by the Hon. Joseph R. Hawley, a Senator from from Connecticut, 16 July 1888, from the Committee on Printing, as substitute for the joint resolution (S. J. Res. No. 97) referred to the committee for the printing of the *Report of the Joint Select Committee on the Newburgh, New York, Monument and Centennial celebration* of 1883, submitted on the 26th of June, 1886.

> *Congressional Record,* V. 19: Part 6, p. 5793; Part 7, pp. 6341, 6735, 6900.
> [*S. Rept. No. 1807 . . . Serial 2525.*]

Joint Resolution (S. J. Res. No. 89)—submitted in the Senate by the Hon. James Donald Cameron, a Senator from Pennsylvania, 4 June 1888, amending and re-enacting the joint resolution approved 14 June 1879, directing the erection of a monument to mark the *birthplace of* George Washington, as amended and re-enacted 26 February 1881.—

> *Journal of the Senate,* p. 914.
> [*Congressional Record,* V. 19: Part 5, p. 4873.]

Resolution—submitted in the House of Representatives by the Hon. T. H. B. Browne, a Representative from Virginia, 16 July 1888, requesting the Secretary of State to inform the House of Representatives what action has been taken under the resolution of the 14th of June 1879, appropriating $3,000 for monuments to mark the *birthplace of* George Washington.—

> *Journal of the House of Representatives,* p. 2363.
> [*H. Mis. Doc. No. 523 . . . Serial 2570.*]

House bill (H. R. No. 1905)—submitted in the House of Representatives by the Hon. Thomas H. B. Browne, a Representative from Virginia, 4 January 1888, for the completion of the *monument to* Mary, *the mother of* Washington, *at Fredericksburg, Virginia.*—

> *Journal of the House of Representatives,* pp. 223, 1077-1078.
> [*H. Rept. No. 937 . . . Serial 2600.*]

House bill (H. R. No. 6146)—submitted in the House of Representatives by the Hon. Robert M. Yardley, a Representative from Pennsylvania, 30 January 1888, in aid of the *Centennial and Memorial Association of Valley Forge, and to secure the Washington headquarters mansion and grounds,* occupied by the Continental Army of 1777.—

> *Journal of the House of Representatives,* pp. 593, 1077.
> [*H. Rept. No. 936 . . . Serial 2600.*]

Petition of the *Homer City Council, Junior Order, United American Mechanics, of Pennsylvania,* praying that the 22nd day of February be made a legal holiday—presented in the Senate, 10 April 1888, by the HON. M. S. QUAY, a Senator from Pennsylvania.

> *Journal of the Senate,* p. 631.
> [*Congressional Record,* V. 19: Part 3, p. 2824.]

Communication from the Committee on the *Centennial Celebration of the Inauguration of* GEORGE WASHINGTON *as President of the United States,* inviting the Congress to participate in the celebration to be held in New York, 30 April 1889—presented in the Senate, 23 April 1888, by the President *pro tempore;* presented in the House of Representatives, 23 April 1888, by the *Speaker.*

> *Journal of the Senate,* p. 697.
> *Journal of the House of Representatives,* pp. 1717-1718.
> [*Congressional Record,* V. 19: Part 4, pp. 3219, 3246-3247.]

Resolution—submitted in the House of Representatives by the HON. SAMUEL S. COX, a Representative from New York, 23 April 1888, for the acceptance of the invitation to the House of Representatives to attend the *centennial celebration of the inauguration of* GEORGE WASHINGTON *in New York City,* 30 April 1889.

> *Journal of the House of Representatives,* p. 1722.
> [*Congressional Record,* V. 19: Part 4, p. 3250.]
> [*H. Mis. Doc. No. 382 . . . Serial 2570.*]

Report—submitted in the House of Representatives by the HON. WILLIAM C. OATES, a Representative from Alabama, 5 June 1888, from the Committee on the Judiciary, to whom was referred the resolution submitted, 23 April 1888, proposing that the House of Representatives accept the *invitation of the Committee on the Centennial Celebration of the Inauguration of* GEORGE WASHINGTON, 30 *April* 1889.

> *Journal of the House of Representatives,* p. 2065.
> [*Congressional Record,* V. 19: Part 5, p. 4911.]
> [*H. Rept. No.* 2441 . . . *Serial* 2604.]

Resolution—submitted in the House of Representatives by the HON. HENRY BACON, a Representative from New York, 23 April 1888, requesting the Secretary of War to transmit to the House of Representatives copies of all reports made to him by the engineers of the War Department or others relating to the present condition of the work on the *monument at* WASHINGTON'S *headquarters, in the city of Newburgh, in the State of New York.*

> *Congressional Record,* V. 19: Part 4, p. 3250.
> [*H. Mis. Doc. No.* 377 . . . *Serial* 2570.]

Report—submitted to the House of Representatives by the HON. WILLIAM G. STAHLNECKER, a Representative from New York, 9 May 1888, from the Committee on the Library, to whom was referred the resolution of inquiry as to the present condition of work on the *Monument at* WASHINGTON'S *headquarters in the city of Newburgh, in the State of New York.*

> *Congressional Record,* V. 19: Part 4, p. 3887.
> [*H. Rept. No.* 2075 . . . *Serial* 2603.]

Letter from the *Secretary of War,* 25 May 1888, transmitting, in compliance with a resolution of the House, a report upon the present condition of the *Monument at* WASHINGTON'S *headquarters in the city of Newburgh, in the State of New York.*

> *Congressional Record,* V. 19: Part 5, p. 4768.
> [*H. Ex. Doc. No.* 336 . . *Serial* 2561.]

Report—submitted to the House of Representatives by the HON. JAMES D. RICHARDSON, a Representative from Tennessee, 24 July 1888, from the Committee on Printing, to whom was referred the Senate concurrent resolution authorizing the printing of the Report *of the Joint Select Committee on the Newburgh, New York, monument and centennial celebration.*

> *Congressional Record,* V. 19: Part 7, p. 6735.
> [*H. Rept. No.* 3022 . . . *Serial* 2605.]

Ordered by the House of Representatives, 28 July 1888: That the report of the Joint Select Committee of Congress on the *Newburgh, New York, monument and centennial celebration of* 1883, submitted on the 26th of June, 1886, be printed as House document.

> *Congressional Record,* V. 19: Part 7, p. 6990.
> [*H. Mis. Doc. No.* 601 . . *Serial* 2576.]

SECOND SESSION OF THE FIFTIETH CONGRESS: 1888-1889

Senate bill (S. No. 3790)—submitted in the Senate by the HON. DANIEL W. VOORHEES, a Senator from Indiana, 8 January 1889, authorizing the purchase of a dressing and shaving table of GENERAL WASHINGTON, used by him during his life and mentioned in his will.—

> *Journal of the Senate,* p. 126.
> [*Congressional Record,* V. 20: Part 1, p. 596.]

Letter of the Acting-Secretary of the Treasury, transmitting an estimate from the Secretary of War of an appropriation for furnishing and maintaining the lodge at the *Washington Monument*—presented in the Senate, 20 February 1889, by the President *pro tempore;* presented in the House of Representatives, 21 February 1889, by the *Speaker.*

> *Journal of the Senate,* p. 352.
> *Journal of the House of Representatives,* p. 581.
> [*Congressional Record,* V. 20: Part 3, pp. 2105, 2164.]
> [*H. Ex. Doc. No.* 149 . . *Serial* 2652.]

Amendment—proposed in the Senate by the HON. GEORGE F. HOAR, a Senator from Massachusetts, 22 February 1889, to be inserted at the end of the Sundry Civil Appropriations bill (H. R. 12008) and to be designated as Section 4: That, in order that the *centennial anniversary of the inauguration of the first President of the United States,* GEORGE WASHINGTON, may be duly commemorated, Tuesday, the 30th day of April, 1889, is hereby declared to be a national holiday throughout the United States.[1]   And, in further

---

[1] Proclamation by BENJAMIN HARRISON, *President of the United States,* 4 April 1889, declaring Tuesday, the 30th of April, 1889, a national holiday.—*Statutes at Large,* 26: 1547.

commemoration of this historic event, the two Houses of Congress shall assemble in the Hall of the House of Representatives on the second Wednesday of December, 1889, when suitable ceremonies shall be had under the direction of a joint committee . . . who shall be appointed by the presiding officers of the respective houses . . . The committee shall invite the *Chief-Justice of the United States* to deliver a suitable address on the occasion . . . And for the purpose of defraying the expenses . . . three thousand dollars, or so much thereof as may be necessary.

> *Congressional Record*, V. 20: Part 3, pp. 2189, 2190.
> [*Statutes at Large*, 25: 980.]

Resolution—submitted in the House of Representatives by the Hon. William J. Stone, a Representative from Kentucky, 28 January 1889, proposing that the United States Congress assemble in the city of New York on the 30th day of April, 1889, and participate in the ceremonies to commemorate the *centennial of* George Washington's *inauguration as first President of the United States.*

> *Journal of the House of Representatives*, p. 357.
> [*Congressional Record*, V. 20: Part 2, p. 1253.]

Resolution—submitted in the House of Representatives by the Hon. Charles S. Baker, a Representative from New York, 2 March 1889, that the Speaker of the House of Representatives designate nine Members-elect to the Fifty-First Congress to attend the *centennial celebration of the inauguration of the first President of the United States to be held in the city of New York on the 30th day of April,* 1889, and to represent the House of Representatives of the United States at such celebration.

> *Journal of the House of Representatives*, pp. 765, 771.
> [*Congressional Record*, V. 20: Part 3, pp. 2648, 2649, 2683, 2717, 2724-2725.]

FIRST SESSION OF THE FIFTY-FIRST CONGRESS:
1889-1890

Resolution—reported to the Senate by the Hon. William M. Evarts, a Senator from New York, 28 March 1889, from the Committee on the Library, to whom was referred the invitation from the committee on the *centennial celebration of the inauguration of* George Washington *as first President of the United States to be held in the city of New York,* 30 April 1889, requesting the Senate to participate in the ceremonies.—

> *Journal of the Senate* (Special Session of the Senate, 4 March 1889—2 April 1889), p. 575.
> [*Congressional Record*, V. 21: Part 1, p. 58.]

Senate bill (S. No. 879)—submitted in the Senate by the Hon. John W. Daniel, a Senator from Virginia, 9 December 1889, for the completion of the *monument to* Mary, *the mother of* Washington, *at Fredericksburg, Virginia.*[1]—

> *Journal of the Senate*, p. 31.
> [*Congressional Record*, V. 21: Part 1, p. 122.]

Report—submitted in the Senate by the Hon. Frank Hiscock, a Senator from New York, 10 December 1889, from the Joint Select Committee appointed to make arrangements for the ceremonies in commemoration of the *inauguration of* George Washington, *the first President of the United States, to be held in the Hall of the House of Representatives, 11 December,* 1889.[2]

> *Journal of the Senate*, p. 33.
> [*Congressional Record*, V. 21: Part 1, pp. 140-141.]

Report—submitted in the House of Representatives by the Hon. Thomas M. Bayne, a Representative from Pennsylvania, 9 December 1889, from the Joint Select Committee appointed to make arrangements for the ceremonies in commemoration of the *inauguration of* George Washington, *the first President of the United States, to be held in the Hall of the House of Representatives, 11 December* 1889.

> *Journal of the House of Representatives*, p. 18.
> [*Congressional Record*, V. 21: Part 1, pp. 132, 140.]

Order of Proceedings on the part of the United States Congress, 11 December 1889, in commemoration of the *centennial anniversary of the inauguration of* George Washington *as first President of the United States.*

> *Congressional Record*, V. 21: Part 1, pp. 144-145, 146-147, 148-153.
> [*H. Mis. Doc. No. 168 . . Serial 2768.*]

Concurrent resolution—reported to the Senate by the Hon. Frank Hiscock, a Senator from New York, 18 December 1889, from the Joint Select Committee on the *Centennial of* Washington's *Inauguration as first President of the United States,* proposing that the thanks of Congress be . . . tendered to the Hon. Melville W. Fuller, *Chief-Justice of the United States,* for the appropriate address delivered by him in the Hall of the House of Representatives on the occasion of the commemoration of the *inauguration of* George Washington, *the first President.*—

> *Journal of the Senate*, p. 50.
> *Journal of the House of Representatives*, p. 74.
> [*Congressional Record*, V. 21: Part 1, p. 214.]

Resolution—submitted in the Senate by the Hon. William Call, a Senator from Florida, 16 December 1889, that 10,000 copies be printed of the address by the *Chief-Justice of the United States* on the *centennial of the inauguration of* George Washington *as first President of the United States.*

> *Journal of the Senate*, p. 45.
> [*Congressional Record*, V. 21: Part 1, p. 176.]

Joint Resolution (H. J. Res. No. 47)—submitted in the House of Representatives by the Hon. Thomas M. Bayne, a Representative from Pennsylvania, 20 December 1889, authorizing the printing of an address by Chief-Justice Fuller.—

> *Congressional Record*, V. 21: Part 1, pp. 339, 521.

[1] See House bill (H.R. No. 903) introduced by Mr. Browne, of Va., 18 December 1889, *Congressional Record*, V. 21: Part 1, p. 258.

[2] The *Joint Select Committee* for arrangements in commemoration of the *centennial of* Washington's *inauguration as first President of the United States,* was appointed under Section 4 of the Sundry Civil Appropriation bill (H.R. 12008), which was approved 2 March 1889. —*Journal of the Senate* (50th Congress, 2nd Session), pp. 377, 548.

Concurrent Resolution—reported to the House of Representatives by the HON. JAMES D. RICHARDSON, a Representative from Tennessee, 13 January 1890, from the Committee on Printing, with the recommendation that it be adopted in lieu of the BAYNE joint resolution (H. J. Res. No. 47), and proposing that 25,000 copies be printed of the *address by* CHIEF-JUSTICE FULLER on the *centennial of the first inauguration* of WASHINGTON *as President.*

> *Congressional Record,* V. 21: Part 1, pp. 521, 540; Part 3, pp. 2428-2429.
>
> [*H. Mis. Doc. No. 168* . . *Serial 2768.*]

Senate bill (S. No. 860)—submitted in the Senate by the HON. JAMES DONALD CAMERON, a Senator from Pennsylvania, 9 December 1889, making an appropriation for the improvement of WASHINGTON's *Headquarters at Valley Forge.*—

> *Journal of the Senate,* p. 30.
>
> [*Congressional Record,* V. 21: Part 1, p. 122.]

Senate bill (S. No. 3544)—submitted in the Senate by the HON. JOHN S. BARBOUR, a Senator from Virginia, 16 April 1890, providing for the purchase of *certain original journals and other relics* of GENERAL GEORGE WASHINGTON.—

> *Journal of the Senate,* p. 234.
>
> [*Congressional Record,* V. 21: Part 4, p. 3417.]

Joint Resolution (H. J. Res. No. 100)—submitted in the House of Representatives by the HON. LOGAN J. CHIPMAN, a Representative from Michigan, 17 February 1890, authorizing the purchase of the *sword worn by* GENERAL GEORGE WASHINGTON *at* BRADDOCK's *defeat.*—

> *Journal of the House of Representatives,* p. 246.
>
> [*Congressional Record,* V. 21: Part 2, p. 1429.]

FIRST SESSION OF THE FIFTY-SECOND CONGRESS:
1891-1892

Senate bill (S. No. 793)—submitted in the Senate by the HON. JOHN W. DANIEL, a Senator from Virginia, 14 December 1891, for the completion of the *monument to* MARY, *the mother of* WASHINGTON, *at Fredericksburg, Virginia.*—

> *Journal of the Senate,* p. 29.
>
> [*Congressional Record,* V. 23: Part 1, p. 44.]

Senate bill (S. No. 1546)—submitted in the Senate by the HON. JOHN W. DANIEL, a Senator from Virginia, 11 January 1892, appropriating $100,000 for the construction of Mount Vernon Avenue.

> *Journal of the Senate,* p. 54.
>
> *Congressional Record,* V. 23: Part 1, p. 241.

Joint Resolution (S. J. Res. No. 102)—submitted in the Senate by the HON. JOHN W. DANIEL, a Senator from Virginia, 19 July 1892, to provide for the construction of a wharf as a means of approach to the *monument to be erected at Wakefield, Virginia, to mark the birthplace of* GEORGE WASHINGTON.—*Approved,* 25 February 1893.[1]
Journal of the Senate, p. 381.

> [*Congressional Record,* V. 23: Part 7, pp. 6429, 6448.]

House bill (H. R. No. 2766)—submitted in the House of Representatives by the HON. ELISHA E. MEREDITH, a Representative from Virginia, 11 January 1892, to commence the construction of the Mount Vernon Avenue.[2]

> *Congressional Record,* V. 23: Part 1, p. 253; Part 2, p. 1775.

House bill (R. R. 7989)—submitted in the House of Representatives by the HON. JOHN H. KETCHAM, a Representative from New York, 7 April 1892, to provide for the purchase of the painting of the house at Mount Vernon by Robert Fulton Ludlow.

> *Journal of the House of Representatives,* p. 278.
>
> *Congressional Record,* V. 23: Part 4, p. 3072.

SECOND SESSION OF THE FIFTY-SECOND
CONGRESS: 1892-1893

Report—submitted in the House of Representatives by the HON. CHARLES T. FERRALL, a Representative from Virginia, 17 February, 1893, from the Committee on the Library, to accompany the Senate joint resolution (S. J. Res. No. 102) to provide for the construction of a wharf as a means of approach to the *monument to be erected at Wakefield, Virginia, to mark the birthplace of* GEORGE WASHINGTON.

> *Journal of the House of Representatives,* p. 95.
>
> [*Congressional Record,* V. 24: Part 2, p. 1744.]
>
> [*H. Rept. No. 2527* . . . *Serial 3142.*]

Resolution—submitted in the Senate by the HON. GEORGE F. HOAR, a Senator from Massachusetts, 14 February, 1893, that on the 22nd of February, current, the anniversary of the *birthday of* GEORGE WASHINGTON, the Senate shall meet at 12 o'clock noon, and after the reading of the *Journal,* shall listen to the reading of WASHINGTON's *Farewell Address* by the Senator from Nebraska, President *pro tempore* of the Senate.

> *Journal of the Senate,* pp. 108, 110, 124.
>
> [*Congressional Record,* V. 24: Part 2, pp. 1565, 1609, 1997.]
>
> [*S. Mis. Doc. No. 52* . . . *Serial 3064.*]

SECOND SESSION OF THE FIFTY-THIRD CONGRESS
1893-1894

Ordered by the Senate, 20 February 1894—on motion by MR. HARRIS, a Senator from Tennessee.

That MR. MARTIN, a Senator from the State of Kansas, be requested immediately after the routine morning business of the Senate on the 22nd instant, to read the *Farewell Address* of GEORGE WASHINGTON, *first President of the United States.*

> *Journal of the Senate,* pp. 91, 94.
>
> [*Congressional Record,* V. 26: Part 3, pp. 2309, 2359.]

---

[1] Also H. R. 6884. 53rd Congress—2nd Session.

[2] The Senate Joint Resolution (S.J.Res. No. 102) was approved during the *second session of the Fifty-Second Congress.*
Journal of the Senate, p. 132.
[*Congressional Record,* V. 24: Part 3, p. 2148.]

House bill (H. R. No. 4958)—submitted in the House of Representatives by the HON. CHARLES E. HOOKER, a Representative from Mississippi, 3 January 1894, making an appropriation for the *Anacostia statue of* WASHINGTON.—

> *Journal of the House of Representatives*, p. 55.
> [*Congressional Record*, V. 26: Part 1, p. 487.]

Joint Resolution (H. J. Res. No. 183)—submitted in the House of Representatives by the HON. ALLAN C. DURBOROW, a Representative from Illinois, 28 May 1894, instructing the officers in charge to keep . . . . the WASHINGTON *Monument* open every week-day from 9 A. M. to 6 P. M., and on Sundays from 9 A. M. to 4 P. M., and on not less than three evenings every week from 7 to 10 o'clock.—

> *Journal of the House of Representatives*, p. 407.
> [*Congressional Record*, V. 26: Part 6, p. 5432.]

FIRST SESSION OF THE FIFTY-FOURTH CONGRESS:
1895-1896

Resolution—submitted in the Senate by the HON. GEORGE F. HOAR, a Senator from Massachusetts, 11 February 1896, that on the 22nd day of February, current, immediately after the reading the the *Journal*, WASHINGTON's *Farewell Address* be read to the Senate by the President *pro tempore*.

> *Journal of the Senate*, pp. 124, 146.
> [*Congressional Record*, V. 28: Part 2, p. 1573; Part 3, p. 2042.]

Senate bill (S. No. 2620)—submitted in the Senate by the HON. JOHN W. DANIEL, a Senator from Virginia, 24 March 1896, to provide for placing a suitable *memorial of* GENERAL GEORGE WASHINGTON *at Washington and Lee University, in Lexington, Virginia.*—

> *Journal of the Senate*, p. 203.
> [*Congressional Record*, V. 28: Part 4, p. 3118.]

House bill (H. R. 3554)—submitted in the House of Representatives by the HON. ELISHA E. MEREDITH, a Representative from Virginia, 9 January 1896, making an appropriation for the *Anacostia statue of* WASHINGTON.—

> *Journal of the House of Representatives*, p. 100.
> [*Congressional Record*, V. 28: Part 1, p. 543.]

Letter of the Acting-Secretary of the Treasury, transmitting a communication from the Secretary of State asking an appropriation for the employment of a watchman to care for the *monument now being erected at the birthplace of* WASHINGTON—presented in the House of Representatives, 6 March 1896, by the SPEAKER.

> *Congressional Record*, V. 28: Part 3, p. 2552.
> [*H. Doc. No.* 284 . . . . *Serial* 3428.]

SECOND SESSION OF THE FIFTY-FOURTH CONGRESS:
1896-1897

Resolution—submitted in the Senate by the HON. GEORGE F. HOAR, a Senator from Massachusetts, 19 February 1897, that on Monday, February the 22nd, current, immediately after the reading of the Journal, WASHINGTON's *Farewell*

JAMES MADISON, A REPRESENTATIVE FROM VIRGINIA, REPORTED IN THE HOUSE OF REPRESENTATIVES, MAY 7, 1789, AN ADDRESS TO PRESIDENT GEORGE WASHINGTON.

Address be read to the Senate by MR. DANIEL, a Senator from the State of Virginia.

> *Journal of the Senate*, pp. 135, 139.
> [*Congressional Record*, V. 29: Part 2, p. 1992; Part 3, p. 2072.]

Letter of the Secretary of State, transmitting a letter from COLONEL JOHN M. WILSON, Corps of Engineers, United States Army, dated 28 January 1897—reporting the completion of the work with which he has been intrusted concerning the erection of the *monument to mark the birthplace of* GENERAL GEORGE WASHINGTON, *at Wakefield, Virginia.*

> *Congressional Record*, V. 29: Part 2, pp. 1634, 1665.
> [*S. Doc. No.* 114 . . . *Serial* 3470.]

SECOND SESSION OF THE FIFTY-FIFTH CONGRESS:
1897-1898

Resolution—submitted in the Senate by the HON. GEORGE F. HOAR, a Senator from Massachusetts, 8 February 1898, that on Tuesday, February the 22nd, current, immediately after the reading of the *Journal*, WASHINGTON's *Farewell Address* be read to the Senate by MR. LODGE, a Senator from the State of Massachusetts.

> *Journal of the Senate*, pp. 92, 120.
> [*Congressional Record*, V. 31: Part 2, pp. 1495, 2014.]

Resolution—submitted in the Senate by the HON. JOHN T. MORGAN, a Senator from Alabama, 22 February 1898, proposing that the Committee on Naval Affairs be instructed to inquire and report whether a man-of-war equal, at least, to any warship in the world, to be named THE GEORGE WASHINGTON, can be built, armed, and commissioned within the period of twelve months, by the use of the facilities of the shipyards, machine shops, mines and forests of the United States wherever the same be found.

> *Journal of the Senate*, p. 121.
> [*Congressional Record*, V. 31: Part 3, p. 2018.]

THIRD SESSION OF THE FIFTY-FIFTH CONGRESS:
1898-1899

Resolution—submitted in the Senate by the HON. GEORGE F. HOAR, a Senator from Massachusetts, 20 December 1898, that on Wednesday, 22 February 1899, immediately after the reading of the Journal WASHINGTON's *Farewell Address* be read to the Senate by MR. WOLCOTT, a Senator from the State of Colorado.

> *Journal of the Senate*, pp. 34, 140-141.
> [*Congressional Record*, V. 32: Part 1, p. 324; Part 3, p. 2171.]

Resolutions—submitted in the Senate by the HON. WILLIAM E. MASON, a Senator from Illinois, 20 January 1899, requesting that the *Farewell Address of* PRESIDENT WASHINGTON be read on Wednesday, the 22nd of February, 1899, or on the day before, in each and all the public schools throughout the United States; in the universities, colleges, and private schools throughout the entire United States; and that the newspapers throughout the United States publish the said address.—

> *Journal of the Senate*, p. 68.
> [*Congressional Record*, V. 32: Part 1, p. 830.]

FIRST SESSION OF THE FIFTY-SIXTH CONGRESS:
1899-1900

Communication from the Great Council of the United States Improved Order of Red Men, inviting the United States Senate to attend the centennial memorial services commemorative of the life and death of GEORGE WASHINGTON— presented in the Senate, 7 December 1899, by the HON. WILLIAM P. FRYE, President *pro tempore*.

> *Journal of the Senate*, p. 29.
> [*Congressional Record*, V. 33; Part 1, pp. 129-130.]

Senate bill (S. No. 1605)—submitted in the Senate by the HON. GEORGE GRAHAM VEST, a Senator from Missouri, 14 December 1899, for the purchase of a *bronze portrait statue of* GEORGE WASHINGTON.

> *Journal of the Senate*, p. 46.
> [*Congressional Record*, V. 33: Part 1, p. 377.]

Resolution—submitted in the Senate by the HON. GEORGE F. HOAR, a Senator from Massachusetts, 30 January 1900, that on Thursday, the 22nd day of February, current, immediately after the reading of the *Journal*, WASHINGTON's *Fare-*

well Address be read to the Senate by MR. FORAKER, a Senator from Ohio.

> *Journal of the Senate*, pp. 107, 155.
> [*Congressional Record*, V. 33: Part 2, p. 1295; Part 3, p. 2059.]

Resolution—reported to the Senate by the HON. THOMAS C. PLATT, a Senator from New York, 12 February 1900, from the Committee on Printing, authorizing and directing the Secretary of the Senate to have printed and bound at the Government Printing Office, for the personal use of Senators, 100 copies of WASHINGTON's *Valedictory Address to the People of the United States*, using for their purpose the form of the same printed in pursuance of a resolution of the House of Representatives adopted on the 22nd day of February, 1837.—

> *Journal of the Senate*, p. 135.
> [*Congressional Record*, V. 33: Part 2, p. 1705.]

Senate bill (S. No. 4142)—submitted in the Senate by the HON. JAMES MCMILLAN, a Senator from Michigan, 11 April 1900, for the purchase of a replica of the *bronze equestrian statue of* GENERAL GEORGE WASHINGTON *by Daniel Chester French and Edward C. Potter.*—

> *Journal of the Senate*, p. 267.
> [*Congressional Record*, V. 33: Part 5, p. 4000.]
> [S. *Rept. No.* 2179 (56th Congress, 2nd Session) . . . . Serial 4065.]

Report—submitted to the House of Representatives by the HON. JAMES T. MCCLEARY, a Representative from Minnesota, 4 June 1900, from the Committee on the Library, to whom was referred the House bill (H.R. No. 5795), introduced by MR. COWHERD, a Representative from Missouri, 10 January 1900, for the purchase of a bronze portrait statue of GEORGE WASHINGTON.[1]

> *Journal of the House of Representatives*, pp. 147, 671.
> [*Congressional Record*, V. 33: Part 1, p. 754; Part 7, p. 6571.]
> [H. *Rept. No.* 1951 . . . Serial 4027.]

Resolution (H. Res. No. 141)—submitted in the House of Representatives by the HON. ERNEST F. ACHESON, a Representative from Pennsylvania, 9 February 1900, providing for the printing of 6,000 copies of the *funeral oration on the death of* GENERAL WASHINGTON, delivered in the German Lutheran Church, Philadelphia, 26 December 1799.—

> *Journal of the House of Representatives*, p. 249.
> [*Congressional Record*, V. 33: Part 2, p. 1685.]

House bill (H. R. No. 10495)—submitted in the House of Representatives by the HON. GEORGE A. PEARRE, a Representative from Maryland, 5 April 1900, to erect a transparent Water's weather case over the *marble statue of* GEORGE WASHINGTON.—

> *Journal of the House of Representatives*, pp. 440, 442.
> [*Congressional Record*, V. 33: Part 4, pp. 3824-3825.]

---

[1] Motion by MR. COWHERD, 27 February 1901, to suspend the rules and pass the bill (H.R. 5795) was not agreed to, and there seems to have been no further action. *Congressional Record* (56th Congress, 2nd Session), V. 34: Part 4, p. 3183.

SECOND SESSION OF THE FIFTY-SIXTH CONGRESS:
1900-1901

Ordered by the Senate, 24 January 1901—on motion by MR. HOAR, a Senator from Massachusetts:

That, unless otherwise directed, on the 22nd day of February in each year, or if that shall be on Sunday, then on the day following, immediately after the reading of the *Journal*, WASHINGTON's Farewell Address shall be read to the Senate by a Senator to be designated for the purpose by the presiding officer.

> *Journal of the Senate*, pp. 103, 105, 197-198.
> [*Congressional Record*, V. 34: Part 2, pp. 1385, 1434; Part 3, p. 2797.]

Report—submitted in the Senate by the HON. GEORGE PEABODY WETMORE, a Senator from Rhode Island, 7 February 1901, from the Committee on the Library, to whom was referred the Senate bill (S. No. 4142), introduced by MR. McMILLAN, a Senator from Michigan, 11 April 1900, for the purchase of a replica of the *bronze equestrian statue of* GENERAL GEORGE WASHINGTON *by Daniel Chester French and Edward C. Potter.*—

> *Journal of the Senate*, pp. 147-148, 175.
> [*Congressional Record*, V. 34: Part 3, pp. 2050, 2442, 2602; Part 4, 3099.]
> [S. *Rept. No.* 2179 . . . Serial 4065.]

Report—submitted in the House of Representatives by the HON. JAMES H. SOUTHARD, a Representative from Ohio, 18 February 1901, from the Committee on Coinage, Weights, and Measures to whom was referred the House bill (H. R. No. 9345), introduced by MR. RIXEY, a Representative from Virginia, 9 March 1900, to provide certain memorial medals for the benefit of the *Washington Monument Association of Alexandria, Virginia.*—

> *Journal of the House of Representatives*, p. 244.
> [*Congressional Record*, V. 34: Part 3, p. 2614.]
> [*H. Rept. No.* 2906 . . . Serial 4214.]

FIRST SESSION OF THE FIFTY-SEVENTH CONGRESS:
1901-1902

Senate bill (S. No. 3618)—submitted in the Senate by the HON. GEORGE GRAHAM VEST, a Senator from Missouri, 6 February 1902, for the purchase of a *bronze portrait statue of* GEORGE WASHINGTON.

> *Journal of the Senate*, p. 138.
> [*Congressional Record*, V. 35: Part 2, p. 1372.]

Senate bill (S. No. 5358)—submitted in the Senate by the HON. JAMES McMILLAN, a Senator from Michigan, 21 April 1902, for the purchase of a replica of the *bronze equestrian statue of* GENERAL GEORGE WASHINGTON *by* DANIEL CHESTER FRENCH *and* EDWARD C. POTTER.—

> *Journal of the Senate*, p. 339.
> [*Congressional Record*, V. 35: Part 5, p. 4464.]

Senate bill (S. No. 4546)—submitted in the Senate by the HON. THOMAS S. MARTIN, a Senator from Virginia, 15 March 1902, to provide for certain souvenir medals for the benefit of the *Washington Monument Association of Alexandria, Virginia.*—*Approved*, 1 July, 1902.

> *Journal of the Senate*, pp. 234, 544, 565, 567.
> [*Congressional Record*, V. 35: Part 3, p. 2819; Part 8, pp. 7778-7779, 7750, 7793, 7794.]

House bill (H. R. No. 8317)—submitted in the House of Representatives by HON. WILLIAM S. COWHERD, a Representative from Missouri, 8 January 1902, for the purchase of a *bronze portrait statue of* GEORGE WASHINGTON.—

> *Journal of the House of Representatives*, p. 192.
> [*Congressional Record*, V. 35: Part 1, p. 530.]

House bill (H. R. No. 11349)—submitted in the House of Representatives by the HON. WILLIAM S. COWHERD, a Representative from Missouri, 14 February 1902, for the purchase of a *bronze portrait statue of* GEORGE WASHINGTON.—

> *Journal of the House of Representatives*, p. 347.
> [*Congressional Record*, V. 35: Part 2, p. 1779.]

House bill (H. R. No. 15111)—submitted in the House of Representatives by the HON. CHARLES F. JOY, a Representative from Missouri, 14 June 1902, for the purchase of the *original Houdon life cast bust of* GEORGE WASHINGTON.—

> *Journal of the House of Representatives*, p. 811.
> [*Congressional Record*, V. 35: Part 7, p. 6835.]

Report—submitted to the House of Representatives by the HON. JAMES H. SOUTHARD, a Representative from Ohio, 25 March 1902, from the Committee on Coinage, Weights, and Measures, to whom was referred the bill (H. R. No. 2766), introduced, 3 December 1901, by MR. RIXEY, a Representative from Virginia, to provide for the coinage of certain memorial half dollars for the benefit of the *Washington Monument Association of Alexandria, Virginia.*[1]

> *Journal of the House of Representatives*, pp. 63, 521.
> [*Congressional Record*, V. 35: Part 1, p. 105; Part 4, p. 3261.]
> [*H. Rept. No.* 1181 . . . Serial 4403.]

SECOND SESSION OF THE FIFTY-SEVENTH CONGRESS:
1902-1903

Ordered by the Senate, 6 February 1903—on motion by MR. GALLINGER, a Senator from New Hampshire, and by unanimous consent, that certain valuable papers relating to the history of the *Washington Monument* be printed as a Senate document.

> *Journal of the Senate*, p. 143.
> [*Congressional Record*, V. 36: Part 2, p. 1776.]
> [S. *Doc. No.* 224 . . . Serial 4436.]

---

[1] This bill was re-introduced (H.R. 16229) in the Second Session of the Sixty-First Congress by MR. CARLIN, of Virginia, 2 December 1909, *Congressional Record*, V. 45: Part 1, p. 287; and again (H.R. 1329), in the First Session of the Sixty-Second Congress, 4 April 1911, *Congressional Record*, V. 47: Part 1, p. 27.

SECOND SESSION OF THE FIFTY-EIGHTH CONGRESS:
1903-1904

Senate bill (S. 3721)—submitted in the Senate by the HON. FRANCIS M. COCKRELL, a Senator from Missouri, 22 January 1904, for the purchase of a *bronze portrait statue* of GEORGE WASHINGTON.[2]

> *Journal of the Senate*, p. 102.
> [*Congressional Record*, V. 38: Part 2, p. 1017.]

Senate bill (S. No. 3802)—submitted in the Senate by the HON. LOUIS E. MCCOMAS, a Senator from Maryland, 25 January 1904, to enable the Joint Committee on the Library to purchase the *sword* of GENERAL GEORGE WASHINGTON from Virginia Taylor Lewis.

> *Journal of the Senate*, p. 111.
> [*Congressional Record*, V. 38: Part 2, p. 1101.]

Message from *Theodore Roosevelt, President of the United States,* transmitting a Report of the Acting Secretary of State relative to the desire of certain citizens of France to present this Government with a *bust* of WASHINGTON *by David D'Angers,* and place it in the Capitol—presented in the Senate, 12 January 1904, by the President *pro tempore;* presented in the House of Representatives, 12 January 1904, by the *Speaker.*

> [*Congressional Record*, V. 38: Part 1, pp. 614, 681, 738.]
> [S. *Doc. No.* 78 . . . Serial 4588.]

Letter from the Secretary of State, transmitting a dispatch from the embassy at Paris reporting the intention of The *Marquis de la Fayette, the Marquis de Grasse,* and other French gentlemen to *present to this Government a bust* of WASHINGTON —presented in the Senate, 28 January 1904, with certain other letters and papers, by the HON. SHELBY M. CULLOM, a Senator from Illinois, with the request that they be printed.

> [*Congressional Record*, V. 38: Part 2, p. 1299.]
> [S. *Doc. No.* 78, No. 2 . . . Serial 4588.]

Joint Resolution (S. J. Res. No. 36)—reported to the Senate by the HON. SHELBY M. CULLOM, a Senator from Illinois, 28 January, 1904, from the Committee on Foreign Relations, accepting a *reproduction of the bust* of WASHINGTON from certain citizens of the Republic of France, and tendering the thanks of Congress to the donors therefor.—*Approved,* 28 April 1904.

> *Journal of the Senate,* pp. 126, 461, 469, 470.
> *Journal of the House of Representatives,* pp. 220, 701, 712, 713.
> [*Congressional Record*, V. 38: Part 2, pp. 1299, 1403; Part 6, pp. 5804, 5824, 5845.]

House bill (H. R. No. 10865)—submitted in the House of Representatives by the HON. IRA E. RIDER, a Representative from New York, 22 January 1904, to provide for placing

2 The bill (S. No. 3721) was reported back to the Senate by MR. COCKRELL, of Missouri, 7 December 1904, and indefinitely postponed. *Congressional Record* (58th Congress, 3rd Session), V. 39: Part 1, p. 46.

in the public schools of the District of Columbia *copies of the bust* of WASHINGTON.—

> *Journal of the House of Representatives,* p. 188.
> [*Congressional Record*, Part 2, p. 1070.]

THIRD SESSION OF THE FIFTY-EIGHTH CONGRESS:
1904-1905

Senate bill (S. No. 5846)—submitted in the Senate by the HON. FRANCIS M. COCKRELL, a Senator from Missouri, 7 December 1904, for the purchase of a *bronze portrait statue of* GEORGE WASHINGTON.—

> *Journal of the Senate,* p. 19.
> [*Congressional Record*, V. 39: Part 1, p. 49.]

Senate bill (S. No. 7009)—submitted in the Senate by the HON. JOHN W. DANIEL, a Senator from Virginia, February 1, 1905, to appropriate a sum of money to the Mount Vernon Avenue Association as assignee of the State of Virginia.—

> *Journal of the Senate,* p. 159.
> [*Congressional Record*, V. 39: Part 1, p. 1669.]

Resolution—submitted in the Senate by the HON. WILLIAM P. FRYE, a Senator from Maine, 14 February 1905, that the Secretary of the Treasury be directed to inform the Senate what was the amount of the *bequest made by* GEORGE WASHINGTON *to the United States for the foundation of the university* and what appropriation was made of it.—

> *Journal of the Senate,* p. 212.
> [*Congressional Record*, V. 39: Part 3, pp. 2513, 2706.]

Letter from the Secretary of the Treasury, 15 February 1905, stating, in response to a resolution of the Senate, 14 February 1905, the amount of the *bequest made by* GEORGE WASHINGTON *to the United States for the foundation of the university,* and what appropriation was made of said bequest.

> *Journal of the Senate,* p. 227.
> [*Congressional Record*, V. 39: Part 3, p. 2706.]
> [S. *Doc. No.* 164 . . . . Serial 4766.]

Ordered by the Senate, 3 March 1905—by request of MR. WETMORE, a Senator from Rhode Island, on behalf of the Joint Committee on the Library:
That there be printed for the use of the Senate, and delivered to the document room, 500 additional copies of the *Report of the Joint Committee on the Library in connection with the presentation of a bust* of WASHINGTON *by certain citizens of France, with two accompanying illustrations.*

> *Journal of the Senate,* p. 316.
> [*Congressional Record*, V. 39: Part 4, p. 3929.]
> [S. *Rept. No.* 4397 . . . . Serial 4778.]

Letter from the Secretary of the Treasury, transmitting a copy of a communication from the Secretary of War, submitting an estimate of appropriation for repairs to the *Washington Monument*—presented in the House of Representatives, 9 December 1904, by the Speaker.

> *Journal of the House of Representatives,* p. 38.
> [*Congressional Record*, V. 39: Part 1, p. 115.]
> [H. *Doc. No.* 84 . . . . Serial 4829.]

FIRST SESSION OF THE FIFTY-NINTH CONGRESS: 1905-1906

Senate bill (S. No. 152)—submitted in the Senate by the Hon. John W. Daniels, a Senator from Virginia, 6 December 1905, to provide for the building of a public avenue on the south side of the Potomac River from the *city of Washington to Mount Vernon.*—

> *Journal of the Senate,* pp. 24, 470.
> [*Congressional Record,* V. 40: Part 1, p. 141; Part 7, p. 6434.]

Ordered by the Senate, 26 June 1906—on motion by Mr. Wetmore, a Senator from Rhode Island, that a communication from the Joint Committee on the Library, transmitting a letter from the French ambassador, together with translation, relating to the volume published by order of the Senate giving an account of the ceremonies on the occasion of *unveiling of the bust of* Washington *presented to Congress by certain citizens of France* be printed in the *Record,* and also as a Senate document.

> *Congressional Record,* V. 40: Part 10, p. 9245.
> [*S. Doc. No. 505 . . . . Serial 4916.*]

House bill (H. R. No. 16674)—submitted in the House of Representatives by the Hon. Theobold Otjen, a Representative from Wisconsin, 13 March 1906, to purchase the *historical art window,* by Maria Herndl, *of* George Washington.—

> *Journal of the House of Representatives,* p. 652.
> [*Congressional Record,* V. 40: Part 4, p. 3759.]

Joint Resolution (H. J. Res. No. 13)—submitted in the House of Representatives by the Hon. J. A. Goulden, a Representative from New York, 4 December 1905, providing for the purchase and placing of Wilson McDonald's *busts of* Washington *and* Lincoln *in the District public schools.*—

> *Journal of the House of Representatives,* p. 50.
> [*Congressional Record,* V. 40: Part 1, pp. 55-56.]

SECOND SESSION OF THE FIFTY-NINTH CONGRESS: 1906-1907

Joint Resolution (S. J. Res. No. 89)—submitted in the Senate by the Hon. Murphy Foster, a Senator from Louisiana, 25 January 1907, authorizing the printing and indexing of the complete orders of General George Washington *during the War of the Revolution.*—

> *Journal of the Senate,* p. 160.
> [*Congressional Record,* V. 41: Part 2, p. 1617.]

Report—submitted to the House of Representatives by the Hon. James T. McCleary, a Representative from Minnesota, 2 March 1907, from the Committee on the Library, to whom was referred the bill (H. R. No. 25853), introduced, 28 February 1907, by Mr. Otjen, of Wisconsin, authorizing the purchase of the *historical art window,* by Maria Herndl, *of* George Washington.—

> *Congressional Record,* V. 41: Part 5, pp. 4313, 4535.
> [*H. Rept. No. 8158 . . . Serial 5065.*]

FIRST SESSION OF THE SIXTIETH CONGRESS: 1907-1908

Senate bill (S. No. 1238)—submitted in the Senate by the Hon. Thomas S. Martin, a Senator from Virginia, 5 December 1907, to re-imburse the *estate of* General George Washington for certain lands of his in the State of Ohio lost by conflicting grants made under the authority of the United States.[1]

> *Journal of the Senate,* p. 45.
> [*Congressional Record,* V. 42: Part 1, p. 173.]

Senate bill (No. 1047)—submitted in the Senate by the Hon. John W. Daniel, a Senator from Virginia, 5 December 1907, to provide for the building of a *public avenue on the south side of the Potomac River from the city of Washton to Mount Vernon.*—

> *Journal of the Senate,* pp. 42, 230.
> [*Congressional Record,* V. 42: Part 1, p. 170; Part 3, p. 2018.]

Senate bill (S. No. 5252)—submitted in the Senate by the Hon. John W. Daniel, a Senator from Virginia, 11 February 1908, to provide for the building of a public avenue on the south side of the Potomac River from the city of Washington to Mount Vernon.

> *Journal of the Senate,* pp. 221, 361, 450.
> [*Congressional Record,* V. 42: Part 2, p. 1802; Part 5, p. 4458; Part 7, pp. 6305-6306, 6435.]
> [*S. Rept. No. 480 . . . . Serial 5219.*]

Report—submitted to the Senate by the Hon. Thomas S. Martin, a Senator from Virginia, 7 April 1908, from the Committee on claims, to whom was referred the bill (S. No. 5252), introduced, 11 February 1908, by Mr. Daniel, a Senator from Virginia, to provide for the building of a *public avenue on the south side of the Potomac River from the city of Washington to Mount Vernon.*—

> *Journal of the Senate,* pp. 221, 361, 450, 936, 939.
> [*Congressional Record,* V. 42: Part 2, p. 1802; Part 5, p. 4458; Part 7, pp. 6305, 6435.]
> [*S. Rept. No. 480 . . . . Serial 5219.*]

Report—submitted to the Senate by the Hon. George Peabody Wetmore, a Senator from Rhode Island, 18 April 1908, from the Committee on the Library, to whom was referred the joint resolution (H. J. Res. No. 124) authorizing the presentation of the *statue of* President Washington, now located in the Capitol grounds, to the Smithsonian Institution.

---

[1] This bill was re-introduced: (S. 8391), by Mr. Martin, of Virginia, 24 May 1910, 61st Congress, 2nd Session, *Congressional Record,* V. 45: Part 7, p. 6840; (S. 3627, in the same session) by Mr. Daniel, of Virginia, 10 December 1909, *Congressional Record,* V. 45: Part 1, p. 75; (S. 2535), by Mr. Martin, of Virginia, 29 May 1911, 62nd Congress, 1st Session, *Congressional Record,* V. 47: Part 2, p. 1597; (S. 1406), 24 April 1913, 63rd Congress, 1st Session, *Congressional Record,* V. 50: Part 1, p. 368; (S. 3137), 7 January 1916, 64th Congress, 1st Session, *Congressional Record,* V. 53: Part 1, p. 494; (S. 351), 4 April 1917, 65th Congress, 1st Session, *Congressional Record,* V. 55: Part 1, p. 193; (S. 1475), 6 June 1919, 66th Congress, 1st Session, *Congressional Record,* V. 58: Part 1, p. 727.—

Journal of the Senate, p. 381.
[*Congressional Record,* V. 42: Part 5, p. 4901.]
[*S. Rept. No. 543 . . . . Serial 5219.*]

Report—submitted to the House of Representatives by the HON. SAMUEL W. MCCALL, a Representative from Massachusetts, 14 February 1908, from the Committee on the Library, to whom was referred the joint resolution (H. J. Res. No. 124) authorizing the presentation of the *statue of* PRESIDENT WASHINGTON, now located in the Capitol grounds, to the Smithsonian Institution.

> *Journal of the House of Representatives,* p. 463.
> [*Congressional Record,* V. 42: Part 3, p. 2051.]
> [*H. Rept. No. 900 . . . . Serial 5225.*]

Joint Resolution (H. J. Res. No. 124)—submitted in the House of Representatives by the HON. JAMES R. MANN, a Representative from Illinois, 31 January 1908, authorizing the presentation of the *statue of* PRESIDENT WASHINGTON, now located in the Capitol grounds, to the Smithsonian Institution.—Approved 22 May 1908.

> *Journal of the House of Representatives,* pp. 399, 463, 609, 933, 943, 950, 968, 981.
> *Journal of the Senate,* pp. 315, 381, 450, 461, 470, 493.
> [*Congressional Record,* V. 42: Part 2, p. 1434; Part 3, p. 2051; Part 4, pp. 3461-3462, 3558; Part 5, p. 4901; Part 7, pp. 6307, 6516, 6592, 6625, 6779, 6893.]

House bill (H. R. No. 16647)—reported to the House of Representatives by the HON. SAMUEL W. MCCALL, a Representative from Massachusetts, 17 April 1908, from the Committee on the Library, for the erection of *a replica of John Quincy Adams Ward's statue of* WASHINGTON.[2]

> *Journal of the House of Representatives,* pp. 431, 730.
> [*Congressional Record,* V. 42: Part 2, p. 1737; Part 5, p. 4896.]
> [*H. Rept. No. 1466 . . . . Serial 5226.*]

House bill (H. R. No. 21210)—submitted in the House of Representatives by the HON. WILLIAM H. STAFFORD, a Representative from Wisconsin, 23 April 1908, authorizing the purchase of the stained-glass painting of GEORGE WASHINGTON by Maria Hendrl.—

> *Journal of the House of Representatives,* p. 828.
> [*Congressional Record,* V. 42: Part 6, p. 5146.]

Resolution (H. J. Res. 140)—submitted in the House of Representatives by the HON. J. ADAMS BEDE, a Representative from Minnesota, 17 February 1908, authorizing the printing of 10,000 copies of the complete orders of GENERAL WASHINGTON during the war of the Revolution.

> *Journal of the House,* pp. 474, 821.
> [*Congressional Record,* V. 42: Part 3, p. 2106; Part 6, p. 5566.]
> [*H. Rept. No. 1568 . . . . Serial 5226.*]

Report—submitted in the House of Representatives by the HON. CHARLES B. LANDIS, a Representative from Indiana, 1 May 1908, from the Committee on Printing, to whom was referred the joint resolution (H. J. Res. No. 140), introduced, 17 February 1908, by MR. BEDE, a Representative from Minnesota, authorizing the printing of 10,000 copies of the *complete orders of* GENERAL WASHINGTON *during the War of the Revolution.*—

> *Journal of the House of Representatives,* pp. 474, 821.
> [*Congressional Record,* V. 42: Part 3, p. 2106; Part 6, 5566.]
> [*H. Rept. No. 1568 . . . . Serial 5226.*]

House bill (H.R. No. 21842)—submitted in the House of Representatives by the HON. MORRIS SHEPPARD, a Representative from Texas, 12 May 1908, for the erection of a suitable *memorial to the mother of* WASHINGTON.[1]

> *Journal of the House of Representatives,* p. 1029.
> [*Congressional Record,* V. 42: Part 7, p. 6170.]

Joint Resolution (H. J. Res. No. 11)—submitted in the House of Representatives by the HON. JOSEPH A. GOULDEN, a Representative from New York, 2 December 1907, providing for the purchase and placing of Mr. Wilson McDonald's colossal *busts of* GEORGE WASHINGTON *and Abraham Lincoln* in each public school building in the District of Columbia.—

> *Journal of the House of Representatives,* p. 9.
> [*Congressional Record,* V. 42: Part 1, p. 24.]

House bill (H. R. No. 5489)—submitted in the House of Representatives by the HON. HENRY D. FLOOD, a Representative from Virginia, 5 December 1907, to re-imburse the *estate of* GENERAL GEORGE WASHINGTON for certain lands of his in the State of Ohio lost by conflicting grants made under the authority of the United States.[2]

> *Journal of the House of Representatives,* pp. 112, 373.
> [*Congressional Record,* V. 42: Part 1, p. 194; Part 2, p. 1314.]

FIRST SESSION OF THE SIXTY-FIRST CONGRESS: 1909

Senate bill (S. No. 3193)—submitted in the Senate by the HON. JOHN W. DANIEL, a Senator from Virginia, 5 August 1909, to provide for the building of a public avenue on the south side of the Potomac River from the city of Washington to Mount Vernon.

> *Journal of the Senate,* p. 183.

---

[2] The bill was re-introduced: (H.R. 2245), by MR. MCCALL, of Massachusetts, 18 March 1909, 61st Congress, 1st Session, *Congressional Record,* V. 44: Part 1, p. 104; (S. 3120), by MR. O'GORMAN, of New York, 15 September 1913, 63rd Congress, 1st Session, *Congressional Record,* V. 50: Part 5, p. 4938.—

[1] This bill was re-introduced: (H.R. 2128) by MR. SHEPPARD, of Texas, 18 March 1909, 61st Congress, 1st Session, *Congressional Record,* V. 44: Part 1, p. 102.—

[2] This bill was re-introduced (H.R. 5266), 26 March 1909, 61st Congress, 1st Session, *Congressional Record,* V. 44: Part 1, p. 391; (H.R 18018), 13 January 1910, 61st Congress, 2nd Session, *Congressional Record,* V. 45: Part 1, p. 618; (H.R. 1533), 4 April 1911, 62nd Congress, 1st Session, *Congressional Record,* V. 47: Part 1, p. 44; (H.R. 19740), 8 February 1912, 62nd Congress, 2nd Session, *Congressional Record,* V. 48: Part 2, p. 1870; (H.R. 6168), 17 June 1913, 63rd Congress, 1st Session, *Congressional Record,* V. 50: Part 2, p. 2072; (H.R. 1459), 6 December 1915, 64th Congress, 1st Session, *Congressional Record,* V. 53: Part 1, p. 41.—

[*Congressional Record,* V. 44: Part 5, p. 4920.]
Referred to Committee on Claims, V. 45; Part 1, p. 668.

Resolution (H. Res. No. 62)—proposed in the House of Representatives by the HON. MICHAEL E. DRISCOLL, a Representative from New York, 22 April 1909:
Resolved, That the Speaker and Members of the House of Representatives accept with cordial thanks the invitation so graciously extended to them by the *Washington Monument Association of Alexandria, Virginia.*[3]

> *Journal of the House of Representatives,* p. 176.
> [*Congressional Record,* V. 44: Part 2, pp. 1477, 1478.]

SECOND SESSION OF THE SIXTY-FIRST CONGRESS: 1909-1910

Statement of the late MR. LAWRENCE WASHINGTON, great-great-grand-nephew of GENERAL WASHINGTON, before the Private Land Claims Committee of the House, 16 May 1910, relative to the bill (H. R. No. 18018) to re-imburse the estate of GENERAL WASHINGTON for certain lands of his in the State of Ohio lost by conflicting grants made under authority of the United States.
> *Printed separately* . . . . G. P. O. 1910.

Report—submitted to the Senate by the HON. GEORGE PEABODY WETMORE, a Senator from Rhode Island, 18 May 1910; from the Committee on the Library, to whom was referred the McCALL bill (H.R. No. 55), *providing for the erection of a memorial arch at Valley Forge, Pennsylvania.*
> *Journal of the Senate,* p. 366.
> [*Congressional Record,* V. 45: Part 6, p. 6442.]
> [*S. Rept. No. 705* . . . . *Serial* 5584.]

House bill (H. R. No. 55)—reported to the House of Representatives by the HON. SAMUEL W. McCALL, a Representative from Massachusetts, 25 January 1910, from the Committee on the Library, providing for the erection of a *memorial arch at Valley Forge, Pennsylvania.*—Approved, 25 June 1910.
> *Journal of the House of Representatives,* pp. 214, 272, 833, 837, 851, 853, 855.
> [*Congressional Record,* V. 45: Part 1, p. 1005; Part 2, pp. 1655-1658, 1684; Part 6, p. 6442; Part 8, pp. 8802, 8958, 9108, 9117, 9119.]
> [*H. Rept. No. 319* . . . *Serial* 5591.]

House bill (H. R. No. 25460)—submitted in the House of Representatives by the HON. HARRY M. COUDREY, a Representative from Missouri, 5 May 1910, to provide for the maintenance of Mount Vernon, Va., and to abolish the admission fee.—
> *Journal of the House of Representatives,* p. 646.
> [*Congressional Record,* V. 45: Part 6, p. 5868.]

THIRD SESSION OF THE SIXTY-FIRST CONGRESS: 1910-1911

House bill (H. R. No. 5266)—reported to the House of Representatives by the HON. E. A. MORSE, a Representative from Wisconsin, 16 February 1911, from the Committee on Private Land Claims, to re-imburse the estate of GENERAL GEORGE WASHINGTON for certain lands of his in the State of Ohio lost by conflicting grants made under the authority of the United States.[4]
> *Journal of the House of Representatives,* p. 317.
> *Congressional Record,* V. 46: Part 3, p. 2743.
> [*H. Rept. No. 2179* . . . . *Serial* 5852.]

FIRST SESSION OF THE SIXTY-SECOND CONGRESS: 1911

Ordered by the Senate, 5 August 1911—on motion *by* MR. HEYBURN, a Senator from Idaho:
That the *last will and testament of* GEORGE WASHINGTON, embracing a schedule of his real estate and explanatory notes thereto, to which are added important historical notes, biographical sketches, and anecdotes, be printed as a public document.
> *Journal of the Senate,* p. 160.
> [*Congressional Record,* V. 47: Part 4, p. 3632.]
> [*S. Doc. No. 86* . . . . *Serial* 6107.]

Resolution (S. J. Res. No. 38)—submitted in the Senate by the HON. HENRY CABOT LODGE, a Senator from Massachusetts, 20 June 1911, permitting the Sons of Veterans, United States of America, to place a bronze tablet in the *Washington Monument.*
> *Journal of the Senate,* p. 103.
> [*Congressional Record,* V. 47: Part 3, p. 2307.]

Report—submitted to the Senate by the HON. GEORGE PEABODY WETMORE, a Senator from Rhode Island, 4 August 1911, from the Committee on the Library, adverse to the Senate joint resolution (S. J. Res. No. 38) permitting the Sons of Veterans, United States of America, to place a bronze tablet in the *Washington Monument.*
> *Journal of the Senate,* p. 159.
> [*Congressional Record,* V. 47: Part 4, p. 3595.]
> [*S. Rept. No. 118* . . . . *Serial* 6077.]

Joint Resolution (H. J. Res. No. 123)—submitted in the House of Representatives by the HON. EBEN W. MARTIN, a Representative from South Dakota, 20 June 1911, permitting the Sons of Veterans of the United States of America to place a *bronze tablet in the Washington Monument.*—
> *Journal of the House of Representatives,* p. 286.
> [*Congressional Record,* V. 48: Part 3, pp. 2339-2340.]

SECOND SESSION OF THE SIXTY-SECOND CONGRESS: 1911-1912

House bill (H. R. 19552)—submitted in the House of Representatives by the HON. DAVID J. LEWIS, a Representative

---

[3] An invitation had been extended to the Speaker and Members of the House by the HON. CHARLES C. CARLIN, a Representative from Virginia, on behalf of the Washington Monument Association of Alexandria, to participate in the celebration of the one hundred and twentieth anniversary of the *first inauguration* of GEORGE WASHINGTON as President of the United States.

[4] *Hearings* on bills relating to the *estate of* GENERAL GEORGE WASHINGTON were held during the Sixty-Second Congress before a Sub-Committee of the Public Lands Committee of the House on March 25 and May 23, 1912.—Printed separately by G. P. O. 1912.

from Maryland, 6 February 1912, to appropriate a sum of money for the restoration of the first American monument to GEORGE WASHINGTON.[1]

> *Journal of the House of Representatives*, p. 273.
> [*Congressional Record*, V. 48: Part 2, p. 1793.]

On motion of MR. CLARKE, of Florida, and by unanimous consent, 22 February 1912, the *Farewell Address to the People of the United States*, 17 September 1796, was read before the House of Representatives on this birthday anniversary of GEORGE WASHINGTON.

> *Journal of the House of Representatives*, p. 346.
> [*Congressional Record*, V. 48: Part 3, pp. 2321, 2322-2325.]

Ordered by the House of Representatives, 22 February 1912— on motion by MR. CULLOP, a Representative from Indiana, that 20,000 copies of WASHINGTON's *Farewell Address to the People of the United States*, 17 September 1796, be printed for the use of Members of the House.

> *Journal of the House of Representatives*, p. 348.
> [*Congressional Record*, V. 48, Part 3, pp. 2339-2340.]

THIRD SESSION OF THE SIXTY-SECOND CONGRESS:
1912-1913

Resolution (H. Res. No. 732)—submitted in the House of Representatives by the HON. DANIEL J. RIORDAN, a Representative from New York, 5 December 1912, to provide for the printing and distribution of WASHINGTON's *Farewell Address to the People of the United States*, 17 September 1796.[2]

> *Journal of the House of Representatives*, p. 28.
> [*Congressional Record*, V. 49: Part 1, p. 196.]

FIRST SESSION OF THE SIXTY-THIRD CONGRESS:
1913

Joint Resolution (H. J. Res. No. 149)—submitted in the House of Representatives by the HON. RICHARD W. AUSTIN, a Representative from Tennessee, 11 November 1913, providing for a gift by the United States to the *Mount Vernon Association of certain relics* of GEORGE WASHINGTON.[3]

> *Journal of the House of Representatives*, p. 341.
> [*Congressional Record*, V. 50: Part 6, p. 5891.]

SECOND SESSION OF THE SIXTY-THIRD CONGRESS:
1913-1914

Statement of the late MR. LAWRENCE WASHINGTON, great-great-grand-nephew of GENERAL WASHINGTON, before a sub-Committee of the Committee on Public Lands, 19 March 1914, during hearings on the bill (H. R. 6168) to re-imburse the estate of GENERAL WASHINGTON for certain lands of his in the State of Ohio lost by conflicting grants made under the authority of the United States.

> *Hearings*—Public Lands Committee of the House— 1914.

Report—submitted to the Senate by the HON. LUKE LEA, a Senator from Tennessee, 8 June 1914, from the Committee on the Library, to whom was referred the SWANSON bill (S. No. 5429) for the purchase of two bronze copies of the *original marble portrait statue* of GEORGE WASNINGTON *by Jean-Antoine Houdon* to be placed in the Military Academy at West Point and in the Naval Academy at Annapolis.—

> *Journal of the Senate*, pp. 256, 323, 391.
> [*Congressional Record*, V. 51: Part 8, p. 7414; Part 10, p. 10008; Part 12, pp. 11893, 11958.]
> [S. *Rept. No.* 585 . . . . Serial 6553.]

FIRST SESSION OF THE SIXTY-FOURTH CONGRESS:
1915-1916

House bill (H. R. No. 11420)—submitted in the House of Representatives by the HON. WILLIAM J. CARY, a Representative from Wisconsin, 12 February 1916, to improve the *birthplace* of GEORGE WASHINGTON.—

> *Journal of the House of Representatives*, p. 326.
> [*Congressional Record*, V. 53: Part 3, p. 2488.]

Ordered by the House of Representatives, 16 February 1916— on motion by MR. RAKER, of California, and by unanimous consent: That on Tuesday next, immediately after the reading of the *Journal* and the disposition of business on the *Speaker's* table, *Washington's Farewell Address* be read.

> *Journal of the House of Representatives*, pp. 340,366.
> [*Congressional Record*, V. 53: Part 3, pp. 2675, 2928.]

Ordered by the Senate, 23 February 1916—by request of MR. SMITH, a Senator from Michigan, that an address delivered at Morristown, New Jersey, before the Washington Association of New Jersey, 22 February 1916, by the HON. HENRY CABOT LODGE, a Senator from Massachusetts, on WASHINGTON's *Policies of Neutrality and National Defense* be printed as a Senate document.

> *Journal of the Senate*, p. 181.
> [*Congressional Record*, V. 53: Part 3, p. 2984.]
> [S. *Doc. No.* 343 . . . . Serial 6952.]

SECOND SESSION OF THE SIXTY-FOURTH CONGRESS:
1916-1917

Senate Resolution (S. Res. No. 297)—reported to the Senate by the HON. JOHN SHARP WILLIAMS, a Senator from Mississippi, 5 February 1917, from the Committee on the Library, transferring *certain papers relating to the death of* GENERAL WASHINGTON from the files of the Senate to the custody of the Librarian of Congress.

> *Journal of the Senate*, pp. 43, 120.
> [*Congressional Record*, V. 54: Part 3, p. 2611.]

---

[1] The bill was re-introduced (H.R. 17469), 24 June 1914, 63rd Congress, 2nd Session, *Congressional Record*, V. 51: Part 11, p. 11073.—

[2] The resolution was re-introduced (H.Res. 63), 21 April 1913, 63rd Congress, 1st Session, *Congressional Record*, V. 50: Part 1, p. 307; (H.Res. 644), 13 October 1914, 63rd Congress, 2nd Session, *Congressional Record*, V. 51: Part 16, p. 16563.—

[3] A bill of similar title (H.R. 15353) was introduced, 3 April 1914, 63rd Congress, 2nd Session, *Congressional Record*, V. 51: Part 6, p. 6213; a joint resolution (H.J.Res. 25) was introduced, 3 April 1917, 65th Congress 1st Session, *Congressional Record*, V. 55: Part 1, p. 170.—

Senate Resolution (S. Res. No. 371)—submitted in the Senate by the HON. WILLIAM ALDEN SMITH, a Senator from Michigan, 22 February 1917, proposing that 1,000,000 copies of WASHINGTON's *Farewell Address to the people of the United States* and his *Farewell Address to the two Houses of Congress* be printed for the use of Members of the Senate and House.

> *Journal of the Senate*, p. 180.
> [*Congressional Record*, V. 54: Part 4, p. 3893.]

Neutrality Proclamation by PRESIDENT WASHINGTON, 22 April 1793—read before the Senate and printed in the *Record*, 23 February 1917, by request of the HON. THOMAS WALSH, a Senator from Montana.

> *Congressional Record*, V. 54: Part 4, 3965.

FIRST SESSION OF THE SIXTY-FIFTH CONGRESS:
1917

Ordered by the Senate, 11 September 1917—by request of MR. POMERENE, a Senator from Ohio, that the addresses delivered at the *tomb* of WASHINGTON, 26 August 1917, by the HON. JOSEPHUS DANIELS, Secretary of the Navy, and *Viscount Ishii*, ambassador extraordinary from Japan, upon the visit to Mount Vernon of the Imperial Japanese War Mission, be printed as a public document.

> *Congressional Record*, V. 55: Part 7, p. 6937.
> [*S. Doc. No. 85* . . . . *Serial 7265.*]

SECOND SESSION OF THE SIXTY-FIFTH CONGRESS:
1917-1918

Ordered by the Senate, 25 February 1918—by request of MR. POMERENE, a Senator from Ohio, that an address delivered by the HON. WARREN G. HARDING, a Senator from Ohio, 22 February 1918, before the Sons of the American Revolution, be printed as a public document.

> *Journal of the Senate*, p. 90 .
> [*Congressional Record*, V. 56: Part 3, p. 2586.]
> [*S. Doc. No. 180* . . . . *Serial 7329.*]

Senate bill (S. No. 3310)—submitted in the Senate by the HON. GEORGE E. CHAMBERLAIN, a Senator from Oregon, 4 January 1918, authorizing the Secretary of State to procure a *portrait of* GEORGE WASHINGTON and present the same to the Military College of the Argentine Republic.—

> *Journal of the Senate*, p. 29.
> [*Congressional Record*, V. 56: Part 1, p. 557.]

House bill (H.R. No. 6966)—reported to the House of Representatives by the HON. HENRY D. FLOOD, a Representative from Virginia, 7 January 1918, from the Committee on Foreign affairs, authorizing the Secretary of State to procure a *portrait of* WASHINGTON and present the same to the Military College of the Argentine Republic.—

> *Journal of the House of Representatives*, pp. 21, 83, 254.
> [*Congressional Record*, V. 56: Part 1, pp. 43, 674; Part 4, pp. 3993,4001.]
> [*H. Rept. No. 233* . . . . *Serial 7307.*]

Ordered by the Senate, 5 July 1918—on motion of MR. OWEN, a Senator from Oklahoma, that the address delivered by PRESIDENT WILSON, 4 July 1918, at the *tomb of* GEORGE WASHINGTON, be printed at a Senate document.

> *Congressional Record*, V. 56: Part 9, p. 8670.
> [*S. Doc. No. 258* . . . . *Serial 7330.*]

THIRD SESSION OF THE SIXTY-FIFTH CONGRESS:
1918-1919

Statement by the HON. PHILANDER C. KNOX, a Senator from Pennsylvania, 3 December 1918, relative to GEORGE WASHINGTON's journey to New England, as President of the United States, in 1789.

> *Congressional Record*, V. 57: Part 1, p. 27.

Ordered by the Senate, 22 February 1919—on motion by MR. GORE, a Senator from Oklahoma:
That the *Declaration of Independence*, and the *Farewell Address to the People of the United States by* GEORGE WASHINGTON, be printed as a Senate document, and that as many additional copies as can be obtained for $500 be printed for the use of the Senate.

> *Journal of the Senate*, p. 169.
> [*Congressional Record*, V. 57: Part 4, p. 4022.]
> [*S. Doc. No. 410* . . . . *Serial 7469.*]

Tribute of WASHINGTON, the Cincinnatus of the West, by George Gordon, LORD BYRON—read into the *Record*, 28 February 1919, by the HON. HENRY CABOT LODGE, a Senator from Massachusetts.

Congressional Record, V.57: Part 5, p. 4521.

Joint Resolution (H. J. Res. No. 429)—submitted in the House of Representatives by the HON. WILLIAM J. CARY, a Representative from Wisconsin, 18 February 1919, for the proposed *purchase of the estate of Mount Vernon by the National Government.*—

> *Journal of the House of Representatives*, p. 215.
> [*Congressional Record*, V. 57: Part 4, p. 3738.]

Resolution (H. Res. No. 592)—submitted in the House of Representatives by the HON. WILLIAM J. CARY, a Representative from Wisconsin, 18 February 1919, authorizing and directing the Committee on Interstate and Foreign Commerce to investigate the *conditions of transportation to Mount Vernon, in Virginia.*

> *Journal of the House of Representatives*, p. 215.
> [*Congressional Record*, V. 57: Part 4, p. 3738.]

SECOND SESSION OF THE SIXTY-SIXTH CONGRESS:
1919-1920

Tribute to GEORGE WASHINGTON *by Abraham Lincoln:* final paragraph of a speech delivered by *Lincoln* in Springfield, Illinois, on the 110th anniversary of WASHINGTON's *birth*, 22 February 1842—read into the *Record*, 23 February 1920, by request of the HON. ADDISON T. SMITH, a Representative from Idaho.[1]

> *Congressional Record*, V. 59: Part 4, p. 3357.

---

[1] The paragraph will be found as quoted in an address by the HON. BENJAMIN K. FOCHT, of Pennsylvania, *Congressional Record*, V. 59: Appendix, p. 8849.

FIRST SESSION OF THE SIXTY-SEVENTH CONGRESS:
1921

Joint Resolution (S. J. Res. No. 67)—submitted in the Senate by
the HON. REED SMOOT, a Senator from Utah, 3 June 1921,
relating to the use of the auditorium of the *George Washington Memorial Building* the erection of which is provided
for—in the act entitled "An act to increase the limit of cost
of certain public buildings; to authorize the enlargement,
extension, re-modeling, or improvement of certain public
buildings; to authorize the erection and completion of public
buildings; to authorize the purchase of sites for public buildings . . . approved March 4, 1913, as amended."[1]

> *Journal of the Senate,* pp. 127, 167, 224, 233.
>> [*Congressional Record,* V. 61: Part 2, p. 2063; Part 3,
>> p. 3010; Part 5, pp. 4747, 5008, 5084.]

Joint Resolution (H. J. Res. No. 42)—submitted in the House
of Representatives by the HON. SCHUYLER OTIS BLAND, a
Representative from Virginia, 12 April 1921, authorizing
and directing the construction of a road from the *monument marking the birthplace of* GEORGE WASHINGTON, *in
Westmoreland County, Va., to the State highway running
from Fredericksburg, Va., to Montrose, Va.—*

> *Journal of the House of Representatives,* p. 65.
> [*Congressional Record,* V. 61: Part 1, p. 175.]

Joint Resolution (H. J. Res. No. 123)—submitted in the House
of Representatives by the HON. JAMES R. GOOD, a Representative from Iowa, 20 May 1921, to provide funds for the
repair of the elevator in the *Washington Monument.—Approved,* 25 May 1921.

> *Journal of the House of Representatives,* pp. 202, 205,
> 215, 219.
>> [*Congressional Record,* V. 61: Part 2, pp. 1562, 1563,
>> 1589, 1592, 1625, 1718, 1774.]

Joint Resolution (H. J. Res. No. 117)—submitted in the House
of Representatives by the HON. JOHN J. KINDRED, a Representative from New York, 12 May 1921, directing the Secretary of the Treasury to acquire, by purchase or otherwise,
the *property on which the tombs and former homes of* PRESI-
DENT WASHINGTON and *President Jefferson are located.—*

> *Journal of the House of Representatives,* p. 187.
> [*Congressional Record,* V. 61: Part 2, p. 1403.]

SECOND SESSION OF THE SIXTY-SEVENTH CONGRESS:
1921-1922

Joint Resolution (S. J. Res. No. 137)—reported to the Senate by
the HON. HENRY CABOT LODGE, a Senator from Massachusetts, 3 February 1922, from the Committee on Foreign Relations, transferring to the custody of the Secretary of the
Smithsonian Institution certain relics now in the possession
of the Department of State.—*Approved,* 28 February 1922.

> *Journal of the Senate,* pp. 85, 101, 102, 107, 110, 112,
> 118.
> *Journal of the House of Representatives,* pp. 161, 165,
> 169, 188.
>> [*Congressional Record,* V. 62: Part 3, pp. 2312, 2776,
>> 2906, 2908, 3038, 3040, 3083, 3181.]
>> [*S. Rept. No.* 487 . . . . *Serial 7950.*]

FOURTH SESSION OF THE SIXTY-SEVENTH CONGRESS:
1922-1923

Concurrent Resolution (S. Con. Res. No. 39)—submitted in the
Senate by the HON. HENRY CABOT LODGE, a Senator from
Massachusetts, 13 February 1923, directing the Sergeant-at-
Arms of the Senate and the Sergeant-at-Arms of the House
of Representatives to place a *floral wreath at the base of the
Washington Monument on* WASHINGTON's *Birthday.*

> *Journal of the Senate,* pp. 161, 168, 178.
> *Journal of the House of Representatives,* pp. 247, 254.
>> [*Congressional Record,* V. 64: Part 4, pp. 3669, 3976,
>> 4195.]

FIRST SESSION OF THE SIXTY-EIGHTH CONGRESS:
1923-1924

Joint Resolution (S. J. Res. No. 85)—reported to the Senate by
the HON. SIMEON D. FESS, a Senator from Ohio, 24 April
1924, from the Committee on the Library, authorizing an
appropriation for the participation of the United States in
the preparaion and completion of plans for the comprehensive observance of that greatest of all historic events, *the
bicentennial of the birthday of* GEORGE WASHINGTON.—
Approved, 2 December 1924.

> *Journal of the Senate,* pp. 164, 313, 376, 462, 472.
> *Journal of the House of Representatives,* pp. 575, 580,
> 706, 711.
>> [*Congressional Record,* V. 65: Part 3, p. 2936; Part 8,
>> p. 7737; Part 9, pp. 9170-9171, 9424; Part 11, pp.
>> 11141, 11204-11206.][2]
>> [*S. Rept. No.* 491 . . . . *Serial 8221.*]

Report—submitted in the House of Representatives by the HON.
DANIEL A. REED, a Representative from New York, 13 May
1924, from the Committee on Industrial Arts and Expositions, to whom was referred the joint resolution (H. J. Res.
No. 199), introduced, 22 February 1924, by the HON. R.
WALTON MOORE, a Representative from Virginia, authorizing an appropriation for the participation of the United
States in the preparation and completion of plans for the
comprehensive observance of that greatest of all historic
events, *the bicentennial of the birthday of* GEORGE WASH-
INGTON.[3]

> *Journal of the House of Representatives,* pp. 269, 522,
> 707.

---

[1] A joint resolution of similar title (H.J.Res. 142) was introduced in the
House of Representatives, 3 June 1921, by the HON. JULIUS KAHN,
a Representative from California.—*Congressional Record,* V. 61: Part
2, p. 2118.—

[2] The Senate Joint Resolution (S.J.Res. 85) was enrolled, presented to the
President, and approved, 2 December 1924—68th Congress, 2nd Session. *Congressional Record,* V. 66: Part 1, pp. 46, 56, 105.

[3] The joint resolution (H.J.Res. 199) was laid on the table. See *S.J.Res.* 85.

[*Congressional Record*, V. 65: Part 3, p. 2977; Part 8, pp. 8496-8497; Part 11, p. 11204.]

[*H. Rept. No. 732 . . . . Serial 8229.*]

Ordered by the Senate, 12 May 1924—by request of MR. CAMERON, a Senator from Arizona, that the Report of Proceedings in the *Washington Monument*, 15 April 1924, upon the dedication of the *Arizona State memorial stone* be printed in the *Record*, and as a Senate document.

Congressional Record, V. 65: Part 7, p. 6973; Part 8, p. 8360.

[*S. Doc. No. 109 . . . . Serial 8243.*]

SECOND SESSION OF THE SIXTY-EIGHTH CONGRESS: 1924-1926

Message from *Calvin Coolidge, President of the United States*, 29 December 1924, with an accompanying letter from the Director of the Bureau of the Budget, transmitting to the Congress a report from the Secretary of State recommending an appropriation for the purpose of securing a *replica of the Houdon bust of* WASHINGTON *for lodgment in the Pan-American building.*

Journal of the Senate, p. 49.
Journal of the House of Representatives, p. 69.
[*Congressional Record*, V. 66: Part 1, pp. 903, 930.]
[*S. Doc. No. 176 . . . . Serial 8413.*]

Message from *Calvin Coolidge, President of the United States*, 17 February 1925, transmitting to the Congress the *First Report of the Commission for the celebration of the two-hundredth anniversary of the birth of* GEORGE WASHINGTON.

Journal of the Senate, p. 211.
Journal of the House of Representatives, p. 283.
[*Congressional Record*, V. 66: Part 4, pp. 4154, 4206.]
[*S. Doc. No. 205 . . . . Serial 8413.*]

Message from *Calvin Coolidge, President of the United States*, 28 February 1925, with accompanying letter from the Director of the Bureau of Budget, transmitting a supplemental estimate of appropriation for the *United States Commission for the celebration of the two-hundredth anniversary of the birth of* GEORGE WASHINGTON.

Journal of the Senate, p. 257.
[*Congressional Record*, V. 66: Part 5, p. 4933.]
[*S. Doc. No. 255 . . . . Serial 8413.*]

Letters written in 1796 and 1798 by *Adelaide-Rosalie Ursula Maussion de la Bastie*, daughter of a young Frenchman who came to America with the *Marquis de la Fayette* during the Revolutionary War—printed in the *Record*, in English translation, 4 March 1925, by request of the HON. C. C. DILL, a Senator from the State of Washington.

Congressional Record, V. 66: Part 5, pp. 1511, 1512, 1513.

House bill (H.R. No. 11799)—reported to the House of Representatives by the HON. ROBERT LUCE, a Representative from Massachusetts, 29 January 1925, from the Committee on

the Library, to secure a *replica of the Houdon bust of* WASHINGTON *for lodgment in the Pan-American building.*—[1]

Journal of the House of Representatives, pp. 142, 173, 261.

[*Congressional Record*, V. 66: Part 3, pp. 2186, 2685; Part 4, pp. 3879, 3929.]

[*H. Rept. No. 1322 . . . . Serial 8390.*]

Communication from *Calvin Coolidge, President of the United States*, 13 February 1925, transmitting a supplemental estimate of appropriation for the fiscal year ending June 30, 1925, for the War Department, for the repair of the elevator in the *Washington Monument*.

Journal of the House of Representatives, p. 248.
[*Congressional Record*, V. 66: Part 4, p. 3695.]
[*H. Doc. No. 629 . . . . Serial 8445.*]

Letter from the *Bureau of American Ideals* relative to the custom of reading WASHINGTON's *Farewell Address to the people of the United States* in the House of Representatives—printed in the *Record*, 4 March 1925, by request of the HON. JOHN E. RANKIN, a Representative from Mississippi.

Congressional Record, V. 66: Part 5, p. 5620.

FIRST SESSION OF THE SIXTY-NINTH CONGRESS: 1925-1926

Joint Resolution of the *Legislature of the State of Montana*, favoring the appointment by the Governor of the State of Montana of a commission to act in conjunction with the Commission appointed by the President of the United States to arrange for a proper observance of the *two-hundredth anniversary of the birth of* GEORGE WASHINGTON—presented in the Senate, 10 December 1925, by the HON. CHARLES G. DAWES, *Vice-President of the United States*.

Journal of the Senate, p. 36.
[*Congressional Record*, V. 67: Part 1, p. 592.]

Ordered by the Senate, 23 February 1926—by request of MR. FESS, a Senator from Ohio, that an address delivered by *Calvin Coolidge, President of the United States*, 22 February 1926, on the subject GEORGE WASHINGTON: *A Great Teacher*, be printed in the *Record*, and as a Senate document.

Congressional Record, V. 67: Part 4, p. 4370.
[*S. Doc. No. 68 . . . . Serial 8557.*]

Editorial under the title *We might honor* WASHINGTON *more by heeding his advice*—read into the *Record* from the *Washington Herald*, 22 February 1926, by request of the HON. COLE L. BLEASE, a Senator from South Carolina.

Congressional Record, V. 67: Part 4, p. 4330.

Joint Resolution (S. J. Res. No. 75)—submitted in the Senate by the HON. CLAUDE A. SWANSON, a Senator from Virginia, 17 March 1926, authorizing certain funds appropriated for the *reservation and monument at Wakefield, Virginia*, to be made

---

[1] The bill (H.R. 11799) was not enacted. See joint resolution (H.J.Res. 64), 69th Congress, 1st Session.

available for certain repairs to existing highways and lanes on said reservation.—

> *Journal of the Senate,* p. 237.
> [*Congressional Record,* V. 67: Part 6, p. 5759.]

Report—submitted to the Senate by the HON. JAMES W. WADS-WORTH, a Senator from New York, 24 May 1926, from the Committee on Military Affairs, to whom was referred the bill (H.R. No. 10131), granting the consent of Congress to the *Wakefield National Memorial Association* to build, upon Government-owned land at Wakefield, Westmoreland County, Virginia, *a replica of the house in which* GEORGE WASHINGTON *was born.*

> *Journal of the Senate,* pp. 373, 375, 431, 460.
> [*Congressional Record,* V. 67: Part 9, p. 9883.]
> [S. *Rept. No.* 910 . . . . Serial 8526.]

Report—submitted to the House of Representatives by the HON. J. MAYHEW WAINWRIGHT, a Representative from New York. 15 April 1926, from the Committee on Military Affairs to whom was referred the bill (H.R. No. 10131), granting the consent of Congress to the *Wakefield National Memorial Association* to build, upon Government-owned land at Wakefield, Westmoreland County, Virginia, *a replica of the house in which* GEORGE WASHINGTON *was born.*

> *Journal of the House of Representatives,* pp. 360, 510.
> [*Congressional Record,* V. 67: Part 7, p. 7553.]
> [H. *Rept. No.* 898 . . . . Serial 8533.]

House bill (H.R. No. 10131)—submitted in the House of Representatives by the HON. S. O. BLAND, a Representative from Virginia, 8 March 1926, granting the consent of Congress to the *Wakefield National Memorial Association* to build, upon Government-owned land at Wakefield, Westmoreland County, Virginia, *a replica of the house in which* GEORGE WASHINGTON *was born.—Approved,* 7 June 1926.

> *Journal of the House of Representatives,* pp. 360, 510, 596, 732, 738, 748, 792.
> *Journal of the Senate,* pp. 373, 375, 431, 460, 467, 500.
> [*Congressional Record,* V. 67: Part 5, p. 5257; Part 7, p. 7553; Part 8, pp. 8625-8681; Part 9, p. 9883; Part 10, pp. 10597, 10756, 10763, 10820, 11460.]

House bill (H.R. No. 8908)—submitted in the House of Representatives by the HON. R. WALTON MOORE, a Representative from Virginia, 4 February 1926, granting the consent of Congress to *George Washington-Wakefield Memorial Bridge,* a corporation, to construct a bridge across the Potomac River. *Approved,* 5 May 1926.[1]

> *Journal of the House of Representatives,* pp. 253, 270, 332, 452, 489, 497, 543, 549, 583, 604, 710.
> *Journal of the Senate,* pp. 200, 262, 279, 303, 304, 331, 347, 364, 444.

---

[1] It does not appear that the bridge provided for in this bill (H.R. No. 8908) is a memorial to GENERAL WASHINGTON; the bill is cited here, because, when built, the bridge will afford direct communication with a region in Virginia inseparably associated with the WASHINGTON family, and with the birthplace of GENERAL WASHINGTON.

[*Congressional Record,* V. 67: Part 3, p. 3339; Part 4, p. 3826; Part 5, pp. 4790, 4792, 4840; Part 6, pp. 6423, 6807; Part 7, pp. 7309, 7341, 7907, 7977-7978, 8082; Part 8, pp. 8468, 8481, 8611; Part 9, p. 10229.]

Joint Resolution (H. J. Res. No. 64)—reported to the House of Representatives by the HON. ROBERT LUCE, a Representative from Massachusetts, 5 January 1926, from the Committee on the Library, to secure *a replica of the Houdon bust of* WASHINGTON *for lodgment in the Pan-American Building.—Approved,* 28 June 1926.

> *Journal of the House of Representatives,* pp. 111,166, 207, 811, 819, 824, 893.
> *Journal of the Senate,* pp. 95, 96, 510, 519, 575.
> [*Congressional Record,* V. 67: Part 1, p. 926; Part 2, pp. 1552, 2310; Part 3, p. 2348; Part 11, pp. 11728, 11799, 11830, 11915, 13092.]
> [H. *Rept. No.* 40 . . . . Serial 8531.]

General Order issued by GENERAL GEORGE WASHINGTON *in New York in July,* 1776, relative to the use of profanity in the American Army—read into the *Record,* 22 February 1926, by request of the HON. WILLIAM D. UPSHAW, a Representative from Georgia.

> *Congressional Record,* V. 67: Part 4, p. 4367.

House bill (H.R. No. 9629)—submitted in the House of Representatives by the HON. BENJAMIN L. FAIRCHILD, a Representative from New York, 22 February 1926, to provide for celebrating the *two-hundredth anniversary of the birth of* GEORGE WASHINGTON by holding an international exhibition of arts, industries, manufactures, and the products of soil, mine, and sea in the city of New York, in the State of New York.—

> *Journal of the House of Representatives,* p. 303.
> [*Congressional Record,* V. 67: Part 4, p. 4369.]

Recipe for making beer, alleged to have been used by GENERAL WASHINGTON—read into the *Record,* 17 February 1926, by the HON. EMANUEL CELLER, a Representative from New York.

> *Congressional Record,* V. 67: Part 4, p. 4170.

WASHINGTON, a poem by HORACE C. CARLISLE—printed in the *Record,* 22 February 1926, by request of the HON. THOMAS J. HEFLIN, a Senator from Alabama.

> *Congressional Record,* V. 67: Part 4, p. 4329.

Joint Resolution (H.R.Res. No. 198)—submitted in the House of Representatives by the HON. S. O. BLAND, a Representative from Virginia, 11 March 1926, authorizing certain funds appropriated for the *reservation and monument at Wakefield, Virginia,* to be made available for certain repairs to existing highways and lanes on said reservation.—

> *Journal of the House of Representatives,* p. 370.
> [*Congressional Record,* V. 67: Part 5, p. 5443.]

Report—submitted to the House of Representatives by the HON. EDWARD M. BEERS, a Representative from Pennsylvania, 24 June 1926, from the Committee on Printing, to whom was referred the concurrent resolution (H. Con. Res. No. 31) providing for the printing of 10,000 additional copies of *Senate Document No. 86*, Sixty-Second Congress, First Session, entitled *Last Will and Testament of* George Washington.

> *Journal of the House of Representatives*, p. 821.
> [*Congressional Record*, V. 67: Part 11, p. 11904.]
> [*H. Rept. No.* 1534 . . . *Serial* 8537.]

Concurrent Resolution (H. Con. Res. No. 31)—submitted in the House of Representatives by the Hon. Addison T. Smith, a Representative from Idaho, 26 May 1926, providing for the printing of 10,000 additional copies of *Senate Document No. 86*, Sixty-Second Congress, First Session, entitled *Last Will and Testament of* George Washington.

> *Journal of the House of Representatives*, pp. 708, 821, 831.
> *Journal of the Senate*, pp. 520, 526.
> [*Congressional Record*, V. 67: Part 9, p. 10148; Part 11, pp. 11904, 11930.]

Report—submitted to the House of Representatives by the Hon. Edward M. Beers, a Representative from Pennsylvania, 24 June 1926, from the Committee on Printing, to whom was referred the resolution (H. Res. No. 263), providing for the printing, with illustrations, of the exercises at the dedication of the *North Dakota State memorial stone in the Washington Monument*.

> *Journal of the House of Representatives*, pp. 626, 821.
> [*Congressional Record*, V. 67: Part 8, p. 9181; Part 11, p. 11928.]
> [*H. Rept. No.* 1535 . . . *Serial* 8537.]

Ordered by the House of Representatives, 24 June 1926—in compliance with the House resolution (H. Res. No. 263), introduced by Mr. Burtness, a Representative from North Dakota, 10 May 1926, that proceedings held in the *Washington Monument*, in the city of Washington, upon the dedication of the *North Dakota State memorial stone* be printed as a House document.

> *Congressional Record*, V. 67: Part 8, p. 9181; Part 11, p. 11928.
> [*H. Doc. No.* 458 . . . . *Serial* 8575.]

SECOND SESSION OF THE SIXTY-NINTH CONGRESS:
1926-1927

Concurrent Resolution (S. Con. Res. No. 28)—submitted in the Senate by the Hon. Simeon D. Fess, a Senator from Ohio, 22 February 1927, that there shall be printed, with illustrations, 75,000 copies of the President's speech before the two Houses of Congress, on this day, relative to the celebration of the *two-hundredth anniversary of the birth of* George Washington.

> *Journal of the Senate*, pp. 198-199, 260.
> *Journal of the House of Representatives*, pp. 315, 382.
> [*Congressional Record*, V. 68: Part 4, p. 4401; Part 5, p. 5368.]
> [*S. Doc. No.* 249 . . . . *Serial* 8709.]

Communication from Calvin Coolidge, *President of the United States*, 21 December 1926, transmitting to the House of Representatives a supplemental estimate of appropriation for the United States Commission for the celebration of the *two-*

John Marshall

A Representative from Virginia, on December 19, 1799, Made an Address in the House of Representatives Announcing the Death of George Washington

hundredth anniversary of the birth of George Washington.

> *Journal of the House of Representatives*, p. 78.
> [*Congressional Record*, V. 68: Part 1, p. 962.]
> [*H. Doc. No.* 608 . . . *Serial* 8734.]

Concurrent Resolution (H. Con. Res. No. 49)—submitted in the House of Representatives by the Hon. Willis C. Hawley, a Representative from Oregon, 29 January 1927, relating to the *two-hundredth anniversary of the birth of* George Washington.

> *Journal of the House of Representatives*, pp. 183, 191.
> *Journal of the Senate*, pp. 116, 117.
> [*Congressional Record*, V. 68: Part 3, pp. 2543, 2550.]

Concurrent Resolution (H. Con. Res. No. 57)—submitted in the House of Representatives by the Hon. John Q. Tilson, a Representative from Connecticut, 22 February 1927, inviting the full co-operation of the legislatures and the chief executives of the respective States and Territories of the United States in the *celebration of the two-hundredth anniversary of the birth of* George Washington.

> *Journal of the House of Representatives*, pp. 310, 315.
> *Journal of the Senate*, pp. 207, 209.
> [*Congressional Record*, V. 68: Part 4, pp. 4459-4460, 4526.]

House bill (H. R. No. 16348)—submitted in the House of Representatives by the Hon. O. J. Kvale, a Representative from Minnesota, 15 January 1927, providing for the preparation, printing, and distribution of pamphlets containing a *biographical sketch* of GEORGE WASHINGTON.

> *Journal of the House of Representatives*, p. 134.
> [*Congressional Record*, V. 68: Part 2, p. 1754.]

FIRST SESSION OF THE SEVENTIETH CONGRESS: 1927-1928

Ordered by the Senate, 12 December 1927—by request of MR. BRATTON, a Senator from New Mexico, that proceedings held in the *Washington Monument*, Washington, District of Columbia, 2 December 1927, upon the dedication of the *New Mexico State memorial stone* be printed as a Senate document.

> *Journal of the Senate*, p. 50.
> [*Congressional Record*, V. 69: Part 1, p. 478.]
> [*S. Doc. No.* 18 . . . . Serial 8845.]

Senate bill (S. No. 3092)—submitted in the Senate by the HON. SIMEON D. FESS, a Senator from Ohio, 8 February 1928, to enable the *George Washington Bicentennial Commission* to carry out and give effect to certain approved plans.—[1]

> *Journal of the Senate*, pp. 166, 211, 349.
> [*Congressional Record*, V. 69: Part 3, p. 2668; Part 4, p. 3581; Part 5, p. 5032; Part 6, pp. 6510, 6630.]

Report—submitted in the House of Representatives, 28 May 1928, from the Committee on Printing, to whom was referred the FESS bill (S. No. 3092), to enable the *George Washington Bicentennial Commission* to carry out and give effect to certain approved plans.

> *Journal of the House of Representatives*, p. 1001.
> [*Congressional Record*, V. 69: Part 10, p. 10459.]
> [*H. Rept. No.* 1915 . . . . Serial 8838.]

Letter from the *George Washington Birthday Association, of Alexandria, Virginia,* inviting the United States Congress to be present in Alexandria, *the home city of* GEORGE WASH-INGTON, 22 February 1928, and witness the parade in honor of GEORGE WASHINGTON's *birthday*—presented in the Senate, 9 February 1928, by the HON. CLAUDE A. SWAN-SON, a Senator from Virginia; presented in the House of Representatives, 10 February 1928, by the HON. R. WAL-TON MOORE, a Representative from Virginia.

> *Congressional Record*, V. 69: Part 3, pp. 2780, 2847.

Joint Resolution (S. J. Res. No. 107)—submitted in the Senate by the HON. DAVID A. REED, a Senator from Pennsylvania, 5 March 1928, authorizing and requesting the Postmaster-General to design and issue a *special postage stamp in honor of the one hundred and fiftieth anniversary of the encampment of* WASHINGTON's *Army at Valley Forge.*—

> *Journal of the Senate*, p. 242.
> [*Congressional Record*, V. 69: Part 4, p. 4065.]

Report—submitted to the Senate by the HON. SIMEON D. FESS, a Senator from Ohio, 5 March 1928, from the Committee on the Library, to whom was referred the SWANSON bill (S. No. 1369), authorizing and directing the survey, con-

struction, and maintenance of a *memorial highway to connect Mount Vernon*, in the State of Virginia, *with the Arlington Memorial Bridge* across the Potomac River at Washington.

> *Journal of the Senate*, p. 241.
> [*Congressional Record*, V. 69: Part 4, p. 4063.]
> [*S. Rept. No.* 469 . . . . Serial 8829.]

Senate bill (S. No. 1369)—submitted to the Senate by the HON. CLAUDE A. SWANSON, a Senator from Virginia, 9 December 1927 (Legislative day, 6 December 1927), to authorize and direct the survey, construction, and maintenance of a *memorial highway to connect Mount Vernon*, in the State of Virginia, *with the Arlington Memorial Bridge* across the Potomac River at Washington.—*Approved*, 23 May 1928.

> *Journal of the Senate*, pp. 43, 241, 248, 499, 504, 522, 532.
> *Journal of the House of Representatives*, pp. 521, 527, 920, 932, 941.
> [*Congressional Record*, V. 69: Part 1, p. 350; Part 4, pp. 4063, 4175, 4376; Part 9, pp. 9378, 9382, 9516, 9449, 9677.]

Report—submitted to the House of Representatives by the HON. JOHN M. ROBSION, a Representative from Kentucky, 28 March 1928, from the Committee on Roads, to whom was referred the bill (H. R. No. 4625), introduced, 5 December 1927, by the HON. R. WALTON MOORE, a Representative from Virginia, to authorize and direct the survey, construction, and maintenance of a *memorial highway to connect Mount Vernon*, in the State of Virginia, *with the Arlington Memorial Bridge* across the Potomac River at Washington.[2]

> *Journal of the House of Representatives*, pp. 86, 609, 920.
> [*Congressional Record*, V. 69: Part 1, p. 80; Part 5, p. 5533; Part 6, pp. 6551-6552; Part 9, pp. 9378-9382.]
> [*H. Rept. No.* 1065 . . . Serial 8836.]

Communication from CALVIN COOLIDGE, *President of the United States*, 23 May 1928, transmitting a supplemental estimate of appropriation for the Department of Agriculture to carry into effect the provisions of the act entitled "An act to authorize and direct the survey, construction, and maintenance of a *memorial highway to connect Mount Vernon*, in the State of Virginia, *with the Arlington Memorial Bridge* across the Potomac River at Washington."

> *Journal of the Senate*, p. 522.
> [*Congressional Record*, V. 69: Part 9, p. 9551.]
> [*S. Doc. No.* 149 . . . . Serial 8871.]

Senate bill (S. No. 4531)—submitted in the Senate by the HON. CLAUDE A. SWANSON, a Senator from Virginia, 22 May 1928, to improve the *birthplace of* GEORGE WASHINGTON *at Wakefield, Westmoreland County, Virginia.*

> *Journal of the Senate*, p. 501.
> [*Congressional Record*, V. 69: Part 9, p. 9429.]

Joint Resolution (H. J. Res. No. 128)—submitted in the House of Representatives by the HON. GEORGE H. TINKHAM, a

---

[1] This bill (S. 3092) was not enacted. See S. 3398, 71st Congress, 2nd Session.

[2] The bill (H.R. 4625) was laid on the Table. See S. 1369.

Representative from Massachusetts, 5 January 1928, making provision for the improvement of the *National Memorial to George Washington in the District of Columbia* by the erection of a suitable base.—

Journal of the House of Representatives, p. 206.
[*Congressional Record,* V. 69: Part 2, p. 1085.]

Resolution adopted by the Brooklyn Chapter of the *American Institute of Architects,* Brooklyn, New York, favoring an appropriation to carry out the *McKim plan for the base of the Washington Monument*—presented in the Senate, 1 February 1928, by the Hon. ROYAL S. COPELAND, a Senator from New York.

Journal of the Senate, p. 149.

House bill (H. R. No. 11208)—submitted in the House of Representatives by the Hon. GEORGE H. TINKHAM, a Representative from Massachusetts, 20 February 1928, providing for engineering and landscape study, preparation of plans, and estimate of cost of *improvement of the base and grounds of the Washington Monument in the District of Columbia.*[1]

Journal of the House of Representatives, p. 444.
[*Congressional Record,* V. 69: Part 3, p. 3309.]

Joint Resolution (H. J. Res. No. 182)—submitted in the House of Representatives by the Hon. HENRY W. WATSON, a Representative from Pennsylvania, 25 January 1928, authorizing and requesting the Postmaster-General to design and *issue a special postage stamp in honor of the one hundred and fiftieth anniversary of the encampment of Washington's Army at Valley Forge.*—

Congressional Record, V. 69: Part 2, 2045.

House bill (H. R. No. 10140)—submitted in the House of Representatives by the Hon. SOL BLOOM, a Representative from New York, 30 January 1928, to commemorate the *two-hundredth anniversary of the birth of GEORGE WASHINGTON* by holding an international exhibition of arts, industries, manufactures, and products of soil, mine, and sea in the Washington Marine Park, Brooklyn, New York.—

Journal of the House of Representatives, p. 322.
[*Congressional Record,* V. 69: Part 2, p. 1222.]

Ordered by the House of Representatives, 14 March 1928—on motion by MR. HAWLEY, a Representative from Oregon, and by unanimous consent: That the address of the *President of the United States* delivered before a joint session of the two Houses of Congress, 22 February 1927, on the *life of GEORGE WASHINGTON and the proposed celebration of the two-hundredth anniversary of his birth* be printed as a House document.[2]

---

[1] MR. TINKHAM, of Massachusetts, re-introduced the bill during the First Session of the Seventy-First Congress: (H.R. 15), 15 April 1929, *Congressional Record,* V. 71: Part 1, p. 27.—

[2] The address delivered by PRESIDENT COOLIDGE before a joint session of the two Houses of Congress, 22 February 1927, as printed in the *Senate Journal* (69th Congress, 2nd Session), pp. 199-203; and, also, as a Senate document: S. *Doc. No. 249 . . . Serial 8709.* No House document has been found.

Journal of the House of Representatives, p. 551.
[*Congressional Record,* V. 69: Part 5, p. 4709.]

House bill (H. R. No. 12807)—submitted in the House of Representatives by the Hon. S. O. BLAND, a Representative from Virginia, 9 April 1928, to improve the *birthplace of GEORGE WASHINGTON at Wakefield, Westmoreland County, Virginia.*

Journal of the House of Representatives, p. 657.
[*Congressional Record,* V. 69: Part 6, p. 6136.]

SECOND CONGRESS OF THE SEVENTIETH CONGRESS: 1928-1929

Senate Bill (S. No. 5616)—reported to the Senate by the Hon. SIMEON D. FESS, a Senator from Ohio, 18 February 1929 (Legislative Day, 15 February 1929), from the Committee on the Library, to enable the *George Washington Bicentennial Commission* to carry out and give effect to certain approved plans.

Journal of the Senate, pp. 199, 179, 244.
[*Congressional Record,* V. 70; Part 3, p. 2438; Part 4, p. 3616; Part 5, p. 4714.]
[S. *Rept. No. 1821 . . . . Serial 8977.*]

Communication from MRS. SUSAN WHITNEY DIMOCK, president of the *George Washington Memorial Association* relative to the erection of the *George Washington Memorial*—read into the *Record,* 20 February 1929, by request of the Hon. CHARLES CURTIS, a Senator from Kansas.

Congressoional Record, V. 70: Part 4, p. 3812.

Ordered by the House of Representatives, 28 January 1929—on motion by MR. SNELL, a Representative from New York, and by unanimous consent: That, on Friday, 22 February 1929, immediately after the reading of *Journal* and disposition of business on the *Speaker's* table, MR. BECK, a Representative from Pennsylvania, may have an hour in which to address the House on the *life and character of GEORGE WASHINGTON.*

Journal of the House of Representatives, p. 156.
[*Congressional Record,* V. 70: Part 3, p. 2391.]

House bill (H. R. No. 16665)—submitted in the House of Representatives by the Hon. JOHN Q. TILSON, a Representative from Connecticut, 28 January 1929, authorizing an appropriation to enable the *George Washington Bicentennial Commission* to carry out and give effect to certain plans approved by said Commission.—

Journal of the House of Representatives, p. 157.
[*Congressional Record,* V. 70: Part 3, p. 2397.]

Report—submitted to the House of Representatives by the Hon. RICHARD N. ELLIOTT, a Representative from Indiana, 14 February 1929, from the Committee on Public Buildings and Grounds, to whom was referred the bill (H. R. No. 15524), introduced, 18 December 1928, by the Hon. LOUIS C. CRAMTON, a Representative from Michigan, for the acquisition, establishment, and development of the *George Washington Memorial Parkway* along the Potomac *from Mount Vernon and Fort Washington to the Great*

Falls, and to provide for the acquisition of lands in the District of Columbia and the States of Maryland and Virginia requisite to the comprehensive park, parkway, and playgrounds system of the National Capital.[3]

> *Journal of the House of Representatives,* pp. 69, 251, 335, 336.
> [*Congressional Record,* V. 70: Part 1, p. 849; Part 4, p. 3490; Part 5, pp. 4613, 4614, 4665, 5086.]
> [*H. Rept. No. 2523 . . . . Serial 8980.*]

Ordered by the House of Representatives, 22 February 1929— on motion by MR. GARRETT, a Representative from Tennessee, and by unanimous consent:
That the address delivered before the House, 22 February 1929, by the HON. JAMES M. BECK, a Representative from Pennsylvania, in commemoration of GEORGE WASHINGTON's *birthday,* be printed as a House document.

> *Journal of the House of Representatives,* p. 299.
> [*Congressional Record,* V. 70: Part 4, p. 4060.]
> [*H. Doc. No. 611 . . . . Serial 9021.*]

FIRST SESSION OF THE SEVENTY-FIRST CONGRESS: 1929

Report—submitted to the Senate by the HON. SIMEON D. FESS, a Senator from Ohio, 20 November 1929 (Legislative day, 30 October 1929), from the Committee on the Library, to whom was referred the SWANSON bill (S. No. 1784), appropriating money for improvements upon Government-owned land at Wakefield, Westmoreland County, Virginia, *the birthplace* of GEORGE WASHINGTON.

> *Journal of the Senate,* pp. 150, 199, 211.
> [*Congressional Record,* V. 71: Part 4, p. 4091; Part 5, p. 5832.]
> [*S. Rept. No. 45 . . . . . Serial 9185.*]

SECOND SESSION OF THE SEVENTY-FIRST CONGRESS: 1929-1930

Senate bill (S. No. 1784)—submitted in the Senate (during the preceding session) by the HON. CLAUDE A. SWANSON, a Senator from Virginia, 1 October 1929, appropriating money for improvement upon the Government-owned land at Wakefield, Westmoreland County, Virginia, *the birthplace of* GEORGE WASHINGTON.—*Approved,* 23 January 1930.

> *Journal of the Senate,* pp. 54, 92, 93, 95, 97, 99.
> *Journal of the House of Representatives,* pp. 101, 168, 174, 180, 192.
> [*Congressional Record,* V. 72: Part 1, pp. 955, 1078; Part 2, pp. 1991, 1995, 2020, 2138, 2169, 2177; Part 3, p. 2266.]

Communication from HERBERT HOOVER, *President of the United States,* with accompanying letter from the Director of the Bureau of the Budget, 25 January 1930, transmitting a sup-plemental estimate of appropriation for improvements upon the Government-owned land at Wakefield, Virginia.

> *Journal of the House of Representatives,* p. 199.
> [*Congressional Record,* V. 72: Part 3, p. 2487.]
> [*H. Doc. No. 272 . . . . Serial 9252.*]

Joint Resolution (S. J. Res. No. 91)—submitted in the Senate by the HON. SIMEON D. FESS, a Senator from Ohio, 3 December 1929, to amend sections 3 and 4 of the act entitled "An act to authorize and direct the survey, construction, and maintenance of a *memorial highway to connect Mount Vernon,* in the State of Virginia, *with the Arlington Memorial Bridge* across the Potomac River at Washington".—*Approved,* 23 January 1930.

> *Journal of the Senate,* pp. 14, 30, 92, 95, 97, 99.
> *Journal of the House of Representatives,* pp. 58, 72, 105, 169, 174, 180, 192.
> [*Congressional Record,* V. 72: Part 1, pp. 31, 305, 541, 1086; Part 2, pp. 1999, 2020, 2138, 2167, 2177; Part 3, p. 2266.]

Report—submitted to the House of Representatives by the HON. GEORGE S. GRAHAM, a Representative from Pennsylvania, 21 December 1929, from the Committee on the Judiciary, to whom was referred the FESS joint resolution (S. J. Res. No. 91) to amend sections 3 and 4 of the act entitled "An act to authorize and direct the survey, construction, and maintenance of a *memorial highway to connect Mount Vernon,* in the State of Virginia, *with the Arlington Memorial Bridge* across the Potomac River at Washington."

> *Journal of the House of Representatives,* p. 105.
> [*Congressional Record,* V. 72: Part 1, p. 1086.]
> [*H. Rept. No. 96 . . . . Serial 9190.*]

Senate bill (S. No. 2708)—submitted in the Senate by the HON. ARTHUR CAPPER, a Senator from Kansas, 17 December 1929, for the acquisition, establishment, and development of the *George Washington Memorial Parkway* along the Potomac River *from Mount Vernon and Fort Washington to the Great Falls,* and to provide for the acquisition of lands in the District of Columbia and the States of Maryland and Virginia requisite to the comprehensive park, parkway and playgrounds system of the National Capital.—[1]

Senate bill (S. No. 3063)—submitted in the Senate by the HON. GUY D. GOFF, a Senator from West Virginia, 9 January 1930, making an appropriation to aid in the construction of the *George Washington Memorial Building* in the city of Washington.—

> *Journal of the Senate,* pp. 69, 75.
> [*Congressional Record,* V. 72: Part 2, pp. 1287-1288, 1488.]

Letter from the *George Washington Birthday Association of Alexandria, Virginia,* inviting the United States Congress to be present in Alexandria on the 22nd day of February, 1930, and take part in the plans to honor the *first President on the*

---

[3] The bill (H.R. 15524) was not enacted. See H.R. 26, introduced by MR. CRAMTON, of Michigan, 71st Congress, 1st Session.

[1] See *H.R. No. 26.*

anniversary of his birth—presented in the Senate, 8 February 1930, by the HON. CLAUDE A. SWANSON, a Senator from Virginia; presented in the House of Representatives, 8 February 1930, by the HON. R. WALTON MOORE, a Representative from Virginia.

> *Congressional Record*, V. 72: Part 3, pp. 3280, 3302.

Senate bill (S. No. 3398)—submitted in the Senate by the HON. SIMEON D. FESS, a Senator from Ohio, 1 February 1930, to enable the *George Washington Bicentennial Commission* to carry out and give effect to certain approved plans.— *Approved*, 21 February 1930.

> *Journal of the Senate*, pp. 115, 132, 151, 154, 160.
>
> *Journal of the House of Representatives*, pp. 248, 281, 288, 298.
>
> [*Congressional Record*, V. 72: Part 3, pp. 2812, 2813, 3278; Part 4, pp. 3897-3899, 3905, 3965, 3966, 4031, 4135.]

Communication from HERBERT HOOVER, *President of the United States*, with accompanying letter from the Director of the Bureau of the Budget, 4 March 1930, (Legislative day, 6 January 1930), transmitting a supplemental estimate of appropriation for the *George Washington Bicentennial Commission* for the fiscal year 1930.—

> *Journal of the Senate*, p. 176.
>
> [*Congressional Record*, V. 72: Part 5, p. 4663.]
>
> [S. Doc. No. 97 . . . . Serial 9219.]

Communication from HERBERT HOOVER, *President of the United States*, with accompanying letter from the Director of the Bureau of the Budget, 10 April 1930, transmitting a supplemental estimate of appropriation for the *George Washington Bicentennial Commission* for the fiscal year 1931.—

> *Journal of the House of Representatives*, p. 442.
>
> [*Congressional Record*, V. 72: Part 7, p. 6995.]
>
> [H. Doc. No. 345 . . . . Serial 9252.]

Communication from HERBERT HOOVER, *President of the United States*, with accompanying letter from the Director of the Bureau of the Budget, 19 May 1930, transmitting a supplemental estimate of appropriation for the *George Washington Bicentennial Commission* for the fiscal year 1931 . . . in lieu of the estimate made on 30 April 1930.

> *Journal of the House of Representatives*, p. 575-576.
>
> [*Congressional Record*, V. 72: Part 9, p. 9255.]
>
> [H. Doc. No. 409 . . . . Serial 9252.]

Report—submitted to the Senate by the HON. ARTHUR CAPPER, a Senator from Kansas, 17 April 1930, from the Committee on the District of Columbia, to whom was referred the CRAMTON bill (H. R. No. 26) for the acquisition, establishment, and development of the *George Washington Memorial Parkway*

. . . .

and to provide for the acquisition of lands . . . .

requisite to the comprehensive park, parkway and playground system of the National Capital.

> *Journal of the Senate*, p. 285.
>
> [*Congressional Record*, V. 72: Part 7, p. 7190; Part 9, p. 9368.]
>
> [S. Rept. No. 458 . . . . Serial 9185.]

Report—submitted to the House of Representatives by the HON. RICHARD N. ELLIOTT, a Representative from Indiana, 18 December 1929, from the Committee on Public Buildings and Grounds, to whom was referred the CRAMTON bill (H. R. No. 26) for the acquisition, establishment and development of the *George Washington Memorial Parkway* . . . . and to provide for the acquisition of lands . . . . requisite to the comprehensive park, parkway, and playground system of the National Capital.

> *Journal of the House of Representatives*, p. 95.
>
> [*Congressional Record*, V. 72: Part 1, p. 926.]
>
> [H. Rept. No. 55 . . . . Serial 9190.]

House bill (H. R. No. 26)—submitted in the House of Representatives (during the preceding session) by the HON. LOUIS C. CRAMTON, a Representative from Michigan, 15 April 1929, for the acquisition, establishment, and development of the *George Washington Memorial Parkway* along the Potomac *from Mount Vernon and Fort Washington to the Great Falls*, and to provide for the acquisition of lands in the District of Columbia and the States of Maryland and Virginia requisite to the comprehensive park, parkway, and playground system of the National Capital.—*Approved*, 29 May 1930.

> *Journal of the House of Representatives*, pp. 95, 212, 556, 586, 592, 595, 655.
>
> *Journal of the Senate*, pp. 113, 114, 285, 349, 372, 373, 431.
>
> [*Congressional Record*, V. 72: Part 1, pp. 926, 1084-1086; Part 2, pp. 1986, 2253; Part 3, pp. 2449-2466, 2708-2724, 2726, 2893; Part 7, p. 7190; Part 8, p. 8848; Part 9, pp. 9368, 9405, 9485.]

Report—submitted to the House of Representatives by the HON. BERTRAND H. SNELL, a Representative from New York, 23 January 1930, from the Committee on Rules, recommending that the resolution (H. Res. No. 132), providing for the consideration of the House bill (H. R. No. 26), be adopted.

> *Journal of the House of Representatives*, pp. 186, 211-212.
>
> [*Congressional Record*, V. 72: Part 2, p. 2253; Part 3, 2705-2708.]
>
> [H. Rept. No. 475 . . . . Serial 9194.]

House Bill (H. R. No. 7393)—submitted in the House of Representatives by the HON. FRED A. BRITTEN, a Representative from Illinois, 12 December 1929, to authorize the preservation, as a national monument, in the District of Columbia, of the *engineering headquarters of* GENERAL GEORGE

WASHINGTON in connection with the execution of the original survey of Washington City.[1]

> *Journal of the House of Representatives*, p. 73.
> [*Congressional Record*, V. 72: Part 1, p. 574.]

House bill (H. R. No. 8358)—submitted in the House of Representatives by the HON. JAMES M. BECK, a Representative from Pennsylvania, 9 January 1930, making an appropriation to aid in the construction of the *George Washington Memorial building in the city of Washington.*[2]

> *Journal of the House of Representatives*, p. 131.
> [*Congressional Record*, V. 72: Part 2, p. 1342.]

House bill (H. R. No. 9153)—submitted in the House of Representatives by the HON. CHARLES A. EATON, a Representative from New Jersey, 25 January 1930, to provide for the commemoration of the military encampment at Middlebrook Heights, near Bound Brook, New Jersey, where GEORGE WASHINGTON *was in camp at the time the United States flag was adopted by Congress, 14 June 1777.*—

> *Journal of the House of Representatives*, p. 197.
> [*Congressional Record*, V. 72: Part 3, p. 2412.]

House bill (H. R. 11489)—reported to the House of Representatives by the HON. LISTER HILL, a Representative from Alabama, 19 May 1930, from the Committee on Military Affairs, to provide for the commemoration of certain military historic events.—[3]

> *Journal of the House of Representatives*, p. 573.
> [*Congressional Record*, V. 72: Part 9, p. 9187.]
> [*H. Rept. No.* 1525 . . . . *Serial* 9192.]

Concurrent resolution adopted by the House of Representatives of the State of South Carolina, 14 January 1930, (the Senate concurring)—authorizing the governor to appoint a Committee to represent South Carolina at the *two-hundredth anniversary of the birth of* GEORGE WASHINGTON—presented in the House of Representatives, 31 March 1930, by the HON. JOHN J. MCSWAIN, a Representative from South Carolina.

> *Congressional Record*, V. 72: Part 6, p. 6197.

House bill (H. R. No. 10177)—submitted in the House of Representatives by the HON. ALLEN T. TREADWAY, a Representative from Massachusetts, 21 February 1930, to provide for the *acquisition by the United States of Mount Vernon, the home of* GEORGE WASHINGTON.—

> *Journal of the House of Representatives*, p. 292.
> [*Congressional Record*, V. 72: Part 4, pp. 4073-4074, 4095.]

Resolution (H. Res. 146)—submitted in the House of Representatives by the HON. JOHN Q. TILSON, a Representative from Connecticut, 7 February 1930, proposing that the session of the House on Saturday, 22 February 1930, the *one hundred and ninety-eighth anniversary of the birth of* GEORGE WASHINGTON, be devoted to a suitable commemoration of that event; and that the House members of the *George Washington Bicentennial Commission* prepare a program and make all necessary arrangements for the proceedings on that day.—

> *Journal of the House of Representatives*, p. 242.
> [*Congressional Record*, V. 72: Part 3, p. 3263.]

Resolution (H. Res. 161)—submitted in the House of Representatives by the HON. JOHN Q. TILSON, a Representative from Connecticut, 21 February 1930, proposing that on Saturday, 22 February 1930, the House meet at 11 o'clock a.m.; that, upon the completion of the reading of the Journal the program for the *celebration of* WASHINGTON's *Birthday* be carried out; and that those who speak have leave to extend their remarks in the *Record.*

> *Journal of the House of Representatives*, p. 291.
> [*Congressional Record*, V. 72: Part 4, p. 4087.]

House bill (H. R. No. 10203)—submitted in the House of Representatives by the HON. JOHN L. CABLE, a Representative from Ohio, 22 February 1930, to authorize the coinage of $3 gold pieces in commemoration of the *two-hundredth anniversary of the birth of* WASHINGTON.

> *Journal of the House of Representatives*, p. 294.
> [*Congressional Record*, V. 72: Part 4, p. 4123.]

Concurrent Resolution (H. Con. Res. No. 23)—submitted in the House of Representatives by the HON. EDWARD M. BEERS, a Representative, from Pennsylvania, 10 March 1930, providing for printing as House document the Proceedings *held in the United States Congress on February* 22, 1930, *in commemoration of the one hundred and ninety-eighth anniversary of the birth of* GEORGE WASHINGTON...

> *Journal of the House of Representatives*, p. 339.
> [*Congressional Record*, V. 72: Part 5, p. 5024.]

Joint Resolution (H. J. Res. No. 368)—submitted in the House of Representatives by the HON. CHARLES A. EATON, a Representative from New Jersey, 14 June 1930, to create a commission to co-operate with the States of Pennsylvania and New Jersey in preparing plans for the construction of the *Washington Crossing Memorial Bridge* across the Delaware *River.*—[1]

> *Journal of the House of Representatives*, p. 700.
> [*Congressional Record*, V. 72: Part 10, p. 10847.]

THIRD SESSION OF THE SEVENTY-FIRST CONGRESS: 1930-1931

Senate bill (S. No. 5644)—reported to the Senate by the HON. SIMEON D. FESS, a Senator from Ohio, 23 January 1931, from the Committee on the Library, to amend the act entitled "An act to authorize and direct the survey, construction, and maintenance of a *memorial highway to connect*

---

[1] Re-introduced (H.R. 9898), 14 February 1930, *Congressional Record*, V. 72: Part 3, p. 3707.—

[2] MR. BECK, of Pennsylvania, introduced a similar bill (H.R. No. 8522). 13 January 1930, *Congressional Record*, V. 72: Part 2, p. 1557.—

[3] To commemorate GENERAL WASHINGTON's encampment at Middlebrook Heights, near Bound Brook, N. J., in 1779.

[1] See *H.J.Res.* 369, introduced on the same date by the HON. HENRY W. WATSON, a Representative from Pennsylvania.

Mount Vernon, in the State of Virginia, *with the Arlington Memorial Bridge* across the Potomac River at Washington," approved May 23, 1928, as amended.—

> *Journal of the Senate*, pp. 119, 268, 272.
> *Journal of the House of Representatives*, pp. 421, 488.
> [*Congressional Record*, V. 74: Part 2, p. 1901; Part 3, p. 2917, 3194; Part 4, p. 4468; Part 6, pp. 5729-5733, 5807, 5830-5834, 5835, 6306.]
> [*S. Rept. No. 1348 . . . . Serial 9323.*]

Senate bill (S. No. 5740)—submitted in the Senate by the HON. ARTHUR CAPPER, a Senator from Kansas, 15 January 1931, to amend subsection (a) of section 1 of the act relating to the *George Washington Memorial Parkway* approved May 29, 1930.—

> *Journal of the Senate*, pp. 96, 231, 323.
> [*Congressional Record*, V. 74: Part 2, 2198; Part 5, p. 5257; Part 7, p. 6951.]

Report—submitted to the Senate by the HON. ROBERT D. CAREY, a Senator from Wyoming, 18 February 1931, from the Committee on the District of Columbia, to whom was referred the CAPPER *bill* (S. No. 5740), to amend subsection (a) of section 1 of the act relating to the *George Washington Memorial Parkway* approved May 29, 1930.

> *Journal of the Senate*, pp. 96, 231, 323.
> [*Congressional Record*, V. 74: Part 5, p. 5257; Part 7, p. 6951.]
> [*S. Rept. No. 1658 . . . . Serial 9323.*]

Senate bill (S. No. 5724)—reported to the Senate by the HON. SIMEON D. FESS, a Senator from Ohio, 3 February 1931 (Legislative day, 26 January 1931) from the Committee on the Library, authorizing the *George Washington Bicentennial Commission to print and distribute additional sets of the writings of* GEORGE WASHINGTON.—

> *Journal of the Senate*, pp. 94, 157, 341.
> *Journal of the House of Representatives*, pp. 245, 255, 306, 488.
> [*Congressional Record*, V. 74: Part 2, p. 2124; Part 4, pp. 3875-3876.]
> [*S. Rept. No. 1450 . . . . Serial 9323.*]

Report—submitted to the House of Representatives by the HON. ROBERT LUCE, a Representative from Massachusetts, 12 February 1931, from the Committee on the Library, to whom was referred the FESS *bill* (S. No. 5724), *authorizing the George Washington Bicentennial Commission to print and distribute additional sets of the writings of* GEORGE WASHINGTON.

> *Journal of the House of Representatives*, pp. 245, 255, 306, 488.
> [*Congressional Record*, V. 74: Part 5, p. 4768; Part 7, pp. 7227-7228.]
> [*H.Rept. No. 2636 . . . . Serial 9327.*]

Senate bill (S. No. 6041)—reported to the Senate by the HON. ARTHUR CAPPER, a Senator from Kansas, 9 February 1931, from the Committee on the District of Columbia, to author-ize an appropriation of funds in the Treasury to the credit of the District of Columbia for the use of the *District of Columbia Commission for the George Washington Bicentennial Commission.—Approved*, 24 February 1931.

> *Journal of the Senate*, pp. 162, 178, 187, 261, 272, 273, 276.
> *Journal of the House of Representatives*, pp. 284, 308, 317, 393, 411, 421.
> [*Congressional Record*, V. 74: Part 4, pp. 3916, 4283, 4510; Part 5, pp. 4763, 4873; Part 6, 5650-5651, 5779, 5816, 5921.]
> [*S. Rept. No. 1550 . . . . Serial 9323.*]

Report—submitted to the House of Representatives by the HON. FREDERICK N. ZIHLMAN, a Representative from Maryland, 13 February 1931, from the Committee on the District of Columbia, to whom was referred the CAPPER *bill* (S. No. 6041), to authorize an appropriation of funds in the Treasury to the credit of the District of Columbia for the use of the *District of Columbia Commission* for the *George Washington Bicentennial Commission.*

> *Journal of the House of Representatives*, pp. 284, 302, 317, 393, 411, 421.
> [*Congressional Record*, V. 74: Part 5, 4873; Part 6, pp. 5650-5651, 5779, 5816, 5921.]
> [*H. Rept. No. 2659 . . . . Serial 9327.*]

Senate bill (S. No. 6103)—submitted in the Senate by the HON. SIMEON D. FESS, a Senator from Ohio, 9 February 1931, to authorize a change in the *design of the quarter dollar to commemorate the two hundredth anniversary of the birth of* GEORGE WASHINGTON.—*Approved*, 4 March 1931.

> *Journal of the Senate*, pp. 179, 182, 338, 344, 345, 347.
> *Journal of the House of Representatives*, pp. 284, 302, 484, 498, 503.
> [*Congressional Record*, V. 74: Part 4, pp. 4284, 4454; Part 5, p. 4764; Part 7, pp. 7210-7211, 7269, 7286, 7394.]

Senate bill (S. No. 6271)—submitted in the Senate by the HON. SIMEON D. FESS, a Senator from Ohio, 17 February 1931, relating to the tenure of Congressional members of the *George Washington Bicentennial Commission.—Approved*, 4 March 1931.

> *Journal of the Senate*, p. 322, 338, 339, 342, 346.
> *Journal of the House of Representatives*, pp. 476, 485, 492, 502.
> [*Congressional Record*, V. 74: Part 7, pp. 6905, 7103, 7212-7213, 7250, 7286.]

Communication from HERBERT HOOVER, *President of the United States*, 25 February 1931 (Legislative day, 17 February 1931) — transmitting, pursuant to law, a supplement estimate of appropriation for the expenses of the *District of Columbia Commission for the George Washington Bicentennial Commission*, fiscal year 1931, to remain available until June 30, 1932.

> *Journal of the Senate*, p. 274.
> [*Congressional Record*, V. 74: Part 6, p. 5917.]
> [*S. Doc. No. 302 . . . . Serial 9347.*]

Senate bill (S. No. 5665)—submitted in the Senate by the HON.
GUY D. GOFF, a Senator from West Virginia, 12 January
1931, to designate the United States Highway No. 50 as
the *George Washington Highway*.—

> *Journal of the Senate*, p. 89.
> [*Congressional Record*, V. 74: Part 2, p. 1974.]

House bill (H. R. No. 15497)—submitted in the House of Representatives by the HON. THOMAS A. JENKINS, a Representative from Ohio, 19 December 1930, proposing to designate the United States Highway No. 50 as the *George
Washington Highway*.—

> *Journal of the House of Representatives*, p. 109.
> [*Congressional Record*, V. 74: Part 2, p. 1169.]

House bill (H. R. No. 16218)—submitted in the House of Representatives by the HON. LOUIS CRAMTON, a Representative from Michigan, 15 January 1931, to amend subsection
(a) of section 1 of an act entitled "An act for the acquisition, establishment, and development of the George Wash-
ington Memorial Parkway along the Potomac *from Mount
Vernon and Fort Washington to the Great Falls*, and to provide for the acquisition of lands in the District of Columbia
and the States of Maryland and Virginia requisite to the
comprehensive park, parkway, and playground system of
the National Capital" approved May 29, 1930.—

> *Journal of the House of Representatives*, pp. 161, 306.
> [*Congressional Record*, V. 74: Part 2, p. 2298; Part 5,
> p. 4768; Part 7, p. 7236.]

Report—submitted to the House of Representatives by the HON.
RICHARD N. ELLIOTT, a Representative from Indiana, 12
February 1931, from the Committee on Public Buildings
and Grounds, to whom was referred the CRAMTON bill
(H. R. No. 16218) to amend subsection (a) of section 1
of the act relating to the *George Washington Memorial
Parkway approved May 29, 1930*.—

> *Journal of the House of Representatives*, pp. 161, 306.
> [*Congressional Record*, V. 74: Part 5, p. 4768; Part 7,
> p. 7236.]
> [*H. Rept. No. 2628 . . . . Serial 9327.*]

House bill (H. R. No. 16299)—submitted in the House of Representatives by the HON. EMANUEL CELLER, a Representa-
tivet from New York, 17 January 1931, for the acquisition
of land in the township of New Windsor, Orange County,
New York, which was occupied as a camp-ground by the
American army during 1782 and 1783, and the creation
there of a national park, in which shall be erected a *perpetual memorial to* GEORGE WASHINGTON on the site of
original camp building.—

> *Journal of the House of Representatives*, p. 166.
> [*Congressional Record*, V. 74: Part 3, p. 2527.]

House bill (H. R. No. 16382)—submitted in the House of Representatives by the HON. GUY E. CAMPBELL, a Representative from Pennsylvania, 20 January 1931, to provide for the

issuing of *postage stamps in commemoration of the two hundredth anniversary of the birth of* GEORGE WASHINGTON.—

> *Journal of the House of Representatives*, p. 176.
> [*Congressional Record*, V. 74: Part 3, p. 2710.]

House bill (H. R. No. 16973)—reported to the House of Representatives by the HON. RANDOLPH PERKINS, a Representative from New Jersey, 14 February 1931, from the Committee on Coinage, Weights, and Measures, to authorize
a change in the *design of the quarter dollar to commemorate the two hundredth anniversary of the birth of* GEORGE
WASHINGTON.—[1]

> *Journal of the House of Representatives*, pp. 278, 326,
> 484.
> [*Congressional Record*, V. 74: Part 4, p. 4424; Part 5,
> p. 4991; Part 7, pp. 7210-7211.]
> [*H. Rept. No. 2668 . . . . Serial 9327.*]

Ordered by the House of Representatives, 18 February 1931—
on motion by MR. TILSON, a Representative from Connecticut, and by unanimous consent:
That on Monday next the House shall meet at 11 o'clock
a.m., and that MR. BECK, a Representative from Pennsylvania, be permitted to address the House for one hour on
the *life of* GEORGE WASHINGTON.

> *Journal of the House of Representatives*, p. 362.
> [*Congressional Record*, V. 74: Part 5, p. 5340.]

Ordered by the House of Representatives, 24 February 1931—
on motion by MR. TILSON, a Representative from Connecticut, and by unanimous consent:
That the address delivered before the House, 23 February
1931, by the HON. JAMES M. BECK, a Representative from
Pennsylvania, in commemoration of GEORGE WASHING-
TON's *birthday*, be printed as a House document.

> *Journal of the House of Representatives*, p. 414.
> [*Congressional Record*, V. 74: Part 6, p. 5864.]
> [*H. Doc. No. 792 . . . . Serial 9367.*]

FIRST SESSION OF THE SEVENTY-SECOND CONGRESS:
1931-1932

Senate bill (S. No. 1306)—reported to the Senate by the HON.
ARTHUR CAPPER, a Senator from Kansas, 19 December
1931, from the Committee on the District of Columbia, to
provide for the incorporation of the District of Columbia,
Commission, *George Washington Bicentennial*.—*Approved*,
18 February 1932.

> *Congressional Record*, V. 75: Part 1, p. 912; 21 De-
> cember 1931, Part 1, pp. 994-995, 4 January 1932,
> Part 2, p. 1274; 8 January 1932, Part 2, p. 1553;
> 1 February 1932, Part 3, p. 3041; 8 February 1932,
> Part 4, pp. 3548-3553; 11 February 1932, Part 4, p.
> 3735; 12 February 1932, Part 4, pp. 3815, 3844; 15
> February 1932, Part 4, p. 3895; 16 February 1932,
> Part 4, p. 4013; 18 February 1932, Part 4, pp. 4209-
> 4210.
> [S. *Rept. No. 10 . . . . Serial 9487.*]

---

[1] The bill H.R. 16973 was laid on the table. See S. 6103.

Report—submitted to the House of Representatives by the Hon. MARY T. NORTON, a Representative from New Jersey, 8 January 1932, from the Committee on the District of Columbia, to whom was referred the CAPPER *bill* (S. No. 1306) for incorporating the District of Columbia Commission, *George Washington Bicentennial.*

> *Congressional Record,* V. 75: Part 2, p. 1553.
> [*H. Rept. No. 32* . . . . *Serial 9491.*]

Senate bill (S. No. 1861)—reported to the Senate by the Hon. SIMEON D. FESS, a Senator from Ohio, 7 January 1932, from the Committee on the Library, authorizing the *George Washington Bicentennial Commission* to print and distribute additional sets of the *Writings of* GEORGE WASHINGTON.—*Approved,* 10 March 1932.

> *Congressional Record,* V. 75; Part 2, p. 1409; 13 January 1932, Part 2, p. 1891; 26 January 1932, Part 3, p. 2715; 28 January 1932, Part 3, p. 2928; 20 February 1932, Part 4, p. 4444; 7 March 1932, Part 5, p. 5415; 8 March 1932, Part 5, p. 5517; 9 March 1932, Part 5, p. 5523; 10 March 1932, Part 5, pp. 5628, 5629.

Report—submitted in the House of Representatives by the Hon. RALPH GILBERT, a Representative from Kentucky, 20 February 1932, from the Committee on the Library, to whom was referred the FESS *bill* (S. No. 1861) authorizing the *George Washington Bicentennial Commission* to print and distribute additional sets of the *Writings of* GEORGE WASHINGTON.

> *Congressional Record,* V. 75: Part 4, p. 4444.
> [*H. Rept. No. 588* . . . . *Serial 9491.*]

Resolution (S. Res. 145)—submitted in the Senate by the Hon. SIMEON D. FESS, a Senator from Ohio, 21 January, 1932: *Resolved,* That *Washington's Farewell Address* be read to the Senate on the 23rd day of February 1932 instead of the 22nd day of such month as provided in the standing order of the Senate relating to the reading of such address.[1]

> *Congressional Record,* V. 75: Part 3, p. 2401; 22 January, 1932, Part 3, p. 2479; 23 February 1932, Part 4, pp. 4475-4479.

Communication from the *George Washington Birthday Association of Alexandria, Virginia,* inviting the United States Congress to attend the celebration in Alexandria, 22 February 1932, in honor of the *two-hundredth anniversary of the birth of* GEORGE WASHINGTON—presented in the Senate, 21 January 1932, by the Hon. CARTER GLASS, a Senator from Virginia; presented in the House of Representatives, 10 February 1932, by the Hon. CLIFTON A. WOODRUM, a Representative from Virginia.

> *Congressional Record,* V. 75: Part 3, p. 2383; Part 4, p. 3680.

Resolution adopted by the *Indiana George Washington Bi-centenary Commission* relative to the distribution of literature by the *United States Bicentennial Commission*—read into the *Record,* 26 January 1932, by request of the Hon. SIMEON D. FESS, a Senator from Ohio.

> *Congressional Record,* V. 75: Part 3, pp. 2701-2702.

Concurrent resolution (S. Con. Res. No. 14)—submitted in the Senate by the Hon. SIMEON D. FESS, a Senator from Ohio, 3 February 1932, granting the consent of Congress for the temporary removal to the Corcoran Art Gallery of certain portraits in the Capitol Building.

> *Congressional Record,* V. 75: Part 3, p. 3328; 5 February 1932, Part 3, pp. 3401-3402; 8 February 1932, Part 4, p. 3531; 18 February 1932, Part 4, pp. 4202, 4245.

Reports—submitted to the House of Representatives by the Hon. RALPH GILBERT, a Representative from Kentucky, 12 February 1932, from the Committee on the Library, to whom was referred the Senate concurrent resolution (S. J. Res. No. 14) granting the consent of Congress for the temporary removal to the Corcoran Art Gallery of certain portraits in the Capitol Building.

> *Congressional Record,* V. 75: Part 4, p. 3845.
> [*H. Rept. No. 429* . . . *Serial 9495.*]

Memorial of the Cambridge Historical Society of Massachusetts held at Craigie House, GENERAL WASHINGTON's *headquarters in Cambridge, Massachusetts,* 22 February 1932, relative to the proposal to erect a *statue to* WASHINGTON *commemorating his taking command of the Continental Army at Cambridge,* 2 July 1775—printed in the *Record,* 5 April 1932, by request of the Hon. DAVID I. WALSH, a Senator from Massachusetts.

> *Congressional Record,* V. 75: Part 7, p. 7462.

Ordered by the Senate, 23 February 1932—on motion by MR. FESS, a Senator from Ohio:
That the address delivered by PRESIDENT HOOVER at the joint session of the Senate and House of Representatives in the House Chamber, 22 February 1932, as well as the address by MR. BECK, a Representative from Pennsylvania, at ceremonies held at the east front of the Capitol, be printed as a public document.[2]

> *Congressional Record,* V. 75: Part 4, 4482; 24 February 1932, Part 4, p. 4591.

Ordered by the Senate, 24 February 1932—
That a cablegram from the BARON WLASSICS, president of the Hungarian Upper House at Budapest, Hungary, to the Hon. CHARLES CURTIS, president of the United States Senate, 21 February 1932, in honor of the bicentennial of our first *President,* be printed in the *Record.*

> *Congressional Record,* V. 75: Part 4, p. 4584.

---

[1] Under authority of Senate Resolution 145, the Chair designated MR. WALSH, a Senator from the State of Montana, to read WASHINGTON's *Farewell Address* on the 23rd of February, 1932.

[2] The order made by the Senate was rescinded 24 February, 1932, by request of SENATOR FESS, of Ohio, in consideration of the House Concurrent Resolution No. 25, which provides for the printing of the Proceedings, 22 February, 1932, in commemoration of the two-hundredth anniversary of the birth of GEORGE WASHINGTON.

Ordered by the Senate, 3 March 1932—

That a cablegram from the presidents of the Senate and Chamber of Deputies of the Dominican Republic to the President of the United States Senate, 22 February 1932, expressing felicitation on the occasion of the bicentennial of the birth of GEORGE WASHINGTON, be printed in the *Record*.

Congressional Record, V. 75: Part 5, p. 5148.

Paragraph from letter revealing how the name of GEORGE WASHINGTON is honored in Uruguay and Venezuela—read into the *Record*, 4 March 1932, by the HON. SIMEON D. FESS, a Senator from Ohio.

Congressional Record, V. 75; Part 5, p. 5238.

Concurrent resolution (S. Con. Res. No. 20)—submitted in the Senate by the HON. SIMEON D. FESS, a Senator from Ohio, 9 March 1932, authorizing the Joint Committee on the Library to accept, on behalf of the United States, the gift of a stone tablet, formerly in Duxbury Hall, Chorley, England, and dated 1622, bearing the conjoined escutcheons of the WASHINGTON and STANDISH families.

Congressional Record, V. 75: Part 5, p. 5527.

Senate bill (S. No. 4204)—submitted in the Senate by the HON. CHARLES W. WATERMAN, a Senator from Colorado, 24 March 1932, to designate a memorial highway to be known as the *George Washington Bicentennial Highway*.

Congressional Record, V. 75: Part 6, p. 6783.

Statement in the Senate by the HON. SIMEON D. FESS, a Senator from Ohio, 24 March 1932, relative to the publication by the *George Washington Bicentennial Commission of the Atlas of George Washington's Travels*.

Congressional Record, V. 75: Part 6, p. 6787.

Letter from FRANKLIN L. BURDETTE, secretary of the West Virginia Society of the Sons of the American Revolution indorsing the proposed plan for a *George Washington Memorial Highway*—printed in the *Record*, 1 April 1932, by request of the HON. MATTHEW M. NEELY, a Senator from West Virginia.

Congressional Record, V. 75: Part 7, p. 7250.

Letter from the HON. SOL BLOOM, *Associate Director of the George Washington Bicentennial Commission* with reference to requests for publications on the *George Washington Bicentennial*—printed in the *Record*, 4 April 1932, by request of the HON. SIMEON D. FESS, a Senator from Ohio.

Congressional Record, V. 75: Part 7, p. 7349.

Letter from EDWIN S. BETTELHEIM, JR., Adjutant General of the Military Order of the World War, inviting the United States Congress to review the parade on the 6th of April, 1932 in honor of those who exposed their lives to the dangers of the battlefield in defense of our national ideals, and honoring the memory of GEORGE WASHINGTON, *first Commander-in-Chief*—presented in the Senate, 6 April 1932, by the HON. DAVID A. REED, a Senator from Pennsylvania.

Congressional Record, V. 75: Part 7, pp. 75-7-7528, 7564.

Letter written by MAJOR O. R. McGUIRE, Finance Reserve, United States Army, 7 June 1932, to the *George Washington Chapter of the Reserve Officers' Association*, in which he pays tribute to GEORGE WASHINGTON as "one of the really great men in the tides of time"—printed in the *Record*, 8 June 1932, by request of the HON. M. M. LOGAN, a Senator from Kentucky.

Congressional Record, V. 75: Part 11, pp. 12284-12285.

Resolution adopted by the *Fort Necessity Chapter*, No. 12, Pennsylvania Society Sons of the American Revolution, Uniontown, Pennsylvania, extending an invitation to the Members of the Senate to be present on the 3rd and the 4th of July, 1932, at the *dedication of the replica of Fort Necessity, the unveiling of tablets, and other memorials of various patriotic organizations*—presented in the Senate, 10 June 1932, by the Vice President.

Congressional Record, V. 75: Part 11, p. 12549.

Concurrent resolution (H. Con. Res. No. 4)—submitted in the House of Representatives by the HON. CLIFTON A. WOODRUM, a Representative from Virginia, 18 December 1931, to provide for the appointment of a joint committee to *make suitable arrangements for the celebration of the two-hundredth anniversary of the birth of* GEORGE WASHINGTON.

Congressional Record, V. 75: Part 1, pp. 792-793; 19 December 1931, Part 1, pp. 922-923, 924, 967; 21 December 1931, Part 1, p. 977; 22 December 1932, Part 1, p. 1136.

House bill (H. R. No. 6741)—submitted in the House of Representatives by the HON. SAMUEL S. ARENTZ, a Representative from Nevada, 4 January 1932, to authorize the coinage of silver 50-cent, 25-cent, and 10-cent pieces in commemoration of the *two-hundredth anniversary of the birth of* GEORGE WASHINGTON.

Congressional Record, V. 75: Part 2, p. 1278.

Concurrent resolution (H. Con. Res. No. 12)—submitted in the House of Representatives, 20 January 1932, by the HON. CLIFTON A. WOODRUM, a Representative from Virginia:

That in commemoration of the two-hundredth anniversary of the birth of GEORGE WASHINGTON *the two Houses of Congress shall assemble in the Hall of the House of Representatives at 11:30 o'clock a. m. on Monday, 22 February 1932;*

That the President of the United States . . . is hereby invited to address the American people in the presence of the Congress . . . ;

That invitations to attend the ceremony be extended to the Members of the Cabinet, the Chief-Justice and associate justices of the Supreme Court of the United States, the Diplomatic Corps, the Chief-of-Staff, the Chief of Naval Operations, the Major-General Commandant of the Marine Corps, the Commandant of the Coast Guard, and such other persons as the joint committee on arrangements shall deem proper.

Congressional Record, V. 75: Part 3, pp. 2342-2343; 21 January 1932, Part 3, pp. 2418-2419, 2468; 22 January 1932, Part 3, p. 2524.

Proclamation by HERBERT HOOVER, *President of the United States,* 1 February 1932, inviting all our people to organize themselves through every community and every association to do honor to the memory of GEORGE WASHINGTON during the period from the 22nd of February 1932 to Thanksgiving Day—printed in the *Record,* 18 February 1932, by request of the HON. JOHN Q. TILSON, a Representative from Connecticut.

> *Congressional Record,* V. 75: Part 4, p. 4245.

Concurrent resolution (H. Con. Res. No. 18)—submitted in the House of Representatives by the HON. SOL BLOOM, a Representative from New York, 8 February 1932, granting the consent of Congress for the temporary removal to the Corcoran Art Gallery of certain portraits in the Capitol Building.[1]

> *Congressional Record,* V. 75: Part 4, p. 3563; 17 February 1932, Part 4, p. 4181; 18 February 1932, Part 4, p. 4245.

Concurrent resolution (H. Con. Res. No. 19)—submitted in the House of Representatives by the HON. SCHUYLER O. BLAND, a Representative from Virginia, 9 February 1932, providing for a wreath to be placed on the grave of the mother of WASHINGTON on the 22nd of February 1932.[2]

> *Congressional Record,* V. 75: Part 4, p. 3630; 15 February 1932, Part 4, p. 3962; 16 February 1932, Part 4, pp. 4014-4015; 18 February 1932, Part 4, p. 4299; 19 February 1932, Part 4, p. 4304.

Report—submitted in the House of Representatives by the HON. LINDSAY WARREN, a Representative from North Carolina, 10 February 1932, from the Committee on Accounts, to whom was referred the concurrent resolution (H. Con. Res. No. 19) providing for a wreath to be placed on the grave of the mother of WASHINGTON on the 22nd of February 1932.

> *Congressional Record,* V. 75: Part 4, p. 3722.
> [*H. Rept. No.* 416 . . . *Serial* 9495.]

House bill (H. R. No. 9596)—submitted in the House of Representatives by the HON. WILLIAM R. EATON, a Representative from Colorado, 20 February 1932, to designate a memorial highway to be known as the *George Washington Bicentennial Highway.*—

> *Congressional Record,* V. 75: Part 4, p. 4444.

Resolution (H. Res. 156)—submitted in the House of Representatives by the HON. ALLEN T. TREADWAY, a Representative from Massachusetts, 20 February 1932, for the purpose of the United States acquiring the property of Mount Vernon.

> *Congressional Record,* V. 75: Part 4, p. 4444.

Concurrent Resolution (H. Con. Res. No. 24)—submitted in the

House of Representatives by the HON. CLIFTON A. WOODRUM, a Representative from Virginia, 22 February 1932, thanking the Governor of the State of Virginia for the statues of GEORGE WASHINGTON and ROBERT E. LEE.

> *Congressional Record,* V. 75: Part 4, p. 4473.

Report—submitted to the House of Representatives by the HON. RALPH GILBERT, a Representative from Kentucky, 1 March 1932, from the Committee on the Library, to whom was referred the concurrent resolution (H. Con. Res. No. 24) thanking the Governor of the State of Virginia for the statues of GEORGE WASHINGTON and ROBERT E. LEE.

> *Congressional Record,* V. 75: Part 5, p. 5059.
> [*H. Rept. No.* 640 . . . *Serial* 9496.]

House bill (H. R. No. 9641)—submitted in the House of Representatives by the HON. DAVID J. LEWIS, a Representative from Maryland, 23 February 1932, to provide for the restoration of the first monument erected in memory of GEORGE WASHINGTON.

> *Congressional Record,* V. 75: Part 4, p. 4580.

Order of Proceedings on the part of the United States Congress at the joint session of the Senate and House, in the House Chamber, 22 February 1932, *in commemoration of the two-hundredth anniversary of the birth of* GEORGE WASHINGTON—printed in the *Record* by request of the HON. HENRY T. RAINEY, a Representative from Illinois.

> *Congressional Record,* V. 75: Part 4, pp. 4449-4451.

Order of Proceedings at the east front of the Capitol, 22 February 1932, *in commemoration of the two-hundredth anniversary of the birth of* GEORGE WASHINGTON—printed in the *Record* by request of the HON. HENRY T. RAINEY, a Representative from Illinois.

> *Congressional Record,* V. 75: Part 4, pp. 4451-4453.

Concurrent resolution (H. Con. Res. No. 25)—submitted in the House of Representatives by the HON. CLIFTON A. WOODRUM, a Representative from Virginia, 24 February 1932, to compile and print, with illustrations, the proceedings at the joint session of Congress in the Hall of the House of Representatives, together with the proceedings at the east front of the Capitol, 22 February 1932, *in commemoration of the two-hundredth anniversary of the birth of* GEORGE WASHINGTON.

> *Congressional Record,* V. 75: Part 4, p. 4665.

Communication from LADISLAS ALMASY, president of the Hungarian House of Representatives at Budapest, Hungary, to the HON. JOHN GARNER, *Speaker of the House of Representatives,* 21 February 1932, in honor of the bicentennial of the birth of GEORGE WASHINGTON—presented in the House of Representatives, 22 February 1932, by the *Speaker.*

> *Congressional Record,* V. 75: Part 4, p. 4453.

Communication, by radio, from the president and secretaries of the Congress of Nicaragua, congratulating the Congress of the United States of North America and the American people on the occasion of the bicentennial of the birth of GEORGE WASHINGTON—presented in the House of Representatives, 29 February 1932, by the *Speaker.*

> *Congressional Record,* V. 75: Part 5, p. 4976.

---

[1] The Senate Concurrent Resolution (S. Con. Res. No. 14) was concurred in by the House, 18 February, 1932, for the loan of portraits of GEORGE WASHINGTON, whereupon the resolution (H. Res. 148) calling for consideration of the House Concurrent Resolution (H. Con. Res. No. 18) was laid on the table.

[2] To carry out the purposes of the concurrent resolution, MR. BLAND, of Virginia, was appointed by the *Speaker,* on behalf of the House, and SENATOR GLASS, of Virginia, was appointed by the President *pro tempore* on behalf of the Senate.

Communication from the president of the Hellenic Chamber at Athens, Greece, expressing to the Congress and the people of the United States, on the occasion of the bicentennial of the birth of WASHINGTON, the admiration felt by the Hellenic Chamber for his noble memory—presented in the House of Representatives, 2 March 1932, by the *Speaker*.

Congressional Record, V. 75: Part 5, p. 5118.

Communication from the presidents of the Senate and Chamber of Deputies of the Dominican Republic to the *Speaker* of the United States House of Representatives, expressing felicitation on the occasion of the bicentennial of the birth of GEORGE WASHINGTON—presented in the House of Representatives, 2 March 1932, by the *Speaker*.

Congressional Record, V. 75: Part 5, p. 5118.

House bill (H. R. No. 11418)—submitted in the House of Representatives by the HON. FREDERICK W. DALLINGER, a Representative from Massachusetts, 18 April 1932, to erect a *statue of* GEORGE WASHINGTON *in Cambridge, Massachusetts.*

Congressional Record, V. 75: Part 8, p. 8449.

Statement, issued 9 May 1932, from the United States Department of State, affirming that GEORGE WASHINGTON was "not only actually and really but also in the most strict legal sense . . . the *first President of the United States*"—read into the *Record*, 11 May 1932, by the HON. SOL BLOOM, *Associate Director of the United States George Washington Bicentennial Commission.*

Congressional Record, V. 75: Part 9, pp. 10040-10041.

Resolution (H. Res. No. 275)—submitted in the House of Representatives by the HON. GRANT E. MOUSER, JR., a Representative from Ohio, 24 June 1932, authorizing the Postmaster-General to cause to be printed a series of memorial stamps in recogntion of the valiant service to this country and the martyrdom of COLONEL WILLIAM CRAWFORD, a native Virginian, and assistant surveyor to GEORGE WASHINGTON.

Congressional Record, V. 75: Part 13, p. 13935.

Concurrent resolution (H. Con. Res. No. 38)—submitted in the House of Representatives by the HON. SOL BLOOM, a Representative from New York, 15 July 1932, authorizing the acceptance of the gift of a stone tablet bearing the *conjoined escutcheons of the* WASHINGTON *and* STANDISH *families* to be placed in the Capitol.

Congressional Record, V. 75: Part 14, p. 15582.

PART THREE

Extracts from the Official Papers and Writings of George Washington
Read Into the Record During Debates in the United States Congress
1789-1932

SECOND SESSION OF THE TWENTY-THIRD CONGRESS: 1834-1835

Message to the Senate under date of 15 April 1794, upon submitting the nomination of JOHN JAY as envoy extraordinary to Great Britain—read into the *Record*, March 2, 1835, by the HON. JOHN QUINCY ADAMS, a Representative from Massachusetts, during debate in the House on the Report of the Committee on Foreign Affairs relative to our relation with France.

Debates in Congress, V. 11: Part 2, pp. 1629-1630.

FIRST SESSION OF THE TWENTY-FOURTH CONGRESS: 1835-1836

Extracts from Annual Messages, under date of the 8th of January, 1790, the 25th of October, 1791, and the 3rd of December, 1793, giving the recommendations of PRESIDENT WASHINGTON to Congress for the national defense, and an historical review showing the policy of the Federal Government, in this regard, under WASHINGTON's *Administration*—incorporated in the *Record*, February 23, 1836, by the HON. THOMAS H. BENTON, a Senator from Missouri, during debate in the Senate on the Fortification Bill.

Debates in Congress, V. 12: Part 1, pp. 595-600.

FIRST SESSION OF THE TWENTY-SIXTH CONGRESS: 1839-1840

Extract from *Letter to* TIMOTHY PICKERING, under date of 27 September 1795, relative to appointment to office—read into the *Record*, May 19, 1840, by the HON. AARON V. BROWN, a Representative from Tennessee, during a speech in the House on freedom of elections and faithful administration of executive patronage.

Congressional Globe, V. 8: Appendix, p. 511.

SECOND SESSION OF THE TWENTY-SEVENTH CONGRESS: 1841-1842

Veto Message, under date of 5 April 1792, upon returning to the Congress the Apportionment Bill according to the first enumeration—read into the *Record*, June 13, 1842, by the HON. JOHN CAMPBELL, a Representative from South Carolina, during debate on the Apportionment Bill under the Census of 1840.

Congressional Globe, V. 11: Appendix, p. 975.

FIRST SESSION OF THE TWENTY-EIGHTH CONGRESS: 1843-1844

Extract from Letter to ROBERT MORRIS, dated Mount Vernon, 12 April 1786, and from *Letter to* JOHN FRANCIS MERCER, 9 September 1796, relative to views on slavery—read into the *Record*, February 23, 1844, by the HON. CHARLES ROGERS, a Representative from New York, during a speech in the House on the right of petition.

Congressional Globe, V. 13: Appendix, p. 316.

Extracts from the *Farewell Address to the People of the United States*, 17 September 1796, relative to views on unity of

Government—read into the *Record*, February 7, 1844, by the HON. GEORGE EVANS, a Senator from Maine, during a speech in the Senate on the tariff.

Congressional Globe, V. 13: Appendix, p. 714.

FIRST SESSION OF THE TWENTY-NINTH CONGRESS:
1845-1846

Extracts from the *Official Papers of* GEORGE WASHINGTON—read into the *Record*, March 5, 1846, by the HON. WILLIAM H. HAYWOOD, a Senator from North Carolina, during debate in the Senate on the joint resolution for giving notice to terminate the convention between the United States and Great Britain relative to the Oregon territory.

Congressional Globe, V. 15: Appendix, pp. 374-375, 376.

Extract from *messages to Congress*, under date of 7 December 1796, relative to the encouragement of manufactures—read into the *Record*, June 18, 1846, by the HON. M. McLEAN, a Representative from Pennsylvania, during debate in the House on the bill proposing to reduce duties on imports.

Congressional Globe, V. 15: Appendix, p. 691.

Extracts from *Messages to Congress*, under date of 8 January 1790 and 7 December 1796, relative to the encouragement of manufactures—read into the *Record*, July 22, 1846, by the HON. SIMON CAMERON, a Senator from Pennsylvania, and July 27, 1846, by the HON. SPENCER JARNAGIN, a Senator from Tennessee, during debate in the Senate on the bill proposing to reduce duties on imports.

Congressional Globe, V. 15: Appendix, p. 1131 and p. 1153.

Extract from *Messages to Congress*—printed in the *Record*, August 10, 1846, in an Address to the People of North Carolina by the HON. WILLIAM H. HAYWOOD, a Senator from that State.

Congressional Globe, V. 15: Appendix, p. 1180, 1181.

FIRST SESSION OF THE THIRTIETH CONGRESS:
1847-1848

Veto Message under date of 28 February 1797, upon returning to the Congress, with his objections, the bill to alter and amend an act entitled "An act to ascertain and fix the military establishment of the United States"—read into the *Record*, June 16, 1848, by the HON. BEVERLY L. CLARKE, a Representative from Kentucky, during a speech in the House on the Veto Power.

Congressional Globe, V. 17: Appendix, p. 746.

SECOND SESSION OF THE THIRTIETH CONGRESS:
1848-1849

Extract from *Letter to* ROBERT MORRIS under date of 12 April 1786, relative to views on slavery—read into the *Record*, February 16, 1849, by the HON. GEORGE A. STARKWEATHER, of New York, during a speech in the House on the Treaty of Peace with Mexico; and by the HON. C. E. STUART, of Michigan, February 26, 1849, during debate in

the House on the bill to establish a territorial government in Upper California.

Congressional Globe, V. 18: Appendix, p. 93 and p. 180.

Extract from the *Farewell Address to the People of the United States*, 17 September 1796, relating to unity of government—read into the *Record*, January 25, 1849, by the HON. R. W. THOMPSON, a Representative from Indiana, during a speech in the House on the question of slavery.

Congressional Globe, V. 18: Appendix, p. 189.

FIRST SESSION OF THE THIRTY-FIRST CONGRESS:
1849-1850

Extract from the *Farewell Address to the People of the United States*, 17 September 1796, relating to the "fatal tendency" of "all obstructions to the execution of the laws"—read into the *Record*, February 8, 1850, by the HON. SAM HOUSTON, a Senator from Texas, the Senate having under consideration the Compromise Resolutions offered by MR. CLAY.

Congressional Globe, V. 19: Appendix, pp. 101-102.

Extract from the *Farewell Address to the People of the United States*, 17 September 1796, in connection with the territorial question—read into the *Record*, March 12, 1850, by the HON. HOPKINS L. TURNEY, a Senator from Tennessee, during debate in the Senate on the President's *Message* transmitting the constitution of California.

Congressional Globe, V. 19: Appendix, p. 296.

Extract from the *Farewell Address to the People of the United States*, 17 September 1796, relating to the "fatal tendency" of "all obstructions to the execution of the laws"—read into the *Record*, April 8, 1850, by the HON. THOMAS H. BENTON, a Senator from Missouri, in connection with his remarks during debate in the Senate on the admission of California.

Congressional Globe, V. 19: Appendix, p. 449.

Extracts from *Letter to* ROBERT MORRIS, under date of 12 April 1786, and from *Letter to* JOHN FRANCIS MERCER, 9 September 1796, relative to views on slavery—read into the *Record*, March 26, 1850, by the HON. SALMON P. CHASE, a Senator from Ohio, during debate in the Senate on the Compromise Resolutions introduced by MR. CLAY.

Congressional Globe, V. 19: Appendix, p. 471.

Extracts from *Letters* revealing views on slavery—read into the *Record*, May 21, 1850, by the HON. ELBRIDGE GERRY, of Maine, and on June 4, 1850, by the HON. K. S. BINGHAM, of Michigan, during debate in the House on the President's *Message* transmitting the Constitution of California.

Congressional Globe, V. 19: Appendix, pp. 608-729.

FIRST SESSION OF THE THIRTY-SECOND CONGRESS:
1851-1852

Proclamation of Neutrality issued under date of 22 April 1793—read into the *Record*, February 9, 1852, by the HON. J. H. CLARKE, a Senator from Rhode Island, during a speech in the Senate on Non-Intervention.

Congressional Globe, V. 21: Appendix, p. 137.

Extracts from the *Farewell Address to the People of the United States,* 17 September 1796—read into the *Record,* February 12, 1852, by the HON. JEREMIAH CLEMENS, a Senator from Alabama, during a speech in the Senate on Non-Intervention.

Congressional Globe, V. 21: Appendix, p. 181.

Letter to THOMAS JEFFERSON, Secretary of State, under date of 12 April 1793, with regard to maintaining a strict neutrality —read into the *Record,* February 26, 1852, by the HON. JACOB W. MILLER, a Senator from New Jersey, during a speech in the Senate on Non-Intervention.

Congressional Globe, V. 21: Appendix, p. 181.

Message to the Senate under date of 8 May 1792, relative to a convention with the government of Algiers for the ransom of American citizens in captivity there—read into the *Record,* March 9, 1852, by the HON. WILLIAM H. SEWARD, a Senator from New York, during debate in the Senate on Non-Intervention.

Congressional Globe, V. 21: Appendix, p. 245.

Message to EDMUND RANDOLPH, Secretary of State, under date of 10 June 1794, transmitting to MR. MONROE, minister to France, instructions relative to the policy adopted by the United States Government toward the French revolution— read into the *Record,* March 22, 1852, by the HON. PIERRE SOULE, a Senator from Louisiana, during debate in the Senate on Non-Intervention.

Congressional Record, V. 21: Appendix, p. 350.

Extracts from *Letters to* ALEXANDER HAMILTON under date of 6th May, 1794, and under date of 8th May, 1796, relative to French *emigres* in the United States during the revolutionary struggle in France—read into the *Record,* March 18, 1852, by the HON. JAMES C. JONES, a Senator from Tennessee, during debate in the Senate on Non-Intervention.

Congressional Globe, V. 21: Appendix, p. 305.

Extract from the *Farewell Address to the People of the United States,* 17 September 1796, relative to institutions for the general diffusion of knowledge—read into the *Record,* March 5, 1852, by the HON. L. D. CAMPBELL, a Representative from Ohio, during a speech in the House on internal improvements.

Congressional Globe, V. 21: Appendix, p. 262.

Extracts from *Writings of* GEORGE WASHINGTON, revealing his views concerning unity of Government—read into the *Record,* March 9, 1852, by the HON. JOHN A. WILCOX, a Representative from Mississippi, during a speech in the House on the Union and States' rights.

Congressional Globe, V. 21: Appendix, p. 284.

Extracts from *First Inaugural Address,* 30 April 1789, and from the *Farewell Address . . .* 17 September 1796, acknowledging the "Invisible Hand which conducts the affairs of men"— read into the *Record,* March 31, 1852, by the HON. ORIN FOWLER, a Representative from Massachusetts, during debate in the House on the Homestead Bill.

Congressional Globe, V. 21: Appendix, pp. 395, 397.

Extracts from *Letters* and from *Messages* to the Congress relative to agriculture and stock-raising, and their prime importance in the up-building of the Nation—read into the *Record,* April 20, 1852, by the HON. EBEN NEWTON, a Representative from Ohio, during debate in the House on the Homestead Bill.

Congressional Globe, V. 21: Appendix, pp. 492, 493.

Extracts from *Letters* relative to views on slavery—read into the *Record,* May 19, 1852, by the HON. JOHN G. FLOYD, a Representative from New York, during a speech in the House on the constitutional relations of the Northern and Southern portions of the Republic growing out of the institution of negro slavery.

Congressional Globe, V. 21: Appendix, p. 588.

Extract from *Messages to Congress* under date of 8 December 1790, relative to the subject of protecting our navigation— read into the *Record,* July 9, 1852, by the HON. GILBERT DEAN, a Representative from New York, during debate in the House on the deficiency appropriations bill.

Congressional Globe, V. 21: Appendix, p. 815.

SECOND SESSION OF THE THIRTY-THIRD CONGRESS: 1854-1855

Text of the *Announcement to the Army of the Alliance with France,* dated at Valley Forge, from the Orderly Book, 6 May 1778—read into the *Record,* February 27, 1855, by the HON. CHARLES W. UPHAM, a Representative from Massachusetts, during a speech in the House on the Joint Resolution requesting the President to tender the mediation of the United States to the Powers engaged in the Eastern War.

Congressional Globe, V. 24: Appendix, p. 253.

SECOND SESSION ON THE THIRTY-SEVENTH CONGRESS: 1861-1862

Extract from *Messages to Congress* relative to the ransom of American prisoners at Algiers—read into the *Record,* March 31, 1862, by the HON. CHARLES SUMNER, a Senator from Massachusetts, during a speech in the Senate on the bill for the release of certain persons held to service or labor in the District of Columbia.

Congressional Globe, V. 32: Part 2, pp. 1450-1451.

FIRST SESSION OF THE FIFTY-SIXTH CONGRESS: 1899-1900

Extracts from the Letters, Speeches, and Messages of GEORGE WASHINGTON, THOMAS JEFFERSON, and ABRAHAM LINCOLN, three statesmen whose guiding hands created and maintained the most beneficent free government known in the world's history—presented in the Senate, 4 June 1900, by the HON. R. F. PETTIGREW, a Senator from South Dakota, with the request that the paper be printed as a public document.

Congressional Record, V. 33: Part 7, p. 6523.
[*S. Doc. No.* 433 . . . *Serial* 3878.]

SECOND SESSION OF THE SIXTY-FIRST CONGRESS: 1909-1910

Paragraph from the *Farewell Address to the People of the United States,* September 17, 1796, relative to "the danger of parties in the state, with particular reference to the founding of them on geographical discriminations"—read into the *Record*, February 22, 1910, by the Hon. Frank Mellen Nye, a Representative from Minnesota, during a speech in the House of Representatives on *Principles of Government*.

Congressional Record, V. 45: Part 2, pp. 2228-2229.

SECOND SESSION OF THE SIXTY-SECOND CONGRESS: 1911-1912

Message to the House of Representatives, under date of 30 March 1796, declining to transmit to the House certain documents relating to the treaty with Great Britain—read into the *Record*, February 10, 1912, by the Hon. Martin Dies, a Representative from Texas, during debate in the House on the Cullop amendment to the bill (H. R. 17595) proposing that . . . before the *President* shall appoint any district, circuit, or supreme judge, he shall make public all endorsements made in behalf of any applicant.

Congressional Record, V. 48: Part 2, pp. 1913-1915.

FIRST SESSION OF THE SIXTY-THIRD CONGRESS: 1913

Extracts from Letters *and* Messages, *quoted by* Edwin D. Mead in his address on the *Principles of the Founders*—and printed in the *Record*, June 13, 1913, by request of the Hon. Richard Bartoldt.

Congressional Record, V. 50: Appendix, p. 202.

FIRST SESSION OF THE SIXTY-FOURTH CONGRESS: 1915-1916

Paragraphs from *Messages* and *Addresses* of President Washington, of John Adams, James Madison, and Andrew Jackson, relative to the Military Establishment—read into the *Record*, 22 May 1916, by the Hon. Charles Bennett Smith, a Representative from New York.

Congressional Record, V. 53, Appendix, p. 1011.

SECOND SESSION OF THE SIXTY-FOURTH CONGRESS: 1916-1917

Proclamation of Neutrality issued under date of 22 April 1793— read into the *Record*, March 1, 1917, by the Hon. Moses P. Kinkaid, a Representative from Nebraska, in connection with the war in Europe.

Congressional Record, V. 54: Part 5, p. 4683.

Extracts from the *Farewell Address to the People of the United States*, 17 September 1796, relative to the policy to be maintained as to the position this Nation should hold with regard to foreign wars—read into the *Record*, March 4, 1917, by the Hon. John D. Works, a Senator from California, during debate in the Senate on the bill (H. R. 21052) authorizing the President of the United States to supply merchantships, the property of citizens of the United States, and bearing American registry, with defensive arms.

Congressional Record, V. 54: Part 5, p. 4998.

FIRST SESSION OF THE SIXTY-FIFTH CONGRESS: 1917

Extract from *Letter to the President of the Congress*, dated at Orangetown, 20 August 1780, relative to conscription as a means to obtain enlistments in the Continental Army—read into the *Record*, April 27, 1917, by the Hon. W. Frank James, a Representative from Michigan, during a speech in the House on the selective draft.

Congressional Record, V. 55: Part 2, p. 1430.

SECOND SESSION OF THE SIXTY-FIFTH CONGRESS: 1917-1918

Proclamation of Neutrality, issued under date of 22 April 1793— read before the House, and printed in the *Record*, February 22, 1918, by request of the Hon. William E. Mason, a Representative from Illinois.

Congressional Record, V. 56: Part 3, p. 2527.

THIRD SESSION OF THE SIXTY-FIFTH CONGRESS: 1918-1919

Excerpts from *Letters* of General Washington and from his *Farewell Address to the People of the United States*—read into the *Record*, 21 February 1919, by the Hon. William E. Borah, a Senator from Idaho, during a speech in the Senate on the *League of Nations*.

Congressional Record, V. 57: Part 4, pp. 3911-3914.

Excerpt from the *Farewell Address to the People of the United States*, 17 September 1796—read into the *Record*, 22 February 1919, by the Hon. James A. Reed, a Senator from Missouri, during a speech in the Senate on the *League of Nations*.

Congressional Record, V. 57: Part 4, p. 4027.

Excerpt from the *Farewell Address to the People of the United States*, 17 September 1796, relative to the policy of the United States with regard to permanent alliances with foreign Nations—read into the *Record*, 9 December 1918, by the Hon. Richard W. Parker, a Representative from New Jersey, during a speech in the House of Representatives on the *League of Nations*.

Congressional Record, V. 57: Part 1, p. 213.

FIRST SESSION OF THE SIXTY-SIXTH CONGRESS: 1919

Extracts from the *Farewell Address to the People of the United States*, 17 September 1796—read into the *Record* by the Hon. John K. Shields, a Senator from Tennessee, during a speech in the Senate, November 17, 1919, on the foreign policy of the United States, and, again, during a speech in the Senate, November 19, 1919, on the treaty of peace with Germany.

Congressional Record, V. 58: Part 9, p. 8628; V. 58; Appendix, pp. 9224, 9226, 9227.

SECOND SESSION OF THE SIXTY-SIXTH CONGRESS: 1919-1920

Extracts from the *Farewell Address to the People of the United States*, 17 September 1796, relative to entanglements with foreign nations—read into the *Record*, April 9, 1920, by the HON. ANDREW J. HICKEY, a Representative from Indiana, in support of his argument against a League of Nations.

Congressional Record, V. 59: Appendix, p. 8972.

Message to the House of Representatives, under date of 30 March, 1796, relative to the treaty-making power of the Government—read into the *Record*, April 9, 1920, by the HON. WILLIAM W. HASTINGS, a Representative from Oklahoma, during debate in the House on the treaty of peace with Germany.

Congressional Record, V. 59: Appendix, p. 8985.

Extracts from *Letters and Opinions of* GEORGE WASHINGTON advocating the draft as the best method to obtain enlistments for war—read into the *Record*, April 9, 1920, by the HON. GEORGE E. CHAMBERLAIN, a Senator from Oregon, during debate in the Senate on the bill (S. No. 3792) to reorganize and increase the efficiency of the United States Army.

Congressional Record, V. 59: Part 6, pp. 5390-5391.

SECOND SESSION OF THE SIXTY-SEVENTH CONGRESS: 1921-1922

Extract from *Letter to the President of the Congress*, dated *Camp Above Trenton Falls*, 20 December 1776,[1] in which GENERAL WASHINGTON states the plight of his Army and appeals to the Congress that "this is not a time to stand upon expenses"—read into the *Record*, 22 February 1922, by the HON. HENRY W. WATSON, a Representative from Pennsylvania, during an address in the House of Representatives on the *Battle of Trenton* and GENERAL WASHINGTON's *conduct of the campaign leading to that engagement*.

Congressional Record, V. 62: Part 3, p. 2901.

Extracts from the *Letter of Congratulation and Advice to the Governors of the Thirteen States*, Headquarters, Newburgh, under date of 8 June 1783—read into the *Record*, February 22, 1922, by the HON. HAMILTON FISH, JR., a Representative from New York, relative to the pending adjusted compensation bill.

Congressional Record, V. 62: Part 3, p. 2908.

Extracts from JARED SPARK's *Life of* WASHINGTON, and from JOHN MARSHALL's *Life of* WASHINGTON—read into the *Record*, June 23, 1922, by the HON. WILLIAM E. BORAH, a Senator from Idaho, in refutation of statements by the HON. THOMAS E. WATSON, a Senator from Georgia, during a speech in the Senate, February 14, 1922, with regard to the attitude of GENERAL WASHINGTON toward a bonus for soldiers.

Congressional Record, V. 62: Part 9, pp. 9243-9244.

Extracts from the *Writings of* GENERAL WASHINGTON, from MARSHALL's *Life of* WASHINGTON, *and from* LODGE's *Life of* WASHINGTON—read into the *Record* on the 23rd of June, 1922, on the 24th of June, 1922, and on the 28th of June, 1922, by the HON. THOMAS E. WATSON, a Sen-

ator from Georgia, during an argument in the Senate to sustain his previous statement, questioned by SENATOR BORAH, of Idaho, that GENERAL WASHINGTON *approved a bonus for soldiers of the Revolutionary Army*.

Congressional Record, V. 62: Part 9, pp. 9244-9245, 9297-9298, 9545-9548.

FIRST SESSION OF THE SIXTY-EIGHTH CONGRESS: 1923-1924

Extract from GENERAL WASHINGTON's *Answer to the Congress on his appointment as Commander-in-Chief*, 16 June 1775—read into the *Record*, March 27, 1924, by the HON. THOMAS L. BLANTON, a Representative from Texas, during debate in the House on the War Department Appropriations bill.

Congressional Record, V. 65: Part 5, p. 5088.

FIRST SESSION OF THE SIXTY-NINTH CONGRESS: 1925-1926

Extract from the *Farewell Address to the People of the United States*, 17 September 1796, relative to the policy to be adopted toward alliances with foreign nations—read into the *Record*, January 15, 1926, by the HON. BERT M. FERNALD, a Senator from Maine, during debate in the Senate on the resolution (S. Res. No. 5) granting favorable advice and consent of the Senate to the adhesion on the part of the United States to the protocol of December 16, 1920, with reservations.

Congressional Record, V. 67: Part 2, p. 2100.

Farewell Address to the People of the United States, 17 September 1796—read before the Senate, January 15, 1926, by the HON. COLE L. BLEASE, a Senator from South Carolina, during debate on the *World Court resolution* (S. Res. No. 5).

Congressional Record, V. 67: Part 2, pp. 2106, 2107, 2108, 2109, 2110, 2111, 2112, 2113, 2114, 2115.

FIRST SESSION OF THE SEVENTY-SECOND CONGRESS: 1931-1932

Recipe for making beer, alleged to have been used by GENERAL WASHINGTON, quoted in a letter from SENATOR HAWES, of Missouri, to SENATOR BINGHAM, of Connecticut—read into the *Record*, 16 January 1932, by request of the HON. MILLARD E. TYDINGS, a Senator from Maryland, during a speech in the Senate on the twelfth anniversary of the Eighteenth Amendment.

Congressional Record, V. 75: Part 2, p. 2113.

Excerpts from letter written by BENJAMIN FRANKLIN, 16 September 1789, to GEORGE WASHINGTON, and from WASHINGTON's reply, dated New York, 23 September 1789—read into the *Record*, 18 January 1932, by the HON. JAMES M. BECK, a Representative from Pennsylvania, in an address before the House of Representatives on BENJAMIN FRANKLIN, *greatest contemporary of* GEORGE WASHINGTON, *and his contribution to the foundation of the American Commonwealth*.

Congressional Record, V. 75: Part 2, p. 2169.

---

[1] Ford: *Writings of Washington*, V. 5: 113, 115-116.

Excerpt from the *Writings of* George Washington together with a tribute to Washington by Abraham Lincoln quoted in an address by the Hon. Charles Curtis, *Vice-President of the United States*, 26 January, 1932, at a meeting of the Chamber of Commerce of Washington, D. C.—printed in the *Record* by request of the Hon. Simeon D. Fess, a Senator from Ohio.

Congressional Record, V. 75: Part 3, p. 2770.

Letters of George Washington and excerpts from his *Messages* to the United States Congress with regard to means of transportation and communication—read into the *Record*, 21 May 1932, by the Hon. Clyde Kelly, a Representative from Pennsylvania, during a speech in the House on the Washington *Bicentennial and Post Office Day, 26 July 1932.*

Congressional Record, V. 75: Part 10, pp. 10859, 10860, 10861.

Excerpts from the *Writings of* George Washington revealing his thought with regard to the *builders of the Republic, the reputation of public men, the triumph of principle, moral virtue in public life, and the duty of those in office at times of crisis*—read into the *Record*, 25 May 1932, by the Hon. Scott Leavitt, a Representative from Montana, during an address at Memorial Services in honor of deceased Members of the House of Representatives.

Congressional Record, V. 75: Part 10, p. 11156.

Excerpts from the famous letter written by General Washington from his headquarters at Newburgh, 22 May 1782, to Colonel Nicola, from his speech to the officers of the Army at Temple Hill, 15 March 1783, and from his letter of congratulation and advice to the Governors of the thirteen States, written from his headquarters at Newburgh, 8 June 1783—printed in the *Record*, 3 June 1932, in an address by the Hon. Hamilton Fish, Jr., a Representative from New York, upon the occasion of the George Washington *Bicentennial Celebration* held at Temple Hill in the State of New York.

Congressional Record, V. 75: Part 11, p. 11906.

Excerpt from letter written by General Washington to the President of the Congress, 28 August 1777, recommending the Count Casimir de Pulaski for the commission of Brigadier-General in the Continental Army—read into the *Record*, 1 July 1932, by the Hon. Samuel B. Pettengill, a Representative from Indiana, during an address before the House of Representatives on Pulaski *and* Washington.

Congressional Record, V. 75: Part 13, p. 14512.

Excerpts from the *Writings of* Geocge Washington relative to the national defense—printed in the *Record*, 9 July 1932, in an address by Commander William Seaman Bainbridge upon the dedication of the Revolutionary Cemetery at *Morristown, New Jersey, headquarters of* General Washington's *Army.*

Congressional Record, V. 75: Part 14, p. 14944.

BROTHERS, HALF BROTHERS, AND SISTER OF GEORGE WASHINGTON

LAWRENCE WASHINGTON

Half brother of George, born at Bridges Creek, Va., 1718, died at Mount Vernon, July 26, 1752.

GEORGE WASHINGTON

1732-1799

ELIZABETH WASHINGTON

Sister of George, born at Bridges Creek, Va., June 20, 1733; married Fielding Lewis, May 7, 1750, died in Culpeper Co., Va., Mar. 31, 1797.

AUGUSTINE WASHINGTON

Half brother of George, born at Bridges Creek, Va., probably in 1720; died there, May 1762. (No portrait of him is known.)

JOHN AUGUSTINE WASHINGTON

Brother of George, born at Mount Vernon Jan. 13, 1735/36 (o.s.), died at Nomini, Westmoreland Co., Va., Feb. 1787.

SAMUEL WASHINGTON

Brother of George, born probably at Bridges Creek, Va., Nov. 16, 1734, died near Charles Town, W. Va., Dec. 1781.

CHARLES WASHINGTON

Brother of George, born at Mount Vernon May 2, 1738, died at Charles Town, W. Va., Sept. 16, 1799.

Selected
George Washington Bicentennial
Addresses

Delivered by

Honorable Sol Bloom

Representative from New York

and

Director
United States George Washington Bicentennial Commission

INTRODUCTION

This compilation of selected addresses made in connection with the nation-wide George Washington Bicentennial Celebration, was prepared to meet the increasing number of requests that followed their delivery. The majority of the addresses were broadcast to nation-wide audiences through the courtesy of the great broadcasting systems.

This section contains a selected number from more than one hundred addresses delivered by Congressman Bloom during the period of the Celebration.

Radio programs have played an important part in the Celebration. In this way every section of the United States has been reached and residents of the remotest districts enjoyed the same programs available to the people in the larger communities. Some of the programs have been delivered for the first time from historic shrines, made sacred by their immortal associations with George Washington.

Addresses were made from Independence Hall in Philadelphia; from Fort Necessity, Pennsylvania; from the home of Mary Ball Washington in Fredericksburg, Virginia; from the old Pohick Church and from Arlington National Cemetery, Virginia; from the home of Francis Scott Key in the District of Columbia; and before the tomb of George Washington at Mount Vernon.

These addresses have been instrumental in helping to make the true character of the Father of Our Country better known throughout the nation. They were designed to inspire patriotism and veneration for that great American whom the nation has honored in this Bicentennial year of his birth.

This Commission desires to acknowledge publicly its appreciation of the cooperation of the National Broadcasting Company and the Columbia Broadcasting Company, and of the many persons and musical organizations that helped make these programs effective.

George Washington Bicentennial Celebration in 1932

An Address on the Preliminary Plans of the Celebration,
Broadcast from Washington, D. C., by the
National Broadcasting Company,
June 15, 1930

To understand George Washington and what he means to America of today, we must think of him as a man and not as an ideal.

As a man we can more nearly take his measure and estimate his greatness. The glamor that has surrounded his name has tended to obscure his human qualities.

It is not my purpose to dwell upon the heroic side of our greatest American. I want to impress upon the people of this country that George Washington was a normal man, subject to normal temptations, normal perplexities, and normal sorrows.

The greatness of George Washington lies in the fact that he surmounted tremendous obstacles and accomplished his purposes through sheer force of character and perseverance.

Let us consider George Washington's career in the order of his outstanding accomplishments.

First, there is the boy, the son of a Virginia farmer, living in the country and having limited educational advantages.

This boy, destined by Providence for such historic achievements, was a normal boy. He was in every sense a good boy, obedient and ambitious. Although he had scant opportunities for schooling, he made the most of what he had.

At an age when other boys are mostly concerned in sports and play, George Washington was seriously devoted to the study of a profession. When barely 16 years old he was commissioned to perform a responsible piece of surveying work which sent him into the wilderness. There he encountered dangers and privations that would have daunted a less sturdy soul. That he performed this work of surveying well, has been shown by repeated re-surveys along the lines he laid down.

We find him again when scarcely of age, commissioned to perform important military and diplomatic exploits into the frontier country.

Inheriting the great estate of Mt. Vernon, while still a young man, George Washington showed unusual interest in the subject of farming. He was among the first scientific farmers in this country. He was the first student of methods of improving live stock, of rotating crops and of diversified agriculture. Had George Washington done nothing more than devote himself to the study of agriculture, he would have been America's pioneer authority on that subject.

Not only was George Washington a farmer, but he was one of the foremost business men of his time. He knew how to make his farms profitable. He had a commercial vision far beyond his contemporaries. He or-

ganized corporations, drained swamps, developed lands, and did a considerable shipping business.

George Washington was the first inland waterways advocate. He actually surveyed and planned waterway connections between the Ohio Valley and the Atlantic seaboard, which he was unable to complete because of the stress of the times.

George Washington looked beyond the boundaries of the original thirteen colonies and his eyes rested upon the Far West as the limits of the future republic. To him, more than to any other man, is due that impetus to foreign trade which has ever been one of America's outstanding business policies.

But George Washington was too great a man to live in the peaceful security of his plantation home. The state of the colonies demanded the resourcefulness, the courage, the calm judgment and the character of its greatest men. George Washington had all of these qualities to a greater extent than any other man upon American soil. He was a natural leader, and instilled into his countrymen that spirit of confidence and devotion, which made the winning of the war of the Revolution a possibility.

It was George Washington who realized more than any man of his time what the freedom of the colonies meant to the men and women who were to come after him. It was his counsel, his judgment and his sure knowledge of men, that guided the infant republic in the formation of our present system of federal government.

In advocating American independence, George Washington staked his life, his property and the interests of his family. He realized, perhaps more than any other man, the hazards and uncertainties of a war for independence.

Great as were George Washington's achievements as a soldier, far greater were his achievements as a statesman and a citizen.

As the first President, he faced problems never faced by any other man. By his wisdom, by his patience, by his persistence, he molded the destinies of the young republic and placed it upon a sure foundation for future growth. As we study the life of this great man there develop new and interesting phases of his character.

Has America sufficiently honored the memory of George Washington? I unhesitatingly say it has not. It is gratifying to every American citizen to realize that the United States is preparing now to express in the most appropriate way possible the honor which is his due.

The Congress of the United States, in recognition of

the Two Hundredth Anniversary of the Birth of George Washington which will be observed in 1932, has created a Commission to formulate plans fittingly to honor his memory.

Congress has asked the Governors of the various states to appoint State Commissions to cooperate with the National Commission. It is the purpose of the Associate Director to make this Celebration nation-wide and all-American.

We have no exposition in mind. There will be no World's Fair, no concentration of material evidences of the nation's growth.

The Celebration will be in the hearts of the people themselves. It will be in the nature of a revival of knowledge of and appreciation for our greatest American, and one of the greatest human beings in all history.

The Federal government has authorized the publication of all of the writings of George Washington, which will be published as a memorial edition in approximately 25 volumes. The great Memorial Boulevard between Washington and Mt. Vernon is under construction and will be one of the most beautiful highways in all the world. A regional park system for the National Capital, unsurpassed in America, is now authorized by Congress as a George Washington Memorial Parkway. This great parkway will include some of the beautiful and historic places with which George Washington has been identified.

Congress has also established Wakefield, Washington's birthplace in Virginia, as a National Monument and will erect upon the site a replica of the house in which George Washington was born.

These are federal projects contributed, or to be contributed, by the Government itself. It is the purpose of the Associate Director to bring the message of George Washington to every church, every home, every school, and every group of citizens in the United States. We want to offer an opportunity to each man, woman and child in America to participate in this national celebration.

In our plans it is proposed to foster and encourage in all parts of the country, local, regional and state celebrations. The people themselves will organize and take part in these celebrations. It is hoped that in 1932, there will not be a school room or school building in the United States without its picture of George Washington. It is hoped that there will not be a school or a church or a home that will not display the American Flag with appropriate reminders of what it means in our national life. It is proposed to hold essay contests, pageants, plays and exercises of similar kinds in public schools. In like manner we want to enlist the cooperation of all the clubs, associations, fraternal organizations and miscellaneous groups of people.

Not only do we want to impress upon the nation its debt to George Washington, but also our debt to other heroes associated with him. We want to remember those splendid men and women, many of them of foreign birth, who offered their lives upon the altar of American independence. We want to remember Von Steuben, De Kalb and the Muhlenbergs. We want to remember Carroll, Barry, Knox and the host of other Irish patriots. We want to remember with gratitude Kosciuszko, Pulaski and other Polish heroes. We want to remember Benjamin Nones, who has been called the "Jewish Lafayette," the Pintos and others of the Jewish race, who offered themselves and their fortunes to the cause of freedom. We want to remember Lafayette, Rochambeau and all that other host of equally heroic men and women of the French, Swedish, Dutch and other European races, who performed their parts so valiantly. Many of them came from across the seas to help the cause of the colonies.

George Washington was the magnet who drew all those brave men to him. George Washington was the man above all others who inspired confidence and devotion among those ragged, hungry and suffering troops who struggled bravely and triumphantly forward under his leadership.

We Americans today still have our differences in origin and in character. We still have our different viewpoints and our different opinions. We still struggle for various ideals and principles, but we can all rally today under the leadership of George Washington, as did those splendid Americans of two hundred years ago.

In honoring the memory of George Washington, there can be no division and no dispute. He is so transcendently great as to continue his influence down through the years. In all the records of his life, in every letter, speech and act, which can be traced to him, there is not one weakness, and but few mistakes. Wherever the flag flies today, those under its protecting folds, should remember that it was George Washington who established that flag and what it stands for. In a world of bitterness, hostility and oppression, George Washington brought freedom and human liberty. Wherever people are free, they should remember those men who gave the world freedom. Wherever there is protection, peace and security, a prayer of thanksgiving should be offered that George Washington lived and wrought.

We of the George Washington Bicentennial Commission have a tremendous responsibility. It is our duty to arouse throughout the nation a proper sense of gratitude to the Founder of the Republic. In this task we cannot act alone. It is for all Americans of all nationalities and creeds, of all conditions and circumstances, to make the year 1932 a year of thought and reverence for the memory of George Washington. He was so intimately associated with all affairs of life, with the church, with statesmanship, with agriculture, with business, with education, with commerce and, in fact every phase of healthful citizenship, that no class of our people can disregard their debt to him.

So let us now dedicate in our hearts the memory of this man. Let us resolve that we shall do him honor and reverence for what he was and what he has given to us. I leave with you this appeal tonight as Americans all, in the freedom and enlightenment which George Washington brought into the world.

George Washington, the Mason

Address Before the Twenty-first Annual Convention of the George Washington Masonic National Memorial Association, Alexandria, Virginia, February 23, 1931

Lives of illustrious men so often concentrate the rays of public attention upon their great deeds that their normal human qualities are obscured.

This is more true of the men of George Washington's time than of our own, for George Washington was not followed by a retinue of news photographers and newspaper correspondents to detail his ordinary acts and, in the modern sense, "humanize" him. Nor did George Washington pose in an absurd and assumed character to popularize himself among the plain people. His every act and deed was a natural one, fitting into the occasion and comporting with the dignity and habits of the man himself.

Also we must remember that more of George Washington's life was devoted to public service than that of any other great man of his time or ours. This meant that not only were his public acts subjects of universal comment, but that he was restricted to a great extent from the exercise of those homely, domestic occupations which as we say, make men human.

From the time he was of age until the day of his death, he was a public character, not from his own inclination, but by the force of those circumstances which called him to a conspicuous place in the nation.

But in all the vast material that has been written concerning George Washington we find a great many references to George Washington the man, the citizen, the neighbor and the farmer of Mt. Vernon. And in all these personal side-lights upon his character nothing shines forth with such distinctness as his love of his fellow men. Nothing seemed to give him greater pleasure than to mingle upon grounds of democratic equality with other men of good minds and good characters. He enjoyed the association of people of intelligence and learning, but he also enjoyed contact with all manner of people from whom he learned much.

The many-sidedness of George Washington may be attributed largely to the fact that he learned the viewpoints of people in all walks of life—the great and the humble, the rich and the poor. From this vast store of information he drew constantly in his administration of the nation's affairs.

If we can disregard for the moment the overshadowing achievements of George Washington and think of him in the simple terms of the man, we will gain an appreciation of his character that can be mentioned in terms of men of our own time.

I have spoken of George Washington's friendliness, of his pleasure in mingling with other men, and this leads me to the consideration of his life as a Mason. Here I must stress the point that so much is said of George Washington the Mason because it interprets the man's moral character. It must be remembered that George Washington was also a member of various other societies of more or less local or specialized interests, and Masonry, if not the only fraternal organization of his time, was at least, the outstanding one.

All of us should bear in mind that this instinct of George Washington for the fellowship of his kind would have led him, in our day, to belong to many other fraternal and civic groups of citizens. And I am sure that most of our prominent clubs and associations would have been proud to number him in their membership were they existing in his day, or he living in their. So that, as a Mason, George Washington assumes a distinct relationship to men of all times and to men's organizations of all kinds.

One of the outstanding phases of George Washington's character was his sincerity. Slow to make any promise or assume any obligation, yet, having made up his mind, he did not deviate from his course.

It is natural, therefore, that upon becoming a Mason, George Washington should have devoted himself wholeheartedly to its sublime standards of moral and spiritual life which so strongly appealed to him.

It is noteworthy that this ancient Craft should have drawn to itself many of the outstanding men of our Colonial and Revolutionary periods. They, too, found in the tenets of Freemasonry, not only an exalted companionship of the mind and spirit, but also a yardstick for judgment of character and moral influence.

Masonry constituted a bond of understanding and confidence which exists today among many fraternal and civic groups, but which in George Washington's time existed only in Masonry itself. So in placing the influence of Masonry upon the life of George Washington we may assume that we are placing the same influence upon the lives and characters of many of those great men of his time who helped him in his tremendous labors in behalf of our country.

As in practically all of the phases of George Washington's life and achievements, there have come down to us Masonic traditions which probably have no truth in fact. Historians have gone astray in portraying the career of this man. One of the most valuable contributions that has been made to history by the United States George Washington Bicentennial Commission has been in correcting errors and portraying the true life of George Washington. Therefore, in his Masonic career, much has been said and much has been written that we know is unintentional error.

It is my purpose, therefore, in this address to touch upon some of the outstanding phases of George Washington's Masonic life in order that there may be perpetuated the truth, as we have found it.

Washington Relics of the Alexandria-Washington Lodge of Free
Masons at Alexandria, Va. The Chair Was Occupied by Washington
as Worshipful Master of the Lodge. The Clock Was in the Room
Where He Died and Was Stopped by an Attending Physician Just
After the Death. The Lights and Hour Glass Are Originals Used
by the Lodge in Washington's Time. The Knife Belonged to George
Washington and Is Traditionally Supposed to Have Been Given to
Him by His Mother When He Was a Boy. The Key of the Bastille
at Paris was Presented to the Lodge by Lafayette in 1825.

George Washington and Masonry began their existence in Virginia at nearly the same time.

True to his life-long habit of prompt arrival, Washington was a little ahead of Masonry in his native state. He was born in 1732 and Masonry was constituted in Virginia in 1733.

As early as 1730, New York, New Jersey and Pennsylvania had Grand Masters. Benjamin Franklin was Grand Master of Masonry in Philadelphia in 1734. Thomas Oxnard, Provincial Grand Master of Massachusetts, is believed to have issued the warrant constituting Fredericksburg Lodge in Virginia in which George Washington took his first step in Masonry, November 4, 1752. He passed to the degree of Fellowcraft on March 3, 1753, and was raised to the Sublime Degree of Master Mason on August 4, 1753.

So George Washington began his Masonic and his military careers at about the same time, for it was in 1753 that Governor Dinwiddie sent him on his first great errand to Fort Le Boeuf to warn the French out of the Ohio Valley.

George Washington spent eight years of his youth on a farm near Fredericksburg. He grew up in that vicinity and was well known to the people of the town. He matured early and had such a reputation for honesty, industry and reliability, it was natural he should have become well acquainted with the members of the Fredericksburg Lodge. It seems inevitable that he should have joined our great fraternity, for the ideals of Masonry, its conception of Divine order and guidance were, of course, a part of his own training and life.

From the time he was raised to the Sublime Degree of Master Mason until his death George Washington was the ideal of our Fraternity. During all the long and burdened years when this great man served humanity and served our great Republic, he never deviated from the lessons he learned within the halls of our fraternity.

When we consider George Washington's life in its fullness can we think of any weakness, any deficiency, anything lacking in his manhood?

Could anyone suggest a trait of character or circumstance of life which would have made him more perfect?

When we think of the young surveyor, treading the pathless wilderness, we know that his every thought and act was of noble purpose. When we think of him as a youthful soldier beyond the Alleghenies, we think of him as a man and a Mason.

When we think of him as a farmer, as a member of the Virginia Assembly, as a member of the Continental Congress, as Commander-in-Chief of the Revolutionary forces, as President of the Constitutional Convention, and finally as President of the United States, we think of him as a Mason, always bringing credit and honor upon our order.

Many noted Virginians of George Washington's time were Masons. Nearly all the great patriotic leaders throughout the colonies were zealous members of the Fraternity, including such names as Benjamin Franklin, Peyton Randolph, John Hancock, James Otis, Roger Sherman, John Jay, Robert Morris, Edmund Randolph, Thomas Jefferson, Robert R. Livingston and John Marshall.

It can be readily understood therefore that through this common tie of Masonry, many of the great men of all the Colonies were enabled to meet a situation which gave all concern.

I am not of the opinion which has been advanced by many other commentators, that Masonry itself exerted an especial influence in the stirring events of George Washington's time. But I am convinced that the fraternal bond which brought the great men of that time together created a confidence, a sense of reliable dependence, among the members of the Craft which enabled them to act with a unity of purpose.

It has been said that Masonry was the one common ground on which the leaders of the colonies could meet. There is perhaps much truth in this from the fact that until the political unity of the colonies was established there was a sharp conflict of opinion upon religion, social order and economic problems which tended to keep the colonies apart.

But when the great men of the time assembled in the atmosphere of brotherhood it was inevitable that there should be developed a better understanding among them of each other's problems and a stronger desire of one to help the other.

It was natural under such conditions that George Washington should have been active in his Masonic life, and through all the fleeting years we catch brief glimpses of him in his Masonic character.

At the outbreak of the Revolutionary War, Virginia had nine legally constituted Lodges. They lost no time in becoming strictly American. On May 7, 1777, five of the nine Virginia Lodges decided to elect a Grand Master for the State and on June 23 of the same year they adopted a resolution recommending that George Washington be named Grand Master of Virginia.

This honor George Washington felt moved to decline. True to his principles he would not undertake any responsibility to which he could not give adequate time and attention. At that period he had all he could attend to as Commander-in-Chief of the Revolutionary Army.

It was a time when the fortunes of the Revolution and the morale of the people were at their lowest ebb. The whole issue of the war hung on George Washington's courage and spirit. He had no time for anything else. So John Blair, afterwards one of the first Justices of the Supreme Court, was made Grand Master of Virginia.

After this period all the Grand Lodges and Grand Masters of the Colonies appointed by foreign jurisdiction, gradually disappeared and a strictly American Freemasonry arose.

When George Washington was inaugurated First President of the United States, Robert R. Livingston, Chancellor of the State of New York and Grand Master of the State, used the Bible owned by the St. John's Lodge of New York City to administer the oath to Washington.

Not much is known of George Washington's activities in Masonry from the time he received his Master Mason's degree in Fredericksburg Lodge in Virginia, in 1753, until the opening of the Revolution in 1775. The priceless records covering this period have been lost, but from 1753 until 1775 Washington probably had few opportunities to visit any organized Masonic body. His time and energy were spent upon the frontier, fighting the Indians and the French. When he settled down to a quiet life at Mount Vernon he was fifty miles from the nearest Masonic Lodge at Fredericksburg.

There can be little doubt, however, that when he went to visit his Mother and his Sister at Fredericksburg, he attended meetings in his home Lodge to greet his brethren. Some of his most intimate friends and associates were members of the Craft. Jacob Van Braam, his early fencing master was a Mason. So were the Weedons and the Mercers. Col. Fielding Lewis, his brother-in-law and John Dandridge, his father-in-law, were Masons.

Washington's deep interest in Masonry is proved in many ways. He could not have received so many honors and attentions from the Fraternity unless he paid attention and honor to Masonry.

The Masons of Virginia wanted him as their Grand Master because he was "Grand Master" at everything already.

In 1779, at a festival at Grand Union Lodge, Reading, Connecticut, the first toast was "George Washington." In the same year a military Massachusetts Lodge was named Washington Lodge and Washington himself was an occasional visitor at their meetings.

At several other meetings of Masonic Lodges during the war George Washington was present.

While the Revolutionary Army was encamped at Morristown, New Jersey, a movement was started to appoint George Washington Grand Master of an American Grand Lodge. The effort fell through only because of the unsettled condition of the times. Washington was nevertheless unanimously endorsed for the position, and it proves that he was foremost in the minds of all Masons.

Soon after the victory at Yorktown, Washington, Lafayette, Marshall and Governor Nelson met and renewed allegiance to the beautiful tenets of Masonry.

All through the later years of the Revolution, the Masons testified their love and respect for Washington. Lodges were named for him, literature was dedicated to him.

He was saluted everywhere not only in America, but abroad, as the most eminent Mason. An American-French mercantile firm, Watson and Cassoul, sent him a present of Masonic ornaments, among which was the famous "Watson and Cassoul" Masonic apron, still preserved by the Craft. One of the most prized relics of Masonry is the Masonic Apron embroidered for Washington by Madam Lafayette.

We may say that the soul of our government and heart of our nation rests on Masonic principles, for President Washington laid the very cornerstone of our National Capitol according to Masonic rites.

As President of the United States George Washington constantly received Masonic honors. On a presidential tour he was welcomed to Newport, Rhode Island, by King David's Lodge of that City. On his famous Southern Tour, Mordecai Gist, his intimate friend and fellow patriot, Grand Master of South Carolina, addressed to him a welcome on behalf of the Masons of

the State. Similar honors and courtesies continued throughout Washington's Presidency.

Washington lent his great influence to the growth and strength of Masonry, but at the same time Masonry influenced George Washington. He freely used Masonic language in his private and state papers. His frequent referencies to the Diety as the Great Architect of the Universe stamp him as a true Mason.

So also his reliance on Divine Support in the hours of stress and trial prove Washington a man whose love for Masonry never waned and whose faith in the Great Architect of the Universe never wavered.

Washington's whole life was an embodiment of the teachings of Masonry. It is seen in his tolerance and fairness and justice. He maintained perfect poise and balance under conditions of strife, rancor, discord and even treason.

He fought no battles of conquest or aggression. He did his best to promote peace and harmony. He seems ever to have had before him the admonition contained in the Apprentice Degree. It may be these teachings which magnified his natural virtues.

He held to an unshakeable belief in the Fatherhood of God and the Brotherhood of Man and these qualities make for international as well as national peace.

Alexandria, Virginia, is most closely associated with the mature career of George Washington. It was his "home town." There he had an office and a town house, although, of course, he spent as little time as possible away from his beloved Mount Vernon. His presence at a number of lodge meetings in Fredericksburg is recorded and he attended a number of public Masonic functions such as the Festival of St. John the Baptist, June 24, 1779, with American Union Lodge at the Robinson House on the Hudson, New York; the Festival of St. John the Evangelist, December 27, 1779, with American Union Lodge at Morris Hotel, Morristown, New Jersey; the Festival of St. John the Evangelist, December 27, 1782, with King Solomon's Lodge at Poughkeepsie, New York; the Festival of St. John the Baptist, June 24, 1784, with Lodge No. 39 at Alexandria, Virginia and the Masonic funeral of Brother William Ramsay, February 12, 1785, at Alexandria.

In 1766 Washington was elected one of the trustees of the City of Alexandria and was interested in the organization of Alexandria Lodge No. 39, becoming an honorary member of the Lodge.

In 1782 six brethren of Alexandria petitioned the Provincial Grand Lodge of Pennsylvania for a Charter; in spite of the fact that the Grand Lodge of Virginia was organized in 1777-8, the Provincial Grand Lodge of Pennsylvania, under the Grand Lodge of England, granted the charter.

The Lodge of Alexandria was chartered in 1783 and met for the first time on February 25, when four of the petitioners and two members of the Grand Lodge of Pennsylvania opened on the Entered Apprentice's Degree, read the charter giving them life and the number 39, and proceeded to exercise jurisdiction "in the borough of Alexandria or within four miles of the same."

Because of some difference in jurisdictional opinion, Alexandria Lodge decided to relinquish its charter under the Grand Lodge of Pennsylvania and to petition the Grand Lodge of Virginia for a charter under its own state authority.

With a desire to honor George Washington, the man and brother Mason, who had achieved so much and stood so high in public opinion, the brethren of Alexandria asked Washington's consent to name him as their first Worshipful Master under the new Charter. That new Charter was granted on April 28, 1788, by Edmund Randolph, Governor of the Commonwealth of Virginia and Grand Master, designating the Alexandria Lodge as No. 22 with George Washington named as Worshipful Master and he was unanimously elected Worshipful Master to succeed himself on December 28, 1788, serving in all about 20 months.

He was inaugurated as President, April 30, 1789, and thus became the first, and so far only brother to be President of the United States and Worshipful Master of his Lodge at the same time.

It was after George Washington's death that the Brethren desired to change the name to the Alexandria-Washington Lodge No. 22, the name which it bears to this day.

Perhaps the outstanding Masonic event in George Washington's life was the laying of the cornerstone of the Capitol of the United States on September 18, 1793. George Washington acted in the official Masonic ceremony as Grand Master pro tem.

And finally, when at the end of his long and most useful life, George Washington closed his eyes to the affairs of this world, December 14, 1799, he was tenderly carried to his last resting place by his brethren of the ancient and noble craft. Thus his career was rounded in perfect Masonic order and Masonry today and forever can rightfully glory in that life which so beautifully exemplified the tenets of our Masonic faith.

And now, to honor the sacred memory of this man, to do all humanly possible to acknowledge his Masonic virtues, we, the living members of the Order, are erecting in this historic City of Alexandria a great temple.

It is a monument built by the Members of the Masonic Fraternity. It is their tribute to George Washington the Man and the Mason.

It is of such sound construction that it should outlast the centuries. It stands on a hill from which can be seen many square miles of land with which George Washington was so closely identified.

Yet, solid as are these granite blocks and marble pillars, we know that they will not and cannot outlast the memory of George Washington. That memory will remain forever green as the sprig of Acacia which will flourish as long as human hearts respond to the nobility of mankind.

Centuries will come and go. These walls may crumble into dust. But the luminous memory of George Washington will flash like a meteor across the firmament of God's Heaven to remind future generations of what he did for humanity; what he gave that men might be free.

AT HISTORIC FREDERICKSBURG

ADDRESS AT A DINNER IN CONNECTION WITH THE ANNUAL MEETING OF THE KENMORE ASSOCIATION,
FREDERICKSBURG, VIRGINIA
MAY 6, 1931

This occasion is one more evidence of an ancient and noble habit of your city.

Fredericksburg is one of the most fortunate communities in the United States. Even in historic Virginia, the native state of George Washington and his forebears, no other city is so closely associated with his personal life.

Although George Washington was one of the most extensively traveled men of his time, so far as his native land is concerned, it is here in this beautiful city that we find those early and formative experiences which had the greatest influence upon his life and career. Here was his early boyhood home. In these streets echoed his footsteps upon the normal activities of youth. Here he went to school, here he formed those enduring friendships which he treasured to the end of his life. Here lived his mother and that domestic circle of which he was so distinguished a part.

In this city lived his sister, in the home that has since become a national shrine.

Whatever the future held for this boy in glory and in attainment; whatever tributes came to him as the greatest man of his time, and surely the greatest man in our Republic, George Washington's heart was ever drawn to your city by the tenderest ties of boyhood memories.

In studying the life of George Washington one is struck by the fact that whenever sterner duties permitted, it was the pilgrimage to this city and these associations that most delighted him. With all of these things you are familiar.

To you George Washington is a living man. He is your neighbor, he is your boyhood associate, he is in spirit still walking your streets, chatting with your people as a familiar friend.

I feel the stimulation of your splendid pride in the reverence which you pay not only to George Washington, but more particularly to the mother of this great man who sleeps near us in hallowed ground.

Many men and women have expressed their tributes to Mary Ball Washington. I can only add my humble expressions of adoration to theirs. I can perhaps but repeat what others have said. Yet after all is there anything more beautiful, more eloquent or more expressive than the simple words upon that beautiful monument raised to her memory, "Mary, the Mother of Washington." Nothing need be added to those words, nothing

One of the Oldest Memorials to George Washington. The Stone Tower, as Restored, Erected on South Mountain, Near Boonsboro, Maryland, in 1827.

First and Unfinished Monument at the Grave of Mary, the Mother of Washington, at Fredericksburg, Va., of which the Cornerstone was Laid by President Jackson, May 7, 1833. The Obelisk on the Ground was Never Placed on the Base.

(Illustration of present monument to "Mary, the Mother of Washington," is shown on page 166.)

could be added that would bring more glory or honor to her splendid womanhood.

Historians and biographers have searched the character of Mary Ball Washington and have laid it before us. But to me there is one commentary that renders needless all that others have said. The character of Mary Ball Washington is summed up and the whole story of her life is told when we say, "She brought George Washington into the world and trained him for life."

That duty was so great and so well performed that I believe America is as fortunate in having possessed Mary Ball Washington, as it was in being blessed with her son. But no one can doubt that from whatever sources George Washington got his intellect, that his greatness and strength of character came from his mother. She gave to him as a heritage the training that equipped him perfectly for the career which Providence held for him.

I believe the historians make too much of the austerity of George Washington's mother. We hear of her stern refusal to let him take to the sea. We hear of the strictness of her rule. But there must have been in her life a rich store of sweetness, of sympathy and of true mother love that has gone unrecorded.

We know this because there was more than duty in George Washington's devotion to her throughout his life. He was devoted to her with all the ardor of his strong nature. He called her the most beautiful woman he ever saw and at the height of his success he was proud to speak of his "revered mother," and at her death rejoiced that she had been so long spared in health and mental activity.

One of his most cherished possessions was the worn copy of the book, "Contemplations Moral and Divine," which had been her constant companion in her quiet hours.

A woman who could inspire such loyalty in her son must have been intensely lovable herself.

I have dwelt upon these more familiar aspects of George Washington's attachment to this city because I wish to impress upon you as citizens of Fredericksburg the importance of the heritage that has been left to you. I also want to impress upon you the fact that the entire country should share with you that generous feeling of proprietorship which you have in these treasured associations.

That opportunity has presented itself in the action of Congress in providing for a nation-wide Celebration next year of the Two Hundredth Anniversary of the Birth of George Washington. The Commission appointed to have charge of this Celebration has been active and the campaign is far advanced. But there is still much to be done. Under the stress of modern conditions of life our fellow Americans have lost touch with our own glorious history. To many people George Washington is not a man, but a tradition.

We want to make him a living human being, and to impress upon the American people some of the feeling of neighborly intimacy which you in Fredericksburg have so nobly preserved.

We want to present George Washington as a man and not as an ideal. As a man he stands forth in all the glory of his character and achievements. As a man he is far greater than the cold and unreal figure upon a pedestal.

Under the direction of Congress it is the duty of the United States George Washington Bicentennial Commission to organize throughout the nation a Celebration in the hearts and minds of the people themselves, in such manner as is most fitting, to the end that his Bicentennial anniversary "may be commemorated in such manner that future generations of American citizens may live according to the example and precepts of his exalted life and character, and thus perpetuate the American Republic."

The Celebration of the Two Hundredth Anniversary of the Birth of George Washington next year is being organized upon the basis of the same dignity and reverence which you feel here in Fredericksburg.

We want the people of America to take part in this Celebration with full understanding of the man they honor. We want them to feel a real sense of this man's having lived, as you have who sense it here.

Just as the feet of George Washington still echo through your streets, we want all America to realize how actual, how human, how normal and yet how great was George Washington.

So we are spreading over the entire country and over the world the full history of George Washington with all the facts of his life as collected and sifted by the eminent historians we have engaged.

We want this Celebration to be what George Washington himself would wish it to be. He would reject the idea of a parade of our material riches in his honor. He would be impatient of glamor and display. But we know that he would wish this tribute to him to come from the hearts of the people—his fellow Americans.

Therefore, we have aimed at no central spectacle, no concentration of ceremony, but wherever the flag of our nation flies today we want Americans all to express in reverence and in love their appreciation of the life and character of the man who brought that flag into being.

It is timely, it is appropriate, that Americans should pause in this fast-living day and think reverently of the man who not only achieved our independence as a nation, but who brought liberty, protection and sound government to those Americans who were to come after him.

It is well that the government of the United States which exists upon the foundation which he laid, should provide for this national tribute in his honor. The Celebration next year will begin February 22 and continue until Thanksgiving Day. Throughout the nation, we are asking men, women and children to organize in their own homes, in their own schools, churches, clubs and other groups special programs to honor George Washington's memory.

The response has been inspiring. Already in thousands of communities preparations are going forward to this end, and we are furnishing to thousands of these groups, programs, plays, pageants, posters, books and similar material to aid them in the preparation of their own ceremonies.

It would be a great pleasure indeed if all of you could visit the headquarters of the United States George Washington Bicentennial Commission in the City of Washington. You would find there such activity, such enthusiasm, and such progress, as would surprise and delight you.

For we are carrying forward the best traditions of Americanism. We are emphasizing in many ways not only the life and character of George Washington, but we are bringing to the American people a vivid picture of the conditions under which he created the monument of his country now stretching from sea to sea.

And may I say that it is always equally inspiring to me to come to this beautiful City of Fredericksburg and here to drink at the fountain of your patriotism, your loyalty and your devotion.

What better influence can be found than to stand upon this historic soil? What loftier sentiments can be experienced than the heart tribute to motherhood as we visit again that hallowed spot where sleeps—"Mary, the Mother of Washington."

MOTHERS' DAY

ADDRESS BROADCAST FROM THE ARLINGTON MEMORIAL AMPHITHEATRE, ARLINGTON NATIONAL CEMETERY, VIRGINIA, ON THE AMERICAN WAR MOTHERS' PROGRAM, BY THE NATIONAL BROADCASTING COMPANY, MAY 10, 1931

Today, throughout our country, we are celebrating Mothers' Day.

Upon this beautiful and solemn anniversary our hearts respond to a common impulse of devotion. From many homes, from many varied occupations, from many conditions of life that occupy our daily thoughts, we experience today upon this sacred occasion the exaltation of the finest of human sentiments.

While we think of motherhood as universal, yet in each one of us there is treasured a shrine of love for that one being to whom we owe our individual homage— our mother.

The heroism of a mother's love—her distinct and individual influence—differs from anything else God ever thought of, for it fixes in permanent outline the future hope of us all.

The honoring of mothers is as old as the human race. We sometimes think of Mothers' Day in our country as being something new, yet festivals and ceremonies of similar kind were common in the dawning period of our civilization. Long before the Christian era something closely corresponding to Mothers' Day was introduced through Greece into Rome, where it was known as the Festival of Hilaria, and appropriately enough was a spring festival. At any rate, we can not claim monopoly of this fine and noble filial sentiment.

As I contemplate the sacrifices and the sufferings of these and all other war mothers I can not refrain from dwelling upon that first American War Mother, who gave her noble son to the service of his country.

Upon a beautiful monument in the city of Fredericksburg, Va., are carved these simple words, "Mary, the Mother of Washington." Beneath that monument lie the remains of that remarkable woman who gave to us the rich heritage of our greatest American. It is to the mother of George Washington that this Nation owes its existence today as a land of liberty and of opportunity.

Not only did Mary, the Mother of Washington, bring into the world a son of rare heredity and character, but we know from research that from his infancy this boy was trained and taught in those high principles of truth, courage, and honor which equipped him perfectly for the great task to which he was to come.

Perhaps, had there been no George Washington, some other man would have arisen who could have carried forward the gigantic task of liberating our country and establishing our form of government. But the one thing we know is that George Washington did fulfill this destiny and that he could not have done so had it not been for the training given him by his mother.

I speak of Mary Ball Washington, the mother of George Washington, as the first American War Mother. My authority for this is the fact that, while there were colonial troops in the field before Washington was appointed Commander-in-Chief, the point is that there was no American Army until George Washington was appointed by Congress to organize it.

Mary Washington lived through those eight years of Revolutionary struggle to witness the final triumph of her son at Yorktown and to meet him again at Fredericksburg on his way from that victorious campaign.

How beautiful and how characteristic was that meeting. George Washington the hero, the conqueror, the liberator stopped at Fredericksburg on his way north from Yorktown especially for the purpose of seeing his mother. Of that meeting in her modest home we have scant record. His visit to the town was probably a quiet one; but there is, nevertheless, a tradition of pomp and circumstance, of a retinue of distinguished generals, both American and French, whom Mrs. Washington greeted. It is a charming, even though apocryphal, story, that of the deference of these warriors and polite foreigners to the mother of their great chieftain, and her courteous and quietly dignified reception of their complimentary attentions.

But when peace was at last established and the Cincinnatus of the West returned to his farm, his first thought was of the duty to his aged parent, the "revered mother by whose maternal hand (early deprived of a father) I was led from childhood." He hastened to Fredericksburg as soon as the weather permitted, in February, 1784, and the rejoicing town made holiday of his presence, with a respectful address, a public dinner, and a grand ball, a celebration which lasted for two days. But the mother had him first as well as last, and a picture of that quiet evening would be one worthy of Mothers' Day. We have a glimpse through the veil of time into that simple scene which brings us into touch with the first American War Mother.

Surely she could not help being proud of this her splendid son whose arrival so honored the town of his youthful associations; and Fredericksburg's acclaim was but one of the many that had greeted his presence and would continue to do so for the remainder of his life. But she was his mother, the nearness and dearness, the divine intimacy, put a check upon her tongue. She did not boast of his achievements; she did not speak of his heroic deeds; she did not refer to any great act of his which drew the admiration and devotion of the world to him. To her he was George, the son, and in all the histories of that time we find but one small reference to any compliment she paid him, and that was when she said:

"George was always a good boy and deserves well of his country."

How modest, how retiring, how beautiful is this renunciation, but we may be sure that love and pride and beautiful attachment warmed the heart of this noble woman when, after her immortal contribution to the world, she rested for a time in the glory of life's setting sun, and passed on.

Today we do well to honor War Mothers. Today we bring to them the Nation's thanks and devotion, and it is well that we do so. Every Gold Star in that glorious constellation of womanhood represents all that could be given—all that could be sacrificed.

But let us not forget those other mothers who have made sacrifices that the world might be made better.

And among those glorious mothers let us exalt that mother who brought into the world the man whose Two Hundredth Birthday Anniversary the Nation celebrates next year in the greatest event of its kind ever held in this or any other country.

The mothers of men are the link between heaven and earth. When we think of our mothers whose noble, unselfish, tireless devotion to us is never dimmed, never destroyed, no matter how far our footsteps wander from the course which they marked out, we are close to the Great Creator of us all.

The constancy of mother love is the divine light which shines upon the world. It is the one trustworthy, unfailing guide that leads us all safely home.

The memory of our mothers is a treasure that grows more beautiful with the years. It is the one thing that we can not forget. It is the one thing that we would not forget if we could.

Whatever the buffetings of fate may be, whatever the sorrows and disappointments we encounter in our life struggle, we can always be sure that somewhere there is one who, although she may be sitting in the shadows, yet waits and watches and prays for our return.

Among all true men and women, every day is mother's day. And if we remember her precepts and are guided by her example, the world will be full of beauty and unselfishness.

To all mothers everywhere let us pay that heart tribute which is due them, but which we more especially owe to ourselves, for no thought of motherhood can come to us without lifting us nearer to God.

MEMORIAL DAY

Address Broadcast From Washington, D. C., by the National Broadcasting Company, May 30, 1931

Memorial Day! A day of memories—the one American holiday which moves us to feelings of solemnity and tender retrospection.

All of our other national holidays are joyful occasions. From New Years until Christmas, they mark a new prospect, the anniversary of some great man's birth, or signalize some outstanding episode of history.

This day is one of sublime dignity, beauty and reverence. It stands upon our calendar to mark the passage of years, of those who have gone from us, and to rekindle in our hearts remembrance of them and what they gave to us.

Memorial Day has long been associated with rites for those who died upon the field of battle in defence of their country, and of ours. It takes nothing from honor to these noble dead, to include as we do today, all of our loved ones who have also passed on.

Reverence for the dead is one of the oldest and surely the most sublime emotion of civilized man. As we pause today to do honor to our departed loved ones, we ourselves are ennobled, our hearts are made purer and our souls come nearer to God.

We who live in a land that is secure, we who have been nurtured in freedom and in equal opportunity, cannot think of those heroes who laid down their lives for our country, without feelings of humility and overwhelming obligation. We cannot think of them without reverence and tenderness and gratitude.

The symbol of our flag is a symbol of sacrifice and glory. Wherever that flag flies today it means more to humanity than any other flag that ever waved in majesty upon the background of heaven. But that flag would not be enshrined in our hearts were it not that it was born in battle and has survived through the turmoil of war.

When it was first unfolded in the free air of liberty, it brought cheer, inspiration and courage to those tattered soldiers of George Washington who were then engaged in that war which established our country and decreed freedom throughout the world.

In honoring that flag we honor all who died that it might survive. In honoring that flag we pay tribute to the hosts of noble men and women who went bravely to their deaths that it might live.

America is known the world over for the splendor of its charities. Our people can hardly wait to attain success before they pour out their wealth in aid of the afflicted, or for founding great beneficial institutions.

But the greatest act of charity, the greatest benevolence ever performed in this land of ours, came from those heroes whose memory we honor upon this occasion.

They gave more than money, something infinitely more precious than riches. They gave all that man can give, when they gave their lives that we who live after them may prosper in a country that is free and enduring.

All that we have and all that we are we owe to these men who offered their bodies to guard their country against encroaching dangers.

Memorial Day is the formal day when we acknowledge publicly the debt we owe them. It is the day when we cease our usual occupations and express from our hearts the love we bear them.

We cannot discharge that debt. Our nation, lasting for all time, could never repay. But we can give that character to our devotion which would please those heroes most. We can express our reverence to them by renewed loyalty to the institutions which they gave us.

No words of mine, indeed no words of any man could add to the immortal sentiments of Abraham Lincoln in his Gettysburg Address which hold true today for every plot of ground where lie Americans who died for their country.

We cannot make more sacred the soil wherein they lie. We can utter no words of gratitude for ears that have long since ceased to hear mortal praise.

Memorial Day is for us and not for them. It is for us to reconsecrate ourselves in patriotism and in devotion to our country's welfare. It is for us the living, to carry forward the torch of freedom so that when we ourselves pass into the Beyond, America's freedom may be more secure.

The services of this day attune our hearts to nobility and honor. As we reverence the dead, so should we remember the living. Out of that ocean of unselfish love, upon which our heroes embarked, let us all feel today that God in His infinite wisdom, has willed that all is well.

Wherever there are living Americans, let us think of all those who fell in the cause of American freedom. We must not forget one of them. We do not honor the heroes of one war alone. In the lengthening record of our history there are many brilliant pages, many pages stained with precious blood.

Let us have in mind today all of our hero dead.

Next year this nation is to celebrate the Two Hundredth Anniversary of the Birth of her greatest son— George Washington. Memorial Day must surely include those starving, ragged, heroes who marched with bleeding feet through the snows at Valley Forge and who died by the thousands in field and camp, for the America that was to come. In honoring the memory of George Washington we are honoring the memory of all those who struggled and sacrificed with him.

The bodies of these heroes are mingled in the democracy of the dust. But their example and their deeds are immortal. Although their very names may have vanished from human memory, the spiritual monument which they erected will last as long as the hearts of humanity beat.

In dying, these men of America gave more than life. They left us more than memory.

It is inspiring to me to think of the millions of our countrymen who are at this moment laying the purest garlands of affection upon the graves of those who have gone. It is our best hope of security that American hearts beat true and that the meaning of this day does not diminish with the years.

Whatever clouds may gather, whatever fears may assail us, we know that our country is sound and that its people are sane.

Love of country is not an image of sentimental imagination. It is as real, it is as vibrant, it is as sacred, as life itself.

That multitude of heroes who gave the last full measure of devotion for their country, did not die for a fanciful ideal. They did not die because of imaginary sentiments. They did not pay with their lives for a lie.

They died for the greatest principle which Divine Providence has placed in the hearts of men. They died for love of their countrymen—love of those who were to come after them.

We cannot honor the memories of these dead by eulogy or by flowers unless we consciously express our own dedication to the principles for which they died.

We who survive them and who benefit by what they did, are sometimes swayed by passions that effect all humanity. We are ambitious, we are striving, we seek individual gain. Sometimes we are ruthless in obtaining what we want. It is the human way.

But from the graves of these honored Americans there comes a message of silent eloquence to admonish us to live more kindly, to deal more justly with our fellow men. That voice must not go unheeded. Patriotism is not vain bluster. It is not the figment of sentimental emotion. True patriotism is that quality of human feeling that safeguards the security and honor of our homes and families, our country and our countrymen. It raises us to the pure air of unselfishness, of kindness, of justice.

Were we to think otherwise would give the lie to all that our heroes died for. It would debase the better natures of us all.

So let us in pride and in beautiful consecration think of this America as an edifice risen from the glory of self-sacrifice. It is ours to defend and to perpetuate.

Let us carry forward this mighty republic and make it better and more worthy of all who have died to preserve its honor and its safety. Let us so live that when the veil of death shall have closed about us, we may join that noble army and face the Great Captain without fear and without reproach.

When for us time shall be no more, may the memories of our lives we leave behind bring to our resting places our portion of those heavenly floral tributes that today spread like God's benediction over the hills and valleys of our beloved land.

GEORGE WASHINGTON AND HIS RELATIONSHIP TO THE SOUTH

ADDRESS FROM WASHINGTON, D. C.,
OVER COLUMBIA BROADCASTING SYSTEM
JUNE 5, 1931

I am asked to say something to you on "George Washington and His Relationship to the South."

No more agreeable subject could be assigned to any one authorized to speak of George Washington. And I doubt if there is another topic more agreeable to Southern listeners.

Historians tell us that George Washington now belongs to the world, that a world-wide humanity now increasingly aware of the benefits it has received at his hands, has taken him to itself.

We in America must rest content with the honor of having presented such a man to mankind.

As the Two Hundredth Anniversary of his Birth approaches, we turn to his character and genius with a new interest, a new attention to every detail of his life.

Search as we may into the life of this man, we do not find one deed or trait to which any of us can take the slightest exception.

There seems to have been no great man of all history so lofty and stainless in every fibre of his being.

The greatness of such a man confers a touch of the same greatness on the people that produced him. We cannot be quite the lost nation that some of our present critics think us, if we can produce from our national existence a figure of the stature and quality of George Washington.

But no matter how great a man may be, no matter how much he may belong to the entire world, that man must have his birth and growth. He must have his starting point from the immediate forebears who gave him his blood, his inheritance, his education and environment. For that reason the American South regards George Washington as its special property.

It takes this proud stand with every right and reason. For three generations before Washington was born, the warm and generous life of the South had shaped and influenced the life and the thought of his ancestors.

Into this same warmth and love of the high and fine things of life, George Washington was born. In the South he passed his boyhood. He mingled with the best of Southern manhood and womanhood. In every way the South, and especially Virginia, put its stamp upon his character, his mental attitude, his ways of thought.

Well may our Southland believe that George Washington is its especial product. For it molded him in its own fine graces, its own high standards of honor, its own patterns of rectitude.

The best authority on the subject of how thoroughly Washington was a Southerner and a Virginian, is George Washington himself.

He never broke into rhapsody over the delights of Southern life. He never critically analyzed the character and the habits of Southern people, as did that other great Virginian, Thomas Jefferson.

George Washington spoke his love of Virginia and the South in more eloquent language than that. Wherever he traveled, wherever he fought, whatever the duties that so often and so long absented him from the place of his birth, he always longed for his home in Virginia, and to that home he hurried the moment that duty permitted him.

In all his travels, through all his critical examinations of American life as it then was, George Washington's heart forever yearned for Virginia and Mount Vernon.

There was his home. There were his beloved acres. There were his friends. There was his Southern wife, whom he loved with such Southern chivalry.

For it was in his home, as the husband, the foster father, the generous host to a world of friends, that George Washington was at his best. There he showed the people among whom he was born and trained all the high traits they had given or taught him—made finer still by contributions from his own noble nature.

In studying the rise and growth of such a man, we can only stand and marvel. When a man so lofty steps forth from the common ranks of mankind, it is as if we were watching the very hand of God, at work in the creation of a miracle.

In the career of such a man, the Omnipotent Hand appears again and again. But for the hand of God, working through the material of what we call destiny, George Washington might have lived as a Southerner and died as a Southerner.

Even the War of the Revolution might not have made him more than a sectional figure, but for one of those workings in other men's minds which strike us, in the long perspective of history, as unmistakably the act of Providence.

Through the instrumentality of John Adams and others of Washington's fellow patriots, this great man of the South was made the leader of all the Revolutionary force and spirit.

In their hearts, the men who made that choice were only solving an immediate practical problem of leadership. We know now what immense consequences flowed from their choice.

Surely the South has honor enough in having bred such a man. If the greatness of George Washington reflects a gleam of the same light on all America, that light shines brightest on the region that harbored his forebears and surrounded his own formative years with its kindness and grace.

But Virginia and the South did more for George Washington than provide him with the traits that made him what he was as the man, the social being.

It gave his genius its first work to do. It provided the tasks that toughened his young manhood's sinews. It sent him on difficult errands that gave him first practice in war and in statesmanship.

The South then regarded itself as the richest and perhaps the most important section of the young country. It had large stakes in the still richer regions to the West and North. It looked with anxious eyes to the safety of its properties. It was determined on the safety of its political rights and liberties.

All these were subject to many grave dangers. Against these threats and enemies, the South meant to be defended. And in that defense it sent George Washington on errands as difficult and dangerous as they were delicate.

How well this mere stripling, this youthful major and colonel, discharged these duties, history now records.

But on one page of that early record, George Washington left an especially brilliant mark.

On Braddock Field, this young Colonial officer salvaged from still worse disaster the pride of the British army, although he was merely a volunteer aide without rank; and he personally snatched his dying superior from the scene of his blunder.

Thereafter not only the South but the entire nation knew that it had in George Washington a man unmatched in personal bravery, unmatched in high resolve, and already a master at lifting a hopeless military situation into the heights of a moral success.

Great as is the honor of having born and bred such a man, greater still is the honor of having given him these tests and proofs of the stuff that was in him.

When his first military assignments had been discharged, George Washington married the love of his heart and became a farmer. He became not simply a farmer, but the most practical, the most progressive, and the most successful farmer of his time.

Throughout his life he showed an almost touching anxiety for the prosperity of Southern agriculture. In the very heat of his military campaigns, he appears to have kept his eyes open to all that went on about him—not omitting the farming methods of other sections of the country.

When victory had been won by his military genius, he still could come home to Mount Vernon with new practices in farming that he sought to impart to his fellow farmers of the South.

Widely traveled as he was, he journeyed oftenest and farthest through the South. Wherever he went his eyes saw everything. Nothing escaped his notice.

As a member of the Virginia House of Burgesses, he helped make the laws of the South, and learned his first lessons in statesmanship.

It was that quiet, impressive individual at Mount Vernon whose urgence brought about Virginia's acceptance of the Constitution, when even Patrick Henry and James Monroe opposed it.

As President of the United States, Washington turned to the South for some of his important Cabinet members—Thomas Jefferson, Edmund Randolph, and Charles Lee, and later Habersham, of Georgia.

Such were the feelings of his heart for his people.

His sympathies encircle the whole of America. But his warmest sympathies and keenest interests seemed always centered on the region and the people of his birth and his youth—the South.

Where his beloved home was, where his fathers slept, there his heart beat highest, there his energies were most lovingly expended.

If the South loved George Washington from the moment of his birth to the moment when the marble at Mount Vernon closed forever over his mortal remains, then the South may be sure from every word that Washington uttered, every deed that he did, that he loved it as much in return, and as long as he lived.

In 1932, the year now closely approaching, this nation which owes so much of its being to the mind, the character, and the iron courage of George Washington, will have an opportunity to express its debt to him, on the appropriate occasion of the two hundredth year since his birth.

George Washington was possessed of a vision that saw farther than any other man of his day. He fought as he did for this country, he thought as he did for this country, because he believed in the greatness it was destined to achieve and enjoy.

But not even George Washington with all his farsightedness could envision the great people we have become—the most courageously pioneering people that ever lived.

Not very long after Washington's death there appeared mechanical inventions that have transformed human life. They have opened avenues to riches never dreamed of before.

We have seized upon those inventions and made the most of them. The result is an America of such greatness that would amaze even Washington. We are rich to a degree that constitutes danger, unless we forget these riches and return to those simple faiths in the fundamentals of human nature, those trusts that guided George Washington in the founding of this nation.

For before these material inventions had appeared

George Washington had given us the greatest invention of all—those principles of government without which we would be nothing.

In thankfulness for what we have, in thankfulness to the man who made all these things possible, let us turn and convert the whole of next year to a tribute to his memory. Even more, let us make it a rededication of ourselves to his trust in men, to his labors for others, for country more than for self.

And in this, let the South, which possesses his sacred ashes, lead the way.

All that George Washington was and did, all that he thought and accomplished, was actuated by that love he bore—that love of his country and his countrymen. It was the underlying motive in all his career.

But in the love he bore to the South, that love took on something more intimate and personal.

So, in additon to all its other claims upon this greatest of all Americans, the South has this last and finest claim —that it received the warmest and deepest share of his personal affections.

That, I think, is at least something regarding "George Washington and His Relationship to the South." It was more than a relationship of great deeds. For under the deeds was the love of a magnificent son for a proud and adoring mother.

NATIONAL SECURITY LEAGUE

Address Broadcast from Washington, D. C., by the Columbia Broadcasting System
June 23, 1931

I am asked by The National Security League to tell you something of an enterprise definitely and vigorously launched by the United States Government about a year ago.

It is different from anything ever before undertaken by any country.

This unique undertaking on the part of our Government is to organize throughout the United States and many other parts of the world, a fitting celebration of the Two Hundredth Anniversary of the birth of the man who did more than any other to make possible our nation and our government—George Washington.

That anniversary comes next year, and it is eminently wise and appropriate that we honor it on a national scale. For this great occasion marks more than the bicentennial of our greatest American. It marks a milestone in the progress of the nation so largely established by him.

In the 200 years since George Washington's birth, this country of ours has achieved a position unparalleled in history. We owe this stupendous progress to the new principles of government laid down by this greatest of our Founders.

It is my privilege and pleasure to tell you how this nation, led by its Government, will next year render its tribute of reverence and gratitude to that benefactor of humanity.

I do so at the invitation of an association of American patriots—The National Security League. But in an enterprise such as this one, of honoring the Father of our Country, I am conscious of addressing a nation of patriots, both within and without this organization.

Next year the whole American people will be one vast security league, newly consecrating themselves to the preservation of their country and the principles of George Washington.

More than a year ago the United States George Washington Bicentennial Commission, authorized by Congress, began the active work of organizing this national tribute.

It was realized that our people would rise in spontaneous honor to George Washington, on the coming anniversary. But the Representatives of the people desired to bring this national impulse into unison and give it singleness of purpose, under the auspices of the Government itself.

The United States George Washington Bicentennial Commission, of which I am the Director, was formed and empowered to do this work.

To give weight and influence to this Commission, the President of the United States was made its chairman, with a membership consisting of the Vice President, the Speaker of the House of Representatives, four members of the Senate, four members of the House of Representatives, and a group of outstanding citizens from various parts of the country.

The coming Celebration we have planned in Washington's honor will be unique in the fact that we have considered no concentration of patriotic activities in any one place.

Instead of bringing the people to some central Celebration, we are taking the Celebration to the people, in their own homes, cities and communities.

This tribute to George Washington in 1932 will begin on February 22, the date of his birth, and will continue until Thanksgiving Day. Every intervening holiday will be marked with special observances appropriate to its relationship with Washington's life and achievements.

During this period of nine months, it is proposed that every man, woman and child living under the American flag shall have some part in honoring the man who made possible that flag and all that it stands for.

The plans for this Celebration are well advanced.

Our first duty and undertaking was to present the facts about George Washington to the people. Washington is the greatest figure in our history, and yet he is the least known. Scholars and historians have delved into every moment of his life, every phase of his career. Yet the American of today needs new realization of

Washington's greatness, a new sense of his service to America and mankind, and a renewed gratitude for all that we owe him.

We of the United States Bicentennial Commission desired to bring to the present generation of Americans a new imprint of the personality of George Washington. We wished to instill into the hearts and minds of our people a new understanding of his life and service, a new sense of our own duty to serve our country in return.

For this purpose we early engaged eminent historians to search out the story of Washington's life.

As these experts have unfolded George Washington's record, our information bureau has spread it forth over the country, for publication in newspapers and magazines. And I am thrilled at the extent to which this material has been published.

It is wonderfully encouraging as evidence of the interest of our people and the spirit and enthusiasm with which they will participate in this Celebration next year. It is evidence that this Celebration will be held where it should be held, and where we wish it to be—in the hearts of a grateful people.

For we are holding no expositions, no parades of our material progress. We are building no new monuments to George Washington.

We want this observance of his birth anniversary to be a reconsecration to his ideals and principles. And we want that reconsecration to be made in every church, home, school, in every individual heart and mind in America.

In order to help the people express themselves in this way, the United States George Washington Bicentennial Commission has also engaged specialists in the preparation of plays, pageants, and other ceremonials. It was thought that one excellent way to bring back the facts and the meaning of Washington's life, was to re-enact it, and see it re-enacted, among the people themselves.

Such spectacles would afford knowledge mixed with pleasure. Better than that, they would provide opportunity for all to take some active part in these honors. These plays and plans and programs are to be made available to all who wish to present them.

How the States and the Territories are swinging in behind the United States Bicentennial Commission in splendid cooperation! Only a few of the States have not yet appointed commissions of their own. In time they will all do so.

It is inspiring testimony to the spirit and the manner in which America will come next year to lay its tribute at the feet of George Washington.

I can not tell you of all the progress that has been made during this past year, and of the progress we expect from now on.

At the present moment I am more interested in what this activity and enthusiasm means.

It means that every good American is swinging back to the old spirit of patriotism. The overwhelming majority of us are one great national security league.

The memory of George Washington is calling us all back to the old principles on which our nation was founded. We all wish to see our country enjoy peace in security. And this occasion of Washington's birth anniversary provides the people with a rallying point for this deep feeling among them.

As I see it, that is the reason why our plans for the Bicentennial Celebration next year have met with such enthusiastic response.

In the mind of George Washington was always dominant that desire to establish national security. In many of his great utterances preserved to us today we find him making use of that word "security" time and time again.

For without security there can be no freedom. Without security there can be no independence. Without security there can be no new nationalism as George Washington understood it.

It was to make our people secure that those early patriots risked their lives, their fortunes and their sacred honor. It was to establish permanent security that thousands of those patriots died in field and camp.

Security is the keynote of all of those dramatic incidents in George Washington's life which made him our greatest American.

Surely never in our history since that immortal day at Yorktown was there greater need of reading into the word "Security" its meaning according to the founders of our Republic.

It is a sense of insecurity that is troubling our country today. It is the vague sense of an unknown danger that creates anxiety among us all.

Security means safety. It means a certain survival and permanence of those safeguards which the founders of our government read into our Constitution.

A security league is an American institution and deserves the honor and consideration which we give it.

But security can never be maintained without strength, without courage and without patriotism. And what we of the George Washington Bicentennial Commission are doing is to help lay a solid foundation beneath our governmental institutions.

The American people owe to George Washington new pledges to keep safe and secure the country he founded for us. I believe a sense of this begins to possess us all.

With the coming of 1932, and the year of tribute to George Washington, I expect to witness such a revival as we never have seen before, of love for country, of new devotion to its security, and a new hatred for every element that would render it asunder.

We Americans of today may have our differences of thought in relation to the problems directly before us. This is a time that invites such differences. It is a period when we are all perplexed with personal worries. We need to be called out of our purely personal interests and reminded of country.

I believe this need is felt by every one of us. We may differ as to creed, policies, and issues. But we can become one people, with a single thought, in a return to established national ideals, and to the great man who more than any other American embodied those ideals— George Washington.

George Washington calls to us to come out of ourselves and become single-minded Americans again. I appeal to every American who hears me to heed that call and join us in honor to the man who set the immortal example in thought and labor for the security of his country.

It is especially appropriate that I make this appeal under the auspices and with the support of a great national organization which has for its sole purpose the promotion of solid American citizenship.

Whether or not you who hear me are members of this Security League, we can all be workers for good Americanism and solid citizenship. We can all be leaders in this movement to turn back to George Washington for inspiration and example.

We all owe to George Washington this offering from our hearts, in the form of a new devotion to country, new pledges to its safety and the realization of its destiny.

I am grateful to the organization of patriots who have asked me to make this appeal, with their support and encouragement. In their name, and in the name of good Americanism, I appeal to all to resolve on some active part next year, that we may display new loyalty to our country, and to the teachings of the great man who did so much to establish this government and this flag—this symbol of our national security, under which we enjoy so many blessings.

INDEPENDENCE DAY

ADDRESS DELIVERED AT INDEPENDENCE HALL, PHILADELPHIA, AND BROADCAST BY THE NATIONAL BROADCASTING COMPANY, JULY 4, 1931

I am standing in Independence Hall, Philadelphia, in what is perhaps the most historic room in America. At the table before me was adopted and signed the Declaration of Independence.

The words I speak on this birthday of the Nation come to you from a microphone standing on the very spot where this Nation of ours was born.

Here, on the anniversary of that day, in this hall where so many remarkable events have taken place, I am permitted to look back from this day of peace and security, of enormous social and political progress, and measure the immense consequences that have arisen from that momentous event that occurred in this room a little more than a century and a half ago.

This extraordinary honor has been accorded me as Director of the United States George Washington Bicentennial Commission, created by Congress to organize among the American people, next year, the Celebration of the Two Hundredth Anniversary of the Birth of George Washington—the man who did more than any other to translate the Declaration of Independence into terms of living reality—the man who did more than any other to place the thirteen struggling colonies on a firm foundation and build them into one great Nation of 123,000,000 people.

It is impossible to conceive of a more direct and dramatic linkage between the present and the past—between this Fourth of July of vast fulfillment and that Fourth of July of gigantic political adventure.

As I stand here where this greatest and strongest Nation in the history of the world had its birth and these beginnings, I am swept with reverence and awe.

I am lost in wonder as I think of the imperishable pages of history that were written here, and the mighty forces of progress that were released here by the wise and steadfast men who shaped at this table before me a new charter of human liberties, and brought into being a new era in human affairs that today is the hope of humanity throughout the world.

Beneath the flag of our country we Americans must pause and realize in our hearts what that flag stands for. It is the living symbol of the blood and tears of those men and women of a bygone age who went gloriously to their graves that our country might live.

Beneath its sheltering folds the dying eyes of countless heroes grew dim and closed forever, a prayer upon their lips for its preservation.

It is for us to carry forward those sacrifices and those ideals. Who knows but what we say today and what we do today may not be translated to that far shore where are gathered the heroes of long-gone years? Who knows but that our account is being written as to how well and how worthily we have kept the faith as Americans?

May God help us to act well our part. May God give us some portion of the courage and devotion which created our country, that we may defend its liberties.

In our enjoyment of these liberties let us remember what they cost. The act performed here by these patriots required more than wisdom, great as it was. It called for another quality which they possessed, and which, please Providence, they have handed on. It called for the utmost in moral and physical courage.

In establishing this Nation they had to fling their defiance in the face of a powerful foe. They knew the risk they took, and that risk was real. On the heads of the men who signed the immortal Declaration of Independence, on the heads of every member of their families, the angry Government they defied placed a price.

Benjamin Franklin's jest was far more grim and truthful than humorous when he warned his fellow signers that "We must all hang together, or assuredly we shall all hang separately."

Yet, reckless of what it might cost them, these patriots pledged to the cause all that they had, and all that they were—"their lives, their fortunes, and their sacred honor."

If, in the list of great names they attached to the Declaration of Independence, we miss the greatest of all—the name of George Washington—it is for good and sufficient reason.

FRAUNCES' TAVERN IN NEW YORK CITY
AS IT NOW APPEARS, ALTERED AND RE-
STORED SINCE REVOLUTIONARY DAYS.
IT WAS BUILT IN COLONIAL TIMES, WAS
THE SCENE OF VARIOUS PATRIOTIC
MEETINGS BEFORE THE REVOLUTION,
AND A RENDEZVOUS FOR CONTINENTAL
OFFICERS DURING THE CAMPAIGN FOR
THE POSSESSION OF NEW YORK CITY—
1776. ITS PROPRIETOR AT THAT TIME,
SAMUEL FRAUNCES, CALLED BLACK SAM,
REMAINED IN THE CITY DURING THE
BRITISH OCCUPATION, BUT THERE ARE
EVIDENCES THAT HE WAS REALLY ONE
OF GENERAL WASHINGTON'S SPIES
THERE. AFTER THE REOCCUPATION OF
THE CITY IN 1783, GENERAL WASHING-
TON BADE FAREWELL TO HIS OFFICERS
HERE DECEMBER 4TH. WHEN GEN-
ERAL WASHINGTON WAS PRESIDENT,
FRAUNCES WAS A PART OF THE TIME
STEWARD AT THE PRESIDENT'S MANSION.
FRAUNCES' TAVERN IN NEW YORK CITY,

While these men wrote at this table George Washington, as Commander-in-Chief of the Continental Army, was already far away on the field of battle.

Already he was fighting the cause of independence before these others had pondered the terms in which that cause should be proclaimed to the world.

Now, we living Americans are witnesses as to how well those patriots planned. The full and rich life we live today attests the greatness of the purpose for which they fought and struggled then.

For the sake of that cause which has made us so great they endured every loss, every danger, and every sacrifice.

And yet, in this vast democracy of Americans today, self-ruled as the patriots planned, far richer than they dreamed, and happy and privileged beyond any people that ever lived, I believe the fathers would find their plans justified, their struggles rewarded, their dreams come true.

Here on this table before me were shaped those liberties and privileges which you and I possess today as citizens of these United States. As I realize this, never have those rights and privileges seemed to me so sacred, so precious, and so real.

If I can I want to bring you into this room and give you a sense of the feelings this scene inspires. I want you to see the vision I see, called up in this birthplace of our country, on this, the anniversary of its birth.

I speak to you through a miracle of modern science, an instrument that symbolizes all our marvelous advances since 1776. Yet I speak in profound humility.

These very advances we have achieved make it all the more needful that we ask ourselves, on this July Fourth, how well we have kept the moral courage of that Fourth of July of 1776—how far are we ready to pledge to our country today "our lives, our fortunes, and our sacred honor."

I am one who believes we can answer that question with pride and respect of self.

I believe we can listen to the whispering voices that echo from these ancient walls without self-reproach. I can but dimly repeople this historic room. Yet my heart beats with new devotion, new love for my country and my fellow Americans, as there passes before my inner vision that procession of patriots.

Here, in this very chair, sat John Hancock, President of the Congress. There, in rows, many others upon that everlasting roll of honor. Fifty-six in all! Immortals! Americans!

Before them I bow in humble respect because of the sacrifices they made. But, my fellow Americans, I am one who believes we have guarded well the great trust they placed in our hands. I believe we have fought the good fight; I believe we have kept the faith.

We live in a day when it is common to hear that our country has lapsed in patriotism. It is said by many to have fallen from the lofty ideals of the founders. It is thought that because we have grown rich we must have grown corrupt.

It is said of us that we are lost in material gain; that we are dead to the spirit that first breathed life into the Nation and is vital to its very existence.

I am not one who believes all patriotism perished here in this sacred hall where it was born. I am not one who believes that all self-sacrifice and devotion to country disappeared with the men who here first practiced those virtues 155 years ago.

I believe these United States of America have grown to be the great Nation they are because we have had throughout the years of our history unfailing generations of patriots. I believe these succeeding generations have always defended American rights and liberties in a way that would earn them the blessings of the patriots of 1776.

We complain that disaffection is abroad in our land. There are those who carp at this Government which has achieved so much. They would rip it to pieces and set up another. It is taken as one more sign that we have slipped from the standards of our fathers.

If we have indifference toward the public interest today, let us remember that in the days of its infancy the cause of liberty had its way to make against a sea of the same troubles.

Valley Forge is the epic story of men who endured every visible hardship for the sake of an invisible cause. Yet now we know that the worst of Valley Forge might have been prevented by men who should have been true to their duties, and instead were not.

Even in those heroic days of the Declaration of Independence, when men of lofty character were winning liberties for future generations at every cost to themselves, there were men who were willing to profit by the sacrifices of these others.

In the dark days of that winter of 1777, John Adams, whose name stands high on the list of Signers of the Declaration of Independence, wrote home from Philadelphia to his devoted wife the bitter and despairing words: "I am ashamed of the times in which I live!"

Would John Adams be more ashamed of the Americans of 1812—the Americans of 1861—of 1898—of the Americans who lie in the fields and the forests of France today?

I can not believe it. The truth of it is that here in this room where I stand the founding of our country was not finished but only begun. Ever since that immortal day we have been busy in founding our Nation. We are still founding our Nation. The great men who shaped the immortal document that once lay on this table before me were not the only ones who have signed it.

The Declaration of Independence is being signed at this very moment by millions of Americans. It is being signed in spirit by every American with a spark of love for his native land. It is being signed in spirit by every American who labors and plans for the larger good of the country. It is being signed in spirit by any American who contributes any humble thing, be it only the digging of a ditch, to the good and comfort of his fellows.

Wherever a devoted American mother toils and denies herself for the preservation and progress of her family she defies an invisible oppressor and writes her own charter of freedom.

I can not believe that the patriots of old would belittle the moral height of that mother and the thousands of Americans she represents. I can not believe we have lapsed so far.

I will not believe that the men who sat here on July 4, 1776, would be deeply ashamed of the record we bring back to them here on July Fourth of this year.

These are some of the feelings inspired by the great memories that will lurk in this chamber forever.

If we have done thus well with the Nation that the fathers placed in our hands, it is only because we have gone back, faithfully and often, and refreshed ourselves at the fountains of inspiration they left us in their deeds and their character.

If this Nation is to go on to a future without an end, it will be only as we and our children come back, again and again, to these memories of the fathers, to their teachings and to their examples.

It should be our only purpose in celebrating the Fourth of July and the adoption of the Declaration of Independence. This year, next year, and forever, it should be the day when we check our course and set our national compass from that glorious star of patriotic purpose which they set in the eternal heaven of human affairs.

As I speak these words our people are in the midst of material difficulties. We are plagued with personal worries. We are afflicted with discontent and threatened suffering. Because of these discomforts we have turned upon each other in bitter recrimination. It is a time that gives rise to violent differences in politics, in business. Our entire system of life is under fire of criticism.

But even in this we only repeat the experiences of the fathers. They also knew what it was to be vexed with divided counsels and violent clashes of interest.

But in the midst of their perplexities they knew what it was to turn to the calm, serene, steadfast courage and judgment of George Washington. And in 1932, I believe, we are going to turn again and rally about him.

I believe that in 1932 the spirit of George Washington will rise from his tomb in Mount Vernon and bring us together again as the living Washington stilled the storms that swept over the days when he lived in the flesh.

I believe this celebration next year of the Two Hundredth Anniversary of the Birth of George Washington is going to afford the American people the greatest national rallying point they ever have had.

I can see this coming. For more than a year the United States George Washington Bicentennial Commission has been guiding and gathering up the Nation's slumbering interest in its greatest man. I have watched that interest come to life and breathe the fire of enthusiastic vitality.

I see in this a nation swept with a single emotion. It is an impulse on the part of 123,000,000 Americans to forget their differences and rally as one about the rock of this great American's character.

Next year, I predict, George Washington will repeat in spirit the great work that a century and a half ago he performed in fact. He will summon all Americans away from their bickerings and their discontent. He will bid them forget themselves and remember their country. He will bid them rededicate themselves to the giving of self for the good of all.

Out of our deathless love for him he will ask us to reconsecrate ourselves to the great and simple principles upon which he and the framers of the Declaration of Independence built this Nation, to last as long as we keep burning the sacred fires of their example and their leadership.

Out from the moving shadows of this impressive room there comes the spirit of courage and peace. That Divine influence which guided the heroes of the past still lives, still exerts its potent guardianship.

The God, our Father, who placed his benediction upon the founders, will not neglect those of succeeding generations if they remain true to American ideals. The shadows whisper this message; this ancient room bears witness to its truth.

To you, my fellow Americans, I appeal over the distances of space to carry this message as I hear it in the mysterious murmurings of this place. Let us live true, let us guard the heritage these Signers of the Declaration have left to us.

Let us honor and preserve all that they stand for, their memories ever strong in our minds, their spirit ever active in our hearts. Thus, in confidence may we look forward to a united America strong and enduring among the nations of the earth.

Invitation to American Farmers

Address for the National Grange,
Broadcast Over National Broadcasting System
August 15, 1931

I deeply appreciate the courtesy of this opportunity to bring to your attention a typical American farmer. He is one you all know and should know well. The man I have in mind might not be called a great farmer in these days of big scale production. He was, however, the leading farmer of his time and a farmer that every other American farmer can understand.

The farmer I have in mind—and among my Southern friends I should, of course, refer to him as the Planter—

was George Washington, who became one of the great soldiers of history, who won our American independence, who directed the writing of the Constitution, who became the first President of the United States and put our Government in motion.

Beyond all question, he accomplished more great historic achievements than any other American. Yet above and beyond all this, that which he loved best of all and upon which doubtless he would wish to base the remembrance of his fellow Americans, was that he loved the soil, and that he was never happier than in pursuing the activities of his farms.

He went through all the typical problems of other American farmers. Droughts and floods ruined his crops and hurt him financially. He had all the disappointments that come at times to every farmer. But like the true American farmer that he was, this man forever tried to improve his farm and his crops, and to find new and profitable methods of making agriculture pay. He tried new kinds of grains, fruits and vegetables and found new ways of tilling the soil. He even invented a combined plow and drill for his own use. He was not only a farmer, but he was an independent, progressive farmer.

He died long ago. But if he could live again he would still be a farmer because he loved farming above everything else—and he did a great number of other things and did them heroically.

But to his dying day he loved his beautiful estate of Mt. Vernon on the Potomac River a few miles south of the city of Washington, beyond any other spot on earth.

Even during his military campaigns, even when he was President, in all the arduous public duties that came to him, and amid all of the tremendous responsibilities from which he never retreated, his mind forever turned back to his beloved farm at Mt. Vernon.

Whenever public duty allowed him he went back to Mt. Vernon. Through all his public career he found time to send frequent letters to his manager at Mt. Vernon, directing the affairs of his fields and of his live stock. Mt. Vernon was a magnet to which his heart turned. There he lies buried in the heart of the beautiful farm he loved so well.

It is most appropriate that when the Congress of the United States decided to organize a nation-wide celebration in honor of the memory of George Washington, his farming activities should form an important part of that celebration.

For we cannot think of George Washington without remembering that he was a product of the soil. He came from a family of farmers. He was born upon a farm. He knew from the labor of his own hands what farming meant.

Throughout the length and breadth of the nation, beginning February 22 next year, and continuing until Thanksgiving Day, thousands of celebrations will be held among the American people in every hamlet, every farming community, and every home in the United States, so that men and women, boys and girls everywhere, will have an opportunity to pay their tribute to George Washington where he would wish it to be —in the hearts of his own people.

I have been asked to give you an outline of this coming Celebration as organized by the United States George Washington Bicentennial Commission, of which the President of the United States is Chairman, and which I have the honor to serve as Associate Director.

During the year and more that this Commission has been at work, our plans have become widely known. We are not giving an exposition, or a show in any one place. We are not asking the people to come to Washington, or to any other place to take part in any ceremony. We are taking the celebration to the people themselves, so that the Celebration of the Two Hundredth Anniversary of the Birth of George Washington next year will be truly a national tribute, among all Americans living under our flag, to that man who did more than any one else to make our flag a reality and our nation great upon earth.

In organizing this nation-wide celebration, we have naturally solicited the active cooperation of all patriotic bodies of citizens. We realized that without such cooperation there could be no successful celebration. We have, therefore, joined with patriotic societies, schools, libraries, churches, clubs and all similar bodies of people so that organization assistance could be given us throughout the nation.

We have felt the need of means by which we could reach the great agricultural people of the country. That means has been supplied by the National Grange and other great organizations of farmers and by the 4-H clubs of boys and girls of the country. We are now working out plans so that the active cooperation of all of these citizens can be secured in promoting the Celebration next year.

Surely if any class of our citizens should be interested in honoring the memory of George Washington it should be those who live upon the farms, and I am convinced that if George Washington himself could influence this Celebration in his honor, he would take no greater delight than in having his name and his services commemorated among the farmers of today.

We are not asking that elaborate preparations be made. We are not seeking or expecting that great sums of money be spent upon any forms of celebration. Rather do we hope that the memory of George Washington will be honored as he would have it honored, in a simple, sincere tribute, among those who love America and those who would see it preserved.

The United States Commission has issued hundreds of thousands of books, posters, plays, pageants, and material of similar kinds upon the life and achievements of George Washington. From our offices in the National Capital we have sent out a steady stream of information concerning the celebration that has reached every nook and corner of our land and has also extended into many other parts of the world. We have prepared plans and programs of celebration for every kind of organization. These plans we have consistently attempted to make simple and inexpensive. In fact, in the vast majority of these celebrations, there will be no expense whatever involved.

Any organization, at its regular meeting, may have an address or a little playlet that will not involve financial expenditure, but will be a valued part of the nation-wide tribute.

In 1932 our Government will issue special George Washington coins and postage stamps. The mint will stamp a special medal to be awarded by the United States George Washington Bicentennial Commission as prizes in oratorical and essay contests in schools and colleges. We are preparing plays, pageants, motion pictures of George Washington's life, radio addresses, posters, booklets and similar material in large quantities which are given away free to the people of the United States so that every group of American patriots may take active part in these honors to the Father of Our Country.

The response of the American people to these efforts we are making is indeed wonderful. Every one of our forty-eight States and our Territories has appointed State and Territorial Commissions to organize the celebration within its boundaries.

All of these people are enthusiastically behind the efforts of the United States George Washington Bicentennial Commission, to make the coming celebration the greatest tribute ever paid a human being in the history of the world.

Next year an entire nation of 123,000,000 people will rise to a new patriotism and a new unity of devotion to country, as we review the labors of George Washington in founding our country and presenting to the world a new model of freedom and opportunity in the enjoyment of life.

I ask every American farmer especially, to join in this mighty tribute to another American farmer who knew from his own experience every trial and yet every satisfaction that comes to those patriots whom he himself would honor the most—those who perform the great work of tilling the soil and feeding the nation. See that your homes, your churches, your schools, join with the millions of other Americans next year in this grand hymn of gratitude to the man to whom we owe nearly all we have and enjoy, in this greatest nation that the world has known.

FORT NECESSITY GROUND-BREAKING CEREMONY

Address Delivered at Fort Necessity, Pennsylvania, and Broadcast Nationally Through Station KDKA, Pittsburgh, Pa., September 29, 1931

We are here to break ground for a national monument long neglected; to perform a duty long overdue.

It pleases me to think that the motive leading us now to the building of this monument comes from the approaching world-wide celebration next year of the Two Hundredth Anniversary of the Birth of George Washington, an enterprise which I have had the honor to advance as Director of the United States Commission created by Congress for that purpose.

The entire nation is aroused to a feeling that the coming Anniversary will serve not only as a measure of George Washington's greatness, but as a measure of our progress as his countrymen. In that feeling we are turning to Washington with a new and burning interest in everything he did, and with a new sense of the great debt we owe him.

So I can say with excellent reason that amid all we do in George Washington's honor next year, the dedication of this monument at Fort Necessity will be one of the most appropriate and outstanding tributes we can pay him.

For here, on this sacred soil, once reddened with patriot blood, George Washington began his labors in our behalf. We, of the United States of today, who stand here, represent the results of what he here began.

In this place George Washington opened the eyes of the world to North America, and stirred two great nations to possess it.

Here he first inspired the Colonies to possess it for themselves.

Where we now stand a boy of 22 changed the map of the world and altered the course of history.

All our own struggles for freedom, for the right to go our own way, came 20 years later. But to this point we may trace all those threads of influence that culminated in the War of the Revolution.

Here, in reality, began the United States of America. And here, in a forge of fire, was welded the courage and the character of a man who chiefly made us what we are.

If ever a few acres of American soil deserve to be marked out forever, it is this site of young George Washington's "Fort Necessity."

With all my heart I congratulate the people of this community, of this State, and of the nation, in liberally contributing to this splendid enterprise. You have allowed no discouragement to stand in your way. Next year we shall dedicate the fruits of your patriotic self-sacrifice, in your gift of this monument to the nation.

But we are here for a purpose beyond ourselves. It is our privilege on this occasion to rewrite American history, as George Washington himself wrote it here, in deeds of blazing valor.

For years historians have regarded Washington's fight at Fort Necessity as a defeat. Washington himself was unaware, at the time, of the real significance of what he had done, and wrote to his brother that he was "soundly beaten."

Now the events that then confused him have cleared. Not only that, we have found long-buried contemporary records, which I am here giving to the country perhaps for the first time.

I am straining no terms of language, I am twisting no facts of history, in pronouncing this fight at Fort Necessity not only a great moral victory for George Washington, but a potential military success.

To understand what he did, let us take ourselves back 177 years. Let us stand here at George Washington's side, facing the tremendous odds that we now know he defied.

It is 1754. Pioneering American settlers have penetrated this region, and so have wakened England and France to what this great wilderness is worth. Now both these nations are reaching for the prize. The French are driving our settlers out and fencing the region off with a line of forts from Quebec to New Orleans.

Virginia's Governor intends to stop this, and the year before sent George Washington, a youth of 21 and almost alone, to warn the French out of this, our territory. It is a miracle for him to come out of the wilderness alive, but he brings back word that the French are determined to stick.

It alarms the Colonies. Some of them act at once. Virginia sends Capt. Trent to build a fort of her own at the forks of the Ohio. Ample forces are to back him up.

George Washington, now a lieutenant-colonel and second in command, heads the vanguard of a few hundred men. He is ordered to stick to defence, but fight if he must. Soon his superior officer dies of an accident, and Washington is in sole command of the expedition —at 22, the age of a West Point cadet.

Early in April he strikes across the Maryland line and over the mountains, cutting his road as he goes—for the supporting artillery that never arrives. Reinforcements of more than 1,000 men are promised him and only a handful ever reach him.

It takes him two months to get a little beyond this place. His food runs short. The only plentiful thing is alarming news.

He learns that the little Virginia fort at the forks of the Ohio has been taken by the French. The meaning of that is war—with George Washington a boy never before in battle, sixty miles from his base of supplies, in a wilderness crowded with enemies, while his provisions vanish, his men tire, and no adequate reinforcements appear. Only the French receive substantial reinforcements.

Against such odds, retreat would not have been a disgrace. Washington chose to fight it out.

It may be that the amazing sense of clear judgment he possessed compelled him to stand. Retreat would have meant the loss of his Indian allies and perhaps the desertion of his men. But I think that what settled the matter was the Washington spirit. Again he was there on a definite errand, and it was the Washington habit to do what he set out to do.

He wrote to his Governor, "I doubt not if you hear I am beaten, but you will at the same time hear that we have done our duty in fighting as long as there was a possiblity of hope."

Those words alone justify this monument here.

He heard of a scouting party of French beyond the Great Meadows and attacked it, killing several including the commander, Jumonville, and taking the rest prisoners except one who escaped to tell the tale. Returning to the Meadows he began the erection of a rough fortification with a palisade which later he named Fort Necessity. This he completes on June 1, and having by reinforcements increased his command to 400 advanced again, meeting almost insuperable difficulties, and failing to receive necessary supplies. When it became known that a superior French force was advancing against him a retirement was decided upon. When Fort Necessity was reached a halt became necessary and here the French and Indian force overtook him. This force has generally been stated to have been about 900, more than double Washington's, and it may have been considerably larger.

Military engineers of today have criticized Washington for planting his fort here in the open, surrounded by woods on higher ground.

He knew his business. He knew French and Indians fought from behind trees. He knew the range of their muskets. He planted himself where his enemies, in order to hit him must leave their shelter and be hit themselves.

Precisely this happened. But only now do we learn the full facts, from accounts at the time, some of them supplied by Washington himself, as published in a remote Colonial newspaper, and buried from sight until now.

On July 3, at 11 o'clock in the morning, one of Washington's sentinels opened fire. It is reported that he killed three Frenchmen before hurrying to the fort. The action was on.

Washington drew up his forces before the trenches, ready to die to the last man, but alert not to be fooled.

At first the enemy kept at long range, hoping to draw Washington's fire. It must have amazed the young colonel not to be charged by an enemy of such strength. Finally he ordered his men behind the trenches to shoot it out, wherever an enemy left his shelter.

For nine hours of a rainy day, until 8 o'clock at night, his men did shoot, and only now do we know that every man in his command accounted for one of the foe. This old newspaper tells us that 300 French and Indians were killed, and large numbers were wounded, although the French acknowledged a much smaller loss.

That is why Washington was further amazed when the French twice called him to parley. Twice he declined, suspecting a trick. Twice he declined the terms presented him and compelled a change. Finally, at midnight, in a driving rain, he did agree to terms that he largely shaped himself.

Washington lost some 30 men killed and 70 wounded, but, again the old newspaper tells us, all that night and part of the next day his enemies were secretly burying their dead and removing their wounded.

In the morning they marched away to the west with all their remaining numbers, while George Washington and his little band trooped east, their drums beating, their flags flying. He had stood off more than twice his number and sent them away, glad to be gone.

Can that be called a defeat?

The immediate consequence of the fight that happened where we stand was to make young Colonel Washington a man discussed all over Europe. The ultimate consequences of what he did here were the retirement of the French, our War for Independence, and the creation of the United States.

Can that be called a defeat?

Do we not rather see the hand of Destiny asserting itself even thus early in the life of the nation, in the fact that George Washington marched his men proudly away from this Fort on a date later to become more memorable still—the 4th of July?

Did I say the hand of Destiny? It was the hand of Almighty God. For never in my heart have I been more convinced of an intervening Providence in the affairs of men, than the conviction which has come to me through a study of the life of George Washington.

From boyhood, until he passed beyond this life, George Washington was an instrument chosen by the Ruler of us all for a career which shaped the history of the world.

Through all his trials, perils, sufferings and sacrifices, he was upheld by that strong consecration to duty which comes only to those chosen of God. In my heart I know that the unseen hand of Divine Providence itself guided the career of this most useful of mortals, and in paying tribute to the life and character of George Washington we acknowledge the source of his greatness and of his power.

George Washington never met defeat. His was a triumphant and successful career, always. What we may term defeats were mere incidents in a chain of sublime achievements.

It is high time we took this battle of Great Meadows out of the shadows of defeat and placed it in the glorious light of triumph and military success.

In raising this monument, we are commemorating more than the glory of arms. We are for the first time truly interpreting the genius of a man and the genius of a people.

It is twice hallowed soil where we stand. George Washington thought so much of these consecrated acres that fifteen years after the battle he bought Great Meadows and kept it until his death.

Next year, on this historic ground, we shall dedicate a monument of stone. Around it, throughout the land and throughout the year, we shall raise a still greater monument—the monument of a nation's gratitude, felt in a nation's heart.

Yet even this is not all we shall have built in George Washington's memory. The greatest of all memorials to George Washington is spoken of by a forgotten biographer, in words that I wish to repeat:

"There is a greater Washington monument, still unfinished but appropriate and significant in all its parts. It covers an area bounded by the lakes and the gulf, the Atlantic and the Pacific. Its final completion may be delayed for centuries, but the quantity of treasure lavished upon it, and the number of workmen employed, increases from year to year; for expense is no object while the country is persuaded that it is perfecting a monument to Washington after Washington's own plans—the United States of America."

So, we the People, are the real memorial to George Washington. Let us see, next year and forever, that we worthily wear his name engraved upon our hearts. Let us truly live according to his precept and example, that the glory of our country may never be dimmed, that our flag may never be dishonored, and that a free, enlightened and happy people may rightfully claim kinship with the immortal George Washington.

George Washington, the Builder

Address Delivered at the Meeting of the National Rivers and Harbors Congress, Willard Hotel, Washington, D. C., December 8, 1931

You have honored me with an invitation to tell you of the celebration that we of the United States George Washington Bicentennial Commission have prepared for America's commemoration in 1932 of the Two Hundredth Anniversary of the Birth of George Washington.

I am going to respond by telling you *how* we are going to celebrate, but first of all *why* we celebrate. And I am going to begin with the reasons why the great occasion next year is of special interest and importance to you members of the National Rivers and Harbors Congress.

For George Washington belonged to your organization a hundred and fifty years before it was formed, and when it consisted of one member. That member was George Washington himself.

What I mean by that is, that George Washington was the first man in America to see the immense importance of transportation. And he set up a drive for improved communication that he kept up with all his energy until he died.

George Washington saw the importance of transportation in two lights—the commercial aspect, and the political. He knew that if the scattered elements of this country were to grow commercially, they needed transportation facilities for the exchange of their goods. He knew that if they were to form a political Union, they needed transportation facilities to bind their interests together.

No man saw this as clearly as George Washington saw it. No other man had traveled over the country so extensively as he had. No man of the time so thoroughly knew and understood the American people and their needs. No man so fully realized that without proper means of transportation, the country would fall apart. And no other man had the everlasting energy to get behind such a movement and put it through.

George Washington had seen all this from his early youth. As soon as he was able to realize anything, he realized the importance of transportation, and the longer he lived the more vigorously he strove for its extension and improvement.

He was not only a strong advocate, he was an organizer. He not only wrote about developing transportation in order to interest other people, but helped to form companies to carry out his ideas. It became one of the great interests and efforts of his life.

I am safe in saying that after the winning of the Revolution, and after the founding of the United States Government, the creation of better roads and waterways was the third major interest in the life of George Washington.

In the reverence we all feel toward George Washington, we are naturally inclined to render him the fullest possible credit for all his endless labors in the building of our nation; but there is no disputing the fact that water and land transportation, as we know it today and are destined to know it in the future, owes everything that it is and will be to the vision and the labors of George Washington. That great credit does belong to him. And let us render it to him in full.

This is the thought I want to develop this evening. And when I speak of George Washington's hand in the development of American transportation, I mean the three forms of it which you include in the three-circled emblem of your organization—River, Road and Rail. All three of them, singly and together, derive straight from the thought and the effort of George Washington—as I think you will agree, when I have sketched in the picture.

By the time George Washington was 19 years of age he was occupied with big problems. He was concerned with big business of the day. He was surveying for one of the biggest landowners of the times, and he was in the confidence of a brother who was interested in the Ohio Company, an organization formed to develop the Great West.

At the age of 21, George Washington saw this great new open country for himself, and had good reason for seeing it. His Governor had sent him on an important errand—to demand that the French troops withdraw from the Ohio territory.

When he was 22, Virginia and the Ohio Company were through with merely telling the French to get out. They sent out armed forces to drive the French out of what was then the Great West, and George Washington was at the head of the troops.

The next year the British sent Braddock to oust the French. In the end the French got out. But the important thing is that George Washington saw two big things that stuck in his mind for the rest of his life.

He saw the enormous riches of Western America, as it was then, and he saw the enormous importance of tapping those riches by means of roads or other means of transportation. And he never forgot what he then had learned.

He had seen Braddock defeated mainly by having to lag and delay while he built a road for his army.

So the lesson of roads, roads, roads, was branded on George Washington's brain while he was still a young man.

From that time on he became the greatest traveler of his time. And wherever he went, the lesson of roads was always present. His Diaries are full of his complaints at the terrible condition of the roads.

When he married and settled at Mount Vernon, and became a farmer, the question of transportation was more than ever brought to his mind, because he had goods of his own to transport. He used the river that flowed past his farms, and here the importance of waterway transportation took a firm grip on his mind.

As early as 1754, he had seen the advantages of water transportation. Now that he was settled at Mount Vernon, he had time to think and do something about it.

Before the Revolution broke out, he was busy with a project to improve the navigation of the Potomac, with an astounding idea for that time—the linking of the Potomac with the Ohio River by means of a portage by land across the mountains of Pennsylvania.

The Revolutionary War put a stop to this for a time. But the War itself only impressed deeper on George Washington's mind the conviction that the country must be united, if it was to last, and that the great need for this was better communication.

In 1783, while the Revolution was still on, he paid his historic visit to northern New York. His outward purpose was to inspect the army posts, as Commander in Chief. In reality he wanted to inspect the proposed route of the Erie Canal, that possible rival of the waterway he long before had planned from the Potomac to the Ohio.

Soon after the Revolution, he set out from Mount Vernon to find the best possible route to tap the rich Ohio Valley.

In a word, he became a Rivers and Harbors Congress all by himself.

Throughout his busy life he remained just that. And as I have already said, he not merely advocated better means of transportation, he everlastingly worked to that end, being the intensely practical man that he was. And it goes without saying that the country has never seen a greater man at the business. With his complete disinterestedness and his high reputation, he probably accomplished more in this way to wake up the country than by the company he formed or the daring engineering works he started, in building canals and deepening rivers.

In 1784, when he got back from this newest trip to the West, he wrote first of all to Governor Benjamin Harrison, of Virginia, urging immediate appointment of commissioners to get busy and survey every mile of the Potomac and the James, from tidewater to their sources, together with every stream tributary to the Ohio, with the ultimate aim of adding the Great Lakes to his scheme of transportation, and Detroit as a great port and outpost of trade.

For the time this was a gigantic scheme of public improvement, but its vastness only encouraged Washington to labor the harder for it. He appeared before committees of the Virginia and Maryland legislatures. He used his great influence and wrote voluminous letters to other influential men. He even looked into Rumsey's contraption that preceded the steamboat.

And he got things going. The Potomac Company came into being, largely because of his efforts, and he invested $10,000 in its stock and served as its president. This project was the construction of the locks and the stretch of canal at Great Falls, on the Potomac, to link his water route from the sea to the Lakes, over the ridges of Pennsylvania. The wonderful locks of this construction still remain to us.

So, if the story of George Washington's work for transportation is a story of struggle, it is also a story of magnificent accomplishment. It was a struggle against indifference, against opposition, against financial handicaps, against the obstacles of Nature itself.

But there is not the shadow of a doubt that the transportation system of America today—by river, by road, and even by rail—has grown from the vision, the planning, and the driving energy of George Washington.

He never lived to see more than the beginnings of what he had achieved. But two years after his death, the Potomac Company paid a 5½ percent dividend. In not many years longer the Chesapeake & Ohio Canal followed the line he laid down. And most astounding of all, in 1834 the Jauniata Canal in Pennsylvania was linked with the West by a portage haul over the mountains at the very point that Washington had picked.

It is all eloquent testimony to the fact that in the power to see and plan on the grand continental scale, George Washington was potentially one of the greatest of engineers, even though he was too busy at other great things to be an engineer in actual practice.

It is true that Stephenson's locomotive and the railroad came after Washington's death. But another eloquent fact remains—that the first practical railroad, the Baltimore & Ohio, ran its line beside the water route to the West laid down not long before by George Washington. He it was who had pointed the way.

And not much later the Pennsylvania Railroad crossed the Alleghenies beside the same portage route that Washington was the first to indicate.

All this George Washington achieved without thought of personal gain, except as he was entitled to benefit as an investor in the enterprise he had founded. Yet, had he been grasping and selfish, he might have made himself enormously rich. As a result of his development of transportation, George Washington's coal lands in Pennsylvania later brought 20 millions of dollars.

He did it all for his country. Behind all of George Washington's mighty efforts to give the country its needed transportation, was the political vision of the great statesman.

All through his life, Washington had seen the need of Union, if the country was to survive. We know the part he played in bringing about that political Union. We know his constant fear of its breaking apart. All through his two administrations as President, George Washington was troubled with the spectre of dis-union. The great Farewell Address is tinged with this foreboding.

This was the other reason, the political reason, why he toiled so hard to see the East and the West, the North and the South, bonded together in ties that began in commercial exchange and ended in political solidarity.

We know, now, how well he succeeded. We are assembled here in the city that he himself founded, and that he placed on this particular spot as a part of his dream of transportation.

He wanted the very capital of government to stand at the head of tide-water and at the beginning of his vast vision of a water route to the West, so that it might grow from the growth of the whole country.

So there is abundant reason why this meeting of the Rivers and Harbors Congress should turn its mind to thoughts of George Washington, the first and the greatest advocate and promoter of America's transportation.

It is why the members of this organization, and why every American concerned for the growth and welfare of his country, should have a personal interest and an active part in the honors we are to pay to this man to whose greatness we owe whatever is great in ourselves and our country.

I have told you some of the reasons *why* you and all America should honor the memory of George Washington. Let me tell you now something of *how* we expect the nation to do so, as planned by the United States George Washington Bicentennial Commission.

Seven years ago, in 1924, Congress took a long look ahead and saw the importance in our national history of the Two Hundredth Anniversary of the Birth of George Washington in 1932. It saw the necessity of planning for a fit commemoration of such an event, and accordingly passed a joint resolution creating the United States George Washington Bicentennial Commission.

It was understood from the beginning that the American people would need no urging in the matter of celebrating the two hundredth birthday of the greatest American. The purpose of the United States George Washington Bicentennial Commission was but to guide and harmonize this national impulse.

As Associate Director of this Commission, I can safely say that we have fulfilled this purpose. With the opening of the celebration now less than three months away, it begins to be clear that next year the American people will rise in the greatest tribute ever accorded any man in all history. I believe I can say, further, that these honors will be of the kind that George Washington himself would approve.

From the beginning we planned no world's fair, no great exposition, no show of our material progress. We had in mind no one central celebration, or group of such celebrations, to which the people would be invited to come.

We planned instead to carry the celebration to the people themselves. Better than that, we planned to let the people themselves do all the celebrating. And that is what they are going to do, in every state, city, and town in the nation, in every country abroad, all over America and all over the world.

Furthermore, this celebration which the people are to undertake is to be held where George Washington would wish them to hold it—in their schools and churches, in their homes, in the hearts of a grateful people. From beginning to end, it is to be an outpouring of the spirit, and not a material show.

Our people have been left to shape in whatever form and manner they please this tribute they are ready to pay to the Father of Our Country. We of the Commission have striven, only, to aid, to suggest, to inform the people, and to offer them plans and programs.

This we have done, and faithfully done. Our first duty to the people was to bring before them George Washington and his history in true human form. To carry out the desire of Congress "that future generations of Americans may live according to the example and precepts of his exalted life and character and thus perpetuate the American Republic."

In order to perform this most important service, the United States George Washington Bicentennial Commission engaged the services of eminent historians who have searched the whole record of Washington's life, from the cradle to the grave. Their findings have been put into brief and readable form, and offered to the people of America in pamphlets, programs and newspaper releases.

In November, the month just closed, more than 20,000 of these sharp and accurate pen-pictures of the real George Washington were published by the newspapers of America.

It has been called "an entire nation sitting in on the greatest history lesson ever taught."

But this widespread publication and reading of George Washington's story means far more than that. It is living proof of the tremendous hold that George Washington still has, and will ever have, on the hearts and minds of the American people.

It means that the people of this country are never tired of hearing of George Washington. It means that they want to draw close to him and understand him. It means that they are glad to discover, at last, that George Washington was not a cold and aloof man, but a human being like themselves. Our people want to love George Washington, and this is what we have enabled them to do, with these intimate, touching glimpses into his warm heart, his busy mind, and his kindly character.

Our whole people are going to turn back to George Washington in 1932 in a new understanding, in a new dedication to the principles he laid down, in a new patriotism patterned after his, in a new willingness to think of country before the serving of self.

It is in such a spirit that we are going to stage the greatest celebration ever held in the history of civilization. During the year and a half that the United States George Washington Bicentennial Commission has been actively at work in organizing this demonstration, I have sat in awe as I watched this spirit grow among our people, until it has become a great national movement. Next year, I predict, the people of America will rally behind George Washington's memory as our forefathers rallied about him in the flesh. I predict that George Washington's spirit will rise and summon this country out of its trials into new triumphs of achievement, precisely as he did when he carried the Revolution to victory, directed the writing of our Constitution, and launched the new Government on its way to greatness. This is something of the national impulse that is destined to express itself when we open this celebration next year.

Just as we planned to hold no one central celebration, in the city of Washington or anywhere else, so we are planning not to confine the celebration to any one day. It will begin on Washington's Birthday, and it will end only on Thanksgiving Day in 1932. And every intervening local and national holiday will everywhere be marked by ceremonies linking that day with the memory of George Washington. What he did for our Country has its part in them all—Patriots' Day, Constitution Day, and every other day of local or national significance.

Congress laid upon the United States George Washington Bicentennial Commission the duty of engaging the cooperation of the States, in this undertaking. This we have done, so that every State now has a cooperating Bicentennial Commission, to transmit to its people the thrill of energy and purpose flowing from the United States Commission as the central clearing-house and power-house of all.

I cannot begin to tell you of all the suggestions and helpful plans that have flowed out in every direction from the United States Bicentennial Commission. It is hard to give you even a comprehensive outline.

But we began with the youngest generation—the children in the kindergarten and the grade schools. We prepared for them new accounts of George Washington to stir their interest, warm their hearts, and quicken their patriotism. We have sent to each classroom of America a large size portrait of George Washington. We have carried the same effort up through the colleges, with complete courses of study in the life and achievements of George Washington.

We have arranged oratorical, essay and declamatory contests on the subject of George Washington's life. We have had designed for use a special medal by a noted artist to be struck off at the United States Mint, as an award to the best pupils and students in these contests.

In order to give the people an opportunity to participate actively in the coming celebration, we have had specialists prepare a large and varied number of plays and pageants picturing Washington's time—all for free distribution to any responsible group. Nothing, we thought, would give our people such pleasure, or serve to bring back more vividly the very scenes and incidents of his life. These have been eagerly sought, from every locality, so that in 1932 the country will be alive with pageantry, brightened by the colors of Colonial uniform and costume, and enlivened by the very music George Washington loved to hear.

Our Post Office will issue twelve commemorative postage stamps of the occasion. Our Treasury Department will issue a special George Washington quarter dollar to supplant the regular coin in 1932.

These are but a few features. The year 1932 will belong to George Washington. The country will belong to him. Our hearts will belong to him. For nine months, 123 millions of people will pour out their praise and gratitude to God for His gift to us and to the world of George Washington, one of the greatest and noblest characters that our Divine Ruler ever created.

HALL CLOCK OF MARY BALL WASHING-
TON, MOTHER OF GEORGE WASHINGTON,
PRESERVED AT KENMORE, THE HOME OF
HER DAUGHTER, BETTY LEWIS, IN
FREDERICKSBURG, VIRGINIA.

THE HOME OF MARY BALL WASHINGTON, MOTHER OF
GEORGE WASHINGTON, IN FREDERICKSBURG, VIRGINIA,
PRESERVED AS A SHRINE. THE HOUSE WAS BOUGHT BY
GEORGE WASHINGTON FOR HIS MOTHER AND HERE SHE
LIVED FROM BEFORE THE REVOLUTION UNTIL HER DEATH,
AUGUST 25, 1789. HER BEDROOM IN WHICH SHE DIED
AND WHERE SHE SAW HER ILLUSTRIOUS SON FOR THE LAST
TIME, IS THE CORNER ROOM WITH THE CLOSED SHUTTERS.

At the Home of Mary Ball Washington

Address Delivered at the Mary Ball Washington Home, Fredericksburg, Va., Broadcast by the National Broadcasting Company, January 1, 1932

I am speaking to the people of the United States from a shrine made sacred by its immortal memories.

I am in the home of Mary Ball Washington, mother of George Washington, in historic Fredericksburg, Virginia. Beside me is an object of special reverence. It is the most precious timepiece in all America. This beautiful "grandfather" clock belonged to Mary Washington and solemnly tolled the passing hours when George and his mother met here in that exalted communion of mother and son.

In a few minutes this clock of artistic design and fully eight feet tall, will strike for the mothers and sons of our country the twelve strokes that will mark the first high noon of 1932, the two hundredth anniversary year of George Washington's birth.

You will hear over the infinite spaces of the air the resonant tones of the very clock that voiced the hour when our greatest American opened his eyes to a waiting world. Those first sweet notes of an historic hour will re-echo through the universe. They will never die away but will continue on and on until the end of recorded time. The impulses of those vibrations surround us today, after two hundred years, and will exert their invisible influences upon us as long as America lives.

When this clock strikes again it will be the voice of history and Destiny itself, calling us back to our own.

I know of no more significant expression of this solemn hour. And surely there could be no more appropriate setting where this reverential act could be staged, than in this bed-room, with the hush of the years upon it, yet vibrant with the echoes of the past.

They crowd upon me—those sweet voices of the dead. I am oppressed and confused by the voices so long silent, that strive to speak again. For every article in this low-ceilinged room bears witness to those touching and dramatic scenes that were enacted here.

I face the colonial fireplace where comfort glowed and which symbolizes the beautiful provision the dutiful George Washington made for his aged and ailing mother. By its side is the low chair where she sat those many, and oft-times lonely hours, thinking of her boy, leading his tattered troops in war. Can we not read in these contemplations the anxiety, the fears, the love and the prayers of that mother who gave to humanity so great a son and who sent him forth with noble self-sacrifice to serve his fellow men?

Here by this window I look out upon scenes perhaps little changed from that day when Mary waited for her son's return.

Out through the garden door I see the Colonial kitchen with its utensils for domestic concerns much as they were when Mary, with her own hands, prepared her boy's favorite cakes. Beyond, through the serene beds of old Virginia flowers I see the box-bordered walks that led to beautiful Kenmore, the mansion home of George's sister, Betty, who kept careful watch upon her mother's comfort when he was far away.

And shortly before the outbreak of the Revolution, he bought for his mother this modest house, among her friends in Fredericksburg, amid the scenes and the people she loved. Here, in this quaint old house in which I speak, he placed her to live out her days in peace.

So our return to this house is sanctified by some of the most beautiful memories of American history. The walls of this house are witness to the most sacred hours in George Washington's life, the hours when he was at his greatest and best—the hours when he came back from war and chambers of State, from stress and turmoil of public life to seek counsel at the knees of his adored mother. This same clock which you will hear measured those precious hours.

When the notes come to you the memory of these scenes in George Washington's life cannot fail to inspire in each heart an exalted feeling of gratitude and love for the mother and the son.

Hardly had George Washington grown to manhood before his countrymen realized his qualities of leadership and gave him important duties and responsibilities, greater perhaps than were ever placed upon the shoulders of mortal man.

I know that the women of America in whose breasts beat the universal heart of motherhood, can realize how Mary Washington longed for her boy. Mothers of America who have lost sons in battle know with what trembling, with what prayerful anxiety, Mary Washington sat here waiting for his home-coming. I know that the mothers of Americans everywhere join with me in the conviction that those prayers which were uttered here in this room to the God of infinite mercy, had their answer then as they have now.

Those prayers gave George Washington to the world. They saved him in time of peril and they have preserved his spirit which surrounds us all at this moment. Here in this house where he placed her to live in comfort, he always returned as often as he could.

He came to see her in sickness and in health. He came to ask as to her comfort. Even when mountainous cares of state came to burden George Washington's mind, and crowded his life with labor, he always found time for a visit to his mother. May we not think with truth that this great man returned here for that spiritual guidance that so influenced his eventful career. May we not feel that he came here because at his mother's knee he felt closer to God.

George Washington resembled his mother in many ways. Mary Washington gave more than a great son to the world—she gave herself.

Something of George Washington, the boy, lived on in George Washington, the man. He never went away on an errand of great importance without first visiting his mother to receive her blessing.

And for the unselfish sacrifice of Mary Washington God rewarded her as no other American mother has ever been rewarded. She saw her son grow tall and strong and she saw him raised to greatness that no other man of our country has ever surpassed. She saw him acclaimed by all the world, adored by his fellow men. And yet to her he was always the son, the boy—her George.

At last it was permitted Mary Washington to greet her son at the end of his physical danger. For here he came after Yorktown. He had won the war of the Revolution. He had made America independent. He had made these United States of ours forever free. He stood at the pinnacle of his greatness—a colossal figure in the world.

Possibly he had seen her when he and Rochambeau passed through Fredericksburg on their way to command at the great siege now so propitiously terminated; but there is a tradition that she had gone beyond the Blue Ridge at the time of Cornwallis's foray and not yet returned. After the siege he had hastened to Eltham to stand at the death bed of his beloved stepson, John Parke Custis; and the sad duties of that disaster attended to, he was again on the road for Philadelphia by way of Fredericksburg and Mount Vernon, accompanied probably only by his military family and escort.

Yet when he came to Fredericksburg, crowned with the laurels of success, his mind, I am sure, went back to the days when he was a little boy and he and his mother were impoverished and obscure. He came here to this house, not with the pomp and glory of the mighty warrior; not as a hero of a grateful people, but as the son. He came alone, on foot.

He had discarded the trappings of command. He was the son. Here at this window through which I am now looking sat the mother, waiting as she had done so many times before, for those familiar footsteps.

Here in this room where I am now standing, with this clock ticking away their all-too-brief time together, they met again. Upon that meeting the veil of time has closed, as too sacred a thing for other eyes to witness.

He came again in February, 1784, under even more auspicious circumstances, for America was at peace at last, recognized by the parent country as an independent nation. He came, as he wrote General Knox, "to pay my duty to an aged mother." But Fredericksburg turned the visit into a celebration, and there was an address and reply, a public dinner, and a grand ball—Fredericksburg's Peace Ball.

When George Washington saw his mother for the last time it was in this room and he was still a greater man, for the people of the United States had demanded with one voice that he be their First President.

Yet he could not assume this office given him with such overwhelming public trust, without first coming here to Fredericksburg, to this little house to receive the blessing of his now fast-failing mother. It was probably the sweetest re-union of their lives and it was God's will that this meeting should be their last.

Mary Washington knew it. A wasting disease was eating her life away. In vain her great son tried to put away her fears and looked forward to seeing her again and again. Mary Washington stilled him with this immortal blessing: "You will see me no more; my great age and disease warn me that I shall not be long for this world: I trust in God that I may be somewhat prepared for a better. But go, George, fulfill the high destinies which Heaven appears to have intended for you; go, my son, and may Heaven's and a mother's blessing be with you always."

These words were only too true. It was not long after this scene that Mary Washington died to the ticking of this old clock.

The whispering voices still crowd upon me. The solemnity of this scene chokes my voice. I can only bow my head in reverence and ask my countrymen everywhere to join in tribute to the memory of the great mother and the immortal son.

To the People of Somerville, Mass.

Address Broadcast from Washington, D. C.,
to Somerville, Massachusetts
January 1, 1932

I congratulate the Mayor of Somerville, its George Washington Bicentennial Committee and all its people for the enthusiasm, the patriotism and the unselfish endeavor they have thrown into their preparations for joining the whole United States this year when America and the world celebrate the Two Hundredth Anniversary of the Birth of George Washington.

As you know, Congress created the United States George Washington Bicentennial Commission, of which I am the Director, for the express purpose of linking together such activities as yours with those of every other city and town in our great country, so that all Americans may honor George Washington this year in one great chorus of reverence and gratitude.

So it has been my pleasure to watch the growth of your plans from the beginning, and I want to say to you now that the people of Somerville, of Boston, and of all Massachusetts and through the East, have set an example to the entire country.

Your section of the United States was honored by the very presence of George Washington at some of the most critical moments of our history. Now you have risen to return this honor by commemorating those historic occasions in ways that are beautiful in their appropriateness.

The whole of the United States may well pause at this instant and listen to what you people of Somerville do and say today. For on the sacred soil which it is your privilege to occupy, occurred one of the most momentous, the most significant, and the most beautiful events in our national existence.

That moment came when George Washington raised on Prospect Hill in Somerville the first flag representing the American people.

It might be said that with that act, George Washington first made us a nation, in giving his patriot countrymen their first rallying point as a united people.

The flag he raised was soon to be made still more faithfully representative of American ideals and American unity. But the banner that Washington first flung forth in the siege of Boston was the first emblem that informed England and the world that here was a people with determination to be free.

You do well to commemorate a moment that lives in our history surrounded with a meaning so profound for us all. I hope the whole nation draws from your example the lesson we all must learn this year—the lesson of new thought for country, a new devotion to the great man who gave of himself so generously to build and make it secure.

I congratulate you all for still another reason, it is because your patriotism has been so eager and so prompt. You have not waited for this anniversary year to grow old before launching these honors to Washington. You have chosen the very first day of 1932.

I see in that the sign of an enthusiasm that I believe fills the entire land.

Throughout the two years that we of the United States George Washington Bicentennial Commission have been planning and preparing this Celebration, I have seen the great heart of America slowly swelling with this new love of our greatest and noblest man. And that love has shown itself in the most far off places. For wherever there are Americans, there also is love for George Washington, and this year it is going to come forth and express itself as never before.

I predict to you, my good friends in Somerville, that all over the United States there is going to be found a new Americanism in 1932 that will rise to match your own.

When schoolboys ask to be allowed to "appropriate" funds to our Commission, when bed-ridden preachers offer us all they have—their prayers—when lonely men in the Arctic Circle hang up George Washington's picture as all they can contribute to this Celebration, you and I know that a tribute is coming from the rest of America.

As if in answer to the common instinct, our people have realized that this year of 1932 is a mighty milestone in their history. We see in this year more than an anniversary measuring two hundred years since George Washington's birth. We see in this year a measurement of our own progress and a test of our character as a people.

We can not think of George Washington without thinking whether we have been true to George Washington. We can not think of what he did for us without asking ourselves how worthy we have been to receive it.

We can not think of his labors to found this nation without asking ourselves whether we have kept that nation safe.

We can not remember the great precepts and teachings he left us, without asking how far we have carried them out.

We can not admire the great example of his character without questioning how much we have been impressed by it.

So this year we are going back to the feet of George Washington and ask him to teach us again. We are going to ask him to lead us once more in spirit, as he led his fellow countrymen in the flesh.

This 200th year since Washington's birth is more than an anniversary; it is going to be a rallying point for these United States to unite in a new dedication to that giving of self to country which first made this nation, and is the one spirit which can keep it eternally secure.

I believe it is a feeling that this is the most important thing in life at this moment that moves these Americans everywhere to unite in this patriotic demonstration. I believe it is this feeling that has stirred the people in your community to be the first to open this year of Celebration. I believe the feeling possesses all America, and will lift it into the greatest tribute ever offered any mortal in history—the gratitude of an entire people, reverently offered to the man to whom they owe their all.

And now I want to leave one last word of congratulation with the good citizens of Somerville and New England. It is because you have not allowed the passing cares and perplexities of these times to deter you from this Celebration of George Washington.

Nothing could be more appropriate, in fact, than that we should turn to George Washington in times like these. Who could better cheer us in present anxieties than the man who endured the winter of Valley Forge, who kept waiting during the long years of the Revolution for the victory at Yorktown that crowned all his efforts and justified all his courage.

The historic truth is that our country was born amid trial, and doubt, and suffering. It is also historic truth that almost the one thing that brought the young nation through these trials triumphant was the will, the invincible determination of George Washington, and his utter refusal to think of defeat.

Now these again are "the times that try men's souls," and it is one more reason for turning back, that we may learn again from George Washington, the lesson of his courage and his faith.

Let us make this year we now enter a year-long resolve, not merely to honor George Washington, but to be like him. If we succeed in that, then our country is safe.

AT POHICK CHURCH

ADDRESS OVER COLUMBIA BROADCASTING SYSTEM FROM POHICK CHURCH, VIRGINIA, SUNDAY, FEBRUARY 21, 1932

On a lovely, rolling hill characteristic of Northern Virginia, is one of the most beautiful and historic shrines associated with the life of George Washington. I am privileged today to stand within the ancient walls of Pohick Church, which is as intimately connected with the life of George Washington as Mount Vernon itself.

Here in the reverential stillness of this sacred place I come as a humble pilgrim, and from this place I have been permitted to broadcast to the nation the thoughts and impressions that come to me.

Virginia is unusually rich in its religious history. Dotted over its area are scores of historic churches dating back from the earliest Colonial days. Of all of these fine mementoes of the time of the established church in the Old Dominion, this building is notable, and one of the outstanding landmarks which the hundreds of thousands of tourists who come to this State during the period of the Celebration of the Two Hundredth Anniversary of the Birth of George Washington, should visit.

We are told that the present Pohick Church is located on land selected and purchased by George Washington in 1767, and is successor to the old Pohick Church, a frame building which stood on King's Highway, leading to Occoquan Ferry, a few miles south, which was built about 1690. It is not only a finely preserved type of Colonial brick edifice, but it has a history, romantic and fascinating. Truro Parish was established in 1732, the year of George Washington's birth, and continued to use the old church until about 1767, when it was decided to build a new one some distance from the old.

The new Pohick Church was ready for occupancy by the Congregation in 1772. George Washington drew the plans for this church and as in other similar plans, he went into great detail, not only designating the proportions, the character and the material, but also the decorations and church furniture. We may be sure that he exercised a potent influence in these matters since he had himself purchased the land upon which Pohick Church is located.

When it was proposed to erect this so-called new church, the argument over its location waxed strong, but Washington ended it by making a survey so complete that it indicated the exact distance which each of the parishioners had to travel as between the new and the old sites. In Washington's surveys this location was shown to be nearer and most convenient for the larger number of the church members.

It must be recalled that George Washington was a vestryman of this parish at the time. As in all things with which he was concerned, George Washington took a deep and active interest in the building and the conduct of this church from the time it was planned until his death.

It must be recalled also that the position of vestryman of a parish in Virginia during the time of the established church was a position of considerable civic as well as religious importance.

However, it is not with this side of the church history that we are concerned today. Our whole attention is centered upon the church itself and the intimate relation which it bore to George Washington, his friends and neighbors.

Pohick Church occupies a site directly upon the highway between Washington and Richmond. It is located about three miles beyond the point where the old road branches off from the highway to Mt. Vernon. Within the church yard surrounded by a brick wall there is about an acre and a half of ground in which are the tombs of the parishioners of long ago.

INTERIOR OF CHRIST CHURCH, ALEXANDRIA, VA., WHERE WASHINGTON PURCHASED A PEW IN 1773, AND WHERE HE FREQUENTLY WORSHIPPED WHEN LIVING AT MOUNT VERNON, EIGHT MILES AWAY.

POHICK CHURCH, VIRGINIA. THE PARISH CHURCH OF MOUNT VERNON, SIX MILES DISTANT FROM THE MANSION. IT WAS BUILT DURING THE YEARS 1767-73 FROM PLANS DRAWN BY GENERAL GEORGE WASHINGTON, WHO WAS A MEMBER OF THE BUILDING COMMITTEE. HE WAS A VESTRYMAN OF THE PARISH FOR TWENTY YEARS. HIS PEW IS NUMBER 28 AS SHOWN BY THE NUMBER UPON THE PANEL UNDER HIS INITIALS. THE PLATE UPON THE LEFT IS ON THE DOOR OF THE PEW AND INDICATES THAT GEORGE WASHINGTON WAS A VESTRYMAN IN 1773.

There is an atmosphere of serene tranquility about this edifice, which impresses us like a benediction, and the gentle breezes move through the old oak trees and whisper of the mystery of time. What a colorful, what a romantic, what a beautiful setting for the quiet and dignified events that took place here during the youth of our country.

One can not come to this placid old house of God without drawing aside in his imagination the curtains of the years to look backward to the days when George Washington, his dear family, his friends and neighbors gathered here to worship.

As I look out through the open doorway to the burying ground that holds the ashes of some of the noblest personages of Virginia's great history, to my mind comes back again that pageant of beauty, of citizenship and of neighborly kindness which was witnessed here on those Sunday mornings long ago.

Let us within the limitations of our fancy place ourselves as members of the Mount Vernon family preparing to come to this meeting place nearly 175 years ago.

It was customary for the family at Mount Vernon to attend church regularly and for the usual guests of whom there were always from two to three, to a dozen, to attend with the family, although none was urged to go. Carriages were provided, of course, and an early breakfast was the rule because it consumed practically a day to attend church and return.

Pohick Church is about six miles from Mount Vernon over the old road, but this six miles which now can be traversed upon a beautiful roadway in a few minutes by automobile, was a formidable journey 175 years ago.

Only those who are familiar with the primitive Virginia roads can realize what travelling meant in those days. The road led through the wood and partly swamp ground. In winter it was usually deep in clay, rutted and difficult of passage, except by carriages drawn by from four to six horses. In summer it was dusty and rough, as little care was given to roadways in those days, for water transportation among the plantations along the Potomac was in common usage for transporting goods and produce.

So the coaches going from Mount Vernon to Pohick Church were sturdily built. Some times there were three or four coach loads of family and friends. Men, women and children of the household and guests, in what we would consider somewhat gay attire for such an occasion, went by coach. The servants and retainers of the estate usually travelled horseback following the coaches, ready to lend assistance in case of need.

The great Washington himself with the beloved Martha and the adopted children of Mrs. Washington usually occupied a carriage by themselves. We the house guests intermingle among the other guests in the two or three carriages of this pilgrimage, and we alight with relief at the gate of this ancient church yard.

Here, as General Washington and his party arrive, are gathered many men, women and children who are upon terms of familiar intimacy with the Mount Vernon family. Walking around to the southern entrance which is in reality the original front, we mark the lovely pedimented portals in gray sandstone.

As we pass through these lovely portals we observe the box pew arrangement drawn by Washington, and note the great pulpit standing at the head of the cross aisle in the middle of the north wall of the church. Proceeding to this point of vantage we inspect the more striking details of the church, and we turn to the altar piece.

We are told that if we could see this in its original condition—for the interior of the church has suffered from the ravages and devastations of war—we would mark the gold-lettered Creed, Lord's Prayer and the Ten Commandments in gold leaf, and the ornaments in the tabernacle and the capitols of the pilasters also covered with gold leaf. The palm leaves and festoon design on the pulpit are also covered with gold leaf furnished by George Washington and his dear friend, George William Fairfax.

Immediately in the center of the cross aisle stands the original fount, made by William Copein. This was taken out of the church during the Civil War and was secreted upon a nearby farm. If we follow the Washington family along the west aisle toward the altar piece, we pause at pews 28 and 29 and know that these pews were owned and occupied by Washington and his family on all occasions of public worship.

The form of that worship then resembled closely the form of worship still familiar to the people of this congregation. The Washington family go sedately to the ancient box pew in which we take our seats. This pew and all others of the church has comfortable cushioned benches partitioned off in rectangular form, so that there are seats on three sides and a small gate leading into the aisle. Upon that gate is still a silver plate bearing the name of George Washington.

We now assume that the beautiful service has closed. The congregation has filed sedately into the outer yard where for an hour or so there will be pleasant neighborhood gossip and much comment upon the affairs of the vicinity. Soon all are gone and we stand alone in the hush of this sacred place, and the shadows come creeping into the corners and back into the gallery which was reserved for humble worshippers.

I wish it were in my power to convey through the miracle of radio, the impression of beauty, of stillness, of solemnity, that enfolds me. Again do I people this beautiful room with the images of those long gone. Again do I hear in imagination the whisperings of those who gathered here to worship an everlasting God, who knows neither time nor place. Again do I see those kneeling figures and heads bowed in prayer that echo back through the years as though 'twere yesterday.

Again do I see the mighty form of General Washington, the Father of His Country, kneeling in humble supplication to his Father on high. In simplicity, in child-like faith, the great man bows in prayer. The soft music of forgotten hymns seems to come to me as the echo of an angel's song and I feel that my humble presence here is as it were a ghost that intrudes upon another era, another state of social order, another age when our history as a nation was beginning.

Gone are those mighty souls who left their indelible impress upon our history and our culture. Gone is the romance, the color, the drama of their sumptuous lives. Gone is the rich bounty of old Virginia, although the inheritance of its hospitality will never fade.

Here I feel that exaltation and an emotion that I cannot express in words. Here lingers within walls hallowed by memory the very scent of the old-fashioned flowers.

To Americans everywhere I would that I had the power of bringing you in spirit to my side. To Americans everywhere I would that you could feel this sacred presence as I feel it now. To the hearts of all humanity I would convey the meaning of this place at this moment, that we could all unite in a common impulse of devotion to our God; to a sense of that ancient neighborly friendliness which was actually part of the old-time religion.

I would that we could join together in the simple hymns they sang; be impressed by the devotions of their day and dedicate ourselves to the sincerity, the simplicity and the beauty of their lives. They are not far away. They seem to be here at my side, and the rhapsody of memory exalts my soul to their worship and to mine, in humility in the presence of our common Creator.

We need it, fellow Americans. We need a return not only to the wisdom, the courage and the character of George Washington, but we need a return to his calm faith in the God of human destiny. We need a new consecration to that morality which guides and stimulates the acts of our daily lives. We need a devotion that surmounts difficulties, that overcomes opposition, that triumphs in the relationship of men with men.

These devoted people who builded this church, who worshipped here in these inspirational surroundings, who set us an example of good living, fine companionship and steadfast honor, would bring us back again into the stream of life as they knew it.

We need the calm, sobering influence of practical religion by which we may set our course, and we need to re-examine these landmarks of public and private decency which point out the undeviating course of justice and kindness and love.

The lessons of this hour are the lessons of simplicity, the lessons of child-like faith, the lessons of the immortality of the soul. Mark it well, "Lest we forget, lest we forget."

I seem to feel as George Washington felt, the influence of all these great sermons that were preached here by men of God. I seem to feel that from every word they spoke there continues an echo that swells into a majestic chorus of Divine praise.

Here the greatest American found companionship with God. Here he received those sacraments that strengthened his character, steadied his purpose and fitted him for the momentous part he played in the epic drama of his time. And there at beautiful Mount Vernon, a few miles away, he sleeps, beside his beloved Martha, to the requiem of immortal adulation of all mankind.

This is God's house and here we know we are close to our Creator, and as we go hence, a glorious recessional of the ancient faith must ring always in our hearts.

Reluctantly, I turn to go. The spell is still upon me. In this mid-winter afternoon the shadows gather early and as I slowly walk toward the world and its concerns, the words of that sweet poem come back to me with a new revelation of truth: "Standeth God within the shadows keeping watch above His own."

An Appreciation

Broadcast Over the Columbia Broadcasting System, February 23, 1932

The great Celebration of the Bicentennial of the Birth of George Washington has been formally opened and from now on interest in the observance of this historic event will gather momentum until its climax and the end of the Celebration on Thanksgiving Day of this year.

Yesterday witnessed the opening of these nation-wide, I should say world-wide, plans which have been maturing for the past two years. We of the United States George Washington Bicentennial Commission of which I have the honor to be the Director, are proud of the overwhelming response of the people of the United States to the work which we have been doing. We are gratified beyond all measure of expression at the cooperation, the sympathetic helpfulness and the deep patriotic feeling that have been exemplified in every part of our beloved land.

I speak from the heart when I say that all of us who have been concerned in this momentous work are deeply touched at the appreciation which has been given to our humble efforts, and we are inspired by the obvious fact that the people of the United States everywhere have rallied to the spirit and purpose of this occasion beyond anything that could have been anticipated.

The events of the past two years have occupied our minds, our hearts and our hands beyond any similar work that was ever undertaken. The beginning of this Celebration yesterday was marked by observances in thousands of towns and cities throughout the nation and in millions of homes and schools and churches. From one end of the country to the other, in our Insular possessions, in foreign lands, wherever Americans reside, there has been exhibited an interest and a wholehearted sentiment of the true American spirit which should hearten every real American living under the protection of our flag.

The Nations of the world joined with us yesterday in paying homage to our great Washington. In practically all foreign countries radio broadcasts were made by the heads of government, statesmen and patriots so that the name of George Washington resounded throughout the world.

The Celebration in the National Capital naturally was the center of immediate interest because here the government itself in the most formal, dignified and magnificent way, paid its tribute to Washington with solemn and beautiful ceremony.

The address of the President of the United States and the singing of "America" by a grand chorus of the entire nation was carried by the miracle of radio to every part of the world. Yesterday the man who still is and ever will be to us, the Father of Our Country, reached the hearts of his people as never before. Today the press of the world tells us how the hearts of humanity responded.

Today it is my proud privilege, through the courtesy of this great broadcasting system to thank the 123,-000,000 Americans who responded so magnificently to this call to a great occasion.

On behalf of the United States George Washington Bicentennial Commission I tender the thanks of this government to our people everywhere and to those across the seas for their interest and their help in this fitting testimonial to the memory of our greatest American.

I can hardly realize what has come to pass. The Celebration has begun in a manner that overwhelms me. It is not only the greatest event of its kind ever held in the history of the world, but it is impossible now to conceive how anything could have been added to this mighty tribute of the people of all countries. The words I speak are hopelessly inadequate to express what I, an American citizen, and lover of George Washington, would like to convey to my fellow-Americans.

No precedent guided us, for no such Celebration was ever attempted by any nation at any time. We set to work with energy and enthusiasm which have not abated during all these months and years of effort.

We were sustained by an unfaltering confidence that Americans were eager to participate in this form of tribute. That confidence grew with the passing of time and with the thousands upon thousands of letters that came to the Commission from all over the world and especially from all over our own country. We were inspired with new confidence, new faith and new energy. I may say truthfully that I do not believe any organization of the government, in time of war or peace has ever given such unstinted service, loyalty and talent as have those who have aided me in the conduct of this mighty enterprise. On behalf of Americans everywhere I want to express my appreciation of this service which is as truly a tribute to Washington as any ceremony or any material monument.

What we witnessed here in the National Capital yesterday was an awakening that gives encouragement to all of patriotic hearts and minds.

When the President of the United States stood in the National Capitol and delivered his wonderful tribute to the memory of George Washington, I felt a thrill I cannot describe. It was what we had worked for, planned for, hoped for, all these years. It was the greatest historical celebration in the life of our country and not at least for another hundred years will there be anything like it. Our dream was realized, our hopes fulfilled and I know that George Washington received the tribute that he would have liked to receive, because it was not in the form of a new monument or material evidence of our growth, but was an expression from the hearts and minds of his people—the people of the United States.

I say this with the pride of an American. I say it with a heart full of gratitude to those who have joined with us in the planning of this great Celebration. We Americans have always loved George Washington, but today we love him with a new revelation of understanding. We love him because we know more about him, and knowing more about him we realize the mighty stature of the man.

What the United States George Washington Bicentennial Commission needed to do was to awaken the love of our people to this new understanding of Washington. It was a mighty task and we are proud to feel that with the support of the people themselves the task has been well done.

Eight years ago far-sighted men in Congress had a vision of just what we witnessed yesterday and took steps to prepare for it.

The program which was launched was broad and comprehensive. It ramified to every corner of the earth and reached every stratum of humanity. When we began our work George Washington was something of a myth —to many, a cold impersonal figure of history, remote and almost unknown. Today there is hardly a man, woman or child in this land of ours but knows a great deal about George Washington. They know something of his mighty character, they know of his services, his sacrifices, his victories and his triumphs of statesmanship. But more than that they know of George Washington as the man. They feel a different sentiment toward him, a nearness, an understanding, a personal love.

From the least known of Americans, George Washington has become one of the best known. We have succeeded in large measure at least, in making him familiar to Americans for what he really was—a simple farmer, like millions of other American farmers—a business man, like many other American business men—a friend worshipped by troops of friends, a father to all the children he knew, a devoted husband, a mighty conquerer without the glamor of ambition, a statesman without selfishness—the ideal American.

I believe that if this Celebration had served no other purpose than in making George Washington understood and loved, it would have been worth all the planning and all the effort.

So I have reason not only to thank the American people for their cooperation, but to congratulate them from the depth of my heart for the long, earnest, self-giving efforts they themselves have put forth to make this memorial to George Washington what it should be.

During these two years of active preparation 60,-000,000 people—half the population of the United States—with half a million committees to lead them, have found the time, the willingness, and the initiative to plan the great tribute which opened in the National Capital yesterday, and in cities, towns and hamlets all over our beloved land.

But it is the 35,000,000 young Americans in our schools and colleges who have touched my heart most profoundly. It was the patriotism of these future generations of American citizens that we wished to awaken first of all to a response in love of country that has stirred me deeply.

The United States George Washington Bicentennial Commission has found it almost impossible to meet the demands for school studies of Washington. We have, however, placed his picture in every one of the 850,000 schoolrooms of the country. We have supplied these schools with literature of all kinds, touching every phase of the life of George Washington. These young people have enrolled themselves with the same enthusiasm in the contests we have arranged through the year for excellence in essay, declamation and oratory on the subject of George Washington and the Americanism he lived and taught.

Nothing could have pleased and touched George Washington himself so much as this overwhelming tribute of affection from these young Americans of to-day. Childless himself, he loved all the children that he could draw near him. Yesterday the children of a later America paid him the same homage of love in song, in parades in every form of exercise.

This tribute from those who will love Washington all their lives and strive to be like him was one of the finest touches to the whole Celebration and I am proud to have had a hand in bringing about a stirring of hearts so deep, so fine and so patriotic.

No greater distinction or self-satisfaction could come to any man, woman or child than to have had a part in this inspiring work.

Throughout the months to come there will be thousands upon thousands of celebrations of all kinds throughout our country. For the most part these will be simple, inexpensive forms of tribute—the kind George Washington himself would most like. I ask the people everywhere and especially the boys and girls to become active in these celebrations, for everyone will have his opportunity.

Let us upon all appropriate occasions find ways of joining in these manifestations of honor to the great American, for in honoring George Washington we honor ourselves; in teaching George Washington we are doing the most important work in the preservation of our common country.

The Date of George Washington's Birth

Explanation of the Date and Day of George Washington's Birth, February 11, 1731, and How It Corresponds With February 22, the Date We Celebrate

Extension of Remarks Made in the House of Representatives February 23, 1932

Reprinted from the Congressional Record *of February 23, 1932*

As we celebrate the Two Hundredth Anniversary of the Birth of George Washington, it may be of interest to consider certain points with reference to our calendar, inasmuch as they have a direct bearing upon the date on which the celebration is to be held.

The use of the Julian calendar in Great Britain and her colonies, including the United States, ended with December 31, 1751, in accordance with an act of Parliament. A part of this act, as contained in Henning's Statutes at Large, Laws of Virginia, volume 1, page 394, is as follows:

"So much of the act of Parliament of Twenty-fourth George II, chapter 23, as relates to the establishment of the new style, is in the following words: 'Throughout all His Majesty's dominions in Europe, Asia, Africa, and America, subject to the Crown of Great Britain, the supputation according to which the year of our Lord beginneth on the 25th of March shall not be made use of after the last day of December 1751, and the 1st day of January next following the said last day of December, shall be deemed the first day of the year of our Lord 1752, and so on, the 1st day of January, 1752, the days of each month shall be reckoned in the same order; and the feast of Easter, and other movable feasts thereon depending, be ascertained according to the same method, as they now are, until the 2d of September in the said year 1752, inclusive; and the natural day next immediately following the said 2d of September shall be called the 14th of September, omitting for that time only the 11 intermediate nominal days of the common calendar; and the natural days following the said 14th of September shall be numbered forward in numerical order from the said 14th of September, according to the order now used in the present calendar; and all acts, deeds, writings, notes, and other instruments executed or signed upon or after the 1st day of January, 1752, shall bear date according to the said new method of supputation, etc.' The section then goes on to provide for the sessions of courts, and so forth, according to the new method.

"With respect to leap years, the second section declares, 'that the years 1800, 1900, 2100, 2200, 2300, or any other hundredth year of our Lord, except only every fourth hundredth year, whereof the year 2000 shall be the first, shall not be bissextile or leap years, but shall be common years, consisting of 365 days and no more; and the years of our Lord 2000, 2400, 2800, and every other fourth hundredth year of our Lord, from the year 2000, inclusive, and all other years of our Lord, which by the present supputation are bissextile or leap years, shall be bissextile, or leap years consisting of 366 days.'"

It is seen from the above that the year 1751 was a short year, in that it began with March 25, and ended with December 31; 1752 was also a short year, in that 11 day dates were omitted in September of that year. That is, no days were designated as September 3 to September 13, inclusive. The day immediately following Wednesday, September 2, was designated Thursday, September 14. There was no interruption of the regular succession of the days of the week.

From the foregoing, and from consideraton of a known error in the Julian leap year rule, it is apparent that on bringing into our present calendar events that occurred between February 29, 1700, and September 2, 1752, both dates inclusive, and "old style," a correction of 11 days must be made because of the 11 dates omitted from September, 1752, and in addition, if the event occurred between January 1 and March 24, inclusive, the year date must be increased by one. For example, George Washington was born on February 11, 1731, according to the calendar in use in Great Britain and her colonies at the time of his birth, but on extrapolating our present calendar back to that time the date becomes February 22, 1732, and we shall celebrate the two hundredth anniversary of his birth on February 22, 1932.

Having been born on February 11, 1731, Washington was 19 years old on February 11, 1750, and 20 years on February 11 of the year following. This would have been 1751, under the old calendar, but the year 1751 ended with December 31, and the following February became February, 1752. Washington's twentieth birthday was, therefore, celebrated on February 11, 1752. In the following September, 1752, 11 day dates were omitted, so that Washington's twenty-first birthday was celebrated on February 22, 1753. From that time onward February 22 has been counted as the anniversary of his birth, and February 22, 1932, will be correctly celebrated as the two hundredth anniversary of his birth.

For many years both before and after the adoption of the Gregorian calendar in this country the practice of "double dating" was customary, or, at least, not uncommon, and sometimes led to confusion. Thus George Washington himself writing to Sir Isaac Heard, Kings Garter at Arms, May 22, 1792, recorded his own birth: "Augustine then married (Mary) Ball, March 6th, 1730; by whom he had issue George, born February 11th (old style), 1732"; meaning 1731/32. This slip has caused some people to claim that he was born in 1732/33.

This practice of double dating was necessary before the adoption in order to avoid uncertainty in official records, correspondence, and especially in documents relating to foreign trade, because of the fact that the Gregorian calendar was in use in Catholic countries from 1582 onward and its use in these countries was recognized in Great Britain and her colonies, although it was not put into effect in Great Britain and her colonies until January 1, 1752. After the adoption, double dating was also used, presumably to eliminate all possibility of confusion which might have resulted from inertia in changing calendars, but the practice soon died out.

Of special interest in this connection is the fact that the Washington family Bible, now at Mount Vernon, records the birth of George Washington in the following manner:

"George Washington, son of Augustine and Mary, his wife, was born ye 11th day of February, 1731/32."

COLONIAL GARDEN TRIBUTE

ADDRESS BROADCAST BY THE NATIONAL BROADCASTING COMPANY
FROM WASHINGTON, D. C.
MARCH 17, 1932

As Director of the United States George Washington Bicentennial Commission, I am invited to launch on this occasion a campaign which is one of the most beautiful and touching honors we can render to George Washington during this year when the nation and the world commemorate the Two Hundredth Anniversary of his birth.

I am asking all those who hear me to plant flowers in memory of George Washington.

In order that this loving tribute, this burst of color from the very earth, shall not be for this year only, you are asked to plant those perennial flowers that bud and bloom year after year, in glorious memorial succession.

Nothing could be more appropriate than such a

tribute. George Washington himself loved scenes of beauty. Time and again in his letters and in his diaries, he tells of pausing, even in the midst of his gravest military anxieties, to admire the beauty of some view, or some locality.

Washington was a gardener himself—a landscape gardener of the first rank in his time. He was a leader in the pleasing work of beautifying his home and the grounds about it, in a State that was famous even in his day for the splendor of its great and beautiful estates.

If you have visited Mount Vernon, or when you do visit Mount Vernon, you have seen there, in every tree and shrub and plant, the magic touch of his hand, creating its serene and peaceful beauty.

Many of the trees that he planted with his own hand are still there, each placed where he knew it would add its cool green color and graceful form to the loveliness of his home.

You will see at Mount Vernon the garden designed and laid out by Washington. There is the mystic maze it amused him to plan—the walks lined with their box-wood—the ivy-draped fences and walls in a curtain of velvet green.

You will see there some of the very flowers he loved to grow—the old and simple blossoms that were as honest and true and unpretentious as he was himself.

Mount Vernon was beautiful because the soul of George Washington was beautiful. It is beautiful today because he coaxed from the bosom of nature, the sweetness and charm to match the sweetness and charm of his own soul.

We do not all possess broad lawns and rolling acres, and the room for rows of blushing flowers. But every patriotic American can plant some floral tribute to George Washington this year, if it is only a geranium pot that he places in the sunshine at his window.

It will be an offering of beauty to a lover of beauty, in a language that speaks across all boundaries of space, and beyond the grave itself. It will be the spirit of America today, exchanging greetings with the spirit of Washington, as if differences in time had disappeared.

The planting of flowers in Washington's name this year will be like covering the fair face of our land with visible symbols of the beauty of Washington's own character and life.

In this growing of lovely things, this covering of the land with a canopy of beauty, I see one more instance proving that Washington's hand is still lifted in blessing over the hearts of our people and the welfare of our country.

In this age of industrialism, and in the rush of material pursuits, we need, as never before, to restore true culture to our lives. We have covered our land with factories, and have covered the sky with the smoke of industry. We live in a day of tremendous accomplishment. In all this there is a beauty of achievement, and enrichment of human life. George Washington would approve all this. Indeed, he largely foresaw it and planned it.

But always he loved to retire to his beloved and tranquil Mount Vernon—to the shade of its trees—the peace of its rolling fields—to stroll through its flowery gardens. And he bids us do the same today.

This broad continent has room for flowers, as it has for factories. Our lives have room for roses and violets as well as for material desires and business aims. We need to give our busy land its needed decoration, with the gifts that nature has placed at our hands, if only we use them.

In so doing we are only turning back to the ways of George Washington, who made himself one of the most prosperous men in America, and still found time to make his home a place to gladden his eye and to rest his soul.

So I hope that every patriotic American who hears me will cooperate in this movement to plant flowers in honor of George Washington and will plant as many beautiful things as he possibly can this Bicentennial year. Plant a garden if you can, if not, only a circle of posies in your dooryard will be a fine tribute to pay to Washington. It will be doing something fine for your country, and it will be doing something fine for yourself.

We of the United States George Washington Bicentennial Commission, want America to be one great garden this year, and for all years to come. We want to see unlovely yards and lots veiled in the petals of buds and flowers. We want all America to be more like George Washington's Mount Vernon.

But to attain this fine spiritual end, practical means are necessary. So I am glad to say to all good Americans who are stirred to go forth with spade and trowel, that we are working to help you, with practical advice and suggestion.

We have working with us the United States Department of Agriculture, American Society of Landscape Architects, the Garden Clubs of America, the Agriculture colleges, and many other floral organizations. The Bicentennial Committees and Commissions in all the States stand ready to do everything possible in promoting this planting of flowers in George Washington's honor.

Experts will tell you of all the varieties of plants and flowers that were loved by Washington or were familiar in his time. They will tell you how to utilize plots of land, how to prepare the soil, how to watch the growth of what you plant—and how to make it a lasting and endless growth, a permanent addition to the loveliness of our land.

I can assure you of a satisfaction in knowing that you are doing something for George Washington, in making your America a happier and more beautiful place in which to live.

One Hundredth Anniversary of the Death of Goethe

Address Delivered in the House of Representatives

March 22, 1932

By HON. SOL BLOOM

Director of the United States George Washington Bicentennial Commission,
and Member of the Goethe Society of America

Reprinted from the Congressional Record, *March 22, 1932*

Mr. BLOOM. Mr. Speaker, I ask unanimous consent to address the House for five minutes on the one hundredth anniversary of the death of Goethe.

The SPEAKER. Is there objection to the request of the gentleman from New York?

There was no objection.

Mr. BLOOM. Mr. Speaker, today marks the one hundredth anniversary of the death of Johann Wolfgang von Goethe. It is only fitting, at a time when the entire world is participating in a bicentennial celebration honoring our George Washington, that we recognize this great date.

It is fitting and appropriate, for a number of reasons, that we pause in our thought of George Washington to turn out attention to the great German poet, philosopher, dramatist, novelist, and scientist.

Far apart as the two men were, in the fields assigned them by the great Creator, the two were alike in many respects.

They were alike, first of all, in being among the very few supreme minds that humanity has produced.

No statesman was greater than Washington. No poet, not even Homer or Shakespeare, was greather than Goethe.

The great German did his work for human advancement in the peace of his study, while the great American wrought the good that he did on the field of battle or in political councils. But in essentials the two men thought alike.

One of Goethe's first dramas concerned itself with the celebration of a great sixteenth century champion of liberty. And in the last great work of his life, the completion of Faust, he raised the hero of that immortal work to the plane that Washington occupied throughout his life—the plane of simple wisdom and disinterested service to one's fellow men.

A survey of Goethe's contributions to human thought, an estimate of what he did for the lifting up of the human heart is the task of scholars and critics. But the person of even limited reading knows something of Goethe's place among the immortals.

So much of human life is gathered up in his varied works—he explored so many human problems, he lighted up so many deep recesses in the human heart—that it is little wonder that critics assign him the honor of having given shape to an entire era of human culture.

Goethe is Germany's pride, as Washington is ours. And the nation which sent to Washington's aid the military genius of Von Steuben and De Kalb, and the loyalty of thousands of German-Americans in Washington's ragged army, deserves the compliment of America's tribute to its chief adornment.

Though Washington and Goethe never met, their purposes ran parallel, their efforts were alike for human good, and the two were one in their counsels of good will.

Could we honor them in any more fitting way than by putting into our everyday relations that same good will, not only among ourselves but with all other nations?

Is it not possible for surface differences between peoples to sleep, as the bodies of these two great men sleep, while the spirit of concord they voiced lives on?

I suggest that in the name of George Washington, whose last public words expressed that spirit, we Americans extend to the German people a fitting return for the honors they have tendered the memory of George Washington in this bicentennial year. [Applause.]

On March 6, under the patronage of President Von Hindenburg, the German Reichstag held a celebration in honor of the George Washington Bicentennial, at which time the walls of that chamber rang with the strains of the Star-Spangled Banner.

Today let us pause and think of their great hero—their gift to civilization—Johann Wolfgang von Goethe. [Applause.]

At York, Pennsylvania

Address Before Veterans of Foreign Wars,
York, Pennsylvania
April 6, 1932

It is my privilege this year to turn the thoughts of the American people toward George Washington on every available occasion.

Outwardly, the reason for this is that we may pay to George Washington the endless honors that are due him, and that have a special timeliness this year, because 1932 is the Two Hundredth Anniversary of his Birth.

But beneath this year of celebration there is an inward and far deeper meaning. George Washington himself would spurn these honors we pay him, as empty and worthless, without this deeper meaning of the words we utter in his praise.

The one way in which we can truly honor George Washington at all is to revive those principles on which he founded our government and our country, and apply ourselves to a new effort in living up to them.

So it is that every other passing anniversary this year is a fit occasion for refreshing ourselves at the fount of Washington's patriotism. Every other memorable moment in our history has its attachment to him. For we would have had no such glorious history, if we had not had Washington in the beginning.

This occasion today, April 6, is the anniversary of that day when our nation was drawn into the recent World War.

It is the day when you who now look toward me, turned your faces to America's enemies and prepared to save your country.

Could there be a closer link between this year and this day, and that former day when George Washington made the same appeal for men to stand with him, facing an enemy of America and willing to suffer and die for the safety of their country?

If George Washington could stand here in my place, I believe the tears would well in his eyes, as they did sometimes when the loyalty of his brave men especially touched him.

The only difference he would see would be the difference between olive drab, and the ancient buff and blue. Under the different uniforms, he would see the same type of American, the same loyal patriot, the same lover of his country, as the men who stayed with him, from Boston to Yorktown and the victorious entry into New York on the heels of the British invaders.

If there is one thing about you that would touch George Washington more than the sameness of you veterans and his devoted Continentals, it would be your vast numbers.

When Washington lived and carried this nation to victory on his own courage and character, nothing tried his courage and his patience more than the problem of raising enough men to fight to victory with him.

He never could collect from the little country that America then was, enough men to make his victories quick and decisive.

He was forced to drag along through eight years of struggle and toil and blood and discouragement. He had to lose bitter battles on Long Island, at the Brandywine and Germantown. He and his nearly naked army had to suffer all the horrors of Valley Forge, and be content with little successes snatched here and there before there came at last that stirring situation at Yorktown that crowned with God's own gift of success the great Commander-in-Chief and his little army in which every man was a hero.

What a leap his heart would give, to see millions of American patriots rush to arms a few years ago, where in his day he sighed in relief when he gained a few thousand more recruits to his ranks!

In 1776, America had a few thousand defenders. In 1917, she had millions to rise and dare a thousand deaths for her safety.

In 1776, war was fought with clumsy weapons. In 1917, the man who came to the defence of his country faced a war made tenfold more horrible by every device that science could invent for the maiming of human bodies and the taking of human lives. Yet millions were ready to meet these dangers. How Washington's heart would go out to you who formed that and other great American armies.

I am sure he would heartily agree with what I say here now—that American patriotism is not dead, but lives as strong as of old.

All honor to the heroes who fought by Washington's side and marched with their bleeding feet through the snow, wherever he ordered them to go. But I contend that love of country did not die and disappear with Washington's men in buff and blue. It lived and flamed again when America once more called to you, her sons of this later day, and placed her destiny in your keeping.

She clad you in different colors, but the hearts that beat beneath your uniforms ran with the same red blood of courage, willing to be shed, if need be, for the nation that George Washington gave us to preserve forever.

You who fought these later battles in the cause of America's safety and in the name of liberty were really fighting for George Washington just as much as if he were to rally and command you.

So we are gathered here in singleness of spirit with the Father of the Land, on soil made sacred by his very presence, and rendered still more holy by our country's history.

About us as we meet here is a city that has grown with America's growth, from struggling Colonial days.

But it was here that history was made when our nation was young and when George Washington himself was alive and already thinking of America's future.

Into this city, a little more than a century and a half ago, Washington rode on one of his frequent travels about the country. He had taken his step-son, Jackie Custis, to New York, to place him in King's College, now Columbia University.

After this happy and peaceful errand, and when he had turned back toward his beloved Mount Vernon, Washington came through Pennsylvania, and stopped at York Town, as it then was called. That was in 1773, while America still was at peace, and nothing distracted Washington from his favorite pursuit of observing the quality of the land and dreaming of the prosperous future he foresaw for his fortunate countrymen.

Then came the struggle for Independence, with its eight long years of doubt and toil and discouragement and suspense. The most powerful nation then on earth had sent its trained and disciplined armies here to keep us enslaved to their king.

During the darkest period in all that anxious time, this city was for nearly a year the capital of the United States. I have said that history has made this sacred soil. Let me tell you why it is made so sacred.

It was here that the Continental Congress sat while George Washington and his army were going through the horrors of Valley Forge.

The powerful foe had driven the Commander-in-Chief to hide his little starving and freezing band in the hills and hollows of that camp which has been forever hallowed by their sufferings.

Before the same all-conquering foe, Congress had been forced to flee from Philadelphia and hold its sessions here.

Had Congress remained in Philadelphia, every member would have been made a prisoner, and might have been hanged as a traitor to the British King. Over the head of George Washington himself hung the same possible fate. He too would have been hanged, if any one of the many efforts to capture him had been successful.

We know what happened instead. Washington lived to triumph over his enemy and establish our land, while a weak but patriot Congress supported him to the best of its power.

But that glorious end of the struggle was far from visible in that winter of 1777 and '78. On the contrary, it looked almost impossible for this impoverished people to conquer the powerful forces arrayed against them.

Here in this city, then a pioneer village, they thought and fought it out—George Washington watching his starving men at Valley Forge, and Congress sitting here and striving to raise the men and the money so sorely needed to win the war.

Into this town Washington sent his despairing and pleading letters from his camp of starvation and distress. Here he told Congress it must somehow feed and clothe and pay his suffering men. Here the heart and the soul of the infant nation was tested as it never has been in all its history. And here American courage won.

So when I compare you patriot Americans of today with the heroes gathered about George Washington, I pay you the greatest compliment that human lips could frame. Now let me add to the compliment by telling you how true it is, and how well deserved.

To you also came the call of service to country in the face of death and danger. To you it meant the same sacrifice that was paid by the patriots of 1777.

Let us never forget what it cost the men of Washington's army to fight at his side. They left their families in danger of want, sometimes in danger of hostile savages. They left their farms to suffer neglect and ruin.

Many of Washington's officers had been well-to-do men, and lost their all in order to serve him. Love of country could rise to no greater heights than that.

But you, too, when you heard the call of your country, laid aside your occupations, your comfortable homes, and the loving embrace of your children, your wives, your loved ones.

You, too, had a menacing enemy to face. When America entered this recent war, that struggle was at the stage of its Valley Forge. The foe appeared to be victorious, with a helpless world at its feet. The heart of humanity was stilled with fear. The fate of the world lay in America's hands, and America was unready and far away.

The only difference between that dark time and the anxious months that Washington had to endure in 1777, was that the danger in 1917 was more fearful, and the cost and the effort needed to meet it was greater still.

Not only that, Washington's men were stimulated to desperate courage from seeing the enemy before their very homes, on their own soil. This later call to American patriotism was to take millions of men thousands of miles to foreign soils, across seas as dangerous as the fields of battle.

This is the very day, fifteen years ago, when many of you heard the call, and prepared to answer it without a murmur.

First came the months of dreary training and drilling the army that had sprung to arms over night and hurried to the great camps hastily prepared throughout the country for it. Then a united nation cheered you on, while you sailed the seas to prove that Americans fight for their high ideals no matter where the threat may rise against them.

The hottest fires of war ever kindled waited to test American courage, American spirit, American endurance and the will to win.

In hardly more than a year from the moment you Americans planted your feet on soil reddened and torn by three years of fire and slaughter, the waves of destruction had been beaten back, the thunder of thousands of mighty guns had been stilled, and once again American might and courage had rendered safe the cause of Liberty and the rights of mankind.

That glorious rounded record you bring here today, on the anniversary of the day when most of you began that record. Here you lay it at the feet of George Washington, on the very ground he once trod, on the very spot where his impassioned appeals for help were heard.

You have only his memory to salute today. The hand of death and a century and a half of change have placed an impenetrable curtain over the great events that occurred when he passed this way. Not all the passionate love we bear him can reach his ears.

But I believe—I know—his spirit is with us here. You who have met here can only mutely lay before him this record of yours, for his equally mute approval. But if some miracle would let us break the grand and solemn silence that reigns where George Washington sleeps—if we could hear his beloved voice once more—I believe we would hear him say:

"Well done, my patriotic Americans. The fire that stirred your fathers to high deeds for a high cause, lives on in you. In you the same soul that made this country, flames on to keep it safe. Raise your sons to receive my blessing, even as I give it in pride to you."

Yes, I believe the great American we honor this year would have more than approval for your deeds, your sacrifices, the risks you ran and the losses you have taken. He would feel every pride in you.

In all the years since Valley Forge, not one thing has lessened the courage of this country, or the constancy of its people. On America's roll of honor, which began early and will never end, you, too, have placed your names in letters that will blaze with the brightest that are there.

But just as George Washington fought and won a war only to issue from it a friend and counsellor of peace, so I believe that you also, who know battle from having faced its perils, are with him in a hatred of its waste and sacrifice of lives.

Washington himself proved what a sublime thing it is to offer one's very life for country—but what a still greater thing it is to live for country. Nobler even than dying for country, is achieving for one's country and adding to its progress.

In that George Washington shone most sublimely of all. And it is along the paths of peace that we need most of all to follow him now.

It may be that not even yet has Almighty God, in his wisdom, lifted the curse of war from the souls of men. It may be that not yet may we hope to have seen the last of carnage and bloodshed. But we do know that mankind has lived up to one of Washington's principles of honor—that only injustice, only the invasion of fundamental human rights, can justify the argument of battle. No longer will the opinion of humanity permit nations to wage wars for mere love of conquest. And George Washington looked forward to a day when enlightened mankind shall have found a way to rule out even the justifiable causes of war.

George Washington not only foresaw that day, he labored to bring it about. As a soldier, he fought to win. As President of the United States he strove for peace.

During his administration this country was under a thousand temptations to enter into the raging disputes of other nations. George Washington underwent some of the bitterest abuse ever heaped on a public officer of this country, in his steadfast and resolute efforts to keep us neutral and aloof. When passions had cooled, when reason returned to men's minds, it was seen that in his labors for peace, George Washington had but added to his greatness.

Today the world is slowly striving toward a goal that George Washington visioned even before the Constitution of the United States was framed and signed. He then expressed a belief in a permanent future world peace, and he stated this belief in a letter to a great French warrior—Lafayette—who had fought with him throughout the Revolution and who knew war as it was known to Washington himself.

In that expression he looked forward to a time when "mankind may be connected like one great family in fraternal ties." He told Lafayette that even then the world was growing less barbarous. The nations were becoming more humanized. The causes for hostility were daily diminishing. And he believed the period was not remote when a free and liberal commerce would take the place of the horrors and devastations of war.

The same man who stated these beliefs could still insist that the best way to avoid war was to be amply prepared for war. The same man who hoped for a future world peace could still insist that the only satisfactory peace was "peace with justice and honor." But he nevertheless hoped and believed that humanity was moving upward towards those principles of international honor and harmony which would one day make war impossible.

Toward that goal George Washington himself strove with all his counsels and teachings, and by his own great example.

So, if it is noble to live for one's country and to strive for our nation's progress, it is noblest and best to follow George Washington's guidance in this exalted purpose.

We could not better honor George Washington, not only this year but in all years to come, than by living for our country in the George Washington way—by living up to his precepts—by "cultivating peace with harmony"; by "observing good faith and justice toward all Nations," just as he has urged us in that greatest state paper ever composed by the hand of man, the Farewell Address.

Let us honor George Washington this year by dedicating ourselves to these counsels he has left. We could not begin this re-dedication at a better time than during this year we have set aside to commemorate the Two Hundredth Anniversary of his Birth. We could not select a more appropriate day than this 15th anniversary of the entrance of our country into the great war for the preservation of world liberty.

In that spirit, and with that high purpose, I invite you who have been warriors in the George Washington spirit, to join with our country this year in its tribute to this great preacher of peace with honor.

You will be like Washington's own veterans, saluting your old Commander. You will be taking a solemn vow for the continued safety of your country—by war only in the last resort, and all the rest of the time through the channels of peace. And so you will be adding a deep and solemn note to the reverence and the affection we pour forth this year to one so well described as "First in war, first in peace, and first in the hearts of his countrymen."

Before the National Security League

Address Delivered Before the National Security League
and Broadcast by the National Broadcasting Company
April 9, 1932

If there is one thought uppermost in the mind of every American today, it is the thought of security— the security of our nation, and the security of every person in it.

It is a time when every one of us is thinking of the welfare of our country, as it relates to us in our daily problems.

Many of us are so disturbed over present conditions that we think no other period in history can compare with this one, in the grave uncertainties presented to us on every hand.

So I am going to draw a comparison between this vast country of ours today, and the very small and struggling country that it was 143 years ago.

The little country I speak of also experienced difficult times. In fact its troubles were so overwhelming that the great men it contained—and they were some of the greatest men that ever lived—were afraid they never could get it going.

That little country had never known anything but pinch and struggle, warfare and discontent.

It had a population of less than 4,000,000, and most of these people were comparatively poor.

It had no general system of taxation. Hence it had no national income. It had no credit, and it was loaded down with debt.

It owed its own soldiers for back pay.

It had no such thing as a national commerce. The trade it once enjoyed had been ruined by war, and independence had cut it off from the chief colonial channels. Its currency had been so debased that it took a wagon-load of money to buy a wagon-load of food.

One section of the country was the rival of all the other sections, and it seemed impossible to get them together into a national plan of action.

In a word, these 4,000,000 people were not a nation, and many people despaired of them ever being one. They were just so many confused individuals and States, wondering as many of us are wondering today—what was coming next?

We think there is a good deal of confusion and chaos today. But we have all the accumulated wealth and experience of the world to draw on, where that little country of the past had none of these things. It had nothing but a passion for security, and I am going to tell you how it got it.

The little struggling country was the United States of America, in 1789, when General George Washington was about to be inaugurated as its First President.

Washington's record up to that time had stamped him as the bravest man in the country. Yet is it strange that when he took the oath of office as President of this untried experiment in government, his hand trembled and his voice shook?

No one realized better than he the terrible task before him—the task of bringing security to a new nation. None saw more clearly than he the possibilities of failure.

It lived down or wiped out every political and economic menace to its safety, and it will do so again, if we follow in the footsteps of the great men and the great leader who brought this nation into being.

You may say that it was easy for the American people of that day to accomplish what they did, because they had George Washington to lead them.

He is as much our leader today.

He left his teachings to us as an immortal possession. And they apply to our present problems as they applied to the problems they solved in those early years of our life.

I am not going to trace George Washington's course and methods, step by step, as he brought the new nation into security. The historians have told that story in eloquent words. George Washington himself has told it best of all, in his own writings.

I am safe in saying that the United States of America owes its existence to two traits in George Washington. They were:

The possession of courage and faith, and a passion for thinking of country first.

George Washington had faith in America and its Americans.

The whole story of his life consists of his acts and thoughts in placing that faith in the service of his country. And one word sums up what he achieved—security. Security for the nation, and for every one in it.

The whole struggle for independence was fought and won on George Washington's physical and moral courage, backed by his faith in his countrymen.

The Constitution of this country was written under his watchful eye and under the inspiration of his courage, and his passion for its security.

He was the center of all the great legislation which was passed during his Presidency, which started this nation in motion on its true and straight course. Every bit of it had for its purpose national security.

To understand what Washington achieved for national security, it must be remembered that he had everything to do for the first time. And no one knew better than he that the whole future of the United States depended on how wisely he made these beginnings.

Presidents who came after Washington have had to appoint one or two justices to the Supreme Court. Washington had to fill that court for the first time— and it was the first great tribunal in history with power to pass on the constitutionality of legislative acts.

Washington had to establish our foreign policy for

the first time. And he had to do this in a world filled with wars and revolutions.

Through all the eight years during which the American people were privileged to have George Washington for their President, his every act was for their perpetual security—their safety as a nation, and the safety of every individual in his rights and possessions.

"Let us have a Government," he said, "by which our lives, liberties and properties will be secured."

And again he said: "Although we cannot by the best concerted plans, absolutely command success, although the race is not always to the swift nor the battle to the strong, yet, without presumptuously waiting for miracles to be wrought in our favor, it is our indispensable duty, with the deepest gratitude to Heaven for the past, and humble confidence in its smiles on our future operations, to make use of all means in our power for our defence and security."

Washington scarcely opened his lips, or touched pen to paper, without pouring forth this passion within him for our national security.

But the greatest gift he left his beloved country is that immortal document—The Farewell Address—in which he sums up all the accumulated wisdom and counsel he has to impart on national security and how to preserve it.

There he tells us in words that will live forever what it is that national security must rest upon. And as always with this simple man, you find these fundamentals simple.

"Observe good faith and justice toward all Nations. Cultivate peace and harmony with all."

But this man who could put things so simply, could think of many things, all necessary to our safety.

He could counsel against "those overgrown military establishments, which under any form of government are inauspicious to liberty, and which are to be regarded as particularly hostile to republican liberty."

And he could add:

"Against the insidious wiles of foreign influence, the jealousy of a free people ought to be constantly awake. . . . The great rule of conduct for us, in regard to foreign nations, is, in extending our commercial relations, to have with them as little political connection as possible. . . . I hold the maxim no less applicable to public than private affairs, that honesty is always the best policy. . . . Harmony, and a liberal intercourse with all nations, are recommended by policy, humanity and interest."

But the same man who so strove to avoid offense to other people and to other nations, was as quick to resent offense to him or to his country. The same man who hoped for permanent world peace and who said "Cultivate peace and harmony," could also say, "To be prepared for war is one of the most effectual means of preserving peace."

What we need is to put those words into action. We need to emulate his courage in facing discouragement. We need to emulate George Washington's unshaken faith in his country. We need to copy his trust in an all-wise Providence.

George Washington believed this country was safe so long as the character of its people was sound and upright.

If we would honor George Washington this year, if we would have our country safe and secure, let us dedicate ourselves again to the simple honesty and patriotism with which he made this nation safe.

UNDER THE CHERRY BLOSSOMS

ADDRESS DELIVERED AT THE TIDAL BASIN, WASHINGTON, D. C.,
AFTER INTRODUCING THE JAPANESE AMBASSADOR,
BROADCAST BY THE NATIONAL BROADCASTING COMPANY,
APRIL 13, 1932

It is rarely the privilege of any American to take part in such an inspiring program as is being presented today beneath this glorious canopy of cherry blossoms in the Nation's Capital.

As I stand here in the presence of this distinguished company to express the inspiring thoughts that come to me, I can, in memory, retrace the years to the fairyland of my childhood. My heart responds to this scene as the most bewitching abode of elfin beauty ever unrolled before human eyes.

Above me, and all about, framing the edges of the lovely Tidal Basin as far as the eye can see, are the most gorgeous, most colorful, blossom-laden trees in all America.

We are here to celebrate the great national cherry blossom season that is famed throughout the world. The

Nation's Capital has given this event peculiar significance. Every Spring as the masses of these famed petals burst into riotous and almost inconceivable splendor, the people of Washington and from all other parts of the country, revel in God's benediction of flowers, spread so generously for our enjoyment and spiritual refreshment.

In this atmosphere of fragrance and of glowing, vital loveliness, who dare question the beneficence of that Providence that spreads such heavenly reflection all about us. Who would deny the Divinity which holds in the hollow of His hand these bright testimonials of His love and remembrance?

You have heard from His Excellency, The Japanese Ambassador, the story of the cherry blossom festival in Japan. He has told us of the significance of this fete and what the blossoms mean to his beauty-loving country. We, in America, have been the beneficiaries of that romantic and poetical nature, and we are fast learning the real meaning of this feast of flowers from those who have adored them for centuries.

We, too, are learning how to understand and appreciate the transcendent influence of this floral baptism that lifts us above the sordid things of life and exalts our souls to God.

Here, we have vivid and impressive proof of that immortality of the good and the beautiful which is the guiding light of human life.

Here, in this significant year which marks the Two Hundredth Anniversary of the Birth of George Washington we stand amidst a scene which would have delighted his soul. I believe that if George Washington should re-visit in human form this city of his dreams, he would pass by every great monument and marble structure and come to the quiet shores of this wonderful Basin, reflecting all about its borders the blossom-laden trees. Here, the deep emotions of the great man would yield in communion with the Giver of all good.

We are in the habit of thinking of George Washington in his more heroic and austere roles. With his name we hear the clash of war or feel the hush of momentous decisions of statecraft. But George Washington loved beauty. He himself has attested to this in his many references to the cultivation of flowers and shrubs and trees upon his beloved estate at Mount Vernon.

There survives to us his own garden of exquisite taste, and floral harmony. We know that George Washington spent many hours in that garden, where the calm, peaceful, uplifting beauty, quieted his soul.

So here in this magnificent capital of the great country which he established, we have come to witness a scene in which his splendid manhood would have found inspiration and delight.

I know of no more appropriate honor we could offer to George Washington than these exquisite flowers that are blooming here today.

It may be that a man's spirit is only that memory of him which lives on as long as there are human hearts to give it a dwelling place. If that is so then Washington's spirit is certainly here. For on this spot are centered some of those things which we know he prized above all others.

Beyond these trees which surround us like an immortal caress, are other trees of similar kind, bordering the beautiful Potomac which Washington loved throughout his lifetime.

It was his river as this is his city. George Washington's own life was one of the most beautiful things that has ever been given to mankind. But one of the elements that made it so, was Washington's love of beauty and his life-long efforts to bring beauty upon the earth about him. He would see that every blossom on these branches is more than a flower. It is a thought, born of God. It is a symbol of peace, as well as a gesture of international good will, from one nation to another.

He wished for the National Capital that it should be magnificent, as well as important. But he also wished that it should be beautiful, as a habitation for the very soul of his people, and these lovely trees of world-wide fame are helping us to make it so.

We think of these trees as blossoming for a short time like a loving garland about this quiet water. But they are blooming forever in the lives of all who have seen them and remember them. They are beautifying human lives wherever they are known.

George Washington would be the first to realize that it is human thought, even more than the hand of nature, which has spread such loveliness here. He would see the literal flowering of one of his fondest dreams—a world dedicated to the cultivation of peace and harmony, and delighting in graceful exchanges.

In these flowers nature has given us her finest language to voice our gladness and our gratitude that George Washington once lived to render all life a nobler thing and to spread good will throughout the world.

That is what I mean in saying that nothing could be more fittingly dedicated to George Washington's memory this year than these ravishing garlands adorning his beloved city in its springtime, and signifying one of his dearest wishes "that mankind be connected like one great family in fraternal ties."

In the name of the United States George Washington Bicentennial Commission, created to lead this country in its honors to George Washington in 1932, I wish to express something that we all know Washington would feel and say on such an occasion—the thanks of his heart to the gracious wife of a later President, and to the Representatives of a friendly nation, for the thought that has brought to our Capital these enrichments—-beautiful for so many beautiful reasons.

At New Bern

Address Delivered at New Bern, North Carolina, April 17, 1932

First, may I ask your permission to express my pleasure at the privilege which has been given me to come to this beautiful place and meet with so many of the patriotic citizens of this community.

It is a rightful boast of this city that it can say with pride, "George Washington passed this way." The people of New Bern of George Washington's time had the pleasure of entertaining President George Washington during his memorable tour of the South in 1791. As descendants of those citizens of that time, it is a fine heritage to know that your ancestors had a part in that ancient ceremony.

In his usual and methodical way, George Washington speaks of his tour of the South and his visit to North Carolina. One entry in his diary will bring a smile to us today and it no doubt mingled amusement with embarrassment to George Washington himself. It was this very month of April in 1791 that he was on his way to New Bern and he writes:

"Wednesday 20th. Left Allans before breakfast, and under a misapprehension went to a Col. Allans, supposing it to be a public house; where we were very kindly and well entertained without knowing it was at his expence, until it was too late to rectify the mistake."

But knowing how proud any American must have felt to have within his home no less a person than George Washington, we can easily imagine how glad Col. Allen was to have such a distinguished guest and how he would try to make George Washington feel at home.

I know there is not one of us today but would not be delighted to have him make a similar mistake in our favor so that we might entertain him no matter what the expense might be.

We know, at least, how glad the people of New Bern were on that memorable occasion to see Washington, for he tells us of the fact in his journal. While he was about it he testified once more to the excellent entertainment he received.

About ten miles from New Bern he ferried across the Neuse River and there he records: "We were met by a small party of Horse; the district Judge (Mr. Sitgreave) and many of the principal Inhabitants of Newbern, who conducted us into town to exceeding good lodgings."

On the next evening he writes "Dined with the Citizens at a public dinner given by them; and went to a dancing assembly in the evening."

That is the spirit and manner in which the 2,000 people of New Bern of 1791 welcomed the First President of the United States and I know that is the spirit in which the citizens of this New Bern of 1932 will honor his memory in commemoration of this two hundredth anniversary of his birth.

The purpose of George Washington on that extensive tour of the South, was to give the people of the United States a sense of being one people, under one friendly and helpful government. And he meant them to acquire that sense of nationality from seeing and meeting and talking with him, their friendly and helpful President.

It seems to me that in this year 1932 we can honor the memory of George Washington in no more appropriate way than to revive this feeling of solid nationality, and if we cannot meet and talk with him, we can, at least, commune with him in spirit and give solemn thought to his great life and teachings.

He is still to us the friendly and helpful President. He is still to us the greatest American who ever lived, and who charted for us a safe course as a nation. In this year 1932 it is particularly appropriate that we acquire a new sense of our solid nationality and the fact that we are one people with one supreme interest at heart—the prosperity and safety of our country. We can show that spirit in no better way than by reverence to the great man who once honored this State and this City with his presence and who, in spirit, presides eternal over our national destiny.

We cannot welcome George Washington to our cities, to public dinners or to dancing assemblies. All that was mortal of George Washington sleeps forever on that beautiful spot beside the Potomac where he loved nothing better than to dispense that warm and generous hospitality which he appreciated so much when tendered him here by your forefathers. But his memory will never die. His teachings will live on and the example of his citizenship will shine on as long as the sun itself.

If we cannot welcome George Washington into our homes, we can still welcome him into our hearts. We can forever keep before us the example of his patriotism; we can forever keep in our minds his teachings; we can forever guide our footsteps by his wisdom.

We not only can do these things, we must do them, if our country is to continue to rise safely on those foundations which George Washington laid in the blood and tears of the Revolution.

This year the nation and the world is pouring out upon Washington's memory all that flood of honor and affection which a new understanding of his life and work has inspired within us. It has been my privilege as Director of the United States George Washington Bicentennial Commission to formulate these great national plans which are reflected now in celebration activities that have awakened the people of the United States and the world. It has been a tremendous task but the inspiration of the work itself has carried us through to success.

There are today in this nation some 800,000 committees actively at work in preparing programs in honor of George Washington. Practically every nation in the world is doing something to add to that flood of honor and affection with which the human race contemplates his life and his work. But the true honor we pay Washington is not to shout loud hurrahs to his name, nor to cry out empty words of praise. The real honor that George Washington deserves is that we bring back into our daily lives something of his self-sacrificing spirit; something of his devotion to country; something of his willingness to think of others before he thought of himself.

North Carolina is doing its part. From many towns, cities and communities in your beautiful state we have the most encouraging reports of celebration activities. I congratulate you upon what has been done and in all earnestness urge you to continued and greater activities. North Carolina, by tradition, by history and by the fine patriotic character of its people, must assume front rank in the great procession of the states of this republic that will honor George Washington in this celebration year of 1932.

We must rise above the selfish passions of the moment and realize that unless we think more of the nation and less of personal gain, the nation itself will suffer and our individual lives will suffer with it.

I believe the American people are filled with this thought. I believe that is the guiding power behind this year of celebration which the people of our country and of the world have prepared in such detail. I believe that many of the ills and anxieties now upon us as a nation have happened because we have gone astray from the simple and unselfish teachings of George Washington.

I believe that the only remedy for our present situation is to return again to the teachings of our immortal Washington. I believe that with a sincere devotion to his practices and ideals and sincere endeavor to follow his guidance we can again return to that normal condition of national life which insures us protection and prosperity.

We have patriots today, many of them, who are steadfast in their unselfish patriotism. We are sometimes confused by the clash of conflicting interests. We are stupefied by alarms and pessimism, but we should ever remember that patriotism is not dead. We should remember that unselfish devotion to country is not destroyed and where we find this devotion and this patriotism we should cherish it and encourage it for in that lies our future safety.

At Washington's First Headquarters

Address Delivered at Ceremony Marking Washington's First Headquarters, Cumberland, Maryland, April 21, 1932

The ceremony of marking this quaint little building today is one of the important contributions to the Celebration honoring George Washington on the two hundredth anniversary of his birth.

Any memorial to George Washington on this spot would be important, for at the original settlement that stood here in pioneer times, he really began his great career.

But between the year 1732, when Washington was born, and the year 1753, when he passed this way on his first momentous errand of statesmanship, all was preparation for what was to follow.

By that time Washington had acquired the little school-room learning that Destiny was to allot him, he had made the acquaintance of those great and good friends who after all were his best teachers.

They had drawn out the solid qualities of manhood with which Nature had endowed him. The most powerful and influential of those friends—Lord Fairfax—had given Washington his first real job, his start in life, as a surveyor.

And the new pursuit had taken Washington into the severest tests of adventure and duty amid the wilds of a young country.

At home he learned the ways of the best human society of his time. At his work he learned the ways of savage man in his savage wilderness.

By his 21st year, Washington was ripe for his real work in the world. The period of youth and preparation was over. His frame was of steel. His character was fully formed. Already, at an age when others are still scarcely more than mere boys, George Washington stood established among all who knew him as a man, strong and hardy in body, sound in judgment, absolutely honest, and equal to any demand that might be made of him.

Destiny had decided that it was time for George Washington to begin his career.

And here, in what is now the city of Cumberland, he began that career. Wakefield is the birthplace of his body. This is the birthplace of his work in the world.

All the great achievements which have made him one of the remarkable men of history, had to have their beginnings. And here where we stand, those beginnings occurred.

There could hardly be a more important spot on the face of the earth than just where we are gathered.

And there could hardly be a more appropriate marker for this spot than the little building upon which this tablet is set and dedicated now.

We who look back on that troubled period know that the shadow of war followed George Washington on the errand that brought him this way in 1753.

George Washington knew only that he was sent upon serious business with a threatening military power. He knew that duty was to take him through 200 miles of wilderness, with danger lurking in every mile, and winter doubling every danger.

It was all he needed to know. The Governor of his Province had placed a grave responsibility in his hands, and he meant to discharge it, whatever the cost to himself.

Twice he came within a hair's-breadth of losing his life on that plunge through the wilderness stretching over the mountains from here. Once he was nearly drowned when the tiny raft that he and Gist constructed with a single hatchet stuck in the ice and Washington was wrenched from his footing and had to fight for his life in the icy waters of the Allegheny.

Not many miles further back, a treacherous Indian had fired a musket at him point-blank, but fortunately had missed the shining mark.

We know now that it was little short of a miracle for any man to cross that dense and hostile forest, and come out alive. No man was ever more in the hands of Destiny than George Washington, and no man was so little aware of it.

In the light of subsequent history we know the gravity of Washington's business with the French commanding officer at Fort Le Bouef, ordered by the Governor of Virginia to remove his forces from what was destined to become the United States.

As it happened that officer's answer opened a chain of events beginning with a war that spread over much of the world, and that ended in the American Revolution, the Independence of America, and the establishment of the United States.

So, if any spot on earth is many times sacred, it is here where we stand today. For here George Washington set in motion the forces that brought this about. Here began the labors of a man ennobled above all others for lifting mankind to a higher life. For this alone it were well that we set this spot forever apart as hallowed soil.

On the foundation of Washington's first errand here, the building of his fame went forward with a rush. Hardly had he returned from merely *warning* the invaders away, when he was commissioned an officer and ordered to *drive* them away.

I need not rehearse the story you know so well. If we of the United States George Washington Bicentennial Commission have done our appointed work, then we have made every school-child aware of George Washington's leap to renown from this point. The cold and distant Washington has been banished, and in his place we have stationed the warm and human Washington, whose entire life of kindness and goodness is an open book.

Today we think of the chapter that deals with the young lieutenant-colonel of 22 who came here in 1754 at the head of a tiny army; sent to capture the French fort where the Monongahela and the Allegheny meet.

We know how the death of his superior gave Washington chief command and responsibility. We know the courage with which he faced hopeless odds in his brave stand at Fort Necessity. Surrounded by enemies

fully three times his number, he had to turn back. But he did it with honor and with flags flying.

It was that stand of George Washington that brought Braddock this way within a year. This little building is to stand here as long as its material shall last to be a reminder of that next historic move—which killed the luckless Braddock but spread still further Washington's sublime personal courage, as the heroic redeemer of Colonial honor.

That fateful day revealed to the people of America that the British soldier was not invincible. It further revealed that America had a born leader. These convictions sank into the public mind, and undoubtedly helped to create that patriotic spirit, that solid public confidence, which led to the Declaration of Independence and the victorious war that established that independence. And it was George Washington who brought this about.

With excellent reason we mark today the starting-point of these great events.

On yet a fourth occasion Washington made this spot important by his presence, when he came here to join the Forbes expedition which finally made the entire western region firmly British—and ultimately American.

When Washington came here a last time on a military errand, he came as President of the United States, and the great career had been nearly rounded to the full circle.

Once again the western end of Pennsylvania, which he knew so well from the days when he fought the Indians and the French in its tangled wilds, called for his firm and masterful grip to set it in order.

The wilderness then was dotted with farms, but the great barrier of the Allegheny Mountains cut off this region from the East. The Ohio and the Mississippi tempted Western Pennsylvania to turn its traffic in that direction, and perhaps set up a separate government institution.

All through his Presidential years, Washington was troubled by this possibility. It was this drift toward secession that made what is known as the Whisky Insurrection such a danger in his eyes.

The new United States was openly challenged by a region that threatened to tear itself loose, and Washington flew to preserve his beloved Union, and keep the Great West safe for America.

For the last time in his life he took the field as head of the army. The new Constitution of the United States made the President Commander-in-Chief of the land and naval forces, and Washington lost no time in exercising his Constitutional authority.

Fortunately the menace was quickly over. An army of 15,000 men, with George Washington in command, was too much for the rebellious westerners. His troops had only to appear on the mountain crests, and the ugly prospect of a civil war had vanished.

But here to this place President Washington came in 1794, and we have his own words to describe the scene, in those direct and simple phrases which only Washington could frame.

He had stopped at Old Town, where, he says, "After

an early breakfast we set out for Cumberland . . . Three miles from the Town I was met by a party of Horse under the command of Major Lewis (my Nephew) and by Brigr. Genl. Smith of the Maryland line, who Escorted me to the Camp; where, finding all the Troops under Arms I passed along the line of the Army; was conducted to a house the residence of Major Lynn of the Maryland line (an old Continental Officer) where I was well lodged, and civily entertained."

How thoroughly Washingtonian that is! Though he now was President of the United States, he nevertheless remembers every old comrade in arms. He remembers such matters as the physical comforts he received from the host who had the honor to entertain him. Busy as he was, and weighted with heavy cares, nothing deserving of his thanks escaped him.

What other thoughts must have possessed this man who noted everything, as he came to Cumberland for the last time before he died!

He now was 62 years of age. Precisely forty-one years had passed, almost to the very month, since that day in 1753 when he left Will's Creek, a mere youth, and plunged into the unknown wilderness on the first mission that began his sublime career.

Now, in 1794, the country he had lived and labored to establish was a recognized member of the world's family of nations. Then it was a thin string of colonies, eager for a little more land to the West, and too weak to grasp it.

Upon his first visit here Washington was hardly more than a boy, unknown outside a circle of friends who had recommended him to his Governor. In 1794 he was a great world figure, revered even by his recent enemies.

Washington spent little time in thinking of himself, but these mighty contrasts cannot have escaped his notice.

He may have scorned to think how his personal fame had grown in those forty years, but he was entitled to draw every satisfaction from the growth of his country.

We are not presumptuous in thinking that he did so, for again he has given us hints in his own language.

After his last visit to Cumberland Washington had moved to the general rendezvous at Bedford. From here, after giving final orders for the advance of the army over the mountains, he returned to his Presidential duties at the national capital in Philadelphia. But true to his habit of noticing everything, he records in his diary these significant words:

"The Road from Cumberld. to this place is, in places, stoney but in other respects not bad. It passes through a valley the whole way; and was opened by Troops under my command in the Autumn of 1758."

So we see that the passing of the years, and the great fruits they had borne, did come to his mind. He tells it himself, in words of quiet but justifiable pride.

So Cumberland had its deep meanings for George Washington.

And what a deep and everlasting meaning he has given to Cumberland!

On this place he conferred the deathless honor of being the crucible in which all the qualities in him were to be forged into greatness, in the white-hot trials of battle and action.

And back to this scene Destiny sent him in the fullness of those powers, as if proud to show what she had accomplished with such materials.

Here the Great Power that directs us all, using a chain of events that reads like a majestic poem, rounded out one of the greatest lives ever lived by a man—from its raw beginnings to its glowing summit.

Such is the honor that belongs to this community—to be forever attached, in this Providential way, to the life-story of that great man. Here is the opening and the closing of the outstanding part of his career. With what proud and deep meaning may the people of this neighborhood say, "George Washington tarried here."

These are some of the feelings that stir us to the depths as we place on this little building the tablet which, though in other words, proclaims that fact—today, tomorrow and forever—"George Washington once tarried here."

The claims of this simple structure to have been the very first of Washington's many headquarters, as we are told, may rest on treasured legend and tradition, rather than upon those sworn and attested documents so precious to the historian. In days to come, some other locality, in proud and friendly rivalry, may discover a similar building, with similar claims to priority.

What does it matter, when we have here all that has earthly interest and importance?

What is of undying interest here is that this hallowed ground, and this privileged community, once enjoyed an association with the living Washington that was especially close, so that his memory is here especially dear.

What is important here is not so much this building, but our coming here to mark it.

By this act we prove, with evidence which cannot be disputed, that the real and the eternal headquarters of George Washington are in the memories of humanity. And what we do in marking this building is to set up another eternal symbol and covenant that so long as the Divine spark of gratitude illumines the souls of men, George Washington will ever live in the hearts of his people.

UNVEILING JOSEPH HEWES MEMORIAL

ADDRESS DELIVERED AT CEREMONY OF UNVEILING MEMORIAL TO JOSEPH HEWES,
"FATHER OF THE NAVY," AT EDENTON, NORTH CAROLINA,
APRIL 28, 1932

I see all about me the pride and pleasure which the good people of this historic city have every right to take on this occasion. But it is my rare privilege to draw from it a pleasure that is probably greater than that felt by any one else who is present.

On the program of the day, I am put down as responding to an address of welcome. I have certainly had a welcome here, that stirs every fibre of my being.

But in turn I bring a welcome and a blessing to you—a welcome that comes to you from the entire United States.

The welcome I bring you is for the important addition you are making here to this tribute our people are pouring forth this year. That is why I may claim to enjoy a pleasure even greater than your own.

I feel all the pride that you feel. And to that is added the pride of all the millions of good Americans in our country. For the unveiling and dedication of this monument to Joseph Hewes, takes appropriate place among the most important of all the celebrations of the year.

Joseph Hewes played a pivotal part in the life and labors of George Washington, whose friend he was. The shining patriot who lived here and forever adorns the history of your city, was far more than a mere passive Signer of the Declaration of Independence.

We have it on the authority of John Adams that Joseph Hewes cast the deciding vote that led to the adoption of that immortal charter of our liberties.

The Continental Congress had already sent George Washington to chief command on the field of battle where our national destiny was to be decided. In the Declaration of Independence it placed in Washington's hands full warrant for all he might be called upon to do, in the winning of our liberties.

Without the vote of Joseph Hewes, that warrant would have been withheld. But with the deciding voice of Hewes, history perfected itself, and George Washington was armed with the last great power he needed—the power of an aroused, united, and flaming public opinion.

And the adoption of the Declaration of Independence was no easy matter. We are told by recorders of that great crisis that for months the question of Independence had been discussed, and always the majority had been against it.

Clouds and uncertainties surrounded that deliberative body. Dangers hovered over it. What happened we have in the words of John Adams himself.

"For many days," says Adams, "the Majority [against the Declaration] depended on Mr. Hews of North Carolina. While a Member one day was speaking and reading documents from all the Colonies to prove that the

Public Opinion, the general Sense of all was in favour of the Measure, when he came to North Carolina and produced letters and public proceedings which demonstrated that the Majority of that Colony were in favour of it, Mr. Hews who had hitherto constantly voted against it, started suddenly upright, and lifting up both his Hands to Heaven as if he had been in a trance, cry'd out 'It is done! and I will abide by it.'"

And then exulting John Adams says, "I would give more for a perfect Painting of the terror and horror upon the Faces of the Old Majority at that critical moment than for the best Piece of Raphaelle."

It is little wonder that George Washington became friendly with a man of such courage.

There is perhaps little that is new that I could impart to you concerning the great patriot who lived here. The people of Edenton are in a position to give rather than receive information, concerning him.

My errand here is rather to give you a sense of how this occasion fits like a jewel into the picture of an entire people. The nation is rendering this year a great tribute to its greatest man, and to all the lofty-minded men and women who either aided him personally, or backed his efforts with that loyal public opinion which John Adams refers to with such exultation.

This year an entire nation takes delight in going over its long and honorable history and feeling at one with its past. It gives us all a new dignity, a new feeling of stability, to turn and take note of our increasing age as a people, and watch the lengthening years stretch out behind us.

It enables us to feel that we are no longer a "young" or "new" nation, but now stand as a fixture among the firmest and strongest nations of human history.

And under all this new pleasure that has come to us, I see a deep and wholesome national instinct. It is more than a mere curiosity as to our history that is turning us back to the past, so that we may say to ourselves again, "Yes, these great men belong to us. They are Americans. We produced them."

We are turning back to them because we know they were leaders who triumphed in a difficult and dangerous time. Now our country, together with the entire world, is in another difficult and puzzling period. We stand confused and anxious. The cry for leadership arises on every hand. We are troubled for our personal fortunes, and some of us, even for our national safety.

So, in the midst of our fears, we have an instinct to turn back and see how Washington and his fellow patriots mastered their trials and discouragements. We feel a need to profit by their example, to study their methods, and refresh ourselves from the spirit of self-giving that made them patriots and made them great.

For many years we have felt that we lived in a wholly new and improved time. We looked upon the America of today, with its marvelous inventions and advancements, as something new in the world. By comparison the America of Washington's time seemed primitive and old-fashioned. It seemed to belong to a day that was past.

I believe that if we were honest enough to confess it, we felt toward Washington himself that, while he was undeniably a great man in his time, he too belonged in the past.

But now we have found that even this most advanced world of today is subject to the same shocks and stresses that have afflicted nations since the world began.

We have found that not all our wealth could save us from uncertainty and fear and distress. We have found that even this scientific time is in danger without the old human virtues of unselfishness, patriotism, thought of country before thought of self.

And so we are moved by a deep and saving instinct to turn back to the great men who practised these virtues and built so great a nation. We feel a need to purge ourselves of the vices of greed and selfishness and forgetfulness of country, that have brought us into loss and confusion, and be filled again with the sublime incentives of the fathers.

In my opinion, nothing else than this profound popular instinct can account for the quiet but great and strong enthusiasm which our people are throwing into this remarkable year-long tribute of respect and reverence to George Washington and his great associates. It is more than a passing jubilee; it is the solemn re-dedication of a people to their ancient standards, and to the mighty souls of old who set us the immortal example of how those standards should be held aloft.

To many of us, no doubt, this return to our ancient history can be hardly more than a refreshing study, an effort to grasp from books and pictures a sense of the reality of our past.

But there are in the country certain privileged places that are the very birth-places of that history. There we get a real feeling of the actuality of those days and their great men. For about us are the houses where they lived and planned, the very churches where they worshipped, the very streets they passed along on their way to business.

This City of Edenton is such a place. It seems to me that here we see America at its very best.

You have here superbly beautiful natural settings and surroundings. You have here traditions of the finest culture, running back to America's very beginnings. You have a record of patriotism that takes its place beside that of any other community in the original colonies.

An honored dweller in this colonial town played a decisive role in upholding George Washington's arm and in establishing the freedom of all the colonies. And into this community President George Washington reached for a member of the Supreme Court, so that the work of Joseph Hewes in molding our national structure was continued by James Iredell, his intimate friend and life-long admirer.

By contributing all this, Edenton fixes itself forever in American history, and by celebrating today the memory of one of her great patriots your city adds, as I say, a touching and important feature to the nation's great program of tribute this year.

And in marking the everlasting memory of one of these men, you are animated, I know, by something of that same wave of national feeling which I have witnessed everywhere else in the country—this turning back to the ancient spirit for that renewal of purpose which we crave and need so much today.

So here, too, the underlying instinct and purpose of this memorable Bicentennial year is being fulfilled.

And so I, who have come here to receive one welcome, bring you another welcome—from an America united this year as never before, rallied as one behind the memory of Washington and of those upon whom he relied for help and support.

Let us remember that while these deeply moving occasions remind us of the dignity of our increasing age, nevertheless America is always new. It is as new today as it was in the days when Washington ordered read to his troops the Declaration of Independence, made possible by the brave and self-sacrificing vote of your famous townsman, Joseph Hewes.

Our nation is ever new because it has new problems to face and to master every day. For that is the law of progress. If we are to march on, we must be prepared to meet new obstacles at every stage. The truth of the matter is that every day every one of us has his own Declaration of Independence to sign. Every day this nation itself must start a new independence.

In the day of Washington and Joseph Hewes, the independence so passionately desired, so defiantly declared and so heroically fought for, was Independence from a foreign political tyranny.

Washington, with men like Joseph Hewes to support him, forever settled that great question.

But today we need Independence from the tyranny of distress, from selfishness, and a hundred enemies within our own borders, that have reduced us to fear and uncertainty.

It is high time that we turned back and learned how the Fathers won their Independence, that we may learn how to win ours.

The man to whose everlasting honor and memory this shaft is unveiled today was the type of man who could vote a saving measure for his country, though he knew that measure might ruin his business. Long before the Declaration of Independence was discussed, Joseph Hewes voted for non-importation of English goods, though his whole fortune depended on his ships and his trade.

Joseph Hewes died at the post of duty. He gave his life to his country as truly as if he had lost it on the field of battle. Frail of body, he devoted himself to brave stands in the council chamber, and there labored with a fierceness of energy that finally killed him. He thus ended a perfect record of service to his country and his fellow countrymen, with the crowning touch of being one of the first members of the Continental Congress to die at his work.

In a letter written while the clouds of the Revolutionary war were gathering, Joseph Hewes tells that he has bought a good musket and a bayonet, and that he would rather fall in action than fade away from his lingering malady.

His wish was fulfilled, though in a different way. He died for country, after labors and achievements that accomplished far more for his people than he could with a musket in the ranks.

It is to the type of patriot represented by your eminent townsman that we are turning back this year, in this national impulse I speak of—this instinct to recapture some of the iron will, the fearless determination, and all the other sturdy virtues that enabled those men to triumph over their dangers and difficulties, so that we may become the masters of ours.

If we would honor Joseph Hewes here, and George Washington everywhere, this year, this is the best way we can do so—by bringing the spirit of 1776 into the problems of 1932.

Upbuilder of his young country's commerce, faithful representative of his countrymen in their provincial assemblies, fearless upholder of their rights in the Continental Congress, Signer of the Declaration of their Independence, first executive head of their navy, wise and experienced legislator—Joseph Hewes was the perfect example of those self-giving men who made possible George Washington's work for America and for humanity.

Your welcome here reflects truly the finest traditions of this beautiful Southland. It is the perpetual tie of that fine hospitality that reaches us and binds us with the past. In this glorious season of vernal beauty when all nature joins in a grand chorus of praise to our All Merciful Creator, your welcome blends with that spirit of friendliness that makes us one with Him.

Those who come here, as I do, for the first time, feel that we have gained a certain enrichment in our lives. There is an impression that will last always, not alone of what you do and say today, but of the atmosphere which shines like a radiance all about us.

I have a new understanding of your love for this place; your yielding to its charms; your local patriotism. And your welcome seems to breathe a sentiment of all those who have gone before you—a welcome to your lives and to your hearts.

So long as that sentiment prevails, so long as we preserve that strong feeling of attachment to our native land, so long will our nation last. In honoring an American patriot we honor our land. This reverent act performed here today seems to me proof that it is our national impulse this year. It speaks out in this noble tribute of respect. It is speaking wherever the memory of George Washington, or any of his co-workers is likewise honored during this two hundredth year since Washington's birth.

I therefore stand here moved as never before, because I believe the feeling here and everywhere else exhibited in America this year, is a proof that our country is safe, because by such very acts as this, it *is* refreshing itself from the men and the principles that brought it into being and gave it life.

I believe in the principles laid down by George Washington.

I believe in the wisdom of his compatriots.

I believe in the Americans of today.

I believe in—America.

Before the Tomb of George Washington

Address Delivered at American Peace Society Ceremony, Before Tomb of George Washington at Mount Vernon, May 2, 1932

This is a place of dreams; a place of reverie; a place of solemn memories. Standing beneath the glory of these majestic trees, before the tomb of him who lies within this ancient vault, we come as humble pilgrims, as children, seeking comfort, inspiration and courage from the great life which ended here.

About us is the quiet, brooding spirit of George Washington. It is the calm spirit, the beautiful spirit, the courageous spirit of the man who gave so much to us. Here we feel in our most sensitive natures the soul of America—the America that George Washington brought into being and which he did all that was humanly possible to preserve after his time by leaving us his precepts and his advice.

I believe that if that long-silent voice could issue from the shadows of this shrine to us, his countrymen, he would bid us have courage, have faith and be strong. I believe that if we attuned ourselves to that infinite spiritual message that we would go from this place with new loyalty and new confidence in our future.

These are dark days for America, but no darker than the days which he experienced and our situation is not as desperate as was his. We must take heart of his courage, faith of his steadfastness and live with his immortal example as a light to our faltering feet.

We are apt to think in these gloomy days that our troubles are mountainous. We are afraid and uncertain. These are qualities which George Washington knew not. For at every point in his life he demonstrated exactly those qualities of mind and heart which we of today should strive to acquire.

The great man who lies within this silent tomb left us more than riches, more than material heritage, more even than the nation which he created, for he left us those guiding principles to answer every national question and to form every national policy within his field of vision. And we are now only beginning to discover how far his vision extended into the future.

His rich and fruitful years brought him a harvest of wisdom which he, in his greatness has left to us. Alert to every important political force and movement of his own time, he traced with unerring instinct the course these forces were to follow in later years and what would be their effect and consequences.

His was not only a great life rounded with the wisdom and the character of a perfect career, but his also was a mind so strongly developed that he looked far into the future and left for us those standards of policy and of life that today, if we acknowledged and followed them, would surely lead us on out of the valley of discouragement and doubt to the shining heights of success and prosperity.

We who have been organizing the great world-wide ceremonies that mark the Two Hundredth Anniversary of George Washington's Birth, have been examining his life, his deeds and especially his opinions with a new interest, and the result has been to discover in him the most powerful intellect that America has yet produced. But intellect without unselfishness is barren; wisdom without charity is empty.

George Washington left us a heritage greater than wealth, greater than station, greater than all the vanities of the world. He left us all of the knowledge and wisdom which he had acquired and which could be applied to the problems of a future America.

These priceless possessions belong to us. They came from the heart and the mind of the man who lived in this beautiful spot and whose bodily remains rest so close to us. Here we come into intimate communion with his life and also with the soul which passed beyond. Here we must feel our dependence upon his wisdom to guide us in our social and political lives as we feel dependent upon the God of Mercy to lead us in our moral lives.

There is not a problem confronting us today, there is not a danger threatening us, that was not in some manner embodied in the vision of this greatest of our people. In so far as our country has remained true to its ideals and safely progressing toward its appointed destiny, it has accomplished this by leaning upon the teachings left to us by this man.

What if George Washington could not foresee the progress in transportation, communication and science that has given this country a different aspect from that which he knew? What if George Washington did not hear the scream of a locomotive, or see airplanes flying over his beloved estate? These are not fundamental influences upon the human heart. They do not in themselves affect the souls of men and women.

The human instincts which George Washington knew so well have remained unchanged amid all this superficial miracle of development, and it is to the hearts of men of his day and for all future days that George Washington made his appeal.

He knew that men's hearts would never change. Men are of restless minds and for this reason George Washington deemed it fit that he should work through the hearts of men to give them a sound, kindly conception of their duties to God, their country and to themselves.

As nearly as it was humanly possible George Washington and his compatriots gave us an unchanging form of Government and we must acknowledge the transcendent wisdom which created that form of Government when we remember that in principle it is exactly the same today as it was when promulgated by the Constitutional Convention over which George Washington presided.

It is because these fundamentals do remain unchanged, and please God, ever will remain unchanged, that we continue to be a nation with unlimited ages of progress before us. But if our future as a nation is to remain secure, we need always to rely on the affectionate and fatherly advice left to us by George Washington and the other great men of his time.

If this Celebration in honor of the Two Hundredth Anniversary of the Birth of George Washington has accomplished nothing else than to direct our minds to a more serious consideration of his rich store of political wisdom, it would have been justified. For in that wisdom lies safety. For in that wisdom lies every national attribute that makes for stability and the happiness of our people.

As a youthful Colonel on his first diplomatic and military errands against hostile forces on American soil, George Washington had impressed upon his mind the need of bringing the scattered colonies together. He saw their need of a new sense of nationalism if they were to live in peace for the future.

As Commander-in-Chief of the Revolutionary Armies he began his twin labors as military leader and as statesman. While saving the colonies themselves, he began that colossal work of welding them into one nation and one people which is today our proud America.

As counselor, advisor and conciliator, he kept a watchful eye upon the progress of the framing of the Constitution upon which he pinned his hopes and desires.

As President, he began the work of creating out of these principles and policies a fabric of government which has outlasted time itself.

We cannot read the record of George Washington's life without realizing that it was a life of continuous struggle. At no time, save the few brief years of his retirement here upon this lovely estate, was George Washington free from care or the burdens of responsibility. These cares and responsibilities were not for himself, but always for his country and his countrymen. Always for others. And in his great heart he thought of us today. Sacrifice, suffering, danger—these were with him during his days and nights.

With devout and yearning hearts we stand here in reverence beside his tomb to catch the fleeting breath of his presence. His message comes to us through that mysterious transmission of spirit that is breathed in the hush of this moment and this place. The infinite peace of God is his. Here his love and his care sustain us in the sure knowledge that he is with us and is pointing the way. He is ever pointing the way. The Commander and the Comrade rides ahead.

If Washington were alive today, would he bow his head in discouragement before the problems which we face? If that inanimate clay which lies in this sacred place should breathe again would George Washington say to us that all is lost? Would he who brought the nation into being fear for its safety after all the years of its glorious history?

I say no!

George Washington, with that steady, inflexible purpose, that judgment and knowledge which he possessed, would calm the turbulent waters of our present unrest and bid us go on to a greater destiny.

That is the spirit of George Washington. That is the soul which we acknowledge here in this quiet spot. No greater tribute could we pay to him who lies within this tomb, than to re-dedicate ourselves to him and to his purposes.

No greater thing could we do for ourselves than to stand here at this solemn hour and say we will go forward with George Washington, and under God's guidance we will achieve, we will succeed, we will preserve that which he gave us.

The benediction of our Creator is here. The peace of God is upon us. We should go forth armed with new courage, new wisdom and new determination. Thus armed we will preserve our country and will keep faith with George Washington.

WHY GEORGE WASHINGTON WAS THE FIRST PRESIDENT OF THE UNITED STATES

EXTENSION OF REMARKS MADE IN THE HOUSE OF REPRESENTATIVES
MAY 11, 1932

Reprinted from the CONGRESSIONAL RECORD *of May 11, 1932*

I doubt if the Members of Congress, or the people of America generally, realize the tremendous service that has been rendered by the United States George Washington Bicentennial Commission in correcting popular historical fallacies and setting forth for the future, the facts in relation to the history of George Washington and his time.

This work of eliminating the false from the true and in setting up unassailable facts of history has been, in a sense, a by-product of the Commission's activities, but its importance is becoming more apparent every day.

To those of us who have been laboring in the almost endless research and publication necessary to bring forth an authentic history of George Washington and his time, it has been astonishing to realize the persistence of error. Almost from the day we started our research service, we were confronted constantly with criticisms, denials and assertions that indicated the general fog, not only in the popular mind, but in the minds of many so-called historians, in relation to this period of our history. We were continually meeting these critics and building up a structure of historical facts that could be relied upon and which would stand for all time as the official record.

It is amazing to note the stubbornness with which a certain number of people contend that Washington's birthday should be observed on the eleventh of February instead of February 22. I have already placed in the Congressional Record a complete statement covering that question and proving beyond any question of doubt that February 22 is the true birthday of George Washington.

Another persistent error is the often repeated assertion that George Washington did not receive a salary as President. By searching the records we have found that George Washington did receive a salary.

Recently another statement has had wide circulation which declares that one John Hanson was the First President of the United States. We have repeatedly denied this and pointed to historical references to sustain our position. It has remained for the State Department of the United States Government to place its final stamp of authority upon the fact that John Hanson was not the First President of the United States, but that George Washington himself was the First President of the United States.

In order to preserve this statement and to correlate it with other important facts which are of official record, I wish to quote a statement issued by the State Department of the United States, May 9, 1932, which says:

"Probably because of the Bicentennial Celebration an unusual amount of interest has been aroused in this country as to who was the first President of the United States. The following is a sample of the reply sent by the Department to the various inquirers:

"Sir: The receipt is acknowledged of your letter of April 23, 1932, in which you enquire 'who is considered the first President of the United States?'

"George Washington was the first President of the United States of America. The office of President of the United States of America was created by express words of the Constitution, which says (Article II, Section I) 'The executive Power shall be vested in a President of the United States of America.'

"George Washington took the oath of office on April 30, 1789, and having been reelected served until March 3, 1797, as it was then considered that the term of office of a President expired at midnight of March 3 although it is now the settled practice that the term expires on March 4, at noon.

"Prior to the Articles of Confederation, which went into force on March 1, 1781, upon the completion of their ratification by the thirteen States, the Continental

Congress chose from time to time presiding officers or 'presidents.' Of these there were seven chosen prior to March 1, 1781. Samuel Huntington, of Connecticut, being then in office.

"Samuel Huntington continued to preside over the session of the Continental Congress then holding until July 10, 1781. He had asked to be relieved of the duties of that office on the ground of ill health and Thomas McKean was elected to succeed him.

"By the Articles of Confederation (Article V) the delegates were to meet in Congress on the first Monday of November in every year and (Article IX) 'the United States in Congress assembled shall have authority . . . to appoint one of their number to preside, provided that no person be allowed to serve in the office of president more than one year in any term of three years.'

"On November 5, 1781, the first Monday in November of that year, 'Congress proceeded to the election of a President; and the ballots being taken, the honorable John Hanson was elected' (Journals of the Continental Congress, XXI, 1100). Thus under the Articles of the Confederation, John Hanson was appointed to preside and held the 'office of president' of 'the United States in Congress assembled.' John Hanson had six successors elected at various dates from 1782 to 1788.

"The names of the various presidents of the Congress prior to 1789 will be found on page 31 of the 'Biographical Directory of the American Congress' (Government Printing Office, 1928) which is available in many public libraries.

"While John Hanson (and sometimes Thomas McKean) has in various writings been spoken of as the 'first president' because of the position which he held under the Articles of Confederation, his office was that of President of the United States in Congress Assembled, and was not the office of President of the United States of America.

"Not only actually and really but also in the most strict legal sense as well, George Washington was the first President of the United States of America."

There is nothing new in the foregoing statement so far as historical research is concerned. The United States George Washington Bicentennial Commission had ascertained these facts many months ago, but it is reassuring to note the State Department's voluntary statement and to feel that this should, and undoubtedly will, put an effective and permanent quietus upon a silly and unjustifiable historical mistake.

Posterity will owe to the United States George Washington Bicentennial Commission a deep debt of gratitude for its studious, earnest and persistent efforts to clarify authentic history. I am convinced that this general subject is of such paramount importance that the Congress of the United States should in some way continue such activities, not only for the Americans of today, but for the generations of Americans yet to come.

Memorial Day at Arlington

Address Delivered at Arlington National Cemetery, Broadcast by the National Broadcasting Company, May 30, 1932

In meeting here today upon this beautiful and solemn occasion, we are responding to a sentiment that reaches deep into the hearts of all humanity.

We are here, again, to express our tribute of respect and gratitude to our hero dead. But these exalted emotions are not restricted to those who are buried here. They encompass the wide range of all our history and all our nation's defenders.

We come not to pay a debt, for the debt we owe and acknowledge here is beyond any human ability to pay. Nor are we here to eulogize the heroes who have gone before. They are beyond eulogy.

We come here to re-consecrate ourselves to the preservation of what they achieved. We are here to pledge in loving remembrance, the true hearts of living Americans, to our countrymen, who gave their lives that our nation might survive.

Those heroes who have gone before are neither high nor low, rich nor poor. In the democracy of death they are made one, and the love we bear them ennobles us and raises before us the radiant symbols of their loyalty and their patriotism.

Many who lie in this vast sacred place were known to us. The record of their lives and their deeds shine forth to brighten the pages of our history. But in other fields, in other acres dedicated to God, heroes lie whose very names do not remain to us.

Those defenders of our land went forth to suffering and to death animated by a single imperishable thought. Whether they were soldiers of a recent war or soldiers of almost forgotten conflicts, we hold them all alike in loving memory and honor.

In this year devoted to the Celebration of the Two Hundredth Anniversary of the Birth of George Washington, it is fitting that we include in these Memorial exercises today a thought and a prayer for the forgotten heroes who achieved our independence, and started our Nation upon its course.

Few records remain to us of the thousands of brave men who followed Washington with a devotion matchless in the history of the world. During that long and terrible winter at Valley Forge alone, many hundreds of George Washington's soldiers died from wounds, disease, and—starvation.

And of all those who sleep upon that historic field in the companionship of immortality, but one grave alone is marked, one name alone stands for all.

It does not in any way detract from our remembrance

of later soldiers that we pause to think of the nameless, forgotten men who were, nevertheless, Americans, and who died for our flag with the same unselfish patriotism as the heroes who lie about us here.

Our eyes fix themselves upon those whose rank and deeds made them especially known, and it is significant that not one of our war heroes is better known than the Unknown Soldier, who stands for all the serried ranks of markers that lie about him here, and in the fields of France, like mortal tears turned to immortal stone.

He stands for those who died in other wars, whose very names are lost behind the misty curtain of the past.

For these unknown there are no flowers today. No bugle calls echo o'er their lonely graves. No mother's grief centers about their resting places. No proud descendants lay flowers upon the earth above them in token of the love we bear them. Their sentinels are the everlasting vigil of the stars. Their requiem is the whispering wind that testifies for all eternity the remembrance of Almighty God.

Let this memorial of ours today reach out to those soldiers whose identity is lost, whose graves the rains have washed away, those blessed patriots who sprang to battle at the living voice of Washington, and who are one with him in the comradeship of immortal glory.

In the memories of this day, in the solemn beauty of this shrine, let us render thanks to our Heavenly Father for giving this country such men—men of today and of yesterday, men of the long, long ago—the noblest manhood of our own America.

FROM THE HOME OF FRANCIS SCOTT KEY

ADDRESS BROADCAST FROM THE HOME OF FRANCIS SCOTT KEY, WASHINGTON, D. C.,
BY THE NATIONAL BROADCASTING COMPANY,
FLAG DAY,
JUNE 14, 1932

Flag Day this year is of particular significance because we are celebrating the Two Hundredth Anniversary of the Birth of that great American who brought our flag into being.

Upon this occasion, therefore, it is appropriate that I speak from the home of Francis Scott Key, whose inspired genius garlanded the "Star Spangled Banner" with sentiments of imperishable glory.

As I stand in this revered old mansion in Georgetown, Washington, D. C., now the property of the Federal Government, and which sheltered the author of our National Anthem, I feel the spell of his transcendent patriotism upon me. I hear re-echoing through the time-stained walls of this historic building, the voice long since gone that first put into articulate form the solemn feeling of his gratitude that the flag was still there.

Before Francis Scott Key wrote his immortal lines, patriotic Americans were powerless to utter the deep emotions that filled them at every sight of the flag and with every thought of the colors that stand for its red-blooded courage, the white, purity of its motives, and the blue of the heaven that has ever been our guide.

In 1812 our country was again in peril because of questions left unsettled by the Revolution, and largely because our young nation had been too busy in establishing itself to prepare adequate defenses. The result was a war with Great Britain that ran for two years against us.

The City of Washington was burned with a loss of the Capitol, the White House and many other public buildings. The President of the United States had been driven from the city. Our shipping had disappeared from the seas. Our humiliation was complete. The fate of the new nation trembled in the balance. It was a question whether the independence of the United States of America would survive.

The whole issue turned on the outcome of one last battle, in the Autumn of 1814. The hope of the nation lay in the City of Baltimore, and the hope of Baltimore lay in the one fort that defended it, with ancient guns and an untrained garrison.

On that fateful Sunday morning in September, 1814, the alarm was sounded through the streets of Baltimore. Cannon boomed from the public square, proclaiming that the enemy ships had entered the Patapsco River and summoning the militia to guard the city.

Thus began the historic attack on Fort McHenry, in which the stout patriots had little to fire at their opponents except nails and scrap iron. We know the issue of that battle now, but while it raged the fighting was desperate, ever at fever pitch, and the victory ever in doubt.

At dusk a great storm cut short the fighting, but at dawn it broke out anew, and fifteen British ships hurled bombs, rockets and solid shot into the ramparts.

All that day and through the ensuing night the conflict continued and every moment of it was watched by Francis Scott Key. He had gone from this home in which I am speaking, to Baltimore and boarded an enemy ship under a flag of truce to arrange for the exchange of a friend who had been taken prisoner. And while the battle raged, he was kept on board ship, himself a virtual prisoner.

From the midst of the attacking fleet he watched the bombardment directed against his fellow Americans. Every shot that left an enemy gun was a blow at his heart. At midnight he witnessed the sending of a detachment from an enemy ship to attack the fort from the rear. Everything dear to him and to his countrymen hung on that movement and its effect on the battle. And over the battle itself hung the black pall, horror and suspense of night.

For Francis Scott Key it was a night of anguish. What would the morning disclose? Would the fort still hold? Would the grand old emblem of red, and white and blue, still float defiantly from the mast of the fort in token of the survival of our country? All night long the poet paced the deck of the ship where he watched, waiting for what the morning would bring.

Then how his heart must have beat in that dramatic moment when the first blush of dawn tinged the eastern sky. With straining eyes he peered through the smoke and fog which momentarily lifted and saw——

There was the flag! The fort still held! The country was safe! In that night of anguish and suspense, in the very midst of shrieking shells and bursting bombs, and in the moment of victory, was conceived our national anthem, "The Star Spangled Banner."

"O say can you see by the dawn's early light" came the question from his heart.

Yes, the flag was still there! Yes, American courage had not faltered! Yes, the oppressor had failed again in a battle to lower that flag forever! Yes, the Star Spangled Banner still waved o'er the land of the free and the home of the brave.

And in reverence to the Giver of all good, Francis Scott Key knelt upon the deck of the ship and returned thanks to Almighty God that the flag was still there.

If ever a song was born of Divine inspiration, it was this song of songs. If ever a man responded to a supreme emotion, it was Francis Scott Key when he set down the words that today are the national anthem of our country and destined for immortality with the flag itself.

The building in which I am speaking was the home of that poet. In this beautiful old city of Georgetown, much older than the National Capital, but now a part of it, Francis Scott Key lived, here on the banks of the lovely Potomac.

All about this house there have been the mutations of progress. But I still see through these windows the Potomac much as it was in his day. On the further side are the verdure clad hills of Virginia, and beyond the sweeping city of our heroic dead, Arlington, while further still are the great radio towers of the government.

Before me rises that magnificent structure which now spans the Potomac River, named in honor of the poet, the Francis Scott Key Bridge. And almost washing the foundations of this house are the placid waters of the ancient canal which was the important method of transportation to Cumberland and the Northwest in the early days of the Capital.

Far off toward the sea-wall of the city, there are airplanes, electric cars and a railway train rushing over a distant bridge. On the Potomac itself are steamers and other craft of many kinds, so that here in this sequestered spot, I see the old linked with the new.

Before me is unrolled the panorama of our life as a nation, and all about I see the flag of your country and mine. Never in all these years of development has there been anything upon our soil as wonderful in its birth, as magnificent in its life as the Star Spangled Banner itself, waving in the glory of our country's progress.

Americans everywhere thrill to the sight of its majestic folds and take comfort in the caressing shadow of its brilliant beauty.

Throughout the world it flies today, triumphant in its undimmed honor, nor ever lowered to an alien foe.

Within these ancient walls now stained with the weariness of the years, this ancient masonry about me, covered with the moss of time, the solemn thoughts that enfold me here are memories—memories of the long ago, memories of our flag and all that it stands for, in all the history of our beloved land.

It was on June 14, 1777, when the Continental Congress passed the resolution which originated that flag. And since that day there has been no permanent change in it, save in the canton which has increased from thirteen colonies to forty-eight states.

Today the same flag which shelters you and me would be recognized by every patriot who has shed his blood for that flag from Brandywine to the present moment.

Today that flag flies from many thousands of staffs, in our own and in foreign lands. It is the bright symbol of human freedom born under its folds and preserved by the millions of Americans whose devotion to it has conquered every enemy and brought victory upon every field.

I am impressed by the solemnity of this hour. I would that through this miracle of science I could bring to my listeners everywhere, the feeling that inspires me as I stand in this ancient shrine, hallowed by the memories and personal associations of Francis Scott Key.

I would that we could all re-dedicate ourselves in devotion and in loyalty to that flag which means so much, not alone to us, but to all the liberty-loving people of the earth.

I would that we could match its purity with the purity of our own lives. I would that we could match its courage with the courage of our people. I would that we could match its meaning with the beauty of the American ideal.

So long as that flag flies, so long will liberty be ours. So long as we look upon its glory, so long will we remember the blood, the tears, the courage and the manhood that brought it into being and preserved it to us.

Through that long and troubled night it flew from Fort McHenry, and in the dawn of that day when Francis Scott Key looked over the water it was still flying, tattered and torn by the shot and turmoil of battle, but still victorious, still our own emblem, still the living symbol of our beloved land.

And as that flag has weathered every storm and survived every peril, so will it continue to lead us on in the pathway of George Washington.

As it has never been lowered in defeat, it will not trail in the dust of our own neglect.

The Ruler of all men guided those minds and hearts that set it in the sky. The God of Nations willed that it should blazen forth upon the background of heaven itself. And we, the living Americans of today, must feel that upon us is the trust laid down by those who looked upon this banner and died happy in the knowledge that it still waved o'er the land of the free and the home of the brave.

In the solemn stillness of this old room I seem to hear the echo of that voice speaking again to the Americans of today and again asking us, his living countrymen, if the flag is still there.

Far up above the distant hills, stand the ramparts of Fort Myer and daily its guns thunder forth to the world that the flag is still there.

At the white marble tomb of the Unknown Soldier, amid the thousands of graves of patriot Americans, the whispering winds bear testimony that the flag is still there.

Down the vista of this majestic city there towers the great monument to Washington giving the answer that the flag is still there.

And beyond from the great noble dome of the Capitol itself comes the signal to all Americans that the flag is still there.

Yes, Francis Scott Key, you may sleep in peace.

We leave the shadows of this shrine, we go forth from the quiet beauty of these memories into the world of affairs, but we leave with you in the spirit which still lingers in this old home, the answer to your question that God rules and the flag of our beloved America is still there.

WASHINGTON THE EVERY DAY MAN

ADDRESS DELIVERED BEFORE THE KIWANIS CLUB AND OTHER CIVIC GROUPS, AT WILKES-BARRE, PA., JUNE 30, 1932

If George Washington were alive today I have no doubt he would be a proud member of such a splendid group as is assembled here. For George Washington not only qualified for the high standards of citizenship which you maintain, but he was the kind of man who would be interested in the advancement of all movements for good citizenship.

It may surprise you to know that George Washington, even in the simple times in which he lived, was a member of several important organizations devoted to the encouragement of knowledge, of culture and better understanding among men.

It is of George Washington, the man, that I would speak to you today. When I say man, I mean our kind of man—the citizen, the business man, the friend and associate of other business men. For George Washington was always a seeker after knowledge and a seeker after the mature opinions of other men, upon all kinds of subjects.

As an engineer he did not possess highly technical knowledge, but he was always anxious to learn and was an intelligent listener, and, what is more, he was an intelligent questioner. As a farmer he was perhaps the best authority on general farming problems of his day. But even so, he conducted a busy correspondence with other farmers here and abroad and was ever alert to learn from their experience.

As a business man, interested in several lines of industry, such as agriculture, shipping, banking and real estate, he was happy to meet with other men devoted to these lines of industry, which moved him to discuss mutual problems in a congenial atmosphere of confidence and esteem.

It is of this man of business, of the common affairs of life, rather than the heroic Washington in his highly dramatic moments, that I would speak to you today. It is difficult for us to imagine from mere reading of history a man of Washington's transcendent personality, sitting with other men, discussing commonplace affairs. Yet we have many instances, most of them cited by Washington in his own writings, where he spent evenings and other times snatched from his busy life, to visit with friends and neighbors and to talk of things in which they were all interested. Not only that, but Washington did not intrude his opinions unless they were asked for, and he was so great that he did not hesitate to acknowledge wisdom in other people, and more than that, to ask advice.

So that we are justified in imagining George Washington here among us, foregathered for good fellowship, for a better understanding and for the benefits which arise from such splendid organizations as are represented here.

George Washington was a man of so many varied interests, so many qualities of manhood, that he was always at home in any group of people. Quiet, dignified, serene, he yet possessed all the human qualities which are summed up in the word "amiable." He was dignified without austerity, quiet without smug self-complacency and wise without egotism. He was in the best sense of the word a good fellow, although he possessed a natural reserve which seldom bent to hilarity or demonstration.

It is comforting to think of Washington in the common denominator of a citizen. As much as we may stand in awe of his superlative military exploits, as much as we may applaud those supreme qualities of statesmanship that made him an outstanding historical figure for all time, we may yet picture George Washington, sitting among us, a fine figure of a man and neighbor, a business man, a substantial citizen, interested in the things in which we are interested, promoting the things which we are promoting, and not too great to be attracted to things of comparatively small concern.

There is one Washington who was in command at the battle of Yorktown, but the same Washington who basked in the applause of the world was not too great or too dignified to spend a night trying to save the life of one of his favorite dogs.

We are now in the midst of the Celebration of the Two Hundredth Anniversary of the birth of this man. Throughout the entire world, honors are being paid to his memory. The United States George Washington Bicentennial Commission was established by Congress to organize and inspire these honors to George Washington in every town, village and hamlet, in every church, school, fraternal and business organization throughout the nation.

In the work of this Commission, of which I have the honor to be the Director, we have had a group of competent historians, delving into every phase of his remarkable life. No other American has had such a keen study made on his every act.

The strong light of investigation has been turned upon every scrap of his voluminous correspondence. We have gone wherever possible to the original sources and it has been one of the chief objects of our Commission to establish a truthful record of that life, free from unsubstantiated tradition, free from prejudice and persistent errors, so that the American people in years to come will have an authentic account of its greatest citizen.

While it is true that a major part of this record is devoted to superlative achievements connected with the winning of our Independence and the founding of our nation, yet I have been struck by the great number of references to George Washington's home life, to his neighborhood life, to his interest in the humbler affairs of those about him. If George Washington had not been the great leader of the Revolution, if his hand had not guided the framing of the Constitution, if he had not been the First President of the United States, he would still have been an outstanding citizen.

It was doubtless pleasant for him to receive the merited applause of his fellow countrymen, but it was equally pleasant for him to shake the hand of his neighbor and wish him well. George Washington, the man, comprehends all of his qualities and all of his character and all of his achievements. But in the vast range of his illustrious career, that which would please him most for us to remember, would be that he was George Washington the farmer of Mount Vernon. That was his pride, his recreation, his place of peace.

There, in his home, surrounded by his family and by his many friends of nearby Virginia, he spent his best, but all too brief hours. There we would have gone to meet George Washington upon terms of association represented by the citizens of this community, and I believe firmly that George Washington would have taken pride in such an exhibition of confidence and esteem among his own kind.

You, who live in this historic valley look back upon a history that is filled with tragedy and with glorious achievement.

Here, in this part of Pennsylvania and upon your northern border, were fought some of the bitterest Indian wars in colonial and early national history.

Following a long controversy over the possession of the lands in this region, one of the most notable incidents of the Revolutionary period occurred. On July 3, 1778, the Indians under Brant and the Tory Rangers under Major John Butler, who had descended upon the valley the first of the month, being certain that Pennsylvania would offer no protection, defeated a motley militia of 400 Connecticut men under Zebulon Butler, near Kingston, in which three-fourths of the defenders were killed or captured and subsequently massacred. The British forces swept through the valley, leaving such a scene of devastation and of murder that this so-called Wyoming Massacre, seems today the supreme horror of the Revolution.

It was in a way the turning point of the Indian-Tory frontier raids, for the next year George Washington sent the famous expedition under Sullivan, that mobilized on the Susquehanna, just above the northern boundary of Pennsylvania, and totally devastated the Iroquois country. This did not entirely end Indian raiding, especially in the Mohawk Valley, but the Iroquois were never able to regain their power.

This is merely an incident in the long list of tragic events that held the stage in this historic region. But we know that George Washington, ever alert for danger and ever mindful of the safety of frontier America, did not hesitate when the time came to strike vigorously and effectively to end the series of horrors enacted here.

Timothy Pickering, the commissioner to effect reconciliation between the warring sections in the valley, had been Adjutant General and Quartermaster during the Revolution, and later was to be Washington's Postmaster General, Secretary of War and Secretary of State.

So that Wilkes-Barre may proudly take its place in the glorious history of a tragic epoch.

In these events we see Washington, both as a Commander and as a far-seeing statesman, using force to bring peace, using wisdom to establish prosperity.

It is appropriate that in this community and in this place, citizens should pause to give thought to the men who not only brought security to your forebears here, but whose influence for peace, for liberty and opportunity, extends throughout the nation and the world.

I am happy for the opportunity of joining with you here upon this occasion. It is an opportunity to take personal part in one of the many local events that carry out the spirit and purpose of the great celebration in honor of the Two Hundredth Anniversary of the Birth of George Washington.

Today the world rings with tributes to George Washington. Today he is acclaimed as the leader in that great school of thought which has overthrown tyranny and instituted human liberty throughout the earth.

The real monument to George Washington is not that superb shaft which rises in the midst of the beautiful park in the national capital. Today the monument to George Washington is not represented by statues, by busts, by paintings, by thousands of books and other material memorials. The monument to Washington that will stand for all time is the monument in the hearts and minds of his people. Its physical expression is our own United States. American sentiment of admiration and of gratitude is the very soul of America itself. But beyond our national boundaries, into the far corners of the world, the effects of his work have brought freedom and a new conception of human relationship among men.

Today in sixty-seven countries of the world we find enthusiastic participants in this great celebration. Do these millions of people in foreign countries pay tribute to Washington as a general? Do they honor him as our President? Do they find in him qualities of exclusive Americanism in which they are not interested?

No, this world-wide tribute to the memory of George Washington goes far deeper than that. He is honored because he has brought liberty to the world. Because he understood the common man and because his great heart responded to the yearnings of the down-trodden and the oppressed.

Never in the history of civilization have so many nations united to honor the hero of a foreign land. And that feeling of reverence and respect is due to those qualities in George Washington's life and character which we are discussing here. The qualities of the man himself.

The United States has responded to this great sentiment in a way that is in many respects marvelous. In a time of uncertainty and of doubt and amid the clouds which are about us, we may well turn to the calm, masterful, confident leadership of George Washington.

He knew the distress of his country, both in war and in peace. He knew what suffering meant to those about him. He faced problems as great as those which we face today, but never for a moment did he doubt that under God our nation would survive. If we today could turn to the immortal lessons which George Washington has left us, if we could be guided by those precepts which have lasted through all our history as a nation, if we could, with the same courage and confidence, press forward with faith in God and a righteous cause, our troubles would vanish and doubts would be dispelled.

George Washington lived a life that was filled with difficulties. Seldom had he a moment that was not heavy with anxiety, not for himself, but for his beloved country. Yes, George Washington knew not only the troubles of foreign tyranny, not only the poverty and misery of his own people, but he knew the hearts of men. He felt the sufferings of others and had he been of less inflexible fibre his own great heart would have burst with anguish. But he knew the responsibility that lay upon him. He knew the faith that was placed in him and he knew that his own courage, his own dependence upon Divine guidance, would be reflected in the courage and faith of those about him.

We catch glimpses of the human George Washington all through his career. To those who think of him only as an austere Commander, let me refer to that hour of anguish during the Battle of Long Island, when George Washington veiled with his cloak the tears that streamed from his eyes at sight of his soldiers being ruthlessly bayoneted by the British Red Coats. Let me refer to those heartbreaking scenes at Valley Forge when the dignified and austere Commander agonized for his troops, and undoubtedly sought the help of the God of us all. And it must be remembered that George Washington never neglected an opportunity of acknowledging his dependence upon Almighty God.

His was a heart full of love for humanity, but when stern duty compelled, he went forward knowing that only by such a course could he justify the cause of American freedom.

I believe that George Washington was our greatest American.

I believe that without his guidance and his sure knowledge of men our freedom could not have been achieved.

I believe that without his religious faith and dependence upon the God of all mercy and power he could not have led us through those terrible years of suffering and of sacrifice.

I believe that the spirit of George Washington is with us today, silently pleading that we forsake all selfishness, all insincerity, all political and moral dishonesty.

I believe that if we as a people would study the teachings of George Washington and try to understand the philosophy of his life that we would be enabled to follow that spiritual leadership out of the maze of trouble into which we as Americans find ourselves.

For George Washington, the man, the friend, the citizen, left us an immortal legacy of advice which is a sure and safe guide in our national life.

Lift up your eyes, fellow Americans. Look upon the glory of your country. Have faith, have courage and be strong. That is the spiritual message that comes from George Washington—the man, who sits with us in unseen council here today.

AMERICAN FARM BUREAU FEDERATION INDEPENDENCE DAY ADDRESS

DELIVERED ON THE
AMERICAN FARM BUREAU FEDERATION NATION-WIDE FARMERS' BICENTENNIAL PROGRAM
NATIONAL BROADCASTING COMPANY
JULY 4, 1932

My fellow Americans, and especially those Americans who form the great body of agricultural producers!

I want to express my deep appreciation for the opportunity given me, through the courtesy of the American Farm Bureau Federation, to join with you today in solemn reconsecration to the welfare of our beloved land.

In spirit I am sitting among you in the thousands of meeting places in which the farmers of America and their precious families are gathered at this hour. In spirit I bring you my humble message of greeting and good cheer, and with us is that great spirit, the spirit of the man whom Americans in loving remembrance will always refer to as the Father of Our Country. And that great spirit of our greatest man belongs especially to you. For he was a farmer—the best farmer of his time. It was as a farmer that he found the few years of peace and tranquillity in a life otherwise crowded with grave national concerns.

I like to give rein to my imagination and visualize George Washington as the farmer of Mount Vernon beside the lovely Potomac. There, amid the calm and quiet surroundings of his homestead, he exemplified the finest qualities of the American farmer. He knew every field, every tree, every animal.

He was not content to follow the agricultural traditions of his time. Always he sought improvement. Always he experimented with crops and soils. Always he sought to raise the standards of his stock. Always he conducted correspondence with farm authorities at home and abroad. And always was his enthusiasm aroused at the sight of good growing crops, neat fences, well-cared-for trees and shrubs and spreading meadows.

When the sun in the glamorous beauty of a Virginia morning rose over the broad waters of the Potomac, his day began. With the first flashing glory of dawn he was astir, and with him came the awakening of all about him. His was the planning mind and the directing hand. Nothing was so small as to escape his keen eye. While demanding industry of those about him, he was not a hard task master. To those who grew old or otherwise incapacitated in his service, he was an indulgent master and provider. Not only did he care for his own family and other dependents, but he never turned a deserving man or woman from his door. His charities were unobtrusive but generous. His private life exemplified the religious principles that influenced his great career.

When the shadows lengthened and the quiet hour of relaxation came, George Washington sat with his family and friends, and watched the play of fading light upon the quiet river. What must it have been to be numbered among that intimate company! What an experience to feel his presence and hear his voice!

George Washington was not all drama and heroics. He was the ideal host, the generous companion, the friendly and sympathetic neighbor.

And, after all, is there anything greater than the friendship and sympathy of a neighbor? Those who dwell in cities have lost almost entirely that finest element of human relationship. But it still survives, and thank God, must ever survive, in the rural neighborhoods and communities of our great nation.

You who are gathered together today represent that neighborhood spirit, that kindness and sympathetic consideration which comes from dwelling close to nature and in the employment of common interests, the serving of common ends and the enjoyment of common labor.

This feeling that I have for rural life is genuine, deep and abiding. You neighboring farmers have a possession far more precious than riches, position or power. It is the expanding of life, the development of elemental human traits in men and women. It makes for sincere and lasting friendships, and those who are privileged to enjoy neighborhood relationships get something from life which must be prized above all other human gifts.

George Washington was the ideal neighbor. I prefer to think of him in that character, although, of course, his transcendent personality, his great deeds of leadership in war and in peace, his service to his country which led him far from home, are the things perhaps best remembered about him.

When the United States George Washington Bicentennial Commission was organized, and I was honored by being made its Director, we had a corps of historians who turned the keen light of research upon every act and every phase of character of this great man.

We have endeavored with the best authoritative assistance, to rescue the life of George Washington from tradition, from myth, from error and from persistent falsehood. We want to preserve for the Americans yet to come a truthful account of the life, the character and the services of George Washington.

In all this mass of material, that which has appealed to me most has been the simpler things, the humbler things in connection with George Washington's personal and private life.

While I stand in awe of George Washington as the military hero, while I bow in humble tribute to his colossal acts of statesmanship, I yet feel closer to the man, when, in reverie, I sit upon the great porch at Mount Vernon of a quiet afternoon and think of him there as the farmer, the husbandman, the neighbor.

How he would delight to be among the farmers of his beloved country today. How his great soul would expand with pleasure to feel the warmth of your love and veneration. And what courage, what strength and what confidence his presence would bring to you in these hours that are clouded with anxieties and confused with difficulties.

George Washington has left us immortal legacies. He has pointed the way for our national security and prosperity. Upon the foundations which he laid our government has expanded until it is one of the greatest powers of the earth. Yet over and above all, is the human George Washington, the neighbor and the man.

The same sun which rises in its glory above the home of George Washington rises upon you and me. The same winds which sang their paeans of peace over the flowers, the shrubs and the trees of George Washington's home, caress us today. The same meadows which spread their fragrant beauty upon the lands of George Washington, are the meadows which gladden your eyes about your own homes. The growing things of the earth still grow as they did in George Washington's time.

The fields still yield their abundance as did his fields at Mount Vernon. The shadows of the passing clouds moved in cooling procession upon his farm as they do upon yours. God in His infinite mercy has willed that nature will ever be as it was in the beginning.

Changes come to our cities. Changes affect our government. Changes have wrought miracles in industrial and commercial development. But still the corn grows, still the wheat ripens and still the trees spread their restful shadows about us as they did when George Washington looked out upon the beauty of the world from the porch at Mount Vernon.

But the earth renews its abundance and it has not changed. Neither have the hearts of men changed. There is still in the world the same love, the same nobility, the same devotion, and—thank Almighty God—the same loyalty which drew to George Washington the love and devotion of his own countrymen.

And who would say that, after all, merciful heaven has not preserved to us the best in life! The sunshine, the gentle rain, the unchanging affection and the loyalty of the human heart, are these not greater than imperial cities? Are they not more important to human happiness than all the miracles of industrial advancement?

Neighborliness is essentially a product of the open air. It is fostered by those who have room to live and love and labor. It preserves to humanity the sweetest and most ennobling qualities of the minds and hearts of our people.

The farmer of Mount Vernon felt this influence more strongly than any other that affected his life. From the turmoil of battle, from the perplexities of the council chamber, he returned to the soil. He looked up into the heaven above him and felt that among the trees and flowers and meadows of his beloved Mount Vernon, he would be nearer to God.

Here he found peace and here upon the banks of the lovely Potomac, lulled to sleep by the flower-scented breezes, he lies in everlasting rest, in the bosom of the earth which in life he loved so well. He sleeps, but his spirit lives on. His spirit is with us today. It brings us the inspiration of hope, of strength, of courage.

In death as in life, he is still the leader. He is still finding the way. Still calling upon us, his fellow Americans to go forward and, as the flag of our country casts its glorious benediction over the peaceful loveliness of Mount Vernon, so within its protecting folds you and I, my fellow countrymen, carry on under the living symbol of that which George Washington left us.

Look up, my fellow Americans, at the glory which shines about you. Look beyond the ground mists of doubt and the fog of uncertainty, into the clean radiance of our own national life, and behold the immortal grandeur of our country, our government, our people. Is it not comforting to realize that, although some functional weaknesses in our government need attention, the structure itself is sound?

Look up, my fellow Americans, at the flag of our country that waves above you. Its glory is undimmed. Its beauty is untarnished. Its symbolism of a united America, is still, as always, strong, courageous, unafraid. Look up at the eternal stars set upon the background of Heaven itself and heed not the passing storm.

America, as always, will stand because it is based upon the immutable foundation of human rights, human freedom, and equal opportunity. The God of Nations who set that symbol in the sky, will not desert it. The Ruler of all who gave strength and purpose and inflexible determination to George Washington and led him through the agony of war and the perplexities of nation building, is still watchful, still merciful, still the protecting Father. And in perfect faith we commend ourselves and our country to Him from whose hands the centuries fall like grains of sand.

ANNIVERSARY OF THE BIRTH OF ADMIRAL COMTE DE GRASSE

ADDRESS OF HON. SOL BLOOM,
INTRODUCING MR. JULES HENRY, CHARGE D'AFFAIRS AD INTERIM, OF FRANCE,
IN A PROGRAM CELEBRATING
THE
TWO HUNDRED AND TENTH ANNIVERSARY OF THE BIRTH OF ADMIRAL COMTE DE GRASSE,
BROADCAST BY THE NATIONAL BROADCASTING COMPANY
FROM WASHINGTON, D. C.
SEPTEMBER 13, 1932

Since February 22, 1932, the United States George Washington Bicentennial Commission has marked for special honor various anniversaries of those patriots who helped George Washington to win the War of the Revolution. We have now come to a date of special significance, the two hundred and tenth anniversary of the birth of the man whose timely action made possible the final blow which brought victory to our arms.

It is well known among students of history that many great men of foreign birth came to America to join George Washington and his patriot army in a glorious but discouraged cause.

Without detracting in the least from the honors due to those other patriots of foreign birth, we may well pause today to give a thought to the man whose unselfish and patriotic impulses, whose prompt and vigorous cooperation, brought victory to the allied armies upon the American continent and forever sealed the liberties of the American people.

Comte de Grasse, a nobleman of France, brought his men and ships to our coast at the extreme of our necessity, and it is well to remember that this great French Commander, not only placed his fighting forces at Washington's service, but his country at the same time sent a large sum of much needed money as a free gift to the American cause.

We must also remember that the Revolutionary War had dragged six years of its course, during which time

the decisive victory to American arms which was necessary to final success.

What must have been the exaltation in the heart of George Washington during these dark hours and after all those long years of war and almost fruitless maneuvering, when there was placed in his hands a letter written by the French Foreign Minister to the French plenipotentiary in America, which said:

. . . "I may say to you M., and you may confide to M. the General Washington exclusively, that M. de Grasse has express orders, after having provided for the safety of our islands, to detach or take the greater part

ADMIRAL COMTE DE GRASSE

Washington's patriot army was almost continuously awaiting the uncertanties of British movements. That army lacked practically everything that an army needed, except courage.

Rochambeau with his French troops had landed on American shores and was cooperating in an attempt at organizing more energetic operations, but George Washington realized the hopelessness of an effort to defeat the pick of British troops upon American soil unless he struck a great decisive blow.

Therefore, in the Spring of 1781, Washington and Rochambeau were cooperating in planning a movement against New York which was held by the British. What would have been the outcome of a determined attack such as they seemed to contemplate we will never know, but it was quite evident that George Washington did not have great faith that such an action would provide

of the fleet to the continent of North America and to lend himself to all operations judged practicable for as long as the season will permit him to remain in those parts. If the Spanish are not in need of reinforcements from our troops, all of them will join you. It will be well that General Washington prepare to make the greatest possible use of this help and that he take measures in advance to assure their subsistence."

The promise of prompt and adequate naval aid concentrating in Chesapeake Bay, in a letter from Comte de Grasse received August 14, turned the entire plan of action.

The proposed attack upon New York was abandoned and the American troops journeyed to Virginia where Lafayette had practically bottled Cornwallis and his Army on the peninsula of Yorktown.

We know that story now and how the British in New

York was misled into expecting an attack while the allied troops hurried to Virginia. We know of the timely arrival of De Grasse and his mighty naval force and how that arrival prevented the rescue of Cornwallis or his escape from Yorktown.

We know of the gratitude felt and expressed by George Washington and his fellow Americans at this magnificent stroke which practically ended the American conflict with the surrender of Cornwallis.

Today as part of the Celebration of the Two Hundredth Anniversary of the Birth of George Washington we pay tribute to the memory of Comte de Grasse. The suggestion that we do this came from Mrs. George Durbin Chenoweth, Regent, Comte de Grasse Chapter, National Society, Daughters of the American Revolution, at Yorktown, Virginia. It is a celebration, jointly, by the French and the American governments and we are honored today by the presence here of the official representative of the French government, Mr. Jules Henry, Chargé d'Affaires ad interim of France, in the absence from our shores of His Excellency, M. Paul Claudel, the French Ambassador.

Before making this introduction, however, I cannot refrain from referring to a recent testimonial of the people of France which is most touching in its significance and which fits so perfectly into the tribute which we are paying to the memory of Comte de Grasse today.

On July 4 last, Baron de Fontenay, President of the Municipal Council of Paris, presented to the Mount Vernon Ladies' Association of the Union, Mount Vernon, Virginia, a painting representing "La Ville de Paris," the flagship of Comte de Grasse, which played such a heroic part in the seige of Yorktown. It is interesting to know that this flagship was thus named because it was presented to Louis XVI by the Parisian people. It was said to be the most beautiful ship of the time and served as flagship of Admiral de Grasse until its magnificent and dramatic end, when ablaze from stem to stern, it sank beneath the waves in the great battle with the English in 1782.

That painting is another and fitting reminder of the historic friendship between the people and governments of France and the United States. It recalls a glorious chapter of our long history and vividly indicates the essential character of the help which France gave to us in our time of need.

I cannot leave this subject without referring to the attitude of George Washington toward Admiral de Grasse after the seige of Yorktown, as indicated by his final expression of thanks to the Admiral.

No one knew or felt more keenly than George Washington the value of the services performed by Admiral de Grasse.

Presumably many of his compatriots, as well as we of today, considered the arrival of De Grasse at Yorktown a happy coincidence, yet Washington knew that this circumstance was directed by that Providence which had guided him and protected his countrymen through all the long years of that terrible war.

De Grasse, it is true, was working under general orders from his government, but had he not been sincerely devoted to the American cause he could easily and conveniently have delayed his action or terminated his service without achieving the glorious results which came with the surrender at Yorktown.

I do not believe that we Americans have ever expressed proper appreciation for the service rendered by De Grasse, and the thought comes to me that I do not remember of having seen or heard of a monument to Comte de Grasse upon American soil.

If that is true, it is a regrettable omission and a neglect that should be promptly and adequately rectified.

In this capital city of the nation where many beautiful monuments stand as memorials to other great foreigners who aided George Washington and his patriot army, there should be a suitable memorial erected to one of the greatest of these men—Admiral Comte de Grasse.

Just recognition of his service has been too long delayed to this French hero whose presence at Yorktown, whose personal interest and strong support, made the victory possible which virtually ended the war of the Revolution.

And now, as Director of the United States George Washington Bicentennial Commission it is my privilege and pleasure to present the Representative of the French government and to express through him, to his countrymen, the lasting gratitude of the United States of America for this supreme act which crowned our Revolutionary arms with success, and brought freedom to our beloved land.

George Washington Laying the Cornerstone of the Federal Capitol at Washington, D. C., with Masonic Ceremonies on September 18, 1793. By De Land.

Masonic Ceremony, September 17, 1932, Re-enacting the Original Ceremony in which George Washington Laid the Cornerstone of the United States Capitol, with Masonic Honors, September 18, 1793. The Modern Ceremony was Conducted Under the Auspices of the Grand Lodge, A. F. and A. M., District of Columbia, with the Original Trowel and Gavel Used by George Washington.

Re-enactment of the Laying of the Cornerstone of the Capitol

Address, September 17, 1932
AT
Ceremony of Re-enactment
of Laying of the Cornerstone of the National Capitol
Which Took Place
One Hundred and Thirty-nine Years Ago.

History is repeating itself today on this spot made immortal by its exalted associations. We are re-enacting a ceremony that in reality marked the beginning of our life as a nation. We are standing at the center of the United States of America. Here, are represented the glory and the authority of our National Government.

One hundred and thirty-nine years ago George Washington stood upon this spot. There was not before his eyes the majestic dome within whose shadows we stand. There was not the inspiring vista of granite and marble which greets our eyes today. But in his vision there was that dream which is realized now.

While George Washington was essentially an idealist, he was, nevertheless, a man of most practical thought and habits. To him the nation which was to grow with the continued liberties of his people, was manifestly a structure of laws, of social development and culture. But he also visualized a nation of progress, of material growth and a government exemplified by the machinery of administration. It was his keen intelligence which projected far into the future the ideals of this Republic. While he stressed always the necessity of Constitutional growth, he yet knew the value of beauty. Therefore, we must feel at this hour that the dreams of George Washington, not only for the political and social development of his nation have come true, but that his ideals of the beauty of this National Capital are being splendidly carried out. We may be sure that as George Washington looked further ahead than most of his compatriots to the physical and political growth of the Nation, he also looked forward to these memorial structures which crystallize and symbolize the soul of the United States.

George Washington laid the first cornerstone of this magnificent Capitol. How appropriate it was that his should have been the hand that spread the mortar upon that occasion. It identifies him with the actual construction of the great building which displays its architectural grandeur before us.

There is being re-enacted here a scene in which George Washington played so noble a part. But more than that, there is being enacted here, and throughout our nation, a re-dedication in the hearts and minds of the American people to those principles of government which are as surely the foundation of our greatness as this granite symbol deposited here today. We are building upon that broader foundation of liberty and of character, the cornerstone of which was George Washington himself.

It is most gratifying to the members of the United States George Washington Bicentennial Commission that this great ceremony should be held in this year in which we are celebrating the Two Hundredth Anniversary of the Birth of George Washington. It is an impressive tribute to our First President that we should so observe this anniversary. For, strong and enduring as is this beautiful building, magnificent as is this great nation of ours, neither the building, nor the nation, can outlive the glory of George Washington himself.

Let us lift our thoughts to Him who watches over our Destinies and to whom we owe all the blessings that have come to us as a nation in all the crowded years of the past. To Almighty God we give thanks for that merciful Providence which guided and protected our infant republic and which today still points the way of safety and of truth.

Even these great columns may crumble into dust, but the name of Washington will live in the world as long as the hearts of men respond to the finest elements in human character. Nations may rise and fall. In the eternal tides of human affairs civilizations may come and go, but as long as liberty shall endure, the name of George Washington will blaze upon the scroll of history in the majesty of everlasting fame.

MASONIC PROCESSION AT THE LAYING OF THE CORNERSTONE OF THE NATIONAL CAPITOL (1793).

MASONIC PARADE IN WASHINGTON, D. C., ON SEPTEMBER 17, 1932, TO COMMEMORATE THE 139TH ANNIVERSARY OF THE LAYING OF THE CORNERSTONE OF THE FEDERAL CAPITOL ON SEPTEMBER 18, 1793.

153rd ANNIVERSARY OF THE DEATH OF CASIMIR PULASKI

ADDRESS OF HON. SOL BLOOM
INTRODUCING MR. WLADYSLAW SOKOLOWSKI, CHARGE d'AFFAIRES AD INTERIM, OF POLAND,
IN A PROGRAM CELEBRATING
THE
COMMEMORATION OF THE 153RD ANNIVERSARY OF THE DEATH OF CASIMIR PULASKI
BROADCAST BY THE NATIONAL BROADCASTING COMPANY FROM WASHINGTON, D. C., OCTOBER 11, 1932.

We may search the pages of history in vain for a more heroic, adventurous and patriotic spirit than that of Casimir Pulaski, whose memory we honor today. This great Polish hero, glowing with enthusiasm for liberty, came from his own distressed land to fight upon our shores for those ideals of freedom that, for the time being, were crushed in his beloved Poland.

Many brave and colorful foreign soldiers were enlisted under the banner of George Washington. Also, many of these were inspired with a passion for the ideals for which the colonists fought. Some of these men of foreign birth contributed important services to our cause and helped to mold out of the untrained, undisciplined, but determined men of George Washington's army, a fighting force which carried on a struggle that was the admiration of the world.

Against the very pick of Great Britain's veteran troops and veteran German mercenaries, these men of America were fitted to contend on grounds of equality, and it was due in large measure to the experienced military experts from other European countries that George Washington was enabled to marshal his forces with effectiveness.

Brigadier General Casimir Pulaski was a dashing and romantic soldier, who had already achieved a reputation for patriotism, heroism and strategy that made him an outstanding figure in Europe. After having seen his father and his brothers treacherously made victims of that conspiracy of Russia, Austria and Prussia to crush and dismember Poland, Pulaski fought upon his native soil, until, having exhausted the last remnant of his strength, he was forced to flee, as Poland lay helpless at the feet of the three conspiring sovereigns.

It was not surprising that the noble Pulaski should be fired with new enthusiasm for freedom in a nation that symbolized something of Poland's heroic struggle. And so he came to us and immediately his devotion to the cause of the colonies, his reckless heroism, his superb horsemanship and his magnetic personality, appealed to the imagination of our own America. Time does not permit a review of the important services which he performed under Washington's leadership. That is all a matter of history.

He was not a soldier of fortune. His love of liberty alone kindled his devotion. He saw in the struggle for American independence an opportunity to pursue that bright vision which had so animated him in his career as a Polish patriot. And he transferred to Washington's service, those remarkable qualities of military genius which everywhere aroused admiration and confidence.

Pulaski joined the Revolutionary army as a volunteer in the Summer of 1777. From that time on he progressively demonstrated his value and became one of the outstanding Commanders of our forces. His glorious martyrdom in the defense of Savannah brought to a dramatic close a career which was matchless in its sincerity and zeal in the cause of human liberty.

Trusted by George Washington, admired by him, and inspiring a devotion that only the comradeship of war can bring about, Pulaski went to his death, dauntless and unafraid. Under direction of Congress, he was sent to South Carolina, and joined Moultrie's force in the defense of Charleston when the British appeared before it. The Governor and the Council of Charleston had already agreed upon terms of capitulation, but General Pulaski went to the Council Chamber to protest against this measure, declaring that as a Continental officer he would defend the City for the United States.

Accordingly, the defense was continued and on the approach of Lincoln's army the British retreated and retired to Savannah. Pulaski was active in the pursuit. In the ill-fated assault on that City, October 9, 1779, Pulaski was wounded in the thigh by a grape shot when trying to arrest the retreat of French soldiers. Two days later, October 11, 1779, after more than two years of service under our flag, Pulaski died on board the ship "Wasp" where he had been taken after being wounded. His body was buried at sea, with simple but impressive ceremony, and his death was lamented universally by the patriots of the Revolution.

Today, upon the 153rd anniversary of Pulaski's martyrdom, we stand with bowed heads in remembrance of that magnificent sacrifice. We reaffirm to Poland and the Polish people our everlasting gratitude for the service which Pulaski rendered to our country.

We have upon the program here today in commemoration of the death of Casimir Pulaski, the distinguished representative of Poland, Mr. Wladyslaw Sokolowski, Chargé d'Affaires ad interim of Poland during the absence from our shores of His Excellency, Mr. Tytus Filipowicz, Ambassador of Poland. Mr. Sokolowski will address you on behalf of his own country and his own people. It is to him, and through him, that I express again the remembrance which the people of the United States will always cherish of his great countryman who came to us in our time of need and who so valiantly and heroically served in our own patriot army.

BRIGADIER GENERAL CASIMIR PULASKI
From an engraving by Oleszczynski

ASIMIR PULASKI was born in the Province of Podolia in the extreme southwest of Poland on March 4, 1747. This section was exposed to continuous incursions of roving marauders, and his father maintained a large band of armed retainers to protect the Pulaski estate. Young Casimir early gained a knowledge of partisan warfare and laid the foundation for the superb horsemanship which later made him a cavalry leader of renown in Europe and America.

Before he was 21, Casimir Pulaski had his taste of regular warfare, serving for six months in the successful defense of Mitau. He continued to fight against Poland's oppressors, becoming known for his courage and valor. His enemies were victorious, however, and Pulaski was forced to leave the country, making his way to Paris. There he learned of the American Revolution and his natural love of liberty led him to apply to Benjamin Franklin for assistance in obtaining a commission in the Continental Army. Franklin wrote the letter requested, which Pulaski presented to George Washington in August, 1777.

Pulaski fought at Brandywine as a volunteer without commission. His valorous conduct in that battle brought recognition from Congress with a commission as Brigadier General in command of all the cavalry of the American Army. After valiant service in the North, which won the praise of his comrades as well as of General Washington, Pulaski was transferred to the South and ordered to join General Moultrie at Charleston. His arrival at that city was welcomed, and he took part in demonstrations against the enemy under General Prevost during the retreat to Savannah. The Americans under Lincoln and the French under D'Estaing laid siege to Savannah and an assault was planned.

A deserter is said to have carried the American plans, in which Pulaski's cavalry had a prominent part, to the British, who prepared for the attack. The assault was not succeeding and in desperation Pulaski led his horse to the attack to stem the tide, but a shot brought him to the ground wounded. Taken aboard a boat in the harbor, he was given every care, but the best was inadequate; gangrene set in, and the gallant Pole died on October 11, 1779. He is believed to have been buried at sea.

THE MOTHER

OF

GEORGE WASHINGTON

RADIO ADDRESS

BY

MRS. JOHN DICKINSON SHERMAN

WASHINGTON, D. C.

MOTHERS' DAY, MAY 11, 1930

ALSO GIVEN ON MOTHERS' DAY, 1932
AT THE WASHINGTON CATHEDRAL
AND BROADCAST NATIONALLY

Mary Ball Washington, Mother of George Washington, Died August 25, 1789. She was Buried Near her Home, Fredericksburg, Virginia, at a Site She Herself had Chosen. The First Monument Over her Grave was Begun in 1833 at Private Expense, but Remained Unfinished (see Illustration on P. 102), and Crumbled. Efforts for a Public Appropriation for a New Monument Failed, and in 1889 the Women of Fredericksburg Formed the Mary Washington Monument Association, Which Developed Into the National Mary Washington Memorial Association, Chartered on February 22, 1890. Women Vice-Presidents Were Appointed for the States to Take Charge of the Movement; the Land was Acquired; Patriotic Societies Took an Interest; a Hereditary Life Membership was Instituted; and the Required Fund for the Monument and Care was Raised. The Cornerstone was Laid on October 21, 1893, and the Structure Dedicated in the Presence of President Cleveland May 10, 1894. The Monument is Fifty Feet High and Comprises a Monolith of Forty Feet, Standing on Bases and Plinth Ten Feet High. The Lower Base is Eleven Feet Square. The Whole Shaft of Fifty Feet is of Barre Granite and the Finest Workmanship. On the Front of the Plinth are the Simple Words: "MARY THE MOTHER OF WASHINGTON," and on the Reverse Side: "ERECTED BY HER COUNTRY-WOMEN." These Inscriptions are Beautifully Cut.

The Mother of George Washington

By Mrs. John Dickinson Sherman

"Mary the Mother of Washington"—These five words, which form the simple inscription on the monument erected to the memory of Mary Ball Washington, are fraught with deep meaning and great significance. They suggest characteristics which the mother of so great a man must necessarily possess; characteristics which by her stoic patience and self-sacrificing devotion were instilled in the heart and mind of her first born, thus laying the foundation for his own future greatness.

Like other mothers of great men, Mary Ball Washington sought divine guidance through prayer and through her Bible and other deeply religious writings. Her associations from early childhood were of a deeply religious nature, for the early settlers staunchly adhered to church doctrine and to the established custom of family prayers.

Mary Ball was imbued with reverence and religious fervor. This supplemented by adequate training in domestic routine and her sense of responsibility for the duties of home life, admirably fitted for the rôle of motherhood.

She represented a fine type of the well-bred colonial Virginia lady with a background of good English ancestry. That she was beautiful and popular in her home community is shown by traditional reference to her as the "Rose of Epping Forest" and the "Belle of Northern Neck." That she was self-contained and content to await the coming of a fitting mate is apparent, for she had reached the age of 24 when she made her choice, and became the second wife of Capt. Augustine Washington.

It was in 1730 that she came as a bride to the Washington home at Bridges Creek, later known as Wakefield, which had been without a mistress since the death of Jane Butler, Captain Washington's first wife and mother of his three children.

Soon after taking possession of her new home the young bride, in making a tour of inspection of the premises, found among the books a much-used volume of Sir Matthew Hale's "Contemplations, Moral and Divine." On turning the pages she read on the flyleaf the name of her predecessor, "Jane Washington." This little reminder of her husband's first wife she accepted with rare good sense, for which she was always noted, and beneath "Jane Washington" she added her own name, "and Mary Washington."

Then she set herself to the task of aiding her husband in the religious training of her young stepsons not yet in their teens, carrying on from their mother's own book the teaching her predecessor had laid down.

As her own children came along they too, were, thoroughly instructed in the principles of the Bible and the Contemplations.

The greatest joy and pride of Mary Washington's life came on February 22, 1732, when her first born was placed in her arms. She chose for her child the name of George in loving regard for her guardian, George Eskridge, an eminent lawyer of Virginia.

A few months later the christening of young George took place in the presence of many friends and relatives, with a full quota of godparents. Mementos of this beautiful and impressive baptismal service may still be seen in the handsome bowl used as a font and the christening robe which are now in the National Museum at Washington.

Of Washington's youth and early relations with his mother we have little but traditions; stories that have their origin more in the known later traits of both mother and son than in any contemporary accounts. But among them are many that are so characteristic that they might well have happened. Thus we are told that Mary Ball Washington wanted this first son of hers to become a minister, but in her wisdom she always sought what was best for him. Also, that from the time little George could toddle his father trained him to sit a horse, to ride, to climb, to jump, to shoot, and to do many athletic stunts, which his adoring young mother must have watched with trepidation though filled with pride at his aptness in learning. The eager delight of the child when his father gave him a little sword brought protests from the mother lest her son crave a soldier's career instead of her choice for him. But she gave way to Captain Washington, who encouraged the soldier tendency, teaching him courage, truthfulness, and always to gage his actions by honor.

Other children came to share her mother care, and always she was especially conscious and prayerful when the guidance and instruction of her children rested upon her, which it did entirely following the untimely death of her husband in 1743.

It is a tradition that it was her lifelong habit to rise at dawn and spend the first hour of the day in silent thought and prayer to prepare herself for the family worship and for the day's events; and that though her eldest son, George, was only 11 when his father died, upon him she placed the old patriarchial duty of saying at table and prayers at night and morning. From this early age his mother expected him to assume and carry such responsibility as the circumstances of life brought to him. Under her pious guidance he could not have evaded any service that she deemed his duty.

Mary Washington personally supervised the management of the large estates in addition to the household duties and the training of her children, and so strong was the influence of her training that all of her children had respect for her decisions. This is exemplified by the account which has been handed down that when Washington was 14 or 15 there was a plan for him to go to sea, whether in a merchantman or as a midshipman can not be said. His mother objected, especially after she had received a letter from her brother in England condemning the plan, and it was abandoned without protest from her obedient son.

Though making no comment of sympathy at the time, his mother knew his sorrow and struggle and shortly afterwards presented him with a new penknife from England which he had long craved, saying, "Always obey your superiors."

This disappointment about going to sea, added to the fact that his father's death had taken away the chance of the English school education that had been given his half brothers, sobered the boy into a realization that he must forego his own career and caused him to listen to and absorb his mother's cultural teachings and led him to consider seriously the set of "Rules of Conduct" a combination of suggestions for proper behavior brought over from England.

Here is one of the rules:

"Associate yourself with men of good quality if you esteem your own reputation; for 'tis better to be alone than in bad company."

With the great responsibility of training and caring for her young family and conserving their inheritances to furnish a proper and sufficient income, Mary Washington became more and more reserved and dignified, to the point of inspiring awe among strangers and ofttimes in her own family. Her children always addressed her as "Honored Madame" in accordance with the extreme formality of the period.

But with all her austerity she was a wise and loving mother who set her face against every diversion in life to devote herself entirely to her children. Her entire interest was centered in and revolved around the care and development of the best that was in them.

George Washington Parke Custis, although too young to have remembered very much of her or to have formed his own opinion of her high character, lived in the home of General Washington from infancy and was fully acquainted with her life. Of her he has written:

"Though apparently endowed with equability of temperament, Mary Washington's nature glowed with a suppressed fervor which transmitted itself to her son and in him became power for endurance, passion for command, ambition to do and to dare in the Colonial wars, spontaneous assumption of leadership, and the natural and easy command of men. This suppressed fire, force or energy or whatever it may be termed, was felt by everybody who contacted either George Washington or his stately mother."

Tradition has given stories of George Washington's boyish pranks and escapades; mostly just boyish carelessness, sometimes only a bit of disobedience to some rule. In these matters Mary Washington stifled her first loving impulse to overlook the matter, requiring the boy to tell his own story. In each case we find her superior wisdom forgiving the act because of the courageous, truthful attitude of her son. She put him and kept him so on his honor that it was not in his code as boy or man to deceive or falsify.

The steady rise of her first born from one position of responsibility to another of leadership was accepted by the "Spartan" mother as a matter of course, as a part of his duty. She is never recorded as praising him. She took his superb valor under fire, his unfailing patriotism, all in his day's work. Her fear for his safety was put aside in the challenge she gave herself—"The mothers of brave men must themselves be brave."

After the Braddock expedition, during which Washington's escape was scarcely less than a miracle, Mary Washington was strenuous in her objections to her son returning to the frontier in command of the Virginia forces placed on guard there. But he wrote her: "Honor'd Madam: If it is in my power to avoid going to the Ohio again, I shall, but if the Command is press'd upon me by the genl. voice of the Country, and offer'd upon such terms as can't be objected against, it wou'd reflect eternal dishonor upon me to refuse it; and that, I am sure must, or ought, to give you greater cause of uneasiness than my going in an honourable Com'd.; for upon no other terms I will accept of it if I do at all."

General Washington's selection to the Presidency, the first Executive of the young Republic, brought no added elation to his mother. It was his duty. She saw nothing else for him to do. When he came to tell her of it, all his future honors were shadowed by her realization that this was her last meeting with the child of her heart. Her mother love sought to enfold him in all her love, protection, and security that her prayers and blessings could invoke.

Among his most cherished family treasures is said to have been his mother's portrait painted in her bridal days, as well as the worn copy of her Contemplations, companion of her quiet hours. This book he kept for his own use until he, too, had no longer need for material things.

Growing into manhood in such an atmosphere, it is not surprising that George Washington was known in his day as the "Defender of the mothers" and the "Protector of the daughters." He has left a heritage of chivalrous conduct in his relations with the women of his immediate family and the circle radiating from his own fireside that has inspired the homage of all ages of every generation since his time.

Never before has there been a more distinct and convincing illustration of the effect of home life on the character of a child and youth than that which surrounded George Washington as he grew into early manhood. The soul of the home became a conscious factor in his everyday life and developed the strength of character, courage, and upright living that made him a shining example of righteous manhood, not alone to the people of that day but to those of all generations.

Mary Ball Washington typifies the highest example of American motherhood and is a most illustrious prototype of colonial home maker. Like Martha of old, she attended well to the ways of her household.

George Washington as a Judge

BY

Hon. R. Walton Moore

(Former President of Virginia Bar Association and former Member of House of Representatives from the Mount Vernon District.)

Reprinted from the
Congressional Record *of March 4, 1932*

George Washington as a Judge

By Hon. R. Walton Moore

Washington was through with school in the ordinary sense of the term when, about 15 years old, he took up his residence with his brother at Mount Vernon. In a letter to his mother attributed to Lord Fairfax, the writer was correct in saying "his education might have been bettered" but correct in predicting, on the basis of his estimate of the youth's unusual qualities, that he "would go to school all his life and profit thereby." In that way certainly no one of the time had more opportunity or was a more intelligent and receptive student. Much has been written of how he was thus trained at almost every step for the great tasks which awaited him, for example, by his service as a young surveyor in a wild and thinly settled region, as a young soldier in the frontier wilderness, as a member of the colonial house of burgesses, and a Member of the Continental Congress.

But the fact seems not to have been at all stressed that for years he was one of the judges of a court possessing extensive jurisdiction and inevitably profited by the contacts and information incident to that service. While it is mainly the present purpose to say something about that one element of the education which the Fairfax letter predicted for him, a further word or so may be permitted with respect to his protracted legislative career as a burgess during the period from 1759 to 1775 and as a Delegate to the first and second session of the Continental Congress. In the House of Burgesses his associates were the ablest and most accomplished Virginia contemporaries, and in Congress the most eminent men of the thirteen Colonies. Of course, not as a speechmaker, but by his industry and wisdom, he won the admiration and confidence of his colleagues. Convincing proof of this is that in 1774 the house selected him as one of the seven Delegates to the first Congress. He was placed in distinguished company. The others were Benjamin Harrison, Richard Henry Lee, Richard Bland, Peyton Randolph, Edmund Pendleton, and Patrick Henry, the last three remarkable lawyers. As to how he was regarded in Congress, there is the testimony of Henry, who was destined to be offered by President Washington the post of Chief Justice of the Supreme Court. Henry, answering an inquiry, said: "If you speak of eloquence, Mr. Rutledge, of South Carolina, is by far the greatest orator, but if you speak of solid information and sound judgment, Colonel Washington is unquestionably the greatest man on that floor."

A recent writer says that when Washington returned to Mount Vernon in 1758, after British rule had been pretty firmly established in the West, he led "the quiet life of a country gentleman." But the life of a man could not have been very quiet who, besides his legislative duties, closely looked after his own large estate and the large estates of his wife and stepson, was busy with the affairs of the church as an energetic member of the vestry of his parish at a time when it had serious official responsibilities, who traveled much in and out of Virginia, and was exceptionally active in political and social relations with the influential people of the Colony. Added to all this, it is clear that not later than the spring of 1768 and thence on until the outbreak of the Revolution, he was a justice of the peace, and as such not only charged with disposing of minor cases, but, along with other justices, was engaged in conducting the business of the county court of his county. As one may see from the court minutes, they were invariably, when holding court, styled "gentlemen justices." Due to the loss of colonial records showing the appointment of justices and the absence here of information understood to be available in England, where there are copies of those records, it is not possible at this moment to determine the precise date when Washington's judicial career started. But there remain two of the Fairfax County court order books covering the period from 1770 to 1775 which, if there were no other reason, are worth examining as an example of the beautiful and still perfectly clear writing of the old-time clerks who wrote up the minutes of the court proceedings.

From these two books it appears that Washington served in the court from 1770 to 1774. It is otherwise shown, however, that his service began prior to 1770. In his accounts are evidences that he began to serve as early as June 1765. Turning to the first volume of his Diaries, which give bare facts with little or no comment, there is this entry under date of April 18, 1768: "Went to court and returned in the evening." Then follow at intervals more than 20 such entries. Now and then they show that the session of the court ran several days. For instance, on June 20, 1769, having been at court the day before, the entry is: "Went up to court again and returned in the evening, with Colonel Mason, Mr. Scott, and Mr. Bryan Fairfax," all of whom were justices. Mason, as we all know, was the author of the Virginia constitution of 1776, which included the Bill of Rights and was the first instrument ever written and promulgated which set up a complete system of government. Though not a practicing lawyer, he was deeply versed in the history and philosophy of the law. He was Washington's near neighbor and friend and one of his most trusted advisors. For instance, the day and evening before the famous Fairfax Resolves were adopted by the citizens of Fairfax in 1774, he and Washington in conference at Mount Vernon agreed on the elaborate statement of the grievances and rights of the colonists which was embodied in the Resolves, and the next day went from Mount Vernon to the meeting at the county seat in Alexandria, at which Washington presided. The last entry in the Diaries relative to the court is June 17, 1774, subsequent to which date Washington was doubtless too much engrossed by affairs affecting the entire country to have much time for local matters.

Along with Mason the 1774 meeting had the benefit of the presence of Robert Hanson Harrison, a learned lawyer, who was a leader of the bar of Fairfax County while Washington was a member of the court. In many a case he had seen Harrison's character and ability tested, and he singled him out as one of a group of great lawyers, among them Marshall and Hamilton, on whom at various stages of his career he was accustomed to rely when the most dependable counsel was needed. Harrison was not only at his side when the Resolves flung defiance at the Crown but at his side as a member of his staff during the Revolution, and when he became President he commissioned him as one of the original appointees to the Supreme Court. Turning again to the Diaries, there is found this interesting entry dated February 6, 1790: "The resignation of Mr. Harrison as an associate judge [he declined the appointment a few days after being commissioned, preferring to be chancellor of the State of Maryland], making the nomination of some other character to supply his place necessary, I determined after contemplating every character which presented itself to my view, to name Mr. Iredell, of North Carolina; . . . I had recourse to every means of information in my power, and found them all concurring in his favor."

The evidence is abundant that no one has had more respect than Washington for the legal profession and that no President has been more solicitous about the importance of the judiciary and the maintenance of its integrity and strength. This is variously indicated. To illustrate, it is indicated by the appointments he made when he took up his duties as President and it is indicated in his letter to Edmund Randolph when he invited him to become Attorney General. "Impressed," he wrote Randolph, "that the due administration of justice is the firmest pillar of good government, I have considered the first arrangement of the judicial department as essential to the happiness of our country and the stability of its political system. Hence the selection of the fittest characters to expound the laws and dispense justice, has been an invariable object of my anxious concern." It can be believed that such a high conception was in no small measure derived from his own participation in the work of expounding the laws and dispensing justice and that this was a factor in the education which it was predicted he would acquire.

In Washington's time, and long before and after, the county court was the most important tribunal in Virginia. While he was serving, with the exception of comparatively trifling cases, it had unlimited jurisdiction of civil cases, law and chancery, of probate matters, and of a large class of criminal cases. It had wide administrative powers touching the fiscal affairs of the county, the construction of public buildings, the laying out and construction of highways, building bridges, providing and operating ferries, the care of orphan children, the licensing of innkeepers and the fixing of their charges. Relative to the last matter, the order books show that periodically the rates to be charged for liquor, the surprisingly many kinds then in use being enumerated, and for lodging and food were determined by the court. Very commonly the final item in the list is, "For a night's lodging, with clean sheets, 6d., otherwise nothing." The trifling nature from our point of view of some of the business of the court can not prevent us from seeing that very much of it was of a kind to require able and discerning men on the bench and lawyers who were representative of the learning and skill of the profession.

Justices for a county were appointed by the governor, not fewer than eight and often more, there being no restriction as to the number. They remained in office indefinitely, and the court recommended appointments to fill vacancies. Without the presence of four no court could be held. The clerk was an appointee of the court and in effect so was the sheriff, though he held his commission from the governor. The justices were not lawyers but nearly always the most prominent and reliable citizens of their county. They received no compensation whatever. They were thought sufficiently compensated by the honor of holding an office regarded as of outstanding importance and dignity, with the opportunity of contributing to the common good by attending to the settlement of small controversies out of court, and in court by taking part in the performance of duties which affected the property and liberty of persons and the general welfare of the public. When the Virginia Constitutional Convention of 1829-30 had under discussion the county court, then composed and having much the same jurisdiction as in Washington's day, Chief Justice Marshall, a member of the convention, said: "It was the truth that no State in the Union had hitherto more internal quiet than Virginia. There is no part of America where less discord, less ill feeling between man and man is to be found than in this Commonwealth, and he firmly believed that that State of things was mainly to be ascribed to the practical operation of our county courts. The magistrates who composed these courts consisted in general of the best men in their respective counties. It was mainly due to their influence that so much harmony existed in the State. His emphatic opinion was that these courts must be preserved." Supporting Marshall's view, another member, Philip P. Barbour, who was appointed to the Supreme Court by President Jackson, said he had practiced in those courts for a quarter of a century and he could say with the utmost truth that his confidence in them had grown with his growth and strengthened with his strength. At the same time Benjamin Watkins Leigh said he had heard of but two instances of corruption in the county courts in 200 years. As to alleged incompetency and ignorance he had seen county courts which were among the ablest tribunals before which he had practiced. Speaking of the type of men who served in these courts, it will be remembered that both Jefferson and Madison were justices; that Monroe, after two terms in the Presidency, accepted an appointment and served as a justice in his county, and that in 1784 the victor of the Revolution was named as a justice for Fairfax County.

That the county court had a central place in the estimation of the public is easy to understand. The population was sparse and the people mainly engaged in agriculture. There were no cities and few villages large enough to be called towns. It was at the county seat when the court was in session that the inhabitants gathered. From several historians, including Fiske, we have this picture: The court day was a holiday for all the country side, particularly in the fall and spring. From all directions came in the people on horseback, in wagons, and on foot. On the courthouse green assembled people of all classes—the hunter from the backwoods, the owner of a few acres, and the great landowner. Old debts were settled and new ones made; there were auctions, transfers of property, and if election times were near stump speaking, when questions pertaining more or less to some real or fancied encroachment on popular liberty of the Crown were apt to be debated. All else aside, as one of the historians has remarked, the county court was one of the main agencies of spreading political education. In every way it was one of the agencies which furthered the education of Washington according to the prediction which had been made.

Perhaps before he had any idea of being identified with the court, Washington must have frequently witnessed such a scene as that just outlined. Such was probably the scene when in his eighteenth year he appeared in the court of Culpeper County to qualify as the surveyor of that county, and such may have been the scene when five years afterwards, on March 19, 1754, he appeared early one morning in the Fairfax court and presented his commission from the governor as lieutenant colonel (he was preparing to set out on the campaign to the West, the year before starting on the fatal expedition with Braddock) and took the prescribed oaths. The courts were not leisurely. In spite of the fact that the justices sometimes had to travel a considerable distance over wretched roads to the county seat, the Fairfax court never convened later than 9 o'clock. Our ancestors seem to have been very industrious in discharging official duties and to have attached high value to the oaths under which they acted. On the occasion just mentioned Washington "took the usual oaths to his majesty's person and government, and took and subscribed the abjuration oath and test," and in Culpeper took also the oath as surveyor. The oath which was subscribed was a disclaimer of belief in the theological doctrine of transubstantiation.

Though a layman, Washington as a member of the court necessarily progressed in his knowledge of the law and of the importance of those who were trained in that profession. That he consulted statutes and law books bearing upon such matters as he was obliged to deal with is reasonably evident from the number of such works listed in the inventory of his estate. It will be plain to anyone who reads the statutes prescribing the jurisdiction and procedure of the courts that he could not have escaped becoming fairly familiar with the rules of pleadings and practice, with the distinction between law suits and chancery suits and the methods of conducting both, with attachment and injunction, with the organization and functioning of grand juries and trial juries, with the means of executing judgments and decrees, with the duties of clerks, sheriffs and other officials. He necessarily became saturated with a good deal of the knowledge and acquired to some extent the habits of mind now assumed to be confined to those who have been equipped for judicial work by long study and then by some experience at the bar.[1] Several years ago in an address lauding the Virginia county court system, the late Holmes Conrad, who was Solicitor General under President Cleveland, not with Washington or any other particular man in view, visualized what occurred when a planter of high character and strong sense, but unlearned in the law, became identified with the court, and in reading what he says we may think of its application to Washington. The difficulties which the new judge encountered at the outset are described. He had difficulty in detecting the real questions involved and in following the testimony and argument, and he distrusted the conclusion which he reached. But "after the novelty wears away, he is able to fix his mind upon the business in hand; he detects and is able to follow the clue which leads him through conflicting testimony. He sees dimly at first, but steadily in the light of conscience he discerns the right and wrong of the case; and now he begins to apprehend and appreciate the arguments of advocates. He feels gaining on him a sense of responsibility and the importance of the work. There is slowly but gradually developing the faculties of his mind, of the powers of which he was before unconscious. He is undergoing a process of education, the effects of which became apparent to himself as also to his friends and neighbors. He is no longer led away by first impressions or whatsoever of the mere surface of matters. He learns to hold his judgment in abeyance until his mind is informed and his conscience satisfied. He goes down from his place on the bench and receives the confidence and manifest respect of the people of his locality."

Whenever it was that Washington qualified as a justice he of course took the same oaths as when he qualified as a lieutenant colonel. In addition, he took a lengthy oath as "justice of the peace" and another as "Justice of the County Court of Fairfax in Chancery." In the former he pledged himself, among other things, to "do equal right to the poor and to the rich after your cunning, wit, and power, and according to law; and you shall not be of counsel of any quarrel hanging before you, and the issues, fines, and americaments,[2] that shall happen to be made, and all forfeitures which shall fall before you, you shall cause to be entered, without any concealment or imbeziling." In the latter oath he was pledged to "do equal right to all manner of people, great and small, high and low, rich and poor, according to equity and good conscience and the laws and usages of his colony and Dominion of Virginia, without favour, affection or partiality." The praise that can be given these "gentlemen justices" is that they lived up to their oaths.

There is no way of knowing the extent of Washington's activities as an individual justice having exclusive jurisdiction of a class of very minor cases. But as he resided in the most populous section of his county and enjoyed everybody's respect and confidence, it is safe to conjecture it must have been considerable and that he always exerted his influence to quiet controversy and promote the tranquil condition for which Marshall thought the county court and those composing it were largely responsible.[3]

Far less is known than could be desired of the proceedings of the Fairfax court during Washington's service. The court papers have long since disappeared and about the only source of information are the two order books already mentioned. Looking at the one of them, which runs from April, 1770, to January, 1772, containing 330 pages, it appears that Washington attended over half of the monthly terms, which was more regular than the attendance of a majority of his colleagues, Mason not excepted. In the period to which the book pertains, hundreds of civil cases were brought and in great variety—actions of debt, trespass, trespass on the case, trover and conversion, detinue, replevin, and

---

[1] His will, prepared a short time before his death, consisting of more than 20 large pages, wholly in his own handwriting, now preserved in the Record office at Fairfax and disposing of the largest estate of that time, tends to show his reliance upon the knowledge of law which he had acquired. Toward the end he modestly says it would be evident "that no professional character has been consulted or has had any agency in the draft."

[2] The old spelling is retained.

[3] In another way he exerted the same sort of influence. As shown by the Diaries he was often chosen and acted as an arbitrator.

ejectment. There was constant resort to attachment. There were suits in chancery, and injuctions were issued to restrain the collection of judgments and prevent irremediable injury. The names of the plaintiffs and defendants are always given and often the names of the lawyers, not only Mr. Harrison heretofore spoken of but others still unforgotten, among them William Grayson, who was to be one of the first United States Senators from Virginia; Benjamin Sebastian, ancestor of one of the first Senators from Arkansas; and George Johnston, who was on Washington's staff in the Revolution. He was the son of that George Johnston, like Mason a neighbor and friend of Washington, and one of the leaders of the Virginia bar, who as a member of the House of Burgesses in 1765, according to Jefferson, who listened to the debate, delivered a powerful legal argument in support of Henry's resolutions condemning the Stamp Tax. The resolutions were carried by a very narrow majority. If Washington was present he undoubtedly gave the resolutions his firm support. The cases were tried by juries unless the defendant failed to appear or waived a trial in that manner, and verdicts and judgments were made payable in tobacco or currency and sometimes partly in each.

Now and then the jurors disagreed after lengthy deliberation, and in one instance a juror was withdrawn and the case continued for "reasons exciting as well the said justices as the said parties"; but the reasons for the excitement are not set out. There were now and then exceptions to the refusal of the court to set aside verdicts, and in a certain case not otherwise notable the bill of exceptions was signed by Washington and sealed with his seal. Delinquent debtors were ordered to be imprisoned and were released after 20 days' confinement upon proof of insolvency. Lawyers were admitted to practice, wills were admitted to probate, letters of administration granted, guardians appointed, and the accounts of fiduciaries passed on. Poor children were directed to be bound out as apprentices and taught trades. There was much done in supervising and enforcing the collection of taxes and making expenditures for local purposes. Relative to ferries there is this entry: "Ordered, that George Mason and George Washington, Gent., be summoned to appear at the next court to give security according to law for keeping the ferries at their respective landings." Both lived on the shore of the Potomac, and ferries were operated across the river to Maryland. The court was required to see to the construction, when needed, and

to the upkeep of the courthouse and jail and warehouses for the storage of tobacco turned in for taxes. In obedience to the statute it had the duty of providing a "pillory, whipping post, and stocks." Notwithstanding, the criminal jurisdiction of the court embraced all offenses except those punishable by death, loss of limb, or outlawry, the order book refers to very few serious offenses. But the court was called on to deal with a great deal of the same comparatively unimportant kind of criminal business which now crowds the dockets of the United States district courts. The order books at the time back of Washington show that many people were charged with not attending their parish churches "within two months last past," with being "idle vagrants," and with "tending of seconds," which meant gathering a second growth of tobacco from the same stalks. The order book now referred to is full of presentments of women for having "base born children," and people for violating the liquor laws and getting drunk, for violating the Sabbath, for failing to list themselves or their property for taxation, of road overseers and other officials for neglecting their duties. There seems to have been a good deal of profanity. A man would be presented for "prophanely swearing by his God one time," or more than one time might be specified, and there was an individual presented for "prophanely swearing by his God five times within three days." Enough has been said to suggest that here was the one nisi prius court operating in a nearly limitless field conducted by picked men who, albeit laymen, necessarily as the years went on, came to know very much of the law applicable to governmental and personal affairs, and the manner of its administration.

Fairfax County was a part of the princely domain called the Northern Neck of Virginia, of which Lord Fairfax was proprietor, embracing what are now more than 20 Virginia and West Virginia counties. He was one of the justices of the county, a special commission empowered "the Right Honorable the Lord Fairfax to act as a Justice of the Peace in all the counties of the Northern Neck;" and on his appearance he was noted at the head of the list as the presiding justice. On the occasion when he and Washington happened to be on the bench together it may be imagined that he was glad to see with his own eyes how constantly there was being verified his prediction quoted at the outset that Washington "would go to school all his life and profit thereby."

I CONSIDER IT AN INDISPENSABLE DUTY TO CLOSE THIS LAST SOLEMN ACT OF MY OFFICIAL LIFE, BY COMMENDING THE INTERESTS OF OUR DEAREST COUNTRY TO THE PROTECTION OF ALMIGHTY GOD, AND THOSE WHO HAVE THE SUPERINTENDENCE OF THEM TO HIS HOLY KEEPING.—*George Washington.*

THE CHARACTER

OF

WASHINGTON

A SPEECH BY

DANIEL WEBSTER

AT A PUBLIC DINNER ON THE 22ND OF FEBRUARY, 1832, IN HONOR OF
THE ONE HUNDREDTH ANNIVERSARY OF THE BIRTH OF
GEORGE WASHINGTON

UNITED STATES
GEORGE WASHINGTON BICENTENNIAL CELEBRATION 1932

The Character of Washington

A Speech by Daniel Webster

On the 22d of February, 1832, being the centennial of the birth of George Washington, a number of gentlemen, members of Congress and others, from different parts of the Union, united in commemorating the occasion by a public dinner in the city of Washington.

At the request of the Committee on Arrangements, Mr. Webster, then a Senator from Massachusetts, occupied the chair. After the cloth was removed, he addressed the company in the following manner:

I rise, Gentlemen, to propose to you the name of that great man, in commemoration of whose birth, and in honor of whose character and services, we are here assembled.

I am sure that I express a sentiment common to every one present, when I say that there is something more than ordinarily solemn and affecting in this occasion.

We are met to testify our regard for him whose name is intimately blended with whatever belongs most essentially to the prosperity, the liberty, the free institutions, and the renown of our country. That name was of power to rally a nation, in the hour of thick-thronging public disasters and calamities; that name shone, amid the storm of war, a beacon light to cheer and guide the country's friends; it flamed, too, like a meteor, to repel her foes. That name, in the days of peace, was a loadstone, attracting to itself a whole people's confidence, a whole people's love, and the whole world's respect. That name, descending with all time, spreading over the whole earth, and uttered in all the languages belonging to the tribes and races of men, will for ever be pronounced with affectionate gratitude by every one in whose breast there shall arise an aspiration for human rights and human liberty.

We perform this grateful duty, Gentlemen, at the expiration of a hundred years from his birth, near the place, so cherished and beloved by him, where his dust now reposes, and in the capital which bears his own immortal name.

All experience evinces that human sentiments are strongly influenced by associations. The recurrence of anniversaries, or of longer periods of time, naturally freshens the recollection, and deepens the impression, of events with which they are historically connected. Renowned places, also, have a power to awaken feeling, which all acknowledge. No American can pass by the fields of Bunker Hill, Monmouth, and Camden, as if they were ordinary spots on the earth's surface. Whoever visits them feels the sentiment of love of country kindling anew, as if the spirit that belonged to the transactions which have rendered these places distinguished still hovered round, with power to move and excite all who in future time may approach them.

But neither of these sources of emotion equals the power with which great moral examples affect the mind. When sublime virtues cease to be abstractions, when they become embodied in human character, and exemplified in human conduct, we should be false to our own nature, if we did not indulge in the spontaneous effusions of our gratitude and our admiration. A true lover of the virtue of patriotism delights to contemplate its purest models; and that love of country may be well suspected which affects to soar so high into the regions of sentiment as to be lost and absorbed in the abstract feeling, and becomes too elevated or too refined to glow with fervor in the commendation or the love of individual benefactors. All this is unnatural. It is as if one should be so enthusiastic a lover of poetry, as to care nothing for Homer or Milton; so passionately attached to eloquence as to be indifferent to Tully and Chatham; or such a devotee to the arts, in such an ecstasy with the elements of beauty, proportion, and expression, as to regard the masterpieces of Raphael and Michael Angelo with coldness or contempt. We may be assured, Gentlemen, that he who really loves the thing itself, loves its finest exhibitions. A true friend of his country loves her friends and benefactors, and thinks it no degradation to commend and commemorate them. The voluntary outpouring of the public feeling, made today, from the North to the South, and from the East to the West, proves this sentiment to be both just and natural. In the cities and in the villages, in the public temples and in the family circles, among all ages and sexes, gladdened voices today bespeak grateful hearts and a freshened recollection of the virtues of the Father of his Country. And it will be so, in all time to come, so long as public virtue is itself an object of regard. The ingenuous youth of America will hold up to themselves the bright model of Washington's example, and study to be what they behold; they will contemplate his character till all its virtues spread out and display themselves to their delightful vision; as the earliest astronomers, the shepherds on the plains of Babylon, gazed at the stars till they saw them form into clusters and constellations, overpowering at length the eyes of the beholders with the united blaze of a thousand lights.

Gentlemen, we are at the point of a century from the birth of Washington; and what a century it has been! During its course, the human mind has seemed to proceed with a sort of geometric velocity, accomplishing, for human intelligence and human freedom, more than had been done in fives or tens of centuries preceding. Washington stands at the commencement of a new era, as well as at the head of the New World. A century from the birth of Washington has changed the world. The country of Washington has been the theatre on which a great part of that change has been wrought; and Washington himself a principal agent by which it has been accomplished. His age and his country are equally full of wonders; and of both he is the chief.

If the poetical prediction, uttered a few years before his birth, be true; if indeed it be designed by Providence that the grandest exhibition of human character and human affairs shall be made on this theatre of the Western world; if it be true that,

"The four first acts already past,
  A fifth shall close the drama of the day;
  Time's noblest offspring is the last";

how could this imposing, swelling, final scene be appropriately opened, how could its intense interest be adequately sustained, but by the introduction of just such a character as our Washington?

Washington had attained his manhood when that spark of liberty was struck out in his own country, which has since kindled into a flame, and shot its beams over the earth. In the flow of a century from his birth, the world has changed in science, in arts, in the extent of commerce, in the improvement of navigation, and in all that relates to the civilization of man. But it is the spirit of human freedom, the new elevation of individual man, in his moral, social, and political character, leading the whole long train of other improvements, which has most remarkably distinguished the era. Society, in this century, has not made its progress, like Chinese skill, by a greater acuteness of ingenuity in trifles; it has not merely lashed itself to an increased speed round the old circles of thought and action; but it has assumed a new character; it has raised itself from *beneath* governments to a participation *in* governments; it has mixed moral and political objects with the daily pursuits of individual men; and, with a freedom and strength before altogether unknown, it has applied to these objects the whole power of the human understanding. It has been the era, in short, when the social principle has triumphed over the feudal principle; when society has maintained its rights against military power, and established, on foundations never hereafter to be shaken, its competency to govern itself.

It was the extraordinary fortune of Washington, that, having been intrusted, in revolutionary times, with the supreme military command, and having fulfilled that trust with equal renown for wisdom and for valor, he should be placed at the head of the first government in which an attempt was to be made on a large scale to rear the fabric of social order on the basis of a written constitution and of a pure representative principle. A government was to be established, without a throne, without an aristocracy, without castes, orders, or privileges; and this government, instead of being a democracy, existing and acting within the walls of a single city, was to be extended over a vast country, of different climates, interest, and habits, and of various communions of our common Christian faith. The experiment certainly was entirely new. A popular government of this extent, it was evident, could be framed only by carrying into full effect the principle of representation or of delegated power; and the world was to see whether society could, by the strength of this principle, maintain its own peace and good government, carry forward its own great interests, and conduct itself to political renown and glory. By the benignity of Providence, this experiment, so full of interest to us and to our posterity for ever, so full of interest, indeed, to the world in its present generation and in all its generations to come, was suffered to commence under the guidance of Washington. Destined for this high career, he was fitted for it by wisdom, by virtue, by patriotism, by discretion, by whatever can inspire confidence in man toward man. In entering on the untried scenes, early disappointment and the premature extinction of all hope of success would have been certain, had it not been that there did exist throughout the country, in a most extraordinary degree, an unwavering trust in him who stood at the helm.

I remarked, Gentlemen, that the whole world was and is interested in the result of this experiment. And is it not so? Do we deceive ourselves, or is it true that at this moment the career which this government is running is among the most attractive objects to the civilized world? Do we deceive ourselves, or is it true that at this moment that love of liberty and that understanding of its true principles which are flying over the whole earth, as on the wings of all the winds, are really and truly of American origin?

At the period of the birth of Washington, there existed in Europe no political liberty in large communities, except in the provinces of Holland, and except that England herself had set a great example, so far as it went, by her glorious Revolution of 1688. Everywhere else, despotic power was predominant, and the feudal or military principle held the mass of mankind in hopeless bondage. One half of Europe was crushed beneath the Bourbon sceptre, and no conception of political liberty, no hope even of religious toleration, existed among that nation which was America's first ally. The king was the state, the king was the country, the king was all. There was one king, with power not derived from his people, and too high to be questioned; and the rest were all subjects, with no political right but obedience. All above was intangible power, all below quiet subjection. A recent occurrence in the French Chambers shows us how public opinion on these subjects is changed. A minister had spoken of the "king's subjects." "There are no subjects," exclaimed hundreds of voices at once, "in a country where the people make the king!"

Gentlemen, the spirit of human liberty and of free government, nurtured and grown into strength and beauty in America, has stretched its course into the midst of the nations. Like an emanation from Heaven, it has gone forth, and it will not return void. It must change, it is fast changing, the face of the earth. Our great, our high duty is to show, in our own example, that this spirit is a spirit of health as well as a spirit of power; that its benignity is as great as its strength; that its efficiency to secure individual rights, social relations, and moral order is equal to the irresistible force with which it prostrates principalities and powers. The world, at this moment, is regarding us with a willing, but something of a fearful admiration. Its deep and awful anxiety is to learn whether free states may be stable, as well as free; whether popular power may be trusted, as well as feared; in short, whether wise, regular, and virtuous self-government is a vision for the contemplation of theorists, or a truth established, illustrated, and brought into practice in the country of Washington.

Gentlemen, for the earth which we inhabit, and the whole circle of the sun, for all the unborn races of mankind, we seem to hold in our hands, for their weal or woe, the fate of this experiment. If we fail, who shall venture the repetition? If our example shall prove to be one, not of encouragement, but of terror, not fit to be imitated but fit only to be shunned, where else shall the world look for free models? If this great *Western Sun* be struck out of the firmament, at what other fountain shall the lamp of liberty hereafter be lighted? What other orb shall emit a ray to glimmer, even, on the darkness of the world?

There is no danger of our overrating or overstating the important part which we are now acting in human affairs. It should not flatter our personal self-respect, but it should reanimate our patriotic virtues, and inspire us with a deeper and more solemn sense, both of our privileges and of our duties. We cannot wish better for our country, nor for the world, than that the same spirit which influences Washington may influence all who succeed him; and that the same blessing from above, which attended his efforts, may also attend theirs.

The principles of Washington's administration are not left doubtful. They are to be found in the Constitution itself, in the great measures recommended and approved by him, in his speeches to Congress, and in that most interesting paper, his Farewell Address to the People of the United States. The success of the government under his administration is the highest proof of the soundness of these principles. And, after an experience of thirty-five years, what is there which an enemy could condemn? What is there which either his friends, or the friends of the country, could wish to have been otherwise? I speak, of course, of great measures and leading principles.

In the first place, all his measures were right in their intent. He stated the whole basis of his own great character, when he told the country, in the homely phrase of the proverb, that honesty is the best policy. One of the most striking things ever said of him, is that *he changed mankind's ideas of political greatness.* To commanding talents, and to success, the common elements of such greatness, he added a disregard of self, a spotlessness of motive, a steady submission to every public and private duty, which threw far into the shade the whole crowd of vulgar great. The object of his regard was the whole country. No part of it was enough to fill his enlarged patriotism. His love of glory, so far as that may be supposed to have influenced him at all, spurned every thing short of general approbation. It would have been nothing to him, that his partisans or his favorites outnumbered, or outvoted, or outmanaged, or outclamored, those of other leaders. He had no favorites; he rejected all partisanship; and acting honestly for the universal good, he deserved, what he has so richly enjoyed, the universal love.

His principle it was to act right, and to trust the people for support; his principle it was not to follow the lead of sinister and selfish ends, nor to rely on the little arts of party delusion to obtain public sanction for such a course. Born for his country and for the world, he did not give up to party what was meant for mankind. The consequence is, that this fame is as durable as his principles, as lasting as truth and virtue themselves. While the hundreds whom party excitement, and temporary circumstances, and casual combinations, have raised into transient notoriety, sink again, like thin bubbles, bursting and dissolving into the great ocean, Washington's fame is like the rock which bounds that ocean, and at whose feet its billows are destined to break harmlessly for ever.

The maxims upon which Washington conducted our foreign relations were few and simple. The first was an entire and indisputable impartiality towards foreign states. He adhered to this rule of public conduct, against very strong inducements to depart from it, and when the popularity of the moment seemed to favor such a departure. In the next place, he maintained true dignity and unsullied honor in all communications with foreign states. It was among the high duties devolved upon him, to introduce our new government into the circle of civilized states and powerful nations. Not arrogant or assuming, with no unbecoming or supercilious bearing, he yet exacted for it from all others entire and punctilious respect. He demanded, and he obtained at once, a standing of perfect equality for his country in the society of nations; nor was there a prince or potentate of his day, whose personal character carried with it, into the intercourse of other states, a greater degree of respect and veneration.

He regarded other nations only as they stood in political relations to us. With their internal affairs, their political parties and dissensions, he scrupulously abstained from all interference; and, on the other hand, he repelled with spirit all such interference by others with us or our concerns. His sternest rebuke, the most indignant measure of his whole administration, was aimed against such an attempted interference. He felt it as an attempt to wound the national honor, and resented it accordingly.

The reiterated admonitions in his Farewell Address show his deep fears that foreign influence would insinuate itself into our counsels through the channels of domestic dissension, and obtain a sympathy with our own temporary parties. Against all such dangers, he most earnestly entreats the country to guard itself. He appeals to its patriotism, to its self-respect, to its own honor, to every consideration connected with its welfare and happiness, to resist, at the very beginning, all tendencies towards such connection of foreign interests with our own affairs. With a tone of earnestness nowhere else found, even in his last affectionate farewell advice to his countrymen, he says, "Against the insidious wiles of foreign influence (I conjure you to believe me, fellow-citizens,) the jealousy of a free people ought to be *constantly* awake; since history and experience prove, that foreign influence is one of the most baneful foes of republican government."

Lastly, on the subject of foreign relations, Washington never forgot that we had interests peculiar to ourselves. The primary political concerns of Europe, he saw, did not affect us. We had nothing to do with her balance of power, her family compacts, or her successions to thrones. We were placed in a condition favorable to neutrality during European wars, and to the enjoyment of all the great advantages of that relation. "Why then," he asks us, "why forego the advantages of so peculiar a situation? Why quit our own to stand upon foreign ground? Why be interweaving our destiny with that of any part of Europe, entangle our peace and prosperity in the toils of European ambition, rivalship, interest, humor, or caprice?"

Indeed, Gentlemen, Washington's Farewell Address is full of truths important at all times, and particularly deserving consideration at the present. With a sagacity which brought the future before him, and made it like the present, he saw and pointed out the dangers that even at this moment most imminently threatened us. I hardly know how a greater service of that kind could now be done to the community, than by a renewed and wide diffusion of that admirable paper, and an earnest invitation to every man in the country to reperuse and consider it. Its political maxims are invaluable; its exhortations to love of country and to brotherly affection among citizens, touching; and the solemnity with which it urges the observance of moral duties, and impresses the power of religious obligation, gives to it the highest character of truly disinterested, sincere, parental advice.

The domestic policy of Washington found its pole-star in the avowed objects of the Constitution itself. He sought so to administer that Constitution, as to form a more perfect union, establish justice, insure domestic tranquility, provide for the common defence, promote the general welfare, and secure the blessings of liberty. Those were objects interesting, in the highest degree, to the whole country, and his policy embraced the whole country.

Among his earliest and most important duties was the organization of the government itself, the choice of his confidential advisers, and the various appointments to office. This duty, so important and delicate, when a whole government was to be organized, and all its offices for the first time filled, was yet not difficult to him; for he had no sinister ends to accomplish, no clamorous partisans to gratify, no pledges to redeem, no object to be regarded but simply the public good. It was a plain, straightforward matter, a mere honest choice of good men for the public service.

His own singleness of purpose, his disinterested patriotism, were evinced by the selection of his first cabinet, and by the manner in which he filled the seats of justice, and other places of high trust. He sought for men fit for offices; not for offices which might suit men. Above personal considerations, above local considerations, above party considerations, he felt that he could not discharge the sacred trust which the country had placed in his hands, by a diligent inquiry after real merit, and a conscientious preference of virtue and talent. The whole country was the field of his selection. He explored that whole field, looking only for whatever it contained most worthy and distinguished. He was, indeed, most successful and he deserved success for the purity of his motives, the liberality of his sentiments, and his enlarged and manly policy.

Washington's administration established the national credit, made provision for the public debt, and for that patriotic army whose interests and welfare were always so dear to him; and, by laws wisely framed, and of admirable effect, raised the commerce and navigation of the country, almost at once, from depression and ruin to a state of prosperity. Nor were his eyes open to these interests alone. He viewed with equal concern its agriculture and manufactures, and, so far as they came within the regular exercise of the powers of this government, they experienced regard and favor.

It should not be omitted, even in this slight reference to the general measures and general principles of the first President, that he saw and felt the full value and importance of the judicial department of the government. An upright and able administration of the laws he held to be alike indispensable to private happiness and public liberty. The temple of justice, in his opinion, was a sacred place, and he would profane and pollute it who should call any to minister in it, not spotless in character, not incorruptible in integrity, not competent by talent and learning, not a fit object of unhesitating trust.

Among other admonitions, Washington has left us, in his last communication to his country, an exhortation against the excesses of party spirit. A fire not to be quenched, he yet conjures us not to fan and feed the flame. Undoubtedly, Gentlemen, it is the greatest danger of our system and of our time. Undoubtedly, if that system should be overthrown, it will be the work of excessive party spirit, acting on the government, which is dangerous enough, or acting *in* the government, which is a thousand times more dangerous; for government then becomes nothing but organized party, and, in the strange vicissitudes of human affairs, it may come at last, perhaps, to exhibit the singular paradox of government itself being in opposition to its own powers, at war with the very elements of its own existence. Such cases are hopeless. As men may be protected against murder, but cannot be guarded against suicide, so government may be shielded from the assaults of external foes, but nothing can save it when it chooses to lay violent hands on itself.

Finally, Gentlemen, there was in the breast of Washington one sentiment so deeply felt, so constantly uppermost, that no proper occasion escaped without its utterance. From the letter which he signed in behalf of the Convention when the Constitution was sent out to the people, to the moment when he put his hand to that last paper in which he addressed his countrymen, the Union,—the Union was the great object of his thoughts. In that first letter he tells them that, to him and his brethren of the Convention, union appears to be the greatest interest of every true American; and in that last paper he conjures them to regard that unity of government which constitutes them one people as the very palladium of their prosperity and safety, and the security of liberty itself. He regarded the union of these States less as one of our blessings, than as the great treasure-house which contained them all. Here, in his judgment, was the great magazine of all our means of prosperity; here, as he thought, and as every true American still thinks, are deposited all our animating prospects, all our solid hopes for future greatness. He has taught us to maintain this union, not by seeking to enlarge the powers of the government, on the one hand, nor by surrendering them, on the other; but by an administration of them at once firm and moderate, pursuing objects truly national, and carried on in a spirit of justice and equity.

The extreme solicitude for the preservation of the Union, at all times manifested by him, shows not only the opinion he entertained of its importance, but his clear perception of those causes which were likely to spring up to endanger it, and which, if once they should overthrow the present system, would leave little hope of any future beneficial reunion. Of all the presumptions indulged by presumptuous man, that is one of the rashest which looks for repeated and favorable opportunities for the deliberate establishment of a united government over distinct and widely extended communities. Such a thing has happened once in human affairs, and but once; the event stands out as a prominent exception to all ordinary history; and unless we suppose ourselves running into an age of miracles, we may not expect its repetition.

Washington, therefore, could regard, and did regard, nothing as of paramount political interest, but the integrity of the Union itself. With a united government, well administered, he saw that we had nothing to fear; and without it, nothing to hope. The sentiment is just, and its momentous truth should solemnly impress the whole country. If we might regard our country as personated in the spirit of Washington, if we might consider him as representing her, in her past renown, her present prosperity, and her future career, and as in that character demanding of us all to account for our conduct, as political men or as private citizens, how should he answer him who has ventured to talk of disunion and dismemberment? Or how should he answer him who dwells perpetually on local interests, and fans every kindling flame of local prejudice? How should he answer him who would array State against State, interest against interest, and party against party, careless of the continuance of that *unity of government which constitutes us one people?*

The political prosperity which this country has attained, and which it now enjoys, has been acquired mainly through the instrumentality of the present government. While this agent continues, the capacity of attaining to still higher degrees of prosperity exists also. We have, while this lasts, a political life capable of beneficial exertion, with power to resist or overcome misfortunes, to sustain us against the ordinary accidents of human affairs, and to promote, by active efforts, every public interest. But dismemberment strikes at the very being which preserves these faculties. It would lay its rude and ruthless hand on this great agent itself. It would sweep away, not only what we possess, but all power of regaining lost, or acquiring new possessions. It would leave the country, not only bereft of its prosperity and happiness, but without limbs, or organs, or faculties, by which to exert itself hereafter in the pursuit of that prosperity and happiness.

Other misfortunes may be borne, or their effects overcome. If disastrous war should sweep our commerce from the ocean, another generation may renew it; if it exhaust our treasury, future industry may replenish it; if it desolate and lay waste our fields, still, under a new cultivation, they will grow green again, and ripen to future harvests. It were but a trifle even if the walls of yonder Capitol were to crumble, if its lofty pillars should fall, and its gorgeous decorations be all covered by the dust of the valley. All these might be rebuilt. But who shall reconstruct the fabric of demolished government? Who shall rear again the well-proportioned columns of constitutional liberty? Who shall frame together the skilful architecture which unites national sovereignty with State rights, individual security, and public prosperity? No, if these columns fall, they will be raised not again. Like the Coliseum and the Parthenon, they will be destined to a mournful, a melancholy immortality. Bitterer

tears, however, will flow over them, than were ever shed over the monuments of Roman or Grecian art; for they will be the remnants of a more glorious edifice than Greece or Rome ever saw, the edifice of constitutional American liberty.

But let us hope for better things. Let us trust in that gracious Being who has hitherto held our country as in the hollow of his hand. Let us trust to the virtue and the intelligence of the people, and to the efficacy of religious obligation. Let us trust to the influence of Washington's example. Let us hope that that fear of Heaven which expels all other fear, and that regard to duty which transcends all other regard, may influence public men and private citizens, and lead our country still onward in her happy career. Full of these gratifying anticipations and hopes, let us look forward to the end of that century which is now commenced. A hundred years hence, other disciples of Washington will celebrate his birth, with no less of sincere admiration than we now commemorate it. When they shall meet, as we now meet, to do themselves and him that honor, so surely as they shall see the blue summits of his native mountains rise in the horizon, so surely as they shall behold the river on whose banks he lived, and on whose banks he rests, still flowing on toward the sea, so surely may they see, as we now see, the flag of the Union floating on the top of the Capitol; and then, as now, may the sun in his course visit no land more free, more happy, more lovely, than this our own country!

Gentlemen, I propose—

THE MEMORY OF

GEORGE WASHINGTON

WE CAST OUR EYES OVER HIS LIFE, NOT TO BE DAZZLED BY THE METEORIC LUSTRE OF PARTICULAR PASSAGES, BUT TO BEHOLD ITS WHOLE PATHWAY RADIANT EVERYWHERE, WITH THE TRUE GLORY OF A JUST, CONSCIENTIOUS, CONSUMMATE MAN!—*Robert C. Winthrop.*

COLONIAL GARDENS

THE LANDSCAPE ARCHITECTURE

of

GEORGE WASHINGTON'S TIME

Prepared by

AMERICAN SOCIETY OF LANDSCAPE ARCHITECTS

PREFACE

THE United States Commission for the Celebration of the Two Hundredth Anniversary of the Birth of George Washington authorized the preparation of this publication on COLONIAL GARDENS and issued it as one of its activities in connection with the George Washington Bicentennial Celebration.

In the compilation of the manuscript, the Commission was aided by the American Society of Landscape Architects, and particularly by certain of its members who have contributed without remuneration those portions bearing upon the particular field in which they are recognized authorities. The chapters on "Mount Vernon and Other Colonial Places of the South" and "Gardens of Old Salem and the New England Colonies" are from the pen of Arthur A. Shurcliff, Fellow and Past President of the American Society of Landscape Architects, and landscape architect associated with the architects in charge of the restoration of Williamsburg. The chapter on "Homes and Gardens of Old New York" has been contributed by Richard Schermerhorn, Jr., Fellow of the American Society of Landscape Architects, and that on "Gardens and Places of Colonial Philadelphia," by Robert Wheelwright, Member of the American Society of Landscape Architects and Professor of Landscape Architecture at the University of Pennsylvania. The final chapter, on "The Colonial Garden Today," has been written by Fletcher Steele, Fellow of the American Society of Landscape Architects and author of *Design in the Little Garden*.

Without the generous help of these contributing authors and the valuable assistance of a Committee of members of the Society, comprising the above with Robert Washburn Beal, Charles F. Gillette, Eugene D. Montillon, and Bradford Williams, under the chairmanship of Albert D. Taylor, this publication could not have achieved its present degree of authenticity.

The task of editing and arranging this material was performed by Bradford Williams, Member of the American Society of Landscape Architects, who has brought to his work an experience gained as Contributing Editor to *Landscape Architecture* and *The American Magazine of Art*.

SOL BLOOM,
DIRECTOR,
UNITED STATES GEORGE WASHINGTON
BICENTENNIAL COMMISSION

COLONIAL GARDENS

MOUNT VERNON
The Home and Garden of George Washington

CHAPTER I

Introduction

Of the many ways of honoring a national figure on the two hundredth anniversary of his birth, none could be greater than to make him live again among us and to find him young in spirit. George Washington could be honored in this way, for in the rôle of farmer, statesman, soldier, or engineer, his memory is as fresh today as his thoughts were clear and his action direct a century and a half ago.

One aspect of the life of George Washington in which he could be re-created with particular appropriateness is that of the country gentleman. From his own diaries and letters we know the minutest details of his life as a planter or farmer as well as gardener. We see him clearly in his home life at Mount Vernon; and in fact, Mount Vernon today is the embodiment for us of George Washington's existence, for in the undying charm of this mansion and its grounds he lives with as much reality and with greater persistency than during the few years of private enjoyment that his life of sacrifice to the public good ever permitted him.

This part of George Washington's life belongs to every citizen. We revere him as a patriot for his generous sacrifice of private life

and interests to an untried cause; as a soldier, for his ability to lead others in defense of this cause; as a statesman, for his understanding in the guidance of a frail vessel through perilous waters. But we feel most closely united to him in his life as a citizen when he shared the same happiness and sorrows of home life that we, two hundred years later, experience today.

Among the never-failing joys of George Washington's private life were his gardens. The management of broad acres at Mount Vernon was both business and pleasure for him, but the arrangement and care of the flower and vegetable gardens and of the grounds in the immediate vicinity of the mansion gave him particular satisfaction. In writing of him as a gardener, we touch on that side of his activities that is most closely akin to the experience of the average citizen today. In him we see an interest and a knowledge of the practical science of horticulture that enabled him to collect and grow in his gardens a wide variety of both native and rare plants; but we find that he also had a love for the beautiful that enabled him to appreciate the orderly arrangement of his grounds and buildings and made him an outstanding patron of the art of landscape architecture or, as it was called at that time, landscape gardening.

One reason, then, for selecting the Colonial Garden as the object of this study is to reveal George Washington, the Planter, as one of the gardeners of his time. The picture of the Colonial Garden that is presented in these pages portrays the garden background of the period as the Virginia Planter saw it in his journeys through the Colonies. Just as he was known in the home of every great soldier and statesman of the time, so was he known in the gardens of his compatriots, as well as abroad. In this we see today another instance of his universality; for the love of growing things is universal throughout the breadth of the land and across the seas.

But a second reason is the example that he set for the citizen of today in the development of his own home at Mount Vernon.

From the early year of his life when he inherited the family home from his brother Lawrence, he maintained the hope that he might develop his house and grounds according to his dignified tastes. During his journeys to the sessions of the House of Burgesses at Williamsburg, or to the Congresses at Philadelphia, or to duties in the more remote colonies of New York and New England, he absorbed impressions from the many handsome places he visited, and when finally he was able to reconstruct the mansion and lay out the grounds in accordance with the prevailing style, he created an establishment that was both suited to the necessary uses of the time and yet possessed all the elements of outdoor enjoyment that are found in the best of the Colonial homes and gardens.

THE EDITOR.

CHAPTER II

The Colonial Garden: Its History and Meaning

Much has been said and written of the gardens of the Colonial period, and yet students of garden art have great difficulty in defining the term "Colonial Garden." In other periods of garden history, we can easily identify the typical development of the time through characteristics common to a number of examples in the period. The term "Moorish Garden in Spain" or "Italian Renaissance Garden" conveys some idea of a particular garden style that has grown up and become recognizable through repeated use of certain principles and characteristics of design.

The gardens of the American colonies were developed under widely divergent conditions of climate and without a common background of social or national characteristics. They developed individually in their own locality. A fusion of types came only as the inherited characteristics of the earliest settlers were modified by long residence in a new country and as means of travel and communication were improved. They were a definite outgrowth of the time and the people, and as such they had their place. With the passing of these conditions, the Colonial Garden passed.

The garden development of the Colonial period can exist for us only in spirit, for today there can be no such thing as a true Colonial Garden. To be sure there are the physical remains of old gardens, and in their glory of old trees and ancient box we can people them with the products of our imagination so that they become alive again in their atmosphere of an inherited past. But the people are changed and the environment is different; even the countryside has undergone an alteration under the influence of the march of time.

The Colonial Garden of George Washington's time was not what we know today as a garden. In most instances there was a definitely segregated enclosed place where plants could be grown free from the inroads of cattle, but in few cases except in later days were these enclosed areas given over purely to out-of-door enjoyment and the cultivation of flowers. In the smaller places seeds were planted in any suitable corner; garden activities, both useful and ornamental, were carried on wherever was most convenient, and it was hard to distinguish the "garden" from any other part

MOUNT VERNON FROM THE WEST
View Across the Vegetable Garden

of the dooryard. On the larger places, where men and means were more available, more ordered effects were attempted; here trees and great hedges were considered part of the garden, and even the mansion and its outbuildings were treated as part of the garden scheme. This meaning of the Colonial Garden must be clear in order to understand the importance of the garden in the thought of the times.

The Colonial Garden of Washington's time played a far more important part in home life than does our garden today. People spent more time at home, partly because conditions were not favorable for travel, and partly because there was little reason for travel. The Colonial home and garden was the center of family life and, as such, it was the place of exchange for social courtesies and of shelter for the traveler. The home was the place of business where all the outdoor activities of the establishment were centered. Outside of the towns it was in the home that you could be certain of finding all people who were not engaged in public occupations or who were not temporarily absent on their business. In the case of the smallest properties, the house, being hot or crowded or inconvenient, must frequently have been unsuited to the entertainment of visitors, and it was natural that some part of the immediate out-of-doors should become a center of the family living during a large part of the year.

The fashions in gardening were more clearly revealed in the house grounds of the well-to-do, for people of "consequence" kept in close touch with England and the Continent,—perhaps more closely in intellectual communion than we today, notwithstanding our improved modes of communication and travel. Building and gardening in 17th-century England and France started with grand scale, long symmetrical vistas and avenues, labyrinths, parterres, and rich decoration.

Similar ideas, but necessarily not so elaborate, appealed to the owners of great estates in the South and as far north as Philadelphia. Houses and outbuildings were laid out symmetrically with long axial avenues and vistas. At times the scale, where topography permitted, was quite as magnificent as in Europe. Cultured travelers from abroad found much to admire in our more splendid Colonial estates, though in detail they could not vie with the palaces of kings.

During Washington's lifetime, due at the end in no small measure to the impetus that his leadership of a revolution for the rights of man inspired, the style changed, for fashion "leapt the fence and saw that all nature was a garden." The park style of landscape architecture came into being with great open meadows, fine trees, distant vistas, and wandering walks and drives. This mode of treating natural scenery was, and has remained, sympathetic to the American people. It was adopted North and South, though mostly in the North, and most successfully along the Hudson River.

Mount Vernon is the typical example of the large Colonial estate in the late days of the Colonies, and there Washington combined the prevailing landscape styles. In his early travels he had found at Philadelphia and elsewhere examples of the 17th-century formal fashion, and if he had made over his grounds at that time it is conceivable that he might have developed a plan of straight avenues and formal parterres of statuary, flowers, and greenery. But he had reached his fifty-second year and had brought the War to a successful conclusion before he began those changes on the grounds that resulted in the form we know today; by then he had seen the newer style of landscape gardening and had decided to adapt it to his own use.

It was Washington's pride to be thought the first farmer in America. In 1773 he had spent fourteen years of his married life at Mount Vernon and, save for repairs that had been made in anticipation of his marriage, the mansion was exactly the same as when he, at the age of fifteen, had taken up his home there with his brother Lawrence. These years of domestic and social life had revealed the limitations of the establishment, and in the autumn of 1773 the carpenters began to carry out his plans for enlarging the building. The changes were not soon completed, however, for it was not until 1778 while Washington was in the third year of his military campaigning that the mansion was raised and its proportions extended to their now familiar shape, the curved and colonnaded covered ways were built, and the portico on the river side was added. One Sunday morning in September, 1781, when pressing ahead of the army which was making a forced march south to join Lafayette at Williamsburg, he stopped at Mount Vernon for the first time in six years, and was rewarded by the first view of his completed mansion.*

On Christmas Eve, 1783, General and Mrs. Washington returned to Mount Vernon from Annapolis where he had laid down his commission on the disbandment of the Continental Army. During the following months—a winter of exceptional ice and snow for the region of the Potomac—Washington laid out his scheme of improvements for the gardens and farms. His diaries of 1785-6 are a running guide to his activities in the adornment of the grounds. As a horticulturist prior to the Revolution, his tastes had been predominantly utilitarian, but as early as 1768 he was beginning to think of beautifying his grounds, for in that year he expressed a wish to have about his mansion house every possible specimen of native tree or shrub that was noted for beauty of form, leaf, or flower. His observation of beautiful Colonial homes and gardens in various sections of the country during the War, together with the contact of cultured people, both Americans and Europeans, had broadened his love of plants to include a feeling for their use and appearance as part of a broad landscape treatment.

On January 19, 1785, he began to lay out his new plan for the West lawn and "serpentine road" with shade trees of many varieties. He then rarely rode through his woods or pastures without remarking some crab, holly, magnolia, or pine that would serve his purpose. In one entry in April he noted that

> the flower of the Sassafras was fully out and looked well. An intermixture of this and Red bud I conceive would look very pretty—the latter crowned with the former or vice versa.

In this same spring he recorded the planting of limes and lindens sent by his good friend Governor Clinton of New York; lilacs, mock oranges, aspen, mulberries, black gums, berried thorns, locusts, sassafras, magnolia, crabs, service berries, catalpas, papaws, honey locusts, a live oak from Norfolk, yews, aspens, swamp berries, hemlocks, twelve horse chestnut sent by "Light Horse Harry" Lee, twelve cuttings of tree box, buckeye nuts brought by him the preceding year from the mouth of Cheat River, eight nuts from a tree called "the Kentucke Coffee tree," a row of shell bark hickory nuts from New York, some filberts from "sister Lewis." His brother John sent him four barrels of holly seeds which he sowed in various

---

* *Mount Vernon: Washington's Home and the Nation's Shrine.* By Paul Wilstach. Indianapolis, Bobbs-Merrill Co., 1916.

parts of the place. But the spring was an exceptionally dry one and he was forced to be absent from home for some days.* He then records that

> Most of my transplanted trees have a sickly look. The small Pines in the Wildernesses are entirely dead. The larger ones in the Walks, for the most part, appear to be alive (as yet), almost the whole of the Holly are dead. Many of the Ivy, wch. before looked healthy and well seem to be declining; few of the Crab trees had put forth leaves. Not a single ash tree has unfolded its buds; whether owing to the trees' decline, or any other cause, I know not. . . . The lime trees, which had some appearance of Budding when I went away, are now withering, and the Horse Chesnut and Tree box from Colo. Harry Lee's discover little signs of shooting. The Hemlock is almost dead, and bereft of their leaves; and so are the live Oak. In short, half the Trees in the Shrubberies, and many in the Walks, are dead and declining.

But Washington was not discouraged, for, as he wrote one of his managers on another occasion,

> I shall begrudge no reasonable expense that will contribute to the improvement and neatness of my farms, for nothing pleases me better than to see them in good order, and everything trim, handsome, and thriving about them; nor nothing hurts me more than to find them otherwise.

* George Washington: Country Gentleman. By Paul Leland Haworth. Indianapolis, Bobbs-Merrill Co., 1915, 1925.

Of all parts of the Mount Vernon estate, the great covered terrace on the river front received more general usage than any other part of the house or grounds. It was the gathering place for the members of the household. It was there that Washington received and entertained great companies of visitors, for his exalted position attracted a constant stream of people who came to pay their respects. No less than thirty windsor chairs were provided to seat them. When inclement weather forbade his usual outdoor exercise in the fields, it was here that Washington paced for an hour before retiring.

Quite apart from the great homes and gardens were the smaller farms and the town houses of the Colonies. In the country, particularly in the North, we have visions of the farm house, situated in the midst of a trimmed grass area and approached through a grove of maples, locusts, or elms. On one side lies the orchard; the long grass beneath the apples invites us to wade knee deep through it. Gigantic lilacs here and there, and perhaps some specimens of ancient box, have come down from earlier Colonial times. On another side a path leads to a garden, box-walled and redolent of the perfume of the box and the sweet-scented old-fashioned flowers.

The town garden was more sophisticated, as befitted the pleasure grounds of those in the seats of culture, and here we find a greater

MOUNT VERNON FROM THE EAST
View Over the Flower Garden

variety of plants. A Boston newspaper of March 30, 1760, gives us the following list of seeds for sale:*

Lavender
Palma Christi
Cerinthe or Honeywort, loved of bees
Tricolor
Indian Pink
Scarlet Cacalia
Yellow Sultans
Lemon African Marigold
Sensitive Plants
White Lupine
Love Lies Bleeding
Patagonian Cucumber
Lobelia
Catchfly
Wing-peas
Convolvulus
Strawberry Spinage
Branching Larkspur
White Chrysanthemum
Nigaella Romano
Rose Campion
Snap Dragon
Nolana prostrata
Summer Savory
Hyssop
Red Hawkweed
Red and White Lavater

Scarlet Lupine
Large blue Lupine
Snuff flower
Caterpillars
Cape Marigold
Rose Lupine
Sweet Peas
Venus' Navelwort
Yellow Chrysanthemum
Cyanus minor
Tall Holyhock
French Marigold
Carnation Poppy
Globe Amaranthus
Yellow Lupine
Indian Branching Coxcombs
Iceplants
Thyme
Sweet Marjoram
Tree Mallows
Everlasting
Greek Valerian
Tree Primrose
Canterbury Bells
Purple Stock
Sweet Scabiouse
Columbine
Pleasant-eyed Pink

Dwarf Mountain Pink
Sweet Rocket
Horn Poppy
French Honeysuckle
Bloody Wallflower
Sweet William
Honesty (to be sold in small parcels that every one may have a little)
Persicaria
Polyanthos

50 Different Sorts of mixed Tulip Roots
Ranunculus
Gladiolus
Starry Scabiouse
Curled Mallows
Painted Lady topknot peas
Colchicum
Persian Iris
Star Bethlehem

In the gardens of the more pretentious houses could be found plants imported directly from the Old World. A page from an old letter written by Mr. Thomas Hancock, well-to-do Boston merchant and uncle of the better-known John Hancock, gives us a pretty picture of these contacts.*

My Trees and Seeds for Capt. Bennett Came Safe to Hand and I like them very well. I Return you my hearty Thanks for the Plumb Tree and Tulip Roots you were pleased to make me a Present off, which are very Acceptable to me. I have Sent my friend Mr. Wilks a mmo. to procure for me 2 or 3 Doz. Yew Trees, Some Hollys and Jessamine Vines, and if you have Any Particular Curious Things not of a high Price, will Beautifye a flower Garden Send a Sample with the Price or a Catalogue of 'em, I do not intend to spare Any Cost or Pains in making my Gardens Beautifull or Profitable.

P. S. The Tulip Roots you were Pleased to make a present off to me are all Dead as well.

New York, Philadelphia, and the Far South were no less active during the Colonial period in their development of garden and home. Let us see in greater detail what were the characteristics of these developments and how they differed one from another.

BRADFORD WILLIAMS.

* Old-time Gardens. By Alice Morse Earle. New York, The Macmillan Co., 1901, p. 33.

* From Bulletin of the Society for the Preservation of New England Antiquities, July, 1926.

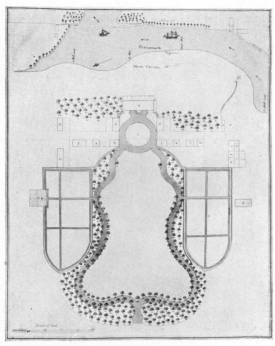

Courtesy of the Library of Congress

Plan

Reference.

a. The Mansion House.
b. Smiths Shop.
c. White Servants appartment
d. Kitchen.
e. Repository for Dung
f. Spinning House
g.
h. Shoemaker & Taylors appartm.t
i. Store House &c.a
k. Smoak House.
l. Wash House.
mm Coach Houses
n. Quarters for Families.
o.o.o Stables.
p.p.p. Necessaries.
q. Green House.
r.r. Cow Houses.
s. Barn & Carpenters Shop.
t. School Room.
u. Summer House.
w. Dairy
xx Kitchen Gardens.

Key to the Plan

The Plan in Perspective, showing Mansion and Gardens from the Southeast

THE PLAN OF MOUNT VERNON

CHAPTER III
Mount Vernon and Other Colonial Places of the South

George Washington and his Virginia neighbors were not commuters or trippers. There were no railroads or fast boats. Horses were the speediest motive power for travel, but they could not make more than seven to nine miles an hour either under saddle or harnessed to the carts, chariots, or coaches. A Sunday afternoon trip on the rough, dusty, or muddy roads of those days did not tempt men to be joy-riders. Travel was the hardest kind of work and it was costly of money and time. The man who was sturdy enough to endure the hardships of travel was either looked up to for his strength, or looked down upon for his folly. He was at best a squanderer of time unless he went on urgent business, and he was a spendthrift unless he roamed like a tramp. Primitive transportation conditions kept men at home. The grandee, as well as the artisan who worked at carpentering, shoemaking, black-smithing, or harness-making, was tied down to life in one place, and that place was home. This confinement was not considered a hardship, because no other kind of life was possible except to the traveler, whose lot was slow and hard.

In the villages and towns a man could find a carpenter or a smith to work for him, and his servants could walk to him. Provisions could be bought at shops. Good books could be borrowed or bought here and there up and down the street. Friends met on the street corners, at the inn, or at church. To the man who lived in the country, however, isolation was inevitable. The need to be a Jack-of-all-trades was universal. The well-to-do man could escape from being a carpenter, blacksmith, or cobbler to his own needs only by creating a community of such helpers in his own dooryard. He must either dip candles and smoke bacon or he must keep men at hand to do that work for him. He could not depend, as we do today, upon the store or upon the mail-order. He could not buy clothes ready made, or machinery, or wheat ready threshed, or flour, shoes, cloth, butter, meat. All must be produced at home.

These conditions of life were common in England as well as in our country in Washington's day. His forbears, when they did not live in villages, were well acquainted with the all-round life of the farm. They had the ability and the knowledge needed to turn their hands to self-sustained labor. In his boyhood Washington lived on a farm. In his ripe manhood he chose a farmer's life at Mount Vernon with full realization of all the labor and cooperation which that life entailed. Farms of great size were called "plantations" in Virginia and the South.

Enough has been said to indicate that Washington's home at Mount Vernon could not have resembled the modern gentleman's place. Our modern gentleman's place reflects the life of a man who has the world at his beck and call through the railroad, motor road, telegraph, telephone, postal system, and a great transportation structure. At Mount Vernon we find vastly more interesting things than a good house, a garage, a barn for horses and cows, an electric water supply, a lawn with a rubber hose, and a garden. We find, as we should expect, a very large acreage of cultivated land and of woodland sufficient to sustain the Washington household and all the workers. In Washington's time there were large herds of sheep and cattle, many draught and saddle horses, swine

and fowls. Over a hundred plantation laborers were engaged in ploughing, cultivating, harvesting, threshing, grinding, smoking meat, pumping water, grooming horses and shoeing oxen, building carts, ploughs, farm gear, making harness, and carrying on all the thousand interesting activities necessary for the support of the laborers and of their master. There were extensive flower and box gardens which were in scale with the needs of the immediate family, but the gardens for produce were in scale with the needs of the hundreds of artisans and laborers and their families. Scores of buildings were needed to shelter these workers, to house the animals, tools, wagons, coaches, and the shops of the carpenters, blacksmiths, cobblers, and overseers.

The modest size of the Washington mansion and its simple practical architectural design attest the caliber of the man who made Mount Vernon a delight to all those, including the humblest, who dwelt there. Washington's interest in the loveliness of Mount Vernon did not absorb him to such a degree as to make him forget its practical use. The skill with which the house and grounds were arranged to meet the needs of the Virginia climate, a hilly topography, and the operation of a great plantation mark him as a man of broad understanding. The needs of a gentle family and of a circle of cultivated friends coming from the ends of the English- and French-speaking world were met also by Mount Vernon, but not to the exclusion of the needs of the great plantation.

The accompanying pictures and the plan of Mount Vernon show the orderly grouping of the mansion and its near gardens and those few plantation buildings which still stand after the lapse of over a century. The stately approach is shown. The trees which were planted by Washington's own hand are shown and they tally in location and in kind with the methodical description of them which he entered in his journals, with notes regarding the weather at the times of planting, the day and month, and the probable usefulness of the species to other planters. Washington was the first American to study farming and gardening from a scientific point of view to increase the yield and to improve the quality.

The mansion was placed on high ground which overlooked the Potomac River and which at the same time permitted an axial view of the house itself to be seen from the straight approach of about a half mile. This high ground was gentle in slope on the side toward the garden, but abrupt on the side toward the stables, coach house, cow yard, and the near pastures. Though moderate in size, the mansion thus overlooked and pleasantly dominated the plantation. This result was not accomplished by bold cutting or filling of the ground or by sacrificing the convenience of the daily life of the great farm. Whether selected by George Washington's father or his older brother Lawrence the site lent itself to all practical needs and also to a stately appearance. Pleasantness of outlook and attractiveness of ground at the very door were found.

The flower or box garden was made on level ground and it conformed along its curved edge to the shape of the approach lawn. On the opposite side the edge of the balancing garden and paddock exactly mated with the curve of the garden. Though

The Flower Garden

The Vegetable Garden

THE GARDENS AT MOUNT VERNON

partly curving, the garden was laid out without an attempt to secure a "natural" effect. Walls, fences, and outbuildings hemmed it in. The paths ran parallel to these. The box hedges and the rows of trees in the garden followed the lines of the paths. Every line was simple and understandable. Today, after all the decades which have passed, its simplicity, its freedom from "smartness," and its intimate relation to its own work buildings and to the mansion make it an appealing vision of use and loveliness. Not striving for attention, it attains the ideals of a garden which was made to satisfy mind and heart.

The widely dispersed arrangement of buildings and gardens at Mount Vernon would not have been practical for use in a cold climate like that of New England, but in warm Virginia buildings are more conveniently used and are more comfortable when widely separated. The symmetrical placing of the wings and outbuildings at Mount Vernon is characteristic of Virginia planning; irregular placing of wing buildings and ells as used in New England was not considered practical or pleasant in Virginia.

If we compare the Virginia places of Washington's time with places in England, the Virginia places were in general as large or larger, somewhat less in cost, less complete in detail, built in many cases for as great permanency, not mellowed by time, of course, or by history, but rapidly mellowed by a bland atmosphere. Virginia houses and outbuildings were often built of brick but not of half-timbered work. Though wood was at hand, brick was generously used for construction. Retaining-walls were rare, but walls for seclusion, if not for privacy, were common. Courtyards were infrequent. Crofts (called "yards") were almost universal. Long axial vistas and long axial approaches were also almost universal in Virginia country places and farms.

The preservation of the mansion, the gardens, and a very large acreage of Mount Vernon has been accomplished. This patriotic achievement has been brought about by a group of ladies, the Mount Vernon Ladies' Association of the Union, who raised the necessary funds for the purchase and who maintain Mount Vernon for the instruction and the delight of the Nation. The United States Government has just completed the construction of a National Parkway leading from Washington to the edge of the Mount Vernon domain. This modern road and the great parking spaces do not enter the interior of the grounds, but they permit visitors on leaving their cars to approach the mansion and the gardens by a walk of two or three minutes.

Symmetry in the placing of outbuildings in Virginia at this Washingtonian period is seen at "Stratford," the ancient Lee place on the lower Potomac. Stratford owes its preservation, first, to the permanence of the brick which forms its massive walls, and second, to the efforts of those who have guarded it as a memorial of the Lee family and of General Robert E. Lee. General Lee knew it well in his early boyhood. In his later life he often referred to his memories of the place with a feeling of tenderness which is strong in Southern men. These men understand deeply the significance of the old plantations in the history of our country.

Reference to a plan of this remarkable place would show the perfect axial balance of the near "kitchen" on the right and the "cottage" on the left. The balance of the "old school" and the "office" left and right on the far side of the mansion is no less striking. In ancient times the Potomac was opened to the view of the mansion by the removal of the trees which now hide the river. The owner of Stratford is the Robert E. Lee Memorial Foundation, Inc., and all of the restoration work is being done under their jurisdiction. A number of other organizations are assisting, among which are the Garden Club of Virginia, the National Society of the Colonial Dames in the State of Virginia, and the United Daughters of the Confederacy.

The old garden which is to be restored was rectangular. No attempt was made in those days to copy that wilderness of woods, brushland, winding path, and irregular pasturage which surrounded the mansion. Pleasure lay in a garden which showed man's control of that wilderness. Around the garden were walls, the many outbuildings, and the impressive towering pile of the mansion. Straight paths, hedges straight or arranged in the simple geometric patterns of those days, straight rows of old-time trees, and flowers of old kinds arranged in the manner of the Southland,—all these were a part of the picture. Box hedges bordered some of the paths. No one could upon other ground copy such a garden or make a new one like it. Without the presence of the old mansion itself, without the facts of the ancient design upon the true site, without the ancient trees, and without the traditions of the Lee family culminating in the affection which General Lee held for this now sacred plot of ground, there could be no garden like this one.

In the reader's mind the question will arise at once as to what were the surroundings and the plans of the small place of the Virginia man of relatively small means at the time of Washington and upon the small plots of ground in towns where there could be no large acreage for development. Brief study shows that all the utility areas and the utility structures which made existence possible to the isolated places are present (on a small scale to be sure), but the buildings for the journeymen carpenters, smiths, and cobblers are absent, because those artisans were available in the town.

In the small lots of the Virginia towns (lots of about 100 feet frontage and having two or three times as great a depth) we find that the house is usually placed about at the middle of the front street line and set back to give a small fenced dooryard. A central door at the back opens upon a path which leads to the rear of the lot and usually abounds with right-angled or nearly right-angled paths branching to lateral buildings always set on or very near the sides of the lot. These buildings include a kitchen combined with a servant's room, a smoke house, dairy, wood house, necessaries, a barn for cows and horses, a hen house and yard, a well-house, and other structures. Sometimes, as shown in the accompanying plan, a fence was arranged across the lot near the house to enclose a garden or a working yard alongside the rear of the house. Sometimes the garden lay near the house. There were usually rows of fruit trees and a vegetable garden. The charm of these small intensively developed places, with widely spread and somewhat symmetrically placed outbuildings, fences, paths, and trees, is manifest. In many towns the use of box in the gardens was almost universal.

Among these small places, as in the great plantations, there was no attempt to secure "natural" appearing grounds by the use of scattered beds of shrubbery, scattered trees, winding paths, or irregular lawns. No attempt was made to build rambling houses of picturesque appearance. Sometimes when the original house became inadequate through the size of a growing family, wings and ells were added. These often varied the symmetry of the original house plan and its elevation. Picturesque building groups thus came into existence, but they came by indirection to meet a need and not

Courtesy of Virginia State Chamber of Commerce

Stratford Hall

A Suggested Restoration of the Garden

STRATFORD

with the aim to make a fanciful or picturesque effect. Similarly a certain departure from symmetry creeps into the gardens, but not by first intention.

Washington's interest in trees and shrubbery did not single him out among Virginians and men of other parts of the South. All Southern men have shown great interest in such matters. The letters of Colonial times and the diaries refer constantly to the names of plants and to their origin. From these scattered sources, from Washington's own journals, and from the ancient plants which we find growing in the old places, we are able to gather lists of trees, shrubbery, and flowers which indicate the flora of the old places. Within the limits of this chapter copies of these lists can not be included.

In general, in Colonial times in the South they depended on the natural flora of the country though they imported some plants from England, France, Spain, and the Mediterranean. In those days, the vast number of plants originating in Africa, China, Japan, and California were unknown. To many persons these horticultural limitations add especial interest to the ancient Southern gardens. Nowadays you will find many who are discarding "modern" flowers, trees, and shrubs in the effort to make their flora correspond to the one with which George Washington and his contemporaries were familiar.

A glance at the generous Southern places with their many buildings for the offices of the household gives a hint of the hospitality of the Southern man. He took pains also to arrange his approaches and to place his gardens with an eye to the good appearance of the house and the pleasantness of home. He built his place with thought for the comfort and the delight of friends. Certainly there is no part of our country in which hospitality shows itself more fully and more sincerely than in the South.

ARTHUR A. SHURCLIFF.

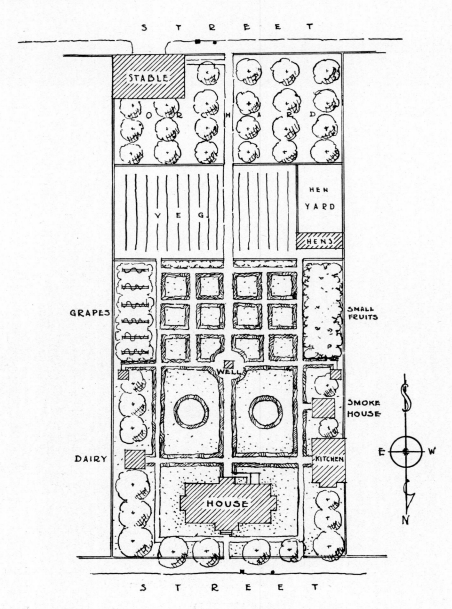

A TYPICAL TOWN PLACE
IN VIRGINIA

CHAPTER IV
Gardens and Places of Colonial Philadelphia

The Eighteenth Century marks a period of prosperity for Philadelphia that might be said to have reached a culmination when the city was selected as the seat of our newly established Federal Government. Located in a country rich in natural resources, and settled by thrifty, industrious people, the community developed rapidly. Commerce, wealth, and culture combined to make it foremost among the cities of the North American colonies, and developed among its citizens that degree of elegance and civility which is ever manifested in a greater regard for gardens as an ultimate expression of culture and refinement.

Colonial Philadelphia was more sparsely built up than our modern suburban towns, and so is comparable to these rather than to a city. Contrary to the tendency of modern suburban zoning laws, Philadelphia houses of Colonial days usually were built directly on the street, although the lots were large, sometimes comprising several acres. High enclosing walls gave the greater privacy desirable for city residences, and the maximum area of the lot was left for the use and enjoyment of the owner. With the growth of the city the gardens have disappeared but fortunately many of the houses are still standing, and bear witness to ancient prosperity.

The view of Washington's residence at 190 (now 528) Market Street gives a good idea of the appearance of old Philadelphia, though it reveals nothing of the arrangement of grounds other than house site and drive entrance. Presumably there was a garden, a stable, and possibly other structures, but we have still to discover landscape plans of this or any other city home and so we must rely upon descriptions to give us an idea of the appearance of the grounds. Washington's residence is gone, but the Powel house,

where he was a constant visitor, still stands. We may never hope to see the replica of the extensive grounds surrounding it adorned with allées and statuary, with orange, lemon, and citron trees and other exotics.

Confining our discussion of town houses to two further examples, one of the earlier, the other of the later Eighteenth Century, we find that Clarke Hall, built about 1700, was laid out "in the old style of uniformity, with walks and alleys nodding to their brothers." Such a description clearly indicates a formal, symmetrical plan. The Bingham house on Third Street above Spruce was built about 1790, after a visit that the owner made to London. A description which says: "The grounds about the house, beautifully diversified with walks, statuary, shade trees and parterres," would indicate gardening of the formal type; while another reference using the term "clump," a familiar form of planting developed under the naturalesque influence of Eighteenth-Century England, indicates an informal arrangement. The lot was of sufficient extent to permit both types of embellishment.

In Germantown the lots were narrow but extended far back in the country for farming purposes. The houses were built close to, or directly on, the one existing street, and a community developed that appeared closely built. Low walls or fences gave enclosure and presented a less conventionalized aspect than did the high garden walls of Philadelphia, but as a type we may class them the same, owing to the constricted character of the grounds in proximity to the houses.

Among the more famous places in Germantown that still retain a portion of their old grounds, "Wister's Big House" (1744), "Cliveden" (1761), and "Wyck" (1690) are the best known.

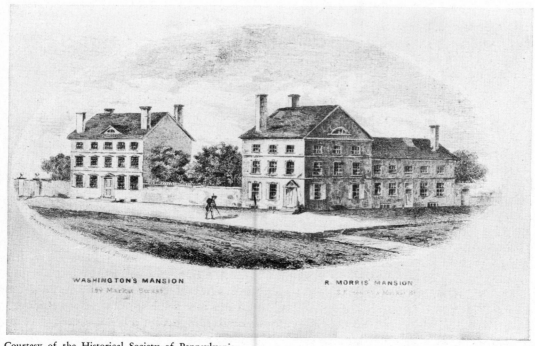

WASHINGTON'S MANSION   R. MORRIS MANSION

Courtesy of the Historical Society of Pennsylvania

Washington's Residence, Philadelphia

"Wister's Big House," Germantown
A Home of the Old Philadelphia Region

Cliveden was the country seat of Chief Justice Chew, but we have no records that give us any satisfactory picture of the grounds as they existed in his day. It is not known when the garden was built at Wyck, but its "old style" suggests greater age than any documentary evidence proves, and we may believe that it existed when Washington lived in Germantown.

While the garden at Wister's Big House, better known perhaps as "Grumblethorpe," has suffered neglect, it was well kept up until comparatively recent years. The squares formed by box-bordered walks are a usual motif of gardens dating from the earlier half of the Eighteenth Century. (An exceptionally well-preserved one is at "Ury House," Fox Chase.) Such gardens were not necessarily flower gardens, but sometimes were used for fruits or vegetables as well. In an old record book are Daniel Wister's notes carefully listing Carnations, Tulips, Narcissus, etc., in accordance with "beds" in which they were planted; so, although we do not know when it was originally built, we have an authentic record for the years 1773-1776.

Scattered widely around the Philadelphia district country places were developed not only for permanent residence but for sojourning. In these we find examples indicating the probability that definite plans were made, but only one actual plan has been found,— that of "Solitude," an estate on the west bank of the Schuylkill about two miles from City Hall. It is now the site of the Zoological Gardens. John Penn, born and bred in England, came to America in 1784, being concerned with family claims. With apparent intent to remain, he built Solitude shortly after his arrival. Penn's taste for the English fashion of landscape gardening is quite evident, with the "ha-ha" wall, the irregular flower garden, the "vista" south of the house, and the clump of trees east of the house. All these features bespeak "Capability" Brown and the "landscape gardeners" of contemporary times in England. Solitude is not American, but many of its English fashions had

already appeared here, and more were destined to hold supremacy in landscape design of the Nineteenth Century. Though essentially foreign, mention of Solitude is warranted if only as a striking example of the lasting quality of planned landscape. The map of Fairmount Park made in 1870 clearly shows the ha-ha wall, the vistas, and the "clump," and the limits of developed property are identical with the original map. The establishment of the Zoological Gardens has destroyed all but the dwelling house.

The same lasting quality of planned landscape is seen in the topographic map of "Mount Pleasant," made in 1870. Mount Pleasant, built in 1761 by John McPherson, on the opposite bank of the Schuylkill and a mile or so higher up, is known as the Arnold Mansion, but Benedict Arnold, though owner, probably never occupied it. The extent of the grounds is quite apparent in the 1870 map, as well as the development of mansion grounds distinct from the farm lands. Full advantage is taken here of the necessity for numerous buildings by grouping them as a termination for the long straight entrance drive. The rows of trees along this drive had lost their regularity of spacing by 1870, but the formality of the scheme is evident. West of the house the contours clearly show the terraced garden which was replanted a few years ago (under the supervision of the Pennsylvania Museum) and so has again assumed a semblance of its original state.

Perhaps no country place was more familiar to Washington than "Belmont," the home of Judge Richard Peters, of the Board of War, during the Revolution. Belmont Mansion is almost directly opposite Mount Pleasant, overlooking a broad reach of the river. Peters inherited this property from his father who, about 1755, erected a new house adjacent to the old one. Apparently the old house faced a garden, and the advantage of this prospect, together with the advantage of relationship to an existing development, may be reason for the close proximity of the two buildings as we see them today. More recent extensions and additions have created a

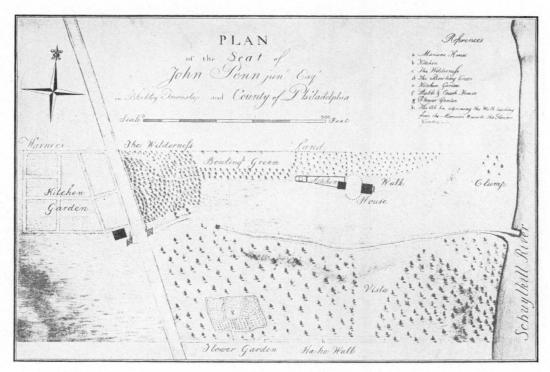

From original in possession of the Historical Society of Pennsylvania

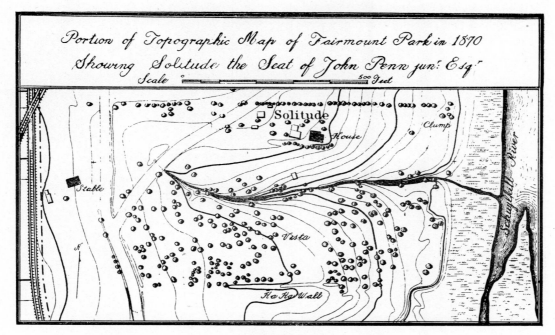

SOLITUDE

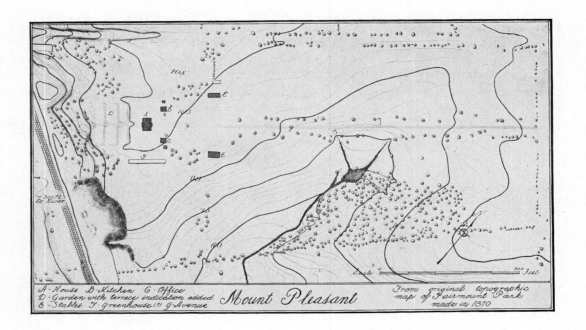

A - House B - Kitchen C - Office
D - Garden with terrace indication added
E - Stables F - Greenhouse (?) G - Avenue

Mount Pleasant

From original topographic
map of Fairmount Park
made in 1870

Courtesy of the Pennsylvania Museum of Art, Philadelphia

The Mansion from the Flower Garden

MOUNT PLEASANT

Clair-voyée on lower terrace of garden
THE GRANGE

confused hodge-podge of structures, and there is almost nothing to indicate how the gardens or grounds were arranged. From old descriptions of the gardens we know that there were two summer houses, a green, a labyrinth, a wilderness, and "a most perfect sample of the old taste of Parterres."* There was also a famous avenue of hemlocks, not less than a quarter of a mile long, which terminated at a masonry obelisk. Extending from the house to the river was another avenue of cherry trees. In all, Judge Peters' taste was evidently one that appreciated the formal manner, rather than the more "modern" fashions, though he included the feature of a "wilderness," a naturalesque type of garden with shrubs and trees.

We can not omit mention of Bartram's Garden, for none of the several arboretums established in the neighborhood of Philadelphia in the Eighteenth Century is so famous or so well preserved. With his chief interest centered in establishing a collection of plants, we doubt whether Bartram considered the arrangement of the grounds as carefully as one less interested in arboriculture. Conventionality is apparent in terraces close by his house, but the general aspect of his property was undoubtedly naturalesque.

An elaborate description remains of the gardens developed by John Cruickshank in 1770 at "The Grange" in Haverford Township.

Nothing could be more picturesque, beautiful and elegant than this highly favored spot. The gardens, the fountains, the Bath in a private garden with walks skirted with boxwood and the trumpet creeper in rich luxuriance overhanging the door and gateways, where the water was so intensely cold that few entered in. The Green houses and Hot houses, the Dairy, the extensive orchards of every variety of fruit; and then the long dark walk seven-eighths of a mile in extent, shaded by tall forest trees, where the tulip poplar abounded, and where the sun scarcely dared to penetrate. On one side a ravine through which a creek flowed, gurgling, and reflecting the sun beams shut out from the dark walk, with the sloping meadows beyond, all presenting a picture never to be forgotten.

Near the beginning of this dark walk Mr. Ross [son-in-law of John Cruickshank] had caused to be constructed, on a spot ten or twelve feet above the walk, a seat capable of holding twenty persons and a place for a table. On the Fourth of July and other warm days of summer he would take his friends there and iced wine would be served. A bell wire, communicating with the house, was arranged to call the servant when wanted and avoid his constant presence.**

The "Bath" was within a building, part of whose walls still stand. The formal garden by the house was in three terraces whose lengths ran parallel to the main prospect from the house. Walks on two terraces were terminated by openings in the high enclosing end-wall, giving a wide view over the country. Such features, known as "clair-voyées," are said to have been introduced to England from Holland in the Seventeenth Century. The Grange was famous for its hospitality, and Washington was numbered among the guests upon one occasion at least, when tradition says that upon his departure he collided violently with one of the gate posts.

In conclusion, we find that, where communities develop with people of similar ideals and a common cultural and religious background, as in Virginia, there is a similarity of expression that is lacking where, as in the district of which Philadelphia was the center, such a miscellaneous assortment of nationalities as Swedes, Welsh, Germans, and English colonize. The religious beliefs of these settlers were even more varied than their nationalities, but the problem of existence created a spirit of community, and a fairly rapid development of an architectural style is apparent.

In landscape design there is less that may be considered typical. The self-dependence which pioneer life imposed upon the people required a greater number of buildings for residence in the country than is the case today, and the Colonists' first concern was the relationship of these to each other and to the site. An orderly arrangement was sought, and this order, related to the irregularities of rolling country, by no means tended toward a symmetrical grouping of buildings. It is questionable whether great consideration

* From the original manuscript letter of Deborah Logan in the possession of the Pennsylvania Historical Society.

** From a letter written by Miss Elizabeth Mifflin, granddaughter of John Ross.

would be given to such architectural grouping where the majority of places were the result of gradual growth with a gradual accumulation of wealth. Such a pretentious development as Mount Pleasant signifies the possession of wealth at the outset and a regard for country living as recreation.

Avenues of trees and formal gardens retained their popularity in a land so close to wilderness, even after the romantic fashions of 18th-century England began to be adopted. In America there was no surfeit of conventionality that cried for relief.

One type of garden alone reappears to a degree that may make us consider it characteristic, although this perhaps belongs more properly to the first half of the Eighteenth Century: the simple box-bordered squares forming a geometrical pattern. At least it combines practical considerations with esthetic possibilities; adaptable to the confines of a small lot, its development was possible with a minimum amount of grading. The square enclosures were large enough to devote to small fruits or vegetables, or could at

any time be transformed into a box-patterned knot or a flower garden; or by the simple expedient of combining a circular central bed with four surrounding square beds, a more effective pattern was developed.

The latter half of the Eighteenth Century witnessed more elaborate developments in landscape design, and of surprising variety. A catholicity of taste is apparent. Earlier tradition has not been ruthlessly cast aside where practical considerations favor conventionality, nor was conventionality of plan enforced where nature offered the greatest opportunities for embellishment in the romantic spirit of landscape gardening.

In the Philadelphia region at least, our forefathers showed discrimination in their gardens that is uncommon today. They accepted that which was sound in the English theories of the Eighteenth Century without discarding the equally sound traditions of earlier Colonial days that harked back to Tudor England.

ROBERT WHEELWRIGHT.

Garden walk on the upper terrace

THE GRANGE

Simple box-bordered squares at "Wister's Big House" in the late 1890's

A box-patterned knot at Ury House, Fox Chase, Pennsylvania

TWO ANCIENT GARDENS OF THE PHILADELPHIA REGION

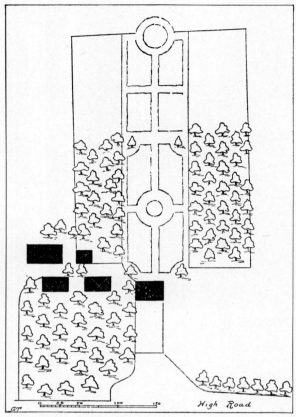

Courtesy of Robert M. McBride & Co.

GARDENS OF
NEW AMSTERDAM

Somerndick's *Bouwerie*

From a "plan of the north-east environs of the city of New York, performed by the order of his Excellency, the Earl of Loudon, &c., &c.,
by Sam'l Holland, 17th Sept., 1757,"
reproduced from *Old-fashioned Gardening*

The White Hall
Governor Stuyvesant's City House

From the *Cosmopolitan*, January, 1892

CHAPTER V
Homes and Gardens of Old New York

The region of New York has always been identified with the richest examples of old-time gardens and country places. In the early days the situation of the city itself was distinctively beautiful. With its wide harbor with long water views, its shores with luxuriant vegetation and thickly wooded slopes, its lowlands with background of rolling country and lofty hills, Manhattan Island had every possible variety of the most attractive scenery. The Hudson River, flowing past Manhattan on the west, one of the most beautiful water courses in the world, has been bordered for many generations with some of the finest country homes to be found in the United States.

In Washington's time New York was easily one of the most consequential settlements in the country. While its size—a population of some 20,000 at the time of the Revolution—had not grown to be impressive, its importance was nevertheless significant. As early as 1748 a visitor (Peter Kalm, the Swedish botanist) mentioned "its fine buildings" and "its opulence." The streets were spacious and most of them were paved. The chief trees were the locust and "Water Beech, or Linnaeus's Platanus occidentalis,"* and there were also many lime (linden) and elm which roofed the sidewalks.

At the time of the Revolution, the greater part of the country places were situated on Manhattan Island bordering the East and Hudson Rivers, though there were a few also on Long Island. In 1774 John Adams, stopping in New York on his way to attend the first Congress in Philadelphia, gave expression to his admiration of the "elegant country seats on the Island."†

The majority of the wealthy citizens of Manhattan were interested in the shipping business, and many lived in considerable luxury. It was an era of particularly good taste and refinement which showed itself in the character of the homes, both in their architectural design and in their outdoor cultivation. Describing this period, an author writes (in 1871): "There was in that day none of the show and glitter of modern times, but with many of the [New York] families . . . an elegance which has never been rivaled in other parts of the country."†

In the time of the early settlement of New Amsterdam, the first home grounds of Dutch New York were naturally of limited scale. The city itself was compressed into a small space, surrounded by a stockade for protection against the Indians. The dwellings were set close to the street line, usually with the gable end fronting the street, and often there was no space between them. The plots were not large and the garden areas were more or less confined. Within such a limited space and in conformity with Dutch precision, the gardens were laid out symmetrically, consisting primarily of straight paths and rectangular beds with perhaps an occasional departure from straight lines to form circular or curved details. The Castello Plan of New Amsterdam, made in 1660, shows occasional garden layouts, some of which have fairly ornate designs, but these plans were probably drawn largely from the artist's imagination rather than from known details. After all, New Amsterdam was primitive, and utility was the most important consideration, means being not abundant to indulge in great luxury or decoration.

In these gardens were planted fruit trees and vegetables, and flowers were planted with them, in some cases perhaps in separate beds, but in others between the vegetable rows. Holland, the most advanced European country of the time, was noted for its cultivation of flowers and fruits, and the ships of the West India Company brought many of them to this country. The love of the Dutch for flowers and their knowledge of them, their tendency toward regular and formal garden design, their preciseness which enabled them to make the most out of the smallest area of ground, —all this undoubtedly had great influence on the later Colonial gardens which followed.

Although Holland relinquished New Netherlands to the English in 1664, the Dutch influence on the home life, architecture, and gardens of the Colony continued well beyond the early part of the Eighteenth Century.

Apart from the simple homes of the average settlers in old New York and the country places of the well-to-do, the institution of the Manorial Estates had a great bearing on the life of the times. In the early settlement of New Netherland, privileges were granted to individuals which would permit them to take up land sixteen miles on one side of the river (Hudson) or one-half that distance on both sides, extending "so far into the country as the situation of the occupiers will permit,"‡—under the condition that each "Patroon" should plant a colony of fifty souls above fifteen years of age. A number of such manors were established along the river, which were remarkable on account of the vastness of their domains, the most noted being those of Van Rensselaer, Van Cortlandt, Livingston, and Philipse. The Van Rensselaer Manor was the only one to be more than temporarily successful, but all of these estates were memorable and their proprietors wielded great influence. Other large land grants were awarded in New York during these early periods, and the homes of their owners were of corresponding elegance.

During the period of Washington many of these manorial estates were still flourishing. In aspect and character they differed to a considerable degree from the plantation estates of the South. The character of the Northern country, especially along the Hudson River, was bolder and more rugged. Apart from the difference in physical characteristics, the Northern system of development was entirely unlike that of the South. While there were slaves in the North, they were comparatively few, and the lands were cultivated principally by tenants. The domestic grounds of the patroons' estates and those of the lesser large-property holders were presumably in most cases laid out after the style of the English Park. The scale was so great, the landscape so imposing, the topography so irregular, that attempts at pronounced formal design in the arrangement of the grounds would have been in most cases incongruous. But what these manor-house grounds lacked in symmetry of design as compared with those of the Southern plantations, they

---

* *Travels into North America.* By Peter Kalm. London, 1772.
† *The Olden Time in New York.* By W. I. Kip. New York, 1872.

‡ *Old-fashioned Gardening.* By Grace Tabor. New York, 1913.

THE OLD MANSION

MAIZELAND

A COLONIAL ESTATE ON THE HUDSON

Courtesy of Doubleday, Doran & Co.

THE PLEASAUNCE, A GRASS-COVERED AVENUE

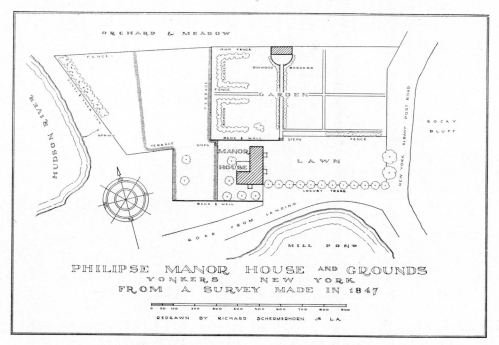

PHILIPSE MANOR HOUSE AND GROUNDS
YONKERS   NEW YORK
FROM A SURVEY MADE IN 1847

REDRAWN BY RICHARD SCHERMERHORN JR L.A.

A garden that Washington often visited

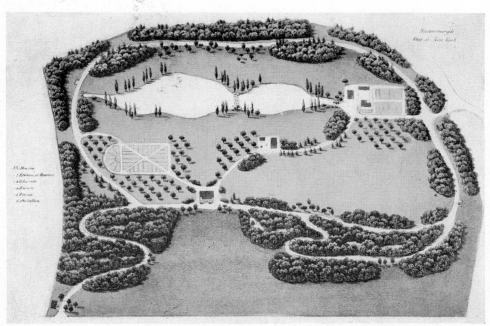

Courtesy of Charles W. Leavitt & Son

The "naturalistic" English style—a place at Duanesburgh, New York, about 1800

TWO COUNTRY SEATS OF THE NEW YORK REGION

made up in their wonderful natural and cultivated woodlands, in their broad sweeping vistas over hill and valley, and in their magnificent space and scale.

While treating in some detail of the homes and gardens of New York during the Washington period, or particularly that just previous to the Revolution, it is necessary to dwell primarily upon the more pretentious country seats because it is of these that we have the clearest record. In their gardening features they were naturally models for the smaller home grounds, and without doubt they influenced the style of gardens in general. During the later Eighteenth Century there was a decided tendency to depart from the formal style then in fashion; instead, the naturalistic English style became popular. Nevertheless, the Georgian type of architecture of the period fostered formal garden design, and this was found in most instances. A description of the main characteristics of some of the more important country places should help to picture the general garden conditions of the period.

In 1745, when the Philipse Manor House grounds (in Yonkers) were improved by the grandson of the original owner, a formal garden with box-bordered paths was laid out adjacent to the house. Every available tree and plant which would grow in the climate was imported and planted. Landscape gardening was the hobby of Frederick Philipse, the third Lord of the Manor, and it is possible that Washington who was a frequent visitor, possibly beginning with his first Northern journey, in 1756, may have recalled the gardens of Frederick Philipse when making plans for the ultimate development of Mount Vernon.

Van Cortlandt Manor contained two individual estates at this time, one located at Kingsbridge and the other at Croton. The original Manor contained 200,000 acres. Both Manor Houses still stand. The former is now within the New York City park system, but the grounds have been changed to such an extent that the original condition can not be traced. The new garden occupies the site of the old one, but obviously can not be similar to it. It is said that in the older garden the terrace on the east was planted with flowering shrubs such as althea, snowball, lilac, and flowering currant, and on the west was planted with apple, plum, and pear trees. Planted across the top of the north terrace to keep the north wind away from the garden, ran a hedge of box trees which grew to huge size. Washington dined at the house in July, 1781, and, on the evacuation of New York by the British, spent a night there in November, 1783, preparatory to riding in to the city.

An old garden still exists on the Van Cortlandt Estate at Croton. While its age can not be exactly determined, it has been called the old Dutch Garden and is probably one of the oldest in this section. Pierre Van Cortlandt, the proprietor of this estate during the Revolution, was a close friend of Washington, who stopped at the house several times, memorably in 1781.

The Beverly Robinson estate opposite West Point on the Hudson should be mentioned owing to the fact of its having been a frequent headquarters of Washington. The mansion was erected in 1750 and the estate contained 60,000 acres, fashioned after the country seats of England with "gardens, lawns, fruit orchards, broad cultivated fields and great deer parks."* Arnold was quartered there.

The Jumel Mansion still exists in the Bronx, facing the Harlem River. It was built about 1765 by Lieutenant Colonel Roger

* *The Homes of America.* By Martha J. Lamb. New York, 1879.

Morris, Loyalist. Morris had been a personal friend of Washington, having fought with him in the French and Indian War. The mansion served as a headquarters for a number of British officers during the Revolution, but was also occupied by Washington at another time. This property is shown on the British Headquarters Map of New York and Environs (1782) where extensive gardens are indicated.

The estate of Sylvester Manor, Shelter Island, at the eastern end of Long Island, was acquired in 1652 by Nathaniel Sylvester, the existing residence being built in 1735. This is an interesting existing example of a Colonial estate, and it has an attractive formal garden with box-bordered beds and hedges. There are fine old trees on the property and wide vistas of lawn flanked by woodland growth. The garden dates back considerably over a hundred years.

Courtesy of *Landscape Architecture*
A boxwood path
Board-Zabriskie Garden, New Jersey

Another old garden of which there is definite record is that of the former Board-Zabriskie House on the Paramus Road, New Jersey, near the New York border, in the heart of an early Dutch settlement. This house was built about 1747 and is of the Dutch Colonial type, showing, however, Georgian influence. Having been recently acquired for Country Club purposes, the grounds and house have been greatly altered. Up to a few years ago, however, there was an interesting old formal garden, with box borders and several interesting garden houses and arbors.

There is also still in existence the old Manice garden in Queens, now the property of the Turf and Field Club, and here is noted a distinctly formal design. The garden is laid out in close conjunction with the house, and while the flower beds take intricate geometrical forms, yet the remainder of the grounds are laid out in the style of the English naturalistic landscape. This garden is known to be over a hundred years old and, with its box borders and other characteristics somewhat like those of Sylvester Manor and others

Courtesy of Doubleday, Doran & Co.
Box-bordered garden paths, Sylvester Manor, Shelter Island

Manice Garden, now part of the Turf and Field Club, Queens, Long Island

GARDENS CHARACTERISTIC OF THE EIGHTEENTH CENTURY

that have been mentioned, a type is pictured which may be a fair representation of the style of the home gardens of the later Eighteenth and early Nineteenth Centuries.

Of the other Hudson River manorial estates little can be said of the gardens, as there is scant existing evidence of their original features. The Van Rensselaer Manor has long since disintegrated, and the last manor house, built in 1765, was moved about thirty-five years ago to Williamstown (Mass.). An early description states that "its simple architectural elegance even now, with its fine park and magnificent trees, gives it an aristocratic air in keeping with the period of high sounding titles and lordly possessions." * The Manor of Rensselaerwyck covered an area of 1000 square miles.† Livingston Manor was partitioned long ago, but several of the old Manor Houses (erected by descendants of the original proprietors) overlooking the Hudson still remain, although their original beauties have largely departed. The original Livingston Manor comprised 160,000 acres.†

As the effects of the War wore off and prosperity and wealth increased, people began again to interest themselves in their gardens and in the development of their country places. At this time the number of good books available on Landscape Gardening had increased, and while the home owners still looked to Europe for guidance in fashioning their gardens and country homes, many of them were their own planners. In some cases, however, it has been shown that master gardeners were brought from Europe to lay out the more pretentious estates.

Pierre Charles L'Enfant, Major in Washington's army during the Revolution and later the designer of the plan of the city of Washington, was perhaps the principal artistic authority of the period immediately subsequent to the Revolution. He made his home in New York for a time, and while the records of his activities in this city are chiefly connected with architecture and land subdivision, nevertheless, as he later is known to have laid out gardens in the South, it is not illogical to believe that he was also consulted in this capacity in New York.

André Michaux, born near Versailles, came to this country from France in 1785, and established a nursery in Charleston, and one in the "Bergen" section, New Jersey (near New York). His influence in horticultural matters was pronounced, and he apparently designed gardens as well, such as that of Richard Varick at "Pros-

pect Hall," in what is now Jersey City, and which was referred to as "containing rare flowers and grotesquely shaped beds and especially one long avenue of imported plum trees."‡

L'Enfant and Michaux were followed after the turn of the century by Joseph Ramée, architect, in 1811, and in 1824 by Andre Parmentier; both engaged in the planning of country places. It is curious to note that these men were French or of French descent, and they must have brought French gardening ideals with them, for L'Enfant was well known to be inclined to formal design, as very likely also was Michaux.

In spite of the considerable general data on this subject, there are no known existing gardens, or complete plans of such gardens, of the New York Colonial period, of which the design may be unqualifiedly placed earlier than the beginning of the Nineteenth Century, although it is safe to believe there was scant difference between those gardens of the early 1800's and those of the half century preceding.

In drawing conclusions from the available data on the Homes and Gardens of Old New York, it is quite apparent that the love of the Dutch for flowers, their experience in horticulture, and their general personal characteristics of orderliness and precision, without doubt influenced the development of a distinct type of garden. This garden, originally a system of regular beds and paths, planted in fruits, flowers, and vegetables, together with the Dutch innate of love for flowers and sense of orderliness, must have affected the style of development of the many noteworthy gardens that appear in Manhattan in Colonial times.

While, in the case of the many pretentious layouts of New York country seats of the Washington period, many favored in design the style of naturalistic English landscape, it is probable that in most cases the grounds immediately adjacent to the house took a formal character largely on account of the Georgian type of architecture then predominant. The gardens themselves were in general box-bordered and in some cases contained beds laid out in geometrical patterns. Probably most of them contained fruit trees, and in some cases vegetables also.

As a concluding thought, it is interesting, first, to remember that Washington visited many of the country seats in New York, especially during the time of the Revolution, and second, to speculate as to how much he may have influenced details of their development or may in turn have been influenced by them in making his plans for Mount Vernon.

RICHARD SCHERMERHORN, JR.

---

* *The Homes of America.* By Martha J. Lamb. New York, 1879.
† *Manors and Historic Homes of the Hudson Valley.* By H. D. Eberlein. Philadelphia, 1924.
‡ *Historic Houses of New Jersey.* By W. Jay Mills. Philadelphia, 1902.

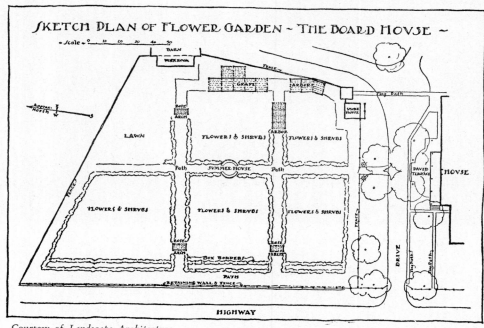

Courtesy of *Landscape Architecture*

An Old Colonial Garden in New Jersey

A SALEM GARDEN

CHAPTER VI
Gardens of Old Salem and the New England Colonies

George Washington's early experience as a surveyor of land and his later experience in military operations made him an observer of topography. The journals of his ordinary travels from Virginia to New England contain many entries regarding the contour of land, its exposure to the sun, the steepness of roads, and other matters of strategic interest to the farmer, to the landscape architect, and to the architect, as well as to the topographer and soldier. In his later years he became a close student of trees. His Mount Vernon diaries abound in the most tireless records of his tree-planting experiments and of his letters to Europe and to New England inquiring about new kinds of plants. If we review the old places of New England as Washington saw them, we must keep constantly before us the facts of topography, exposure, soil, and vegetation.

The New Englander, like the men of the South, based the planning of places and gardens on the remembered plans of the fatherland of England. Fortunately for us, however, the memory of the old places across the Atlantic was not always accurate. Moreover, the Colonists were not ready to sacrafice their comfort in a new bleak land to the mere copying of English traditions,

though these were revered. Thus, fortunately, the New England places and gardens present many interesting departures and adaptations even though the "feeling" of the designs is English. Naturally enough, the adaptations which were made by New Englanders were not the same as those made by Virginians, because the climate and building materials, as well as the manners and the customs, were not the same in these distant parts of our country.

If we compare the New England places of Washington's time with places in England, the New England places and gardens were in general smaller, less in cost, much less elaborate in detail, and not built for great permanency; they have not been mellowed by the centuries of time and history, or by the bland atmosphere of the Old Country. New England houses and outbuildings as a rule were not made of masonry, or exposed half-timbered work, or of brick. Wood was at hand in unlimited quantities and therefore it was commonly used for construction in New England. Retaining walls were rare. High walls for privacy were almost unknown. Courtyards, crofts, long axial vistas, and long axial approaches were rare even in the largest country places of New England.

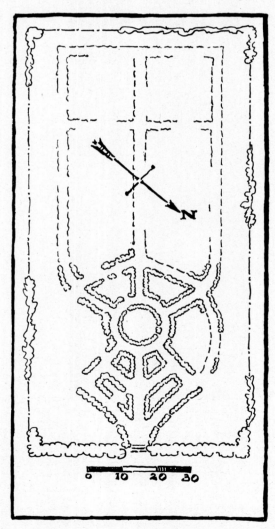

Figure 1. An ancient box-garden

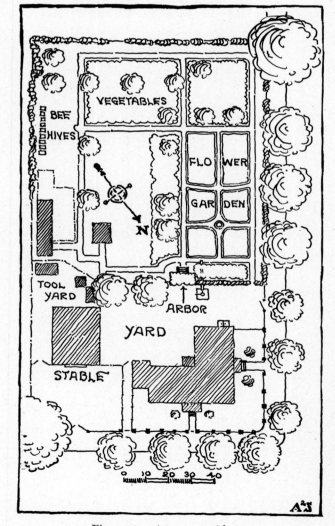

Figure 2. A town residence

GARDEN PATTERNS OF THE REGION OF OLD SALEM

A portion of the farm group

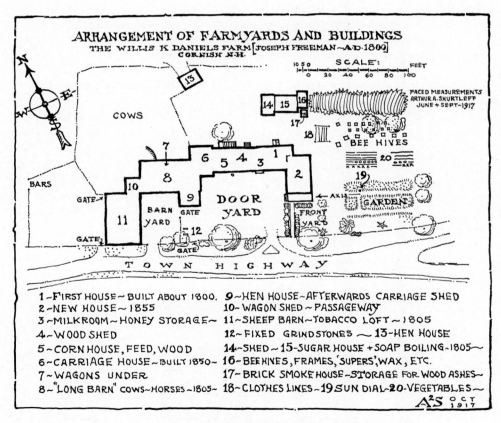

ARRANGEMENT OF FARMYARDS AND BUILDINGS
THE WILLIS K DANIELS FARM [JOSEPH FREEMAN ~A.D. 1800]
CORNISH N.H.

1~FIRST HOUSE~BUILT ABOUT 1800.   9~HEN HOUSE~AFTERWARDS CARRIAGE SHED
2~NEW HOUSE~1855   10~WAGON SHED~PASSAGEWAY
3~MILKROOM~HONEY STORAGE~   11~SHEEP BARN~TOBACCO LOFT~1805
4~WOOD SHED   12~FIXED GRINDSTONES ~ 13~HEN HOUSE
5~CORN HOUSE, FEED, WOOD   14~SHED~ 15~SUGAR HOUSE + SOAP BOILING~1805~
6~CARRIAGE HOUSE~BUILT 1850~ 16~BEE HIVES, FRAMES, "SUPERS", WAX, ETC.
7~WAGONS UNDER   17~BRICK SMOKE HOUSE~STORAGE FOR WOOD ASHES~
8~"LONG BARN" COWS~HORSES~1805~ 18~CLOTHES LINES~19 SUN DIAL~20~VEGETABLES~

A NEW ENGLAND FARMYARD

In comparing New England places and gardens with those of Virginia and the South in Washington's time, we must remember the colder climate of New England with its long winters, the more searching winds, the lower sun, the more broken and stony soil, the less dependence upon agriculture. Under these conditions the New Englander placed his buildings near together; a widely spaced arrangement was out of the question for reason of the cold and the deep snow. Thus he was forced into a thrift of space and of work which was not wholly unnatural to his temper. The New England man, by and large, did not understand long vistas, long axial approaches, symmetrically placed buildings, axially placed gardens. The climate and the soil ran counter to them. Therefore the English traditions regarding these desirable things lapsed to the number of exceptions sufficient to prove the rule.

The climate of New England made an isolated though well-rounded life like that of the Southern plantation much more difficult. True, there were isolated farms in New England, but as a whole the farms were nearer to one another than in the South and nearer to the villages, towns, and to the mills. The places were built close to the highways for convenience in the deep snow season when the towns "broke out" the highways with ox ploughs. For reasons of comfort men of great wealth also built near the highways and usually in or near the outskirts of the towns. In the isolated farms the smoke house, cobbler's shop, milk house, carpenter's shop, the weave house (usually an attic room), and other utility structures were built; but with the very small opportunities to get labor, all the structures were small and were often combined under very few roofs. Naturally, therefore, the New England places were small, compact, unsymmetrical; but because of these very limitations they were exceedingly interesting in the records of our Colonial times.

Let no one think there was gloom in the gardens of this land of long winters and of consequent thrift. Far from it. When April came the earliest wild flowers were later than the common flowers of the gardens. Long before the countryside came into leaf the dooryards were blooming with the honeysuckles, the azaleas, and the cornels which had been brought from England to these shores. Then followed the glory of the plum, cherry, pear, apple, lilac, and quince. Delights of this kind were later than the same delights in Virginia, but in New England they came one by one from April through June and not with a rush through a shorter season. The early New England pictures, the needlework, the May Day customs, the curious laconic poetry, even the terrible sermons hot with a fire lacking in the sun, portray a love for gardening and for flowers which was the more intense because of the cold winters and the austere doctrine which, with all their goodness, nipped it somewhat while making it real.

Old Salem, Massachusetts, is mentioned in the title of this brief paper not because it was unique among New England towns, but because it is typical (like Marblehead, Newburyport, Portsmouth, Windsor, Greenfield, Hatfield, and a score of others) in possessing Colonial places which have come down to us from the time of Washington, with some of the ancient glamour of interest and charm still clinging to them. The students of those times well know their ignorance of the exact lineaments of the ancient places. We are all in danger of being far too sure that what we attribute to the old layouts actually existed in the old days. In this dilemma we are safer in describing the oldest of the places as they existed according to measurements as recent as a third of a century ago, than to attempt to go back a century and a half by imagination, where far less complete records are available.

Scattered through New England are many old houses which have been kept in a fair state of repair, and which, therefore, have survived wind, rain, and snow since Colonial times. Few of these old buildings still possess the ancient ells, sheds, barns, gardens, fences, pumps, and other structures which once stood near at hand. Money and care have not been available to keep those lesser structures in repair and they have fallen to ruin and to dust. Few of the ancient trees of Colonial times have survived, few of the shrubs, and fewer of the flowers. The hedges of the garden paths have vanished, and the paths have become lost in the grass sod. I shall pass by the depleted places of this type and refer the reader to places richer in material even though later. The assumption is made that these places have retained much of their ancient appearance and have copied an earlier mode of the same locality.

The accompanying plan (see page 211) of the John Freeman farm, built before 1800, shows a typical New England farm group of the usual irregular plan. The composition faces south. All the out-buildings, except the shed, sugar house, and smoke house, can be reached from within-doors. The pattern of the garden, the position of the beehives, and all the other appurtenances are shown. The driveway's three contacts with the town highway show to what large extent this farmer, like his neighbors, depended upon the highway for his most intimate approach. The cold climate of Cornish, New Hampshire, restrained the Daniels family from extensive gardens, but the love of flowers and the efforts to secure an orderly axial and rectangular relation to the house is expressed. The hen-house (see 13 on the plan) is turned exactly south to secure the maximum sun in the winter. The wings of the house also extend toward the south to receive the warmth. The heavy planting of trees at the north was arranged to break the force of the winds.

The Marblehead plan (see page 213) shows an axial approach on the north and a curious attempt to secure an axial approach on the south. The lofty site of the building on a series of terraces is indicated by the cross sections. By placing the stable on the main highway it was possible for the inhabitants of the house to reach the best traveled highway in the winter without removing snow from the more impressive northern approach. The zigzag alignment of steps and paths at the west side of the house indicates the frugality of the New Englander, who built these steps where they would conform most closely to the topography. He was willing to make a detour to save costs and to secure convenience. To many students of design this was a fundamentally good quality in the New Englander, but to others designs of this type express a want of vision. The nearness of the pastures and of the orchards to the house also expresses frugality and good common sense. The space allotted to gardens here is very small.

Plans on page 210 illustrate garden patterns from the Salem-Newburyport-Portsmouth region. Figure 2 shows the practical arrangement of a service yard adjacent to the coach house and stable behind the mansion. From this yard an arbor gives entrance to the gardens which are not axially placed, except in relation to this arbor. The garden patterns are all rectangular and relate in the most frugal and delightful way to the boundaries of the lot. All these places are in the towns, so the boundaries are relatively small and rectangular. There is no effort at display here. The grounds were arranged conveniently for the pleasure of the family and to secure the least cost for upkeep. Page 214 shows a characteristic long narrow garden having a wisteria arbor, but in other respects having no relation to the house. The loveliness of this New England place is well expressed by this plan. The names of some of the flowers are indicated and the extraordinary simplicity of the layout. The intimate garden near the corner of the house is bordered with box, which, however, does not thrive in northern New England without much protection. In some of these gardens the patterns of the ancient box gardens which have been overrun with grass and weeds and whose designs were discoverable a third of a century ago have disappeared. A glance at a design of this kind (see Figure 1, page

210) shows the carefree gesture of the layout as far as classic precedent is concerned, but the result is of unusual interest.

Privacy was secured in the Colonial gardens that are illustrated on pages 210 and 214 by the use of board fences, five to six feet high, placed on the property lines and unadorned with pilasters or lattices, or any other modern devices to break the plainness and to add to the first cost and the upkeep. As a rule, all interesting gardens of these old types are provided with high fences. Where there are no gardens, there are generally no high fences.

In considering all these early Colonial layouts, the reader must remember that automobiles and all their paraphernalia were un-

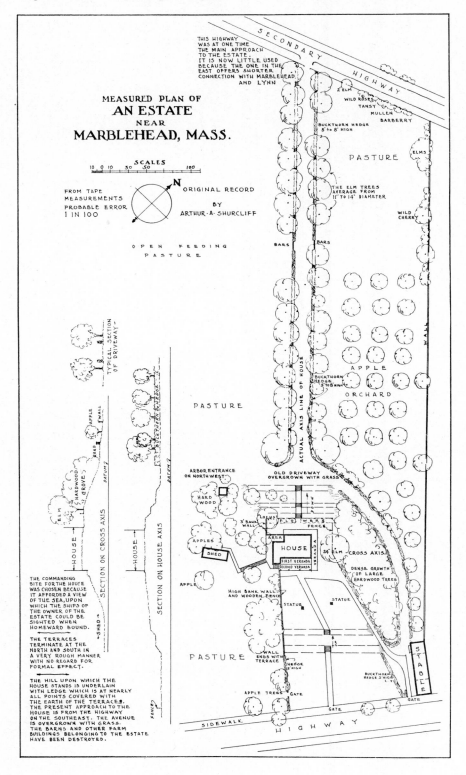

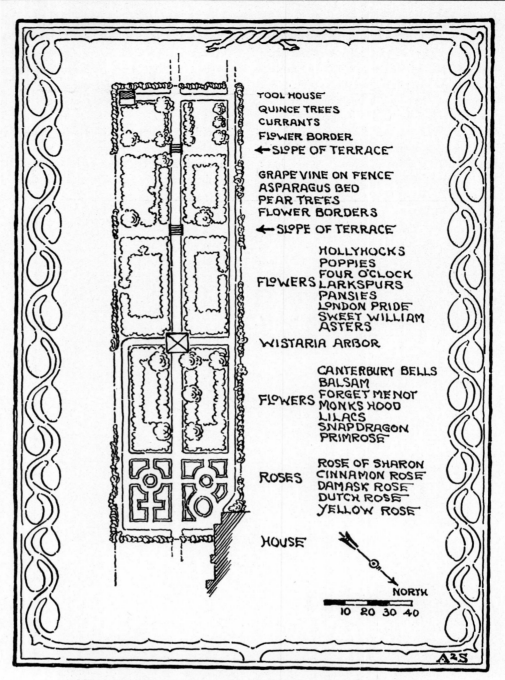

TOOL HOUSE
QUINCE TREES
CURRANTS
FLOWER BORDER
← SLOPE OF TERRACE

GRAPE VINE ON FENCE
ASPARAGUS BED
PEAR TREES
FLOWER BORDERS
← SLOPE OF TERRACE

HOLLYHOCKS
POPPIES
FOUR O'CLOCK
FLOWERS LARKSPURS
PANSIES
LONDON PRIDE
SWEET WILLIAM
ASTERS

WISTARIA ARBOR

CANTERBURY BELLS
BALSAM
FORGET ME NOT
FLOWERS MONKS HOOD
LILACS
SNAP DRAGON
PRIMROSE

ROSE OF SHARON
CINNAMON ROSE
ROSES DAMASK ROSE
DUTCH ROSE
YELLOW ROSE

HOUSE

NORTH
10 20 30 40

A NEW ENGLAND FLOWER GARDEN OF COLONIAL DAYS

known. Small turning spaces were adequate for the horse-drawn vehicles of those times. Only small quarters were needed for the carriages and for the animals. The buildings, sheds, and turning spaces were not considered ugly, but were made frankly a part of the equipment of the home and were kept in good condition by men who took pride in the home grounds. The small courtyards were often paved with cobblestones when such material could be had from ships using stone ballast and coming without full cargoes from foreign ports.

The hospitality of the New Englander was genuine and hearty, but the student will understand that hospitality in its widest sense could be practiced more generously by the men of Virginia and the South, who lived in a less austere climate and who were enabled, therefore, to provide more liberally for comfort both within and

without doors. George Washington enjoyed northern hospitality on many occasions and it made a deep impression upon him. During his journeys in New England, he spent much time in country places where delightful grounds lay spread out for his enjoyment.

As we view the field of Colonial life of country and town embracing the South and New England, we constantly see the figure of George Washington. He moves northward and southward always with understanding of men and environments. It is not strange that the history of these far-flung parts of our country cannot be written without constant reminders of the broad sympathy and the knowledge possessed by Washington. He wished to be known as a practical surveyor and a planter. Recognized ability in these fields was a forerunner of his fame in the more unusual and wider labors to which the country later called him.

ARTHUR A. SHURCLIFF.

CHAPTER VII
Colonial Gardens of Charleston and the Far South

On a peninsula formed by the junction of the Ashley and the Cooper Rivers, some seven miles inland from the South Carolina coast, Old Charleston developed its own civilization in the New World. The original settlers—Cavaliers and gentlemen adventurers from England, and Huguenot refugees from France—brought with them a grace of living which blossomed individually under a warm southern sun. Isolation on the north by dense forests and by the perils of the voyage around Cape Hatteras, on the west by unfriendly Indians, and on the south by the Spaniards, promoted an independence of thought and action which has made Charleston homes and gardens distinctly individual among those of the thirteen colonies.

When Washington arrived at Charleston on May 2, 1791, he found a city which compared favorably with those he had seen to the north. In the homes of the citizens he perceived on the one hand an aristocratic quality which had come over in the inner consciousness of the Cavalier stock and had found expression in dignified mansions, formal gardens, and great gateways; but this dignity had been softened by life in a subtropical climate which, under the necessity of making provision for coolness, had developed an ease of living. Spacious verandas protected the houses from a burning sun, high ceilings encouraged a circulation of air indoors, and large windows with lattice blinds admitted the prevailing breezes while warding off unwelcome heat.

The characteristic type of house with which Charleston of the post-Revolutionary period is associated—a three- or four-story structure, one room wide, on a deep lot with sometimes little more than a fifty-foot frontage—occupied a north corner of the property with one narrow end at the sidewalk edge. The broad front of the building, faced by a two- or three-story veranda, thus enjoyed both the garden which lay before it and the prevailing southern wind. A high wall of brick and wood along the street assured complete privacy; but where it joined the house it grew in dignity and height to include a door that served as the main entrance to the place. This doorway, with a dignified architectural treatment, opened directly onto the street end of the veranda; the house itself was entered only by an entirely separate door that led in from the middle of the veranda. Frequently the house was elevated so that the main living rooms were raised above the ground floor; in this case the street door opened onto a stairway that led up to the veranda which overlooked the garden below.

Contemporary chronicles of Washington's time describe for us the charm of these walled gardens with their grass lawns, shade-giving trees, and fragrant vines and flowers of the South. Yet the area was not all given over to garden, for at the back were the kitchens, quarters for servants, storage space, and the stables. An impressive feature of many of the old places, even in the small houses, is the pair of large gate posts in the street wall, flanking the entrance to the stable court.

Outside of Charleston a number of villages and country places had been developed by Washington's time. A description of one of these places, at Goose Creek, remains to us in an old letter which relates a visit to

several very handsome gentleman's seats, at all of wch we were entertained with the most friendly politeness. The first we arrived at was Crowfield, Mr. Wm. Middleton's seat, where we spent a most agreeable week. The house stands a mile from but in sight of the road, and makes a very handsome appearance; as you draw nearer new beauties discover themselves; first the beautiful vine mantling the wall, laden with delicious clusters, next a large pond in the midst of a spacious green presents itself as you enter the gate. The house is well furnished, the rooms well contrived . . . From the back door is a wide walk a thousand feet long, each side of wch nearest the house is a grass plat ornamented in a serpentine manner with flowers; next to that on the right hand is what immediately struck my rural taste, a thicket of young, tall live oaks, where a variety of airy choristers poured forth their melody . . . Opposite on the left hand is a large square bowling green, sunk a little below the level of the rest of the garden, with a walk quite round bordered by a double row of fine large flowering Laurel and Catalpas—wch afford both shade and beauty. My letter will be of unreasonable length if I don't pass over the mounts, wilderness, etc., and come to the boundary of this charming spot, where is a large fish pond with a mount rising out of the middle the top of wch is level with the dwelling house, and upon it is a Roman temple. On each side are other large fish ponds, properly disposed wch form a fine prospect of water from the house—beyond this are the smiling fields dressed in vivid green.*

Farther up the rivers were the great plantations surrounded by rice fields and blue gum and cypress swamps. Often the houses were set up on high brick foundations as a precaution against rising of the river in freshet times, while the outbuildings for servants were set off in a grouping of their own. On other plantations, the houses, not impressive in themselves, though often situated on high bluffs whence they commanded views over mile after mile of rice fields, were surrounded by lawns, gardens, and meadows, with woodlands in the rear. The diary of a traveler through these parts in 1785-1786 records pleasure at the

opportunity of seeing the different plantations in (this) vicinity . . . They are chiefly rice plantations and of course there prevails a sameness thro the whole—but still there is a variety in regard of buildings, avenues, walls and gardens. There is a common taste for improvements of this kind among the planters here about.†

Farther south, the first settlement at Savannah was established in 1733 when large grants of land were made on condition that each grantee bring ten able-bodied men to cultivate the mulberry tree. From the earliest times the typical one-story plantation house with high basement and long sloping roof to shade the wide verandas became established on the high wooded bluffs bordering the wide salt rivers of the Savannah district. When silk culture proved unsuccessful, the high lands bordering the salt rivers were given over to cotton, and rice was planted on the fresh-water banks. Now that rice cultivation has been largely discontinued, many places have been deserted; but great avenues of live oaks draped with gray Spanish moss, masses of evergreen shrubs, holly trees, and the ancient mulberries, suggest the attractive home that the late eighteenth-century Savannah plantation afforded.

---

* *Historic Houses of South Carolina.* By H. K. Leiding. Philadelphia, J. B. Lippincott Co., 1921. p. 24.
† *Ibid.*, p. 47.

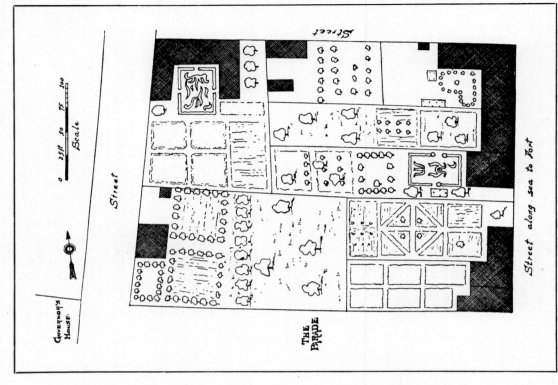

From *Old-fashioned Gardening*

A BLOCK OF RESIDENCES ACROSS FROM THE GOVERNOR'S HOUSE

The gardens were walled and were entered through the houses
or through covered passages from the street

By permission of Robert M. McBride & Co.

THE GOVERNOR'S HOUSE AND GARDENS

The double line of trees provided a shaded walk from which to
view the central parterre

PORTIONS OF PLAN OF ST. AUGUSTINE, 1763

It must not be forgotten that gardening on this continent during Washington's lifetime was not confined to the thirteen colonies. Still farther south, when America had been known for little more than a hundred years, two small Spanish settlements had been established: St. Augustine in Florida (1565), and Santa Fe (1604-1608) in the southwest. According to the custom of all Spanish colonization, soldiers and priests went together, and it is not likely that much time could have passed before the Jesuit fathers were cultivating their gardens; indeed we have an account of Sir Francis Drake's visit to St. Augustine in 1583 when, finding that the Spanish resented his coming, he "burned their buildings and destroyed their gardens." Sixty-five years later St. Augustine had been rebuilt to a town of three hundred householders with "a flourishing Monastery of the Order of St. Francis, with fifty Franciscans," which was probably the finest and the best garden of the community.

In 1763, at the time of the cession of Florida to the English, the Governor's gardens were "stocked with rare ornamental plants, trees, and flowers."† The accompanying plan shows the mansion fronting the Parade or public square, and opening at the back to a formal walled garden facing the sea. The central portion contained square beds of flowers and, immediately adjoining the house, a design which was probably executed in box according to the prevailing fashion in Spain. At either side a double row of trees running the length of the garden offered a shady walk which overlooked the central parterre. Presumably there were very few native plants used, since the settlers in a new world would have wished to make their gardens as like those in Spain as they could.

Another community where gardens developed during the Eighteenth Century was New Orleans. Here, only fourteen years before Washington's birth, the French had planted a post which grew into a town of some size. In 1762 France transferred Louisiana to Spain, in whose hands it remained for nearly forty years until its return to France in 1800. Spanish ownership might not have been so significant in the history of the homes and gardens of the city if a disastrous fire in 1780 had not destroyed a large part of the residential section; for as the city was rebuilt it took on a Spanish aspect in its adobe or brick walls, arcades, inner courts, ponderous doors and windows, balconies and white or yellow lime-washed stucco. The newer houses, however, were of brick, sometimes of two stories, but generally one story high with small narrow balconies projecting over the sidewalks. The following description suggests some of the living conditions which confronted the New Orleans residents of 1799:

> One of the most disagreeable features of the city in those early days was the condition of the streets in which not a stone had been laid. A wooden drain served for a gutter . . . and the street between the sidewalks was alternately a swamp and a mass of stifling dust. Wagons dragged along, with the wheels sunk to the hubs in mud . . . The city was lighted by means of oil lamps suspended from wooden posts, from which an arm projected. The light only penetrated a very short distance, and it was the custom always to use lanterns on the street. The order of march, when a family went out in the evening, was first a slave bearing a lantern; then another slave bearing the shoes which were to be worn in the ball-room or theatre, and other articles of full dress that were donned only after the destination was reached, and last, the family.
> There were no cisterns in those days, the water of the Mississippi, filtrated, served as drinking water, while water for common household needs was obtained from wells dug on the premises. Some houses possessed as many as two of these wells.*

In contrast to the rude streets were the quaint old Spanish courtyards of the houses, fresh and cool, with sunlit pavements across which palms, olives, and magnolias cast their shadows. These were the gardens of the Colonial period and we find their modern counterpart in the courtyards of the old French Quarter of New Orleans today.

Gardening in the Southwest during the Eighteenth Century flourished in the Missions of the Franciscan fathers which extended in a long line from Mexico north through Texas and Arizona to San Francisco. The *padres* who took part in the northward march of Spanish expeditions from Mexico founded posts in San Antonio (1720-1731) and throughout the region to the west, but the best-known establishments are those that stretched at intervals along five hundred miles of the California coast. From their beginning in 1769 the California Missions provided shelter for the traveler and a welcome from the little community that developed around each until the time of their dissolution (1826-1846) by order of the Mexican Government. Without skilled artisans, the builders drew on their memory of the churches with which they were familiar in Spain, and, under the force of the local conditions, evolved a distinctive type of architecture. One of the characteristic features of the Mission was the patio, a large garden area, usually with a fountain, palms, and fruits such as the orange, lemon, and lime, surrounded by buildings. Planned primarily for defense against outlaws, unfriendly Indians, and marauders from pirate ships, the patio become eventually a council chamber, living room, and kitchen garden. There were other gardens too,—in the open but protected by cactus hedges,—and acres of vineyards.

Within the limitations of this chapter it would not be appropriate to speak of the early gardens of the north central and western part of the continent, nor of the manorial establishments of the seigneurs in the St. Lawrence Valley, but it should be remembered that there were homes and gardens in these regions during the lifetime of George Washington that are worth our study.

BRADFORD WILLIAMS.

† *Old-fashioned Gardening.* By Grace Tabor. New York, Robert M. McBride & Co., 1925. p. 22.

* *Historical Sketch Book and Guide to New Orleans and Environs.* Ed. and comp. by several leading writers of the New Orleans press. New York, 1885. p. 14.

Photograph by Paul J. Weber

OLD COLONIAL HOUSE WITH MODERN DOORYARD GARDEN

The Mission House, a memorial to Mr. and Mrs. Joseph H. Choate,
in Stockbridge, Massachusetts

CHAPTER VIII
The Colonial Garden Today

The Colonial Garden filled a want in its time, and is now a thing of the past. We cannot bring it to life today except in our imagination or our memory of what has gone before. And yet there is a subtle quality that pervades the homes and gardens of the Colonial period that we should be able to catch and transpose to our own use,—an indefinable spirit of the design that, when translated into modern terms, will create a Colonial garden that is appropriate to our life today.

George Washington, the farmer, loved the land and the fullness thereof, but as a home-owner he loved the isolated privacy of his own garden and grounds, where he created beauty and comfort for his friends, his family, and himself. There he found contentment, and in so doing pointed out the way for us to follow. We, too, can use the principles that Washington followed, and can find in the Colonial home grounds where he found his inspiration the answer to some of our own problems of home and garden building.

Large or small, North or South, certain characteristics were noticeable in all Colonial gardens. First, they were useful in that they furnished food and drink,—herbs, vegetables, and fruits. Only rather lately has fashion separated the decorative "flower garden" from the useful vegetable garden. Washington did better. His box-edged flower garden is balanced by the vegetable garden, which is not merely useful but is made ornamental with carefully placed walls, paths, lines of grapes, and boxwood. Neat rows of vegetables, bush fruits, and fruit trees, when prettily arranged and edged with flowers, are capable of giving strong esthetic satisfaction to the seeing eye. Our Colonial forebears knew that use and beauty can and do go hand in hand.

A chief feature in the home surroundings, both South and North, was the "yard,"—a generally useful place close to house and outbuildings, where all sorts of work and quiet recreation were concentrated. Wood chopping in one corner, sun-cooking preserves in another, linen bleached in the middle, churning under a grape arbor at one side,—a hundred forms of industry were carried on here. And during the noon hour or at dusk it offered a protected spot in which to gather for talk of the day's doings. At Mount Vernon, Washington created "a village" of small buildings grouped closely about the mansion, and in this "yard" that the Master inspected every morning between his rising hour of four and his breakfast at seven, his servants concentrated their multitudinous duties pertaining to the care of a great plantation.

This general principle of usefulness applies as appropriately today as ever it did in Washington's time. The grounds and gardens of every American home should be useful. Good fruit from trees and bushes, nuts to crack for the trouble of gathering, vegetables for the table (many of which, like asparagus and rhubarb, require almost no attention from those who lack time for gardening), flowers to enjoy,—these are both useful and ornamental purposes to which the house surroundings can be devoted. For those who have other interests than gardening, we can lay out game courts. Some games can be played in small areas, such as Badminton. An enclosed yard for little children is a joy to them and a comfort to their mothers. And above all, work can be done more efficiently in a well-ordered yard. Today we spend less time chopping wood and churning. Our

yards have too frequently dwindled to small areas used for drying clothes. On the other hand, we have found many new chores which could best be done in an enclosed, neatly arranged yard, and we should make more immediate use of this Colonial inheritance.

Another guiding principle of the Colonists in laying out their grounds was economy in the use of land and in providing for ease ease of maintenance. The country was hot and dry in summer, then as now, but they had no garden pipes and hose. Consequently it was convenient, on this account as for others, to have the more choice growing things in gardens close to the house where wellwater, first used for washing and bleaching, could be finally disposed around the precious plants; or else to grow them on slopes in orderly terraces falling away from cisterns where rain water was thriftily conserved. On the smaller places such gardens were naturally compact and neatly joined, one to another. Lawns were definitely set apart and, on modest places where labor was more needed for other things, reduced to a minimum. For there were no lawn mowers: grass was cut by hand scythes, or was kept mowed by cattle. The lower part of the great tree-lined vista down to the river from the east front of Mount Vernon, separated by a sunk wall from the immediate house lawn, gave Washington much concern until he hit upon the happy idea of keeping it mowed by browsing deer.

There is every reason, too, for our following the Colonial good sense in economical arrangement of land for use and maintenance. The best plan is to concentrate the areas where similar work is done. Vegetable, flower, and fruit gardens should adjoin each other or be actually combined in one useful and attractive unit. Service areas, garage, tool sheds, cellar and kitchen doors, etc., should be near together,—all opening on the enclosed "yard" if possible. When a place is orderly and practical in arrangement it is economical to maintain. Lastly, there should be no meaningless, useless places. Too often one sees some land back of the garage or beside the house or between garden and property line which is, strictly speaking, neither part of lawn or garden nor put to any definite use. This is wasteful. Better plant an apple tree than nothing.

A third characteristic of the Colonial Garden is the inclusion of every comfort to induce people to go out of doors and live in the open. Among the most important comforts was privacy. Walls, in Virginia and Pennsylvania, alternated with hedges and fences to separate the garden from the outer world. Fences of palings and solid boarding served the same purposes in the North. In large places "the private garden" was even an inner, especially enclosed part of the general garden treatment. Mount Vernon, the homestead, was hospitably open to all who knocked; but Washington was forced by the crowds of people who came to pay him respect in his later years to set aside certain portions of his grounds for his own comfort and privacy, as private house rooms were reserved to special uses.

Not the least of outdoor comforts in the Colonial home was the provision of suitable garden structures for pleasure and for useful ends. Wide paved grape arbors, cool vine-clad summer houses or fragrant bowers, and benches in shade or sun for choice according to the weather were the scenes of many restful garden hours. On

Photograph by Paul J. Weber

MODERN ADAPTATION OF COLONIAL GARDEN WITH BOX-EDGED ROSE BEDS
Residence in Simsbury, Connecticut

the purely useful side there were hives for the ever-interesting honey bees, deep arched woodsheds, and the well-sweep with cool refreshment near at hand.

People who live in their gardens must be able to retire in them as to the walled-in rooms of a house. Many of us in these democratic times have forgotten this fact which was obvious to George Washington. If a high wall or fence around the "out-door living room" would be too expensive or for any reason unwise, then grow a good high hedge of lilac in the North, or tree box in the South. Get some really comfortable garden chairs and benches. Set a flat stone under their legs if they sink in the ground,—or make a little brick platform. Have a place in the shade an' one in the sun, protected from too cold winds. Have other places where the lightest breezes can slip under the trees without obstruction in sweltering weather. Keep water fresh in a bird bath or a water lily tub that the family pets can drink from. There will always be comfort and diversion in such a garden, shut away from the outside world.

In all things, both Northern and Southern Colonists had a real sense of the comely and appropriate. They liked precision and orderliness, probably all the more in contrast with their enveloping enemy, the wilderness, which must have seemed unkempt and disorderly to them. They possessed a marked sense of balance and

good proportion. They preferred sun and air rather than stiffly architectural arrangement.

To plan square garden beds bounded by walks from which one can see and attend to plants is rather a human and universal tendency than a strictly Colonial one. To have these beds regularly edged with hedges of box is, however, almost a distinctive trait of early American gardens. It is a sensible idea, as the separation between path and bed is difficult for the gardener to handle from week to week. It is typically Colonial, too, to run these paths through, around, and across the vegetable gardens, cutting them into plots. The paths themselves were frequently bordered by flower beds and small fruit trees, making a most successful combination of ornament and use that we might more often attempt nowadays. Near the house these garden plots were subdivided into small pattern beds for pot herbs and flowers. Thus the various features of the gardens were unified in idea, yet varied and separated one from another in practice. In any event, the exact size and shape of these gardens was rarely imposed solely by the esthetic sense of the gardener. The shape and size of the lot on which they were placed seems to have played its own, by no means minor, role in the design.

So it should be today. We start, as gardeners always have, with ideas of squares, rectangles, and curves. But we are growing rigid

Photograph by Paul J. Weber

THE COLONIAL GRAPE ARBOR TODAY

An outdoor terrace in Connecticut where meals can be served

in our conceptions, one fears; at any rate, one hears of a "true" line, a "true" circle, as if it were more virtuous than a bent line or an oval shape. The Colonists adjusted their forms gracefully to existing objects: used them as opportunities to create changes and varieties in designs that otherwise might have been too prim. So should our side paths follow property lines regardless of "true right angles." Where symmetrical patterns are wanted, stick to the plan where possible; but if the garage gets in the way, yield the design to the inevitable. Get around as best one can, and then go on again. Instead of unsightliness, the result is fairly sure of having unexpected charm. For it shows common sense and ability to make the most of what we have—both agreeable qualities.

At Mount Vernon, George Washington used wood and brick, which were common materials for houses and gardens in Virginia. In Pennsylvania, they often made houses, barns, and walls of stone; in New York, of brick and wood; and in New England they worked mostly with wood. It makes little difference what materials we use today. Usually it is best to continue garden objects, such as walls or fences, summer houses, and tool sheds, of the same stuff that the house is built of. At any rate, even when different they can be painted or white-washed to get a harmony of color throughout.

During Washington's lifetime the horizon of the average gardener was immensely widened in the realm of plant material. During the "Dark Ages" and until some time after this country was settled,

the use of plants for medicine, flavoring, etc., was overwhelmingly dominant. Indeed the first English book in which the pleasures of gardening received attention equal to its usefulness is generally considered to be Parkinson's *Paradisi in Sole, Paradisus terrestris,* published in 1629. Gradually interest grew in the broader aspects of horticulture. Nurseries were started near New York and Philadelphia. Explorers went to the ends of the then known world to find new plants and trees. The public followed the experiments of introduction with keen interest. Seeds from home gardens had always been part of the pioneer's equipment. The qualities of American plant material were observed and enjoyed. Interchange of plants among friends was a common courtesy. Washington received new material from travelers and Europe. Is it too much to believe that he himself presented to Lafayette the American elm which the Frenchman planted, now standing at the edge of the moat by his old home at "La Grange"?

Today we are far more fortunate than were the Colonists, in that we have nurseries on every hand to furnish us with a wealth of plant life that they never knew. Washington's manner of using plants still remains, however, as an object lesson to us. He studied them all, tried such new material as he could get, watched it to discover its best uses, and then recommended it to others. We have so much about us today as to seem confusing; but to offset this profusion, we have far better scientific knowledge and more useful sources of information than ever our ancestors had.

FLETCHER STEELE.

Photograph by Paul J. Weber

FRONT YARD GARDEN WITH DESIGN COPIED FROM COLONIAL ORIGINAL

The Mission House, Stockbridge

SOME REFERENCES TO AMERICAN COLONIAL GARDENS*

GENERAL

BLANCHAN, NELTJE. The old-fashioned garden. (*In* her The American flower garden. New York, Doubleday, Page and Co., 1909. p. 45-65. Illus.)

CAPEN, OLIVER BRONSON. Country homes of famous Americans, New York, Doubleday, Page and Co., 1905. 176 p. Illus.

EARLE, ALICE (MORSE). Old time gardens, newly set forth. New York, The Macmillan Co., 1901. 489 p. Illus.

HUBBARD, HENRY VINCENT, and THEODORA KIMBALL. An introduction to the study of landscape design. New York, The Macmillan Co., 1917. 406 p. Illus., plates.

KIMBALL, FISKE. The beginnings of landscape gardening in America. (*In* Landscape architecture, July, 1917; vol. 7, p. 181-187. Plans.)

LAMB, MRS. MARTHA J., *ed.* The homes of America. New York, D. Appleton & Co., 1879. 256 p. Illus.

LOCKWOOD, ALICE G. B., *comp. and ed.* Gardens of colony and state. Vol. I: Gardens and gardeners of the American colonies and of the republic before 1840. Compiled and edited for the Garden Club of America. New York, Charles Scribner's Sons, 1931. 464 p. Illus., plans.

LOUDON, J. C. Gardening in North America. (*In* his Encyclopaedia of gardening. London, Longmans, Green and Co., 1871. p. 329-341. Illus.)

LOWELL, GUY. American gardens. Boston, Bates & Guild Co., 1902. [40 p.] Plates.

Park and garden pioneers, a little known company of early American writers. (*In* Park international, Nov., 1920; vol. 1, p. 243-244.)

SCHERMERHORN, RICHARD, JR. Early American landscape architecture. (*In* Architectural review, Apr., 1921; vol. 12 (new), p. 105-111. Illus.)

TABOR, GRACE. Old-fashioned gardening: a history and a reconstruction. New York, McBride, Nast and Co., 1913. 263 p. Illus., plans.

REGION OF VIRGINIA

BALDWIN, FRANK CONGER. Early architecture of the Rappahannock valley. (*In* Journal of the American Institute of Architects, Nov., 1916; vol. 4, p. 448-454. Illus., plan.)

* Compiled in Library of Schools of Landscape Architecture and City Planning, Harvard University, for the American Society of Landscape Architects, Committee on George Washington Bicentennial.

BIBB, ALBERT BURNLEY. The gardens and grounds of Mount Vernon, Virginia. (*In* House and garden, Oct., 1902; vol. 2, p. 459-473. Illus., plans.)

BROWN, GLENN. The message of Mount Vernon. (*In* Garden and home builder, July, 1927; vol. 45, p. 461-467, 517. Illus.)

(The) Colonial homesteads of the James River, Virginia. (Brochure series of architectural illustrations, Nov., 1901; no. 11, whole number. Illus.)

DAVIS, E. GORTON. An example of early American landscape architecture. (*In* American landscape architect, Dec., 1929; vol. 1, no. 6, p. 28-33. Illus., plans.)

FOWLER, LAWRENCE HALL. "Hampton," an old colonial mansion and gardens at Towson, Maryland. (*In* House and garden, Jan., 1903; vol. 3, p. 41-48. Illus., plans.)

HAWORTH, PAUL LELAND. George Washington: farmer. Indianapolis, Bobbs-Merrill Co., 1915. 335 p. Illus.

KIMBALL, FISKE. A landscape garden on the James in 1793. (*In* Landscape architecture, Jan., 1924; vol. 14, p. 123.)

————. The gardens and plantations at Monticello. (*In* Landscape architecture, April, 1927; vol. 17, p. 172-182. Illus., plans.)

LAMBETH, WILLIAM ALEXANDER, and WARREN H. MANNING. Thomas Jefferson as an architect and a designer of landscapes. Boston, Houghton Mifflin Co., 1913. 122 p. and 23 plates. Illus., plans.

LEE, VIRGINIA. "Reveille": a white brick Virginian house that has watched two hundred years of history go by its doors. (*In* House beautiful, Nov., 1929; vol. 66, p. 547-551, 594. Illus.)

MORRISON, BENJAMIN YOE. The garden of our first president. (*In* Garden and Home Builder, July, 1927; vol. 45, p. 468-471, 513, 518. Illus.)

SADLER, ELIZABETH HATCHER. The bloom of Monticello. Richmond, Va., Whittet & Shepperson, 1926. 31 p. Illus.

SARGENT, CHARLES SPRAGUE. The trees at Mount Vernon. Reprinted from 1926 Annual report of the Mount Vernon Ladies' Association of the Union. The Association, 1926. 16 p. Plan (folded).

SHOULTS, WORTH E. The home of the first farmer of America. (*In* National Geographic Magazine, May, 1928; vol. 53, p. 603-628. Illus.)

SHURTLEFF (SHURCLIFF), ARTHUR A. The design of colonial places in Virginia. (*In* Landscape Architecture, April, 1929; vol. 19, p. 163-169. Plans.)

WILSTACH, PAUL. How and of what the early houses were built. (*In* Country Life in America, January, 1931; vol. 39, No. 3, p. 62-65. Illus. Part III of series Potomac Landings.)

—— ——. Domestic Life Outdoors. (*In* Country Life in America, March, 1921; vol. 39, No. 5, p. 55-57. Illus. Part V of series Potomac Landings.)

—— ——. Mount Vernon: Washington's Home and the Nation's Shrine. 4th ed. Indianapolis, The Bobbs-Merrill Co., 1930. 301 p. Illus.

—— ——. Tidewater Virginia. Indianapolis, The Bobbs-Merrill Co., 1929. 326 p. Illus.

REGION OF PHILADELPHIA

Account of the Bartram Garden, published in "The Horticulturist" in 1850; revised and corrected by the author, and now printed for the Central Fair in aid of the U. S. Sanitary Commission, 1864. 11 p. Illus.

CLARK, BERTHA A. Bartram's Garden, the First Botanical Garden in America. (*In* House Beautiful, March, 1917; vol. 41, p. 205-207, 262-263, 266. Illus.)

DOWNING, ANDREW JACKSON. Historical Notices. (Section 5. *In* Theory and Practice of Landscape Gardening Adapted to North America With a View to the Improvement of Country Residences, With Remarks on Rural Architecture. Ed. by H. W. Sargent. New York, Orange Judd Agricultural Pub. Co., 1865. 7th ed. p. 554-556. *Also in* ed. revised by F. A. Waugh. New York, 1921.)

HINDERMYER, GILBERT. "Wyck," an Old House and Garden at Germantown, Philadelphia. (*In* House and Garden, November, 1902; vol. 2, p. 549-559. Illus., plans.)

WESTCOTT, THOMPSON. The Historic Mansions and Buildings of Philadelphia. Philadelphia, Porter & Coates, c. 1877. 528 p. Illus.

WHEELWRIGHT, ROBERT. The Garden at "Goodstay." (Wilmington, Del.) (*In* Landscape Architecture, October, 1929; vol. 20, p. 5-11. Illus., plan.)

WRIGHT, LETITIA E. (Mrs. W. R.) The Colonial Garden at Stenton, described in old letters. Read at first annual meeting of Garden Club of America, May 1, 1913. New York, The Club, 1916. Unpaged. Illus.

REGION OF NEW YORK

EBERLEIN, HAROLD DONALDSON. The Manors and Historic Homes of the Hudson Valley. Philadelphia, J. B. Lippincott Co., 1924. 327 p. Illus.

—— ——. Manors and Historic Homes of Long Island and Staten Island. Philadelphia, J. B. Lippincott Co., 1928.

KIP, W. I. The Olden Time in New York. New York, G. P. Putnam's Sons, 1872.

MOTT, HOPPER STRIKER. The New York of Yesterday. New York, G. P. Putnam's Sons, 1908. 597 p. Illus.

SCHERMERHORN, RICHARD, JR. Country Places of Old New York. (*In* Journal of the Horticultural Society of New York, February, 1923.)

SINGLETON, ESTHER. Social New York Under the Georges, 1714-1776. New York, D. Appleton & Co., 1902. 407 p. Illus.

—— ——. Dutch New York. New York, Dodd Mead & Co., 1909.

TRYON, THOMAS. An Island Garden from 1652. (*In* Country Life in America, July, 1916; vol. 30, p. 19-21. Illus.)

WHEELWRIGHT, ROBERT. Notes on a Colonial Garden. (*In* Landscape architecture, October, 1913; vol. 4, p. 12-20. Illus., plans.)

REGION OF NEW ENGLAND

BRAYTON, ALICE. A Seventeenth Century Garden, Tiverton, Rhode Island. (*In* Bulletin of The Garden Club of America, July, 1923; No. 12, new series, p. 56-61.)

KIMBALL, FISKE. An American Gardener of the Old School: George Haussler, born 1751, died 1817. (*In* Landscape Architecture, January, 1925; vol. 15, p. 71-75. Illus.)

ROOT, R. R., and G. R. FORBES. Notes Upon a Colonial Garden at Salem, Mass. (*In* Landscape Architecture, October, 1911; vol. 2, p. 16-20. Illus., plans.)

SHURTLEFF (SHURCLIFF), ARTHUR A. A New Hampshire Farm Group of 1805. (*In* Landscape architecture, October, 1917; vol. 8, p. 19-22. Illus.)

—— ——. Some Old New England Gardens. (*In* New England Magazine, December, 1899.)

SLADE, DANIEL DENISON. The Evolution of Horticulture in New England. New York, G. P. Putnam's Sons, 1895. 180 p.

WHEELWRIGHT, ROBERT. A Maine Homestead of 1786. (*In* American Landscape Architect, January, 1931; vol. 4, p. 35-39. Illus.)

THE FAR SOUTH

ANDERSON, MARY SAVAGE. Savannah's Old Plantations. (*In* Bulletin of the Garden Club of America, January, 1930; vol. 7, p. 13-20. Illus.)

HAMPTON, EDGAR LLOYD. The Architecture of California. (*In* House and Garden, February, 1927; vol. 51, No. 2, p. 104-105, 154, 156. Illus.)

Historical Sketch Book and Guide to New Orleans and Environs. Edited and compiled by several leading writers of the New Orleans press. New York, Will H. Coleman, 1885. Illus.

HOLDER, CHARLES FREDERICK. The Gardens of the Missions. (*In* House and Garden, January, 1909; vol. 15, p. 3-8. Illus.)

JAMES, GEORGE WHARTON. The Patio in Mission and Modern Buildings. (*In* Indoors and Out, August, 1907; vol. 4, No. 5, p. 232-238. Illus. Part 4 of series The Mission Style in Modern Architecture.)

LEIDING, MRS. HARRIETTE (KERSHAW). Historic Houses of South Carolina. Philadelphia, J. B. Lippincott Co., 1921. 318 p. Illus.

PIPER, NATT. The California Missions: Their Early History and Their Architecture. (*In* Pencil Points, September, October, and November, 1929; vol. 10, p. 611-618; 691-698; 753-760. Illus., plans.)

SMITH HARVEY P. The Charm of Old San Antonio. Monograph series, 1931; vol. 17, No. 4, whole number. Illus.

THE COLONIAL GARDEN TODAY

BOTTOMLEY, MYRL E. The Design of Small Properties; a book for the home owner in city and country. New York, The Macmillan Co., 1926. 233 p. Illus., plans.

GOODWIN, ISABEL M. G. Gardens of Old Georgetown. (*In* House Beautiful, October, November, December, 1927; vol. 62; January, February, 1928; vol. 63, p. 369-372, 424; 526-527, 576-577; 661-663, 697; 36-37, 84-86; 155-201, 204-205. Illus., plan.)

STEELE, FLETCHER. Design in the Little Garden. Boston, Atlantic Monthly Press, 1924. 124 p. Illus. (The little garden series.)

———— ————. Mission House, the Oldest House in Stockbridge. (*In* House Beautiful, July, 1930; vol. 68, p. 26-33. Illus.)

TABOR, GRACE. Reproducing the Old-fashioned Garden. (*In* Old-fashioned Gardening; a History and a Reconstruction. New York, McBride, Nast & Co., 1913. 263 pages. Illus., plans.)

———————

A great fund of information, covering all parts of the country, is available in the United States Department of Agriculture Bulletins and the various State Agriculture Department and Experiment Station publications. Students will find constantly new material in books, magazine articles, and the published work **of** horticultural societies, arboretums, botanic gardens, garden clubs, etc.

THE MORE I AM ACQUAINTED WITH AGRICULTURAL AFFAIRS, THE BETTER I AM PLEASED WITH THEM; INSOMUCH THAT I CAN NO WHERE FIND SO GREAT SATISFACTION AS IN THOSE INNOCENT AND USEFUL PURSUITS. IN INDULGING THESE FEELINGS, I AM LED TO REFLECT HOW MUCH MORE DELIGHTFUL TO THE UNDEBAUCHED MIND, IS THE TASK OF MAKING IMPROVEMENTS ON THE EARTH, THAN ALL THE VAIN GLORY THAT CAN BE ACQUIRED FROM RAVAGING IT, BY THE MOST UNINTERRUPTED CAREER OF CONQUEST.

—*George Washington.*

THE MUSIC

OF

GEORGE WASHINGTON'S TIME

BY
JOHN TASKER HOWARD
EDITOR, MUSIC DIVISION

THE MUSIC OF GEORGE WASHINGTON'S TIME

By JOHN TASKER HOWARD, *Editor, Music Division*

PREFACE

Music played an important part in many of the celebrations arranged to commemorate the Two Hundredth Anniversary of the Birth of George Washington. It was fitting, therefore, that the United States Commission for the Celebration of the 200th Anniversary of the Birth of George Washington should offer to the people of the United States, authoritative and comprehensive information on the music of Washington's time—music written in his day to extol his virtues and to commemorate his achievements; songs and pieces known and performed in eighteenth century America; and music associated with historic events and personages.

In publishing and distributing this booklet it is our aim to give correct and interesting information, not only on the origin of our first national airs, but also on musical conditions in early America, the influences that shaped our musical life, and most important, the relation of music to the events of the period. It is earnestly hoped that these pages will be helpful in suggestions to those arranging musical programs, and to all who wish to learn of the important part that music played in our beginnings as a nation.

ACKNOWLEDGMENTS

In presenting the material in these pages the author wishes first to make acknowledgment to those who have been helpful in his work of research and gathering data. While it would be impractical, because of limited space, to name all those who have been helpful with kindly suggestions, there are a number who have been of especial assistance and whose names should be mentioned: at the Library of Congress, Carl Engel, Chief of the Music Division, and his assistants, Walter R. Whittlesey and W. Oliver Strunk; R. W. Gordon, in charge, Archive of American Folk-Song, at the Library of Congress; Richard G. Appel, Chief of the Music Division of the Public Library in the City of Boston; Carleton S. Smith, Chief of the Music Division of the New York Public Library; and librarians at Harvard University, Massachusetts Historical Society, Library Company of Philadelphia, and the Historical Society of Pennsylvania.

A number of individuals have been particularly helpful, among them Edward Hopkinson, great-grandson of Francis and grandson of Joseph Hopkinson; Mrs. L. D. Redway of Ossining, New York; as well as several private collectors of musical Americana—J. Francis Driscoll of Brookline, Massachusetts; Joseph Muller of Closter, New Jersey; Arthur Billings Hunt of Brooklyn, New York; Abbe Niles of Forest Hills, Long Island; and Henry C. Woehlcke of Philadelphia, in whose collection was found the original manuscript of the *Toast* to Washington, by Francis Hopkinson.

Music publishers have kindly cooperated in supplying lists of music in their catalogues, and it is upon information they have supplied that Chapters II and III are based—the catalogues of *Authentic Eighteenth Century Music in Modern Editions* and of *Modern Music Commemorating George Washington, or Otherwise Appropriate for Use in Washington Celebrations.*

Thanks are also due to Thomas Y. Crowell Company of New York for permission to use some of the material contained in the author's book, *Our American Music.*

J. T. H.

I. The Music of George Washington's Time

1.

THE MUSICAL BACKGROUND

Musical Conditions in Early America

To understand the music of George Washington's time, it is necessary to know musical conditions in America from the days of the first settlers to the end of the eighteenth century. Although there was little music here in the years immediately following the first coming of the white men, it is not correct to assume that there was no considerable musical life in the Colonies by the time our nation asserted and won its independence. True, our ancestors were largely dependent on musical importations from abroad; yet concerts, ballad operas, and musical evenings in the home were frequent in the principal cities from 1750 on.

There were several attitudes toward music in America's infancy. In New England the muse of song had a difficult road to travel. She was viewed suspiciously by the Puritans, who at first would allow no musical instruments, and would tolerate singing only as an aid to divine worship, and then only after bitter arguments as to the propriety of singing Psalms in church.

In New York, Pennsylvania and the South, music and secular diversions were more welcome than in New England, although the Quakers in Pennsylvania considered plays, games, lotteries, music and dancing alike, and advised all their members to have nothing to do with them.

To our present knowledge, there were no native-born composers of music until the time of Francis Hopkinson (1737-1791), signer of the Declaration of Independence, treasurer of loans during the Revolution, Judge of the Admiralty of Pennsylvania, and a great cultural influence in eighteenth century Philadelphia. Hopkinson, a friend of George Washington, is credited with being the first American composer, and we shall hear later of his songs, which were charming and reflective of the musical style and taste of the period, even though they may have lacked individuality.

The manuscript book containing Hopkinson's first song bears the date 1759, one hundred and fifty years after the Jamestown colony was first established. The next composer to appear was James Lyon, (1735-1794), a clergyman who wrote a number of hymns, anthems and psalm tunes. In 1770, the year Beethoven was born, William Billings of Boston (1746-1800) published a book called the *New England Psalm Singer,* in which he included a number of his own compositions, among them some "fuguing pieces", as he called them, crude attempts at the fugues of the masters. Billings had little training as a musician, but he was important for his desire to be original, and for the undoubted vitality he put into his own music, and that of his colleagues.

Soon after the appearance of Hopkinson, Billings and Lyon, other native composers appeared, and while none of them achieved anything that could be considered great, they planted the seeds of a native musical product which has developed to our own day. One of these musicians, Oliver Holden, published in 1793 a hymn-tune that has had continued life, and is known throughout the world—*Coronation,* sung to the words, "All hail the power of Jesus' name".

Throughout the eighteenth century there had of course been foreign musicians in America, who had come from abroad, and because of their superior training had exerted a strong influence on our musical life. In Bethlehem, Pennsylvania, the Moravian colony which was settled in 1741 enjoyed music that was unknown elsewhere in America. Intense music lovers, these Germans brought their instruments and their voices with them, and their orchestras and choruses performed the works of the masters in a manner worthy of the music. When Washington visited Bethlehem in 1782, he was serenaded by the trombone choir. Yet these Moravians were sufficient unto themselves, and mingled little with their neighbors. Their culture had but slight influence on the rest of America.

After the Revolution more foreign musicians came to our shores and by the time of the French Revolution they immigrated in wholesale quantities. Better trained than the native Americans, they naturally took our musical life into their own hands, and their works soon took the place of American compositions on concert programs. Of course, most of the foreigners eventually became Americans themselves, and their descendants tday can boast a long line of American ancestors; but for the time being they stifled much of our native effort in music. Many of these artists were English, some of them French, a few were Germans, although the great influx of German musicians belongs to the next century—in 1848, at the time of the revolutions in Central Europe.

Early Concerts

The first public concert in America, of which we have record, was held in Boston. This was in 1731, at a time when the New England ban against secular music was gradually being lowered. The affair, "a Concert of Music on sundry Instruments", was held in "the great room" at Mr. Pelham's, an engraver, dancing master, instructor in reading and writing, painting upon glass, and a dealer in the "best Virginia tobacco". A few years later the selectmen of Boston allowed Fanueil Hall to be used for "Concerts of Musick", and by 1754 there was a concert hall at the corner of Hanover and Court Streets, where concerts of "Vocal and instrumental Musick to consist of Select Pieces by the Masters" were given. After Boston, the next American city to enjoy a concert was Charleston, South Carolina. Then came New York, where in 1736 there was advertised a "Consort of Musick, Vocal and Instrumental, for the benefit of Mr. Pachelbel, the Harpsichord Part performed by Himself. The Songs, Violins and German Flutes by Private Hands."

If contemporary records are to be trusted, Philadelphia heard its first advertised concert in 1757, when John Palma offered an affair "at the Assembly Room in Lodge Alley", January 25th.[1] Yet it seems altogether likely that there were concerts in the Pennsylvania city before this time, for Philadelphians were cultured, and, except for the Quakers, fond of amusement. There was a dancing master in the city in 1710, and dancing was taught in its boarding schools as early as 1728.

Except for the interval of the Revolution, when the Continental Congress passed a resolution "to discourage every species of extrava-

---

[1] Palma followed this with another concert March 25th. In Washington's ledger, March 17th, the following entry appears—"By Mr. Palma's Tickets 52s 6."

gance and dissipation . . . exhibition of shows, plays and other expensive diversions and amusements" (1774), concerts were offered regularly in the principal cities during the last half of the century. Their programs contained many works that are forgotten today, yet there were a number of standard pieces which are still being played on concert programs. Handel, Haydn, and, in the closing years of the century, Mozart, were well represented, and the overtures of the London Bach—Johann Christian (son of Johann Sebastian)—were played often.

Typical programs of the period shows a variety of compositions. In 1769 an Italian resident of Philadelphia, John (Giovanni) Gualdo offered this characteristic list:

ACT I.

Overture composed by the Earl of Kelly.
'Vain is beauty, gaudy flower' [sung] by Miss Hallam.
Trio composed by Mr. Gualdo, first violin by Master Billy Crumpto.
'The Spinning Wheel', by Miss Storer.
A German flute concert, with Solos, composed by Mr. Gualdo.
A new symphony after the present taste, composed by Mr. Gualdo.

ACT II.

A new violin concerto with solos, composed by Mr. Gualdo.
A Song by Mr. Wools.
A Sonata upon the Harpsichord, by Mr. Curtz.
Solo upon the Clarinet, by Mr. Hoffman, junior.
Solo upon the Mandolino, by Mr. Gualdo.
Overture, composed by the Earl of Kelly.

Many of the concert programs offered names and works that are still standard musical fare. Here is a typical example from a subscription series advertised in Philadelphia in 1792, while Washington was president, and the Pennsylvania city the national capital:

ACT I.

Grand Overture of Haydn, called la Reine de France

[The first movements of symphonies were sometimes offered as "overtures." This was no doubt the first movement of Haydn's Paris Symphony No. 4, "La Reine", composed in 1786.]

Song	Mrs. Hodgkinson
Quartetto composed by Mr. Gehot	
Concerto Violoncello	
(composed by the celebrated Duport)	
Sinfonia	Bach [Johann Christian Bach]

ACT II.

Quartetto	Messrs. Reinagle, Gehot, Moller and Capron

[While the name of the composer was not given, this may have been a Quartetto by Pleyel, presented again at a later concert of the series by the same performers.]

Song	Mrs. Hodgkinson
Sonata Piano Forte	Mr. Moller
Double Concerto, Clarinet and Bassoon	Messrs. Wolf and Youngblut
Overture	Reinagle

Other concerts of the series offered standard works as well as original compositions by the performers. Such names as Stamitz, Gretry,

Vanhall, Boccherini, Pleyel, Martini and Handel are encountered recently.

Haydn was represented by symphonies, piano sonatas, an occasional trio, and numerous "overtures" and "finales", probably first and last movements, respectively, of symphonies. Mozart's name does not appear as often as that of Haydn, but there are references to his piano sonatas, and other works. Handel was performed frequently; the *Messiah* was first presented in New York in 1770. Many concerts in America offered selections from the *Messiah,* and often when a chorus was available, the "Hallelujah" Chorus would be sung, sometimes "with an accompaniment of kettledrums". The overtures to Handel's oratorios were favorites—such works as *Samson,* and the opera, *Otho.* The march from *Judas Maccabeus* was often performed.

Washington, known to be a frequent concert-goer, must have been familiar with much of the music performed in his day. O. G. Sonneck in his essay on "The Musical Side of Our First Presidents", has traced a number of concerts which Washington is known to have attended, and has described their programs. Still another program is particularly interesting, for it was offered in Philadelphia in the Spring of 1787, four days after the Constitutional Convention had assembled. (May 25.) Under the date of May 29th Washington noted in his diary that he "accompanied Mrs. Morris to the benefit concert of a Mr. Juhan". The *Pennsylvania Packet* printed the program of Mr. Juhan's concert:

ACT 1st.

Grand Overture	Martini
Song	Reinagle
Solo Violin (newly composed)	Juhan

ACT 2nd.

Overture to the Deserter [a ballad opera, by Monsigny]

Concerto Flute	Brown
Sonato Piano Forte	Reinagle
Concerto Violoncello	Capron

ACT 3rd.

Concert Violin	Cramer
Sonata Guittar	Capron

(By desire) the Overture to Rosina [ballad opera, by Shield]

The works of Reinagle on this program are of especial interest, for Reinagle was one of the most important musicians who came to America from Europe in the latter eighteenth century. Several of his works have recently been reprinted in modern editions, and it is evident that while he was no great genius, he was nevertheless a well equipped musician, possessed of taste and imagination. Before coming to America in 1786 he had been an intimate friend of Carl Philip Emmanuel Bach. It is generally supposed that he was engaged as the music teacher of Washington's step-grand-daughter, Nelly Custis.

Reinagle was important also as a theatrical manager, for in 1793, in association with Thomas Wignell, he built and managed the Chestnut Street Theatre in Philadelphia, which presented brilliant seasons at the nation's capital during Washington's second administration. Washington was always a lover of the theatre, and attended it frequently from his early manhood in Virginia, where plays were given at Fredericksburg and Williamsburg.

The theatre and music were inseparably associated in eighteenth century America, for many of the theatrical performances were bal-l-operas—plays interspersed with music, somewhat like our present-y musical comedies. Often, too, the actors would sing popular songs tween the acts of the drama.

The Beggar's Opera, by Gay and Pepusch; Rosina, by Shield; The ountaineers, by Arnold; Love in a Village, by Arne and others; o Song, No Supper, by Storace, were among the favorites. The ngs from these plays were also the popular songs of the day, and any of them were traditional ballads.

Popular Songs in the Eighteenth Century

It is not possible even to estimate the age of any of the so-called merican folk-songs, although it is probable that a number were in istence before 1800. On the other hand, the popular music of the ghteenth century is well-known. The literature of peoples' songs nsisted largely of English ballads and songs, some of them intro-iced in the ballad-operas. Many of these songs are still current, and is not difficult to re-enact the singing of Washington's time.

The famous tune of Green Sleeves is very old, some authorities te it from 1580, so it must have been known in America during ashington's boyhood. The Vicar of Bray appeared in ballad-operas om 1728:

The Vicar of Bray

Girls and Boys Come Out to Play appeared in the ballad-opera lly, a sequel to the Beggar's Opera, in 1729:

Girls and Boys Come out to Play

Old King Cole announced his appearance in Gay's Achilles in 1733 with this tune:

3

Old King Cole

Rule Brittania was highly popular in the colonies before the Revolution. Dr. Arne composed the music in 1740, and it was well-known in America within a few years after this date. Sally in Our Alley has had an honorable career in America as well as in England. The words have been sung to two tunes, the first dating from 1719, and composed by Henry Carey:

4

Sally in Our Alley

Henry Carey

About 1760, however, Carey's tune seems to have been discarded, and since that time the verses have been sung to a tune known earlier as The Country Lass:

5

Sally in Our Alley

Tune used after 1760

The Girl I Left Behind Me has always been popular with fife and drum corps. Authorities differ as to its age; some think it originated about 1758, while others date its English origin as late as 1778. The stirring tune of The British Grenadiers was also popular in America. The age of this air is unknown, although there is reason to believe that it originated in England in the Elizabethan period. There are frequent references to it on American concert programs, from as early as 1769.

Drink to Me Only With Thine Eyes, as a poem, is very old, for its author, Ben Jonson, lived from 1573 to 1637. No doubt it has been known as a song for several centuries, but the present tune cannot safely be dated before 1780. It was frequently sung in America after 1790.

O, Dear, What Can the Matter Be started its American vogue in the closing years of the eighteenth century. Different authorities date its English origin from 1780 to 1792, and American references to the song date from its publication in Shaw's *Gentleman's Amusement* in 1795.

This is but a brief list of some of the English songs popular in Washington's time which are still known today. Doubtless he was familiar with them, for he went to concerts and the theatre, and also enjoyed the playing of music in his own home. While he probably played no instruments nor sang himself, he nevertheless provided instruments and a musical education to his step-children and step-grand-children. At Mount Vernon there are still preserved several music books which belonged to the Washington household; two of them were owned by Martha Parke Custis, the daughter of Martha Washington, who died in 1773. One of these bears the signature of Martha Custis, and the date 1769. It is entitled:

> Harpsichord or spinnet—Miscellany, being a Graduation of Proper Lessons from the Beginner to the tollerable Performer. Chiefly intended to save Masters the trouble of writing for their pupils. To which are prefixed some Rules for Time. By Robert Bremner.

Included in the contents are a *Lesson* by Lully, a *Gavotte* (in F) by Corelli, and a few popular airs of the period—such tunes as *Maggy Lauder* and *God Save the King.*

The other book belonging to Martha Custis was entitled *New and Complete Instructions for the Guitar.* It contained a number of dances of the period, minuets, cotillions, and such country dances as *The Hay-Makers Dance,* and many popular airs; among them *Here's to the maiden of bashful fifteen, I winna marry ony mon,* and others.

Three of the music books at Mount Vernon belonged to Eleanor Parke (Nelly) Custis, and among their contents are six sonatas by Nicolai (Nos. I to VI inclusive), *Overture de Blaise et Babet* by Dezede, adapted for the Piano Forte, the score of Goldsmith's *The Hermit,* set to music by James Hook, and three piano sonatas by G. Maurer.

The Dances of Washington's Time

Dancing was a popular diversion in eighteenth century America, and Washington himself was particularly fond of it. In early manhood, during the Revolution, and in the years of his presidency he attended many "assemblies." He enjoyed such affairs to his last days, and it was only in 1799 that he was compelled to write to the managers of the Alexandria Assembly:

> Mrs. Washington and myself have been honored with your polite invitation to the assemblies of Alexandria this winter, and thank you for this mark of your attention. But, alas! our dancing days are no more. We wish, however, all those who have a relish for so agreeable and innocent an amusement all the pleasure the season will afford them.

The minuet and the gavotte were the formal dances of Washington's time. European composers were of course using these forms for movements of their suites and their sonatas, notably Haydn and Mozart. Martini and Boccherini supplied many such dances, and the latter's charming *Minuet in A* is still a favorite. (This was composed in 1771, and first published abroad in 1775.)

Composers in America, too, wrote prolifically for dancing. In 1770 Gualdo, in Philadelphia, advertised his *Six New Minuets, with Proper Cadences for Dancing.* The Library of Congress has an autograph collection of dance tunes by Pierre Landrin Duport, a dancing master of the day who was also an excellent musician. Among these pieces are a *Fancy Menuit* "DANCE BEFORE GENL. WASHINGTON, 1792", and a *Fancy Menuit with figure Dance by Two young ladies in the presAnce of Mrs. Washington in 1792. PHILA."* Alexander Reinagle was among the composers who wrote minuets and gavottes.[1]

There are frequent references also to the sarabande and the allemande, although strictly these belong to an earlier period. The waltz was probably not current in America until the close of the century, for it did not make its appearance in Central Europe until 1780, and was not used in England and France much earlier than 1791 or 1792. One of the earliest American references to the waltz was the publication of a *Dance for Waltzing,* issued by George Willig of Philadelphia, somewhere between 1795 and 1797.

Reels and country dances were equally, if not more popular than the more formal minuet and gavotte. There are dozens of contemporary references to reels, jigs, country dances, and the contre-dance or quadrille. One of Washington's favorite dance tunes was *Successful Campaign*[2], which was also one of the popular marches of the period.

The Hay-Makers Dance was a favorite tune:

The Hay-Makers Dance

Musical Instruments

By Washington's time a variety of musical instruments was used in America. As early as 1761 Washington ordered a spinet from abroad. The harpsichord, and later the piano-forte, were found in many homes, and were used at concerts.[3] Violins and 'cellos were well-known, and the so-called German flute was as necessary to perfect eighteenth century gentleman's outfit as his wig or powdered hair.

The concert programs of the day give an idea of the instruments that were most used, for many of them announce the instrumentation of the orchestras that performed, as well as the instruments used by soloists. We have already learned that Gualdo's concert in 1769 offered solos on the violin, the German flute, the clarinet, the harpsichord, and the mandolino. Earlier than this, however, is an account

---

[1] The Dupont minuets, and the minuet and gavotte by Reinagle are included in *Music from the Days of George Washington,* published by the United States Commission for the Celebration of the 200th Anniversary of the Birth of George Washington.

[2] Included in *Music from the Days of George Washington,* published by the United States Commission for the Celebration of the 200th Anniversary of the Birth of George Washington.

[3] Pianos were manufactured in America in 1774.

the music played in the church at Bethlehem, Pennsylvania, on Christmas Day, 1743. The instruments used included the violin, the viola da braccio, the viola da gamba, flutes, and French horns. One of the earliest references to trombones comes from Bethlehem, when in 1754 a number of them were brought from Europe. It is recorded that one night in 1755 a number of trombonists at Bethlehem warded off an Indian attack by playing chorales. Trumpets, too, were known in America at an early date in the eighteenth century.

It has sometimes been stated that wood-wind instruments, the oboe and the bassoon especially, were not used to any extent until the latter part of the century, but this is not accurate, for there are early references to such instruments. In 1757 the *Pennsylvania Gazette* announced that Mr. Charles Love, an actor, was wanted in Virginia for running away from a gentleman of that state with a "small white horse", and "a very good bassoon".

In 1786 the proprietor of the Pennsylvania Coffee House in Philadelphia announced

> that by desire of several gentlemen, he has proposed for the summer season to open a Concert of Harmonial Music, which will consist of the following instruments, viz.

> Two clarinets   Two bassoons
> Two French horns   One flute

Another item from a later date indicated the standard type of orchestra used at concerts. At an affair at Oeller's Hotel, Philadelphia, 1796, a supplementary orchestra of amateurs was used to augment the *concertino*, or small band of soloists which was constituted thus:

> First violin and leader of the band . Mr. Gillingham
> Principal violoncellos   Mr. Menel
> Double Bass   Mr. Demarque
> Principal Hautboy [Oboe]   Mr. Shaw
> Tenor [Viola]   Mr. Berenger
> Bassoon and trumpet   Mr. Priest
> Horns   Messrs. Gray and Homman
> Violins   Messrs. Daugel, Bouchony,
>   Stewart and Schetky

Sometimes large orchestras were assembled for festivals, one of them particularly is worthy of comment—a charity concert in 1786 promoted by an English musician in Philadelphia, Andrew Adgate, performed by a chorus of 230 and an orchestra of 50.

There are several instruments at Mount Vernon which belonged to the Washington family—a flute, a citra or guitar, and the harpsichord which Washington bought for Nelly Custis. These were the instruments most often found in homes, and on which young people as well as adults were taught to play. Several passages from two letters of a young New England girl of twelve years, who was studying at the school in Bethlehem, told her parents of her musical education. They were written in 1787:

> There are about thirty little girls of my age. Here I am taught music both vocal and instrumental. I play the guitar twice a day; am taught the spinet and forte-piano, and sometimes I play the organ.

She also told of the music at the Bethlehem church services:

> They sing enchantingly, in which they are joined with the bass-viols, violins and an organ. To call the people into chapel four French horns are blown, with which you would be delighted. . . . After we are in bed, one of the ladies, with her guitar and voice, serenades us to sleep.

She described the Moravian Christmas celebration:

> We began with music. There were four violins, two flutes, and two horns, with the organ; which altogether sounded delightfully. The children sang one German and eight English verses. . . . Many of the neighboring inhabitants came to visit us. . . . We entertained them with music.

Military Bands of the Revolution

There are many contemporary references to the military bands of the day, and there has been much discussion as to what they consisted of. It is probable that they were not the brass bands of our generation, but were rather fife and drum corps. John C. Fitzpatrick, in his book, *The Spirit of the Revolution*, presents a number of arguments to support this theory, and he also describes the function of fifes and drums in the Continental Army. Instead of the bugle, the drum was used for military orders, with such signals as the Reveille, the General, the Assembly, the Retreat, and the Taptoo which became Taps. Many of the flute books of the period are filled with marches, scored for two flutes, which would seem to indicate that flutes, and in the case of army bands, fifes, were used in two-part arrangements.

There are only a few references to contradict the belief that fifes and drums were the sole instrumentation of American bands in the eighteenth century, especially during the period of the Revolution. Among these is an account of a concert conducted by Josiah Flagg of Boston, with a program of "vocal and instrumental musick accompanied by French horns, hautboys [oboes], etc., by the band of the 64th Regiment." This was in 1771, and of course the 64th Regiment was a British organization, not American. It is known that Flagg organized a band himself, but there is no account of the instruments it contained.

The printed version of a *Federal March*, played in Philadelphia in 1788, contained directions for "trumpets." This, however, was several years after the Revolution.

An interesting item is found in an edition of Kotzwara's sonata, *The Battle of Prague*, "adapted for a full band" by J. G. C. S[c]hetky, published in Philadelphia in 1793. The word "band," however, is misleading, for the edition has parts for basso, violino, and cannon ("to be played on a drum"). The piano score has directions for horn call and trumpet.

No doubt hautboys were sometimes used with the fifes, although the 1756 account of

> The Philadelphia Regiment consisting of upwards of 1000 able bodied effective men [who] after being review'd and performing the manual Exercise [marched] thro' the town in Three Grand Divisions . . . with Hautboys and Fifes in Ranks. . . [and] Drums between the third and fourth Ranks,

referred to an English rather than an American regiment.

Yet the music of the fife and drum, if these were indeed the only instruments used in Continental bands, was often stirring, and inspired soldiers to action. The old English tunes, *The Girl I Left Behind Me*, *The British Grenadiers*, as well as *Yankee Doodle* and the marches of the day were widely played by the fifers. The drum major and the fife major were persons of distinction in the army.

2.

MUSIC ASSOCIATED WITH HISTORIC EVENTS

The Music of Pre-Revolutionary Episodes

The Music of Pre-Revolutionary Episodes

A chronological account of the music that originated in Washington's time forms something of a history of his career and of American events generally. During his boyhood and early manhood, Washington heard chiefly English music. Of English patriotic airs, *God Save the King* was probably composed in England in 1740, and was no doubt known in the colonies soon after that time. *Yankee Doodle* originated either in America or in England while Washington was a young man, for the common tradition regarding Dr. Schuckburg, who composed verses to the tune, and played a joke on the Yankee troops at Albany, dates from 1758, during the French-Indian Wars.

The year 1759 saw the composition of the first known song by a native American composer, for that is the date marked on the manuscript book containing Francis Hopkinson's *My Days Have Been so Wondrous Free.* It is altogether fitting that this charming amateur should have been the first American composer of music, for, as we have already learned, he was a man active in political and cultural affairs.

The events of the French-Indian War were commemorated with music. *A Thanksgiving Anthem,* by William Tuckey, an English musician resident in New York, was performed December 8, 1760, in Trinity Church, "before his Excellency General Amherst, on his return to New York from the conquest of Canada." The Peace of Paris, by which France ceded to England all of Canada and, with the exception of New Orleans, all of her region east of the Mississippi, was accomplished February 10, 1763. In the same year we find a number of musical celebrations to mark the event. On May 17th, at the College of Philadelphia, there was performed an *Exercise, Containing a Dialogue and Ode,* "on occasion of the peace," written by "Paul Jackson, A.M.", for solo voice and chorus. On September 28th, the senior class of Nassau Hall delivered an original *Dialogue on Peace,* "interspersed with music," at its anniversary commencement. A number of years later, in the *Pennsylvania Magazine* of March 1775, a song was printed to commemorate the *Death of General Wolfe,* who fell during the taking of Quebec in 1759.

The music of this period shows the loyalty of the colonists. Even at a time when there were tremors of discord with England, poets and composers publicly paid homage to the sovereign and to the mother country. At the commencement of the College of Philadelphia, May 23, 1761, the students performed *An Exercise Containing a Dialogue and Ode,* written and set to music by Francis Hopkinson, "sacred to the memory of his late gracious Majesty, George II." The next year Hopkinson wrote another *Ode and Dialogue* for the commencement, "on the accession of his gracious Majesty, George III." Little did Hopkinson know that more stringent enforcement of the obnoxious Navigation Acts would be ordered in 1764, or that in 1765 the Stamp Act Congress would find it necessary to publish a "declaration of rights and grievances."

There were other musical testimonials to the greatness of Britain. The *Ode on the Late Glorious Successes of His Majesty's Arms and Present Greatness of the English Nation,* published by William Dunlap in Philadelphia in 1762, may have called for music, and it is highly probable that James Lyon composed the music for *The Military Glory of Great Britain,* "an entertainment given by the late candidates for bachelor's degree, held in Nassau Hall, N. J., September 29, 1762."

Songs Showing Early Resentment of England's Attitude on Taxation

In 1765 we begin to find references to the colonies' resentment of their treatment by England. One of the earliest was a ballad called *American Taxation,* written soon after the ship Edward arrived in New York bearing news of the passage of the Stamp Act.

There are many references in Revolutionary history to the tune *The World Turned Upside Down,* and we shall learn later that Cornwallis' troops are supposed to have surrendered to its strains. There is, however, considerable confusion as to what tune was played on various occasions. In 1767, the year of the Townshend Acts, which laid duties on important commodities for the support of a British army in America, and of the law suspending the New York Assembly, an anonymous poet contributed to the *Gentleman's Magazine* a poem entitled *The World Turned Upside Down,* or *The Old Woman Taught Wisdom,* intended as "an humble attempt to reconcile the parent and her children, made by a peace-maker to Great Britain and her Colonies," an entirely different poem than the English verses with the same title. Later, when the words were printed on a music sheet, they were adapted to the English tune, *Derry Down.* Chappell, in *Popular Music of the Olden Time,* gives this tune in the following version:

Derry Down

Der-ry down, down, hey, der-ry down.

With the exception of the refrain, which was omitted, the peace making verses could be easily sung to this melody:

Goody Bull and her daughter together fell out,
Both squabbled and wrangled, and made a ———— rout,
But the cause of the quarrel remains to be told,
Then lend both your ears, and a tale I'll unfold.

The old lady, it seems, took a freak in her head,
That her daughter, grown woman, might earn her own bread;
Self-applauding her scheme, she was ready to dance;
But we're often too sanguine in what we advance.

In vain did the matron hold forth in the cause,
That the young one was able; her duty, the laws;
Ingratitude vile, disobedience far worse;
But she might e'en as well sung psalms to a horse.

Young, froward, and sullen, and vain of her beauty,
She tartly replied, that she knew well her duty,
That other folks' children were kept by their friends,
And that some folks loved people but for their own ends.
 . . . .
Alas! cries the old woman, and must I comply?
But I'd rather submit than the huzzy should die;
Pooh, prithee be quiet, be friends and agree,
You must surely be right, *if you're guided by me.*

Unwillingly awkward, the mother knelt down,
While her absolute farmer went on with a frown,
Come, kiss the poor child, here come, kiss and be friends!
There, kiss your poor daughter and make her amends.

Dickinson's "Liberty Song," and its Parodies

John Dickinson of Delaware is generally credited with being the author of the first patriotic song composed in America. Dickinson was an ardent patriot, even though he did at first oppose the Declartion of Independence, because he doubted the policy of Congress "without some percursory trials of our strength." He had long been active in public affairs—a member of the Pennsylvania Assembly in 1764, and of the Congress of 1765. It was in 1768 that he contributed his *Liberty Song* to the *Boston Gazette*. Here are a few of its verses:

> Come join hand in hand, brave Americans all,
> And rouse your bold hearts at fair Liberty's call;
> No tyrannous acts shall suppress your just claim,
> Or stain with dishonor America's name.

Refrain:—　In Freedom we're born, and in freedom we'll live;
> Our purses are ready,
> Steady, friends, steady,
> Not as *slaves*, but as *freemen* our money we'll give.

> Our worthy forefathers—let's give them a cheer—
> To climates unknown did courageously steer;
> Thro' oceans to deserts, for freedom they came,
> And, Dying, bequeath'd us their freedom and fame.

Refrain:—　In Freedom we're born, etc.
> All ages shall speak with amaze and applause,
> Of the courage we'll show in support of our laws;
> To die we can bear,—but to serve we disdain,
> For shame is to freedom more dreadful than pain.

Refrain:—　In Freedom we're born, etc.

The final stanza shows that at this early date there was no thought of disloyalty to Britain:

> This bumper I crown for our sovereign's health,
> And this for Brittania's glory and wealth;
> That wealth, and that glory immortal may be,
> If she is but just, and we are but free.

Refrain:—　In Freedom we're born, etc.

Dickinson's song was set to an English tune, *Hearts of Oak,* which was composed by Dr. William Boyce, and made its first appearance in a ballad opera in 1759:

Hearts of Oak
with the words of the Liberty Song

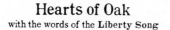

Soon after the *Liberty Song* was printed, a parody appeared in the *Boston Gazette*:

> Come shake your dull noddles ye pumpkins, and bawl,
> And own you are mad at fair Liberty's call
> No scandalous conduct can add to your shame,
> Condemned to dishonor, inherit the fame.

Refrain:—　In folly you're born, and in folly you'll live,
> To madness still ready,
> And stupidly steady,
> Not as men, but as monkeys, the tokens you give.

The patriots were ready with a rejoinder to this tory taunt, and *The Parody Parodised,* or the *Massachusetts Liberty Song,* was published not only in America, but appeared in the *St. James Chronicle*, London, in November, 1768:

> Come swallow your bumpers, ye tories, and roar,
> That the sons of fair Freedom are hamper'd once more;
> But know that no cut-throats our spirits can tame,
> Nor a host of oppressors shall smother the flame.

Refrain:—　In freedom we're born, and, like sons of the brave,
> We'll never surrender,
> But swear to defend her,
> And scorn to survive, if unable to save.

> Let tyrants and minions presume to despise,
> Encroach on our rights, and make freedom their prize:
> The fruits of their rapine they never shall keep:
> Tho' vengeance may nod, yet how short is her sleep!

Refrain:—　In freedom we're born, etc.

> Not the glitter of arms, nor the dread of a fray,
> Could make us submit to their chains for a day;
> Withheld by affection, on Britons we call,—
> Prevent the fierce conflict which threatens your fall!

Refrain:—　In freedom we're born, etc.

In these years various overt acts were gradually leading the Colonies and England to the inevitable struggle. March 5, 1770, saw the Boston Massacre, and soon afterwards an anonymous British sympathizer circulated this song on a broadside, adapted to the *Derry Down* tune:

> You simple Bostonians, I'd have you beware,
> Of your Liberty Tree, I would have you take care,
> For if that we chance to return to the town,
> Your houses and stores will come tumbling down.
> 　　Derry down, down, hey derry down.

> Our fleet and our army, they soon will arrive,
> Then to a bleak island, you shall not us drive.
> In every house you shall have three or four,
> And if that will not please you, you shall have half a score.
> 　　Derry down, down, hey derry down.

The Boston Tea Party occurred in December, 1773, and soon a number of songs were devoted to the subject of tea—*The Taxed Tea, Virginia Banishing Tea,* and *The Blasted Herb.*

Early in 1775 the British Parliament rejected the petition of the Colonies, and declared that a state of rebellion existed in America. The Continental Congress appointed Washington head of the American army on June 15. As yet there was officially no thought of independence from England, but a number of the song poets made no attempt to hide such possibilities. Here is a song to the *Derry Down* tune written in 1775:

> What a court hath old England, of folly and sin,
> Spite of Chatham and Camden, Barre, Burke, Wilkes and Glynn!
> Not content with the game act, they tax fish and sea,
> And America drench with hot water and tea.
> 　　Derry down, down, hey derry down.

There's no knowing where this opposition will stop;
Some say—there's no cure but a capital chop;
And that I believe's each American's wish,
Since you've drench'd them with tea, and depriv'd 'em of fish.
    Derry down, down, hey derry down.

Three Generals [1] these mandates have borne 'cross the sea,
To deprive 'em of fish and make 'em drink tea;
In turn, sure, these freemen will boldly agree,
To give 'em a dance upon Liberty Tree,
    Derry down, down, hey derry down.

Then *freedom's* the word, both at home and abroad,
And ———— every scabbard that hides a good sword!
Our forefathers gave us this freedom in hand,
And we'll die in defence of the rights of the land.
    Derry down, down, hey derry down.

Yankee Doodle Becomes an American Song

The battles of Lexington and Concord resulted in at least one important capture by the Colonial troops, for it was at this time that *Yankee Doodle* became an American song. Since the days of the French-Indian War the song had been used by the British to make fun of the colonials, "in their ragged regimentals." The term "Yankee" was indeed an insulting epithet when Captain Preston hurled it at the crowd during the Boston Massacre. One of the favorite pastimes of the British troops had been to gather in front of the New England churches and sing *Yankee Doodle* while the church-goers were singing their Psalms. Then, in 1775, when Lord Percy led the reinforcements out of Boston on the 18th of April, bound for Lexington to help those who had gone before them to capture John Hancock and Samuel Adams, they kept step to the strains of *Yankee Doodle*. When the British retreated from Lexington and Concord, affairs were in a complete turnabout, for the Yankees appropriated the song for themselves, and sang it back at the British as they fled. Since then it has been an American song.

It is difficult to determine what words to *Yankee Doodle* may have been sung on various occasions, for there are so many different sets of verses. The stanza that is best known today:

> Yankee Doodle came to town
>   Riding on a pony
> Stuck a feather in his cap
>   And called it macaroni

may have originated as early as 1764, for the word *macaroni* probably refers to the fop or dandy who was a member of an affected class of Englishmen about 1760.

Possibly the British marched to Lexington singing the following words, for they refer to their specific errand:

> Yankee Doodle came to town
>   For to buy a fire lock;
> We will tar and feather him
>   And so we will John Hancock.

Washington's arrival at the Provincial Camp near Cambridge, July 2, 1775, may account for a reference in one of the most widely current sets of Yankee Doodle verses. O. G. Sonneck believed that the famous "Father and I Went Down to Camp" words were composed by a Harvard student, Edward Bangs, at the camp either in 1775 or 1776:

> Father and I went down to camp,
>   Along with Captin [sic] Gooding:
> There we see the men and boys
>   As thick as hasty-pudding.

Chorus

> Yankee Doodle keep it up,
>   Yankee Doodle dandy;
> Mind the music and the step,
>   And with the girls be handy.

———————

> And there we see a swamping gun,
>   Large as a log of maple,
> Upon a duced little cart,
>   A load for father's cattle.

> And every time they shoot it off,
>   It takes a horn of powder,
> It makes a noise like father's gun,
>   Only a nation louder.

> And there was Captain Washington,
>   And gentlefolks about him;
> They say he's grown so tarnal proud.
>   He will not ride without 'em.

> He got him on his meeting clothes,
>   Upon a slapping stallion;
> He set the world along in rows,
>   In hundreds and in millions.

There were other verses in similar vein. Many have supposed that because this doggerel derided the Americans, it must have been written by an Englishman, or at least by a British sympathizer. Sonneck took an opposite view:[1]

> [The text] is so full of American provincialisms, slang expressions of the time, allusions to American habits, customs, that no Englishman could have penned these verses. . . . To be a British satire on the unmilitary appearance of provincial American troops . . . the verses would have to be derisively satirical, which they are not. They breathe good-natured humor and they deal not at all with the uncouth appearance of American soldiery, but with the experience of a Yankee greenhorn in matters military who went down to a military camp and upon his return narrates in his own naive style the impressions made on him by all the sights of military pomp and circumstance.

Yankee Doodle became the battle song of the Revolution. It was sung by the troops and played as a march by their bands of fifes and drums. Throughout the war it faithfully lived up to one of the stanzas sung to its strains:

> Yankee Doodle is the tune,
>   That we all delight in;
> It suits for feasts, it suits for fun,
>   And just as well for fightin'.

Adaptations of "God Save the King"

Until 1776 *God Save the King* was the national anthem of the British Colonies, as well as of England. The complete break with the mother country came with the Declaration of Independence, and of course her national hymn ceased to be ours. But the tune was current throughout America, and it was but natural that it should be adapted to new words by American patriots. One of these sets of verses may

---

[1] Burgoyne, Clinton, Howe.

[1] In Report on "The Star Spangled Banner," "Hail Columbia," "America," "Yankee Doodle," by O. G. Sonneck; Library of Congress, 1909; Gov't. Printing Office.

possibly be dated as early as 1776. It refers to Washington's command, and to the death of Montgomery, who fell in the 1775 campaign against Quebec:

> God save America
> Free from despotic sway
> 'Till time shall end
> Hushed be the din of arms,
> And to fierce war's alarms;
> Show in all its charms
> Heaven born peace.
>
> God save great Wasihngton,
> Fair freedom's warlike son
> Long to command.
> May every enemy,
> Far from his presence flee,
> And many grim tyrant
> Fall by his hand.
>
> Thy name Montgomery,
> Still in each heart shall be
> Prais'd in each breast.
> Tho' on the fatal plain
> Thou most untimely slain,
> Yet shall thy virtue's gain
> Rescue from death.

The last verse of the version from which this copy was taken (in a manuscript book dated 1796) must have been written after 1778, when the French alliance was completed:

> Last in our song shall be
> Guardian of liberty
> Louis the king,
> Terrible god of war
> Plac'd in victorious carr [sic]
> Of fame and of Navarre,
> God save the King.

In 1779 the following song appeared in the *Pennsylvania Packet,* written "by a Dutch lady at the Hague, for the sailors of the five American vessels at Amsterdam":

> God save the Thirteen States!
> Long rule th' United States!
> God save our States!
> Make us victorious;
> Happy and glorious;
> No tyrants over us;
> God save our States!
>
> To our fam'd Washington,
> Brave Stark at Bennington,
> Glory is due.
> Peace to Montgomery's shade,
> Who as he fought and bled,
> Drew honors round his head,
> Num'rous as true.
> *etc., etc.*

In 1776, while the British were occupying Boston, her neighbor, Connecticut, expressed her encouragement with this song, published in the *Connecticut Gazette:*

> Smile, Massachusetts, smile,
> Thy virtue still outbraves
> The frowns of Britain's isle,
> And rage of home-born slaves.
> Thy free-born sons disdain their ease,
> When purchased by their liberties,

On March 17 Washington compelled Howe to evacuate Boston, and the field of military operations moved from New England. The soldiers of the New England army sang their congratulations:

> Sons of valor, taste the glories
> Of celestial liberty.
> Sing a triumph o'er the tories,
> Let the pulse of joy beat high.

One of the many verses, probably added later, referred to the Hessian troops:

> Let them rove to climes far distant,
> Situate under Arctic skies,
> Call on Hessian troops assistant,
> And the savages to rise.

The lyrics and ballads of these years refer constantly to stirring events. The Battle of Trenton, Burgoyne's proclamation on June 20, 1777, and his defeat at Saratoga in the same year, provided plenty of material for the poets of the day. In 1778 Francis Hopkinson wrote his famous poem, *The Battle of the Kegs,* satirizing the alarm of the British as they destroyed the powder kegs the Americans had floated down the Delaware to annoy British shipping. This, presumably, was sung to the tune of *Yankee Doodle.*

It was in 1778 also that Hopkinson wrote the words and music of his *Toast* to Washington. The words appeared in the *Pennsylvania Packet* of April 8 and the music was recently found in a manuscript book in Hopkinson's handwriting.[1] The *Toast,* with its music, was printed in 1799, for Benjamin Carr of Philadelphia published it in that year together with *Brother Soldiers, All Hail,* "a favorite new patriotic song in favor of Washington." The music of this latter song was the *Washington March* No. 1.[2]

Billings' "Chester"

William Billings' *Chester* has been termed the "Over There" of the Revolution, and while *Yankee Doodle* was no doubt the most used marching song, *Chester* was certainly sung by the troops throughout the Continental Army. Billings had originally written the melody as a hymn-tune, but when his second book, *The Singing Master's Assistant,* appeared in 1778, it contained *Chester* as a war song, with new words:

Chester

William Billings

Let ty-rants shake their i -- ron rod And slav-'ry clank her gall-ing chains, We'll fear them not; we trust in God, New England's God for-ev-er reigns.

---

[1] The *Toast* is published in modern form by the United States Commission for the Celebration of the 200th Anniversary of the Birth of George Washington.

[2] Page 239.

Howe and Burgoyne and Clinton, too,
  With Prescott and Cornwallis join'd,
Together plot our overthrow,
  In one infernal league combin'd.

When God inspired us for the fight,
  Their ranks were broke, their lines were forc'd,
Their Ships were Shelter'd in our sight,
  Or swiftly driven from our Coast.

The Foe comes on with haughty Stride,
  Our troops advance with martial noise,
Their Vet'rans flee before our Youth,
  And Gen'rals yield to beardless boys.

What grateful Off'ring shall we bring,
  What shall we render to the Lord?
Loud Hallelujahs let us Sing,
  And praise his name on ev'ry Chord.

The unsuccessful attempt to capture Rhode Island by Count D'Estaing of the French forces and the American General Sullivan, in August 1778, led the British, or their sympathizers, to attempt the recapture of *Yankee Doodle*, with these verses derisive of the Americans:

From Lewis Monsieur Gerard came,[1]
  To Congress in this town, sir,
They bow'd to him and he to them,
  And then they all sat down, sir.

Begar, said Monsieur, one grand coup,
  You shall bientot behold, sir;
This was believ'd as gospel true,
  And Jonathan felt bold, sir.

So Yankee Doodle did forget
  The sound of British drum, sir,
How oft it made him quake and sweat,
  In spite of Yankee rum, sir.

He took his wallet on his back,
  His rifle on his shoulder,
And vow'd Rhode Island to attack,
  Before he was much older.

In dread array their tatter'd crew,
  Advanc'd with colors spread, sir,
Their fifes played Yankee doodle, doo,
  King Hancock at their head, sir.

As Jonathan so much desir'd
  To shine in martial story,
D'Estaing with politesse retir'd,
  To leave him all the glory.

He left him what was better yet,
  At least it was more use, sir,
He left him for a quick retreat,
  A very good excuse, sir.

The Music of Yorktown

The battle of Yorktown, and the final surrender of Cornwallis, October 19, 1781, was duly commemorated in song. *Yankee Doodle* was inevitably one of the tunes that were used. One of the songs was playful:

Cornwallis led a country dance,
  The like was never seen, sir,
Much retrograde and much advance,
  And all with General Greene, sir.

---

[1]Gerard was the minister from France; the first minister from any nation to the United States.

Greene, in the South, then danc'd a set,
  And got a mighty name, sir,
Cornwallis jigg'd with young Fayette,
  But suffer'd in his fame, sir.

Quoth he, my guards are weary grown
  With footing country dances,
They never at St. James's shone,
  At capers, kicks or dances.

His music soon forgets to play—
  His feet can no more move, sir,
And all his bands now curse the day,
  They jigged to our shore, sir.

Now tories all, what can ye say?
  Come—is this not a griper,
That while your hopes are danc'd away,
  'Tis you must pay the piper.

The Scotch tune, *Maggie Lauder,* supplied the music for *Cornwallis Burgoyned:*

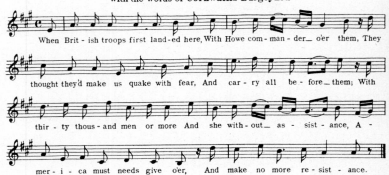

Maggie Lauder
with the words of Cornwallis Burgoyned

When Brit-ish troops first land-ed here, With Howe com-man-der-o'er them, They thought they'd make us quake with fear, And car-ry all be-fore-them; With thir-ty thous-and men or more And she with-out-as-sist-ance, A- mer-i-ca must needs give o'er, And make no more re-sist-ance.

But Washington, her glorious son,
  Of British hosts the terror,
Soon, by repeated overthrows,
  Convinc'd them of their error;
Let Princeton, and let Trenton tell,
  What gallant deeds he's done, sir,
And Monmouth's plains where hundreds fell,
  And thousands more have run, sir.

Cornwallis, too, when he approach'd
  Virginia's old dominion,
Thought he would soon her conqu'ror be;
  And so was North's opinion.
From State to State with rapid stride,
  His troops had march'd before, sir,
'Till quite elate with martial pride,
  He thought all danger's o'er, sir.

But our allies, to his surprise,
  The Chesapeake had enter'd;
And now too late, he curs'd his fate,

And wish'd he ne'er had ventur'd,
For Washington no sooner knew
  The visit he had paid her,
Than to his parent State he flew,
  To crush the bold invader.

When he sat down before the town,
  His Lordship soon surrender'd,
His martial pride he laid aside,
  And cas'd the British standard.
Gods! how this stroke will North provoke,
  And all his thoughts confuse, sir!
And how the Peers will hang their ears,
  When first they hear the news, sir.

Be peace, the glorious end of war,
  By this event effected;
And be the name of Washington,
  To latest times respected;
Then let us toast America,
  And France in union with her;
And may Great Britain rue the day
  Her hostile bands came hither.

Reference has already been made to the music played on the occasion of Cornwallis' surrender. John Fiske, the eminent historian, presents an interesting account of the scene.[1]

The British army became prisoners of war, subject to the ordinary rules of exchange. The only delicate question related to the American loyalists in the army, whom Cornwallis felt it wrong to leave in the lurch. This point was neatly disposed of by allowing him to send a ship to Sir Henry Clinton, with news of the catastrophe, and to embark in it such troops as he might think it proper to send to New York, and no questions asked. On a little matter of etiquette the Americans were more exacting. The practice of playing the enemy's tunes had always been cherished as an inalienable prerogative of British soldiery; and at the surrender of Charleston, in token of humiliation, General Lincoln's army had been expressly forbidden to play any but an American tune. Colonel Laurens, who now conducted the negotiations, directed that Lord Cornwallis's sword should be received by General Lincoln, and that the army on marching out to lay down its arms, should play a British or a German air. There was no help for it; and on the 19th of October, Cornwallis's army, 7,247 in number, with 840 seamen, marched out with colours furled and cased, while the band played a quaint old English melody, of which the significant title was "The World Turned Upside Down"!

It is well known that the American bands responded with *Yankee Doodle,* the tune that had been hurled at them in derision up to the time of Lexington and Concord. But the identity of *The World Turned Upside Down* is not so easily established. We have already read of the verses that were adapted to *Derry Down,* and the following is the version of a tune that appears in Chappell's *Popular Music of the Old Times,* under the title *When the King Enjoys his own again:*

11

The World Turned Upside Down

A number of titles were used for this tune, and *The World Turned Upside Down* was among them. It is, however, not established that this is the tune that was played at Yorktown, although it was known to be popular in Revolutionary times.

Shortly after Yorktown, in November, there occurred in Philadelphia the performance of a work that may logically be considered the first American opera. This was an "oratorical entertainment," an allegorical-political opera or dramatic cantata, consisting of an overture, arias, ensembles and choruses in praise of the American alliance with France—the work of the eminent Francis Hopkinson.[2] Although

---

[1] *The American Revolution,* by John Fiske, Vol. II, pp. 282-3: Boston, Houghton, Mifflin & Co.

[2] Sonneck, in *Francis Hopkinson and James Lyon,* calls attention to the fact that while the libretto was printed anonymously in the *Freeman's Journal,* it was signed "H" when it was reprinted years later in the *Columbian Magazine.* This fact, added to Sonneck's discovery of a fragment of a manuscript in a copy of the second volume of Hopkinson's collected poems and prose, seems to establish his authorship of *The Temple of Minerva* beyond reasonable doubt.

the music is not extant today, the libretto was printed in the *Freeman's Journal* December 19, 1781, with the explanation that it had been performed "by a company of gentlemen and ladies in the hotel of the minister of France in the presence of his Excellency General Washington and his lady."

Music to Celebrate Peace with England

The peace which was finally concluded September 3, 1783, following the separate preliminary treaty with England of November, 1782, was celebrated in many ways, and inevitably in song. In 1784 Abraham Wood of Worcester, Mass., advertised *An Anthem on Peace,* his own composition, as "published and sold by him at his house in Northborough, and at the Printing Office in Worcester." As late as 1785 (July 29), a performance was advertised for the theatre in Philadelphia of *Peace and Liberty,* "a grand serenata . . . consisting of recitation, recitative, airs, and choruses. The parts . . . selected from the works of Thompson, Sterne, etc. etc. The music, vocal and instrumental, composed by Handel, Arne, Tenducci, Fischer, Valentino, etc."

Nor were those who had fallen in battle forgotten. Successive issues of the *Pennsylvania Journal* of December, 1784, advertised a performance of "Lectures (Being a mixed entertainment of representation and harmony)," in which the opening number would be a *Monody to the memory of the chiefs who have fallen in the cause of American liberty (the music of which is entirely new) adapted to the distinct periods of the recital.* The entertainment was to conclude with a *Rondelay,* "celebrating the Independence of America. Music, Scenery and other Decorations."

The Washington Marches

The year 1784 is important because it is the earliest to which any of the historical *Washington's Marches* has been traced. It is highly probable that at least one of these marches was of Revolutionary origin, and was played by the army fife and drum corps. For many years Sonneck was inclined to the belief that they originated at a later date, and in his most extended analysis of their probable origins, he was extremely doubtful of their association with the Revolution.[1] Since writing this account (1905) he discovered in the *Massachusetts Spy* (Worcester), issue of May 27, 1784, mention of a *Washington's March* that was played at a concert in Philadelphia on May 8 of the same year. This makes the Revolutionary origin of one of the marches not only possible, but probable. It is not, however, an easy matter to determine which of the several pieces was played.

The march which is today generally referred to as *Washington's March* runs as follows:

12

Washington's March No. 1

---

[1] O. G. Sonneck: *Francis Hopkinson and James Lyon*—pp. 96-104.

A second march is commonly designated as *Washington's March at the Battle of Trenton.*

The numbers, 1 and 2, by which these marches are designated in these pages, are purely arbitrary, for our own purposes of examination; they do not assume that one or the other is necessarily the older.

It is of course unsafe to base any conclusions upon the evidence of prints and manuscripts extant today, for some item that comes to light tomorrow may upset theories based on circumstantial evidence. Yet the early prints that are available, and the many manuscript collections in libraries and private collections are tempting to those who enjoy the unravelling of mysteries.

It has generally been assumed that March No. 1, as we have termed it, is the older of the two, largely because later editions of March No. 2 give it the title of the *President's New March.* This is not a tenable theory, for both of the marches have been termed the *President's New March* or the *New President's March* on occasion. No printings of either march have been found which may safely be dated earlier than 1794. An undated volume of miscellaneous *Marches and Battles* in the Ridgway Branch of the Library Company of Philadelphia, contains March No. 1 as *Washington's March,*[1] and No. 2 as *Washington's*

Washington's March No. 2

March at the Battle of Trenton. Sonneck ventured 1794 as a possible date for this collection of marches. In 1794 or 1795 March No. 1 was printed "at G. Willig's Musical Magazine" in Philadelphia, "as performed at the New Theatre."

While there may have been discovered no prints of March No. 2 earlier than this issue of March No. 1 by Willig, two manuscript items in the Library of Congress are of extreme interest, and possibly of importance. One of these is *Henry Beck's Flute Book,* a manuscript volume of marches and popular airs scored for flute solo and sometimes for two flutes. On the first page of this volume is a pencil date, 1786. If this date is plausible, it would probably indicate the year in which the copying was begun, and the fact that some of the later tunes are known to have originated after 1790 would show that the work of transcribing covered a number of years.

In the early part of the book, on page 50, is a piece called *General Wayne's March,* which is none other than our March No. 2, commonly called *Washington's March at the Battle of Trenton.* This may prove

[1] As part of *America and Brittania, Peace.* "A New March composed by R. Taylor (and so arranged as to Harmonize perfectly with Washington's March played both together.)" Taylor came to America in 1792, so this publication must be dated after that time.

nothing, or it may prove a great deal, but it does tend to weaken th belief that March No. 1 is the older. General Wayne, of course, wa the Mad-Anthony Wayne who added to his reputation by stormin Stony Point in 1779. The question whether this march was originall written to commemorate Wayne, and later adapted to honoring Wash ington, provides material for interesting speculation.

Whatever the origin, and whatever the precedence, these two march were played, published, and reprinted for years. Often they were bot included on the same sheet of music. The following table shows th parallel appearances of the two marches well into the nineteenth cen tury:

	March No. 1	March No. 2
1786 (?)		*General Wayne's March* (Beck's Flute Book.)
1791 (?)		*Genl. Washington's Mar* (in a Mss. Book in the L brary of Congress.)
1794 (?)	*Washington's March* (in undated collection of *Marches and Battles*; see text above.)	*Washington's March at t Battle of Trenton* (in u dated collection of *March and Battles*; see text above
1794—5	*Washington's March,* as performed at the New Theatre, Phila. (G. Willig's Musical Magazine.)	
1797		*Washington's March at t Battle of Trenton,* as part James Hewitt's *Battle Trenton* Sonata.
1798 (?)	*The New President's March,* (New York; J. Paff's Music Store.)	*Washington's March* (Ne York; J. Paff's Music Store
1798—1801		*Washington's March* (N. Y Geo. Gilfert, 177 Broadway
After 1798		*General Washington's Mar* (Boston, G. Graupner, Franklin Place.)
1799	*Brother Soldiers, All Hail* ("a new patriotic song in favor of Washington", to the tune of *Washington's March*: Phila., Benj. Carr.)	*Washington's March* (in Be lamy's Band Book, Mss. L brary of Congress, scored two treble clefs and one ba clef.)
1799—1800	*The New President's March* (N. Y., J. Hewitt, 23 Maiden Lane.)	*Washington's March* (N. Y J. Hewitt, 23 Maiden Lane
1802	*Washington's March* (in the *Flute Preceptor,* or *Columbian Instructor,* improved by R. Shaw, Philadelphia.)	*President's New March* (the *Flute Preceptor,* etc.)
Ca. 1805	*Washington's March* (in the *Compleat Tutor for the Fife,* Phila., Geo. Willig.)	*Washington's March* (in Collection of *Favorit Marches,* arranged for t flute and violin. N. Y., Hewitt's Musical Repositor 59 Maiden Lane.)
After 1805		*Washington's March* (in Wi lig's *Instruction for the Ge man Flute.* Phila., G. Wi lig's Musical Magazine, 1 Chestnut Street.)
1808		*General Washington's Mar* (in the *Village Fifer,* No. arranged for two fifes. E eter, N. H.)

	March No. 1	March No. 2		March No. 1	March No. 2
1814—16	*Washington's Grand March* (Phila., A. Bacon & Co., 11 So. 4th Street.)		1844—57		*Washington's March* (Boston, Oliver Ditson.)
1815—18	*Washington's March* (scored for 2 flutes and piano in *The Martial Music of Camp Dupont,* arranged by Raynor Taylor, Phila., Geo. E. Blake, 13 So. 5th Street.)		1846—7		*Washington's March* (arr. as a duet for the Pianoforte by M. Hall, N. Y., Firth Hall & Pond, 239 Broadway.)
1818	*Washington's March*[1] (in *Amerikanische National-Marsche fur das Piano-Forte.* Leipzig, C. F. Peters.)		1847—51	*Washington's March* (Phila., E. Ferrett & Co., 40 So. 8th Street.)	
After 1819		*March at the Battle of Trenton,* (Phila., Geo. Willig, 171 Chestnut Street.)	Ca. 1852		*Washington's March* (N. Y., Firth, Pond & Co., 1 Franklin Square.)
Before 1820	*Washington's March* (Phila., G. E. Blake.)	*Washington's March at the Battle of Trenton* (Phila., G. E. Blake.)	1854	*Washington's March* (with brilliant variations, Ch. Grobe, Phila., Lee & Walker, 722 Chestnut St.)	
After 1820		*Washington's March* (N. Y., N. Thurston.)	1858	*Washington's March* (arrangement for orchestra in J. W. Moore's *Star* collection, Boston, Oliver Ditson.)	
182(?)	*Washington's March* (Baltimore, G. Willig.)	*Washington's March at the Battle of Trenton* (Baltimore, G. Willig.)	1861	*Washington's March* (in *American Medley,* Ch. Grobe, Boston, Oliver Ditson.)	
Ca. 1830		*Washington's March* (Mss. arrangement for brass band by Chas. Zeuner, Library of Congress.)	1863—1877	*Washington's Grand March* (N. Y., Wm. Pond & Co., 547 Broadway.)	*Washington's March* (N. Y., Wm. Pond & Co., 547 Broadway.)
After 1832	*Washington's Grand March* (N. Y., Firth & Hall, 1 Franklin Sq.)	*Washington's March* (N. Y., Firth & Hall, 1 Franklin Sq.)	Before 1864		*Battle of Trenton March* (N. Y., S. T. Gordon, 538 Broadway.)
Before 1833		*Washington's March* (Boston, C. Bradlee, Washington St.)	1864—9	*Washington's March* (N. Y., S. T. Gordon, 706 Broadway.)	*Washington's March at the Battle of Trenton* (N. Y., S. T. Gordon, 706 Broadway.)
1834—9		*Washington's March* (N. Y., Atwill's, 201 Broadway.)	1876	*Washington's Grand March* (arr. by Septimus Winner, Boston, Oliver Ditson Co.)	
Before 1836	*Washington's Grand March* (Arr. for the Spanish Guitar by J. B. L'Hulier, Phila., Geo. Willig, 171 Chestnut St.)				
184(?)		*Washington's March* (Boston, G. P. Reed, 17 Tremont Road.)			
1842	*Washington's Grand March* (and the *National Melody, Yankee Doodle,* with variations, for the Spanish Guitar, Phila., Geo. Willig.)				
After 1843		*Washington's March* (Boston, C. H. Keith, 67-69 Court Street.)			

This parallel list shows a number of things, principally the enormous and continued popularity of both marches, evidenced by the many editions extending to the latter part of the nineteenth century. Also, according to the number of printings that the author has tabulated and examined, March No. 2 was issued more often than No. 1. Another apparent fact is interesting—March No. 2 has been named *Washington's March* far more often than it has been called *Washington's March at the Battle of Trenton.*

While these two marches seem to have had the widest distribution, there were of course other Washington Marches, quick-steps, *Washington Guard* quicksteps, etc. One of these further marches is worthy of comment:

[1] Following the publication abroad of these American marches, the following review appeared in the *Allgemeine Musikalische Zeitung* (Leipzig), September 13, 1820:

These may well be the first musical compositions from North America to reach the Old World! As is well known, there is little demand there for artists (mechanical artists excepted), and of late they have even been expressly warned against immigration. It is therefore not surprising that these marches should not rank very high as musical compositions *per se.* Nor is it any more surprising that these pieces, having arisen and grown popular in that country, where utility is of course considered the principal, if not the sole requirement, should be most practically devised for the purpose at hand—as marches, for marching, in all sorts of march-time; and that in answering the broader requirements, the stimulation of courage and the warlike disposition in general, more attention should have been paid to the outward character of the music (fanfares and trumpet movements) than to the inward. In all these respects (if not in others) the reviewer finds the present work really interesting and believes that others will find it so too. . . .

14

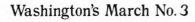

Washington's March No. 3

This piece may be of little importance, for few prints of it are extant. It was included in the *Complete Fifer's Museum* (printed in Northampton, Mass., 1807) and in 1825 it was issued in sheet music form by J. T. Siegling of Charleston. Yet there is at least one fact that renders it worthy of consideration. While *Genl. Wayne's March* (identical with our March No. 2) appears on Page 50 of *Beck's Flute Book*, this third march is found on page 12 of the same collection, with the title, *General Washington's March*. March No. 3 may therefore have a claim to an early Revolutionary origin, even though it dropped from view far sooner than the others.

The authorship of none of these Washington Marches has been established, although there have been many claims on behalf of Francis Hopkinson as the composer of one of them. The following item appeared in the January, 1859, issue of the *Historical Magazine*:

> . . . I have . . . reason to believe that the "Washington March" generally known by that title . . . was composed by the Hon. Francis Hopkinson, senior, having seen it in a manuscript book of his own handwriting among others of his known compositions.   J. C.

"J. C." may have been Joseph Carr, a music publisher, well qualified to make such a statement, but unfortunately none of the Hopkinson manuscript books now extant, even the recently discovered book containing the *Toast* to Washington, contain any trace of a *Washington's March*. Hopkinson's authorship must rest upon tradition until further evidence is available.

Miscellaneous Songs in Honor of Washington

The songs of the years following the Revolution show to what a great extent Washington was idolized. A "New Song" which appeared in the *Philadelphia Continental Journal* of April 7, 1786, was adapted to the tune of *God Save the King*:

> God save great Washington
> His worth from ev'ry tongue
> Demands applause:
> Ye tuneful powers combine,
> And each true Whig now join
> Whose heart did ne'er resign
> The glorious cause.

On the occasion of the General's birthday in 1786, the "adopted Sons" performed a work especially written for the event—an *Ode on the Birthday of his Excellency George Washington*"; "celebrated by the Adopted Sons at the Pennsylvania Coffee House in Philadelphia, composed by a member of that society". The words, which were printed in the *Pennsylvania Packet* two days later, hailed Washington as a patron of music—

> "Parent of soothing airs and lofty strains—"

In the same year William Selby, an English musician of Boston, composed an *Ode in Honour of General Washington*, performed at a concert in that city, April 27.

The "Federal March" to Celebrate the Ratification of the Constitution

From May 25 to September 17, 1787, the Constitutional Convention held its stormy sessions in Philadelphia. By June 6, 1788, ten of the States had ratified the document and "come under the Federal roof". July 4 of that year was a gala day in Philadelphia, duly commemorated in music, for Alexander Reinagle contributed the *Federal March* which was "performed in the grand procession", "composed in honor of the ratification of the Federal Constitution by Ten of the States".[1]

[1] In 1898 the *Federal March* was revived, when it was played in Philadelphia, October 27, during a military parade before President McKinley.

15

Federal March

Alexander Reinagle

Maestoso

In the Fall of 1788 another work was advertised, celebrating the same subject—the *New Constitutional March* and *Federal Minuet*, "composed by Mr. Sicard, adapted to the pianoforte, violin and German flute".

Francis Hopkinson Dedicates Eight Songs to Washington

In the same year Francis Hopkinson published the eight songs that he dedicated to George Washington. The father of our country wrote many charming letters, but few were more gracious than that addressed to Hopkinson, accepting the dedication:

> . . . But, my dear Sir, if you had any doubts about the reception which your work would meet with—or had the smallest reason to think that you should meet with any assistance to defend it—you have not acted with your usual good judgment in the choice of a coadjutator, for . . . what alas! can I do to support it? I can neither sing one of the songs, nor raise a note on any instrument to convince the unbelieving. But I have, however, one argument which will prevail with persons of true estate (at least in America)—I can tell them that it is the production of Mr. Hopkinson.

While there were actually eight songs in the collection, the volume was entitled *Seven Songs*, and contained under the last number a footnote explaining that the author had decided to include it after the title page had been engraved. The titles of the songs, as well as their poetic and musical content, show the influence of the contemporary English style: *Come, fair Rosina, come away; My love is gone to*

FEDERAL MARCH—(Continued)

; Beneath a weeping willow's shade;[1] Enraptur'd I gaze; when my
elia is by; See, down Maria's blushing cheek; O'er the hills far away,
the mirth of the morn; My gen'rous heart disdains, the slave of love
be; and The trav'ler benighted and lost, o'er the mountains pur-
es his lone way.

Hopkinson sent a copy of the collection to Washington, and an-
her to his friend Thomas Jefferson, who was then in Paris. In his
tter to Jefferson the composer said he thought that the last song, "if
ayed very slow, and sung with Expression", was "forcibly pathetic—
least in my fancy". Jefferson thought so, too, for he replied:

I will not tell you how much they have pleased us, nor how
well the last of them merits praise for its pathos, but relate a
fact only, which is that while my elder daughter was playing
it on a harpsichord, I happened to look toward the fire & saw
the younger one all in tears. I asked her if she was sick? She
said "no; but the tune was so mournful".

nd that, we may be sure, was indeed a compliment!

Music of the Inaugural Tour

On February 4, 1789, the electoral college chose Washington as
the first president of the United States. On April 14 he received
official notification at Mount Vernon, and immediately started his
memorable journey to New York, where he was inaugurated April 30.

The music of these times shows his travels and his triumphs. As
he passed beneath the Triumphal Arch erected on the bridge at Trenton (April 21) he was greeted by a *Chorus*, "sung by a number of
young girls, dressed in white, decked in wreaths and chaplets, holding
baskets of flowers in their hands." The words, by Richard Howell,
were a welcome and a tribute:

> Welcome mighty chief! once more
> Welcome to this grateful shore:
> Now no mercenary Foe
> Aims again the fatal blow.
> Aims at thee the fatal blow.
>
> Virgins fair and Matrons grave,
> Those thy conquering Arms did save,
> Build for *the* Triumphal Bowers
> Strew, ye fair, his way with flowers,
> Strew your Hero's way with flowers.

"As they sung these lines", the contemporary account continues, "they
strewed the flowers before the General, who halted until the Chorus
was finished. The astonishing contrast between his former and actual
situation *on the same spot*—the elegant state with which the Triumphal Arch was adorned at the time, and the innocent appearance of
the white-robed Choir, who met him with his gratulatory Song, made
a lively and strong Impression on his mind."

C. E. Godfrey, in an article in the *Trenton Sunday Advertiser*,
December 29, 1912, proved conclusively that these verses were sung
at Trenton to the Music of Handel's *See the Conquering Hero Comes*,
from *Judas Maccabeus*. In connection with this article Godfrey
printed Howell's words with the Handel music, thus showing that it
was entirely possible to sing them to this composition. The use of
several notes for a single syllable was thoroughly characteristic of the
period.

A few months later (September 22) the program of the New York
Subscription Concert offered a number which was advertised as "a
chorus to the words which were sung as Gen. Washington passed the
bridge at Trenton—The music now composed by Mr. Reinagle." This
setting is probably identical with the published *Chorus Sung before*

General Washington, "as he passed under the triumphal arch raised at the bridge at Trenton, April 21, 1789. Set to music and dedicated by permission to Mrs. Washington by A. Reinagle. Price ½ dollar. Philadelphia. Printed for the author, and sold by H. Rice, Market Street." Yet it is clear that Reinagle's was a later setting; not the music used at Trenton.

The President's March

It is not known what music, if any, was played at Washington's inauguration ceremony, when he delivered his famous inaugural address in Federal Hall, New York. It may have been at this time, however, that the famous *President's March,* later used by Joseph Hopkinson as the music for *Hail Columbia,* came into being, although it is generally assumed that the piece was not composed until after 1790.

17

The President's March

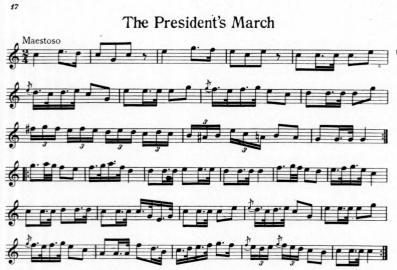

For years a controversy has been waged on the authorship of the *President's March,* and claims have been advanced for Francis Hopkinson, Philip Roth, and Philip Phile. Hopkinson's authorship has never been seriously considered by authorities, and Roth's is impossible to verify. Sonneck believed that Phile's claim was established beyond reasonable doubt by the appearance, a number of years ago, of an unnumbered page in the collection of former Governor Pennypacker of Philadelphia. This page had evidently been torn from an engraved music collection, and it bore two marches. One of them was the *President's March* by Pheil, the other a *March* by Moller. The latter piece indicates that the sheet belonged to one of the publications issued by the firm of Moller and Capron in Philadelphia in 1793.

Whoever wrote it, and whenever it first appeared, the *President's March* was the most popular piece of the early days of the United States. It was played on all occasions, by bands and orchestras. Leaders of the music in the theatres could not avoid playing it, for often their rendering of classics was interrupted by cat-calls and demands from the gallery for the *President's March.*

The 4th of July in 1789 was doubly celebrated, for not only was it the annual observance of the Declaration of Independence, it was the country's first Fourth as a nation. This was indicated by an *Ode for American Independence,* printed in the *Massachusetts Magazine* of July 1789—the words by Daniel George, the music by Horatio Garnet. The first verse refers to the Declaration of Independence, and its signing by Massachusetts' son, John Hancock:

18

The next three verses recount the history of the Revolution, fro Burgoyne's defeat at Saratoga, to the surrender of Cornwallis at Yor town. The sixth verse deals with the present situation:

> Now from Mount Vernon's peaceful shades again,
> The Hero comes, with thousands in his train:
>   'Tis Washington, the Great
>   Must fill the chair of state,
>   Columbia cries:
> Each tongue the glorious name re-echoes to the skies.

Refrain: Fly, swift, wing'd fame, etc.

The final stanza hails Washington and peace:

> Now shall the useful arts of peace prevail,
> And commerce flourish, flavor'd by each gale;
>   Discord, forever cease,
>   Let Liberty and Peace,
>   And Justice reign;
> For Washington protects the scientific train.

Refrain: Fly, swift, wing'd fame, etc.

Music Performed During the New England Tour of 178

From October 15 to November 13 Washington was occupied wi his famous tour of New England. When he arrived in Boston, O tober 24, he was greeted at the Triumphal Arts by the singing of Ode to Columbia's Favourite Son, performed by the Independe Musical Society:

19

Ode to Columbia's Favourite Son

There view Columbia's Favourite Son,
   Her Father, Saviour, Friend and Guide!
There see th' Immortal Washington!
   His Country's Glory, Boast and Pride!

In the Christian Advocate of February 22, 1900, a piece of music was printed which was called Holden's *Ode to Washington.* Oliver Holden was the composer of *Coronations,* the famous hymn-tune. This Ode is of particular interest because of the explanatory note, signed by Benjamin B. Davis of Brookline, which prefaced the printing of the piece in the *Advocate:*

> Desirous of perpetuating the memory of Washington, I wrote this music from memory, of an Ode sung October 24, 1789, on the occasion of President Washington's arrival at the Old State House, Boston. Having learned it from my Father in 1805 when ten years of age, he being one of the Chorus singers.

With the exception of minor variations, this *Ode,* written from memory by Mr. Davis, is identical with the *Ode to Columbia's Favourite Son* "sung by the Independent Musical Society," and printed anonymously in the October 1789 issue of the *Massachusetts Magazine.* This seems to establish Holden's authorship.

At the Stone (King's) Chapel, three days after the welcome at the State House, another *Ode* was performed "before the President of the United States of America," the words "by Mr. Brown of Boston":

Recitative

Behold the man! whom virtues raise
   The highest of the patriot throng!
To him the muse her homage pays,
   And tunes the gratulory song.

Air

Illustrious Visitant! design'd
   By heaven's invincible decree
T'enoble and exalt the mind,
   And teach a nation to be free;

Welcome, thrice welcome to the spot;
   Where once thy conq'ring banners wav'd,
O never be thy praise forgot,
   By those thy matchless valour sav'd.

Other works were issued at the time of Washington's Boston visit, one of them an *Ode to the President of the United States,* "By a Lady. The musick set by Mr. Hans Gram." Gram was a German musician who had come to Boston to live, and the *Ode* was printed in the *Massachusetts Magazine* of October 1789, on the page immediately following the *Ode to Columbia's Favourite Son.*

In the following years there were many tributes to Washington in music and song. Samuel Holyoke, a New England psalmodist and compiler of hymn collections, published in 1790 a song, *Washington,* which praised the hero's part in the struggle for liberty. *Washington's Counsel Forever Huzza!* was the title of a song "written, composed and to be sung by Mr. Clifford," in the comic opera, "The Farmer," at the Charleston Theatre on January 22, 1794. *Washington,* a song written by Mrs. Pownall, a favorite actress and songwriter of the period, was advertised as part of a concert given in Boston, August , 1794. *A Song on General Washington,* by Alexander Juhan, printed with a set of six songs in 1794, commenced with the allegorical line:

"On the white cliffs of Albion, reclining sat fame—"

Mrs. Pownall wrote and sang another song in tribute to Washington in 1796—*Washington and Liberty.* It was performed after the play at the City Theatre in Charleston on the President's birthday.

Songs in Honor of Other Revolutionary Characters

Other historical characters of the day were commemorated. When Lafayette returned to America in 1824 and 1825 many songs and instrumental pieces were written in his honor, but some were composed in the latter eighteenth century too. *Young's Vocal and Instrumental Miscellany,* published in Philadelphia in 1794, contained *Lafayette,* "a new song". When John Hancock died in 1793, there was published a Sonnet, "for the fourteenth of October, 1793. When were entombed the remains of his Excellency John Hancock, Esq., late Governor and Commander in Chief of the Commonwealth of Massachusetts. The music taken from an oratorio by the famous Groun of Berlin. The lines written and adapted by Hans Gram, Organist of Brattle Street Church, in Boston."

A number of songs were devoted to Major André,—*Major André Complaint,* printed at Carr & Co.'s Musical Repository in 1794; *Major André,* a song which appeared in *American Musical Miscellany* (1789), and several others.

In the final decade of the century much music was written which harked back to the Revolution. Descriptive "sonatas," and "overtures" were very popular in those days, and composers tried to write music which would be descriptive of events and scenes, much in the fashion of modern writers of so-called "program" music. One of these pieces achieved considerable vogue in America, *The Battle of Trenton,*[1] a sonata for pianoforte dedicated to General Washington, and first published in 1797. The composition was the work of James Hewitt, an English musician who came to America in 1792 and became active in the musical life of New York and Boston. The various sections of this piece were elaborate in their descriptiveness:

> Introduction—The Army in motion—General Orders—Acclamation of the Americans—Drums beat to Arms.
> Attack—cannons—bomb. Defeat of the Hessians—Flight of the Hessians—Begging Quarter—The Fight Renewed—General Confusion—The Hessians surrender themselves prisoners of War—Articles of Capitulation Signed—Grief of Americans for the loss of their companions killed in the engagement.
> Yankee Doodle—Drums and Fifes—Quick Step for the Band —Trumpets of Victory—General Rejoicing.

Much music of a general patriotic nature was written and published in these years. Benjamin Carr's *Federal Overture,* first played at the Cedar Street Theatre, Philadelphia, September 1794, was important because its published version (1795) is the earliest known printing of *Yankee Doodle* in America. Several popular airs were included in the Overture—*Marseilles hymn; Ca Ira; O dear, what can the matter be?; Rose tree; Carmagnole; President's March,* and *Yankee Doodle.*

Reinagle's *America, Commerce and Freedom* was frequently sung. It praised the life of the sailor, and toasted American shipping. This song was published in 1794, and was advertised as "sung by Mr. Darley, junior, the Ballet Pantomime of The Sailor's Landlady."

There were other "Federal Overtures." In Providence, Rhode Island, the *New Federal Overture* "composed by Mons: Leaumont" was advertised for performance at the New Theatre (1795). P. A. Van Hagen, in Boston, composed a *Federal Overture* which was played at the Haymarket Theatre in October, 1797.

One of the most elaborate works was the setting by James Hewitt of some verses by a Mr. Millns, *The Federal Constitution and the*

---

[1] Included in *Music from the Days of Geo. Washington,* issued by the United States Commission for the Celebration of the 200th Anniversary of the Birth of George Washington.

President Forever, "adapted to the joint tunes of *Washington's March* and *Yankee Doodle.*" This was published in 1798. A few of the stanzas suffice to show the author's good intentions, if not his skill as a poet:

> Poets may sing of their Helicon streams,
> Their Gods and their Heroes are fabulous dreams;
> They ne'er sang a line
> Half so grand, so divine,
> As the glorious toast,
> We Columbians boast,
> The Federal Constitution boys, and Liberty forever.

> Montgomery, Warren still live in our songs,
> Like them our young heroes shall spurn at our wrongs—
> The world shall admire
> The zeal and the fire
> Which blaze in the toast
> We Columbians boast
> The Federal Constitution and its advocates forever.

> Fame's trumpet shall swell in Washington's praise
> And time grant a furlough to lengthen his days;
> May health weave the thread
> Of delight round his head—
> No nation can boast
> Such a name—such a toast—
> The Federal Constitution boys, and Washington forever.

The Stormy 1790's

The years after 1790 were trying for the young American republic. The French Revolution started in 1789. In 1793 France was at war with Prussia, Austria and England. On April 22 of that year Washington made his famous proclamation of neutrality, but there was a strong element in this country who thought we should go to war with England on the side of France, to repay the French for their aid in our struggle for independence. In the same year "Citizen Genet" arrived in Charleston and proceeded thence to Philadelphia as Minister from France. He did all he could to undermine Washington's attitude of neutrality, and his recall was demanded.

England began to seize the American ships in French trade, and the Jay treaty of 1794 effected merely a compromise with Great Britain on neutral trade. After John Adams began his presidency, France commenced raids on American shipping in reprisal for the Jay Treaty and other actions contrary to the old alliance. The French Directory seemed determined to take as overbearing an attitude towards America as she was taking against the small states of Europe. In the notorious "X.Y.Z." affair of 1797, our ministers to France were so insulted and humiliated that Adams declared: "I will never send another minister to France without assurances that he will be received, respected and honored as the representative of a free, powerful and independent nation."

Preparations were made for hostilities, and during the next few years an actual state of war existed with France, although it was never formally declared. There were a few minor naval engagements. On July 4, 1798, Washington was appointed commander-in-chief of the military forces of the nation.

It is necessary to know these events if we are to understand the many references to contemporary affairs in the music of the closing years of the century, for the songs of the day were closely associated with the history of the times. In the early 1790's a number of songs appeared pertaining to the French Revolution. One of them was by the English composer, Storace, entitled *Captivity,* "a ballad supposed to be sung by Marie Antoinette during her confinement." The American edition of this song was published by Carr in Philadelphia in 1793. Another of Carr's publications in the same year was "favorite sonato by Elfort," *The Bastile.* Then, too, there were American printings of the *Marseillaise, La Carmagnole and Ca Ira,* stirring songs of the French Revolution.

"Hail Columbia"

Nearly all of the patriotic music of 1798 and 1799 related to our break with France. *Hail Columbia* is the most important song of that time, because it has lived to our own day, and until the Spanish American War it shared honors with the *Star Spangled Banner* as our national anthem. The music of *Hail Columbia* is the *President's March,* and the words were written by Joseph Hopkinson, son of Francis Hopkinson. Hopkinson later told how he came to write *Hail Columbia:*

"Hail Columbia" was written in the summer of 1798, when war with France was thought to be inevitable. Congress was then in session in Philadelphia, debating upon that important subject, and acts of hostility had actually taken place. The contest between England and France was still raging, and the people of the United States were divided into parties for the one side or the other, some thinking that policy and duty required us to espouse the cause of "republican France," as she was called, while others were for connecting ourselves with England, under the belief that she was the great preservative power of good principles and safe government. The violation of our rights by both belligerents was forcing us from the wise and just policy of President Washington, which was to do equal justice to both but to part with neither, and to preserve an honest and strict neutrality between them. The prospect of a rupture with France was exceedingly offensive to the portion of the people who espoused her cause, and the violence of the spirit of party had never risen higher, I think, not so high, in our country, as it did at that time upon that question.

The theatre was then open in our city [Philadelphia]. A young man belonging to it [Gilbert Fox], whose talent was high as a singer, was about to take a benefit. I had known him when he was at school. On this acquaintance he called on me one Saturday afternoon, his benefit being announced for the following Monday. His prospects were very disheartening; but he said that if he could get a patriotic song adapted to the "President's March" he did not doubt a full house: that the poets of the theatrical corps had been trying to accomplish it, but had not succeeded. I told him I would try what I could do for him. He came the next afternoon, and the song, such as it is, was ready for him. The object of the author was to get up an American spirit which should be independent of, and above the interests, passions and policy of both belligerents, and look and feel exclusively for our honor and rights. No allusion is made to France or England, or the quarrel between them, or to the question of which was most in fault in their treatment of us. Of course, the song found favor with both parties, for both were American, at least neither could disown the sentiments and feelings it indicated. Such is the history of this song, which has endured infinitely beyond the expectation of the author, as it is beyond any merit it can boast of except that of being truly and exclusively patriotic in its sentiment and spirit.

"Adams and Liberty"

Another song, *Adams and Liberty,* was important for several reasons. It was one of the songs of the 1798 trouble with France, it showed the temper of the time, and it used for its music the English tune, *To Anacreon in Heaven,* now the melody of the *Star Spangled Banner.* This music has been attributed to Samuel Arnold, an Englishman who was composer to His Majesty's Chapel and the compiler of many ballad operas, but it is more probable that it was composed by John Stafford Smith, Arnold's successor at the Chapel Royal, about 1775. The song became known in America soon after it was written, and as a drinking song it became the official lyric of the several Anacreontic societies in this country. From 1797 the tune appeared in many versions, generally adapted to patriotic words.

In June, 1798, the Massachusetts Charitable Fire Society, at its banquet in Boston, sang a song it had commissioned Robert Treat Paine to write for the occasion. This was *Adams and Liberty,* and tradition has it that Paine received $750 for his copyright. The author's name was originally Thomas, but not wishing to be confused with the freethinker of that name, he petitioned Congress to allow him to assume the name of his father, a signer of the Declaration of Independence, Robert Treat Paine.

The words were intensely patriotic:

> Ye sons of Columbia, who bravely have fought,
>   For those rights, which unstain'd from your Sires have descended,
> May you long taste the blessings your valor has bought
>   And your sons reap the soil, which your fathers defended,
>   Mid the reign of mild peace,
>   May your nation increase,
> With the glory of Rome, and the wisdom of Greece;

Refrain: And ne'er may the sons of Columbia be slaves,
    While the earth bears a plant, or the sea rolls its waves.

> Should the tempest of War overshadow our land,
>   Its bolts could ne'er rend Freedom's temple asunder;
> For unmov'd at its portal, would Washington stand,
>   And repulse with his breast, the assault of his Thunder!
>   His sword, from the sleep
>   Of its scabbard, would leap
> And conduct, with its point, every flash to the deep.

Refrain: For ne'er shall the sons, etc.

> Let Fame to the world sound America's voice;
>   No Intrigue can her sons from their Government steer;
> Her pride is her Adams—his laws are her choice,
>   And shall flourish till Liberty slumber forever!
>   Then unite, heart and hand.
>   Like Leonidas' band,
> And swear to the God of the ocean and land,

Refrain: That ne'er shall the sons, etc.

Another song of 1798 linked the two heroes of the day, and referred to Adams at the head of the government, and Washington in command of the military forces. This was *Adams and Washington,* by P. A. Van Hagen, junior, printed in 1798 at the composer's "Musical Magazine," in Boston, where, we learn from the sheet music, "may also be had the new patriotic songs of Washington & Independence, Hail Patriots All, Our Country is our Ship, the Ladies Patriotic Song." Whatever the poet may have lacked in literary gifts, he made up in enthusiasm:

> Columbia's brave friends with alertness advance
>   Her rights to defend in defiance of France
> To volatile fribbles we never will yield,
>   While John's at the Helm, and George rules the field.

One of the stanzas referred to the tribute demanded of our ministers to France, a tribute that amounted to a bribe:

> By paying those vultures large tributes in gold,
>   I should think our dear country in some measure sold:
> Columbia the fair, they can ne'er overwhelm,
>   While George rules the field, and her John's at the helm.

The naval battles with France, minor engagements though they were, found record in music. *The Constellation,* companion of the *United States,* the *Constitution* and other frigates of our navy, overtook and captured the French boat *L'Insurgent.* Soon Gilbert Fox, who had been the first to sing *Hail Columbia,* presented at the theatre in Philadelphia another new song, *Huzza for the Constellation.* Truxtun, captain of the *Constellation,* was commemorated with *Truxtun's Victory,* a song "written by Mrs. Rowson" and published by Van Hagen in Boston in 1799. *General Pinckney's March* "composed by Mons. Foucard" and played at Charleston in 1799, honored the General Pinckney whom Washington had appointed as one of his chief subordinates when he accepted the post of commander-in-chief.[1]

Music Composed to Mourn the Death of Washington

Nothing shows more forcibly how greatly Washington was loved by his countrymen during his lifetime than the deep sorrow of the nation when he died, December 14, 1799, and nothing proves this sorrow more effectively than the many dirges and elegies which were

20

Dead March and Monody

Benjamin Carr

composed immediately after his passing away. Twelve days after he died, Benjamin Carr had ready for performance a *Dead March and Monody* which was performed at the memorial services held in the

---

[1] Pinckney was also the minister whom France had refused to receive, as well as one of the X. Y. Z. commissioners, credited with the "not a cent for tribute" slogan, which some authorities claim he did not say.

Lutheran Church in Philadelphia. This music was printed soon after, and it was truly dignified and in keeping with the character of the man it honored. It is interesting to note how much this piece reflects the European music of the period. It is reminiscent of the style of the later Haydn, and it seems to anticipate Beethoven, who at this time was only twenty-nine, and little known in America.

New England paid many musical tributes, among them *Hark from the Tombs, etc.*, and *Beneath the Honors, etc.*, adapted from Dr. Watts and set to music by Samuel Holyoke, A.M. Performed at New-buryport, 2nd of January, 1800. The day on which the citizens unitedly expressed their unbounded veneration for the memory of our beloved Washington.

Van Hagen composed *A Funeral Dirge* "on the death of General Washington," and Abraham Wood commenced his *Funeral Elegy,* "on the death of General George Washington. Adapted to the 22d of February" with the lines:

"Know ye not that a great man hath fall'n today?"

Oliver Holden contributed several works to the memorial services. His anthem, *From Vernon's Mount Behold the Hero Rise,* was per-formed as "part of the tributory honors to George Washington" held at Old South Meeting House in Boston, January, 1800. He also wrote a *Dirge,* "or Sepulcral Service memorating the sublime virtues and distinguished talents of George Washington. Composed and set to music at the request of the Mechanic's Association, for performance on Saturday the 22 inst." (February, 1800). Holden is also known to be the composer of a collection of *Sacred Dirges, Hymns and An-thems,* "commemorative of the death of General George Washington, the guardian of his country and the friend of man. An original com-position by a citizen of Massachusetts."

Yet, as we have seen, it was not alone at his death that Washington was extolled by music. His talents, his achievements, and the esteem and gratitude of the whole American people were sung throughout his whole career.

DEAD MARCH AND MONODY—(*Continued*)

20 con.
Monody— Sung by Miss Broadhurst
Slow

Sad are the ti - dings ru - mour tells, a grate - ful peo - ple
mourn his___ end. A - midst the_brave and just he__ dwells, A
na-tion's fa-ther and its_friend.

2.

With honor crown'd mature in age
He fell the wonder of mankind
Laden with laurels left the stage
Nor leaves alas! his like behind.

3.

Seated in bliss supreme on high
O spirit dear attend our pray'r.
Our guardian angel still be nigh
Make thy lov'd land thy heav'n care.

II. A Catalogue of Authentic Eighteenth Century Music In Modern Editions

1. MUSIC PUBLISHED AND DISTRIBUTED BY THE UNITED STATES FOR THE 200TH ANNIVERSARY OF THE MIRTH OF GEORGE WASHINGTON

MUSIC FROM THE DAYS OF GEORGE WASHINGTON

(Printed as a complete collection)

MILITARY AND PATRIOTIC

The President's March . . . . Philip Phile (d. 1793?)
    (Arranged by James Hewitt)
Washington's March . . . .
General Burgoyne's March . . . .
Brandywine Quick-Step . . . .
Successful Campaign . . . .
The Toast (1778) (to Washington) . . . . Francis Hopkinson
                                      (1737-1791)
The Battle of Trenton, a Favorite Historical
    Military Sonata, Dedicated to General Wash-
    ington (1797) . . . . .James Hewitt
                                        (1770-1827)

CONCERT AND DANCE MUSIC

Sonata (First Movement) . . . . Alexander Reinagle
                                        (1756-1809)
Minuet and Gavotte .Alexander Reinagle
Two Minuets (Danced before General and Mrs.
    Washington) (1792) . . . . .Pierre Landrin Duport
Rondo (1787) . . . . .William Brown

SONGS AND OPERATIC MUSIC

Beneath a Weeping Willow's Shade (From the
    "Seven Songs" dedicated to Washington)
    (1788) . . . . .Francis Hopkinson
Delia (1793) . . . . .Henry Capron
The Mansion of Peace (1790?) . . . . .Samuel Webbe
                                        (1740-1816)
Lullaby (1792) (From the Opera "The
    Pirates") . . . . .Stephen Storace
                                        (1763-1796)
The Bud of the Rose (1782) (From the Opera
    "Rosina") . . . . .William Shield
                                        (1748-1829)
The Wayworn Traveler (1793) (From the
    Opera "The Mountaineers") . . . . .Samuel Arnold
                                        (1740-1802)

The following are issued separately:

ALBUM OF MILITARY MARCHES

(Containing)

The President's March . . . . Philip Phile (d. 1793?)
General Washington's March . . . .
General Burgoyne's March . . . .
Brandywine Quick Step . . . .

Successful Campaign . . . .
Washington's March at the Battle of Trenton . .

DANCE MUSIC

(Containing)

Minuet and Gavotte .Alexander Reinagle
Two Minuets (Danced before General and
    Mrs. Washington) (1792) . . . . .Pierre Landrin Duport

THE TOAST, TO GEORGE WASHINGTON

By Francis Hopkinson

2. MUSIC ISSUED BY MUSIC PUBLISHERS

KEY TO PUBLISHERS

ADL —Alfred D. Liefeld,
    303 McCance Block,
    Pittsburgh, Pa.

AM —Alexander Maloof Music Co.,
    712 Carnegie Hall,
    New York City

AMP —American Music Publishers,
    528 S. Dearborn St.,
    Chicago, Ill.

AMC —Alfred Music Company,
    145 West 45th Street,
    New York City

APS —Arthur P. Schmidt Co.,
    120 Boylston Street,
    Boston, Mass.

AS —Albert Shutt,
    1226 Jackson Street,
    Topeka, Kans.

ASB —A. S. Barnes & Co.,
    67 West 44th Street,
    New York City

BC —Boosey & Co.,
    113 West 57th Street,
    New York City

BMC —Boston Music Company,
    116 Boylston Street,
    Boston, Mass.

CCB —C. C. Birchard & Co.,
    221 Columbus Avenue,
    Boston, Mass.

CF —Carl Fischer, Inc.,
    56 Cooper Square,
    New York City

CFS —Clayton F. Summy Co.,
    429 S. Wabash Avenue,
    Chicago, Ill.

CWH —Charles W. Homeyer,
    458 Boylston Street,
    Boston, Mass.

EA —Emil Ascher, Inc.,
    315 Fourth Avenue,
    New York City

EBM —E. B. Marks Music Co., Inc.,
    223 West 46th Street,
    New York City

EEH —Eldredge Entertainment House,
    Franklin, Ohio

ELB —E. L. Bohal & Co.,
    Ashland, Ohio

ET —E. Toldridge,
    The Farragut,
    Washington, D. C.

FMP —Forster Music Publisher, Inc.,
    218 S. Wabash Avenue,
    Chicago, Ill.

GS —G. Schrimer, Inc.,
    3 East 43rd Street,
    New York City

GW —Gene Weller,
    Roseville, Ohio

HMC —Hatch Music Company,
    611 Washington Street,
    Boston, Mass.

HSG —Hamilton S. Gordon, Inc.,
    33 East 21st Street,
    New York City

HTF —H. T. FitzSimons Co.,
    23 East Jackson Blvd.,
    Chicago, Ill.

HWG H. W. Gray Company,
    158 East 48th Street,
    New York City

IMP —International Music Publishing
    Co.,
    1611 Great Northern Bldg.,
    Chicago, Ill.

JF —J. Fischer & Bro.,
    119 West 40th Street,
    New York City

JRF —Jas. R. Fennell,
    3350 Perry Avenue,
    Bronx, New York City

JFO —James F. Oates,
    1609 D Street, S.E.,
    Washington, D. C.

KK —Kay & Kay Music Publishing
    Corp.,
    254 West 47th Street,
    New York City

LaT —Charles H. LaTourette,
    Princeton, N. J.

LPC —Lorenz Publishing Co.,
    Dayton, Ohio

MM —Miller Music Co.,
    62 West 45th Street,
    New York City

MMC —Manus Music Company,
          145 West 45th Street,
          New York City

MPC —Mulwerhof Publishing Co.,
          Milwaukee, Wis.

MPO —M. P. Opie,
          Olney, Md.

MW —M. Witmark & Sons,
          1650 Broadway,
          New York City

NMB —National Manuscript Bureau,
          333 West 52nd Street,
          New York City

OD —Oliver Ditson Company,
          178 Tremont Street,
          Boston, Mass.

PP —Paul-Pioneer Music Co.,
          119 Fifth Avenue,
          New York City,

RJ —Ross Jungnickel, Inc.,
          122 Fifth Avenue,
          New York City

RK —Ruebush-Kieffer Co.,
          Dayton, Va.

SBS —S. Brainard Sons,
          c/o E. B. Marks Music Co.,
          223 West 46th Street,
          New York City

SF —Sam Fox Publishing Co.,
          Cleveland, Ohio

SMC —Southern Music Co.,
          Washington, D. C.

TH —Theodore Henckels,
          2006 Columbia Road, N.W.,
          Washington, D. C.

TP —Theodore Presser Co.,
          1712 Chestnut Street,
          Philadelphia, Pa.

TSD —T. S. Denison & Co.,
          Chicago, Ill.

USGW—United States Commission for
          the Celebration of the 200th
          Anniversary of the Birth of
          George Washington,
          Washington Building,
          Washington, D. C.

WGB —Will George Butler,
          State Normal School,
          Mansfield, Pa.

WJ —Walter Jacobs, Inc.,
          120 Boylston Street,
          Boston, Mass.

WMC —Willis Music Co.,
          137 W. 4th Street,
          Cincinnati, Ohio

W-S —White-Smith Music Publishing
          Co.,
          40 Winchester Street,
          Boston, Mass.

THE MUSIC THAT WASHINGTON KNEW

With an historical sketch by William Arms Fisher. A Program of Authentic Music, vocal and instrumental, with historical data, for the use of Schools, Musical Societies, Music Clubs and Historical Celebrations. OD

CONCERT SONGS COMPOSED IN AMERICA

Pioneer American Composers
    A Collection of Early American Songs, edited and augmented by Harold V. Milligan. APS (Two Volumes)

Seven (8) Songs, by Francis Hopkinson.
    Dedicated to George Washington, edited and augmented by Harold V. Milligan. APS

Colonial Love Lyrics, six songs by Francis Hopkinson.
    Edited and augmented by Harold V. Milligan. APS

The First American Composer, six songs by Francis Hopkinson.
    Edited and Augmented by Harold V. Milligan. APS

Benjamin Carr
    Willow, Willow, in *Pioneer American Composers*, Vol. I APS

James Hewitt
    The Twin Roses, in *Pioneer American Composers*, Vol. II APS

Francis Hopkinson
    Beneath a Weeping Willow's Shade, in *Seven Songs*, and in *The First American Composer* APS
    Come, Fair Rosina, in *Seven Songs*, and in *The First American Composer* APS
    Enraptured I Gaze, in *Seven Songs*, and in *Colonial Love Lyrics* APS
    The Garland, in *Colonial Love Lyrics* APS
    Give Me Thy Heart, in *Colonial Love Lyrics* APS
    My Days Have Been So Wondrous Free, in *The First American Composer* APS
    My Generous Heart Disdains, in *Seven Songs*, and in *The First American Composer*, APS
    My Love is Gone to Sea, in *Seven Songs*, and in *Colonial Love Lyrics* APS
    Ode From Ossian's Poems, edited and harmonized by Carl Deis GS

    O'er the Hills, in *Seven Songs* and in *The First American Composer* APS
    See Down Maria's Blushing Cheek, in *Seven Songs*, and in *Colonial Love Lyrics* APS
    The Traveller Benighted, in *Seven Songs*, and in *The First American Composers* APS
    With Pleasures Have I Passed My Days, in *Colonial Love Lyrice* APS

Victor Pelissier
    Dry Those Eyes, in *Pioneer American Composers*, Vol. II APS
    Return, O Love, in *Pioneer American Composers*, Vol. I APS

Alexander Reinagle
    I Have a Silent Sorrow, in *Pioneer American Composers*, Vol. I APS
    Jerry's Song, (From "The Volunteer"), in *Pioneer American Composers*, Vol. II APS

Raynor Taylor
    Cupid and The Shepherd, in *Pioneer American Composers*, Vol. I APS
    The Wounded Soldier, in *Pioneer American Composers*, Vol. II APS

Timothy Swan
    The Soldier's Farewell, in *Pioneer American Composers*, Vol. I APS

P. A. Von Hagen
    Gentle Zephyr, in *Pioneer American Composers*, Vol. II APS
    May Morning, in *Pioneer American Composers*, Vol. II APS
    Monody, in *Pioneer American Composers*, Vol I APS
    The Pride of Our Plains, in *Pioneer American Composers*, Vol I APS

J. Willson
    I Knew by the Smoke, in *Pioneer American Composers*, Vol. II APS

CONCERT SONGS FROM ABROAD, KNOWN IN AMERICA

Michael Arne (1740-1786)
    The Lass With the Delicate Air, edited by Max Spicker GS

Thomas Arne (1710-1778)
    Blow, Blow, Thou Winter Wind, edited by Max Spicker GS
    Under the Greenwood Tree GS
    When Daisies Pied, and Violets Blue GS
    Where the Bee Sucks, (Ariel's Song in "The Tempest"), edited by Max Spicker GS

G. B. Buonancini
    L'Esperto Nocchiero (O Why is the Pilot) GS
    Per La Gloria D'Adoravi (For the Love my Heart Doth Prize) GS

Henry Carey (?)
    Sally in Our Alley, arranged by Harry R. Spier JF
    Sally in Our Alley GS

Charles Dibdin
    Blow High, Blow Low, in *Reliquary of English Songs*, collected and edited by Frank Hunter Potter GS
    The Lass that Loves a Sailor, in *Reliquary of English Songs* GS

A. E. M. Gretry
    Je Romps La Chaine (From the Opera "L'Amant Jaloux") (1778) edited by F. A. Gaevert GS
    Songe Enchanteur (Dream Most Enchanting) GS

Handel, G. F.
    Angels Ever Bright and Fair GS
    Honor and Arms (from the oratorio "Samson") GS
    O, Ruddier Than the Cherry (From "Acis and Galatea") GS
    Ombrai Mai Fu (From the Opera "Xerxes") GS

G. B. Lully
    Bois Epais (Woods So Dense) GS

Giovanni Martini
    Plaisir d'Amour (The Joy of Love) GS

G. B. Pergolesi
    Se Tu M'Ami (If thou lovest me) GS

Antonio Sacchini
    Se Mai Piu Saro Geloso (Should I Doubt Again My Loved One) GS

See key to music publishers.

William Shield
The Friar of Orders Gray GS
The Thorn, in *Reliquary of English Songs* GS

Anonymous
The Bee, harmonized by Samuel Endicott, in *Three Melodies of Revolutionary Times* CWH
The Charms of Floramel, harmonized by Samuel Endicott CWH
He Stole My Tender Heart Away, harmonized by Samuel Endicott, in *Three Melodies of Revolutionary Times* CWH
The Heavy Hours, harmonized by Samuel Endicott CWH
Queen Mary's Farewell to France, harmonized by Samuel Endicott, in *Three Melodies of Revolutionary Times* CWH
Sheep in Clusters, harmonized by Samuel Endicott CWH

ARRANGEMENTS FOR CHORUS

Mixed Voices
When Daisies Pied and Violets Blue, Michael Arne, arranged by Augustus Barrett KK
When Icicles Hang by the Wall, Thomas Augustine Arne, arranged by Augustus Barratt KK
Where the Bee Sucks, Thomas Augustine Arne, arranged by Augustus Barratt KK

Men's Voices
When Icicles Hang by the Wall, Thomas Augustine Arne, arranged by Augustus Barratt KK
Where the Bee Sucks, Thomas Augustine Arne, arranged by Augustus Barratt KK

Women's Voices
Where the Bee Sucks, Thomas Augustine Arne, arranged by Augustus Barratt KK

ENGLISH BALLAD OPERAS

The Beggar's Opera, Gay-Pepusch, new version arranged by Frederic Austin BC
Polly, Gay-Pepusch, edited and arranged by Clifford Bax and Frederic Austin BC
No Song, No Supper, Storace BC
Rosina, Shield BC
Love in a Village, Bickerstaffe BC

PIANO MUSIC COMPOSED IN AMERICA

The following are included in *A Program of Early American Piano Music*, edited by John Tasker Howard. JF

James Bremner
Trumpet Air

Benjamin Carr
Rondo (from overture to "The Archers")

John Christopher Moller
Sinfonia

John Palma
Lesson

Alexander Reinagle
Sonata, E Major

Raynor Taylor
The Bells

INSTRUMENTAL MUSIC FROM ABROAD

Johann Stamitz
Trio, No. 5, B Flat GS
See also symphonies, overtures, quartets, sonatas, etc., by Johann Christian Bach, Haydn, Mozart, etc., in catalogues of standard publishers.

RELIGIOUS MUSIC

William Billings
The Lord is Risen Today, for mixed voices, arranged by Joseph Clokey JF

James Lyon (1735-1794)
The Lord Descended from Above, for mixed voices, arranged by James Clokey JF
Gott ein Herrscher Aller Heiden (God is Great), seven part motet from the Ephrata Cloister. Mixed chorus, arranged for six parts by James Clokey JF
Old Hundred, traditional hymn-tune, sung by the first settlers in America. As mixed chorus in any standard hymnal.
Old Hundred, violin solo arranged by Gustav Saenger GS
Ye Olde New England Psalm Tunes, mixed chorus, edited by Wm. Arms Fisher OD

MARCHES

From the Days of George Washington, for band and orchestra, either small or large, arranged by Adolph Schmid, including the following: GS

The President's March
Washington's March
General Burgoyne's March
Washington's March (At the Battle of Trenton)
Roslyn Castle (Marcia Funebre)
Quick Step (Band March)
Successful Campaign
Brandywine Quick Step
Yankee Doodle (Original Version)
Yankee Doodle (Modern Version)
Finale (apotheosis) *President's March*

President's March
See *Hail Columbia* (Historic National Airs)
Washington's March, piano solo HSG
Washington's March at the Battle of Trenton, piano solo HSG
The Girl I Left Behind Me, band arrangement WJ

BOOKS CONTAINING INSTRUCTION FOR HISTORIC DANCES

American Country Dances, by Elizabeth Burchenal GS
American Indian and Other Folk Dances, collected by Mary Severance Shafter ASB
Dances, Drills and Story Plays, by Nina B. Lamkin TSD
Dances of Our Pioneers, by Grace L. Ryan ASB
Folk Dance Music, by Elizabeth Burchenal and C. Ward Crampton GS
Gilbert Dances, by M. B. Gilbert GS
Gymnastic and Folk Dancing, by Mary Wood Hinman ASB
An Introduction to the English Country Dances, by Cecil J. Sharp HWG
Natural Dance Studies, by Helen Norman Smith ASB
Newman Album of Classic Dances, by Albert W. Newman TP
Rhythms and Dances for Elementary Schools, by Dorothy La Salle ASB
Three Old American Quadrilles, collected and edited by Elizabeth Burchenal BMC

HISTORIC NATIONAL AIRS

America

Words written in 1832, but tune known in eighteenth century as music for *God Save the King*.
CHORUS
Mixed
America, SSA, arranged by Walter H. Aiken BMC
America, (My Country 'Tis of Thee), arranged by Gustav Ascher HSG
America, (My Country 'Tis of Thee), arranged by Geoffrey O'Hara JF

See key to music publishers on pages 249 and 250.

America, arranged by Rhys-Herbert   JF
America   BMC
MEN'S VOICES
　America, arranged by W. Rhys-Herbert   JF
PIANO SOLO
　My Country 'Tis of Thee, arranged by Henry Weber   WMC
　America, arranged by George Smith   CF
VIOLIN AND PIANO
　America, arranged by Lowell Tracy   W-S.
　America, Overture on National Airs, arranged by Theo. M. Tobani
　　CF
　America, a fantasia, arranged by Louis Kron and Gustav Saenger
　　CF
ORCHESTRA
　America, Overture on National Airs, arranged by Theo. M. Tobani
　　CF
　My Country (America), a scenic fantasy, arranged for symphony
　　orchestra by Mortimer Wilson   JF
ORGAN SOLO
　American Fantasy, on the theme *America, composed by Roland
　　Diggle*   W-S

HAIL COLUMBIA

(Music of the *President's March*)

CHORUS
　Mixed
　　Hail Columbia, arranged by W. Rhys-Herbert   JF
　　Hail Columbia, arranged by N. Clifford Page   OD
　　Hail Columbia, arranged and harmonized by J. P. Weston   W-S
　　Hail Columbia, arranged by S. T. Gordon   HSG
　Women's Voices
　　Hail Columbia, arranged and harmonized by John H. Brewer   GS
　Men's Voices
　　Hail Columbia, harmonized by Max Vogrich   GS
　　Hail Columbia, arranged by W. Rhys-Herbert   JF
　　Hail Columbia, arranged and harmonized by J. P. Weston   W-S
VOCAL SOLO
　Hail Columbia, arranged by S. T. Gordon   HSG
PIANO SOLO
　Hail Columbia, arranged by Henry Weber   BMC
　Hail Columbia, fantasietta by T. Bissell   HSG
VIOLIN AND PIANO
　Hail Columbia   W-S
　Hail Columbia, arranged by Louis Kron and Gustav Saenger   CF
ORCHESTRA
　Grand American Fantasia (Hail Columbia), arranged by Theo. M.
　　Tobani   CF

THE STAR SPANGLED BANNER

(Words written in 1814, but music sung in latter part of eighteenth
century to the words, *To Anacreon in Heaven*)
VOCAL SOLO
　The Star Spangled Banner, harmonized by Walter Damrosch   GS
　The Star Spangled Banner, Service Version   OD
CHORUS
　Mixed
　　The Star Spangled Banner, harmonized by Clarence Dickinson
　　　HWG
　　The Star Spangled Banner, arranged by S. T. Gordon   HSG
　　The Star Spangled Banner, arranged and harmonized by Geoffrey
　　　O'Hara (SAB)   JF
　　The Star Spangled Banner   W-S
　　The Star Spangled Banner, arranged by W. Rhys-Herbert   JF
　　The Star Spangled Banner, prepared and harmonized by Geoffrey
　　　O'Hara (8-part)   JF

Women's Voices
　The Star Spangled Banner, arranged by W. Rhys-Herbert   JF
Men's Voices
　The Star Spangled Banner, prepared and harmonized by Geoffrey
　　O'Hara   JF
　The Star Spangled Banner, arranged by W. Rhys-Herbert   JF
PIANO SOLO
　The Star Spangled Banner, arranged by Henry Weber   WMC
　The Star Spangled Banner, piano version by Joseph Hofmann
　The Star Spangled Banner, arranged by George Smith   CF
ORGAN SOLO
　The Star Spangled Banner, arranged by Ira B. Wilson   LPC
VIOLIN AND PIANO
　The Star Spangled Banner, arranged by Lowell Tracy   W-S
　The Star Spangled Banner, arranged by Louis Kron and Gust
　　Saenger   CF
FOUR VIOLINS
　National Airs, introducing *The Star Spangled Banner*, adapted
　　A. E. Harris   CF
BAND
　The Star Spangled Banner, Service Version, arranged by Walla
　　Goodrich   OD

YANKEE DOODLE

VOCAL
　Yankee Doodle, solo or duet and chorus, arranged by S. T. Gord
　　HSG
　Yankee Doodle, chorus of mixed voices, arranged by F. C.   OD
PIANO SOLO
　Yankee Doodle, (March)   HSG
　Yankee Doodle, arranged by Henry Weber   WMC
　Yankee Doodle, arranged by George Smith   CF
　Yankee Doodle, with variations by "A Lady"   HSG
　Yankee Doodle, arranged by William Gooch   W-S
VIOLIN AND PIANO
　Yankee Doodle, arranged by Louis Kron and Gustav Saenger
　Yankee Doodle, arranged by J. Denbe   CF
　Yankee Doodle, arranged by George Lowell Tracy   W-S
　Yankee Doodle, arranged by Emil Levy   CF
BAND
　Yankee Doodle   WJ

POTPOURRI AND COLLECTIONS CONTAINING HISTORICAL NATIONAL AIRS

CHORUS
　The Columbia Collection of Patriotic and Favorite Home So
　　WJ
　The Everybody Sing Book, edited by Kenneth Clark   PP
　Grand Army War Songs, edited by Wilson G. Smith   SBS
　Patriotic Medley, arranged by H. L. Heartz   W-S
　Patriotic Songs of the U. S. A., edited by Frank Damrosch   GS
　Six National Airs, arranged by Ambrose Davenport   W-S
　Songs of Dixie, arranged by Collin Coe   SBS
　Songs of the People   RK
　Songs of Our Nation   WMC
　The Star Spangled Banner, Hail Columbia, America, in Stanb
　　Edition, edited and arranged by Frederic H. Ripley and H.
　　Heartz   W-S
PIANO SOLO
　Centennial Echoes, arranged by Henry Dora   HSG
　Familiar Melodies for Piano, arranged by T. L. Rickaby   HMC
　Our War Songs   SBS
　The Star Spangled Banner, Hail Columbia, Yankee Doodle,
　　ranged by E. Mack   HSG
　U. S. Patrol, introducing *Yankee Doodle*, and *The Star Spang
　　Banner*, composed by Harry A. Peck   W-S

See key to music publishers on pages 249 and 250.

VIOLIN AND PIANO

Fantasie Pratriotique No. I, composed by Gustav Saenger   CF
God Save the King (America) and *Hail Columbia*   W-S
Mammoth Collection, Songs of the World, arranged by Louis To-caben   CF
Old Treasures, arranged by George Brayley   CF
The Young Artist, transcribed and arranged by Victor Hammerel JF

CELLO AND PIANO

Recreations for Young 'Cellists, Book I, arranged by Anton Hegner   CF
Recreations for Young 'Cellists, Book III, arranged by Anton Hegner   CF

ORCHESTRA

American National Melodies, arranged by Emil Ascher   EA
Ever-Ready Series No. I For Special Occasions, arranged by J. A. Browne   AMC

Jacobs Evergreen Collection, arranged by R. E. Hildreth   WJ
The Little Folks Own Orchestra, compiled and arranged by Griffith Lewis Gordon   WMC
National Melodies, edited and orchestrated by Chas. J. Roberts CF
Old Glory Selection, arranged by J. Seredy, mandolin arrangements by J. Tocaben   CF
U. S. A. Patrol, arranged by Otto Langley   W-S

BAND

American National Melodies, arranged by Emil Ascher   EA
The Columbia Collection of Patriotic and Favorite Home Songs, arranged by R. E. Hildreth   WJ
Jacob's Evergreen Collection, arranged by R. E. Hildreth   WJ
U. S. A. Patrol, arranged by Otto Langley   W-S
Hail Columbia and *Yankee Doodle*   WJ

III. A Catalogue of Modern Music Commemorating George Washington, or Otherwise Appropriate for Use in Washington Celebrations

COMPOSITIONS WRITTEN FOR THE UNITED STATES COMMISSION FOR THE CELEBRATION OF THE TWO HUNDREDTH ANNIVERSARY OF THE BIRTH OF GEORGE WASHINGTON

SONG OF FAITH

A Choral Ode by JOHN ALDEN CARPENTER

Published by G. Schirmer, Inc., New York, N. Y. Chorus copies for actual use in official celebrations may be obtained from the headquarters of the Commission.

GEORGE WASHINGTON BICENTENNIAL MARCH

By JOHN PHILIP SOUSA

Published by Sam Fox Publishing Co., Cleveland, O.

FATHER OF THE LAND WE LOVE

A Song by GEORGE M. COHAN

Published by the United States Commission for the Celebration of the Two Hundredth Anniversary of the Birth of George Washington.

MUSIC COMMEMORATIVE OF GEORGE WASHINGTON AND HIS TIME

VOCAL SOLO

Father of the Land We Love, song by Geo. M. Cohan   USGW
The Birthday of Washington, a song with recitation, edited by Walter H. Aiken   BMC
Honor to Washington, music by William J. Oates, words by James F. Oates   JFO
Lead Us On, Washington, song, words and music by John Richard Mullen, Geo. C. Hofer and Alex P. Werner   MPC
National Ode to George Washington, words and music by Edward L. Bohal   ELB
Washington, words and music by Chas. H. LaTourette   LaT
Washington Birthday March, march song, words and music by Mary Pickens Opie, published by M. P. Opie, Olney, Md. Available also for band and orchestra.

CHORUS

Mixed

Song of Faith, a choral ode, by John Alden Carpenter   GS
All About George Washington, words and music by Alan Gray Campbell   EEH
America's Memory (Commemoration of George Washington) by Michael Herrmann   AMP
Fair Land of Washington, arranged by N. Clifford Page   OD
Father of the Freeman's Nation, music by Henry Walter, words by Frederick Manley   CCB
George Washington, the Father of Our Country, music by Ira B. Wilson, libretto by Edith Sanford Tillotson   LPC
The Glorious Name of Washington, arranged by William Arms Fisher   OD
Hail Brave Washington, music by Kane Powers, words by Lizzie Dearmond   BMC
Homage to Washington, words by Dorothy Rose, music by Franz C. Bornschein   CCB
The Land of Washington, composed by John Carroll Randolph OD
Lead Us On, Washington, song, words and music by John Richard Mullen, George C. Hofer and Alex P. Werner   MPC
Lexington Ode, music by Schubert-Felton, words by G. A. Brown TP
Mount Vernon Bells, arranged by B. Clifford Page, music by Stephen C. Foster   OD
National Ode to George Washington, words and music by Edward I. Bohal   ELB
Ode for Washington's Birthday, music by L. van Beethoven, arranged by N. Clifford Page   OD
The Spirit of '76, music by Ira B. Wilson, libretto by Dorothy Summerau   LPC
Washington, words by David Stevens, music by Samuel Richards Gaines   CCB

Women's Voices

George Washington "February", (Unison); Music by Mrs. R. R. Forman, words by Gertrude L. Knox   JF
Homage to Washington, words by Dorothy Rose, music by Franz Bornschein   CCB

See key to music publishers on pages 249 and 250.

National Ode to George Washington, words and music by Edward L. Bohal ELB

Our Washington, music by Sybil Ann Hanks, poem by Clinton Scollard HTF

Washington, words by David Stevens, music by Samuel Richard Gaines CCB

Children's Voices

Father of Liberty, (Unison), a march song. Music by Charles J. Roberts, words by Irving Cheyette CF

The U. S. A. in Rhyme and Lay, (Unison), verses and music by Helen Cramm BMC

Men's Voices

Homage to Washington, words by Dorothy Rose, music by Franz C. Bornschein CCB

National Ode to George Washington, words and music by Edward L. Bohal ELB

Our Washington, music by Sybil Ann Hanks, poem by Clinton Scollard HTF

Washington, words by David Stevens, music by Samuel Richard Gaines CCB

PIANO SOLO

Colonial Dames, a govotte, by J. F. Zimmerman TP
Colonial Dames, by Frederick Williams TP
Colonial Dance, by R. G. Rathburn TP
Colonial Dance, by Charles M. Tait TP
Colonial Days, by R. Goerdeler TP
Colonial Days, introducing "Virginia Reel", by R. S. Morrison TP
George Washington Bicentennial March, by John Philip Sousa SF
Martha Washington, by Eugene Wyatt BMC
The Minute Men, by Albert Stoessel BMC
Washington's Birthday, introducing *Yankee Doodle*, by George L. Spaulding TP

VIOLIN SOLO

Colonial Dance, by M. Greenwald TP

TWO VIOLINS, OR VIOLIN AND PIANO

Colonial Days, by M. Greenwald TP

ORCHESTRA

Father of the Land We Love, by Geo. M. Cohan USGW
George Washington Bicentennial March, by John Philip Sousa SF
Father of His Country, march, by E. E. Bagley WJ
First in Peace, (George Washington), march, by James M. Fulton OD
Lead Us On, Washington, by John Richard Mullen, Geo. C. Hofer and Alex P. Werner MPC

BAND

Father of the Land We Love, by Geo. M. Cohan USGW
George Washington Bicentennial March, by John Philip Sousa SF
Father of His Country, march, by E. E. Bagley WJ
Father of Liberty, march, by Charles J. Roberts CF
First in Peace, (George Washington), march, by James M. Fulton, OD
Lead Us On, Washington, by John Richard Mullen, George C. Hofer and Alex P. Werner MPC
A Great American, by Lieut. Charles Benter, arranged by Mayhew Luke MM

CANTATAS

MIXED VOICES

Braddock's Defeat, by Henry P. Cross OD
George Washington, words by Romanie Van De Poele, music by J. V. Dethier CCB
The Goddess of Liberty, by Camille W. Zeckwer TP
The Minute Man, by Franz C. Bornschein OD
Our First Flag, by E. S. Hosmer OD
Paul Revere, book, lyrics and music by May Hewes Dodge and John Wilson Dodge WMC
Paul Revere's Ride, by Carl Busch OD

The Phantom Drum, music by James P. Dunn, poem by Freder H. Martens JF

The Spirit of '76, music by Ira B. Wilson, libretto by Doro Summerau LPC

The Tale of the Bell, music by William Lester, words by Freder H. Martens JF

Washington, music by R. Dean Shure, book by Edward C. Pot JF

MEN'S VOICES

The Liberty Bell, by William G. Hammond OD
Our Colors, music by Charles Gilbert Spross, text by Caroline L TP

WOMEN'S VOICES

The Mischianza, music by Camille Zeckwer, words by Richard Beamish CF

CHILDREN'S VOICES

George Washington, the Father of Our Country, music by Ira Wilson, libretto by Edith Sanford Tillotson LPC

OPERETTAS

MIXED VOICES

Home and Native Land, by Will H. Ruebush and John W. W land RK

CHILDREN'S VOICES

Mixed

Betsy Ross, or The Origin of Our Flag, music by George L. Spau ing, book and text by Jessica Moore MW

The Lost Locket, music by Mrs. R. R. Forman, words by Gertr Knox Willis TP

Mount Vernon, music by R. Spaulding Stoughton, book by Fr erick H. Martens OD

Washington's Birthday, book, lyrics and music by Lina Lor WMC

When Betsy Ross Made Old Glory, words and music by M Orita Wallace WMC

When Washington was a Boy, words and music by John Mok CFS

Boys' Voices

Charter Oak, music by Edward Johnston, book by Edith M. B rows JF

Old Glory, by Anthony J. Schindler JF

RELIGIOUS MUSIC

VOCAL SOLO

God Save Our President, music by W. Franke Harling, words W. Franke Harling and Frank Conroy HWG

O Beautiful My Country, (Bass) by Mark Andrews HWG

CHORUS

American Army Hymn, music by Mark Andrews, words by A Eastman Cross HWG

George Washington Processional music by George B. Nevin, wo by Lillian C. Nevin OD

God of Our Fathers, music by Eugene W. Wyatt, words by J. Hopkins HWG

God of Our Fathers, arranged to the music of the *Inflamma* from Rossini's *Stabat Mater*, words by William Smedley HW

God Save America, music by W. Franke Harling, words by Franke Harling and Frank Conroy HWG

God Save Our President, music by W. Franke Harling, words W. Franke Harling and Frank Conroy HWG

Great God of Love, For This Our Land So Free, melody by C. Vallee, arranged for chorus by A. Jury HWG

Peace Hymn of the Republic, music by Walter Damrosch, wo by Henry Van Dyke HWG

A Prayer For Our Country, music by W. R. Voris HWG

We Lift Our Hearts, O God To Thee, music by A. Bernard, wo by Right Reverend B. B. Ussher BMC

VIOLIN SOLO

Old Hundred, arranged by Gustav Saenger CF

See key to music publishers on pages 249 and 250.

IV. MUSICAL PROGRAM SUGGESTIONS FOR BICENTENNIAL CELEBRATIONS

1. SUGGESTED MUSIC TO BE USED FOR PROGRAMS FOR THE NATION-WIDE CELEBRATION IN 1932 OF THE TWO HUNDREDTH ANNIVERSARY OF THE BIRTH OF GEORGE WASHINGTON

(Published and distributed by the United States Commission for the Celebration of the Two Hundredth Anniversary of the Birth of George Washington.)

Note:—Selections marked * are printed in "Music from the Days of George Washington," published and distributed by the United States Commission for the Celebration of the Two Hundredth Anniversary of the birth of George Washington. Selections marked † may be found in the first chapter of this booklet.

PROGRAM ONE——FAMILY RELATIONSHIPS OF GEORGE WASHINGTON

* *Beneath a Weeping Willow's Shade*—Francis Hopkinson (A song written by Francis Hopkinson, signer of the Declaration of Independence, and dedicated to Washington)
* *Sonata,* for pianoforte, first movement—Alexander Reinagle
* *Rondo* (for piano)—William Brown
  (Concert pieces of the latter 18th century)

PROGRAM TWO—HOMES OF GEORGE WASHINGTON

* *The Mansion of Peace*—Samuel Webbe (English song well known in America)
* *Sonata*—Reinagle
* *Rondo*—William Brown

PROGRAM THREE—YOUTH AND MANHOOD OF GEORGE WASHINGTON

The British Grenadiers
Rule Brittania
God Save the King
Green Sleeves
  (English songs sung in America during Washington's youth and manhood. They may be found in many standard collections.)
†*Girls and Boys Come out to Play*
†*The Haymaker's Dance*

PROGRAM FOUR—THE MOTHER OF GEORGE WASHINGTON

* *Lullaby*—Stephan Storace
* *The Mansion of Peace*—Samuel Webbe

PROGRAM FIVE—GEORGE WASHINGTON, THE MAN OF SENTIMENT

* *Beneath a Weeping Willow's Shade*—Hopkinson
* *The Bud of the Rose*—William Shield (An English song written in 1782 and sung in the ballad opera "Rosina," which was frequently performed in this country)

PROGRAM SIX—GEORGE WASHINGTON, THE MAN OF ACTION IN CIVIL AND MILITARY LIFE

* *The Battle of Trenton* (An historical military sonata for piano, dedicated to General Washington by James Hewitt)
* *Washington's March*
* *The Toast* (to Washington)—Francis Hopkinson

PROGRAM SEVEN—GEORGE WASHINGTON, THE CHRISTIAN

Old Hundred (This is the oldest tune sung by the colonists which has survived to the present day. The Puritans and Pilgrims brought it with them from abroad and sang to it the words of the One Hundredth Psalm. Today it is used for singing the Doxology)

Coronation—Oliver Holden (This stirring tune was composed in 1793 by Oliver Holden, a New England composer who wrote a number of odes in honor of George Washington. The hymn-tune "Coronation" has always been sung to the words of "All Hail the Power of Jesus' Name.")

Both of these hymn-tunes may be found in any standard collection.

PROGRAM EIGHT—GEORGE WASHINGTON, THE LEADER OF MEN

* *The Toast*—Francis Hopkinson
* *The President's March*
* *Washington's March*

PROGRAM NINE—THE SOCIAL LIFE OF GEORGE WASHINGTON

* *Successful Campaign* (A country dance tune, said to be a favorite of George Washington)
* *Minuet and Gavotte*—Alexander Reinagle (It is commonly supposed that Reinagle was engaged by Washington as the music teacher for his adopted daughter, Nelly Custis)
* *Two Minuets* (Danced before General and Mrs. Washington)—Pierre Duport

PROGRAM TEN—GEORGE WASHINGTON, THE BULDER OF THE NATION

* *President's March*
* *Washington's March*
* *The Toast*

PROGRAM ELEVEN—GEORGE WASHINGTON, THE PRESIDENT

* *The President's March*—Philip Phile (It is generally supposed that the *President's March* was written shortly after Washington's inauguration as President, to take the place of the *Washington's March* of Revolutionary times)

PROGRAM TWELVE—THE HOMEMAKING OF GEORGE AND MARTHA WASHINGTON

* *The Wayworn Traveller*—Samuel Arnold (This song, composed in 1793, is known to have been a favorite of Washington)
* *Delia* (song)—Henri Capron
* *Sonata For Pianoforte*—Reinagle

2. MISCELLANEOUS PATRIOTIC MUSIC ESPECIALLY SUITED TO CLUBS, COLLEGES AND PATRIOTIC ORGANIZATIONS

(See also *A Catalogue of Authentic Eighteenth Century Music in Modern Editions,* and *A Catalogue of Modern Music Commemorating George Washington, and Otherwise Appropriate for use in Washington Celebrations*)

VOCAL SOLO

Father of the Land We Love, by George M. Cohan USGW
Allegiance, words and music by Albert Shutt AS
All Hail America, music by Albert D. Liefeld, words by Walter E. Schuette ADL
American Consecration Hymn, music by Francis MacMillen, poem by Percy MacKaye CF
America, Our Own Our All, music by Joe Hahn, words by J. B. Strauss FMP

See key to music publishers on pages 249 and 250.

Dear Old Flag, words and music by L. Z. Phillips　SMC
Dear Old Glory, words and music by Bernard Hamblen　HWG
Flag of My Country, music by J. C. Beckel, words by David Bates　HSG
Flag of My Home and Heart, words and music by E. Toldridge ET
Flag of the Free, by Harrison Millard　HSG
God's Country, words and music by Frank Sheridan, arranged by Christopher O'Hare　KK
Honor to Washington, music by William J. Oates, words by James F. Oates　JFO
Just a Bit of Cloth, but It's Red White and Blue, words and music by Harry C. Eldredge　EEH
Land O'Mine, music by James G. MacDermid, words by Wilbur D. Nesbit　FMP
Lead Us On, Washington, song, words and music by John Richard Mullen, Geo. C. Hofer and Alex P. Werner　MPC
My Own Red White and Blue, words and music by Jas. R. Fennell JRF
National Ode to George Washington, words and music by Edward L. Bohal　ELB
O Beautiful, My Country, music by Mark Andrews　HWG
O Glorious Emblem, words and music by Thomas O'Neill　TP
Old Glory (A Patriotic Song of America), music by Homer N. Bartlett, words by Thomas J. Duggan　CF
Old Glory I Salute You, words and music by Vaughan De Leath CF
Our Country, O Land of Glory, music by Rossini, arranged by W. Ethelbert Fisher　WMC
Our Flag, music by William J. Guard, words by Frank Lawrence Jones　CF
Our Own America (We Trust in Thee), words and music by Bernice E. Comey　NMB
Song of the American Eagle, words and music by Gene Weller GW
There's Magic in the Flag, words and music by George L. Spaulding HMC
United States of America, (My Country), words and melody by Michael Herrmann　AMP
Washington Birthday March, words and music by Mary Pickens Opie　MPO
Washington, words and music by Chas. H. La Tourette　LaT

CHORUS
Mixed
Song of Faith, a choral ode, by John Alden Carpenter　GS
Allegiance, words and music by Albert Shutt　AS
America, music and words of verses 1 and 4 by Theodore Henckels, words of verses 2 and 3 by Henry Van Dyke　TH
America, music by Leo Ornstein, words by Frederick Martens　CF
America, music by Charles A. Chase, words by Samuel F. Smith, BMC
America Dear Land of Hope, verses An Ancient Irish Melody, Chorus by Walker Gwynne DD, Harmonized by W. Y. Webbe HWG
American Army Hymn, music by Mark Andrews, words by Allen Eastman Cross　HWG
The American Flag, words by Joseph Rodman Drake, music by Carl Busch　HWG
American Consecration Hymn, music by Francis MacMillen, poem by Percy MacKaye　CF
American Hymn (Speed Our Republic), words and music by Matthias Keller, edited by I. Meeks　WMC
America, the Beautiful, music by Herbert C. Peabody, words by Katherine Lee Bates　HWG
America's Memory (Commemorative of George Washington), by Michael Herrmann　AMP
America, My Land, music by John Wilson Dodge, words by May Hewes Dodge　WMC
Braddock's Defeat, by Henry P. Cross　OD
Columbia, music by W. W. Nusbaum, words by R. E. Rose　WMC

Columbia, Columbia, arranged by D. F. E. Auber　TP
Dear Old Glory, words and music by Bernard Hamblen　HWG
Democracy, music by Carrie Jacobs-Bond, words by William Mil Butler　BMC
The Flag is Passing By, music by Reginald Barrett, text by Henry Holcomb Bennett　TP
Father of the Freeman's Nation, words by Frederick Manley, musi by Henry Waller　CCB
Flag of My Land, music by Charles A. Chase, words by T. A Daly　BMC
Freedom's Flag, words and music by J. Harold Powers　WMC
For Thee America, music by Alexander Maloof, words by Elizabet Serber Freid　AM
George Washington, a cantata, words by Romanie Van De Poele music by J. V. Dethier　CCB
George Washington Processional, music by George B. Nevin, word by Lillian C. Nevin　OD
The Goddess of Liberty, a cantata, by Camille W. Zeckwer　TP
God of Our Fathers, arranged to the music of the *Inflammatu* from Rossini's *Stabat Mater*, words by Wm. Smedley.　HWG
God of Our Fathers, music by Eugene W. Wyatt, words by J. H Hopkins　HWG
God's Country, words and music by Frank Sheridan, arranged b Christopher O'Hare　KK
God Save America, music by W. Franke Harling, words by W Frank Harling and Frank Conroy　HWG
God Save Our President, music by W. Franke Harling, words b W. Franke Harling and Frank Conroy　HWG
Great God of Love, For This Our Land so Free, melody by C La Valle, arranged for chorus by A. Jury　HWG
Hail, Brave Washington, music by Kane Powers, words by Lizzi Dearmond　TP
Homage to Washington, words by Dorothy Rose, music by Fran C. Bornschein　CCB
Land O'Mine, music by James G. MacDermid, words by Wilbu D. Nesbit　FMP
Land of Our Hearts, music by George Whitefield Chadwick, poem by John Hall Ingham　BMC
The Land of Washington, by John Carroll Randolph　OD
Lead Us On, Washington, song, words and music by John Richar Mullen, Geo. C. Hofer and Alex P. Werner　MPC
Let Freedom's Music Ring, words and music by Wellington Adam EBM
Let the Hills with Song Resound, music by Brinley Richards words by W. J. Baltzell　TP
Lexington Ode, music by Schubert-Felton, words by G. A. Brow TP
Long Live America, words and music by Will George Butle WGB
Long Wave Old Glory, by R. M. Stults　TP
Lord Howe's Masquerade (A Revolutionary Legend), by N Clifford Page　OD
The Minute Man, a cantata, by Franz C. Bornschein　OD
My America, by Frank Peer Beal　BMC
My Country 'tis of Thee (a new setting to the poem "America") by E. S. Lorenz, words by S. F. Smith　LPC
National Ode to George Washington, words and music by Edward L. Bohal　ELB
'Neath the Flag of the U. S. A., words and music by Risca Wil liams　WMC
O Columbia We Hail Thee, arranged by L. S. Leason　TP
Old Glory (A Patriotic Song of America), music by Homer N Bartlett, words by Thomas J. Duggan　CF
Old Glory, by Kate McCurdy　WMC
Old Glory I Salute You, words and music by Vaughn De Leath arranged by Palmer Clark　CF
Our Country, O Land of Glory, music by Rossini, arranged b W. Ethelbert Fisher　WMC

See key to music publishers on pages 249 and 250.

Our Country Festival Choral March, words and music by George F. Whiting   TP

Our First Flag, by E. S. Hosmer   OD

Our Nation, words and music by George R. Young   WMC

Our Native Land, music by William Lester, words by John R. Wreford   CF

Our Pledge to U. S. A., music by M. H. Greulich, words by Luke S. Murdock   WMC

Our United States, arranged, harmonized and orchestrated by Leopold Stokowski, words by Edward W. Bok   TP and CF

Paul Revere, a cantata, book, lyrics and music by May Hewes Dodge and John William Dodge   WMC

Paul Revere's Ride, a cantata, by Carl Busch   OD

Peace-Hymn of the Republic, music by Walter Damrosch, words by Henry Van Dyke   HWG

The Phantom Drum, a cantata, music by James P. Dunn, poem by Frederick H. Martens   JF

The Pilgrim Fathers, music by Percy E. Fletcher, words by Felicia Hemans   HWG

A Prayer for Our Country, music by W. R. Voris   HWG

Song to the Flag, music by John Geo. Boehme, words by Estella Clark, arranged by Palmer Clark   CF

The Tale of the Bell, a cantata, by William Lester, words by Frederick H. Martens   JF

Thru All The Land, music by Gounod, arranged by Christopher O'Hare, words by E. S. S. Huntington   KK

To America, music by Cecil Forsyth, words by Alfred Austin   HWG

The Unfurling of the Flag, music by John Hopkinson Densmore, words by Clara Endicott Sears   BMC

The United States of America, words and music by L. B. Cochran   WMC

Washington, a cantata, composed by R. Dean Shure, book by Edward Potter   JF

Washington, words by David Stevens, music by Samuel Richard Gaines   CCB

We Love Thee, America, by Ruby Barrett Carson   WMC

...en's Voices

The American Legion, music by J. Sebastian Matthews, words by William Adams Slade   HWG

Dear Old Glory, words and music by Bernard Hamblen, arranged by Mark Andrews   HWG

Democracy, music by Carrie Jacobs-Bond, words by William Mill Butler   BMC

Homage to Washington, words by Dorothy Rose, music by Franz C. Bornschein   CCB

Land of Our Hearts, music by George Whitefield Chadwick, words by John Hall Ingham   BMC

Land O' Mine, music by James G. MacDermid, words by Wilbur D. Nesbit   FMP

Liberty Bell, a ballad cantata, by William G. Hammond   OD

My America, by Frank Peer Beal   BMC

National Ode to George Washington, words and music by Edward L. Bohal   ELB

O Native Land, music by Alfred Wooler, words by S. E. Mekin   WMC

Our Washington, music by Sybil Ann Hanks, poem by Clinton Scollard   HTF

Our Colors, a cantata, music by Charles Gilbert Spross, text by Caroline Lord   TP

The Song of Freedom, music by G. Ad. Uthmann, text by C. L. Seelbach   TP

Washington, words by David Stevens, music by Samuel Richard Gaines   CCB

...omen's Voices

God's Country, words and music by Frank Sheridan   KK

Homage to Washington, words by Dorothy Rose, music by Franz C. Bornschein   CCB

Land of Our Hearts, music by George Whitefield Chadwick, words by John Hall Ingham   BMC

Land O' Mine, music by James G. MacDermid, words by Wilbur D. Nesbit   FMP

My America, by Frank Peer Beal   BMC

The Mischianza, a cantata, words by Richard J. Beamish, music by Camille Zeckwer   CF

National Ode to George Washington, words and music by Edward L. Bohal   ELB

O Columbia, Columbia Beloved, music by Donizetti, arranged by Viano   WMC

Our America, words and music by Anna Case   TP

Thru All the Land, music by Gounod, arranged by Christopher O'Hare, words by E. S. S. Huntington   KK

Washington, words by David Stevens, music by Samuel Richard Gaines   CCB

Organ Solo

Liberty March, by J. Frank Frysinger   TP

Piano Solo

Allegiance, by Albert Shutt   AS

Orchestra

Father of the Land We Love, by Geo. M. Cohan   USGW

Allegiance, by Albert Shutt   AS

American Eagle March, by John Geo. Boehme   CF

American Rhapsody, by George F. W. Bruhns, arranged by Ross Jungnickel   RJ

American Patrol, by F. W. Meacham   CF

The American Sentinels March, music by Joe Hahn, arranged by Harry L. Alford   FMP

America Our Own, Our All, music by Strauss and Hahn, arranged by Charles L. Johnson   FMP

Cruiser Harvard (march), by Gustav Strube   MMC

Land O' Mine, by James G. MacDermid   FMP

Lead Us On, Washington, song, words and music by John Richard Mullen, Geo. C. Hofer and Alex P. Werner   MPC

National Heroes' March (U. S. A. Battle March), by George F. W. Bruhns, arranged by Ross Jungnickel   RJ

Our National Honor (March), by Wm. Grant Brooks, arranged by Julius S. Seredy, mandolin arrangement by L. Tocaben   CF

Overture Americana, by M. L. Lake   CF

Song of the American Eagle, by Gene Weller, orchestra arrangement by Charles J. Johnston   GW

United Liberty March, by F. H. Losey, arranged by Seredy-Tocaben   CF

Washington Birthday March, words and music by Mary Pickens Opie   MPO

Band

Father of the Land We Love, by Geo. M. Cohan   USGW

Allegiance, by Albert Shutt   AS

American Bugler, by M. L. Lake   CF

American Consecration Hymn, music by Francis MacMillen, poem by Percy MacKaye, arranged by M. L. Lake   CF

American Fantasie, by Victor Herbert, arranged by Julius Seredy   CF

The American Sentinels March, by Joe Hahn, arranged by Harry L. Alford   FMP

America Our Own, Our All, by Joe Hahn   FMP

Cruiser Harvard, by Gustav Strube   MMC

Dear Old Flag, by L. Z. Phillips   SMC

A Great American, by Lieut. Charles Benter, arranged by Mayhew Lake   MM

Lead Us On, Washington, by John Richard Mullen, Geo. C. Hofer and Alex P. Werner   MPC

March "Patriotic", compiled by George Rosey, arranged by J. C. McCabe   MMC

See key to music publishers on pages 249 and 250.

Old Glory, I Salute You, by Vaughn De Leath, arranged by Chas. J. Roberts CF

Patriots and Pioneers, by Joseph Meinrath, arranged by H. O. Wheeler FMP

United States of America (My Country), by Michael Herrmann MH

Washington Birthday March, by Mary Pickens Opie MPO

3. MISCELLANEOUS PATRIOTIC MUSIC ESPECIALLY SUITED TO JUNIOR ORGANIZATIONS (SCHOOLS, CLUBS, BOY AND GIRL SCOUTS, ETC.)

(See also *A Catalogue of Authentic Eighteenth Century Music in Modern Editions,* and *A Catalogue of Modern Music Commemorating George Washington, or Otherwise Appropriate for Use in Washington Celebrations.*)

VOCAL SOLO

Father of the Land We Love, by Geo. M. Cohan USGW

All About George Washington, words and music by Alan Gray Campbell EEH

All Hail America, music by Albert D. Liefeld, words by Walter E. Schuette ADL

America, words by Frederick Martens, music by Leo Ornstein CF

Dear Old Flag, words and music by L. Z. Phillips SMC

Dear Old Glory (Key of C), words and music by Bernard Hamblen HWG

Flag of My Home and Heart, words and music by E. Toldridge ET

God's Country, words and music by Frank Sheridan, arranged by Christopher O'Hare KK

Honor to Washington, music by William J. Oates, words by James F. Oates JFO

Just A Bit of Cloth, but It's Red, White and Blue, words and music by Harry C. Eldredge EEH

Land O' Mine, music by James G. MacDermid, words by Wilbur D. Nesbit FMP

Old Glory, I Salute You, words and music by Vaughn De Leath CF

Our Own America (We Trust in Thee), words and music by Bernice E. Coney NMB

There's Magic in the Flag, words and music by George L. Spaulding HMC

Washington, words and music by Chas. H. LaTourette LaT

CHORUS

Mixed

Song of Faith, a choral ode, by John Alden Carpenter GS

The Banner of the Free, music by Brinley Richards, words by E. R. Latta, edited by Walter H. Aiken WMC

Betsy Ross, or the Origin of Our Flag, an operetta, music by George L. Spaulding, book and text by Jessica Moore MW

Charter Oak, an operetta, music by Edward Johnston, book by Edith M. Burrows JF

Father of Liberty, a march, music by Charles J. Roberts, words by Irving Cheyette CF

The Father of Uncle Sam, words and music by Harry C. Eldredge EEH

The Flag Is Passing By, music by Reginald Barrett, text by Henry Holcomb Bennett TP

For Thee, America, music by Alexander Maloof, words by Elizabeth Serber Freid AM

God's Country, words and music by Frank Sheridan, arranged by Christopher O'Hare KK

Hail Brave Washington, music by Kane Powers, words by Lizzie Dearmond TP

Hail the Flag, an anthem, dedicated to Girl and Boy Scouts of the U. S., words and music by James E. Ryan IMP

Hail to the Flag, music by J. A. Jeffrey, words by Charles Henry Arndt TP

Let the Hills With Song Resound, music by Brinley Richards, words by W. J. Baltzel TP

Lexington Ode, music by Schubert-Felton, words by G. A. Brown TP

The Lost Locket, an operetta, words by Gertrude Knox Will music by Mrs. R. R. Forman TP

Mount Vernon, an operetta, music by R. Spaulding Stoughton book by Frederick H. Martens OD

Old Glory (Or The Boys of '76), an operetta, by Anthony Schindler JF

Old Glory, by Kate McCurdy WMC

One Land United, text and music by Paul Bliss WMC

Our Country's Flag (Unison) music by J. Truman Wolcott, te by Mrs. Florence L. Dresser TP

Our Flag (The Stars and Stripes) a cantata, music by George Root, words by Lydia Avery Coonley TP

Our Presidents (unison) words and music by Frank L. Bristo WMC

Our United States (unison) original melody by C. F. Van Re words by Edward W. Bok, arranged, harmonized and orche trated by Leopold Stokowski TP

Paul Revere, a cantata, book, lyrics and music by May Hew Dodge and John Wilson Dodge WMC

The Pilgrim Fathers, music by Percy E. Fletcher, words by Feli Hemans HWG

Song of the Stars and Stripes, music by A. J. Boex, words by A B. McAvoy WMC

The Unfurling of the Flag, music by John Hopkins Densmo words by Clara Endicott Sears BMC

Thru All the Land, music by Gounod, arranged by Christoph O'Hare, words by E. S. S. Huntington KK

Washington's Birthday, an operetta, book, lyrics and music Lina Loring WMC

When Betsy Ross Made Old Glory, a playlet, words and music Maud Orita Wallace WMC

PIANO SOLO

American Cadet (march) by Eugene Edgar Ballard FMP

Boy Scouts March, by Henry Purmont Eames FMP

Patriots and Pioneers, by Joseph Meinrath FMP

Waving Flags (military march) music by Al Caradies, arrang by Leo Oehmler TP

VIOLIN AND PIANO

America Forever (march), by Robert Widdop W-S

Red, White and Blue, arranged by Louis Kron and Gustav Saeng CF

'CELLO AND PIANO

Recreations for Young 'Cellists, Book II, arranged by Anton He ner CF

ORCHESTRA

Father of the Land We Love, by George M. Cohan USGW

The American Sentinels March, by Joe Hahn, arranged by Har L. Alford FMP

America, Our Own, Our All, by Strauss and Hahn, arranged Charles L. Johnson FMP

George Washington Bicentennial March, by John Philip Sousa

The Little Folks Own Orchestra, compiled and arranged by Gr fith Lewis Gordon WMC

BAND

Father of the Land We Love, by George M. Cohan USGW

The American Sentinels March, by Joe Hahn, arranged by Har L. Alford FMP

America Our Own, Our All, music by Joe Hahn FMP

Father of Liberty (march), by Charles J. Roberts CF

George Washington Bicentennial March, by John Philip Sousa

A Great American, by Lieut. Charles Benter, arranged by Mayhe Lake MM

Old Glory, I Salute You, by Vaughn De Leath, arranged by Char J. Roberts CF

Patriots and Pioneers, by Joseph Meinrath FMP

See key to music publishers on pages 249 and 250.

GEORGE WASHINGTON

AS A FRIEND AND PATRON

OF MUSIC

INTRODUCTION

THIS excerpt "George Washington as a Friend and Patron of Music" is a great tribute to General Washington, and his fondness for and interest in things musical. His greatness inspired the composition of many Odes in his honor, and the music composed following the Revolution shows to what a great extent he was idolized, and that music played its part in the memorable achievement of the birth of our nation.

> *"Let us with awe and reverence breathe*
> *The mighty name of Washington*
> *And in the deathless splendor leave*
> *It shining on."*

George Washington as a Friend and Patron of Music

*Taken from "The Musical Side of Our First Presidents,"
contained in "Essays in Music" by the late O. G. Sonneck,
former Chief, Music Division of the Library of Congress.*

[*By Permission of G. Schirmer, Inc., Music Publishers*]

For generations the life of George Washington has been described mainly from the standpoint of a man of public affairs. In the reading of biographies the conclusion is almost forced on us that all our early Presidents took interest in nothing but politics. How absurd such a notion is appears from the several "true" lives that have come to light in recent years. Indeed, the lesser sides of their character, their private life, their fancies and foibles, must be made to frame the historical picture if we would feel ourselves in the presence of human beings instead of political automatons. A modest nook in the biographical edifice should be reserved for music. To be sure, it will not be filled with the manuscripts of concertos or of operas written in competition with crowned composers. The musical items to be gathered from the writings of George Washington and from other historical sources are few. Yet they are sufficient to throw interesting sidelights on our early musical history.

The "General," as his contemporaries used to call George Washington, was, in the true sense of a much-abused term, a gentleman of the world. Some persons severely criticized him for this attitude, but, on the whole, his mode of living only served to endear him to the hearts of a people not willing to be over-ascetic or to condemn the niceties of life as temptations of Satanas.

MUSIC WRITTEN IN HONOR OF WASHINGTON

Certainly there is an affinity between this and the fact that George Washington's praise was sung in countless songs. In fact, there were very few patriotic poems of those days which did not wind up with the glorification of his beloved personality. The musicians, too, contributed their share of worship, and the literature of music written in his honor is not a small one, comparatively speaking. I allude, for instance, to the numerous Washington marches, one of which, the "President's March," was immortalized by furnishing the tune to Joseph Hopkinson's "Hail Columbia." Then again our first operatic effort on allegorical-political lines, Francis Hopkinson's "Temple of Minerva" (1781), was practically a panegyric on Washington. But in this connection the first cyclus of songs written and composed by a native American is of particular interest. I mean the "Seven Songs for the Harpsichord or Forte Piano" (Philadelphia: 1788), by Francis Hopkinson, the first American composer. They were dedicated to George Washington, and in his graceful letter of acknowledgement, dated Mount Vernon, February 5, 1789—by the way, one of the very few documents in which he shows a humoristic vein—our first President writes:

> "I can neither sing one of the songs, nor raise a single note on any instrument to convince the unbelieving.
> "But I have, however, one argument which will prevail with persons of true taste (at least in America): I can tell them it is the production of Mr. Hopkinson."

WASHINGTON DID NOT PLAY HIS MUSICAL INSTRUMENTS

This statement destroys once forever the legend that Washington knew how to "raise" the tones of the flute and violin. If we find in his earliest account books the entry, "To cash pd. y° Musick Master for my Entrance, 3.9.", this probably refers, to use the words of Paul Leicester Ford, to the singing master whom the boys and girls of that day made the excuse for evening frolics. But the statement interferes not with the fact that George Washington was fond of dancing and music. We know from George Washington Parke Custis's "Recollections," edited by Mr. Lossing, that the "General" was conspicuous for his graceful and elegant dancing of the minuet.

There is a natural connection between the love of dancing and the love of music, and an unmusical person would never have been sincerely admired for the elegant dancing of the minuet. But we possess more direct evidence to prove our point.

MUSIC OF THE THEATER

Mr. Custis also recollects that Washington used to visit the theater five or six times a season, if circumstances allowed it. This statement finds more than a corroboration in Washington's ledger and diary which he kept from time to time. Mr. Paul Leicester Ford made copious use of these sources, important not only for the study of the "true" George Washington but also for the history of the drama in Virginia and Maryland, in his masterly monograph on "Washington and the Theatre," published in 1899 by the Dunlap Society. From this book we may glean that the General, especially in his younger days, would purchase "play tickets" three, four, and five times a month. Certainly a convincing proof of his fondness of the theater. Now, we must remember the peculiar character of the American stage of that period. The actors would take a part in a drama of Shakespeare or Sheridan tonight and would sing in fashionable ballad-operas the next, or even the same, evening, if they were given as "afterpieces." In addition, hardly a performance passed without some Thespian's singing popular songs or arias between the acts, and instrumental music was played at the theaters very much as it is today. Consequently, nobody with ears to hear could escape music if he ventured into a theater. Had George Washington been indifferent to the charms of music, he certainly would not have cared to listen to operas. This, however, he did and continued to do until two years before his death. By combining the theatrical entries in his diary with the dates of performances at New York, Philadelphia, and elsewhere, we learn that he was familiar with such ballad-operas as "The Poor Soldier," "Cymon and Sylvia," "Maid of the Mill," "The Romp," "The Farmer," and "Rosina."

A WASHINGTON RELIC

Among the miscellaneous Washington relics in the United States National Museum is an English-keyed zither owned by Nelly Custis. The body of the instrument is pear shaped, with sounding board of fir, and back, sides, and neck of maple. The sounding board is decorated about the edge with a painted circlet of green leaves. A circular hole in the sounding board is filled in with an ivory piece which has six small holes across the center and is decorated in open work with the initials "E. P. C." and with small designs. The instrument is fitted with twelve steel strings. On one side of the bridge is a keyboard with six keys, which actuate six hammers, the heads of which rise through the top between the bridge and the neck and strike the underside of the strings. The mechanism of the keyboard is fitted in a drawer located within the body of the piece. This zither was presented by Washington to Eleanor Parke Custis as a birthday gift.

THE ARMONICA INVENTED BY BENJAMIN FRANKLIN

We find these entries for expenditures made at Williamsburg, Virginia, while serving as Burgess:

[1765] "Apr. 2, By my Exps. to hear the Armonica, 3.9."
[1767] "Apr. 10, Ticket for the Concert, 5s."

Of course, the armonica was not the wretched instrument boys and sailors maltreat nowadays, but "the musical glasses without water, framed into a complete instrument capable of thoroughness and never out of tune," as Philip Vicker Fithian (in 1774) called the then world-famous invention of a no less illustrious person than Benjamin Franklin. Whom George Washington heard perform on the armonica we know not, as it seems impossible to trace the two concerts mentioned.

During the War for Independence the Commander in Chief had but scarce opportunity for attending plays, concerts, and the like. Still, a few occasions are on record. For instance, he was the guest of honor when Luzerne, the minister of France, celebrated the birthday of the Dauphin in July, 1782, with a concert, fireworks, a ball, and a supper. But the entertainment given by the minister in December, 1781, is by far more interesting to the students of "Americana." Under date of December 19, 1781, the *Freeman's Journal*, Philadelphia, reported:

"On Friday evening of the 11th inst. his excellency the minister of France, who embraces every opportunity to manifest his respect to the worthies of America, and politeness to its inhabitants, entertained his excellency general Washington and his lady; the lady of general Greene, and a very polite circle of the gentlemen and ladies, with an ele-

THE MUSIC ROOM AT MOUNT VERNON

A PROMINENT FEATURE OF THE MUSIC ROOM IS THE HARPSICHORD WHICH GENERAL WASHINGTON PRESENTED TO NELLY CUSTIS. THE STOOL ACCOMPANYING THE HARPSICHORD IS AN ORIGINAL WHICH BELONGED TO NELLY CUSTIS. A FLUTE, ALSO A ZITHER, OR GUITAR, MAY BE SEEN ON TOP OF THE HARPSICHORD.

gant Concert, in which an Oratorio, composed & set to music by a gentleman whose taste in the polite arts is well known, was introduced and afforded the most sensible pleasure."

Mr. Ford certainly would have added in his charming style a few appropriate remarks had he known that this so-called "Oratorio" was identical with Francis Hopkinson's allegorical operatic sketch celebrating the Franco-American alliance and entitled "The Temple of Minerva." I discovered their identity when studying certain manuscripts of our Revolutionary poet.

RESTRICTIONS AGAINST DRAMA

It is a peculiar coincidence that of the two allusions to opera to be found in Washington's diary, one should again deal with a sequel to "The Poor Soldier." During the Federal Convention at Philadelphia in 1787, he made the following entry on July 10:

"Attended Convention. Dined at Mr. Morris's. Drank Tea at Mr. Bingham's and went to the Play."

By investigating the newspapers we are enabled to add to this meager statement:

"*Spectaculum Vitae*: At the Opera House in Southward This evening the 10th July, will be performed a Concert in the first Part of which will be introduced an entertainment, called the Detective, or, the Servants' Hall in an Uproar. To which will be added a Comic Opera in two acts, called Love in a Camp, or, Patrick in Prussia. . . ."

A curious advertisement, but familiar to the students of early Philadelphia papers. Its explanation is simple enough. The Quakers did their best to suppress all the theatrical entertainments after the war and would stop short of concerts only. The managers were forced to find a way out of the dilemma, and they evaded the law by giving performances under all sorts of disguises like the above. The most ingenious was that of "Hamlet" as "a moral and instructive tale" as "exemplified in the history of the Prince of Denmark."

George Washington is stated to have opposed the narrowminded restrictions against drama, and this is given somewhere as the main reason why he "went to the play" three times in rapid succession during the Federal Convention. At any rate, he went, and if he was brought into contact with the modern English music of his day, on July 10, he was carried back to the classical period on July 14. The "*Spectaculum Vitae*"—in the innocent disguise of a concert—presented on that day:

"An opera called the Tempest, or the Enchanted Island (Altered from Shakespeare by Dryden). To conclude with a Grand Masque of Neptune and Amphitrite: With entire new Scenery, Machinery, etc. The Music composed by Dr. Purcell."

CONCERTS OF MUSIC

But George Washington not only attended sham concerts. We know from various historical sources that he also went to regular concerts. Again, it is his ledger that furnishes the most valuable clues in this direction. In 1757 we find the entry: "March 17th —By Mr. Palmas Tickets, 52.6." Mr. Ford remarks:

". . . presumably an expenditure made in Philadelphia during the officer's visit there to meet Lord Loudoun; but whether the tickets were for the theatre or for a lottery cannot be discovered. The second entry is more specified, being to the effect: 'April 27—By Tickets to the Concert, 16.3.' "

Information may here be added, overlooked by Mr. Ford. In the first place, it appears from the *Pennsylvania Gazette* that said Mr. Palma was a musician, his Christian name being given as John, probably, the anglicized form of the Italian "Giovanni." This John Palma gave a concert in Philadelphia at the Assembly Room in Lodge Alley on January 25, 1757. I find no further allusion to him, but it presumably was he who advertised in the *Pennsylvania Journal* on March 24, 1757:

"By Particular Desire. To Morrow Evening, in the Assembly Room precisely at 7 o'clock, will be a Concert of Music.

"Tickets to be had at the Coffee-House at one Dollar each."

Is it too far-fetched to argue that George Washington purchased 52s. 6d. worth of tickets in advance for this concert? If not, then this concert would be the earliest on record as attended by the future Father of Our Country. Otherwise it would be the one for which he purchased tickets on April 27, but to which I found no further allusion.

WASHINGTON'S FAVORITE OPERA

Washington's favorite opera seems to have been William Shield's "The Poor Soldier," first performed at London in 1783 and two years later introduced into the United States. At least Charles Durang, in his "History of the Philadelphia Stage" (partly compiled from the papers of his father, John, a ballet dancer in Washington's days), says so, and he adds that "The Poor Soldier" was often acted at the President's desire when he visited the theater.

We also know from Dunlap's "History of the American Theatre" that he witnessed the first performance of "Darby's Return" on November 24 (or December 9), 1789, at New York. This ballad-interlude, written by Dunlap as a sequel to "The Poor Soldier," in which Darby after various adventures in Europe and in the United States returns to Ireland and recounts the sights he had seen, was for years very popular. Of the first performance the author tells us this amusing story:

"The remembrance of this performance is rendered pleasing from the recollection of the pleasure evinced by the first President of the United States, the immortal Washington. The eyes of the audience were frequently bent on his countenance, and to watch the emotions produced by any particular passage on him was the simultaneous employment of all. When Wignell, as Darby, recounts what had befallen him in America, in New York, at the adoption of the Federal Constitution, and the inauguration of the President, the interest expressed by the audience in the looks and the changes of countenance of this great man became intense. He smiled at these lines alluding to the change in government:

" 'There, too, I saw some mighty pretty shows;
A revolution, without blood or blows;
For, as I understood, the cunning elves,
The people, all revolted from themselves.'

"But at the lines—

" 'A man who fought to free the land from woe,
Like me, had left his farm, a soldiering to go,
But, having gain'd his point, he had, *like me,*
Return'd his own potato ground to see.
But there he could not rest. With one accord
He's called to a kind of—not a lord—
I don't know what. He's not a great man, sure,
For poor men love him just as he were poor.
They love him like a father, or a brother,

Dermot

As we poor Irishmen love one another.'

"the President looked serious. And when Kathleen asked—

" 'How looked he, Darby? Was he short or tall?
"his countenance showed embarrassment, from the expectation of one of those eulogiums which he had been obliged to hear on many occasions, and which must doubtless have been a severe trial to his feelings; but Darby's answer that he had not seen him, because he had mistaken a man 'all lace and glitter, botherum and shine,' for him, until the show had passed, relieved the hero from apprehension of further personality, and he indulged in what was with him extremely rare, a hearty laugh."

NELLY CUSTIS PLAYS HER GRANDFATHER'S FAVORITE OLD MELODY

It is highly probable that Alexander Reinagle, like Capron and Brown, excellent European musicians settled at Philadelphia, was engaged to give Nelly Custis harpsichord lessons. George Washington had presented to his adopted daughter a fine instrument at the cost of a thousand dollars—it is now at Mount Vernon in the drawing room—and it was one of his great pleasures to have Nelly sing and play to him such songs as "The Wayworn Traveller," with which he kept her constantly supplied. To poor Nelly, however, the instrument became one of torture, for her grandmother made her practice upon it four and five hours a day, as her brother tells us in his "Recollections."

Few as these glimpses are into George Washington's private life, they will have sufficed to show that he was not indifferent to music, and that he by no means "appears more as a patron or an escort to the ladies than as a lover of music," as Mr. Toner has it in his "Excerpts from Account Books of Washington."

WASHINGTON A CONCERT GOER

In a similar manner George Washington may be traced as a concert goer until the year 1797, from Charleston, S. C., up to Boston. At Boston, in October, 1789, while on his New England tour, he was treated to a so-called "Oratorio" under circumstances described in Sonneck's book on "Early Concerts in America," and Jacob Hilzheimer narrates in his diary that he was present "with his lady" at a concert in the Lutheran Church at Philadelphia on January 8, 1791. At Philadelphia the President entered in his own diary, under date of May 29, 1787:

". . . accompanied Mrs. Morris to the benefit concert of a Mr. Juhan"—not Julian, as Mr. Ford erroneously gives the name.

At Charleston, S. C., in May, 1791, the President entered:

". . . went to a Concert at the Exchange at wch. there were at least 400 ladies the number & appearance of wch. exceeded anything of the kind I had ever seen."

And on June 1, 1791, at Salem, N. C., a Moravian settlement:

"Invited six of their principle people to dine with me—and in the evening went to hear them sing & perform on a variety of instruments Church music."

And February 28, 1797, *Claypoole's American Daily Advertiser*, Philadelphia, announced that:

"The President and his family honor the Ladies' Concert with their presence this evening."

In order to give an idea of the kind of music our first President would hear on such occasions, I quote from the *Pennsylvania Packet*, June 4, 1787, the remarkable program of Alexander Reinagle's concert, which Washington, according to his diary, attended on June 12:

ACT I

Overtures . . . . Bach

(Of course the "London" Bach, not Joh. Seb.)

Concerto Violoncelle . . . . Capron
Song . . . . Sarti

ACT II

Overture . . . . André
Concerto Violin . . . . Fiorillo
Concerto Flute . . . . Brown

ACT III

Overture (La Buona Figliuola) . . . . Piccini
Sonata Pianoforte . . . . Reinagle
A new Overture . . . . Reinagle

(In which is introduced a Scotch Strathspey)

Music from the Days
of
George Washington

COLLECTED AND PROVIDED WITH
AN INTRODUCTION BY

CARL ENGEL
Chief, Division of Music,
Library of Congress

———

THE MUSIC EDITED BY

W. OLIVER STRUNK
Assistant, Division of Music,
Library of Congress

———

WITH A PREFACE BY

HON. SOL BLOOM
Director
United States George Washington Bicentennial Commission

❀

UNITED STATES
GEORGE WASHINGTON BICENTENNIAL COMMISSION
Washington, D. C.

PREFACE

THE United States George Washington Bicentennial Commission is issuing this selection of eighteenth century music as an important contribution to the general program for observing the Two-Hundredth Anniversary of the Birth of George Washington, in 1932.

It is proper in the formation of a general program for the celebration that music should be given a conspicuous place in the detail of ceremonies and observances. A great amount of music suitable for the purpose is available, in a variety of forms, including some that has been especially written for the occasion. But music dating from the days of George Washington himself is rare and can be found only in libraries and historical collections.

This Commission, therefore, has considered it helpful and appropriate to issue, for distribution, this collection of eighteenth century music intimately connected with the historic period of our national origin.

The sincere and strong character of this music accords well with the rugged simplicity from which sprang the faith and vision that laid the foundation of our Republic.

SOL BLOOM
Director
United States George Washington
Bicentennial Commission

INTRODUCTION

IT required the solemn celebration of the two-hundredth anniversary of George Washington's birth to prepare this volume of music. The collection could, and properly should, have been compiled before this. If it does not reveal musical treasures hitherto unknown or of great price, it clearly reflects a whole epoch—of foremost importance in the history of our nation—an epoch which loudly resounded with the tumult of war, but not to the exclusion of more peaceful strains. Fife and drum did not silence harpsichord and flute. And while the occasion has governed the choice, the music represented here is not entirely of an "occasional" character, seeking apologetic shelter under merely "historical associations."

Such associations, of course, exist in the majority of cases. As befits the purpose, they are directly or indirectly connected with George Washington. The soldier has been ranked with Frederick the Great and the first Napoleon. Of the illustrious trio, only the Prussian King had decided musical tastes and talents. But both Napoleon and Washington valued music as an indispensable adjunct to military, social, and religious functions; and neither of the two was spared the numerous and varied musical tributes paid to his person and glory, in accordance with the fashion of the times.

When Dr. Charles Burney, the English historian of music, visited Prague, capital of Bohemia, in 1772, he wrote: "A great part of the town is new, as scarce a single building escaped the Prussian batteries and bombardment during the blockade, in the last war." Frederick's military feat moved an otherwise unremembered composer to write a piece for the piano entitled "The Battle of Prague," enormously popular among the least bellicose of musical amateurs far into the first half of the eighteenth century. Napoleon's spectacular victory at Marengo was similarly illustrated in tones, and many editions of this battle-piece were published, not only in Europe but in the young United States. True to form, an American composer, James Hewitt, was inspired by Washington's signal achievement at the battle of Trenton to write an elaborate

"historical military Sonata," first printed anonymously in 1797.

As the late O. G. Sonneck has pointed out in a study of "The Musical Side of Our First Presidents," George Washington, man of the world that he was, did not shrink from attending concerts, dances, or performances of the then prevailing English ballad-operas. Personal modesty, however, may have made these musical events a little irksome, whenever they turned into personal ovations. At least there is a curious account in the German periodical, "Magazin der Musik" (Vol. II, 1784), edited by Carl Friedrich Cramer, telling of a concert given in Philadelphia in 1783, which was attended by General Washington. The concert was to have ended with the singing of an "Ode" written in his honor. When he learned of this, he is said to have taken leave before the concert was over. We are therefore left to wonder what were Washington's real feelings when, on April 21, 1789—on his journey to New York for his inauguration as first President—he was greeted at Trenton[1] by "a white-robed choir who met him with the congratulatory song"[2] before a triumphal arch erected on the bridge that spanned the Assanpink Creek. Washington handsomely thanked "the matrons and young ladies" for their musical offering. On this occasion the narrow bridge left no other means of progress or egress.

It is certain that Washington liked good company; and company of any sort, in his day, meant musical accompaniment. If it were argued that such public attendance, in an official capacity, did not necessarily prove Washington to have been a lover of music, there would remain the fact that apparently he listened with enjoyment to the playing and singing of his adopted daughter, Nelly Custis, in the family circle at Mount Vernon. Arnold's "The Wayworn Traveller," tradition says, was one of the songs with which she delighted him most often during the last quiet months of his own eventful journey.

[1]See "The New Jersey Journal and Political Intelligencer," Elizabeth, N. J., May 6, 1789; cf. also Dr. C. E. Godfrey's article in "Trenton Sunday Advertiser," Dec. 29, 1912, pages 19 and 20.

[2]The words by Major Richard Howell, adapted for the occasion to Handel's chorus "See, the conqu'ring hero comes," and later published with music specially composed by Alexander Reinagle.

Washington attended Christ (Episcopal) Church in Alexandria. It is not likely, however, that he joined in the hymns. He avowed himself incapable of raising a note; and he probably was too considerate of the proprieties—if not too musical—to add one more discordant voice to a choir which probably suffered no lack of them.

Practical considerations have limited the selection of music offered in this volume. Nevertheless, it may claim to present a fairly complete cross-section of the secular music that was heard in America during the latter half of Washington's life. Purely political songs (such as "The Battle of the Kegs," sung to the tune of "Yankee Doodle," or "Adams and Liberty," adapted to the convivial air of "Anacreon in Heaven" composed by the Englishman John Stafford Smith, long before Francis Scott Key wedded to it his poem known as "The Star-Spangled Banner") have been purposely excluded. So has religious or church music, of which there existed almost as many different kinds as there were denominations or sects in a country that gave freedom of worship to all of them. Some of these church hymns (as, for instance, the fine tune "Coronation" by Oliver Holden [1765-1844] of Charlestown, Mass., which is now sung to the hymn beginning "All hail the pow'r of Jesus' name!") are still in use, or have been especially collected and are easily available.[1] Of both a religious and patriotic character was the hymn known as "Chester,"[1] the words and music of which were written about 1778 by William Billings [1746-1800], tanner and "singing-master." It was a great favorite among the Continental troops in the North and South. The thirst for freedom in some of these revolutionary composers extended to strange liberties which they took with the laws of musical harmony as then established.

*   *

*

A few words of comment on the music contained in this volume may be helpful. The first part comprises samples of patriotic and military music. They date from the Revolutionary and post-Revolutionary periods. "The President's March" was probably composed by Philip Phile, a German music-teacher, who settled in Philadelphia after 1771. The earliest known edition of this march was published about 1793; which does not mean that it may not have been composed and in use before that year, since most of this military music was copied and re-copied by hand, as is shown by numerous manuscript tune-books of the time that have come down to us, in many of which this march is recorded, thus proving its immediate and wide-spread popularity. Upon this popularity was conferred a degree of permanence when, in 1798, Joseph Hopkinson wrote for it his poem "Hail, Columbia!", which has become one of our most stirring national airs.

The next number, "Washington's March," was also called "Washington's Grand March" and "The New President's March." It is not impossible that this is the oldest among the several variants of Washington marches, since references to it have been found in American newspapers as early as 1784. But its seniority is not absolutely established. Nor has there been brought to light, so far, any convincing proof that this march was written by Francis Hopkinson [1737-1791], the first native-born American composer and one of the signers of the Declaration of Independence, a man of such manifold gifts and signal accomplishments that it seems only natural to see in him the author of something which he certainly had the skill and ability to write. There is no doubt, however, concerning Hopkinson's authorship of the words and music of "The Toast." The poem was printed in the "Pennsylvania Packet" on April 8, 1778. Apparently the earliest and only printed issue of the music and words was not brought out until 21 years later, when Benjamin Carr, the Philadelphia publisher, advertised it in the Philadelphia newspapers, in March, 1799. It was issued jointly with "Brother soldiers, all hail! A favorite new patriotic song in honor of Washington," the words of which were adapted to "Washington's March." There will be another reference to Hopkinson later.[2]

---

[1]See "Ye olde New England psalm-tunes, 1620-1820, with historical sketch by William Arms Fisher, Boston, Oliver Ditson Co., 1930; *cf.* also "American writers and compilers of sacred music," by Frank J. Metcalf, **The Abingdon Press, New York and Cincinnati, 1925.**

[2]A copy of this extremely rare publication is in the music collection of the Boston Public Library.

A manuscript copy of the words and music of "The Toast" marked "composed by F. H. Esq.," once part of the library of Michael Hillegas [1729-1804], the first Treasurer of the United States, was accidentally found in 1931 by Mr. Edward Hopkinson, a descendant of Francis, in the Philadelphia shop of Henry C. Woehlcke, where Mr. John Tasker Howard kindly copied it for use in this collection.

"General Burgoyne's March" is taken from a manuscript band book in the Library of Congress, inscribed "The property of the Bellamy Band, June 1799," the Bellamy in question being probably Col. Samuel Bellamy of Hamden, Conn. The name of a British General as title of the march is indication of its origin. It also shows that the American army bands had evidently no scruples about appropriating a good tune, even if it happened to be the enemy's. The same applies to the "Brandywine Quick-Step" (the engagement that gave the march its name was fought between General Howe and Washington on Sept. 11, 1777), which remained popular with American bands for some years, since it was still included in Blake's "The Martial Music of Camp Dupont," a collection of military tunes published in Philadelphia after 1815.

"Successful Campaign" appears in Thompson's, the London publisher's, "Twenty-Four Country Dances for the Year 1769" with the title "Successfull Campain; or, Bath Frollick." The Bath referred to, was, of course, the fashionable English spa. In connection with this tune, Dr. John C. Fitzpatrick, the editor of Washington's papers and eminent authority on all matters pertaining to his life, has recorded the following characteristic incident:

"When the French army arrived at Rhode Island, the Continental drums were thrown somewhat in the background by the more showy bands of Rochambeau's force. On Washington's visit to Newport in March 1781, to confer with the French commander, the French officers arranged a ball in his honor. They decorated the ballroom with flags, swords, drums, streamers and all the fanciful color that the army possessed, and George Washington opened the ball by request. He danced the first number with Miss Margaret Champlin, one of the reigning belles of Newport, and, as the signal was given, the French officers took the instruments from the hands of their musicians and flourished the opening strains of "A Successful Campaign," which piece Miss Champlin had chosen as the one with which the ball should open.

"It proved a prophetic choice for, eight months afterwards, the two generals present at that Newport ball finished a successful campaign by forcing the surrender of Cornwallis at Yorktown. . . ."[1]

Reference has already been made to Hewitt's Sonata, entitled "The Battle of Trenton" and dedicated to Washington. It is neither better nor worse than a great many similar descriptive pieces of the period, by means of which the player

[1] John C. Fitzpatrick, "The Bands of the Continental Army," in his *Spirit of the Revolution*, p. 173.

sought to procure for the delicate sensibilities of the tender sex, assembled in the drawing-room, the thrill and emotions attendant upon the bloody clash of arms. The "Washington's March" introduced in this Sonata is usually called "Washington's March at the Battle of Trenton" (found also under the titles of "The President's New March" and "General Wayne's March"). This military Sonata crosses the border-line into the second group of pieces, which comprises samples of the kind of music that Washington and his contemporaries heard at concerts and social gatherings.

* *
*

In Washington's diaries and account books there are numerous entries which permit a fair idea of what sort of musical affairs he was apt to attend. One such concert in particular—given by Alexander Reinagle in Philadelphia, on June 12, 1787—is notable for its program, which follows:

ACT I.

OVERTURE . . . . [John Christian] Bach
CONCERTO VIOLONCELLO . . . . Capron
SONG . . . . Sarti

ACT II.

OVERTURE . . . . André
CONCERTO VIOLIN . . . . Fiorillo
CONCERTO FLUTE . . . . Brown

ACT III.

OVERTURE (La Buona Figliuola) . . . . Piccini
SONATA PIANOFORTE . . . . Reinagle
A NEW OVERTURE (in which is introduced
    a Scotch Strathspey) . . . . Reinagle

Alexander Reinagle (of Portsmouth and London), William Brown (*recte* Wilhelm Braun, of Cassel, and probably a former member of a Hessian Band!), and Henri Capron (of Paris?), the three composer-performers who appeared as soloists, contributed much to musical life in America during the last years of the eighteenth century. On the concert programs of Washington's time composers' and performers' names were often indiscriminately interchanged; it is therefore impossible to say with certainty whether Reinagle and his friends played original compositions. But it is more than likely that the "Sonata Pianoforte" that figures on this program was one of four such works, which, in the composers's handwriting, are now in the Library of Congress. The first movement of one of these Reinagle Sonatas, not hitherto published, is here included. The manuscript is not dated, but the notation "Philadelphia" indicates that it was written after 1786, the year of Reinagle's arrival in this country. Brown is represented by the first of his "Three Rondos for the Piano Forte or Harpsichord" (1787), dedicated to Francis Hopkinson.

From a Library of Congress manuscript in the autograph of Pierre Landrin Duport (a French dancing-master who fled from Paris after the storming of the Bastille, July 14, 1789, and emigrated to the United States) are taken the four dances that complete the second group of pieces. Their titles, as written by Duport himself, are "Minuetto & Gavott, Compos'd by Alxr. Reinagle Esqr.," "Fancy Menuit Dance before Genl. Washington 1792," and "Fancy Menuit with figure Dance by Two young Ladies in the presance of Mrs. Washington in 1792. Phila." Let us trust that the gentleman's choreography was better than his orthography.

The first place among the vocal pieces chosen has naturally been accorded to one of the most attractive of the eight songs that Francis Hopkinson, in 1788, dedicated to Washington as a mark of his affection and esteem. "This little Work . . . is such as a Lover, not a Master, of the Arts can furnish," Hopkinson writes in his letter of dedication. "I am neither a profess'd Poet, nor a profess'd Musician; and yet venture to appear in those characters united; for which, I confess, the censure of Temerity may justly be brought against me. . . . However small the Reputation may be that I shall derive from this Work, I cannot, I believe, be refused the Credit of being the first Native of the United States who has produced a Musical Composition. If this attempt should not be too severely treated, others may be encouraged to venture on a path, yet untrodden in America, and the Arts in succession will take root and flourish amongst us." Washington's gracious letter of acceptance is too characteristic not to merit another reprint in full:

Mount Vernon Feby 5th, 1789.

Dear Sir,

We are told of the amazing powers of Musick in ancient times; but the stories of its effects are so surprising that we are not obliged to believe them, unless they had been founded upon better authority than Poetic assertion—for the Poets of old (whatever they may do in these days) were strangely addicted to the marvellous,—and if I before *doubted* the truth of their relations with respect to the power of Musick, I am now fully convinced of their falsity—because I would not, for the honor of my Country, allow that we are left by the ancients at an *immeasurable* distance in everything,—and if they could sooth the ferocity of wild beasts—could draw the trees & the stones after them—and could even charm the powers of Hell by their Musick, I am sure that your productions would have had at least virtue enough in them (without the aid of voice or instrument) to soften the Ice of the Delaware & Potomack—and in that case you should have had an earlier acknowledgment of your favor of the 1st of December which came to hand but last Saturday.—

I readily admit the force of your distinction between "a thing *done*" and "a thing *to be done*"—and as I do not believe that you would do "a very bad thing indeed" I must even make a virtue of necessity, and defend your performance, if necessary, to the last effort of my musical abilities.—

But, my dear Sir, if you had any doubts about the reception which your work would meet with—or had the smallest reason to think that you should need any assistance to defend it—you have not acted with your usual good judgment in the choice of a Coadjutor;—for, should the tide of prejudice not flow in favor of it (and so various are the tastes, opinions & whims of men, that even the sanction of Divinity does not ensure universal concurrence) what, alas! can I do to support it?—I can neither sing one of the songs, nor raise a single note on any instrument to convince the unbelieving.—But I have, however, one argument which will prevail with persons of true taste (at least in America)—I can tell them that *it is the production of Mr. Hopkinson.*

With the compliments of Mrs. Washington added to mine, for you & yours

I am—Dear Sir
Your most Obedt and
very Hble Servant
Go. Washington.

Hopkinson's song is followed by "Delia, a New Song," composed by the Henri Capron already mentioned as having performed before Washington in Philadelphia. "Delia" was first published in Philadelphia, in 1793, as part of Moller and Capron's second "Monthly Number." A copy of a later edition, issued by Willig of Philadelphia about 1800, is among the music contained in certain volumes which were once the property of Ann Washington (Mrs. Bushrod Washington) and used by her at Mount Vernon.

The four remaining songs are all of English origin. Even though the United States had gained political independence, it continued for long to be indebted to Europe for musical fare.

The first of these four songs, Samuel Webbe's "The Mansion of Peace," is a gem of the purest water. That it was so great a favorite in America as to have gone through several editions, speaks well for the musical taste of Washington's contemporaries. It figures on at least two programs of which we have a record: a concert at Corre's Hotel, New York, on Jan. 7, 1794, and a concert at Oeller's Hotel, Chestnut Street, Philadelphia, on April 8, 1794.

The last three numbers are excerpts from three ballad-operas which achieved great success in their day. Shield's "Rosina" (first London performance in 1782, first American performance in 1786) and Arnold's "Mountaineers" (first London performance in 1793, first American performance in 1795) were given by wandering troupes in New York, Boston, Providence, Hartford, Philadelphia, Baltimore, New Orleans, and other cities. The "Lullaby" from Storace's "Pirates" (first London performance in 1792, and apparently not given in America as a whole) was a great "drawing-room favorite."

*   *

*

Since it is the aim of this collection to satisfy practical and current needs, these have been occasionally permitted to outweigh purely historical considerations. Thus the arranger has taken the liberty of making excisions in both the Sonata by Hewitt and the Rondo by Brown. In the movement from the Reinagle Sonata, on the other hand, he has adhered closely to the composer's autograph—apparently written in haste—making only such non-essential changes and slight corrections as Reinagle himself would presumably have made before letting his work go into print. In all other instances the best available original version has been made the basis of the accompaniment or harmonization.

The variety offered by the pieces contained in even this small collection should suffice for purposes of furnishing incidental music to patriotic pageants and plays,[1] or of providing material for historical programs. No doubt, the times that are mirrored in this music were more heroic and of a vaster import than their musical reflection appears to us today. And yet, we must remember that simple airs and songs of the people have sometimes decided the destinies of nations. The birth of our own nation was thus heralded and accomplished. The music that played its part in that memorable achievement is therefore sure of a lasting place in our hearts.

CARL ENGEL
Chief, Division of Music
Library of Congress

---

[1]The military and patriotic marches of this collection, including several contained in the Hewitt Sonata, have been published in arrangements for both orchestra and band by G. Schirmer (Inc.), New York.

TABLE OF CONTENTS

The President's March

Arranged by
James Hewitt (1770-1827)

Philip Phile (d. 1793?)

Washington's March

The Toast
(1778)

Francis Hopkinson (1737-1791)

General Burgoyne's March

Tempo di Marcia

Brandywine Quick-Step

Successful Campaign

The Battle of Trenton

"A Favorite Historical Military Sonata Dedicated to General Washington"

(1797)

(abridged)

Introduction

Lento

James Hewitt (1770-1827)

The Army in Motion

Più vivo

General Orders

Acclamation of the Americans

Drums Beat to Arms

Washington's March (at the Battle of Trenton)

Maestoso

The American Army crossing the Delaware

Ardor of the Americans at Landing

Trumpets sound the Charge

Attack
Presto

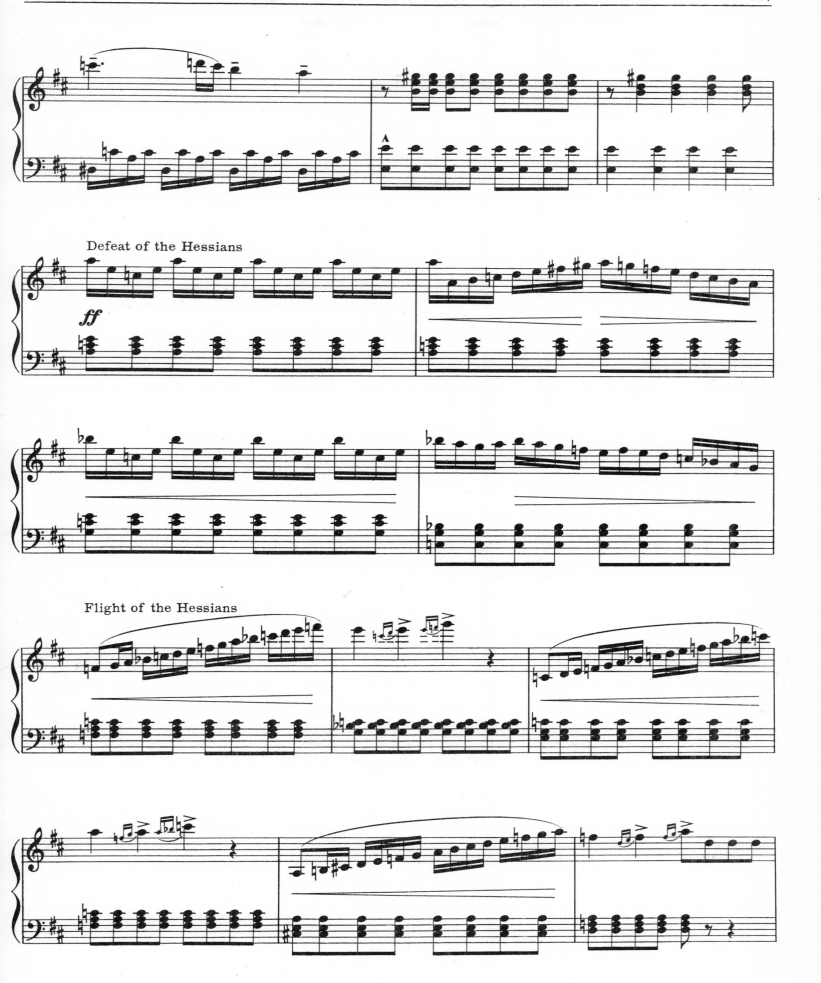

Defeat of the Hessians

Flight of the Hessians

The Hessians begging Quarter

The Fight renew'd

General Confusion

The Hessians surrender themselves Prisoners of War
Andantino semplice

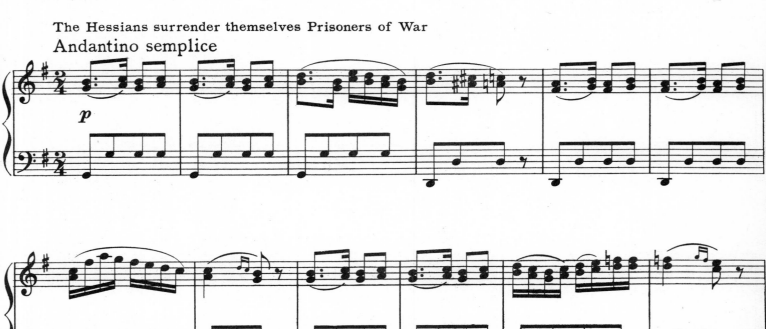

Roslin Castle

Grief of the Americans for the Loss of their Comrades killed in the Engagement

Lento con espressione

Yankee Doodle
Drums and Fifes

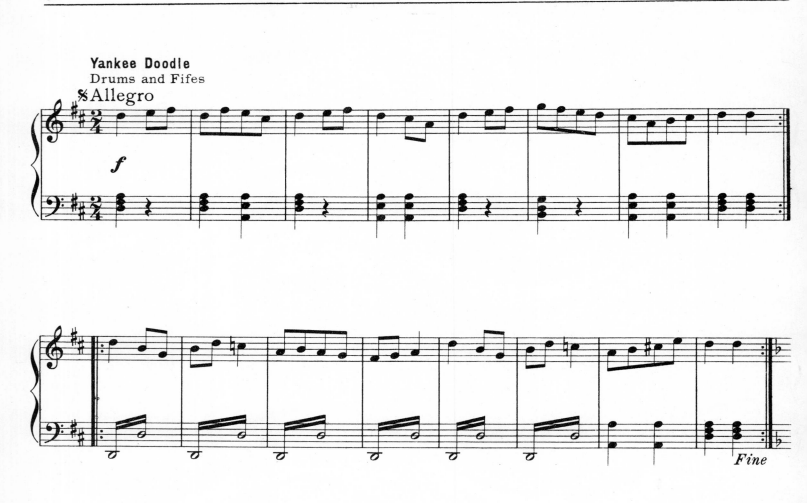

Quick-Step for the Band

D.C. al 𝄋

Trumpets of Victory

poco riten.

General Rejoicing
Allegro

Sonata

(First movement)

Alexander Reinagle (1756-1809)

Allegro con brio

Minuet and Gavotte

Minuet

Tempo di minuetto lento

Alexander Reinagle (1756-1809)

Gavotte

Two Minuets

Minuet danced before General Washington

(1792)

Pierre Landrin Duport

Tempo di minuetto

Fine

Trio

D.C. al Fine

Minuet danced before Mrs. Washington

Tempo di minuetto

Fine

Trio

D.C. al Fine

Rondo

(1787)
(abridged)

William Brown

poco marc.

Beneath a Weeping Willow's Shade

(From the "Seven Songs" dedicated to George Washington)

(1788)

Francis Hopkinson (1737-1791)

Be-neath a weep-ing wil-low's shade She sat and sang a - lone,_____ Be-

Fond Ech - o to__ her strains re - ply'd, The winds her sor - rows bore,_____ Fond

neath a weep - ing wil - low's shade She sat__ and sang a -
Ech - o to__ her strains re - ply'd, The winds her sor - rows

lone;   Her hand up - on__ her heart__ she laid, And
bore;   A - dieu dear youth, a - dieu,__ she cry'd, I

plain - tive was__ her moan,__ And plain - tive was__ her moan.__
ne'er shall see__ thee more,__ I ne'er shall see__ thee more.__

The mock-bird sat up-on___ a bough,   The mock-bird sat up-on___ a bough And lis-ten'd to___ her lay,___ Then

to the dis-tant hills he bore__ The dul-cet notes a - way,_____ Then

Delia

(1793)

Henri Capron

Soft pleas - ing pains un - known be - fore My beat - ing bos - om__
Some-times at mid - night do I stray Be - neath in - clem - ent__
O tell ye shades that fold my fair And all my bliss con -

feels_____ When I be - hold the bliss - ful bow'r Where dear - est De - lia
skies_____ And there my true de - vo - tion pay To De - lia's sleep-seal'd
tain,_____ Ah why should ye those bless - ings share For which I__ sigh in

dwells,   That
eyes;   So
vain,   But

When I be-hold the__ bliss-ful bow'r Where
Some-times at mid-night do I stray Be -
Ah__ why should ye those bless-ings share For

p

tr

dear-est___ De - lia dwells, That way I dai - ly
neath in-clem-ent skies, So pi-ous pil-grims
which I___ sigh in vain, But let me not re -

drive, I dai-ly drive__ my__ flock,__ Ah
roam, So pil-grims night-ly__ roam,__ With
pine, At fate, at fate__ re-pine,__ And

hap - py vale, Ah hap - py vale, There look and wish, and while I look My
trav - el faint, With trav - el faint, To kiss a - lone the clay - cold tomb Of
griefs im-part, And griefs im-part, She's not your ten - ant, she is mine, Her

sighs in - crease the gale.
some lov'd— fav - 'rite saint.
man - sion— is my heart.

When I be - hold the bliss - ful bow'r Where
Some-times at mid - night do I stray Be -
O tell ye shades that fold my fair And

dear - est De - lia__ dwells,_____ There look and wish, and
neath in - clem - ent__ skies,_____ And there my true de -
all my bliss con - tain,_____ Ah why should ye those

while I look My sighs in - crease the gale,__ My__
vo - tion pay To De - lia's__ sleep - seal'd eyes,__ To__
bless - ings share For which I__ sigh in vain,__ For__

sighs in - crease the gale.
De - lia's sleep-seal'd eyes.
which I__ sigh in vain.

The Mansion of Peace

(1790?)

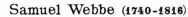

Samuel Webbe (1740-1816)

Andante

Recit.

Soft Zeph-yr, on thy bal-my wing

Thy gen-tlest bree-zes hith-er   bring,

Her slum-bers

guard   some hand di - vine,   Ah watch her with a care like mine.

Affettuoso

rose,   a   rose,   from her   bos - om has   stray'd;___   I'll
las   sil-ly   rose,_____   sil - ly   rose, hads't thou   known___   T'was

p legato

seek to__ re - place   it,   to re - place   it   with   art;   A -
Daph - ne that   gave   thee,   that__ gave thee   thy   place,

But   no,   no, no,   'twill her slum-bers in - vade,   I'll
Thou   ne'er,   no ne'er,   from thy sta - tion hads't   flown;   Her

cresc.

wear   it   (fond   youth)____ next   my   heart.
bos - om's   the   man - sion   of

dim.

2.

peace.

p

f

Lullaby

(from the Opera "The Pirates")

(1792)

Stephen Storace (1763-1796)

Peace-ful

slum-b'ring on the o-cean, Sea-men fear no dan-ger nigh; The winds and
wind tem-pes-tuous blow-ing, Still__ no dan-ger they de-scry; The guile-less

The Bud of the Rose

(from the Opera "Rosina")

(1782)

William Shield (1748-1829)

mouth, which a smile, de - void of all guile, half o - pens to view, Is the bud of the rose, is the bud_ of the rose_ in the morn-ing that blows, im - pearl'd with the dew, im - pearl'd with the dew, the bud_ of the rose, im - pearl'd with the dew.

The Wayworn Traveller

(from the Opera "The Mountaineers")

(1793)

Samuel Arnold (1740-1802)

Faint and wear-i-ly the way-worn trav-el-ler___
Tho' so mel-an-chol-y day has past__ by,__

plods un-cheer-i-ly, a-fraid to stop,
'twould be__ fol-ly now to think on't more;

Wan--d'ring drear-i-ly, a sad un-rav-el-ler___
Blithe and jol-ly, he the can holds fast__ by,__

of the__ ma-zes tow'rd the moun-tain's top;
as he's__ sit-ting at the goat-herd's door;

Doubt - ing,   fear - ing,   while his course he's   steer - ing,
Eat - ing,   quaff - ing,   at past la - bours laugh - ing,

Cot - ta - ges ap - pear - ing,   as he's nigh to drop,___
Bet - ter far by half___ in   spir - its than be - fore,___

Oh,   how brisk - ly then the   way - worn   trav - el - ler___
Oh,   how mer - ry then the   rest - ed   trav - el - ler___

threads   the___ ma - zes tow'rd the   moun - tain's   top,
seems   while sit - ting at the   goat - herd's   door,

Oh, how brisk-ly then the way - worn trav - el - ler___
Oh, how mer - ry then the rest - ed trav - el - ler___

threads the_ ma - zes tow'rd the moun - tain's top.
seems while sit - ting at the goat - herd's door.

IN all history no other human being has merited and received such universal homage as George Washington; nor has any other human being, in the full light of his character and achievements, been so fortunate in escaping criticism and engendering controversy. It is fitting, therefore, that the government of the United States, which he did more than any other man to establish, should promote in 1932, the nation-wide celebration in his honor. This celebration is not intended to add new glories to Washington's name, or place one new leaf in the laurel crown of immortal reverence which his memory inspires. That would be impossible.

The thought behind this Celebration of the Two-Hundredth Anniversary of the Birth of George Washington, is to benefit the living by reviving in the minds and hearts of the American people a just appreciation of the part played by George Washington and his great compatriots in inaugurating a new era of political and social independence that has spread throughout the world.

Responding to this appeal the people of America and other countries have joined with enthusiasm in the plans for celebrating the Bicentennial of Washington's birth. Americans are again learning the lessons of their own history. They are again placing proper values upon the sacrifices and patriotic devotion of the men and women who "brought forth on this continent a new nation, conceived in liberty and dedicated to the proposition that all men are created equal."

By reviving among us the lessons of our national life, by fresh consecration to the fundamentals of the newer freedom of mankind that has shed the glory of equal opportunity upon a world of strife and social and political oppression, by stirring among us all a more exalted appreciation of the priceless heritage left us by the founders of the Republic, the *United States Commission for the Celebration of the Two-Hundredth Anniversary of the Birth of George Washington*, seeks to carry to successful fulfillment the charge laid upon it by the Congress.

FATHER *of the* LAND WE LOVE

WRITTEN FOR THE AMERICAN PEOPLE

BY

GEORGE M. COHAN

TO COMMEMORATE THE

TWO HUNDREDTH ANNIVERSARY

OF THE BIRTH OF

GEORGE WASHINGTON

PAINTING CONTRIBUTED BY JAMES MONTGOMERY FLAGG

The Story of Washington

"FIRST IN WAR"

George Washington was truly "First in War," not from any militant disposition of his character, but because of his environment and the times in which he lived.

Born at Bridges Creek, Virginia, February 22, 1732, upon a plantation known later as Wakefield, the boy inherited the blood and stamina of those early colonial pioneers who were almost constantly armed and alert against the invasion of warlike enemies. It was the same blood and stamina that inspired the pioneers of America everywhere to push outward and establish homes amid hostile surroundings.

When George Washington was seven years old, the family moved to a farm on the Rappahannock River, opposite the town of Fredericksburg. It was in this locality that George began his schooling, which consisted principally of reading, writing and arithmetic.

When he was eleven the first great tragedy came into George's life. His father died. Three years later he wanted to join the British Navy, but his mother persuaded him to give up this idea. Shortly thereafter he went to live with his half-brother Lawrence at Mount Vernon, who had inherited the estate from his father. He soon became deeply interested in surveying and assisted in surveying the lands of Lord Fairfax, whose home, Belvoir, was only a few miles distant. At sixteen he made a month's surveying journey beyond the Alleghenies.

The military career of Washington began when he was twenty-one. He was commissioned by Governor Dinwiddie to deliver a message to the French on the Ohio, who were encroaching upon what was then Virginia territory. His subsequent activities during the Braddock campaign are all well known.

At the age of twenty, Washington came into possession of Mount Vernon through the death of his half-brother Lawrence, and the latter's daughter.

In 1759 he married Martha Dandridge Custis and brought her to Mount Vernon which was their home the remainder of their lives, and where he died, December 14, 1799.

George Washington was not only "First in War," but he was among the very first to be prepared for war in the event that England persisted in her crushing attitude toward the colonies.

Washington was one of the leading members of the First Continental Congress.

When called to serve in the Second Continental Congress, he said: "It is my full intention to devote my life and my fortune to this cause."

Upon assuming command of the American Army at Cambridge, July 3, 1775, he solemnly vowed that he would fight until America gained its liberty. This was the beginning of seven years of warfare that was destined to change the history of the world, and bring happiness and prosperity to millions of people.

Never in all history did a commander conduct a war under such discouraging

---

IN all history no other human being has merited and received such universal homage as George Washington. Nor has any other human being, in the full light of his character and achievements, been so fortunate in escaping criticism and engendering controversy. It is fitting, therefore, that the government of the United States, which he did more than any other man to establish, should promote in 1932, the nation-wide celebration in his honor. This celebration is not intended to add new glories to Washington's name, or place one new leaf in the laurel crown of immortal reverence which his memory inspires. That would be impossible.

The thought behind this Celebration of the Two Hundredth Anniversary of the Birth of George Washington, is to benefit the living by reviving in the minds and hearts of the American people a just appreciation of the part played by George Washington and his great compatriots upon the stage of history at a time when human liberties were at their lowest ebb, and in inaugurating a new era of political and social independence that has spread throughout the world.

Responding to this appeal the people of America and other countries have joined with enthusiasm in the plans for celebrating the Bicentennial of Washington's birth. Americans are again learning the lessons of their own history. They are again placing proper values upon the sacrifices and patriotic devotion of the men and women who "brought forth on this continent a new nation conceived in liberty and dedicated to the proposition that all men are created equal."

By reviving among us the lessons of our national life, by fresh consecration to the fundamentals of the newer freedom of mankind that has shed the glory of equal opportunity upon a world of strife and social and political oppression, by stirring among us all a more exalted appreciation of the priceless heritage left us by the founders of the Republic, the *United States Commission for the Celebration of the Two Hundredth Anniversary of the Birth of George Washington*, seeks to carry to successful fulfillment the charge laid upon it by the Congress.

"FIRST IN THE HEARTS OF HIS COUNTRYMEN"

conditions. But discouragements to this hardy pioneer meant nothing. His first work was to convert an aggregation of 16,000 men, mostly farmers, into a disciplined fighting machine.

His next big job was so to arouse the love and patriotism of his soldiers for the cause for which they were fighting, that they would be willing to endure hunger, sickness, disease, and go shoeless and well-nigh naked.

In a short time Washington drove the enemy out of Boston and took a position before New York. When the British thought they had him cornered there, he quietly moved his army of 10,000 across the river. His retreats were as annoying to the enemy as his victories. He could always turn a defeat into a reason for more determined fighting.

Today all the world applauds his midnight crossing of the ice-flowing Delaware and the dramatic battle of Trenton, where he surprised the Hessians and won a victory that electrified the nation.

The Battle of Monmouth, in New Jersey, has a remarkable place in history. The fight was almost lost through the disobedience of General Charles Lee. Washington discovered his unsoldierly conduct in time to snatch victory from defeat.

The Battles of Brandywine and Germantown will always be remembered for the remarkable generalship displayed by Washington.

Military geniuses throughout the world have ever marveled at the brilliant success of Washington's manoeuvering across New Jersey.

From Valley Forge, during the winter of 1777-78, Washington wrote

Congress saying of his soldiers: "Their marches might be traced by the blood of their feet." There was never a finer example of the loyalty of soldiers to their leader.

On October 19, 1781, Washington, for all time to come, became a world-figure in military history. That was the day that Cornwallis surrendered at Yorktown. That was the day that America forever won her political and industrial freedom from the oppressing land beyond the sea. It was the true beginning of the United States of America.

And then came peace and quiet. Cannons ceased to roar. Muskets occupied a place of honor behind the kitchen door. Swords were hammered into scythes. Old war horses were hitched to plows and wagons. Crops were planted. Houses and barns were repaired. Churches and schools were put in order.

Washington again became the outstanding American farmer. He was happy at his beloved Mount Vernon, beautifying his estate, enriching his fields, improving his crops and livestock, and doing everything possible to bring happiness and contentment to his loved ones.

The wise and far-seeing statesmanship of Washington was clearly and effectively shown in his last circular letter to the governors of the states, dated June 8, 1783, shortly before resigning his commission. This is a most remarkable document. It contained what he considered the necessary requirements for the very existence of the country.

Always a wise citizen, he kept a watchful eye on the ship of state. It was no great task for this versatile man to change from soldier to statesman. When the time came to place the struggling young country on a more permanent foundation, Washington was made President of the convention which

---

"FIRST IN PEACE"

framed the Constitution under w we now live. His advice and diplor were invaluable.

And now it was time to elect a P dent. Washington was unanimo chosen. How he got Congress to f tion, how he appointed a cabinet, he created our courts, how he es lished our entire governmental chinery, and how he won the h and respect of the entire civilized w has long been a matter of history.

Why was George Washington "I in the Hearts of his Countrymen" why does he continue to hold place?

Because, he was courageous enoug go to war with one of the most po ful nations on earth for the freedor his own country. He built an a out of the raw material that cam him from the farms and the to He held this army together through most unbelievable hardships, and it he outmanoeuvered and defeated s of the best generals of which Eu could boast. By his own exampl patient, dogged determination he spired his men to persevere in the of privation and discouragement.

Because, after independence had won he gave one of the finest exam of patriotic generosity that the w has ever known. He laid aside sword and the commission which placed him at the head of a great a and voluntarily returned to the qui his beloved home. He sought no ho or personal glory. When he saw country free he asked nothing f her, but unostentatiously resumed happy life of a private citizen w had been interrupted by the war.

Because, when the Constituti Convention was called to frame a government, he yielded to the im tunities of his countrymen and bec a delegate to that meeting. He immediately elected president of Convention. During those stormy sions when sectional and other di ences divided the delegates so that existence of the Union was threate Washington exerted a powerful in ence for compromise that cannot over-estimated.

Because, as First President of United States, he started this cou on her career as one of the greatest tions in all history. It has been that the framers of the Constitu created the Presidency of the Ur States with George Washington in r as the ideal man for the office.

Because, he possessed the qualitie leadership and knowledge of men inspired confidence among all classe people. Faith in him was well-universal. Complete understanding isted between him and the people. general conduct was such as to hold affection of the public. He was one man in the country who co harmonize all factions and bring together in the adjustment of impor measures. He quietly and effecti overcame the contentious elem which sought to create national dist ances.

Because, in addition to all this was kind, helpful, considerate and erous. In private and public life he above reproach. He lived and died voted and faithful to his high idea true American manhood.

To Commemorate the Two Hundredth Anniversary of the Birth of George Washington

Father of the Land We Love

Written for the
American People

George M. Cohan

ISSUED BY THE UNITED STATES GEORGE WASHINGTON BICENTENNIAL COMMISSION, WASHINGTON, D. C.

ev -'ry day with les - sons done, They sing their song of Wash - ing - ton, A
ev - er drums be - gin to roll, With - in the na - tion's heart and soul, A

song of love that reach - es near and far: _____
pat - ri - ot - ic some - thing seems to say: _____

CHORUS

First in War, First in Peace, First in the hearts of his

coun - try - men That is the sto - ry of Wash - ing - ton,

Father of the Land We Love.

Father of the Land We Love.

FIRST READING OF THE DECLARATION OF INDEPENDENCE

WAKEFIELD, VIRGINIA BIRTHPLACE OF GEORGE WASHINGTON

MOUNT VERNON

THE SURRENDER OF CORNWALLIS

THE FIRST INAUGURATION

THE CAPITOL

ISSUED BY UNITED STATES GEORGE WASHINGTON BICENTENNIAL COMMISSION

George Washington and Education

AN ADDRESS BY

President Calvin Coolidge

BEFORE THE

DEPARTMENT OF SUPERINTENDENCE,
NATIONAL EDUCATION ASSOCIATION

WASHINGTON, D. C.

FEBRUARY 22, 1926

IN THE REVOLUTION AND IN THE PERIOD OF CONSTRUCTIVE STATESMANSHIP IMMEDIATELY FOLLOWING IT, FOR OUR GOOD FORTUNE IT BEFELL US THAT THE HIGHEST MILITARY AND THE HIGHEST CIVIC ATTRIBUTES WERE EMBODIED IN WASHINGTON, AND SO IN HIM WE HAVE ONE OF THE UNDYING MEN OF HISTORY——A GREAT SOLDIER, IF POSSIBLE AN EVEN GREATER STATESMAN, AND ABOVE ALL A PUBLIC SERVANT WHOSE LOFTY AND DISINTERESTED PATRIOTISM RENDERED HIS POWER AND ABILITY——ALIKE ON FOUGHT FIELDS AND IN COUNCIL CHAMBERS——OF THE MOST FARREACHING SERVICE TO THE REPUBLIC.

Theodore Roosevelt.

GEORGE WASHINGTON AND EDUCATION

*An Address by President Calvin Coolidge before the Department of
Superintendence, National Education Association,
Washington, D. C., February 22, 1926*

Reprinted from the Journal of the National Education Association, April, 1926*

Ladies and Gentlemen:—It is doubtful if anyone outside of certain great religious teachers ever so thoroughly impressed himself on the heart of humanity as has George Washington. No figure in America has been the subject of more memorial tributes and more unstinted praise. And yet the subject never seems to be exhausted and the public interest never seems to be decreased. The larger our experience with affairs of the world, the more familiar we become with his life and teachings, the more our admiration enlarges, and the greater grows our estimation of his wisdom. He represented the marvelous combination of the soldier, the patriot, and the statesman. In the character of each he stands supreme.

As a brave soldier he won the Revolutionary War. As an unselfish patriot he refused to use the results of that victory for his own benefit, but bestowed them all on his fellow countrymen. As a wise statesman, gathering around him the best talent of his time, he created the American Republic. All the increasing years only reveal to us how universally great he was. If to set a mark upon the minds of men which changes the whole course of human events is teaching, then Washington ranks as a prince of teachers.

The world is not the same as that into which he was born on that February day in 1732. It is a better world. The stately march of civilization which has since advanced so far, has proceeded in a course which he marked out. The imposing edifice of human progress which has since been raised so high rests to a large extent upon the foundations which he wrought. To those who wish more civilization and more progress there must be a continuing determination to hold to that course and to maintain those foundations. If any doubt what benefit these have been, they have but to compare the present state of America especially, or even of the rest of the world, with what it was when Washington was born.

History seems to indicate that he led and directed a transformation that was growing with an increasing strength over western civilization. The fires of the Middle Ages had burned out. The reaction from the days of Cromwell had run its course in England. The glory of the old régime in France was declining. The power of Spain was shifting to other hands. But while the old was passing the new had not yet begun. Materially and spiritually, things were at a low ebb in the Old World. It has been described as a time

"when poetry sank into dull prose; when philosophy rarely soared above the material or the purely logical; when the only earnestness existing took the direction of greed or self-indulgence;

when the public service was corrupt; when public morals were licentious and when common language was profane."

The finances of the people were in a disordered condition. It was distinctly a transition period in America. The early settlers who had come from the old country had passed away. A very large proportion of the inhabitants of the Colonies, estimated by some as nearly 90 percent, was native born. The pioneer crusading fervor was gone. The new awakening had not come. The attachment to those institutions that are represented by an order of nobility was breaking down. Both in the Old World and in the New the ancient aristocracy was crumbling; but the modern democracy had not yet arisen. An era was approaching which was to give less and less attention to kings and more and more attention to the people. In that era Washington was to be the heroic figure.

No doubt the most powerful influence which was working to establish the new order was the revival of religion. This movement had been started in England by John Wesley and George Whitefield in 1729. It was distinctly an effort to reach the common people. They went down among those who were not otherwise reached, preaching the gospel. In America, Jonathan Edwards led two revival movements, culminating in 1742. Whitefield came to this country and preached to great congregations during this period, and the followers of Wesley sent Bishop Asbury here in 1771. These religious activities were distinctly popular movements. They rested on the theory that every human soul was precious. They resulted in a leveling process; but it was not a leveling down, it was a leveling up. They raised every person that came under their influence to a higher conception of life. A new recognition of spiritual worth gave to all humanity an increased importance.

Another very predominating influence, supplementing religion and flowing from it, was education. This movement was not new in the Colonies but it increased in volume after 1732. It has been claimed that the Reformed Dutch Church of New York founded an academy in 1633 and that the Boston Latin School was established in 1635. In the same year Boston took action in a town meeting to support a school, and in Connecticut and Rhode Island schools were opened within a few years. In Philadelphia, New Jersey, Maryland, Virginia, and South Carolina, and other Colonies, early action was taken to provide schools, but the effort was not followed up so assiduously as it was in New England, where the clergy were very active in its promotion. This influence was seen in the first compulsory school law in America, which was passed in Massachusetts in 1647.

"... . it being one chief project of the old deluder Satan to keep men from the knowledge of the Scriptures,"

---

* Also printed as a congressional document under title: *Washington: A Great Teacher*.

the preamble recited, the General Court ordered that each township "after the Lord hath increased them to the number of 50 householders shall then forthwith appoint one within every town to teach all such children to write and read."

Towns of 100 families were required to have a grammar school and a teacher able to prepare youths for the university. Penalties were fixed for the violation of this law.

In 1732 there were already three colleges in America—Harvard, William and Mary, and Yale—with a combined attendance which is estimated at about 275 students.

The intellectual awakening that went on between that time and the opening of the Revolutionary War could not be more plainly revealed than by the establishment during that period of only a little over forty years of no less than ten additional colleges. Then were laid the beginnings of such great institutions as Pennsylvania, Princeton, Columbia, Brown, and Dartmouth. When it is remembered that a knowledge of the truth has always been the maker of freedom, this remarkable quickening of the religious and intellectual life of the Colonies in these years just prior to the Declaration of Independence becomes of enormous significance. Rightly considered, it would have been an ominous warning to the British Government that America had long since begun to think for itself and unless justly treated would soon begin to act for itself.

While this intellectual and spiritual awakening was taking place during the youth and maturing years of Washington, he benefited by it not so much from taking part in it as in later directing the results of it. Although he lived in one of the most populous and perhaps richest of the Colonies, popular education around him was still undeveloped. Newspapers were almost unknown in the New World and permanent and regular lines of transportation did not exist. About the only regular visitors to his Colony were foreign tobacco traders, dealers in fur, and peddlers. The clergy were almost the only professional class. The people were very largely engaged in agriculture.

At an early age, however, Washington was placed under the instruction of a tutor, who seems to have confined his teaching to the most rudimentary subjects. When he was eleven another man took charge of his education and began to instruct him in the fundamentals of the forms of business. Some of his copy books of that day are still in existence. There is evidence that he was taught some Latin, but his preliminary education was virtually completed when he was thirteen years old. Paul Leicester Ford says:

The end of Washington's school days left him a good cipherer, a bad speller, and a still worse grammarian; but fortunately the termination of instruction did not by any means end his education.

After this he studied surveying and pursued that occupation for several years. This was an exacting calling, training him in accuracy. But when he was fifteen he came into close contact with Lord Fairfax, a cultured gentleman of sixty years, who had a considerable library. His diaries of that period show him reading English history and essays in the *Spectator*. But these early opportunities constituted only the beginning of his education, which he continued in one form or another almost to the end of his days. His experience, his power of observation and absorption finally overcame this lack of early training, so that in his later days his writings, correct in form and taste, adequately revealed the great strength of character which he had developed.

Perhaps because of his own early experience he was the more solicitous for the members of his family. To one who was charged with the care of John Parke Custis, he wrote as follows:

In respect to the kinds, and manner of his studying, I leave it wholly to your better judgment—had he begun, or rather pursued his study of the Greek language, I should have thought it no bad acquisition; but whether [if] he acquire this now, he may not forego some more useful branches of learning, is a matter worthy of consideration. To be acquainted with the French tongue is become a part of polite education; and to a man who has the prospect of mixing in a large circle absolutely necessary. Without arithmetick, the common affairs of life are not to be managed with success. The study of geometry, and the mathematics (with due regard to the limites of it) is equally advantageous. The principles of philosophy, moral, natural, etc., I should think a very desirable knowledge for a gentleman.

His practical interest in education in his later life was further manifest by his accepting the position of a chancellor of William and Mary College in 1788.

In religion he conformed to the practice of his time. It is related that he was baptized when two months old and probably attended church regularly until he was sixteen. From that time until 1759 he was largely engaged in expeditions. After his marriage and settlement at Mount Vernon he was made vestryman in two parishes, for one of which he was instrumental in erecting a building. While he was not a constant church attendant, he was a constant contributor and always gave respectful consideration to the religious beliefs of others. He was tolerant in all things.

The mature opinion of Washington upon the importance of the intellectual, moral, and religious forces of the Nation is not only revealed by his actions, but is clearly set forth in his statements. He looked upon these attributes as the foundation which supported the institutions of our Republic. This opinion was most forcibly expressed in his farewell address, where he said:

Of all the dispositions and habits, which lead to political prosperity, religion and morality are indispensable supports. In vain would that man claim the tribute of patriotism, who should labor to subvert these great pillars of human happiness, these firmest props of the duties of men and citizens. The mere politician, equally with the pious man, ought to respect and to cherish them. A volume could not trace all their connexions with private and public felicity. Let it simply be asked where is the security for property, for reputation, for life, if the sense of religious obligation *desert* the oaths, which are the instruments of investigation in courts of justice? And let us with caution indulge the supposition that morality can be maintained without religion.

—Whatever may be conceded to the influence of refined education on minds of peculiar structure—reason and experience both forbid us to expect, that national morality can prevail in exclusion of religious principle.

'Tis substantially true, that virtue or morality is a necessary spring of popular government. The rule indeed extends with more or less force to every species of free government. Who that is a sincere friend to it can look with indifference upon attempts to shake the foundation of the fabric?

The policies of Washington always had a national outlook. He warned his country against sectionalism. He promoted internal improvements calculated to bring together different parts of the Nation. When he came to the consideration of the problem of training the youth of the country he was not only in favor of education for its own sake, but sought to make it contribute to the national spirit. Believing thoroughly in American ideals and in the American Union, it early occurred to him that a national university would be beneficial both by the power it would have to present the principles on which the Republic was founded, and the power it would have to resist provincialism, by creating a forum for the exchange of ideals through a student body drawn from all quarters of the Nation. It is said that he expressed this thought soon after he took command of the Continental Army at Cambridge. He referred to it in a general discussion of the subject of education in one of his early messages to the Congress, in which he said:

Nor am I less persuaded, that you will agree with me in the opinion, that there is nothing which can better deserve your patronage than the promotion of science and literature. Knowledge is in every country the surest basis of public happiness. In one, in which the measures of government receive their impression so immediately from the sense of the community, as in ours, it is proportionably essential. To the security of a free constitution it contributes in various ways; by convincing those who are intrusted with the public administration, that every valuable end of government is best answered by the enlightened confidence of the people; and by teaching the people themselves to know, and to value their own rights; to discern and provide against invasions of them; to distinguish between oppression and the necessary exercise of lawful authority, between burthens proceeding from a disregard to their convenience and those resulting from the inevitable exigencies of society; to discriminate the spirit of liberty from that of licentiousness, cherishing the first, avoiding the last, and uniting a speedy but temperate vigilance against encroachments, with an inviolable respect for the laws.

Whether this desirable object will be best promoted by affording aids to seminaries of learning already established, by the institution of a national university, or by any other expedients, will be well worthy of a place in the deliberations of the legislature.

And in his farewell address he again uttered this same thought as follows:

Promote, then, as an object of primary importance, institutions for the general diffusion of knowledge. In propor-

tion as the structure of a government gives force to public opinion, it is essential that public opinion should be enlightened.

He urged it more strongly in a letter to the Commissioners in the District of Columbia in 1795, and finally he declared in his will—

That as it has always been a source of serious regret with me to see the youth of these United States sent to foreign countries for the purpose of education, often before their minds were formed or they had imbibed any adequate ideas of the happiness of their own, contracting too frequently not only habits of dissipation and *extravagence,* but principles unfriendly to Republican Governm't and to the true and genuine liberties of mankind, which thereafter are rarely overcome.—For these reasons it has been my ardent wish to see a plan devised on a liberal scale which would have a tendency to spread systamatic ideas through all parts of this rising Empire, thereby to do away local attachments and state prejudices as far as the nature of things would, or indeed ought to admit, from our national councils— Looking anxiously forward to the accomplishment of so desirable an object as this is, (in my estimation) my mind has not been able to contemplate any plan more likely to effect the measure than the establishment of a University in a central part of the United States to which the youth of fortune and talents from all parts thereof might be sent for the completion of their education in all the branches of polite literature—in arts and sciences—in acquiring knowledge in the principles of politics and good government— and (as a matter of infinite importance in my judgment) by associating with each other and forming friendships in juvenile years, be enabled to free themselves in a proper degree from those local prejudices and habitual jealousies which have just been mentioned and which when carried to excess are never failing sources of disquietude to the public mind and pregnant of mischievous consequences to this country.

And he therefore made a bequest to the National Government on condition that it cooperate in carrying out his wish for a national university.

His desire for the increase of knowledge was further elaborated and reiterated in his will. In that instrument he even provided for educating the slave children which he set free. He made bequests to two academies besides that for the founding of a national university. Although the Congress failed to cooperate, so that this wish was never carried into effect as he had contemplated it, yet the city of Washington has been made the seat of no less than ten colleges and universities, and the larger institutions all over our country are more national than local in precepts and teaching.

While there has been agitation lasting almost up to the present day for a national university, if the idea ever prevails it will probably not be an institution devoted to the regular collegiate courses, but one for postgraduate and original research work, for which there are such abundant sources and opportunities already located in the Capital City. The Federal Government, however, has not been remiss in the support of advanced learning and of vocational training, for which it has appropriated more than $90,000,000 in the last thirty-five years, while for general educational purposes it has donated about 95,000,000 acres of the public lands.

The country at large has not failed to follow the precepts of Washington. From the three institutions of higher learning in existence at the time of his birth the number has grown to 913, with a total enrolment of over 664,000 students and over 56,000 teachers, an endowment of nearly $815,000,000, and a property value of over $1,000,000,000. Our elementary and secondary schools have expanded until they provide for more than 26,000,000 pupils and require over 822,000 teachers. In 1912 the total amount expended yearly for all educational purposes was about $706,000,000. This has been increasing with great rapidity, until in 1924 it reached $2,400,000,000. The source of this enormous expenditure, so far as public money is concerned, is almost entirely from the local and state governments.

This represents the result which has been secured by the carrying out of some of the most important policies of our first President. It should be noted that these are the policies of peace. They are based on a desire for intellectual and moral enlightenment. They are the only means by which misunderstandings, suspicions, hatreds, and wars can finally be eradicated from the earth. They are the foundation of order, of law, and of an advancing civilization. It is these elements of domestic tranquility and foreign harmony that Washington helped to build into the structure of our institutions. There is no other structure on which they can rest.

Envy, malice, uncharitableness, class jealousies, race prejudices, and international enmities are not realities. They do not abide. They are only the fictions of unenlightened comprehension. Those who preach them are not safe advisers and not sound leaders. Nothing but discord and disaster at home and abroad can result from following these policies. Washington was the antithesis of all this. His writings and teachings breathe a higher, broader purpose, a more inspired leadership. No man clung more tenaciously to what he believed was right, or was prepared to make greater sacrifices in its support. But he viewed the right as a universal principle, to be applied not only to himself but to others, not only to his own state but to the Nation, not only to his own countrymen but to foreigners. There was nothing about him of the small American.

He believed our own political institutions were superior to those of other countries, but he never preached hatred of all things foreign and he made large concessions in the negotiation of treaties for the settlement of disputed questions which were for the advantage of foreign nations. He believed that obligations were mutual; that what we expected to receive we should be ready to give, both in the field of citizenship and in the larger domain of international relations. He clung to the realities. That was his greatness.

Washington has been known as one of the most practical of leaders. He was not emotional. He was possessed of that broad comprehension of a situation which made his judgment eminently sound. With the possible exception of the field of Monmouth, when disobedience to his orders amounting almost to treachery was losing the day, history always reveals him as calm, cool, and collected. He always knew what he was doing. He was not a sentimentalist. But he was a man capable of deep and abiding affection and of exalted and inspiring ideals. He loved his country with an abounding devotion. He lavished upon it a wealth of genius.

We are wont to think of him as a military commander and a civil administrator—as a man of public affairs. He was surpassingly great in all of that. But he was very much more. He wished to see his country not only materially prosperous and politically successful, but beyond that, and above it, he wished to see the intellectual, moral, and spiritual life of the people developed. This is the side of Washington to which too little attention has been given. He did not fail during his lifetime to give the most painstaking thought to these subjects. In his Farewell Address he solemnly warned his countrymen that these are the foundations on which rest all American institutions. More than that, they are the foundations on which all civilization must rest. It is as an expounder of these great principles that he performed the greatest service for the world.

Our country has prospered, our Government is secure. But that prosperity and that security flow from the school and the church. They are the product of the mind and the soul. They are the result of the character of the American people. Through and through Washington is the great example of character. He sought to besow that heritage upon his country. We shall fail in our estimation and understanding of him unless we remember that during his lifetime he helped to build a place of religious worship; in his will he provided for institutions of learning, and in his Farewell Address he emphasized the spiritual values of life. But what he did was even more eloquent than what he said. He was a soldier, a patriot, a statesman; but in addition to all these he was a great teacher.

ORATIONS AND ESSAYS

OF THE

GEORGE WASHINGTON BICENTENNIAL NATION-WIDE ORATORICAL, ESSAY, AND DECLAMATORY CONTESTS IN SCHOOLS AND COLLEGES

IT is through the schools and colleges of the country and the national literature that the heroes of any people win lasting renown; and it is through the same agencies that a nation is molded into the likeness of its heroes. . . . What a reward is Washington's! What an influence is his, and will be! One mind and will transfused by sympathetic instruction into millions; one character, a standard for millions; one life a pattern for all public men, teaching what greatness is, and what the pathway to undying fame.

CHARLES W. ELIOT.

Compiled by

HAZEL B. NIELSON
Director of Educational Activities

GEORGE WASHINGTON COMMEMORATIVE MEDAL

Obverse

Reverse

Showing the obverse and reverse of the official Commemorative Medal designed by Mrs. Laura Gardin Fraser and selected by the special committee of the United States George Washington Bicentennial Commission, for use in the Celebration of the Two Hundredth Anniversary of the Birth of George Washington. This medal was awarded to the winners in the National and State Bicentennial Declamatory, Essay, and Oratorical Contests; the gold medal to the national winners, the silver medal to each state winner, and the bronze medal to the contestant placing second in the state contest

Nation-Wide Bicentennial Contests

ONE of the most far-reaching and satisfactory educational activities undertaken by the United States George Washington Bicentennial Commission was the Nation-wide Series of Educational Contests. The plan of organization for these contests included a Bicentennial Committee in each state appointed by the State George Washington Bicentennial Commission with which the United States George Washington Bicentennial Commission cooperated. To each State Contest Committee was left the details of organizing its contests. Through the untiring efforts of these State Committees the success of the State and National Contests was achieved.

The Nation-wide Series of contests open to bona fide students of all public, private, and parochial schools was organized in three distinct types of Contest—Declamatory Contests in the elementary schools, Essay Contests in the high schools, and Oratorical Contests in the institutions of higher learning.

Provisions were made for a *Declamatory* Contest for each grade of the elementary schools with a school, county, district, and state contest to determine the best declaimer in each state. The Declamatory Contest was confined to the State-wide Contest for students of the seventh and eighth grades. The extent of the contest for students of grades one to six was determined by the superintendents and teachers in the local schools.

The declamations were selected from a printed pamphlet prepared and issued by the United States George Washington Bicentennial Commission, containing forty-four different selections suitable for the first eight grades, respectively. The selections were chosen largely upon the recommendation of more than five hundred teachers and supervisors to whom requests were made for their choice of prose and poetry relating to George Washington. The names of the elementary pupils who received places in the State Declamatory Contests are found on page 402.

The next division of this series, the *Essay* Contest, Nation-wide in scope of competition, was open to all high school students. The subjects for the essays were limited to a list of eight submitted by high school teachers of English and History. The essay selected as the best in each school competing in the High School Essay Contest in each State was placed before a State Jury of Awards. These essays were submitted to the Federal Commission where the National Jury of Awards passed upon the competing state essays. The essay awarded first place in each State Essay Contest appears in this publication and the names of the students who were given second and third places.

This National Jury of Awards was composed of Dr. William J. Cooper, Commissioner, United States Office of Education, chairman; Senator Hattie W. Caraway, of Arkansas; Congresswoman Florence P. Kahn, of California; Mr. Joy Elmer Morgan, Editor of the Journal of the National Education Association; and Dr. Albert Bushnell Hart, Historian of the United States George Washington Bicentennial Commission. The first award in the National Contest was given to Miss Betty Ann Troy, of Sacred Heart Academy, Stamford, Connecticut, and on August 4 President Hoover presented the Official George Washington Commemorative Gold Medal to Miss Troy.

The *Oratorical* Contest, another division of this Nation-wide series, was open to all college and university students with a State, Regional, and National Contest to determine the National winner. The subjects for the orations were taken from a list of ten prepared by college teachers of English and History. The oration of each college student who was given first place in each State Oratorical Contest is included in this publication. The names of the regional winners appear in the program of the National Oratorical Contest. The first award in the National Oratorical Contest held in Washington, D. C., June 24, was given to James R. Moore, of Washington and Lee University, Lexington, Virginia. The Jury of Awards for this National Oratorical Contest included Miss Anne Madison Washington, descendant of the Washington family; William Tyler Page, Executive Secretary of the United States George Washington Biceneninal Commission; Ira C. Bennett, publisher of the Washington Post; Hon. Joseph W. Byrns, Representative from Tennessee and member of United States George Washington Bicentennial Commission; and Dr. John C. Fitzpatrick, editor of the Definitive Writings of George Washington and recognized as one of the leading authorities on the life and times of our First President. This publication contains the orations by the state winners and the names of the students who received second and third places in the state contests.

The United States George Washington Bicentennial Commisison presented the Official George Washington Commemorative Medal in silver and bronze to the students who won first and second places in each State Contest of the series. A Certificate of Award was presented to the student who won third place in each State Contest.

The Official George Washington Commemorative Gold Medal was presented to Betty Ann Troy in the National Essay Contest, and to James R. Moore in the National Oratorical Contest.

In the long and arduous campaign of planning and organizing these various Nation-wide Educational Contests, the United States George Washington Bicentennial Commission has been most fortunate in having the services of Miss Hazel Belle Nielson, Director of Educational Activities. Miss Nielson has served with energy and ability and possesses high qualifications for the task. To her belongs the principal credit for the success which has made the Commission's work among the school children of America conspicuous.

SOL BLOOM,
DIRECTOR,
United States George Washington
Bicentennial Commission

Regional Oratorical Winners at the White House

President Hoover receiving the nine regional winners in the National Oratorical Contest at the White House, June 24, 1932. At the right of the President is Honorable Sol Bloom, Director of the United States George Washington Bicentennial Commission. The contestants (left to right) are as follows: J. Milton Richardson, Fred Couey, Donald Holand, James R. Moore, Margaret G. Degnan, Martin J. Tracey, Bryson Hays, Felicien Lozes, and John W. Crawford

George Washington Bicentennial National Oratorical Contest

DEPARTMENT OF COMMERCE AUDITORIUM
WASHINGTON, D. C.
EVENING OF JUNE 24, 1932
Under the Auspices of the
UNITED STATES GEORGE WASHINGTON BICENTENNIAL COMMISSION
WASHINGTON, D. C.

The National Bicentennial Oratorical Contest, conducted in the colleges and universities throughout the country, was promoted in the States by the State Contest Committees, which cooperated with the Federal Bicentennial Commission. The winning contestants of each State Oratorical Contest competed in the Regional Oratorical Contests. The successful regional representatives participating in the National Bicentennial Oratorical Contest appear below.

PROGRAM
HONORABLE SIMEON D. FESS, Presiding
MUSIC—United States Navy Band Orchestra

ORATIONS
(The order of speaking, determined by lot, is as listed below)

"WASHINGTON: NATION BUILDER"......................James R. Moore
Washington & Lee University, Lexington, Virginia.
East Central Region.

"FIRST IN PEACE"...............................Felicien Lozes
Loyola University, New Orleans, Louisiana.
South Central Region.

"THE SPIRIT OF WASHINGTON"......................Martin J. Tracey
Fordham University, New York City.
Middle Atlantic Region.

"WASHINGTON: EXEMPLAR OF AMERICAN IDEALS".....Margaret G. Degnan
New Haven State Normal School, New Haven, Connecticut.
Northeastern Region.

"WASHINGTON: EXEMPLAR OF AMERICAN IDEALS"....J. Milton Richardson
University of Georgia, Athens, Georgia.
Southeastern Region.

"THE SPIRIT OF WASHINGTON"......................John W. Crawford
Northwestern University, Evanston, Illinois.
Central Region.

"WASHINGTON: NATION BUILDER".....................Donald Holand
University of North Dakota, Grand Forks, North Dakota.
North Central Region.

"FIRST IN PEACE"...................................Fred Couey
Colorado State Teachers' College, Greeley, Colorado.
Southwestern Region.

"GEORGE WASHINGTON'S UNDERSTANDING OF MEN"........Bryson Hays
Columbia University, Portland, Oregon.
Northwestern Region.

MUSIC—United States Navy Band Orchestra

DECISION OF JUDGES—The decision of the five judges will be tabulated according to the low-point-total system, and the contestant receiving the lowest score will be declared the winner.

PRESENTATION OF AWARD—By Honorable Sol Bloom. The Official George Washington Commemorative Gold Medal will be awarded to the National winner.

MUSIC—United States Navy Band Orchestra

JUDGES—Joseph W. Byrns, Representative from Tennessee and Member of United States George Washington Bicentennial Commission; Miss Anne Madison Washington, a descendant of the Washington family; Ira E. Bennett, Editor, The Washington Post; William Tyler Page, Secretary, United States George Washington Bicentennial Commission and author of "The American's Creed"; Dr. John C. Fitzpatrick, Editor of the Definitive Writings of George Washington and one of the leading authorities on the Life and Times of our First President.

JAMES R. MOORE
of Washington and Lee University

Winner of the National Oratorical Contest,
who was awarded the official George Washington Commemorative Gold Medal

Washington College Building of Washington and Lee University, Lexington, Virginia.

The orations and essays presented in the Nation-wide Series of Educational Contests in connection with the activities of the Bicentennial Celebration of the Anniversary of the Birth of George Washington reflect great credit upon the instruction that these young people have received in the educational institutions of our country. The history of the United States and the development of its form of government present a most inspiring illustration of the movement of human progress. The fine contributions made by these young men and women show an understanding and appreciation of our national history that are most encouraging to those striving for the stability and advancement of our American institutions. Studies in the history and government of our country should be greatly stimulated by these thoughtful productions. The high standards of citizenship being taught in our schools and colleges give assurance of that intelligent leadership that will guarantee the integrity and the safety of our American civilization in the years to come.

JOSEPH ROSIER, *President, National Education Association.*

ORATIONS

First Place Awards in the State Bicentennial Oratorical Contests in Colleges and Universities

The first nine orations were awarded first place in the regional contests and were delivered by the regional winners in the National Oratorical Contest in the City of Washington, June 24, 1932. Following these orations, beginning with Alabama, appear the orations of the other state winners. The orations are printed as received without editing out minor historical errors.

Washington: Nation Builder

JAMES R. MOORE

Somerset, Kentucky

WINNER OF THE NATION-WIDE COLLEGE ORATORICAL CONTEST

Washington and Lee University, Lexington, Virginia

Representative, East Central Region

The world has produced only one George Washington. It is fitting in this year 1932 that the United States of America pay to to the Father of Our Country the honor he deserves. The Bicentennial Celebration in honor of America's greatest hero is worldwide. Americans everywhere, no matter what their creed or color, will join in a common tribute to their fellow citizen and patriot, George Washington. It is our desire to make him live anew in the hearts and minds of the American people. We would not visualize him as some half-mythical demigod, but rather as a courageous, strong, patient, intensely human person. We would visualize him as a man who worked, played, studied; sacrificed, fought, suffered; and lived to foster our infant republic into being.

That infant republic of yesterday is today one of the greatest governments on the earth. It is with a deep sense of gratitude that we who are enjoying the privileges afforded by this magnificent political organization, realize that no one man did more toward building the nation, than did George Washington. Whether our minds go back to the stormy days of the revolution, or picture the trying difficulties of the loosely organized confederation, or recount the critical days of the newly formed Union, we behold Washington as the dominant figure. It is the sterling character of Washington which went into the very fiber of the Nation, thus, we may aptly term him: "Nation Builder."

When the artist took brush in hand and painted Washington as he crossed the Delaware, and as he weathered the severities of a bitter winter at Valley Forge, and finally, when he received the surrender of Cornwallis at Yorktown, there were glorified for us certain dramatic moments in the life of this man. But can we look behind the paintings and see Washington as he actually was, in many of those disappointing moments, when his spirit must have been tried to the point of breaking, as he led his ragged woodsmen through the dark and dreary days of the revolution. When we look at him under such conditions as these, and see the manner in which he met such adversities, then we can realize what he accomplished in the building of the nation.

At the very outset of the struggle, he was faced by the best troops of Europe, while he had to rely on a raw militia, who elected their own officers and carried on war as they pleased. There was no commissary department, no uniforms, no arrangements for gunpowder or cannon. Furthermore, he had to deal with a Congress which was utterly ignorant of the needs and details of war and which represented a people without money, without arms, without allies or credit, and torn by selfish interests. Amid all this confusion and utter lack of organization, Washington was called upon to defend the thirteen colonies against the mightiest military power in Christendom.

But this lack of equipment and general preparedness for war was not the only obstacle Washington had to overcome.

As the war dragged on, the spirit of the soldiers tended to weaken. The forces under Washington's command had to undergo such unendurable miseries and privations that there was always danger of wholesale desertion. In addition to this, the Commander-in-Chief had to face actual treason in his ranks. When his efforts did not bring immediate success, sharp and bitter personal attacks were hurled against him. Toward the end of the struggle, the defeats which every army must at times suffer, tended to break the morale of the people at home. It was in the face of such difficulties as these, that the courageous and intrepid spirit of Washington held the army together, and kept alive the determination of the people to complete what they had begun. If you will picture Washington as he crossed the Delaware, personally directing his campaigns, or, if you will picture him at Valley Forge, actually experiencing the hardships and privations which the men of his army had to endure, then we will see Washington as he really was, a dynamic figure immersed in the building of a nation.

When the war was ended, we might well have expected the General to retire, content with the contributions which he had already made to his country. But, with the welfare of the people foremost in his heart, he carried on in peace as he had carried on in war. Now that freedom had been won, it must be retained and the stability of the newly formed union must be assured. The West must be developed and connected with the East. A strong central government which would hold the thirteen colonies together must be created. The devastating war had temporarily wrought utter demoralization of society, politics, and public opinion. The Continental Currency had degenerated. The debts of the new nation were staggering. Our credit abroad was insecure. Our foreign relations were muddled. And the petty quarrels and jealousies which arose when the enthusiasm of the war had subsided, threatened to wreck all that had been won. In short, there was no concerted plan which the states could follow to promote their general well-being. Washington saw clearly the imperative need for Union and that task he set himself from the day he resigned from the army until the day he was inaugurated President of the United States. Thus it was Washington who started and nurtured that great movement which culminated in the Constitution and the Union of the States. No other man could have done this, for no one had the personal influence necessary to arrest public attention. Thus we must again think of Washington as a nation builder.

Everyone recognizes the part Washington played in the building of the nation when the colonies were in the throes of revolution. No one denies the tremendous significance of his efforts during the trying days of the loosely organized Confederation. But now that the Colonies had formed a Union, and Washington had been raised to the highest office in the land, his greatest work in the building of the nation was yet to be done. When after the ceremonies of the first inaugural were over and the shouts and cheers of the populace had died away, Washington pondered deep and long the problems which lay before him. He knew that every move he would make would be watched by critical eyes, and that his every action would be subjected to the most careful scrutiny. As yet, there was no precedent to be followed, for this was a new and untried experiment. Nothing existed but a Congress and a President. There were no departments, no Supreme Court Judges, no Cabinet members, no funds, and no financial resources. What should be the mode of conduct and etiquette of the President? What should be the relation of the President to the Senate, or to foreign ministers or to the public at large? For example, what was Washington to do when the minister of France desired to have personal access to the President and even discuss matters of business with him? Here at the very outset, he could "have lowered the dignity of the Presidential office by a false idea of republican simplicity," or he could have adopted a policy of cold seclusion on the one hand or of pompous ostentation on the other. In the face of such problems as these, Washington preserved the dignity and respect due his office, yet, at the same time, managed to give free access to everyone entitled to it.

During his terms of office, he had to handle the gravest of situations, on the outcome of which depended the strength and success of the new nation. The acute Indian problem must be handled with firmness, yet with rare intelligence; the question of whether the National government should assume the state debts threatened internal harmony; and the establishment of a National Bank caused great controversy. The most insidious problem of all was the Whiskey Rebellion in Western Pennsylvania. Those self-willed Scotch-Irish frontiersmen were determined to have their own way and resist the collection of a national revenue on distilled products. Here was the first direct challenge to the new government. It had to be answered, and on the answer hung the fate of the untried union, for, if insurrection within its own borders could not be put down, then the new experiment had failed.

Washington met the challenge squarely, and, at the proper moment, moved fifteen thousand militia men into Western Pennsylvania, and with one bold stroke crushed the resistance completely.

The solution of these internal difficulties was not the only service Washington rendered in the building of the nation. There was constant danger of foreign entanglements. Trouble lurked in our relations with the three greatest powers of the time, France, England, and Spain. Should our young Nation side with the cause of liberty in the French Revolution? Should the United States tolerate the British impressment of our seamen? Could the new government establish free access to the Mississippi without antagonizing Spain? The story of Washington's policy need not be retold. His one great aim was to avoid foreign entanglements, and, if humanly possible, maintain peace, so that the new nation might develop the continent and, in that manner, rise to National greatness.

As we look back and review the part played by Washington in the building of the nation, we cannot help but have a keener sense of his greatness. Some may have shown as much zeal in the winning of our freedom. I doubt it. Others may have labored as ardently in forming an enduring Union. We don't know them. A few may have equalled Washington in constructive statesmanship. None surpassed him. But as to courage, vision, and leadership displayed in the moulding of a disorganized people into a strong and democratic government, no one approached him. Fortunate indeed was America to have at its inception such a man as Washington. The Personal Empire of Napoleon had crumbled before he died in exile in St. Helena, but the work of Washington still endures.

First in Peace

FELICIEN LOZES
New Orleans, Louisiana

*Loyola University, New Orleans, Louisiana
Representative, South Central Region*

FELICIEN LOZES

We are celebrating this evening, the Bicentennial of the birth of a man who stands foremost among the patriots of the world, not only as the liberator, but also as the Father of His Country.

As the sun rises out of the East, and slowly but surely rescues the world from the oppression of darkness, as it heralds the nativity of a new day, so did this man rise out of the darkness of a struggling nation, to rescue it from the oppression of tyranny, and make possible the ringing of the bell that joyously announced to the universe that a new nation was born. And as that sun in its flaming course across the sky, gives strength and vigor to the living things of earth, so did this man prove to be the source of light for new ideals, and the vital spark that enkindled a new hope for a nation in travail. Again as that sun, receding in the Western sky, grows larger and gleams forth in all its majesty and splendor just before it drops beneath the horizon, bidding adieu to the world, so did this man, nearing the end of his transit on the orb of life, shine in his greatest glory and splendor in the years just before he bade Farewell to the nation to which he had given life and strength.

I am referring to the man, who great as a military leader, was even greater as a peace leader; to the man whose sun shone in its greatest glory just before it set, who as a peace leader stands on the topmost pinnacle of greatness,—to George Washington, "First in Peace."

In an analysis of the meaning of peace, we find that it is not a state of lethargy, not a state of lackadaisical dullness; that it is not that servile submission which is shown externally when the heart and mind are in rebellion; that it is not merely the absence of a state of war. But we learn from the philosopher, that peace is simply, "the tranquillity of order,"—the quiet and smooth functioning of an ordered social system.

In studying the life of Washington, we find that he was not a pacifist, not one who claims that all war is wrong; but that he was a sincere seeker after real peace, one who admits the lawfulness of war in a just cause as a means of securing and insuring peace.

Even as a general in the Revolutionary War, Washington proved himself to be a sincere seeker after peace. He was fighting for the right to establish order in place of the chaos that existed in pre-revolutionary days. Even before his resignation as Commander-in-Chief of the Colonial Army, he declared that among the things essential to the welfare of the new nation were, "the adoption of a proper peace establishment; and, . . . the prevalence of that pacific and friendly disposition among the people of the United States."

But when the Revolutionary War was won, the Declaration of Independence consummated, chaos still existed. The establishment of order was the first step. Again Washington was the leader. He took the first step in the establishment of order when he served as president of the Constitutional Congress, a position that demanded the prudence, sagacity, and wisdom of a Solomon. Conflict and chaos reigned on all sides. Yet he wisely chose the golden mean between the conflicting theories of Hamilton and Jefferson, and choosing the better points from the theories of other members of the convention, he left to posterity a masterpiece of political acumen, the Constitution of the United States, the system or order by which the new nation was to be governed.

Order was now established. Next came the monstrous task of establishing the tranquillity of that order. For only where there is order plus the tranquillity of order can it be said that real peace exists. And again the duty fell to Washington. As first president of the United States he assumed the task of putting into effect the theories of the new order, a task which called for even more moral courage than any which taxed his physical courage during those bleak days at Valley Forge. Criticisms were hurled at the new government from all sides. Some states refused to recognize it. Washington himself came in for his share of the abuses. This disorder and chaos reached its peak during the latter part of his second term as president. Revolution raged in France. England was caught in the maelstrom, and war was declared between the two nations. French propaganda had been circulated throughout the colonies, and all America was fired to the highest pitch of sympathy for France. Yet Washington remained firm in his stand that the tranquillity of order should prevail. With a marvelous insight to the future, he saw that the hope of America's progress and power lay in a policy of neutrality. And so he boldly issued the proclamation of neutrality, and though it was at first greeted with storms of protests, ultimately his wisdom was apparent to all. And so, in the course of time, peace, the tranquillity of order was established.

As a military man, therefore, George Washington made it possible for this nation to consummate its Declaration of Independence from foreign power; as a peace leader, he laid the foundations upon which the nation might grow.

As he laid down his sword at the conclusion of the Revolutionary War, to pick up the quill of state, he found a nation without a government, thirteen scattered states, and a heterogeneous mass of people, all with conflicting opinons; when he bade farewell to that country, he left a united nation with a government—a democratic government—a government by the people, that was really a government and not an anarchy. He found a nation in chaos; he left a nation in order. He brought about the tranquillity of order, the unruffled perfection of peace. The "Sun" of Washington had shone in its greatest glory—he bade Farewell to his nation.

Farewell? Washington has not said farewell. In the words of a great orator, "Washington counts more for the life of America today than at any time when leading her armies or occupying her presidential chair. He is the ideal by which her life must be directed, if she is to fulfill her providential mission among the nations." And so we see that there is still a need for the spirit of Washington on this Bicentennial of his birth. Only recently on the Eastern front, Mars belched forth his fire that threatened the world. In Europe the deadly vultures of Communism and Bolshevism are gnawing at the vitals of the social organism. Here in America an economic war is corroding the foundations of the nation. While from above the majestic countenance of the man who was "first in peace" gazes down and awaits our reply. Let us hope that the present leaders of this nation, on this Bicentennial of the birth of its first leader, may become imbued with the same wisdom, sagacity, and unselfish patriotism that were his characteristics. Let us hope that the spirit of that face above us, the spirit of the man who was "first in peace" may reign in the hearts and minds of our present day leaders; that they may guide us from our present chaotic state of military and economic war, to the state of universal peace, as did Washington guide the infant nation from the state of war, to the state of peace,—to the tranquillity of order.

Then, then, will that majestic countenance deign to smile down in approbation, then may this nation go ever onward, out, out, into the purple twilight of the future, not carving its record with the sword, but illuminating the pages of history with the adornments of enduring peace.

The Spirit of Washington

MARTIN J. TRACEY

New York City

Fordham University, New York City
Representative, Middle Atlantic Region

MARTIN J. TRACEY

During the days when America was young, and hero worshipers thronged our land, a magnificent, flawless statue, reminiscent of the stone gods of Greece, was chiseled out of marble and looked upon as an idol of perfection. As time flew by, some of the descendants of the same idealists gradually changed until they reached that stage wherein they constructed an entirely new image. This statue resembled a gay, carefree gentleman of the Eighteenth Century, who possessed no great intellectual powers, but who was capable of many human weaknesses. Both statues were images of the same person. Yet, in reality, that person was neither. For George Washington was not a demigod, not a carefree gentleman of the Eighteenth Century, but he was a true, real man.

If Washington had been a man capable of many human weaknesses which he could not overcome, history could not say of him: "He carried into public life the severest standards of private morals." Were he a perfect man, he could not have erred as history also reveals. Each is partially true, but the whole truth is: Washington did perform good deeds, Washington did make mistakes. In the truly representative picture, great eye, grim jaw, and gripped lips do what granite can to give you the real master—and so a man! He was not a cold, lifeless statue, but a real, red-blooded man. The body of that man has perished but the spirit lives on loved by all men.

As a real, true man, Washington was most active. Yet, not by his actions is he immortal, but by his spirit. For as Emerson tells us, "We cannot find the smallest part of the personal weight of Washington in his exploits." Through his deeds, Washington might easily be condemned. For it could be said that he was not a great general like Caesar and Frederick the Great, since he never won a major conflict. It could be held that he was not a great political thinker, since the crowning achievements of his Presidency were jewels from the mind of Hamilton. But, going behind these actions, what stands out? The fact that Washington was the soul of the Revolution and without him it would have perished at its birth, the fact of a courage that never faltered; the fact of a cool judgment that developed into a ripe, sane wisdom; the fact of a patriotism that never stooped to the thought of self-glorification. With such a spirit did Washington carry the nation through long, dreary hours, black with defeat and treason to a peak high and mighty in the universe. Not by his deeds but by his spirit has Washington made himself to history not only an indispensable man but an indispensable memory.

Although the spirit of Washington is mighty, it is not built on genius. His spirit is made up of moral integrity, courage, and sound judgment—in a word, manhood. Had it been otherwise the name of Washington might have passed away with his body. For in that age were born Madison, Hamilton, Adams, Henry—all men of great talent and prodigious minds. In such company Washington, as a man of genius, might have been completely overshadowed. But Washington was more than a genius. As he himself said so humbly, "Integrity and firmness are all I can promise. These, . . . shall never forsake me, although I, may be deserted by all men." Had he been a genius he might have wrecked the new nation upon the rocks of brilliancy after the fashion of Napoleon and Alexander the Great. Where the genius of his contemporaries failed, the spirit of Washington triumphed. For when the Confederacy fell apart like a "rope of sand," it was not the genius of Eighteenth Century minds, but it was the spirit of Washington that cemented the nation under the Constitution into that everlasting rock that stands today in undying tribute to the great spirit of a great man.

Strange as it may seem, this spirit was not peculiar to Washington alone. It was born in Eternity and will live for all Eternity because it is the spirit of true manhood. In George Washington, this spirit of manhood found its greatest exemplar on the American soil, since he perfected himself in its fundamental virtues. Down through the ages this spirit has lived and has been rebuffed by men. Today, in modern America, speed and laxity have somewhat unbalanced man's moral life. Today, as never before, the spirit of Washington, that exemplar of true manhood, cries out for Twentieth Century Americans to balance their moral life by upholding sound judgment, courage, and moral integrity. That spirit cries out with a remedy for the present depression in Washington's words: "Of all the dispositions and habits, which lead to political prosperity, Religion and morality are indispensable supports." That spirit cries out for honesty in politics, a straight forwardness in business uprightness in the treatment of labor. That spirit cries out again in the language of Washington: "Why quit our own to stand upon foreign ground?—Why, by interviewing our destiny with any part of Europe, entangle our peace and prosperity in the toils of European ambition, rivalship, interest, humor, or caprice?" Washington is dead, but his spirit still lives—the same now as it was two hundred years ago. And now as then, it is calling the American people to aid their country by building up their own individual morality. That spirit cries out not for a law-fearing, but a God-fearing America.

Well might many men attempt to defame such a powerful spirit lest it too readily lay hold of the minds of true Americans. Yet —such men forget that Washington's contemporaries stamped him as Jefferson said: "A wise, a good, a great man!" Scientific historians reveal that Washington was not a genius but at the same time they steadfastly maintain that he is among the noblest of noble Americans. Even if some scientific historians should discover flaws in Washington's actions it is an established fact that the spirit of Washington was great and still is great. Every flaw, every defect which the spirit of Washington has conquered adds more honor, more glory to the sterling Character of an unimpeachable man.

Too often, perhaps, many people condemn praise of Washington as old antiquated, and hence annoying and useless. But the sun is old in time. Yet, each morn as it brightens the eastern sky that same sun is new, and glorious to behold. Like the sun the spirit of Washington is old in time, because it began in Eternity. Like the sun, that spirit is new, glorious, because each time we behold it there surges up within us new hope, new vigor, new inspiration to avoid what is un-American and to do what is American. For the spirit of Washington is ever old, ever new, ever capable of furnishing a model for every type of American life.

For over a century and a half, not only America but the world at large has honored the spirit of our First President. His spirit of manhood has placed him not above men, not below men, but on a level with all men. They revere him because they see in him the perfection of that manhood which they themselves can at least approach. As an idol of perfection Washington the Statue will crash and perish; as a carefree gentleman Washington will fade away, "unwept, unhonored, and unsung." But as a true, red-blooded man, tingling with life, the spirit of Washington lives, now and will live for all time. For, that spirit is Eternal, that spirit inspires all men to a greater moral and practical life, to a more noble and American life, that spirit immortalizes one man, and for us, one man alone—George Washington.

Washington:
Exemplar of American Ideals

MARGARET G. DEGNAN
Derby, Connecticut
State Normal School, New Haven, Connecticut
Representative, Northeastern Region

MARGARET G. DEGNAN

Every great nation has certain ideals which are characteristic of that nation alone. The average American has standards of clean living, clean thinking, and worthwhile doing as his ideals. Thus the ideal American would be a man who is physically fit, mentally awake, and morally straight; a man who is honest, righteous, and cheerful; a man of integrity, a leader of men.

Such a man was George Washington—one of the noblest characters in our history. He was humble, charitable, and courageous; but each of these traits alone would not have made him great. A noble character is a combination of elements, and it was the combination of many virtues that glorified Washington.

William E. Lecky has said of Washington: "He was in the highest sense of the word, a gentleman and a man of honor, and he carried into public life the severest standards of private morals." We know that honesty was vital to him. He believed that every man must be honest to live a happy life. This honesty embraced not merely actions, but thoughts and opinions as well. In a letter to James Welch, Washington once said: "To contract new Debts is not the way to pay old ones." When a lad of thirteen, he drew up a code of behavior. The wisdom revealed in this code far exceeded his thirteen years. Even at so young an age, George Washington planted the seed of honesty in his own heart when he said: "Undertake not what you cannot perform but be Careful to keep your Promise." Washington was a man of integrity. No private interest nor dislike could alter a decision which his natural wisdom and justice had previously rendered.

Coupled with this rugged honesty was a peaceful, almost meek nature. We may be sure of this, because it has been proved that Washington never drew his sword except in defense of public safety. Governor Wilbur L. Cross, of Connecticut, recently said of Washington: "Washington, as President, relied not on the sword but on public opinion as the source of all lasting power. Calm, serene, just, and humane, he won in equal measure the glories of peace and the glories of war."

Despite overwhelming success and rapidly increasing popularity, Washington remained simple and modest. When he first took his seat in the Virginia Assembly, he was so embarrassed, according to Edmund Randolph, that while he was blushing and stammering in an attempt to acknowledge his enthusiastic reception, the speaker relieved him by saying: "Sit down, Mr. Washington, your modesty is equal to your valor, and that surpasses the power of any language I possess."

One of the traits that helped to make Washington a great man was his courage. Stories of his indomitable courage and success against odds are numerous. We know how he held his men together at Valley Forge in the winter of 1777 and 1778, in the face of discouraging and unbelievable hardships; how he brought them out in the spring stronger than ever in spirit and in discipline. That was more than a duty, more than a light task. How many of those men must have wanted to die, must have prayed to have their hunger and starvation, their frozen bodies relieved by the long and peaceful sleep of death. It takes courage to live—courage and strength and hope and humor. And courage and strength and hope and humor have to be bought with pain and work and prayers and tears. George Washington suffered pain with his men. That memorable picture of his crossing the Delaware is ample proof of this fact. He worked with a will, not over his men, but with them. He prayed at night that relief might come to the suffering men in his charge; and he cried out to God in his own mental anguish for guidance in the surrounding confusion. The courage which was flung about him as a mantle was indeed sorely tried, but found to be invulnerable.

With the traits of honesty, integrity, peacefulness, modesty, and courage, the ideal American must have wisdom in order to know how to use his other virtues. The wisdom with which George Washington led his men to one victory after another is equalled only by that with which he guided this country during his presidency. It was his knowledge and foresight that had trained his Virginians to fight. It was his judgment that saved them when, with General Braddock, they were attacked by Indians near Fort Duquesne. General Braddock had commanded the army to fight out in the open, while the Indians were safe behind the trees. When Braddock was mortally wounded, Washington took command and ordered the few hundred remaining men to take to the trees as the Indians were doing. Surely such a deed is not the action of a man of ordinary intelligence.

We have been thinking of Washington as a military leader and a political leader, rather than as a human being. We are apt to forget that great men, and even ideals, are human after all. One of the most attractive characteristics of a real human being is cheerfulness. The ideal American would enjoy life, radiate good cheer, would play as well as work, would have a sense of humor, and dissipate gloom. George Washington fairly breathed contentment; he had a kind and a loving disposition, and a generous appreciation of others. Nature made him great; he made himself virtuous. His highest ambition was the happiness of mankind; his noblest victory, the conquest of himself.

Though an ideal is usually a star shining in the distance, George Washington has brought our ideal, the American ideal, nearer and nearer to us. If we let that star take on new meaning, it will represent integrity, honesty, peacefulness, modesty, courage, and wisdom. It takes little imagination to see in place of that star the familiar face of George Washington, exemplar of American ideals.

Washington:
Exemplar of American Ideals

J. MILTON RICHARDSON, JR.

Rivoli, Macon, Georgia

University of Georgia, Athens, Georgia
Representative, Southeastern Region

J. MILTON RICHARDSON, JR.

Among all the great names that have adorned and enriched the history of America, there is no more majestic figure than George Washington. To paint that majestic man's full length portrait or adequately portray the qualities that gave him greatness and the virtues that make him immortal, I cannot. But with you I can reverently sit at his feet and listen to a story that will arouse within us lofty aspirations and cause us more diligently to seek the old paths of high endeavor and manly honor.

It is not my purpose to indulge in extravagant or indiscriminate eulogy, but if possible to give a judicial estimate of a great man who was the most commanding figure in a fierce and eventful national crisis.

George Washington began life well. He had a clean boyhood with no tendency to vice or immorality. He formed no evil habits which he had to correct and forged upon himself no chains which he had to break. His life was as transparent as the light that shone about him; his heart was as open as the soft skies that bent in benediction over his country home. George Washington, first of all, exemplified the ideals of the "American Boy."

As a military leader Washington's fame is written with eternity's pen of diamond point upon the triumphs of genius. George Washington was the best American soldier of his day. He had the genius for patience, the instinct for strategy, and the capacity for making the most of limited resources with the courage of a lion and the cunning of a fox. Washington marshalled the crude, untrained, inexperienced American farmer into a veteran and supplied by discipline the lack of experience.

There is a certain glamour that gathers about a military hero which commands our admiration but too often evokes extravagant praise. One who braves the shout of battle and wins the chaplet of victory is unconsciously invested with a halo more brilliant than the crown of any civilian, however great his accomplishments or magnificent his gifts. And so it is with Washington. We are too prone to allow Washington the soldier to overshadow Washington the civilian.

Whatever of imperishable lustre Washington's genius may have shed upon our arms, he rendered a far nobler service to liberty when as presiding officer he guided and controlled in large measure the deliberations of the Constitutional Convention. But for the confidence that his colleagues had in his sterling character and peerless patriotism we now know that the Constitutional Convention would have dissolved in strife. Debate was animated; jealousies existed; rivalry contended; the convention was barely held together by the strength of a thread.

Through these months of doubt, anxiety, and fear, Washington sat patient and forbearing; and, by the very force of moral grandeur, he moulded contraries into concord.

Just as without Washington's genius the Revolutionary War would have probably been lost, just as without his counsel the Constitutional Convention would never have agreed to a plan of government, so without his influence the instrument of government would never have been ratified by the thirteen original states. For the first time Virginia refused to follow the leadership of the eloquent Patrick Henry and harkened to the voice of Washington, ratifying the Constitution by the narrow margin of ten votes.

The hearts of a grateful people turned once more to Mount Vernon and chose Washington to be the Chief Magistrate of the Nation. Surrounded by Hamilton and Jefferson, by Randolph and Knox, Washington launched this government upon the untried and uncharted waters and for eight years guided its course. As the president of this storm-cradled nation Washington faced problems and solved them; he met difficulties and surmounted them, he wisely and resolutely and in defiance of public clamor refused to allow this nation to enter the entanglements of the crowned heads of Europe which threatened to draw us into tragedy and ruin. Having steered the Ship of State for eight years Washington retired into private life at the very pinnacle of earthly glory.

Washington stood for certain things of which we stand in desperate need today. In the gloom of today, when men are hopeless of the present and doleful of the future, Washington looms forth as a lighthouse to guard us from dangerous rocks and guide us into port.

Washington had a passion for the law and we have become the most lawless nation on earth. In the Farewell Address, that last will and testament of the Father of His Country to the people that he loved better than life, he eloquently expressed this sentiment: "This government . . . has a just claim to your confidence and your support.—Respect for its authority, compliance with its Laws, acquiescence in its measures, are duties enjoined by the fundamental maxims of true Liberty." Would that this thought might be engraved upon the heart of every American citizen!

Washington stood for faith and confidence, and today the absence of both is taking its toll in human misery and economic ruin. In the discouragement found on every hand it should cheer men's souls to remember the soldier who, retreating, often defeated, never faltered in faith until victory was his reward.

Washington believed in the potential power of religion and today America is threatened by the blight of religion. Washington said that the only basis for public prosperity is religion and morality, and religion is the only security for morality.

Let us on Washington's anniversary day learn some lessons in patriotism from this great American. Let us replight our faith in the principles of constitutional liberty to which he was devoted. Let us repledge our allegiance to the flag of the country for which he fought and resolve to make Washington in deed as in name the exemplar of American ideals.

Greatest of Americans, leader of our armies, expounder of our political creed, Pilot of the Ship of State, the exemplar of American ideals, we shall ever speak his name with reverence and cherish his memory with patriotic pride. Marvelous, many-sided, masterful man, his name will grow in lustre and his figure will become more majestic as the decades ripen into centuries and the "stories of time melt into the music of eternity."

The Spirit of Washington

JOHN W. CRAWFORD
Oak Park, Illinois
Northwestern University, Evanston, Illinois
Representative, Central Region

John W. Crawford

As you have undoubtedly guessed from what our Chairman and the preceding speakers have said we are here tonight to honor George Washington. Strange, is it not, that this Two Hundredth Anniversary of his Birth should find the nation he created in the midst of difficulties very similar to those which he himself encountered? Perhaps in reviving the memory of Washington we may perceive what we need in this present hour of crisis. For, in that other dark period of our history America was fortunate indeed in finding the courage of the patriot, the insight of the statesman, the dignity and confidence of the administrator, all in one great leader,— George Washington.

When Washington arose in the Continental Congress, attired in the blue and buff of a Virginian colonel, it was a signal that the hour for action had come; that a new nation was about to be born. On the eve of the great conflict it was Patrick Henry who said, "If you speak of solid information and sound judgment, Colonel Washington is unquestionably the greatest man on that floor." The confidence of the people in Washington summoned him forth as Commander-in-Chief of the Continental Army. He at once measured the magnitude of the work and unflinchingly faced the facts. The patriotism of the American people he well knew. He also knew that with an untrained, undisciplined army he was about to face the best troops in Europe. The phantom Congress, torn by local self-interests, without credit, and fearing the strength of a central army, had no power to act. But the cause for immediate action was not wanting—the English troops surrounded Boston! What did Washington do? Out of this chaos he brought forth an efficient and well distributed army. To Congress he taught the need and details of war organization. Unceasingly he pleaded with the jealous governors and colonies for support. His plan of war was clear. His small army could not fight great battles until it was better supplied with arms and provisions. For nine years he

worried the enemy, pausing only to snatch a signal victory that raised the courage and hope of the American people. So when the little half disbanded army was in retreat, Washington commanded them to turn, and with one bold stroke wrested a two-fold victory from the panicky enemy. Thus Washington gave to the soldiers, to the Congress, and to the people, the finest and most effectual of all lessons—the example of courage, loyalty, and self-sacrifice.

But the superiority of Washington's character and genius as a patriot and soldier was to become more exalted as a statesman in the formation of the Constitution. The object of war achieved, no one foresaw more clearly than Washington the magnitude of the problems confronting the country. There was a vast unguarded frontier, rich, unclaimed! Above all was the need for a stronger union. The bitter experience and hard facts of war had taught Washington the vital need and value of union, for the grim spector of disunion lurked behind him as he rode from Cambridge to Yorktown. There was the restlessness and open rebellion of a sullen and unpaid army demanding redress from a poverty stricken and helpless Congress. There were the jealousies of the states, repugnant to the idea of a higher order of central government. All these were allied against him, yet passionately did he seek to save that liberty for his people which he had just won. To Hamilton he wrote, "It is clearly my opinion, unless Congress have powers competent to all general purposes, that the distresses we have encountered, the Expense we have incurred, and the blood we have spilt . . . will avail us nothing." To the governor of every state he ardently urged the necessity of a stronger central government. The same appeal went to the army. It was a general's last order by which he made each soldier a pioneer in the cause of the union. With a conviction that left nothing to be added he pleaded thus with his men: "—that, unless the principles of the Federal government are properly supported, and the powers of the Union increased, the honor, dignity, and justice of the nation will be lost forever." A plan for commercial agreement between Maryland and Virginia, drawn up at Mount Vernon, was the first practical step in the formation of our Constitution, for it led directly to a summons for a national convention to meet at Philadelphia for the purpose of rendering the Constitution of the Federal Government adequate to the exigencies of the Union. Washington was elected chairman of this convention. Here, behind the closed doors of the same hall in which was signed the Declaration of Independence, met the advocates of the two great opposing political philosophies. On the one hand the exponents of the Confederacy and state individualism; on the other, those who strove for the Union and national security. For four long months of hope and despair, debate and compromise, patience and anxiety, the steady hand of Washington guided the convention until the work had been accomplished. A great charter of liberty had been written, the Constitution of the United States.

But the new Constitution was yet to be ratified, and arranged against it were the pride and jealousy of the states, the distrust of central power, and the ambition of leaders. Moreover, lawlessness was abroad in the land; products without markets, currency without value, and men without work. For the third time Washington arose to the call of his country,—not as the patriot-soldier of the Revolution, not as the statesman of the convention, but as chief executive of the United States. It was the weight of his great name and the assurance that he would be the first president which was the deciding factor in securing the adoption of the new Constitution by the states. It was John Lamb, the able leader of the opposition who said, "For to no other mortal would I trust authority so enormous." When we realize what it meant to take thirteen hostile, half-starved, petty commonwealths and mold them into one united republic, and when we further realize the difficult task of organizing the new government in accordance with the general principles of the Constitution, of rescuing an infant nation from the impending bankruptcy, of establishing, in the face of a social upheaval in Europe, a definite foreign policy, then we become aware of his magnetic power, his executive ability, and the breadth and soundness of his statesmanship.

More than a century has passed since he last walked among men, yet can we not say that his great leadership is the fundamental need of our day? The dark cold days of Valley Forge are not far from the bleak and hopeless days of 1932. The mad conflict between personal and local interest and the common welfare rages today as it did a century and a half ago. Trade is strangled, credit is paralyzed, factional strife increases, governments are inactive and helpless. Dare we any longer be indifferent to these facts? No! We cannot wait for the dove to return with the olive branch, for the floods to recede, and for peace to be born again. The interests of men and nations are interwoven into the complex fabric of the world. There are two alternatives, either we are to fall upon our neighbor in selfish hatred or we are to be drawn together by the bonds of love and a common enterprise. Into these darkened moments of peril, misgivings must radiate the courage, the foresight and the confidence of a Washington. We need today a Washington with an unselfish and courageous conviction who will change our politics from a racket to a service! A Washington of sincere statesmanship who will promote an irresistible moral force for peace: a Washington of foresight and action who will recognize our nation's recovery in a cooperative will of the world: a Washington with a far-reaching conception of statesmanship who will work out a righteous solution to the great problem of starvation in a land of plenty. Into the homes of our people, into the schools of our youth must be infused those ideals which are broad enough to see beyond personal and local interest, to embrace a finer, a more intelligent interpretation of the great problems of personal success, national welfare, and international understanding.

Washington: Nation Builder

DONALD HOLAND

Grand Forks, North Dakota

University of North Dakota, Grand Forks, North Dakota
Representative, North Central Region

DONALD HOLAND

Late in 1783, Washington bade farewell to his generals and resigned his position as Commander of the Continental Armies. It was the end of a military career so adorned with victories and so glorious in its achievements that it could have added splendor to the Napoleonic accomplishments. He then journeyed to Mount Vernon where he had intended to spend the remainder of his life in the quiet and comfort on the banks of the Potomac. For the first time in nearly ten years, he would be able to enjoy the private home life for which he had yearned so longingly. For once his own time would be at his own disposal. The following excerpt is taken from a letter to Lafayette: "I have not only retired from all public employments, but I am retiring within myself, and shall be able to view the solitary walk, and tread the paths of private life, with a heartfelt satisfaction." During the next few years he amused himself about his estate—planting trees, beautifying in general, and tending to private business.

But this could not be for long. Little did that great soldier and statesman then realize that one of his most important tasks yet lay before him.

It remained for an incident to occur late in 1786 which shocked the country to its very foundation and made Washington see the necessity of a strong central government. A group of farmers living on the hilly, rocky soil of Massachusetts could stand their impoverishment no longer. The war had driven them deeply into debt. They decided that if they could overthrow the British government, they could certainly overthrow the government of Massa-

chusetts. So under General Shays the same men who fought at Bunker Hill shouldered the muskets with which they shot down the picked British soldiers, and reduced four counties to a state of anarchy. The condition was truly serious, for with disorder in one state, what could prevent it from spreading to the others? The thirteen independent American states faced democratic ruin.

The instant that Washington heard of this outbreak he turned to his household and said that this settled it—that a strong central government was necessary.

The scene next shifts to the State House in Philadelphia Friday morning, May 25, 1787. Delegates representing nine states to the Federal Convention had assumed their respective places when Robert Morris rose and nominated George Washington to preside over the convention. A vote followed and as a result, Washington was ushered to the president's chair.

And so, at the age of fifty-five, did this great hero, who had so ably borne the burdens of revolutionary leadership, come to be the presiding officer of one of the most distinguished assemblies recorded in history—the assembly which drafted the Constitution of the United States of America!

Responding to the call of the Federal Convention meant the beginning of a new career. It meant—Father of a Country endowed with high ideals of peace and freedom. It meant First President of a nation destined to attain formidable heights as a world power.

Following the all-summer session of the convention came finally the adoption of the Constitution. It provided for a president selected by a group of electors. The inevitable followed, and on the ensuing April 30th, Washington assumed his role as chief executive of the new-born nation.

As president during the crucial period of early development, he served with such capability that for those who like to build imaginary halls of fame, I say: you may well be proud of the little niche reserved for the Father of Our Country. No better man could have been chosen from the point of view of honesty, fair-mindedness, dignity, and faithfulness. He had a superior quality of commanding obedience, and everyone, whether Federalist or Anti-Federalist, trusted him. Truly, no better man could have been chosen to set up standards for that perpetual stream of successors!

As chief executive he exhibited a sagacity of insight, a firmness of purpose, and a power of execution,—qualities envied by all business men.

Now I would not attempt further to glorify the name and character of Washington. They are so radiant and so glittering in themselves that even Abraham Lincoln was led to utter the following statement: "Washington is the mightiest name of earth—long since mightiest in the cause of civil liberty, still mightiest in moral reformation. On that name no eulogy is expected. It can not be. To add brightness to the sun, or glory to the name of Washington is alike impossible. Let none attempt it. In solemn awe we pronounce the name, and in its naked deathless splendor leave it shining on."

We can, however, deal with the more definite and understandable outgrowths of that character. Let us look for a moment upon the seemingly forgotten trials of that period of organization. The Articles of Confederation had failed. And we too often forget that it was their unfinished tasks—mind you—the problems which they could not meet with which this new government had to contend. Then there was the problem of government organization with all its ramifications into the judicial, administrative, and legislative departments;—of establishing a revenue suitable to the entire country,—foreign relations involving adjustments with several countries were yet in a premature stage,—and the financial problems including payment of debts, establishment of banks, and the levying of taxes remained untouched.

This in its way presents the paramount issues of the day. Yet, friends, I am utterly failing to present the situation as it really was. For it did not mean merely sitting in council to discuss these things. It did not mean merely the passage of laws and statutes. No, the respect of our people for government had previously been uprooted. This must be renewed—then those laws and statutes could be enforced. But this you will agree was no easy matter for even today, more than one hundred fifty years later, we are still combating that sinister foe—lawlessness. Yes, herein lay the test of the new government.

Should success crown the efforts of the convention all would be well. But should failure prevail—should this experiment prove to be futile—there would be two possibilities, disunion or an American Monarchy. Either would have been a confession of shattered hopes.

But I need not linger here. For we all know that during Washington's two terms as president, the government was established upon a basis coveted by many abroad. The experiment had proved a success upon first try! The seed of a democracy destined to grow had been sown!

I need only cite for you the sharply contrasting conditions at the end of Washington's eighth year. Amidst appalling obstacles the authority of the government had been firmly established; a sound credit created; and a floating debt funded in a perfectly satisfactory manner. The difficulties involved in the establishment of a system of internal taxation were completely removed. Funds were provided for the gradual but total extinguishment of the public debt. The agricultural and commercial wealth of the country soared to almost unbelievable heights. Our foreign difficulties had been reconciled. And the various war-like Indian tribes toward the Mississippi had been taught to respect peace with the new nation.

Yes, a new government had been created and was prospering.

True, our democracy today has its problems. An economic depression, and a political campaign with all its bitterness among our people over major issues, are upon us. But after all how minor are these things in comparison to the actual basis of the Government! They remind me of two small children quarreling in the upstairs nursery room of a huge colonial mansion. And yet our people are one in their respect and admiration for the *foundation* of that colonial structure, our government.

For today, to change the figure, that government stands as an aged tree, spreading its branches from coast to coast shading and protecting you and me. The winds of ill-fortune may whistle through its boughs and winters cold may test its strength. But let us be true husbandmen and dedicate our lives to its perpetuation that it may live on as a living monument to the memory of George Washington.

First in Peace

FRED COUEY
Trinidad, Colorado
Colorado State Teachers College, Greeley, Colorado
Representative, Southwestern Region

FRED COUEY

Ladies and Gentlemen: We are gathered here to commemorate the Two Hundredth Anniversary, not of a costly war, not of a cataclysmic political upheaval, not even of an outstanding individual, but of our great symbol of patriotism—our national hero, George Washington.

There are those in the epics of every people who have a value quite apart from the historical facts: France has her Joan of Arc; England, her King Arthur; America, her Washington! These heroes become legendary figures, around them crystallize the ideals of a people. And so, as the reverence of two centuries has made Washington a legend, as a legend we must accept him.

The scene has been laid with the slow care of two hundred years, and the player, for there is but one actor, moves across the stage with set directions. Shall we watch the play? Look! the curtain rises; the events unfold before us.

A country struggling in its birth agonies calls out, "A leader! A leader!"—from the background there steps one, fearless, quick to command, able to control. Comes the stir of drums, the privations of Valley Forge, the breathless procession of campaigns, the climax of the first act—America is born!

The scenes have passed quickly; the action has been powerful; the actor has done well. We applaud, then search our program: We read, "The second and final act shall be a tableau depicting our actor in the midst of the mightiest task in the history of these United States." Our curiosity is aroused. Surely no task could crown the achievements of the first act; surely no quiet tableau could evoke greater technique than those fiery battle scenes. Then, from one side Time steps forward. He speaks: "Let the rolling drums be silent; let the armies be forgotten; let the general fade into the great landowner, and behold the symbol, the great intangible abstraction that is, to us, George Washington." He steps back; the curtain rises. There stands Washington across the threshold of our country, and in his hands he holds the finished Constitution and the Farewell Address, and beneath his feet lie calmness and peace, and above the war clouds of destruction are a blot on the far horizon. The curtain falls—our play is done.

And so we depart, impressed by the deeds, by the character of this mighty legend, and not regarding him as a man, but as an instrument. And it is altogether fitting that we do this, for Washington's humanity has been covered by the slow debris of two hundred years, his deification is denied by the warm outlines that remain of the once sharply—defined leader, and his degradation is absurd in the face of the records of his justice, prudence, honesty, and fearlessness.

We are fortunate in having as our national hero a man who has withstood the most penetrating and the most scurrilous attack, and who has emerged above his belittlers by the quiet strength of a great character. And we have said that the greatest thing this man has done was the successful culmination and maintenance of a national peace. You may ask, and justifiably, "Were not these greater: a military force created out of country lads, France persuaded to reinforce our tiny navy, the surrender of Lord Cornwallis, the refusal of dictatorship?"

In answer, let me take you back to November of seventeen hundred eighty-three. The war is over; the army, disbanded. The Articles of the Confederation loosely control the thirteen colonies, Congress is in debt $38,000,000 and there is no executive power to collect the taxes levied by the Legislature. For six years this condition persisted, until the country is as Washington said, "little more than the shadow without the substance." And it is this panorama which greets Washington's inaugural eye: a country desolate, indebted, quarrelling, uncontrolled, unable to endure and powerless to change. And yet from this infantile monstrosity, Washington produced the prodigy—America. Are we not, then, justified in giving the First in Peace precedence over the First in War? Can we not, in these blustery times, profit by his rules? I tell you, we can profit much by them. Never in our national life has there been a period when we so seriously needed to know the precepts of peace. In the light of the recent Far-Eastern embroilments, it is highly pertinent that we review the principles practiced by our Advocate of Peace and reapply them to our national policy. Therefore, I repeat it, we need to know the four cardinal points of Washington's philosophy which were calculated to make us, as a nation, First in Peace.

What, then, are these principles which shall set us aright with Japan and England and the imposing array of the League, without at once losing our international prestige? They are as simple as they are universal: preparedness, unity, honesty, and prudent isolation. Let me say it again, this platform of peace: preparedness, unity, honesty, and prudent isolation.

Considered dispassionately, the first adequate national defense is perhaps paramount. As the strong man does not have to fight to maintain his position, and his mere opposition often quells the insurgent fighting, so may a nation strong and powered to fight have the influence necessary to stifle many wars at their very conception. Vast military machines as odious to us as intricate political rings but adequate national preparedness is a thing as vital as our very independence itself.

The need for unity was shown in our Civil War and in the World War, but can not our parties learn a further lesson of united voting, our business the law of cooperative world marketing?

And should I speak of honesty and legal fairness? Should I speak of honesty, in a day when the very cornerstone of our judicial system—trial by jury—is being worn smooth by perjury among the people, when a Dwight Morrow is almost singular in his generation of statesmen? Of greed and graft, of protested bootlegging, of criminal lawyers, Washington could and would say much.

And, as for the last, prudent isolation, or as Washington called it, "calm and sane alliances, not swayed by either love or hate, but by economic necessity, sympathy and humanity," have we not had proof of its value in the snarls of the Holy Alliance and the Triple Entente, which involved all Europe in a fatal and bloody war? We cannot have complete isolation now, for being the great creditor nation of the world, we are financially involved everywhere, but we can have prudent isolation, we can have our executives free to follow their highest convictions of right and free to adopt a highly flexible foreign policy.

And so I present you with the four tenets of Washington's peace, and I lay them before you as a challenge that you may remember them and apply them wherever possible: first, maintain the tools of war—be prepared; second, promote the widest integration—be united; third, stamp out graft and lawlessness—be honest; fourth, be prudent—avoid meddling in alien implications.

So let us, with Washington's four great precepts as our guide and Peace our goal, uphold our nation as a bulwark of civilization, a mighty refuge for the prostrate nations of the world, a beneficent influence in the path of humanity. May not these fundamental truths, which have underlaid our national policy for two hundred years, prove of equal value in this period of economic and diplomatic stress? May not they revitalize a world statesmanship that quibbles and rants while imperialism stalks in the dark corners of the world?

God, grant that from the swelling folds of Old Glory peace and harmony may be spilled across the world spreading everywhere those glorious tenets we have learned from our great and legendary hero —George Washington, First President of the United States!

George Washington's Understanding of Men

BRYSON HAYS

Multnomah, Oregon

Columbia University, Portland, Oregon

Representative, Northwestern Region

BRYSON HAYS

George Washington was to make a public appearance. The square was crowded with a curious multitude— anxious to see what manner of man was this who had led the colonies to freedom. As he took his place on the platform silence fell upon the multitude. The assembled citizens scanned him carefully. They were looking at a tall, powerful man, dignified of bearing, with cold, blue eyes and a nose, aquiline and prominent. He possessed all the qualities of leadership which men demanded. Yet the people seemed to feel a lack of a certain something. This man could not be human. But now the quiet was broken by the voice of a small boy who wanted a closer look at his hero. His

demand became so insistent that a way was cleared through the throng, and the lad with his embarrassed mother approached Washington. He scrutinized him carefully and turned to his mother and exclaimed, "Why, he's only a man."

Washington's cold dignity melted away, and with an appealing smile he replied, "Yes, my boy, I am only a man after all."

Here is the hidden secret of the greatness of Washington, the leader of men. He was a man, not a cold, superhuman creature. His understanding of the hearts of men, his knowledge of character and worth, lift him high as a leader; for without the gift of knowing men, without sympathizing and loving them, it is doubtful if he would now be "first in the hearts of his countrymen."

But the passing centuries have somewhat dimmed the real picture of the man. They have shrouded him with mists of unreality, they have clothed him with traits of character which have slowly but surely removed him farther from our reach. By placing George Washington upon the peak of cold chastity they have de-humanized an intensely human man.

It is not difficult to understand why Washington was preeminent as a leader when we analyze his character. He had a real sympathy and love for his men. When the continental army was wintering at Valley Forge he sent message after message to Congress, begging, pleading, yes even demanding sufficient food and clothing for the ragged hungry troops. It was he who covered his face with his cloak and wept at the sight of his men in Fort Washington bayoneted by the British soldiers. His soldiers knew his deep and real love for them, and they placed their very lives in his hands.

Coupled with his general understanding of men was Washington's true understanding of character and worth. It is said that only one man, Benedict Arnold, ever completely deceived him. He entrusted young Lafayette with the command of the troops who were to harry the great Cornwallis; delicate tasks were confided to the impetuous Mad Anthony Wayne. History proves that his judgment was right.

Few of us today realize that Washington's temper was violent. Early in life he conquered this demon and held it in the iron bonds of self-control. How many times his leadership would have suffered, how many a delicate scheme would have come to naught had not this fierce temper been controlled by his indomitable will!

As men study the portrait of the Father of Our Country, there are some who fail to see in it the picture of a man who could have real affection or tenderness for his fellow-men. But let us look at this scene for a moment. The Revolution is over and the time has come for Washington to say a last farewell to his staff. They are gathered around him, each reluctant to be the first to say farewell. Finally, General Knox steps forward and offers General Washington his hand. They look at each other for a moment in silence, and then Washington takes Knox in his arms and with tears streaming down his cheeks, fondly kisses him. As each officer steps up in turn, the brave Washington with the strong love of a father and yet with all the tenderness of a mother, affectionately embraces him. For some men, men would gladly live; for such a man as this, men will gladly die. Love, the handmaid of respect and admiration, was the service, and is today the reward that such a soul commands.

Again and again throughout his entire public career we find understanding of men and sympathy with their views, averting crises and smoothing the many difficulties so unavoidable to the life of a new and young nation. His choice of cabinet officials, his whole-hearted support of Hamilton, his masterly handling of the fiery French envoy, his private correspondence with Lafayette and his own relatives, reveal a depth of human understanding and an almost unlimited feeling for the frailties of mortals which none but a true human could possess.

Still this man has been pictured as a super-mortal, a man without human warmth, emotion or love. How could such a man have held together the warring factions of the Colonial days, commanded the respect of his soldiers, and the love of all of his fellowmen if he were cold and aloof—in a word, if he were not a man, with all the virtues, and many of the weaknesses of his fellowmen?

George Washington's understanding of men! That human trait, born of the fact that he was man himself, reveals to us the true Washington, pulsating with life like our own; it fixes his fame, not on the mythical picture of a super-human, but on the reality of a man among men.

Let us put aside the old picture of Washington, the demigod, and put in its place the true image of a human like ourselves, but with a finer knowledge of character, a fuller understanding of human impulses and emotions. Let us sketch him in his true colors, a warm human personality with the beautiful human virtues of his kind, together with its frailties, and the noble inspiration of Washington will continue to live. In times of stress and strife his understanding and love of men will guide us; his spirit will whisper wise counsels into the ears of our statesmen; our people, through a definite conception of his love and sympathy for mankind, will feel his presence, encouraging, directing, and drawing them to safety and peace through his understanding of men.

[OTHER STATE WINNERS]

Washington: Exemplar of American Ideals

MARGARET ALLEN WALLIS
Talladega, Alabama
Alabama College, Montevallo, Alabama

The romantic myth of George Washington has been exposed. Zealous investigators have stripped from the national hero every shred of sentimental tradition; they have ruthlessly laid bare every discrediting detail of his personal conduct. He no longer appears as a straight-laced, flawless gentleman, or majestic figure. He has become a human being, yet to the American people he is still a hero. The nation as a whole has with undiminished enthusiasm recently entered into the celebration of his birth. Particular stress has been put on the event by those in best position to feel the pulse of the nation. Shopkeepers and department store managers have featured it in window displays. Teachers have planned and eager children have executed great Washington pageants. The character and achievement of Washington have repeatedly been the theme for leading editorials. Even college students have put aside their multiplicity of duties and forgetting their pose of worldly-wise indifference have whole-heartedly entered into the celebration. Indeed, the living Washington remains the most vivid and dynamic figure of American history.

How shall the historian of the future explain this fact? Why does the childhood of today so confidently revere the memory of George Washington? Why is it that today when men wish to inspire, in the highest sense, they select phrases from his Farewell Address? Why is it that Washington, in spite of obscuring time, in spite of adverse criticism, in spite, indeed, of much seeming American cynicism, still remains first in the hearts of the people?

Let us recall just what manner of man the living Washington is —and was. Despite his inheritance, that of a wealthy and aristocratic Virginia gentleman, Washington was always a tremendous worker, a worker who accomplished things. He supervised his farm, wrote all the letters of his large correspondence, kept his own books carefully and precisely, served in the Virginia House of Burgesses, and in both Continental Congresses. In none of these services do we see him in the position of an orator. Yet he always took a definite stand on current questions and then backed his decision by open enterprise. In all his achievements we may say of him that he was a man of vision, certainly, but had he been merely a man of vision without drive he would not occupy the place in the hearts of American people which he today holds. Men of vision are, to us, dreamers. Dreamers we may admire but never revere. This combination of vision and force carried him successfully through those first years of the presidency. Those were years of stupendous toil, years demanding tremendous initiative. The first

presidential term of the United States was a period of marvelous achievement due largely to the extraordinary capacity and initiative of our First President.

The term courageous has justly been attached to the name of Washington. He understood full well when he took his place at the head of the continental troops that a lost cause would mean that he would be branded as a common traitor and be dealt with accordingly. There was, however, a restraint and a strategy in his expositions of courage. His sense of balance and his calm judgment were responsible for the fact that he never fought aimlessly and therefore not futilely. It has been said that Washington displayed his utmost capacity as a general, that he and his men proved themselves victorious during the winter they spent in Valley Forge— during those times that tried men's souls. It was there that his soldiers became convinced of his persistent aggressiveness which could not be daunted. It was there that laboriously he formulated his plans for the coming attack. It was there that through his kindly leadership, his determined stand, his obvious fighting always for causes, he set for all times a standard of action for American soldiers.

Although fundamentally a fighter, Washington had few enemies. This too was possible because he fought for and against policies rather than against personalities. He was, indeed, always a philosopher, pondering both those matters which pertained to him personally and the questions that came to him in the discharge of public duty. His philosophy dominated the critical hours of his career. Emphasis on other aspects of that career has sometimes reduced the credit granted him as a statesman; yet not less strategic than his services as Commander of the American forces was his contribution to the cause of representative government in the Constitutional Convention. As a philosopher, believed to be sane and just, he was elected chairman of that convention and as a philosopher, in its closing hours, he saved the Constitution from defeat. The strongest strand of his idealism was his attitude toward public service. Always he offered his abilities to the nation asking no reward whatsoever. Because he was a philosopher, without ostentation, he was able to set an enduring pattern as a great public servant.

Washington's philosophy was not that of a speculative thinker. There was a quality in this philosophy which marked him off as distinct from speculative thinkers. His broad understanding of armies and of government seems to have been based first of all upon a deep, sympathetic understanding of men. In his lifetime Washington stood before the people of the colonies and later of the United States as surveyor, farmer, statesman, general, and president, but first and always as a man who allowed heart to enter his every transaction. His indignation at the criminal carelessness that led to Braddock's defeat was not the disappointment of a soldier so much as it was the protest of a great-hearted friend of soldiers. When he accepted the appointment as Commander-in-Chief of the Colonial Armies, his declaration that he did not consider himself equal to the task impressed those who heard it as issuing not so much from a sense of lack of skill as from a sense of the human values represented in their enterprise. Finally, the reverberating appeal of his Farewell Address which he referred to as the counsels of an old and affectionate friend have been treasured by the American people ever since because they have thought that they read in the cadences of that speech the rich music of a great understanding and sympathy.

Washington maintains steadfast claim to the position of first in the hearts of his countrymen. He stands out for us as a combination of Adams, Franklin, Jefferson, Hamilton, Lincoln, and Lee. We see in each of these men certain traits which we particularly admire. We find in Washington something of the incessant activity of Adams, the calm capacity for business of Hamilton, the idealism of Jefferson, the philosophy of Franklin, and the profound sympathy of Lincoln and Lee. If we take the leaders of the past (and also those of today) whom we most highly respect and locate the specific quality on which we base this respect, we will find, in almost every instance, that Washington was the possessor of the same quality. Beyond this, if we look, as in a mirror, carefully into our innermost selves penetrating the source of our highest ideals we will realize that the traits we find there closely resemble those for which Washington is revered. He is indeed the great exemplar of American ideals.

The Spirit of Washington

CLARENCE FLOOD

Jerome, Arizona

State Teachers College, Flagstaff, Arizona

We are gathered here today to remember, to cherish, and to profit by the spirit of Washington—the spirit of the first great American, known to us not only through the annals of history, but through a personal influence bequeathed us from father to son through the generations. Every age has its hero, but the cold judgment of time seldom leaves one who lives in the very affection and love of all, after ages have passed away. It is true the records of the deeds of the great are many, their heroic valor, the lifelike pictures of them cover history's pages—their accomplishments are known to all, but their memory cannot boast an abode in our hearts as well as in our minds. The sculptor's chisel, the historian's pen labor untiringly to record the mighty battles of Alexander the Great, of Caesar, and of other great aggressors whose ambitions were no less than to subdue and subject the world. Blood and tears shed for their glory—agonies endured for their ambition! Those heroes remain in our minds, indeed, yet only as colossal exemplifications of force and murder. But the memory of Washington is in our hearts. His battles were greater battles than theirs, against greater odds, for a far grander and holier cause—not to conquer and rule a world, but to stem the flood of "man's inhumanity to man," and to erect from the ashes of war a new nation. That nation is today in the darkest hours of peace.

Therefore it may well be considered significant that this Bicentennial Celebration of the birthdate of Washington should fall on this momentous year of 1932. We are today facing one of the most critical periods that has ever tried the patriotism, the ingenuity, and the courage of the American people. The nation is in turmoil—repeated demonstrations of revolt against our political structure are running together in a treacherous undercurrent. And so it seems not only fitting but fortunate, that at this Bicentennial Celebration, if only for a second, we should pause in our headlong plunge; we should rest from the exigencies of our government long enough to review the life and principles of a great man who lived through another critical period of our history. We are met to remember and to profit by the spirit that rallied a nation in the hour of public disasters, by the spirit that amid the storm of war shone as a beacon light to guide the people, by the spirit that attracted to itself a whole nation's confidence—the Spirit of Washington.

The American people are today facing a problem—we are confronted by dangers that imminently threaten us. It is the sacred duty of the people of this nation to face these difficulties, to realize their importance, and to eliminate them in the practical and conquering spirit of Washington. Washington was confronted with the stupendous and seemingly impossible task of freeing thirteen disorganized colonies from the yoke of the powerful British Empire. His ability to face a difficult and awe-inspiring situation from a practical standpoint, and his genius in the application of common sense principles were taxed to no less an extent in the Revolution than in the critical days prior to the adoption of the Constitution. The problem of that Critical Period was the establishment of a government without a throne, without an aristocracy, without castes or privileges, and this government was to be extended over a vast country of different climates, different interests, and different habits. Washington's ability to cope with trying situations was tested beyond our comprehension when we considered that this proposed government, an entirely new experiment, was crowned with success even in the limited time of his Presidency. Friends, we too can crown with success our efforts toward economic and political regeneration if we but attack our problems in the practical and conquering Spirit of Washington.

The people of the United States today more than at any other time in the history of this great nation since Washington need men who are willing to work for the good of the whole—men who will not sacrifice to political party that to which mankind is entitled. Do we fully realize that the United States of America in this very year, 1932, is in dire need of patriotic men—men free from personal ambition, men not seeking for self-aggrandizement? Is it asking too much for men today to give of their time, to sacrifice their thought and talent—even to give freely of their personal fortunes, to count as their reward only that bright but flickering hope that the United States shall be a better nation because of their sacrifices? Yet in those very sacrifices for the nation, Washington points the way for us. Those miserable days of the Revolution, climaxed by the deepening shadows of Valley Forge only begin to disclose the magnitude of Washington's spirit of self-sacrifice. Needy and suffering soldiers received upward of 20,000 pounds, every bit of ready cash that Washington could draw from his neglected estate. In the days of the Critical Period Washington gave freely of his commanding talents. To this gift he added a disregard of self, a spotlessness of motive, a steady submission to every public duty. In these days Washington devoted his time and energy to encourage a stronger central government than that provided by the Articles of Confederation. He worked untiringly for the more orderly establishment of those liberties which he had so largely won. So earnest was he in building a great nation that he sacrificed the individual differences of his native state, Virginia, to the creation of a more perfect union. As President of the United States, Washington adhered solely to a policy for the strengthening of the newly established government—his personal ambition was smothered by his enlarged patriotism. He had no favorites, he rejected all partisanship that could have led to affluence and wealth, and acting honestly for the universal good his reward was the universal love. That universal love that we proclaim for Washington because of his spirit of self-sacrifice shall become a sacrilegious, idle boast unless we too protect our political greatness through individual sacrifice.

America today is once more at the crossroads. Present conditions affirm that we have concluded another era in industrial and political experimentation. We are about to launch these United States upon a new movement for better or for worse. If today we can visualize the America of tomorrow as the embodiment of those principles of economic opportunity for all and a well regulated democracy, not only in name but also in truth, we shall be exercising no more than the spirit of Washington—no more than his love for our native country. The immortal words of Daniel Webster portraying Washington's love for America still ring true—"We are met to testify our regard for him whose name is intimately blended with whatever belongs most essentially to the prosperity, the liberty, the free institutions and the renown of our country." For Washington to cherish a generous love for a nation whose doom seemed inevitable at times exemplifies that he was above all a man of character and ideals. For Washington to visualize those thirteen disorganized colonies as a powerful nation embracing the principles of human liberty and free government testifies that his visions and hopes were not those of the common clay nor of the vulgar great. What America has need of in our present crisis is a spark from the brilliant spirit of Washington to kindle the potential American spirit that can guide us through the critical days of 1932.

George Washington has been buried a great number of years. Our institutions, our political organization, our social problems, and our international relations are of a different magnitude from those of his day. Washington and the time in which he lived are day by day fading into the horizon of the past. The name of Washington has been immortalized and again it has been slandered, but the spirit of Washington must be cherished by every true American even more in the future than in the past.

I have come here today not to make a schoolboy's attempt at declamatory eloquence, not to exaggerate the historical importance of 1776 and the days that followed. Rather I have come here to plead with you that our national integrity rests only upon the spirit of courage, the spirit of individual sacrifice, and inspired vision. Friends, I attest by everything that is sacred without being profane, that that spirit is the Spirit of Washington. Washington's ability to conquer in a stupendous crisis is a challenge to Americans of the present day. Washington's spirit of personal sacrifice for the good of this nation should either make us ashamed, or inspire us to greater heights than we have reached. Washington's vision of a great nation and his untiring efforts to create that nation should inspire in us a vision of a new and greater America, should kindle in us the effort to transform the America of 1932 into a nation worthy of its founder. Courage, sacrifice, and vision will today just as surely as in Washington's day lead us in triumph out of these darkest hours of peace.

The Spirit of Washington

ROSS BORDERS

Independence, Kansas
The College of The Ozarks, Clarksville, Arkansas

The three outstanding things known about Washington today are that he is the Father of Our Country, that he could not tell a lie, and that he once used a hatchet very disastrously on a cherry tree.

During the recent Two Hundredth Anniversary of Washington's Birthday the American Tree Association attempted to remedy the third one of these facts by planting ten million trees to take the place of the one cut down by George so many, many years ago. The second one of these facts is still being wondered at by the small American boy even though he soon quits attempting to equal it. The first one of these facts is being accepted more fully each day by the average American citizen.

May I present three other facts about this great man which have had a much more wholesome influence upon the character of American civilization than the three I have just mentioned? It has been said of Washington that he was "first in war, first in peace, and first in the hearts of his countrymen." This Two Hundredth Anniversary has awakened in us a train of reflections on what Washington achieved for us and how we have taken advantage of the privileges and opportunities offered to us because he championed the cause of freedom and the rights of humanity.

It was not Washington's natural inclination to be militaristic. He was not of the military type. It was a national emergency that made him a military genius. Carlyle has said that the entire history of mankind has centered around the lives of certain great men and women, that every crisis in the history of civilization has been met by the courage of an individual who dared to brave the opposition and lead his people into the paths of freedom and happiness. Thus it was that Washington in the crisis of national life braved the anger of the Mother country and led our ancestors to a glorious victory. Napoleon was born a military genius and used this ability to wreak his vengeance upon innocent people who stood in the way of his vaulting ambition. Thrones tumbled at his behest, millions of people died for his glory, tears were shed and hearts were broken that he might live in regal splendor. No wonder Bob Ingersol said of him: "I had rather been a French peasant and gone down to the tongueless silence of the dreamless dust than to have been that imperial impersonation of force and murder known as Napoleon the Great."

How different the plaudits of Washington to be called the Father of His Country. His early life was spent amid the quiet of a colonial farm community. He did not choose war but the life of a surveyor. He never considered leading a military career. He much preferred the peace and security of his home to the turmoil and strife of war. Yet when war became inevitable, when it became certain that the Mother country was determined to enforce her iniquitous demands, Washington was ready to use his utmost strength to prevent the catastrophe. When he was called to serve in the first Continental Congress he said: "It is my full intention to devote my life and fortune to the cause we are engaged in, if needful."

I need not repeat to you his marvelous achievements during the Revolutionary War—how he successfully fought the British, winning many battles in the face of overwhelming odds, Princeton, Monmouth, Brandywine, Germantown, and finally Yorktown. All these names bring memories of desperate fighting, of intelligent maneuvering, of astute generalship. All the world is still wondering at his crossing the Delaware. And finally at the surrender of Yorktown he was crowned by the entire world the leading military genius of all time. Unto the end of time the world will tell the story of Valley Forge and praise the great general who could inspire his men with courage and devotion.

Let us not, however, dwell on the military accomplishments of Washington. The greatest quality of his manhood at which the world still marvels is not his military genius but his utter simplicity. When the war closed he returned to the quiet of Mount Vernon where he could rest and be contented with the joys and comforts of home. He did not demand political recognition. He expected no laurels for his achievements. In fact he refused, yea, spurned the offer of kingship. He desired to be left at home with his growing crops and ripening harvests. Truly he could well have been that simple farmer described by Henry W. Grady as the ideal American with "barns and cribs well filled and the old smokehouse odorous with treasure."

But not long was he to enjoy this pastoral quietness. Soon he was called as a delegate to the Constitutional Convention. When the Constitution was finally drafted and sent to the different states for adoption Washington wrote many articles in favor of its adoption. Again, when this task was accomplished, he returned to the simplicity of farm life. These acts of unselfish devotion to the American cause coupled with his refusal to seek any honors at the hands of his country have made him first in the hearts of his countrymen. When he accomplished the freedom of his country he asked nothing from her but without pomp resumed the respected life of a private citizen.

Still again his country called him, called him to the highest honor in the gift of the American people. It has been said that the framers of our Constitution created the office of our chief executive with Washington in mind as the ideal president. Certain it is that no man since has graced that mighty office with greater intellectual ability, with a keener insight into the intricacies of governmental procedure, with more zeal for service to humanity, and with a stronger determination to shape legislative practices to secure the greatest blessings for the greatest number of people.

I thus present for your consideration a great military genius who dared to go to war with the most powerful nation in the world in the cause of freedom, a general who could take inexperienced troops and so inspire and train these same troops that they would voluntarily fight to the finish even though their weapons were crude, their ammunition limited, their food scarce, their clothes ragged, and they left their footprints in blood on the frozen ground.

I present to you a statesman who could frame a Constitution initiating a new and untried form of government based upon principles that up to that time had been considered detrimental to good government, a statesman who could set up a form of government based upon this Constitution in an unsettled country, with inexperienced helpers and so shape its policies that even after a lapse of more than one hundred years it is still known as a "government of the people, by the people, and for the people."

But greatest of all I present to you a man who while possessing the potentialities of human frailties, yet was able to overcome not only his own selfish weaknesses but could inspire others to do likewise, a man who believed firmly in the observance of the Golden Rule, who practiced neighborly kindness, who never placed his own selfish desires above the welfare of his fellow man, who was kind and considerate to everyone with whom he came in contact.

He has been the inspiration of many loyal hearts to progress upward and the despair of those less courageous souls who could see no hope of ever climbing within hailing distance of his incomparable character. We need more men today to strive to reach his station. We need to point to Washington today as the emblem of upright manhood and encourage our children to study his life in an effort to make theirs more beautiful and useful. We do not need a greater army and a greater navy. We do not need a larger supply of gold piled mountain high in the vaults of our nation, but we do need a more consecrated manhood and womanhood, a youth taught and nurtured in the spirit of Washington. Our nation should cry out to the mothers of our land in the voice of the poet:

> "Bring me men to match my mountains,
> Bring me men to match my plains,
> Men with empires in their purpose,
> And new eras in their brains;
> Bring me men to match my prairies,
> Men to match my inland seas,
> Men whose thought shall have a highway
> Up to ampler destinies;
> Pioneers to clear thought's marshlands,
> And to cleanse old errors fen;
> Bring me men to match my mountains,
> Bring me men."

Washington: Exemplar of American Ideals

JEROME J. DOWNEY

Washington, D. C.

Georgetown University
Washington, D. C.

America stands, today, on the threshold of a new era in her history. On every side she must meet the challenge of those who threaten her social, political, and economic welfare. It is fitting then, during this Bicentennial year of the Father of Our Country that we should consider the two factors that have raised America to a position unsurpassed by any nation of the world. Those factors, which will always inspire Americans to lofty sentiments of patriotism, are the Constitution of the United States, our American theory of government, and George Washington, the exemplar of our American ideal of patriotic citizenship.

In that stirring message, the Declaration of Independence, America proclaimed to the world her doctrine of liberty, equality, and freedom. In that message was conceived the feeble flame of Democracy which today is the beacon and guide of all liberty-loving people. Yet to perpetuate those ideals of government after the chaos of the Revolution, required consummate skill and judgment. A nation lacking credit, her industries paralyzed, the Articles of the Confederation proven inadequate, and even anarchy was rearing its ugly head awaiting an opportune moment to strike. From colonies united against the common foe, dissolution and disintegration was draining the life blood of the Sovereign Government. Yet imbued with the same spirit and courage that carried the first American citizen through the dark days of the Revolution, they accepted the challenge against their national existence.

As though divinely directed, a convention presided over by George Washington handed to posterity the great Constitution of the United States. Never, in the history of the world has there been a system of government so devised whereby the controlling forces of the nation were so skillfully adjusted to meet the needs of such a great people and so vast a Republic. Breathing the very basic principles of democracy, by guaranteeing the will of the majority, but protecting the rights of the minority, the Constitution was framed so that to no branch of the law-making body was there a delegation of absolute authority. By the system known as the "check and balance" the powers of the government are so evenly distributed between the legislative, executive, and judicial bodies that each in its own capacity guarantees justice to all. Although maintaining the supremacy of the Federal government, the sovereign states are given certain inviolable rights upon which the Federal government cannot encroach.

With respect to the private citizen the Constitution draws her mantle of protection about the humblest citizen and guarantees him in well-defined terms the sanctity of life, liberty, and property. It has been demonstrated time and again that when selfish and fanatical interests helped by unwise laws threatened to sweep away these inalienable rights, the Constitution has stood like a mighty Gibraltar preventing its accomplishment.

Still this American theory of government would have been but a hollow shell to be crushed by the pressing hands of time if there was not breathed into it the spirit of Washington. The Constitution needed a personality which would illustrate in a practical way the theory of American Democracy. And this personality was supplied by George Washington, the soldier, the statesman, the man. It is precisely because we can find these qualities in the Father of Our Country that we can point to the growth and perpetuation of American ideals during all the years of our history.

Washington was essentially a man of Christian principles, of noble qualities, of penetrating wisdom. Look back with me on the events of his life. There is one which stands out above all others. It is at Valley Forge where the hardships, the suffering, the starvation, the death among a battered army beggars description. And there is Washington—alone—kneeling in prayer on the snow—entrusting the fate of an army, yes, the destiny of a nation to God. That was the spirit of America. That was America's answer to a national crisis. That was the shining example of American citizenship.

See again the character of Washington as the statesman, the leader of the people. The nation was young, but politics were old. Foreign nations sought to entangle the new republic in the mesh of alliances; the country itself was being torn asunder by political leaders; Hamilton advocating federal supremacy; Jefferson staunchly demanding complete state sovereignty. And Washington joined the hands of these political enemies and guided the new Ship of State through the troubled sea of domestic and foreign turmoil. What nation today can point to a man who more eminently exemplified the character of his people, who more successfully directed a new-born nation in the path of justice, equality, liberty as did George Washington? What man can claim more perfect piece of statecraft than the Farewell Address of Washington?

Yet today we are challenged by those who would discard our American ideals as so much dross; who would overthrow many of the social, economic, and political principles which have always been cherished by true and loyal Americans. We are in the midst of economic depression; crime was never more widespread, the family, the very foundation of society is threatened; foreign troubles seek to entangle us; Democracy itself is challenged. Will our lawmakers answer the challenge the way Washington dictated in his Farewell Address? Will political parties disregard self-ambition and seek only the common good? Will the American citizen realize his duty to protect our principles and ideals?

We are recipients of a precious heritage, bought and paid for in the blood of patriots. America, destined to occupy a higher pedestal in the hall of civilization, relies on us, her subjects to fulfill the sacred trust. Let us answer the challenge of today and with Washington as the exemplar of American citizenship, let us press on to greater achievements, newer triumphs, undying glory.

The Spirit of Washington

WILLIAM A. McRAE, JR.

Jacksonville, Florida

University of Florida, Gainesville, Florida

We are gathered here today to do homage to a man whose radiant life was begun two centuries ago. We are gathered here to bear witness to our sense of its magic and its power.

Little can be said concerning the incidents of his life which is not already well known to all of us. Though known, we do not tire of hearing these familiar stories told again. Like a song, well known and loved, the stories of the harrowing days of the Revolution and the early years of our Republic ever strike a familiar chord in our hearts. But, with the passing years, the figure of Washington has become less and less real to us. He is too often thought of only in terms of the serious-miened Gilbert Stuart portrait. Let us pause for a moment, and breathe the breath of life into that grave countenance. Can we not see him smile as he views the canvas of the painter which portrays him in so staid a mood? Can we not see him smile again as he writes, "The skill of this Gentleman's Pencil, will be put to it, in describing to the World what manner of man I am."

Washington was a man of feeling and sentiment. He was likewise a man of dignity and reserve. We cannot, moreover, look to his conduct on public occasions or at state dinners to get an intimate glance into his heart, to appreciate him as an individual. Let us, rather, look to his gracious refusal to accept pay for his services as Commander-in-Chief of the Continental Army, an act so spontaneous and so untainted with personal motive that it has, ever since, been the object of unbounded praise; an act so magnanimous that it was the subject of one of the splendid poems of Lord Byron.

Let us but call to mind those bitter winter days at Valley Forge. See the unhoused, scantily-clad, half-starved army, shivering in the midst of December's cold and snow, uncheered by any recent victory, regarded with disapprobation by the very Congress which should have been giving aid! It was then that the mettle of every soldier was put to the supreme test. But, how truly, during these trying days, did the patriot, the inspired leader, rise above the mere soldier. His dauntless spirit would not know defeat. His sympathy for the tattered citizen soldiery, his understanding of their hardships, and his willingness to share those hardships, engendered in his men a perfect confidence in the wisdom, the courage, and the ability of their Commander-in-Chief.

During this period, Congress was misled into believing that the Continental Army was not sufficiently active, that the Commander-in-Chief was inefficient. Hear him as he fearlessly and frankly answers these criticisms: "I can assure those gentlemen," said he in a letter addressed to Congress, "that it is a much easier and less distressing thing to draw remonstrances in a comfortable room by a good fireside, than to occupy a cold, bleak hill, and sleep under frost and snow, without clothes or blankets." Little wonder it is that his men loved him, honored him, obeyed him.

The War of the Revolution had lasted till the energies and resources of the Confederacy were well-nigh exhausted. The morale was at a critically low ebb. Congress, torn by factions, hampered by jealousy and treachery, was a constant source of embarrassment to Washington. Many of the generals, unable to endure the calumnies heaped upon them, resigned from the army. When Cornwallis finally surrendered in October, 1781, the joy which spread throughout the country knew no bounds. Everywhere could be heard the cries, "The War is over!" . . . "The Country is free!"

The joy of the moment was soon displaced by the appalling realization that the Confederacy lacked permanent organization. But how could this organization be accomplished? Washington! Yes, Washington, the hero of the Revolution was the man, above all others, who could best head the new organization. And now, what kind of an organization would it be? A kingdom, thought some. Yes, a kingdom founded on principles similar to those existing in England. A proposal was forthwith conveyed to Washington, now retired from the army and living at Mount Vernon, indicating the inherent weaknesses of republics, and arguing strongly for a kingdom with him as its regal head. His response was immediate, conclusive, indignant. "No occurrence in the course of the war," said he, "has given me more painful sensations, . . . you could not have found a person to whom your schemes are more disagreeable." It defies our imagination to picture what the history of our country would be had Washington been swayed by a lust for power and glory into accepting and promoting this idea.

Again, let us see him on the memorable occasion when he bade farewell to his mother before departing for his inauguration as President of the United States. He must leave for New York on the morrow. He had galloped up from Mount Vernon to spend an hour with the woman he revered in the weakness of her old age as when her will had overruled the boy's plans of a career. He found her in her chamber, alert in mind and serene in spirit, but so altered in appearance that his heart misgave him. Concealing his dread, he began to speak cheerfully of his intention, as soon as public business could be disposed of, to return to Virginia and to see her again. She stayed him there with the steady voice and feeble hand. This would be their last meeting.—She was old.— She would not be long for this world. Then, laying the wasted hand on the head bowed to her shoulder, she told him that Heaven's and his mother's blessings would always be with him. As he stooped for a parting embrace, she felt him slip a purse into her hand. She put it back, raising her head with the old time pride. "I do not need it," she said. "My wants are few." Time passed, but he lingered to plead tenderly, "Whether you think you need it or not, for my sake." On many occasions did he show this tenderness for his mother, and throughout her long and useful life he ever manifested deference and respect for her opinions.

We ask, then, wherein does the greatness of Washington lie? It lies first in his humanity. It lies in the splendid equipoise of his powers, his remarkable versatility. He was a rare, yes, a crowning genius of balance and proportion.

In this day when there are those who call themselves biographers, and who seek glory for themselves by maliciously defaming and exaggerating the weaknesses in the giants of the human race; at a time when such an air of cynicism seems to be the order of the day, it is striking to note that the most that has been said of Washington is that he was a mere victim of propitious circumstances. However true this may be, however true it may be of all men of genius, the fact remains that he was a victim who was also a master; a master who, among the great masters of world history, has few equals and no superiors. Does not the pathos and the tragic tenacity of the winter at Valley Forge recall to your minds Hannibal upon the Alps? Does not the loyalty of his untrained and ragged New England soldiers remind you of the loyalty of the Roman legions to their great leader, Julius Caesar? Does not the fearlessness of the Trenton campaign awaken thoughts of William the Conqueror at Hastings? Does not his benignant, healing, and just administration as President inevitably invoke thoughts of Alfred the Great? And yet, who, among these men, was as versatile as Washington?

Wherein does the greatness of Washington lie? It lies in his honesty, his uprightness, his integrity. It lies in his perfect sense of patriotism, pure and unblemished. Rising above the pettiness of his day, towering above the pettiness of those who would seek to drag him to the level of the base or the commonplace, he remains the Washington beloved of all admirers of true greatness.

Wherein does his greatness lie? It lies in the thorough nobility and loftiness of his character.

We hear him then speak these prophetic words, "The game is yet in our own hands; to play it well is all we have to do." "Nothing but harmony, honesty, industry, and frugality are necessary to make us a great and happy people." How admirably has the United States fulfilled this prophecy. How great would have been the joy of its Chief Founder could he have known that some day the United States would be what it is today: a nation of millions of happy families, a nation of splendid schools and universities, a nation of active, beneficent, and noble churches—a land of plenty. How great would have been his joy could he have known the place which the United States would some day hold among the nations of the world. And yet again, when we pause to consider the titanic economic and governmental problems which our statesmen have as yet not solved; when we reflect that there is current today, all too frequently, an abuse of trust in public office; when we further reflect that, throughout our country there is, all too frequently, a reckless disregard of the law, we repeat the words of Washington as words prophetic of our nation as it is today: "The game is yet in our own hands; to play it well is all we have to do." "Nothing but harmony, honesty, industry, and frugality are necessary to make us a great and happy people."

Note—The oration, "The Spirit of Washington," by Ralph Olmstead, of Minidoka, Idaho, representing the University of Idaho, Moscow, Idaho, was not available for publication.

Washington: Exemplar of American Ideals

IRWIN LUTHI
Canyon City, Colorado

Kansas State Teachers College, Pittsburg, Kansas

To the north, in the Black Hills of South Dakota, there is being chiseled out of the solid granite and stone of one of those mighty cliffs, facial likenesses to America's greatest characters of bygone days. Among these is the stern face of George Washington, gazing immutably into the distance, a nation's latest tribute to her founder; a memento that through the ages shall remain unblemished and untarnished despite the adverse storms of nature. As remains this monument, so remains the name and spirit of Washington, unblemished and untarnished, despite the adverse storms of society.

Washington, the renowned, no! I care not to add one leaf to the crown of immortal reverence that his name inspires. Washington, the man! Ah, yes! Stripped of all the gorgeous costumes of praise, jewels of admiration, veils of worship, left only in his naked simplicity.

Today we live in a world faced by far greater difficulties than even that faced by the patriots of '76 whose bones now lie mingled with the soil from Georgia to Maine. We see our world faced by conditions of poverty and human need. War looming ominously on the horizon, and in the face of these things to view Washington as the masterful man of the ages; the conquering hero; would be but fool's play and to no avail, for these things like prints in the sand fade and vanish, but the true spirit of Washington, the thing that was responsible for all he accomplished, like that great stone face itself, lives on forever. May America ever realize that Washington was the man of the hour, yea, and of the ages, called to create a nation, and to bequeath to posterity a just and lasting impression of national character.

We vision Washington in that familiar picture, amid the snow-clad and tattered tents of Valley Forge, kneeling in the snows of winter and lifting his prayers to Almighty God for assistance. Again we see him as he took over the reins of Government as the First President of our infant nation, before that great assembly of delegates in fervent prayer that forever that recognized power might guide the destinies of their nation. True, Washington was born in riches, blessed by his inheritance with great means, a country gentleman, opportunity to live a life of leisure, and yet, we see him leave it all, stoop to the hideous hardships of the Revolutionary period, grasp a struggling, groping nation of people, trampled in the very mire of domination, and lead them on to a golden sunrise. May God grant, I only ask, that we might have men and women today who will respect the deity of God as exemplified by Washington. Yes, and men who, like Washington, though born in riches, reared in leisure, see fit to address their message not to the rich and powerful, but to prepare a feast of simple humility, of noble justice, of unwavering truth, and invite the sons of democracy to partake.

After the work of Washington in the service of his country was completed he retired to his beautiful Mount Vernon home on the Potomac where he soon was to pass from the land he loved. It was a bitter cold December night, outside the wind howled in blizzard proportions. Inside lay George Washington, breathing his last breaths of life; it was then that, when his faithful secretary, Lear, endeavored to give him ease that once brawny hand of Washington was raised in protest and he said, "I am afraid I shall fatigue you too much; well, it is a debt we must pay to each other." And then that hand fell. Ah, my friends, that hand which had led armies on in the face of overwhelming odds, that hand which had stilled the radicalism of law makers, now reached up to portray the true sympathy and tenderness of Washington.

It was with steadfast hope, with grim determination set upon the face of Washington as he stood in his little ship and faced the rapids, the whirlpools, the angry waters of the raging Delaware River, and it is with that same steadfast hope, grim determination that America must stand in her Ship of State to face the rapids, the whirlpools, the angry waters of the mighty political and social crisis of 1932. America! Arise! Rebuke the storms, and doing so with a spirit that was Washington's there will be a great calm.

Washington the Courageous

J. R. GILLESPIE
St. Albans, West Virginia

Asbury College, Wilmore, Kentucky

Courage is that quality of a person which enables him to meet danger when he could run away; to assume responsibility when he could shirk; to stand for an ideal when it is unpopular; and to struggle on when the possibility of his reaching a goal is slight. It is not that dare-devil spirit of walking up to the mouth of a cocked cannon! However, it may mean walking into the jaws of death when a principle is at stake. As the giant oak sends its roots far into the earth, so does genuine valor make its way deep into the physical, the mental, and the moral fiber of a man's being. It is not easily shaken by the storms of adversity.

Who could be a more noble example of courage than George Washington? Cradled and reared in the highest of moral ideals, he not only scaled the mountains of vision, but braved the hardships of American primeval life. Can you imagine a sixteen-year-old boy going into the wilderness, sleeping by brushwood fires at night in the land of savages, and facing the hostility of these unfriendly Indians to survey a vast unexplored estate? The accomplishment of this task was no accident, for the consistency with which Washington, the Virginia Cavalier, faced dangers proved that his achievements were not mere chance. He was not schooled in a protected nursery, but in the open country where "Indians war-whooped and wild beasts prowled." From such native terrors he sucked the strength that fitted him for the destiny that Providence had decreed for him in military and state affairs.

Picture a twenty-one-year-old youth, with his boyish love for adventure all aglow, as he led a band of Virginian warriors over wild and tangled trails to warn the French who were settling on the English claim of the Ohio Valley. This unprecedented responsibility proved to be only another stepping stone for this bold youth who rapidly advanced to the heights of military leadership.

Who could have been better prepared to aid the British General, Braddock, who was unacquainted with the methods of Indian warfare? After the frightful defeat and death of Braddock, behold Washington riding in the midst of a dispirited army rallying it to fight on! When the ambushed enemy shot two horses from under him, he did not hasten to shelter from the angry storm of bullets, but mounted a third horse and continued. The four shots which pierced his coat did not even graze his courage. Though inconsiderate of consequences to himself, the deadly perils of the French and Indian conflicts became shield and buckler to Washington during the Revolution. To the arms of the Commander-in-Chief, they were sinews of iron that empowered him, Samson-like, to throw off the galling yoke of England.

American independence was so burned in his heart and mind that there was no shadow of a question whether Americans were to be freemen or slaves. He was so firmly convinced that America should not be shackled and reduced to a state of servitude from which no human efforts could then deliver her, that he unhesitatingly led an impoverished handful of Colonists against the greatest nation on earth. He dedicated his all to the struggle: a happy home, and one of the largest and richest estates in the Colonies from which, when necessary, he drew heavily—yes, even life itself was consecrated to press the cause of his country's freedom!

Not only was Washington fearless in battle even in the face of death, but he was the soul of democracy. Though born an aristocrat, unlike many a general, he did not thrust his army into the hottest of the fight while he himself stayed back from the danger zone. At the battle of Yorktown, when the atmosphere was alive with whizzing bullets, one of the aides who was anxious and disturbed about the safety of Washington, told him that the place was perilous. In this tense situation, Washington's quiet answer was, "You are at liberty to step back." This calm, cool, courage was contagious. What rugged Colonist would not willingly face the smoking muskets of the tyrannical Red Coats?

Though untutored in any college, Washington was a genius in judgment. He knew when his hour had come, and his dauntless will would defy the raging forces of nature to follow his intuition. Recall a ragged, disheartened army, too weak to risk battle, trapped by the enemy on the banks of an ice-filled river. The British army, thoroughly confident of its victory, settled down for the night to wait until morning to take its helpless prey. But imagine the amazement of the English, when they arose at day-break, to find that the foxy Washington and his shattered troops had forced their way across the angry Delaware River and escaped. When, a few days later, the far-seeing Washington braved the treacherous waters again, and put the British to flight, Frederick the Great said that it was one of the greatest feats in the annals of military history!

As great and as enduring as was the physical and mental courage of the Father of Our Country, he, perhaps, would have given up his almost hopeless task if he had not been girded with moral virtues that were founded on a faith in God which strengthened as they were exercised by impossible situations. Let us get a glimpse of a most trying winter as Washington himself saw it. His men were without clothes to cover their nakedness; without blankets to lie on; they could be traced in the snow to their winter quarters by the blood which oozed from their bare, frost-bitten feet. His men were almost as often without the bare necessities of life as they were with them—they were without food, without houses or huts to shelter them until they could be built. What did he do? Desert privation and slip away home to boundless luxury? No, he had the courage of humility: he fell at an altar in the temple of the woods where a hidden Quaker, overhearing his plea for divine help, prophesied aright his final victory.

Washington also had to face the additional trials of conspiracy, ambition, cowardice, and treason among his generals. From these

came a series of petty, malignant persecutions that Deity alone could have emboldened him to meet with patient endurance.

Then there was the loss of battles wherein many of the raw, undisciplined, and even mutinous recruits would break under fire and leave the field to the enemy. Although the British often defeated his men, they could not whip the general. Washington, strongly confident that an invisible Host was with him, remained as calm in defeat as was his wont in victory.

Again, when weak, vacillating Congressmen plotted his downfall, calumniated his motives, disparaged his abilities, and "deliberately with-held from him absolute necessities while demanding of him utter impossibilities," although depressed and anxious, "He was not perturbed out of measure, inasmuch as he believed himself to be in direct relation with an authority which was superior to Congress." This Supreme Power was his strength, his fortress; the rock in which he trusted; his courage and his deliverer.

After the firing of the last musket, in the eight-year struggle, Washington had the fortitude to take up a program of reconstruction. As soon as he had hung his sword on the wall, he was called to don executive robes and begin the Herculean task of welding an indestructible union out of a group of scattered and at times antagonistic Colonies. He was urged to seize the impotent government, and backed by the support of his army, bind the group of struggling colonies into a monarchy with himself as king. However, Washington made it clear that no scheme to establish a monarchy in America would ever receive his support. "When fortune flung to him a crown, he flung the bauble back," and enthroned a government "of the people, for the people, and by the people." We honor that noble spirit, who unlike Caesar, could whole-heartedly reject the crown, and place the scepter in the hands of the governed. Rich in our God-given republic, heaven forbid that we should ever lose our dearly bought heritage which is now seductively threatened from within.

Real danger is lurking. We cannot coax ourselves to believe that the Red Communism which has sneaked out of Russia is harmless. It is now creeping into China, India, Germany, many other nations, and even into the United States. New York City, alone, has 100,000 Reds. Their pernicious propaganda is alluring in these days of universal unrest, when depressions are threatening all nations with decadence. National and international leaders, as they try to resuscitate their lifeless countries need the indomitable spirit of the selfless Washington. For eight years, his office and labors of state were not for his own interests, but for the general welfare. He was a man of destiny who felt the moral compulsion to serve a cause rather than self.

We know not what others may do, but, "We are more determined than were Americans in Washington's day to maintain our existing political system." For to lose democracy would mean that liberty would be only a memory. Americans would be reduced to a state of serfdom—driven by an iron hand of violence. "Italy may have her Mussolini; Russia her Stalin; and Jugoslavia may return to her king; but on this Bicentennial of Washington's birth, we recommit ourselves to the maintenance of the republic which" was so daringly founded and ably defended by George Washington the Courageous.

The Spirit of Washington

VIRGINIA RANDOLPH

Dillon, Montana

Montana State Normal College, Dillon, Montana

An aged Indian chieftain speaking of George Washington in a moment of inspiration said, "There is a something bids me speak in the voice of a prophecy. Listen! The Great Spirit protects that man and guides his destinies. He will become the chief of nations, and a people yet unborn will hail him as the founder of a mighty empire!"

Even now we are met—that generation then unborn, to honor and revere George Washington. His name stirs our thoughts, our dreams, and our reverence of the past, upon whose firm foundations rest our very existence. Sometimes it is with a stillness and a reverence that I think of the great men whose unselfish, loyal, and patriotic spirits laid the foundations of our nation, bequeathing to us a noble heritage which might otherwise have been but a Utopian dream.

A nation is no stronger than the fibers of its countrymen. If those fibers are brittle, easy to snap, or so soft as to be bent by the least passing friction, that nation can attain no heights. How thankful we may be that behind the strength and security of our Nation is the fiber of inspiring manhood. America's true citizens are the lighted constellation above us—and in that constellation, a continuous, unbroken illumination is the spirit of immortal George Washington!

Years have attested this fact. When the stream of time flows on, ever deepening and strengthening the opinion of a people for a man, bringing him immortal vitality in the eyes of his countrymen, then we realize the true nobleness of his character. A sneer, an undercurrent, may find its way to the surface and seek to pull him down, but in the end it is only a riffle on the surface of public opinion. It weakens and fades away. Thus at the expiration of two hundred years from his birth, we still cherish the memory of George Washington. Something in his spirit has caught the imagination of mankind.

We think of him at once as the great general who fought successfully a discouraging and trying war; as our First President, advising and helping a struggling young nation; as an eminent statesman, and a great public man. But rather than dwell on the political aspect of his greatness which we all profoundly respect, let us catch a glimpse of that true heroic spirit which has ever remained a radiating force in American life.

Too often George Washington seems to us a mere graven image, a cold and lifeless statue, put away on some distant pedestal to be admired but not understood. How little of the true spirit of the man is caught in that indifferent, austere picture!

Let us see George Washington as a man—in everyday life dealing with family, friends, and associates. Let us see him as an American citizen, and as these pictures come before us, let us watch for these qualities of true manhood which have endeared George Washington to the hearts of his countrymen.

One man said, "Poor men love George Washington just as if he were poor; they love him as a father or a brother." Indeed his thoughtful consideration for others and his commanding manner "not only endeared him to his friends but commanded the admiration and respect of his opponents." Throughout all of his career men showed unwavering trust in him. He made deep and lasting friendships and inspired the confidence of those about him by proving himself always a true friend to a friend.

Let us shift our scene to an old-fashioned, stately ballroom. The place is at Fredericksburg after the surrender of Cornwallis, and a great gathering of officers and admirers are there to pay tribute to the General. A path is made in the gathering—the crowd is silent. Washington is entering, ushering in his sweet and stately mother to introduce her to his many friends. George Washington as a son was always tender, thoughtful, and appreciative. From earliest manhood his mother was a faithful source of solicitude to him, and he was ever desirous of making her comfortable.

A third picture comes before us—George Washington as a husband. George and Martha Washington journeyed through four decades of life together, always taking the atmosphere of serene and contented home life where duty called them. Throughout all of his career he showed the profoundest respect and consideration for her. Cares nor duties of public life, distressing and burdensome as they sometimes proved to be, never made him less thoughtful of her nor took him away in spirit from his home life. He pos-

sessed the admirable ability of being able to devote himself wholeheartedly to matters of state and business; yet, never failing to give kindly thoughts to his home and those whom he loved.

Thoughtful, considerate as a friend, son, and husband—a lover of home and its beauties of contentment; nevertheless he felt the stern call of hardship, danger, and action, and exhibited a strength of will and undaunted courage that were potent factors in our Nation's fight for liberty.

We see him as a young man being called by Governor Dinwiddie to take a letter through the French and Indian country. One man had already given up the mission because of its grave dangers, but Washington is said to have never known or exhibited fear. We see him witnessing the horrors of Braddock's defeat, with two horses shot beneath him and four bullets through his coat, a test of the steel courage that was to reach its greatest heights in the war to come.

How familiar we are with the trying scenes of the American Revolution; the heroic crossing of the ice-filled Delaware on a dark and stormy night—the feverish struggle to maintain the American Army during the cruel hardships of the winter at Valley Forge; the long discouraging months when every victory seemed to be checked by a worse defeat. Here Washington's spirit rose supreme. Thirteen struggling colonies held loosely together by a disjointed Congress would many times have scattered the army disastrously, but Washington's courage and indomitable will held the fragments together and wrung victory under conditions that would have crushed the spirit of any man whose will was not of the strongest fiber. How well that Indian chieftain spoke when he said that George Washington would become the founder of a mighty nation!

Let us turn another leaf of his character and see him as an American citizen. His busy life as a farmer, plantation owner, surveyor, general, and Commander-in-Chief of the armies never rendered him too occupied to study thoughtfully and seriously our public questions. "He attended every civic duty with the same careful attention he gave to those of his military life and his career as a statesman, even to riding ten miles to the nearest polling town to vote, because he believed it his duty to do so."

His spirit breathes the essence of patriotism! His country came foremost before every other consideration. When he desired more than all else the peace and contentment of his home and family at Mount Vernon, he roused to our country's call! For Glory? For money? These thoughts were the farthest ones from the mind of George Washington. In answering this call he sacrificed comfort and placed on his shoulders the burdens and cares of a new nation which he loved above all else. He detested those who put self before country and said, "No punishment is too great for the man who can build his greatness on the ruin of his countrymen." How well this might be applied to the trend of modern times when the desire for wealth has traversed so many other considerations. That lifeless enigma has seeped into the hearts of countless American citizens, crowding out the uplifting thoughts of unselfish patriotism which build a nation. The cold, material considerations are not vital nor can they make a life, and a nation built on them will crumble and fall—a mirage of greatness, built on empty scheming dreams. Never before in her history has America sent forth a more urgent call for men and women with spirit and character enough to defeat the empty strife of living for materialism. Our nation must be guided by unselfish, loyal, and public-spirited citizens who are willing to give freely of their time, their intelligence, their vigor, and their innate high ideas to perpetuate real America!

We pause to reflect. George Washington stands not aloft and cold as an austere idol, but rather a vital, red-blooded ideal of manhood whose spirit lives today in the hearts of true American citizens. We have seen glimpses of him in life exhibiting seven virtues of true manhood; a friend to a friend, a thoughtful son, a tender husband, a patron of the beauties and peace of home, a man among men with dauntless courage, a fire that burned even in the depths of bleakest discouragement; strong will power, and above all a true American citizen of the fiber that builds a nation.

Those seven virtues make up the spirit which even now radiates from every corner of America. There must be American men now with those same virtues, that same steel fiber, and it is in them to do for our nation today, racked as it is with cares and baffling problems the same that George Washington did for our nation one hundred fifty years ago.

Under the guidance of God may they take upon them the cares of our nation and exhibit those same noble qualities which shall ever perpetuate the spirit of George Washington!

Washington: Exemplar of American Ideals

BERNARD MERGEN

Sparks, Nevada

University of Nevada, Reno, Nevada

In our modern code of living, it is the inherent right of man to enjoy the fundamentals of self-government, to establish for himself the ideals so sacred to the human soul. Since the beginning of time, man has had some sane desire to better himself for the task for which the Almighty so placed him. Through a world of darkness and years of progress, man has ceaselessly toiled to accomplish that end. Heroes have made history on the battlefield, men have perished in the eternal struggle for supremacy, battered by the gods of fortune.

Many of the scholars of yesterday have matched their wisdom against the inevitable. Volumes have been compiled for the want of the individual. Thousands have raised their voices in protest to the untouchables who destroyed man's march of progress. Through another series of dark ages, man struggled for freedom and enlightenment, only to be quelled by an engulfing stream of tyranny and oppression. As a result they sought their happiness in a newly discovered land, only to have that happiness snatched from them by the whims of a selfish King. Then—as if looking toward the east in the dim hours of morning—a light appeared, in the form of a true AMERICAN; an American who possessed a character far superior to that of any man the world has ever known. His love for his country was laid broad and deep in the eternal truths of morality. A martyr for a suppressed people—an individual man among men—a savior by the name of WASHINGTON!

Brought up in a lonely aristocratic family on a Virginia farm, he established in himself the perfect manliness—the courage—and the self-reliance—that led a liberty-loving people, for over forty years of public service. He had but a mediocre education, but at some time in his early life some one instilled in him the moral precepts which fastened themselves deeply into his soul.

Perhaps it would appear to some that George Washington was nothing more than a great soldier, and the First President of our Republic. Those are all good people who recognize him in that way, but they are people who have had not the opportunity to study profoundly the qualities and deeds of the man. Much new material has come to light since the time of the secondary reader and the wisdom of the country school teacher. More attention has been paid to WASHINGTON'S greatness in fields other than war. We have uncovered more fascinating facts, and we find in doing so that his versatility challenges us. He was an excellent business man; a genius on the battlefield; a superb President; and an equally great statesman! Back of all this, he was a kind, sympathetic, and gracious man! Although he was a graduate of no school, he valued education above all other ordinary things in life, and today one of our greatest institutions of learning is the outgrowth of his superior foresight.

A thousand times we have asked: "Whence this superb character? What are the qualities which made Washington predominant among men?" From the pages of history and biography, we glean our answer. Piece by piece we fill in the parts, until at last we have a combination of traits that leave us awed in the presence of the whole. He possessed a courage yet to be equalled. He had a power to win the hearts of men, which still remains unexplained. He controlled a sense of duty and good judgment that are difficult to find in the character of any one man. His courage was demonstrated by the defeat of Braddock and hurled in the face of both England and America. He showed it many times over when he turned certain defeat into victory by the true AMERICAN spirit which prevailed over him. He proved his power to win the hearts of men, by keeping an army of home-loving men together for over a period of six months. It has often been said that had Napoleon, before he conquered Italy, penetrated the forests of Ohio, or attempted to hold a frontier ruled by scalping parties, for several years, with a mere handful of men, his pride might still have been, as the Venetian envoy wrote, "His dominant reaction." Washington's sense of duty and good judgment were qualities of outstanding importance to the nation, on which rested the destiny of a loyal people.

In 1775 Washington took over command of the Continental Army. It was at this time the eyes of the world were turned his way. The diaries he left never recorded his personal thoughts or feelings, but we find that as far back as 1765 he wrote letters to friends in England, denouncing the Stamp Act, and told how such a miscarriage of justice was causing a discussion of principles in the colonies. He was constantly striving to bring about right in all its glorious surroundings. To the English merchants who advocated the repeal of the Stamp Act we have his own words of thanks "for their opposition to any act of oppression."

His power and worth of character first enabled him to secure help from the French during our war for independence. It was his excellent foresight which allowed him to establish the United States of America on equal footing with the powers of Europe. It was his innate spirit of freedom that first told him that an administration must be acquired to meet the demands of the grave situation. He was satisfied that the acts of the British Parliament were no longer governed by justice, and that they were trampling on the American rights and liberties. He had heartily wished that the dispute had been left to posterity to determine, yet when the crisis did arrive, he had the fortitude to establish himself as a leader and guide a grateful people to everlasting liberty!

It is altogether fitting at this time to bring to the attention of the American people the character, the achievement, and the perseverance of a man whose name has been on the lips of every individual in the United States—yes, and on the lips of every student of government in the entire world! Let us at this time refresh our memories with the blood of the Revolution—the triumph of Congress—and the emancipation of man and woman. Then, let us at this time give our humble honor to the man who was responsible in placing us on the pinnacle of everlasting peace—and equality among men!

Washington The Courageous

FRANCIS D. BURKE

Norman, Oklahoma

University of New Mexico, Albuquerque, New Mexico

A great philosopher once told us that thousands of men breathe, move and live, pass off the stage of life, and are heard of no more. We wondered why. He told us that they did not partake of good in this world, and none were blessed by them; none could point to them as the means of their redemption; that not a line they wrote, not a word they spoke, could be recalled; and so they perished; their light went out in darkness and they were remembered no more than insects of yesterday.

I come before you this evening, my friends, to discuss a man whose deeds and character stand alone in their grandeur, alone like some star that has no fellow in its celestial realm of greatness; a man who left behind him a monument of virtue that the storm of time can never destroy; a man who wrote his name forever upon the hearts and minds of the American people, and whose exalted character challenges the admiration and the homage of mankind.

Far be it from me to presume to render a just tribute to this great man, and I will ask that you deal charitably with my presumption if I propose to describe the character of George Washington the Courageous, when every scene in that remarkable career has been traced hundreds, yea thousands of times, by the most brilliant and illustrious pens and tongues of our land.

Ah, my friends, the courageous character of Washington, who can describe it worthily—modest, generous, just—self-denying and self-sacrificing; achiever and preserver of liberty, founder and guardian of his country, father of his people—brave, fearless, heroic. What attribute could be added to that consummate character to commend it as an example above all other characters in merely human history.

I do not forget that there have been other men, in other days, in other lands, who have been called upon to command larger armies, to grapple with as complicated and critical affairs, and to offer solutions to problems that had baffled the ingenuities of men for ages. May gratitude and honor be ever upon their persons and upon their names. But we do not estimate Miltiades at Marathon, Brian Boru at Clontarf, or William of Normandy at Hastings, by the number of forces which they led. Nor do we gauge the glory of Columbus by the *Nina*, *Pinta*, and *Santa Maria*, with which he ventured so heroically upon the perils of an unknown sea. Some circumstances cannot occur twice, some occasions cannot be repeated, some names cannot be surpassed in the assertion of their individual preeminence. The glory of Columbus shall never be equalled until there be new worlds to discover, and the courage of Washington shall remain unique and peerless until American independence shall require to be achieved again or the foundations of constitutional liberty to be laid anew.

Is there one among us here today, upon whose mind and heart is not written indelibly the story of Valley Forge! The trials and tribulations of those zealous patriots of Seventy-six, from the time the Minute Men fired that "shot heard around the world" to that memorable day at Yorktown when the lofty banner of Britain bowed to the Stars and Stripes of the States, will be the supreme test and standard of courageous fighting men, throughout the countless aeons of eternity.

But if I might venture to discriminate, I would say that it was in those conflicts of opinion that succeeded the Revolution that the courage of Washington most displayed itself. For it was then that peril thickened in its most subtle forms, that rival passions burned in intestine flames, that crises came, demanding a wider reaching and far greater courage than may be exhibited in war, and a higher heroism than may be displayed in battle. And when the mighty voice of that courageous Washington spoke forth those principles of truth and tolerance and justice and freedom, it reached the uttermost boundaries of the world. And that mighty voice will forever be heard in the wilderness and chaos of the human maelstrom.

As the beloved English poet, Byron, once wrote:

> "Where may the wearied eye repose
> When gazing on the great,
> Where neither guilty glory glows,
> Nor despicable state!
> Yes, One—the first, the last, the best,
> The Cincinnatus of the West,
> Whom envy dared not hate—
> Bequeathed the name of Washington,
> To make men blush there was but One!"

While we contemplate with admiration the mighty influences which surround us today, and which demand our cooperation and our guidance, let our hearts overflow with gratitude to that patriot who handed down to us this great inheritance. Let us strive to achieve that lofty standard and to measure our integrity and our patriotism by our nearness to it or our departure from it.

Ah, my friends, well did Abraham Lincoln speak for all Americans when he said, "To add brightness to the sun, or glory to the name of Washington is alike impossible. Let none attempt it. In solemn awe we pronounce the name, and in its naked deathless splendor leave it shining on."

The Spirit of Washington

OWEN KING, JR.
Aberdeen, South Dakota

Northern Normal and Industrial School, Aberdeen, South Dakota

A sculptor, inspired by a great ideal, fashioned a monument for the marvel of mankind. As he saw his creation grow he became so lost in the magnitude of the task, that he reared it to the sky, forgetting that the world of men about him could not see and appreciate his masterpiece. The great work of art was lost in the clouds of the sculptor's imagination and the real monument was forgotten.

Such has been the hero worship accorded George Washington. In the one hundred thirty-odd years since his death the real Washington has faded into an idealism given him by succeeding biographers until today we are facing a hero worship unparalleled in American history. His body was buried in a simple grave at Mount Vernon; but the American people have laid him away in a mausoleum darker and more difficult to excavate than the pyramids of the Pharaohs.

Statues have been dedicated for the purpose of preserving his likeness for posterity. Historical writers have made him a demigod and the vital spirit of the great man has been entirely obscured by the vaporous clouds of sentimentality which have been thrown about him by his admirers.

George Washington was at heart an ordinary citizen. He did not wish to be a hero; yet this very trait of simplicity in his character made him a man to be trusted with great undertakings. A wealthy Virginia planter, he was elevated to world prominence, and became the democratic leader of a new republic, the creator of an ideal in government. Yet with all this glory and honor the man was as much amazed by the greatness of the task he had accomplished as by the tumultuous praises that beat upon his ears. He had given so unselfishly to the cause for which he labored that he had been unaware of giving. To relate historical data about his life is not my purpose today, as it would be triteness in itself. You, my friends, know his biography—every detail has been published. It is of another phase of his influence that I would speak—namely the spirit of Washington as it has come down to us through the ages.

How well that spirit might be imitated today by our politicians and so-called national leaders. He was a man who served his country without pay and risked his life that the oppressed citizens of a colonial empire might live. The man who served mankind, that he might save them, has given us an ideal that it would be well for us to follow. Unmindful of the criticisms and insults heaped upon him by his contemporaries, he found a people in need and he gave aid unsparingly. Seldom before had men served but for their own glory, but this man served only that he might save his fellow men.

Certain profiteering political leaders have robbed the helpless in our nation until today our citizens are facing an economic crisis. Starvation and destitution have been brought on by cleverly maneuvered legislation which has given advantages to the wealthy few and has ignored the needy. The only thought of these men has been selfish advancement politically and financially. Would that these leaders might follow the example set by our First President. Let them serve the people without thought of selfish reward. Let them serve that they may save our citizens from the plight in which they now find themselves. Let them place the welfare of the nation and its people before every other consideration. If this is done we shall find a way out and a stronger and better union will emerge.

The problem of law enforcement is facing the American people today. Washington emphasized the absolute necessity of law enforcement when he said, "All obstructions to the execution of the Laws, all combinations and associations, under whatever plausible character, with the real design to direct, control, counteract, or awe the regular deliberation and action of the constituted authorities, are destructive of this fundamental principle, and of fatal tendency."

Today we have organized combinations and associations whose design is to counteract the laws of this nation. Groups of men defy our legal statutes. Our second largest city is controlled by the denizens of an underworld. Allied with these persons are men whose sworn duty it is to uphold the law. When gangs and political groups unite to contaminate such Federal action as the Eighteenth Amendment; when underworlds exist and thrive on penal inefficiency; when kidnappings cause parents to resort to gangsters for aid; and lawyers conduct litigation with the success of their client rather than justice as their primary aim; then it is time for law-abiding citizens of this democratic nation to rise up and demand that the ideals for which their early forbearers fought be upheld by solemn oath and righteous achievement.

The citizens of our country stand aghast and pay tribute to the racketeer. We fear to take a stand that will stop defiance of the law. We encourage them by our very cowardice.

How different a story was told at the beginning of our government. Just as much danger was imminent then—just as great a task faced Washington during the Whisky Rebellion, but a courage and bravery to see constituted authority control, inspired him to quell the uprising and make the men of that generation realize that the new government and its laws were supreme.

What we need in this country today is the spirit of courage and bravery that will cause men to act. Let us incorporate in our lives that spirit of courage and demand that the laws of the land be enforced without fear, and that constituted authority be recognized rather than racketeer anarchy.

Not alone in domestic affairs has the spirit of our First President been a guiding hand, but in international dealings as well we may profit by his words. In his Farewell Address he says, "Against the insidious wiles of foreign influence, . . . the jealousy of a free people ought to be *constantly* awake, since history and experience prove that foreign influence is one of the most baneful foes of republican Government. But that jealously to be useful, must be impartial."

How true this is today! The profiteer with capital invested in foreign securities would have us see only one side of the controversies which arise. In the Orient today we can not show excessive partiality. There are two sides to every conflict. Let us seek a middle course and be influenced by the words of Washington in our international dealings. He said, "The great rule of conduct for us, in regard to foreign Nations, is, in extending our commercial relations, to have with them as little *Political* connection as possible." He realized that commercial relationships are necessary to the welfare of a commonwealth, but that political alliances involve the people of a country in wars and conflicts of another nation's making.

Not independent isolation should be sought, but a thorough understanding of international alliances and their consequences must be the guide of this nation in dealing with other countries.

Thus the problem of applying the principles of Washington to our government confronts you, the citizens of the United States. You have wandered away from the precepts and practices of your forefathers. Your legislative assemblies have become the servants of a privileged minority. Men serve, not for the good of their fellow men, but for their own personal glory and avarice. Your laws have become a travesty on justice. Crime runs rampant in the underworlds of your cities. You have permitted mercenary

ambitions to warp the ideals of the founder of this nation. In your greed for wealth you have neglected the principles and precepts for which Washington stood—ideals that would make this nation a fit place for decent law-abiding citizens to live. Such scandals as the Tea Pot Dome would have caused Washington to rise up in righteous wrath and denounce them without fear of political downfall.

The spirit of the great leader demands that you, the citizens of this country, awaken to the responsibilities which face you. You must no longer allow your citizens to be coerced, your courts to be made a jest of, and your Constitution violated. Rather shall law and order prevail and the rights of the individual be protected.

If you follow this guidance, then this nation will grow and prosper and in the dimness of tomorrow will ride the spirit of the Father of His Country—guiding—preserving and ever keeping watch above his own.

The Spirit of Washington

JOE WILLIAMS WORLEY

Johnson City, Tennessee

State Teachers College, Johnson City, Tennessee

That the world's crises develop leaders stands beyond dispute. The breath that blows from a people's needs creates the spirit that fires and impels those leaders. Two hundred years ago, our forefathers, crushed by the tyranny of England, hindered by the petty colonial jealousies of several racial and commercial groups, stood in days of darkness.

How to bring harmony out of the discord that prevailed, to produce strength from weakness, and to create resources where they did not exist, were the tasks that faced Washington at the beginning of the Revolution. How he succeeded, despite the difficulties that beset his path, will always remain a marvel to historians of those times. But that strange, indefinable, intangible something that always marks "the man of the hour" prevailed, and the spirit of Washington has won for him an enduring fame throughout the succeeding ages.

At the time of the war when the Colonial army was almost disorganized, Washington stood serene amid the storm, sending his clear, calm voice o'er the tumult, inspiring hope and courage when both seemed madness. Never before did such destinies hang on a single man, for it was not the fate of a people, but the fate of human liberty the world over which rested on the issue of that struggle.

In the very beginning when the Stamp Act began to be enforced, Washington was among the first to raise his voice in defense of Colonial rights. He was ready at all times to peril his life in Liberty's behalf. Although opposed to war, he proclaimed that no man should scruple or hesitate a moment to raise arms in defense of so valuable a blessing as liberty. When in 1774, a day of fasting and prayer was appointed in sympathy with the people of Boston, Washington wrote in his diary, "Went to Church and fasted all day."

From that time until he bade farewell to the army, he moves before us in the majesty of virtue and courage, whether bowed in prayer in behalf of country, or planning in his mind the moves of his brave army; whether retreating before the overwhelming numbers of the enemy, or exhorting his tired squadrons to the charge, whether lost in anxious thought as his eyes seek in vain for some ray of hope amid the gloomy prospect which surrounds him; or guiding his fragile craft through the broken ice of the angry Delaware; whether galloping into the deadly volleys of the enemy to restore confidence to the wavering spirits of his footsore soldiers, or wearing the wreath of victory which a grateful nation placed upon his brow;—the spirit of Washington is immutably written into every line of our nation's birth-story.

When at last the colonies were freed from England's domination, a greater problem arose to confront the leaders of that day. An almost insuperable task it was, to blend into a unified and harmonious whole, plans of men sprung from widely differing backgrounds, representing groups of opposing interests and filled with conflicting ideals of government. The halo of history clusters 'round that little group of men who, pursuant to the call of Washington, met in Liberty Hall, Philadelphia, in 1787, to give to their people, and to the world at large, the greatest contribution that ever sprang from the brain of man.

After months of weary compromises, at last came that hour when General Washington announced that the product of their labors was ready to be signed. As man after man affixed his signature to that document, the venerable Franklin, with finger pointed to a sun painted above the presiding officer's chair, arose, and with the vision of a prophet proclaimed, "As I have been sitting here all these months, I have often wondered whether yonder sun is a rising or a setting sun, but now I know it is a rising sun." And Washington wept. Such was the spirit of solemn sincerity in which he wrought.

Elevated and returned to the helm of the country he had led on battle-field and through council-hall into the list of the nations of the world, Washington guided the newly-formed state through the perilous years of infancy. And at the expiration of eight years, this Cincinnatus of the western world refused the offer of another term, fearing that if he accepted, the fruit of his labors for democracy would be eaten by the worm of monarchy. In his Farewell Address, he broke down and wept, dampening his officers' brows with his tears as he bade them good-bye. Such was the character of the man who molded from wilderness this nation which ere long was to be foremost in world affairs.

As the decades have heaped into an almost century and a half of our national existence, and have seen his country stretch from a mere fringe of sparsely settled communities along the Atlantic Seaboard, westward to the Pacific, and onto the isles of the seas; have seen her leaders take their places in the world's council-halls and market places; have felt her political ideals permeate the soul of mankind; have placed her name on the lips of those that thirsted for human rights—the vision that fired the spirit of our Washington has been justified.

With torch aloft, blazing the way to this land of opportunity, stands our Statue of Liberty. About her hovers a shadowy host of those who have played well their parts to give to earth's broken bodies and hungry hearts a haven and a hope. Above her broods a spirit intangible, calling to American youth to dedicate its life to the preservation of that priceless heritage, the spirit of Washington.

Today we are met in commemoration of the Bicentennial anniversary of the birth of him who has been so aptly termed, "first in war, first in peace, and first in the hearts of his countrymen." About us the storm clouds gather and settle down into a darkness that tries men's souls. Doctrines are rife and isms rampant that strike at the very sacredness of our government and would seek to paralyze its agencies. Public officials have proved unfaithful to trust and have shaken the confidence of our citizenry in their institutions. Indifference on the part of the electorate has too often resulted in incompetency and dishonesty in high places. Public office has been prostituted to private gain and public money has flown like wine down a broken press.

Needed is the vision of a Franklin to (yet) see a rising sun, and the spirit of a Washington to lead on to a glory that may yet be.

"God give us men, a time like this demands strong men,
Great hearts, true faith and ready hand,
Men whom the lust for office does not kill,
Men whom the spoils of office cannot buy,
Tall men, sun-crowned, who live above the fog,
In public duty and in private thinking."

The Spirit of Washington

MARY LYNN ORGAIN

Temple, Texas

Temple Junior College, Temple, Texas

The people of America are familiar with the high points in Washington's life. Our hearts are thrilled with patriotism when we think of the winter he and his heroic men spent at Valley Forge. We know, that as first president, he guided our young nation safely and sanely through perilous years. But to know and appreciate the spirit of Washington, we must appraise the man himself.

George Washington has been idolized to almost God-like proportions. In late years we have seen, too, an attempt to tear down his goodness and greatness. We well know that Washington was not a god, nor was everything he said and did the perfect thing. But we do know that his personality is the outstanding one of his nation.

Notwithstanding the abrasions of time, it is significant that after two centuries Washington comes to us with his glory brighter and more lasting. His own conception of self-control was identical with the familiar Biblical injunction, "He that ruleth his spirit is greater than he that taketh the city." This, George Washington completely fulfilled.

He had an ardent temperament, and strong passions. His constant effort was to check the one and subdue the other. This he was able to do because his contact with men in every walk of life was marked with the consistency of dignity, which was not so much the dictates of his native good sense and judgments as it was the fruits of long and unwearied discipline of self.

Another fruit of the spirit of Washington was his unselfishness and kindness. His unselfishness is revealed even in his early life, when, as a boy of eleven, he found himself without the guidance of his good father. The father and older brothers had had the very best education England and the Colonies could offer. But the youthful boy, who loved his books devotedly, gave up his dream of an academic education to learn a trade to help support his widowed mother. At the age of sixteen, he was earning a livelihood as a young surveyor under Lord Fairfax. There was never a complaint from the lad because he had sacrificed his fondest ambition; namely, that of acquiring an education, but he gave of himself heart and soul to his work.

Deprived of systematic schooling, he secured much knowledge by self-education. The clear, distinct style of Washington's writings, and the classical allusions of his work, make us know that although Washington was not a university trained, nor a college bred man, he came to be a man of culture. He acquired a remarkable library. The keynote of his conception of knowledge he explained thus: "I conceive a knowledge of books is the basis upon which other knowledge is to be built." His own example of self-education should be an inspiration to every youth and adult alike. Washington, in his unselfishness, had for his measuring rod of greatness, the one and only true standard, that of service. Truly, he embodied the concept of the Master of men, whom he so humbly worshipped. "He that would be greatest among you, let him be the servant of all." Why are we honoring Washington today, two hundred years after his birth? Why has this great Nation paused to honor him? The answer comes ringing down the ages—because of inestimable, invaluable service of an unselfish, patriotic, God-fearing man.

Seventy-five years ago, Edward Everett, in his famous address on the character of Washington, brought out the fact that Washington's greatness was due more to his common sense and moral balance than to any other one thing.

In this time of general depression, an age of nervous tension and speed, the necessity for balance is obvious. The world has always suffered, more or less from lack of balance. Since in the rush and hurry of life today, we are in danger of having taken from us, normal balance, which is necessary if we are to endure and be happy, it seems prophetic that we should come back to Washington and his moral balance.

When we speak of Washington's patriotism, his courage and his loyalty are inseparably bound up with it. Without actual experience in directing operations of war on an extended scale, without adequate equipment for his troops, without a strong government or treasury of even reasonable strength, he was summoned, from a peaceful home to the battlefield. Through almost insurmountable difficulties, with a patience and a courage that bordered on the superhuman, he led a small and undisciplined body of men taken suddenly from the ordinary walks of life, to final victory against the best trained legions of Europe fighting in behalf of the foremost nation of the globe at that time. In triumph and in disaster he was alike steadfast and serene; in official conduct and in private intercourse his every act was free from the slightest taint of intemperance, immorality, or corruption. No slaughter of helpless foes, nor deeds of cruelty dimmed his fame. The only reward he desired for his services was the gratitude of his country.

As oratory finds its most beautiful expression from the gifted tongue of Demosthenes; as painting reaches its zenith at the hands of the master, Raphael; as dramatic art attains its loftiest peak in the plays of Shakespeare; as philosophy achieves its most scholarly reasoning from the teachings of Aristotle; as music scales its highest pinnacle in the oratorios of Handel, the operas of Mozart, the sonatas of Beethoven; so human conduct finds its most glorious expression in the spirit and deeds of Washington.

Today, more than a century after his death, the interest and the love of earth's increasing millions are centered in his memory.

Washington's greatness was of that sort which we all can share. His virtues were of a kind that in degree we too may possess. No more fitting ideal of manhood could have been chosen for this Nation. His one desire of serving well his country and his fellowmen, his faithfulness through victory and discouragement, these traits of the spirit give Washington a unique place among the world's heroes.

George Washington is indeed first in the hearts of his countrymen. His purity of purpose stands unimpeached, his steadfast earnestness and his sterling honesty are our priceless examples. We love the man. We call him, "The Father of Our Country," and in Lincoln's words sum up the splendid traits that mark him apart: "Washington is the mightiest name of earth—long since mightiest in the cause of civil liberty, still mightiest in moral reformation. On that name no eulogy is expected. It can not be. To add brightness to the sun, or glory to the name of Washington is alike impossible. Let none attempt it. In solemn awe we pronounce the name, and in its naked deathless splendor leave it shining on."

The Spirit of Washington

NOEL COOK

Oceana, West Virginia

West Virginia University, Morgantown, West Virginia

On the twenty-second of February, 1732, there was born in Westmoreland County, Virginia, a child who in the annals of American history might well have been given the sobriquet of the great Corsican soldier, "the child of destiny." That child, christened George Washington, grown to manhood, was destined to lead his people in a grand march against tyranny and oppression, a grand march which would terminate in the creation of a state, the champion of free government over two continents. For the erection of that state some would give Washington complete credit, reasoning that the man makes the times. Others would deny him the fullness of that honor, contending that the times make the man. A truer premise would be that the times afford the oppor-

tunity for the man. What he will be will in a great measure rest with his intellect, his traditions, his character, and his strength of will. No more fitting analogy of this truth can be drawn than the contrasting careers of George Washington and Napoleon Bonaparte.

George Washington; Napoleon Bonaparte! Could one choose two more celebrated national heroes? And yet could one find two leaders whose paths in public life were more widely divergent? The opportunities presented to each were identical, but the products were as widely separated as the poles.

Each upon his advent into public affairs found an undercurrent of civil strife in the government that was to reach its climax in revolution. The people were revolting against the existing tyranny of monarchy, an age of wrong and oppression. The newer theories of organized society that had been slowly growing through the centuries had established firm root in the minds of the populace. They needed only leadership. Our two heroes adequately afforded that leadership. They had proven themselves capable men, and were vested with immense power, and high position. They were trusted to lift their countrymen from the whirling chaos into which they were plunged. How each kept faith with that trust is what will hold him high to the coming generations or mark him with eternal shame. But here at the threshold of power their similarity fades from out our sight, never again to be observed. What caused that likeness to disappear? Why did not their lives follow like channels, under such similar conditions? The answer lies within the personalities of the men, for they were by nature not akin. Posterity shall judge them in the only way it knows,—by their action.

Napoleon was a marauder, a glamorous adventurer. His life was given to the quest of power, not for any useful purpose to which he might direct it, but for the sheer glory of possession. Cool, calculating, and ambitious, every act was duly considered for his self-aggrandizement. He knew no law he could not break. To him the institution of the state was nothing except as it helped or hindered his ambition; freedom was nothing, and the lives of men were nil unless they served to feed that rapacious appetite for fame and glory. He made his way to empire, as the orator has said, "over broken oaths and through a sea of blood," to find it emptiness and vain glory. In the end even his mighty genius could not stay the fate of a tyrant. He was forced to lay aside that crown he had set upon his head with his own hands, for the ignominy of St. Helena. He was the victim of his own nature. The underlying principle of his life was selfishness. He builded falsely, about his own false self, ignored truths and principle, and when he crashed his empire crashed with him. The results were inevitable as the laws of the universe. He shall be remembered only through the archives of history, and not as a creator, but as a destroyer; not as a father, but as a betrayer of his country; not as a patriot, but as an adventurer, an exploiter.

But as ruthlessly as Napoleon destroyed, as ardently Washington builded. When he was a betrayer of his country, a usurper, a scheming designer, Washington was a patriot, a statesman, a servant of the people. When Napoleon fell from his dizzy height the light of his empire went out forever, but when Washington retired from public life his state lived on, prospering through the years to champion the ideals for which he stood. When Napoleon died in exile, far from the land he had despoiled, there were few to mourn save the weeping willows 'neath which he was buried. But when Washington passed, the flags of the world were lowered to half mast, and a nation mourned as a child would mourn the passing of its father.

Why did Washington succeed, when the other failed? Why is he enshrined in the hearts of his countrymen, and the other hated? The answer is that Napoleon stood for the man,—Washington for a principle. Wisdom, energy, unselfish devotion, and reverent patriotism are the qualities that marked him for a leader. But there was something deeper, something subtler, something lending purpose to those virtues. Washington was the living symbol of a sentiment, a growing feeling for democracy, a more rational conception of the state and government. Perhaps the men of his time never realized it, perhaps he did not fully conceive of the movement he represented, but to us looking through the perspective of two hundred years he is the spirit of liberty of representative government blossoming into full flower. In him we see the culmination of centuries of thought. The final outgrowth was in a man who would give those ideas impetus.

A new country where land was to be had for the taking, where men breathed a spirit of freedom, where the rigors of life made it imperative that a man be measured by his ability to combat the forces of nature, furnished a fertile field for democracy. Soon the old order ceased to bear its fruit, democratic ideas crept in, and imbedded themselves deep in the lives of the settlement. The people needed but a leader, a strong, active leader, and they would follow him to the utmost bounds, to the dearest sacrifice, to attain their ideals. Thoroughly imbued with the spirit of the times, Washington became that leader. Others might deal abstractly with those philosophies, but his was to do. His life was lit by a dream, a dream of a great nation fostering those ideals he believed so conscientiously. To the realization of that dream he turned all the magnificent power of his mind and body. Those visionary qualities, that imagination, linked inseparably with his spirit of sacrifice for the ideal, make of him more than a man,—they make of him a spirit, the moving spirit of the embodiment of those ideals. But the embodiment of those ideals into an independent government was no simple task. There were the thirteen independent colonies to unite in a common purpose; there was a well-trained, well-equipped army to combat; there was his own raw, undisciplined, ill-equipped army to meet it; there were sectional rivalries to allay;

there was the problem of financing the struggle; there were petty jealousies and ambitions to be snubbed; and finally, even if success crowned his efforts, there was the machinery of the new government to be set in order. The boundless energy, the foresightedness, the spirit of conciliation with which Washington met these problems is a matter for the historian, but what is less known and little appreciated is his own bitter struggle to achieve these things. When the soldiers grumbled for their pay; when his officers vied for fame and glory; when the people doubted their commander; when the flare for independence waned, how much simpler it would have been to lay down his own arms and go home. But in the spirit of one who labors in a righteous cause, he struggled on until the task was finished. Then when the struggle was over, when his efforts had been crowned with victory, in the spirit of a Cincinnatus he turned from the glamor and the shout and went home to the arms of a loving wife, claiming no greater reward than the common good brought to all.

Today he sleeps a few miles below the city bearing his name, where the waves of the Potomac kiss the shores and murmur a perpetual requiem about his tomb. The true American at the tomb of Washington will ponder on the glorious heritage he has left us, and consider his own obligation to pass on that heritage unimpaired. Here rests the dust of one of the noblest men who ever lived, and he was great because he consecrated all the magnificent powers of his body, mind, and soul to the utmost performance of his duty. He needs no stately sepulchre, for he is enshrined in our hearts, and his monument is our Country.

FACSIMILE OF CERTIFICATE OF AWARD
FOR ALL TYPES OF CONTESTS

The Other State Winners
in the Bicentennial Oratorical Contests

TOP ROW (left to right)—Bernard Mergen, Nevada; Irwin Luthi, Kansas; Clarence Flood, Arizona; Francis D. Burke, New Mexico.

MIDDLE ROW—Margaret Allen Wallis, Alabama; Mary Lynn Orgain, Texas; Virginia Randolph, Montana.

BOTTOM ROW—Owen King, Jr., South Dakota; William A. McRae, Jr., Florida; J. R. Gillespie, Kentucky; Ross Borders, Arkansas; Joe Williams Worley, Tennessee.

Photographs Not Available—Jerome Downey, District of Columbia; Ralph Olmstead, Idaho; Noel Cook, West Virginia.

Students Awarded Second and Third Places in their Respective State Oratorical Contests

Alabama

Gerald Loggins, State Teachers College, Florence
William Hardie, Spring Hill College

Arizona

Don Graves, University of Arizona
Lynn Tenney, Gila College

Arkansas

John William Hammons, Hendrix College
Billie Murray, El Dorado Junior College
Franklin Wilder, Fort Smith Junior College

Colorado

Lucille Riede, Loretto Heights College
Delbert Ross, University of Denver

Connecticut

Mamie Garamella, New Haven State Normal School
Marjorie Brett, New Haven State Normal School

District of Columbia

Seymour Mintz, George Washington University

Florida

Charles Brooks, Rollins College
Glen Hutchinson, Southern College

Georgia

Searcy S. Garrison, Mercer University
Brainard Currie, Augusta Junior College

Idaho

M. Elizabeth Henry, Lewiston State Normal School

Illinois

Glen Seidenfeld, Lake Forest College
Charles Seidenspinner, Wheaton College

Kansas

Charles Stevens, Washburn College

Kentucky

Frederica Puryear, Nazareth Junior College
Sam Beckley, Eastern Kentucky State Teachers College

Louisiana

Frances Trim, Louisiana State University
Henry Pierson, Louisiana State Normal College

Montana

Mary Moore, Montana State College of Agriculture and Mechanic Arts

Nevada

Elwin Jeffers, University of Nevada
Donald E. Butler, University of Nevada

New York

Abraham S. Guterman, Yeshiva College
Mary Gleason, D'Youville College

North Dakota

Donovan Sutton, Jamestown College
Erling Groth, State Teachers College, Mayville

Oregon

Richard Blandau, Linfield College
Carl Johnson, Oregon Agricultural College

South Dakota

Walter Slocum, South Dakota State College of Agriculture and Mechanic Arts
Lyle Wirt, University of South Dakota

Tennessee

Esther King, Milligan College
Thomas Dallam Morris, University of Tennessee

Texas

Margaret Jordan, East Texas State Teachers College
Ralph Elliott, Austin College

Virginia

Jenilee Knight, State Teachers College, Farmville
W. R. Stevens, Emory and Henry College
P. S. Trible, Virginia Polytechnic Institute

West Virginia

Elaine Avington, West Virginia Wesleyan College
Ina Sinclaire, West Virginia Wesleyan College

President Hoover Honors the Winner of the National Essay Contest

President Hoover presenting the official George Washington Commemorative Gold Medal, August 4, 1932, to Miss Betty Ann Troy, Stamford, Connecticut, who was awarded first place in the National Essay Contest conducted in the High Schools of the Nation. To the right of Miss Troy is the Honorable Sol Bloom, Director of the United States George Washington Bicentennial Commission, who presented Miss Troy to the President

ESSAYS

First Place Awards in the State Bicentennial Essay Contests in High Schools

The essay which appears first in this group was given the National Award.   The essays are printed as received without editing out minor historical errors.

The Many-sidedness of George Washington

BETTY ANN TROY

Sacred Heart Academy, Stamford, Connecticut

Winner of the Nation-wide High School Essay Contest

WARRIOR

ADVENTURER

SPORTSMAN

HOME-MAKER

INVESTIGATOR

NATION-BUILDER

GENERAL

TRUSTEE

OFFICIAL

NATIONAL HERO

Has any other one man so distinguished himself in fields so varied, so apparently incongruous, as has our Washington?   Let us review his career.

WARRIOR was he from earliest youth!   Even as a child, he never tyrannized over others, yet no one was found brave enough to tyrannize over him.   He inherited his power of demanding obedience from his Spartan mother, a masterful woman possessing a temperament not admitting of contradiction.   His definite military tendency was early discovered by his father, who implanted in his mind the germ of the high moral standards which characterized his later fighting.

As an ADVENTURER, Washington takes precedence, even in those pioneer days when all men were necessarily adventurers.   An experienced surveyor at sixteen, he accepted the man-sized task of exploring and surveying a pathless and heretofore untravelled wilderness.   The hardships and dangers which confronted him were enough to tax the courage of inured frontiersmen, but in every emergency, his good judgment, fearlessness, and endurance enabled him to triumph.

However, with Washington, it was not a case of "all work and no play"—he was a keen and proficient SPORTSMAN.   His superb horsemanship, his ardor and skill in the hunt, and above all, his sense of fair play won for him the friendship of Lord Fairfax, which friendship was a dominating influence in Washington's character formation.

But it is as HOME-MAKER that we find the most satisfying Washington.   That a man with dominating qualities should attain pre-eminence in public life is ordinary, but that such a man lead an ideal home life is exceptional.   Whether he was at Mount Vernon, or in camp quarters, to which he brought Mrs. Washington whenever possible, or in the executive mansion, he succeeded in establishing a cheery, homey, Christian atmosphere.   Regularity and hospitality formed the keynote and resulted in the happiness of the Washington household.

Furthermore, he was a progressive gentleman-farmer, indeed, an enthusiastic INVESTIGATOR of agricultural operations.   Always seeking new and better farming methods, and unceasingly experimenting until he could build up a satisfactory theory, he was America's first scientific farmer.   Unable to appeal to a Department of Agriculture, he made personal tests of plowing, treatment of seeds, rotation of crops, and other experiments.

Not all of Washington's time was devoted to personal pursuits, however; much of it was consigned to political affairs, but how clean were his policies, how unselfish, his aims!   When we needed a NATION-BUILDER, Washington was ready for the task.   Unless we had had a man to bring the war to a successful issue, to spurn the crown and instead found a Republic, to form and enforce the laws of this new-born Republic, the Declaration of Independence would have been fruitless, and the ideal of the Colonists would have been slain at birth!

As a GENERAL, he was able, resourceful, invincible.   Even the most prejudiced biographers admit that without Washington's bold and skillful moves, the cause of the Revolution would have been lost.   He created an army out of the coarsest material and nurtured the inspiration that developed into the "spirit of '76."   A past-master at strategy, he surpassed in military ability all the generals that the English could send against him.   He stood the tests of criticism, disloyalty, treason.   In fine, he brought triumph out of chaos!

Even before his election to public office, Washington was TRUSTEE of our nation.   The destiny and welfare of America were confided to him as Commander-in-Chief; the solution of the problem of the Colonies, who were "states subject to nobody," lay in his hands; his rejection of the proffered crown decided the foundation of a Republic; the outcome of the Constitutional Convention rested with him, its most influential member; finally, the establishment of unity in the Infant Republic was entrusted to him as President.

In Washington, we find a capable OFFICIAL, a model executive.   Throughout his term as head of the nation, he faithfully kept his oath to "preserve, protect, and defend the Constitution."   He exhibited the greatest integrity and firmness; his singular courage enabled him to accomplish his decisions in the face of great difficulty.   His views on morality and religion, which he professed to have received from his mother, account for the greatness of character which was responsible for his success.

America may well be proud of her NATIONAL HERO!   She may present him to her citizens as the "model citizen"; she may unblushingly compare him to national heroes of other countries.   Washington has stood the test of time.   He is still supreme!

Washington's Balance of Character

HERMAN PFAFF
Birmingham, Alabama

Phillips High School, Birmingham, Alabama

Perhaps the most accurate opinion regarding the balance of a man's character is that formed by a careful analysis of his reactions, mental as well as physical, to both commonplace and critical situations. Some of George Washington's wisest and noblest thoughts and actions seem to have sprung spontaneously from his inherent sublimity of character; in other cases a decision respecting a principle, or a course of behavior, was arrived at only after long hours filled with uncertainty and self-conquest. But Washington's every tenet and every action seems to have been determined by a certain balance in the constituent elements of his character.

Washington was born and bred in a society refined and courtly of manner. During young manhood he lived the rough life of the wilderness surveyor, scout, and soldier in close comradeship with men utterly disdainful of all social formalities. The result of these strikingly different environments was to produce a man of rare poise in his valuation and usage of arbitrary customs. In the words of Henry Cabot Lodge: "He [Washington] neither overvalued nor underrated social conventions, for he knew that they were a part of the fabric of civilized society, not vitally important and yet not wholly trivial. . . ."

Washington was a slave holder. Yet he was not certain of the justice of the practice, even though it had a salutary effect on both slave and master when the latter was a gentleman of high principles. Even so, the institution of slavery seemed to him to be a necessary part of the economic and social structure of the South. Washington did not advocate general emancipation, nor did he free his own slaves; for he recognized that such measures would precipitate violent economic, moral, and social disorder. Call this a "straddling" position, if you will; nevertheless, it was in accord with the opinions of the most enlightened men of the day, and it bespoke a fine balance and broadness of character.

During his career as soldier and statesman, it was many times necessary for Washington to appoint men to positions of great public responsibility. In his life as a planter, it was extremely important that his private servants be trustworthy. And at every period of his life he had hosts of personal friends. Yet he who so acutely judged the character of others, had in his own character just the right proportions of the conflicting feelings of a natural trust and a cultivated caution toward all mankind, and was so unaffected by the abuse of foes or the flattery of schemers or the praise of friends that there is but one case (that of Benedict Arnold) where one whom he implicitly trusted wilfully betrayed the confidence.

The blending of his many admirable traits of character to form a character even more admirable in its entirety is well illustrated by Washington's conduct on his being selected by the Continental Congress to lead the American Army. It is said that when John Adams arose and recommended him to the Congress for that position that the modest Washington, who was present, blushingly withdrew from the chamber. It seems perfectly sure that Washington himself—and of all the Congress, himself alone—sincerely doubted that he possessed the requisite ability in military affairs. Yet it is equally certain that he felt a pleasant glow of pride withal. Without a doubt, also, Washington was perfectly cognizant of two unpleasant facts: namely, that the success of the Colonists' arms was doubtful, even improbable; and that in the event of their failure he would be reviled, possibly hanged, as a traitor. He also realized that in a personal nature he had little to gain and much to lose by his acceptance of the command; he was to receive no monetary reward for his services, his estate would suffer from neglect, and he must exchange all the manifold pleasures of his life as a country gentleman for the hardships of camp life. Yet, even in the

stress of all these varied feelings, he did not hesitate for long, but accepted the commission with such a mixture of diffidence and self-respect, of a full realization of all difficulties and a firm faith in a just Providence, and of a keen sense of self-sacrifice and a ready willingness to serve that all noble men loved him and looked to him for leadership.

Yes, it might truly have been said of George Washington that

"... The elements
So mix'd in him, that Nature might stand up
And say to all the world, 'This was a man!' "

Washington's Balance of Character

SYLVIA POSTERT
Lowell, Arizona

Loretto Academy, Bisbee, Arizona

It is the duty of every American citizen to commemorate the immortal name of Washington. The year 1932 is bringing with it many memorials in celebration of the Bicentennial of George Washington's birth. To say that we are proud to claim such a man of character as our own is but mildly expressing our thoughts. Here I can truly use the words of Lord Byron:

"Where may the wearied eye repose
    When gazing on the Great;
Where neither guilty glory glows,
    Nor despicable state?
Yes—one—the first—the last—the best—
The Cincinnatus of the West,
    Whom envy dared not hate,
Bequeath the name of Washington,
To make men blush there was but one!"

Washington's character may want some of the poetical elements which delight and dazzle the multitude; however, he possessed fewer inequalities and a rarer union of virtues than ever fell to the lot of man.

When a mere boy, Washington composed a set of rules of conduct, which ended with the words: "Labor to keep alive in your Breast that Little Spark of Celestial fire Called Conscience." Washington made his country's cause a conscientious matter. We recognize this at every stage of his eventful career.

An incident revealing his pure generosity is shown in a letter to his wife in which he says: "You may believe me, my dear . . . when I assure you, . . . that, so far from seeking this appointment, I have used every endeavor in my power to avoid it, not only from my unwillingness to part with you and the family, but from a consciousness of its being a trust too great for my capacity."

During his presidency this occasion brought to light his unselfishness and wisdom. He found the duty of administration so strenuous that he determined to retire at the end of his first term of office, but the success of the new government was not assured, and he was asked to take again the chair of president. So he disregarded his own feelings for those of the people.

As Commander-in-Chief of the army, Washington's poise, strength, and courage are unquestioned. When given command of the army, he accepted it upon terms characteristic of his self-sacrificing patriotism, rather than upon those of Congress. His magnetic personality attracted people; his wisdom won their respect. But beyond all this, his tact, or one might say his spirit of toleration, his genuine patriotism, his deep belief in a permanent union of the States, have made him an outstanding figure among nations.

That innate quality of kindness which gives men irresistible magnetism was another of Washington's characteristics. While at Winchester with his feeble army of ill-fed and ill-clothed men, the town was attacked by Indians. Many of the soldiers were killed. The women came to him with their babes in their arms begging him to save the children. Washington wept bitterly, sorry that he could do no more than he was doing. He was bitterly assailed—every outrage inflicted by the Indians was charged to his negligence or incompetency, but such criticism gave strength to heroic patience.

This kindness of disposition had its source in a refined natural modesty. More than once, when he found himself a target for hostile criticism, his retiring disposition and modesty made him wish to yield place to other men. When John Adams, who described Washington as "discreet, and virtuous, no ranting, swearing fellow, but sober, steady and calm" proposed him to Congress as the only leader who—because of skill, fortune, and excellent character—could unite the interests of the Colonies, then so discordant, Washington, who happened to sit next the door, showed his usual modesty, and dashed into the library. The pages of Adams' diary are besprinkled with these telling words, "character," "modesty," "firmness," "calm," "deliberate."

Yet when withdrawn from his retreat Washington began a career which redounds to his eternal credit. Infallible judgment, complete devotion, perfect balance, utter unselfishness, faith, hope, and charity went to make up the majestic manhood of our First President.

Let us now turn aside from the soldier and statesman, bearing the burdens of war and government and view the man in his lighter moments. Some think Washington hard and cold, or perhaps superhuman marble, whereas his laughter and tears have either been omitted or so botched in the telling that one can feel little or no understanding of either his woes or his gayety. Instead of being what most people believe him to have been—a man of majestic aloofness from ordinary feelings—Washington was one of the most emotional men that ever lived. He revealed his tenderness when returning home on one occasion and finding his step-daughter dead, he threw himself on his knees before her bed and sobbed for an hour.

Washington's character would lack that perfect balance one admires so much were it to want his sense of humor. He himself tells an anecdote which took place during the siege of Boston. The British made several false sallies which caused much unnecessary scurry. During one of these General Greene could not find his wig, and of course he could not appear on the battle-field without such a necessary article. He paced before his men in a fashion very unbecoming a general and repeated, "Where is my wig? Where is my wig?" Finally, General Charles Lee said, "Your wig is behind the mirror." When Greene dashed to the mirror and saw his wig on the back of his head, his expression was so comical that Washington laughed until he fell over on the sofa.

When we place his sterling qualities in the balance, we find the traits which make up the character of a noble, loyal, patriotic citizen. Bitter trials and crushing disappointments failed to destroy his trust in his Creator and in his fellow citizens.

Let us take him as our Model American Citizen and strive to the utmost to imitate his integrity, his unswerving devotion to his Country. Truly, we must say with the poet:

"A leader, trusted and strong and sure;
A heart that was noble and brave and pure,
Fearless to dare and firm to endure;
Charity; Faith in God secure;
Our hero, Washington."

The Many-sidedness of George Washington

GERTRUDE SCHUSTER

Pilot Grove, Missouri

St. Scholastica Academy, Fort Smith, Arkansas

It is difficult to estimate the true greatness of the man whose birth two hundred years ago is a date upon which the future of

nations hung. George Washington has been lauded and berated alternately by historians and critics. The praises have redounded to the glory of those who gave them, the criticisms have lessened the esteem of those who condemned; but both praise and blame have left him where he was in his own time, and will be as long as America lasts—immortalized in the hearts of his people.

Cold and flawless he has been pictured to us, with no weakness to pity, no oddities to scoff at, no injustices to deplore. Yet there was no mystery about this outstanding character of history. For George Washington the sportsman, the soldier and statesman, the land-owner and home-lover, was also the man. Singularly elevated indeed was his character—admirable is his strength of achievement, but lovable is the human heart which guided all his deeds.

His mental qualities were his highest type of greatness. We know in what they consisted—wisdom which could not be deceived, judgment that never failed, vision that saw into the future, understanding which produced the life and glory of a nation. His was the mind of the Revolutionary War—he was its leader and counsellor—his perseverance and fortitude were its inspiration and support.

There were more brilliant types of genius than his during that period. There were other forces that contributed to the glory of the war—but its grandeur came from Washington.

It was not his achievement in any one duty that singled him out from his contemporaries and made him an example to posterity. It was his faithful performance of every task. Each part of his life has a definite bearing on the whole. Washington was a sportsman, and from his earliest boyhood he loved the out-of-doors and the exercise of those magnificent physical qualities with which he was so generously endowed. He derived from the hunt not only a keen enjoyment, but also a sense of fair play and true sportsmanship which stood him in good stead in the days when he was the "fox" and Cornwallis the hunter. The same sportsmanlike qualities made him a magnanimous victor when at last the battle was his.

Washington was a soldier—how much a great soldier we know from the masterly skill with which he led an undisciplined people to victory. He was a statesman, whose wise guidanace was the nation's main stronghold in the stormy days of the early United States. Calm and clear of judgment, he aroused the admiration of foreign countries, and the undying confidence of the public, although critics assailed him even in his time.

But while state and soldiery claim him, Washington belongs first to the home-lovers and land-owners. The Washingtons were a family who loved peace and retirement and our First President was no exception. On his beloved Mount Vernon estate he spent the happiest days of his life, among his loved family and in the occupation of a farmer. His greatest teacher was the land—it was his first love. More than military skill, more than presidential honors he valued it, and with a pen which never wrote what could be questioned or regretted, he himself said:

"How much more delightful . . . is the task of making improvements on the earth, than all the vain glory that can be acquired from ravaging it, by the most uninterrupted career of conquest."

A deep love of Nature is the outgrowth of a kind, deep-feeling heart. Love of social companionship and response to friendship is another. Because Washington was schooled in restraint and kept his temper under control, he has been thought of as heartless—peerless indeed, but with the perfection of marble—lacking the fire of life and love. Yet no one can adequately analyze the inner workings of his soul. Then let his deeds be the judge, for their noble worth was actuated by his heart, as was the great mind subject to its ruling.

He had the basic qualities of gentility, even as a lad of sixteen, when he pored over "Rules of Civility." Reverence for a Higher Being, respect for women, integrity and honor—all made his character as immortal as the deeds which placed him in history. He was more than soldier and general. He was more than statesman—more than first citizen of the land, he was a gentleman.

Washington's Balance of Character

ROSE ADELE GIANELLA

Chico, California

Holy Names Central High School, Oakland, California

Washington, in his haven of eternity, has probably long since revolted against the desecrations of scholars and schoolboys alike. His spirit has been worn so threadbare by ingenious moralists who constantly reiterate the epic of the cherry tree to uplift the younger generations that we hesitate to molest him further by discussing his moral character. However, there is one quality of character which Washington evidenced that we might well discuss both for the sake of edification and emulation—his balance of character.

The confidence which Washington possessed was that of a man who would tolerate no wavering doubt, and allow no question of indecision to linger in his mind. His confidence was that of a man whose physical life burned more brightly perhaps than his spiritual life, for he never knew the nameless doubts which haunt the inner life. No adverse array of circumstances could challenge or overcome his splendid confidence. In the face of apparently insurmountable vicissitudes, he remained ever resolutely determined and implicitly confident. Washington was a man of courage, but not of daring—he was willing to brave untold hardships along well-trodden paths but he had not enough of the adventurer's spirit to follow the great unknown in quest of spiritual heights. For an example of this, we have the occasion of his being told of his possible succession to the office of the chief executive of the land. After hearing the speaker through, he was obsessed by innumerable and gigantic doubts of his own ability. Nor could any one question the sincerity of his sentiments. This was the same man who had evidenced such splendid faith in himself and in his fellowmen by his perseverance in the position of the Commander of an army of undisciplined, unruly men, despite the difficulties involved. A man who is both valorous and humble has indeed a balanced character and because of this balance we find apparently antithetical qualities compatible in Washington.

In contrast to his grave decorum and austere manner, we find his gallantry and fondness for the ladies. In him was that strange union of aloof dignity and hearty comradeship. The grave manner incumbent on him because of his high honor and rank was never violated, but, in spite of it, we find him a favorite with the ladies, and have a record of two of his happy though unsuccessful courtships. This grave, dignified, almost super-man was as susceptible to human passions as any one. While stopping at the house of a friend for rest and refreshment on an official business trip, he experienced the pangs of a great love—overnight he wooed and won the Widow Custis. That a man of Washington's gravity and severity should delight in dancing seems incongruous; nevertheless, the evidence to prove that he did is trustworthy.

Washington was a man slow to think yet quick to act—he relied on the virile mind of Alexander Hamilton to prompt him to act sagely and with keenness of discrimination on many occasions. However, having weighed a question and confirmed his judgment, he chafed at delayed action, knowing the futility of indecision and hesitancy. His judgment was unerringly accurate. Consider the Constitution of the United States which was created under the guidance of the Father of Our Country—does it not bear witness to his sagacity and foresight?

Devotion to duty inspires respect for others, obedience to law, forgetfulness of self. Devotion to duty was the keynote to Washington's life, moral and spiritual; it is a sublime tribute to the man to say that he was uncompromisingly faithful to his ideals. It is an indication of his moral integrity and dauntless valor of soul. Yet this righteous Washington was not without a saving sense of humor. For proof of this we have the story of the joke he played at an official ball. It seems that while he was the President he captured the belle of the ball one evening and danced with her, dance after dance, to the evident dismay of the young gallants who naturally could not compete with the President for the young lady's favor.

Having considered Washington from these varied aspects, we find him a man who could retain his spiritual equilibrium through difficulties; a man of moral balanace. He combined the quality of superb self-confidence with that of profound humility, the ability to suspend his judgment with the faculty of swift and decisive action; though grave in manner when decorum demanded, he knew the necessity of recreation and social good fellowship; all through life, his devotion to duty, while exacting sometimes, never suppressed his sense of humor. We find him a leader of men and a master of himself.

George Washington: Statesman and Soldier

EDWIN VAN CISE

Denver, Colorado

East High School, Denver, Colorado

George Washington was born in an aristocratic Virginia family, of English descent, mannerisms and patriotism. His love for England is shown in his eagerness to serve and in his activities in the Seven Years' War, in which he played no small part. As a colonel on Braddock's staff and as second in command, he saved the British and Virginians from annihilation at the hands of the French by a masterful retreat from the banks of the Monongahela. From this point on, he was the foremost soldier in Virginia, supervising and commanding her militia and outposts on the frontier.

In the Virginia House of Burgesses, some time later, he was very conservative and made very few speeches. Gradually, however, his love for England waned because of its attitude in the colonies. His sense of justice drew him away until he became much interested in the tendencies of the time, although he did not advocate independence except as a last resort.

In 1774, his patience gave out, and he rose in the Virginia provincial convention and said, "I will raise one thousand men, subsist them at my own expense, and march myself at their head for the relief of Boston."

He was elected by Virginia to represent her in the first Continental Congress. His activities here were disappointing, for he took very little part and said nothing. However, his presence was a steadying influence on some of the fiery young men gathered to consider America's troubles.

Although not a member of the Second Congress, he was much interested in its doings. When the Colonies came to blows with the mother country, Washington, because of his known ability and because political expediency called for a Virginian, was appointed Commander-in-Chief of the Continental armies.

The General skillfully drove the British out of Boston, but then the Americans, retreating through New York and on through New Jersey, were defeated time after time. However, like a wild cat at bay, Washington turned suddenly, pounced on the Hessians at Trenton, and worked back to New York.

Following a disastrous year—disheartening defeats in Pennsylvania—Washington retired to Valley Forge. This winter was the hardest one for the cause to bear, a strain and torture on the men that was terrible, and the time when Washington himself almost acknowledged defeat. When spring came, nevertheless, his little army was fit and ready for whatever was asked of it.

The turning point in the war had been reached; and, despite setbacks in the South, with the aid of France, the net was drawn around Cornwallis, forcing his surrender. The General's work as a soldier was over, but his greatest services were just beginning.

After four years of quarreling, a convention was called, which was presided over by Washington. A Constitution which has been the model for the later republics of the world, was framed and later ratified by the states.

Elected as the first president of his country, he assumed the tremendous task of changing thirteen quarrelsome, bickering colonies into one prosperous, contented nation. In organizing his cabinet he procured the services of both Jefferson and Hamilton, men of widely differing ideals and views of government, but absolutely essential to the inauguration of the republic.

So the United States bank was established, a tariff was placed on imports, the United States government took over the states' debts, and the continental dollars were redeemed at face value. Due to the fact that Jefferson favored France and Hamilton England, Washington issued the proclamation on neutrality, written by John Jay and Edmond Randolph. Even now this doctrine is used as a powerful argument against international entanglements. It is acknowledged that, but for this, America would have been engaged in two ruinous wars which would have crushed the new republic. Yet the chief executive conceded nothing to either England or France and even refused to accept the minister of the tricolor, Genet.

While Washington's honesty incited some criticism, and all during his administration he was the object of severe charges and unfair statements; nevertheless, when he left the Presidency, he had the whole-hearted support and love of all his countrymen.

When Washington retired, he left, not a radical, little, troublesome group of states, but a united country, well on the way to financial independence, recognized and respected by Europe, and with a well-defined policy of non-intercourse and non-interference with the affairs of other nations.

George Washington, The Farmer at Mount Vernon

ELIZABETH ALLEN

South Jacksonville, Florida

Landon High School, Jacksonville, Florida

The very name, George Washington, always brings a picture to our minds of an erect figure on horseback, viewing a vast army. Or perhaps he is visualized on a platform delivering an address or behind a massive desk absorbed in the duties of his country as a president. Still behind these there is another picture that very few people realize existed. This picture is George Washington as a farmer, which shows an entirely different view of his character.

While Washington was still fighting in the French and English Colonial War, Lawrence, his eldest brother, died leaving him Mount Vernon with all its land and slaves. Soon after the struggle was over Washington married Mrs. Martha Custis, a very wealthy widow. It was then that he settled down to farming at Mount Vernon.

Having greatly increased his estate since his marriage, he then had about eight thousand acres of land. One half of this was timber land or uncultivated lawns, but about four thousand acres were in tillage, and managed directly by Washington himself. The cultivated lands lay in five farms, each with its appropriate set of laborers directed by an overseer.

During Washington's long absences from home the whole farm was under a general superintendent. At these times each of the overseers was required to make a weekly written report to the superintendent, containing a minute account of everything done on the farm in the course of the week. This included the condition of the stock and the number of days' work performed by each laborer. These reports were recorded in a book by the superintendent who then sent the originals in a weekly letter to General Washington. A weekly answer was returned which was usually a letter of four pages, sometimes of twice that length. He carefully prepared this from a rough draft, wrote it neatly and then had a press copy taken of it.

The rotation of crops in his numerous fields was arranged by himself for years beforehand. Before the Revolution, tobacco and wheat were the staple products of his plantations. The wheat was ground to flour on the estate and what was not wanted for home consumption was sold at Alexandria or shipped from the river. Usually the tobacco was shipped directly to Liverpool, Bristol, or London. At these times part of the returns were always received in English manufactures. In the latter part of his life, however, Washington gave up the culture of tobacco because it was exhausting to the soil and unfavorable to the health of his laborers.

The management of a large estate under such a system necessitated it being run on a somewhat commercial basis. Invoices of the articles to be exported and orders for the articles to be received in exchange had to be made out with mercantile exactness. Account books had to be kept and an extensive correspondence carried on. All this labor was performed by Washington with his own hand, and with remarkable precision and neatness.

He had inherited a plantation cultivated by slaves, and their number was largely increased by the dowry of his wife. The whole number belonging to the estate of Washington in his own right, at the time of his decease, was one hundred and twenty-four.

His correspondence with a friend shows him to have been strict and vigilant, but at the same time a kind, just, and considerate master. He was no more careful of his own interests than of the health and comfort of his dependents. As early as 1786 he had formed a resolution never, unless compelled by particular circumstances, "to possess another slave by purchase."

When at home, every afternoon Washington mounted his horse and rode out over his vast fields and personally inspected the crops, talked with his slaves, and attended to all their needs. Even the day before he was taken ill with acute laryngitis, of which he died, he rode out in a snow storm for this daily inspection. These actions show that he was always interested in whatever he undertook and that he went the limit to see that all was done right and that no improvements could be made.

George Washington: Statesman and Soldier

ETHEL MAE BEAVERS

Atlanta, Georgia

Commercial High School, Atlanta, Georgia

Winter. 1777. Bleak, snow-covered hills give scant shelter to the weary American army huddled together in the narrow gorge called Valley Forge. Here and there are small groups of ragged, barefoot soldiers gathered round tiny campfires, trying to thaw out frostbitten hands and feet. For weeks they have subsisted on unpalatable flour cakes and water. They have slept on the cold, damp ground, with only a thin, tattered blanket for cover.

In the nearby farm house, which serves as headquarters, Washington is trying valiantly to devise some plan of obtaining relief for his gaunt, worn men. At dusk, he steals away to a secluded spot on the frozen hillside to pray for guidance, for success. Washington, The Soldier!

The heart of Washington never failed, his spirit never wavered. His purpose was firm.

Few other generals have performed more campaigns that were such masterpieces of strategy. At Princeton, he built large campfires, then marched around and attacked the unsuspecting British at daybreak. At Trenton, he crossed the ice-blocked Delaware to surprise the carousing Hessians. At Brooklyn, he used masked batteries and presented a fierce row of round, black spots painted on canvas that, from the city, looked like the mouths of cannon. It is said that he also sent a note threatening to fire these cannon, on which the enemy hastily withdrew.

Washington fought on valiantly in the face of frequent defeat, State squabbles, incapable subordinates, and bickerings of the people at large. Repulse meant only fresh resolve, and hardship only more splendid rewards of triumph.

No man of sound judgment would doubt that George Washington was one of the greatest of the world's generals. A general comparable with Hannibal, with Caesar, and with Napoleon. His career gives one a sense of harmony and proportion, yet withal, one is fascinated by those elements of sublimity one feels when viewing a character so elevated above the common tide of humanity.

No other president has dominated his administration more completely than did Washington. No other president has been better fitted to steer the ship of state.

From an early age, he had to rely on himself, so he attained to that self-discipline which is indispensable to a political leader. His early experiences as a surveyor, and as a soldier fighting the Indians, gave him a true conception of democracy. His social position as an aristocratic planter put him in touch with that English past from which the new nation could not break entirely. Washington had not a single conspicuous weakness. All in all, he was a statesman well equipped to set all social and political precedents.

Dignity, steadfastness, uprightness, serenity, benignity, wisdom—these are the characteristics of Washington's statesmanship, whether applied to his stern policy of neutrality toward revolutionary France, or his cordial acceptance of the financial measures of Hamilton, or his noble efforts to reconcile his cabinet, or his prompt crushing of the Whiskey Rebellion.

Such a rare combination of noble traits constituted a genius comparable with Alfred the Great or Sophocles. His mind was great and powerful. Though not unusually quick, neither could it be termed slow. He listened to all suggestions, carefully weighed and sifted them, and selected the best.

Jefferson said of him, "His integrity was the most pure, his justice the most inflexible, I have ever known; no motives of interest or consanguinity, of friendship or hatred, being able to bias his decision. He was, indeed, in every sense of the word, a wise, a good, and a great man."

His unparalleled genius as a general made him "first in war," his dignity and steadfastness as a statesman made him "first in peace," and the inspiration of his noble character makes him "first in the hearts of his countrymen."

Washington's Influence on Our Life Today

ELIZABETH ARCHER

Honolulu, Hawaii

Sacred Hearts Academy, Kaimuki, Honolulu, Hawaii

It is doubtful if a man since the dawn of the Christian era has had any greater effect, morally, politically, and materially, upon the development of a nation and a people, than has the "Father of His Country" upon the development of the United States and the American people.

This effect is due in part to a tradition of greatness and goodness thrown about the memory of Washington by the magnitude of his services to the nation at a critical period in its history. The influence of this tradition impresses our people and urges them to greater efforts in contributing to the welfare of the country today.

One of the most lasting and beneficial influences of Washington is derived from the multitude of legends built around his life which acts as a tremendous moral incentive to the American youth of the present time. There is no more effective means of inculcating

the principles of truth and straightforwardness in the American boy than the renowned "cherry tree" incident. This is merely one of many examples reflecting the noble personality of Washington. However, this one anecdote stands as a paragon for a vast majority of the nation's juvenile population who desire to imitate him; it sets forth an ideal whose influence is splendid in spite of the sporadic and unpopular attempts of iconoclasts to tear it down, as in the recent case of Mr. Hughes' biography.

Washington's influence upon the political growth of the United States is still preponderant in many ways. We feel it more directly and unquestionably throughout the Constitution, in the framing of which he probably had the greatest part next to James Madison.

The fundamental principles embodied in this great document are still successful and effective after the test of nearly one hundred fifty years. In addition to this part in the writing of our organic law, a number of official utterances of Washington which have never been inserted in our jurisprudence, still have sufficient power to defy the efforts of even our greatest contemporary leaders and override them. His famous declaration against "entangling alliances" made in his Inaugural Address, is one such phrase; and it has had, most likely, a deciding influence in keeping the United States out of the League of Nations.

Washington realized that if the United States was to remain a living nation, it must from the first be an expanding and united republic. One of his greatest reveries was the vision of a mighty empire from the Atlantic Ocean to the Mississippi River, and thence to the Pacific. The distinguished leader was a man, however, with much forethought. He realized that adequate means of communication and transportation with the chief centers of population and trade were needed in order to unify, colonize, cultivate, and develop the new nation. As our First President, he endeavored to convince the officials of our growing democracy that especially the uninhabited interior regions depended upon efficient methods to insure their future importance. Through his early surveying, Washington acquired a splendid knowledge of the perils of frontier life and he also learned to judge land from numerous standpoints of value as farm land, land proper for grazing cattle, locations for mills, and sites for towns. His surveys are so true and so skillful that, even though he lacked implements, they bear the test of modern times and are often used for reference today.

He, thereby, laid a plan upon which the future generations could construct our great republic.

Therefore, now that over a century has elapsed, we glory to say that "The Father of Our Country" has set up a most inspiring character for all subsequent generations to follow. His personality stands permanently as a high ideal to attain, while our strong government and our sound economic system remains an immortal memorial, the fruit of his keen insight.

Small wonder is it that, in this Bicentennial Celebration, the Nation takes an elated pride in honoring the man who secured for us the Blessings of Liberty and cast an undying influence over our glorious United States and its people.

George Washington, The Farmer at Mount Vernon

BETH ILLUM

Malad City, Idaho

Malad City High School, Idaho

For fifteen happy years George and Martha Washington lived in great style on a typically Southern estate known as Mount Vernon. Though Washington had other plantations—Muddy Hole, Dogue Run, Mill Run, and the Neck Plantation, he loved this beautiful old Southern estate which he inherited from his half-brother, Lawrence.

Washington was a gentleman farmer, raising almost all of the food that appeared on his table, some food coming from neighboring plantations. Farming was Washington's hobby, and he took much delight in managing his eight thousand acres which were divided into five farms and woodlands. Most of this ground was under cultivation, tobacco being the main crop. Very early Washington realized that the rotation of crops, that of tobacco followed by Indian corn the following season, would in time ruin the fertility of the soil. With this in mind, he made many experiments, some of which were successful. As the years passed, Washington gradually changed his main crop from tobacco to wheat, though the latter was not as profitable as the former. From the records we find that in 1769 he sold 6,241 bushels of wheat. Most of this was sent to the West Indies, but enough was kept out for a generous food supply. Later, Washington operated two mills, thus always having plenty of work for his laborers. I might add that he also had a fishery and a ferry and spent many pleasant hours fishing. One experiment which he made in wheat was to find just how short to cut the stems of the wheat and at what time of the year was best to cut it. In another experiment he mixed soil, sand, marle, mould, clay, and manure in recorded mixtures in a box containing ten compartments. In each compartment he planted three grains each of wheat, oats, and barley. This experiment he began in April of 1760. He also made several experiments to prevent wheat rust and also to kill the pesky Hessian fly.

At first Washington did not have much information about agriculture, but, being a broad-minded man, he could not let ignorance interfere in any way with his activities. He progressed rapidly, and soon we find him raising corn, oats, barley, rye, buckwheat, hay, and alfalfa, which he called lucerne, all of which he used for domestic consumption. By this time, the number of his animals had increased. He also raised the common vegetables—roots and legumes. He did not raise cotton, but he did raise flax and hemp.

He was enthusiastic over breeding a new stock of horses which he could use for light work and another breed which he could use for heavy work. He discovered that oxen and mules were good steady workers and that they did not require as much care and food as horses. Whether he finally obtained his new stock of horses is not known.

He tried out many new ideas in landscape gardening. He was constantly on the lookout for precious bulbs, flowers, shrubs, and trees. He planted, experimented, and watched eagerly for results.

Early Washington realized the advantages in improving farm machinery, farming methods, and farm equipment His first experiment with machinery was in making a plow to suit his requirements. He also made a barrel drill which proved very useful. At about this time, he realized that since the War his plantations were in need of a general manager. From time to time he had engaged a relative, but on May 31, 1786, he engaged James Bloxham, who, though from England and not used to building up soil, finally learned how to farm on a large scale in America. Though he was President of the United States, Washington called on Baron de Polnitz on January 22, 1790, to see a threshing machine in operation. Not being satisfied with the English model, Washington worked upon a plan for one that would have all the best points of the English model plus points required for American operation in America. The thresher was finally built in 1797. A little later, however, a better model was placed on the market. Washington, ever ready to adopt a better thing, discarded the machine which was his own invention. In 1788, Washington built a round brick barn, the plans of which were drafted with the helpful suggestions of Arthur Young.

By 1798, the fame of George Washington as a husbandman, as an agricultural expert, and as a large-scale farmer had spread over the country. Richard Parkinson, a wealthy English farmer, came to see Washington's much-talked of plantations.

George Washington will be remembered for the following paragraph which he wrote in 1788 to Marquis de Chastellux: "For the sake of humanity it is devoutly to be wished, that the manly employment of agriculture, and the humanizing benefit of commerce, would supersede the waste of war and the rage of conquest; and the swords might be turned into ploughshares, the spears into pruninghooks, and, as the Scripture expresses it, 'the nations learn war no more.'"

Had the financial leaders of the world from 1914 to 1918 been as far-sighted as was Washington, as much interested in agriculture, our basic industry, we would have had no World War. Had our national leaders in the last two years been as self-sacrificing, and as interested in the practical affairs of life as was Washington, we would not now be suffering from economic disaster. Let us praise and emulate the citizen and "Father of Our Country," George Washington.

Washington's Balance of Character

FRANCES GALATI

Belleville, Illinois

Notre Dame Academy, Belleville, Illinois

Have there been soldiers more skilled in the technique of warfare? Statesmen more sagacious in the councils of the nations? Diplomats keener-minded in international affairs than Washington? Perhaps. But history has produced no one, in whom the aggregate of manly traits blended so perfectly and formed so complete a balance as in the Father of Our Country.

This happy harmony of attributes was the result of heredity, environment, training, and personality. Bereft at an early age of a sturdy, provident father; reared by a noble, Christian mother who governed with the finesse of a seasoned diplomat, brought to manhood in an environment of rural isolation and as a member of the Virginian aristocracy possessed of landed and human dependencies, Washington was spared the emasculating influences of doting elders, crowded cities, and effeminate courts.

Jovial humor under due restraint, a sense of power, a spontaneous assumption of leadership, and an ambition for adventure were some of the powers that Washington brought to the surveyor's task, at the age of twenty-one. His struggle with impassable forests and unfordable rivers improved his superb physique and augmented his native self-reliance. It did more. It granted him a vision of America—a vision which he sought to realize in his supreme capacity as nation-builder.

The success of his mission to the Ohio and his blunder and surrender at Fort Necessity proved his undaunted courage in refusing no necessary risks and his sane caution in attempting no unnecessary ones. Though grieved at Braddock's defeat, it later afforded him the supreme assurance that British forces were not invincible.

A rapacious soldier? No. The sound of whistling bullets which charmed him in his first battles palled, and he became the victim of "a deadly sorrow" at the tears of panic-stricken women and the gaunt fear of men beating their way back through their own lines, like frenzied animals. Yet with the vision of a future nation rising continually in his mind, he steeled himself to so admirable a control of his horror of war that he could see an undisciplined army at Valley Forge starve and freeze and all but perish, that the nation might be born. Congress' faith in him sustained his courage. Ah, the tragedy of it! Congress bickered over the little money he asked, and gave ear to petty plots made to remove him. But the war went on. Yes, it was finally won and a nation was conceived and brought to life not by force of men and arms, but by the power of one man's balance of character.

What incomparable poise marked his renunciation not only of a salary for his services in the war but of a proffered sceptre! What an admirable self-mastery in again relinquishing his congenial, carefree life among the Virginian gentry for the onerous duties of a nation-builder! And in the exercise of his executive duties, what an assemblage of talents, stifling even envy itself!

Washington's cool judgment that ripened to a rare wisdom, his unvarying fortitude, his manly restraint of powerful impulses in the midst of harassing annoyances, his serenity in defeat, his equanimity in victory, and his unfaltering trust in the loving Providence of God rank him easily as history's nonpareil. Yet in his character was integrated not only of the admirable but also of the lovable traits to which our nature is heir. However Ween's biography transfigured him, and Stuart's portraits chiseled him, Washington was intensely human. Never was a son more reverently devoted and more proudly fond of his mother; never did a husband cherish his wife more tenderly; never did a father watch more providently over his own or loved them more affectionately than Washington cherished and loved the children of Martha Custis. He who laughed at a joke until the tears coursed his cheeks, wept with tenderness at the absence of a friend, and sobbed without restraint over the grave of his loved ones. With his perfect self-confidence was blended a courteous consideration for the opinions of others. He was the soul of tenderness to the weak; the acme of intolerance to the cowardly. He was the humblest of citizens and the proudest of statesmen. Indeed, the symmetry of his life was astounding

"..., and the elements were
So mixed in him that Nature might stand up
And say to all the world, 'This was a man!' "

The Many-sidedness of George Washington

MARTHA SPILLE

Union City, Indiana

Union City High School, Indiana

George Washington was a man who seized opportunities. His education was not of the best, but he studied diligently and made a conscientious search for the knowledge he wished to acquire. Firmly grounded in the necessary principles, he rose steadily from one position to another, and left to us all the remembrance of a life of many things well done.

Washington's first desire was to become a sailor; but as his mother advised him against such a plan, he took up the study of surveying. At fourteen years of age, he made his first surveys and a little later went into the wilderness to measure land. His love of outdoor life and of adventure helped him to overcome much of the unpleasantness of his surroundings. His remarkable knowledge of mathematics, combined with concentration and perseverance, made him an outstanding surveyor for that time. As there was a great demand for skilled surveyors in this still uncharted land, Washington became county surveyor at twenty-one years of age. Even later when he had other work, his knowledge of surveying was indispensable to him; in fact, if he had never taken up a different occupation, this work would have made him successful.

It was not long until his military ability was recognized, and he was appointed district adjutant of the militia. Here he was aided by his knowledge of the country and of the Indians. He was self-confident, resourceful, and utterly fearless. As a soldier in the French and Indian War, he showed a remarkable knowledge of military affairs and sound judgment at all times.

Engrossed as Washington was in military affairs, he was no less capable as a colonial statesman. He was a member of the Virginia Council and a member of the House of Burgesses for fifteen years. When Patrick Henry was asked who the greatest man in the General Congress was, he replied, "If you speak of eloquence, Mr. Rutledge of South Carolina is by far the greatest orator; but if you speak of solid information and sound judgment, Colonel Washington is unquestionably the greatest man on the floor."

When affairs between Great Britain and America came to such a sudden dramatic climax that war was declared, George Washington entered into a period of his life for which he had long prepared. He accepted the position as Commander-in-Chief of the army, and began his work without hesitation. The soldiers were untrained and poorly equipped; the winters were long and cold. The Commander-in-Chief bore the suffering and struggled ahead. Now he retreated deftly from the enemy; now he crept forward stealthily and surprised them; always he worked with strategy and care, bearing criticism as he knew he must. Though his manner seemed stern and cold, the ragged soldiers knew that it but partially covered the sympathy and kindness he felt for them. Thus a master in the art of war—a magnificent leader of men—he led the army to such a well-planned victory at Yorktown, that he is now ranked as one of the leading generals of all time.

Even while working for his country, Washington found time to become an excellent farmer. He rotated his crops and beautified Mount Vernon with lovely gardens and trees. Moreover, when he was confronted with the problems of caring for his vast acres, he was a keen business man. He was ever a promoter of ideals, a patron of education, and a leader in philanthropy.

Washington has served his country well: a young government surveyor, a soldier fighting Indians, a colonial statesman, a Commander-in-Chief. As he himself said, he had grown old and gray in the service of his country. And now, when a leader was needed, faces of trusting, thankful people turned eagerly toward him. He was prepared for the office and highly deserving of this final honor—the Presidency. It was his duty to lay down the first principles, to establish the necessary reserve and respect for the President, to appoint the Cabinet, and to establish a social system. So well did he perform these duties, that thirty presidents have since followed his example.

Born two hundred years ago this year, a leader in war for justice, the First President in peace—a versatile man who performed many necessary and enduring services for Liberty and the Union—that was George Washington.

Washington's Influence on Our Life Today

JESSIE HINES

Menlo, Kansas

Pleasanton High School, Pleasanton, Kansas

Washington, the builder, such is the appellation of the "Father of Our Country." There could be no word better adapted to describe this famed leader.

Washington began his career of building a great nation as a surveyor and engineer. By his prowess as a soldier and military commander he cleared away the debris of restriction and ill-will. Because of his remarkable ability as a statesman he was chosen to select, organize, and direct those fitted to begin laying the foundation of the new country. With his unerring judgment, Washington chose as his co-workers four skilled workmen who at once set about hewing the rocks for a monument to sound national credit. Quietly and surely, with careful deliberation and unfailing wisdom this immortal man builded, cementing the rocks so precisely and so knowingly cementing them with patriotism and nationalism, with confidence and simplicity. Washington was very careful that the primary stones should be only those which could withstand the storms of ages and yet remain unscathed.

After eight years, during which a precedent for all other leaders was set, Washington gave over his position to his successor. Before leaving, however, he—with his far-seeing vision—instructed how best to carry on the delicate work, which was to create a new nation.

In his address to Congress, February 22, 1932, President Hoover said, "Upon these foundations of divine inspiration laid by our forefathers, and led by Washington, our nation has builded up in this century and a half a new system unique to the American people. . . . This destiny of national progress was clearly foreseen by George Washington. . . . His far-flung dreams have come true and he lives today in his works, in the names of our towns or cities and our states, and in the affectionate reverence of us who so immeasurably benefit by his wisdom."

After retiring to a well-earned life of quiet, Washington still did not cease his constructive activities. He was one of the first American agriculturists to practice systematic crop rotation. We can truthfully say that Washington's improvements in agriculture were the first steps toward our highly specialized methods of today.

As a social figure Washington was cultivated, refined, and dignified. Many of our rules of etiquette are derived from his rules for behavior. In nearly every vocation we see something which has been improved and enriched by Washington's zeal and sterling character. Of him Calvin Coolidge says, "His ways were the ways of truth. He built for eternity. His influence grows. His stature increases with the increasing years. In wisdom of action, in purity of character, he stands alone. We cannot estimate him. We can only indicate our reverence for him and thank the Divine Providence which sent him to serve and inspire his fellow men."

Not only our own nation, but also all other nations have felt the influence of Washington's guiding hand. The government, unique and steadfast, which he originated has been successfully imitated by republics the world over. "If we work upon marble, it will perish; if we work upon brass, time will efface it. If we rear temples, they will crumble to dust. But if we work on men's immortal minds, if we impress on them high principles, the just fear of God, and love for their fellow-men, we engrave on those tablets something which no time can efface, and which will brighten and brighten to all eternity." No words could be more true, more characteristic of Washington than these, spoken in tribute to him by another immortal American builder, Daniel Webster.

Our international negotiations, our governmental achievements, our political campaigns, our social relations, even our very lives are being molded daily by the influence held before us in the life of our own George Washington. "Legacy to America from these troubled years, he is,—apart, from independence itself—the noblest heritage of all," writes James Truslow Adams.

George Washington, the ever present standard of attainment, the awe-inspiring doer of great things, we revere him; we love him. Washington was a builder of men, of nations, of ideals. He is a builder; he will ever be a builder as long as man inhabits this wondrous earth.

Washington's Balance of Character

ELVIS STAHR

Hickman, Kentucky

Hickman High School, Kentucky

Present trends and present needs in our country make it eminently fitting, upon this Two Hundredth Anniversary of his Birth, that the young and old of America should be called upon to study and evaluate anew the life of that greatest American, George Washington.

In him we find one of the most perfectly balanced characters in history. His marked success in all his varied undertakings was made possible by the possession of a character fitted to carry out any task and to overcome all obstacles.

Washington's patriotism was the fire, which—tended by an all-powerful sense of duty—led him from his peaceful farm first to lead the armies of his country to victory in a long, hard war; and again to shoulder the burden of the presidency of a nation founded

upon principles till then untried. His patriotism was his supreme motivating power. He himself said, "The love of my country will be the ruling influence of my conduct."

And yet, if Washington had not been patient to the last degree, thoroughly courageous, but withal prudent; if he had not had steely determination and inspiring leadership; and had he not possessed perseverance that never gave way to despair, and resourcefulness which could wrest victory from defeat, he could not have victoriously led the few undisciplined, ill-paid, and ill-equipped militia against Britain's highly trained armies. Every school child knows that while many of the soldiers were deserting, and the country was despairing, Washington planned and executed a brilliant Trenton campaign; and that while his enemies were plotting his downfall in Congress, he was drilling his soldiers in the snow at Valley Forge. But how aptly are his perseverance and resourcefulness shown by such instances as these.

At the close of the Revolution, with unparalleled unselfishness and modesty Washington resigned his commission and retired to his farm. Unlike Alexander, Cromwell, and Napoleon, he fought not for himself, and, when supreme power could have been his almost for the asking, he, with duty done and victory won, went back home to peaceful citizenship. "His own self-mastery," says one historian, "was a living example to democracy. No more fitting ideal of manhood could have been chosen for the new republic. The absence of a mean ambition, the one desire of serving well his country and his fellow-men, the faithfulness that could not be driven from its task through jealousy or resentment—these were the traits that gave him a unique and solitary place among the world's heroes."

On his farm, Washington showed thrift, foresight, and ability. He once rejected an expensive dish of shad, saying that he would not suffer his table to set such an example of extravagance. He quit the raising of tobacco, foreseeing that it would soon exhaust the soil, and took up rotation of crops and scientific farming. His love of beauty was shown by his artistic landscape gardening, in which, being an ardent Mason, he used Masonic designs.

He maintained a hospitable home, enjoying all the social activities of that day. It may be hard to realize that Washington, a traditionally august personage, was, as has been proven by late biographers, intensely human. He liked dancing, riding, and following the hounds. He was not the prig that legend might lead us to suppose him, and his anger, once roused, was devastating. It is related that at a cabinet meeting, word having come to his ear that he was being accused of wanting to be king, he pounded the table and shouted "that *by God . . .* he had rather be on his farm than to be made *Emperor of the world.*"

Washington had a high code of manners and morals, and was a deeply religious man. An old Quaker told of finding him in prayer in a wood near Valley Forge. Washington's tact and wisdom enabled him to harmonize the sectional differences in the Constitutional Convention, and to establish the different branches of the new government, as he started the Ship of State on its hitherto uncharted course. The confidence of the people in his virtue and his power was a bulwark of strength to him, and his highest reward.

His farewell to the army showed his love and gratitude. Those who knew him found him a warm, affectionate friend; and yet he brought to the conduct of state affairs the dignity he felt to be their due.

In honoring Washington, we honor America, for in his character are epitomized those qualities which Americans admire, those ideals which Americans cherish.

After the test of two hundred years, Washington comes down to us a well-balanced, noble character. Each succeeding generation finds fresh inspiration, not only in what he did, but in what he was —a strong, wise, and patriotic leader on the one hand; on the other, a friendly, sports-loving, home-loving Virginia Farmer. Dignity did not obscure kindliness; courage was tempered with prudence and wisdom; and patriotism could never separate him from a yearning for home and loved ones.

George Washington, The Farmer at Mount Vernon

MARY BELLE HATCHER

Longstreet, Louisiana

Longstreet High School, Louisiana

That we think only of George Washington as a statesman and soldier and often times forget him as a farmer is not wholly our fault. Popular history has pictured him to us in no other way.

Nothing is clearer from Washington's own writings than that farming was his real vocation and chief joy. The greater part of his life was spent on the farm; most of his writings were devoted to scientific farming. It was from soil and not politics that he accumulated one of the largest fortunes of his day.

Washington always went when the duties of military leadership called him and after the campaign was over he laid down the burden with genuine relief hastening back to his beloved fields.

In 1788 before he became President he wrote to Arthur Young of England: "The more I am acquainted with agricultural affairs, the better I am pleased with them; insomuch that I can no where find so great satisfaction as in those innocent and useful pursuits." Even after his first campaign he expressed the same satisfaction upon his return to his farm.

At the age of eleven he received a two-hundred-eighty acre farm from his father's estate; at the age of twenty he added to it by purchasing one thousand acres more. He inherited a two-thousand-five-hundred acre estate from his half-brother. At this time he married Martha Custis, an elegant and wealthy widow and received the legal title to her estate. At the age of thirty Washington possessed thousands of acres of land to which he continued to add until late in life.

He imported a patent plow, made the invention of a barrel plow, built on English plans the largest and most convenient barn in this country. He constructed and improved a machine for gathering clover seed and another for raking up wheat, all of which were at least fifty years ahead of the times.

He gave the closest attention to seed selection; imported and tried out alfalfa, clover, rye, barley, peas, and vetch. He experimented with steeping his wheat seed in brine and alum to prevent smut and to determine the exact stage at which wheat should be cut. He even counted the various types of seed in a pound, so as to better know the amount to sow per acre.

Washington was also a skillful horticulturist. At Mount Vernon he planted the widest variety of fruits as apples, peaches, pears, cherries, quinces, and pecans. Many of these trees he grafted himself. In 1768 he made an effort to transplant specimens of every native tree and shrub noted for beauty of form, leaf, or flower.

Washington was a pioneer in the raising of livestock. He was the first to introduce the mule to America. The King of Spain heard he was interested in mules so he sent him a magnificent jack which he named "Royal Gift."

Washington, the farmer, was the first great American conservationist. His never ceasing study was the conservation of soil and for methods of all kinds to save and improve his land. He recognized the sacred obligation of every man to preserve for future generations the earth's natural resources. To the day of his death he was a pattern of progressiveness, open-minded, inquiring and eagerly seeking every means of improving his produce and his methods.

As Washington was quietly passing away what image do you imagine flitted through his mind in those last confused hours? Did he toil again through the western wilderness, sleeping under the stars, plunging into the icy waters of winter rivers? Did he rejoice again in the whistle of bullets as he did in the tumult of Braddock's disastrous fight? No. His thoughts turned to the homely plantation life, his slaves who were so often indolent and careless, his cattle which he had striven so hard to breed up to the best European standards, his crop projects, already formulated for the next three years.

Washington's last days and hours were as he wished them spent, not as a general, not as a statesman, but as a farmer.

George Washington, The Farmer at Mount Vernon

ELEANOR BOUNDS

Laurel, Maryland

Laurel High School, Maryland

George Washington, well known as a great statesman and soldier, was really a farmer at heart. He followed a military and public career merely because of a sense of public duty and from necessity at his country's call. Washington derived more satisfaction and pleasure from farming than from the applause and honors given for his distinguished service on the field of battle or in public life. Farming was the only occupation he really loved.

When George Washington was only twenty years of age, he came into possession of Mount Vernon through the death of his brother, Lawrence, which was soon followed by Lawrence's only living child. His inheritance of two thousand seven hundred acres was soon increased to eight thousand acres because of his extreme interest in agricultural pursuits. These eight thousand acres were divided into five farms with an overseer to manage each and a general superintendent over all. When the owner was absent and during his last years, the superintendent took charge; but at other times the work was planned by Washington, himself. There were also employed a number of slaves and white servants who did the work on the plantation. Among them there were weavers, carpenters, brickmakers, blacksmiths, shoemakers, and millers. Washington kept track of all his labor force, personally supervising the work by riding daily the seven-mile circuit of his estate.

This great agriculturist found that raising only tobacco, as other Virginia planters did, exhausted the soil; therefore, he went in for diversified farming. The crops included wheat, flax, hay, clover, buckwheat, rye, maize, turnips, and potatoes. He was constantly on the search for new varieties and species of plants and grains. Washington always kept in touch with English growers to secure better plants, and even his friends saved seeds for him. If they proved satisfactory and practical from his experiments, they were put into general use. He was the most progressive farmer of his day.

Besides using varieties of plants, Washington used other methods to build up the fertility of the soil. Crop rotation was regularly practiced on his estate. He experimented with manures to learn which would produce the best possible results to certain plants. Muck from the bed of the river was even used on some fields. These methods were found to be highly beneficial to the soil and were used extensively.

Washington bought the newest improved farm machinery that was offered in his day. That did not stop his efforts to improve it for one day when he found a plow unsatisfactory, he constructed another to better suit his purpose. He also invented a so-called barrel plow, which was more like a drill than a plow. Washington was very far advanced in agriculture for his day.

Stockraising also interested the "Master of Mount Vernon." He took special pride in his horses, for he spent much time fox-hunting on his estate. He kept the best strains of horses and cattle which had been introduced in Virginia. Not content with just the animals usually kept by Virginia farmers, Washington experimented with new stock. He found that mules could be used at an advantage as work animals. Very few farmers then kept sheep, but Washington gave much attention to them, improving the breed so as to produce more wool than any other stock raiser.

This great farmer's interest in agriculture is shown in his diaries. They record many details of his farming operations at Mount Vernon—chiefly—the varieties of seed planted, the different ways of fertilizing the soil, the growing condition, and the work done by his laborers. When Washington made a presidential tour of New England in 1789, he described in his diary the scenery, products and manufacturers of that section, conditions of the farms and roads, and the methods used for farming. It is strange to note that he kept no record of political events; this fact shows that his greatest interest was in agriculture.

Thus Washington, the statesman and soldier, was also a great agriculturist. If we follow his example in our methods of farming, we will be successful farmers, even though we cannot be famous statesmen or soldiers also.

George Washington: Statesman and Soldier

ELLEN GALLAGHER

St. Louis, Missouri

St. Philomena Technical School, St. Louis, Missouri

Washington! What wonderful pictures are released on memory's screen by that magical name—pictures of scenes dominated by the majestic presence, the magnetic personality of the Father of His Country! Cambridge, Boston, Trenton, Princeton, Valley Forge, Yorktown with intervening activities appear before our mental vision as the film unrolls, each scene pregnant with the far-reaching deeds of the valiant soldier, the intrepid General who was appointed by Heaven for the stupendous work of delivering his Country from the despotism of foreign rule, and of placing her among the nations of the earth.

From the day when Washington was chosen Commander-in-Chief of the Continental Army, the Revolution rested on his shoulders. Had any other man been selected history would probably have a different story to relate as the result of the Revolution. For Washington was the Man of the Hour, a great general gifted with wonderful self-control and penetrating judgment, and capable of bold, swift, decisive action, as he proved in his hard fought campaigns.

After the heroic struggle between the United States and Great Britain was ended and the British troops recalled, Frederick the Great sent a portrait of himself to General Washington bearing these remarkable words: "From the oldest General in Europe to the greatest General in the world."

Washington's conduct throughout the Revolutionary War,—his wisdom, his sagacity, his resourcefulness, his strategy, the wonderful magnetism that enabled him to hold together his army, insufficiently clothed and fed—and often mutinous—verified this striking eulogium.

Frederick had followed with keenest interest the movements of the "American Fabius" whose superior skill and brilliant strategy set at naught the much vaunted prowess of the British Army. England had sent her most experienced generals to conquer Washington, and to crush the Colonists. Howe, Burgoyne, Clinton, Cornwallis, and Carlton strove in turn to out-general him and each was compelled to acknowledge defeat and to surrender. The testimony of Frederick was not needed to prove Washington's superiority over the generalship of his contemporaries. His own marvelous achievements decided his rank as a military leader in the history of Nations.

As first Executive of the nation, to Washington fell the work of launching our Ship of State, in the accomplishment of which he proved himself a constructive statesman of the highest order. He had no precedent to guide him. It was part of his task to establish precedents for the guidance of the nation; to mold into an indestructible union thirteen jarring, antagonistic states, each legislating for its individual welfare to the exclusion of all its neighbors.

By sheer force of his indomitable will and immense capacity for hard work, Washington drew a stable government out of political chaos, and placed it among the nations, imparting to it some of his own stability of character, thus challenging the admiration of the world.

History records the well-nigh insuperable difficulties he had to surmount in making the Constitution a fit instrument for the establishment of peace and order. During the eight years that covered his administration, Washington gave force and direction to the written principles of the Constitution and proved how practical a document it is in its application to the affairs of government and of men.

When Washington by his sagacious statesmanship secured the adoption of the Constitution, he cemented the union which has made the United States a powerful nation and put all mankind in his debt forever; for the Constitution has proved the bulwark of every God-given right dear to the human heart, and of every principle that the American Revolution upheld. Not in vain is he credited with saying to the framers of the Constitution: "Let us raise a standard to which the wise and honest may repair. The event is in the hand of God."

With remarkable discernment Washington read and understood men. This quality gave him the ability of choosing among them and placing them where they could exercise their talents to the highest advantage—a power which is absolutely essential to the great soldier or statesman. His comprehensive views of men and of political affairs combined with his quick discrimination between the true and the false, all stamp him as an eminent statesman.

His Farewell Address shows his penetrating foresight of the perplexing problems that call for solution today. Indeed Washington seems to have been gifted with prophetic vision in those last hours of his official life and he voiced the counsels of an "old and affectionate friend" while still vested with the authority that rightfully claimed the respectful attention of his countrymen.

Setting aside the historical facts back of this Address, a thoughtful reader cannot miss the appeal of the great national principles which it embodies, nor can he escape the feeling that he is in the presence of a great and magnetic personality.

As time folds away the years with their fleeting events in the ponderous book of eternity, posterity gazing down the long vista, gets a true perspective. In the dim distance shadowy forms of departed greatness flit wraithlike before the cinema and vanish, while in the foreground illumined by the radiant flood-light, stands Columbia's peerless soldier and statesman—George Washington.

The Many-sidedness of George Washington

LECLERC PAGE

Butte, Montana

Washington Junior High School, Butte, Montana

Two hundred years ago, in the remote little district of Westmoreland County, Virginia, a boy was brought into the world—a fun-loving, sportsmanlike boy, skilled in athletics and seemingly, exactly like his friends. Yet in his manhood, this boy was to become the founder and guiding spirit of a Nation, and the most revered of the world's sons.

That boy was George Washington. Never has a name existed that excites a greater, a more profound show of love and homage than that of the Father of His Country. A great tenacity and determination, a love of country and devotion to duty so intense that life itself was as nothing when weighed in the balance, a wonderful mind, unprejudiced in its decisions, and a strong, firm belief in the principles of liberty, democracy, freedom, equality, and justice, led Washington on toward the marvelous goal which he attained and which he has kept, regardless of attempts to put a taint upon his name. The benevolent, almost fatherly kindness with which Washington treated his men, the perseverance with which he forged ahead to the completion of every task, no matter how small, his wonderful service to our country, and the pure, spotless characteristics to which he himself ever held true, have through the years been held aloft as the highest possible standards of American manhood and citizenship. They have won for him lasting fame, and the passionate, undying devotion of the people of one of the greatest nations of the world.

Washington during his lifetime acted as soldier, statesman, farmer, surveyor, nation-builder, and President. In all of these walks of life he excelled, proving himself to be what others thought him to be—a leader among men, a thinker of unrivalled integrity, a spirit so magnanimous that to grant his slightest wish was an honor.

It is probable that the people of the world know most about Washington's life as a soldier. His wonderful valor, bravery, and daring, and the complete forgetfulness of self have lived through the years as the highest attainments of militarism, never yet rivalled by the accomplishments of another.

But as a statesman, too, Washington was great. A quiet man, he little liked to publicly express his views; but his influence was the guide which determined the destiny of the colonies and of the Nation.

As farmer and surveyor, he was always foremost in his line, ever ready to accept new ideas, and susceptible to all suggestions that he believed were aids to progress and betterment.

Nation-builder and President! These words seem to hold a strange charm when connected with the name of Washington. Without him, the thirteen poorly united Colonies would never have become the powerful country we know today. To Washington we owe the freedom, the equality, the very existence of our land. In the words of Jefferson, "The crystallized utterances of Washington became the pillars, the foundation, upon which a nation was builded."

But even above Washington's achievements as soldier and statesman, above his services as Nation-builder and President, come his splendid qualities as a friend. "He who gained the friendship of Washington had a friend upon whom he could rely even unto death."

Unlike many great men, Washington did not care for pomp and ceremony, or for the honors showed him by the people. The dearest of his possessions were his home and family, and never was he so happy as when he could wander at leisure around the grounds of his beautiful estate, Mount Vernon. On being informed of his election to the presidency he said, "I had hoped to spend the rest of my life here with my family, away from the strife of political life; but I sacrifice all to my country."

"First in war, first in peace, first in the hearts of his countrymen," Washington remains the greatest man the world has ever known.

Washington himself belongs to the ages; but his country, the land of the free, endures in ever-increasing splendor, and the memory of Washington's pure and noble life shall never die in the hearts of his people.

Washington's Balance of Character

KATHERINE O'BRIEN

Carson City, Nevada

Carson City High School, Nevada

Never in any period of history has there been such a character as George Washington. The fame of this great man has spread to the most distant corners of the earth; yet this fame is not entirely due to his achievements, for his character remains a source of inspiration to everyone.

Even as a child, George Washington had a remarkable character. Enlightened by religious and educational teachings in a home of pleasant environment, he early in life awoke to a conscious knowledge of character and its attributes. Honor was instilled in him by his father, while from his mother he acquired that precious characteristic, strong self-reliance. Very adventurous and fiery in his youth, he laid the foundations for that courage which was later to become so strong that it could endure hardships, long continued suspense, and real agony.

Truthfulness was perhaps the most outstanding and generally stressed attribute of this great man. Even as a small boy, Washington was unusually truthful. It is the heritage of every American to know and profit by the wonderful examples he set forth. Later on, in service to his country, Washington's truth developed into that unparalleled asset, justice. Many, many times as the soldier, the Commander-in-Chief, or the President, he was forced to meet uncertain situations and never once did he fail to render justice. Washington abhorred favoritism and at all times showed his sagacity in judging people truly for their worth.

Religion played an important part in Washington's life. Numerous and difficult though his trials were, they only served to strengthen his belief and faith in the eternal God. Having learned the fundamentals of religion while he was very young, Washington in his later years became very devout. Never did Washington become a radical in his religious views. In fact he was as tolerant and broadminded in this respect as in any other. He acknowledged and respected all religions, severely condemning any refractory attitude on the part of soldiers or officers who were inclined to mock at certain religious ideas. By his own example, Washington strove to impress and inspire his soldiers and direct their minds towards moral and religious thoughts and actions. One may well understand how strongly this ethical side of George Washington had been developed by reading his "Farewell Address to the Armies of the United States." This great masterpiece, a true expression of Washington's character, embodies in it his real spirit of Christianity and brotherly love.

Washington's high sense of responsibility, as well as his energy and devotion to his country was thoroughly proved when he became the Chief Executive. Many times he voluntarily underwent fatigue, both mental and physical, just because he felt that it was his duty. No one could have been more patriotic than was Washington. His foremost desire was to become a peaceful farmer and to live in obscurity. In spite of this, however, he devoted most of his life to patriotic service. Little did he wish to remain President for a second term. Yet, because he felt that his country needed him, he again submitted to the nomination.

Aside from political duties, Washington had qualities destined to make him very popular. He was superb in his unselfishness and considered it his chief duty to make everyone about him as happy as possible. True friendship, in his estimation was a priceless asset, while he valued character above all else. By his gracious manner Washington won all hearts to him and at all times proved himself most kind and reliable.

During the whole of his life, Washington never lost zeal in his search for knowledge. He respected all ideas, and sought advice from every source. Although elaborate customs and styles were prevalent during the Revolutionary period, Washington shrank from any ostentatious display and showed quite a bit of diffidence in accepting high positions.

Washington respected and honored his mother, adored children, and was generous in every respect. He had a very strong will and had developed his self-control to the utmost of his ability. He always insisted upon strong self-discipline and was usually reserved when his deeper emotions were involved.

It was not circumstances which made Washington great. It was the manner with which he met these circumstances. Washington was not a perfect man, yet he proved himself so loyal, so zealous, and so sincere in all of his struggles and dealings with life that he shall ever remain the idol of the American people—the inspiration of the nation!

The Many-sidedness of George Washington

PHILIP HINDES

South River, New Jersey

South River High School, New Jersey

The conception of George Washington that we are given when in the grades is one that portrays a remarkably truthful perfect specimen of manhood. Somehow or other, this does not meet with our approval. We sympathize with "Honest Abe" Lincoln much more when the grade teacher tells us of his early struggles and many hardships, admiring him more and more as we learn of his later life. As we grow up, we become duly acquainted with the fact, however, that although Washington was a man truly worthy of the praise and adulation which America accords to his memory, he was not the God-like individual placed on a pedestal which ideal we were led to believe in in our younger years. In fact, some of us are surprised and even secretly pleased to find that George Washington was only a human after all.

As the title of this theme suggests, there were many sides to our First President. It is extremely gratifying to us to know that George had his failings as all of us and that he had his bad points as well as his good ones. Let it be understood, however, that his good qualities outweighed the bad qualities by such an exceedingly large margin that there can be no possible doubt as to his greatness. No one is perfect. George Washington wasn't either. It seems that some of the present-day biographers grasp the opportunity for notoriety by giving us bigoted, nonsensical, startling unproportionate pictures of this great hero's life. They can be dismissed with this thought in mind. When Calvin Coolidge was asked by reporters of what he thought of such books, he looked out of his office window at the monument to Washington, brilliant in the sunlight, 555 feet high, and said after a moment's thought, "Do you see that obelisk over there? Well, it's still standing." Now let us get on to some of these different sides of Washington. Most of the ones set down here are the good ones chiefly because, despite the present-day commentators, those compromise the make-up of Washington's manyfold activities and consequently, his character.

George Washington was a statesman, president, soldier, and leader. He was a surveyor, courtier, and dispenser of justice. He was a father, host, and friend. George was a farmer, huntsman, slaveholder, sportsman, and athlete. He danced very well, dressed carefully, and was a great practical joker at the expense of others. He was a lover of display which, as one might expect, plunged him more than once into debt. Reading each one of these carefully and meditating slowly over them, we come to realize more fully the wide scope of this national hero. Truly it took a man of great ability to fulfill each one of these as successfully as George Washington did.

As a statesman and president, we come to appreciate more and more as the years go by, the wise sagacity and remarkable foresight possessed by the First President of the United States. With a firm and everguiding hand did he rule this country for a goodly number of years until he chose to retire from public life and even at the end of his career, he handed to us his immortal Farewell Address whose content was and still is increasingly ingenuous in its advice. Those words of entangling alliances, international relations, etc., will live on forever in our country's history.

What greater soldier and leader have we had than Washington? We owe more than we can say to his ever-abounding perseverance and courage in the face of defeat. Recall to your mind that winter in Valley Forge and the surprise attack at Trenton at a time when almost certain downfall seemed inevitable. If those two examples are insufficient, remember the Battle of Brandywine, where, although he was defeated, Washington showed his true mettle. Again think of the ragged handful of followers he had which, largely due to his genius, defeated England's trained troops.

When a young man, he served as a surveyor, leading a rugged life, braving many dangers in Indian territory. As a courtier, father, host, and friend, George Washington showed the other side of himself: gentle, true, sympathetic, loving, and courteous, he is placed in the highest class of colonial gentlemen.

Farming took up a good deal of George's time in his later life while at all times he was fond of hunting and athletics, being a very capable athlete himself if we are to believe only one-half of the feats credited him. Even his enemies always credited him as being a thorough sportsman. When such happens, there certainly *is* ground for praise and glorification. The word "sportsman" takes in a good many fine attributes that some of us would like to be able to achieve.

No rich man of those times went without his slaves and Washington, as an acute business man, was an extensive slaveholder and made good profits thereof. It is hard for us to consider such as an asset, but had we lived in those days, we would have severely criticized him if he had not actively engaged in that business. Fair in all his dealings, he achieved a reputation for being a true dispenser of justice. Lack of space prevents a lucid explanation of the latter fact.

With all these activities, he found time to keep a diary, dance very well, play host to his many friends, and elaborate great schemes of display. What a wide range indeed did this man have within his span of life. There have hardly been any in the world's history who have successfully coped with so many deeply widespread participations. Therefore do we pay him due credit.

In our closing sentence, we can sum up all the foregoing with this statement: Truly may we call George Washington "The Father of Our Country."

George Washington: Statesman and Soldier

SAM MONTOYA

Pena Blanca, New Mexico

Pena Blanca High School, New Mexico

"An able commander, he wrested liberty from tyranny. A statesman, he helped evolve a stable government from political chaos. Wisdom, patience, tolerance, courage, consecration to the righteous cause, animated his every act. Ambition and opportunity never tempted him from the narrow path of honor."

George Washington, the man whom the above words praise so highly, early prepared himself for his future famous career; for while yet a boy, he was adjutant-general with the rank of major in the Virginia militia. His strong character was shown to still greater advantage, when later he was chosen to carry an important message to the French, and in spite of the great hardships and accidents encountered, successfully performed his task.

Shortly after his return from this journey, Washington was appointed lieutenant-colonel of the only regiment which Virginia controlled. With half of this regiment Washington routed a small band of the enemy on the Ohio. On the death of the colonel, being placed in command, he united the regiment and at Great Meadows ordered the construction of a fort named Fort Necessity. Here he was outnumbered by the French, and, because of the lack of ammunition, surrendered; but through skillful work was allowed to retire with his arms.

This genius for turning defeat into victory was shown also in the campaign of 1754. During the attack in the Pennsylvania Forests Braddock fell with about a thousand soldiers, and it was only the gallant conduct of young Colonel Washington, whose horse was shot under him twice, and whose uniform was pierced with bullets, that saved the retreat from utter rout and panic.

In 1774 Washington was chosen as a delegate to the First Continental Congress. Many great men were there—the Adamses,

Franklin, Jefferson, and others—but Patrick Henry said: "If you speak of solid information and sound judgment, Colonel Washington is unquestionably the greatest man on the floor." When offered the position as Commander-in-Chief of the Continental Forces, Washington replied that he could not perform such a great task. However, he finally consented, although he refused to accept pay for his services.

Even against such great difficulties as desertion of men, lack of supplies, and jealous rivalry, Washington showed himself an excellent leader. Besides carrying on the war, he had to persuade Congress and the thirteen colonies to furnish men and supplies.

Washington's fame as a soldier does not rest on the battles he fought but on his brilliant tactics, his patience, and perseverance; for instance, his retreat across New Jersey, the attack on the enemy at Trenton and Princeton, his vigorous resistance against the British entrance into Philadelphia, and the terrible winter spent at Valley Forge; where in spite of great hardships, failure to get supplies, and the discouragement of the people, he still kept his position. Even Cornwallis complimented Washington upon his "unsurpassed performances" during the war.

Had Washington died after this great event, his title as the Father of His Country would have been secure. But his great services during peace made him a recipient of greater honors.

When the movement for "forming a more perfect union" began, Washington responded and once more gave his services for the benefit of his country. None but the far-seeing wisdom of Washington could detect the dangers which beset the newly-formed nation. Through his influence the convention met in Philadelphia in 1787 to revise the Articles of Confederation. During the session his hand guided the work of that notable meeting. Afterwards Washington continued to work for the ratification of the Constitution by the states, and only through his untiring efforts was the consent of the people obtained.

As the Constitution provided for a president, Washington was unanimously elected; and, to the task of setting the new government into operation, was added the organization of the various departments advocated by the Constitution. He made successful appointments throughout his administration. He exerted his enduring influence in establishing a mildly protective tariff, in establishing the First National Bank, and in stopping the Whiskey Rebellion.

Before his retirement he issued his famous Farewell Address; giving advice which, if kept, would avert from us all serious trouble, namely, in one word to be a nation, to be Americans, and to be true to ourselves. A greater soldier and a better statesman cannot be found; therefore Washington is and continues to be "First in War, First in Peace, and First in the Hearts of His Countrymen."

The Many-sidedness of George Washington

KATHLEEN O'HARE

Cleveland, Ohio

Convent School, Syracuse, New York

"To be ranked with the noblest of any age"

Other nations have at different times produced heroes, warriors, and men of noble character, but at the time of the American Revolution, America realized a ruler of supreme power—one whose fame has left an indelible mark on the memory of every citizen of the United States. To survey the sixty-seven years of Washington's life, it seems as if no other American has had a career filled with so many events. We can picture him at duty in the cities and in the wilderness, in battles and at councils, his intercourse with a diversified crowd of foreign noblemen, native neighbors, squabbling statesmen, starving soldiers, Indian chiefs, and negro slaves—each party he treated with an equal interest, always acting on principle,

completely abnegating every self-advantage for the good of the American people, refusing to receive anything in return beyond the respect and gratitude of his fellow citizens. Truly he loved his fellowmen!

The majority of people, when thinking of Washington, imagine him a stern, rigid, solemn, and rather retired gentleman, but the true American is thrilled to believe that this far off figure, this man of patriotic splendor, this self-sacrificing devoted president was a convivial man, with a hearty laugh, a deep sense of humor, and an all-embracing sympathy for all living things; to make him seem more realistic he was also a man with a white hot temper.

Washington's strongest and most prominent characteristics were stability, determination, kindness, and cheerfulness. When he was left to support his mother and the younger members of his family he had to sacrifice many pleasures that other boys of his age enjoyed because he knew he must fit himself for his responsibilities, therefore many hours were devoted to intense indoor study. This necessitated isolation from his youthful companions. It was while he denied himself the "finishing" of college at home or abroad that he received the "finishing" from an unexpected source. He came under the influence of a civilization more finely civilized than England, more courteous and more restrained than the Eighteenth Century England knew.

Washington's school copy book dated 1745 reveals one hundred and ten rules of civility. With these rules for a standard the lad chiseled out of his impetuous nature the man to whom the world bows in admiration.

These rules played the most important part in his life, and affected everyone with whom he came in contact. M. D. Conway says, regarding the influence of these rules upon Washington's character: "In the hand of that man of strong brain and powerful passions once lay the destiny of the New World—in a sense, human destiny. But for his possession of the humility and self-discipline underlying his Rules of Civility, the ambitious politicians of the United States might today be popularly held to a much lower standard."

It does seem rather a misfortune that the American girl and boy of today should be told the untrue story of the hatchet and cherry tree when so much benefit could be derived from George Washington's original copy book.

The year of 1759 finds Colonel Washington married. One might say that this was his first chance to enjoy leisure since the days in which he pored over his copy book. The six short tranquil years at home, before being called back to public duty were such a contrast to the troublesome ones ahead of him. This peaceful time permitted a deep growth in character. During these few years of solitude he was able to follow his inclinations, his private tastes, and to enjoy his domestic life. Washington always preferred the quiet way of acting and of living; therefore, he moved constantly in simplicity and humility, that balanced and wholesome ease of spirit, which when it appears among those who must be showing off "shines like a quiet star upon fireworks."

At sixty-seven, just as at twenty-seven, he was still shrinking from all praise, in spite of honors won. This humility, simplicity, nobility, and kindness of spirit, are characteristics that strike a flashing spark of life and allow us to see along the dim, dark distance, the true heart of our noble Washington.

George Washington's Sense of Duty

FRANK McKEE

Gastonia, North Carolina

Gastonia High School, North Carolina

Did George Washington measure up to the requirements of a good citizen with a keen sense of duty? In reading over the lines below let us see whether Washington had a sense of duty. Let us see whether he really deserves the honors which have been heaped upon his name. A good citizen has three main obligations: his duty to his country, his duty to himself, and his duty to his God. Let us see whether Washington met these obligations of good citizenship.

Washington was fully conscious of his duty to his country. This was proved by his actions in the French and Indian War and in the Revolutionary War. Among the names of all the heroes who answered this country's call, George Washington is the name which stands foremost. His name has been famous for one hundred and fifty years and will be remembered for centuries to come. We all know the story of Washington as a soldier through the stories of his heroic behavior at Valley Forge, at Yorktown, and at many other battlefields.

After the British had departed, Washington wished to return to a quiet life at Mount Vernon; but when called to sit at the framing of the Declaration of Independence, he again left his estate and wife because of his sense of duty toward his country.

During the years of his Presidency George Washington strove faithfully to build up this great republic. The idea that everyone liked Washington and the things he did is absurd. He received many criticisms; many people worked against him, and he was very glad to return to his home at Mount Vernon after eight years of faithful service. When offered another four years of presidency, he showed a true spirit of democracy by refusing.

George Washington did not consider his duty to his country fulfilled until he had done his duty by his fellow-men. During the fateful winter at Valley Forge Washington did all that a human could do to comfort and help his men. When the men were sick, weary, bare-footed, and in rags, he suffered with them. The men loved him, and would follow him anywhere. Washington was a leader. His spirit alone won many battles for America. Washington always obeyed the Golden Rule faithfully, always realizing his duty to his fellow-men. Self-composure was another one of the traits which endeared him to his fellow-men.

Washington also realized his duty to himself. Washington was not a born leader; no man is. "Success can only come from hard work" must have been the motto which Washington used as a guide through life. As a boy of seventeen he was struggling through the wild country of southern Virginia to lay a surveying line which still remains. A little while later he was an officer in the British expeditions to Ohio. Washington formed a set of rules for proper conduct when only thirteen years old. These things prepared him for the struggle for independence and for the years as president.

Washington faithfully observed his duty to God. When only a lad, he formed a prayer for strength, for purity, and for forgiveness of sins. In the darkest moments of American history this prayer was on his lips.

Through all this only one thing is seen: that we do not have to strive to be perfect, but only to be more like George Washington, the model citizen. Love, honor, courage, and response to the call of duty helped to make George Washington the man he was. No one can deny that it was Washington's sense of duty to his country and his fellow-men, to himself, and to his God, which made him "First in war, first in peace, and first in the hearts of his countrymen."

The Many-sidedness of George Washington

EDNA MAE SKAAR

Berg, North Dakota

Williams High School, Croff, North Dakota

Grand and many-sided as were the phases of Washington's character, we have no difficulty in understanding them. He was no veiled prophet. Simple, natural, and unaffected, his life lies before us, a fair and open manuscript which all may read.

He represented in public life the marvelous combination of the soldier, the patriot, and the statesman. In the character of each he stands supreme. Behold him in 1775 taking leave of his family and hastening to the relief of his country. Watch him as he transforms a band of rustics into an army. Follow him to the battlefield and see him first into danger and last out of it. Go with him to the Constitutional Convention and listen as he joins the battle that clears the way for our Constitution. Stand by his side as he guides the ship of our infant republic through the first stormy years of its long voyage. Enter his home during the last peaceful days of his life at Mount Vernon. Then, and only then, can we see and understand to the utmost the many-sidedness of his character.

Knowledge of his family relationship during his youth and manhood is also necessary to an understanding of his character. Loving, dutiful, and thoughtful, he gave his parents obedience as a boy. As a young man he gave his mother's wishes respectful attention, and at the pinnacle of fame he paid tribute to the hand that led him to manhood. To his wife he gave forty years of tender care and devotion.

"He was of extraordinary nobility, purity of purpose, and great practical wisdom. Many individuals may have surpassed him in extent of wisdom, depth of knowledge, or brilliancy of character." Patriots of equal purity may have devoted their lives to the service of their country and some may have exhibited a moral example as pure and unblemished. Chieftains superior to him may have led armies to victory as loyally and as courageously, but in no one known to fame have we found all these elements blended as abundantly and as harmoniously as in Washington.

Courage, physical and moral, was a part of his nature. At all times and under all conditions he rang true to the note of splendid manhood. Faith, also, was an outstanding trait of his character. To know the depth and intensity of the divine fire that burned in his breast we must go back to the dark and icy days at Valley Forge. When desertions were many and when his men went hungry and left bloody footprints on the snow, he was not perturbed out of measure for he felt that he was in direct relation with an Authority that was higher than the Continental Congress.

A moral quality, his humility, secured for him a long unbroken opportunity for advancement in the activities of leadership. He never appeared as a man aiming at prominence or power, but rather as one under an obligation to serve a cause. The people trusted him implicitly in war and peace "as one who would never forget his duty or his integrity in the sight of his own greatness."

His enemies as well as his friends bore evidence of his honesty. In the words of Jefferson, "His integrity was the most pure I have ever known. No motive of interest or friendship or hatred was able to bias his decisions."

In viewing the many-sidedness of his character, Henry Cabot Lodge said: "I find in him [Washington] a marvellous judgment which was never at fault, a penetrating vision which beheld the future of America when it was dim to other eyes, . . . a will of iron, an unyielding grasp of facts, . . . I see in him too a pure and high-minded gentleman of dauntless courage and stainless honor, simple and stately of manner, kind and generous of heart."

The records of human greatness contain no other character so elevated and spotless as a monument of moral supremacy, individual greatness, and unsullied worth. Its blended rays of virtue, wisdom, and modesty rival the soft glow and mingled beauties of the rainbow.

The many-sidedness of Washington's character—his uncompromising truth, his self-control, his devout reliance on God, his priceless gift of leadership, his purity, his intense loyalty to his country and his ideals, his humanity, generosity and justice blending harmoniously with his sound judgment, and valor equalled only by his modesty, made up a character which the world fearlessly challenges for a parallel.

Washington's Influence on Our Life Today

IRENE E. SOEHREN

Dallas, Oregon

St. Helen's Hall, Portland, Oregon

Great nations are always proud. America, with her untold wealth and resources is a great nation. She has a right to hold her head high among the nations of the world. But she must be proud only of the right things. Vast resources and wealth can never replace great men. History shows that a nation must inculcate its principles into the lives of its leaders. If it fails to do this, it will die for lack of ideals and worthy aspirations.

Yet we often excuse our failure to emulate the greatness of our leaders by saying that their paths were lighted by the fire of genius, that they were endowed with a super-human knowledge and wisdom, that they were thus enabled to reach heights of perfection we can never hope to attain. Thus we endow them with the characters of gods rather than of men, and convinced of the futility of our attempts to reach the shining goal they have set, we scorn those faculties we possess as unworthy and content ourselves with obscurity instead of fame. The nation forgets that those principles for which her ancestors fought are the underlying principles of our republic today, and that the characters and the policies of her early leaders are as vital now as they were two centuries ago.

Today the name of Washington has become synonymous with the highest American ideals. It is a name that stands for patience and modesty, truth and honor, courage and patriotism. It is the name of a man who sacrificed personal desire that these United States might be forever free. We who have inherited this freedom have also inherited the principles of George Washington.

Life is the great teacher. If we can discover nobility in the lives of others, it will teach us to make our own noble. Our understanding of how great men have faced danger and struggled will help us to conquer in our own struggles.

From his distinguished ancestors, Washington inherited a high code of honor, a life of truth, and a deep sense of justice and duty. From them, also, came an inherent faith in God—an unshakable belief in a merciful and all-divining Providence. To his mother he owed his simple dignity, steadfast courage, and ability to command.

Washington received only a rudimentary, colonial education. Loving knowledge, he learned by observation and experience. The training which prepared him for his great calling was purely American. Thus George Washington was the Son before he was the Father of His Country. He loved the superior culture of the Old World. He admired its refined aristocracy—its ancient code of chivalrous courtesy and unstained honor. Yet when the crucial test came, it was not these shadowy, romantic traditions of a forgotten past that he acknowledged, but a new ideal—a new creed for a New World.

Washington's standards as a gentleman were irreproachable. These standards were not merely refinement, nobility, and education, but also kindness, hospitality, and generosity. Guiding him always was conscience, bidding him be fair, just, and helpful. To-day, when the laws of courtesy seem forgotten, we may well remember Washington, who so perfectly embodied these principles. Modern youth has declared a second War of Independence—a rebellion against restraint and formality. There is a tendency to throw convention to the winds and seize upon the sensational and novel. Our daughters often forsake the ideal of feminine grace and charm, and our sons disdain the gallantry of other days. We admire culture abroad; we ignore it at home. But the example of George Washington, gentleman, keeps always before us a worthy ideal.

Intelligence is required to recognize intelligence, and it takes a great mind to see the workings of God. Washington, in his triumphs and failures, acknowledged an Intelligence greater than his own. His belief in a Supreme Being was deep and constant. Early in life he was taught by his mother to "Remember thy Creator in the days of thy youth." He was taught forbearance, self-denial, and modesty—stern lessons which we of a carefree age too willingly forget. But these lessons made a lasting imprint upon Washington and have today become the heritage of American youth.

Washington, the statesman, combined personal integrity and moral principle with intense loyalty. With singleness of mind and heart, he served his country, and with a foresight and vision we cannot readily understand, counseled her to preserve peace at home and abroad. Undoubtedly, he foresaw the entanglements that would result from foreign alliances. At any rate, his influence upon our national policies has been tremendous, and, in times of stress like the present, his counsels are our surest guide.

Two centuries have passed since the birth of Washington, but two centuries have not sufficed to dim the glory or obscure the splendor of that immortal name. As long as America stands, a monument to liberty and democracy, that name shall also stand. As long as Americans exist upon the face of the earth, that name shall be revered and honored. As long as freedom and justice prevail, it shall be remembered. And so, with Lincoln, ". . . In solemn awe we pronounce the name [of Washington], and in its naked deathless splendor leave it shining on."

The Many-sidedness of George Washington

ELINOR RITTENBERG

Charleston, South Carolina

Ashley Hall, Charleston, South Carolina

An impressive fact about the leaders of the American Revolutionary period is the diversity of their greatness. George Washington was no exception. He excelled not in one field but in several. As family man, farmer, soldier, citizen, President, leader in religious affairs, patron of education, philanthropist, business man, master of Mount Vernon—in each of these roles he displayed characteristic energy and success.

A beautiful study of Washington is found in his relationship to people about him. From boyhood to Presidency he gave his mother obedience and filial respect; he often expressed his obligation to her for his career. To his wife he gave forty years of love and tender care; to her children and grandchildren a lifelong devotion and concern which could not have been greater had they been of his own flesh and blood.

With the ambition to become America's first farmer, he became the foremost planter of his day. He introduced crop rotation, new methods of planting, and modern machinery on his farms. As soldier and statesman he did his duty; as farmer he achieved his heart's desire.

The basis for Washington's prominence in history is his military career. His experiences in surveying and in journeying to the Ohio, in frontier campaigns and under Braddock and Forbes, prepared him for his prominent and responsible place in the Revolution. As Commander-in-Chief of the American forces he was superb. From Cambridge to Yorktown he suffered with his men. In many a crisis only his unquestioned leadership and superior judgment averted disaster.

After the war he aided in framing the Constitution and stabilizing the future of the nation whose independence he had assured. As burgess, Freemason, vestryman, justice, trustee, state representative, he served faithfully and well, a conscientious and public-spirited citizen. When in dire need of a leader for their newly-established republic, his fellow citizens paid him their highest tribute—they unanimously elected him their first President. His administration was wise and impartial, with one underlying theme—the good of the entire nation, not only then but in years to come.

As a good Christian Washington possessed deep reverence for God and respect for his religious matters. Through his diaries and letters, models of good style and poor spelling, his abiding faith in God is revealed. Knowing the need of his men for religious support he provided in his orders for services, appealed for chaplains for the army, and attended church himself whenever possible.

Throughout his life Washington was a patron of education. He established the first free school in Alexandria, Virginia, and left in his will funds for an American university. Although his own education had been a painfully haphazard affair, by his extraordinary powers for intellectual self-development he became one of the best-educated men in the Colonies.

Educating many children out of his own pocket was only one of Washington's philanthropies. The extent of his charities is unknown, as they were not a matter of record, but it is certain that, always responsive to the genuine need of friend or stranger, he constantly helped others to help themselves by most practical means.

Washington has so often been presented to the world as soldier and statesman that his business genius has been underemphasized. In spite of the fact that he devoted one-third of his life to exacting public service, he left at his death one of the largest estates then existent, and a record which places him among the foremost American pioneers of finance. Far-sighted beyond his contemporaries he furthered enterprises which developed transportation and industry, commerce, and colonization.

Upon his retirement to private life General Washington assumed the duties of the master of Mount Vernon. The hospitality and high living of his house were renowned, but he was the magnet which drew the throngs to its doors. He now held unquestioned supremacy in the hearts of his people and, after a life of service to them, was left to enjoy his remaining years in peace and happiness, a model American citizen.

George Washington: Statesman and Soldier

RALPH GLENN

Sioux Falls, South Dakota

Washington High School, Sioux Falls, South Dakota

The question whether Washington was the greater as a statesman or as a soldier is still an open one. Surely he was truly a great man in both capacities. Although he was a member of both Continental Congresses, his work as a statesman actually began later. When the disorders due to the weakness of the Articles of Confederation made a new government necessary, everyone looked to Washington because he favored a strong centralized union. "Washington's personality, his kindness, his tact, his spirit of toleration, his genuine patriotism, his deep belief in a permanent union of states made him an outstanding figure at the great Constitutional Convention of 1787 and the logical head of our new government." It was thought that, since Franklin was the other candidate for president of the United States, it would be a great honor bestowed on Washington to have Franklin nominate him. It had been planned to carry this idea out, but Franklin was taken sick just before the convention; consequently, Franklin requested Robert Morris to nominate Washington. This was done and Washington was unanimously elected president, showing his popularity in all the states.

While Washington was undoubtedly elected president on the strength of popularity won in prosecution of the Revolutionary War, he was now to show himself a kindly and wise counselor in peace. Many of the policies which he formulated are still in use at the present time. Washington emphasized the necessity of union, the dangers of sectionalism and factional or party conflicts, the importance of prompt obedience to all laws, and the imperative necessity of the maintenance of public credit. Though France had helped us in the Revolutionary War, he opposed entering an alliance with that country and warned the people against all permanent or entangling alliances. These policies were not popular with the people. He was criticized and abused by many. Later events, however, demonstrated his far-seeing wisdom and the accuracy of his analysis of conditions. Washington founded his decisions upon wisdom, not upon emotions or the impulse of the moment.

Washington's military career is one of the most brilliant in history. It actually began when he was made aide-de-camp to Braddock on the fatal expedition against Fort Duquesne. It was here that he showed those brilliant fighting qualities which afterward made him so famous. When Braddock fell wounded, Washington was left in command. He ranged the whole field on horseback, a target for every Indian bullet, as he tried to rally the frightened troops. Two horses were shot from under him and four bullets pierced his coat. Yet he fought on. Gallantly he tried to save the rest of the British army from annihilation. When he saw that the battle was lost, he brought his Virginia rangers off in fair order.

Because of deeds like this, the Second Continental Congress unanimously elected him Commander-in-Chief of the Colonial Army of the Revolutionary War. On July 3, 1775, under the famous elm of Cambridge, he drew his sword and officially took command. Washington's task was a difficult one. He had practically no army, equipment, or supplies. He couldn't raise money. A weaker man than he would have failed. Washington, however, kept his faith in Divine Providence, and, by his strength of character and power over men, he held his army together through almost incredible hardships and privations. Thus, through Washington's inspiration and Von Steuben's drilling, the army emerged stronger in spirit and discipline than ever. "Bravery, patriotism, common sense, the ability to make use of every bit of information that came his way—these were the qualities that distinguished him." He was a fighter, a soldier every inch of him. He not only had no fear himself, but he couldn't understand fear in others. Nothing aroused his anger so much as to see his troops scatter and flee. More than once, seeing his troops break wildly before the enemy, he would shout at them with cries of rage and beat them back into line with his sword. Sometimes his men fought through fear of his wrath, but more often because of their affectionate admiration for him. "This ability to lead men against overwhelming odds, to their death if need be, this fighting zest and indomitable bravery gave Washington success as a commander." He would not admit defeat, and he had a method of turning disaster into profit. No one knew better than he the value of strategy, and no one was more skilled at deceiving the enemy. It was this rare military genius that brought the war to a successful close.

After the war, when he was bidding farewell to his officers, Washington, who usually was so dignified and reserved, was overcome with emotion. His voice broke and he could hardly speak. His farewell address was simple, but beautiful: "With a heart full of love and gratitude, I now take leave of you. I most devoutly wish that your latter days may be as prosperous and happy as your former ones have been glorious and honorable." Then he requested all to come and shake his hand. Silently they obeyed. How they loved their great Commander!

Thus to the end of time Washington will be honored both as a soldier and as a statesman. To the end of time also will Americans unite in that beautiful eulogy spoken at his funeral: "First in war, first in peace, and first in the hearts of his countrymen."

George Washington's Sense of Duty

DAVID CHEATHAM

Pulaski, Tennessee

Central High School, Pulaski, Tennessee

The history of every nation begins with her heroes; the Hebrews had their Moses, Rome had her Augustus Caesar, France had her

Philip II, England had her Alfred the Great, and America had her Washington.

Lincoln said, "Washington is the mightiest name of earth. . . . On that name no eulogy is expected. It can not be. To add brightness to the sun, or glory to the name of Washington is alike impossible. Let none attempt it. In solemn awe we pronounce the name, and in its naked deathless splendor leave it shining on."

When Washington's country asked him to command the poorly-equipped and raw American recruits against the well-equipped and well-trained troops of England, Washington did not ask, "What will be my recompense? What will be the opportunities for immortal glory?" but gave the simple and sincere answer, "I do not think myself equal to the command I am honored with." and assured Congress that he did not expect pay for his services. Was not this a fatherly love for his country?

As a true father protects his off-spring from their enemies, so Washington unsheathed his sword and drove from American soil despotism, the enemy of American liberty.

Now the Colonies had independence, the Colonies had liberty. What would thirteen conflicting, jealous, envious, and suspicious commonwealths become? What would come forth from this state of chaos? Again the country called her father, Washington. Again he responded. Washington was unanimously elected chairman of the Constitutional Convention: when he is credited with having said, "Let us raise a standard to which the wise and honest can repair, the event is in the hands of God." And out of that convention came, "We, the people of the United States, in order to form a more perfect union, establish justice, insure domestic tranquility, provide for the common defense, promote the general welfare, and secure the blessings of liberty to ourselves and our posterity, do ordain and establish this Constitution for the United States of America."

Now the Colonies were to become a coalition, a federal union, a oneness of states. Who was to be the executive? Who was to furnish the parental guidance for the infant nation? Who was to be the embodiment of the spirit of that nation? Again the immortal character of Washington illumines the horizon. And with the unanimous election of Washington as First President of the United States, there dawned a new day of liberty, of equality, and of Constitutional Government.

Now came eight of the most perfect years of public service in the annals of our country. Washington had no predecessor; he had no precedent to guide him, but he established a precedent that has lasted until our day. Washington's appointments were based on capacities for service and were given with contempt for favoritism. He established our national credit both abroad and at home. His foreign policy was to avoid entangling "our peace and prosperity in the toils of European ambition." His domestic policy was the Constitution.

At the end of his second term Washington was the most popular man in America. He could have received from the hands of the American people a kingly crown but instead he gave them his Farewell Address.

Washington's trial in the army, his contacts with other nations, the intermingling of his mind with his contemporaries gave him an unparalleled knowledge of the problems of American Democracy, and his native ability gave him the solution which he crystallized in this Farewell Address. Between the lines we see his unselfishness, his justice, his vision, his wisdom, his loyalty, his faith, and his Christian character. If for no other reason we would remember him for his fatherly advice in this message.

John Milton said of Oliver Cromwell, "War made him great, peace greater." So it was with Washington.

Standing alone in his preeminence, fixed forever in the hearts of his fellow countrymen, the great southern gentleman then returned to Mount Vernon but remained the oracle of the American people.

Caesar, the conqueror of men, died by the hands of men uttering, "Thou too, Brutus!" Napoleon, the conqueror of nations, died the prisoner of the English nation babbling of battle fields and carnage. But these conquerors had selfish ambitions while our unselfish

Washington, the conqueror of despotism and the father of American liberty, died calmly uttering the sublime words, " 'Tis well."

So passed the life of our immortal Washington, but as long as the hearts of mankind shall love liberty, so long will the spirit of Washington prevail.

George Washington: Statesman and Soldier

EDNA DATO

Houston, Texas

Sam Houston Senior High School, Houston, Texas

As Father Time slowly throws his scythe over his shoulder and totters disdainfully down life's highway, it is with renewed interest that we commemorate this year to the most idolized figure in American History,—the soldier, the statesman, George Washington.

Only when one learns the personal traits of that most human personage, does one appreciate him. His nature was well balanced, and his disposition one of equanimity. However, he was given to excessive anger, when once aroused. In civil life, he was very deliberate; in military life, his instinctive courage guided his actions.

At sixteen, still a youth in age, but a man in physical bearings, he accepted the position of surveyor for Lord Fairfax. Three years he spent in the wilderness, obtaining from this experience his philosophical views of life. He learned to conquer his violent temper, and to acquire the calm and serenity it breathes.

By 1753, the French had taken possession of the Ohio Valley, and the French and Indian War was raging. Washington, at the age of twenty-one, having previously been appointed a major in the Virginia militia, was sent as an armed messenger to warn the French to withdraw.

Washington was a born soldier. Always as a boy, he listened breathlessly to tales concerning war. Before he reached the age of twenty, he was famous the country round for his fearlessness. His success as a soldier may be attributed to his patriotism, common sense, and the ability to make use of every circumstance. As a soldier, he made use of his knowledge of statesmanship also. He saw behind the manipulation of armies the winning and losing of battles, the political effect and the bearing of a military campaign upon the welfare of the country in general.

Washington's composition of "Six Rules of Strategy" contained one rule that he illustrated one Christmas night in severe winter. Crossing the Delaware to Trenton, New Jersey, and taking the British by surprise, he made the Americans a Christmas present of some several thousand Hessians. His rule was—never do what the enemy want you to do.

When he received from General Braddock the invitation to join his ranks as a colonel, Washington felt highly honored, but association with the English proved that he was considered inferior in all respects because he was a colonial.

We are all acquainted with the facts of the outcome of Braddock's efforts; how he paid no heed to the young colonel's advice; and, as a result, was defeated and slain. Washington learned from this incident the valuable lesson that the colonials were better adapted to fighting in the new world than the English troops.

Again at Valley Forge, he turned disaster into joy for his country. After that devastating, unmerciful winter was terminated, Washington emerged with disciplined troops, instead of the scattering army, that the country expected.

When his military work was concluded, and the responsibility of constructing political ideals and molding the form of a nation was placed upon his shoulders, Washington planned wisely and well; thus launching an adequate, new government.

His theory that the nation would progress only by the discontinuation of party strife was illustrated in the composition of his cabinet. Its members were leaders who voiced the opposing views that divided the country at large.

Washington, assuredly, was not the first to conceive the idea of independence, but it was upon him that the task of making that independence genuine and durable fell. It was through his accomplishments as Commander-in-Chief that this supposed independence was acquired. However, in the eyes of the Colonists, it existed only as far as victory in warfare was concerned. Was this really independence within the nation itself, this divided allegiance among the states? There was difference of origin, activities, interests; all were mutually distrustful and jealous. Using all of his diplomacy and superior wisdom, it was Washington, who was responsible for the leavening of malice among the states into mutual interest.

No one but Washington, with his experience as a soldier and a statesman, and his ever constant marks of a gentleman, could have guided and led his country on to the road of progress. There could have been no better choice for the first president of the United States.

It was because he was free from all party trammels, strong in his nationalism, that he was able to plan so wisely for the future of the country, that he had done more than anyone else to establish.

The Many-sidedness of George Washington

EVELYN YOUNG

Heber, Utah

Wasatch High School, Heber, Utah

The name of Napoleon has gone down in history as the greatest of soldiers, but he was a soldier only. Hamilton will be remembered as a statesman, and Jefferson, as a builder. The early Greek has been upheld as a standard of physical culture and development. The pilgrim is reverenced for his faith and devotion to God; the pioneer, for his perseverance in conquering new lands. How great then is the name, and how long will live the memory of the man who is the embodiment of all of these—George Washington the soldier, statesman, farmer, Christian, and builder.

Years of surveying, as well as time spent in the French and Indian wars had fully prepared him for military leadership. A perfect physical structure, radiating energy, vitality, and endurance made it possible for him to become the great general that he was. Very early in life he learned the use of a sword and firearms, along with acquiring great skill in horsemanship. To be a soldier was an inherited tendency, gained from a long line of fighting ancestors.

As leader of the army, he showed unflinching courage, determination, and an unwavering purpose. He was wise in choosing positions for attack or retreat, and in using every possible means of strategy to keep the English from knowing the extreme weakness of the army. Thus many times it was saved from ruin.

As a statesman, Washington exhibited the same fine qualities which made him famous as a military leader. His judgment in choosing his co-workers was remarkable, both from the standpoint of help to himself and keeping peace between the two rapidly growing political parties. His profound wisdom displayed itself in his ability to guide the Ship of State over many dangerous periods, to keep the new nation peaceful at home and respected abroad.

Washington's foresight had a decided influence upon the advancement of this nation. His powerful mind, looking into the future, and seeing the greatness of undeveloped resources which his country held in store, formulated plans for the building up of transportation, communication, commerce, and colonization to meet the needs of a rapidly growing nation.

It has been said that the Federal Constitution originated at Mount Vernon, nor was this altogether wrong for Washington was among the first to see the inadequacy of the Articles of Confederation, and visualize means for improvement. In an early

speech to Congress he declared three things necessary to a successful government: "First. An indissoluble union of the States under one federal head. Secondly. A sacred regard to public justice. Thirdly. The adoption of a proper peace establishment; and, Fourthly. The prevalence of that pacific and friendly disposition among the people of the United States."

Such crystallized utterances as these, and his sincerity of action became the foundation on which the new nation was built. The people of the states had such explicit faith in him, that they proclaimed him their president with one accord.

One thing which attributed most to the success of this great leader—which aided him through so many perilous places in battle, and in the affairs of State—was his faith in God. At all times he showed the traits of a true Christian. When in deep trouble he called on God for help; when victorious, he gave thanks to Him. Every great act or important decision of his life was preceded by prayer.

Although Washington was a surveyor, soldier, statesman, commander, and president, he was primarily a farmer. During the six years he was away from Mount Vernon, he kept in touch with the estate and was keenly interested in the cultivation of his farms. He always looked forward to the time when he could retire to his home and live the life of a simple farmer. He inherited his love of land from his English forefathers, and called farming his chief amusement.

A famous writer once said, "Great is the man who can do a thing to perfection, but still greater is he who can do all things well." Unknowingly he was paying tribute to the Nation's first and greatest hero—George Washington.

George Washington, The Farmer at Mount Vernon

MARY ELIZABETH LAWSING

Randolph, Vermont

Randolph High School, Vermont

Nearly every periodical this year is running an article about Washington. Yes, I'll have to admit that he was a great general, and, yes again, that he was a great president—but just where was the real George Washington? Was it his main ambition to command an army or father a nation?

In magazine articles we find that it is human nature to try to pick flaws in a public character, or else to gild it with a complete set of all human virtues. By exploring reliable sources of information we discover that Washington "had an almost fanatical love of farming." He regarded leading the Continental Army to victory and piloting a new nation through its first growing pains, as unavoidable interruptions to his true vocation—farming.

A proof of his agricultural genius would seem to be that he became wealthy by farming the none too fertile acres of Mount Vernon while most of his neighbors remained poor. Let us make a visit to his farm as it was in his day, to see if we can discover reasons for his prosperity.

Our conveyance, a carriage with leather thorough-braces instead of springs, is drawn by a fine span of horses driven by a negro coachman, who is also our guide. In approaching Mount Vernon we pass through much standing timber. On the widely scattered plantations are large fields of tobacco, but in many of them the plants look stunted and starved. We see large gangs of slaves working with the tobacco. The mansion houses we pass often look run down, but on nearly every estate we see beautiful saddle horses.

When our coachman informs us that we are entering the Washington estate we notice that the universal fields of tobacco have been replaced by luxuriant fields of wheat, corn, turnips, and hay. Pointing to a large sixteen-sided brick barn, our guide says that "Massa" George himself designed and built it. Inside is a circular threshing floor made in sections which allow the flailed grain to drop into bins below. The barn was built so that threshing would not be dependent on the weather.

"Thar's Massa George now!" In one of the fields we see an erect figure on horseback, wearing drab clothes, a broad-brimmed white hat, carrying a hickory switch and riding under a large umbrella attached to his saddle-bow by a long staff. And now the mansion itself comes into view, on a bluff overlooking the beautiful Potomac.

These buildings show no signs of the prevailing poverty! There are greenhouses and gardens. We learn that the whole establishment is carried on as a vast experiment station or agricultural laboratory. With seeds and theories collected from England and many of the colonies, Washington, as pioneer farmer of the day, carries on much research work with both plants and animals. We have space for but a few illustrations.

Having obtained one thousand grains of Good Hope wheat, he planted rows two feet apart, with seeds six inches apart in the row, in order to produce the greatest increase possible. He is very much interested in wheat and has found a way to protect it from rust. He is the first farmer in America to employ rotation of crops and fertilizers to any great extent. Observing that tobacco impoverishes the soil, he grows only enough to serve as a medium of exchange.

We see a herd of cattle and several large flocks of sheep, but our interest is focused on a trio of Spanish asses that the King of Spain presented to Washington, and another of a lighter type from the Isle of Malta presented by Lafayette. Washington devotes much time and attention to improving mules and fully expects that the mule will replace the horse in America because of its longevity and cheapness of maintenance. Washington's success as a farmer may be largely attributed to his careful management. When he was at home the whole estate was under his daily personal supervision, and while he was away he mailed weekly instructions to and received weekly reports from his competent managers. Realizing the expense and inefficiency of slave labor, he put all his slaves under military discipline. In his last address to Congress, hoping that his words would have weight both then and later, Washington expressed his deepest desires for his country. Among the things advocated was the creation of a Board of Agriculture.

Washington, so many-sided, excelled along so many lines that it is difficult to decide in which way he most benefited his country. But certain it seems to me that the qualities which made him a successful farmer made him also the successful general and president.

The Many-sidedness of George Washington

ELIZABETH WALTON

Clifton Forge, Virginia

Clifton Forge High School, Virginia

"Every genius is an impossibility until he appears." Here we have Thomas Carlyle's conception of a genius: an unbelievably remarkable person whom an incredulous world is forced to accept. Naturally, such persons are few; yet Washington attained such excellence in so many fields that the impossibility of it reaches into unfathomable depths. However, his qualities of genius as a military leader, a statesman, and a private citizen are well known to all students of history. The memory of the bravery and valor displayed in that fateful battle against Fort Duquesne, the firmness and idealism with which Washington presided at the Constitutional Convention, and the tender love which he held for his mother will linger in the hearts of the American people for years to come as expressions of a character which achieved greatness in many fields.

Washington stands out preeminently as a military figure. Had the task of leading a group of men, a group which could not yet be termed an army, men who could not be called soldiers, against the formidable, well-trained, splendidly equipped army of a ranking nation fallen to any man other than Washington, the result of that struggle probably would have been quite different. In Washington the Congress had found a man possessed of wonderful judgment and self-control, yet capable of quick, bold, decisive action; a man who had the courage to undertake the impossible and succeed as Washington did when he crossed the Delaware on that memorable Christmas Eve. Here was a general who commanded the highest respect, and yet to whom the lowest wretch of a soldier could unfold his burden.

If General Braddock had allowed his young aide-de-camp to carry out his request that he be allowed to lead ahead a scouting party of the Virginia Regulars, a different story might have been told of the ill-fated expedition at Fort Duquesne. The wise judgment of the young man seemed almost uncanny. Military tactics seemed a natural course for Washington. As a boy he had delighted in playing soldier. His whole life gleamed with military splendor; and he had what has justly been termed "military bearing."

The opportunities for serving his country were greater than ever in the period immediately following the Revolutionary War. It was Washington who was a leader in "the critical period of American history." Washington realized that under the weak government provided for by the Articles of Confederation the nation was standing ready for a plunge into an abyss that meant destruction; and it was he who invited commissioners to Mount Vernon to settle a commercial disagreement between Maryland and Virginia. There he clearly pointed out the necessity for a union in fact as well as in name. He supported the Annapolis Convention which strongly emphasized the need of a union and urged that a larger general convention be held to discuss the matter.

The honor of being presiding officer at the Constitutional Convention was accorded Washington, and in that capacity he ably served. Many writers give to Washington more than to any other one person the credit for the formation of the national Constitution, a document acclaimed far and wide for its conciseness, its completeness, and its ability to fulfill the needs of all ages. Through the entire document runs the spirit of the man who spent many hours puzzling over its intricacies.

As president of the nation Washington had the opportunity to use his powers of statesmanship, and because of those powers the present nation rests upon firm foundations of democracy, liberty, and honesty with ourselves and with other nations. Washington exploded the theory that a military leader cannot ably serve his country as its chief executive. Realizing the vast horrors and the futility of war, he entertained no desire for it, and exercised the same infallible judgment which had won victories in the Revolution.

After his retirement from public life, Washington lived quietly at Mount Vernon as a private citizen. A generous host, an honored master, and the beloved head of his household, he endeared himself to everyone. Who would ever have thought that this man who took joy in farming, in his correspondence, and in the social pleasures of country life, had been a dashing officer, rough and ready to charge the enemy? He was constantly thinking of other people; he educated his nephews, had a hand in making a match for Nellie Custis, and was a leader in philanthropy; his many charities will probably never be known. He gave freely to individuals and to educational institutions.

Farming and writing were Washington's chief diversions. In him the student finds one of America's first experimental agriculturalists, always trying to improve his crops, on the watch for any improvement in implements, avoiding disease among his plants, and finding his recreation with nature. In addition to his diary of business accounts, Washington's correspondence kept him occupied a good part of his time. A joy in his home life is portrayed by all of his biographers, and it may well be said of him that he made as great a success of simply living at home as he did in serving his country.

Thus we find Washington at once a leader, yet willing to be led; a soldier and a statesman, at ease in the midst of a raging battle with bullets darting on all sides, and at ease in the midst of a battle with words flying like bullets; a servant of his country, and a master too; a private citizen living on a country estate, and the chief officer of the land receiving homage from all sides. America proudly accepts Washington for what he was—a loyal military patriot, an honest, far-seeing statesman, and a kind neighbor—whose combined achievements mark him as a rare phenomenon among world leaders, a many-sided genius.

Washington's Influence on Our Life Today

SUSIE L. ROLEY

Washougal, Washington

Washougal High School, Washington

With the exception of the Biblical characters, there is probably no personality of the past whose influence is more strongly felt in the United States at present than that of George Washington. This influence is felt in a multitude of different ways; and the busts, portraits, etchings, speeches, and dedications which are seen so abundantly about us are only the external manifestations of a tradition which has its roots deep down in the heart of every American.

As an establisher of political precedent, as a model of ethical character and an example of admirable statesmanship, Washington has left a record which stands well the wear of years, and will probably never be entirely erased.

Being an exponent of the great cause of independence, Washington proved the compatibility of aristocracy and democracy. Coming of a family of wealth and impeccable social standing, Washington showed his faith in the judgment of the less fortunate, though more numerous commoner. In this present period of bitter competition between the moneyed class and the laborer, it is well that the school child, as well as the adult, has always before him this classical example of mutual trust and benefit between the groups.

Certain authors have lately published works derogatory to the character of George Washington. While deplorable, this literature has probably had little real influence on the thinking public. The glorious tradition of Washington's integrity, his wisdom, executive ability, and great good common sense, lives on.

The progressive quality of his thinking is shown in the fact that he strongly favored education for the masses when such an idea was generally scorned by his own social group and considered impractical by the common people. It was through his influence and diligent efforts that the first free public school was established in the state of Virginia. It occurred to him that a public which was to be endowed with the privilege and responsibility of governing itself wisely and well, must be prepared in some measure for this task from youth. Again, he no doubt saw that public education would be fertile soil for the growth of the freedom-through-democracy which he so ardently championed. The public school as it is today, though far from ideal, substantiates these arguments, so radical in Washington's day.

Washington's rare sympathy, his dogged determination, and force of character are all shown vividly in the Valley Forge incident so well known to every school child. They all played an important part in the winning of a cause as dear to every one of us as to those starved, ragged, brave soldiers. Had he been less loved, less competent, less determined, the great war might have had a very different outcome. And there are very few of us, regardless of how worldly, who do not admire intensely this steadfastness and integrity of purpose, this staunchness of character.

At a time when great decisions must be made; when plans must be made which would vitally affect people for hundreds of years; when stands must be taken and adhered to; when internationally important treaties negotiated, Washington displayed his unparalleled statesmanship. Always open-minded, Washington listened to the arguments of many factions, weighed them carefully, and acted accordingly. He surrounded himself with men of outstanding ability and was advised by them. The work done by this group, than which a greater assemblage has never been known, is still held in great respect by statesmen of today. Much of it still affects our daily lives. In their solicitousness for the newly found freedom they did much to insure that freedom to us, hundreds of years later.

So, as evidenced by the numerous remembrances, the cherished legends, the revered traditions and precedent, Washington is still a very influential personality in modern civilization. Goldsmith said, "An honest man is the noblest work of God," and certainly the Deity was at His best when he bequeathed to a needful world the super-man, George Washington.

In recognition of all this, it seems that George Washington's influence on our lives today may be considered comparable to the influence of the gardener on his garden when he plants his seed, gives it fertile soil in which to grow, a trellis upon which to climb and then passes on, leaving it to be tended by his posterity, knowing that he has done well a great deed.

George Washington's Sense of Duty

VERA BROYLES

Princeton, West Virginia

Princeton High School, West Virginia

"America has furnished to the world the character of Washington. And if our American institutions had done nothing else, that alone would have entitled them to the respect of mankind," Webster tells us.

That character, the greatest ever known to Americans, was dominated throughout by a sense of duty, a patriotism which placed him first during his entire lifetime.

A sense of duty is based mainly on one's ideals—the root and source of all the good that is in man. Carlyle says, "Great men, taken up in any way, are profitable company." And certainly the most profitable way to study great men is to concentrate on their ideals.

As a man possessed of ideals and purposes, George Washington is perhaps unsurpassed in the history of the world. He had the purpose of reaching the pinnacle of greatness of mind and thought; the purpose of freeing his people from oppression; and the purpose of leading that same people to a greater degree of equality, fraternity, and trust and justice in humanity. He possessed the ideal of democracy, the ideal of brotherhood, and the ideal of liberty. He became the leader of a people whose ideals and purposes were a bit hazy, but who had the common hatred of tyranny in every form; and here was a man who had the inspiration to guide them into paths of practical justice and equality.

Washington's sense of duty would first make him an American. And after all, what is it to be an American? It is to believe in America and American people. It is to have an abiding and moving faith in the future and destiny of America—something above and beyond the patriotism which every man whose soul is not dead within him feels for the land of his birth. It is to be national and not sectional; independent and not colonial. It is to have a high and true conception of the possibilities of America, and to work with loyalty and truth to the fulfillment of that ideal.

Has any other man fulfilled these requirements more completely or fully than George Washington? Has any man ever lived who has served the American people more faithfully, or with a higher and truer conception of what this new nation was to become?

And yet, this is the man whom Mr. Clarence King omitted when he said, "Abraham Lincoln was the first American to ever reach the lonely height of immortal fame. Before him, in the narrow compass of our history, were but two preeminent names: Columbus the discoverer, and Washington the founder; the one an Italian seer, the other an English country gentleman."

That same sense of duty, that patriotism which would not be quieted, caused Washington to turn traitor to England, our mother country. He took an army of twenty thousand men, who were raw, inexperienced sons of farmers and mechanics, and instilled into them the principles of discipline and patriotism. With this raw material he struggled through the eight years of war, under privations and hardships that would have crushed any save an indomitable spirit.

"He had the spirit of a ruler,
 And the station of a ruler. Well for us
It was so! Few can rule themselves,
Can use their wisdom wisely.
Happy for the whole where there is one
         among them that can be a center
And a hold for many thousands;
That can plant himself like a firm column
For the whole to lean on safely."

And the whole of America did lean on Washington during the era referred to in Revolutionary history as "the critical period." From the presidency of the convention that formed the Constitution he went into the presidency of the government which that convention brought into being, and in all that followed, his one guiding thought was to make the American people independent in thought and policy as the Revolution had made them independent politically.

That is George Washington—our first and greatest American, the Commander-in-Chief of the Continental Army, our First President, and our immortal hero, enshrined forever in the hearts of Americans.

"Sleep softly—under the stone.
 Time has its way with you there
 And the clay has its own.
 Sleep on, O brave hearted, O wise man,
 That kindled the flame—
 To live in mankind is far more than to live in a name.
 To live in mankind—far—far more than to live in a name."

Washington's Influence on Our Life Today

HELEN MILLS
Wheatland, Wyoming

Wheatland High School, Wyoming

George Washington—his humanity will never be forgotten—his services will never be fully estimated—his policies will never lose their force—they have become the very substance of America and of American ideals and beliefs. Not only was he the most versatile man of the age, but the influence that he wielded in the fields of education, agriculture, and government was built upon so sound a basis that the passage of years has added only to its strength.

Although denied a full education, Washington was one of the foremost advocates of education in America. He said, "The best means of forming a manly, virtuous and happy people, will be found in the right education of youth.—Without this foundation, every other means, in my opinion, must fail." To accomplish this end he instituted the first free schooling in Alexandria, Virginia, contributed to the education of his step-children and friends, and left bequests to colleges and universities.

George Washington was one of the first Americans to realize the basic need for progressive agriculture. In knowledge and practice, he was years ahead of his countrymen. He introduced crop rotation and soil fertilization, invented new farm machinery, increased the wool production of his sheep, and conducted experiments in the control of plant diseases and insects. American farmers would be far behind their present advanced stage had Washington not imbued their forbears with the spirit of progress.

It was Washington who led the way to independence and secured for us that territory which is now the home of thousands of American citizens. He was not a revolutionist, but when it became necessary to defend the Colonists' rights, Washington led in the movement. His force lay, not in oratory; his service was more fundamental, for it was his "solid information and sound judgment" that brought him recognition as "the greatest man on the floor" of the Continental Congress. And when war came, Washington with his financial generosity, his inspiring character, and his military genius brought victory for the American cause—victory which would have been impossible without him.

To Washington we owe much of the credit for the form of our government today. Congress had drawn up the Articles of Confederation during the war, and they soon became operative. So manifold were their weaknesses, however, that with many enthusiasm for democracy waned, and a longing for a monarchial government grew up. Some one even suggested to Washington the idea that monarchy might be stronger, and one can little doubt that with his far-reaching influence he could have brought about the establishment of such a government, and made himself the king. Instead, he was very displeased, but realizing the many defects of the existing government, he urged a convention to deal with the problem. When that convention met in 1787, he was chosen presiding officer. His most influential act during the session was the deliverance of one of his rare speeches. It rang with nobility, and patriotism and won the delegates to high standards in forming the new constitution.

Even Washington's lesser governmental actions were so respected that their influences are still powerful. His custom, while President, of calling in the heads of the various governmental departments to advise him, developed under his successors into the President's Cabinet. His refusal to accept a third term in that office made such an impression that from that day, few presidents have attempted a second reelection, and those few have failed. His advice against entangling foreign alliances in the "Farewell Address" is responsible for the non-membership of the United States in the League of Nations.

An old chieftain, gazing with a prophet's eye into Washington's future, once said:

"Listen! the Great Spirit protects that man and guides his destinies. He will become the chief of nations, and a people yet unborn will hail him as founder of a mighty empire."

And we, that people, striving for words of acknowledgement, can only say with Lodge:

"I see in Washington a great soldier who fought a trying war to a successful end impossible without him; a great statesman who did more than all other men to lay the foundations of a republic which has endured in prosperity for more than a century. I find in him a marvellous judgment which was never at fault, a penetrating vision which beheld the future of America when it was dim to other eyes, a great intellectual force, a will of iron, an unyielding grasp of facts, and an unequalled strength of patriotic purpose."

Students Awarded Second and Third Places in their Respective State Essay Contests

Alabama
    Lillian Hinson, Murphy High School, Mobile
    Homer R. Jolley, Spring Hill
Arizona
    John Farnsworth, Phoenix Union High School, Phoenix
    Robert Jeter, Ray
Arkansas
    Mary Medearis, North Little Rock
    Wilma Sturdivant, Pine Bluff
California
    Alice Macrae, Academy of the Holy Names, Pomona
    Mathilda Cummings, St. Andrews High School, Pasadena
Colorado
    Edward Lyons, Regis College High School, Denver
    Benjamin Laposky, St. Mary's High School, Colorado Springs
Connecticut
    Grace Hickey, Mount St. Joseph's Academy, Hartford
    Callista Begnal, Waterbury Catholic High School, Waterbury
Florida
    Jeff Rhyne, Jackson County High School, Marianna
    Florida Madison, St. Cloud
Georgia
    Mildred Flury, Commercial High School, Atlanta
    Helen Brooke Ruck, Commercial High School, Atlanta
Hawaii *
Idaho
    Dawna Cox, Soda Springs
    Helen Banaka, Lewiston
Illinois
    Elizabeth Ann Salisbury, Wheaton Community High School, Wheaton
    Robert Sass, Morgan Park Military Academy, Morgan Park, Chicago
Indiana
    Harold Cooper, Arsenal Technical High School, Indianapolis
    Mary Nan Coxen, Reitz High School, Evansville
Kansas
    Maxine D. Lewis, Marysville High School
    *
Kentucky
    Eleanor Marks, LaSalette Academy, Covington
    Dorothy McDonald, Frankfort
Louisiana
    Elizabeth Pickett, Melville
    Janet LaCombe, Junior High School, Baton Rouge
Maryland
    Nancy Lankford, Laurel
    Dorothy Voris, Laurel
Missouri
    Margaret Hightower, Walker
    Pearlie Carter, Emma D. High School, Goodson
Montana
    James Thompson, Chinook
    *

Nevada
    Gerrit Roelof, Senior High School, Reno
    Jean McElrath, Wells
New Jersey
    Grace Stimson, Bogota
    Ruth Lake, Hackettstown
New Mexico
    Margaret Joanne Smith, Loretto Academy, Santa Fe
    Marjorie Seawalt, Lovington
New York
    Frances Carpenter, Cheesebrough Seminary, North Chili
    Betty Illmer, Cortland
North Carolina
    Maria Tucker, St. Mary's School and Junior College, Raleigh
    Thomas Worth Crowell, Newton
North Dakota
    Maynard Burk, Juanita
    Clarice Benson, Edmore
Oregon
    Margaret Froman, Gilliam County High School, Condon
    Helen Jane Brown, Jefferson High School, Portland
South Carolina
    Florence Grahl, Parker High School, Greenville
    Mary Wertz, Saluda
South Dakota
    Kathleen Malloy, Scenic
    Beth Steffen, Hitchcock
Tennessee
    Kathleen Wettstein, St. Cecilia Academy, Nashville
    Nell Frances Callahan, Cathedral High School, Nashville
Texas
    William Barney, Central High School, Fort Worth
    Mildred Hodges, Austin High School, El Paso
Utah
    Howard E. Silliman, Green River
    Charles Ball, Eureka
Vermont
    Gertrude Barry, Cathedral High School, Burlington
    Leone Gould, People's Academy, Morrisville
Virginia
    Cecilia Schroth, St. Mary's Academy, Alexandria
    Mary Chappell, Portlock High School, Norfolk
Washington
    Vincent Anderson, Roosevelt High School, Seattle
    Margaret Winterhalter, Queen Anne High School, Seattle
West Virginia
    Virginia Thomas, Fairmont
    Gladys Tennant, Shepherdstown
Wyoming
    Grace Kawamoto, Sheridan
    Eugene Olson, Pine Bluffs

_____
* Names not reported at time of publication.

GROUP III
DECLAMATIONS
Students Awarded First, Second, and Third Places in the State Declamatory Contests in the Elementary Schools

Alabama

B. L. Machen, Albertville
Mary Lindon, Leeds
Saranel Burford, Minor School, Birmingham

Colorado

Joseph Stein, Cathedral School, Denver
Estees Potter, Cherry Hills, Littleton
Charles Bitzer, Steamboat Springs

Connecticut

Herbert E. Bailey, St. Joseph's Cathedral School, Hartford
John Gorman, St. Mary's School, New London
Harold Lackman, J. I. Scranton School, New Haven

Florida

Joseph Gibeault, Memorial Junior High School, Orlando
Sadie Brown, Kirby-Smith Junior High School, Jacksonville
Margaret Salley, Florida High School, Tallahassee

Idaho

Anna Mae Malberg, Twin Falls
Vernon Harris, Lewiston
Weldon Purcell, Idaho Falls

Illinois

Agnes Anthony, Beaverville
Roland Berndt, Whittier School, Oak Park
Charline Eddleman, Junior High School, Pinckneyville

Kentucky

Virginia Gibson, Monticello
Martha Valentine, Maysville
Mildred Coley, Shelbyville

Louisiana

Nora Eskridge, Baker
Helen Story, Mansfield
Winifred Gonzales, Joseph Maumus School, Arabi

Montana

Raquel Davis, Vida
May Brumley, Havre
Ruth Kelly, Dillon

New Mexico

Melva Jane Reed, Five Points School, Albuquerque
Louise White, Steins
Jean Cox, Carrizozo

North Carolina

John Williams, Wentworth
Mary Lynn Fox, Silver City

North Dakota

Betty Hanson, Larimore
Leonora La Brash, Jamestown
Bernice Hande, Rhame

Oklahoma

Ruth Welch, Okmulgee
Doris McManus, Putnam City
Barbara Gamble, El Reno

South Dakota

Raymond Gormley, Huron
Betty Heggelund, Deadwood
Donna Jeanne Smith, Centerville

Tennessee

Harris Abrahams, Tarbox School, Nashville
Jessie Clay Orr, McDowell School, Columbia
Sarah Hancock, Lebanon
† Linewood Graves, Kingsport
† Anita Fleming, Mount Pleasant
† Thomas Adair, Nashville

Texas

Tom Davis, Junior High School, Austin
Dan Grover, St. Gerard's School, San Antonio
Lillian Schroeder, Brownwood

Virginia

Clifton Kreps, James Monroe School, Norfolk
Peter Pauls Stewart, East End Junior High School, Richmond
Lee Montgomery, Newport News High School, Newport News

Washington

Earl Woodbury, Washington School, Bremerton
Clinton Lemmon, Oakville
Dallas Williams, Carl Puckett Junior High School, Kelso

West Virginia

Elizabeth Moyer, Williamson
Margaret Crigler, Cassville
Betty Morissey, Bluefield

Wyoming

Jack Schwendiman, Deaver
Bob McBride, Buffalo
Dorothy Rae Speas, Casper

---

† Winners in contest in colored schools.

ORGANIZATION AND REGULATIONS

OF THE

DECLAMATORY, ESSAY,

AND

ORATORICAL CONTESTS

OF THE

UNITED STATES GEORGE WASHINGTON
BICENTENNIAL COMMISSION

Prepared by

HAZEL B. NIELSON

Director of Educational Activities

PREFACE

THIS pamphlet, ORGANIZATION AND REGULATIONS OF THE DE-CLAMATORY, ESSAY, AND ORATORICAL CONTESTS OF THE UNITED STATES GEORGE WASHINGTON BICENTENNIAL COMMISSION, describes the working organization for the contests; the regulations, including type, scope, and time of the contests; the topics for selection of subjects; the commemorative medals of award; and contains facts on reference material, also a list of selected books relating to George Washington, and the membership of each State Contest Committee.

The pamphlet which was prepared for use in the Declamatory Contests in the elementary schools, contains selections of prose and poetry relating to George Washington, arranged according to grades. These selections were chosen from those submitted by educators from many states. The pamphlet was furnished to the schools enrolling in the Declamatory Contest, which terminated with a state contest.

The Nation-wide series of Educational Contests touched every type of school. The teachers and students whether in a one-room school or a great university had the privilege of being a part of this Nation-wide activity.

THE WHITE HOUSE

WASHINGTON

December 21, 1931,

TO THE TEACHERS AND YOUTH OF OUR LAND:

Celebration of the two hundredth anniversary of the birth of George Washington brings to our million teachers and thirty-two million school children a special incentive to fresh study of the formative period of the nation. So rich and vivid is the record that the founders live again in the epic of laying the foundations of the republic. Washington as the central figure kindles our imagination as the embodiment of the courage, idealism and wisdom which transformed scattered and dependent colonies into a free and independent nation. The heritage of freedom which we enjoy had its beginning in the spirit and deeds of Washington. The study of that bright page of our history will quicken our patriotism and deepen our devotion to the land we love.

Herbert Hoover

KINDLE NEW FIRES OF PATRIOTISM

WHAT an opportunity is yours in 1932 to instill in the minds and hearts of the youth of our land an appreciation of the personality, character, and ideals of George Washington! A hundred years will pass before such an opportunity is again given to the people of the United States to join in a united effort in paying tribute to Our First President.

George Washington believed in education. He became well educated although he did not have the opportunities or privileges in youth which we have. He learned by travel, by study, by thinking things out for himself, and by doing—never throwing the responsibility on another.

The United States George Washington Bicentennial Commission seeks to open every avenue of expression in the Nation-wide Celebration of the Two Hundredth Anniversary of the Birth of George Washington. The activities are many so that the people of this Nation may find various ways in which to express their appreciation of the services of the greatest of Americans. One of the avenues open to the students is the Nation-wide series of Educational Contests.

SOL BLOOM,
Director,
UNITED STATES GEORGE WASHINGTON
BICENTENNIAL COMMISSION.

NATIONAL CONTESTS

NATIONAL contests had their beginnings thousands of years ago. They had their origin in devotion to country and in the stimulation and cultivation of physical prowess so necessary at the time for the preservation of the State. But mental culture is as much a national need as muscular development and in the Olympic and other great contests of the old Greeks the powers of mind and body were both displayed.

We moderns are less in need of physical power and skill than our forbears but we are not less in need of knowledge of our past history and of the problems of our national and international life. Patriotism means far more than clannish sentiment and explosions of gunpowder. It meant far more to George Washington; and it is highly appropriate that, in this year 1932, we should bring to the attention of our school children the high qualities of the Father of His Country and the large ambitions for that country which he had in mind.

WILLIAM JOHN COOPER,
Commissioner,
UNITED STATES OFFICE OF EDUCATION.

The Spirit of George Washington

"The best means of forming a manly, virtuous and happy people, will be found in the right education of youth.—Without this foundation, every other means, in my opinion, must fail."—George Washington.

STUDENTS OF THE UNITED STATES OF AMERICA

Dedicate yourselves to a study of George Washington during the Bicentennial year, and make your contribution of appreciation

Seek to make the spirit of George Washington your companion this year.

Plan to take part in this Nation-wide Celebration.

Inspire to action your school companions for a full enlistment in the school contests honoring George Washington.

Read to gain a better understanding of the life and achievements of Washington as surveyor, engineer, frontiersman, business man, farmer, writer, soldier, commander, statesman, and the First President of the United States.

Improve to the fullest every opportunity to express the principles of George Washington.

Try to make your tribute to George Washington worthy of his ideals and his service to his country.

Regulations

STATE CONTEST COMMITTEE

APPOINTMENT

Made by each State George Washington Bicentennial Commission.

MEMBERSHIP

Listed on pages 411-416.

PURPOSE

To organize and conduct the series of contests—declamatory, essay, and oratorical—in each state.

To serve as medium of contact between the United States George Washington Bicentennial Commission and the schools.

To secure cooperation of organizations interested in school contests and avoid duplication of effort.

STEPS IN ORGANIZATION OF CONTESTS

Conducted by State Contest Committee.

Division of state for elimination contests.

Arrangement of time for elimination contests.

The United States George Washington Bicentennial Commission suggests that all local elimination contests be held in a school or community prior to February 22, 1932.

Selection of Jury of Awards within state.

Give special attention to selection of competent judges. The presiding officers and judges in any contest should be disinterested persons.

Determine order of speaking in Declamatory and Oratorical Contests by lot.

Mark on the scale of ten, using low-point-total system in judging.

Selection of State Awards.

United States George Washington Bicentennial Commission will present the official George Washington Commemorative Medal to the state winners in the three state contests—Declamatory, Essay, and Oratorical.

Note explanation regarding awards under Types of Contests.

Other awards, within states to be chosen and provided by state and local committees.

TYPE AND SCOPE OF THE NATION-WIDE SERIES OF EDUCATIONAL CONTESTS

The Series of Contests will include the following divisions:
Declamatory contests in elementary schools
Essay contests in high schools
Oratorical contests in institutions of higher learning

These contests are open to bona fide students of all public, private, and parochial schools.

Every student entering a contest must register in accordance with regulations furnished by the State Contest Committee.

Closing date of entry determined by State Contest Committee.

Schools participating are expected to meet the expenses of their contestants.

DECLAMATORY CONTEST IN ELEMENTARY SCHOOLS

The United States George Washington Bicentennial Commission has prepared a pamphlet containing selections of prose and poetry relating to George Washington. The contestants in the Declamatory contest must choose their selection from this pamphlet, which will be distributed to the teachers of the schools where students enroll in the Declamatory contest.

The Declamatory contest will include a local, district, and a state contest. All local and district elimination contests, as well as state contests, shall be held according to regulations and organization of state determined by State Contest Committee.

Open to all grades grouped as follows:

    (1) Grades 1 and 2
    (2) Grades 3 and 4
    (3) Grades 5 and 6
    (4) Grades 7 and 8

The extent of the contest for students of grades 1, 2, 3, and 4 will be determined by the superintendents and teachers.

District contests for grades 5 and 6.

State contests for grades 7 and 8.

Note page 407 for information on Jury of Awards.

Speaker marked upon three points: delivery, voice and gestures, and interpretation.

The United States George Washington Bicentennial Commission will award the official George Washington Commemorative Medal in silver to the student winning the state declamatory contest; to the winner of second place the official medal in bronze, and to the student in third place a certificate of award.

ESSAY CONTEST IN HIGH SCHOOLS

Essay contest will include a local, district, state, and a national contest. All elimination contests within the state shall be according to regulations determined by State Contest Committee.

Closing date of entry for state contest determined by State Contest Committee.

Closing date of entry for national contest April 19, 1932.

    Essay awarded first place by State Contest Committee may compete in the national contest.

    The essay must be received by April 19, 1932, at the School Contest Division, United States George Washington Bicentennial Commission, Washington Building, Washington, D. C.

Selection of subjects must be from the following:
    George Washington, the Farmer at Mount Vernon
    George Washington's Spirit of Sportsmanship
    George Washington: Statesman and Soldier
    George Washington's Sense of Duty
    Washington's Balance of Character
    The Many-sidedness of George Washington
    George Washington, the Friend
    Washington's Influence on Our Life Today

Regulations to be observed by contestants in essay contest:
    Contestant must state in writing, "This essay is my original production and is not copied from any source except as indicated by quotation marks."
    Essays must be written on one side of the paper only. If possible the essay should be typewritten.
    A sealed envelope attached to each essay must contain the name, school, and home address of the student. This must be countersigned by the teacher or principal of the school.
    Essay should be not less than 600 words in length, nor more than 750 words.
    No essay will be returned.
    Note page 407 for information on Jury of Awards.

The United States George Washington Bicentennial Commission will award the official George Washington Commemorative Medal in silver to the student winning the state essay contest; to the winner of second place the official medal in bronze; and to the student in third place, a certificate of award.

To the winner in the national essay contest the United States George Washington Bicentennial Commission will present the official George Washington Commemorative Medal in gold.

ORATORICAL CONTEST IN INSTITUTIONS OF HIGHER LEARNING

Oratorical contests will include a local, district (if arranged by State Contest Committee), state, regional, and a national contest.

All elimination contests within the state shall be according to regulations arranged by State Contest Committee.

The student winning first in each state shall compete in the Regional contest.

Regional elimination contests arranged by United States George Washington Bicentennial Commission in cooperation with State Contest Committees. Time and place to be announced.

The student winning in the Regional contest shall compete in the National contest.

National contest to be held in Washington, D. C. Time to be announced.

The orations must be on any one of the following subjects:
    Washington the Courageous
    Washington and the West
    Washington the Man of Business Vision
    Development of George Washington's Military Ability
    George Washington's Understanding of Men
    Washington: Nation Builder
    First in Peace
    Washington: Exemplar of American Ideals
    George Washington, a World Figure
    The Spirit of Washington

Regulations to be observed by students entering this contest:
    The work of each student must be original. The winner in each elimination contest must give the same oration in the next higher contest.
    The orations will be limited to twelve minutes
    Note page 407 for information on Jury of Awards.

The United States George Washington Bicentennial Commission will present the official George Washington Commemorative Medal in silver to the student winning the state oratorical contest; to the winner of second place, the official medal in bronze; and to the student in third place, a certificate of award.

To the winner in the National oratorical contest the United States George Washington Bicentennial Commission will present the official George Washington Commemorative Medal in gold.

REFERENCE TO MATERIALS
Issued by the United States George Washington Bicentennial Commission

It is important that authentic information be given students participating in the contests.

When a school reports the number of students registered in the nation-wide series of educational contests, available material will be sent.

Pamphlet of *Selections Relating to George Washington for Declamatory Contests in the Elementary Schools.* For use of teachers.

Forty-eight Papers of the Twelve George Washington Programs. Papers based on material gathered from many authors, telling of the life, character, and experiences of George Washington.

Honor to George Washington and Reading about George Washington. Fifteen pamphlets included in this series with a list of selected authorities in each present authentic facts about different aspects of the life of George Washington. Pamphlet No. 15 of this series, "Classified Washington's Bibliography," divided into four parts, compiled by the American Library Association.

Handbook of the George Washington Appreciation Course. Prepared for the use of students in institutions of higher learning, teachers, and study groups. Course divided into twelve units, dealing with the life and achievements of George Washington and outstanding features of the Nation's Capital. References in each unit to the historical material issued by the Commission are in chronological order.

Suggestions and Outline of the George Washington Appreciation Course. Contains brief outline of the twelve units of the course and general objectives and aim.

SELECTED BOOKS RELATING TO GEORGE WASHINGTON

Out of the hundreds of volumes relating to George Washington and his service to his country the following will be especially accurate, interesting, and generally available:

1. ADAMS, JOHN. *Works.* Vols. II, III, IX. (Boston, Little Brown, 1850-1854.)

2. ANDREWS, CHARLES M. *Colonial Folkways* (*Chronicles of America*, Vol. IX). (New Haven, Yale University Press, 1921.)

3. ANDREW, CHARLES M. *Colonial Period.* (N. Y., Holt, 1912.)

4. AVERY, ELROY M. *History of the United States and Its People.* Vols. V-VII. (Cleveland, Burrows, 1908-1910.)

5. BAKER, WILLIAM S., ed. *Early Sketches of George Washington.* (Philadelphia, Lippincott, 1893.)

6. BAKER, WILLIAM S. *Itinerary of George Washington from June 15, 1775, to December 23, 1783.* (Philadelphia, Lippincott, 1892.)

7. BAKER, WILLIAM S. *Washington After the Revolution.* (Philadelphia, Lippincott, 1898.)

8. BEER, GEORGE L. *British Colonial Policy, 1754-1765.* (New York, Macmillan, 1907.)

9. BELCHER, HENRY. *First American Civil War,* 2 vols. (New York, Macmillan, 1911.)

10. BEMIS, SAMUEL F. *Jay's Treaty.* (New York, Macmillan, 1923.)

11. BEVERIDGE, ALBERT J. *Life of John Marshall.* Vol. II. (Boston, Houghton Mifflin, 1916.)

12. BOWEN, CLARENCE W. "Inauguration of Washington." (*Century Magazine,* vol. 37, 1889.)

13. BOWERS, CLAUDE G. *Jefferson and Hamilton.* (Boston, Houghton Mifflin, 1925.)

14. BRACKENRIDGE, HENRY M. *History of the Western Insurrection in Western Pennsylvania.* (Pittsburgh, W. S. Haven, 1859.)

15. BROOKS, ELBRIDGE S. *True Story of George Washington.* (Boston, Lothrop, 1895.)

16. BRYAN, WILHELMUS B. *History of the National Capital.* Vol. I. (New York, Macmillan, 1914.)

17. CALLAHAN, CHARLES H. *Washington the Man and the Mason.* (Washington, 1913.)

18. CHANNING, EDWARD. *History of the United States.* Vols. III, IV. (New York, Macmillan, 1912-1917.)

19. CONWAY, MONCURE D. *Barons of the Potomack and the Rappahannock.* (New York, Grolier Club, 1892.)

20. CONWAY, MONCURE D. "English Ancestry of Washington." (*Harper's Magazine,* vol. 84, 1891.)

21. CONWAY, MONCURE D., ed. *George Washington and Mount Vernon.* (Brooklyn, Long Island Historical Society, 1889.)

22. CORBIN, JOHN. *Unknown Washington.* (New York, Scribner, 1930.)

23. CUSTIS, GEORGE W. P. *Recollections and Private Memoirs of Washington.* (Philadelphia, William Flint, 1859; other eds.)

24. EARLE, ALICE M. *Child Life in Colonial Days.* (New York, Macmillan, 1899.)

25. EARLE, ALICE M. *Home Life in Colonial Days.* (New York, Macmillan, 1898.)

26. EARLE, ALICE M. *Old Time Gardens.* (New York, Macmillan, 1901.)

27. EARLE, ALICE M. *Stage-Coach and Tavern Days.* (New York, Macmillan, 1900.)

28. EARLE, ALICE M. *Two Centuries of Costume in America.* 2 vols. (New York, Macmillan, 1903.)

29. EARLE, SWEPSON. *Chesapeake Bay Country.* (Baltimore, Thomsen-Ellis, 1923.)

30. FISHER, SYDNEY G. *Struggle for American Independence.* 2 vols. (Philadelphia, Lippincott, 1908.)

31. FITZPATRICK, JOHN C. *George Washington, Colonial Traveller, 1732-1775.* (Indianapolis, Bobbs-Merrill, 1927.) (Also, *George Washington Himself,* to be issued in 1932.)

32. FORD, PAUL L. *True George Washington.* (Philadelphia, Lippincott, 1896.)

33. FORD, WORTHINGTON C. *George Washington.* 2 vols. (New York, Scribner, 1900.)

34. FROTHINGHAM, THOMAS G. *Washington, Commander in Chief.* (Boston, Houghton Mifflin, 1930.)

35. GERWIG, GEORGE W. *Washington, the Young Leader.* (New York, Scribner, 1923.)

36. GIBBS, GEORGE. *Memoirs of the Administrations of Washington and John Adams.* Vol. I. (New York, Van Norden, 1846.)

37. GIST, CHRISTOPHER. *Journals.* (Pittsburgh, Weldin, 1893.)

38. HAMILTON, JOHN C. *History of the Republic of the United States of America as traced in the Writings of Alexander Hamilton and his Contemporaries.* 7 vols. (New York, Appleton, 1857-1864.)

39. HAMILTON, STANISLAUS M., ed. *Letters to Washington.* 5 vols. (Boston, Houghton Mifflin, 1898-1902.)

40. HAPGOOD, NORMAN. *George Washington.* (New York, Macmillan, 1901.)

41. HARLAND, MARION. *Some Colonial Homesteads and their Stories.* (New York, Putnam, 1897.)

42. HART, ALBERT B. *Formation of the Union, 1750-1829.* Rev. ed. (New York, Longmans Green, 1925.)

43. HART, ALBERT B. *George Washington: Reading with a Purpose.* (Chicago, American Library Association, 1930.)

44. HATCH, LOUIS C. *Administration of the American Revolutionary Army.* (New York, Longmans Green, 1904.)

45. HAWORTH, PAUL L. *George Washington, Country Gentleman.* (Indianapolis, Bobbs-Merrill, 1925.)

46. HEATH, WILLIAM. *Memoirs.* (Boston, Thomas & Andrews, 1798; later eds.)

47. HENDERSON, ARCHIBALD. *Washington's Southern Tour, 1791.* (Boston, Houghton Mifflin, 1923.)

48. HERBERT, LEILA. *First American, His Homes and His Households.* (New York, Harper, 1900.)

49. HILL, FREDERICK T. *On the Trail of Washington.* (New York, Appleton, 1910.)

50. HOWARD, GEORGE E. *Preliminaries of the Revolution.* (*American Nation,* Vol. VIII.) (New York, Harper, 1905.)

51. HULBERT, ARCHER B. *Colonel Washington.* (Marietta, Ohio, Western Reserve University, 1903.)

52. HULBERT, ARCHER B. *Historic Highways of America.* Vols. II-V. (Cleveland, Clark, 1902-1903.)

53. HULBERT, ARCHER B. *Washington and the West.* (New York, Century, 1905.)

54. IRVING, WASHINGTON. *Life of George Washington.* 5 vols. (New York, Putnam, 1855-1859; later eds.)

55. JERNEGAN, MARCUS B. *American Colonies, 1492-1750.* (New York, Longmans Green, 1929.)

56. JOHNSON, BRADLEY T. *General Washington.* (New York, Appleton, 1894.)

57. KITE, ELIZABETH S. *L'Enfant and Washington, 1791-1792.* (Baltimore, Johns Hopkins Press, 1929.)

58. LEAR, TOBIAS. *Letters and Recollections of George Washington.* (New York, Doubleday Page, 1906.)

59. LECKY, WILLIAM E. H. *American Revolution.* (New York, Appleton, 1898.)

60. LEE, CHARLES. *Lee Papers.* 4 vols. (New York Historical Society, *Collections,* 1871-1874.)

61. LITTLE, SHELBY. *George Washington.* (New York, Minton Balch, 1929.)

62. LODGE, HENRY C. *George Washington.* 2 vols. (*American Statesmen.*) Rev. ed. (Boston, Houghton Mifflin, 1898.)

63. LOSSING, BENSON J. *Home of Washington.* (New York, Virtue & Yorston, 1871; earlier eds.)

64. LOSSING, BENSON J. *Life of Washington.* 3 vols. (New York, Virtue, 1860; later eds.)

65. LOSSING, BENSON J. *Mary and Martha, the Mother and Wife of George Washington.* (New York, Harper, 1886.)

66. MACE, WILLIAM H. *Washington, a Virginia Cavalier.* (Chicago, Rand McNally, 1916.)

67. McKAYE, PERCY. *Washington the Man Who Made Us.* (New York, Knopf, 1919.)

68. McMASTER, JOHN B. *History of the People of the United States.* Vols. I, II. (New York, Appleton, 1883-1885.)

69. MARSHALL, JOHN. *Life of George Washington.* 5 vols. (Fredericksburg, Va., 1926; first pub. 1804-1807.)

70. MEADE, WILLIAM. *Old Churches, Ministers, and Families of Virginia.* 2 vols. (Philadelphia, Lippincott, 1857.)

71. MITCHELL, S. WEIR. *Youth of Washington.* (New York, Century, 1904.)

72. MOORE, CHARLES. *Family Life of George Washington.* (Boston, Houghton Mifflin, 1926.)

73. NELSON, WILLIAM. "American Newspapers of the Eighteenth Century as Sources of History." (American Historical Association, *Report for 1908*, Vol. I.)

74. OGG, FREDERIC A. *Opening of the Mississippi.* (New York, Macmillan, 1904.)

75. OSBORN, LUCRETIA P., ed. *Washington Speaks for Himself.* (New York, Scribner, 1927.)

76. PITT, WILLIAM. *Correspondence with Colonial Governors.* Edited by Gertrude S. Kimball. 2 vols. (New York, Macmillan, 1906.)

77. PRUSSING, EUGENE E. *Estate of George Washington, Deceased.* (Boston, Little Brown, 1927.)

78. PRUSSING, EUGENE E. *George Washington in Love and Otherwise.* (Chicago, Covici, 1925.)

79. ROOSEVELT, THEODORE. *Winning of the West.* 4 vols. (New York, Putnam, 1889-1896.)

80. ROWLAND, KATE M. *Life of George Mason.* (New York, Putnam, 1892.)

81. SAWYER, JOSEPH D. *Washington.* 2 vols. (New York, Macmillian, 1927.)

82. SCHAUFFLER, ROBERT H., ed. *Washington's Birthday.* (New York, Moffat Yard, 1910.)

83. SCHLESINGER, ARTHUR M. *Colonial Merchants and the American Revolution.* (New York, Columbia University, 1917.)

84. SEELYE, ELIZABETH. *Story of Washington.* (New York, Appleton, 1893.)

85. SMITH, HELEN E. *Colonial Days and Ways.* (New York, Century, 1900.)

86. SMITH, WILLIAM H. *St. Clair Papers.* 2 vols. (Cincinnati, Clarke, 1882.)

87. SPARKS, JARED. *Life of George Washington.* (Boston, Tappan & Dennet, 1842.)

88. STANARD, MARY N. *Colonial Virginia.* (Philadelphia, Lippincott, 1917.)

89. STRYKER, WILLIAM S. *Battles of Trenton and Princeton.* (Boston, Houghton Mifflin, 1898.)

90. STRYKER, WILLIAM S. *Battle of Monmouth.* (Princeton, Princeton University Press, 1927.)

91. THACHER, JAMES. *Military Journal During the American Revolutionary War.* 2d ed., rev. (Boston, Cotton & Barnard, 1827.)

92. THAYER, WILLIAM R. *George Washington.* (Boston, Houghton Mifflin, 1922.)

93. TOWER, CHARLEMAGNE. *Marquis de La Fayette in the American Revolution.* 2 vols. (Philadelphia, Lippincott, 1895.)

94. TREVELYAN, SIR GEORGE OTTO. *American Revolution.* New ed. 4 vols. (New York, Longmans Green, 1905-1912.)

95. TREVELYAN, SIR GEORGE OTTO. *George the Third and Charles Fox.* 2 vols. (New York, Longmans Green, 1912-1914.)

96. VAN TYNE, CLAUDE H. *Founding of the American Republic.* Vols. I, II. (Boston, Houghton Mifflin, 1922-1929.)

97. VOLWILLER, ALBERT T. *George Croghan and the Westward Movement.* (Cleveland, Clark, 1926.)

98. WASHINGTON, GEORGE. *Diaries.* Edited by John C. Fitzpatrick. 4 vols. (Boston, Houghton Mifflin, 1925.)

99. WASHINGTON, GEORGE. *Rules of Civility.* Edited by Charles Moore. (Boston, Houghton Mifflin, 1926.)

100. WASHINGTON, GEORGE. *Writings.* Edited by Worthington C. Ford. 14 vols. (New York, Putnam, 1889-1893.)

101. WATERS, HENRY F. *Examination of the English Ancestry of George Washington.* (Boston, New England Historic Genealogical Society, 1889.)

102. WHARTON, ANNE H. *Social Life in the Early Republic.* (Philadelphia, Lippincott, 1902.)

103. WHIPPLE, WAYNE, ed. *Story-Life of Washington.* (Philadelphia, Winston, 1911.)

104. WILSON, WOODROW. *George Washington.* (New York, Harper, 1896.)

105. WILSTACH, PAUL. *Mount Vernon.* (Garden City, N. Y., Doubleday Page, 1916.)

106. WINSOR, JUSTIN. *Narrative and Critical History of America.* Vols. VI, VII. (Boston, Houghton Mifflin, 1887-1888.)

107. WISTER, OWEN. *Seven Ages of Washington.* (New York, Macmillan, 1907.)

MEMBERSHIP OF STATE CONTEST COMMITTEE

ALABAMA

Mrs. B. L. Parkinson, Montgomery.
Dr. Danylu Belser, University.
Mrs. Mary Moore McCoy, Alabama College, Montevallo.

ARIZONA

State Commission

Hon. C. O. Case, Secretary, State Supt. of Public Instruction, Phoenix.

College

Dr. Homer L. Shantz, Chairman; President, University of Arizona, Tuscon.

Dr. Harvey L. Taylor, President Gila College, Thatcher.

Mary T. Boyer, Head, Dept. of English, Arizona State Teachers College, Flagstaff.

High School

E. W. Montgomery, Chairman; Principal Phoenix Union High School, Phoenix.

E. Q. Snider, Principal High School, Yuma.

J. E. Carlson, Jr., Superintendent of Schools, Douglas.

Elementary School

Dr. Herman E. Hendrix, Chairman; Superintendent of Schools, Mesa.

Mrs. Laura Hopper, Wall County School Superintendent, Prescott.

George J. Peak, Assistant Superintendent of Schools, Tucson.

Arkansas

Mrs. L. D. Reagan, Chairman, 1921 Schiller Avenue, Little Rock.

Mrs. D. W. Woodhouse, Publicity, 181 Allis Street, Little Rock.

College

Gen. Heber L. McAllister, President, State Teachers College, Conway.

High School

Dr. A. M. Harding, Director Extension Division, State University, Fayetteville.

Mr. Marvin Owens, Supervisor High Schools, Department of Education, Little Rock.

Elementary

Mr. W. F. Hall, Supervisor of Schools, State Department of Education, Little Rock.

Miss Annie Griffey, Assistant Superintendent of Schools, Little Rock.

California

Hon. Vierling Kersey, State Supt. of Public Instruction, Sacramento.

Colorado

Dr. George Willard Frasier, Chairman; President, State Teachers College, Greeley.

Mrs. Lucy Cason Auld, Secretary; Deputy State Supt. Public Instruction, Denver.

Mr. Charles E. Greene, Director of Research, Denver Public Schools, Denver.

Rev. F. Gregory Smith, St. Mary's Church, Littleton.

Connecticut

Mr. Charles M. Larcomb, Supt. of Schools, Bloomfield.

Dr. James McConaughy, President Wesleyan University, Middletown.

Mr. Clarence P. Quimby, Principal South Manchester High School, South Manchester.

Mr. N. H. Batchelder, Principal Loomis Institute, Winsdor.

Miss Elizabeth M. Bennett, Principal Barnard School, South Manchester.

Father Austin Francis Munich, Supt. State Parochial Schools, Hartford.

Delaware

Dr. H. V. Holloway, State Supt. of Public Instruction, Dover.

Florida

Dr. B. C. Riley, Dean of Extension, University of Florida, Gainesville.

Mrs. Ruth L. Riley, University of Florida, Gainesville.

Miss Bernice Ashburn, Instructor in Extra-Mural Activities, University of Florida, Gainesville.

Mr. H. P. Constans, Professor of Speech, University of Florida, Gainesville.

Georgia

Mrs. Julius Talmadge, Athens.

Mrs. Julian McCurry, Athens.

Mrs. Mell Knox, Social Circle.

Mrs. Max Land, 975 Myrtle Street, N. E., Atlanta.

Mrs. M. R. Redwine, Athens.

Idaho

Mr. John I. Hillman, Secretary, State Education Association, Sonna Building, Boise.

Mr. Ray M. Berry, Blackfoot.

Mr. W. E. Goodsell, Meridian.

Mr. Irl Roper, Roberts.

Miss Isabelle Lindsey, District No. 1, Kellogg.

Miss Lola Berry, District No. 2, Lewiston.

Mr. Aldyne Breneman, District No. 3, Emmett.

Mr. John F. Estes, District No. 4, 130 10th Avenue, E., Twin Falls.

Mr. George A. Pearson, District No. 6, Route No. 3, Rexburg.

Illinois

Mr. Francis G. Blair, State Supt. of Public Instruction, Springfield.

Mr. William J. Bogan, Supt. of Schools, 460 S. State Street, Chicago.

Mrs. William J. Sweeney, Rock Island.

Mrs. Thomas J. Dixon, Oak Park.

Miss Bertha Provine, Taylorville.

Dr. William Hudson, President, Blackburn College, Carlinville.

Mr. Edward J. Tobin, County Supt. of Schools, 1122 Court House, Chicago.

Judge Ross C. Hall, 120 S. LaSalle Street, Chicago.

Mr. Paul N. Angle, Monmouth.

Mrs. Eli Dixon, Roseville.

Mr. Walter Dill Scott, President, Northwestern University, Evanston.

Mr. Robert M. Hutchins, President, University of Chicago, Chicago.

Dr. Harry W. Chase, President, University of Illinois, Urbana.

Miss Evangeline C. Hursen, 19 South LaSalle Street, Chicago.

Mrs. Maude Maury Laurence, 935 N. Academy Street, Galesburg.

INDIANA

Mr. Paul C. Stetson, Supt. of City Schools, 150 North Meridian Street, Indianapolis.

Mr. William N. Otto, Shortridge High School, Indianapolis.

Mr. Grover Van Duyn, State Department of Education, Indianapolis.

Miss Winifred Ray, President, Indiana Teachers of Speech, Wiley High School, Terre Haute.

Mr. Raymond H. Myers, Coach of Oratory and Debate, Bloomington High School, Bloomington.

Mr. Darrell Gooch, Coach of Oratory and Debate, Lebanon High School, Lebanon.

IOWA

Mr. K. D. Miller, Supt. Fort Dodge Public Schools, Fort Dodge.

Mr. W. S. Miller, Supt. Reinbeck Public Schools, Reinbeck.

Miss Edna Gibbs, Supt. Adair County Schools, Greenfield.

Superintendent Clark Brown, Clinton Public Schools, Clinton.

Miss Lucy Hobbs, Head, Dept. of English, Sioux City High School, Sioux City.

Professor L. B. Schmidt, Iowa State College, Ames.

KANSAS

College

W. A. Lewis, President, Fort Hays College, Hays.

High School

Supt. M. E. Pearson, Kansas City.

Supt. Neal W. Wherry, Holton.

Supt. W. L. Rambo, Paola.

Supt. Clyde O. Davidson, Columbus.

Supt. Charles A. Hall, Marion.

Supt. J. J. Yoder, Marysville.

Supt. J. S. Morrel, Beloit.

Supt. W. M. Richards, Dodge City.

Supt. W. R. Potwin, McPhearson.

Elementary School

†Mr. George A. Allen, Jr., State Supt. of Public Instruction, Topeka.

KENTUCKY

Dr. Wellington Patrick, Director of Extension, University of Kentucky, Lexington.

Dean William S. Taylor, Dept. of Education, University of Kentucky, Lexington.

Mr. James H. Richmond, State Supt. of Public Instruction, Frankfort.

LOUISIANA

Mr. W. A. Sisemore, Assistant State High School Supervisor, Dept. of Education, Baton Rouge.

* Chairman of State George Washington Bicentennial Commission.
† Deceased.

Mrs. George P. Meade, Gramercy.

Mrs. Richard K. Boney, Tallulah.

Miss Mary Mims, Baton Rouge.

Dr. W. W. Tison, President, State Normal College, Natchitoches.

MAINE

*Hon. Clarence C. Stetson, Bangor.

MARYLAND

*†DeCourcy W. Thom, Maryland Trust Building, Baltimore.

MASSACHUSETTS

Prof. Walter J. Campbell, Springfield.

Mrs. Carl L. Schrader, Belmont.

Mr. Alexander Brin, 251 Causeway St., Boston.

MICHIGAN

*Dr. Randolph G. Adams, University of Michigan, Ann Arbor.

MINNESOTA

Mr. Ross N. Young, Marshall High School, Minneapolis.

MISSISSIPPI

Mrs. R. C. Gaddis, Laurel.

Mrs. Frank Gowdy, Meridian.

Mrs. Calvin Brown, Oxford.

Mrs. Bailey Schumpert, West Point.

Miss Marion McNair, Jackson.

Mrs. R. N. Somerville, Cleveland.

Mrs. Roy Andre, Gulfport.

Mrs. W. T. Johnson, Grenwood.

MISSOURI

College

Prof. Wilbur E. Gilman, University of Missouri, Columbia.

Dr. E. L. Hendricks, President, Missouri State Teachers College, Warrensburg.

Sister Marietta, St. Teresa Junior College, Kansas City.

High School

Supt. W. S. Smith, Excelsior Springs.

Miss Jessie Via, Rolla.

Sister M. Loretta, Rosati-Kain, St. Louis.

Elementary School

Mrs. Effie I. Bess, West Plains.

Professor C. F. Scotten, Sedalia.

MONTANA

Miss Elizabeth Ireland, State Supt. of Public Instruction, Helena.

Dr. Melvin A. Brannon, Chancellor of the University of Montana, Helena.

Mr. Norbert C. Hoff, President Mount St. Charles College, Helena.

Mr. M. P. Moe, Montana High School Supervisor, Helena.

Miss Regina Kohten, Rural School Supervisor, Helena.

Mr. R. J. Cunningham, Secretary, Montana Education Association, Helena.

Nebraska

*Hon. Charles W. Bryan, Governor of State of Nebraska, Lincoln.

Nevada

Hon. Walter E. Clark, President, University of Nevada, Reno.

Supt. B. D. Billinghurst, City Supt. of Reno Public Schools, Reno.

Mr. Charles W. Priest, Supt. City Schools, Carson City.

New Hampshire

Mr. Walter M. May, Deputy State Commissioner of Education, Concord.

Professor Harlan M. Bisbee, University of New Hampshire, Durham.

Mrs. Eulelah Blodgett, Elementary School Teacher, Hanover.

Mr. Edwin S. Huse, Keene Normal School, Keene.

Miss Katherine McLaughlin, Elementary School Principal, Laconia.

Mr. Leonard S. Morrison, Superintendent of Schools, Whitefield.

Mr. William Y. Morrison, Headmaster, Central High School, Manchester.

Mr. Clarence C. Sanborn, Headmaster, High School, Portsmouth.

New Jersey

Mr. Harold White, Deputy State Commissioner of Education, Trenton,

New Mexico

Mrs. Georgia L. Lusk, State Supt. of Public Instruction, State House, Santa Fe.

Chief Justice H. L. Bickley, Supreme Court, Santa Fe.

Mrs. David Chavez, Regent, Santa Fe Chapter, D. A. R., Santa Fe.

Miss Isabel L. Eckles, City Supt. of Schools, Santa Fe.

Mr. George I. Sanchez, Santa Fe.

Mr. E. Dana Johnson, Santa Fe.

New York

Miss Harriet Mills, State Capitol, Albany.

North Carolina

Hon. A . T. Allen, State Supt. of Public Instruction, Raleigh.

Mr. Tyree C. Taylor, Raleigh.

Mrs. O. Max Gardner, Raleigh.

Mrs. Alfred W. Williams, Raleigh.

Hon. Fred Morrison, Raleigh.

Mrs. Frank Johnson, Statesville,

---

* Chairman of State George Washington Bicentennial Commission.

Mrs. Hugh Perry, Louisburg.

Mr. Cale Burgess, Raleigh.

North Dakota

Miss Beatrice Johnstone, Extension Division, University Station, Grand Forks.

Miss Lillian E. Cook, Director and Librarian, State Library Commission, Bismarck.

Mr. Clarence Robertson, Supt. of City Schools, Jamestown.

Mr. John A. Page, State High School Inspector, Bismarck.

Mr. H. K. Jensen, County Supt., Morton County, Mandan.

Ohio

Hon. B. O. Skinner, Director of Education, Columbus.

Mr. C. D. Everett, Principal, North High School, Columbus.

Mr. E. L. Porter, Columbus.

Mr. F. E. Reynolds, Secretary, Ohio Education Association, Columbus.

Mr. Roy Reichelderfer, Ohio School of the Air, Columbus.

Mr. E. R. Wood, Chairman Scholarship Tests, Columbus.

Oklahoma

Liaison Member

Mr. J. A. Holley, State Capitol of Oklahoma City, Oklahoma City.

College

Mr. Ned Shepler, President of State Press, Lawton.

High School

Mr. T. M. Beaird, University of Oklahoma, Norman.

Elementary School

Mr. W. E. Wrinkle, El Reno.

Oregon

Hon. C. A. Howard, State Supt. of Public Instruction, Salem.

Dr. Carl C. Doney, President, Williamette University, Salem.

Dr. John B. Horner, Corvallis.

Pennsylvania

*Hon. Thadeus S. Krause, 1420 Chestnut Street, Philadelphia.

Rhode Island

*Governor Norman S. Case, Providence.

South Carolina

Mr. Henry O. Strohecker, 9-A Rutledge Avenue, Charleston.

South Dakota

General Education Committee

Mr. Alvin Waggoner, Chairman, President, State Board of Regents, Philip.

Mr. E. C. Giffin, State Supt. of Public Instruction, Pierre.

Mr. N. E. Steele, Ex. Secy. South Dakota Education Association, Sioux Falls.

College

Dr. Herman G. James, President, University of South Dakota, Vermillion.

Dr. C. W. Pugsley, President, State College of Agriculture and Mechanics Arts, Brookings.

Dr. C. C. O'Hara, President, State School of Mines, Rapid City.

Dr. Earl A. Roadman, President, Dakota Wesleyan University, Mitchell.

High Schools

Mr. W. I. Early, Prin. High School, Sioux Falls.

Mr. G. G. Warner, Pres. South Dakota Press Association, Gregory.

Mr. R. V. Hunkins, Supt. City Schools, Lead.

Mrs. Gertrude Flyte, Secy. South Dakota P. T. A., Gann Valley.

Grade School

Dr. C. G. Lundquist, Pres. S. D. School Officers Assn., Leola.

Mr. D. C. Mills, Secy. Young Citizens League, Pierre.

Mrs. Myrtis Gruhn, County Superintendent of Schools, Aberdeen.

Adah Minard, Teacher, City Schools, Watertown.

TENNESSEE

Mr. H. F. Srygley, Supt. of City Schools, Nashville.

Mrs. Benton McMillin, Richland Avenue, Nashville.

Professor A. M. Harris, Vanderbilt University, Nashville.

Mrs. Willard Steele, State Regent D. A. R., Chattanooga.

Mr. C. E. Rogers, Supt. of City Schools, Johnson City.

Mrs. Eldran Rogers, State Pres. P. T. A., Memphis.

Prof. J. W. Brister, State Teachers College, Memphis.

TEXAS

Mr. John E. Rosser, 707 Browder Street, Dallas.

College

Dr. S. H. Whitley, President, East Texas State Teachers College, Commerce.

High School

Mr. R. L. Paschal, Principal Central High School, Fort Worth.

Elementary School

Miss Gladys Little, Second Assistant State Supt. of Public Instruction, Austin.

UTAH

Hon. C. N. Jensen, State Supt. of Public Instruction, Salt Lake City.

Dr. George Thomas, President, University of Utah, Salt Lake City.

Dr. E. G. Peterson, President, Agricultural College of Utah, Logan.

Mr. Mosiah Hall, Supt. of Rehabilitation, Salt Lake City.

Mr. S. B. Neff, Head, Dept. of English, University of Utah, Salt Lake City.

Prof. N. A. Pedersen, Prof. English and Speech, Utah State Agricultural College, Logan.

Mr. E. E. Greenwood, President Utah Education Assn., Midvale.

VERMONT

†Professor Walter H. Crockett, Burlington.

Professor Arthur W. Peach, Northfield.

Professor F. W. Tupper, Burlington.

Mr. Walter J. Coates, North Montpelier.

Mrs. Oscar H. Rixford, East Highgate.

Mrs. Caleb Lamson, Brattleboro.

Mrs. Abner V. Freer, Brandon.

Mrs. Julius Wilcox, Rutland.

Mrs. Guy B. Horton, Montpelier.

Mrs. F. B. Welling, Jr., North Bennington.

VIRGINIA

Dr. Francis P. Gaines, President, Washington & Lee University, Lexington.

Dr. J. A. C. Chandler, President, William & Mary College, Williamsburg.

Dr. Charles G. Maphis, Dean, University of Virginia, Charlottesville.

Dr. J. D. Eggleston, President, Hampden Sydney College, Hampden Sydney.

Dr. Sydney B. Hall, State Supt. of Public Instruction, Richmond.

Hon. Robert Gilliam, Jr., Petersburg.

High School

Mr. Charles H. Kauffman, Secy. Virginia High School League, University of Virginia, Charlottesville.

Elementary School

Mr. J. H. Montgomery, Executive Director, Virginia Cooperative Education Assn., Grace-American Bldg., Richmond.

WASHINGTON

Mr. Walter F. Meier, Northern Life Tower Building, Seattle.

WEST VIRGINIA

Prof. Wilbur Jones Kay, Dept. of Public Speaking, West Virginia University, Morgantown.

Miss Myra Neffen, State Supervisor Rural Schools, Charleston.

Mr. Dan H. Perdue, State Supervisor High Schools, Charleston.

Miss Rose McGraw, Washington, D. C.

WISCONSIN

* Senator Walter H. Hunt, River Falls.

---

* Chairman of State George Washington Bicentennial Commission.

† Deceased.

WYOMING

    Mrs. Katharine A. Morton, State Supt. of Public Instruction, Cheyenne.

    Mr. Thomas E. Kuiper, Buffalo.

    Mr. Raymond H. White, Douglas.

    Mr. A. H. Dixon, Torrington.

    Mr. E. D. Bloom, Kemmerer.

    Mr. O. L. Liming, Basin.

ALASKA

    Mr. W. K. Keller, Territorial Commissioner of Education, Juneau.

    Hon. Luther C. Hess, Fairbanks.

    Hon. Grover C. Winn, Juneau.

    Mr. John H. Dunn, Juneau.

    Mr. Thos. D. Jensen, Nome.

    Mr. B. H. Barndollar, Anchorage.

    Mr. J. D. Harlan, Fairbanks.

DISTRICT OF COLUMBIA

    Mr. Isaac Gans, 7th and Pennsylvania Ave., N. W., Washington.

    Mr. J. Leo Kolb, 1237 Wisconsin Avenue, N. W., Washington.

    Mr. Douglas Bement, Asst. Professor of English, George Washington University, Washington.

    Dr. George F. Bowerman, Chief Librarian, Public Library, Washington.

Selections Relating to George Washington

for

Declamatory Contests

in the

Elementary Schools

Compiled by

HAZEL B. NIELSON

Director of Educational Activities

Preface

—

THIS pamphlet, SELECTIONS RELATING TO GEORGE WASHINGTON FOR DECLAMATORY CONTESTS IN THE ELEMENTARY SCHOOLS, contains selections of prose and poetry suitable for the Declamatory Contests in the elementary grades of the public, private, and parochial schools. This material is divided into four groups, arranged according to grades.

The general regulations which governed the Declamatory Contest are included. This contest terminated with a state contest, the organization of which was left to the State Contest Committee, appointed by the State George Washington Bicentennial Commission.

It is a pleasure to acknowledge the kindness of those who responded to requests for choice selections of prose and poetry relating to George Washington. The selections for this pamphlet have been chosen from those submitted by educators from many states, as the best type of literature to be used in a Declamatory Contest to impress upon the minds of the youth the citizenship of George Washington. Two hundred years have not dimmed his glory. This varied collection affords an opportunity of enriching the memory with the true character and worth of the Father of Our Country.

Grateful acknowledgments are made to the following publishers and authors for the poems here represented:—D. Appleton & Company—William Cullen Bryant, *The Twenty-Second of February;* T. S. Denison & Company—Collection from Marie Irish; E. P. Dutton & Co., Inc.—Eliza W. Durbin, *Our Washington;* Houghton Mifflin Company—Oliver Wendell Holmes, *Ode For Washington's Birthday*—James Russell Lowell (extract from *Under the Old Elm*)—John Greenleaf Whittier, *The Vow of Washington;* Lothrop, Lee & Shephard Co.—Sam Walter Foss, *I'm the Little Red Stamp;* Harriet Monroe—*Washington;* The Overland Monthly—John A. Prentice, *Washington;* Mr. George M. Sangster—Margaret E. Sangster, *Washington's Birthday;* Child Life—Nancy Byrd Turner, *Washington;* Youth's Companion—Hezekiah Butterworth, *Crown Our Washington.*

State Contest Committee

Appointment

Made by each State George Washington Bicentennial Commission.

Purpose

To organize and conduct the series of contests—declamatory, essay, and oratorical—in each state.

To serve as medium of contact between the United States George Washington Bicentennial Commission and the schools.

To secure cooperation of organizations interested in school contests and avoid duplication of effort.

Steps in Organization of Contests within State

Conducted by State Contest Committee.

Division of state for elimination contests.

Arrangement of time for elimination contests.

The United States George Washington Bicentennial Commission suggests that all local elimination contests be held in a school or community prior to February 22, 1932.

Selection of Jury of Awards within state.

Give special attention to selection of competent judges. **The** presiding officers and judges in any contest should be disinterested persons.

Determine order of speaking in Declamatory and Oratorical Contests by lot.

Mark on the scale of ten, using low-point-total system **in** judging.

Selection of State Awards.

United States George Washington Bicentennial Commission presents the official George Washington Commemorative **Medal** to the state winners in the three state contests—Declamatory, Essay, and Oratorical.

Note explanation regarding awards under Types of **Contests.** Other awards within states to be chosen and provided by **state** and local committees.

Type and Scope of the Nation-Wide Series of Educational Contests

The Series of Contests will include the following divisions:

Declamatory contests in elementary schools

Essay contests in high schools

Oratorical contests in institutions of higher learning

These contests are open to bona fide students of all public, private, and parochial schools.

Every student entering a contest must register in accordance with regulations furnished by the State Contest Committee.

Closing date of entry determined by State Contest Committee.

Schools participating are expected to meet the expenses of their contestants.

Declamatory Contest in Elementary Schools

The United States George Washington Bicentennial Commission has prepared this pamphlet containing selections of prose and poetry relating to George Washington. The contestants in the Declamatory contest must choose their selection from this pamphlet, which will be distributed to the teachers of the schools where students enroll in the Declamatory contest.

The Declamatory contest will include a local, district, and a state

contest. All local and district elimination contests, as well as state contests, shall be held according to regulations and organization **of** state determined by State Contest Committee.

Open to all grades, grouped as follows:

(1) Grades 1 and 2
(2) Grades 3 and 4
(3) Grades 5 and 6
(4) Grades 7 and 8

The extent of the contest for students of grades 1, 2, 3, and 4 will be determined by the superintendents and teachers.

District contests for grades 5 and 6.

State contests for grades 7 and 8.

Speaker marked upon three points: delivery, voice and **gestures,** and interpretation.

The United States George Washington Bicentennial Commission will award the official George Washington Commemorative Medal in silver to the student winning the state declamatory contest; **to** the winner of second place the official medal in bronze, and **to the** student in third place a certificate of award.

Early Celebrations of George Washington's Birthday

Tuesday, February 22, 1791

At Philadelphia: "*February* 23.—Yesterday being the Anniversary of the Birth-Day of THE PRESIDENT OF THE UNITED STATES, when he attained to the 59th year of his age—the same was celebrated here with every demonstration of public joy. The Artillery and Light-Infantry corps of the city were paraded, and at 12 O'clock a federal Salute was fired. The congratulatory

Compliments of the Members of the Legislatures of the Union—the Heads of the Departments of State—Foreign Ministers—**Officers,** civil and military of the State—the Reverend Clergy—and **Strangers** and Citizens of distinction, were presented to the President on **this** auspicious occasion."—*Gazette of the United States.*

Wednesday, February 22, 1792

At Philadelphia: "*February* 23.—Yesterday both Houses of Congress walked in Procession to wait on the President of the United States to congratulate him on the anniversary of his Birth Day. . . . The officers of the militia of the City, Liberties and Districts of

Philadelphia paid their respects in a body and there was also a military parade, with firing of guns and ringing of bells."

—*Dunlap's American Daily Advertiser.*

Selections For Group I

(*Grades 1 and 2*)

LAND OF WASHINGTON

My country is America, my flag red, white,
    and blue,
And to the land of Washington I ever will
    be true,
So wave the flag and wave again
And give three loud hurrahs
For our beloved America and for the stripes
    and stars.

           ·Anonymous.

OUR VERY BEST

To be *as great* as Washington,
We could not if we would,
And so we have made up our minds,
To try to be as good.

           · ·Anonymous.

A YOUNG PATRIOT

I'm just a very little boy:
    I never fired a gun,
I never lead an army,
    Like brave George Washington.
And though like him I may not fight
    To set a people free,
I'll try to be as brave and true,
    As kind and good as he.

           Alice Jean Cleator.

TO WASHINGTON

The flag of Washington
    Is the flag for me,
And to its stars and stripes
    I'll ever loyal be.

Today the flag we raise
    In honor of the name
Of our dear Washington,
    And his undying fame.

        Collection of Marie Irish.

SO SHALL I

Washington loved his flag,
    And so do I;
I'm happy when I see
    Its colors fly.

Washington stood by this flag,
    And so shall I;
I will guard it that disaster
    Shall not come nigh.

Washington honored this flag,
    And so shall I;
I'll strive to make it the greatest
    Beneath the sky.

        Collection of Marie Irish.

WASHINGTON'S SUCCESS

Washington when but a youth
From duties did not shirk,
But at whatever task he met
He diligently went to work.

        * * *

He did not wait with yearning
For a soft and easy snap,
Nor sigh with vain impatience
For a place in Fortune's lap.

      · Collection of Marie Irish.

WASHINGTON'S BIRTHDAY

'Tis splendid to live so grandly
    That, long after you are gone,
The things you did are remembered,
    And recounted under the sun;
To live so bravely and purely
    That a nation stops on its way,
And once a year, with banner and drum,
    Keeps its thought of your natal day.

        Margaret E. Sangster.

RULES OF CIVILITY AND DECENT BEHAVIOR

When George Washington was a young boy he studied rules of behavior. I have learned four of his rules.

Rule 1: Every Action done in Company, ought to be with Some Sign of Respect, to those that are Present.

Rule 4: In the Presence of Others Sing not to yourself with a humming Noise, nor Drum with your Fingers or Feet.

Rule 6: Sleep not when others Speak, Sit not when others stand, Speak not when you Should hold your Peace, walk not on when others Stop.

Rule 8: At Play and at Fire its Good Manners to Give Place to the last Commer, and affect not to Speak Louder than Ordinary.

Rule 22: Shew not yourself glad at the Misfortune of another though he were your enemy.

Rule 65: Speak not injurious Words neither in Jest nor Earnest Scoff at none although they give Occasion.

Rule 73: Think before you Speak pronounce not imperfectly nor bring out your Words too hastily but orderly & distinctly.

Rule 77: Treat with men at fit Times about Business & Whisper not in the Company of Others.

Rule 82: Undertake not what you cannot Perform but be Careful to keep your Promise.

Rule 84: When your Superiors talk to any Body hearken not neither Speak nor Laugh.

Rule 89: Speak not Evil of the absent for it is unjust.

WASHINGTON FAMILY

Selections For Group II

(Grades 3 and 4)

I'M THE LITTLE RED STAMP

I'm the little red stamp with George Washington's picture;
    And I go wherever I may,
To any spot in George Washington's land;
    And I go by the shortest way.
And the guns of wrath would clear my path,
    A thousand guns at need,
Of the hands that should dare to block my course,
    Or slacken my onward speed.

Stand back! Hands off of Uncle Sam's mail!
    Stand back there! Back! I say;
For the little red stamp with George Washington's picture
    Must have the right of way.

Sam Walter Foss.

WASHINGTON

No heroes of the ancient time
    With Washington compare,
No statesman of the days of yore
    Displayed such wisdom rare.

* * *

May this great land of ours be true
    To what he said and taught,
And keep his words in memory fresh
    With rarest wisdom fraught.

To patriots all his honored name
    An heirloom has become—
A beacon light to all who seek
    True freedom's peaceful home.

A star of hope in peace and war
    Will be our Washington,
To those who guide the Ship of State
    With favoring gales to run.

* * *

The friends of freedom everywhere,
    In this broad land we tread,
Agree to honor Washington—
    His fame still wider spread.

At each recurrence of the day,
    With joy we'll celebrate
The praises of our foremost man,
    Our chieftain, wise and great.

Thomas M. Menihan.

WASHINGTON

Hail, patriot chief, all hail: Historic Fame
In purest gold hath traced thy glorious name!
Earth has Niagara, the sky its sun,
And proud mankind its only Washington.

He lives! ever lives in the hearts of the free;
The wing of his fame spreads across the broad sea;
He lives where the banner of freedom's unfurled,
The pride of his country, the wealth of the world.

The character of Washington—in war, in peace, and in private life, the most sublime on historical record.

William H. Prescott.

WASHINGTON'S BIRTHDAY

'Tis splendid to live so grandly
    That, long after you are gone,
The things you did are remembered,
    And recounted under the sun;
To live so bravely and purely
    That a nation stops on its way,
And once a year, with banner and drum,
    Keeps its thought of your natal day.

'Tis splendid to have a record
    So white and free from stain
That, held to the light, it shows no blot,
    Though tested and tried amain;
That age to age forever
    Repeats its story of love,
And your birthday lives in a nation's heart
    All other days above.

Margaret E. Sangster.

WASHINGTON

He played by the river when he was young,
He raced with rabbits along the hills,
He fished for minnows, and climbed and swung,
And hooted back at the whippoorwills.
Strong and slender and tall he grew
And then, one morning, the bugles blew.

Over the hills, the summons came,
Over the river's shining rim.
He said that the bugles called his name,
He knew that his country needed him,
And he answered, "Coming!" and marched away
For many a night and many a day.

Perhaps when the marches were hot and long
He'd think of the river flowing by,
Or, camping under the winter sky,
Would hear the whippoorwill's far-off song.
Boy and soldier, in peace or strife,
He loved America all his life!

- Nancy Byrd Turner.

RULES OF CIVILITY AND DECENT BEHAVIOR

George Washington copied 110 rules on conduct in an exercise book. Washington lived up to these rules. They should be studied by all boys and girls who want to be polite, kind, just, and loyal as Washington. I have studied many of them, but will recite six.

Rule 5: If you Cough, Sneeze, Sigh, or Yawn, do it not Loud but Privately; and Speak not in your Yawning, but put Your handkerchief or Hand before your face and turn aside.

Rule 14: Turn not your Back to others especially in Speaking, Jog not the Table or Desk on which Another reads or writes, lean not upon any one.

Rule 28: If any one come to Speak to you while you are Sitting Stand up tho he be your Inferior, and when you Present Seats let it be to every one according to his Degree.

Rule 29: When you meet with one of Greater Quality than yourself, Stop, and retire especially if it be at a Door or any Straight place to give way for him to Pass.

Rule 35: Let your Discourse with Men of Business be Short and Comprehensive.

Rule 39: In writing or Speaking, give to every Person his due Title According to his Degree & the Custom of the Place.

Rule 40: Strive not with your Superiers in argument, but always Submit your Judgment to others with Modesty.

Rule 50: Be not hasty to believe flying Reports to the Disparagement of any.

Rule 54: Play not the Peacock, looking every where about you, to See if you be well Deck't, if your Shoes fit well if your Stockings Sit neatly, and Cloths handsomely.

Rule 81: Be not Curious to Know the Affairs of Others neither approach those that Speak in Private.

Rule 108: When you Speak of God or his Atributes, let it be Seriously & [with] Reverence. Honour & Obey your Natural parents altho they be Poor.

Selections For Group III

(Grades 5 and 6)

WASHINGTON,
The Brave—the Wise—the Good;

WASHINGTON,
Supreme in War, in Council, and in Peace:

WASHINGTON,

Valiant	Discreet	Confident
without	without	without
Ambition;	Fear;	Presumption:

WASHINGTON,
In Disaster, Calm; in Success, Moderate; in All, Himself:

WASHINGTON,
The Hero, the Patriot, the Christian,
The Father of Nations, the Friend of Mankind;
who,
When he had won All, Renounced All;
and sought,
In the Bosom of his Family and of Nature,
Retirement;
And in the Hope of Religion,
Immortality.

Inscription at Mount Vernon written and left by Dr. Andrew Reed, an English
Philanthropist, in 1833.

WASHINGTON'S BIRTHDAY

All honor to that day which long ago
Gave birth to him who Freedom's cause
    espoused;
Who, by his ardor in the sacred fight,
The fire and strength of patriots aroused;
Who knew no master, save that One divine
Whose strength was his, who knew no fear,
    save one—
The fear of doing wrong! All hail the day
That gave to Freedom's cause George Wash-
    ington.

Years come and go, and generations fall
Into the dust. The world its heroes gives.
They step upon the stage, then pass away
And are no more, but Freedom ever lives.
And while it lives, and while its banner
    bright
Is upward flung into the golden sun,
Within the heart of every freeman's child
Will live that honored name, George Wash-
    ington.

Then honor to the day that gave him birth,
For it is also Freedom's natal day.
Let all who worship Freedom's cause stand
    forth
And to his memory their homage pay.
And let each loyal son the work take up—
For, know ye, Freedom's work is never
    done—
And greater, grander, build the edifice
Begun so long ago by Washington.
                    Arthur J. Burdick.

MOUNT VERNON, THE HOME OF WASHINGTON

There dwelt the Man, the flower of human
    kind,
Whose visage mild bespoke his nobler mind.

There dwelt the Soldier, who his sword ne'er
    drew
But in a righteous cause, to Freedom true.

There dwelt the Hero, who ne'er killed for
    fame,
Yet gained more glory than a Caesar's name.

There dwelt the Statesman, who, devoid of
    art,
Gave soundest counsels from an upright
    heart;

And, O Columbia, by thy sons caressed,
There dwelt the Father of the realms he
    blessed;

Who no wish felt to make his mighty praise,
Like other chiefs, the means himself to raise;

But there retiring, breathed in pure renown,
And felt a grandeur that disdained a crown.
                    William Day.

OUR WASHINGTON

O Son of Virginia, thy mem'ry divine
Forever will halo this country of thine.
Not hero alone in the battles' wild strife,
But hero in ev'ry detail of thy life.

So noble, unselfish, heroic, and true,
A God-given gift to thy country were you;
And lovingly, tenderly guarding thy shrine,
Columbia points proudly, and says: "He is
    mine."

Thy courage upheld us, thy judgment sus-
    tained,
Thy spirit stood proof when discouragement
    reigned,
Thy justice unerring all bias withstood,
Thy thought never self, but thy loved
    country's good.
And thy country will never, till time is no
    more,
Cease to cherish the sleeper on yon river's
    shore;
And every fair daughter and ev'ry brave son
She will tell of the greatness of her Wash-
    ington.

O hero immortal! O spirit divine!
What glory eternal, what homage is thine!
Forever increasing will be thy renown,
With the stars of Columbia that gleam in
    thy crown.
The God who guards liberty gave thee to
    earth,
Forever we'll honor thy heaven-sent birth.
E'en heaven itself has one gladness the more,
That our hands shall clasp thine on eternity's
    shore.

Then sleep, sweetly sleep, by the river's calm
    run;
Thy fame will live on in the land thou hast
    won;

To Potomac's soft music then slumber
    serene,
The spirit of freedom will keep the spot
    green;
And so long as time echoes the hour of thy
    birth,
We will pay loving tribute and praise to thy
    worth,
And pledge to keep spotless the freedom
    you gave,
And the land that is hallowed by Washing-
    ton's grave.

Eliza W. Durbin.

THE GLORY OF WASHINGTON

To Americans the name of Washington will be forever dear,—a savor of sweet incense, descending to every succeeding generation. The things which he has done are too great, too interesting, ever to be forgotten. Every object which we see, every employment in which we are engaged, every comfort which we enjoy, remind us daily of his character.

Every ship bears the fruit of his labors on its wings and exultingly spreads its streamers to his honor. The student meets him in the still and peaceful walk; the traveler sees him in all the smiling and prosperous scenes of his journey; and our whole country, in her thrift, order, safety, and morals, bears inscribed in sunbeams, on all her hills and plains, the name and glory of Washington.

Timothy Dwight.

WASHINGTON'S BIRTHDAY EVER HONORED

Welcome, thou festal morn!
Never be passed in scorn
    Thy rising sun,
Thou day forever bright
With Freedom's holy light,
That gave the world the sight
    Of Washington.

Unshaken 'mid the storm,
Behold that noble form—
    That peerless one—
With his protecting hand,
Like Freedom's angel, stand,
The guardian of our land,
    Our Washington.

Traced there in lines of light,
Where all pure rays unite,
    Obscured by none;
Brightest on history's page,
Of any clime or age,
As chieftain, man, and sage,
    Stands Washington.

Name at which tyrants pale,
And their proud legions quail,
    Their boasting done,
While Freedom lifts her head
No longer filled with dread,
Her sons to victory led
    By Washington.

Now the true patriots see,
The foremost of the free,
    The victory won,
In Freedom's presence bow,
While Sweetly smiling now
She wreathes the spotless brow
    Of Washington.

Then, with each coming year,
Wherever shall appear
    That natal sun,
Will we attest the worth
Of one true man to earth,
And celebrate the birth
    Of Washington.

George Howland.

TO THE MEMORY OF WASHINGTON

Our Washington is no more! The Hero, the Sage and the Patriot of America—the man on whom in times of danger, every eye was turned, and all hopes were placed—lives now, only in his own great actions, and in the hearts of an affectionate and afflicted people. . . .

More than any other individual, and as much as to one individual was possible, has he contributed to found this our wide spreading empire, and to give to the western world its independence and its freedom. . . .

Having effected the great object for which he was placed at the head of our armies, we have seen him convert the sword into the plowshare, and voluntarily sinking the soldier in the citizen. . . .

We have seen him once more quit the retirement he loved, and in a season more stormy and tempestuous than war itself, with calm and wise determination, pursue the true interests of the nation and contribute, more than any other could contribute, to the establishment of that system of policy which will, I trust, yet preserve our peace, our honour and our independence.

Representative John Marshall—Remarks introducing Resolutions to the Memory of Washington in the House of Representatives, December 19, 1799.

LETTER IN MEMORY OF GEORGE WASHINGTON

With patriotic pride, we review the life of our Washington, and compare him with those of other countries who have been preeminent in fame. Ancient and modern names are diminished before him. Greatness and guilt have too often been allied; but his fame is whiter than it is brilliant. The destroyers of nations stood abashed at the majesty of his virtue. It reproved the intemperance of their ambition, and darkened the splendor of victory. . . . Let his country-men consecrate the memory of the heroic General, the patriotic Statesman, and the virtuous Sage; let them teach their children

never to forget that the fruit of his labours and his example, are their inheritance.

Senate of the United States—Letter Addressed to President Adams, December 23, 1799.

RULES OF CIVILITY AND DECENT BEHAVIOR

In the Library of Congress at Washington is preserved the school exercise book of George Washington in which he copied 110 Rules of Civility and Behavior before he was sixteen years old. These rules had an influence upon the conduct of George Washington. The rules are plain, sensible facts which we should know and live up to in our every day life. Our class has studied them and I have chosen seven.

Rule 41: Undertake not to Teach your equal in the art himself Proffesses; it Savours of arrogancy.

Rule 44: When a man does all he can though it Succeeds not well blame not him that did it.

Rule 48: Wherein you reprove Another be unblameable yourself; for example is more prevalent than Precepts.

Rule 49: Use no Reproachful Language against any one neither Curse nor Revile.

Rule 56: Associate yourself with Men of good Quality if you Esteem your own Reputation; for 'tis better to be alone than in bad Company.

Rule 68: Go not thither, where you know not, whether you Shall be Welcome or not. Give not Advice whth [without] being Ask'd & when desired [d]o it briefly.

Rule 74: When Another Speaks be attentive your Self and disturb not the Audience if any hesitate in his Words help him not nor Prompt him without desired, Interrupt him not, nor Answer him till his Speec[h] be ended.

Rule 79: Be not apt to relate News if you know not the truth thereof. In Discoursing of things you Have heard Name not your Author always A [Se]cret Discover not.

Rule 86: In Disputes, be not So Desireous to Overcome as not to give Liberty to each one to deliver his Opinion and Submit to yᵉ. Judgment of yᵉ. Major Part especially if they are Judges of the Dispute.

Rule 88: Be not tedious in Discourse, make not many Digressions, nor rep[eat] often the Same manner of Discourse.

Rule 109: Let your Recreations be Manfull not Sinfull.

Rule 110: Labour to keep alive in your Breast that Little Spark of Ce[les]tial fire Called Conscience.

LETTER BY GENERAL GEORGE WASHINGTON

Addressed to the Governors of All the States at the End of the War

(Extract)

I now make it my earnest prayer, that God would have you, and the State over which you preside, in his holy protection; that he would incline the hearts of the citizens to cultivate a spirit of subordination and obedience to government; to entertain a brotherly affection and love for one another, for their fellow citizens of the United States at large, and particularly for their brethren who have served in the field; and finally, that he would most graciously be pleased to dispose us all to do justice, to love mercy, and to demean ourselves with that charity, humility, and pacific temper of mind, which were the characteristics of the Divine Author of our blessed religion, and without an humble imitation of whose example in these things, we can never hope to be a happy nation.

FAREWELL ADDRESS

To the People of the United States by President George Washington—1796

(Extract)

Observe good faith and justice towards all Nations. Cultivate peace and harmony with all.—Religion and Morality enjoin this conduct; and can it be that good policy does not equally enjoin it?—It will be worthy of a free, enlightened, and, at no distant period, a great nation, to give to mankind the magnanimous and too novel example of a People always guided by an exalted justice and benevolence.—Who can doubt that in the course of time and things, the fruits of such a plan would richly repay any temporary advantages, which might be lost by a steady adherence to it? Can it be that Providence has not connected the permanent felicity of a Nation with its virtue? The experiment, at least, is recommended by every sentiment which ennobles human nature.—Alas! is it rendered impossible by its vices?

FAREWELL ADDRESS

To the People of the United States by President George Washington—1796

(Extract)

Citizens by birth or choice of a common country, that country has a right to concentrate your affections.—The name AMERICAN, which belongs to you, in your national capacity, must always exalt the just pride of Patriotism, more than any appellation derived from local discriminations.—With slight shades of difference, you have the same Religion, Manners, Habits, and political Principles.—You have in a common cause fought and triumphed together. The Independence and Liberty you possess are the work of joint councils, and joint efforts—of common dangers, sufferings and success. . . .

This government, the offspring of our own choice uninfluenced and unawed, . . . has a just claim to your confidence and your support.—Respect for its authority, compliance with its Laws, acquiescence in its measures, are duties enjoined by the fundamental maxims of true Liberty.—The basis of our political systems is the right of the people to make and to alter their Constitutions of Government.—But the Constitution which at any time exists, 'till changed by an explicit and authentic act of the whole People, is sacredly obligatory upon all.—The very idea of the power and the right of the People to establish Government, presupposes the duty of every individual to obey the established Government.

THE VOW OF WASHINGTON

The sword was sheathed! in April's sun
Lay green the fields by Freedom won;
And severed sections, weary of debates,
Joined hands at last and were United States.

* * *

How felt the land in every part
The strong throb of a nation's heart?
As its great leader gave, with reverent awe,
His pledge to Union, Liberty and Law!

* * *

That pledge—the heavens above him heard,
That vow—the sleep of centuries stirred;
In world-wide wonder listening peoples bent
Their gaze on Freedom's great experiment.

* * *

Thank God! the peoples' choice was just,
The one man equal to his trust;
Wise beyond lore, and without weakness good,
Calm in the strength of flawless rectitude!

* * *

His rule of justice, order, peace,
Made possible the world's release;
Taught prince and serf that power is but a trust,
And rule alone, that serves the ruled, is just.

* * *

Land of his love! with one glad voice
Let thy great sisterhood rejoice,
A century's suns o'er thee have arisen and set,
And, God be praised, we are one nation yet.

* * *

Then let the sovereign millions, where
Our banner floats in sun and air,
From warm palm-lands to Alaska's cold,
Repeat with us the pledge a century old!

John Greenleaf Whittier.

Read in New York, April 30, 1889, at the Centennial Celebration of the Inauguration of George Washington as the first President of the United States.

Washington Resigning His Commission at Annapolis December 23, 1783

Selections For Group IV

(Grades 7 and 8)

THE TWENTY-SECOND OF FEBRUARY

Pale is the February sky,
  And brief the midday's sunny hours
The wind-swept forest seems to sigh
  For the sweet time of leaves and flowers.

Yet has no month a prouder day,
  Not even when the summer broods
O'er meadows in their fresh array,
  Or autumn tints the glowing woods.

For this chill season now again
  Brings, in its annual round, the morn
When, greatest of the sons of men,
  Our glorious Washington was born.

Lo, where, beneath an icy shield,
  Calmly the mighty Hudson flows!
By snow-clad fell and frozen field,
  Broadening the lordly river goes.

The wildest storm that sweeps through space,
  And rends the oak with sudden force,
Can raise no ripple on his face,
  Or slacken his majestic course.

Thus 'mid the wreck of thrones, shall live
  Unmarred, undimmed, our hero's fame,
And years succeeding years shall give
  Increase of honors to his name.
            William Cullen Bryant.

CROWN OUR WASHINGTON

Arise—'tis the day of our Washington's
      glory,
  The garlands uplift for our liberties won;
Oh sing in your gladness his echoing story,
Whose sword swept for freedom the fields
      of the sun.
        Not with gold, nor with gems,
        But with evergreens vernal,
And the banners of stars that the continent
      span,
Crown, crown we the chief of the heroes
      eternal,
Who lifted his sword for the birthright of
      man!

He gave us a nation; to make it immortal
  He laid down for Freedom the sword that
      he drew,
And his faith leads us on through the up-
      lifting portal
  Of the glories of peace and our destinies
      new.
        Not with gold, nor with gems,
        But with evergreens vernal,
And the flags that the nations of liberty
      span,
Crown, crown him the chief of the heroes
      eternal,
Who laid down his sword for the birthright
      of man!

Lead, Face of the Future, serene in thy
      beauty,
    Till o'er the dead heroes the peace star
      shall gleam,
Till Right shall be Might in the counsels of
      duty,
    And the service of man be life's glory
      supreme.
        Not with gold, nor with gems,
        But with evergreens vernal,
And the flags that the nations in brother-
      hood span,
Crown, crown we the chief of the heroes
      eternal,
Whose honor was gained by his service to
      man!

O Spirit of Liberty, sweet are thy numbers!
    The winds to thy banners their tribute
      shall bring,
While rolls the Potomac where Washington
      slumbers,
    And his natal day comes with the angels
      of spring,
        We follow thy counsels,
        O hero eternal,
To highest achievement the school leads the
      van,
And, crowning thy brow with the ever-
      greens vernal,
We pledge thee our all to the service of
      man!
            Hezekiah Butterworth.

CHARACTER OF WASHINGTON

Washington had more to do with the formation of the constitution than our enthusiasm for other phases of the great work
he did for his country usually makes prominent. He fought the battles which cleared
the way for it. He best knew the need of
consolidating under one government the colonies he had made free, and he best knew
that without this consolidation, a wasting
war, the long and severe privations and sufferings his countrymen had undergone and
his own devoted labor in the cause of freedom, were practically in vain. The beginning of anything like a public sentiment
looking to the formation of our nation is
traceable to his efforts. The circular letter
he sent to the governors of the States, as
early as the close of the War of the Revolution, contained the germ of the constitution;
and all this was recognized by his unanimous
choice to preside over the convention that
framed it. His spirit was in and through it
all. . . .

I have referred only incidentally to the
immense influence and service of Washington in forming our Constitution. I shall not
dwell upon his lofty patriotism, his skill and
fortitude as the military commander who

gained our independence, his inspired wisdom, patriotism, and statesmanship as first
President of the republic, his constant love
for his countrymen, and his solicitude for
their welfare at all times. The story has
been often told, and is familiar to all. If
I should repeat it, I should only seek to present further and probably unnecessary proof
of the fact that Washington embodied in
his character, and exemplified in his career,
that American sentiment in which our government had its origin, and which I believe
to be a condition necessary to our healthful
national life.

  Grover Cleveland—*Character of Washington,* Southern Society, New York, February 22, 1890.

WASHINGTON AND EDUCATION

It is doubtful if anyone outside of certain
great religious teachers ever so thoroughly
impressed himself on the heart of humanity
as has George Washington. No figure in
America has been the subject of more memorial tributes and more unstinted praise.
And yet the subject never seems to be exhausted and the public interest never seems
to be decreased. The larger our experience
with affairs of the world, the more familiar
we become with his life and teachings, the
more our admiration enlarges, and the greater
grows our estimation of his wisdom. He
represented the marvelous combination of the
soldier, the patriot, and the statesman. In
the character of each he stands supreme.

As a brave soldier he won the Revolutionary War. As an unselfish patriot he
refused to use the results of that victory for
his own benefit, but bestowed them all on
his fellow countrymen. As a wise statesman, gathering around him the best talent
of his time, he created the American Republic. All the increasing years only reveal
to us how universally great he was. If to
set a mark upon the minds of men which
changes the whole course of human events
is teaching, then Washington ranks as a
prince of teachers.

  Calvin Coolidge—*Washington and Education,* National Education Association,
Washington, D. C., 1926.

CHARACTER AND POSITION OF WASHINGTON

No nobler figure ever stood in the forefront of a nation's life. Washington was
grave and courteous in address; his manners were simple and unpretending; his
silence and the serene calmness of his temper
spoke of a perfect self-mastery; but there
was little in his outer bearing to reveal the

grandeur of soul which lifts his figure, with all the simple majesty of an ancient statue, out of the smaller passions, the meaner impulses of the world around him. What recommended him for command as yet was simply his weight among his fellow landowners of Virginia, and the experience of war which he had gained by service in Braddock's luckless expedition against Fort Duquesne. It was only as the weary fight went on that the colonists learnt little by little the greatness of their leader, his clear judgment, his heroic endurance, his silence under difficulties, his calmness in the hour of danger or defeat, the patience with which he waited, the quickness and hardness with which he struck, the lofty and serene sense of duty that never swerved from its task through resentment or jealousy, that never through war or peace felt the touch of a meaner ambition, that knew no aim save that of guarding the freedom of his fellow countrymen, and no personal longing save that of returning to his own fireside when their freedom was secured. It was almost unconsciously that men learnt to cling to Washington with a trust and faith such as few other men have won, and to regard him with a reverence which still hushes us in presence of his memory. Even America hardly recognized his real grandeur till death set its seal on "the man first in war, first in peace, and first in the hearts of his fellow countrymen."

John Richard Green—*Short History of the English People.*

ODE FOR WASHINGTON'S BIRTHDAY

Welcome to the day returning,
  Dearer still as ages flow,
While the torch of Faith is burning,
  Long as Freedom's altars glow!
See the hero whom it gave us
  Slumbering on a mother's breast;
For the arm he stretched to save us,
  Be its morn forever blest!

Hear the tale of youthful glory,
  While of Britain's rescued band
Friend and foe repeat the story,
  Spread his fame o'er sea and land,
Where the red cross, proudly streaming,
  Flaps above the frigate's deck,
Where the golden lilies, gleaming,
  Star the watch-towers of Quebec.

Look! The shadow on the dial
  Marks the hour of deadlier strife;
Days of terror, years of trial,
  Scourge a nation into life.
Lo, the youth, becomes her leader!
  All her baffled tyrants yield;
Through his arm the Lord hath freed her;
  Crown him on the tented field!

Vain is Empire's mad temptation!
  Not for him an earthly crown!
He whose sword hath freed a nation
  Strikes the offered sceptre down.

See the throneless Conquerer seated,
  Ruler by a people's choice;
See the Patriot's task completed;
  Hear the Father's dying voice!

"By the name that you inherit,
  By the sufferings you recall,
Cherish the fraternal spirit;
  Love your country first of all!
Listen not to idle questions
  If its bands may be untied;
Doubt the patriot whose suggestions
  Strive a nation to divide!"

Father! We, whose ears have tingled
  With the discord-notes of shame,—
We, whose sires their blood have mingled
  In the battle's thunder-flame,—
Gathering, while this holy morning
  Lights the land from sea to sea,
Hear thy counsel, heed thy warning;
  Trust us, while we honor thee!
      Oliver Wendell Holmes.

COMMEMORATIVE ADDRESS BEFORE CONGRESS

Will you go with me to the banks of the Monongahela, to see your youthful Washington, supporting, in the dismal hour of Indian victory, the ill fated Braddock; and saving by his judgment and his valour, the remains of a defeated army, pressed by the conquering savage foe? or, when—oppressed America nobly resolving to risk her all in defence of her violated rights—he was elevated by the unanimous voice of Congress to the command of her armies? . . .

Who is there that has forgotten the vales of Brandywine—the fields of Germantown —or the plains of Monmouth? Everywhere present, wants of every kind obstructing, numerous and valiant armies encountering, himself a host, he assuaged our sufferings, limited our privations, and upheld our tottering Republic. . . .

Possessing a clear and penetrating mind, a strong and sound judgment, calmness and temper for deliberation, with invincible firmness and perseverance in resolution maturely formed, drawing information from all, acting for himself, with incorruptible integrity and unvarying patriotism: his own superiority and the public confidence alike marked him as the man designed by heaven to lead in the great political as well as military events which have distinguished the era of his life. . . .

First in war, first in peace, and first in the hearts of his countrymen, he was second to none in the humble and endearing scenes of private life: Pious, just, humane, temperate, and sincere; uniform, dignified, and commanding; his example was as edifying to all around him as were the effects of that example lasting.

To his equals he was condescending; to his inferiors kind, and to the dear object of his affection exemplarily tender: Correct throughout, vice shuddered in his presence,

and virtue always felt his fostering hand; the purity of his private character gave effulgence to his public virtues. . . . Such was the man for whom our nation mourns.

Representative Henry Lee—Oration before Congress, December 26, 1799.

WASHINGTON

Soldier and statesman, rarest unison;
High-poised example of great duties done
Simply as breathing, a world's honors worn
As life's indifferent gifts to all men born;
Dumb for himself, unless it were to God,
But for his barefoot soldiers eloquent,
Tramping the snow to coral where they
    trod,
Held by his awe in hollow-eyed content;
Modest, yet firm as Nature's self; unblamed
Save by the men his nobler temper shamed;
Never seduced through show of present good
By other than unsetting lights to steer
New-trimmed in Heaven, nor than his steadfast mood
More steadfast, far from rashness as from
    fear;
Rigid, but with himself first, grasping still
In swerveless poise the wave-beat helm of
    will;
Not honored then or now because he wooed
The popular voice, but that he still withstood;
Broad-minded, higher-souled, there is but one
Who was all this and ours, and all men's—
    WASHINGTON.

James Russell Lowell—Extract from *Under the Old Elm*, read at Cambridge, July 3, 1875, on the Hundredth Anniversary of Washington's taking command of the American Army.

WASHINGTON

When foolish kings, at odd with swift-paced Time,
Would strike that banner down,
A nobler knight than ever writ or rhyme
Has starred with Fame's bright crown
Through armed hosts bore it free to float
    on high
Beyond the clouds, a light that cannot die!
  Ah, hero of our younger race!
  Strong builder of a temple new!
  Ruler, who sought no lordly place!
  Warrior, who sheathed the sword he drew!
  Lover of men, who saw afar
  A world unmarred by want or war,
  Who knew the path, and yet forebore
  To tread, till all men should implore;
  Who saw the light, and led the way
  Where the gray world might greet the
    day:
  Father and leader, prophet sure,
  Whose will in vast works shall endure,
How shall we praise him on this day of days,
Great son of fame who has no need of praise?

How shall we praise him? Open wide the
  doors

Of the fair temple whose broad base he laid.
Through shining halls a shadowy cavalcade
Of heroes moves on unresounding floors—
Men whose brawned arms upraised these
    columns high,
And reared the towers that vanish in the
    sky—
The strong who, having wrought, can never
    die.

    Harriet Monroe—From the *Columbian Ode,* read and sung at the Dedication of the World Columbian Exposition, Chicago, October 21, 1892.

WASHINGTON

Our Nation's birth gave history your name,
    Recording on its pages your great deeds.
No hesitation marred when duty came,
    No clouds obscured from you your coun-
        try's needs.
Pure were the thoughts you planted in man's
    heart,
    Nor is your harvest fully garnered yet;
Still grows and thrives the tree that had its
    start,
    In hallowed ground with honest purpose
        wet.
Each passing day your wisdom is revealed,
    Each added year some richer promise gives;
Your presence led our fathers in the field,
    Your spirit leads us still to that which
        lives
In Liberty and Peace, for which you fought
To gain Eternity, the goal you sought.
        John A. Prentice.

WASHINGTON'S BIRTHDAY

'Tis splendid to live so grandly
    That, long after you are gone,
The things you did are remembered,
    And recounted under the sun;
To live so bravely and purely
    That a nation stops on its way,
And once a year, with banner and drum,
    Keeps its thought of your natal day.

'Tis splendid to have a record
    So white and free from stain
That, held to the light, it shows no blot,
    Though tested and tried amain;
That age to age forever
    Repeats its story of love,
And your birthday lives in a nation's heart
    All other days above.

And this is Washington's glory,
    A steadfast soul and true,
Who stood for his country's honor
    When his country's days were few,
And now, when its days are many,
    And its flag of stars is flung
To the breeze in defiant challenge,
    His name is on every tongue.

Yes, it's splendid to live so bravely,
    To be so great and strong,
That your memory is ever a tocsin
    To rally the foes of the wrong;

To live so proudly and purely,
    That your people pause in their way,
And year by year, with banner and drum,
    Keep the thought of your natal day.
        Margaret E. Sangster.

LETTER BY GENERAL GEORGE WASHINGTON

Addressed to the Governors of All the States at the End of the War

(Extract)

There are four things, which, I humbly conceive, are essential to the well-being, I may even venture to say, to the existence of the United States, as an independent power.

First. An indissoluble union of the States under one federal head.

Secondly. A sacred regard to public justice.

Thirdly. The adoption of a proper peace establishment; and

Fourthly. The prevalence of that pacific and friendly disposition among the people of the United States, which will induce them to forget their local prejudices and policies; to make those mutual concessions, which are requisite to the general prosperity; and, in some instances, to sacrifice their individual advantages to the interest of the community.

These are the pillars on which the glorious fabric of our independency and national character must be supported. Liberty is the basis; and whoever would dare to sap the foundation, or overturn the structure, under whatever specious pretext he may attempt it, will merit the bitterest execration, and the severest punishment, which can be inflicted by his injured country.

FAREWELL ADDRESS

To the People of the United States by President George Washington—1796

(Extract)

The Unity of Government which constitutes you one people, is also now dear to you. —It is justly so;—for it is a main Pillar in the Edifice of your real independence; the support of your tranquillity at home; your peace abroad; of your safety; of your prosperity in every shape; of that very Liberty, which you so highly prize.—But as it is easy to foresee, that, from different causes, and from different quarters, much pains will be taken, many artifices employed, to weaken in your minds the conviction of this truth; —as this is the point in your political fortress against which the batteries of internal and external enemies will be most constantly and actively (though often covertly and insidiously) directed, it is of infinite moment, that you should properly estimate the immense value of your national Union

to your collective and individual happiness; —that you should cherish a cordial, habitual, and immoveable attachment to it; accustoming yourselves to think and speak of it as of the Palladium of your political safety and prosperity; watching for its preservation with jealous anxiety; discountenancing whatever may suggest even a suspicion that it can in any event be abandoned, and indignantly frowning upon the first dawning of every attempt to alienate any portion of our Country from the rest, or to enfeeble the sacred ties which now link together the various parts.

FAREWELL ADDRESS

To the People of the United States by President George Washington—1796

(Extract)

Of all the dispositions and habits, which lead to political prosperity, Religion and morality are indispensable supports.—In vain would that man claim the tribute of Patriotism, who should labour to subvert these great Pillars of human happiness, these firmest props of the duties of Men and Citizens.—The mere Politician, equally with the pious man, ought to respect and to cherish them.—A volume could not trace all their connexions with private and public felicity.—Let it simply be asked where is the security for prosperity, for reputation, for life, if the sense of religious obligation *desert* the oaths, which are the instruments of investigation in Courts of Justice? And let us with caution indulge the supposition, that morality can be maintained without religion.—Whatever may be conceded to the influence of refined education on minds of peculiar structure—reason and experience both forbid us to expect, that national morality can prevail in exclusion of religious principle.—

'Tis substantially true, that virtue or morality is a necessary spring of popular government.—The rule indeed extends with more or less force to every species of Free Government.—Who that is a sincere friend to it can look with indifference upon attempts to shake the foundation of the fabric?

Promote, then, as an object of primary importance, institutions for the general diffusion of knowledge. In proportion as the structure of a government gives force to public opinion, it is essential that public opinion should be enlightened.

CHARACTER OF WASHINGTON

A true friend of his country loves her friends and benefactors, and thinks it no degradation to commend and commemorate them. The voluntary outpouring of the public feeling, made today, from the North to the South, and from the East to the West, proves this sentiment to be both just and natural. In the cities and in the villages, in the public temples and in the family circles, among all ages and sexes, gladdened voices today bespeak grateful hearts and a freshened recollection of the virtues of the Father of his Country. And it will be so, in all time to come, so long as public virtue is itself an object of regard. The ingenuous youth of America will hold up to themselves the bright model of Washington's example, and study to be what they behold; they will contemplate his character till all its virtues spread out and display themselves to their delighted vision; as the earliest astronomers, the shepherds on the plains of Babylon, gazed at the stars till they saw them form into clusters and constellations, overpowering at length the eyes of the beholders with the united blaze of a thousand lights. . . .

A hundred years hence, other disciples of Washington will celebrate his birth, with no less of sincere admiration than we now commemorate it. When they shall meet, as we now meet, to do themselves and him that honor, so surely as they shall see the blue summits of his native mountains rise in the horizon, so surely as they shall behold the river on whose banks he lived, and on whose banks he rests, still flowing on toward the sea, so surely may they see, as we now see, the flag of the Union floating on the top of the Capitol; and then, as now, may the sun in his course visit no land more free, more happy, more lovely, than this our own country!

Daniel Webster—*Character of Washington.* Speech, Washington, D. C., February 22, 1832.

NATIONAL MONUMENT TO WASHINGTON

In the whole history of the world it may be doubted whether any man can be found, who has exerted a more controlling influence over men and over events than George Washington. To what did he owe that influence? How did he win, how did he wield, that magic power, that majestic authority, over the minds and hearts of his countrymen and of mankind? In what did the power of Washington consist? . . .

But it was not solid information, or sound judgment, or even that rare combination of surpassing modesty and valor, great as these qualities are, which gave Washington such a hold on the regard, respect, and confidence of the American people. I hazard nothing in saying that it was the high moral element of his character which imparted to it its preponderating force. His incorruptible

honesty, his uncompromising truth, his devout reliance on God, the purity of his life, the scrupulousness of his conscience, the disinterestedness of his purposes, his humanity, generosity, and justice,—these were the ingredients which, blending harmoniously with solid information and sound judgment and a valor only equalled by his modesty, made up a character to which the world may be fearlessly challenged for a parallel. . . .

The Republic may perish; the wide arch of our ranged Union may fall; star by star its glories may expire; stone after stone its columns and its capitol may moulder and crumble; all other names which adorn its annals may be forgotten; but as long as human hearts shall any where pant, or human tongues shall anywhere plead, for a true, rational, constitutional liberty, those hearts shall enshrine the memory, and those tongues shall prolong the fame, of George Washington!

Robert C. Winthrop—Oration delivered at the Laying of the Corner-stone of the National Monument to Washington, July 4, 1848.

WASHINGTON'S MONUMENT

For him who sought his country's good
In plains of war, 'mid scenes of blood;
Spent the warm noon of life's bright day,
Who in the dubious battle's fray,
That to a world he might secure
Rights that forever shall endure,
    Rear the monument of fame!
    Deathless is the hero's name!

For him, who, when the war was done,
And victory sure, and freedom won,
Left glory's theatre, the field,
The olive branch of peace to wield;
And proved, when at the helm of state,
Though great in war, in peace as great;
    Rear the monument of fame!
    Deathless is the hero's name!

For him, whose worth, though unexpress'd,
Lives cherished in each freeman's breast,
Whose name, to patriot souls so dear,
Time's latest children shall revere,
Whose brave achievements praised shall be,
While beats one breast for liberty;
    Rear the monument of fame!
    Deathless is the hero's name!

But why for him vain marbles raise?
Can the cold sculpture speak his praise?
Illustrious shade! we can proclaim
Our gratitude, but not thy fame.
Long as Columbia shall be free,
She lives a monument of thee,
    And may she ever rise in fame,
    To honor thy immortal name!

Anonymous.

National Monument to Washington

One tribute to his memory is left to be rendered. One monument remains to be reared. A monument which shall bespeak the gratitude, not of States, or of cities, or of governments; not of separate communities, or of official bodies; but of the people, the whole people of the nation;—a National Monument, erected by the citizens of the United States of America. (Winthrop, Robert C.—*Addresses and Speeches,* Vol. I, p. 71.) (Oration, Laying the Corner-Stone of the National Monument to Washington, July 4, 1848.)

(Not for Declamation Contest)

WASHINGTON THE NATION-BUILDER

BICENTENNIAL POEM

Written especially for the
CELEBRATION OF THE TWO HUNDREDTH ANNIVERSARY OF THE BIRTH OF GEORGE WASHINGTON

By

EDWIN MARKHAM

Author of "The Man With the Hoe"

A Spartan mother called him into Time,
And kindled duty in him as a flame;
While he was schooled by the primeval hills
Of old Virginia—schooled by her mighty woods,
Where Indians war-whooped and the wild beast prowled.
His name was written on no college scroll;
But he drank wisdom from the wilderness.
The mountains poured into his soul their strength,
The rocks their fortitude, the stars their calm.

He grew a silent man;
Yet carried on all roads
The lofty courtesies, the high reserves.
He seemed to know, even in this noise of time,
The solemn quiets of Eternity.
But fiery energy, a live crater, slept
Under that mountain calm; yet never blazed
Into a passion, save in some black hour
When craven souls betrayed the people. Then
He was all sword and flame, a god in arms.

With the heart of a child, the wisdom of a sage,
He toiled with no self to serve.
He grew in greatness, year by luminous year
Until he carried empire in his brain.
Yet if no Cause, no high commanding Cause,
Had called him to the hazard of the deed,
None would have guessed his power
To build a nation out of chaos, give
To her the wings of soaring destinies.
But at the Hour, the People knew their Man,
The one ordained of Heaven, ordained to stand
In the deadly breach and hold the gate for God.

And when the Scroll was signed and the glad Bell
Of Independence echoed round the world,
He led his tattered host on stubborn fields,
Barefoot and hungry, thru the ice and mire—
Thru dolors, valors, desperations, dreams—
Thru Valley Forge on to world-startling hours
When proud Cornwallis yielded up his sword.
And all the way, down to the road's last bend,
Cool Judgment whispered to his listening mind.
Where there was faltering, he was there as faith;
Where there was weakness, he was there as strength;
Where there was discord, he was there as peace.

His trust was in the Ruler of Events—
In Him who watches. He could say, "The ends
Are in God's hands. I trust,
But while I trust I battle." In this creed,
His soul took refuge and his heart found rest.
When, after Yorktown, all the guns were husht,
Still was our Chieftain on a battle line,
Fighting old laws, old manners, old beliefs.
He fought the outworn old,
And lit new torches for the march ahead.

Life tried his soul by all the tests of time——
By hardship, treachery, ingratitude;
Yes, even by victory and the loud applause.
When fortune flung to him a crown, he flung
The bauble back and followed the People's dream.
He turned from all the tempters,
Stood firm above the perils of success——
Stood like Monadnock high above the clouds.

He did the day's work that was given him:
He toiled for men until he flamed with God.
Now in his greatness, ever superbly lone,
He moves in his serene eternity,
Like far Polaris wheeling on the North.

This Bicentennial Poem, by Edwin Markham, appears in Vol. I, Literature Series, but is repeated here because it was a part of the declamatory material for elementary schools.

A display of original work exhibited by the Seventh Grade, Junior High School, Atlantic City, New Jersey, in celebration of the George Washington Bicentennial

TYPICAL SCHOOL PROGRAMS
of the
George Washington Bicentennial Celebration

FROM many thousands of reports of Bicentennial Celebration activities in the schools of the United States, brief selections have been made, and are printed in this folder, to indicate the scope and value of this work. The purpose is not to indicate the *number* of such programs but rather their *character*.

Nothing that has been accomplished in the whole range of Bicentennial Celebration activities has been more productive, or has met with more enthusiastic response, than the appeal to school children, and the effect of this endeavor will make a lasting impression upon American citizenship in years to come.

Here, as upon other occasions, this Commission expresses its profound appreciation for the earnest and generous cooperation of school authorities and teachers everywhere. They made the outstanding success of this activity possible.

TYPICAL BICENTENNIAL PROGRAMS
North, South, East, and West, They Celebrate

Washington Program, Roosevelt School
Chisholm, Minnesota

PROGRAM	CHILDREN PARTICIPATING
Drum Corps	6
Introduction:	
Washington	10
Crown Our Washington	
The Glory of Washington	
United States as an Independent Power	
Washington's Address to His Troops	
The Story of Our Flag	
George Washington	
The Flag Goes By	
Songs of Washington Built on Bugle Calls	36
Dedication of the Picture of Washington	11
Dramatization	8
"Young George Washington"	
Games and dances included	
Minuet	8
A Hunting We Will Go	8
Yankee Doodle	10
Draw a Bucket of Water	16
Flag Drill	10
Topics:	
The Fame of Washington	
The Faith of Washington	
The Unselfishness of Washington	5
The Character of Washington	
The Memory of Washington	
Acrostic and Songs	29
Dramatization: "The First Flag"	8

The George Washington Bicentennial at Audubon School
428 Broadway, New Orleans, Louisiana

Singing of America	The School
Soldier Boy March	The Kindergarten
A Children's Dance	
The Making of the Flag, A Poem	Group of three Children
George Washington	Recitation by three Children
The Story of our Border	Explanation of Washington Frieze made by the Class
A Boy's Privilege	Recitation by three Children
Washington's Birthday	Recitation by Group
Washington and Peace	By Pupils
Patriotic Songs	Sung by Departmental Grades
Washington, Patron of Education	By Group
Maxims of Washington	Group of Pupils
1732-1932: Contrasts	A Lantern Picture Story Group of Pupils
March to Flagstaff	School and Visitors
Raising of New Flag	In charge of Committee of Boy and Girl Scouts
Pledge to Flag	
Star Spangled Banner	
Dedication of George Washington Magnolia Tree	
Dedication of Mount Vernon Garden planted under Direction of Mr. James M. McArthur, Public School Director of Nature Study and School Gardening	

Program On Birthday of George Washington
Nashmead, California

Practically all the population attended consisting of eighteen adults and eight school children.

Salute to the Flag
Song—America
Address—On Life of Washington
Anagram—With stories of Washington
Unveiling of Washington's picture and Children's Salute—"We salute you Washington"
Reading—Washington and Lincoln
Reading—Columbus and Washington
Reading—The Commander-in-Chief
Recitation—What Do We Plant When We Plant a Tree
Reading—Washington the Man
Talk—Appreciation of Washington
American's Creed
Outdoors in School Yard
Planting of Five Trees— { Three Elms / Two Arizona Ash Trees

George Washington Program, Twelve Rural Schools
Field Day Activities on Grounds of San Marcos School
San Marcos, California

Flag Salute	
Star Spangled Banner	School Chorus
Washington as a Boy	Richland
There are many Flags	School Chorus
Rhythm Band	Rincon
Washington as a Youth	Richland
Minuet	Cle Mar, Oakdale, Twin Oaks
Harmonica Band	Orange Glen
Washington as a General	Pomerado
Hail Columbia	School Chorus
Washington as President and Citizen	San Marcos
Mt. Vernon Bells	School Chorus
Rhythm Band	San Pasqual
America the Beautiful	School Chorus

Program on the 200th Anniversary of Washington's Birthday
Sacred Heart School, Highland Falls, N. Y.

Prayer for Civil Authorities
Chorus—"Father of the Land We Love"   School
Salute to the Flag
Recitations   By the First Grade
    "Six Little Girls"   "The Hatchet Story"
    "Somebody"   "I'll Try"
Second Grade—Recitation: "The New George Washington"
Acrostic: "Something About George Washington"
Third Grade—Song: "Hail to the Father of Our Country"
Recitations: "I Would Tell of Washington"
    "All Hail to Thee, Great Washington"
Fourth Grade—Recitations: "The Story of Our Flag"
    "The Flags of Washington"
Chorus—"O Columbia, the Gem of the Ocean"   School
Fifth Grade—Recitations: "Life's Journey"
    "The Thirteen States"
Sixth Grade—Class Recitation: "Washington's Birthday"
Essay: "Washington"
Seventh Grade—Sayings of Washington
    Characteristics of Washington
Musical Drill—"The Minute Men" Boys of 5th, 6th and 7th grades
Address   Rev. D. W. Sheeran
Grand Chorus—"The Star Spangled Banner"   School

Orange County, N. C., Schools Report
County Activities In Celebration of the Washington Bicentennial

THE Washington Bicentennial Commission is one commission that has been appointed that the teachers and school children of this county at least thoroughly approve of. There hasn't been any money in the county this year. So we knew that big programs and celebrations were out of the question but all the schools have had several small programs and each grade has made a study of the life of Washington some time during the year and they have enjoyed these no little.

Thanks to the Commission much valuable reference material and many good suggestions have been available. This material has been properly bound or mounted and put into the materials file of each of our large schools and also in the central files in the county office.

The children have carried on some rather good studies of Washington; and the activities growing out of these have been very interesting.

They wrote books—
Biographies of Washington,
History of the Travels of Washington,
Washington's Private Life,
Washington's Contribution to Our Country.
They made the books and illustrated them.
They wrote and produced Colonial Plays.
They collected pictures and mounted them or assembled them in books.

They depicted the life of Washington in friezes and wall hangings.

They modeled and carved busts of Washington.

They built and furnished replicas of Mount Vernon.

They gave assembly programs.

Some of them took trips to the Washington Country, and upon their return gave little lectures on the Life of Washington to other grades or other schools.

They have collected interesting colonial pieces for their school museums.

They had Washington Exhibits.

All of this has taught the history of early life of our Country as nothing else could have and the materials collected by the children and teachers are in our school files and libraries for use for many years to come. So the work will go on.

Commencement Exercises in each Elementary School in the county centered around the Life and Work of Washington. Several were very good.

The County Officials have encouraged this work as much as they could by sending out mimeographed suggestions and questions for study and music for choruses and school bands. Examples of some of this material are included with this brief report.

MARY HYMAN, *Supervisor,*
Orange County Schools, North Carolina.

Letters From Two Prominent Educators

NICHOLAS MURRAY BUTLER
BROADWAY AT 116 STREET
NEW YORK CITY

Southampton, N. Y.
August 29, 1931.

Hon. Sol Bloom
House of Representatives
Washington, D. C.

My dear Congressman:

I am glad to see the handbook of the George Washington Appreciation Course and have no doubt whatever that it will be widely used and do an excellent service in turning the attention of the present generation to a study of George Washington, his character, his public service, his ideals and his permanent influence. As the years pass, it becomes more and more clear that the fathers of this nation were a group of men of first importance in the history of civilization and all that that word means. We cannot study their personalities, their words and their deeds too long or too earnestly.

With cordial regards, I am,

Faithfully yours,

NICHOLAS MURRAY BUTLER.

NMB:MB

UNITED STATES
DEPARTMENT OF THE INTERIOR
OFFICE OF EDUCATION
WASHINGTON

ADDRESS REPLY
THE COMMISSIONER OF EDUCATION

September 18, 1931.

Hon. Sol Bloom,
Washington Building,
Washington, D. C.

Dear Mr. Bloom:

I have just found time to look over the handbook of the George Washington Appreciation Course, which with other pamphlets accompanied your letter of September 1.

I am struck by the orderly arrangement, the convenient division of materials, and the accuracy of information. I believe the book will be a very great help to teachers and others in making preparation for proper commemoration of the bicentennial of Washington's birth.

Cordially yours,

W. JOHN COOPER,
Commissioner.

COMMENTS ON EDUCATIONAL ACTIVITIES
OF THE BICENTENNIAL CELEBRATION
From Executives, Superintendents, and Teachers

State Department of Public Instruction
Oklahoma City

What I particularly wish to commend with reference to the materials which have been distributed by your Commission is the sincere and successful attempt to state the facts in plain and understandable English without the glamor and mystery that sometimes attaches itself to literature dealing with the lives of the great.

J. ANDREW HOLLEY,
Chief High School Inspector.

* * * * *

Syracuse, New York

It is a splendid thing for the country that your Commission has been as active as it has in stimulating educational contests and other activities that are developing in all of our people a proper appreciation of Washington's character and what his life has meant to us through the years in the building of this Nation.

HUGH P. BAKER,
Dean, The New York State College of Forestry.

* * * * *

Yankton College
Yankton, South Dakota

In this connection permit me to thank you for the very wonderful material you have prepared and sent out. We have been greatly impressed by your literature, and assure you that we stand ready to cooperate with you in every possible way until the close of the bicentennial period.

G. W. NASH, *President.*

* * * * *

Puukolii, Lohaina, Maui, T. H.

Our principal, Mr. Butler, and the pupils of the seventh and eighth grades want to thank the George Washington Bicentennial Commission for the materials and the information that they have sent us. We are thankful to have these because now we have better programs and we have learned more about George Washington. We want to know about him because it is more interesting while reading or listening to the one who is telling the story about his life.

(Mas.) SENMATSU ASHITO.

* * * * *

North Woodstock, New Hampshire

I wish to report to the Commission that all of my twenty-eight schools have taken part in a Bicentennial Celebration during the present year. The programs varied a great deal but all were enjoyed by the public who attended.

ALONZO J. KNOWLTON,
Superintendent, Supervisory Union Schools, No. 33.

* * * * *

Elizabethtown College, Elizabethtown, Pennsylvania

We appreciate your promptness in sending literature and the wholesome, broad-minded spirit of Washington that is being instilled in our American citizenry through the work of your Commission.

LAVINIA C. WENGER,
Professor of History.

* * * * *

Chaska, Minnesota

May I thank you for the material suitable for celebrating the Washington Bicentennial. This material was distributed among the sixty-three rural teachers of Carver County, and they are now making good use of it.

ESTELLA L. ELKE,
Carver County Superintendent.

* * * * *

Baker University, Baldwin City, Kansas

My course in the Summer School here which we call the "George Washington Appreciation Course" is attended by more students than any other in the Department.

THOMAS L. HARRIS,
Department of History.

Bay County, Michigan

The Bicentennial program was carried on in Bay County, Michigan, last year, consisting of both individual projects and county-wide work. For instance, each school did some work on Washington Posters, Washington Booklets. Appropriate Washington programs were held, both in school by the school children and evenings by both school children and parents. In some places, evening programs were held and consisted purely and simply of Washington Bicentennial material.

EARL S. GOODMAN,
Bay County School Commissioner.

* * * * *

Fairmont State Teachers College, West Virginia

I think that you are doing a real service in promoting the Bicentennial, and believe that the educational program you are sponsoring is the most successful educational project the government has ever undertaken. My course on George Washington is increasing in popularity. . . . I will very much appreciate an answer to this letter, and assure you that I am very grateful to you for the cooperation you have given me to date in the matter of material and other teaching aids.

I. F. BOUGHTER,
Head of the History Department.

* * * * *

Rock Hill Public Schools
Webster Groves, Missouri

On behalf of my faculty and student body, I wish to express to you our sincere appreciation for the splendid material you recently sent us, on George Washington. I consider your material the most inclusive and practical I have ever seen and am confident it will be an inspiration to teachers, students and community leaders throughout the Nation.

T. H. CUSHMAN, *Principal.*

* * * * *

Boston Public Schools
Washington Irving Intermediate District
Roslindale, Massachusetts

I have been much pleased with all the material which you have sent me and I assure you it has served as an inspiration to the boys and girls of our school. Some of them have built up quite remarkable collections of writings and pictures pertaining to George Washington. It lends itself finely to the Art Appreciation classes where each has his individual collection of masterpieces of art. They have surprised me in the zeal they have shown in making collections of pictures from the life of Washington.

BERTHA L. PALMER.

* * * * *

Saint Meinrad's Abbey, Saint Meinrad, Indiana

Moreover, please favor us with two or more copies of the Handbook for the Appreciation Course.

I realize that this is asking a good deal, but I regard this book as the greatest help to the teacher, and one which will induce our overworked English professors here to throw themselves more readily into the work of shaping their programs for the coming year. The Handbook makes the work very simple and provides indispensable outlines for their aid.

REVEREND VICTOR DUX, O.S.B.

* * * * *

The Glendale Junior-Senior High School
Glendale, Ohio

The suggestions for programs, the lists of pageants and plays, the bibliographies, and the many pages of biographical and historical matter which the officers of your Commission have published in such convenient form, will prove invaluable in our programs for the coming fall months.

LOUISE C. ROBB, *Principal.*

University of Florida
Gainesville, Florida

We are glad if you feel that our efforts have added anything to this Celebration. We have been happy to have a small part in it, and believe that under the leadership of your Commission a very splendid program has been put on over the country generally. I believe that the observance has had a profound educational effect, not only upon our children, but upon the adult citizenship of the country.

JOHN J. TIGERT,
President.

* * * * *

State Department of Education
Sacramento, California

The year has been a noteworthy year in that the tendency of our citizens to react in terms of emotional responses to economic conditions and to general social and political unrest has been, we feel, very greatly stabilized and controlled by the reaction of our young people as they have had their thinking tuned to the eminent American, George Washington, Father of Our Country who during days fraught with much more hazard than are the present ones saw us through, and so our young people reacting to the teaching and the stress of emphasis resultant from the Washington Bicentennial have had great opportunity which they have met with success and which has involved them in a translation of Washington's life into present day conditions.

V. KERSEY,
Superintendent of Public Instruction.

* * * * *

University of Kentucky
Lexington, Kentucky

At this time, may I express my high appreciation of the work of the George Washington Bicentennial Commission for the splendid work it has done. To emphasize the importance of the ideals of George Washington in the lives and ideals of American people, is a distinct contribution to American life and culture.

WELLINGTON PATRICK,
Director, Department of University Extension.

* * * * *

Capitol Building
Richmond, Virginia

Enclosed please find copies of the program of our state-wide declamatory contest. It was quite successful and all of us are enthusiastic about the results.

I was present at the State Contest and noted that the winners and their parents were delighted with the beautiful commemorative medals which your Commission so generously provided.

Your Commission is to be congratulated on conceiving this contest and on the way in which you have promoted it.

J. G. POLLARD, *Chairman,*
Virginia George Washington Bicentennial Commission.

* * * * *

State Education Department
Albany, New York

I am grateful for your letter of October 14 and for the exceedingly helpful materials you have sent me from time to time. I have given instructions that these materials shall be kept in a special file available to my associates and as a part of the permanent record of this office. As the years pass, they will be of increasing importance to the cause of Elementary Education.

May I congratulate you and your associates on the interest you have created and on the contribution you have made to our national, social and civic consciousness.

J. CAYCE MORRISON,
Assistant Commissioner for Elementary Education.

* * * * *

The University of Montana
Helena, Montana

I think much interest in the life of George Washington has been developed among the young people of the public schools and I know

that there was great interest manifested in our two collegiate unit which conducted the local contests and there was an exceedingl fine reaction to the effective presentation of the two able oration given by our Montana representatives at the state meeting. . .

May I thank you for your kindness in forwarding to this office th interesting and valuable material mentioned in your letter of Jul 8th? You have done a very distinguished work in carrying on thi great national project, and I am sure you must have high satisfac tion as the conclusions of the contests have been reached wit such admirable results.

MELVIN A. BRANNON,
Chancellor.

* * * * *

Inglewood, California

I listened with intent interest to the broadcast tonight of Mr Moore's oration on "Washington: Nation Builder." Having onc been a competitor for regional honors in a similar contest in 192? conducted for high school students by various newspapers through out the country, I can frankly say that the selection of Mr. Moore' oration is one of the outstanding pieces of contemporary literatur of the present day.

I sincerely believe that if the masses of the country would becom more interested in "nation building," there would be fewer home in stress today. I congratulate Mr. Moore.

SHERMAN T. WARE.

* * * * *

Mandan, North Dakota

Of the many contests we have participated in during the last nineteen years in this county I am fully convinced that the one conducted by the George Washington Bicentennial Commission wa the most outstanding as concerns educational value and having such a splendid National Organization has given to the entire students of the Nation a great deal of value.

H. K. JENSEN,
Morton County School Superintendent.

* * * * *

Harrisville, West Virginia

We competed with Calhoun County in the Regional Contest. I am of the opinion that this work has been worth while and that the schools throughout the Nation have made a wonderful record in helping to honor the birth of such a Great American.

I shall feel very grateful to you for any material that will aid the teachers of our country in helping to teach children the value of the life of this honored citizen of the past.

SIMON D. GOFF,
Ritchie County School Superintendent.

* * * * *

State Normal School
Danbury, Connecticut

You have sent us a great deal of most interesting and valuable material for some time past. We have read and used a great deal of it and we are grateful indeed for having had it. I have myself felt that this type of commemoration was the best that could possibly be had—designed as it has been to make this great man better known to his countrymen.

L. D. HIGGINS,
Principal.

* * * * *

MacMurray College
Jacksonville, Illinois

The student body enjoyed these activities and the local college committee and the President counted it a pleasure to work with the Commission at Washington to this end. On more than one occasion a student told the writer that Washington had at last really lived to her. The work of the Commission I am sure has served to quicken the sensibilities of the American people to the great debt this nation owes to George Washington. I congratulate your Commission upon the fine work done.

ROB ROY MACGREGOR,
Professor of History.

FLAGS OF
AMERICAN LIBERTY

On the following two pages is shown a colored chart of the "Flags of American Liberty." This chart illustrates Local Flags, Pine Tree Flags, Rattlesnake Flags, and Regimental and other Battle Flags of the American Revolution; also various stages (more or less traditional) in the development of the National Ensign.

RICAN LIBERTY

RATTLESNAKE FLAGS OF AMERICAN REVOLUTION

SEAL OF THE PRESIDENT
The personal seal of the President. The device is used in the President's flag on a field of blue with a white star at each corner of the flag. It is also shown in bronze in the floor of the entrance corridor to the White House.

SOUTH CAROLINA NAVY ENSIGN
Another form used on early ships, especially South Carolina state vessels.

WESTMORELAND BATTALION FLAG
Ensign of a Pennsylvania battalion raised in Westmoreland County by John Proctor in 1775

FIRST STARS AND STRIPES
There was no official land flag during the Revolution: the circle of stars is the traditional form.

AG OF TODAY

y Act of Congress, April 9, 1818)

STARS AND STRIPES

ISTORIC ADDRESS BY
ADCAST JUNE 17, 1931, FROM
SE, PHILADELPHIA, PA.

y, those who gaze upon its pro-
n its creation there was brought
llation of states, but a new prin-
g and My Flag which George
first bright banner of unstained
stined for a vast new Liberty.
National History, that Flag has
ever been lowered to the enemies
Country Almighty God has been
dignity, and the significance of
me today, there is the guiding
nce which has willed that all
d."

HER BATTLE FLAGS
N REVOLUTION

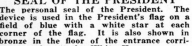

AMERICAN NAVY JACK
One form used in early navy.

GADSDEN FLAG
So called because Christopher Gadsden presented such a flag to the South Carolina Provincial Congress. Commodore Esek Hopkin's broad pennant, hoisted by Lieut. John Paul Jones on the "Alfred" early in 1776, was probably like this.

BEDFORD FLAG
Standard of Minute Men at Concord; meaning "Conquer or Die."

CULPEPPER MINUTE MEN FLAG
Motto taken from famous speech of Patrick Henry, March 23, 1775—"Give me liberty or give me death."

FORT MOULTRIE FLAG
First American flag of the South, sometimes without the word "Liberty". The emblem Sgt. Jasper nailed to the staff June 28, 1776.

JOHN PAUL JONES' STARRY FLAG
The flag of the "Bon Homme Richard"; probably originally had a thirteenth star.

NEW YORK REGIMENT FLAG
Originally of Col. Gansevort's Regiment, of Fort Stanwix fame. Flag also at siege of Yorktown, 1781.

THE STAR SPANGLED BANNER
Flag that inspired immortal lines of poem of Francis Scott Key; Emblem of our National Anthem, fifteen stars and fifteen stripes, ordered by act of January 13, 1794.

CONNECTICUT FLAG
Color differed with the regiment. One of the first regimental flags; almost identical with the state flag of today.

RHODE ISLAND FLAG
Carried at Trenton, Brandywine, and Yorktown as regimental standard of Rhode Island troops. Originally without canton; date of addition uncertain.

FLAG OF THE THIRD MARYLAND
Carried at Cowpens, January 5, 1781.

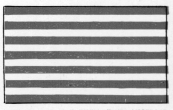

MERCHANT AND PRIVATEER ENSIGN
Probably one of the origins of the Union Flag. Striped flags were common on the seas before the American Revolution.

NE
NT
d of
au's
t by
phold
berty.

ROYAL DEUX PONTS
Flag of courage and loyalty carried at Siege of Yorktown.

FIRST PENN.
Thompson's riflemen, later First Penn. Regiment.

TALLMADGE'S DRAGOONS
Carried at Brandywine, Germantown, and Monmouth.

HANOVER FLAG
Adopted by the Hanover Township (now in Dauphin County, Pa). Riflemen; probably in 1775.

EUTAW STANDARD
Flag of Col. William Washington's Cavalry at Cowpen and Eutaw Springs.

FLAGS OF AMER

PINE TREE FLAGS OF AMERICAN REVOLUTION

UNION OR CONTINENTAL FLAG
Hoisted January 1, 1776, at the siege of Boston. Origin and authority not known, but designed primarily for naval use.

BUNKER HILL FLAG
Pine (fir) tree flag, also with a red field; both forms may have been at Bunker Hill.

PINE TREE FLAG
A second form, with Cross of St. George eliminated.

PHILADELPHIA LIGHT HORSE
Flag of Washington's escort (part way) to command Continental Army, 1775.

EARLY NAVY ENSIGN
Used by Washington's Fleet (1775) and Massachusetts.

LIBERTY TREE FLAG
A popular form, originating from the liberty (elm) tree in Boston.

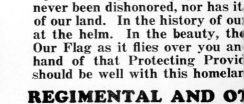

GREAT SEAL, UNITED STATES
Adopted by Continental Congress June 20, 1782. Displayed at embassies, legations and consulates. Affixed to commissions of cabinet officers, ceremonious communications to heads of foreign governments, proclamations, etc.

AMERICAN FL

EN. WASHINGTON'S GUARD FLAG
The Guard organized in 1776 of troops from all colonies.

PINE TREE—RATTLESNAKE FLAG
This form brought together pine tree design of New England and more southern rattlesnake emblem.

LINKED HAND FLAG
Thirteen mailed hands grasping thirteen links of an endless chain. Exhibited at the Centennial as a Newburyport, Mass., flag.

(*This flag was formally adopted*

THE STORY OF THE

EXCERPTS FROM AN
HONORABLE SOL BLOOM, BRO
THE BETSY ROSS HOU

"Wherever this Flag flies toda
tecting folds must realize that i
into being not only a new conste
ciple of government. Your Fl
Washington won for us, is the
honor to float over a people d
Upon all the glorious pages of ou
never been dishonored, nor has it
of our land. In the history of ou
at the helm. In the beauty, the
Our Flag as it flies over you an
hand of that Protecting Provic
should be well with this homelar

BENNINGTON FLAG
Associated with victory at Battle of Bennington, August 16, 1777, under General John Stark.

FIRST NAVY STARS AND STRIPES
In absence of specific arrangement of stars in the resolution of Congress, June 14, 1777, it is probable that in the naval flag the stars were in the form of the crosses of St. George and St. Andrew.

BUCKS OF AMERICA
Flag of a post-Revolutionary colored company of Boston, initialed J. G. W. H. for Hancock and Washington.

TAUNTON FLAG
Raised at Taunton, Mass., 1774. British union with American watchwords—"Liberty and Union".

FLAG OF FRANCE
Adopted 1794. It was the white standard of the Bourbons that was carried by Rochambeau and De Grasse.

PULASKI STANDARD
Made by Moravian Sisters, Bethlehem, Pa., for Count Pulaski's corps.

REGIMENTAL AND OT
OF THE AMERICA

BEAVER FLAG OF NEW YORK
Symbol of the colony from the seal of New Netherland. Said to have been carried by armed ships, 1775.

WEBB'S REGIMENT
Probably a guidon of several Connecticut regiments.

SECOND NEW HAMPSHIRE REGIMENT FLAGS
These two flags carried by one regiment were captured at Fort Anne by the British; probably the only captured flags of the American Revolution now in existence.

WHITE PLAINS
Apocryphal battle flag from contemporary English engraving.

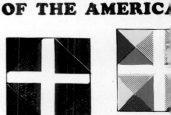

GATINOIS REGIMENT
After Yorktown known an "Royal Auvergne."

**SAINTO
REGIM**
A standa
Rochamba
army se
France to
American

SAMPLES OF BRAILLE PRINTING FOR THE BLIND

AS ISSUED BY THE

BRAILLE DEPARTMENT

OF THE

UNITED STATES GEORGE WASHINGTON
BICENTENNIAL COMMISSION

In Charge of
MISS DOROTHEA E. JENNINGS

INTRODUCTION

O N the following pages are samples of Braille printing for the blind, together with the translations, which demonstrate the type of material for the blind which was issued by the Braille Department of the United States George Washington Bicentennial Commission. This department was organized to carry the advantages and features of the Celebration to the visually handicapped and blind people of the nation, through the medium of embossed print.

Among the publications of the Commission which were published in Braille are the following pamphlets of the "Honor to George Washington" series: Frontier Background of Washington's Career, Washington the Colonial and National Statesman, Washington and the Constitution, Washington as President, Washington the Military Man, and Washington the Business Man (2 volumes). "George Washington Year by Year" was also published in Braille, as well as the "Music of George Washington's Time" (2 volumes) and the song by George M. Cohan, "Father of the Land We Love."

This Braille material was distributed to schools for the blind, Braille classes, and Braille Libraries and reading rooms, throughout the United States.

SAMPLE OF BRAILLE PRINTING FOR THE BLIND

Prepared by the Braille Department of the

UNITED STATES GEORGE WASHINGTON
BICENTENNIAL COMMISSION

(Translation is given below)

PLANS AND PURPOSES OF THE

GEORGE WASHINGTON

BICENTENNIAL COMMISSION

IN RECOGNITION OF THE 200th ANNI-
VERSARY OF GEORGE WASHINGTON'S BIRTH THE
CONGRESS OF THE UNITED STATES
CREATED BY A SPECIAL ACT IN 1924 A
GEORGE WASHINGTON BICENTENNIAL COM-
MISSION TO FORMULATE PLANS TO FITTINGLY
HONOR HIS MEMORY.

SAMPLE OF BRAILLE PRINTING FOR THE BLIND

(Continued)

(Translation is given below)

IN THIS ACT ITS DUTIES ARE OUTLINED AS
FOLLOWS:
FIRST, TO CREATE INTEREST IN THE
CELEBRATION;
SECOND, TO FORMULATE AND EXECUTE
PLANS FOR THE CELEBRATION SUCCESS;
THIRD, TO COLLECT AND DISSEMINATE
ALL THE INFORMATION POSSIBLE ABOUT
GEORGE WASHINGTON AND HIS TIMES.
IT WAS ALSO PROVIDED THAT THE STATES
OF THE UNION SHOULD BE, AND THE GOVERNMENT
OF FOREIGN COUNTRIES COULD BE, INVITED
TO PARTICIPATE IN THE CEREMONIES.

SERMONS

ON

GEORGE WASHINGTON

*This Section Contains a Number of Sermons, Prepared at the Request of
the United States George Washington Bicentennial Commission
by Ministers of Various Denominations in Different
Sections of the United States.*

FOREWORD

THE SERMONS ON GENERAL GEORGE WASHINGTON contained in this section have been prepared by ministers of churches of various denominations, located in different sections of the United States.

They were written at the request of the United States George Washington Bicentennial Commission, with the thought that they would be helpful to pastors in the smaller cities, towns and rural sections where extensive research facilities are not available, as well as of interest to all ministers, even though they be located where such facilities are available.

The Commission has reprinted the various sermons as they were prepared and takes this opportunity to extend its appreciation to those who have contributed to this volume.

THE INSPIRATIONS OF A GREAT LIFE

By ALBERT W. BEAVEN

President, THE COLGATE-ROCHESTER DIVINITY SCHOOL
Rochester, New York

Text: Genesis 50:26—"So Joseph died, and they embalmed him, and he was put in a coffin in Egypt."

The tremendous contribution made by Joseph to the development of the Hebrew people in the time of their sojourn in Egypt is well known. After his death, as the text points out, they placed his body in a coffin in Egypt, but instead of leaving it there permanently, they kept it ready for removal at any time when they should return to their promised land. This accorded with the pledge which Joseph had exacted of them. That "coffin in Egypt" not only became a memorial to the service which had been rendered the children of Israel by this outstanding personality, but also remained a challenge to the nation to prepare itself for a new period of advance.

It is a mark of strength when a nation is able not only to memorialize the great lives lived in its past, but to make those great lives become truly, for the present, inspirations to new achievement.

This is what America has done with many of her heroes, and it is particularly what is now proposed in connection with the celebration of the two hundredth anniversary of the birth of George Washington. I want to emphasize here certain beneficial results which I believe may come from it, results which we greatly need to have brought about.

First of all I refer to the need for injecting into our contemporary life a larger appreciation of the values of the past. Today we tend to be supercilious in our attitude toward yesterday. We make fun of it. We use words such as "Puritan" and "Victorian" as terms of reproach, with little emphasis upon the great contributions that came through those periods. Youth, in particular, eulogizes the present and looks with a sort of patronizing air upon things gone by, as though to be old fashioned is the unforgivable sin. While youth may exhibit this attitude more openly, a large number of adults are afflicted with the same short-visioned worship of the contemporary.

This tendency to undervalue the personalities and achievements of yesterday may be partly a by-product and partly a cause of the bitter cynicism in our present literary life. Contemporary literature has been marked by extreme iconoclasm. "Idol smashing" has been a favorite form of literary sport. Every personality that stood out above the crowd was naturally a target for these writers. There has been an almost ghoulish glee in the attacking of the heroes of our past and the snatching of the halos from their brows. Notice the attacks on Lincoln and Beecher, and in view of this celebration we all are particularly conscious of the various attacks on the great personality we now honor—our first president—George Washington.

In attempting to appraise the value of the criticisms made against him, we need to place it against the mood of our particular time. Undoubtedly, during the World War we carried idealism to a great height. We more or less worshiped the great personalities who were leading us, and refused to see any of their weaknesses. Criticism was restrained and adulation stimulated.

In the period which followed, it was natural that the pendulum should swing the other way. A time of disillusionment was upon us. Criticism was unleased and critics began hurling their darts. Practically every great idol of the war was dethroned, and as part of this general attitude of disillusionment we developed our present school of literary cynics. They were tempted to extremes, also, because in a time when the general mood was one of reaction against idealization, the more harsh and stark the criticism, the more it was talked about and the better it sold.

We are now happily passing out of this period of what may be called "buzzard literature," but we should not forget, when we try to evaluate the critical biographies of a man like Washington, that many of those recently put out are strongly tainted with the flavor of literary muck-raking which has been popular in the past decade.

This is not to deny that there have been elements of truth that have come to the surface in this time of "realism" in writing. No one would doubt, I think, that we probably had tended to overidealize our great men and that a fair historical approach to their lives would result in painting in more of the drab colors and not simply displaying the gold and crimson of hero worship. But when we admit this we are in no sense admitting that anything has been proved which in any way lessens the value and propriety of such a celebration as we are now having, to honor and perpetuate the memeory of this great American personality, George Washington.

The important thing for us, however, is to realize that such a mood of criticism can spread until it actually robs our generation of one of its most valuable assets, namely, the inspiration it can and should receive from the great figures of its past. We cannot permanently hurt Washington, but we can hurt ourselves. A generation that alienates itself from its past is a generation that has been weakened at a fundamental place. Progress comes by keeping the values of yesterday as well as adding the achievements of the future. We do not argue here for a slavish adherence to the things that were said and done by Washington, as though he had a finality of wisdom. If we were to do this we might duplicate the unfortunate history of science in relation to Aristotle, where the worship of the man practically prevented the development of the very thing for which he stood but we do believe profoundly that the preserving of a sense of gratitude for service rendered, the keeping alive of the memory of heroic actions, and the study of the statesmanlike foresight of the great men of the past, are means by which national greatness is assured.

To waste the memories of a great life is as foolish as it is to waste other national resources. There is no future which is not related to the past. Trees do not grow in mid-air; they send their roots into the ground. So the tree of our national future must be rooted in the solid ground of our past accomplishment.

A great personality is an achievement, in any age. Such a

445

thing is not so easily attained that it can be ignored when that is once accomplished. When we think of the vast number of people who have the chance to do it but whose lives are dismal nonentities when they have finished, the contrast makes the importance of a personality like that of George Washington all the more vivid.

It was a blessing of Providence to us as a nation that we had so splendid a person, with so fine a character, to guide us in the formative period of our national life. Exceedingly valuable was it also that his experience had developed him along so many lines. An engineer of ability, an agriculturist of note, a soldier of prominence and a statesman of world-wide fame, he helped to mold our infant republic in a fashion which places every citizen of this republic under permanent obligation. Like the children of Israel, we should not only put him in a "coffin in Egypt," but we should see to it that as we move on toward the further development of our national life we take with us consistently the memories of his accomplishments as an inspiration for the greater tomorrow.

It is important, also, that a man who occupies this outstanding position in the history of our national life should be a man whose life is a high-grade exhibition of moral and religious values. It is entirely possible for a nation to have as its heroes men who, while they may be effective along the lines of statesmanship or military ability, may nevertheless give such an exhibition of immorality and irreligion as to cast the sinister shadow of their own attitude across the national life. America is fortunate in that its outstanding men, such as Washington and Lincoln, have been men whose attitude toward great moral questions has been invariably wholesome, and whose attitudes toward religion has been constructive.

It is not necessary to claim perfection for our heroes, nor to state that a man like Washington did not act in ways that were customary in that time but about which we now have a more acute social conscience. He was undoubtedly human and affected by the standards of his time. But after we have admitted these limitations, there yet is exhibited in Washington a character which for rugged honesty, truthfulness, and high idealism is not frequently surpassed among men of his time or of any other time.

Washington saw far more clearly than do many men of today the value of moral character and spiritual idealism to the state. Listen to these words of his Farewell Address:

"Of all the dispositions and habits, which lead to political prosperity, religion and morality are indispensable supports. In vain would that man claim the tribute of patriotism, who should labor to subvert these great pillars of human happiness, these firmest props to the duties of men and citizens."

"And let us with caution indulge the supposition that morality can be maintained without religion. Whatever may be conceded to the influence of refined education on minds of peculiar structure, reason and experience both forbid us to expect, that national morality, can prevail in exclusion of religious principle."

It would be an exceedingly wholesome thing if many men who today ridicule Washington could appreciate as did he the necessity for moral idealism. He realized, as we need to do, that moral character is a fundamental requisite in a democratic society. Confidence in government, in a democracy or a republic, varies in direct proportion to our confidence in the character of the leaders who are in positions of responsibility.

Morality is to society what cement is to concrete. It is that integrating power which binds the various individual particles together. It makes the stable foundation upon which can be erected the institutions of society. Take out the confidence which is created by moral leadership, and democracy goes to pieces as truly as does a building reared upon concrete out of which cement has been left.

There are those today who look upon morality or immorality as a purely individual matter. Actually, immorality is a public nuisance. Badness always assesses its bills against goodness. It can never be a matter of indifference to good people, because it never lets good people alone. It is not content to carry on its own evil doings and then care for the results; it goes off and lets honesty carry the burden of its dishonesty, and purity suffer as the result of its impurity.

The first man who was electrocuted in New York state, we are told, cost approximately $100,000 to society. No one of us thinks for a moment that he paid the bills, nor do we think that his parents paid them, nor do we think there is a "criminal foundation" somewhere which comes around annually to pay such obligations. The fact is, of course, that that law-breaker and all law-breakers leave the bills for their law-breaking to be paid by the law-abiding citizen. This is a parable that runs all through society. Goodness always carries its own burdens, and the burdens of badness as well. The honest tax-payers carry the burden of the grafters, the tax-dodgers, and the criminals who break the laws and crowd the jails and penitentiaries. It is always so. Washington saw that the creating of moral fiber in the citizenship was an essential industry, and he wrote this conviction in large type both in his life and in his speech. We do well to emphasize this today.

He saw a further thing, which many a self-admittedly wise person is too shortsighted to see today, namely, that if you want to produce character, you can produce a better quality and a larger quantity of it as a by-product of religious conviction than you can in any other way. "Let us, with caution, indulge the supposition," said he, "that morality can be maintained without religion." The fact is that men act in moral ways not primarily because of reasons from without, but because of reasons from within. If a man is honest only because it is the best policy, he will be dishonest when it is not. By religion, you put back of one's moral action the most majestic ideas the mind of man is capable of conceiving, the ideas of God, eternity, and immortality. By religion, you give a man the most perfect example of the moral life in Jesus Christ. By religion, you enable a man to add to his own best powers the resources of the spiritual universe in living as he should live. When a man deals with his God, when he believes that a certain code of action is right because the blessing of God will attend it, because he owes it to his God to act in that fashion, when he deals with that God eternally on the basis of his actions here, then you have a reason for creating permanent moral attitudes which cannot exist when a man is simply taking his cue from his own personal desires or from the morals of his time.

Our particular day finds many of its would-be literateurs indulging in the composition of epitaphs for the grave of religion.

But unless we mistake the signs of the times, we can see indications which already show the disgust with which youth and others are turning from the cold and heartless irreligion of modern materialism and atheism, and turning back to explore again that vast area of experience of spiritual inspiration which has come to the race through the Christian religion. We are at the dawn of a time when Washington's emphasis upon the central importance of religion is to have a new and larger significance.

Finally, Washington has a message for our day because he was the great exemplar in contributing the element of moral and spiritual idealism to citizenship. It is this very element which we lack now, and for the lack of it we have all kinds of diseases plaguing us in our civic and national life. Just as a patient who is anæmic may have this malady show up in various external symptoms, so the toleration of crime and racketeering, the indifference to malfeasance in civic office, the prostitution of the courts of justice, the gay and debonair air with which citizens of high position unite in breaking our laws—all these and more show that in our citizenship ideals we are suffering from a species of moral and spiritual anæmia. We need an inoculation of moral vigor in the veins of our citizenry.

Washington evidenced his power to do this for the men of his day, when he stressed by life and word that citizenship meant responsibility as well as privilege. This is the essence of the Christian ideal as to the attitude of the individual toward the group. When I ask only "What do I get in privileges?" I take a pagan point of view, but when I ask "What can I contribute to it?" I am essentially Christian.

Washington enjoyed the privileges, but he continually paid the price, and assumed the responsibilities of his citizenship. Whatever the cost, he went straight ahead. It is that attitude which makes a nation great. Such an attitude will make efficient any form of government.

Today one is discouraged by the number of citizens of high position who seem to measure their advance in political life not by the amount of responsibility they carry, but by the favors they can get by political pull. They know and they work this judge or that district attorney, or the boss who can pull the string which enables them to avoid the consequences of illegal action; and they gloat over this power. A man who takes this attitude is a parasite. If everyone followed his course of action the very institutions on which he depends for protection would be wrecked. We need a few summons to take up the responsibility of our citizenship, a call that will shame the mere privilege hunters. It is a wholesome thing that in this day we can lift again in the midst of our national life, the kind of standards for which Washington stood, and proclaim that high moral conviction and genuine appreciation of the deep religious foundations of life are essential to good government. The memories of that great life which will be made vivid again by this celebration will do for us what the "coffin in Egypt" did for the children of Israel. May it be a constant challenge to that finer American citizenship of the future toward which we look.

WASHINGTON, THE INSPIRED WORKMAN

By REVEREND W. HERBERT BURK, D.D.

Founder and Rector of the WASHINGTON MEMORIAL CHAPEL
Valley Forge

"And I have filled him with the spirit of God, in wisdom, and in understanding, and in knowledge, and in all manner of workmanship, to devise cunning works, to work in gold, and in silver, and in brass, and in cutting of stones, to set them, and in carving of timber, to work in all manner of workmanship." (Exodus 31:3, 4, 5).

These words come home to us with a new significance as the Nation commits itself to the commemoration of the Bicentennial of the Birth of George Washington. They marked a national event in the far distant past of the Hebrew people. To that Nation's life and thought was to be added the Tabernacle to give order and beauty to worship, to deepen the national consciousness of the presence and power of Jehovah. For this there must be vision, and to the vision must be united the skill to make the vision abide. For this great work the artist must be called and endowed. Out of all the Nation, Bezeliel was chosen to be the architect of the Tabernacle, its designer and fabricator. To his natural gifts Jehovah added the gift of his Spirit, saying, "And I have filled him with the spirit of God, in wisdom, and in understanding, and in knowledge, and in all manner of workmanship. To devise cunning works, to work in gold, and in silver, and in brass, and in cutting of stones, to set them, and in carving of timber, to work in all manner of workmanship." (Exodus 31:3, 4, 5.) It was certainly a marvelous equipment for the task, one of the greatest so far set before the Nation. And yet at best the task was to meet a temporary condition imposed by the nomadic life of the Hebrew people. Beyond it was to be another life, a larger and more highly developed life, with its own needs, its own conditions, and for this the Tabernacle would be necessarily inadequate. Inevitably the Hebrew people were moving toward that future stage of settled occupation of the Promised Land. The goal was assured by God. The marvel is that God so richly endowed the architect of the temporary Tabernacle. It is a wonderful encouragement to man in any worthy endeavor. If Bezeliel be given the Spirit of God for his task, will not God more richly endow those to whom greater tasks will be committed?

Instinctively we turn from the task of the architect and builder of the Tabernacle to the Builder of a Nation and we turn with high hopes from Bezeliel to Washington. Those hopes of spiritual endowment will be more than realized in the man destined by God to be the leader in the building of a New Nation in the New Land. First and foremost we will see that God was the real architect and builder in the later age as He was in the far remote past. It is His Spirit which gave life and being to the Republic as it was in the Hebrew Nation. His love, His guidance, His vision, and His power are as manifest in America as they ever were in Canaan. Washington was as divinely selected, endowed and blessed as any man in the world's history.

None of those who gathered for a baptism in the old Virginia in 1732 had any idea of the significance of that service when the son of Augustine Washington and Mary Ball, his wife, was consecrated to the service of God. Was that the 5th of April or the 30th? It is too bad that none of the Godparents have left us any information, but Mr. Beverly Whiting and Captain Christopher Brooks and even Mrs. Mildred Gregory, his Godparents, failed to enlighten posterity on the Baptism of George Washington. The fact is after all the most important, that is that in Baptism George Washington was consecrated for the service of God and of his fellowmen.

One of the most momentous events in the life of Washington was the death of his father. This occurred when he was only eleven years old. Great as the personal loss was, it had much to do in the preparation of George for his life work. It threw him upon his own resources and gave to life a seriousness which he never lost. It also had much to do with his association with Lord Fairfax, an association of the highest value and greatest importance. As the surveyor of Lord Fairfax, Washington at the age of sixteen became the pioneer of America. He opened the way to the West and made ready for the westward faring of the American people. At twenty-one he was serving as an ambassador of England, in America, bearing to the representatives of France, in America, the demand that France withdraw its citizens and soldiery from the Ohio valley. His preservation, even at this early period of his eventful life, he counted an act of Providence. He served not only as an officer in command of troops, but acted also as the chaplain of his men when the Governor denied his request for a chaplain.

According to the records of Fairfax County, Virginia, George Washington entered upon a most important era of his life on February 15, 1763, when "He took the oaths according to Law, repeated and subscribed the Text and subscribed to the Doctrine and Discipline of the Church of England, in order to qualify him to act as a Vestryman of Truro Parish." He had been elected Vestryman on the 25th of October in the previous year, taking the place of "William Peake Gent, deceased," as the parish register states. His service as a vestryman must have been approved by his associates for on October 3, 1763, he was made one of the wardens for a year, the other being George William Fairfax. By this action Washington was put in the forefront of the religious life of his country and that meant that he assumed a leadership in the worship of God.

This is a point which few students of Washington's life consider, yet his religious faith on this account is better attested than that of many of his fellows. It is a matter of official record, not a family tradition, nor even a parish record. This is of the utmost importance when one stops to think of the prominence of the man or of the hostility of his detractors.

As a Church Warden his first important duty was in relation to church building. The Church Wardens were to advertise for plans and bids for a Church to be erected "at or near the Old Falls Church," for which the Parish was to be taxed "30,000 pounds of tobacco," which was "to be sold for cash by the Church Wardens for the highest prices they can get."

On the 28th of March, 1763, Washington was at a Vestry meeting at Falls Church, where it was decided that the old Church should not be repaired, but that a new one should be built. The next year some of the members of the Parish of Truro petitioned the House of Burgesses Court to divide the Parish by the creation of another Parish to be named Fairfax. By this division Washington was placed in the new Parish of Fairfax, in which he was elected a vestryman March 28, 1765. This division was unfair to the old Parish, so a new bill was passed and after its passage we find Washington was again in his old Parish, and of course he was re-elected vestryman. Naturally all this was of the deepest interest to Washington, and his record of the whole business seems to indicate that he had a hand in the equitable division which was finally effected. In 1767 the Vestry of Truro Parish met and resolved to build a new Church, Washington being present and advocating a new site. To determine the location of the new Church Washington made a survey showing the location of the houses of the residents with the distances marked. The map won the day for the new location of the Church. "April 7, 1769, the Vestry resolved that the Honorable George William Fairfax, George Washington & Mr. Edward Payne do view and examine the building from time to time, as they or any three of them shall see fitting, to whom the undertaker is to give notice when the different materials are ready." Thus for the second time Washington took his place as a church-builder and Pohick Church stands today as a monument of the ability of Washington as a business manager, but infinitely more it stands as a monument of his reverence and devotion. Nor should it ever be forgotten that while the Creed, the Lord's Prayer and the Ten Commandments were to be painted in black, it was Washington and George William Fairfax who gave the gold leaf for these fundamentals of our Holy Religion to be illumined in gold on the walls of Pohick Church.

At the request of the Vestry Washington imported: "A cushion for the pulpit and Cloths for the Desks & Communion Table of Crimson Velvett, with Gold Fring"—"as also two Folio Prayer Books covered with blue Turkey Leather with Name of the Parish thereon in Gold letters." When the pews were sold, following the custom of the day, Washington bought Pew No. 28 for £16. The adjoining pew was sold to Fairfax at the same price. The Washington and Fairfax Pews brought the highest sum bid for the Pews in Pohick Church. These Pews were just in front of the Communion Table, in the very front of the Church. Later he bought the next pew. When Christ Church, Alexandria, was built, Washington bought Pew No. 5 in Christ Church, again paying the highest price, £36.10.

There is such a determined effort to deny Washington's religious faith that we should note Washington's services as a Vestryman. Dr. Goodwin has pointed out that "During the eleven years of his active service from February, 1763, to February, 1774, thirty-one "Vestries" were held at twenty-three of which he is recorded as being present. On the eight occasions when he was absent, as we learn from his Diary or other sources, once he was sick in bed, twice the House of Burgesses, of which he was a member, was in session, and three other times certainly, and on the two remaining occasions probably, he was out of the

County." We should add in all fairness that time and again Washington drove the long distance to attend a meeting of the Vestry, when through the negligence of his associates, there was no quorum and of course no meeting was held.

These Vestry-days formed one of the most important factors in the life of the most honored man in America. They were the days of training for the later and larger services of liberator and ruler. They were days consecrated to the worship of God and the service of his fellows. Those too were the days of love and marriage and it should never be forgotten that the only surviving letter of Washington to his fiancee ends with this prayer, "That an all-powerful Providence may keep us both in safety is the prayer of your ever faithful and affectionate friend." That prayer was answered and the marriage took place on January 6, 1759, a marriage richly blessed with love and happiness.

This lover's prayer is a type of Washington's prayers, prayers that are spontaneous, the expression of a soul in tune with the Infinite. In resigning his Commission as Commander-in-Chief of the Army of the United States, his prayer was one "commending the interests of our dearest country to the protection of Almighty God, and those who have the superintendence of them to His holy keeping."

June 1, 1774, was a day of intercession and prayer for peace between England and America. On that day Washington wrote in his diary: "Went to Church and fasted all day." At Gulph Mills the Army spent the day before its march to Valley Forge in thanksgiving and prayer, as it did on May 6, 1778, in gratitude to God for the French Alliance. In appointing the hour for the Sunday services in the brigades, he said: "While we are zealously performing the Duties of good Citizens and Soldiers, we certainly ought not to be inattentive to the higher Duties of Religion. To the distinguished Character of Patriot it should be our highest Glory to add the more distinguished Character of Christian." With these words we must place the tribute to religion which he included in his farewell address: "Of all the Dispositions and Habits which lead to political Prosperity, Religion and Morality are indispensable Supports. In vain would that Man claim the Tribute of Patriotism who should labor to subvert these great Pillars of human happiness, these firmest props of the Duties of Men and Citizens." These are the words of no scorner of religion. They represent the sincere judgment of one who has walked with God and has beheld His mighty works, and has been blessed with His Presence.

Out of his sixty or more prayers and benedictions the outstanding utterance is his prayer for his Country and your Country, for his Nation and your Nation. In writing from Newburgh to the Governor of each State, he wrote his heart's prayer in these words: "I now make it my earnest prayer, that God would have you, and the State over which you preside, in his holy protection; that he would incline the hearts of the citizens to cultivate a spirit of subordination and obedience to government; to entertain a brotherly affection and love for one another, for their fellow citizens of the United States at large, and particularly for their brethren who have served in the field; and finally, that he would most graciously be pleased to dispose us all to do justice, to love mercy, and to demean ourselves with that charity, humility, and pacific temper of mind, which were the characteristics of the Divine Author of our blessed religion, and without an humble imitation of whose example in these things, we can never hope to be a happy nation." What a prayer that is! What a revelation it is of the patriot who breathed its petitions to the God Whom he served!

Today a grateful Nation unites to honor George Washington. The land resounds with the story of his many services, his great achievements, his marvelous successes. The great Republic stands as the monument of his life and labors. He lived to see something of his mighty work. He gave the praise to God.

Washington saw the history of his Nation as did the writer of the Book of Leviticus, and nothing better attests his religious character, "for as many as are led by the Spirit of God, they are the sons of God." (Romans 8:14.) In his letter to General Armstrong March 11, 1792, he said: "I am sure there never was a people who had more reason to acknowledge a divine interposition in their affairs, than those of the United States; and I should be pained to believe, that they have forgotten that agency, which was so often manifested during our revolution, or that they failed to consider the omnipotence of that God, who is alone able to protect them." In reviewing the movements of the Revolution he wrote to General Nelson, August 20, 1778: "The hand of Providence has been so conspicious in all this, that he must be worse than an infidel that lacks faith, and more than wicked, that has not gratitude enough to acknowledge his obligations."

That is Washington's condemnation of you and of me, and of all the people of this great land if we this day and hour do not bow in reverence and in deep gratitude to Almighty God, our Heavenly Father, for our Nation, its history, its institutions. The deeper our knowledge of its history, the greater our appreciation of its institutions and their significance, the greater will be our debt of gratitude that above all else He called Washington to be His servant, and endowed him with His Spirit that he might build not a tabernacle, but a Republic for the blessing of the human race. So God has called every man, woman and child to some service, higher or lower, and He has given to each a measure of His Spirit. The Bicentennial of Washington's Birth therefore comes to us a challenge to deeper consecration of soul and body and to higher service to our Country and our God.

WASHINGTON, THE MAN

By REVEREND EDWARD O. CLARK

Chevy Chase, Md.

"Quit you like men; be strong."—I Cor. 16:13

There is no need to add fulsome praise to the name of George Washington; that name shines resplendent in its glory. But there is need of knowing Washington the man, Washington as he was among the men of his day,—not a sainted paragon, something other than human; nor yet an ambitious schemer given to vicious pleasures; but a man, strong, capable, courageous, a man who in the face of duty never cringed, and in the example he left to posterity, none need be ashamed.

In his well-rounded manhood rather than in the formal routine of ecclesiastical performances, is the true religion of Washington to be discerned. And it seems not too much a stretch of the imagination to believe that the heart within him would have warmed greatly to the words of the Apostle Paul to the men of Corinth, "Quit you like men; be strong." These words are truly fitting of him. In innumerable ways Washington quit himself a man. His was a courageous spirit, and it is important that we should truly reveal the man he was to the world; for time has served to make him unreal, a sort of demi-god; and sentimentalism has greatly obscured the essential qualities of his manliness.

A man of vitality—Washington's character is essentially typified in his strong splendid physique; over six feet in height, muscular in body, he was impressive in personality. As he was physically strong, so were his interests concerned with that which was vital in life. He had no time for the merely academic or theoretical phases of things, much less for that which was dead in its complaisant formality. His education was of the practical sort and mostly self-attained. We know how he learned surveying in the frontier regions of Virginia, how he got what military technique he possessed in the hard school of the Braddock defeat and in the French and Indian encounters; how he gained an essentially trained outlook upon the problems of life through actual contact with life problems. His actual schooling was very little; his education was truly profound.

Throughout his life we see how he was always concerned with issues and duties which were dominant and vital: his concern in the protection of the colony of Virginia from the Indians; his interest in the government of the colony as a member of the House of Burgesses; his fondness for managing his plantation estates; his conduct of the colonial forces in the Revolutionary War; his services in the Constitutional Convention and later as the First President of the nation; in all of these varied situations Washington was the realist. He never lost sight of the ideal, but he always remembered the practical aspects of every situation; hence his success.

Caricature and compliment—In contrast with the true picture of the rugged manhood of Washington, we have the early caricature by Parson Weems. In his early "Life" he was portrayed as a precocious boy and a sentimentally pious saint who could not sin. Historically it is agreed that the cherry tree episode has no foundation in fact. From one point of view it is a caricature. From another point of view, whether true or false, it is a compliment to the integrity of Washington's manhood. Certainly it is unlikely such a tale would have been told of one known to have been lacking in integrity; and had it been told, would never have survived, unless it was somehow fitting. That such a tale was told of Washington is, therefore, a tribute of his sterling honesty and unquestioned integrity. Such qualities were part of his "quitting himself a man."

A vital faith—We see, also, how his interest in religion was from the practical rather than the formal point of view. That he was a Churchman and attended Divine services with varying regularity throughout his life, is known to all. His interest in religion, however, was in the influence for a moral life which faith exerts and in the inner spiritual satisfactions of belief in an over-ruling All Wise Providence. For religion as a perfunctory observance he had little time, as shown from an excerpt from his journal of a Sabbath spent at a tavern in Connecticut. He wrote: "A meeting-house being within few rods of the door, I attended morning and evening service, and heard very lame discourses from a Mr. Pond." His interest was in sermons that were not "lame," but which touched life in a vital way.

Perhaps the most spontaneous expression of his early faith in God is to be found in one of those revealing sentences from a letter written to Mrs. Martha Custis shortly after their engagement. He was in the midst of stern duties in the frontier regions and wrote, "That an all-powerful Providence may keep us both in safety is the prayer of your ever faithful and affectionate friend." In religion as in moral character he nobly quit himself a man.

A man of mastery—The will to succeed was strong in Washington. Success early became a habit with him. The story of his attempt to break in his mother's famous colt only to have the high-spirited colt fall dead under him, is a tribute, whether true or not, to the unflexing will of the man. Such a story was at least possible with Washington; he was not a weakling.

He first of all learned a self-mastery of strong passions and high temper which not alone reveal his greatness; but which contributed not a little to his real success, as a leader of others. In regard to the common customs of the day, Washington was a child of his times. We need neither hide nor apologize for his drinking of wine and other alcoholic beverages, his pleasurable pastimes of fox-hunting, dancing, card playing. They were in his life whether we like them or not, and for my part, judging not from today, but from his own day, they cast no opprobrium upon him, but serve rather to reveal the man he was. The significant thing, however, is that he never allowed such pleasurable indulgences to gain the mastery. When we consider the virility well within bounds, is a lasting testimony to his self-control.

His leadership—Having gained a mastery of himself he was in a position to lead the armies of the colonies through to a successful termination of the struggle. The story of the Revolutionary War is too well known for repetition. Many factors entered into the final outcome, but above them all was the strong, self-reliant, unselfish personality of George Washington. Almost unknown outside of Virginia, when given the command of the colonial armies, and selected somewhat on the basis of conflicting jealousies, he soon won the loyalty of the soldiers, the esteem of other leaders, and the confidence of the people to a remarkable degree.

This habit of the mastery of self and of situations which he had established in his own life brought him patience in dealing with a contrary Congress, and perseverance in continuing the long-drawn-out struggle. Nowhere are the essential qualities of manliness manifest to better advantage than in Washington's actions under the fire of unjust criticisms, as in the Conway Cabal, or amid the jealous contentions and traitorous behavior of some of his officers, or in the face of discouraging prospects of victory. Men of lesser caliber under such conditions would have quit the command many times over. That he did not do so is a lasting tribute to his greatness.

That habit of mastery of self is further seen when he was willing to later forego the personal delights of home life at his beloved Mount Vernon to the repeated call of service for his country. He confessed that it was a sense of duty alone which led him to attend the Constitutional Convention in Philadelphia in 1787. And again when he took the heavy burdens of the First President of the new nation, he consulted not his own selfish interest, but his duty, and once having determined that, straightway set forth to discharge it. It is a significant fact that in the forty-seven years of his occupancy of Mount Vernon, nearly one-half of that time was spent in the service of his country, for which he received no real compensation; while, on the other hand, during the Revolutionary War alone through the depleted income from his estates, due principally to his absence, he lost approximately fifty thousand dollars. Here was the victory of moral unselfishness. And of those who differed from him, not one dared to impugn the high nobility of his motives. He quit himself a man.

A man of vision—No one would say that of the large number of the early American leaders any were lacking in vision, and yet among them Washington stands foremost in the clarity with which he foresaw real issues and coming events. He thoroughly believed in the American colonies and foresaw both a great people and a great nation in the offing. Acting upon this foresight he sought early to develop the then western lands of the Ohio Valley much to the amazement of people generally who did not expect the nation to expand thus.

On many moral questions he manifested an advanced mind above that of many contemporaries. It is true he was a slave-holder, for the institution was then part and parcel of colonial life; but he manifested a humane consideration for his slaves to an uncommon degree and in his will gave freedom to those he held in his own right. Writing of his own state, Virginia, he said, "I could wish from my soul that the Legislature of this State could see the policy of a gradual Abolition of Slavery; it would prevent much future mischief." In this his vision was only too clear.

On the subject of education he was much advanced in his views. He showed much interest in and concern for the education of his stepson and his step-grandson, writing detailed letters to them concerning the subjects desirable. He made annual contributions to schools and academies. One desire close to his heart was for the establishment of a university at the National Capital.

A man's man—Summing up the true character of Washington, we find him to be in all respects a man; human indeed, with the characteristic desires, longings, pleasures of mankind generally; but in addition, we find him through a long and varied life acquitting himself with strength, with courage, with self-control, and with a native capacity for leadership such as has been true of few men. We find him manly in his moral idealism as he was practical in his grasp of concrete problems; and throughout his career unselfish in motive and far-visioned in outlook. No wonder the nation unites to pay tribute to the sterling qualities of manliness which he so nobly embodied.

GEORGE WASHINGTON

By DR. HENRY H. CRANE
Malden, Massachusetts

Any selection of foremost Americans, if it is to be taken at all seriously, must of necessity place in a pre-eminent position the name of him who will forever be called "the Father of His Country." Any person, or people, would naturally think highly of the man who brought him or them into being, for the recognized prerogative of parenthood everywhere is to be the object of veneration. But never was reverence and esteem more richly merited by any parent than by this man "who died childless that a Nation might call him father." It is no empty platitude, but the expression of a great truth, when it is said that George Washington is, in the minds of most Americans at least, "first in war, first in peace, and first in the hearts of his countrymen."

Unless the foremost judges of Washington's own day and likewise those of every period since have grievously erred, we are perfectly justified in saying that he was actually one of the great figures of the world, not only because of the brilliancy of his achievements and the triumph of his ideals, but also because of the moral majesty of his manhood and the unimpeachable integrity of his character. Washington stood supreme, unique, above the rest of his contemporaries by general consent, despite the fact that his age was blessed with an unusually large number of master minds. Says Lord Bryce, that very competent judge of statesmen, "Washington stands alone and unapproachable, like a snow peak rising above its fellows, with a dignity, constancy and purity which have made him the ideal type of civic virtue to succeeding generations . . ."

But with all these unqualified encomiums we are likely to over-paint the picture, and instead of revealing a man of flesh and blood, there is danger of producing a cold and lifeless image, rather forbidding and false. This is precisely what has happened in a great many instances. To multitudes Washington is virtually a demigod, with scarcely any of those endearing human qualities which bring him near to us. It is rather difficult to become acquainted with an "unapproachable snow peak." As we approach it our emotions may be sublime, but also cool. For this very reason, perhaps, many have come to think of our first president as Mount Washington, rather than Mr. Washington; and his deepest appeal—that of his humanity—is denied us.

As a reaction against this "Washington myth," and in order that we might become really acquainted with our first great national hero, a considerable number of books, pamphlets and magazine articles have appeared of late professing to give us the "real" Washington. Some of these publications have been reverent and wise; others, as is to be expected, are crude and disproportioned. The would-be iconoclasts have had an uproarious time smashing numerous traditional notions about our first president.

Certain so-called sophisticates, by exagerating and exploiting the foibles and frailties of the man, have sought to lower him to the level of worse than moral and mental mediocrity; but these human hyenas have succeeded in nothing other than revealing their own perverted predilections.

Altogether the result of this very modern and thorough historical study has been most beneficial, in that it has released Washington, the man, from a fictitious and cramping perfection which prevented those correct estimates of him which more than ever justify us in placing him in a supremely great position among the noble spirits of the earth.

The standards we have rather arbitrarily set up, whereby we are seeking to measure the greatness of each man who might qualify as one of the five foremost Americans, serve to show Washington's pre-eminence most readily. We have said that to determine a man's greatness we must ask (1) what he was, i.e., the quality of his character; (2) what he dreamed, i.e., the reach and directions of his aspirations; and (3) what he did, i.e., the extent and value of his accomplishments as seen in the number of lives affected, the significance of the interests involved and the permanence of his achievements.

With reference, then, to what he was, we may say that despite the fact that he was not "the blameless boy who never lied, the priggish youth over whom pedantic moralists have luxuriated, the faultless man, cold as moonlit marble," whom some biographers have developed, he was, nevertheless, one of those rare pictures in the gallery of heroes whose character shines through his face, whose very nature was large and kingly, who could not have been undistinguished, who was, in the truest and highest sense of the word, a thoroughbred. He will always shine as one of the great white lights of history.

It is not necessary to recount the details of his life, so familiar to everyone; but certain great characteristics should be enumerated. And first of all, mention should be made of the perfect POISE, the beautiful BALANCE of his life. All extremes are evidences of weakness; all excesses are manifestations of madness. Poise, when dynamic and not static, means power; proportionateness implies proficiency. In Washington no one quality protruded in his make-up at the expense of another. He had ambition, but it was never stained by unworthy compromise. He had strength, but it was never allowed to run over into vindictiveness nor cruelty. He had daring, but it was never evidenced in any foolhardiness. He was a rich man, but he lived simply and realized the responsibility of his possessions. He was a gentleman, but he was never snobbish in his bearing. He was a patriot, but he was never smirched with the jealousies and quarrels of partisanship. He was a churchman, but no one ever accused him of hypocrisy. He was conservative without being reactionary. He was liberal without being radical. He was wise without being academic. He was steadfast without being stubborn. He was an idealist, yet possessed of a restraining practicality. He was vastly endowed with common sense.

Incidents illustrating these various virtues are known to everyone at all familiar with the life of this great man. In boyhood, young manhood, maturity and old age the same sterling quality of balance or poise was ever evident. When we think of the tumultuous times in which Washington lived—an age of revolution, of violent passions and desperate measures—we can come to a fuller appreciation of the significance of the utterance of the great historian, Green: "The foundations of the whole world were shaken, but not the understanding of Washington." The fact is the difficulties which confronted the nation as it was struggling for birth, the problems which were presented to the agonized father of the country cannot possibly be described. The whole land was shaken with petty strife; individualism was running riot; sectional differences were vociferously and viciously evident; the war scarcely over when the horrors of the French revolution burst upon Europe, and fanatics shrieked aloud that America should participate in the European embroglio; everywhere confusion, consternation. But amid all the upheaval and storm there was one man who remained poised, serene, sure and by the magic of his personality he held the people fast to the great ideal.

Many great men were necessary in those times that tried men's souls; one man was indispensable. Says George William Curtis: "Hamilton was the head, Jefferson was the heart, John Jay was the conscience, but each one of these separate qualities may truthfully be said to have had even more signal expression when they were all united in the single character of Washington."

Another outstanding characteristic of our first president was his PATIENCE. Patient with his mother, whose rather whimsical and often petulant demands were of considerable embarrassment to him all through his life; patient with his soldiers and his officers, whose weakness and obstinacy sorely tried him; patient with his superiors, whose stupidity and folly at times well nigh cost him his life; patient with the Continental Congress, whose wranglings and pettiness would have driven lesser men mad; patient with the country as it slowly struggled into selfhood as a nation. Perhaps there is no one thing that betokens greatness more readily than patience, that is real patience, not its spurious counterfeit that is actually nothing other than indifference. For where there is true patience there is deep PURPOSEFULNESS and a sense of POWER sustained by a high FAITH. And certainly these qualities were sublimely evidenced in the life of Washington, and so clearly that they need no illustrations to substantiate them.

So we might continue to enumerate those virtues that made

him great. Feeling with the people, always, he did not follow them, maintaining his independence of thought no matter what public opinion might be. He was a born leader. Conscious of his power, he was quiet, never striving nor crying out as do those who are impotent and feel they must pretend to possess that which they lack. He knew and trusted those cosmic spiritual forces that exert themselves in due season—so he could wait, without impatience. He impressed his contemporaries, as he has impressed posterity, with the sense of steadfastness—he seemed rooted and grounded in God. Having no vanity, he sought no praise and hence was never offended. He always felt he had more of the good things of life than he could possibly have deserved.

Living in a certain self-sufficient aloofness, his apparent isolation was yet warm and attractive, for he was keenly alive to human relationships and influences. He loved. He laughed. He wept. He suffered. He cared. Bitterness, cynicism, and pessimism, which are tempters of pettiness, he never harbored in his strong, brave heart. Confidence, cheer, hope and an unquenchable optimism abounded in him, for these are always the by-products of greatness.

But the golden secret of Washington's greatness, the twin virtues that more than all else made him what he was, seem to me to be his downright INTEGRITY, and his upright FAITH IN GOD. He was a bond slave to his great convictions of right, truth, justice. As a youth he copied in his rules of conduct, "Labor to keep alive in your breast that little spark of celestial fire called conscience." And he succeeded well in his appointed task, for the flame of that divine fire was never dimmed. So men everywhere *believed* in him, they *trusted* him, they had *confidence* in him, and they *followed* him. Washington was a spiritual giant in soul stature. He was great by virtue of what he *was,* the quality of his character.

And what shall we say of his dreams, the reach and direction of his aspiration? This man whose vision inspired a whole new continent of people to dream of independence, cohesion and nationhood, saw with the eye of the soul the glory and the grandeur of a people who could and would govern themselves. He dreamed a democracy—and it came into being.

The nature and extent of his achievements are so vast, so far-reaching, that they cannot be compressed into the limitations of any formal enumeration and description.

From the days of his boyhood to the time of his demise he was above all else a doer of deeds. It has been supposed that Washington knew few hardships, that his training was enveloped in the comparative ease of a well-to-do Virginia planter's household where help was plentiful and the owner's wants anticipated. The fact is, he deliberately chose to live his life in the open where, by hunting, fishing, swimming the streams, exploring and camping in the woods, he hardened himself for those subsequent battles of life which no hothouse variety of humanity could ever hope to cope with. For three years and more Washington toiled at the profession of surveying, which in those early days was a most taxing task requiring much courage and perseverance as well as skill. Having received instruction in the manual of arms, fencing and sword exercise, and proving himself at an early date an able soldier, he was selected by Governor Dinwiddie not only to take that dangerous trip to the outpost of the French Possessions, but he was subsequently assigned to an important post in the war with France and her Indian allies. These exacting engagements helped to fit him for the larger duties of Commander-in-Chief of the Continental forces in those most critical days of the American Revolution, and the signal services rendered in that capacity are well known to the world.

But Washington's most enduring achievements were those which followed the War. Its success, to be sure, elevated him beyond all his fellow soldiers and statesmen in the confidence and esteem of the nation. They unanimously elected him the presiding officer of the convention which met at Philadelphia in May, 1787, to draft a constitution for the new republic. Here his services were absolutely invaluable. The states still had rival rights and divided interests. They were frightfully jealous of one another. He wrote to Madison that the separate states were "Thirteen Sovereignties pulling against each other." He felt there must be some bond to unite all in common interest—to make them in fact as well as in name United States.

It is in the capacity of the great unifier of our nation that his most significant contribution is to be found. The single, outstanding, cohesive force that eventually broke down the destructive devisiveness between the various colonies and welded them into a nation was nothing other than the personality of George Washington. From the first he was the one great unifying force. None other than he could have held the colonies together from the outset of the great struggle for independence. It was he who guided them safely past the rocks and shoals on which the frail vessel of colonial unity threatened so frequently to go to pieces. By the example of his own selfless devotion to the great cause in which he believed so sincerely, he held all together in that great common enterprise, and his grip was strong enough to withstand the perpetual attacks of particular partisanships. He, more than any other man or force, held the colonies together during those critical years that intervened between the Revolution and our constitutional government. When the Articles of Confederation proved more and more inadequate and Congress sank into increasing impotence and deserved popular contempt, when devisive influences were rife and the Old World looked with avidity for the speedy collapse of the American experiment of democratic and federal government, Washington stood in the midst of all this storm and strife like a tower of strength, unmoved and immovable.

Again, in the varying and conflicting groups that took shape and power at the Constitutional Convention, it was the influence of Washington that enabled that body to proceed with its work and ultimately achieve its end. Others may have had more to do with the shaping of the Constitution, with its outline and phrasing and form, but he was the one and only indispensable member of the Convention without whom it would surely have broken up in disaster.

Then again, during those disturbed and doubtful months of debate over the ratification of the Federal Constitution, it was Washington, and he alone, who held the country together. Had it not been for the popular confidence in him, it is practically certain that the Constitution would have failed of ratification. Patrick Henry, in his violent attack upon the Constitution as the surrender of the sovereignty of the State of Virginia, found Washington's endorsement of the scheme the one stubborn fact which he could not overcome.

But the glory of Washington's achievements as leader in the revolutionary and constitutional struggles must not allow us to overlook the immensely valuable services he rendered during the closing years of his life in an even wider and more significant cause. The last great effort of Washington was to hold the new nation here erected to a lasting friendship with the great nation from which it had severed itself. Here again he served as a bond to hold firmly together those elements which were speedily tending to fly apart and which the good of humanity demanded should be kept in concord and unity. His firm advocacy of a policy of goodwill between the United States and Great Britain brought upon him hostile attacks of criticism, but history has rendered a verdict of unstinted approval upon the wisdom of his course. In all history there is scarcely a finer example of far-sighted steadfastness in the fact of popular opposition than that revealed in the last years of Washington's life of service. It is a question if his chief crown of glory as a peacemaker be not that demonstration of far-sighted, large-minded international statesmanship which led him to hold steadily neutral between France and England. He knew that he had fought not the British people, but a system which misrepresented them. He was big enough and true enough to see straight even amidst the distorting forces and the passions of war. He saw clearly that the good of America and the good of the world demanded the closest possible relations of goodwill and cooperation between Great Britain and the United States.

Washington left many a rich and valued heritage to the people of this country. It is doubtful if any of them is worth more—it is certain that no one of them is more vital and valuable just now—than this noble, steadfast example of the spirit which holds together men and forces, groups and nations, thus making and maintaining peace. It is no wonder that Washington is, in tradition and in fact, the symbol of union. His loyalty and his vision were not limited by the narrow provincialism of his day. He saw past partisanship to patriotism, and past patriotism to a passion for humanity.

When at last Washington prepared to leave the presidency, in that memorable Farewell Address to the American people, he spoke these words which we should ponder deeply and hold to heart: "It will be worthy of a free, enlightened, and at no distant period a great nation, to give to mankind the magnanimous and too novel example of a people always guided by an exalted justice and benevolence."

As we seek to do honor to "The Father of our Country," what better tribute can we pay him than to follow out the implications of his injunction? About the world today many denizens and peoples are asking anxiously if America is to play in the future that kind of a role prescribed by her first President. Never has mankind stood more in need of a magnanimous example of a people guided by justice and benevolence. It is a great gain for this country, and for the world, that the man whose thoughts are so large a part of the national tradition should have in his final and greatest expression brought such a message to his people. Washington is still the reminder of America's duty to herself and the symbol of her place in the world.

"BEHOLD THE UPRIGHT"

Delivered by the
RT. REV. JAMES E. FREEMAN, D.D., LL.D.

Bishop of Washington, at the National Cathedral, Washington, D. C.
Text: Psalms 37.37. "Mark the perfect man and behold the upright."

As we see him through the mists of the multiplying years, the character of Washington becomes more appealing and more luminous. Among the greatest names chronicled on history's enduring page, his, by the consent of nations, stands among first. He endures, not alone because he was the first and foremost of great patriots, but because his life in itself incarnated those principles that make for fame and immortality. An eloquent Irishman has said concerning him:

"No country can claim him, no age appropriate him
—the boon of Providence to the human race—his fame
is eternity, his residence, creation."

Carthage had her Hannibal, Rome her Caesar, Prussia her great Frederick, France her Napoleon, England her Norman conqueror, but the consensus of history gives Washington a place more unique and more transcendent than that held by these mighty masters of events. Not as great a statesman or as skillful a general as others who went before, his place in history is secured by attributes and qualities of more excelling worth, and

no less an authority than Lord Brougham gives him place among the greatest the world has known.

Had America produced nothing more than the extraordinary characters of Washington and Lincoln, her existence as a nation would be justified to the world.

Judged in comparison with his remarkable contemporaries, he occupies the foremost place in this group of heroic men. Fisher Ames, who sat with him in the pew in St. Paul's Church, New York, on the day of his inauguration, wrote of him: "I was present in the pew with the president, and must assure you that, after making all deductions for the delusion of one's fancy in regard to characters, I still think of him with more veneration than for any other person."

The most exacting critics of the period through which he moved accord him a higher place than that enjoyed by any of his associates. Hamilton gave us our banking system, Jefferson our Declaration of Independence, Marshall our system of jurisprudence; Franklin, Jay, and Monroe our international policies, but Washington gave us our character as a nation and as a people. It has been given to few men in the course of human events to so indelibly stamp their personality upon the life and characteristics of a nation. To no other than Washington do we accord the proud distinction, "Father of his Country."

The mighty shaft erected to his memory in the capital of the nation is symbolic of the symmetry, proportions, and stateliness of his character. We think of him as the man of the hour, whose high achievements knew little of hindrance. We fail to reckon with his adversities, the stern and at times violent opposition to his course, or the enemies that obstructed and sought to defeat his aims. All these he had, and like other great leaders, they are to be considered in appraising his life and lofty attainments.

It might be safe to affirm that the gateway to all opportunity is beset with difficulties. It is of little worth to us as a nation that we cherish the name and deeds of this greatest of Americans, unless we are prepared to emulate his virtues and to maintain those high standards for which he stood. Nothing is cheaper than praise, nothing more costly than emulation. Here was one whose simplicity of life, singleness of purpose, fidelity to obligations, private and public, and strong Christian virtues, constitute at once the ambition and despair of succeeding generations. Moulded as if by the finger of God, this stately figure survives all criticisms, triumphs over all adverse judgments, defies the effacing touch of time and holds without dissent or challenge the love and veneration of each succeeding age.

From his hands we received our heritage, by our hands it is ours to preserve it. Said the author of the "Weal of Nation": "To dilute the quality of our natural manhood is a sad and beggarly prostitution of the noblest gifts conferred upon a people. Who shall respect a people who do not respect their own blood?" This query is a searching one for every true patriot who seeks to perpetuate those institutions transmitted to us by the fathers of the republic. Calling the nation to higher ideals, the late Bishop Potter of New York declared: "If there be no titular royalty in this country, all the more need is there for personal royalty. If there be no nobility of descent, all the more indispensable is it that there should be nobility of ascent."

When patriotism comes to be but the expression of political ambition, or the "last refuge of scoundrels," it has marked the period of its decadence. It is of little worth that we sing:

"My country 'tis of thee,
Sweet land of liberty,"

unless we are prepared to make sacrifices to maintain that liberty untarnished and unsullied. If we would continue as a nation, we must do more than chronicle the names of our patriots in bronze and marble, we must make their principles vital forces in the life of our time. If a lust for wealth is outstripping love of country, if selfish indifference characterizes our attitude toward civic duty and obligation, then the praise of our heroes is but the certain evidence of our disloyalty to all that they held dear and is an indictment of our selfish abandonment of their ideals.

Our growth has been unparalleled and our proud place in the sisterhood of nations so unrivalled that at times we betray a conceit and assurance wholly unworthy of us. It is undoubtedly true that the extent of our territory, the heterogeniousness of our population, the complexity of our ever increasing urban problems, together with our vast accumulation of wealth, render us susceptible to the machinations of the demagogue and his political chicanery, and to the envy and ambitious designs of those whose ways are alien to our ideals and institutions. At possibly no time in our history have we been more open to these malign forces than in the more recent years. The very unrest and widespread disorders that characterize the life of the world today compel us to adhere more rigidly to the dictum that, "Eternal vigilance is the price of liberty."

A fresh recognition in this Bicentennial year of the gifts and qualities of Washington furnishes abundant opportunity for a closer study of his character and a better understanding of the principles that motivated and governed him. No such study can be regarded as adequate that leaves out of reckoning the strong virtues that adorned and enriched his life. We do not venture to maintain that his character was without flaw, or that in the many and various capacities in which he served he was wholly free from error in judgment. He was human like other men, and his modesty so great that one of his associates on an occasion said to him: "Mr. Washington, your modesty equals your valor, and that surpasses any language that I possess." There is no occasion that, in our estimate of this unusual man, we should hold him blameless; on the other hand, the long years in which he has withstood the white light of an exacting criticism, he has held without diminution of interest and praise his proud place as the highest exemplar of American manhood and American ideals.

Fundamentally and essentially, Washington was a deeply religious man. Even those who have studied his life most critically have not denied him this distinction. His reverence for God and his devotion to spiritual ideals, are conspicuous in the record of his public and private life. He weighed issues, reached decisions and acted in accordance with the dictates of his conscience. To him, love of country was necessarily related to love of God. His relation to the Protestant Episcopal Church was intimate and at times official. At Pohick he served with singular fidelity on the vestry, and the story of his relation to this parish and to Alexandria discloses his deep and unfailing interest in the essential place the Church occupies in corporate and individual life. In his farewell address he warns his people in these memorable words: "Let us with caution indulge the supposition that morality can be maintained without religion."

No study of his career or of the motives that governed him is adequate or consistent, that leaves out of consideration the strong religious impulses that determined his action. To his mind religion was the indispensable and stabilizing element in private and public life. The need for emphasizing this today has never been greater. America in particular has recently emerged from a period in which her search for things material and her passion for prosperity rendered her for the while immune to spiritual ideals. Her people had come to believe that the security and continuing power of the nation resided in the accumulation of riches and the possession of treasure. Her temples of commerce, her ever increasing industries, her proud position as the creditor nation of the world had intoxicated her with a sense of her own inherent power and capacity to endure. Suddenly, and without warning, this dream of empire, this sense of immunity to ills that afflict other peoples has been dissipated, and the proud republic has been humbled. The miseries and misfortunes of the elder world, America has been compelled to share. In the face of such a grave and critical situation we are compelled to turn again to those sources of power that have made and preserved us a nation. We have learned at frightful cost that all true attainment is not to be purchased in the market places of the world. We have been sobered and rendered more reflective by the stern events of recent years.

It is well that this notable Bicentennial anniversary should come to us in such a period. It compels us to re-examine and re-study the sure footings on which the fathers builded the republic. They trusted in something more than statesmanship, something more than strength of arms, something more than the genius and cunning of the trader; they believed that only as the nation served with fidelity the God in whom they trusted and maintained those virtues that guarantee life, liberty, and the pursuit of happiness would it continue stable and secure.

In the notable group that constituted the leadership of that early period, a group wholly representative of genius, of chivalry, and of statesmanship, Washington stands quite alone and supreme. That he and his compatriots, in the face of seemingly insuperable difficulties were able to lay the foundations of a republic that in design and purpose was utterly unique, witnesses to a quality of greatness that finds few if any parallels in human history.

We may be standing today in one of those great transition periods where far reaching changes are impending. It may be that we have come to the beginning of a new era that is to be marked by sweeping changes in customs, habits, and institutions that have resisted the forces that for generations have been arrayed against them. It is unquestionably true that newer and severer tests are being applied and new and strange theories of government advanced. At such a time it behooves us to regard with meticulous care those principles whereon the republic was builded, and to study afresh the motives that dominated the men who gave the republic its character.

There are those in our commonwealth who would part company with systems, institutions, and ideals transmitted to us from the past. To such, Washington and the noble band that surrounded him are but figures, however picturesque, that belong to an age wholly unrelated to our own. As the stately minuet has no longer its appeal, so the virtues and ideals that marked the period of its vogue find no consistent place in this later age of accelerated movement, machinery, and steel. Their hands are dead and powerless that once in other and plastic days moulded and fashioned the young Republic. Their ways, their habits, their outlooks and their ideals, can find no place of accommodation in this modern, colorful period in the world's history. Can we unthinkingly accept such an affirmation or believe such an evaluation of our most creative period? We think not. No

matter what later and striking changes we have witnessed, nor yet what our esteem of our place in the sun may be, it is clearly evident, more so today than ever, that nations rise or fall by the estimate they place upon spiritual ideals as related to their domestic, social, industrial, and political concerns. Whatever the foibles may have been that characterized the men of Washington's period, and they were not impeccable, one thing is conspicuously true concerning them; namely, they had a deep reverence for sacred and holy things and they recognized that the source of all virtue and of all security resides in an obedient recognition of God's laws. This is wrought into every state paper and characterizes every action of this noble band. The gulf that divides us from this generation of heroic men may seem wide and deep, but adherence to the high ideals and purposes that marked their conduct and devotion to the state is our surest warrant of security, peace, and continuing power. The recognition of the immutable laws of God, unfailing allegiance to those fundamental principles of life given to mankind by Jesus Christ, these we may not ignore or neglect, except to our peril. We shall only add further confusion to our present distracted country, if we at this time acclaim with high praise the valorous deeds of Washington and forget his ringing call to a service that involves sacrifice in the maintenance of those principles upon which this American Republic was builded. Nothing alien to our traditions may assume to govern or control us in our course or determine for us our relation to problems at home or abroad. This is no affirmation of a policy that is insular in its designs and aims, it is adherence to those institutions, ideals, and purposes that are inherent in our system and peculiar to our conception of government. At such a time as this the guiding hand and pervading spirit of Washington are sorely needed in our life. No new and fantastic conceits born of a passion for change must stay our ship of state or deflect it from its chosen destiny. "Thy wise men were thy pilots," was spoken to a nation of old. Even so we turn again today, away from the blatant cries of those who would alter our course, and with renewed devotion and assurance claim the guiding hand of him who firmly held the helm in days when our frail bark was putting out over strange and unknown seas.

Once again we reverently invoke the God of our fathers and avow ourselves loyal to all that is implied in American institutions and American ideals. We repeat, with increased emphasis, —no unhallowed or alien hands shall deflect us from our course as we proudly turn to him who, trusting in God, gave us our chart and set our prow in those deep and secure channels that must ultimately bring us to the haven where we would be.

Washington and the American Tradition

By RABBI ABRAM SIMON, Ph.D.
Washington Hebrew Congregation, Washington, D. C.

The other eleven months of the calendar may well covet the proud distinction which February enjoys as the birth month of Washington and Lincoln. In the presence of our two towering personalities, we may pause for a fresh intake of hope, courage, and pride. Washington and Lincoln, shining peaks of the eastern and western mountain systems, homes of the watersheds where trickling streams wind their silvery and fertilizing paths over the broad areas of our land and culture! Peaks, surrendered by many other glistening eminences, drawing the heart of admiration upward, assure us that they rest, as they must, upon the mighty shoulders of large and spreading ranges of American citizenry.

Washington (and our concern now is only with him) is more than a mere individual. He expresses an epoch. Great by right of inherent genius, he is, nevertheless, the inevitable culmination of historic forces which stretch back through the decades. The high adventure of the early pioneers, the moral fervor of Pilgrim and Puritan, of Quaker and Cavalier, the growing pains of political emancipation, the Boston Tea Party, find their irresistible answer in the Declaration of Independence, in the birth of the United States of America, and in the majestic leadership of a God-given Washington. The next half century of increasing population, of new states added to the Union, of sprouting industries, agriculture and education, finding its body, Laocoon-like, encircled by the sinuous serpent of slavery, calls to the western prairies for her humble son, the rail splitter, to drive the last nail in the coffin of human slavery.

The third leader, at present unnamed, will incarnate the last seven decades. It is essentially one of a reunited America, of labor risen to dignity and power, of woman advanced to economic and political equality, of industry's blazing furnace filling the ships that ply the seven seas, of her unfurled flag respected everywhere, of her answer to Cuba's call, her opening wide the windows of Japan, her refusal to be paid in terms of money for her humanity to China, her pouring forth of millions across the Atlantic to safeguard the freedom of the seas, and which now places its sacramental signature to the protocol of a World Court of International Justice. From Lexington through Lincoln to Locarno is an inevitable march of American idealism against bondage to political despotism, against the thraldom of human chattel, and against the curse of international aggression.

These three eras of the continuous flux of American political and moral sagacity express themselves in written documents, namely, the Mayflower Pact, the Constitution of the United States, the Emancipation Proclamation, and what will be our new Declaration of International Interdependence. But alongside of this Written Law flows the Unwritten Law, just as luminous, just as prideful, and just as interpretive of the American spirit. It is a great and glorious tradition, not static nor stagnant, but throbbing with healthy confidence, vital, fluid, burning in the breasts of every loyal son of our forty-eight states. It stirs in our blood; it is regnant in our consciousness. We feel it; we act in its spirit oft unconsciously. We know its appeal, sacred, authoritative, rising at times to the dignity of a moving presence, warning, directing, and inspiriting.

In view of all that I have said, what is the great American Tradition? As I view it, it is composed of three intertwining and unbreakable strands.

First. The American citizen is equal to the highest responsibility of the expanding ideal of Democracy. Our Government is born of, and rests on, the will of the people. The capacity of our citizens to understand and to interpret political history from Washington's time to the present day cannot be questioned. Political institutions may change, as change they inevitably will, but our ability to meet the rising tide of political necessity remains an inviolable endowment. It is part of our mentality.

We have gone far away from the day when American Democracy can be called an experiment. Our form of Government, with all its firmness and elasticity, has touched the chancelries of the world, and floods the home of the humblest individual in lands across the Atlantic and Pacific with the sunshine of a newer hope. Every great leader in our country has pinned his faith, on the integrity, the intelligence, and the loyalty of the people. That high faith has not been misplaced.

We resent any imputation that our Democracy is but a thrusting upward of mere mediocrity. Lincoln's leadership is an unanswerable argument. We resent the imputation that our Democracy does not win the whole-hearted loyalty, even unto supreme sacrifice, of the lowliest individual here. We resent the imputation that the self-governing ability of the people of America inspires a lack of respect for authority and a courting of revolution and political sabotage. The heart of the American rings true to America. He rejoices in a personal sovereignty within the heart of the national sovereignty.

It is easy to adopt an ostrich policy. A hasty glance at European political conditions should stir us to serious contemplation. Reaction has set in, and with it the disillusion of democratic hopes. Europe is in the grip of dictators or small coalitions of absolute power. What this portends to the United States it is difficult to put in accurate phrase. At present, depression is disturbing. Yet if "boring from within" breeds discontent in the masses; if an economic crisis should bring in its train the clash of classes, increasing unemployment and starvation, we shall hope to find our representative form of government pulling itself up to its giant strength to withstand the shock. Now is the time to be warned. Now must we devise wholesome social legislation that will maintain the morale of the workers, and stabilize it for any emergency.

This dower of the unwritten law does not conflict, but it actually and truthfully interprets the written law. It is the unwritten law to which we must always appeal for a respect for the Constitution. I say to you, American citizenship can be trusted. The average citizen loves his country too dearly to submit to a new slavery, and yet I dare add that there will be no lessening of American loyalty if the great moral power of this nation is flung across the Atlantic to lessen the possibility of the next war. It is the next war which we must prevent by the heroism of constructive peace. Without any misleading of her glorious past, or any loss of present or future prestige, America should throw the whole weight of her titanic persuasion and declare "War shall be no more."

The second strand of this tradition is woven of the rights of conscience. Religious liberty is a sacred American doctrine. It is home grown, of pioneer extraction. Favoring winds may have carried the seed from abroad, but here it flowered into majestic maturity. The fathers of the Constitution bought religious liberty at too high a price to have it vitiated by any movement, any class, any legislation, or any intolerance.

The right to believe involves the right to disbelieve. A man's atheism may be as dear to him as my love of God is to me. This does not mean that we hold religion of little concern. On the contrary, America believes that religion is an essential ingredient in her civilization. Holding firmly to the doctrine of a separation of Church and State, our government expects the Church to train its youth and adults in the joyous responsibility and in the moral values of life, liberty, and the pursuit of happiness. Just because of its necessity, its free and full development must be unhindered. Intolerance ought not to find an inch of space in free America to strike root. The more truly religious we are, the less will bigotry divide us. If America is a sectarian enterprise, the fathers of the Republic have been betrayed. America is an adventure in Brotherhood. We stand for it. We stand by it, difficult though it may be to realize constantly its blessings and duties. Someone told me the story that Mr. Grumbles, with rather weak eyes, was constantly giving vent to his discontent. A woman, a neighbor, came into his room and without listening to him began to clean the windows, pull up the blinds, when suddenly old Grumbles said, "My eyes are worse; my eyes are worse; I cannot see. Pull down the blinds."

Oh, no, religious liberty means to pull up the blinds. The light that stares in from the window may at first be a glare, but we shall become at once accustomed to the new light that pours in through the windows of science and art and the mutual relationship of people of different faiths. Pull up the blinds, and let us look through the windows into one another's eyes, and into one another's souls; and looking into one another's souls, we will find that the things on which we agree are so many, and those upon which we disagree are so few; we will find that real liberty will be the bridge over which we will come to understand one another better.

The third element in this tradition is the American love of home. Across the Atlantic we are still accused of being a people of greed, of materialism, and of the arrogance which success engenders. And yet we know that there is as much domestic affection, chivalry, disinterestedness and idealism here as obtain anywhere in the world. America is a nation of home lovers. Any one who was abroad with the soldiers during the World War knows that the sentimental ballad was their favorite. More im-

portant than any question of tariff or tax is the integrity of the home. We must set our faces like steel against any force or fashion that would tend to quench the hearth fires.

Unfortunately, the American home is being invaded by an old paganism. There are conditions in our social environment and industrial milieu which give us pause and concern. Sometimes I fear that the moral fiber is becoming flabby. The increase of divorce, trial marriage, infidelity, the exaggerations of flaming youth, the conscienceless break of social convention, and the commissions of old sins dressed in fancy garb are indications that the old domestic props are in danger. Too many of our homes are so crowded with furniture as to leave no room for love. Women in the new-fangled cult want self-expression to get rid of the mid-Victorian customs. I do not wish to romanticize about the mid-Victorian age, or grow sentimental, but I do feel that something of the old chivalry between the sexes, something of that fine domesticity ought to come back to us; I tell you I should dread the bankruptcy of the American home. American virility is proportionate to the strength and purity and inviolability of the American home.

Home chivalry is a tradition in our country. It is the stuff of which true patriotism is made, and we must see to it that wobbly morality, lack of parental control, contempt for wholesome restraint shall no longer eat into the vitality of our domesticity. Fathers are abdicating their thrones, and mothers resigning their position as spiritual educators because it is so easy to throw the educational responsibilities upon the public school and the Sunday School.

I do not believe that the American home is attacked by so-called alienism. Let us not attribute the vices, which an industrial civilization engenders, to the immigrants who have come hither. They, too, will fight to the last ditch, for wife and child and home.

This is the great American tradition, a three-fold cord which must not be broken. This tradition underlies our American idealism. To remain true to this tradition is the best honor that we can pay the heroes of our country. What the great wars in our land have wrought, peace must preserve. To us, as men, as husbands, as fathers, as wives, as mothers and sisters, the thought and the principle of the great American tradition, namely, our capacity to meet the strain, the joy and the responsibility of our representative form of Government, the loyalty to religious liberty, and the stability and integrity of our homes become and are the very essence of the idealism which we must manifest. This tradition is our heritage. It is the unwritten law in our hearts, and beats with every pulse throb of our souls.

These three strands find their firmest weave in the warp and woof of Washington's mind and heart. Mighty interpreter of America's capacity for political liberty and democratic institutions, doughty champion of religious liberty, warmest advocate of the serenity and the peace of the domestic fireside, he is for us—THE AMERICAN TRADITION.

The Thoroughness of Washington

A Sermon by the
RT. REV. THOMAS FREDERICK DAVIES, D.D.
Bishop of Western Massachusetts

George Washington was always a very real person to me. When my father became Rector of St. Peter's Church, Philadelphia, he had two parishioners who remembered General Washington. Our house was but a few squares from Independence Hall. In the pew opposite ours in St. Peter's Church was a hassock, covered with faded yellow damask, on which Lady Washington had been wont to kneel. At the house of a neighbor, Mr. Bushrod Adams, I was sometimes allowed, as a boy, to hold General Washington's watch and seals.

It would be exceedingly difficult to answer the question, what was Washington's greatest quality? As one reviews his life, so many great qualities appear. On the occasion of Washington's death, Talleyrand, French Minister of Foreign Affairs, spoke of his courage, his genius, his nobility, his virtues, his greatness, his unassuming grandeur, his wisdom, his unselfishness.

As I study his life again, the quality that most amazes me is the thoroughness of Washington. From his boyhood to his death it keeps appearing. It shows in his careful penmanship, in the accurately formed letters of his faultless handwriting. It appeared over and over again in his care for detail. He was most particular as to his dress. His servants were clad in proper livery. All his appointments for fox-hunting were traditional and correct. George Washington was a fine horseman, but one does not always realize how much thought went into his horsemanship. The make of his bridle, the quality of his saddle-girths, ways of mounting, all these received careful attention. His harnesses had to be the best of their kind. His hounds were most carefully bred, and his horses unsurpassed in Virginia. Magnolia, his road-horse, was a full-blooded Arabian; while Blueskin, Ajax, Valiant and Chinkling, were all high-bred hunters. All this, I believe, was not so much because of a taste for luxury, but rather because of a desire to have everything thoroughly well done.

When one's eye falls upon the surveyor's tripod, now in the library at Mount Vernon, one's mind goes back to that adventurous survey of the lands of Lord Fairfax, which George Washington made at the age of sixteen. The work was well done, and it is of very great interest to read in Mr. Lodge's Life of Washington that these early surveys "were considered of the first authority, and stand unquestioned to this day. . . . It was part of his character, when he did anything, to do it in lasting fashion, and it is worth while to remember that the surveys he made as a boy were the best that could be made."

Young Washington was a keen observer, and made accurate reports. "And so this boy," wrote Woodrow Wilson, "learned to show in almost everything he did the careful precision of the perfect marksman."

At the age of twenty, Washington had to undertake the management of a large estate, and it was extraordinary how intimate a knowledge of it he acquired. "He knew," writes his biographer, William Roscoe Thayer, "every foot of its fields and meadows, of its woodlands and streams; he knew where each crop grew, and its rotation." All through his life he took the keenest interest in the Mount Vernon estate, and brought it to a high point of fertility and productiveness. In his diary for April 14, 1760, a most interesting instance occurs of Washington's thoroughness in agricultural experiments. He had a box made with ten compartments, and in each of them he placed a different mixture of soil. "In each of these divisions," he writes, "were planted three grains of wheat, three of oats, and as many of barley—all at equal distances in rows, and of equal depth. . . . Two or three hours after sowing in this manner, and about an hour before Sunset I watered them all equally alike with water that had been standing in a tub about two hours exposed to the sun."

He had even that sort of thoroughness that seeks to undo things wrongly done. I find an instance of this in his diary for November 10, 1785: "There having fallen so much rain in the night as to convince me that the Straw which I had placed between the ceiling and the wall of my Ice House, must have got wet, and being in some doubt before of the propriety of the measure, lest it should get damp, heat, and rot; I had it all taken out, leaving the space between unfilled with anything."

After his marriage, Washington undertook the education of his step-children, Martha and John Parke Custis, with what a biographer calls "characteristic thoroughness and solicitude." Realizing that his own education had been imperfect, he set about making it more thorough, and we find him writing to his agents in London, Robert Cary and Company, to send him books on history, biography, and government.

When General Washington took command of the army at Cambridge, he had to organize, equip, and train it, and the thoroughness of his methods made something like disciplined troops out of raw and untrained recruits. Washington became a great General, but it is not always remembered how hard he had studied tactics in the early days at Mount Vernon. Even during the suffering of that terrible winter at Valley Forge, Washington was looking ahead and planning a new and better organization of his forces.

"Nothing," says Senator Lodge, "was ever finished with Washington until it was really complete throughout." After the surrender of Lord Cornwallis, the country was tired of war, and inclined to relax. Not so Washington. It was then that he wrote to Congress that this was the very time for energetic action: "If we follow the blow with vigour and energy," he writes, "I think the game is our own."

His principles were not for political effect, but for application, and affected the life of his own household, where he would allow (in 1769) the use of no article (except paper) taxed by Parliament to raise revenue in America.

During the eight years and eight months he was away at war, he did not forget his accustomed charities at home, and wrote to Lund Washington, his manager: "Let the hospitality of the house with respect to the poor be kept up. Let no one go hungry away."

Washington had a way of looking ahead and thinking things through. After the war was won, he wrote to Theodorick Bland about making the Union firm: "We have now," he wrote, "a National character to establish." He knew that the British were right when they said that if the independent states were left to themselves, they would soon go to pieces. The idea of Union grew in his mind, and, as he looked ahead, the ideal of a strong, centralized government rose before him. Towards this he bent his energies—consultations, discussions, letters—all were made to further the constitutional idea. Nothing has interested me more than to learn that in the period between his resignation as Commander-in-Chief and his election as President, Washington made a study of classical constitutions—of Greece, of Rome, of the Amphictyonic Council, of the Helvetic, Belgic, and Germanic States. Coming to the Presidency totally inexperienced in civil administration he set himself thoroughly to understand the task before him. Always he kept looking into the future, and planning to perfect the Union.

Of course, during the Revolutionary War and his terms as President, Washington could be very little at Mount Vernon, yet it was never without his care. Every week, if possible, he prepared a long letter covering several closely written pages, and giving extraordinarily full and detailed directions as to the management of his estate. In his sixty-eighth year he prepared a table for his overseers on the rotation of crops. It is a large document in his own hand, and remains, says Mr. Wilstach, "one of the testimonials to his genius for organization and detail."

His "Farewell Address" to Congress delivered in September, 1796, is ranked by William Roscoe Thayer "among the few supreme utterances on human government." It was not the inspiration of a moment, but the fruit of long and thorough preparation, discussed in part some years before with Madison, and submitted in outline to the criticism of Hamilton.

I have not been trying to write another Life of Washington, but only to collect some examples of his extraordinary thoroughness. A pathetic instance of that occurred in his last illness. His Secretary, Tobias Lear, has left us an account of Washington's willingness to do everything his physicians recommended, so far as he could. When Mr. Rawlins had bled him, Washington thought a sufficient quantity of blood had not been drawn, and managed to gasp out "more!"

President Wilson speaks of Washington's old policy of Thorough. It was more than a policy, it was a part of the man. "Whether it was breaking a horse," says Mr. Lodge, "or reclaiming land, or fighting Indians, or saving a state, whatever he set his hand to, that he carried through to the end." Or again, "No man had done or given so much as Washington, and at the same time no other man had his love of thoroughness." I believe that under God it was largely due to this quality of his that the United States of America came into being.

It is a quality on which the Gospel is not silent. The righteousness our Lord required was a thorough righteousness, exceeding the formal righteousness of the scribes and Pharisees. He looked not only upon the outward act but upon the inner state of mind from which it proceeded. Perhaps the most thorough-going demand ever made upon men was to love their enemies. The standard Jesus Christ required was not excellence in this or that direction, but the perfection of our Father in heaven. The Sermon on the Mount is in effect a Sermon on Thoroughness.

Is not this a quality pre-eminently needed in American life and citizenship? The manufacturer who turns out flimsy articles, has often brought upon us the reproach, so commonly heard in Europe, that American goods are made to sell, not to wear.

The passage of laws without sufficient thought as to whether they can be enforced, or as to their ultimate effect upon the sacredness of Law, the maintenance of order, and the morals of the people, is an offense against that Thoroughness that looks far ahead.

The trend of American Education, as seen by many, is to give a smattering of many subjects and a thorough knowledge of none. It is said that our people are being educated for times of prosperity and activity, but not at all for times of adversity or leisure. Any system of Education that is without a spiritual background, is bound to be incomplete.

American Art has dabbled superficially in the attempt at prettiness to the neglect of any intellectual or spiritual meaning. Most of all are we failing to develop the art of arts, which should be the most beautiful and perfect of all, the art of Home Life.

Our penal system, which drives men to the use of narcotics and murderous mutiny, leaves them without hope, and fails of reformation, is as unscientific and ineffective as it is brutal and degrading.

The citizen who does not take the trouble to cast his vote, or who does so without having informed himself of the issues at stake, or of the character, record and fitness of those nominated, sins against the Thoroughness which made this Nation, and which can keep it wholesome and sound.

The man or woman who does not plan and labor to make his or her community as thoroughly clean, and orderly, and healthy, and sweet, and beautiful, and happy as possible, is not a thoroughly good citizen.

The workman who is not trying to do his job as well as it can be done, is not the sort this country needs.

The employer who looks only to his profits and not at all to the well-being of his employees, is not a thoroughly good American business man.

The brand of statesmanship that consists in much eloquence and small performance, as well as the type of citizenship that seeks to leave others to bear the common burden, may well take to heart that short speech made by Washington in the Virginia Convention in Williamsburg in 1774—a speech declared by Mr. Lynch to be the most eloquent that ever was made: "I will raise one thousand men, subsist them at my own expense, and march myself at their head for the relief of Boston."

In a Democracy such as ours the stability of the Nation depends upon the integrity of its citizens, and consequently crimes are not only offenses against the Law, but disloyalties to our Country. In such a Democracy each citizen must be in his degree politician and statesman, judge, legislator and executive. We must all take our part in our Country's affairs, and remember that we cannot wholly delegate responsibility to our representatives. We should have a stronger and sounder Nation, if every citizen would make his own those far-reaching words of Washington's, spoken about the planting of grain: "It is a fixed principle with me, that whatever is done should be well done!"

WASHINGTON

By DR. SOLOMON B. FREEHOF

K. A. M. Temple

Chicago, Ill.

In this imperfect world, nothing is perfect. No sky remains unclouded. No tree grows up without some scar; and no fruit without some touch of decay. In this imperfect world no human being ever attains perfection. Therefore, when we study the lives of great men, we must take for granted that they are human and therefore imperfect. We do not delude ourselves with notions of their perfection but granting their human weaknesses we seek in them those fragments of divinity which awaken our adoration and may ennoble our lives.

Therefore, while we would grant in principle that George Washington was not the perfect ideal which earlier biographers first lovingly pictured him to be, we nevertheless must voice a protest against the mood of recent biographical description of his life and work. There seems to be a cynical desire current among many literary men today not merely to point out inevitable imperfections, but to leave the definite implication that there is hardly any nobility left in those men whom humanity has been accustomed to adore. Perhaps this is due to a certain mob spirit which loves to take belated vengeance against those noble souls whose very nobility makes the mob aware of its own coarseness. These destructive biographies put on the cloak of science by claiming to use the methods of psychoanalysis in unearthing the sins and the weaknesses of the men of the past. It would not be amiss, therefore, since such attempts have been made with regard to Washington, to say a word about the unscientific nature of all such investigations.

Psychoanalysis, when practiced by a scientific physician, is a highly technical and extremely difficult process. The analyst must study every expression of the patient. He must not be misled by the mere words which the patient uses but must try to delve back of the words into unspoken thoughts and hidden desires. With the patient before him day after day for perhaps six months, the analyst tries to decipher the soul, and even then he frequently fails. If, then, the task is so difficult, even with the patient before us, how can we possibly presume to psychoanalyze a personality, dead, let us say, a century, of whom we have only the written word or public utterances on state occasions? The desires and the dreams and the imaginations of such a man were hidden even from his contemporaries and now constitute a sanctuary in which we can no longer penetrate. Any attempt to psychoanalyze great men of the past has therefore no scientific basis. It is not psychoanalysis but charlatanry.

We may therefore dismiss on principle all such attempts to uncover the inner life of Washington. Yet, we must not regret the fact that the inner personality of Washington is now hidden from us forever. This is inevitable and we must accept it. But at least his deeds live and can still be honestly judged. Even with regard to his character as revealed in his deeds many irresponsible speakers and writers have been pleased to cast slurs. We are told for example that Washington had no inner life, that he had no imagination, no ability to grasp abstract ideas, that he was just a plodding peasant type of mind, rooted in the obvious and in the practical things of life. This rather bitter conclusion has been arrived at by a study of Washington's diary in which he lists carefully all the material possessions on his Virginia farm.

It is true we can not be sure enough of Washington's inner life to refute completely so confident a description. But there is one bit of evidence at least which reveals him to be a man of sensitive judgment and profound understanding of humanity. As a Rabbi I am interested in the relationship of Washington to the Jews. He wrote a letter to the Jews of Newport, R. I., in which letter a profound insight in his character may be gained.

The Jews of Newport, R. I., were of Spanish-Portuguese origin. They belonged to that proud section of Jewry which produced poets, philosophers, merchant princes, and statesmen in Moorish and Christian Spain. They suffered martyrdom for their faith, enduring the tortures of the Inquisition. They fled from Spain to Portugal. In Portugal once more they were subjected to the rack and the fagot. They fled from Portugal to Holland, from Holland to Brazil in the new world, and from Brazil to New York, and thence to Newport, R. I. After the American Revolutionary War was won these Jews wrote a letter to the first President of the United States. They were naturally anxious about their future. Would they at last find justice, rest, and opportunity in this New World? Or would the horrors of the past be repeated? In their anxiety they wrote a letter of greeting to Washington. If Washington had merely written a formal note in reply, it would not have been to his discredit, for how could a Virginian gentleman ever be expected to visualize the tragic anxieties and the stubborn courage of the fugitive Jews in Rhode Island? If Washington were just the plodding gentleman farmer which some biographers depict him to be, his letter to these people would have been unimaginative, and of no historical significance. Yet, his letter reveals a tenderness of understanding and a refined beauty of spirit. The letter concludes with these words:

"All possess alike liberty of conscience and immunities of citizenship. It is now no more that toleration is spoken of as if it was by the indulgence of one class of people that another enjoyed the exercise of their inherent natural rights. For happily the government of the United States which gives to bigotry no sanction, to persecution no assistance, requires only that they who live under its protection should demean themselves as good citizens, in giving it on all occasions their effectual support. . . . May the children of the stock of Abraham who dwell in this land, continue to merit and enjoy the good-will of the other inhabitants; while 'everyone shall sit in safety under his own vine and fig-tree and none may make him afraid.' May the Father of all mercies scatter light and not darkness in our paths, and make us all in our several vocations useful here, and in his own due time and way everlastingly happy."

This letter has the natural eloquence of the soul. Only a man of profound understanding and delicate imagination would have thought of quoting from their own Scriptures a phrase assuring them in the words of the Prophet Micah of their security and their future. If we had no other document but this we could justly worship the nobility of this great soul.

Besides unwarranted sneers at Washington's spiritual qualities, certain biographies brush away as insignificant all his material accomplishments. They say that he was a very poor general, that he foolishly fought in the European system of using armies as machines instead of the native American system based upon the mobility of Indian warfare; that he therefore lost many battles unnecessarily; that he was a poor statesman; that he initiated no new legislation nor developed any new governmental principles. All this is very strange. He is said to be a poor general, and yet he won a long and arduous war; a poor statesman yet during his two terms a group of mutually suspicious colonies were welded into a united nation, the first firmly established republic in modern history. Those who find in Washington only dullness and prosaic plodding must be puzzled at the tremendous accomplishments of his career.

It is evident that chance and opportunity are never in themselves sufficient to account for great accomplishment. In all consistent achievements the inner powers of man constitute an indispensable element. One man will squander the finest opportunity while another will find the spiritual strength by which to conquer even the most hostile circumstances. Since therefore, Washington achieved victory against a great military power, and since he built the colonies into a nation, it is reasonable to suppose that he possessed much more ability than disillusioned biographers are inclined to grant.

The ability which Washington possessed was of a type which in our modern mood is not easily understood, nor fairly appreciated. Just what that ability was can be seen in contrast between the Greek and the Roman peoples. There is no doubt that the Greeks possessed exceptional genius. Within three centuries they produced the most brilliant galaxy of marvellous men that ever shone in the firmament of human experience. Yet for all that genius the Greek nation was weak, disorganized, and the easy victims of the first strong conqueror. The Romans are said to have no genius at all. They had no exceptional generals, yet they organized victory; they had no great physicians, yet they were the first to establish hospitals and works of public sanitation;

they had no genius in science, yet their engineering is still one of the wonders of the world. With all its flashing genius, Greece was just a flickering torch blazing for a moment soon to be extinguished; while Rome with no outstanding genius built an empire which is still the foundation of modern Europe.

What the Romans possessed was much more important than genius. They had character, patience, understanding, responsibility, seriousness of purpose; all these traits characterized the Roman people and were the true foundation of their social structure. Genius is spectacular and evokes worshipful adoration; character is constructive and unites men to common effort.

Washington's greatness was the greatness of character. When, during the Revolutionary War, colleagues mocked him and plotted against him he was dignified and patient. When defeat broke the courage of those about him he remained unbroken and brave. When suffering became unendurable for his fellow Americans, he endured with magnificent fortitude; and when the war was finally won and he became President of the new United States, his self-abnegation and stability won the hearts of his countrymen, and evoked in all the colonies the traits of character which were the spiritual basis of the Republic.

An exceptional military genius might have won the War sooner, but had he become president might have used his power to be more than President. Every student of American history knows how easily Washington might have established a new monarchy had he so desired. But Washington was just what the country needed. In an arduous war he was patient and brave and in an experimental government he was reliable and self-forgetful. His character won him his permanent place in the affections of his fellow citizens. When he travelled through the States during his Presidency his very presence gave stability and strength to the nascent republic.

Let pseudo-scientific biographers seek to deprecate all that Washington was and did. They reveal thereby the destructive irreverence of their own mood. The average American, without deifying Washington, will always find in him those elements of inner strength and spiritual dignity wherein all who are creative in business and profession feel their psychic kinship. Washington's character built this republic. The continued influence of that character will ever maintain it.

A LEADER AND COMMANDER OF THE PEOPLE

(A Sermon on the Bicentennial of George Washington's Birthday)
By DR. HUGH THOMSON KERR
Pastor of the SHADYSIDE PRESBYTERIAN CHURCH
Pittsburgh, Pennsylvania

Text: "Behold, I have given him for a witness to the people, a leader and commander
to the people."—Isaiah 55:4

We are judged by our admirations. We are what we aspire to be. We are judged by the heroes we worship. Our ideals are the reflections of great personalities. A nation whose people visit the resting place of Lenin or the shrine of Confucius or the tomb of Napoleon reveals to all the world the secret springs of its life. It proclaims to posterity its hopes and aims by the names it immortalizes in its Westminster Abbey, its Roll of Honor, its Val-Halla, its Hall of Fame.

When the Hall of Fame for great Americans was founded by New York University a thousand names were presented for first honors and from these, twenty-nine were elected and the first name chosen was that of Washington. That was in 1900. If the election were to take place today, two hundred years after his birth, or if it were to take place two thousand years from now, who among us could doubt the result? Such unanimity and enthusiasm is the best evidence that the moral health of the nation is sound and that America will carry on in truth and loyalty to those ideals which called her as a nation into being. Who can imagine that George Washington can ever be repudiated? As long as rich and poor, conservative and radical, young and old respond to the challenge of his character our land is forever secure.

I.

What is there about Washington that makes this appeal? What is there about his character and life which makes it possible for the Church, as well as the nation, to celebrate him in song and story two hundred years after his birth? Lord Bryce, that discerning British scholar and statesman, in his study of "Modern Democracies," says of Washington that he "set a standard of courage, calmness, dignity and righteousness by which every public man's conduct was to be tried." He goes on to say that the leaders of American life, and above all Abraham Lincoln, the next great name in our Hall of Fame, were inspired by the life and character of Washington and that after the tragic struggle that divided the nation during the Civil War Washington's memory was a bond of union, honored and cherished by North and South alike. There is something in that. He stands alone, a unifier belonging to no group, no party, but the supreme leader and commander of all the people. What is there about his memory that gives his name immortality?

II.

First of all we recognize that it was given to him to be a pioneer. He is rightly called the father of his country. It may be that in the Providence of God some other man would have raised up to do what he did, but history records that it was Washington who led America up and out into nationhood. That alone would distinguish him. Every great movement is enshrined in a personality. No one individual creates an era in history but it is nevertheless true that great world movements come to flower in a great name. Other names swing like stars around that name as round a central sun. In electricity it is Edison. In science it is Darwin. In astronomy it is Copernicus. In discovery it is Columbus. In medicine it is Pasteur. In jurisprudence it is Blackstone. In democracy it is Washington. Washington takes his place with Moses, with Alfred, with Caesar, with Alexander, with Cyrus but we do not apply to him the epithet of Great.

He is the symbol of what America was and is and will be. Ask yourself the question, What is America? and when you have answered the question you have looked into the face of Washington. There is, in the Smithsonian Institute, a brass medallion which contains the Declaration of Independence. It can be read by one standing in front of it without difficulty but when one steps to the side and looks he sees no word. The words fade out and he sees clearly the face of Washington. It is a true symbol.

III.

We press our enquiry further. What is there about the character of this man of destiny to win our admiration and our abiding loyalty? We rejoice first of all in his moral wholesomeness. No whisper of dishonor, no touch of the drab, no suspicion of littleness or meanness stains the page that tells the story of his life.

Modern commercialized writers have sought to remove him from his high pedestal but his monument still stands four-square, the center of the nation's admiration, pointing heavenward. When he was yet a lad he wrote in his copybook the golden words, "Labor to keep alive in your breast that little spark of celestial fire called conscience." He, himself, fanned that spark into a flame both in private and public life and his name was kept unsullied from youth to age. That fact is the nation's best asset and this commemoration will miss much of its worth if it does not recall and dedicate the leadership of America to this dominant characteristic of his great life.

Do you wish an example of high honor and tender devotion? Then read the words in his last Will and Testament which freed the slaves he had owned, and especially read, "To my mulatto man, William (calling himself William Lee) I give immediate freedom, or if he should prefer it (on account of the accidents which have befallen him, and which have rendered him incapable of walking or of any active employment), to remain in the situation he now is, it shall be optional in him to do so; in either case, however, I allow him an annuity of 30 dollars during his natural life, which shall be independent of the victuals and clothes he has been accustomed to receive, if he chooses the latter alternative; but in full with his freedom, if he prefers the first; and this I give him as a testimony of my sense of his attachment to me, and for his faithful services during the revolutionary war."

Do you wish an example of filial affection and tender solicitude? Then read the record of his interviews with his mother and her implicit trust in him. Do you wish an example of charm and an understanding spirit of youth? Then read how he wears the uniform chosen for him by youth and beauty. Do you wish an example of unspoiled humility in the midst of honors unparalleled? Then read his hesitation in accepting place and position and his reluctance at carrying responsibility. Honors did not spoil him. Criticism did not sour him. Age did not deflect him from those sweet and sane principles of life which formed his character.

John Morley tells us that William E. Gladstone sent a message saying that on the following morning he would worship in the Tabernacle and hear London's greatest preacher, Charles Spurgeon, preach. Mr. Spurgeon replied that he would be happy to have him in his Church and added the words, "While we believe in no man's infallibility it is restful to believe in one man's integrity." This is how we feel in regard to Washington.

IV.

When we press the matter further we are brought face to face with the sacrificial patriotism that puts us to shame in these days of drab morality. The patriotism of Washington was born of fearlessness and the love of liberty. As the heir of conservative tradition, born in comfort, living the life of a gentleman, knowing nothing of poverty, he nevertheless chose the hard path of service and sacrifice. He was something of a radical, but a radical in the true meaning of the word.

Speaking in the Senate Chamber not long since, one of our Senators said, "George Washington and Abraham Lincoln were the radicals of their time. If it be said of Washington that he belonged to the property owning class, how can we explain his failure to join the Tories? What shall we say of his devotion to his ragged, suffering soldiers at Valley Forge? A man does not endure such suffering and such danger except his heart be stirred by a deep passion for a great cause. His monument is this great Republic and its future. His monument is at last in the hearts of the people the world around who love liberty and who devote their lives to duty and truth."

To understand the springs of his patriotism we need only read his addresses which mark the path of his increasing influence. Perhaps one quotation, and a familiar one, will serve our purpose. In his Farewell Address to the people of the United States in the year 1796 he said, "Of all the dispositions and habits which lead to political prosperity, Religion and Morality are indispensable supports. In vain would that man claim the tribute of Patriotism, who should labor to subvert these great pillars of human happiness, these firmest props of the duties of Men and Citizens. The mere Politician, equally with the pious man, ought to respect and to cherish them. A volume could not trace all their connections with private and public felicity. Let it simply be asked, Where is the security for property, for reputation, for life, if the sense of religious obligation desert the oaths which are the instruments of investigation in Courts of Justice? And let us with caution indulge the supposition that morality can be maintained without religion. Whatever may be conceded to the influence of refined education on minds of peculiar structure, reason and experience both forbid us to expect that national morality can prevail in exclusion of religious principle."

How humiliating it is in the light of these lofty moral principles to feel that lawlessness and secularism have taken up their abode in our social order. We have heard President Hoover say "There has been a subsidence of the moral foundations of the nation." And we have seen no one rise up to challenge his indictment. We have heard former President Coolidge say, "A government which does not enforce its laws is unworthy of the name of a government" and yet we go on in the faith that somehow as a nation we are destined to immortality.

As far back as 1909 we heard the late Chief Justice Taft say, "It is not too much to say that the administration of criminal law in this country is a disgrace to our civilization, and that the prevalence of crime and fraud, which here is greatly in excess of that in European countries, is due largely to the failure of the law and its administration to bring criminals to justice." And yet we suffer the things complained of to continue. We have been caught in the blinding storm of the destruction that wasteth at noonday. When a nation is young and emerging out of the shadows of obscurity, painfully struggling up the slope, it is beset with many dangers and temptations such as come from weakness, timidity and isolation but the real danger comes to a nation when it has found for itself a place in the sun and has reached the summit and discovered its strength.

The secularizing spirit, which has laid hold upon all the world, has had its grip upon America. We have thought in these latter days so much of "things" that other values have been obscured. Dean Inge says that if a person spends sixteen hours a day dealing with "things" and five minutes thinking about God it will not be strange if "things" seem two hundred times more real than God.

V.

When we think of Washington after the years have gone, we see his face in clearer light and we see how strongly religion ruled his life. How could it be otherwise? He was cradled in the atmosphere of religion. He came of a long line of loyal church-men. His great great grandfather was a clergyman of the Church of England and his mother was baptized into a fine religious devotion. When he made his farewell visit to his mother she commended him to God and to the high destiny which Heaven appeared to have intended for him saying, "Go, my son, and may Heaven's and a mother's blessing be with you always." His messages are radiant with religious faith and hope. His orders to the Army have the uniform touch of a man of God. His first inaugural leaves no doubt where he put his trust. "No people," he says in that memorable address, "can be bound to acknowledge and adore the invisible hand which conducts the affairs of men more than the people of the United States. Every step by which they have advanced to the character of an independent nation seems to have been distinguished by some token of providential agency. . . . These reflections, arising out of the present crisis, have forced themselves too strongly on my mind to be suppressed. You will join with me, I trust, in thinking that there are none under the influence of which the proceedings of a new and free government can more auspiciously commence. . . . We ought to be no less persuaded that the propitious smile of Heaven can never be expected on a nation that disregards the eternal rules of order and right, which Heaven itself has ordained."

The strong and unhesitating testimony which he gave to the churches of America, that sent to him deputations expressing the loyalty of the churches, leave no doubt in our minds as to his devotion to organized religion. To the Methodist Episcopal Church he said, "I implore the Divine benedictions on ourselves and your religious community." To the Baptist churches he said, "I have often expressed my sentiment that every man conducting himself as a good citizen, and being accountable to God alone for his religious opinions, ought to be protected in worshiping the Deity according to the dictates of his own conscience." To the Presbyterian churches he expressed the opinion that no man could prove untrue to the civil community, and at the same time be a true Christian. To his own Protestant Episcopal Church he said, "It would ill become me to conceal the joy I have felt in perceiving the fraternal affection which appears to increase every day among the friends of genuine religion. It affords edifying prospects, indeed, to see Christians of different denominations dwell together in more charity, and conduct themselves in respect to each other with a more Christian-like spirit, than ever they have done in any former age, or in any other nation."

He was not only religious in his thought but he was loyal in his life to the Church. He was a man of prayer, an officer in the Church, living and dying in the faith of a glorious immortality. There are many people who have a vague and fluid religion who refuse to relate it to the Church and to organized religious activities. Washington believed in making his religious life real and found in the Christian Church a place of worship, of inspiration and of service. Willard L. Sperry puts his finger on this truth when he says, "Man is not yet so transfigured that he has ceased to keep the window of his mind and heart open towards Jerusalem. The abstract proposal that we worship at any place where God lets down the ladder is not yet an adequate substitute for the deep desire to go up to some central sanctuary where the religious artist vindicates a concrete universal in the realm of the spirit.

Henry Cabot Lodge, in his analysis of the character of Washington, discovered the secret springs of his versatile and victorious life, in his religious faith. "He had the same confidence in the judgment of posterity that he had in the future beyond the grave. He regarded death with entire calmness, and even indifference, not only when it came to him, but when in previous years it had threatened him. He loved life and tasted of it deeply, but the courage which never forsook him made him ready to face the inevitable at any moment with an unruffled spirit. In this he was helped by his religious faith, which was as simple as it was profound. He had been brought up in the Protestant Episcopal Church, and to that Church he always adhered, for its splendid liturgy and stately forms appealed to him and satisfied him. He loved it too as the Church of his home and his childhood. Yet he was as far as possible from being sectarian, and there is not a word of his which shows anything but the most entire liberality and toleration. He made no parade of his religion, for in this, as in other things, he was perfectly simple and sincere. He was tortured by no doubts or questionings, but believed always in an overruling Providence and in a merciful God, to whom he knelt and prayed in the day of darkness or in the hour of triumph with a supreme and child-like confidence."

VI.

Today we are facing new issues, unknown and undreamed of to Washington, and we can do no better thing than to make a pilgrimage to his shrine. There was nothing complex or elaborate in his political philosophy. He was not, what we would call today, a shrewd politician. He believed in a few simple political principles, a few simple moral postulates, a few authoritative religious sanctions, and he believed them always and everywhere, in war and in peace, in life and in death. Perhaps today there stands beside him, in imagination and affection, some obscure American lad who is dedicating his life to those things for which Washington gave the last full measure of his devotion, and he will be the leader of the morrow for which we all pray.

"Earth listens for the coming of his feet;
The hushed Fates lean expectant from their seat.
He will be calm and reverent and strong,
And, carrying in his swords the fire of song,
Will send a hope upon these weary men,
A hope to make the heart grow young again,
A cry to comrades scattered and afar;
Be constellated, star by circling star;
Give to all mortals justice and forgive;
License must die that liberty may live."

THE SPIRIT OF WASHINGTON

A Sermon by the

REV. CHARLES EDGAR LIEBEGOTT

St. Paul's Lutheran Church
Akron, Ohio

George Washington stands alone and supreme among the great and noted men of America. No name written on the page of our country's history is so illustrious and bright as the name Washington.

He has been imbedded with reverence in the heart of every loyal American and enshrined with love in the soul of this great people. Compare him as we may with other great souls who have added to America's fame and glory and each of them fall beneath the plane of greatness on which stands the Father of his Country. Not alone, however, in the soul of America has Washington been enshrined but he has become a hero among the people of the world and at his feet the people of all nations of the world lay the wreath of the unfading flowers of adoration and veneration and love.

If we were to speak one word which would symbolize all that is great, honorable and beautiful in America, it would be the name of Washington. Speak his name across the vast dominion of America; let hills and vale resound; let the deepest valley and the highest crag catch the sound and as it falls upon the ear of busy America there will come a hush as before us rises the figure of this great personality, who shall never die as long as this great republic stands. Speak his name and a hundred million voices will resound, "Hail mighty chief and hero of our land; thy fame shall never die." The foundations of the Alleghenies may be shaken and destroyed, the sun-kissed peaks of the rockies may crumble in the dust; the waters of the mighty Mississippi may dry up but the name of Washington shall still be set on foundations which can not be shaken or destroyed.

But what unseen force took this man, what unseen hand lifted him to so lofty a place in a nation's history and inscribed his life and name on the imperishable monument of democracy. In his day there were other men who might have been lifted from obscurity and sent down the path of honor and fame. Was it only blind chance that laid a hand on George Washington and lifted him to the pedestal of greatness and laid at his feet the wreath of love and devotion? Was it the power of wealth that caused him to be adored by the poor as well as by the wealthy? Was it political and social prestige that upraised him until his star shone forth to grow brighter as the years grow old? Was it his own personal desire for power and a selfish motive to satisfy a selfish life that sent him forth to blaze his way through a nation's history and compel a great people to revere him?

We can not look to any of these forces as having raised a single soul to greatness and set the star of fame in the constellation of the great and mighty of earth. Chance did not destine this man to be great, for chance has never moved men upward. Wealth, political and selfish powers have alas sent the world and men into the way of blood and death.

As we eliminate one by one the forces and powers which have raised men to a so-called position of greatness, we are driven to the conclusion that the great Creator prepared and sent forth into the life of this nation, George Washington, as truly as He prepared and sent forth Moses to lead Israel to the promised land.

The life record of Washington declares that he was a man prepared for a day like this. No man could have done the work which he did save that he was led of God and no man could have cast aside the popular clamor to become an imperial ruler, save he whose heart was prepared to lead a people into political and civil liberty. View Washington's life as it stands forth amid a great people and every ray of light thereof will reflect back into a life that served unselfishly his fellowmen, with no thought for self but the good of every man, woman, and child, who should breathe the air of freedom, was the motive which accentuated him to serve and to give his best, his all, for his countrymen. On this fact rests the undying greatness of Washington and placed around his service there shines a halo that never dims.

For what produces true greatness, lasting honor, and undying fame to one's life if it is not the securing, of "peace and good-will," by unselfish service, for the common good and welfare of one's fellowman.

What Washington did for America bears testimony that his love for his country was greater than his love for power and fame, which might have been secured through a way of lesser hardship and sacrifice but he chose the way of sacrifice with no thought of greatness, that his country and his countrymen might be set free from political tyranny and enjoy the blessings of God as a free and noble people.

When his country called him to be the Commander-in-Chief of the Continental army he laid aside his wealth, the privileges and benefits thereof and willingly accepted the responsibility and all the hardships and privations so characteristic of a soldier's life in that day. This act alone is worthy of emulation, for if wealth has an inherent power to bestow blessings and give peace and happiness, then Washington had a right to accept the blessings of wealth and enjoy its privileges. His possessions had been acquired honestly and honorably. No taint of fraud or corruption was to be found thereon. Owner of a great estate, well equipped and located, he might have accepted these things as his right to enjoy, but not so, his country had called, his fellowmen were looking for him to lead them to victory and he accepted his task and faced its responsibilities as all true Americans do. We can find in this act nothing which would suggest the idea that Washington accepted the leadership of the army for the purpose of either safeguarding his wealth or acquiring greater possession should the victory be his.

We can find, however, as we see the sum total of his devotion to his country, this truth, which shines brighter as the years pass by, that he risked his all that his fellow-citizens by and through his service might secure the wealth and blessings of liberty, which always have and always shall be prosperity and peace. A greater love for one's Country has no citizen than he who is willing to lay down all for his Country's good.

Again we see the nobility of his character expounded in word and deed as he advocated political freedom for the colonies.

Washington had an influence and powerful contacts which no doubt would have secured for him many a political favor if he had allied himself with the mother country. Perhaps most men in Washington's position would have reasoned that the best protection for property and the greatest political spoils were to be had by remaining on the side of the well established and more secure government of England, rather than on the side of a people who were launching out on a new adventure in political freedom. But Washington was a Son of the New Land, he was an American rather than a politician. Love and devotion rose higher than reason could rise, and as he looked into years unborn and saw a people free, happy and prosperous, he chose well as he chose the way of struggle to gain the ideal. He was among the first as a member of the first General Congress to raise his voice in behalf of freedom even though it were by the sword. He accepted as a trust his call to lead one of the poorest equipped, poorest trained armies that ever took the field of battle. Privation, rebuke, starvation and even desertion followed hard in his steps but never once did he turn back. With an implicit trust in God he knew that right would win and that his cause was just. Look at that camping ground of Valley Forge; see the half-fed, ragged, ill-supplied army which he was leading. If Washington had been seeking his own ends surely this would have been the place and the conditions thereof which would have justified him to surrender to England. If men on either side ever thought that he would give up the cause, they were now surely convinced that Washington would go on until the cause had been won, for only he with a resolute heart could go through such a crisis as a victor and Washington did. What brought him through, steadied him and moved him onward;— nothing less than the sublimity of a great conviction. At last the victory was won, the sword laid down, a farewell to his loyal troops and his face was set towards Mt. Vernon. He asked nothing for his service. He desired no favoritism. He asked for no spoils of war, for what he had done was but the execution of an outward act, expressing a heart's desire for the welfare of his country and her citizens. The end had been gained and he was well content to turn the newly secured blessing of freedom over to the people to enjoy. But such a man could not retire to the hills of peace for there still was a work for him to do. New problems arose, difficulties were many and a leader there needed to be, and who but Washington could lead on in the way of construction.

It was here, it seems to me, where the very incarnation of all that is sacred and holy in the name of America was revealed in the soul of Washington. Colonel Nicola wrote him and suggested that he seize the army and rule the land which he had redeemed, and thus bring order out of chaos. But Washington refused to capitalize the confidence of his fellow-citizens and use it for selfish ends. One word and he might have become the King, the Emperor, the Dictator of America, but the word was never spoken.

As we look back over the illustrious and glorious history of America we are convinced that in this refusal of Washington there was revealed the high ideal that would govern America.

Can we not say today that it has? The heart and the spirit and ideal of Washington is always revealed in our dealings with the nations of the world.

It is revealed as we see America, year after year striving to utilize her wealth, and power for the good of all. Not a president or a great leader of America has ever usurped their delegated power for selfish ends, but, catching the Spirit of Washington, have given their best in service that the example of Washington might live on, namely, that genius and power and fame are not to be compared to the moral excellency of love, devotion and service for one's country. An example worthy to be emulated by all both great and small in positions of public trust.

Lastly, Washington recognized that America would stand among the nations of the earth as a great nation as long as America would maintain the ideal of her founders and so he declared that religion and morality are indispensable to a nation's welfare. His biography speaks of a man of faith and trust in God. Faithfully attending divine worship even amid the trying days of the war. Relying on the guidance of God at all times, as the hills and trees of Valley Forge could well declare, he went forward in faith. He lived a life that none can gain say for the record bears testimony that he was not subjected to the moral vices of his day. As we see his life in the highest realm of human experiences, that of religion and morality, we need not wonder that when his conviction, that right must win, was tested in the cauldron of war, that he stood firm and true, at last to have the laurels of victory crown his work. He stood in his day the very incarnative of those principles of religion and morality for which the Pilgrim Fathers dared the sea and the venture of a new cause to establish and inculcate them in a new government under the guidance of God. From him has flowed those ideals and principles, the guide of every true and loyal American, which have made America truly great these many years. The spirit of Washington shall never die, but when worlds cease to revolve and stars cease to shine his spirit shall be seen in ages unborn to have been a reflection of the Christ, "who came not to be ministered unto but to minister." America, bear thou witness before the great and mighty. Bear thou witness to the humble and the poor, Washington our servant has become the greatest of all Americans.

Then: "Unfurl the banner to the breeze, the glorious stripes and stars!
Remember what it meant to those who perished in our wars!
The trumpet's peal, the rattling drum, the shrill tones of the fife,
Revive the fading memories of days of bloody strife.
Remember freedom's priceless cost, remember those who died,
Place Bunker Hill and Arlington, in memory, side by side.
Chant once again the old sea song, the little Mayflower band
Sang years ago, with bowed, bared heads, on Plymouth's barren sand.
Kneel once again and kiss the Rock, on which our Fathers prayed,
And raised the Temple Beautiful, on sure foundations laid.
But keep a niche in Freedom's shrine, for Freedom's favorite Son,
The wise and silent patriot, Beloved Washington!"

WHAT WASHINGTON WON

By DANIEL A. POLING, D.D., LL.D.
THE MARBLE COLLEGIATE REFORMED CHURCH, New York City
February 24, 1929

Text, Proverbs 22:1: A good name is rather to be chosen than great riches and loving favour rather than silver and gold.

This Washington won, a good name with loving favor. Time has not amended the judgment of Henry Lee, "First in war, first in peace, and first in the hearts of his countrymen." Of his unique place Abraham Lincoln added eloquent testimony when he said, "To add brightness to the sun or glory to the name of Washington, is alike impossible. Let none attempt it. In solemn awe pronounce the name, and in its naked, deathless splendor leave it shining on." And that the conclusion of his fellow countrymen had more than casual assent in the minds of the world, is confimed by Lord Byron's "The first, the last, the best, the Cincinnatus of the West."

"O noble brow, so wise in thought!
O heart so true! O soul unbought!
O eye so keen to pierce the night,
And guide the ship of state aright!
O life so simple, grand and free;
The humblest still may turn to thee.
O king uncrowned! O prince of men!
When shall we see thy like again."

Thus sang Mary Wingate in a veritable ecstacy of fervor.

A good name with loving favor is Washington's today and forever. His name is of the quality that comes from nothing less than character. No sudden rise in political or social fortune was responsible for it, nor was it based upon mere reputation. Character, substantial and enduring, gave and gives the name of Washington its pre-eminence.

Perhaps the character of the Father of his country received its supreme test in the reaction of the peace which followed the victory at Yorktown, and the acknowledgment of Independence. Certainly the wisdom of the first president of the United States, the forbearance of his statesmanship, the genuineness of his patriotism in the more laborious if less spectacular processes of an uncertain and a troubled peace, were as great as those martial qualities which made the Virginia planter the victorious commander-in-chief of the Continental armies.

Not only did he survive the after-revolutionary period of reconstruction with fame unimpaired, but returning to private life, he added to the luster of his name, as he passed, in quiet dignity along the path of uncrowned American citizenship to this throne of immortality.

Three men among us have borne the supreme responsibilities of government in crises somewhat similar: Washington, Lincoln, and Wilson. Lincoln went to his coronation at the close of the first of the three stages. The world will always believe that the reconstruction period, so-called, which followed the Civil War, was shot to its demoralization by the bullet that sent Lincoln to his death in Ford's theater. Always we must envision our first national martyr as he would have been in the stern times of a troubled peace, and in those quiet days of home life beyond, toward which he ever looked with wistful eyes.

The great man who has so recently gone from us, is too close to his ordeals and his contemporaries to be made the subject of historical comparisons. Unlike Washington, who survived unimpaired, and Lincoln who died, he fell with a mortal wound that withdrew him from active leadership, while it left him mentally fully alive. With time the only competent judge for Woodrow Wilson's spirit and deeds, we salute him now as the first American who both challenged and captained the morality of the world.

Of the three Americans who served their day and generation,

in times somewhat similar, in crises vast, momentous beyond all others, in the nation's history, George Washington alone of the three, humanly speaking, finished his work, completed his career, rounded his life. An intervening providence called Lincoln after Appomatox, and halted Wilson after Versailles. Only the inscrutable eye of God can measure the trail hence-forward they would have followed. But the path of Washington lies under the eyes of the world, a highway undisturbed by fatal violence, and completed through vicissitudes of every sort, to the end of its human destiny. Serene and unhastened; the escutcheon of his shield unsoiled by the darkest experiences of the vast ordeals through which his honor fought, his eternal place already fixed in the hearts of his countrymen, and in the life of the world, he took his last couch as quietly as the humblest citizen who has ever found in death the Christian's great adventure.

Let us examine the claim of our text more closely. A good name is rather to be chosen than great riches, and loving favor rather than silver and gold. The implication is that silver and gold, in certain values at least, do not assay 100 per cent; that even in the pure metal there is a certain alloy; that their purchasing power is limited. And even to a casual, a superficial thinker, the sound basis for the implication becomes quickly apparent.

Of itself, money and its equivalents can do absolutely nothing more than purchase bodily comforts, and be the means of bettering conditions; and as to bettering an individual's or society's condition, money may be the means of making conditions for the individual and for society worse. Temporal wealth is potentially always as much a menace as it is a blessing, and always it is to persons and governments a temptation to selfishness and profligacy. God pity the poor man, or the rich man, who puts his confidence in riches—the one to squander his life in a mad rush after them, and the other to impoverish his soul by trying to feed his immortal spirit upon them.

It is the speaker's observation, that great riches, particularly riches easily and quickly gotten, are frequently closely companioned by great vices, as well as by the very thing they widely gamble against—unhappiness. On the other hand, character and happiness, even with poverty, go together. Not even sorrow and pain, defeat and temporal turmoil, can separate them. Only a little while ago I heard a very rich man say, "Pity the poor rich man!" and though he spoke jestingly, I was not the only hearer who detected more than humor in his voice.

Pity the poor rich man. Ah, but keep a false note out of the sermon here, Mr. Preacher. Envy him, too. Envy him his opportunity to do good; to distribute blessings. It takes character to be both righteous and rich. God does not allow all of us to be tempted by riches, for it is written, you will remember, that he will not suffer us to be tempted above that we are able to bear, and also that with the temptation he will make a way of escape.

But men and women there are—those who have found happiness not in riches but with riches; who have financed worthy causes as Morris pledged the way of the Revolution; who have braided silver cords to hang a tyrant, and paved with gold the upward path of freedom. When I look out upon New York, walking her streets, climbing her stairs, listening to her many tongued voices, smelling her international odors, pondering her problems and coveting her heart and her life for Jesus Christ, I

pray among my first prayers, "O God, give us more men fit to be trusted with silver and gold, and give to them the riches of the world that the world may be made rich, in the blessings of opportunity." And when I pray that prayer, I think first of New York, because I try to think in the spirit of One who sat above an ancient city and wept because of its selfishness and sin, and the doom that these would bring upon it; because I try to think in the spirit of Him who told the friends who were to work after Him, "to begin where they were."

The wise writer of the proverbs of Scripture could not give first place to silver and gold, because he knew that the world's experience had proven them incapable in themselves of supplying happiness and virtue, capacity and knowledge, wisdom among men and favor with God; because his own experience had found them to be a path away from these greater values, as well as a means to them. Aye, and more, because he was bound to testify that riches walked always with anxiety and suspicion; well companioned, frequently, by a peculiar and isolating pride, while they carried a golden trumpet that enticed both the weak and strong to self-indulgence and cynicism.

As to Washington, who will say that great riches were responsible for his great name? Of him it may be said that silver and gold did not deprive him of loving favor; that they even became a means of blessing in his hand, as indeed they have added to the comfort and happiness of a vast number in all generations. But the character of Washington which issued in his life, in his colossal ministry of patriotism, gave him what he holds today—first place in the hearts of his countrymen. And this character made his temporal possessions a moral asset and not a moral liability. His portion of the "great riches" which are cold and lifeless until used, and which may be so used as to become a curse, he turned to the account of justice and liberty.

But more specifically, why is a good name so greatly to be desired? Why is loving favor so rich a reward? First of all, because they have life in themselves; because they are personal; because they are nearer to us than property. Money lies in the pocket; these live in the soul, and always better an empty purse than an empty heart.

Secondly, because a good name gives a man his final social status. An individual who is rated a millionaire financially in the community where he lives, may be listed as a rascal and a miserable miser by his neighbors, while about his humble tenant may grow up all the generous traditions of Longfellow's "Village Blacksmith." Great names—names great by the distinctions of earth, may carry either social approval or disapproval, or they may wear the double crown, as did Washington. In history's stern school where moral judgments are deliberately reached, Washington has been found both good and great.

And a good name with loving favor is richer than riches, because it is human. The brightness of silver and gold is only a surface glow, a reflected light. Money cannot say, "I trust you." "I love you for your own sake." And there are some men and women in the world who are never quite sure they have heard those generous words spoken in sincerity, for always they have lived in the suspicion created by their stocks and bonds. If it were necessary to choose, who would not say, "better be poor and have friends, than be rich and friendless." Character—character which is personality—character which is you—character alone brings direct and satisfactory blessings. Yes, the writer of Proverbs is right; he is eternally right: "A good name is rather to be chosen than great riches, and loving favor rather than silver and gold."

How are they won? How did Washington win them? First of all, they are won; never are they a gift. Nor are they ever, finally, an inheritance. I may receive at birth and carry to the age of accountability my father's good name, and the loving favor of my mother, and what unspeakable boons to those who possess them they are! But as my parents won theirs by generous thinking and right living, so must I win mine. The contribution of my character, of my life, to the good fame of my house, may be either honor or dishonor, bane or blessing, but it will be mine.

George Washington had in all the temporalities of life and in his own body, a running start for a good career. He was well born; clean blood coursed his veins; he was perfectly environed; the generations of his family behind had given him a social status second to that of no man in the new world. But these things, priceless though they are, did not win for him his good name and great. Aaron Burr and Benedict Arnold had all of these advantages, too. Royal birth, great riches, physical prowess and social distinction, have been the inheritance of many a man who has become in his own right a moral and social outcast. No, George Washington, with full credit to the great wealth of his inheritance, won the name with which our lips salute him, and the loving favor with which he commands our hearts.

He won it by unselfishness; by desiring nothing of gain for himself, and by pouring his own spirit through his inspired leadership into the morale of his armies and into the affairs of the infant republic. In one of his great utterances he declares "Let us impart all the blessings we possess or ask for ourselves, to the whole family of mankind." What modern disciple of brotherhood, what present day statesman of the new and more Christlike international order, could say with greater eloquence more than this? Lafayette, in speaking of his beloved friend when the news reached him of Washington's death, testified, "In my idea he is the greatest man for I look upon him as the most virtuous."

George Washington won his good name with loving favor by completely surrendering himself to a cause worthy of such a surrender; a cause so worthy that in addressing it no man had given aught until he had given all—his plantation and his savings; his security of person; his hope for social advancement; his ambitions of every sort, were laid in full knowledge of the risk and of their value, upon Freedom's young and trembling altar, and it was because he so emptied himself of self that fame has found so large a room in which to store her treasures of remembrance.

And, intimately associated with this sublime quality of unselfishness, is the fact that Washington seems to have faced no circumstance, to have been challenged by no ordeal, no attack of foe, no treachery of friend, in which he was less than the master of himself. "More than all, and above all, Washington was master of himself," has written Charles Francis Adams. "If there be one quality more than another in his character which may exercise a useful control over the men of the present hour, it is the total disregard of self when in the most elevated positions for influence and example."

Nor would we approach completeness for even so brief a study of so great a life, were we to fail of placing emphasis upon his generosity—particularly his generosity in dealing with his foes. What pride Americans have in the memory of Grant at Appomatox, when to gallant Lee he returned the shining sword no defeat could dishonor, and in the memory of Lincoln, whose fine soul could not countenance the triumphal entry of Richmond, and in the memory of the conqueror of Conwallis, who addressing his victorious troops at Yorktown, refused to triumph over the fallen foe, but called upon his men to attend divine services "with that seriousness of deportment and gratitude of heart which the recognition of each reiterated and astonishing interpositions of Providence demand of us."

But above every other quality named or that might be named, above all the qualities that have won for the Commander-in-Chief of the Continental armies, and the Father of his country, the world's loving favor, and first place in the hearts of his countrymen, I wright tonight his faith in God. The power of George Washington's life was the authority of his soul. His strength and poise and wisdom came not from his massive form, nor from his courageous heart, nor out of his majestic head. They came from God. If you would view the field where Washington won; if you would come upon the secret of his greatness, if you would hold the key of his immortal destiny, do not go to Cambridge, where so earnestly he took his high command, nor to Long Island, nor to Trenton, nor to Yorktown, nor to Mount Vernon, where on holy ground he waits the rallying of the judgment, but go as I went again this afternoon to the ancient treasury building, which stands in Wall Street, with old Trinity looking down upon it through a mist of years, and see the figure of a man, a man of the ages kneeling in the snows of Valley Forge, holding council with the Captain of his salvation. George Washington's final appeal was not to the courts of kings, but to the throne of Heaven.

> "Never to see a nation born,
> Hath been given to mortal man,
> Unless to those on that summer morn
> Gazed silent when the great Virginian
> Unsheathed the sword whose fatal flash,
> Shot union through the incoherent clash
> Of our loose atoms crystallizing them,
> Around a single will's unpliant stem
> And making purpose of emotion rash.
> Out of that scabbard sprang as from its womb,
> Nebulous at first, but hardening to a star,
> Through mutual share of sunburst and of gloom.
> The common faith that makes us what we are."
>
> —*Lowell.*

THE RELIGIOUS LIFE OF GEORGE WASHINGTON

By NOEL PORTER

Arch Deacon of California, San Francisco, California

Text Ps. 84:5   "Blessed is the man whose strength is in Thee; in whose heart are Thy ways".

Personality is the most majestic thing in the universe. The worlds are the outflashing of personality. Back of the universe itself is the Supreme Personality.

Now a great personality is the result of conscious contact with the Divine, for the greatness of any man is but the greatness of God in him.

Take Abraham Lincoln. What was the secret of his power? The picture on the monument at Springfield comes to mind. It shows the boy Abe, lying before the log fire, writing with a piece of charcoal in the flickering light of his mother's hut. Underneath the picture are these words: "At any rate I'll study and get ready, then maybe some day the chance will come." When the chance came he was ready.

We need to remember how in his farewell address to his fellow citizens at Springfield, in the simplest way he asked their prayers, that God might help him perform his great task.

There was David Livingstone found in the heart of Africa dead beside his couch with the ink scarcely dry on these words that interpreted his vision: "God bless all men everywhere who help to heal this open sore of the world".

When we think of Theodore Roosevelt we recall that all through Harvard he taught a Sunday School class, while at Oyster Bay he attended the services of the Episcopal Church, joined the men's club and often took up the offering on Sundays.

Then there is George Washington whose 200th anniversary the whole country is celebrating. We are apt to think of him as the Father of our Country, as the great Patriot, as the Hero. The other day I read an article dealing with George Washington "The Business Man". But now I want you to consider with me his religious life, for therein we may find the secret of his real greatness. For how true are the words of the Psalmist: "Blessed is the man whose strength is in Thee; in whose heart are Thy ways".

1. *There was the Boyhood of Washington.* It was hallowed by Godly parents. As we see the holy influences that surrounded his boyhood we catch a glimpse of his future greatness. For as Milton said: "The childhood shows the man as morning shows the day". And we must begin with his Godly mother, for as the source lies back of the river, as the sun overhangs the million beauties of nature, as the atmosphere lends itself to the trilling voices of birds in the springtime of the year, so the mother stands back of her child, breathes through the child, is the source of the child's greatness.

Who was Augustine? A saint, plus his mother.

Who was John Wesley? A statesman evangelist, plus his mother.

Who was Abraham Lincoln? A great human redeemer, plus his mother.

Who was Phillips Brooks? A great preacher, plus his mother. And it was his mother who when he was a boy sent him little love-notes such as this "Be true to your Savior dear Phillip, remember the sacred vows you have taken; be true to them, and true and lasting success will be yours".

And so the story runs. You have heard it many times before. It is old, very old—as old as the heart of God, as old as the deepmost genius of the universe, and yet, it is enchantingly, movingly, fascinatingly new. Motherhood is the greatest thing in the world.

As a boy I remember being taken to some of the great art galleries of the old world. There are gathered pictures of war and peace, of love and hate, of tragedy and despair, of victory and defeat. Every now and then as you go round the walls you come to place where the marble has been worn away by the tread of many feet. Multitudes have stood there; men, women and children, who know little about art, have stood before certain pictures as before sacred shrines. And invariably it is a woman's picture that the artist has painted, and invariably she holds a sweet, glad, wondersome child. Motherhood is the greatest thing in the world.

Washington learned to pray at his mother's knee; by her side he walked to church and learned to love God and the prayerbook service.

Washington illustrated the words of the Wise Man in his boyhood: "Remember now thy Creator in the days of thy youth".

At 13 years of age the boy copied in a kind of journal over 100 maxims, including these:

"Let your recreation be manful, not sinful".
"When you speak of God and His attributes, let it be seriously and with reverence".
"Honor and obey your parents, although they be poor".
"Labor to keep alive in your breast that little spark of celestial fire called Conscience".

Washington was shot through and through with a certain boyish soundness. He was a sturdy, imaginative, aspiring, manly **youth.**

When he was commissioned at 21 to carry despatches to the Commander at Fort Le Boeuf it is traditionally stated that he went to receive his mother's farewell kiss, and that going forth on his arduous task, Mary Washington said to him: "My son, neglect not the duty of secret prayer".

His parents were Godly people. Good parents make for noble children. It matters little what kind of a house our children live in, or what kind of clothes they wear, or how much money we leave them when we die. If we have not revealed to them as the rib and backbone of God's universe those eternal verities of righteousness and truth and purity and love, we have been a bane to our children and not a blessing.

And we can not teach righteousness by mere words. We may teach our children the Ten Commandments until they know them by heart; we may moralize as much as Lord Chesterfield did to his son, but if we ourselves worship mammon instead of God; if we steal and call it business, if we lie cleverly to avoid some little social unpleasantness, then the chances are that our children will lie and steal and be infidels as well. For righteousness is an atmosphere; it is color, tone, spirit, life.

George Washington owed a great deal to his early training, for his parents realized the truth of these words of the Psalmist of old: "Blessed is the man whose strength is in Thee, in whose heart are Thy ways".

2. *Then there is the Personal and Public Religious Life of Washington.* Washington gave his soul a chance. There have been few more loyal churchmen than George Washington. Again and again in his diary and journals we find record of his being in the house of God.

George Washington was baptized in our Church. A number of years ago in speaking to the children of a Church School in Southern California, I emphasized this fact that George Washington was a Churchman and had been baptized in our Church. One little girl was deeply impressed, and on her return home her mother questioned her as to what she had learned at Church School that morning. "Something wonderful, mother," she replied, "What do you think? Dr. Porter baptized George Washington!"

When General Braddock died from the wounds received at his defeat, was he to be denied a Christian Burial? Disorganized by the terror of the retreat, their General dead, no chaplain available, circumstances seemed against Christian ceremony. Then it was that George Washington, 24 years of age, is said to have acted as lay reader and read the Christian burial service over Braddock's body rather than have that honored dust given back to Mother Earth with no words of solemn farewell.

Another scene is from the opening of the Continental Congress at Philadelphia in 1774. The officiating clergyman offered a prayer and we are indebted to John Adams for a description of the scene, in a letter to his wife some days later:

". . . the extempory prayer, filled the bosom of every man present." Irving adds, "Washington was kneeling. . . ." Washington was kneeling!

God can answer our petitions whether we be standing, walking, lying, sitting or kneeling. Yet somehow I like to read that Washington was kneeling. I have never read of a nation, or an individual, going to perdition on its knees.

Then there is the beautiful, even though apocryphal, story of the trying days at Valley Forge, when Washington, the Commander-in-Chief, had recourse to the God of Nations. The Tory Quaker, Isaac Potts, tells us that going through the woods near headquarters he heard sound of a human voice. Following the lead of the tone he came at last to a natural bower of ancient oaks. There he beheld Washington on his knees in prayer. Returning home Potts spoke to his wife and said: "I have this day seen what I never expected. Thee knows that I always thought that the sword and the Gospel were utterly inconsistent, and that no man could be a soldier and a Christian at the same time. But George Washington has this day convinced me of my mistake, and I feel that God will work out through him a great salvation for America."

While in Washington attending the General Convention it was my privilege to visit Christ's Church, Alexandria, Virginia. There was I shown the pew in which George Washington sat. He also had a pew in the little church at Pohick not far from Mount Vernon, where he was a vestryman for years. In talking with one of the present vestrymen at Alexandria after the service, he told me that recently they had looked up the minutes of the old vestry meetings at Pohick to ascertain what kind of a churchman George Washington had been. Out of 23 vestry meetings the record showed that he had attended at least 18.

His regularity in church going is certainly an example for us today. He found strength and inspiration in the services of the sanctuary. So may we. And we too will come to a clearer vision of the Master's face and realize the truth of these words of the Psalmist: "Blessed is the man whose strength is in Thee; in whose heart are Thy ways."

3. *Finally Washington manifested the spirit of the Cross of Jesus Christ—the spirit of self sacrifice and unselfish service.*

During the time Washington lived there was another great general in the person of Napoleon. Napoleon was a greater military genius, but Washington was a greater man. France can never repay Napoleon for rescuing her from the hands of the despoilers; yet while he waded through the seas of blood he thought only of a crown and a bauble for his son.

Washington waded through blood and hunger and privation for his country's sake and when it was done he asked no reward save to be left alone on his Virginia farm. Napoleon asked for a crown and received nothing; Washington asked for nothing and received a crown.

Here then is the secret of real greatness. Little men are anxious lest they bloom unseen and waste their sweetness on the desert air, but the truly great can afford to wait, knowing this law that nothing worth while is ever lost.

"Thou shalt know Him when he comes
Not by any din of drums,
Nor by the vantage of His airs,
Neither by His gown nor His crown,
Nor by anything He wears."

But this is sure and certain certificate, he forgets self and serves others.

The way to greatness is through unselfish service. We need to remember that the greatness of America lies not in the vastness of its domain, nor in the numerals that witness to its wealth. Character alone determines national greatness. At the core of our national life there must be honesty and integrity and unselfish service.

Let us then as loyal churchmen and loyal Americans take to heart this message from the life of George Washington. Let us stand for the spirit of Brotherhood and Fellowship and Self-sacrifice, that is, willing to give up in order that it may lift up. Let us go forth in his spirit and we shall know the truth of these words of our text:

"Blessed is the man whose strength is in Thee; in whose heart are Thy ways."

A PLEA FOR THE HEROIC IN AMERICAN CITIZENSHIP

By THE REVEREND HAMILTON SCHUYLER, Litt.D.

Honorary Canon of TRINITY CATHEDRAL
Trenton, New Jersey

And the Lord said unto Gideon, by the three hundred men that lapped will I save you,
and deliver the Midianites into thine hand.—Judges VII, v. 7.

Gideon had been summoned by God to become the leader of the Israelites in liberating them from the galling yoke of the Midianites, by whom they had been for many years mightily oppressed. Against the forces of the invaders, who are described in the narrative "as grasshoppers for multitude and their camels without number, as the sand by the seashore for multitude," Gideon had succeeded in assembling a bare two and thirty thousand men. Even this vastly inferior number was declared by God to be too great for the purpose, and Gideon was bidden to proclaim in the ears of the people that whoever was fearful or afraid should straightway depart and return home. Twenty-two thousand accordingly departed, leaving only ten thousand men to confront the vast army of the Midianites. Again the Lord declared that the number was too great, and directed Gideon to bring the people to water and note their behavior. "The Lord said unto Gideon, everyone that lappeth of the water with the tongue as a dog lappeth shalt thou set by himself, and likewise everyone that boweth down upon his knees to drink." Three hundred men out of the ten thousand lapped the water, the rest following the other method, Gideon was directed to retain only the three hundred and to dismiss the others.

"And the Lord said unto Gideon, by the three hundred men that lapped will I save you, and deliver the Midianites into thine hand."

In the self-restraint thus revealed by their action, the three hundred demonstrated their fitness to fight the Lord's battle. In their eagerness to meet the enemy they did not stop to gratify their natural desires to the full. They wasted no time in lying down to drink, but as they ran forward merely refreshed themselves a little, and quenched the edge of their thirst. They almost forgot their own bodily needs in their haste. They were content to subordinate their personal comfort to the pressing business before them. The nine thousand seven hundred who adopted the more leisurely method, who seized the opportunity freely to slake their thirst, were doubtless valiant men. They had heard the words of Gideon commanding those who were afraid or fearful should depart, and they had stood firm while two-thirds of their countrymen had gone back. But here was a test of earnestness, of self-discipline, for which they were not prepared. They were thirsty from their long, dry march. Here was water; why should they not drink their fill? There could be no harm in satisfying a natural craving. Automatically they obeyed the predominant impulse and thus revealed their true character. Their zeal and steadfastness were not pitched in the heroic key, and so God discarded them as unfit instruments for the accomplishment of his purpose. To the three hundred men only who lapped was it given to defeat the host of the Midianites and win for Israel the great victory.

The story of Gideon and the three hundred is one of the most thrilling in the history of any people. If it be purely legendary,

as the higher critics assume, it is yet a legend that, like the story of Thermopylae, has the power to kindle the imagination and awaken the generous admiration of all lovers of the heroic in mankind. Its practical significance for us today lies in the great truth which it enshrines, namely, that the purposes of God are carried out not by the many, but by the few; that it is individual character that counts, not force of numbers; that the instruments by which God's victories are won are chosen according to a process of elimination, whereby the fit are separated from the unfit or the less fit. This is a principle which we are quick enough to recognize in theory; indeed, the whole history of God's dealings with mankind, as set forth in the Bible, plainly proves that such is the divine method. Abraham, Moses, Joshua, Gideon, David, were chosen as special vehicles to carry out the divine purpose regarding Israel. Of the twelve tribes it was Judah only whose identity was preserved and from whom the nation took its name. The family of Jesse was selected to perpetuate the royal line and it was a humble virgin of that stock who became the mother of the world's Redeemer. Of the thousands of Jews, twelve men were selected as foundation stones of the spiritual Israel. Upon one man, Paul, was laid the task of converting the Gentiles and vindicating the ecumenical character of Christianity.

As we study the history of the Christian Church we find the same principle prevailing. It was Athanasius against the world during the Arian Heresy, and it was the truth which Athanasius stood for which finally prevailed and became the accepted creed of Christendom. The various reformations which the Church has known were mainly the work of individuals. It was always the few, and not the many, who came to the rescue and saved the day. It was the man or the men in whom there burned a single-minded devotion to truth, who scouted the thought of personal comfort, and cared nothing for popular approval or disapproval, who won the victory and laid mankind under a lasting debt of gratitude.

We can see illustrations of the same principle of salvation by the heroic few in the history of races and nations. Upon a single personage, Charlemagne, devolved the tremendous task of rebuilding the fabric of civilization in Europe after the downfall of the Roman Empire. It was Alfred the Great by whose sagacity and patriotism the scattered Saxon tribes were consolidated into a unity out of which sprang the English nation. It was through the heroism of Joan of Arc, that France was able to expel a foreign invader and win back the kingdom to its rightful ruler. It was owing to the faith and courage of William of Orange, that the Netherlands won civil and religious liberty. It was a little band of exiles fleeing from injustice and oppression in their own country who brought to these shores the seeds of the civil and religious liberty which we enjoy today.

It was Washington and his few compeers whose hearts were

fired with a hatred for tyranny and oppression, to whom we are indebted for the establishment of this American nation. It needed the presence and example of these men, their outspokenness, their undaunted courage, their willingness to risk their own lives and fortunes, to inspire the Colonies with a determination to throw off the British yolk. As we interpret the history of those critical times we have to acknowledge that it was a few individuals with Washington at the head through whom the impulse and the encouragement came to initiate and carry through to a successful issue and against frightful odds the great cause which they had at heart.

It has become the fashion today in some quarters to depreciate and disparage the characters of these men and to deny that their public lives were marked by loyalty to a high purpose and by an absence of self-seeking. This tendency to find blots and blemishes in revered names is doubtless due to a reaction against the unreasoning idealization which formerly prevailed. But surely, to idealize a benefactor is better than to indulge in carping criticism and to exaggerate the debt we owe to such, if that be possible, is nobler than to begrudge the praise that is fairly due.

There are those, we are well aware, who in their ignoble zeal to drag down the great to the common level, would not leave even Launcelot brave or Galahad pure. Surely we are right in cherishing the memories and glorifying the lives of those who by their patriotism and faith founded the nation.

To the few, not to the multitude, is our gratitude properly expressed. Those who fought in the ranks were doubtless many of them brave and deserving men, but they could have accomplished nothing had there not been leaders like Washington to arouse their enthusiasm and direct their energies. The heart and brains of any movement are found in a few individuals. The rank and file are merely the body and hands.

It is not necessary to idealize the characters of the founders of the nation in order to appreciate the benefits they won for us and to pay them our meed of gratitude and admiration. They were men of like passions to ourselves. Doubtless they had their full share of the faults and frailties common to humanity and to the age in which they lived. That the motives which led them, or some of them, to take the stand they did were not exclusively those of the purest altruism we may concede, but when all is said it is at least certain the main incentive was unselfish and patriotic. In the event of an unsuccessful issue they would doubtless have been called upon to pay the penalty of death for treason, and no man can give stronger proof of his devotion to a cause than his willingness to risk his life for it.

The salvation of the multitude is always due to the courage and faith of the few. Although we are ready enough to grant the truth of the general principle, we are slow in learning the practical lesson which it involves. I am pleading for the heroic in citizenship, for the giving to the common welfare of that which is best and noblest in us. I am speaking of self-sacrifice, not merely of duty. The appeal to a sense of duty is not an appeal to what is highest in humanity, and, while it may be efficacious in getting things done, it commonly leaves men cold. To the hero spirit it is not duty, but the joy of self-sacrifice that inspires to action. The three hundred men that lapped were not thinking of their duty, but rather were consumed by the fire of an ardent patriotism. An appeal to a man to do his duty is really an appeal to enlightened self-interest and can evoke little enthusiasm. There is in every man a potential hero and it is to him the appeal should be made.

"If we assist you what will you give us?" was asked of a certain patriot who was seeking outside help for his country in overthrowing a tyrannical government. "What will I give you?" he replied; "I will give you sufferings, wounds, imprisonments, death and victory." "We will go with you," was the response.

To demand from ourselves and from others less than the heroic in citizenship is to degrade the claims of patriotism. To ask little is to get little. To be content with half-hearted efforts and desultory labors is to invite them; whereas, to set and exact a high standard in patriotism is to draw to the service of the State all those who are earnestly minded and whose labors will be those of love. It is true, doubtless, that only the few will rise to the high level of which I am speaking, but those few, if they be forthcoming, will be sufficient to save the nation. Though the call comes to all, the glorious privilege of heroism will be grasped by those only who possess the true spirit. The majority as always will be content to live their lives ingloriously upon the lower levels. Having declined the opportunity of becoming heroes the commonplace and the conventional will be their portion forever. Respectability, not heroism, will be the goal to which they attain. The twenty and two thousand of Israel who tacitly acknowledged themselves lacking in courage and departed to their homes, find their counterpart in the vast majority of us today, who hesitate and go back when the crisis comes.

Indolent and fearful they will have no part or lot in the matter. The progress of civic righteousness will owe nothing to them. They may be honest men and law-abiding citizens, but they are not of the stuff which heroes are made. It is left for the few nobler spirits upborne by a sublime courage and self-forgetfulness, reckless of personal consequences, to fight the battle for righteousness and save the day for their country.

But more than mere courage is required of those who enlist in the battle waged against the forces of unrighteousness which seek to destroy the integrity of the State. The hero must have courage, of course, but he must also have other virtues. Primarily he must be endowed with a spirit of lofty self-sacrifice. He must be willing for the success of the cause which he has embraced to subordinate to it all personal considerations. He must forget self-interest and think of nothing save the matter in hand.

The ten thousand who remained after the twenty and two thousand had departed were courageous men. They were determined to face the issue. They promised well, but the true mettle was not in them. When the opportunity was presented to test their fortitude, to tell whether they would subordinate their personal comfort and interest to the cause they had espoused, their true characters were made manifest. The ten thousand in stopping at the stream and lying down to drink their fill, proved that they were unfitted for the high enterprise before them, and they were accordingly discarded. They were estopped from taking any further part in the warfare. They were put aside as unworthy vessels.

How often we see good men, courageous men, whose motives seem of the best and purest, who nevertheless fail in the accomplishment of their purpose, because of some appetitie or passion which they are unable to control: the lust for power or popularity, the unwillingness to be included in a despised minority, the obstinacy which clings to a personal preference, the pride which refuses to yield the first place to another. How many great enterprises have been ruined on account of little defects of character among those to whom the work has been committed. How many noble projects have come to nought through the unwillingness of the leaders to subordinate their own feelings and preferences to the cause to which they have pledged themselves.

George Washington properly epitomizes in his own person the highest and truest ideal of a great national hero, not for his intellectual gifts or military genius, though these were considerable, but rather because of his moral qualities, his unswerving constancy to a lofty aim, his willingness at all times to subordinate his military and political fortunes to the single task of serving his country. Physical courage and the resolution to endure hardship he shared with many others, but where he was unique was in his pure selflessless, his determination to allow no false pride or vainglorious ambitions to abate his disinterested efforts to promote his country's weal. His whole career proves that his dominating thought was the vindication of a great principle, of which he was merely the instrument. The cause was always first and all personal considerations were subsidiary.

As compared with other eminent national heroes in whom personal and political ambitions were mingled with patriotic ardor, Washington must be awarded the preeminence. William of Orange, Oliver Cromwell, Napoleon Bonaparte, and Wellington and even Lincoln, great as they were and notable as were their services to their respective countries, were all morally less great than he, for all to some extent at least were plainly actuated by a double motive, whereas Washington knew but one. Eliminating self, he gave himself without stint to the cause he had embraced. In peace as in war it was ever the same—his country was first and all else was secondary.

But it is not alone or chiefly in war or other dramatic crises of national life that the need is felt for heroic men. In a time of profound peace as at present the call for such is equally imperative. I need not point out to you the dangers and perils which today threaten the well-being and integrity of the State. "Eternal vigilance" as we are reminded, "is the price of safety." If we have no cause to fear any foe from without, if we may lightly dismiss the thought of any foreign enemy invading our land, if the consciousness of our strength and resources tempts us scornfully to deride the idea of suffering humiliation in war at the hand of any nation, we must yet surely realize that there are malign forces at work in the commonwealth which threaten to disturb our peace and to disrupt our institutions. These dangers can only be met and overcome by leaders and statesmen who are animated by the purest ideals of patriotism, who are conscious of a high mission and content to serve the State without any thought of self. We need men who are equally above the blandishments of an arrogant plutocracy and indifferent to the specious applause of the proletariat, men of high moral courage, who pursue a straight course, unmoved by favor or by fear.

As in the past the State was preserved by the few and not by the many, so undoubtedly it will be in the future. As formerly self-seeking and indolence, cowardice and faithfulness, depleted the ranks of the patriots, so it will be again. As in the case of Gideon, the Lord will save the State, indeed is now saving the State, by a faithful remnant. The individual is still the instrument whereby He works mightily.

The practical application of these remarks lies in the fact that to each one of us personally there comes the call to rise to a heroic stature, to the end that in our day and generation God may use us for our country's good. The need is urgent, the faithful are few.

"And the Lord said unto Gideon, by the three hundred men that lapped will I save you, and deliver the Midianites into thine hand."

The Greatness of Washington

By THE REV. FREDERICK F. SHANNON, Litt.D., LL.D.
Minister of CENTRAL CHURCH
Chicago, Illinois

And I was with thee whithersoever thou wentest, and have cut off all thine enemies out
of thy sight, and have made thee a great name, like unto the name of
the great men that are in the earth.—2 Sam. 7:9.

Human greatness finds varied expressions in different ages. But always, when we strike into the quick of true greatness, certain qualities are as invariable as the law of gravity itself. Washington, who belongs to the small band of great men of the first order, is a striking illustration of this principle. With all their initiative and force of character, such men are ringed about with the golden fire of Providence. They may come from following the sheep, like David, from the wilderness, like Lincoln, from the chisel, like Angelo, from the counting room, like Bagehot, from the University, like Wilson, or from the farm, like Washington; it makes little difference whence they come and when they come—they come, they speak their word, they do their deed, they go. Having gone, they leave the world somewhat different. Yet, in perspective, it is our privilege to understand that racial and national leaders are distinguished by a large and wise providentialness. This is one of the many reasons why, as we approach the 200th birthday of Washington, we may profitably reconsider the secret of the greatness that went into the making of our chief Founding Father.

Now Washington, as I wish to show this morning, does not belong to what we ordinarily term the galaxy of genius. He was not intellectually dazzling, like Hamilton, nor brilliantly learned, like Jefferson, nor overwhelmingly eloquent, like Patrick Henry. Yet Washington had, in combination, a set of intellectual and moral qualities which lift him, head and shoulders, above any of these men. The distinctive characteristic of Washington, it seems to me, is a certain wise old wisdom that dwells at the heart of things, that patiently waits for the rare human who can be entrusted with her secret, her mystery, and power. When he comes along, Mother Wisdom adopts him as her very own. He may be terribly misunderstood, outrageously mistreated, but, nevertheless, he leads a kind of charmed life. In spite of all adverse circumstances, he takes his place, whether as a shepherd of sheep or a shepherd of men, among those who wear "a great name, like unto the name of the great men that are in the earth."

Before turning to some of the qualities which distinguish Washington, it may be worth while to consider the evolution of the word "greatness." I used to have a noble friend; he was one of the most widely read men that it has ever been my good fortune to know. Moreover, he was a thinker as well. If we are so inclined, it is both easy and delightful to read, as well as profitable. But to think, really and seriously to think—this is indeed one of the most difficult tasks ever set for mortals. Some great thinkers are not necessarily great readers; yet, wherever you have a proper focus of the reading man and the thinking man, you have a combination of the factors entering into greatness.

Now my friend held that there are three stages in the evolution of the idea of greatness. First of all, there is the stage of force; the stage symbolized, for example, by Nimrod in the Old Testament; or, all through history, by the men of sheer power, exponents of ruthless, unbridled force. Then, very much higher indeed, is the stage of intellect. Here we enter the realm of genius—the men of intellectual daring and variousness, whose minds fairly flash with lightnings of thought even as storm-wracked midnights flash with electric splendors. But the highest stage of all is the stage introduced by our Lord and Master—the stage of goodness, the stage of wise, just, and righteous character. Here we are in the presence of the imponderables, which, ultimately, have a fashion of pushing the pretentious, noisy things out of the way. Definitely linked with God, this third type of great man, alive with the majesty of morality, has the right of way. Packed with the irresistible force named goodness, which is the secret of those who serve and fear the living God, he knows what he is about and goes about it with a nameless, irresistible might and spell. Therefore, let us think of Washington as a kind of individual and social solvent. Just as the chemist employs a substance in solution, so Washington is the embodiment of definite individual and social solvents which may be immensely valuable in face of the tremendous problems confronting America and the modern world.

There is a misconception of him which makes him a kind of statue on a pedestal—cold, austere, unemotional, dispassionate. Long prevalent, this misconception was not held by those who knew him face to face. Search out the testimony of those who were close to him, and they leave the impression that underneath his calm, unruffled surface there was a raging energy, a white-hot fire sometimes terrible in its fierceness, and more than one man knew what it was to be burned by the heat thereof. That fire burned away the walls of many who were imprisoned by the superficial; it destroyed the pretentious burdens weighing heavily upon those who dared to strut in his presence.

Yes, under that calm exterior is character that challenges the admiration of all who are capable of the admirable; within those raging fires there was a soul that held him in splendid leash, a mind that said to his passions, "Thus far shalt thou go, and no farther." There was a governor, a self-control, at the center of his being which made the circumference of his life sublime. Whether in public or private, this quality was always in ascendancy. Living within forty years of Washington's death, W. E. H. Lecky, the British historian, says:

"He never acted on the impulse of an absorbing or un-calculating enthusiasm, and he valued very highly fortune, position, and reputation; but at the command of duty he was ready to risk and sacrifice them all. He was in the highest sense of the words a gentleman and a man of honor, and he carried into public life the severest standard of private morals. It was at first the constant dread of large sections of the American people that if the old government were overthrown, they would fall into the hands of military adventurers and undergo the yoke of military despotism. It was mainly the transparent integrity of the character of Washington that dispelled the fear."

Here, then, is an invaluable tradition, rooted in fact, that should be revered and reproduced not only in America, but in the life of mankind.

In the light of Washington's magnificent self-control, our generation has much to learn and practice. With all our getting, we seem not to have gotten the power and wisdom of self-control. Just what is the catchword of our time? Is it not this: "Do as you please! Let yourself go! A short life, and a merry one!" And we are told, in some quarters, that this is the "new liberty" which has been discovered quite recently. Well, nobody but a fool calls it new; and nobody but the morally insane calls it liberty. To be plain, just how new is this attitude, and just how liberating as well? "Let yourself go!" Why, that cry is as old as Babylon, as Nineveh, as Tyre, Yes, and every whit as deadly as the centuries-old graveyards in which their civilizations lie entombed. But not only the Babylonians said that; not only the Greeks and Romans. The first decades of the twentieth century were saying it also. By letting itself go, humanity kindled a fire in 1914 which burned across the world—a fire which was not extinguished until the blood of thirty-five millions of human beings was poured upon it.

As your friend, let me say this to you: The "let-your-self-go" philosophy inevitably leads the disciples thereof to hell. And that is not all; it places them in hell while they are on the way. For the hell I have in mind is not a creation of medievalism; it is the living hell of hatred, jealousy, lust, secularism, fatigue, shattered nerves, and, finally, the despair that exclaims, "What is it all about, anyway?" It is not the old fire-and-brimstone hell; rather it is the hell of the new psychology all dressed up in the old materialism and nowhere to go but into the abyss of its own futility.

Here is the illustration employed by one of the behaviorists. He thinks of man, in his own words, "As an assembled organic machine ready to run." There is your automobile, with its wheels, tires, differentials, gas engine, body. Now the automobile is good for certain kinds of duties. In a similar way, John Doe, this organic animal, is composed of certain parts named head, arms, hands, trunk, legs, feet, toes, and nervous, muscular and glandular systems. He, too, this mechanical John Doe, is good for certain jobs. In making the comparison, Watson remarks, almost naively,

"I mean nothing very difficult by this." Yet, as Doctor Bridges says in his brilliant volume, "Taking the name of science in vain," there is one factor Mr. Watson strangly overlooks in his illustration of the automobile, and that is—the driver. After all, what is your automobile without a driver? Moreover, how did your automobile come to be without a mind? That, rejoins the behaviorist, is perfectly simple—"the body is the mind." Without even a smile or a twinkle of their humorous eyes, they tell us that this is the new and true interpretation of man's place in the universe. How new? In the seventeenth century John Locke, father of the sensational system of philosophy, said, "There is nothing in the mind which was not first of all in the senses." To which Leibnitz, philosopher and mathematician, replied, "Nothing—except the mind, or intellect, itself."

Now, some people would like to believe that they are just non-moral, irresponsible machines. Doing as they please here, they will not have to be pleased hereafter because they conclude, there is nothing about which to be either pleased or displeased. Sugar-coat it verbally as we may, this is what it all amounts to. How personal responsibility was, is, and shall continue to be the mark of moral worth in man. It was so of Washington; it is so of every human who has the moral mettle to stand upon his own feet and realize what Amiel called the "life of perpetual achievement." To do this calls for self-control.

I would like to express this thought as carefully as I may: While his magnificent self-control is in the active Washington, his fine obedience is uttered through the passive Washington. True, he had his grandly active and positive side, as all great natures have; but he had, also, a nobly passive side. In a word, Washington not only acted, but was acted upon.

Recently I had a letter from a gentleman in Denver. He says that he would like me to buy a Napoleonic clock which he owns. He insists that it is a splendid specimen of clock-making of the period; that Napoleon himself had it made and presented it to a certain European king. Now, if this gentleman should happen to be listening this morning, I wish to say in reply: If I could have the finest Napoleonic clock ever made, I would not give it space in my house. I might admire its workmanship; I might even sell it and devote the proceeds to worthful ends. But I have so little admiration of Napoleon and the brutality he personifies that, for me, a kind of curse rests upon the things associated with his name. With all his intellectual power, his statecraft, his military genius, he was one of the outstanding egotists of history, selfish to the core, who made himself the center of the mean and heartless little universe in which he lived.

What was Napoleon obedient to? What did he worship? What did he bow before? Nothing—save his own colossal self-conceit. Washington, on the other hand, was obedient to the highest he knew. Dynamically active, he was acted upon. Obey the law of a force, says the philosopher, and the force will obey you. Obey the living God, says morality and religion, and there is a holy and beautiful sense in which God can not help obeying you. In league with him, determined to do his will at all costs, loving what God loves and hating what God hates, you and God are united in "cooperative goodness." And it is through human obedience, not otherwise, that this redemptive reality is established between the Divine and the human.

Now is there anything finer than to see Washington, the great commander, commanded? There is a story that back in the old Virginia town a servant had told his mother that her illustrious son, worn and tired, had put up at the village tavern. "Go tell George to come here instantly," was the command issued by his venerable and queenly mother, Mary Washington. And he obeyed, instantly, masterful man that he was. Unfolding his six feet and more of flesh and blood, just about that which constituted the lineal proportions of Abraham Lincoln, he moved toward his commanding mother with the majesty of an uncrowned king. Show me the man or woman who has something within that compels obedience to the lofty and true, and I will show you the divinest creation within the universe. Show me, on the other hand, men and women who just "let themselves go," and I will show you the most sinister social plague-spots in the modern world. Within Washington's self-control, and, indeed, growing out of it, came the stimulus that responded, not to animalism and immorality, but to humanity at its best.

Consider the sense of obedience that steadied him at Valley Forge. It was a period that tried Washington's very soul. Not only the distressful conditions in the army weighed upon him, but the criticism, fault-finding, and abuse of certain citizens almost crushed him. It was then, we are told, that his faith actually and temporarily wavered. After a long struggle with himself, he wrote his resignation. General Knox came in the cabin which Washington used as his headquarters. He saw the resignation; he also saw a white-handled penknife, the gift of his mother. She had given him this knife, says a biographer, when George was a boy, and "counseled him always to be respectful to his superiors." Seeing, on that fateful day, the sorely tried leader and knife which he carried from childhood, General Knox fingered the keepsake for a time and then gently slipped it into Washington's hand. The great man flushed, and he clenched it. Half an hour later, Washington threw his resignation into the devouring flames of the fireplace. "He would 'obey his superiors,' who, in this case, were the colonists fighting for American freedom."

Here, then, is the heart of the matter. Freedom, in the individual and social order, is possible only through obedience to the highest. Make no mistake, this is a cornerstone of the real world, which can not be removed—except to crush the human beings who undertake to remove it. Recently, in a university center, a teacher recalled what the head of the department of psychology had said to his class: "If any of you students think you have a mind, or soul, you have no business in my class." After the statement had become public property, a citizen of the community, who happened to be a journalist, asked the professor if he had been correctly quoted; whereupon the citizen was told that "it was none of his business." After telling me the story, the scholar asked, "What do you think of that?" I answered somewhat as follows: "If true, it is just a sample of the unpsychologic idiocy which inevitably results when the antipsychologic idiot 'makes up his windpipe that he has no mind.' "

Imagine a Washington produced by such academic inanity, not to say asininity! Imagine any normal human nourished upon such drivel! Imagine good citizenship built upon such a mental mudsill! Imagine moral ruggedness growing out of such a vitiated atmosphere! The fact is: This whole situation is your business, my business—indeed, the business of everybody who believes in genuine education and the quality of human beings such education produces. But it is set down as surer than fate and steadier than gravity that education based upon the mechanistic concept of life issues in character that is neither wise nor great. On the contrary, it makes for brazenness, lawlessness, upstartishness, the unhappiness which ends in despair, and, sometimes, in suicide. "The citizens of the future who are now in our schools," says a greatly educated American, "should be taught with utmost care and thoroughness that their own rights can be made secure only by constant respect for and observance of the rights of others."

This is the seed-principle that Washington dropped into the furrows of our national career at its very beginning: Sow the seed of self-control in the fields of individual and social life and a fine crop of growing, obedient humans must be the result; on the contrary, sow the dragon's teeth of a mechanistic philosophy and not only armed men must spring up, but men armed with weapons of self-destruction. Is it not somewhat paradoxical, after all, for a nation to maintain an army and navy for defense against foreign foes, when all the while, deadly foes are at work within to destroy not only nationality, but even the idea of morality itself. And they make a living out of it—not a life, not something big with final values, because they dogmatically assert that there is, properly speaking, no such fact. We are but foam-bubbles on the stream whose waves are heredity and environment, stimulus and response, nerves and neurons—just irresponsible murderers and misguided morons; or, perhaps, individual robots and social Punch-and-Judies. In due time the bubbles burst and—well, what of it?

At the other extreme is the spineless humanism which asserts, "All the world needs is to cheer up and get on its toes." Perhaps a better remedy would be for some of us to shut up and get down on our knees. May the good Lord deliver America from the mental and moral libertine, on the one hand, and from the screaming, ineffectual reactionary on the other! Life is too serious, personal responsibility is too poignant, self-choice is too far-reaching, to be treated with either sardonic laughter or intellectual incompetence. The living God is not interested in being academically patronized as the Infinite. Perhaps or defended as an obsolete nonenity; the fact that God in Christ is living and active means that men and nations must go the way God is going or perish. "Let us with caution indulge the supposition," says Washington, "that morality can be maintained without religion." Both Samuel and Washington are in accord in the religious reality which declares, "Behold, to obey is better than sacrifice, and to harken than the fat of rams." Yes, obedience to the Supreme is better even than the sacrifice of soldiers upon the altars of patriotism, better than the fat of the rams of a godless prosperity which never fails to cave in upon itself.

Response and stimulus are very much in the air of our time. We are tempted to forget, however, that there is response to the low and the high, that there is stimulus from the devilish and stimulus from the divine. Just now, emphasis seems to be placed upon the low; we conveniently ignore the high. Washington, in making his imperishable record of duty, was all the while responding to the call of the supreme.

It requires moral mettle to do that. No human who comes to close grips with duty but is severely tested; there is no other way out for moral beings in a moral universe. Washington withstood this terrible test—not only on physical battlefields, but on the inner, decisive battlefields as well. At a cabinet meeting in 1793 he is reported to have said that he would rather be in his grave than in his present situation; that he had never but once repented having wavered the moment of resigning his office, and that was every moment since. Once before, in 1782, he shone resplendent in the light of duty. Discontented with the existing government, a party making Colonel Nicola its spokesman, believed that the remedy was in some kind of monarchy, with a large infusion of the one-man power. Washington was, of course, to be that man! O no—not he! Like a smoldering fire, his indignation burns quietly but not the less hotly in his measured words of reply. "I am much at a loss," he says, "to conceive what part of my conduct could have given encouragement to an address which to me seems big with the greatest mischiefs which can befall my country."

Thus, like all achieving humans, Washington climbed the arduous hills of duty. Sometimes the load was heavy, but he never quailed or faltered. In face of duty, bauble of temporal power—the title of "King George of America"—held no lure, no appeal whatever. "To persevere in one's duty and be silent," he said, "is the best answer to calumny."

In this relation, another fact must not be overlooked—and that is the conscience which inspired Washington's self-control, obedience, dutifulness. "Labor," he wrote in his copybook, "to keep alive in your breast that little spark of celestial fire called conscience." What is conscience? Certainly, it is more than consciousness; for consciousness seems to begin down among the plant-animals, reaches a higher stage in the simian, and, highest of all, the Christ-like human. Conscience is consciousness in full bloom—toward God, toward self, toward society. It is one of the imponderables which must be reckoned with, both here and hereafter. It may be seemingly ignored and, apparently, anodyned out of existence. Nevertheless, conscience invariably asserts itself, inevitably wakes up, and speaks with "a thousand several tongues." Mencken's plea is that he and his school shall take their stand with the aristocrats, becoming "free spirits, each holding himself responsible only to his own notions." Here, verily, is innocence abroad in the modern world and embodied in a modern of the moderns! Hold ourselves responsible only to our own notions? Why, there is just one fatal objection to it: It can't be done,—that is, finally done. This little spark of celestial fire refuses to be blown out by any winds whatsoever. The very winds that would blow it out only blow it into fiercer heats of searching judgment-day reality. True, the behaviorist may deny the existence of consciousness and conscience, of mental life in any form. But let us calmly remember, as the philosopher and scholar reminds us, that in doing so the behaviorist "invalidates and discredits the very powers by which he essays to establish his conclusions. He uses logic to annihilate logic, and reasons that reason is an unreality." Set over against such mental and moral contradiction hear Washington's lofty conclusion of the whole matter: "The consciousness of having attempted faithfully to discharge my duty, and (to win) the approbation of my country, will be recompense for my services." Such sublime behavior can not be explained by behaviorism. For both the divine and the human move tremendously within this tremendous man; and the two forces are interpreted by Mary Blake Woodson, in her "Wee Washington":

> "What do he see?" his mammy said, "alooking off so far?"
> How could she know wee Washington was looking at a star?
>
> "Don' play with shadders, honey chile," his old black mammy said.
> How could she know he grasped at stripes that lay across his bed?
>
> "Don' eat so much," his mammy said, "kase gemmen folks don' gorge.
> How could she know that he could starve, and stick, at Valley Forge.

> "Let's warm your foots, close by de fire," his old black mammy said.
> How could she know his feet would march when all the fires were dead!
>
> "How squar' he jaw," his mammy said, "he won' min' none at all.
> How could she guess that that square jaw would save a nation's fall!
>
> How could she know, while rocking him, so wee, with tender love.
> He'd use stars, stripes, cold, hunger, grit, to make a nation of!

SERMONETTE ON GEORGE WASHINGTON

By RT. REV. ERNEST V. SHAYLER
Bishop of Nebraska

History is built around the lives of great men. Out of their spiritual and patriotic service to human kind grow the real values of character which they bequeath to succeeding generations. Never are these statements more true than when applied to the thoughts and deeds which cluster around the life of George Washington in the genesis of these United States. Without disparagement to those others who, in the formative and realizing days of our infant republic, shared with him in brain and in brawn, in spirit and in action, none equals in glory the service of that hero and patriot whose anniversary we now celebrate.

An inheritance of gentle blood endowed him with the chivalry and courtesy which ever marked his expression. The possession of a superior intellect satisfied his inherent thirst for knowledge. His physical equipment produced a manly bearing that made him the masterful soldier that he was. The love of romance led him into charming deeds of devotion and was crowned by a serene domesticity which made his home life the center of happy social activities.

Upon the broad acres of his plantations he began to learn that capacity in leadership of men which served him so well as Commander-in-Chief of our army. His speech was meticulous and graceful, his well-chosen words of tongue and pen revealed mastery in the realm of letters whether expressed in private correspondence or in public document. His character was a rare combination of fortitude, courage and heroism constantly portrayed through an indomitable will guided by a quickened conscience. His willingness to sacrifice self and to forego pecuniary rewards marked him as the most magnanimous of men. His breadth of vision lifted him above all pettiness and partisanship into the clear realm of a true patriotism, and his fidelity to a sacred cause was unswerving and the choice possession of his soul until he breathed his last.

It is not difficult to discern the cause and origin of these rarely combined elements of character. Seldom did George Washington pen a document or render public speech but that he committed himself and his cause to Divine Providence. Upon that eternal, impregnable support he based his life, his career, his cause. His life was compassed with the Divine, which issued in Christian conduct through the exercise of Christian virtues, and has become immortalized. Through the record of his years of worship and service as a communicant and vestryman of the little Virginia Church may be traced that inner stream of the Spirit which emerged in that mighty flood of deeds of devotion and sacrifice. His life was a constant witness to God and his character was moulded to the principles of Christ.

Two hundred years ago was his natal day. But to the end of our national existence and to the end of international civilization his fame will endure and his name will be held in veneration. This nation owes to him a debt of gratitude which it never can pay. The youth of today and men of tomorrow may inbreathe inspiration from his living memory. The rulers of this and every land may well follow in his footsteps, and all who believe that true democracy can run its course by following Divine guidance may rejoice with grateful hearts for the life of George Washington.

America's Calvary

A Sermon by
REV. FULTON J. SHEEN, Ph.D.
Catholic University
Washington, D. C.

The really worthwhile things of life and history have generally involved something costly and painful to the doer. All the great truths of the past which have illuminated human thought, all the lofty examples of heroes and saints who have invigorated human effort, all the inspiration of poets and patriarchs that has steeled hearts and strengthened holy resolves—all have been, more or less, dearly paid for by moral, mental or physical suffering. Each truth has its martyr, although the martyr may be unseen.

Nature looked at superficially seems to say that death and sufferings are ruins, but looked at more profoundly, death has seemed to be the prelude of life, and suffering the condition of purification. Like the legal impurities of the old tabernacle, the errors and miseries of the world are purged with blood. Unless the grain of wheat falling to the ground die to its outer shell, it remains alone and does not spring up into the blade and the harvest.

> "The fall doth pass the rise in worth;
> For birth hath in itself the germ of death,
> But death hath in itself the germ of birth.
> It is the falling acorn buds the tree,
> The falling rain that bears the greenery,
> The fern-plants moulder when the ferns arise.
> For there is nothing lives but something dies,
> And there is nothing dies but something lives,
>   Till skies be fugitives,
> Till Time, the hidden root of change, updries
> Are Birth and Death inseparable on earth;
> For they are twain yet one, and Death is Birth."

The prototype of the seeds that fall to the ground only to find their new life in the full grain, as well as the prototype of all those who go down to the death of their lower selves in order to relive the larger freedom of the spiritual, is the Son of God on Calvary, Who, from a gibbet where He was unfurled like a wounded eagle, proclaimed a solemn and awful paradox of life; that unless there is a Good Friday in our lives, there will never be an Easter Sunday; unless there is a Cross there will never be an empty tomb; unless there is a scourged body there will never be a glorified body; unless there is a burial there will never be a resurrection; for death is the antecedent of life, and apparent defeat the condition of victory.

Our country was born according to this law, for there was blood shed at its birth, and pain suffered at its first seeing the light of day, for only upon its battlefields which had been "dunged with rotten death" could there bloom and blossom the white lily of liberty. That we might be most conscious of how strictly and rigidly the American nation submitted to this law, and was in labour at its birth, it behooves us now and then to recall in our mind's eye the sufferings of a General and the pains of his soldiers in giving to a new hemisphere the resurrection of a new liberty through and by the crucifixion of a Good Friday. No one could contemplate the sufferings of Valley Forge without thinking of it in terms of blood. If snow were as lasting as stone, we would today read its history, not in the ink upon pages, but in the blood upon snow. Consider Washington as he sat, unconquered by the defeats of war, reviewing his fast dwindling army at Valley Forge. In the piercing northern weather, his men were destitute and in rags. Blanketless, shelterless, coatless, shoeless, they huddled together in the freezing air, drawing their muskets across their bony shoulders, and with empty stomachs and sickened hearts, they longed for the comfortable home fires they had left, and vaguely wondered how long it need be before they returned to them. With nothing to cover their bodies, with nothing to sustain their courage, with only Washington to instill hope into their souls, wasting away from exposure, starvation and disease, we can only marvel at the forebearance which carried these early American sons through the dark and awful winter of 1777, the Good Friday of American liberty.

It is highly improper that as a nation we ever grow unmindful of the great price that had to be paid for the purchase of our freedom. And yet there is danger that we do forget, and on the occasion of this Bicentennial it is necessary that we renew the law that operated at Valley Forge, and long before it at Calvary, and prepare ourselves to purchase still greater liberty by the restraint which the law enjoins. If that law received an universal approbation throughout our country, we might more readily realize that political rights might sometimes be moral wrongs, and that the true leader of men is not one who feels the pulse of his constituents to give them what they want, but rather one who feels their pulse to give them what they need. If we understood the law rightly, we would be less afraid of public opinion, rather making it than following it. We would have little use or respect for those citizens or politicians who are afraid to condemn a dominant error or a triumphant vice: and who fear not to strike where justice demands, conscious that right is right if nobody's right, and wrong is wrong if everybody's wrong.

If our nation then is ever to become not only the economic, but the moral leader of the world, it will do so by the cultivation of the spiritual truth which brought it into being; it will lose patience with men whose sails are open to every wave of popularity, and take courage in those who let the broad stroke of their challenge ring out on the shield of the world's hypocrisies. We have the germ of moral leadership in our birth. We are started right, and if we are to unfold, true to all the beautiful spiritual ideals which inspired our birth, if we are to achieve that greatness which comes by the subjection of that which is low to the domination of that which is high, if we are to become great, not in the savage sense of being physically powerful, but in the spiritual sense of realizing that the things that make a millionaire do not necessarily make a man—if, I say, we are to become all that our infancy and youth have promised and inspired, then we will look upon our War of Independence, and its leader in suffering, not as a Revolution, but as a Redemption.

GEORGE WASHINGTON AND THE SECOND MILE

Sermon by
REV. JAMES I. VANCE, D.D.
Pastor of the FIRST PRESBYTERIAN CHURCH
Nashville, Tennessee

"Whosoever shall compel thee to go a mile, go with him twain."—Matthew 5:41

This is the way the Man of Galilee measures men. He measures them with the second mile. Of course, one must go the first mile before he can go the second. He must be just before he is generous. He must do his duty before he attempts the heroic. But if he is to lead his fellows in a great crusade and earn a place among the immortals, he must do more than his duty. He must live in the second mile. "Whosoever shall compel thee to go a mile, go with him twain."

The first mile is law. The second mile is grace. The first mile is what law compels us to do. The second mile is what our hearts prompt us to do. In the first mile one claims his rights. In the second mile he surrenders his privileges. The first is the mile of citizenship. The second is the mile of patriotism. The first is the mile in which life is protected. The second is the mile in which life is laid down. In the first mile man rules. In the second he serves.

Our country is preparing to celebrate the two hundredth anniversary of its greatest citizen. At Wakefield in the Virginia tidewater country, on February 22, 1732, George Washington was born. Recently I visited the lovely spot where the river slips quietly down to the bay where the new house to take place of the old home that was burned is nearing completion. I tried to visualize the bit of sky and land which first greeted the sight of the greatest of Americans.

The early history of our country was to a large extent the history of a dominant personality. Able and sagacious men were associated with Washington, but the country turned to him as the ablest and most sagacious of them all, and his ideals of statesmanship, his conceptions of government and his views on public questions rapidly became a part of the United States. In 1789 there were only three million people in our nation, one-fifth of whom were negro slaves. If Washington had been other than he was, America would not be today what it is.

Let us try to measure him with the second mile, not by law, but by service; not by statistics, but by statesmanship; not by what duty demanded and position compelled, but by what a great love for his country and his fellowmen prompted him to do.

There can be no doubt but Washington was deeply religious. He was baptized in the Episcopal Church. Beyond all doubt, he was a sincere believer in the Christian faith. It was the practice of his life to attend public worship whenever possible. He prayed, and relied on the efficacy of prayer and the help of Divine Providence for success in the serious undertakings which devolved upon him. He declared that: "Reason and experience both forbid us to expect that national morality can prevail in exclusion of religious principle."

At eleven years, as the eldest son at home, on the death of his father, he led the family prayers. He attributed his escape in encounters where he repeatedly risked his life to the "miraculous care of Providence." He looked upon life as a trust from his Maker, and it was to be exercised not for selfish gain or personal honor, but for the glory of God and the good of his fellow-men. He went the second mile.

This tendency in his life started with his mother. There was something old-fashioned and chivalrous in his treatment of her, and there was something masterful in her treatment of him. There is the story of the plan in his youth for a maritime career, possibly a midshipman's warrant. All preparations were made, and he was about to sail, when his mother changed her mind. It must have been a great disappointment to the adventure-loving youth, but without a murmur he accepted his mother's decision as to his career, and gave up the life of a sailor, years later to become the first President of the United States. After the war Washington delivered an address at Fredericksburg and spoke proudly of his obligations to his "revered mother." She spoke to her son of old times and old friends, "but of his glory not a word." She saw him still as her son, and he never forgot that she was his mother. She saw him in the second mile, and he accepted her ideal of life and lived it to the day of his death.

The same spirit showed itself in his treatment of the other members of his family and of the kindred of his wife. He was among them not as the powerful leader of a great nation, a man of world distinction whose name was to be acclaimed through centuries, but as a kinsman, deeply interested in the small affairs of their daily lives. He paid their debts, and repeatedly helped them out of financial difficulties. There were many of them, and in a generous way he carried them all. When one of his nephews was threatened with consumption, his uncle's purse supplied what was needed. To the young widow and her children he opened Mount Vernon, saying: "You can go no place where you will be more welcome," and added: "The offer . . . was made to you with my whole heart." Washington had no children of his own, but during his life he assumed the expenses of nine of the children of his kin. It was not something he was compelled to do. It was just his way of living in the second mile.

This characteristic of the great Washington showed itself in all his dealings with his fellow-men. He was human and companionable. One night after a battle he and Lafayette slept under the same blanket and talked long into the night. When Lafayette languished in prison during the French Revolution, it was funds from Washington which supplied the pressing necessities for Lafayette's wife and son. He did the same for the family of General Nathanael Greene, left in embarrassed circumstances at the close of the war.

General Washington was a slave holder, but he was opposed to slavery. He said: "I am principaled against this kind of traffic in the human species." He was the kindest of masters. A clause in his will directed "upon the decease of my wife it is my will and desire that all slaves which I hold . . . shall receive their freedom." In 1791, not counting the house servants, there were more than a hundred and fifty "hands" on the Mount Vernon place. Speaking of the burden of caring for so many hungry mouths, Washington said: "It would really be to my interest to set them free rather than to give them victuals and clothes." He was not so much their master as their provider. They were his slaves, but he was their servant, for in his treatment of them he did more than he was compelled to do. He lived in the second mile.

While mingling on terms of easy friendship with the great families of that day in Virginia, and equal among the best, Washington was thoroughly democratic in all his relations with his neighbors, and ever of easy approach. He thought of others. He gave to Tilghman the honor of carrying to Congress the news of the surrender of Cornwallis. He gave to Humphreys, another aide, the distinction of bearing the standards captured at Yorktown, at the same time commending him "for attention, fidelity and good service." He did not allow the ingratitude of Alexander Hamilton or the bitter attack of Tom Paine or the base duplicity of the Conway cabal to embitter him or make his unmindful of the service he might render to others. A tribute to the humanness in Washington's personality was humorously paid him in an impromptu song rendered in a play which Washington witnessed during his presidency:

" . . . with one accord
He's called to be a kind of—not a lord—
I don't know what, he's not a *great* man, sure,
For poor men love him, just as he were poor,
They love him like a father or a brother,
As we poor Irishmen love one another."

This was the way the people felt about Washington. He was a man of unmistakable dignity, of great composure and poise, but there was a friendliness about him that came from his belief that position meant service. He was living his life in the second mile. He was not thinking of the power he possessed as president, but of the opportunity and obligation for service which came to him in the lofty place to which the people of his country had lifted him. Such was the statesmanship of Washington. He thought of other nations. His diplomacy was the diplomacy of the Golden Rule. He said: "To administer justice to, and receive it from, every power with whom they are connected will, I hope, be always found the most prominent feature in the administration of this country." In stressing the four things which he regarded as essential to the well-being of the country, he emphasized "the sacrifice of individual advantages to the interest of the community." He spoke of the nations of the earth as "one great family," and declared that human nature cries aloud for "a general peace." These were great words for a soldier to utter in an age that knew no way but war. Washington was more than a politician. He was a patriot.

His effacement of self-interest in love for country is revealed in his refusal to take any compensation for his long and laborious services in the Revolutionary War. While his salary as president was $25,000, he spent all of it and probably more in connection with expenses involved in the duties of his office, and this career of high idealism, of lofty patriotism, of unselfish love of country and devotion to the cause of freedom he climaxed when he spurned the suggestion that he be made king. Colonel Lewis Nicola had been selected to approach Washington in 1782. Speaking of the weakness of republics, he ended by saying:

"I believe strong arguments might be produced for admitting the title of king, which I conceive would be attended with some material advantages."

Washington's reply was an immediate and emphatic rejection of the idea. It was written on May 22, and the exactness of the copy which Washington kept was certified by Humphreys and Trumbull, his aide and secretary. He said: "With a mixture of great surprise and astonishment I have read with attention the sentiments you have submitted to my perusal. Be assured, sir, no occurence in the course of the war has given me more painful sensations than your information of there being such ideas existing in the army as you have expressed, and I must view with abhorrence and reprehend with severity. For the present, the communication of them will rest in my own bosom, unless some further agitation of the matter shall make a disclosure necessary. I am much at a loss to conceive what part of my conduct could have given encouragement to an address which to me seems big with the greatest mischiefs that can befall my country. If I am not deceived in the knowledge of myself, you could not have found a person to whom your schemes are more disagreeable. . . Let me conjure you, then, if you have any regard for your country, concern for yourself or posterity, or respect for me, to banish these thoughts from your mind, and never communicate as from yourself or anyone else a sentiment of the like nature."

Such was the man who two centuries ago was born at Wakefield, and who became the first president of these United States. He has been pronounced the noblest figure that ever stood in the forefront of a nation's life. In nothing was he greater than in this element of service. Let us hope and pray that among the blessings which may come to us as a result of the observance of the two hundredth anniversary of Washington's birth, there will be a recovery and revival of the patriotism of the second mile.

GEORGE WASHINGTON,
A MAN OF FOUR DIMENSIONS

By REV. FREDERICK J. WEERTZ
ST. JOHN'S EVANGELICAL LUTHERAN CHURCH
Des Moines, Iowa

Ephesians 3:17-19: That ye . . . . may be able to comprehend with all the saints
what is the breadth, and length, and depth, and height . . .
and to know the love of Christ.

The apostle speaks of a four-fold life in Christ Jesus. It is the all comprehensive life of a well-rounded man, and may be fittingly applied to the life of the man whose life we now commemorate.

I. Length. The length of a man's life in years is no criterion of greatness. Not how long, but how much does one live in this brief span called Life ? The Word of God tells us Methuselah lived to be 969 years of age. The longest-lived human on earth. Perhaps that was all that was to be said about this man's life who grew to be as old as the Sequoia tree of California. There is no outstanding achievement recorded. No battle won. He erected no eleemosynary or educational institution that would perpetuate his memory. He healed no sick, wrote no poems, composed no verse or song that would bring cheer to rising generations. He made no contribution politically worth mentioning. No doubt there was nothing else to write, but that which pertained to length of years. Life to some is a monotonous existence, to others it is a sacred gift of God, an opportunity to rise from valleys of obscurity to heights not yet attained.

There is so much in the life of George Washington that makes the pulse-beat quicken. He lived such a well balanced life, which had much of the pure gold in it. Nature endowed him for great a task. The world admires a fine specimen physically. Scripture speaks glowingly of the ruddiness of her Davids, the purity of her Josephs. All accounts agree that George Washington was of imposing presence. Six feet in height, two hundred pounds or more in weight, calm of countenance, pure in heart—a man to be reckoned with. A man of ideals, one whom Tennyson would classify as a man "whose strength was as the strength of ten because the heart was pure."

Washington was a born fighter—not by choice but necessity. He loved the quietude of rural life; however it was not his lot to live a life of peace for a far-seeing providence had a different plan for him, so that this land could become a refuge for all nations. Yes, the dangers of the wilderness had to be faced, and the shackles of tyranny had to be broken. "There were giants in the land," and as God called Joshua of old to conquer Canaan, I feel Washington was called to liberate the Colonists and lay that strong foundation upon which we are building today.

The world has always been interested in the man "who fights the good fight." It detests one who gets into a brawl. At twenty, the young man was made an adjutant general of a military district of Virginia. At twenty-three he was a volunteer in the Virginia forces serving valiantly in Braddock's campaign. At twenty-six, when psychologists tell us a man's habits are well formed, we find him commanding the advance guard of the expedition which captured Fort DuQuesne, renamed Fort Pitt.

Honors and fame followed, but he sought neither. At this point, which was a critical one in his career, he may well have basked in the light of accomplishments of the past. He asked no favors, abhorred the life of a demi-god, sought no publicity, but retired to private pursuits for the next sixteen years. This sterling character after having served his country so well, went back to the less romantic, nevertheless heroic task of developing the natural resources of his native state. He was as clear in his thinking of following in the strict path of duty as a man could possibly be. What he did was done well; it was a life at its best. Each added year found life unfolding itself as a healthy growing flower, which when overtaken by death in the sixty-seventh year was cut down in full bloom.

II. Depth. Out in our western country we have a river called the North Platte, the beauty of which can not be disputed. It has length and breadth, but no depth. It is shallow. The Chicago river is less attractive in natural beauty, but it carries on its bosom the commerce of the seas. In Washington we find combined the traits of strength of mind, beauty and depth of character. Greatness in one field does not signify success in others. Some men are brilliant in public, but dull at home; yea, they may even be devils. There was something noble in his attitude toward the home. When I speak of this relationship, I refer to his early as well as to his married life. The child that learns obedience in the home has mastered one of the greatest problems. In this he laid a sure foundation that when the storms and winds of life beat upon him he stood the test. "Honor thy father and thy mother, that it may be well with thee, and thou mayest live long on the earth" is an ancient command of God. Though little is said of his early life, he learned well the lesson of implicit obedience. No man can rule others who can not rule himself. "He grew in favor with God and man." The first commandment of the Decalogue with promise was literally fulfilled in his life. His entire being was inseparably linked with that of his mother's. At the crossroads her influence counted heavily. Adventure and romance are powerful factors that every youth must reckon with. The glamor of the sea beckoned him, but when his plan was contrary to the wish of the mother heart, magnificently he acquiesced. Romance gave way to duty—duty to mother and home.

History has convinced us that when he made his decision, it proved a turning point for all that was good. The future held much in store. If America continues to produce Washingtons and other great leaders, she must have great homes and mothers.

All lovers of homes find in Mount Vernon upon the Potomac that which charms us most. The marriage vow when taken was kept sacred until death. What a lesson to this age when divorces are so easily secured. No nation is stronger than its homes. Divorce destroys! This is one of the greatest blots on American life. The spirit of love predominated in Mount Vernon. The home was a home where Christ was a welcome guest, as that home was in Bethany. Everything centered itself around a lofty idealism. The home to all the world is a gem artistically, and an inspiration to noble men and women ideally.

"But everywhere where love abides
And friendship is a guest,
That is home, and home sweet home to me
For there the heart can rest."

Home at its best is a miniature heaven, and Mount Vernon has enshrined itself in the hearts of mankind.

No man is ever equipped to do his best when harassed by domestic difficulties. Washington's home to him was an anchor, a refuge in every storm. No matter what troubles had to be met, he could give to the world that calm leadership that reflected the heart and spirit of Mount Vernon. As our great mountains of the West, whose summits bask in the light of the sun, but upon whose bosom the storms rage, so was Washington, the calm, serene leader, because there was an outer reflection of that inner home.

He was a conservative, though an unusually fine business man. He well knew that a dollar was of no greater value than the honest effort put back of it. We shall grow in depth of character only as we re-emphasize those homely principles which made his life so outstanding. Washington was a great man because he was a good man. When one sounds the depths of his life, there are no false notes to be found. We commend him to our children today for his depth of conviction and the noble simplicity that characterized his entire life.

III. Breadth. In Washington we have epitomized the leadership of his generation. All ages are known by its leading men. When God called Moses to become the liberator of the Jews, this man felt himself incompetent for the task. Washington with that same keen insight, felt his limitations. His letters show during his service in Congress, that he was never under any delusions concerning the taxation struggle. He expected war. When Congress, after the fights at Lexington and Concord, resolved to put the nation in a state of defense, the unanimous selection fell to Washington, who became commander-in-chief of the armed forces of the United Colonies. Refusing any salary, he accepted the position, asking every gentleman in the room, however, to remember that he did not believe himself equal to the task. He reiterated this belief in private letters to his wife.

It is at this point that his life is so interesting. He not only recognized his strength, but his shortcomings. If humility and willingness to serve are essentials to outstanding leadership, then Washington qualified. Where human strength ended, the Divine began! Herein we find him to be a lion in courage. Once he thought a question through, no power could stop him from carrying his purpose to a conclusion. Gladly would he have continued to live at peace after sixteen years of tranquility at Mount Vernon, but the hour had arrived when new vistas of service dawned.

His survival of the year 1776 was a miracle! His service under Braddock was but a skirmish compared to those agonizing days. Those days were the beginnings of Washington's Gethsemane. Those were the hours when he won the great victories over self, and over others which were to make him such a powerful factor. No man of ordinary fibre could have withstood this terrific onslaught from all angles.

When he took command of the army, he faced all conceivable opposition, both at home and abroad. The Colonial poverty, the exasperating annoyances, the selfishness and stupidity that cropped out again and again for the most part from patriotic followers, were enough to have broken the heart of most men. These bitter experiences completed his training. If he was not a great man when he went to Cambridge, he was a general and a statesman in the finest sense when he drove the British out of Boston in March, 1776. From that time on until his death he was the foremost man on the continent.

Fittingly and lovingly we call him the Father of Our Country. No greater tribute could ever have been paid than to ascribe to him the name of "Father." All the degrees of learning could never have been a substitute for that word. When our Lord and Master taught the disciples the prayer perfect, reverently He said, "Our Father, Who art in Heaven." All learning, all science can never fully comprehend the meaning of this simple word "Father." A child can understand it, eternity itself will be necessary to reveal the breadth of this familiar term. It carries with it all the tenderness of heaven and earth. We do stand on Holy ground this centennial period, and may God help us ever to remember as a people the rock from which we were hewn.

IV. Height. The real height of any man's life is not measured in feet and inches, but in the upward look—the intent of the human soul. George Leigh Mallory, the intrepid climber of Mount Everest, who afterward perished amidst its enternal snows, was once asked when in America, "Why do you want to scale Mount Everest?" His reply, so characteristic of any doer of deeds, was, "Because it is there." Washington was not content with the commonplace; his was a growing soul.

All of his life he was a member of the established Church. Retiring from the Presidency in 1797, Washington resumed his plantation life with the companionship of his loving wife and family, and the care of his slaves. No man with Washington's Christian spirit could long endure slavery. Christianity is the world's greatest equalizer. At the Lord's Table and in the sight of God, all men are alike. Superficial barriers can not long exist. True to a fine idealism, he resolved sometime before his retirement, never to obtain another slave and "wished from his soul" that his state could be persuaded to abolish slavery.

To understand God's love for the world we must stand beneath the cross of Calvary. To understand this great man's love for liberty, we must stand with him on the sacred ground of Valley Forge. No picture can be dearer to the hearts of Americans than that winter of 1777-78. No blessing can ever come without sacrifice and suffering. Moments like those make us appreciate our blessed heritage.

It is said on reliable authority that Clemenceau upon one occasion called upon Marshal Foch when the latter was in the attitude of prayer during the darkest days of the World War. Though the mission demanded that an immediate conference be held, the statesman commanded that the Marshal was not to be disturbed while at prayer. "Let him alone," said Clemenceau, the pronounced unbeliever, "Foch is always a stronger man after prayer." It is unbelief's tribute to the efficacy of prayer. In prayer Washington rose to his sublimest heights. He never was ashamed to be found in the attitude of prayer. No man can conquer life's enemies without destroying them unless the love of God is in the soul. Cæsar had his Brutus, Washington his Benedict Arnold, and in such leadership we find sublimity on the one hand, and the degradation of the human soul on the other. In that lone hour when Washington's cup of grief was filled to the brim with all human suffering and want, this man appeared. All these circumstances went to show that there was a superhuman hand to sustain him; a strength that came from God alone.

Washington was a Christian gentleman to the end. There were no theatrical adieus when he went down into the valley alone. As a minister, I have never known a man on his death bed to regret the fact that he had served God. A man to die right must live right. It does matter how one dies! As the shades of night encircled themselves around Washington for the last time, there was that calmness of soul that had always been evident in his life! He was still climbing upward. The end was but the prelude to eternal dawn!

WASHINGTON'S SPIRIT MUST LIVE

By REVEREND FRANKLIN CLARK FRY

Pastor, EVANGELICAL LUTHERAN CHURCH OF THE HOLY TRINITY
Akron, Ohio

Matthew 10:39. He that findeth his life, shall lose it; and he that loseth his life for
My sake, shall find it.

Theodore Roosevelt never wrote more astute nor more ardently patriotic words than these, which, flashing indignation, introduce his essay on "Washington and Lincoln—The Great Examples":

"There is nothing sillier and more mischievous than to dull the conscience with lofty sentiments which cloak ignoble failure to perform duty; or to praise the great men of the past for what they did in the past and yet refuse to act in similar fashion in the present. Lip-loyalty to Washington and Lincoln costs nothing and is worth just exactly what it costs. What counts is the application of their principles to the conditions of to-day."

Before we indulge in adulation of that noble man, the peerless leader of heroes, who did more than any other to bring our nation into being, we shall do well to give earnest and sober heed to this admonition. If the eloquence of our praise of him must be in emulation of his life, we should first inquire wherein the greatness which we celebrate, and which in some humble measure we would appropriate, consisted.

Many have the grotesque, though usually inarticulate, most frequently even subconscious, belief that the eminence of the illustrious personalities of earlier ages and the significance of all the mighty trends of preceding history are alike derived from their relation to us to-day. Naively enough—and this is a common opinion—they conceive that the course of the centuries has toiled laboriously up to the summit of excellence which we occupy and has there paused, so that the merit of all that has gone before must be assessed in the light of its effect on what has eventuated in these times. To be sure, such an uncritical and self-flattering view of the continuous ascent of history with the present as its triumphant achievement, to which all else is to be gauged as contributory and preparatory, involves an unwarranted and provincial-minded disparagement of the past and anyone to hold it must be pathetically lacking not only in perspective but in a sense of humor as well. Yet, I suppose, men have ever complacently regarded themselves as "the heirs of all the ages" in a sense which makes that inheritance seem not only a consequence but, by subtle inference, the deliberate purpose of the previous experience of mankind. And the present is no exception! If anything, the fault has been aggravated by the self-importance of our contemporaries. Nor has Washington been exempt!

When modern Americans laud Washington as the "Father of His Country," their accent is apt to be upon the last word of the epithet rather than the first. "First in war, first in peace, first in the hearts of his countrymen" (declaimed, as we Lutherans are thrilled to remember, from the pulpit of Zion-St. Michael's Lutheran Church, Philadelphia, by "Light Horse Harry" Lee at Washington's Congressional funeral in that historic edifice) infers, of necessity, that there are those who come after, but for it to be made to seem that the glory of the succession is in them and is reflected from them upon him who was first is a perversion which should be rebuked. In celebrating the bicentenary of the First President's birth, men of this disposition are indirectly, and to me offensively, glorifying twentieth century America, so much of the life of which is a travesty upon the spirit of this man. When they are not idealizing him, making him at the same time both more and less than human, and so removing from themselves the disconcerting summons of his example to unselfish patriotism, to higher devotion to the welfare of all men as a principle of citizenship, and to the abatement of insatiable and frequently rebellious self-interest, they count it ample renown for him that he had the distinction of initiating the government which in our day has become preponderant among the peoples of the world.

But if the greatness of Washington does not emerge from his relation to us, neither is it to be confused with the physical bigness of the forces with which he dealt, unlike much which passes for personal eminence today. Certainly it is not to be ascribed to the unforeseen and unpredictable immensity of territory, natural resources, and population of the America of a later day. We have become so imbued with the thought of the vastness of our land that we recall with what approaches incredulity that it was not always thus, specifically not in the time of Washington. If the fame of a general is dependent upon the numbers of his troops, the master strategist of the battle of Trenton does not deserve to be ranked even as a brigadier. The Continental Army at Valley Forge mustered only a few thousand men and the United States itself contained fewer than four million people when President Washington took the oath for the first time. The new nation, far from being a dominant world power, had precariously established its independence after skirting disaster—the margin almost continuously being the genius and devotion of this man—for five years, and at the end only with the potent help of France. Politically, it was chaotic; economically, it was insignificant. It may be that never has a single mighty personality done so much to found a nation, has so literally carried a nation on his shoulders as did Washington the American democracy. It is calumny to ascribe the greatness of Washington to anything external to himself, to make it a creation of fortuitous circumstances, adventitious and accidental, belonging not to the essential spirit of the man but imputed to him by benefit of a bigness which did not exist until after he was long dead. Had America remained a child among the nations in size and in power, its illustrious progenitor would still merit an exalted place among those honored and gratefully extolled by humanity. His was a spiritual greatness. The springs of it were in himself. The dimensions of it were the height and breadth and depth of his soul.

"Washington, the brave, the wise, the good. . . . Valiant without ambition, discreet without fear, confident without presumption. . . . The father of nations, the friend of mankind; who when he had won all, renounced all"—so reads that well-known inscription at Mt. Vernon. In its fervent, majestic simplicity and with its true discernment of the quality of his life which invested him with an eminence which, because nothing not inherent in his own character bestowed it, no reappraisement of the conditions of his achievement and no reversal of the subsequent career of the nation can ever therefore take away, it bids us pause and ponder. Quite the opposite of the vainglorious ambition and aspiration to prestige and power which are native to less noble spirits and are even counted laudable among them, the constant and conscious motive of Washington's prodigious labors as commander-in-chief and President was subservience to the common good.

Selflessness and renunciation are to be attributed no more, rather less, to his final forbidding of his partisans—which is tantamount to saying, of his nation—to secure to him a life tenure of authority either as President or, as some insisted, as king than to the whole course of his patriotic, public service. Indeed, although the reasons which he sincerely advanced and by which alone he permitted his decision to be governed had to do only with the national welfare and with his convictions as to the means most conducive to its permanence, Washington's ultimate retirement to the placid, congenial life of his well-beloved Mt. Vernon accorded more with his own long-cherished desires than had his assumption of any of the anxiety-laden responsibilities of his active years.

In a measure that is scantly appreciated, Washington lived outside of himself, for the good of other men, many of whom distrusted and disparaged him for his recompense, rather than to please himself. His patriotism militated against his own advantage; his honors led him away from his preference. Wealthy and aristocratic, he was secure even as a young man in the possession and enjoyment of all the physical good which he ever wanted. He needed no Revolution to avenge his wrongs nor to improve his station. All that Revolution could do to him would be to hazard and menace what was already his and to disturb his chosen, pleasurable manner of life. It exchanged the comforts of Mt. Vernon for the stark privations of the field. It exiled him from his family and his friends and disrupted intercourse with the land of his fathers.

To his selection as commanding general of the insurrectionists, he acceded reluctantly and the personal side to his exultation at the triumphant conclusion of the war was his unconcealed gratification at the prospect of resuming at last what he had foregone so long. If anyone can ever justly plead his right to be relieved of a further surrender of his personal interests and of further interference with the disposition of his life according to his own wishes or if anyone can ever honorably contend that his duty to his nation has been discharged and his contribution made so that its future obligations should fall upon others, surely that man was Washington then. Yet, when in its extremity America summoned him to the arduous and often ungrateful task of becoming its first President and of translating the document which it had adopted, the Constitution of the United States, into substantial institutions, he forsook his own pleasure and preference for eight more years, which he must have anticipated would be most of his remaining time on earth, and lived again for the benefit of his fellows.

The immortality of this man, so far as this world and his abiding influence here are concerned, was in the immersion of his life in the common good and in the defense and perpetuation of an ideal which he esteemed not only for himself but for mankind. He subjected himself, all he was and all he had, to what he was profoundly convinced is the righteous purpose of God for human liberty and justice and virtue. He made his life to flow with that tide which sweeps on to eternity, overwhelming and obliterating all vain perverseness in its course which contrives the base advantage and exaltation of any man in contempt for the well-being of others and in contravention of the divine intent. No encomium is more sublime nor more unstrained when spoken of him, that which was true also of his Lord and of all the nobility of the spirit, than that in losing his life, he found it.

Shall we not then do most worthy honor to the illustrious Washington and perpetuate his exemplary spirit most effectually in the America of our day by incarnating and diffusing his selflessness and devotion to the welfare of the nation, even when it means for us, as it did for him, an abridgment of our convenience or self-gratification? Is it not mockery to give pretentious homage to the life he lived and to continue to forswear his spirit?

We are not men of Washington's stature nor can we impress upon the destiny of a nation the lineaments of a single personality as did he. In the immensity and complexity of our national life, the weight of the individual seems infinitesimal. Men lose the sense of the consequence and the sacredness of the example and influence of every citizen. There is far less incentive to give over destructive greed and baleful self-indulgence and there is correspondingly less of a rewarding sense of virtue in such renunciation. The ominous result, which is to be seen on every hand, is that too many men, not regarding the obligations of citizenship, are debasing the nation into an instrumentality for fulfilling their own desires. They conceive of it as an entity apart from themselves which they can exploit or ignore or flout. In that direction lies decadence and the collapse of democracy, for democracy has no integrity nor even power to survive in itself.

It is the sum of what we, its participants, contribute of that which is precious to us to the common store and what we abjure for the good of all. It is the losing of life by each that all may find its fullness.

Washington's spirit must live. His United States will not long survive it.

SERMON ON THE TWO HUNDREDTH ANNIVERSARY OF THE BIRTH OF GEORGE WASHINGTON

By THOMAS F. GAILOR, D.D.
Bishop of the EPISCOPAL CHURCH IN TENNESSEE

Text: "They shall bring the glory and honor of the Nations into it."—Revelation, XXI, 26.

This text is an appropriate subject for our meditation, when we are commemorating the birth of our National life and renewing our loyalty as citizens of the Republic.

The American Nation is still in its childhood, not yet one hundred and fifty years old, and only recently beginning to be self-conscious, realizing its personal destiny; and that growth of national self-consciousness has come only through suffering and sacrifice, in ways of which our fore-fathers did not dream.

This is what critics of American life and government complain of, as one of them has said:

"The typical American has no sense of State; not that he is really unpatriotic; but he has no perception, that his business activities and his private employments are constituents in a large collective process, and that they affect other people and the world forever, and cannot, as he imagines, begin and end with himself."

In plain English we are accused of being dominated by such a passion for individual success, that we take no thought for the success of the whole; that, while we are ready—most of us anyhow—to defend and perhaps fight for that freedom under the Flag, which secures to us safety and opportunity—freedom and opportunity to do our own work in our own way—yet we have little or no loyalty to the Government, because it is the Government, and to the laws of the organized State, because it is the State. Our commercial achievements, it is said, and the supremacy of mere commercial standards of life and education have not tended to create and develop genuine patriotism.

It is worth while, therefore, to consider the meaning and value and responsibility of national life; its challenge to the individual citizen; and the principles that must guide in making it a help and blessing to ourselves and to the world.

No nation in history, perhaps, owes its existence so preeminently to the courage, devotion and foresight of one man as does the United States. And certainly no nation can boast of a Founder, whose character in private and public life has so splendidly sustained the criticism of four generations. As Mr. Gladstone said: "Among all . . . public characters of extraordinary nobility and purity" Washington stands supreme.

I refer to Washington, because, I believe, he left two legacies

to his countrymen, besides the example of his noble and unselfish life. His first legacy was his religious faith. In his Farewell Address he declared his firm conviction, that the stability of the Republic would depend upon the maintenance of the moral standards of the people, and said: "Whatever may be conceded to the influence of refined education upon minds of peculiar structure, reason and experience both forbid us to expect that national morality can prevail in exclusion of religious principle." His second legacy was his belief in the National Idea. As a prophetic statesman, looking into the the future, he saw the heterogeneous elements of our population welded into one mighty whole, and, as a recent critic says, he ventured to use the word nation and advocate the national idea long before nine-tenths of the people saw that they were bound to become a nation or desired to be one. Today that dream of Washington has been fulfilled and all Americans are responding with more or less earnestness to the privilege and responsibility of the national life.

However, the national idea has not won its way except through blood and sacrifice. It has been a slow and reluctant growth in the minds and hearts of our people; and in God's providence the wars in which Americans have taken part have done more to bind us together as one people than a central government, or a common language, or a common territory. Thus God hath brought good out of apparent evil and hath made the wrath of man to turn to His praise.

But I hear someone say: "Is not the true religious ideal the obliteration of all racial and national lines in the unity of humanity? and is not the maintenance of national patriotism a contradiction of the Christian theory of the brotherhood of man?"

And my reply to that is, that the nation is only a larger individual person, and in the Christian scheme the individual must lose himself to find himself, that is, his true self development is accomplished by his surrender in unselfish service; and so it is with the nation. When Our Lord said: "Nation shall rise against Nation," He set His approval upon the natural political structure of human society, of which the family and the nation are the indestructible units; and every attempt of men to make the Kingdom of God, or its concrete expression, the Christian Church, usurp the place and authority of the nation has been destructive to public and private morals. Humanity indeed, in God's sight, is one; but every advance it has made has been dependent upon the development of national aspirations. When Tennyson sang:

"When the war drum throbs no longer
And the battle flags are furled,
In the Parliament of man,
The Federation of the world,"

it was "Federation" he dreamed of, not the abolition of national life. Indeed it would be a gray and stupid and monotonous world, from which all national inspiration of patriotism and all national incentives to self-expression were removed. No; God's lofty idealism regarded the nation as an individual, whose existence was justified by its consciousness of the obligation of service; that it should not be a hermit or a profiteer among the nations, but accept its blessings of freedom and civilization as in trust for all the world; and to give forth, in justice, mercy and good will an encouragement to every people on the earth. Brethren: Let us thank God that we are Americans; that under His protecting care the "little one has indeed become a thousand, and the small one a strong nation"; and let us welcome the responsibility, and each one do his part, to work and pray, that the American type of manhood and womanhood,—in our political and social,—yes, in our industrial and religious life, may grow to such nobleness and genuineness of character, that it may contribute to the world some great and true ideals.

———

There is a real American tradition, declared by our fathers and fought for on many stricken fields, and consecrated by the blood and sacrifice of many heroic Americans. Daniel Webster expressed it in his speech at the laying of the corner-stone of the addition to the National Capitol on July 4th, 1851.

"Freedom of the individual; equal opportunity; representative government; supremacy of law, created by the people through their representatives; without any crowns or thrones or titled aristocracies, or privileged classes; and a written constitution, defining and restraining the powers conferring upon the government." These are American principles, and they are still worth living for and dying for.

First then: Freedom of the individual and supremacy of law.

We can hardly be said to have succeeded in realizing fully either of these traditions. On the contrary, we are painfully aware of a sad lack of reverence for law, as such, among citizens of all classes; and the condition is not improved but rather aggravated by groups of people, who show their distrust of our courts by organizing themselves into bands of Regulators to enforce the laws they favor. It would almost seem that some reformers are in collusion with law-breakers to spread distrust and disrespect for constituted authority.

We seem to have forgotten that liberty is an earned degree and involves a solemn responsibility. What I mean is that freedom cannot be conferred upon a people by mere legislative enactment. It has to be won and earned by men who have shown the capacity to exercise it; and the task of the statesman today is to keep a free people from forgetting the discipline and self-restraint by which freedom has been won and by which it must be maintained. It is often true that a man who inherits a fortune without working for it is tempted to become a spendthrift and a failure; and so it is with liberty. In the hands of the undisciplined and incapable it becomes as the Bible says a "cloak of maliciousness."

But the safeguard of liberty is the sense of the obligation of service. That also is the redemption of democracy, which may be a very vulgar thing, and which may also be a very noble and splendid thing, if exercised by a people who have a profound conviction of the obligation to devote their gifts and powers to the public service. And this means fellowship. This means freedom from blind partisanship, and the willingness to know and understand the other man's point of view—to see things, as he sees them, to know life as he knows it. And today we are sharing in the awakening of the public conscience, which says that business and politics must be made moral, and that the test of any government or religion or industry is the character and quality of the men and women it is producing. So the State—that is organized public opinion—is interfering with individual liberty. It repudiates the notion that free government means the right of the strong man and the wicked man to take advantage of and despoil the weak man under the form of law; and that therefore there are certain kinds of labor, and certain forms of trade, and certain ways of doing business that are not to be tolerated.

Of course the development of individual character and the freedom of individual opinion are essential to the success of a democracy; and any restriction of the liberty of the individual must be based upon principles of justice and fair play, and the ascertained welfare of all the people, and not a concession to the prejudice of any group or class.

As to the other elements in our American tradition, as Mr. Webster described it, "Law made by the people through their representatives" and the inviolable safeguard of a written constitution, there are, it seems to me, deplorable tendencies today to do away with the representative character of our government and to treat the constitution as a suit of old clothes, to be patched and altered, whenever a sufficiently well organized force of opinion can be brought to bear upon it.

———

To meet and counteract these tendencies, which threaten the continuance of our American tradition of government, we need today, I believe, above all other things, a campaign of education, and that, not a mere utilitarian system of acquiring sufficient knowledge to make a success of a business or profession,—which is not education at all,—but an education that includes a recognition of the moral and spiritual values of life. Prof. Huxley once said that it was "better for a boy to starve to death—better for himself, better for his family, better for the country—than that he should grow up to be a thief and a liar, and impure and dishonorable." But Washington struck the higher note when he said. "The stability of the Republic depends upon the moral standards of the people, and those moral standards are most sure when based on religious faith"; or as a great Frenchman expressed it: "The great conservative and progressive factor in human civilization is the belief in God."

Yes; knowledge indeed is power; but it may be selfish and unscrupulous power,— a power to injure and not to save;

"Who loves not knowledge? Who shall rail
Against her beauty? Who shall fix her pillars?
Let her work prevail.
But what is she, cut off from love and faith,
But some wild Pallas, from the brain
Of demons? Fiery hot to burst

All barriers, in her onward race
For power? Let her know her place
She is second, not the first."

And next to the education of our people in moral ideals of life and duty, which I believe can be accomplished only by the teaching of religion, is the effort to create in the minds and hearts of our citizens the sense of personal responsibility. It is the greatest word in the English language. The sweetest word is "HOME," but the greatest word is responsibility, as Daniel Webster said; and here again is the challenge of religious faith.

Finally, Brethren: Let us believe in and love our country—believe in it and work for it, not merely that it may be rich and prosperous and powerful, but in order that in every quality that makes a nation great it may be a consecrated servant and benefactor of mankind.

For here is the meaning and purpose and justification of the Christian Church—not to weaken nor destroy the faith in the nation and national patriotism, but to consecrate that patriotism and enrich it with wider service to humanity,—holding ever before our minds the glory and the beauty of that Kingdom of God, which transcends all boundaries and limitations of race and country; assuring us of the inevitable victory of the love of the All Father, to which the cross bears witness; until we all come, in the unity of the faith and of the knowledge of the Son of God unto the perfect man, the measure of the stature of the fullness of Christ.

"Who is he, that born of woman
Ever wholly can escape
From the lower world within him
Mood of tiger and of ape?
Man as yet is being made
And ere the crowning age of ages
Shall not eon after eon pass
And touch him into shape.

All about him still the shadow;
Yet, while races flower and fade,
Prophet eyes may catch a glory,
Ever gaining on the shade;
Till the peoples all are one
And their voices blend in choric
Alleluia to the MAKER,
It is finished. Man is made."

SERMON ON GEORGE WASHINGTON

By REV. PETER GUILDAY, Ph.D.
Professor of Church History, THE CATHOLIC UNIVERSITY OF AMERICA
Washington, D. C.

Wisdom conducted the just man . . . through the right ways, and shewed him
the kingdom of God . . . made him honorable in his labors
and accomplished his labors—*Wisdom,* x, 10.

No other text in Holy Writ summarizes so admirably the life story of George Washington, the Father and Founder of the American Republic.

All along the highroad of his public career when first, at the age of twenty-one, he was sent by the Governor of Virginia to northwestern Pennsylvania to warn the French against further encroachment upon English colonial soil, up to the moment forty-six years later, when he departed from this life at Mount Vernon (December 14, 1799), Wisdom walked by his side as an angel of light, of truth, of courage, and of justice.

Rectitude or the knowledge of right and clean living became his portion long before his maturity began. Truth and justice belonged to him as his most cherished possessions; and in all his dealings with his fellowmen, whether as platation owner, as soldier, as captain and general, and as president of the nation, was the spirit of truth present in his mind and heart. Honorable in all his actions, Washington never failed to refer to Almighty God, to Divine Providence, to Heaven's Assistance, to the Source of all Public and Private Blessings, to the great Governor of the Universe—the phrases are all his own—whatever success came to him in the performance of those duties which patriotic love of country had placed upon his shoulders.

Wisdom guided him especially through the maze of anxieties created by the enemies of his leadership at every stage of the strong conflict which ended in our independence. The victim to sectional intrigues and personal ambitions, to forgery, to treachery, and to personal abuse, Wisdom kept George Washington safe from his enemies in order that our land might come into being and take its rightful place among the nations of the world.

During the critical period which set in after the victory of the American and allied troops at Yorktown that great October day in 1781, the unity of the States dissolved; men were boldly asking whether the Revolution were a blessing or a curse. In this most perilous time Washington again led his nation to victory as president of the Constitutional Convention in Philadelphia.. Wisdom never deserted him during those stormy days from May to September, 1787; and the determined weight of his sturdy honest character, even though he said but little in that momentous assembly which conquered the hazardous state of the cause of our liberty, accomplished more than any one single influence in the Convention to create "a more perfect union, to establish justice, insure domestic tranquillity, provide for the common defense, promote the general welfare, and secure the blessings of liberty to ourselves and to our posterity."

Wisdom led him step by step to the highest office in the nation, and on April 30, 1789, the sceptre of rulership over the United States of America was placed in his hand. Through eight years of reconstruction of our battered forces—economic, military, political and financial—in spite of a recrudescence of the older enmities, this time fiercely personal and in some respects unspeakable, Wisdom brought him sublime power against those that would oppress him, and gave him finally in death the glory of immortal fame.

The varied qualities of Washington's character, of his unique personality, and of his exalted attitude toward life itself were so singularly blended in the Father of our country that no nation since his day has denied to his memory the highest praise. Other ages and other lands have had their liberators, great captains who led their peoples on the field of battle and in the assembly halls to victories that shall never be forgotten while history remains to record their triumphs. But Washington stands apart from these. His glory it is to belong not to his own age and his own people, but to all ages and to all climes. His name, as Daniel Webster said a century ago (February 22, 1832), "descending to all time, spreading over the whole earth, and uttered in all languages belonging to the tribes and races of men, will forever be pronounced with affectionate gratitude by every one in whose breast there shall arise an inspiration for human rights and human liberty."

When the news was brought from Mount Vernon on December 15, 1799, that George Washington had passed away, the Senate of the United States declared that "ancient and modern names are diminished before him; greatness and guilt have too often been allied, but his fame is whiter than it is brilliant; the destroyers of nations stood abashed at the majesty of his virtue."

Time moves swiftly, and our children will be holding in solemn manner less than a score of years from now the one hundred and fiftieth anniversary of Washington's death, as we today are joyfully celebrating the bicentennial of his birth. To them, as to all succeeding generations, the dominant thought will then be, as it is today with ourselves, whence came this man's greatness? The ideal patriot, the supremely model citizen of our Republic, the founder of a government which "changed mankind's ideas of political greatness"—wherein lies the secret of his heroism, of the noble symmetry of his life?

It is a secret not hard to discover. If, honestly and sympathetically we search the records of Washington's life, we shall find that it is fundamentally his sincere dependence upon Almighty God and his love for his fellowmen. We are not inclined in these days to dwell much upon the religious motives which dominated the careers of our great leaders; and yet, without understanding Washington's Christian faith, his whole life becomes an enigma. For, as has been justly said it was this faith which was "the foundation of his greatness, the source from which his many noble traits and virtues flowered, the power that ennobled his motives strengthened his will, guided his judgment, enlivened his actions, and secured his success."

During his earlier career before the days of the American Revolution, Washington's life was that of a Christian gentleman. We know of his loyalty to the services of the church, to which he belonged, during his youth and early manhood; and there are too many instances of his religious zeal during the battles of the Revolution, of his zealous attention to the spiritual wants of his soldiers, and of his own devotion to prayer in the crisis, for any honest American to deny to him this unique glory of a childlike and constant dependence upon our Almighty Father for the success of the great cause of liberty. These indications of his Christian spirit in times of stress are but a shadow to the generous display he makes of his faith in God and in Divine Providence in his writings, letters, official messages and documents. All along the years of his public political life from 1783 when he resigned his commission as commander-in-chief of the victorious American army, to 1789, when he accepted election to the presidency of the United States, and from that year until his last testament to the nation—the Farewell Address of September 17, 1796— there runs in unmistakable language a constant reverential appeal to Almighty God to preserve the union which had been won at such great cost to keep alive in the hearts of America's citizens the realization of their supreme dependence upon Divine Providence for the security of our national life and for the continued blessings of peace and prosperity.

In his noble letter of June 8, 1783, to the Governors of the States of the Union, in which he makes such a strong appeal for a more perfect and indissoluble union under one federal head, it is to Providence and to Heaven that he gives credit for our opportunity for political happiness—an opportunity he says, fairer than any other nation has been favored with; and he reminds us that Heaven's vengeance would surely follow upon any flagrant instance of injustice in the conduct of public policy. "I now make it my earnest prayer," he writes at the end of this letter:

> that God would have you, and the State over which you preside, in his holy protection; that he would incline the hearts of the citizens to cultivate a spirit of subordination and obedience to government; to entertain a brotherly affection and love for one another, for their fellow-citizens of the United States at large, and particularly for their brethren who have served in the field; and finally, that he would most graciously be pleased to dispose us all to do justice, to love mercy, and to demean ourselves with that charity, humility, and pacific temper of mind which were the characteristics of the Divine Author of our blessed religion and without an humble imitation of whose example in these things we can never hope to be a happy nation.

Washington's first official act as President after taking the oath of office on April 30, 1789, was to bow down reverently and to kiss the Bible upon which his hand rested while Chancellor Livingston read the oath. That same day in his first inaugural address to Congress, without any misgivings or faltering he avowed publicly that the rise of the American Republic was due to the divine stream of Providential design for the betterment of the human race; and he stressed the necessity of our realizing that the preservation of the Republic depended upon the "indissoluble union between virtue and happiness, between duty and advantage, between the genuine maxims of an honest and magnanimous policy and the solid rewards of public prosperity and felicity." He warned his listeners that "the propitious smiles of Heaven can never be expected on a nation that disregards the eternal rules of order and right, which Heaven itself has ordained."

For over one hundred and forty years our presidents have issued an annual call to the nation for prayer and recognition of God's rule over us in conformity with Washington's proclamation of our first national Thanksgiving Day. "I do recommend and assign Thursday, the 26th day of November next," he wrote:

> to be devoted by the people of these States to the service of that great and glorious Being who is the beneficent author of all the good that was, that is, or that will be; that we may then all unite in rendering unto Him our sincere and

humble thanks for His kind care and protection of the people of this country previous to their becoming a nation; for the signal and manifold mercies and the favorable interpositions of His providence which we experienced in the course and conclusion of the late war; for the great degree of tranquillity, union, and plenty which we have since enjoyed; for the peaceable and rational manner in which we have been enabled to establish constitutions of government for our safety and happiness, and particularly the national one now lately instituted; for the civil and religious liberty with which we are blessed, and the means we have of acquiring and diffusing useful knowledge; and, in general, for all the great and various favors which He hath been pleased to confer upon us.

There is a stateliness about his diction when he speaks of Almighty God which is seldom seen in our day, and no man can mistake the profound reverence of the heart which voiced its faith in such phrases as the Great Arbiter of the Universe, the Omnipotent and Supreme Being, Sovereign Ruler of the Nation, God our Benign Parent, Divine Munificence, and the words which occur most often—Divine Providence.

Nowhere is this fact seen to better advantage than in his reply to the different religious congregations and communities which addressed him in felicitation during his first year of his presidency.

In all this there was no deceit; no pretence. Washington was never ostentatious in his profession of belief in God or in his devotional life. But that deep abiding sense of dependence upon the Creator is visible in all his public utterances. His early education, his pioneer days in the wilderness of the frontier, his life in the mountains, along the streams and under the stars, begot in him an honest forthright religious sincerity and humility which place him apart from the other Founders of our Republic. In all that he wrote there is not a solitary word which reflects the current deism of the times.

To the address from the Lutherans of Philadelphia, Washington replied (April 20, 1789) that even in the presence of the grave danger that his fellow countrymen might impatiently expect too much at the outset of our organized government, he felt confident of the direction of God, since "the same Providence which has been visible in every stage of our progress . . . gives us cause to hope for the accomplishment of all our reasonable desires." To the general Assembly of the Presbyterian Church (May, 1789), he reiterates "the profession of my dependence upon Heaven, is the source of all public and private blessings," and he thanks those who wrote to him for their prayers "to Almighty God for his blessing on our common country," and upon himself, "the humble instrument which He has been pleased to make use of in the administration of its government." To the Bishops of the Methodist Episcopal Church, he wrote that same month: "It always affords me satisfaction, when I find a concurrence in sentiment and practice between all conscientious men in acknowledgments of homage to the great Governor of the Universe . . . I must assure you in particular that I take in the kindest part the promise you make of presenting your prayers at the Throne of Grace for me, and that I likewise implore the divine benedictions on yourselves and your religious community." To the Baptists, Washington wrote:

> If I could have entertained the slightest apprehension that the constitution framed in the convention, where I had the honour to preside, might possibly endanger the religious rights of any ecclesiastical society, certainly I would never

have placed my signature to it; and, if I could now conceive that the general government might ever be so administered as to render the liberty of conscience insecure, I beg you will be persuaded, that no one would be more zealous than myself to establish effectual barriers against the horrors of spiritual tyranny, and every species of religious persecution. For you doubtless remember, that I have often expressed my sentiment, that every man, conducting himself as a good citizen, and being accountable to God alone for his religious opinions, ought to be protected in worshipping the Deity according to the dictates of his own conscience.

In his letter to the Quakers, Washington repeated these sentiments regarding religious liberty and equality, assuring them that the freedom enjoyed by the people of these States of worshipping Almighty God agreeably to their conscience, is not only among the choicest of their blessings but also of their rights. And to the Roman Catholics in the United States, in reply to their congratulatory address, Washington's optimistic forecast of our national prosperity "under the smiles of Divine Providence," includes not only a just recogntion of civic duty but also a strict adherence to the policy of religious freedom as enshrined in the Constitution. He refers to the French alliance in this reply and to the fact that, without the aid of that Catholic nation, independence would have been well-nigh unattainable:

> As mankind become more liberal they will be more apt to allow that all those who conduct themselves as worthy members of the Community are equally entitled to the protection of civil Government. I hope ever to see America among the foremost Nations in examples of justice and liberality. And I presume that your fellow-citizens will not forget the patriotic part which you took in the accomplishment of their Revolution, and the establishment of their Government, or the important assistance which they received from a Nation in which the Roman Catholic faith is professed.

One last letter—out of hundreds—may be cited: that to the Hebrew Congregation of the City of Savannah, written in May, 1790, in which Washington sums up with remarkable conciseness the long and weary years of sorrow in the history of Jews. "May the same wonder-working Deity," he says:

> Who long since delivered the Hebrews from their Egyptian oppressors, and planted them in the promised land, whose providential agency has lately been conspicious in establishing these United States as an independent nation, still continue to water them with the dews of Heaven, and to make the inhabitants of every denomination participate in the temporal and spiritual blessings of that people whose God is Jehovah.

Many other evidences of practical Christian spirit of George Washington might be given from his private and public correspondence. A final citation will suffice, from his Farewell Address (September 17, 1796) to his "friends and fellow-citizens": the people of the United States. As a last will and testament few official documents in our history have had so profound an influence upon the public life of the nation. While the document, precious in American history, was not wholly his own, there is no mistaking the following passage as coming from his pen:

> Of all the dispositions and habits which lead to political prosperity, religion and morality are indispensable supports. In vain would that man claim the tribute of patriotism who should labor to subvert these great pillars of human

happiness, these firmest props of the duties of men and citizens. The mere politician, equally with the pious man, ought to respect and to cherish them. A volume could not trace all their connections with private and public felicity. Let it simply be asked, Where is the security for property, for reputation, for life, if the sense of religious obligation desert the oaths, which are the instruments of investigation in courts of justice? And let us with caution indulge the supposition that morality can be maintained without religion. Whatever may be conceded to the influence of refined education on minds of peculiar structure, reason and experience both forbid us to expect that national morality can prevail in exclusion of religious principle.

Such then, is the potent and significant lesson of Washington's deeply religious and moral character as a Christian gentleman, a valiant soldier, a prudent and patriotic statesman. No other leader in the history of the world can lay claim to the title: Father and Savior of his Country, with more justice than George Washington. Shining out as a guiding star to all who could penetrate the depths of his success, there will ever be the fact that no man in all our national annals displayed more wisdom in times of peace as well as in times of war. It is as though in the words of Holy Writ, Washington pledged to himself in the earliest days of his career that he would take Wisdom "to live with me, knowing that she will communicate to me of her good things, and will be a comfort in my cares and grief. For her sake I shall have glory among the multitude and honour with the ancients, though I be young . . . Moreover, by means of her I shall have immortality: and I shall leave behind me an everlasting memory to them that come after me." (*Wisdom— viii-13*)

On that national day of requiem, February 22, 1800, when all the churches of the land at the request of Congress held solemn commemoration of his passing to the great beyond, the first Bishop of the Catholic Church in this country, John Carroll, described Washington's character in words that caught the nation's heart. After stating that never again in our national history would we encounter a man in whom were united so many virtues, Dr. Carroll said:

Washington beheld from his retirement as the Jewish legislator from the summit of Mount Phasga, the flourishing prosperity of his country. Health sweetened his repose and rural occupations; his body and mind retained their usual vigour. We flattered ourselves with the expectation of his continuing long to retain them: Joy beamed in our hearts, when on every annual revolution, we gratefully hailed this, his auspicious birthday. But alas! how dark is the cloud that now overshadows it! The songs of festivity converted into the throbs of mourning. The prayers of thanksgiving for his health and life changed into lamentations for his death! Who feels not for him, as for his dearest friend, his protector, and his Father? Whilst he lived, we seemed to stand on loftier ground, for breathing the same air, and inhabiting the same country, and enjoying the same constitution and laws, as the sublime, magnanimous Washington. He was invested with a glory, that shed a lustre on all around him. For his country's safety, he often had braved death, when clad in her most terrific form: he had familiarised himself with her aspect; at her approaching to cut the thread of his life, he beheld her with constancy and serenity; and with his last breath, as we may believe from knowing the ruling passion of his soul, he called to heaven to save his country, and recommended it to the continual protection of that Providence, which he so reverently adored. May his prayer have been heard! May these United States flourish in pure and undefiled religion, in morality, peace, union, liberty and the enjoyment of their excellent Constitution, as long as respect, honour, and veneration shall gather round the name of Washington; that is, whilst there shall be any surviving record of human events.

How fortunate we are, we of this present day, to possess in the Founder of our nation one whose whole life from the cradle to the grave was so thoroughly infused with the spirit of faith in God, with the spirit of hope for the unfaltering influence America would have in the continual betterment of mankind, and with the spirit of charity towards all which has made our Republic a haven of happiness to all who came here to enjoy the blessings of liberty.

We have not been unmindful of Washington's supreme share in establishing our nation. Although his fame has grown with the years, grown to such an extent that our eulogies seem to falter, every loyal heart in the United States will ever beat with renewed allegiance to our ideals at the mention of Washington's name. No higher tribute to his memory has ever been given than that spoken by John England, Bishop of Charleston, one of those remarkable sons of Ireland who have been so intimately interwoven into the spiritual progress of our Republic. With his words this message may well conclude:

Fellow-citizens! I can speak no eulogy of Washington. Though separated from this world, he lives in the center of our hearts; his name is a talisman of power, the watchword of freedom, the emblem of patriotism, the shout of victory. It casts around us a halo of glory, for it continues to receive the homage of Mankind. There have been many sages, there have been many heroes, there have been many legislators— there is but one Washington.

Centennial Celebration of Washington's Inauguration

Speech of
HON. PETER HENDRICKSON
Battery D Armory, Chicago, 1889

We stand today upon the summit of the centuries; we look back over the past and we look forward into the future, and on this auspicious day we would reason together and give an account of the faith we have in the future of the republic. Your presence here, the look of gladness and devotion which is pictured on the thousands of faces in this vast assembly, and the festal feeling with which the whole atmosphere of the day seems charged, bear testimony to the fact that the day is one of joy and not of grief.

It is the conditions and the circumstances of today that pronounce judgment upon the century that is past, and the century makes us look with reverence upon the intellects and characters of the men who have shaped it. Reverence is the noblest activity of the human mind. In this reverence there is an element of fear which guards our minds from presumption and our lips from uttering rash speech. In this reverence there is hope which gives buoyancy to the whole being. In this reverence there is affection, which is the power that moves the world and makes men invincible.

These feelings gathered into one by the rays of light from a hundred years of history, and finding their focus in this day and hour, we sum up in one word, Patriotism. And if this day has any significance any more than a mere merry-making, it is to find the ground and basis for this feeling of patriotic devotion and give it expression in grand unison of heart and voice.

Patriotism! What is it? Is it a myth invented by some enthusiast? Patriotism may be called localized philanthropy, but it is more than this—something that eludes definition, something that we are cognizant of when we sing, "I love thy rocks and rills, thy woods and templed hills." Patriotism is both a principle and a passion, harmonized and controlled by intelligence. Its foundation is knowledge, its active principle is love of man, and its scope is our country. Patriotism is not a plant of accidental growth; like all virtues it must be cultivated and nurtured to become strong. Of this, too, there is a spurious article as well as a genuine. There is a cultured plant and there is a weed. That patriotism which consists merely in upholding and defending your country and its institutions because they are yours, may have its uses, but it is based on false principles and degenerates into mere passion. The imitation is rooted in selfishness, the genuine in self-sacrifice. The weed is luxuriant in foliage but meager in fruitage. How to nurture this plant of patriotism so that it may be at once fragrant in the bloom and abundant in fruit should be the first aim and the persistent effort of the citizens who understand the responsibility imposed by free institutions.

You will pardon me, I trust, Mr. Chairman, if I should have misapprehended the true purpose of this great national anniversary. We are today dropping wreaths upon the graves of the heroes of a hundred years ago, but we are doing this not to add luster to their fame only; our minds are more in the present and the future than in the past, and what we do today should be a testimony to future generations of the sense of duty and responsibility with which we accept the inheritance of the century that is past, and of the solemn care with which we transmit the treasure into the hands of the centuries yet to come. We therefore in mind take the present and the future generations by the hand and lead them back over the hundred years that are past, and while we learn we would also teach a lesson from the fountain and source of our liberties and our laws.

George Washington and the Federal Constitution! The two are inseparable. When the lips have named the one, the thought has embraced the other. Wherever liberty is considered a boon and order is thought better than anarchy, the name of Washington is revered and the Federal Constitution respected. Washington was not an angel. Washington was not a demon. George Washington was a man. No angel has ever governed a state; no demon has founded a dynasty or an empire. These are the works of men, and in our day it has come to pass that men are judged by their works and not by the adulations of enthusiasts or the railleries of irreverent fault-finders.

Nothing but a weak mind and a small soul can ever approach the character of Washington without reverence. No name or fame in history stands less in need of being surrounded by the halo of sainthood, and no character can be less harmed by the scrutiny of impartial criticism. No American patriot will ever be humbled by the necessity of drawing the veil of charity over the life or the record of the Father of his Country. These are facts, the contemplation of which should fill our minds with humility and our hearts with gratitude.

The Federal Constitution is, in the words of Gladstone, "the most wonderful work ever struck off at a given time by the brain and purpose of man." It is the greatest work of constructive statesmanship known to the race. The homage which is today everywhere accorded to this Constitution is not due to its age, but to its adaptibility and power. The ideal republic of Plato is hoary with age; its ingenious structure has been the delight of scholars and poets for many centuries, but it has never commanded the loyalty and homage of a people. The symmetrical system of Locke is twice as old as our Constitution, but it has never enjoyed a celebration or an anniversary. These were babes born out of due season, founded on fancy and elaborated by the imagination. The progress of mankind is tentative; step by step we find our way through the tangles of history. No invention and no system that has not sprung from present needs and solved pressing difficulties have ever been useful to man. Washington was great because he filled a great place, the Constitution is great because it has solved a great problem. It was the product, not of speculation, but of experience. It is for their services that we love and cherish both Washington and the fundamental law of the republic.

There is that in man which forbids his full appreciation of any gift unless he knows its cost. If you would inculcate the lessons of patriotism, if you want the citizen of the future to love the institutions under which he lives, if you want him to appreciate the value and responsibility of citizenship, you must show him what it has cost. You must teach him the agonies of its birth, you must conduct him to its cradle and show him the perils that surrounded its infancy and point out to him the calamities from which he has been rescued. No lesson in patriotism, no instruction in statesmanship can be better than a study of the history of the five years from the conclusion of peace to the adoption of the Federal Constitution.

Never have the destinies of a great future hung more tremblingly in the balance than when that memorable assembly gathered at Philadelphia in the month of May, 1787, to begin the work which should secure a more perfect union between these states. The magnitude of the task and its beneficent fruits will be seen when we reflect that a union between these thirteen feeble states was as much dreaded and feared then as is disunion today. Massachusetts and Rhode Island were as jealous of their neighbors and more unwilling to give up their sovereignty to a general government than were South Carolina or Louisiana in the days of nullification and rebellion.

The five years from 1783 to 1788 are the saddest and darkest in our history. Anything approaching to that now would be called anarchy, and with fear and trembling it was so recognized then. The Continental Congress was despised and discredited, had been driven out of Philadelphia by a handful of riotous soldiers whom neither state nor city authorities could control. There were no funds with which to pay the defenders of our liberties or provide for any common need. We were ridiculed and mocked at by all the powers of Europe; even France was ashamed of having aided us to achieve an independence which we were incapable of enjoying. There were men who had struggled to sever the bond which united them with England, who now in the fact of this future regretted their vain sacrifices and toil, and wished themselves back under the sheltering wings of the mother country. These little states who had learned to sing the songs of freedom and of self-government were yet ignorant of the sentiment of union which today is the pride of every American and the only guaranty of the future of the republic. I am not drawing a fancy picture. I am not exalting the present at the expense of the past when I say that you can raise more funds for a common object in the city of Chicago today than you could in the thirteen states one hundred years ago yesterday.

Now what is it that has secured to us this contrast? What is it that has harmonized 60,000,000 people from all quarters of the globe and made them one in spirit and hope under a union that is loved and respected by all? It is this charter of our liberties, this pillar of our national temple, and this rock on which we rest—the Federal Constitution. And who gave us this Constitution? I answer it was not the people of the states, it was not the Continental Congress. Next after the "divinity that shapes our ends," it was George Washington. So much did these liberty-loving thirteen states fear a union, that it was not till it became known that George Washington was chosen delegate that many of the states would have anything to do with the Constitutional Convention. So great was the power of his fame even then that

it created confidence and courage all over the country. Where Washington would take the lead it was safe to follow. Does any one say Washington was not a statesman as well as a soldier? I answer: there is one element without which no amount of learning and genius can make a statesman, and that is courage and moral conviction. This it is which made the Constitution what it is and has kept it where it is, and that element in it is due to Washington more than to any other man. Washington presided over the convention and his character was its foundation and defense. Listen to the words which, according to a member of the convention, he uttered when delegates began to propose half measures. In that solemn and decisive moment he rose from his seat and pointed out the only course of safety. "It is too probably," he said, "that no plan we propose will be adopted. Perhaps another dreadful conflict is to be sustained. If, to please the people, we offer what we ourselves disapprove, how can we afterward defend our work? Let us raise a standard to which the wise and honest can repair; the event is in the hand of God." Is there no statesmanship in this? Is there a man in this assembly who would be afraid to trust his destiny to a convention presided over by such a man? Washington was first in peace as well as in war. This is no idle phrase. Let it never pass our lips unless our hearts give it its full meaning and our voice its due emphasis.

But Washington, though chief, was not alone. We should do injustice to the memories of the past and to our sense of right if we did not today remember with gratitude the names of Benjamin Franklin, James Madison, Alexander Hamilton, Thomas Jefferson, John Jay and the Adamses and the Pinckneys, and other immortal men who, both in and out of the convention, did so much to erect this noble structure, and prepare the minds of the people for its acceptance.

But we should also do injustice to the people of these colonies if we did not recognize the fact that what in the outset proved the greatest obstacle to the Union was in the end its safety, its rock of defense. Intense love of self-government, rooted in experience and cherished by patriotic devotion, was the first characteristic of the people of the colonies. The obstacle which this presented was the fact that each man's patriotism was centered in his own state, his loyalty wholly absorbed by his own local government. An unseen, unlocalized and indefinable union presented no image to them but that of a foreign tyrant. The great work of the Constitution was to create a new centre for this strong affection and transfer it from the government of the colonies to the government of the Union. It was to enlarge the mind and expand the affection. To create the conviction that my colony was not my country, but only a part of it. It was to get the inhabitant of Massachusetts, of Delaware, of Virginia, to rise to the grand conception that his Fatherland was not a colony, but a continent. That he was not first and foremost a Virginian or a New Yorker, but an American. That the colonies had fled from common troubles, had sought a common refuge and had freed themselves from a common oppressor in order to gather under the aegis of a common government and become not many small but one great empire. How grand was this thought and how all-important was the change!

And here, too, let us remember that the great power which alone could make such transformation was the fame and name of Washington. As the presiding genius of the convention he created confidence. As the first head of the new government, as the common centre of the new and larger Fatherland, he drew the hearts of the people from the old allegiance to the new. Here let us behold the greatest work ever performed by mortal man, here let us realize the true significance of this solemn day, and humbly uncover our heads in the presence of the sublime spirit and character of Washington, which even today presides over the destiny of the republic.

But while the Federal Constitution is the central pillar of this noble temple whose first century of life terminates today, there are other forces without whose support it may be doubted whether the structure would have withstood the storms. It was the vastness of the territory which made it so difficult for the colonies to conceive of the Union in the sense in which it presents itself to our view. The Constitution could not unite and harmonize material interests so different and so diverse. Without a material bond to unite and hold them together the unity of mere law would be inefficient. This material bond was at this moment in the throes of birth. At the very time when the Constitutional Convention was seated at Philadelphia, the first steamer was launched on the Delaware River. The Federal Constitution and the steam engine are the great twin products of Anglo-Saxon intelligence and enterprise. It may well be doubted whether either, without the aid of the other, would be active forces in Chicago today. The Constitution was born in the nick of time. The planets were in the right conjunction, and the twins were born under the star of hope. If it were not for the steam engine you and I might not be here, and wherever we might be and whatever we might be doing we should not be celebrating the adoption of the Constitution. It was by this marvelous coincidence that the bond of law was supplemented by a bond of intercourse to which we are indebted for what we are today.

But there is a third pillar in the structure, without which political and material bonds would be torn asunder. That pillar is the public school. I would not say one word here that on this day of harmony and common joy should arouse any prejudice or the slightest murmur of dissent, but I should do violence to my most settled conviction if I did not say that the public school, a common education for the young, under the same teachers, on the same benches and in the same classes for all children and youth, not of the laborers only, but of rich and poor, the native and the foreign, of all creeds and of all colors, is as essential, is as vital to the stability of this nation and to the lasting happiness of the people as the Constitution and the steam engine combined. It was possible to unite the colonies into one because they were young and pliable and devoted to a common teacher and master. It will only be possible to melt so diverse a population together into common love and devotion to the same institutions by accustoming them to live and play and act together without prejudice and distinction in the tender years of childhood and youth. These are the gifts of the century that is gone, and these are the pillars of the Union and the guaranty of fraternal friendship through centuries to come. The Constitution will change in the course of the future as it has changed in the past, for it is not a dead carcass or a fossil, but a living law, and this change will be a growth, not in the direction of curtailing popular government, but of expanding it; not by taking power from the people, but by giving larger power to the people. But remember this, that larger power will never be safe in the hands of the people without a large intelligence and a common intelligence, and this intelligence for all without distinction and without exception.

There are weak and ignorant men who even today affect to believe that this Constitution is an experiment, and the perpetuity of the Union an unsolved problem. Let them not desecrate the sacred precincts of the second century of our national existence with this malady of doubt. Has not this Constitution and this Union borne its test? Has it not grown strong by adversity? Has it not conquered not only the arms, but the hearts of doubters and foes?

Classic fable tells us that when Hercules was born he, too, inherited the hate of the divinity of doubt and opposition. When the infant giant lay in his cradle the malignant goddess sent two serpents to press their deadly venom into the breast of the sleeping infant. But the infant was not asleep. He stretched forth his right hand and his left, and in his giant clutches he choked the vile reptiles in the dust and returned to placid repose. So has the Constitution triumphed over the divinity of hate. Her reptiles came to his infant cradle. The black serpent of slavery on the one hand the green serpent of disunion on the other, and the youthful giant arose and in one hand he seized the black serpent and in the other the green serpent, and he bruised their heads against the rock, and buried their vile bodies in the dust forever. Is there any one here that doubts?

And this Constitution is ours and in joyous echo I hear the word "ours" coming from every state, from every county, from every hamlet and from every fireside today in this goodly land. It fills the American heart everywhere from Maine to the farthest point of Florida, and from the Golden Gate to the Atlantic, and in every breast there is forgiveness, fraternity and affection. If this Constitution has borne the strain of the century that is past, may we not today, in joyful assurance, hand it down to the centuries that are to come and bid them guard it with the same jealous care and the same intelligent devotion which has attended it in the past? We have faith that the future will not be found wanting. Washington was a hopeful man, for he was sound and healthy in body and mind. The Constitution was born of this hope, and with faith it is handed down to the future. We know full well that the whole brood of hateful serpents is not dead. The divinity of discord is still sending forth her progeny to perplex the children of men. Some of them are even now pointing their venomous fangs at the young state and its Constitution. We can see their slimy heads in the grass. There is the serpent of corruption and fraud, the serpents of spoil and plunder, the serpent of monopoly, the serpent of sectional jealousies, the serpent of anarchy, the serpent of strife between the rich and the poor, and, more than all, the old serpent with its hundred heads and its thousand fangs, the snake that destroys the heart and the conscience and the home, the old dragon of strong drink. We are not blind to their dangers, but we stand here calm in the faith that the same giant will stretch forth his hand and one by one crush their heads under his heel, and when the next great centennial of this day shall dawn the joyful shouts will rise from the lips of hundreds of millions: "We have performed the task which you set us one hundred years ago."

George Washington—
The Symmetry of His Character

A Sermon by

REVEREND EDWARD M. JEFFERYS, S.T.D.
Rector of St. Peter's Church, Philadelphia

Text: "And he that spake with me had for a measure a golden reed.
And he measured the city with the reed.
And the city lieth foursquare.
The length and the breadth and the height thereof are equal."

—Revelation XXI : 15-16

The famous English orator and versatile writer, Lord Brougham, in comparing Washington with Napoleon, spoke of the former as "The greatest man of our own or any other age." And when the news of Washington's death reached Europe, foreign fleets and armies paid solemn tribute to his greatness. And even since his death the world in general has been eagerly according him an outstanding position among the greatest heroes of history. And why?

The armies which he commanded were eventually victorious, but as a strategist he does not rank with the greatest of the world conquerors. He was a statesman, but he does not stand out pre-eminently conspicuous in the realm of statecraft. He was a great patriot, but he did not surpass in patriotism some of his own and other times. He was good, but he did not monopolize the greatness of goodness. He was a Christian gentleman, but in spirituality he did not outshine the apostles, prophets and martyrs of the ages.

Washington was not, as Lord Brougham considered, "The greatest man of any age," because of any particular characteristic equipment or achievement, but because, like the Ideal City, "The length and breadth and the height" of him were "equal"—because he was, as a great Jewish prophet said of the Lord's Sanctuary, "Foursquare round about." The greatness of his character was the greatness of symmetry. From whatever point "Round about" it, we may examine it, his character bulks not only large, but also in equal dimensions.

Many of the world heroes have been abnormal, unbalanced, even fanatical. They have had one-track minds, and have been top-heavy or lop-sided, but Washington's personality stands out pre-eminently conspicuous for its poise and symmetry.

He was *human* in the length and breadth of the meaning of the term. Most of us are more than satisfied that he was not, as the primer school-books once represented him, a prig and a prude. He loved his home and his family. He was hospitable, and enjoyed the hospitality of others. He loved his friends and was generous to his enemies. He appreciated the amenities of life, but was at home in the great open spaces and in the depths of primeval forests. He liked dancing, and games, and the theatre; liked to fish and hunt and follow the hounds. He loved his horses. Jefferson said of him that he was "The best and most graceful horseman of his age." He was a successful farmer. He made good in his chosen profession of surveying. He was an exact accountant, and conscientious and scrupulous in his business. He did not hesitate to follow St. Paul's advice to his friend

and fellow-worker, and used a little wine for his stomach's sake. On occasion he used emphatic language. As a soldier he knew how to obey without question: As a commander he exercised an iron discipline. He became a successful general. The close of the Revolution with the capture of Yorktown was a brilliant piece of military strategy. He loved peace, but he was a good fighter. After his baptism of fire, he wrote to his brother, "I have heard the bullets whistle; and believe me, there is something charming in the sound." He enjoyed a good dinner, and loved life, but when he was dying he said, "I die hard, but am not afraid to go." He read the good books that were available to him, and wrote widely influential letters. And according to Patrick Henry, no man in the Continental Congress was his equal for "solid information and sound judgment." Unquestionably he was a very great President, and a modest, self-denying, self-sacrificing patriot. And the civilized world has acclaimed him, and is still acclaiming him as one of the greatest figures in all human history.

A man without religion is abnormal, unbalanced. He is abnormal in the realm of life, as a man who is colour-blind or tone-deaf is abnormal in the field of vision or audition. Man is a religious being. His religious instinct is one of the chief characteristics which differentiate him from the brutes that perish. To be without it is to be one-sided, incomplete. Human nature in its entirety, in its perfection, instinctively demands God. As Voltaire said, "If there were no God, it would be necessary to invent Him." A foolish person is an unbalanced person, and, as the Hebrew poet said, it is "the fool that hath said in his heart, there is no God."

Because he was so well-balanced, so symmetrical, Washington was a religious man. Certain recent writers, following imagination rather than historical records, have portrayed a Washington without religion. Their portrait is objectionable because it is not true. It seems to be inspired by a wish to make out a case against religion rather than by any wish to write history.

Washington was a man of prayer, in his home, in the field and in the House of God. He was a devoted member of the Episcopal Church. He also held office in the same, serving his parish as a vestryman. And when occasion arose, through the absence of the Rector, he would as lay-reader conduct the services of the church. It was his habit to keep the Lord's Day religiously. That he did so, even when away from home, moving from place to place, is abundantly proved by the number of colonial churches scattered through the country which still treasure the evidence that he worshipped in them for longer or shorter periods. Although he was a loyal member of the church of his forefathers, he was broad-minded enough, when there was occasion, to attend the services and accept the ministrations of other Christian bodies. For Washington's private and public religious life there is ample proof, such clear proof that no "literary ghoul" will ever be able to rob the American people of Washington, the Christian gentleman.

The Founder of Christianity set before His disciples an appallingly high ideal. He said, "Ye shall be perfect, as your Heavenly Father is perfect." Some would translate "complete" instead of "perfect," but such a translation does not make the ideal less appalling. The ideal, however, may not be so discouraging as it appears or sounds.

The geometric figures which connote for us most vividly the idea of completeness, perfection are the square, the cube, the circle, the sphere. And it is to be noted that a small square, cube, circle or sphere can be in its little way as complete or perfect as a large one, even an infinitely large one. It would appear, therefore, unless we are to feel that the Christian ideal is hopelessly out of reach, that Christ was thinking in terms of *symmetry* rather than in those of *magnitude*. He was asking his followers to shun the unbalanced, the one-sided, the unsymmetrical in the process of character building, and to aim at a foursquare or well-rounded moral and spiritual development, a cubical or spherical character.

It is only too true that many who have professed and called themselves His disciples have been unbalanced, fanatical, morally and spiritually deformed; in defiance, that is, of His ideal of completeness or perfection.

It is also only too true that many of those whom the world has agreed to immortalize and enshrine in its Hall of Fame have been monstrously misshapen, magnificent perhaps on some one side, but hideous and repulsive on other sides.

Among such "immortals," you will find patriots, whose public lives were irreproachable, but whose private lives were highly reprehensible. You will find among them artists, musicians, painters, sculptors, whose works are sublime, but whose manners and morals savoured of the gutter. You will find conquerors who have lived to glorify themselves on their own lands, but have brought red ruin to other peoples and other lands. In a word, you will find bigness and grandeur mixed with littleness and meanness. And so among these immortals, when we look for beauty of character, we find too often abnormality; when we look for spirituality, we find fanaticism; when we look for moral leadership, we find thinly disguised tyranny; when we look for patriotism, we find self-seeking; that is, we find monstrosity where we look for symmetry; incompleteness instead of perfection, deformity and disfigurement instead of squares, cubes, spheres or character.

What a relief it is, therefore, when in the Hall of Fame we turn towards the "Immortal Washington" and find his beauty of symmetry! He holds the first place in the hearts of our citizenry, and a glorious place in the estimation of the whole world, not because he was a successful commander, and nothing more; not because he was our first and greatest President, and nothing more; not because he loved his country as few have loved it, and nothing more; not because he was a fine figure of man on foot or on horseback, and nothing more; not because he was a gentleman in the truest meaning of the term, and nothing more; but because with all these he revealed himself a real man, because the length and breadth and height of his character were equal. His is the immortality of symmetry. At home, on his farm, in the forest, in camp, in battle, in the forum, in the curule chair, in peace and war; on his knees, on his death bed; he manifested a winsome manhood. And for this, and not for any one virtue, however noble; not for any one trait, however fine; not for any one achievement, however brilliant; for any office, however exalted; but rather for the equilibrium and completeness of his *life*— are we, and not only we, but also men of other lands, ready to proclaim him the greatest of the Great.

GEORGE WASHINGTON AND THE TEST OF TRUE GREATNESS

By BISHOP A. W. LEONARD, D.D., LL.D.
Resident Bishop, BUFFALO AREA, METHODIST EPISCOPAL CHURCH

"Whosoever of you will be the chiefest, shall be servant of all." (Mark 10:44.)

In his recent book entitled "Guidance from Francis Thompson in Matters of Faith" the author, Dr. John A. Hutton, in commenting on the "Sister's Songs" says, "The greater the man is the more solitary and outstanding is his fundamental experience."

Hegel, the Philosopher, conveyed the same underlying idea when he said—"The condemnation which a great man lays upon the world is to force it to explain him."

These statements are so descriptive of George Washington that we might easily believe the authors had him in mind when they made them. There is no character in all American history about whom so much has been written. It is not possible to mention his many traits of character or catalogue his unmatched achievements. The fact remains that for well nigh two hundred years men, the world over, have been trying to account for the almost preternatural endowments of body, mind and spirit of him who came to be known as the "Father of his country." If a man's greatness is to be registered according to the efforts men make to explain him, then Washington is rightfully classified among the greatest of earth. He stood solitary and alone for nearly a century. Again and again men have become almost feverish in their efforts to explain him.

"The antiquarian, the historian, and the critic have exhausted every source, and the most minute details have been and still are the subject of endless writing and constant discussion. Every house he ever lived in has been drawn and painted; every portrait, and statue, and medal has been catalogued and engraved. His private affairs, his servants, his horses, his arms, even his clothes, have all passed beneath the merciless microscope of history. His biography has been written and rewritten. His letters have been drawn out from every lurking place, and have been given to the world in masses and in detachments. His battles have been fought over and over again, and his state papers have undergone an almost verbal examination. Yet, despite his vast fame and all the labors of the antiquarian and biographer, Washington is still not understood,—as a man he is unfamiliar to the posterity that reverences his memory. He has been misrepresented more or less covertly by hostile critics and by candid friends, and has been disguised and hidden away by the mistaken eulogy and erroneous theories of devout admirers."

The biographies of Washington, and they are legion, usually deal with one or more of the following phases of his life:

Washington, his boyhood and youth; Washington the man, the soldier, the statesman, the President, the patriot, the private gentleman, the man of affairs and the Christian.

In the limitations of this discourse I shall refer briefly to the boyhood and youth of Washington; to Washington, the man; and to Washington, the Christian.

The early period of Washington's life,—his boyhood and youth,—has caught the imagination of the world. From the boy and girl in the country school to the greatest of statesmen and historians, Washington's early life has made a most unusual appeal. There was a directness of march, from obscurity to fame, the like of which is seldom found in the lives of other great men. This branded him a child of destiny. He was born at Bridges Creek Plantation in Westmoreland County, at ten o'clock in the morning of February 22, 1732. The house in which he was born was destroyed by fire. The Potomac was not far away from it and primitive clearings in the tangled forests broke the landscape here and there. Little did the Washington family think on that eventful morning of what was actually happening to them and to the world in the birth of that little babe. His father died when George was but eleven years of age.

In those days it was the custom of wealthy Virginia planters to send their sons to England to complete their education. His half-brothers Lawrence and Augustine, who were fourteen and twelve years older than himself were in this respect the favored sons of the family. The death of the father doubtless interfered with such plans being carried out for George. Whether or not that was the case, he was sent to a field school in the neighborhood, where he was taught to spell, to read, to write and to cipher. He later attended a school of somewhat higher grade where he devoted most of his time to the study of mathematics. He early showed that he had unusual ability in that line of study.

Although his school privileges were quite limited he was fortunate in having a Godly mother who was endowed with a rare degree of practical good sense. She was a devoted Christian and well possessed of a decisive and well-balanced character who inspired love and at the same time enforced in the family circle marked obedience to parental authority. Washington came by his ardent but impulsive temper honestly for those were strong traits in his mother's character. His remarkable mastery of himself, in the crises of his later life, as well as those crises of national and international importance in which he figured so conspicuously, undoubtedly reflects credit upon the mother who had him in her school training during his most impressionable years. Through her own Christian life and the teachings she imparted, George learned what many have never learned and that is the art of keeping the body in subjection. His love of truth, his generous and noble acts won the confidence of all who knew him and gave him a place among the fellows which only virtue can secure.

In the Library of Congress there may be seen the very book in which he drew his first exercise in surveying. The diagrams show the great care exercised by the young student in those early days and are prophetic of that which came to be a recognized trait of his character.

His mother inculcated in the mind and heart of her son those Christian principles which opened the way for him to appreciate the significance of the words,—"In all thy ways acknowledge Him and He shall direct thy paths."

As early as sixteen he started out to make his own way in the world, and at that early age gave himself to surveying the frontiers of Virginia. His measurements as a surveyor were so accurate that they are even to this day consulted by authorities.

He grew and developed amidst the conditions and was environed by the moral and social standards of the time in which he lived. He entered enthusiastically into the sports of the day, was fond of horses, and of great physical strength.

Through his brother Lawrence who had served in the Cartagena Expedition under General Wentworth and Admiral Vernon, George learned of the advantages and excitements of a seaman's life and there is evidence that arrangements were made for him to go to sea (possibly as a midshipman), but influenced by a letter from her brother the youth's mother is supposed to have withdrawn her consent.

Washington was fortunate in having the benefit of many refining influences. He became an intimate and trusted friend of the Fairfax family, who reflected in their western home the refinement, culture and many of the customs of the English aristocracy of that time. Lord Fairfax was an English nobleman, a contributor to the *Spectator*, a polished gentleman and a bachelor. When young Washington met him, he was past fifty years of age and possessed in Virginia an incredible estate comprising not fewer than five million acres. That was more land than there is in the entire State of New Jersey. In later years the State of Virginia entered a series of lawsuits against the heirs of Lord Fairfax, the latter being represented and defended by no less a person than John Marshall, afterwards Chief Justice of the Supreme Court of the United States. In time the lands passed out of the possession of the Fairfax heirs.

Woodrow Wilson said Lord Fairfax was "a man strayed out of the world of fashion . . . a man of taste and culture, he had written with Addison and Steele for the Spectator."

In addition to the wonderful influence exerted over Washington by his mother and Lord Fairfax, the benign influence of his brother Lawrence should not be overlooked. Until his death he cared for his young brother with a solicitude which was characterized by a paternal care as well as a fraternal love. Such knowledge as Washington had in the art and science of military warfare was, undoubtedly, secured through instruction by his brother Lawrence's associates.

Although only fifteen years of age when he met Lord Fairfax, he had the appearance and bearing of one much older. He wore a thirteen shoe and Lafayette said that his hands were the largest "I have ever seen on a human being." He was six feet, two inches in height, had grey-blue eyes and his hair had a tinge of reddish brown.

His meeting with Lord Fairfax may be regarded as the boundary line between Washington the youth, and Washington the man.

From this one his rise to prominence and leadership was meteoric. For the next ten years he was destined to live a life of almost wild adventure. During that decade he was surveying, exploring, fighting Indians and the French, with now and then a return to civilization.

Fairfax employed him to survey his vast estate. In 1749 he received a commission as public surveyor and during the next three years he spent the summer months following his profession in the regions of the Alleghanies, and especially on the immense tracts of land owned by Lord Fairfax. Surveyors were not plentiful, remuneration was large, and by practising rigid economy the young surveyor acquired property by purchase years before he reached his majority. The qualities of character which he displayed during this period gained him a good name and a solid reputation. He thus early won the admiration and esteem of the leading men of the colony.

At twenty-one he went on a journey through the wilderness to a French military post that challenged control in the West. At twenty-two he was in charge of an expedition against the French.

Governor Dinwiddie chose him as a special agent, on the eve of the French and Indian War, to carry a message to the French commandant on the Ohio, in which he demanded of him his reasons for invading territory belonging to England. Amidst hardships and difficulties that called for the greatest physical and moral courage Washington delivered Governor Dinwiddie's letter to the French commandant at Fort le Boeuf, about twenty miles south of Lake Erie and returned to the capital of Virginia in the month of January, 1754.

Braddock made him a member of his staff when he was but twenty-three. Following that ill-fated expedition he was for over two years in command on the frontier.

He was only twenty-six when he led the Virginia troops of Forbes army through the wilderness and occupied Fort Duquesne, which is now Pittsburgh.

It is not the purpose of this discourse to present an outline of Washington's military career. The events above are mentioned for the purpose of showing how rapidly he came into prominence.

On January 6, 1759, George Washington married Martha Custis. He was then almost twenty-seven years old and Mrs. Custis somewhat older.

Some of the early biographers of Washington may have erred in representing him as a being of such superhuman excellence that they failed to portray the man as he was. During the celebration in 1932 of the Two Hundredth Anniversary of the birth of George Washington ample opportunity will be afforded to separate the wheat from the chaff so far as criticism is concerned. Quite recently it has become the fashion for some writers to do

their utmost to discredit the established reputations of great men who, having passed into the Great Beyond, can no longer defend themselves. One biographer says that he has "no desire to belittle Washington" but on the same page with this disclaimer makes the very interesting statement that, "Washington possessed only ordinary intellectual ability." In this same connection he also says,—"The truth is that he was entirely devoid of original ideas. He had no overpowering intellectual urge, no passion for making novel mental combinations. He was without mysticism, without fancy. In the dim regions of his soul there were no lonely beaches where the ocean of infinity sent its rolling surf. His ideas were all plain, conventional and as familiar to the perception as slabs of granite. He never announced a belief in anything that was not already believed in by many other people. Although he assisted in forming the American Government there is not a single important feature of the Government structure that was contributed by him."

This is a very sweeping statement and if we were to believe all that is implied we should be compelled to conclude that Washington was a man of less than average intellectual ability.

It is true he did not have the advantages of higher education which were afforded his brother Lawrence and in the accepted sense of the term he was not a scholar. But in the face of all the facts nothing could be more unfair than to discount his intellectual attainments because he was not what men call scholarly.

His library consisted of more than twelve hundred volumes chiefly on agricultural and military topics. The latter no doubt included a considerable amount of history.

Undoubtedly Washington was one of the most versatile as well as one of the best informed men of his time. He early formed the habit of keeping a diary and of recording in almost minute detail the more important happenings of the day. While he was not faultless as a speller, he was known for his magnificent handwriting. There are in existence not less than twenty thousand letters which have to do with the personal life of Washington, most of which were written and signed by himself. He was the first authorized engineer in the colonies and, therefore, in the United States. He assisted in the making of Braddock's Road, which became the first highway west of the headwaters of the Potomac. The Baltimore and Ohio Railroad made use of the very routes he suggested across the mountains. He was interested in the origins of steam navigation, laid out the Potomac River improvement, which was the predecessor of the Chesapeake and Ohio Canal, and had a part in draining the Dismal Swamp.

Albert Bushnell Hart is authority for the statement that Washington "was among the first to suggest the possibility of a canal along the lines of the present Erie Canal from the upper waters of the Hudson to the Great Lakes and he added the suggestion revived by President Hoover, that there should also be a system of canals connecting the Great Lakes with the Ohio River and its tributaries."

It is the plan of the George Washington Bicentennial Commission to publish the writings of George Washington in twenty-five volumes. These volumes will not include his diaries. His unusual contacts with people of education and culture, his interest in the education of the Custis children, and his personal solicitude for the education and training of a large number of others, his contributions to encourage free schooling, and his plan for the development of a national university, made him a leader in the more important educational movements of his day.

When, therefore, Washington is branded as a man of "only ordinary intellectual ability," . . . "devoid of original ideas," . . . and with "no overpowering intellectual urge" the proof for such statements rests with the accuser. In the face of all that was accomplished through Washington's intellectual ability, including some of his State papers which rank among the greatest of their kind, it is inconceivable that any one could bring as scathing a criticism against Washington as the one to which reference has been made.

The detractors are not satisfied with their efforts to discredit the intellectual ability of Washington, but have gone a step further and have with abashless audacity endeavored to besmirch his moral character. The so-called "George Washington Scandals" consist of four stories containing more or less distinct charges against the moral life of the Father of his Country. Three of these stories rest upon, "foundations of cloud with superstructures of smoke." In the face of the most searching scholarship, all persons not possessed of morally depraved minds are compelled to classify these stories as apochryphal.

The fourth story having to do with "the so-called letter of invitation to Mount Vernon in which, it is claimed, the allurements of an octoroon slave-girl are set forth as an inducement for the visit" is so completely answered and the baseness of it is so completely revealed in the pamphlet written by Dr. John C. Fitzpatrick, entitled, "The George Washington Scandals" that it is not possible to add anything to what that pamphlet contains.

Although a man of unsual endowments and achievements he was very human. A man must always be judged by the times in which he lived. There were moral standards and social customs characteristic of the colonial period. Fancy and colorful dress for both men and women was the mode. Washington and his family were never behind in the styles of the day. It is said that at his wedding he wore a suit of blue cloth, the coat of which was lined with red silk and ornamented with silver trimmings. His waistcoat was of embroidered white satin, his knee buckles were of gold and his hair was powdered.

The wedding dress of Martha Washington consisted of a satin quilted petticoat, over which there was a heavily corded silk overdress. She wore a necklace of pearls and on her shoes were diamond buckles.

Washington was a good horseman, was fond of horse racing, participated occasionally in games of chance. He attended the theatres, was fond of fox-hunting, and was frequently present at country balls. He was a moderate drinker and his home was a center of social life. He took special delight in the entertainment of friends at his own fireside. Such things were a part of the life of that day.

He was nevertheless a man of sterling character. He possessed a strong will but was a pattern of self-discipline and of self-control. He was known everywhere for his integrity, fortitude, steadfastness and courage.

In that masterful work, "The Rise of American Civilization" by Beard and Beard, the authors ask the pertinent question,— "How then was it possible for the thirteen states, weak and divided in councils, to effect their independence in the test of arms?" To this question there is the following significant answer: "In the enumeration of the items that go to make up the

answer, all historians agree in assigning first rank to the personality of Washington, commander of the weary and footsore Continental army that clung to the cause to the bitter end. Mythology, politics, and hero-worship did their utmost to make a solemn humbug of that amazing figure, but his character finally survived the follies of his admirers and even the thrusts of his detractors made in their reaction to idolatrous adulation. Washington was a giant in stature, a tireless and methodical worker, a firm ruler yet without the ambitions of a Caesar or a Cromwell, a soldier who faced hardships and death without flinching, a steadfast patriot, a hard-headed and practical director of affairs. Technicians have long disputed the skill of his strategy; some have ascribed the length of the war to his procrastinations; others have found him wanting in energy and decision; but all have agreed that he did the one thing essential to victory—he kept some kind of an army in the field in adversity as well as in prosperity and rallied about it the scattered and uncertain forces of a jealous and individualistic people."

Woodrow Wilson in his "History of the American People" supports this view. "The first thing to be done was to give the new government dignity, vigor, and preeminence, lest it should inherit the taint of contempt which had fallen on the Confederation. It was the office and authority of the president, rather than the increase in the powers of Congress, that constituted the chief difference between the new government and the old. It was to be a government which could not only make laws, but execute them also; and Washington knew that no small part of its efficacy and prestige must depend upon him, its Executive. 'I walk,' he said, 'upon untrodden ground. There is scarcely an action the motive of which may not be subjected to a double interpretation. There is scarcely any part of my conduct which cannot hereafter be drawn into precedent'."

No less a man than Washington could have accomplished the desired end.

To achieve such results a man must believe in God and in himself, and Washington did both. A character such as his cannot be explained on any superficial grounds. It didn't just happen.

He was a Christian. Born of Christian parentage, reared in a Christian enclosure, Christian principles governed the impulses of the Father of his Country.

There are many evidences of the fact that Washington was a Christian. When a little less than two months old he was presented for baptism and received that rite at the hands of a clergyman of the Protestant Episcopal Church, of which Church he was a member at the time of his death.

In her account of the life of Washington, Little is authority for the statement that in 1747, at the age of fifteen years he was Godfather to a child in baptism. In 1748 at the age of sixteen he was Godfather to his niece, Frances Lewis. In 1751 at the age of nineteen, to his nephew, Fielding Lewis, his sister's first child, and his mother was Godmother. In 1760 at twenty-eight he again became sponsor for another nephew, Charles Lewis.

The dominant Church at that day was "the Established" or Episcopal Church. The old vestry book of Pohick Church has this entry: "At a Vestry held for Truro Parish, October 25, 1762, ordered, that George Washington, Esq., be chosen and appointed of the Vestry-men of this Parish, in the room of William Peake, Gent. deceased."

The court records show that, "At a Court held for the County of Fairfax, 15th February, 1763,—George Washington, Esq., took the oaths according to Law, repeated and subscribed the Test and subscribed to the Doctrine and Discipline of the Church of England in order to qualify him to act as a Vestryman of Truro Parish."

It is, therefore, evident that he became one of the "twelve most able and discreet men of the Parish."

His diaries reveal the fact that he and his family attended the Church services. He was more regular in his Church attendance after his marriage than before.

He was a man of prayer. After the death of the only daughter of Mrs. Washington on June 19, 1773, he wrote to a relative: "The sweet, innocent girl entered into a more happy and peaceful abode than any she had met with in the afflicted path she hitherto has trod."

He prayed before and after great occasions. In Barnes' history are these words,—"Who can tell how much of the subsequent brilliant success of the American armies was in answer to prayers of the American General at Valley Forge? To the latest times it will and should be a subject of the deepest interest that the independence of our country was laid, not only in valor and patriotism and wisdom, but in prayer. The example of Washington will rebuke the warrior or the statesman who never supplicates the blessing of God on his country. It will be encouragement for him who prays for its welfare and its deliverance from danger."

From his wide observation and experience Washington hoped for the day that would witness the emancipation of the slaves.

He once remarked, "Not only do I pray for it on the score of human dignity, but I can clearly forsee that nothing but the rooting out of slavery can perpetuate the existence of our union by consolidating it in a common bond of principle."

He was great because he served. He has forced the world to explain him. All acclaim him one of earth's greatest and even those who would rate him below Hamilton or Jefferson in political

wisdom join with those who pay tribute to his unselfish devotion to duty, especially to the cause of independence, to his courage, his moral integrity, his sublime hopefulness under defeat, his strong will and his abiding faith in Almighty God. Times without number he counted not his life dear unto himself that he might serve his country.

It is said that when Greece was at the height of her power, Herodotus visited on one occasion the Olympian games. After a little while he was recognized and the multitudes broke loose and bearing him upon their shoulders carried him around the arena crying—"Let us honor the man who has written our history."

It is fitting and proper that America should honor, on the Two Hundredth Anniversary of his birth, the memory of the man who in a very real sense has made our nation possible.

Ella Colter Johnston has expressed in an unusual way the secret of Washington's greatness:

"Throughout the ages men have sought to rise
    To heights of greatness and to peaks of fame,
    Thinking to carve an everlasting name
By conquering the weak, whom they despise,
And by mere strength of arms to tyrannize
    The world till it shall bow down to acclaim
    Them as all-powerful. This their only aim.
Sadly they fail—though they may win the prize.

Who would have power which none can overthrow,
    But which shall last through all eternity,
    Must conquer hearts by selfish service; then
The world will gladly on that one bestow
    Its never-ceasing praise; for only he
    Is great who greatly serves his fellow-men."

Jesus said, "Whosoever of you will be the chiefest, shall be the servant of all." Mark 10:44.

This is the test of true greatness and George Washington met the test.

GEORGE WASHINGTON
PIONEER, PATRIOT, AND PRESIDENT

A Sermon by

REV. WILLIAM CARTER, D.D., LL.D.

Pastor of The Throop Avenue Presbyterian Church, Brooklyn, N. Y.

Preached for the 200th Anniversary of Washington's Birth, Brooklyn, February 21, 1932

Text: Psalm 25:21. "Let integrity and uprightness preserve me: for I wait on Thee."

History sometimes centres in a movement and sometimes in a man, but the only history that is of permanent value to present or future generations is that which centres in men and movements which, in their turn, are centred in an inerrant and Omnipotent God.

The race is not always to the swift nor the battle to the strong. It is a false philosophy that the purse proud and arrogant have too long been indulging in, which says: "Might makes Right!" The truer philosophy, attested by the facts of history, is: "Right makes Might!" No otherwise can you explain the victory of

Washington and those embattled farmers against the power and might of England's glory on land and sea, as they went on conquering and to conquer, from Lexington to Yorktown, and gave at last this new Republic to the world.

This newer movement for life and liberty in character and action had, indeed, within it the three-fold essential for success and permanency: It had men who were brave, movements that were just and, above all, a God that is inerrant and all powerful —One who ever strengthens the arm of Right and makes it to prevail over all the enemies of Truth and Justice.

There were movements that were sufficient, without doubt. Movements positive and negative; movements just and unjust: "Navigation Laws," "Writs of Assistance," "The Stamp Act," "The Boston Port Bill," "The Non-Importation Agreement," and "The Tea Tax" leading to the most stirring of all these movements—"The Boston Tea Party."

There were men in plenty, also; men like Otis, Adams, Hancock, Henry, Jefferson, Franklin and Hamilton—men with liberty in their hearts and a Republic in their brains; but of all the men there was one outstanding far beyond the rest; of all the movements there was one that included everything: The movement was Liberty! The man—George Washington!

God never calls a man to a great national crisis without some preparation for it—either conscious or unconscious. Abraham Lincoln was prepared through his Puritan and Quaker ancestors' hatred of slavery. Cromwell by his musing amid the fens of Huntington on his own and England's wrongs. William the Silent was prepared by his training in all the arts of War in the Court of Charles the Fifth which he was afterwards to use so disastrously against Spain and Philip, the son of that same Charles, as he fought against them for his own Netherlands.

Wherein and whereby, then, did Washington receive his training? Without any apology or platitudinous maunderings, we can concisely say: He got it at his mother's knee; in a Christian home where family prayers and devotion to God were his daily benison and blessed prerogative.

To all the titles of our subject then, this morning, we must add that basic word: "Christian." George Washington was a Christian Pioneer; a Christian Patriot; a Christian President. That added adjective is the only explanation of his success. The guiding principle of his life—whether conscious or unconscious—was that prayer of David's: "Let integrity and uprightness preserve me; for I wait on Thee."

Born in the softer and more sensuous atmosphere of the South, he nevertheless was born with a legacy of reverent love for truth and righteousness and a holy love of God. Reared in comfort, he was yet reared to "endure hardness as a good soldier of Jesus Christ." He was reared with thoughtfulness for others; to be able to suffer for conscience sake; to sacrifice himself for others needs.

One writer has truly said: "Whereas Lincoln steadily rose from nothing to his place beside Washington, Washington laid down almost everything men usually cherish to find his place on our highest pedestal." "His ways were the ways of Truth," says Calvin Coolidge. "In wisdom of action; in purity of character, he stands alone."

At sixteen, this young aristocrat became a pioneer—a Christian pioneer—roughing it in the woods; enduring hardness as a good solder while surveying new lands for Lord Fairfax—carving new empires from the wilderness.

At twenty he was made District Adjutant General of the Militia of Virginia, with the title of Major.

At twenty-one, he was sent on a diplomatic mission to the French invaders of the Ohio, a dangerous journey in itself, in those pioneer times, as well as a difficult task to perform.

At twenty-three, because of his gallant defense of Fort Necessity, which he built, and conduct in the disastrous Braddock Expedition, he was made Commander-in-Chief of the forces on the Virginia frontier. It was during his command on the frontier

that he first issued his orders that divine services be held each Sabbath for the soldiers. He urged attendance upon these on his officers and set the example to all by his own attendance, an example he was to set in the same orders issued at Valley Forge and on all of his campaigns.

Yet, some say he was not a Christian! Books have been written to prove it, whose names I will not here mention to their author's shame. One minister, in a New Jersey Church, has refused to hold a patriotic Service in his church today, because he holds that George Washington was not a Christian! Yet, the records in the County Court of Fairfax, Virginia, state that on the 15th of February, 1763, "George Washington, Esq., took the oaths, according to Law, repeated and subscribed to the Doctrine and Discipline of the Church of England," as a Vestryman of the Anglican Church of the Parish of Truro! Yet, he surveyed himself the land for the Pohick Parish Church; was Chairman of the Building Committee; gave the largest sum for its erection and contributed the largest sum, annually, for its maintenance! Yet, his pew was the nearest to the Communion Table for which he had given, with George William Fairfax, the gold to glorify those sacred vessels. Yet, he was most constant in his attendance on its services and a most faithful worshipper!

God give to these new critics the nearest view of Thomas Jefferson, who voiced in it the opinions of his contemporaries: "The whole of his character was in nothing bad, in few points indifferent and in its mass perfect!"

So great and outstanding, indeed, was his character that, even in his pioneer days, he was spoken of by the Rev. Samuel Davies, President of the College of New Jersey, now called Princeton University, in a public sermon, as "that heroic youth whom, I cannot but hope, Providence has preserved for some important service to his country."

Yes, God was preserving him in integrity and uprightness for greater things. Retiring to his Mt. Vernon home after the French and Indian Wars, he was called time after time to serve in the Colonial Assembly of Virginia, which was to prepare him for Statesmanship as he had already been trained for War.

Called to the First Continental Congress, when England became rapacious and oppressive, Patrick Henry, who journeyed with him from Virginia, said of him: "He was the greatest of us all." He had, underneath his calm exterior, some of Patrick Henry's fire. Writing to Robert Mackenzie, formerly a fellow colonial officer and now a captain in the British Army, he says with bursting indignation that if these policies of the English Parliament are followed "More blood will be spilled . . . than history has ever yet furnished instances of in the annals of North America." Again, when England had refused petition after petition of the Colonists, Washington cried with fervid, patriotic wrath: "Shall we after *this* whine and cry for relief?"

No, the crying for relief had now passed. The cry must now be changed to the call to arms. Relief could only come through the arbitrament of War. The patriot flamed. Like William the Silent, Washington was now ready to turn his arms against those who had instructed him in their use. He became the flaming, soul fired patriot. He stirred the Continental Congress with his passion—not so much in public address, as in private conversation. He impressed himself upon all as a leader worthy to be followed. The people and the Congress knew his worth. He had been tested, tried and trained for just such times as these. They knew that he was ready to sacrifice himself, as he had done before. They knew that he was ready to die, if thereby his country might live. Yet when Adams suggested the vote that was to make him Commander-in-Chief of the Continental Armies, this man who was not afraid to face death for his country's cause, was afraid to face the praise of his fellow-men and left the room in embarrassment. In accepting the appointment, he said that he felt there were many better men than himself to lead the Cause and that they had made a mistake in choosing him, but if they felt that there was no other ready to accept such a task, he was willing to lead to the best of his ability.

There is no time here to go into all the long drawn out details of that struggle from the Siege of Boston to Yorktown. To tell the battles, sieges, fortunes that he passed would try your patience —perhaps as much as his was tried! Let it suffice to say that his was not the path of any conquering hero. His was a soul tried as by fire. He met with opposition not only in the field among his enemies but also in the camp, the Congress, and among those whom he had counted his closest friends.

The Congress that had so enthusiastically voted him the place was too weak to support him in it. Arnold's treason almost broke his heart. Conway's Cabal to place Gates in command was enough to make him lose his faith in man, himself, and God. Valley Forge's horror was enough to break any proud spirit that trusted in himself alone. Washington held on because he held on to God. In integrity and uprightness he held fast to God because he trusted in Him. Ill fortune, defeat, calumny, privation, starvation, failure dogged the footsteps of this indomitable man who would not give up, who never acknowledged failure, because his Shibboleth was that of that other Christian warrior and patriot, David: "Let integrity and uprightness preserve me; for I wait on Thee!" He waited on God and on October 19, 1781, at Yorktown of his own Virginia, that God of battles gave the trusting Christian, patriot, warrior, at long last, a victory that set the Stars and Stripes of a new nation aflame throughout the world. Love and loyalty for God and native land had won the field!

In these days of cynicism, of materialism and radicalism, it is becoming too much the fashion to sneer at the finer feelings and sentiments of life and ban them, or damn them as pious platitudes and snivelling sentimentalities. Nevertheless, there are two supreme loyalties in life: Loyalty to God and Loyalty to our Land. These are first and foremost. All others, dear as they are, are secondary and subservient. Love is the keynote of loyalty; Patriotism is the keynote of both: Love of country. Loyalty to a Cause. Patriotism for the Patria—for the Fatherland and God.

> "Breathes there a man with soul so dead,
> Who never to himself hath said:
> This is my own, my native land?
> Whose heart hath ne'er within him burned,
> As home his footsteps he hath turned,
> From wandering on a foreign strand?
> If such there breathe, go mark him well;
> For him no minstrel raptures swell;
> High though his titles, proud his name.
> Boundless his wealth as wish can claim,—
> Despite those titles, power and pelf,
> The wretch, concentred all in self,
> Living shall forfeit fair renown,

> And, doubly dying, shall go down
> To the vile dust from whence he sprung,
> Unwept, unhonored, and unsung."

Beware of a man who scoffs at his own country. Beware of the man who jeers at Patriotism. Love of country was called not so many months ago, by a minister in a New York pulpit, "Damnable National Patriotism!" He may be a great minister but he certainly is not a great Patriot! Patriotism is Loyalty. Loyalty is Love. For this cause a man will leave father and mother, wife and children and give himself to death that his country may live. For this cause wives and mothers will willingly send their husbands, sons and dear ones forth to battle for their country's cause, for the preservation of national integrity, the safety of their homes, their honor and every high and holy ideal. "Damnable National Patriotism?" Wives and mothers, husbands, sons and brothers all cry out in protest: "Nay! It is the highest, holiest love, next to the love of God, within the human heart!"

This is what sent Washington forth as a pioneer and a patriot. This is what elevated him to the Presidency of the land he had saved. This is what elevated him to become what "Light Horse Harry" Lee declared him to be: "First in War, First in Peace, and First in the hearts of his countrymen."

Such a Patriot could not hide himself. If he buried himself in the wilderness the world would make a footpath to his door. Retiring to Mt. Vernon, once more, after the war was over, he again was called to lead the nation in the construction of a fitting Constitution. Made President of that Constitutional Convention he held contentious factions in check and, more than any other, calmly and wisely formulated laws for the land of which he was, already, being called the Father.

His contemporaries gave Washington his rightful place. They were nearest to him. They knew him best. Jefferson said: "He was the only man in the United States who possessed the confidence of all." Patrick Henry said the same thing, as did those of other lands. Kossuth, the great Hungarian patriot, said: "Let him who looks for a monument to Washington look around the United States. Your freedom, your independence, your national prosperity and your prodigious growth are a monument to him."

Listen also to James Bryce that great English Ambassador, Statesman and Historian: "Washington stands alone and unapproachable, like a snow peak rising above its fellows into the clear air of the morning, with a dignity, constancy, and purity which have made him the ideal type of civic virtue to succeeding generations?"

Calvin Coolidge has put it still more tersely and succinctly in this one pregnant sentence: "His was the directing spirit without which there would have been no independence, no Union, no Constitution, and no Republic."

Yes, Washington was a great Statesman as well as a great pioneer and Patriot. His choice for the Presidency was the natural choice of men who knew his worth. There was no other choice to make. He stood, like Saul of old, head and shoulders above his fellows.

Called to the highest office in the land he had saved, whose laws he had formulated out of factious strife, he ruled for eight years of two successive terms, welding the distracted States into a nation. His was no sinecure. He still had factions to fight.

He still had enemies to conquer. With Hamilton he worked out a financial system that conquered the depression following the War and paid the debts of the people and also to other nations out of a Treasury that had been much depleted. He put down the Whiskey Rebellion that was threatening civil War and showed the country that it must respect its own laws—a lesson that we today ought to take much to heart. He established Law and Order and, his task accomplished, gladly laid down the burden he had assumed and retired, like a modest hermit, again to his Mt. Vernon hearth and home, though they had begged him to continue in the Presidency which he might have held until death claimed him.

He was an ideal Statesman. No self seeking gnawed him. He had no greater ambition than to serve where others refused. They offered him a Kingship through Col. Nicola, speaking for his fellows, but he indignantly, indeed, with great wrath, refused to consider it. They offered him a third term as President and this also he refused. He never seemed to have an ulterior motive. He served as General without pay, though it had been voted him, sending in only his bills to cover his expense.

He was a Christian idealist. His thought was ever for others and for the high purposes of God and his native land. His was a national patriotism. Others, today, boast of their Internationalism. They are the kind of Internationalists who seem to think their own country always wrong and other countries always right. He rejoiced in the progress of other nations along righteous lines, knowing that all such progress led to the success of other nations but, as a patriot should, he loved his own country best. He knew his Bible well enough to know that: "If any provide not for his own, and specially for those of his own house, he hath denied the faith and is worse than an infidel." He knew that every righteous, progressive movement must start, as Christ said the Gospel must start: "Beginning at Jerusalem"—beginning first at your own home! Then it may spread, as he has caused the influence of this nation to spread, in beneficence and blessing, to the uttermost parts of the world. It is such a patriotism as this that needs a new birth today!

"Death loves a shining mark." He was not old, as we count age. He had not reached the three score years and ten. He was still hale and vigorous enough to go about his farm and fields and attend to the business of his wide spreading estate. But, his country called him again. France threatened War. Adams, then President, called him back to head the Army of the United States as Commander-in-Chief, saying: "There will be more power in your name than many an Army."

He accepted, as he had before, modestly, and yet willing to serve his country in its need. He immediately began laying plans for the threatened conflict, but stipulated that he should not take the field before the actual conflict. So he continued to be a farmer as well as lieutenant-general and commander-in-chief during the last year and a half of his life. Thus came mid-December, 1799, when in the wind and sleet of a stormy day he went afield, as usual, looking over the necessary work of the day. Two days later he died—died like a soldier, true to his self-imposed duty to the last. He who had faced death so many times was not afraid to face it now. He knew that he was dying, yet he said: "I am not afraid." His last words were: "It is well!"—and with those words upon his lips he passed to his reward.

Yes, Washington, mighty Father of a new Republic: "It is well!" It is well with the Republic which has grown from thirteen Colonies and States to a widespread nation of forty-eight lusty, prosperous commonwealths. It is well with Liberty, gained by such heroic deeds as thine and maintained by others in 1812, in 1861, in 1898 and 1917, by valiant and courageous men full worthy of their noble sires! It is well with the Flag, that precious emblem that thou didst first unfurl to the breeze and which has ever stood for Liberty and Righteousness and never yet has been stained by dishonor or defeat! It is well and ever will be well with all of us as long as we abide by thy principles and trust in thy Lord and thy God!

"God of our fathers, known of old
Lord of our far flung battle line,
Beneath whose awful hand we hold
Dominion over palm and pine,—
Lord God of Hosts, be with us yet,
Lest we forget—lest we forget!"

George Washington

A Sermon by

NATHAN KRASS

Congregation Emanu-El of the City of New York

The bicentennary of Washington's birthday comes to us in the midst of critical times. We were on the high road to peace and prosperity. Science opened the doors of new marvels. The population of the United States of America was on the verge of a new epoch. Then, of a sudden, we found ourselves lost in chaotic, bewildered conditions. Instinctively, we are yearning for a great leader, a man who will kindle the imagination of the public, inspire confidence, put hope into the hearts of the despondent. Would a Washington were here to lead us into the promised land. Lord Brougham said the test of progress is the veneration of Washington. As long as we value Washington properly idealism

will endure. When we have done with the ideals which inspired the birth of a new nation, the decline of American civilization is at hand. The tendency of mankind is to glorify or deify its heroes. Thus myths are created and perpetuated. Historians, jealous of the flawless characters of its heroes, make plaster saints out of them and leave a legacy that may truly corroborate the definition of history, pithily put "history is a lie agreed upon." The humanity is stripped and unreality is clothed in the vestments once donned by these historic personalities. Styles change in history as elsewhere. In our day we have noted the critical process at work in the realm of biography. A new school of historians has not scrupled to lay bare all facts even at the risk of marring a favorite idol and dethroning a popular divinity. Not content with removing the errors of history, they pile ridicule and contempt upon the worthies of yesterday. Impatient of these myth makers they fly to the other extreme and find fiction, legend, and fable as the ingredients of the classic characterizations. Every short-coming they find they magnify. Every foible they exaggerate. Reverence is thrown to the winds and the heroes are hurled from their pedestals. None escapes. The Father of his country has not been spared. Legends are tributes to the love of a grateful people. Imagination has warmed cold facts and has transfigured them.

The George Washington of popular tradition has withstood the ruthless blasts and has emerged a finer, greater, more inspiring personality. There were great men in those days. And he looms the most resplendent of them all.

Another great President said that Washington is a name to conjure with. He was superlatively versatile. Soldier, patriot, statesman, these are well known. But there are profundities which we lose sight of because we stress the non-essentials. Strange as it may seem we live by ideals. We pay tribute by recognizing them even though we may observe them in the breach.

Washington was first and foremost a liberal. He had no narrow vision of politics or religion or statesmanship. He believed in the rights of man. He felt that kingship is an anachronism. Kinship with man must supplant kingship among rulers. He believed that the people should have a voice in government and that hereditary officialdom should be not tolerated. He may have been a great soldier but his broad vision will more likely lead to immortality. There was a time when Washington was considered perfect. He possessed every virtue. He never did wrong. Then came the iconoclasts and unearthed blemishes. He made no claims to infallibility. His speeches and letters are filled with homely and wholesome wisdom. But because one may find an argument to bolster some favorite theory one need not clamor for Washington's support. He was not always right. His solution was not always the correct solution. He himself builded a monument more lasting than cherry trees. He was a great liberal. Religion was to him a matter between man and his maker. The Moslem was protected in his faith just as the Jew and the Christian. Church and state should be forever separated. Each person should be permitted to delve into the secrets of his own heart without let or hindrance. Sumptuary legislation was obnoxious to him for he felt that in matters of taste each human being is entitled to have preferences. Traditionalists who interpret their bibles literally forget the clear memento that it is not so much that which enters our mouth as that which comes out of it which defiles.

Washington did not feel that the new world was isolated. He believed that the old international quarrels should not be fomented and that the new world should refrain from taking sides. But this does not mean that America should not look after its own welfare, even though it should treat with magnanimity the other nations.

Washington was an unselfish man. He did not seek personal aggrandizement. He sought the welfare of the people. He felt that the new republic must be nurtured and he set himself to the task of helping it grow. He might have been king. He might have been perpetual president. The temptations were strong, but he withstood them all. He had honor and glory. He had the adoration of the public. He loved the esteem of a grateful people. Yet he was unselfish. In our present critical condition what illumination the first president sheds! The country needs great men. Sacrifices must be made. We must turn to real leaders. Self-seeking must be parked until stability is once more established and security once more assured. Our legislators may eulogize the name of Washington but what boots it unless they profit by his example? We need more wisdom and fewer laws. Officers must think in terms of the republic and not in terms of partizanship. Frenzied finance has been an affliction. We must put humanity above the dollar. Property must serve man—not man property. The wealthy must make not charity their watchword but justice. This country is rich in material wealth; let none be poor. Washington did not dilly dally. He took drastic measures. Inspired by his leadership let us be men.

Washington loved his home. The present method of living too oft precludes the transmutation of the home into a sanctuary. Migratory folks do not make good home bodies. Moralists are warning us of the disintegration of the home. As we sing praises to the name of Washington let us extol him because he loved his home and express the hope that millions will follow his illustrious example.

Washington lived in a simpler world than we do. His problems were not our problems. We must not look for his guidance in detail but for his inspiration. Most things change. But certain things remain unchanged. Human nature is to all intents and purposes unaltered. Greed, chicanery, deceit were the same in Washington's days as they are in ours. If we admire our first president let us use him as a model. It is futile to make of him a paragon of virtue. God's attributes need not be couched in terms of Washington. The assets and liabilities should be measured one against the other. The most critical historian will admit that Washington was not perfect; nevertheless, his shortcomings were far less than his good points. He was a man of remarkable common sense. He had a sane and sound outlook and wisdom inhabited his house. A little less greed and a little more fairness, a little less deceit and a little more honesty and many of our problems would be solved. Noblesse oblige. Rules, policies, legislation, are of no avail. We need truth in the inward heart.

Washington is an inspiration, because so many things that baffle us puzzled him not. As the sun lifts the mists and shows the way so Washington seems to dispel the fog and light penetrates. He was no doctrinaire. He was a soldier, but did not glorify war. He was a pacifist but did not let this stand in his way when he had to fight for the rights of America. He respected all religions, but did not permit sectarianism to dominate. He believed in peace, but warned the nation that good fellowship makes for greater happiness provided protection was guaranteed. He was a real statesman because he tore the heart out of a difficulty and did not get confused. He believed that an ounce of prevention was worth a pound of cure, and did not let problems accumulate. He did not waver, but went on going right and fearing no one.

He was a man of action. He saw the goal and he marched right through. He was given to contemplation, but he never let inaction take command. He was a hero. He suffered with his soldiers, and cheered them on. Privation hardened, not weakened him. He did not cry over spilled milk, but made the future compensate for the past. He was a patriot not a chauvinist. Well might we heed his monition. Too many in our generation have mistaken the words and used them as synonyms. Two hundred years have flown since Washington first moved a mighty man on this sublunar sphere. America commemorates the birthday of the Father of his country. Millions of tributes will be recited. Let us not lose ourselves in words. Let oratory not be enough. Ideals make the race move forward. Quickened by the immortal Washington let us rededicate ourselves to carry on the things which will redound to the welfare of our land, bring peace to mankind, and make for a better, a healthier, and happier world.

WASHINGTON'S WORTH TO AMERICA

RIGHT REVEREND CHARLES E. WOODCOCK, D.D., LL.D.
Bishop of the EPISCOPAL CHURCH *in Kentucky*

The glory of children are their fathers; Proverbs 17:6

Memory is the gratitude of the heart that treasures and keeps alive our appreciation for the names and deeds of those whom we delight to honor. So long as high personal character and notable public service exert powerful influence among men, so long will a grateful people continue to commemorate sons worthy of renown. Of those entitled to our unfailing gratitude and commemoration none, in this whole land, ever will outrank George Washington. We do not attempt to praise him, but we do desire to keep him in loving and grateful remembrance. Our praises cannot advance his fame nor brighten his honor. His character, his personal worth, his inestimable service remain forever his imperishable monument—"records that defy the tooth of time."

When someone lightly remarked that "History is the place where great men go to be forgotten," he obviously overlooked all those faithful, loving hearts that refuse to leave the name of Washington to the unfeeling custody of history; for history has no conscious function that it may exercise. To us, and those who come after us, belong the precious right and privilege of perpetuating his great name and his heroic deeds. We rejoice in keeping his memory green and in rendering to him the homage of grateful hearts—hearts that never will permit his name to die. Hearts that will enshrine his name throughout succeeding generations; for in keeping the name of Washington, his fame and his deeds are forever safe from oblivion.

Epochs are born when great men come to the surface with personalities and powers equal to the demand of great emergencies. In this land a sore need had arisen in the cruel invasion of the rights and liberties of the colonists. When, after long and unwarranted aggression in which appeals went unheard and protest brought no relief; when, in desperate straits, protest "changed remonstrance into murmur and murmur into resistance"; when, at length, the storm broke and the heavens came crashing down upon a people, in such calamitous days to whom could these feeble folk look for a captain of their cause? Who and where was the champion of their rights and liberties—"his arm a fortress and his name a host?" Called to defend his country, Washington served in the hour of her sorest need without reward and with courage, loyalty and sacrifice unsurpassed in any land, for any cause, by any man. "None but himself could be his parallel."

Others have felt and expressed their appreciation of this outstanding leadership. The great historian, William E. H. Lecky, pays to our great countryman this high tribute:

"Washington had his full share of disaster, but it may be truly said of him that his military reputation steadily rose through many successive campaigns, and before the end of the struggle he had outlived all rivalry and almost all envy. For several years, usually in the neighborhood of superior forces, he commanded a fluctuating army, wretchedly armed, wretchedly clothed and sometimes in imminent danger of starvation. Unsupported for the most part by the population among whom he was quartered, and incessantly thwarted by the jealousy of Congress, he kept his army together by a combination of skill, firmness, patience and judgment which has rarely been surpassed, and he led it at last to a signal triumph."

By another distinguished writer, Justin McCarthy, we have this enconium:

"The war that gave the world a new nation and a republic greater than Rome added one of the greatest names, perhaps the noblest name, to the great captains of the earth. No soldier of all those that the eyes of Dante discerned in the first circle, not even 'Cæsar, all armored with gerfalcon eyes,' adorns the annals of antiquity more than George Washington illuminates the last quarter of the eighteenth century."

Again another historian, Richard Henry Green, pays our indomitable leader this high praise:

"No nobler figure ever stood in the forefront of a nation's life. * * * It was only as the weary struggle went on that the colonists discovered, however slowly and imperfectly, the greatness of their leader, his clear judgment, his heroic endurance, his silence under difficulties, his calmness in the hour of danger or defeat, the patience with which he waited, the quickness and hardness with which he struck, the lofty and serene sense of duty that never swerved from its task through resentment or jealousy, that never in war or peace felt the touch of meaner ambition save that of guarding the freedom of his fellow countrymen, and no personal longing, returning to his own fireside when their freedom was secured. It was almost unconsciously that men learned to cling to Washington with a trust and faith such as few other men have won and to regard him with a reverence which still hushes us in the presence of his memory."

These gracious and generous eulogies, be it noted, come not from Americans, but from our cousins over seas who recognized and proclaimed one who is first in the hearts of his own countrymen.

In George Washington we find far more than his fame as a military leader. We hold him in deep veneration for the selflessness of his unwearied service and the value of his great personality. He is not dead but alive in our undying memory and affections. His voice is silenced in the cold embrace of the grave; but still speaks to us through the noblest American ideals and the highest American manhood. He yet lives, and will forever survive, in the best type of American honor and public service. Can we rightly speak, therefore, of one as dead whose personality vibrates in our national life and destiny and whose character is repeated in all who give to their country those willing sacrifices that are never measured by regrets? We never shall understand Washington nor appreciate him until we strive to reproduce in ourselves the noble attributes that crowned his life.

It is most fitting, therefore, that we stress and commemorate, at this time, the value and influence of Washington's exalted service to this land. Think of what he is giving to America today in the influence upon millions of hearts inspired and upheld by his example and ungrudging service. We have forever with us the imperishable heritage of a living personality. Whatever dangers threaten whatever distress or calamities befall us, whatever may strike at our foundation and institutions, let the spirit of our unconquerable leader animate and sustain us. We shall do well to remember that in the midst of appalling hardships, opposed by superior forces, facing mutiny and treason, surrounded by those whose hearts failed them for fear, unsupported by a timid and vacillating Congress, it was Washington who stood unmoved, undaunted and invincible. He stands forth as the most gallant and the most intrepid of leaders. Brave beyond measure, he dedicated all his powers to his country's cause to which he pledged his life, his fortune and his sacred honor. As we follow his leading it becomes "a day for gods to stoop and men to soar."

We are indebted as much to Washington for his civic service as for his military renown. Who can fully estimate the great contribution that he made to his country in the hazardous days following the revolution? For there is as much honor and patriotism in living for one's country as in dying for her. Peace may be as searching a test of citizenship as war. Without Washington's incomparable leadership and statesmanship in the chaotic days succeeding the war the gravest disaster might have ensued. Few have realized, to the full extent, that America owes as much to Washington in peace as in the great struggle for her liberty. In the dark, uncertain days coming after victory when the new-born republic burst her swaddling bands, but had not found her strength nor determined her policy, it was Washington's guiding hand that steered her course through many tortuous and stormy channels. In the formative days of our nation he encountered tasks greater, perhaps, than the burdens and exactions of war. Here his super abilities seem as resplendent and equal to emergencies as in the revolution. Overcoming the origi-

nal obstructions, allaying controversies, firmly uniting the people, winning contentious parties and hostile factions to the necessities of a new-born country, he blazed the trail and illuminated the pathway of our national destiny. "Born for his country and the world, he never gave up to party what was meant for mankind."

We have it in our power to honor the name of Washington in ways superior to the loftiest eulogy. It is to live as he lived, to serve our country as he served, so that our commemoration shall not be in mere sentiments but in deeds and emulation.

Product of the ideals of the cavalier and of the passionate love of liberty of the pilgrims, have we in our day departed from the ideals and institutions of our forefathers? In this age where, often, "the anarchy of speculative thought is almost a harmony compared with the chaos of moral ideals," in times when agitation and unrest reveal the dregs, and when peace has not yet clarified the turbid flux of disturbed and portentious conditions, have we in any way betrayed the trust transmitted to us or in any way forfeited our birthright?

A much needed reminder in our times is to be recalled to a keen loyalty to our inheritance. We have been bequeathed a precious legacy, baptised with fire and consecrated by sacrifice; it is in our keeping today to pass it on, unimpaired, to our children tomorrow. If we would preserve our traditions, we must translate them into the living thought of today and interpret them through our own character in personal service and loyalty to the land which we have inherited. If we would maintain our institutions, it must be by respect for and loyal obedience to law. We have no political rights which do not involve personal obligations. A nation's strength is no greater than the average character, loyalty and obedience of her citizens. Her honor is no safer than the honor of those who serve her and defend her charter and her liberties. If we have no veneration for the past, if we revere not the exploits of our fathers and voice not the praise of those who bore the brunt, then we shall become a nation incapable of producing heroes.

> "Words are but breath,
>   But where great deeds are done
> A power abides
>   Transferred from sire to son."

Every citizen has a contribution to make to his country. He is unworthy who withholds. That contribution was best illustrated by Washington; namely, an undying patriotism. Let us be sure that we clearly understand what this means. Patriotism is no mere sentiment, it is not the cant of the demagogue and charlatan. Some have robbed it of its true meaning by their profanation. Patriotism is no fugitive impulse, no occasional hysteria, no fine glow of feeling that evaporates before stern demands and heroic sacrifices. "Like snow upon a river, a moment white then gone forever." We must not profane it nor mutilate it by the limitations that we put upon it. We may not be able fully to define it, but we may personally experience it. Patriotism is an undying, imperishable principle, a passionate, selfless love of country. It is faith and love and trust. It is a faith and love so deep and so sure that it freely suffers distress without ever feeling distrust. Who can tell all that it is? It is hope, it is life, it is service and it is experience. He who has not experience will never understand. For some it may be death, for others it may be service, and for all it is unquestioned fealty and loyal obedience. What matters it what the demand if what we fulfil be to save the life of our nation and keep her soul bright? Our patriotism lacks integrity if it does not contribute something definite and lasting to the resources of America. "Take away patriotism and the soul of the nation has fled." For us there is but one liberty, the liberty to do right; for all our liberty is in exact proportion to our obedience to law.

Finally, we owe to Washington a tribute for his religious example and practice. He never was afraid to acknowledge his dependence upon Divine guidance. He never was ashamed to associate himself with the religious life of his community. He did not hesitate to take his part and do his share in the Church of which, for many years, he was a faithful member. His religion was of a manly type, and he found in it guidance and support in the hour of his deepest need. He could, and did, "Trust God, see all, nor be afraid." We take as witness his own words: "No people can be bound to acknowledge and adore the Invisible Hand which conducts the affairs of men more than the people of the United States. Every step by which they have advanced to the character of an independent nation seems to have been distinguished by some token of providential agency."

Let the welfare of our country have an inmost place in our hearts. If we would uphold our political rights and religious freedom, let us merit and exalt them. If we would endow this land, but not with gold; if we would make her strong, but not by army and navy alone; if we would uphold her honor in the eyes of all nations, not because of her area, her material resources and her unbounded wealth; then let this be a land where the poorest shall have their full rights and the richest no undue and unfair advantage. Let this be a land where law is revered, where the rights of man are respected and the honor of woman is safe. A land where God is loved, adored and served. Then may we pray:

"God give us men;
The man who never fails his brother,
The man who never shames his mother,
The man who stands for country, home and God."

RELIGIOUS LIBERTY

By RABBI DAVID PHILIPSON, D.D.
Cincinnati, Ohio

I am departing from my usual custom of taking the text for my sermon from the Bible. In place thereof I shall found my words upon a remarkable utterance of the mighty man whose life and achievements are being proclaimed and honored in this bicentenary year throughout the length and breadth of our land. In the year that George Washington was elected president of these United States there were comparatively few Jews in the country. There were all told but six Jewish congregations; namely, in Newport, Rhode Island, New York, Philadelphia, Richmond, Charleston, and Savannah. These congregations addressed letters of felicitation to the first president on the occasion of his inauguration. These letters are three in number; the congregations of Newport and Savannah each addressed an individual communication while the other four combined to send a joint missive of congratulation. Washington answered these messages in dignified manner. The opening sentence in the reply to the joint communication of the congregations of New York, Philadelphia, Richmond, and Charleston shall serve as my text. This golden sentence reads as follows: "The liberal sentiment toward each other which marks every political and religious denomination of men in this country stands unrivalled in the history of nations."

In a conspicuous place in beautiful Fairmont Park, Philadelphia, there stands a sculptured marble group, the work of the famed American Jewish sculptor, Moses J. Ezekiel. The group expresses the idea of Religious Liberty chiseled into stone. The Genius of Liberty is represented by a stately female figure standing in the center of the group. In the rim of the Phrygian cap which adorns her head are set thirteen stars, symbolical of the thirteen colonies that formed the thirteen original states. At her right stands a boy clinging to her for security; the boy with pure glance directed upward embodies the Genius of Devotion looking to the Genius of Liberty for protection. At the left of the central female figure we see the eagle, the bird of freedom, clutching in its talons a serpent, representative of the spirit of intolerance.

The glorious thought which the artist expresses through this sculpture; namely, liberty protecting religious devotion on the one hand and freedom stifling intolerance and prejudice on the other, is a true representation of the spirit of our government as conceived by the immortal founders, Washington and his confreres, and as continued by such of their successors as grasp the intent of the American principle of religious liberty.

The commanding idea of the right of every man to think as he will, aye, what is more, to worship as he will, was first carried into full execution here in our United States. Here was a government founded without an established church. Here was first realized that prime prerequisite of full religious liberty; namely, the separation of church and state. One of the greatest boons which the newly founded republic of the West conferred upon this world at large was the testimony it gave that together with full political freedom there was possible full religious liberty.

I believe it may be said without fear of contradiction that the fairest jewel in the crown that decks Columbia's brow is religious liberty. One of the chief causes of the unhappiness and misery of thousands has been religious fanaticism and bigotry. Religious intolerance has slain victims by tens and hundreds of thousands. Religious intolerance accused the early Christians of burning Rome in the days of Nero and caused the death of hundreds of these poor unfortunates. Religious intolerance persecuted the Quakers and the Catholics in England. Religious intolerance slew thousands of Protestants on St. Bartholomew's Day in France and drove them from that country into exile. Religious intolerance was the moving cause of the horrible massacres of the Sicilian vespers. Religious intolerance exiled thousands of unoffending Jews and Moors from Spain. Religious intolerance threw central Europe into an all destructive, all consuming Thirty

Years War between Protestants and Catholics; religious intolerance has been one of the greatest curses, if not the greatest, that has afflicted mankind far more than any other agency; it has excited the passions of men to the highest pitch, and has been the fruitful cause of much of the hatred which has blackened the pages of the history of human relations. Religious intolerance invented the tortures of the Inquisition. Religious intolerance lit the funeral pyres whose flames ascending higher and higher at last devoured with greedy tongues the poor helpless victims of this Inquisition, whose only crime lay in the fact that they differed in religious belief from the dominant church. The cruelty and bloodshed that can be traced throughout the centuries to religious intolerance indeed proves the truth of the poet's line that man's inhumanity to man has made countless thousands mourn.

Even in this country in the early days, this intolerant spirit showed itself. The Quakers were forbidden to enter Virginia. They were hanged in Massachusetts. Roger Williams was driven from Massachusetts and founded the colony of Rhode Island because he protested against the union of Church and State. Most of the original thirteen colonies made church attendance compulsory and inscribed blue laws in their statute books. Religious liberty, as we now understand it, was unknown during the colonial period. When, however, in the fullness of time, the Declaration of Independence was proclaimed, a new era in the history of mankind began. When, after the victorious struggle with Great Britain, the United Colonies established themselves into a free government, then did it dawn upon the minds of the great statesmen who fathered the new state in the commonwealth of nations that full freedom required religious as well as political liberty. The first note was struck when Thomas Jefferson submitted in the General Assembly of Virginia his proposition entitled "An Act to Establish Religious Freedom" which was carried in 1785. This historic document contained these words: "Be it enacted by the General Assembly that no man shall be compelled to frequent or support any religious worship, place or ministry whatsoever, nor shall be enforced, restrained, molested, hindered in his body or goods, nor shall otherwise suffer because of his religious opinions or beliefs. But all men shall be free to profess and by argument to maintain their opinions in matters of religion and that the same shall in no wise diminish, enlarge or affect their civil capacities." Precious words! Even today after a lapse of one hundred and fifty years they can not be improved upon as a definition of full religious liberty. This sentiment was written into the United States Constitution some years later in the famous First Amendment—"Congress shall make no law respecting the establishment of religion or prohibiting the free exercise thereof."

Because of this provision this country became the refuge of the oppressed, the down-trodden and the persecuted of every creed; here every man may profess any religious opinion subject to one condition only, that he interfere not with the religious worship and opinion of others. True, there have been attempts now and then on the part of bigoted religionists to overturn this fundamental American principle; there have been occasional outbursts of sectarian prejudice and hatred like the Know Nothing movement in the nineteenth century, but these were not endorsed by the bulk of the people and they vanished in the course of a few years like the mist before the rising sun. For the most part, men and women of diverse religious beliefs have dwelt here in amity even though now and then the serpent of intolerance has lifted its head and shown its fangs and spat forth its venom. Despite all the heart burnings of these gloomy days in this most troubled year, religionists of all kinds and degrees are dwelling side by side in peace. The cry of the bigot is stilled and the voice of the fanatic is not heard except at rare intervals. Protestant, Catholic, and Jew are joining in great enterprises like Good Will movements and meetings for better understanding. Such good will and better understanding are the logical outcome of the pioneer planting of the seed of religious liberty by the founders of our government. I feel that there is nothing of greater importance to be stressed in this bicentenary year than just this. Religious liberty is the capstone of the great massive column of political freedom. I am reminded of another unforgettable utterance of the soaring spirit whose memory we are delighting to honor:—"The Government of the United States gives to bigotry no sanction, to persecution no assistance and requires only that those who live under its protection should demean themselves as good citizens in giving it on all occasions their effectual support." Such being Washington's attitude, it is not surprising that this supreme leader, great in thought as in deed, and free in deed as in thought, should have shaped the course of this government as the protagonist of civic and religious freedom more than any other one individual.

Therefore it is particularly mete when we commemorate his mighty achievements to refer particularly to the great boon conferred on mankind when he and his co-workers made this nation the leader in the march of the peoples who have since then proclaimed freedom of religious worship and right of opinion. There is indeed something sublime and inspiring in a country-wide jubilation such as we are participating in this year. Here in this most cosmopolitan of lands, in free America, which has taken under its protection men from all parts of the world for no other reason than they are men seeking freedom, is it not glorious to think of the millions united in a mighty celebration commemorative of the firm establishment of civic and religious liberty? Christian and Jew, believer and unbeliever, conformist and nonconformist, all laying aside their differences of creed and opinion, in order to celebrate together as a united people doing homage to our country's first citizen. The high doctrine of the right of men without distinction of rank or station to life, liberty, and the pursuit of happiness had been placed upon the statute books first in this land. The enlivening breath of freedom was wafted from these Western shores across the waters. Carried into the effete monarchies of Europe, it succeeded by virtue of its life giving force in clearing away much of the rubbish through the medium of the French Revolution, that spectacular conflagration which ushered in the new era in Europe and followed so closely upon the unfurling of the banner of universal freedom here, for on the fifth day of May seventeen hundred and eighty-nine took place the meeting of the States General in Paris, the first step in the government of the New France whose watchwords were the famous triad, Liberty, Fraternity, Equality.

The message that sounded so powerfully in this land one hundred and fifty years ago, the message that came as a revelation to the rest of the world, the tolling of the Liberty Bell with its inscription "proclaim freedom throughout the land and to all the inhabitants thereof" rang forth glad tidings indeed. During the intervening years that message has penetrated to the far corners of the earth. Freedom has achieved many victories, but the complete triumph has not yet come. Mankind is still on the way with eyes directed to the coming of the day when from one earth's end to the other the American ideals will be realized,— that in spite of all their differences men are one in their humanity.

Yes, this is the American ideal! and animated by this ideal all our people from whatever quarter of the world they may have come originally, from fair France or gloomy Russia, from sunny Italy or from icebound Norway, from absolutist Germany or from free England, from seagirt Ireland or from mountain enchained Switzerland, all are now gathering in meeting places throughout these United States as Americans of many origins, to do honor to the Father of our common country and to give thanks that this haven of peace for the oppressed and persecuted of earth had been opened at a time when it was so welcome and so necessary.

Hither men fled from political tyranny and religious persecution. Here the complete separation of church and state had been achieved at one bold stroke. This separation has been a guiding star of the government's policy. All religious denominations are here alike tolerated. What such denominations do within their own church confines is no one's concern but their own, but when, as has happened now and then, they aim to branch out and force their peculiar views upon others, when they presume to command free individuals "this may you do and this not," then must a halt be cried. Such action in any form is the antithesis of the fundamental principle of our government. The real lovers of this country can be none too careful lest there be removed any one of the mighty foundation stones; and the entire spiritual edifice, whereon the ages have labored and in which men of whatever belief or creed have made thir home, fall and crumble into ruin.

Yes, none too jealously can the rights of free thought, free speech, and free worship be guarded and every attempted subversion thereof be repelled by all the friends of American liberty. Our own convictions and our own beliefs may never blind us to the rights of others. Protestantism, Catholicism, Judaism or any other ism may propagate its doctrines freely and undisturbed, but none may attempt to force its own peculiar doctrines and observances upon the government or any of its branches in the separate states. The history of European governments demonstrates only too clearly the danger of identifying the state with any one special form of religion. The real welfare of the people demands a complete separation of church and state lest the tenets of a state church cripple the working of the state as the fatherland of all its citizens of whatever religious persuasion they may be.

This land has stood as a model to all the earth because of the perfect tolerance that marks its attitude toward all its citizens. As two parallel streams flowing along peaceably side by side, each pursuing its own course, the two never mingling, must Church and State continue in this country as they have in the century and one half that has rolled by, the century and one half that has witnessed this land throw off the swaddling clothes of the babe until now it stands a very colossus among the nations of the earth. This glorious result would never have been reached had it not been that there has not been tolerated by the government at large the infringement of the rights of any man as far as religious freedom of thought is concerned. So marvelous a career as our Republic has run was possible only in such an atmosphere of freedom. May this free spirit spread from zone to zone, and from clime to clime. May all men everywhere be brought under its influence so that in time the day may have come when North shall tell it unto South and East proclaim the glad word to the West, "persecution has disappeared from the earth, religious liberty has become universal, men's hearts are knit together in love and all men dwell together in peace and security under the protection of the spirit of Religious Liberty."

THE RELIGIOUS UNDERTONE IN THE LIFE OF GEORGE WASHINGTON

By SAMUEL JUDSON PORTER, D.D., Litt.D.
Pastor, First Baptist Church, Washington, D. C.

Preached on February 28, 1932

Acts 13:36—"After he had served his own generation by the will of God, he fell asleep."

The colonial period in the history of our country was a season of planting and growth which came to flower in the events which culminated in the signing of the Declaration of Independence. In 1748, at Aix-la-Chapelle, the ancient capital of Charlemagne and the site of that monarch's tomb, a treaty was concluded which ended the Austrian War of Succession in which all the great powers of Europe, on one side or the other, had been engaged. The treaty which terminated this war of eight years' duration left the different countries with nearly the same possessions as before, but with many points unsettled which proved the cause of strife for years to come. Humanity had suffered without beneficial results. In his history of the United States George

Bancroft closes the colonization section by contrasting the formulators of this treaty with an unknown American youth, who had been born by the side of the Potomac, beneath the roof of a Virginia planter. No academy had welcomed him to its shades, no college crowned him with its honors; to read, to write, to cipher—these had been his degrees in knowledge. At sixteen he set out to make an honest living by hard work. "Himself his own cook, having no spit but a forked stick, no plate but a large chip," he roamed over the spurs of the Alleghanies and along the banks of the Shenandoah, alive to nature, living among skin-clad savages with their scalps and rattles, or uncouth immigrants who scarcely knew how to speak English; rarely sleeping in a bed and glad of a resting place on a little hay, straw, or fodder. "This strippling surveyor in the woods . . . contrasted strangely," says the historian, "with the imperial magnificence of the Congress of Aix-la-Chapelle. And yet God selected none of those diplomats, not a monarch of the house of Hapsburg nor of Hanover, but the Virginia stripling, to give an impulse to human affairs; and as far as events can depend on an individual, had placed the rights and destinies of countless millions in the keeping of the widow's son."

With Bancroft's belief that Washington's career was divinely destined many students of human affairs agree, among whom was T. DeWitt Talmage, at one time pastor of the First Presbyterian Church of this city. In a notable sermon on "The Upper Forces" he said: "Washington himself was a miracle. What Joshua was in sacred history, the first American President was in secular history. The world never saw his like, and probably never will see his like again, because there probably never will be another such exigency. He was let down by divine interposition. He was from God direct. I do not know how anyone can read the history of those times without admitting that the contest was decided by the upper forces."

A prime principle in religion is belief in the will of God concerning one's life, finding that will, and conforming to it. In his pivotal hour on the road to Damascus, Paul asked, "Lord, what wilt thou have me to do?" In Gethsemane Jesus cried, "Father, not my will, but thine, be done." Who that knows Washington can avoid the conclusion that here in this man was not an accident but part of a plan contrived in heaven. Kipling sings:

> "Who clears the grounding berg,
> And guides the grinding floe,
> He hears the cry of the little kit fox,
> And the lemming in the snow."

Washington believed that such a clearance and such a guidance followed him through his days. Unlike King Cyrus of whom God said, through the prophet Isaiah, "I have called thee by thy name, and girded thee, though thou has not known me," Washington seemed so conscious of the divine protection and control that his whole being appeared as one continued act of faith in the intelligent and moral order of the universe. At the age of twenty-three he counted the bullet holes in his coat after Braddock's disastrous defeat and acknowledged, with common-sense practicality, that a power higher than man had saved him. At the beginning of the war for independence, having accepted the commission which placed him in command of the army, in a letter to his wife he unbosomed his inmost thoughts: "I have used every endeavor in my power to avoid it, . . . from a consciousness of its being a trust too great for my capacity, . . . but . . . as a kind of destiny . . . has thrown me upon this service, I shall hope that my undertaking it is designed to answer some good purpose. I shall rely . . . confidently on that Providence which has hitherto preserved and been bountiful to me." During the dark days of the revolution, writing to a friend about what he called "the strangest vicissitudes" of his struggles around White Plains he says: "The hand of Providence has been so conspicuous in all this that he must be worse than an infidel that lacks faith, and more than wicked that has not gratitude enough to acknowledge his obligations." Having begun his duties as commander in chief with a dedication and avowal of confidence in "the patronage of Heaven," at the close of the war

he resigns his commission with a prayer: "I consider it an indispensable duty to close this last solemn act of my official life by commending the interests of our dearest country to the protection of Almighty God, and those who have the superintendency of them to his holy keeping."

Thus in his career as soldier and likewise as statesman, his character and his calling matched each other. Character is the voice that sings the song; calling is the instrumental accompaniment. Every man should learn to combine the two in a beautiful harmony. This Washington did as but few others have ever been able to do. From his own statements we are compelled to feel that he consciously fell in with what he thought was God's plan for his life. As a picture fits its frame, as a swan fits the lake on which she swims, as the river conforms to the channel in which it flows, as a planet glides along its appointed orbit; or, in the phrase of England's greatest nature poet, as a wild duck fits "her gleaming nest of golden leaves inlaid with silver down," so the greatly successful life fits into God's plan for it.

Obedience is the first law of our being. Washington was a challenging example of obedience to God's law for his life. No man obeys perfectly, otherwise we should not need a merciful Saviour to recover us from our sins. Washington was not perfect; but in its larger outline and forward sweep his career obeyed a divine impulsion. He did not spring into life a perfect and impossible man, as has been so often ludicrously represented. On the contrary, he was educated by the fiery trial of circumstances; but the metal came out of the furnace of experience finely tempered, because it was by nature of the very best and with but little dross to be purged away. From his heart Washington was truly and deeply religious. His convictions became more intense through the influence on his character of the tremendous events of his life. Think of the lonely pioneer paths he trod, of the upheavals through which he passed. Surely his soul was beaten into shape under the hammers of God. As he looked back upon the thick-set dangers through which his course had been steered, we know, from his own words, that he could not but feel that he had been sustained by "the all powerful Guide and Dispenser of human things."

A brilliant historian has said: "General Washington is known to us, and President Washington. But George Washington is an unknown man." These pungent words urge a closer study of the man himself. In making a study of Washington for the famous statue which he produced, M. Houdon was profoundly impressed with the magnificent and well-nigh perfect proportions of Washington's features and form, surpassing those of any other man whom the artist had ever observed. A similar study of the man's moral and spiritual qualities will reveal a corresponding symmetry in his character. Behind the statuesque figure of history, there was a strong, vigorous man in whose veins ran warm, red blood, in whose heart were stormy passions and deepest sympathy for humanity, and who was informed throughout his being with a resistless will. He was the most absolutely silent great man that history can show. His letters and speeches fill many volumes but they are profoundly dumb as to himself. Miss Custis writes: "He was a silent, thoughtful man. He spoke little generally; never of himself. I never heard him relate a single act of his life during the war. I have often seen him perfectly abstracted, his lips moving; but no sound was perceptible." While the veil of his silence is not often lifted, and never intentionally, now and then there is a glimpse behind it, and by stray sentences and in little incidents the real man is revealed; and when we are thus permitted to look at the true proportions of his massive personality we clearly see in George Washington what John Richard Green, the English historian, pronounced him to be—"the noblest figure that ever stood in the forefront of a nation's life."

Washington was not a metaphysician, not an analyzer of creeds, not a doctrinal hairsplitter; his religious faith grew out of his experience in action. He made no parade of his religion, for in this as elsewhere, he was perfectly simple and sincere. No man more thoroughly believed in the governing Providence of a just and almighty power; "and as a chemist knows that the leaf, for its greenness and beauty and health needs the help of an effluence from beyond this planet, so Washington beheld in the movements of nations a marshalling intelligence, which is above them all, and which gives order and unity to the universe." In his first inaugural address, with a voice deep and tremulous, and his whole form shaking with emotion he expressed "fervent supplications to that Almighty Being who . . . presides in the councils of nations, . . . that his benediction may consecrate to the liberties and happiness of the people of the United States a government instituted by themselves." Personally he was tortured by no doubts or questioning, but believed always in a personal God, to whom he knelt and prayed, in the day of darkness or in the hour of triumph, with a supreme and childlike faith. In a wonderful way he lived for the future, revealing the same confidence in the judgment of posterity that he had in the future beyond the grave. He regarded death with entire calmness, not only when it came to him, but when in previous years it had threatened him.

The entire undertone of his life was essentially religious. Among the influences which assuredly contributed to the religious element in his character a few may be mentioned. He had a praying mother who was gifted with good sense and a strong will. She was sober-minded, dignified, affectionate, and ruled her kingdom well. To the last she retained a profound hold upon the dutifulness of her son. There are indications that his half-brother, Lawrence, whose estates George inherited, was a man of a religious turn of mind, for whom George had a great deal of affection and admiration, and who strongly influenced the lad for good, during his formative years. There are evidences that his wife was a help to him, and not a hindrance, in matters religious. As a child he was taken to church and must have been influenced by the services. The rural church in those days was not a great institution, as the world counts greatness, and yet in the truest sense it was then, and is today, the most potent and persistent agency for righteousness and character building that America has ever known. In it are the seed-plots of our national greatness and strength.

"A little thing, this church? Remove its roots,
Ossa upon Pelion would not fill the gap."

At sixteen he went into the wilderness as a surveyor, and continued in this pursuit for three years, where the forests trained him, in meditative solitude, to freedom and largeness of mind; and nature revealed to him her obedience to serene and silent laws. "If you want a truly religious man," says Cooper in "The Pathfinder," go to sea, or go into the woods. When alone in the forest, I seem to stand face to face with God; all around me is fresh and beautiful, as it came from his hand. The woods are the true temple after all, for there the thoughts are free to mount higher even than the clouds." These sylvan influences were assuredly not lost on Washington.

Placed upon the largest theater of events, at the head of the greatest revolution in human affairs, mindful of the limitations under which he must advance and the oppositions that he must meet, he was so driven for refuge and resource to belief in God, that trust in the divine overruling power formed the very essence of his character. Washington was a man of action; his creed appeared in his life; he would mobilize for his task not alone the impedimenta and physical equipage of warfare, but the imponderables of the spirit.

Washington's religion revealed itself in life. "By their fruits ye shall know them," said Jesus. Under this test Washington stands forth resplendent in the common relationships of life, as well as in the broader relations. In his home at Mount Vernon he gave an example of calm benevolence, hospitality, peace, and purity of life, which I saw eloquently symbolized last spring in the serenity of a robin's nest brooded over by the mother bird in a lilac bush in Martha Washington's flower garden. His devotion to his wife was sublime; her miniature likeness he wore on his breast from the day of his marriage till his death. No shadow ever rested on their married life, and when the end came Mrs. Washington only said, "all is over now. I shall soon follow him." Having none of his own, he took to his heart his wife's children; later taking two of the grandchildren and watching over them with rare tenderness and love. Those of his own household know best the genuineness of a man's religion; in his family Washington was loved for his goodness, even by the servants.

He was generous and sympathetic in an unusual degree. During the French War, when the people on the frontier were the victims of Indian depredations, Washington, pleading for re-enforcements, wrote: "The supplicating tears of the women and moving petitions of the men melt me into such deadly sorrow that, I solemnly declare . . . I could offer myself a willing sacrifice to the butchering enemy." Such sentiments of concern for the welfare of others were not exceptional but characteristic, and frequently occur in his communications to the Congress during the period of the Revolution.

He had been brought up in the Episcopal Church and loved it as the church of his home and childhood. After marriage he attended services at Pohick and later at Christ Church in Alexandria, when at home, on an average of once a month. Both were distant from Mount Vernon so that it was something of a journey to reach them by coach, and we find entries in his diary of his being prevented from attending, by the carriage being away, and by his starting and having the carriage break down on the road. There are a few instances of illness and once he was kept at home by toothache. In religion as elsewhere whatever his hand found to do he did with enthusiasm and purpose. In Truro parish, of which he was a vestryman, a warm discussion arose as to the proper site of Pohick Church. Washington and George Mason led respectively the opposing forces, each contending that the site he preferred was more convenient for the larger number of parishioners. After much debate and no conclusion, Washington appeared at a vestry meeting with a mass of statistics. He had measured the distance from each proposed site to the home of each parishioner and found, as he demonstrated, that his choice of location was actually nearer to more people than the other. It is needless to add that he carried his point, that the spot he desired was the one to be chosen, so that Pohick Church stands there to this day—witnessing that the best way to settle disputes, religious and others, is to get at the facts impartially and abide by them.

Washington was versatile and practical. He knew how to meet emergencies and to make use of such means as were at hand. After Braddock's defeat at Fort Duquesne, having escaped without a wound but with four bullets through his coat and two horses shot down under him, the young officer rallied the routed fugitives and carried the dying general from the field. Four days later he laid Braddock's body in the grave and perhaps conducted the funeral service over the dead. With him religion was a reality in the quiet of the home or on the field of battle. On June 1, 1774, the day the Boston Port Bill went into effect, he attended the services appointed for prayer and noted in his diary that he "went to church and fasted all day." The governor of Virginia might well have reflected that when men of the George Washington type began to fast and pray all day on account of political misdoings, something must soon come to a show down. And when the war did come, religion still held a place in his scheme of thought, as the following order shows: "The Commander-in-Chief directs that divine service be performed every Sunday at 11 o'clock. . . . While we are zealously performing the duties of good citizens and soldiers we certainly ought not to be inattentive to the higher duties of religion. To the distinguished character of Patriot it should be our highest glory to add the more distinguished character of Christian." He was putting religion above patriotism even in the life of the soldier. Said Edith Cavell just before she went out to death: "Patriotism is not enough."

In the political sphere Washington's religion shone not as a borrowed ray but with a steady glow breaking from within. They say of Giotto that he introduced goodness into the art of painting; Washington carried it with him to the camp and the cabinet, and thereby set up a new criterion of human greatness. He never faltered in his faith in virtue, he stood fast by what he knew to be just; free from delusions; never dejected by fear of difficulties and perils that loomed before him; but drawing the promise of success from the justice of his cause, he moved forward in his course with fixed aim and steady purpose. It has been said that, "Integrity was so completely the law of his nature

that a planet would sooner have shot from its sphere than he have departed from his uprightness, which was so constant that it often seemed to be almost impersonal." Jefferson writes: "His integrity was the most pure, his justice the most inflexible I have ever known, no motives of interest or consanguinity, of friendship or hatred, being able to bias his decision."

When the final ordeal came which tries the professions of all, his claim was not found invalid. On his deathbed, after nearly twenty-four hours of struggling for breath, he placed the final seal of courageous manhood upon his life and went to meet his Maker with faith unshaken. "I felt from the first," he whispered, "that the disorder would prove fatal, but I am not afraid to go." Brave in life; unafraid in death. In these last words from his lips lies the worth of his religion to George Washington.

Referring to the elaborate preparations in progress in the Capital City for the Washington bicentennial celebration some one remarked facetiously that George Washington must be coming to town. It is more than the truth. He is already here in the hearts of a half million people—his spirit broods over the city he founded and the nation he loved. He is even so always coming to town! I visualize him, not riding over the grand highway that links Mount Vernon with the Nation's Capital in contrast with his coach of one hundred and fifty years ago laboriously drawn along the muddy Virginia roads of that period, but along the radiant avenues of immortality—overarched by the palms of undying renown, he moves, while moral triumph sits upon his brow and moral grandeur shines from his face. He rides in a golden chariot whose name is duty. Its wheels are truth and righteousness; the steeds which draw it are reverence for God and love to man. The weapons of his warfare are faith and integrity. He is driving, ever driving toward the sunrise of endless day, with the light of eternal dawn upon his brow. Let us hail and follow him—still our worthy leader!

"Follow light and do the right, for man can half control his
    doom,
Till we see the deathless angel seated in the vacant tomb."

I feel that Shakespeare's description of the king who should be worthy to succeed Queen Elizabeth would finely fit our own great Washington:

"Wherever the bright sun of heaven shall shine,
    His honor and the greatness of his name
Shall be, and make new nations. He shall flourish,
And, like a mountain cedar, reach his branches
To all the plains about him:—our children's children
Shall see this, and bless Heaven."

WASHINGTON, THE VALOROUS

By REV. EDGAR DeWITT JONES, D.D.
Minister, Central Woodward Christian Church, Detroit, Michigan

"A mighty man of valor." I. Sam. 16:18.

This is a Scriptural phrase popular in Old Testament times. It is applied to Gideon, who with his famous band made history; it is used with reference to Kish, the sturdy father of Saul, the first King of Israel; it is applied to David, who while still a lad achieved a reputation for courage; it is applied to Naaman, the Syrian general, who was born to command, and in First Chron-

icles there is a reference to valorous men of Arvad who "hang their shields upon the walls." To be valorous is to be brave, chivalrous, honorable, steadfast, generous, even to a foe. This American nation has known many valorous citizens, men of high courage, faith, and fortitude, and none more so than the great Virginian, George Washington!

Two hundred years have passed since Washington's birth, and one hundred thirty-three years since his death. The master of Mount Vernon has stood the ordeal well. All but deified in the years following his death, placed upon a lofty pedestal by hero-worshipping biographers, he became to the second and third generation, little more than a steel engraving, lofty, alone, and aloof. More recently the iconoclastic school of biographers has had its day and Washington has been taken from his pedestal, his foibles, and petty vanities, exalted out of proportion, yet neither extreme panegyrist, nor zealous iconoclast, has dimmed the splendor of Washington's fame or taken one iota from the glory of his achievements. A mighty man of valor, Washington was, is now, and ever shall be.

BACKGROUND AND BIRTH

The background and birth of George Washington are familiar to every student of American history. He came of gentle breeding. He was a landed proprietor, a slave owner, a fox hunter, a gentleman used to formal functions. He belonged to a privileged class. To be the leader of the American experiment meant that he had to rise out of his environment, mount above his class preferences and privileges. This is a terrible test and few can meet it. It is easier to conquer the environment of poverty and obscurity, than it is to become victor over good fortune, delightful surroundings, turn one's back on rank and ease, and assume the burden of a people's cause. The glory that is Washington's is partly due to the fact that he surrendered his pleasant relations with the favored few in order that he might serve the many and to experience thereby the inevitable ingratitude of an unheeding and unknowing multitude.

"It is good to bear the yoke in youth," avers the author of Lamentations. The youth of Washington was distinguished by self-discipline, privation, much out of door life, and no little experience as a pathfinder. As surveyor, and young soldier, he learned self-reliance, how to manage difficulties, and developed a resourcefulness that afterward stood him well in hand. There was nothing "soft" in Washington's early life. He was not pampered or spoiled. He was reared in the social amenities that belong to his school of gentility, but he was not shielded or spared. He knew what it was to make his bed out in the open under the cold stars on a bleak winter night. He slept in rude shacks and cabins that were not over clean. He cut his way through tangled thickets, climbed rugged mountains, and counted it all in the day's work. There is something ennobling in this kind of training, something Spartan, and thoroughly religious in the discipline of youth, the mastery of one's self and circumstances. No assessment of Washington's greatness can be adequately made that does not give consideration to his having borne the yoke in youth.

Washington was brought up in a school of good manners. He was taught courtesy, gallantry. The word "gentleman" meant much to him. His one hundred and ten rules of civility bear scrutiny. Here is a cluster of them.

"Let the gesture of thy body be agreeable to the matter of thy discourse."

"Sleep not when others speak."

"Read no letters, or books, or papers in company."

"Labor to keep alive in your heart that little spark of celestial fire called conscience."

It would be profitable to trace the effect of these maxims on Washington's character. Deportment ranked high in his estimation. The amenities of life were part of his social creed. He conducted himself in all of his relations with men, women, children, servants, public and private assemblies, upon a high plane of invariable courtesy, grave and thoughtful consideration. Even toward his opponents he was just and kind. A democracy is not supposed to make over much matters, and to belittle those amenities that soften life's asperities. I say "not supposed," for there is an aristocracy of good manners that rightly belongs to a democracy. There is something to be said for Mr. Clifford Raymond's comment: "Washington was an aristocrat. When the United States runs out of his breed it will be out of luck."

IN WAR AND PEACE

The army attracted Washington as a young man. There was much in the soldier's life that appealed to his youthful ambitions. He came by this naturally, for back of him were generations who deemed the soldier's career full of honor and glory. Later in his more mature years he thought war a calamity, became a peacemaker, and his fondest wish, not only for this nation but for all nations, was "peace on earth and good will among men." As the commander of the American troops in the War of the Revolution, Washington was a soldier by necessity and a valorous commander. Military experts may differ as to whether Washington belongs with the mighty military captains of the world. Certainly he was not a Napoleon, a Caesar, or a Charlemagne. He was something more than a military strategist. He took a small body of poorly equipped and inadequately trained soldiers and fashioned them into a fairly effective instrument of battle. It was the good fortune of that army to have Washington at its head. Without him the rigors of Valley Forge would never have been endured. It was his fortitude, capability, and sheer force of character, that held this army together amidst privation, hardship, mutterings of mutiny, and public discouragement, together with political efficiency and often the sheer disloyalty of political chieftains.

As statesman, the valor of Washington was ever in evidence. He was not a constructive thinker in the realm of fundamental and structural politics. He contributed no original ideas to the constitution, yet by the strength of his character, and the power of his personality imparted serenity, strength, and encouragement to the Hamiltons, Franklins, and Madisons, who were destined to do the structural work in that notable convention. He was not a partisan. He brought Jefferson and Hamilton into his Cabinet knowing that they represented different political schools of thought, because he believed the young republic needed their great genius. As he grew older Washington acquired more and more the knack of getting along with men of different types and viewpoints. He brought dignity to the new government, and just enough form and ceremony to save it from swinging out pendulum-like to an informality that might deteriorate into something worse in years to come. The young government seemed stable because Washington was at the head of it, a mighty man of valor presiding over the destinies of the young republic. As one views Washington, so great and grand, in those formative years of the nation, and the people revering him, a famous phrase of the Old Testament comes to mind: "My father, my father, the chariots of Israel and the horsemen thereof."

FAMILY LIFE

Washington was essentially a home man. He loved Mt. Vernon with a very great love. Over and over again in his correspondence and diary he uses the Biblical phrase "vine and fig tree" when referring to Mt. Vernon. He was never so happy as when there. His early morning ride astride a good horse out over the plantation, the sight of his dogs frolicing about his heels, the survey of his crops from seed time to harvest, the superintendency of shipping the produce of his plantation, the stroll through the garden, alongside the box hedge rows, the entertainment of guests at Mt. Vernon, the delightful meals and accompanying conversation at the table, the marked interest in his step-children and other relatives—all these distinguished and haloed Washington's life at Mt. Vernon.

As a family man, Washington's life is full of charm and loyalty. Never having had children of his own he interested himself in the children of his relatives and was almost constantly, for the greater part of his middle and later life, helping some member of the family group. His nieces, nephews and cousins, all seemed to have some claim upon his mind and heart. Martha Washington was a demure and sturdy matron who possessed many admirable qualities. She fits snugly into the lovely picture in Proverbs 31, of "a worthy woman." Life held little for her when the General went out of it and the story of her sitting at a window where she could look out upon his grave for the rest of her days rings true. Memories of Mt. Vernon are fraught with a high type of domesticity, generous hospitality, and a well stocked and well managed plantation—an attractive picture.

Washington was very human. He possessed an innate love of ceremony. "Pomp and circumstance" appealed to him. He loved the feel of good clothes, and graced fine garments admirably. He was naturally a little vain, and recognizing this vanity as a weakness he sought hard to overcome it. He was anything but sentimental, soft, or easy going, yet his emotions were deep and when stirred were impressive. Arnold's treason left its marks upon his soul. The discourtesy of General Charles Lee wounded him deeply. The deceit of Conway added to his discomfort. The plight of Major André grieved him so that he was almost overcome with emotion. He bore himself like a father toward his aide Colonel Hamilton when that young man was little short of insolent. The strange doings of General Gates perplexed him, and the ingratitude of his countrymen toward the close of his second term caused him anguish. He behaved beautifully toward General Greene in the famous Yorktown campaign, making sure that full credit be given him for his heroic service in the south. Yet he had his lighter side. He enjoyed a bowl of punch. He liked the theatre and attended a play whenever he could. He delighted to dance the minuet. He was an inveterate diner out. He loved to ride with his hounds and he liked a horse race. He was not much of a reader, yet was well informed. He wrote a neat hand and when he took pains his literary style was unusually good. He was most methodical in his habits, kept a daily journal, noted the weather, made a record of all his crops, and their progress at various stages, also the birth of puppies and other live stock.

George Washington is a preeminent example of the greatness and influence of character. Compared with his contemporaries he was not their equal in some respects. He lacked the brilliance and creative mind of Alexander Hamilton. He did not possess the versatility and charm of Thomas Jefferson, nor the philosophic wisdom and sense of humor of Benjamin Franklin. He did not have the venturesome political faith of Samuel Adams, nor the expansive and daring mind of George Mason, his neighbor and friend. But in the realm of nobility of character and sheer force of personality, he surpassed them all. Wherever he sat was the head of the table. Coming into his presence, strangers meeting him for the first time, old acquaintances, friends and neighbors, recognized instinctively the greatness of the man.

There is a story which is characteristic, even though it cannot be verified, that a group of his neighbors and friends of many years, waiting for him in the vestry of Pohick Church, agreed that they would not arise when he came in, a custom that they had followed for years without exactly knowing why. Good-naturedly they agreed that there was no particular reason for their getting to their feet every time Washington appeared and found them seated. So they waited, fully of the mind to greet the General as they sat at ease. Suddenly he appeared, and at once every man arose. There was something in the character of their neighbor which evoked this tribute of respect—call it personality, magnetism, or what you will.

Was He A Christian?

Was Washington a religious man? Or, more to the point, was this valorous American a Christian? He was an Episcopalian, and a vestryman of Pohick Church near Mt. Vernon. During his presidency he attended church with a good deal of regularity, though his presence at a communion service is doubtful. It was his custom to retire at the time of holy communion, although his wife invariably remained to participate in the memorial supper. Some of his biographers have explained Washington's reluctance to partake of the communion because he could not reconcile his bloody business as a soldier with participation in the sacrament. This is interesting, but we have no such explanation over Washington's signature. The Rev. M. L. Weems, in his famous though discredited biography, endeavored to make Washington out as an exemplary Christian, pious, thoroughly orthodox, a paragon of doctrinal regularity, but in order to do this he drew freely upon his imagination and disregarded facts with abandon. The truth is the General was reticent upon the subject of personal religion.

Perhaps nothing so reveals a man as his correspondence and diaries, especially the latter. The publication of Washington's diaries is a comparatively recent event, and has thrown a flood of light upon his mind, attitude, habits, likes, and dislikes. These diaries cover the period from 1748 to 1799. They teem with references to his social life, the many dinners he attended, what he ate and drank, his plantation, his horses and dogs, numerous business deals, the plays he patronized; but the myriad pages throw no light on his political or religious views. There are no references to the Bible, prayer, or theology. One of Washington's latest biographers, Mr. W. E. Woodward, claims that the most thoroughgoing search of the General's voluminous correspondence, diaries and public documents does not reveal a single use of the phrase "Jesus Christ". This omission of itself may or may not be important, but it does appear to be characteristic.

It is interesting to contrast with Washington's journal, that of Samuel Pepys, the famous English diarist. Pepys was a constant attendant upon church services, a listener to many sermons, a sermon taster of note. Scarcely a Lord's Day passes without a reference to the church service, the preacher, his text, topic, and how he handled his theme. The case of Pepys indicates that it is possible for one to be a very regular attendant upon religious services without being deeply religious. I hope I do the memory of Mr. Pepys no injustice when I say that, although a faithful public servant, he does not seem to have been either devout or highly ethical in personal conduct. On the other hand, Washington, whose lack of constant attendance upon religious services was as conspicuous as Semual Pepys' fidelity to them, is, in my judgment, the more religious of the two, of a much finer fiber, more conscientious and self-sacrificing.

With regard to General Washington's religion, somewhere between the attempt on the one hand to make him a loyal church man, devout, greatly interested in religious matters, and on the other, the endeavor to portray him as wholly uninterested in religious matters, and unrelated to them in personal conduct and business—I say, somewhere between these two extremes will the truth be found. Certainly he was not critical of religious institutions; on the contrary, he praised them highly. My own conclusion in this aspect of Washington's life, after the reading of many books and the poring over his diary and correspondence, is that, like Lincoln, Washington was not a "technical Christian" and that theologically his views did not differ greatly from those of Jefferson and Franklin.

If by the term "Christian" is meant conformity to the accepted doctrinal standards of his day, habitual reading of the Bible, daily devotions and regular attendance on public worship, then Washington could scarcely be called by that name. If, however, by "Christian" is meant one who believes in a directing providence, the "our Father who are in heaven" of Jesus, and the two laws or commandments that Christ affirmed to be fundamental, "Love of God and love to one's fellow man"; who confesses an obligation to high ideals of honor, justice, truthfulness, and gives himself in sacrificial leadership in behalf of a mighty cause; if reverence for things religious, magnanimity of mind, and generosity of heart—if these constitute a Christian, Washington richly deserves the title. The year following Washington's death, President Timothy Dwight, of Yale said, "If he was not a Christian, he was more like one than any man of the same description whose life has hitherto been recorded."

There can be no doubt but that Washington believed in the beneficent blessings of a religious faith, and the steadying, conserving influences of the institution of the church upon the people. Always he stood for law and order. In public papers, he was not slow to express himself on the subject of religion and morality and the following extract from one of his most famous addresses is evidence of how sincerely he viewed religion as a stabilizer and inspirer of mankind.

"Of all the dispositions and habits, which lead to political prosperity, religion and morality are indispensable supports. In vain would that man claim the tribute of patriotism who should labor to subvert these great pillars of human happiness, these firmest props of the duties of men and citizens. The mere politician, equally with the pious man, ought to respect and cherish them. A volume could not trace all their connections with private and public felicity. Let is simply be asked, where is the security for property, for reputation, for life, if the sense of religious obligation desert the oaths, which are the instruments of investigation in courts of justice? And let us with caution indulge the supposition that morality can be maintained without religion. Whatever may be conceded to the influence of refined education on minds of peculiar structure, reason and experience both forbid us to expect that national morality can prevail in exclusion of religious principle."

Valorous throughout life, Washington with fortitude and serenity faced death. Mercifully, he was not long ill. He rode around his plantation on a snowy day in December, caught cold, had a severe attack of quinsy with complications, suffered dreadfully and in a day and a night was dead. But he showed no weakness or fear in those long hours of suffering. He was calm, composed. He knew that his time had come. He said to Dr. Craik, "I die hard, but I am not afraid to go". He insisted that a colored servant standing at the foot of his bed through a long, weary vigil be seated. He bade his faithful physician not to put himself out for his sake. "I pray you," he said, "Let me go off quietly." And so passed his "strong, heroic soul away."

In the month of August 1826 Daniel Webster delivered in Faneuil Hall, Boston, his impressive oration on the passing of Thomas Jefferson and John Adams. He concluded his tribute to these two luminaries of the revolutionary period with a reference to that heroic group who made the Revolution a success. It is a grand passage. The "godlike Daniel" was never more eloquent. Upon reaching his peroration he said:

"If we cherish the virtues and the principles of our fathers, heaven will assist us to carry on the work of human liberty and human happiness. Auspicious omens cheer us. Great examples are before us. Our own firmament now shines brightly upon our path. Washington is in the clear upper sky."

With this high tribute we are agreed. "Washington is in the clear upper sky." There is a singularity in his career, a glory of character, a splendor of spirit, that sets him apart. There were giants in those days, men to match the mountains; but above them all, in the clear upper sky is this towering character, this mighty man of valor, George Washington.

One thing more: When Washington made his last tour through the Northern States, and had reached the vicinity of Portsmouth, the question was asked, "What title shall we give him?" The venerable Dr. Haven replied with this quatrain which may well close this sermon:

"Fame spread her wings, and with her trumpet blew;
Great Washington is near! What praise his due!
What title shall he have? She paus'd, and said,
Not one, his name alone strikes every title dead."

A mighty man of valor, indeed!

Sermon on the Life of George Washington

By REV. JOSEPH BAER BAKER, D.D.
York, Pa.

Text: "Let the man of God come again and teach us." Judges 13:8

When Webster, upon the death of Adams and Jefferson, spoke of them as having taken their place in the great American constellation of immortals, in whose clear upper sky was Washington, he proved himself a poet as well as a statesman and voiced a sentiment as sublime as it is true.

On this great occasion, the two hundredth anniversary of his birth, we shall honor him best and help ourselves most by praying anew the prayer of Menoah, that "the man of God may come again and teach us."

Let the man of God come again and teach us

The Priceless Value of A Good Foundation

No one ever had a better opportunity to slight his work than Washington did when he surveyed beyond the Blue Ridge Mountains in his youth. His instruments were crude and he had no reason to believe that his markings would be closely checked for many years to come; yet today his record stands as a paragon of professional accuracy and technical skill. His character and his fame rest, like the monument that bears his name, upon a foundation that is deep and broad. He built upon a rock, and fitted the unseen foundation stones of his career as carefully as he laid the plans for his army and cemented the members of the new government together. Washington moved in a straight line from his youth to his death and the direction of that line, like the palm tree's, was toward the sky. He had no weeds of slovenliness, no wild oats of dissipation, no thistles of duplicity to pull out. He sowed the kind of wheat he expected to reap.

Anything but the best was foul to him. While he was away in the Revolution and again as Chief Executive, his property and his fields were allowed to deteriorate, and immediately, upon his return, each time, he set about rejuvenating farms and meadows so that they might yield the best and not the common brand of grass and grain. All this thoroughness was already presaged, in fact guaranteed, in the conscientious accuracy of his youth.

Let the youth of America dip deeply into the youth of Washington in this memorable year. Let them read his Rules of Conduct, ponder upon his industry, marvel at his courage, bow at his reverence. Let them come to his youth as to a hill-top fountain; come with big buckets and dip in often and fill them to the brim each time.

Let the man of God come again and teach us the

Beauty of Sacrificial Service

He was a planter by birth, training, and choice. He loved fields, gardens, cattle, and all the thousand and one associations that cluster about waving grain, singing birds, lowing kine, and sylvan scenes. Yet, for his country, he made himself a pilgrim and an exile the greater part of his life, giving up the spacious acres and the palatial mansion on the Potomac for a tent and the old army trunk that still waits at the foot of his bed for hands that will never come again.

But his sacrificial service went beyond mere absence from home. Every school boy knows the stories of the horses that were shot beneath him, of the holes that bullets pierced in his hat and coat, of the Indian guide who walked a few paces ahead of him and deliberately fired upon him. Again and again he was Abraham and Isaac rolled into one, and, tho spared the actual shedding of blood, as the patriarch was of old, God counted it to him for righteousness just the same.

To his loneliness and danger he also added in the most positive manner the sacrifice of a wageless service. When the eight years of Revolution were over he took not a penny for his services except actual expenses.

It was this perfect abandonment of every vestige of personal gain that made the common people so glad to follow him and gave them such perfect confidence in his counsels.

Away back in 1774 at Williamsburg, in the Virginia Convention, he is reported to have said: "I will raise one thousand men, subsist them at my own expense and march myself at their head for the relief of Boston." That flashed out the spirit of Washington like a meteor and undoubtedly added fire to Patrick Henry, who, the following year, thrilled the colonies with his immortal declaration.

It is high time that we recall him from his grave to teach us anew what unselfish public service is.

"God give us men! A time like this demands
Strong minds, sound hearts, true faith and ready hands.
Men whom the lust of office does not kill,
Men whom the spoils of office cannot buy,
Men who possess convictions and a will,
God give us men."

Let the man of God come again and teach us also the

Immense Significance of Tendency

By many signs, some more obvious and some less obvious, England showed a lordship over the colonies which, to say the least, had a tendency to shackle the very liberties which the first colonists came here to establish. One thing led to another until the Stamp Act called for a tax for the purpose of having the colonies share in imperial expenses.

This would not have pauperized the colonists and none knew this better than Washington; but he knew at the same time that it was the camel's note in the tent and that if it were not promptly ejected the whole camel would soon be in. The principle involved was so menacing to him that he offered his life to counteract it.

The greatest part of his farewell address to the American people at the close of his second term of office is shot thru with the same fear, and he warns his countrymen again and again to beware of party strife and sectionalism. He had the prophet's uncanny vision of things to come, and saw across the years as others see across the street. Let the man of God make us more concerned about tendencies, the tendencies to hysteria, to prodigality, to superficiality, to indifference, to Godlessness.

The appreciation of a tendency is a guard rail at the top of a precipice which is always better than an ambulance at the foot of it.

Let the man of God come again and teach us to

Venerate Our Laws

The population of the United States seems to be made up at present of three types of people—those who flout the laws, those who insist on selecting their own laws, and those who honor all law.

Washington, tho not a lawyer, had nevertheless an appreciation of law, and reached Alpine heights when he said in his farewell address:

"This government, the offspring of our own choice, . . . has a just claim to your confidence and your support. . . . The Constitution which at any time exists, till changed by an explicit and authentic act of the whole people, is sacredly obligatory upon all. The very idea of the power and the right of the people to establish government presupposes the duty of every individual to obey the established government."

None knew better than Washington the weakness of human nature and the fallibility of human judgment, yet he knew also that in the long run humanity would with a drastic and inevitable finality legislate for the best interests of all and that it would therefore result in the greatest happiness to all if all would honorably obey all law.

Let us ponder upon these salutary words anew; let us brood upon them until they flow in our blood, ring in our speech, live in our thought.

In the beautiful words of Lincoln: "Let reverence for the laws be breathed by every American mother to the lisping child that prattles on her lap; let it be taught in schools, in seminaries, and in colleges; let it be written in primers, spelling books and in almanacs; let it be preached from the pulpit; proclaimed in legislative halls, and enforced in courts of justice. And, in short, let it become the political religion of the nation; and let the old and the young, the rich and the poor, the grave and the gay of all sexes and tongues and colors and conditions, sacrifice unceasingly upon its altars."

Washington calls the nation to this worship.

Let the man of God come again and teach us

The Magnificence of A Solid Faith

Ella Wheeler Wilcox said:

"I will not doubt, tho sorrows fall like rain,
  And troubles swarm like bees about a hive;
I shall believe the heights for which I strive
  Are only reached by anguish and by pain;
And tho I groan and tremble with my crosses,
  I yet shall see, thru my severest losses,
        The greater gain."

Washington did. He lost more battles than he won, but he won the war and that was everything. He won the war because he never doubted. When the redcoats sneered at his farmer soldiers in New England, when he lost to Howe on Long Island, when his militia ran from Kips Bay, when he retired from White Plains and was hounded thru upper New Jersey, when cabals worked against him in Congress and in the army, his faith in his integrity, his cause and his country stood out in the sky like invincible Everest. This solitary faith of war days was as magnificent in the civic days that followed.

When France, during his second term, entered upon her Reign of Terror and declared war upon England, thousands upon thousands in America felt that America owed it to France to help her in her struggles, in return for the assistance France had given us. They not only felt it; they declared it from the housetops. Washington, however, was opposed to such action. For this opposition he was roundly flayed by many editors and called an "ingrate to France" and "tool of England." As on previous occasions Washington paid no public attention to his detractors. He knew that their horizons were just beyond their feet and that their prickly plants of scorn would soon wilt under the scorching sun of international events. Resisting an enemy is easy, but to resist a friend on principle takes a man of force. Washington had it, and that is why today he is acknowledged by all to be not only the Father of his Country but the Father of the Army and of the Constitution as well.

Let us learn from him to stand alone, if the inner monitor in the light of facts directs us to, and to stand alone as he did, with that silence that envelops one with triple steel. This was never more necessary in these days when national and international hook-ups can manufacture public opinion almost over night. It still remains true as in the days of old that if we are true to ourselves we cannot then be false to any man.

Because Washington was true to his ideals and never doubted, all the nations of the earth now know something of the sweetness of liberty and most of them know it as well as we do. Millions have followed the rod of his faith to the promised land as the multitude followed the rod of Moses. None but God knows whither our faith will have led our descendants two centuries hence. Ours is but the task to do and dare.

Let the man of God come again and teach us

The Value of A Good Woman

Washington, like Moses and Timothy, Jonathan Edwards and Garfield, was woman-bred. Having lost his father at eleven and having received only the scantiest rudiments of a school education his early training was from his mother. That dignity and courtesy, that exactness and courage, that resourcefulness and honor, that faith and reverence that made it so easy for him to master men while serving them must have resulted in part at least from this training.

In addition to a godly mother he was blessed with a queenly wife, whose wealth of soul surpassed her wealth of lands, as "daylight doth a lamp."

When Washington left Mt. Vernon with Patrick Henry and Edmund Pendleton in 1774 to attend the first Continental Congress in Philadelphia, Martha Washington said as she bade them goodbye: "I hope you will all stand firm. I know George will. God bless you." He wore a miniature portrait of his wife suspended from his neck from the day of his marriage to the day of his death, but her faith in him and her quiet confidence in God meant more to him than a thousand portraits. He only visited Mt. Vernon twice during the entire Revolution, but her love, her letters and the sweet memories of her charm and trust surrounded him with an inner guard more impenetrable and protective than any that he ever chose from his soldiers, and she was at headquarters with him during part at least of each winter.

The benediction of these two noble women upon the life of Washington ought to kindle in the breast of every mother and wife a new joy in their privilege and a new reverence in its discharge.

Kitchen economy adds wealth to any man, but when the ruler of the home adds to that a regnant faith she gives to her husband and her children a fortune that cannot be measured; "her price is far above rubies."

Let the man of God return again and teach us

The Need and Value of Religion

A few literary men have lately belabored themselves considerably in trying to convince Americans that Washington was a very worldly man and had only a dim sense of religion and no religious feeling. If they mean by religion an enthusiasm for doctrinal niceties, or monastic routine, or modern parish practices, we quite agree with them; but what right has a man to demand gracefulness in a life-guard battling with billows or in a fireman rushing thru the halls of a burning building. There are times when all that there is to religion is action, and most of Washington's life was cast into such days. "By their fruits ye shall know them."

Recall his deeds. When he and his men had to beat a hasty retreat over the East River to escape capture by Howe, Washington went over in the last boat. When his bedragged army went into winter quarters at Valley Forge he established his men before he established himself. When Gates with the aid of a clique in Congress planned a Canadian expedition without Washington's consent and had Lafayette appointed to command it, Washington placed no obstacles in the way, even tho the whole procedure was a phase of the opposition to himself. When he was called, after he retired to his beloved Mt. Vernon the last time, to organize an army again for what seemed like an impending war with France, during Adams' term of office, Washington accepted and proceeded to Philadelphia for consultation and planning.

"As my whole life has been dedicated to the service of my country in one shape or another, for the poor remains of it," he said, "it is not an object to contend for ease and quiet."

If these things be not the signs of a man of God and the evidences of true religion then we know not what religion is.

But Washington religion was not entirely in the field of conduct. He knew too well the need of reinforcements to try to carry on without frequent communication with the base of sup-plies. The Divine Base was all the more appealing to him because the military base was often so pitifully poor and intermittent.

Whether or not Washington prayed at Valley Forge in the manner in which Isaac Potts declared, there is as much reason to believe that he did pray at Valley Forge as there is to believe that Lincoln prayed in Washington and Foch in Paris under the heavy weight of their titanic burdens. No man knows the need of prayer like the man who has millions and centuries hanging upon his decisions.

Washington not only attended worship regularly himself when he could, but again and again issued orders that his soldiers should. Even in the wild delirious moments following the surrender of Cornwallis he asked that services of thanksgiving be held and "that the troops not on duty should universally attend, with . . . seriousness of deportment and gratitude of heart."

When he was in York and he found old St. John's of his own faith closed, he went over to Zion Reformed Church and sat reverently through a whole German service, though he understood not a word. Let his detractors match that before they push their scurrilous pens any further.

Furthermore, Washington had what many moderns do not seem to sense, a profound appreciation of the need of religion as a steady underlying base for all permanent social service as well as for morality.

In that noblest of all American political instruments, his farewell address, when, like the Son of God, he seemed to take his own into an upper room, Washington said:

"Let us with caution indulge the supposition that morality can be maintained without religion. Whatever may be conceded to the influence of refined education on minds of peculiar structure, reason and experience both forbid us to expect that national morality can prevail in exclusion of religious principle."

A hundred years ago Webster in his centennial speech expressed the wish that this farewell address might be distributed and read by every American. The need is even greater today, for we are one century more removed from the man of God who wrote it.

Let us turn anew to the God of Abraham, Isaac and Jacob, the "Mighty to Save," the "Ancient of Days," in whom Washington trusted, to whom Washington prayed, whom Washington worshipped.

"Hither to the Lord hath led us."
"Lord God of Hosts, be with us yet,
Lest we forget, lest we forget."

"Let the man of God come again and teach us."

The Man of Mount Vernon

By REV. MARSHALL WINGFIELD
Of Cincinnati, Ohio

In the year 1842 Abraham Lincoln delivered an address commemorative of the birthday of the Father of our Nation. As he brought his oration to an end he gave utterance to these now classic words:

"Washington is the mightiest name of earth—long since mightiest in the cause of civil liberty; still mightiest in moral reformation. On that name no fitting eulogy can be expected. . . . To add brightness to the sun or glory to the name of Washington is alike impossible. Let none attempt it. In solmen awe we pronounce the name and in its naked, deathless splendor leave it shining on."

If no fitting eulogy on the name of Washington could be spoken on the one hundred and tenth anniversary of his birth, how much more is it impossible today, after the passing of almost another century has set the seal of its high approval upon his fame? The remorseless spirit of the hour-glass and scythe dims the lustre of many names, but the name of Washington shines brighter and brighter unto the perfect statesmanship.

Even in the early days the Man of Mount Vernon was seen to tower above his contemporary statesmen of the Republic, and now, like the great shaft in the Capital City which bears his name, and which seems to grow taller as the spectator sails down the Potomac, the figure of Washington assumes more colossal proportions as we pass down the stream of time. When a few more decades shall have passed he will fill the whole horizon of early American history.

It would be easy to devote the entire period allotted to this address to eulogy, but it will be far more profitable for us to inquire into those forces and factors which made the fame of Washington secure.

The initial step in such an inquiry brings us before the question of his heredity. Oliver Wendell Holmes declared that "No great life can be interpreted or appreciated without due consideration to the ancestral forces behind it." This may be undue emphasis on heredity, yet we do well to consider the bearing of his ancestral heritage upon the rich and fadeless fabric of his life. We know, of course, that there is a sense in which all men are not born free and equal; that the sins as well as the virtues of the fathers may be visited on the children for many generations. There are certain hereditary strokes of character by which a family may be as clearly distinguished as by the most pronounced physical features. Hereditary rank may be an illusion, but hereditary tendencies to virtue or vice cannot be denied. All that has been acquired, impressed, or altered in the organization of individuals during the course of their lives is preserved by generation and transmitted to the new individuals which spring from those who have experienced these changes. Hence the intelligent person is keenly aware of Bishop Warburton's observation that "good breeding is a thing none disparage save those who have it not, nor is it an occasion of boasting save by those who have nothing else to be proud of."

This truth is somewhat sobering to the thinking being, even painful, and yet it is not without its attractive phase. For if evil tendencies are bequeathed from parent to child, even so may a predisposition to virtuous ways be passed on from generation to generation.

Washington drew from the blood of his forefathers that element of gentleness which made him a gentleman. His was not the over-vaulting ambition which would mount to glory at the expense of the feelings of others. The story of the youthful plan to go to sea, and its abandonment when he saw what distress such a course would bring to his widowed mother, has only a slender basis; but it is too characteristic of the thoughtfulness for the feelings of others which characterized his whole life, to be discarded entirely. After he surrendered his commission at the end of the Revolution, he hastened, as soon as the weather permitted, to Fredericksburg, Virginia, to visit his "revered mother".

We are told that he was the soul of gentleness in his home, not reserving his smiles and courtesies largely for outsiders, as the manner of some is. All at Mount Vernon loved the evening which was the children's hour. Even during his Presidency, Washington found time to write letters to his youthful relatives, and to go out of his way to express the tenderness of his great nature. Mencius, the philosopher, said that "the great man is he

who does not lose his child's heart." According to this standard Washington was great. His kindness to little children he extended to dumb animals. The sorrel horse which had borne him on many battlefields he turned out to perpetual and unsaddled freedom in the meadows of Mt. Vernon. Likewise many of his faithful black slaves were pensioners on his bounty.

Never did he turn deaf ears to the ancestral voices which called him to be a gentleman. In him was illustrated the truth that:

> "The bravest are the tenderest—
> The loving are the daring."

Washington's environment, no less than his herity, played a part in the shaping of his character. He was not the product of the rectic life of the feverish city. It may be true that "the converse of cities sharpens the wit" but God speaks to men in the solitudes. A roll call of the great men of all ages would show that the majority of them came out of the silences. It is not to be doubted that greater dreams came to Washington in the heart of the wilderness he surveyed than would have come to him upon the Broadways of the world's great cities. "Solitude," said Disraeli, "is the nurse of enthusiasm, and enthusiasm is the parent of genius." Far from "the maddening crowd's ignoble strife" Washington found time to possess his soul of a serenity which deserted him not in the midst of battle shock and the awful orchestra of war. In the quiet valleys of the Rappahannock and Potomac and in the unsurveyed wilderness to the west, he heard nature sing such songs as are drowned by the voice of the city.

But heredity and environment alone cannot account for George Washington. Indeed these forces cannot account wholly for any noble character, for nobility of character comes chiefly from that force within which highly resolves and nobly determines. The son of a noble ancestry, and of good environment, is not great save as he appropriates his heritage by the exercise of his will, for it is within the kingdom of the human will that man comes to greatness. In Washington,

> The star of an imperial will,
> Shone splendid in his breast,
> Serene and resolute and still
> And calm and self-possessed.

Washington willed to know himself, to control himself, and this determination brought his life to sovereign power. Recent biographers have commented on his temper, forgetful of the truth of the old proverb that, "Temper is one of the sinews of the soul; and he that lacks it hath a maimed mind." The passion we call temper, when controlled, ministers richly to life. Strange it is that we pity temper in men and praise it in metal, when one without it is as dull as the other. Aristotle was near the truth when he declared that, "The only trouble with temper is that men exercise it on the wrong grounds, or with the wrong people, or in the wrong way, or for too long a time." It is true that "we do well to be angry at times," but let us not mistake the times. Concerning this phase of Washington's life, Woodrow Wilson said:

"The soldierly young planter gave those who knew him best the impression of a singular self-restraint and self-command. They deemed him deeply passionate and yet could never remember seeing him in a passion. No doubt he had given way to bursts of passion often enough in camp and on the march, when inefficiency or cowardice angered him hotly. There were stories to be heard of men who had reason to remember how terrible he could be in his wrath. But he had learned in the very heat and discipline of such scenes how he must curb and guard himself against surprise, and it was such trials of self-command that made him the finely poised man he became."

In the language of an unknown poet:

"He governed his passions with absolute sway,
    And grew wiser and better as the years wore away."

At no point in his life did this phase of character show to better advantage than under the misrepresentation and calumny which assailed him. He experienced the truth of Shakespeare's words, "Be thou chaste as ice or pure as snow, thou shalt not escape calumny." He yearned for peace and tranquility, and expressed his desire in these beautiful words:

"I am gliding down the stream of life and wish that my remaining days might be undisturbed and tranquil; and conscious of my integrity, I would willingly hope that nothing would occur tending to give me anxiety; but should anything present itself in this or any other problem, I shall never undertake the painful task of recrimination, nor do I know that I should even enter upon my justification. My temper leads me to peace and harmony with all men, and it is peculiarly my wish to avoid all feuds or dissensions with those who are embarked in the same national interests with myself, as every difference of this kind must be injurious in its consequences."

But this dearest wish of his heart was denied him. However, be it said to his everlasting honor, that when assailed he refused to retaliate in kind, nor did reproach and criticism cause him to swerve from his chosen course.

His character was so completely baptized in the Stygian waters of a great purpose, that not one vulnerable spot remained. In the midst of glory he spurned the vulgar greed for fame, and in the chill winter of calumny he held his head high against the storm. His defeats had their victories no less renowned than his triumphs. In his darkest hours he set an example for his countrymen which shall be to the end of time the inspiration to a larger and nobler national life.

In this day when all wise men are decrying narrow nationalism, the message contained in his Farewell Address sounds more like the voice of the future than the voice of the past:

"Observe good faith and justice toward all Nations. Cultivate peace and harmony with all. Religion and Morality enjoin this conduct; and can it be that good policy does not equally enjoin it? It will be worthy of a free, enlightened, and, at no distant period, a great nation to give to mankind the magnanimous and novel example of a people always guided by an exalted justice and benevolence. Who can

doubt that in the course of time and things, the fruits of such a plan would richly repay any temporary advantages, which might be lost by a steady adherence to it? Can it be that Providence has not connected the permanent felicity of a Nation with its virtue? The experiment, at least, is recommended by every sentiment which ennobles human nature."

Such was the exalted statesmanship of the Man of Mount Vernon. How refreshing are these words when the spirit of partisanship tempts men who were born for the universe to so narrow their minds that they give up to party what was meant for the whole human race. Party spirit, like the spirit of religious sectarianism, blinds the eyes of men to the highest interests of humanity causing them:

"Always to vote at their party's call,
    And never to think for themselves at all."

Pope was not far afield when he said, "Party spirit is, at best, the madness of the many for the gain of a few."

And now what are the practical lessons which come to us from reflecting on the life of the Man of Mount Vernon? First of all we are reminded, or should be reminded, that Washington's life is incomplete. Our generation and the generations to follow, must undertake its completion. In the beginning of this address I quoted Lincoln's famous eulogy, the burden of which was that it is impossible to add to Washington's glory. Beautiful rhetoric but wholly untrue in the highest sense. If Washington is the Father of this Republic, as we say, and if the glory of the father is enhanced by the glory of the children, then we can, by our faithfulness to his ideals, add glory to his name and greatness to his fame.

As the architect lives and grows on in the growing splendor of the cathedral he designed but never saw completed, so our illustrious forefathers live on and come to a nobler completion in us. For we are co-workers with those who have gone before, just as the workmen who complete the temple are co-workers with him who designed it centuries before. Remoteness in time cannot affect unity of service.

As co-workers with Washington we are to aspire to that life which exalts a nation, and shun the way which is a reproach to any people. By so living and striving we shall assure all mankind that:

The star of his spirit shall never decline,
But shall shine eternally bright.
We shall add our rays to its glory divine
And all nations shall walk in its light.
His challenging words shall resound near and far
Calling men to a glorious quest,
And the wise and the good shall follow the star—
Liberty's star of the West.

George Washington and Religious Liberty

By THE REV. D. de SOLA POOL, Ph.D.

Sermon Preached in the Spanish and Portuguese Synagogue Shearith Israel,
Central Park West and Seventieth Street, New York City,
on Sabbath Tetsavveh, Adar 13, 5692,
February 20, 1932

"And thou shalt make holy garments for Aaron thy brother for splendor and
distinction." Exodus 28:2

In what special raiment of splendor and distinction shall we clothe our great leader George Washington, whose birth we commemorate this day?

In this shrine of peace, his memory shall not be arrayed with blustering threat of "boom of gun and beat of drum . . . and march of men at arms." Nor would we here invoke the blatant jargon of the patrotic speech that would derogate from the calm nobility of his name written indelibly in the records of America and in the heart of mankind. Nor need we paint once more the picture of George Washington as the soldier, the statesman, the "high minded gentleman of dauntless courage and stainless honor, simple, and stately of manner, kindly and generous of heart," the man of unflinching patriotic purpose, the man of vision as to the future of America.

Rather, in the spirit of this Synagogue, which for close upon three hundred years has known how to combine simply, naturally and without protestation, an unswerving loyalty to Jewish traditions with an unquestionable loyalty to America, we would use this historic occasion to speak of that religious liberty, so vital to us as Jews, which George Washington helped to write into the very fabric of American institutions.

In his days, religious liberty as we now know it was not a well understood, conventional policy. It was a daring revolutionary departure from the universally accepted order. In all Europe, and throughout the New World also, there were established state churches. In this land, too, notwithstanding the pioneer efforts of Roger Williams, Jefferson, Madison and Washington, many of the clergy belonging to the faith of the majority were zealous in endeavoring to see their Church constitutionally recognized and the colonial establishment continued in the new States. To their sincere piety, the state should naturally be, as it was everywhere else, the ally of the universal claims and missionary spirit of the Church. Had not that tradition been set up in this land by the Puritan Fathers when they established here not so much a state as a church policy expressing itself through the forms of a state?

The results of that union of Church and State are all too well known. Those very Puritan Fathers who had sought these shores as a refuge from the intolerant discriminations exercised by a dominant majority Church in the Old World, in their turn here exercised the same discriminations against those whom they regarded as dissenters.

Long before the time of George Washington, Spinoza had asked "what policy more self destructive can any nation follow than to regard as public enemies men who have committed no crime or wickedness save that of freely exercising their intelligence," and, we may add, save that of freely exercising their conscience. Yet this danger existed a century and a half ago in this land, notwithstanding the strong sectarian differences in the religious denominationalism of the thirteen states. Against this danger, George Washington took a firm, determined and consistent stand. Churchman though he was, he could not understand a concept of national liberty which gave physical freedom without spiritual freedom. He declared:

> The cause of American liberty is the cause of every virtuous American citizen, whatever be his religion or descent.

He who had led the fight for liberty understood the words of Leviticus (25:10) cast on the Liberty Bell, "and you shall proclaim freedom throughout the land to all the inhabitants thereof" as meaning freedom of conscience as well as political freedom.

In the eyes of George Washington, this complete spiritual as well as civic liberty had to be not a grudged or a gracious concession, but a right. It was not to be toleration exercised by a privileged majority, it was to be religious equality. Again and again he expressed himself in this vein, as when he wrote to the United Baptist Churches:

> Every man conducting himself as a good citizen, and being accountable to God alone for his religious opinions, ought to be protected in worshipping the Deity according to the dictates of his own conscience.

To the new Swedenbogian Church in Baltimore he wrote words guaranteeing immunity for all religions, together with an assurance that there should be no religious test for holding office:

> In this enlightened age and in this land of equal liberty, it is our boast that a man's religious tenets will not forfeit the protection of the laws, nor deprive him of the right of attaining and holding the highest offices that are known in the United States.

To us Jews, most memorable of all are the words occurring in the greeting extended to George Washington in August, 1790, by our sister Jewish community of Newport, Rhode Island, and Washington's reply. In that greeting, Moses Seixas wrote:

> Deprived, as we have hitherto been, of invaluable rights of free citizens, we now—with a deep sense of gratitude to the Almighty Disposer of all events—behold a government erected by the majesty of the people, a government which gives no sanction to bigotry and no assistance to persecution, but generously affording to all liberty of conscience and immunities of citizenship.

To this statement, Washington, in part quoting the very phrases used by the Jewish community of Newport, replied with the immortal words:

> All possess alike liberty of conscience and immunities of citizenship. It is now no more that toleration is spoken of as if it was by the indulgence of one class of people that another enjoyed the exercise of their in-

herent natural rights. For happily the Government of the United States, which gives a bigotry no sanction, to persecution no assistance, requires only that those who live under its protection should demean themselves as good citizens, . . .

As the President of the Constitutional Convention, Washington labored to translate these broad, and what were then novel and revolutionary, sentiments, into constitutional principles. His attention was forcibly drawn to this issue by Jonas Phillips, a leading member of this congregation. In a memorial presented to Washington as President of that Constitutional Convention, Jonas Phillips asked that there should be no religious discrimination under the federal constitution which was being drafted:

> Then the Israelites will think themselves happy to live under the government where all Religious Societys are on an Equal footing:

and he added with prophetic insight:

> I solicit this favor for myself my children and posterity, and for the benefit of all the Israelites through the 13 United States of America.

In the result, in the first federal constitution adopted in 1787 these classic words were built into the foundation principles of this republic:

> No religious test shall ever be required as a qualification to any office or public trust under the United States.

Yet this did not prove to be a sufficient safeguard. For conscientious observers of the seventh day Sabbath were still fined and imprisoned for working on Sunday. When this fact was brought to the attention of George Washington, he wrote:

> If I had had the least idea of any difficulty resulting from the Constitution adopted by the Convention of which I had the honor to be President when it was formed, so as to endanger the rights of any religious denomination, then I never should have attached my name to that instrument. If I had any idea that the general government was so administered that liberty of conscience was endangered, I pray you be assured that no man would be more willing than myself to revise and alter that part of it so as to avoid religious persecution.

These soothing words were not the suave insincerity of a professional politician, but the sincere conviction of an honest man. Washington encouraged James Madison to draw up the Bill of Rights amending the Constitution, containing the words,

> Congress shall make no law respecting an establishment of religion or prohibiting the free exercise thereof.

Washington probably went still further, for we find included in the treaty with Tripoli the negotiation of which was under his administration, the statement that:

> The government of the United States of America is in no sense founded on the Christian religion. The United States is not a Christian nation any more than it is a Jewish or a Mohammedan nation.

By this definite statement Washington hoped, as he informed the Baptists of Virginia:

> to establish effectual barriers against the horrors of spiritual tyranny, and every species of religious persecution.

This was no mere local American triumph of religious freedom. For the precedent of this stand taken by the Father of our country made it easier in later years for European states to free themselves from alliance with a Church, and thereby to create freedom and equality for Jews and adherents of other minority religious groups living within their borders.

Washington himself took more than one occasion to give public and eloquent demonstration of his own utter freedom from religious prejudice, and his convictions that in this new America all religions must stand on a footing of equality, as when at his inauguration as first President of the United States the whole clergy of this city, including, as we recall with pride, Gershom Mendes Seixas, the Minister of this Congregation at the time, took official part in the parade and epoch-making ceremonies.

It was his hope that the eradication from the statute book of all trace of bigotry would rapidly be followed by its exorcism from men's hearts. Indeed, as he wrote to the Catholics:

> As mankind become more liberal, they will be more apt to allow that all those who conduct themselves as worthy members of the community are equally entitled to the protection of civil government.

In like manner, in his letter to the Jewish community of Savannah, Georgia, he expressed his rejoicing that

> a spirit of liberality and philanthropy is much more prevalent than it formerly was among the enlightened nations of the earth, and that your brethren will benefit thereby in proportion as it shall become still more extensive.

Alas that his roseate belief has been so bitterly belied, and that a century and a half after he wrote these noble words the great majority of our brethren of Israel in other lands are cowering or crushed under social segregation, political discrimination, economic boycott, calculated persecution or bloody violence. When we turn our saddened eyes away from some countries which show these hideous manifestations of man's unholy hatreds in the name of religion, we can with the more devout thankfulness praise God for George Washington.

The words he wrote to this Congregation and to the Jewish community of Philadelphia, Richmond and Charleston, are still gloriously true.

> The liberal sentiment toward each other which marks every political and religious denomination of men in this country stands unparalleled in the history of nations.

The recent appointment to the Supreme Court of the nation of a son of Shearith Israel by popular acclaim and professional demand as well as by presidential choice, is brilliant testimony that the great heart of America still beats true to the principle of equality before the law for citizens of every religious affiliation.

But this great principle for which George Washington stood so strongly, bravely and unflinchingly is not yet fully granted by lesser men with narrower hearts. Eternal vigilance is the price of religious liberty. We must still be on our guard against those who, without daring openly to advocate an overthrow of the constitution, would yet undermine it by a thousand insinuating ways of giving to our government, our public schools, and all our institutions a sectarian character in the pattern of a dominant Church. We must still exercise unresting vigilance against attempts to give such preference to any one denomination in this country as would reduce the adherents of other faiths to a status of more or less tolerated inferiority. We must still exercise unwearying vigilance against the hydra-headed monster of bigotry. We must still combat any violation of the American spirit of George Washington and of the constitution, and preserve our America from any disrupting intolerance within our own borders, whether it be the intolerance of religion or the intolerance of irreligion. Any who may flaunt that constitutional civic liberty and liberty of conscience which we recall today as among the most precious gifts bequeathed to this country by George Washington are untrue to this country. In the measure that we Jews of the United States stand resolute and indomitable to save our beloved country from those whose open or insidious abridgement of religious liberty would besmirch and detract from America's greatness, in that measure shall we be paying our truest tribute of homage to the glorious and immortal memory of the great liberator and protagonist of religious freedom, George Washington.

Let us pray, adapting the very words of Washington:

Almighty God, we make our earnest prayer that Thou wilt keep the United States in Thy holy protection, that Thou wilt incline the hearts of the citizens to cultivate a spirit of subordination and obedience to government, to entertain a brotherly affection and love for one another and for their fellow citizens of the United States at large.

Uphold Thou our government which gives to bigotry no sanction and to persecution no assistance. . . . May the children of the stock of Abraham who dwell in this land, continue to merit and enjoy the good will of the other inhabitants, while everyone shall sit in safety under his own vine and fig-tree and there shall be none to make him afraid.

Sermon on the Bicentennial of the Birth of George Washington

Delivered at the Cathedral, St. Alban's Mount, Washington, D. C.   July 3, 1932

By THE REVEREND S. PARKES CADMAN, D.D., LL.D.
Radio Minister of the Federal Council of Churches of Christ in America

Text: "And a man shall be as an hiding place from the wind, and a covert from the tempest; as rivers of water in a dry place, as the shadow of a great rock in a weary land."—(Isaiah XXXII:2)

I

A. Though the first Isaiah did not attain the prophetic height of Jeremiah's announcement of the New Covenant, he notwithstanding surpassed all Israel's prophets in his mastery of sacred discourse, and the magical resonance of his classic passages. His unfaltering faith in the dominion of the Spiritual over the temporal was combined with his realism as a statesman, his intuition as a saint, and his creative imagination as a seer. That he accomplished what he did against formidable odds, was an achievement worthy of the greatest men of any age.

B. It is therefore appropriate that in this Cathedral, which symbolizes the strength and spaciousness of Isaiah's personality and message, we should commemorate on the eve of our natal day as a Republic, the character and services of another statesman and hero who exemplified the prophet's principles, and was instructed by his precepts.

C. The Messianic Commonwealth associated with the text is still to seek, but it is the nearer because of Washington's devotion as one of its connecting links. Nations governed by aristocracies of character, upheld by enlightened, virtuous democracies, versed in justice and equity, solidified in a common good, and delivered from the atavistic diabolisms of armed conflict, may seem nothing more than an ecstatic mirage on the low dim verge of humanity's horizon.

II

A. The world's collapse traceable to turpitude, chicanery and betrayal; to the lust of acquisition and for illicit pleasure; may seem to forbid the consideration of an Ideal Commonwealth as untimely and inopportune. Is not the churl still abroad, the fool still vocal, the inarticulate still dumb? Indeed, they are, and so they were in Isaiah's vexed and despairing era. Yet his experience of the past kindled his hopes for her future, and our bequest in Washington is so munificent that we, too, can well afford to believe that the God who gave him to us will not suffer His great servant's work to be devastated.

B. Notwithstanding every violation of trust or excitation of prejudice and passion, national and international rectitude and peace are perceptibly more clearly defined and available because of the Virginian gentleman, soldier, patriot and magistrate we have met to honor. His origin and career form an impressive comment on the central teaching of the text: that the extraordinary individual is the favorite channel of God's guidance; the solution of problems otherwise insoluble, the essential nucleus of mass movements for betterment.

C. Washington's singular and exalted fame reveals once more the indispensability in every age and under any political system, the sheer indispensability of those elect spirits who clarify the public mind, animate its mind, sanitate its conscience, and without whose cooperation our boasted democracies are as sheep having no shepherd.

III

A. He was in outward respects typical of his era, and in his hidden qualities typical of the best of all past eras. His first stage was fashioned by the formal thinking and practical tendencies of the eighteenth century. His whole development in its maturity was molded by a thousand years of Anglo-Saxon life and law, and of Norman boldness and initiative. Cautious conservatism and breathless adventure blended in his blood. His farther backgrounds merge into the vistas of Jewish theocracy, Greek political thinking and Roman legalism, which are the headwaters of modern civilization's healing stream.

B. If Washington was not the mythical demigod portrayed by his earlier eulogists, neither did he leave to his keenest censors any posturings, meannesses, or self-interested motives to be exposed. Now, when his humanization is restored to us, and we know that he too was mortal, he continues to be for us and for the race "as the shadow of a great rock in a weary land". To him all eyes turned after Yorktown's surrender, and the ratification of the Constitution. He alone commanded the victories of peace, no less renowned than those of war.

C. He alone could effectively silence factious clamor and rebuke partisan extremes. He alone was entrusted with the unprecedented prerogatives of the Presidency. In none of the thirteen States was any other name than his considered for that office, and to no other candidate would they have handed over the executive functions of the Federal Government.

IV

A. Yet after his unanimous election, which he reluctantly accepted, he became the object but not the victim of an irrational storm of abuse, and villification. Thus began the shameful chapter in our annals inscribed by the calumniator, which is not yet sealed in the oblivion it merits. Denounced as "a snob", "a monarchist", "a tyrant", and even as "a traitor"; his precision, and sobriety were caricatured; his wisest measures perverted. Intrigues and conspiracies beset his administrative path.

B. His name and labors suddenly became sacrosanct after his decease, when many who denied him their sympathetic response while he was alive, tried to make amends by asserting a spurious beatification for him when he was dead. Their tardy tributes ushered in the pseudo biographies which left him lifeless as moonlit marble.

C. The tremendous emotions seething under his customary self-mastery; the fact that though his morals were above the level of his social group, he was no precisian: these and other essentials to his adequate appraisal were ignored. Those who have endeavored to interpret him forgot that his period sorely needed not only political but social readjustment, an educational program equal to the necessities of newly enfranchised citizens, and above everything else, a religious rebirth in spiritual righteousness and compassion.

V

A. In truth, it was Edmund Burke's sublime eloquence, George Washington's majestic being and John Wesley's divinely inspired evangelical zeal, which stayed the destrictive reactions of revolution in English-speaking nations. From their incomparable exertions thus displayed, we may trace the reintegration of those peoples which is still in process; and already offers to mankind one of its finest demonstrations of independence, fraternity, and freedom coordinated by law.

B. Hence, authoritative Britons have praised Washington's epoch-making contribution to the evolution of constitutional government, not only here, but in their own Empire. The largest, most pregnant result of the conflict of 1776 and onward, is the vindication of that government by the crucial tests imposed upon all methods of sovereignty. What remains to be done is in the hand of God, and Time's ameliorating drift.

C. How was it that Washington stood out as the great man of his age, and one of the greatest of all ages? The answer is not found in his intellectual gifts. His contemporaries, Frederick of Prussia, Napoleon the First, Chatham, Fox, Jefferson, Hamilton, Franklin, Adams, and Marshall surpassed him in profound meditation and facilities of expression.

VI

A. It was the very essential we lack that distinguished and lifted him up forever. He was always nakedly true to himself, and more concerned for his conscience than for the opinion of others. He had the moral valor to be what so few are, proudly aloof from the prejudices and passions besieging him. Lord of himself, and the tranquil warrior for truth and right, as he understood these, his unswerving allegiance to duty became the best traditions of his blood.

B. His unyielding integrity entitles him to our grateful remembrance. It made him indeed, "a hiding place from the wind, and a covert from the tempest," a patrician of the Kingdom Isaiah anticipated, "in which dwelleth righteousness."

C. Shall we not keep the Ideal Commonwealth, Washington pre-figured, steadily before our beggared and prostrated age? It has hitherto survived to produce him. Human frailty and disaster have not obliterated Isaiah's vision. On the contrary, at its central flame of hope and assurance, the just and the good have successively relit their lamps.

For we but jest with the memory and the fame of this mighty man if while we praise him with our lips, we give him the lie by our actions. So long as the unfit and the predacious despoil us, we are unclean in the radiant presence of our first Chief Magistrate.

VII

A. If one factor rather than any other stands forth in this dilemma, it is that the individual citizen must foster the intellectual, ethical and religious resources of the nations of the world. Upon him rests the final responsibility for its desirable progress. By him its collective welfare is preserved. "A man" is to be more than our mass movements and herd instincts allow. When he falls below the standard, and what should be rock is sand, social disaster is at our heels.

B. Hence the question is always imminent, and of much more vital consequence than emotional, political essemblies—"how can human nature be elevated above the plane of weakness, ignorance and wrongdoing?" Nothing is decided well until that inquiry is satisfied. Neither education nor legislation can introduce the millenium. The gap between their specifics and national cleanliness, honor and consistency, is apparent. Were Washington here today, I am convinced he would remind us that because we have forgotten this is God's country and world, we have lost the personal character which determines our weal. That is the collapse which mothers all other failure.

C. For Washington could not conceive abandoning his convictions, or hesitate at any sacrifice in their behalf. Can we say this of ourselves? If so, Heaven be praised! If not, why not? Let us, therefore, in God's enablement, renew our allegiance to whatsoever is pure, true, lovely and good report, and pattern ourselves after this grave and matchless servant of the nation. Blessed in him is the Motherland of his forebears; the Republic he brought to birth and baptized in the noblest precedents, and blessed be the Lord our God, who in His benevolent wisdom, gave us George Washington.

WASHINGTON SUPREME

Delivered by

DR. STEPHEN S. WISE, RABBI

OF THE FREE SYNAGOGUE, *New York, and President of the Jewish Institute of Religion in honor of Washington's Bicentennial Celebration, before a Joint Session of the Legislature of State of Rhode Island at Providence.*
February 22, 1932.

"Washington stands out as the supreme figure, in any event, one of the two supreme figures of American history. His statues may be defaced, but his stature can not be lessoned by present-day scribblers who are not interested in revealing the true inwardness of Washington but satisfied, apparently, to disclose the littlenesses and the meannesses of themselves. The debunking process in historical writing can have no relation to the sure fame and name of Washington. That he was less than a perfect mortal has been known too long to give any occasion for concern touching his place in history. This whole so-called "debunking" seems to be little more than an incurable inferiority complex in action, which can not lift its possessor up and is equally ineffective in pulling down the object of its envy and venom. It is well for these gentlemen to learn that there are some figures in history whose place is unassailable by the scribblers. Such figures are Washington and Lincoln, Adams and Jefferson, Hamilton and Franklin.

The supremely interesting thing in connection with the group of men who presided at the founding of the republic is the intellectual and moral stature which distinguished them. It were more than a miracle if that notable company of men had produced a less enduring work. The greatest of them all was Washington who sometimes seems an all but impeccable Roman figure outwardly and inwardly until one comes to think of him as first among his fellows; namely, the supreme example of the American aristocrat. The first of American aristocrats forever proved the folly of the notion that there is no compatibility between the American and the Aristocrat. And, in truth, the Puritan was no less completely the aristocrat than the cavalier. Lincoln, in his rugged, homely, back-woods way was just as truly an American aristocrat and an American gentleman as Washington himself.

What the counsels of Washington would be at this time it is, of course, difficult to say. But one thing is sure—the literalism must be avoided in any interpretation of what might be the mind and counsel of Washington in this hour. Let it be remembered that we can not know what Washington's counsels would be if we think of him as having stood still since the day of his death, 132 years ago. We can not know where he stands. We can know where he would have stood if he were himself and if he had marched forward, as he marched straightforward throughout his days. Surely, it is not unfair to invoke the counsel and, indeed, the shade of Washington in an hour which finds democracy mocked and derided, which find the political sophisticates of our day questioning the validity of the very bases of our political and social democracy. We know it to be true with respect to every so-called democratic or parliamentary government, which either abandoned the parliamentary form of government or is upon the verge of doing so, that the governments of Europe, which have foresworn the parliamentary or congressional system of government, have not, for the most part, made any real experiment in the great field of democracy. Their impatience with the imperfections of democracy grows out of their unfaith, at all times, in its value and validity.

The impatience of some people with the democratic processes ought to serve as a rebuke only to those who imagine that, from the beginning, our American democracy was a finished and perfect achievement instead of being no more than a most humble and tentative and, indeed, imperfect experiment. Such an experiment our American democracy remains, and will long remain, though, indeed, as the most hopeful of all experiments in the world-wide area of government and self-government. To lose one's faith in democracy is, it appears to me, tantamount to treason to the faith of Washington, to the faith and works of Lincoln. What American democracy needs is a dignity of mood, an elevation of tone and a majesty of spirit which, indeed, are for the most part wanting, not because of the lowly masses but because of the impatient arrogance of the classes.

The great question of the hour is, what would be the counsel of Washington in relation to the urgent foreign problems of our nation. To cite his warning against "permanent" alliances will little avail us. There are alliances that are entangling. There are alliances that may be disentangling. There are enslaving and liberating alliances. When Washington uttered his classic warning against this peril, it must be remembered that the American republic had just freed itself from the entanglement of an alliance of domination with the Mother country. The Atlantic had come to be conceived as the highway between national freedom and extra-national domination. In the day of Washington, permanent alliances meant alliances with nations far off, which alliances could be negotiated only after long lapses of time and through the services of remotely stationed ministers and ambassadors.

Today, the Foreign Office or State Department of our nation transacts the larger part of its great and pressing business all but directly and immediately with the remotest capitals of earth. America was bidden by Washington to keep itself aloof from alliances lest these and the freedom of America bring about some coalition of power against its independence. The danger of America losing its political and national freedom no longer stands.

In any decision touching our nation's conduct in its domestic or foreign affairs, let it be borne in mind that the business of America is not business, as was falsely said some years ago by a successor to George Washington—that the business of America is not even marked America; the business of America is to live and go from strength to strength and bless the whole human family. To the counsellors of timidity, let the answer be made that Washington was not a fearful, "stay-at-home," that Washington was not a cowardly reactionary. He was a great, daring, far-seeing pioneer, and the intellectual and political and spiritual pioneering of him and his comrades alike in arms and in Congress created the nation we love.

THANKSGIVING BLESSINGS

NATIONAL GRACE
Written by RIGHT REVEREND JAMES E. FREEMAN,
Bishop of the Diocese of Washington, Washington, D. C.

(1). For these and all Thy gifts, dear Heavenly Father, we give Thee thanks. As we enjoy them make us mindful of the needs of others, and continue to our nation and people Thy favor and protecting care. Amen.

NATIONAL THANKSGIVING PRAYER
Written by REVEREND PETER GUILDAY, Ph.D.,
Of the Catholic University of America, Washington, D. C.

(2). Almighty and Eternal God, from Whose throne above cometh every best gift and every perfect gift, we bless Thy holy Name this day of National Thanksgiving for the merciful Providence which Thou hast bestowed upon our Land and upon our People.

We thank Thee especially today for the Liberty, Justice and Equality won for us a century and a half ago under the leadership of George Washington, who, throughout his career as Citizen, Soldier and first President of our Republic, taught us the supreme lesson of holding fast to those abiding supports of all good government—Religion and Morality.

We pray Thee, Father of Mercies and God of all Comfort, our only Help in time of need, to grant us the grace to follow always in the footsteps of Washington in Uprightness and Integrity of Life, in Patience and Perseverance under sorrow and trial, in Loyalty to American idealism and in a childlike Profession of belief in Thy Divine Providence over us.

We pray Thee, O God of Might, Wisdom, and Justice, through Whom authority is rightly administered, laws enacted, and judgments decreed, to assist with Thy holy spirit of Counsel and Fortitude the President of our country, the Governors of our States, the Members of the Legislatures and of Congress, all Judges, Magistrates and other officers appointed to guard our political welfare, that they may be enabled to discharge the duties of their respective stations to the greater honor and glory to Thy Name.

We recommend likewise to Thy unbounded Mercy, all our brethren and fellow-citizens throughout the United States, that they may be blessed in the knowledge, and sanctified in the observance of Thy most holy law; that they may be preserved in the Union of the Spirit and in that Peace which the world can not give; and after enjoying the blessings of this life, be admitted to those which are eternal. Amen.

NATIONAL THANKSGIVING PRAYER
Written by DR. JAMES SHERA MONTGOMERY,
Chaplain, House of Representatives of the United States

(3). Thou who dwellest in the heavens and earth; Thou who holdest up the soul of the nation and sufferest it not to be moved—unto Thee we pray. Fill our souls with exceeding gratitude and let all the people praise Thee. We thank Thee for our Country, with its broad lands and fertile vales. Thou hast crowned us with honor and given us a responsibility in the moral sovereignty of the world. O God, a rich sentiment has set apart this hour. We pause to pay tribute to him whose dust sleeps on the historic banks of the Potomac. A Republic, undergirded by the best blood and over-arched by Thy Providence, adjourns in memory of him who was first in war and first in the hearts of his Countrymen. The heart of every lover of liberty, every dreamer of the finest ideals of free institutions goes out in praise to Thee. Bless abundantly our land and may its watchwords ever be intelligence, equal opportunity and justice to all. We beseech Thee to allow no discord to mar our national brotherhood, but may all seek to serve all. O soften labor, refine learning and draw all men toward the highest levels of wisdom, knowledge and culture. Open wide Thy sheltering arms to all and enfold our homes in the infinite stretches of Thy mercy and love, and unto Thee be eternal praises. Amen.

NATIONAL GRACE
Written by RABBI ABRAM SIMON, Ph.D., D.H.L.,
Of the Washington Hebrew Congregation, and President of the Board of Education, Washington, D. C.

(4). Heavenly Father, Fountain of all good, we raise our heart in praise to Thee for the blessing of our daily bread. May our appreciation inspire in us the spirit of helpfulness to those who are less fortunate than we are. We thank Thee not only for the food which sustains our body but also for the spiritual nourishment of life, liberty and the pursuit of happiness. We pray that the exalted services of George Washington may come to us as heavenly Manna to nourish our faith in Thee and loyalty to our beloved nation. For the bread of nature's bounty sweetened by the toil of man, and for the living waters of freedom we give Thee our ceaseless gratitude. Praised be Thy holy name. Amen.

A Collection of
George Washington Poetry

Compiled by

BEATRIX REYNOLDS

AND

JAMES GABELLE

FOREWORD

IT HAS been the great experience of my life to serve as Director of the Federal Commission created by Congress to lead the people in celebrating this year the Two Hundredth Anniversary of the Birth of George Washington. While I have ever been a worshipper of the man whom all Americans are privileged to regard as the Father of their Country, this experience has given me a still more intimate knowledge of his life and character, and a still greater respect for his noble achievements. It has thrilled me to see the whole American people rise to this new knowledge and greater love for George Washington, inspired by the Bicentennial Celebration.

The Bicentennial year was one long testimony to that new love, expressed in every variety of form. This collection of the poetry which lives like a wreath of laurel about his memory is but one more touching expression of the new affection in which Washington has come to be held. Since it is the poet's function to put into more beautiful words the thoughts that fill us all, I heartily commend to all good Americans this collection of inspired sentiments in praise of George Washington.

SOL BLOOM,
Director,
United States George Washington
Bicentennial Commission

A Collection of George Washington Poetry

George Washington

Anonymous

Only a baby, fair and small,
  Like many another baby son,
Whose smiles and tears comes swift at call;
Who ate, and slept, and grew, that's all—
  The infant Washington.

Only a boy like other boys,
  With tasks and studies, sports and fun;
Fond of his books and games and toys;
Living his childish griefs and joys—
  The little Washington.

Only a lad, awkward and shy,
  Skilled in handling a horse or gun;
Mastering knowledge that, by and by,
Should aid him in duties great and high —
  The youthful Washington.

Only a man of finest bent,
  Hero of battles fought and won;
Surveyor, General, President,
Who served his country, and dies content—
  The patriot Washington.

Only—ah! what was the secret, then,
  Of his being America's honored son?
Why was he famed above other men?
His name upon every tongue and pen—
  The illustrious Washington.

A mighty brain, a will to endure,
  Passions subdued, a slave to none,
A heart that was brave and strong and sure,
A soul that was noble and great and pure,
A faith in God that was held secure—
  This was George Washington.

Epitaph on Washington

Anonymous

The defender of his country,—the founder of liberty,
  The friend of man,
History and tradition are explored in vain
  For a parallel to his character.

In the annals of modern greatness
  He stands alone;
And the noblest names of antiquity
  Lose their lustre in his presence.
Born the benefactor of mankind,
  He united all the greatness necessary
To an illustrious career.
  Nature made him great,
  He made himself virtuous.
Called by his country to the defense of her liberties,
He triumphantly vindicated the rights of humanity,
  And, on the pillars of National Independence,
  Laid the foundation of a great Republic.

Twice invested with Supreme Magistracy
  By the unanimous vote of a free people,
  He surpassed, in the Cabinet,
  The glories of the field,
And, voluntarily resigning the scepter and the sword,
  Retired to the shades of private life;
  A spectacle so new, and so sublime,
Was contemplated with profoundest admiration,
  And the name of Washington,
  Adding a new lustre to humanity,
Resounded to the remotest regions of the earth.
  Magnanimous in youth,
  Glorious through life,
  Great in death;
His highest ambition, the happiness of mankind;
  His noblest victory, the conquest of himself,
Bequeathing to posterity the inheritance of his fame.
  And building his monument in the hearts of his
  Countrymen,—
He lived—the ornament of the Eighteenth Century;
  He died, regretted by a mourning world.

Man and Mountain

CLARIBEL WEEKS AVERY

A distant mountain range is always blue.
The varying green that ripples round its base,
The lines of ledge that seam its rugged face,
The silver brooks—all fade to violet hue
So men of other days are lost to view
Beneath the common badge that marks the race.
Most men, not *all!* In any time or place,
Some names are ever honored, ever new.

As high above each blue-clad lesser height,
Against the morning red or evening dun,
Some mighty peak stands forth in startling white,
Aloft, aloof, while ages come and go,
So shines the memory of Washington,
Unspotted as the mountain's crown of snow.

Washington in Wall Street

Arthur Guiterman

Sublime, where traffic's billions beat
A nation's wealth about his feet,
He stands; upon the surging street
    He looks benignly down.

He hears the distant, wall-hid sea,
The silver chime of Trinity,
And, voicing passion, grief, or glee,
    Our million-throated town,

And up and down our tasks we ply
With rapid step and heedless eye,
Alert alone to sell or buy;

    But when the day grows dim,
When evening brings its sweet release
From toil and care, when tumults cease,
When twilight crowns his brow with peace,
    The children come to him.

Rejoicing, free, in a careless grace
They climb the massy granite base;
Unawed they view that noble face,
    They swarm the brazen knees

Whose polished surface now denies
The gray of age that artists prize;
But more than art is all that lies
    In love of such as these.

What matters race, or hue or creed
Though born to wealth or born to need,
Or sprung of poor plebeian seed
    Or proud patrician stem,

From lowly hut or lordly hall—
By these his land shall rise or fall.
His hand outstretched above them all,
    Their father blesses them.

Washington

Thomas Marshall

No heroes of the ancient time
    With Washington compare,
No statesman of the days of yore
    Displayed such wisdom rare.

May this great land of ours be true
    To what he said and taught,
And keep his words in memory fresh
    With rarest wisdom fraught.

To patriots all his honored name
    An heirloom has become—
A beacon light to all who seek
    True freedom's peaceful home.

A star of hope in peace and war
    Will be our Washington,
To those who guide the Ship of State
    With favoring gales to run.

· · · ·

The friends of freedom everywhere,
    In this broad land we tread,
Agree to honor Washington—
    His fame still wider spread.

At each recurrence of the day,
    With joy we'll celebrate
The praises of our foremost man,
    Our chieftain, wise and great.

Washington

May Folwell Hoisington

The golden rays of hallowed glory shine
    Upon his name who waived aside a Crown;
And with unfaltering courage, half-divine,
    From failure and defeat brought forth renown.

O Washington, with mind so crystal clear
    Thy thought leaped far ahead and shaped our days,
Wise General of a Nation's hopes, and Seer
    Of future hours . . . thine is the crown of bays!

Washington

Harriet Markham Gill

Oh, Washington, thy noble life
Was like a lantern held by God.
Your acts, like rays of healing light,

Glorified the ground you trod.
Your simple nobleness of soul
Enfolded like a mother's arms,
And drew to you the country folks
Who tended isolated farms;
And won for you respect of seers,
And statesmen far and near;
That shed a glory down the years,
And makes your name so doubly dear.
Oh, Washington, from some high plane
Keep faith with us today. And give
Of higher wisdom you have learned
That we a richer life may live.

Our Washington

C. H. Harrington

Air "Maryland, My Maryland"

O, Washington, great Washington!
Hail to our bravest, noblest son!
In thee, God gave a leader true
To guide our ship, to dare, to do!
Potomac's shores and Vernon's slopes
Gave to the world new dreams, new hopes;
Fate marked this valiant country youth
To fight for freedom, love and truth!

On farm and field he gathered strength,
And wrought full well until, at length,
He led his soldiers, brave and bold,
Through battle's fire and winter's cold.
He gave himself, his heart, his wealth,
For scant reward, and shattered health;
Withstood the thrusts of greed and scorn,
To serve a nation newly born!

O, gift sublime! O, worthy one—
While ages roll, and tides and sun,
Men shall revere thy matchless name,
And add new lustre to thy fame!
O, Washington, great Washington!
Hail to our bravest, noblest son!
In thee, God gave a leader true
To guide our ship, to dare, to do!

Acrostic

The Rev. Samuel Tomb, 1800

G lorious as the orb of day,
E xpelling darkness with his ray;
O h all the nations shedding joy;

R efound his virtues,—spread his fame,
G rateful record th' illustrious name;
E v'ry tongue his praise employ.

W hat nation's round this spacious earth
A dorned by such an Hero's birth?
S hall we not then his death bemoan
H ail him! Ye angels, on his way.
I llume his path, AUTHOR of day.
N ote him, ye Seraphs, round the throne.
G o Down, my soul,—lament thy loss,
T hy mournful country fits in tears,
O n every heart his NAME emboss;
N or let it be effaced by years.

Washington in Art

Gaetano Federici

Carrachi's bust of Washington has the appearance of a Roman commander.

Canova's seated figure recalls the Gattamelata of Donatello.

Trentanove's bust with very close cropped hair reminds one of a Greek philosopher.

Greenough's colossal statue has the appearance of an Olympian Jove.

To George Washington

Robert C. Winthrop

I

Illustrious names in each successive age,
Vying in valor, virtue, wisdom, power,
One with another on the historic page,
Have won the homage of the little hour
Which they adorned, and will be cherished still
By grateful hearts till time shall be no more;—
But, peerless and supreme, thy name shall fill
A place apart, where others may not soar,
In "the clear, upper sky," beyond all reach
Or rivalry; where, not for us alone
But for all realms and races, it shall teach
The grandest lesson History hath known,—
     Of conscience, truth, religious faith and awe,
     Leading the march of Liberty and Law.

II

Yes, century after century may roll,
And bury in oblivion many a name
Which now inspires the lip or stirs the soul,
Giving brave promise of an endless fame;—
Yet still the struggling nations from afar,
And all in every age who would be free,
Shall hail thy great example as the star
To guide and cheer the way to Liberty:—
A star which ever marks with ray serene,
The path of one who from his earliest youth
Renounced all selfish aims, whose hands were clean,
Whose heart was pure, who never swerved from truth;
To serve his country and his God content
Leaving our union as his monument.

To Washington

Elkanah East Taylor

It does not matter now if slow or fleet
Goes the heart's beat,
Or if a tear
Blurs the bright eye of him who lingers here
To read the name engraved upon the stone.
Soldier and sleeper, fighting days are done,
And who shall say
How valiantly on some dark hill one day
You met the foe, waved high the flag of Truth,
Endangered youth,—
With faltering breath
Fought that near victor, Death,
That from defeat might come a final gain
To recompense your pain.

Like the great Martyr, you devoted life
That hate and greed and strife
Be vanquished, and to bring that day
Of brotherhood when Life would tread the way
Linked arm and arm with Love and Truth,
And when each lusty youth
Would know a sure surcease
From war's red harvest and could live in peace.

Oh, sleeper, soldier, is your dream denied,
Or is the dream come true . . . and are you satisfied?

Washington, The Lonely Man

Annie Southerne Tardy

Companioned by grim loneliness, he missed
    The dearest joy of earth. Pledged mind and heart
To common weal, he yet could not resist
    The urge to live his inmost life apart.

Home did not bring the happiness that might
    Have been for him, had unkind fate but smiled,
Though life went on its quiet way, despite
    His solitary soul, unreconciled.

Alone in bitter war, though some would fain
    Have sought the heights of generalship which he,
With clear unselfish vision could attain,
    To lead the weary road to victory.

Alone in war's tumultuous aftermath,
    He only, showed the wise and lasting good;
No hand but his could clear the tangled path.
    No heart assume his country's fatherhood.

No one too high to do him reverence,
    No one so loved as this American
Who was his country's safe and sure defense,
    Yet Washington was still a lonely man.

Washington's Statue

Henry Theodore Tuckerman

The quarry whence thy form majestic sprung
    Has peopled earth with grace,
Heroes and gods that elder bards have sung,
    A bright and peerless race;
But from its sleeping veins ne'er rose before
    A shape of loftier name
Than his, who Glory's wreath with meekness wore,
    The noblest son of Fame.
Sheathed is the sword that Passion never stained;
    His gaze around is cast,
As if the joys of Freedom, newly gained,
    Before his vision passed;
As if a nation's shout of love and pride
    With music filled the air,
And his calm soul was lifted on the tide
    Of deep and grateful prayer;
As if the crystal mirror of his life
    To fancy sweetly came,

With scenes of patient toil and noble strife,
  Undimmed by doubt or shame;
As if the lofty purpose of his soul
  Expression would betray,—
The high resolve ambition to control,
  And thrust her crown away!
O, it was well in marble firm and white
  To carve our hero's form,
Whose angel guidance was our strength in fight,
  Our star amid the storm!
Whose matchless truth has made his name divine,
  And human freedom sure,
His country great, his tomb earth's dearest shrine,
  While man and time endure!
And it is well to place his image there
  Upon the soil he blest:
Let meaner spirits, who its councils share,
  Revere that silent guest!
Let us go up with high and sacred love
  To look on his pure brow,
And as with solemn grace he points above,
  Renew the patriot's vow!

Elegy on the Death of George Washington

Rev. Peter Whitney, A.M.

Set to Music by Captain Abraham Wood, sung in Northborough and Many other places in 1800

Know ye not that a great man hath fallen to-day.
Yeah we know it, Yea we know it, Yea we know it.
Hold thou thy peace.
Mourn, mourn, mourn, mourn, O, Americans for
  WASHINGTON'S no more.
"Reft his dear fword beneath his head;
Round him his faithful Arms fhall ftand;
Fix his bright Enfigns on his bed,
The guards and honors of our land.
Fair liberty in Sables dreft,
Write his loved name upon his Urn,
WASHINGTON; the fcourage of Tyrants paft,
And awe of Princes yet unborn.
Glory with all her lamps fhall burn,
And watch the warrior's fleeping clay,
'Till the laft triumphs of the day.
Great Soul we leave thee to thy reft;
Enjoy thy Jefus and thy God,
Till we, from bonds of clay releas'd,
Spring out and climb the fhining road,

"Earthly cavern, to thy keeping
We commend our brother duft,
Keep it fafely foftly, fleeping,
'Till the Lord demand thy truft.
Sweetly fleep, dear Saint, in Jefus,
Thou with us fhalt wake from death;
Hold he cannot, though he feize us
We his power defy by faith.
Jefus, thy rich consolation,
To thy mourning people fend;
May we all, with faith and patience,
Wait for our approaching end.

The Trip to Cambridge

(JULY 3, 1775)

Unknown

Tory balladists found rich material for their rhymes in the undisciplined and motley army of which Washington was the head. Due, however, to the commanding personality of the great commander there were very few attacks leveled at his head. We herewith present one of the few that have survived.

When Congress sent great Washington
  All clothed in power and breeches,
To meet old Britain's warlike sons
  And make some rebel speeches.

'Twas then he took his gloomy way
  Astride his dapple donkeys,
And traveled well, both night and day,
  Until he reach'd the Yankees.

Old mother Hancock with a pan
  All crowded full of butter,
Unto the lovely Georgians ran,
  And added to the splutter.

The rebel clowns, oh! what a sight!
  Too awkward was their figure.
'Twas yonder stood a pious wight,
  And here and there a nigger.

Upon a stump he placed (himself),
  Great Washington did he,
And though the nose of lawyer Close,
  Proclaimed great Liberty.

The patriot brave, the patriot fair,
  From fervor had grown thinner,
So off they march'd, with patriot zeal,
  And took a patriot dinner.

What He Means To Me

Phyllis-marie Arthur

Let other praise his statesmanship and tell
  The glory he has for his country won.
  On what he means to me I humbly dwell.
  I feel that would please George Washington.

Besides the thrilling tales of Mother Goose,
  I learned the story of the cherry tree.
  And that's the tale that I most always choose,
  When teaching my two children honesty.

His military prowess was revealed
  To me as o'er my college desk I bent.
  Now I recall his courage on the field
  When dark skies frown their black discouragement.

Oft as I work to fill the cookie jar,
  I see his noble face there on the wall,
  Smiling upon the laundry calendar.
  Saying, it seems to me, "I've suffered all."

My son who has a stamp collection buys
  The first stamps of the Washington issue.
  My daughter who is fashionable now cries
  That every frock must be red, white or blue.

Even their father plants a little tree
  Mild evenings when the day's hard toil is done.
  These are the humble things he means to me.
  I feel that it would please George Washington.

Washington

Noureddin Addis

Fear brooded o'er the land, and stygian
Black clung the pall of dread upon men's lives,
That tyrant hand had forged anew strong gyves
To re-enfetter hearts that for a span
Of years had known that joy elysian
Is liberty. And up from homes and hives
Of industry prayers rose to Him who strives
Within us ever; that God might call a man!

In Philadelphia that magic year
A congress, Washington among the rest,
Deliberated. Since history began
Such gathering was ever without peer,
Which mustering at liberty's behest
Spoke Heaven's choice. Thus did God call a man!

Now redly through that cloud of dark dismay
Leapt thunderbolts of war; as dread suspense
Yielded to certitude. A struggle tense
And ruthless gulfed the world; and some gave way
To moan, "You know not British pluck," while gay
Hearts quailed for fear that out of indigence
And want, America might perish—hence
"We do not know . . . against them we are clay."

As well have stormed in rage against the tides
As Washington. He knew and stood like steel,
Assured that Heaven did battle for the right.
His simple faith outweighed the world besides,
Assured that God warred for the commonweal,
America—great freedom's neophyte.

Peace came at last: America breathed praise.
Those fearful years of war had taken toll,
Scribing immortal thousands on the scroll
Of tragedy and loss. A world ablaze
With freedom, kindled of those deathless days,
Did reverence the name of yon great soul,
George Washington, who from that motley whole
Wrought unity—a light to nobler ways.

Ended the storm, the warfare done. Acclaim
Had not puffed up the land that bore the palm;
Nor yet the soldier-statesman to whom all
Old earth paid tribute. Neither could the fame
Which rang round all the globe molest his calm
Awaiting now serenely God's last call.

Washington

OUR COUNTRY'S PRIDE AND FAME

Henry Felton Huse

Man of the out-of-doors who loved
  The trails through forests wide;
Afoot, ahorse, at home was he
  From dawn till eventide.

Self-disciplined in character,
  With faith and brotherhood;
Throughout the years, from first to last,
  He sought the common good.

Vision was his America!
  A nation great and free;
Time, talents, leadership he gave,
  That it might come to be.

Illustrious! With love we speak
　　His great and honored name;
The first among Americans,
　　Our country's pride and fame.

Washington the Beloved

Leroy Elmer Bentley

It was bitter cold.
And he, on bended knee,
Prayed as never soldier prayed.
And those of his fold
In the wood, they understood
In bare feet and garments frayed.

Washington

Isabelle V. Hayward

Genius has written, lesser scribes extolled
　　His virtues, Artist's, skilled, have done their
　　　　part
To give the perfect semblance of his face,
　　But not for us to know the hero's heart.

Those inmost questionings whence came the grave
　　Decisions—Onward, on, nor count the cost,
Or calmly waiting guidance of his faith—
　　Delaying warily, lest all be lost.

If he knew faithless moments of despair—
　　He was but human, yet took stern command
Of self, and with a higher courage led
　　His fellow patriots on to firmer stand.

Maybe he visioned all that freedom meant—
　　Felt in his heart the fires of victory glow—
Perhaps he prayed for strength to bear defeat—
　　He may have fought more battles than we
　　　　know.

But freedom won, he served the land he saved,
　　Wise in counsel that unrest might cease,
And to his country through the strife of war
　　He brought the crowning victory of Peace.

For Liberty

Lyman Bradley

Great Washington sat in council.
A sentry came and whispered low,
A message for that general's ear alone.
He rose, and with some hasty words
Excused himself, and left the room.
Hamilton, Lafayette and Green
Eyed each other in deep concern
As if to ask: "What can this mean?"

A drummer boy lay dying.
Sore wounded, he moaned his life away.
His eyes brightened as he beheld
His chief bend over him.
"I knew you'd come, sir," he gasped.
"I wanted to see you so,
To speak to you face to face.
Tell me, sir, shall we one day
Be free?"

"Under God, we shall," the leader said,
Laying his hand in silent
Benediction
Upon the clotted and fevered brow.

"Thank God! I die for liberty,"
The boy cried out in gladness
Raising himself, he gave his Chief
A fervent, long salute,
Then fell back—dead.

Elegaic Verses

John Searson, 1800

On the decease of His Late

Excellency,

The Illustrious and Ever-Memorable

Great and Good
George Washington,
Of Immortal Memory.

Oh! is he gone and left behind
Millions to mourn him in their mind;
With agonizing hearts they cry,
Alas! must our great gen'ral die!

Physic alas! could do no good,
No, no, nor all our earthly food;
O death thou sparest none that live,
But to thee all our lives must give.

See angels guard the good man's bed,
Because to heav'n he's surely fled:
To heav'n from earth, he took his flight,
Angels his guard and their delight.

Hero Immortal

James M. Stewart

Hero immortal! Who, the bards among,
    Shall, with fit eulogy, the theme prolong?
To worthier harp the triumph should be sung,
    To grand career the minstrels' thought and song.

If to thy honor were a shaft to rise,
    In classic grace beseeming thy renown.
The glorious marble should invade the skies,
    With Heaven's eternal sunlight on its crown.

Leader of men! in every mood sublime!
    Thy wisdom taught thee to be truly free;
And thus thy life, adown the stream of time,
    Passed on, like tranquil river to the sea.

'Tis well! thy latest words when leaving earth;
    For death alone could be thy greater gain;
And wise men deem thee, when they measure worth
    One of the few that have not lived in vain.

Beloved! Revered! What time the orb of day
    Shall cease to circle Earth with path of flame;
When stars shall leave the sky and pass away,
    And Heaven's historian read the roll of fame;

The angel of the trump, on pinions spread,
    Shall to the worlds proclaim the great award:
A crown of light auroral for thy head,
    Gemmed with the brightest jewels of the Lord.

Mount Vernon! Washington! Once more I press,
    With fancy's feet, the laws he loved so well;
Again I turn the noble dust to bless,
    And list the requiem of the passing-bell!

Soft is the bed whereon a patriot lies!
    His memory rich whose name to honor moves!
He sleeps serenely, who has won the prize!
    He rests in virtue whom the Lord approves!

Masonic Hymn

George Richards

*Composed for the funeral obsequies; and sung at
St. John's Church, December 31, 1799*

At God's imperial, high decree,
Our Master sleeps in dust;
His Brethren bend the prostrate knee;—
Thy WILL, O GOD is just.

That Will, GRAND MASTER, MOST SUBLIME!
Lent him to guide our way;
When darkness wrapp'd COLUMBIA'S clime,
And veiled the LIGHT OF DAY.

That WILL beyond the storm of war,
Our Masters steps conveyed;
Our BROTHER left his trophied car,
And fought Mount Vernon's shade.

In War, in peace; in War again,
COLUMBIA'S voice is heard;
A master, Brother, cried AMEN,
And bowed to Adams' word.

His Godlike courfe of glory run—
HEAV'NS ROYAL ARCH sublime;
'Mid MORN'S bright star and Light's full Sun,
Enthrone his foul divine.

IMMORTAL MASTER, Brother, hail:
Adieu, farewell, adieu;
The Caffia sprig, in Glory's vale,
Is bathed in VIRTUE'S dew.

Washington

Rev. Dennis O'Crowley

Thou gallant Chief whose glorious name
Doth still adorn the Book of Fame:
Whose deeds shall live while freemen prize
The cause for which the Patriot dies,
Long to Columbia may'st thou be
The beacon light of Liberty.

A Jeweled Name

Myra Belle Dungan

A jewel blazing brighter with each sun—
A dazzling name is thine, O Washington!
Our country ill could spare thy noble worth,

Although a foreign shore might give thee birth.
Like Moses, you the side afflicted took,
The tyrant's hand and power of terror shook;
Another David, shared the camp and field
Till strong, embattled hosts were forced to yield.
Then, armed with right, your feeble Gideon band
Banished the proud oppressors from our land.
For "not by might and not by power" 'tis said,
But by the Lord Jehovah wast thou led.
We honor thee—thy manhood, courage, skill,
Self-sacrifice, indomitable will,
Thy statesmanship, so masterful and strong
That even proud England sings thy praises long;
Erects at last a monument to thee,
Her debt acknowledged—thy true loyalty.
And we, who knew thee better, still shall sing
Thy praises down the centuries as they ring.
Though other heroes hold exalted place,
Thy name, the first, our nation's page shall grace;
Recounted worth each year add greater glow,
Because "first in our hearts"—'tis ever so.

George Washington

Schuyler E. Sears

The leader of a little haggard band
Dared to confront trained armies of a king;
So valiant was this leader's compassing
That soon, a hero, he possessed the land,
And snatched its freedom from despotic hand
And placed it 'neath the strong peace-angel's wing.
Since then the nations fairest tributes bring
To crown him "Father of his Country" grand.

We should not think alone of victories gained,
Nor should we think alone how he endured
In those historic conflicts one by one;
But we should think of that great faith unfeigned
And help from heaven his righteous cause secured—
That faith in God and man made Washington.

Mount Vernon

Grace Evelyn Brown

*(After George Washington's death, Martha changed her room
to a small one at the top of the house, because its
window looked out on George's tomb.)*

That window—Martha's. When her lord had died
She soon forsook the larger lower room;
For this small attic looked out on his tomb.

Across the grass to where the waters glide,
She gazed upon his sepulcher beside
Those ancient trees, while roses dropped their bloom.
Great clouds disperse and lofty stars still loom
Above the years that mortal dreams denied.

Yet now she seeks no more his honored dust
In that dark silent place above the river.
The little window, blank, forgotten lies;
For love meets love because it always must.
In that old garden, light as moonbeams quiver,
Their presence merges into raptured skies.

Washington

Edwin Thomas Whiffen

A tower—a light upon a shouting sea
Of blowing war and faction—till it shone
The small dawn of the larger day to be—
This tower—this light in darkness—Washington.

December 1783

B. Phillip Freneau

*Occasioned by General Washington's Arrival in Philadelphia,
on His Way to His Residence in Virginia*

The great unequal conflict past,
  The Briton banished from our shore,
Peace, heaven-descended, comes at last,
  And hostile nations rage no more;
From fields of death the weary swain
Returning seeks his native plain.

In every vale she smiles serene,
  Freedom's bright stars more radiant rise,
New charms she adds to every scene,
  Her brighter sun illumes our skies.
    Remotest realms admiring stand,
    and HAIL the hero of our land:

He comes!—the Genius of these lands—
  Fame's thousand tongues his worth confess,
Who conquered with his suffering bands.
    And grew immortal by distress:
    Thus calms succeed the stormy blast,
    And valor is repaid at last.

O WASHINGTON!—thrice glorious name,
  What due rewards can man decree—
Empires are far below thy aim,

And sceptres have no charm for thee;
    VIRTUE alone has your regard,
    And she must be our great reward.

O say, thou great exalted name!
    What Muse can boast of equal lays,
Thy worth disdains all vulgar fame,
    Transcends the noblest poet's praise.
        Art soars, unequal to the flight,
        And genius sickens at the height.

For States redeem'd—our western reign
    Restor'd by thee to milder sway,
Thy conscious glory shall remain
    When this great globe is swept away
        And ALL is lost that pride admires,
        And all the pageant scene expires.

The Unrevealed

Louise Crenshaw Ray

Upon tradition's walls are hung
A score of portraits which reveal
The patriot who is first among
His country's great—a man of steel

And wisdom; first alike in war
And peace. We see him elderly,
Distinguished, distant as a star;
Or looking back to battles, see

Him in a hail of bullets, lead
His men to victory—a bold,
Intrepid warrior. We read
Of Princeton, Valley Forge, the cold

And starving ranks who followed him
Across a river's icy span
To freedom. Then the pictures dim . . .
We know but half of any man;

The man disclosed is great and wise
Though half is hidden from our view;
What if our minds could visualize
The Washington whom no man knew?

The Cornerstone

Beatrix Reynolds

Just a wholesome lad
    Simple, full of fun,
Active, gay and blithe,
    The little Washington.

Just a tall young man,
    Eager for his work
In the unknown wilds,
    Where the dangers lurk.

Just a soldier who
    Fought and kept his head,
And saved his regiment
    Though Braddock lay there dead.

Just a leader then
    Who knew the way he trod
Would bring annihilation
    Without the help of God.

Thus a statesman wise
    Had grown to be our guide
In building these United States—
    And he has never died!

From "Age of Bronze"

Lord Byron

Washington's a watch-word such as ne'er
Shall sink while there's an echo left to air.

Washington

Rosa A. Langtry

He kneeled alone upon the snow and prayed;
    Great things are shown to man in solitude,
The anguished spirit, tortured, broken, flayed,
    By God's grace, flames its fires of brightest good.

The wind shrieked from the hills at Valley Forge,
    A note of freedom in its ceaseless cry;
He heard it not, upon his soul, the scourge
    Of war, gray as the sky, hung heavily.

Though chilled by icy blasts that struck afresh,
    He ceased not, low, his intercessions rose;
Drawing their rags across their cankered flesh
    Up stood his starving men to face their foes.

The world is quiet now, my lamp is dim,
    My dog, relieved from charge of kine and sheep,
His supple body rests, and lax of limb,
    He lies beside me, on the rug, asleep.

The clock in happy reminiscent mood,
Singing each quarter hour its lulling chime,
Joins in my rituals of gratitude,
Builded along the journeyings of Time.

These are my acres, this my peaceful Home,
My country's gift to my forebears and me,
Assigned by battle lines, and blood dipped foam,
Won by the sons of war on soil and sea.

Washington

Jessica Morehead Young

We realize the greatness as time flies,
Of Washington, the many perils trace,
The dangers in the wilderness, to face.
The chieftain's arrows, as concealed he tries
To take the life of him who was so wise
And showed such courage, in each trying place.
He tempered justice with a kingly grace
To enemies, herein his greatness lies.

He loved his friends, his family and his home,
And when not battling for his country, there
He planted trees, and vines, and tilled the loam;
Left to posterity Mount Vernon,—where
He lived and died, the greatest of them all;
Who never failed to heed his country's call!

Washington

Nell Mace Wolfgang

We speak his name with reverence
And sing his noble name in song,
He who belongs to the ages—
But walks now with the busy throng.
He's "The Father of His Country"
And justly earns his honored name
As the hero of all masses
Who constantly repeat his fame.

And our nation's firm foundation
Was proudly built with his insight,
Which will prosper from his vision
Of truth, honor, justice and right.
Oh, noble name of Washington—
Whose well earned glory cannot die!
As it lives through countless ages
And on through every battle cry!

The Light Perpetual

James Gabelle

George Washington
Is a beacon
Light
Across a dark
And stormy sea;
Sending
A ray of hope
To every
Storm-tossed
Soul.

A Man!

Clinton Scollard

About his brow the laurel and the bay
    Was often wreathed,—on this our memory
        dwells,—
Upon whose bier in reverence today
    We lay these immortelles.

His was a vital, virile, warrior soul;
    If force were needed, he exalted force;
Unswerving as the pole star to the pole,
    He held his righteous course.

He smote at Wrong, if he believed it Wrong,
    As did the Knight, with stainless accolade;
He stood for Right, unfalteringly strong,
    Forever unafraid.

With somewhat of the savant and the sage,
    He was, when all is said and sung, a man,
The flower imperishable of this valient age,—
    A true American!

Tribute to Washington

From a London Newspaper

Great without pomp, without ambition brave,
Proud, not to conquer fellow-men, but save;
Friend to the weak, a foe to none but those
Who plan their greatness on their brethren's woes,
Aw'd by no titles—undefil'd by lust—
Free without faction—obstinately just;
Warm'd by religion's sacred, genuine ray,
That points to future bliss the unerring way;
Yet ne'er control'd by superstition's laws,
That worst of tyrants in the noblest cause.

To George Washington

(Pater Patriae)

Clarence L. Haynie

You sleep in majesty beside the stream,
　　Whose rippling music echoes endless praise;
On earthy couch you realize the dream
　　Whose glow illumined all your humble ways.
At Valley Forge you knelt for us in prayer,
　　And fought your way to victory and fame;
You kindled love of country's brilliant flare,
　　And all the world pays homage to your name.

You taught the beauty of eternal truth,
　　And surveyed paths through tangled solitude;
Your early life inspires the heart of youth
　　To heights beyond this earthly interlude.
You wrote our country's newest, brightest page,
And gave us freedom of our heritage.

Washington

Lillian Winters

Long years have passed since first you fought
And from the chaos you have wrought
A country.　Heaven blest.
As time rolls on it stands the test, of years.
It's people, noble race, mid cheers and tears
Stands staunch in time of need and without fear.

Had you but known your effort would have gained
A country rich in blessings, rich in fame
As stands today.　Your dreams achieved
Far passed your power to perceive.
We stand in awe on this your day of birth
And praise God for this country, on this earth.

Washington Crosses the Delaware

December, 1776

Clinton Scollard

That night upon the Delaware
　　Their horns the wild Valkyries blew
As though the legions of despair
　　Swept the impending heavens through.
The Fates and Furies rode the air
That night upon the Delaware.

The ice-pack gnawed the sodden banks,
　　Sundered and rocked the middle stream;
There ran a murmuring through the ranks
　　As at some dread, foreboding dream.
Amid the crunch of splintering planks
The ice-pack gnawed the sodden banks.

The trees seemed wan and wizened ghosts,
　　And groped the mists with shriveled hands;
Weird was that gathering of hosts,
　　The massing of those tattered bands.
On those inhospitable coasts
The trees seemed wan and wizened ghosts.

Yet valorous their victory
　　That gray and grim December dawn;
What quenchless fires of destiny
　　Burned in his breast who led them on!
For us, and for futurity,
How valorous their victory!

"George Washington We Honor You"

J. Milton Swartz

(Tune—"The Son of God Goes Forth to War")

　　George Washington, we honor you,
　　　　And gather on this day:
　　For the dear old Red, White and Blue
　　　　You started on its way.
　　A mighty Nation founded true,
　　　　Triumphant over fray,
　　Your Spirit ever guides us through,
　　　　We to you homage pay.

　　All Hail, the Nation's greatest son,
　　　　From whom much wisdom came,
　　We sing your praises Washington
　　　　And shout with loud acclaim.
　　To you, America's noblest one
　　　　Who built with sword and flame,
　　And as through centuries, we run
　　　　We will revere your name.

　　Two hundred years, we celebrate
　　　　Your birth with greatest pride,
　　In every town, in every state
　　　　And o'er the Nation wide:
　　Unfurl all banners, curb all hate
　　　　Let Patriotism ride,
　　And Washington, forever great
　　　　Oh be our constant guide.

Young Washington

Arthur Guiterman

(*The Embassy to the French Forts, 1753*)

Tie the moccasin, bind the pack,
Sling your rifle across your back,
Up! and follow the mountain track,
    Tread the Indian Trail.
North and west is the road we fare
Toward the forts of the Frenchmen, where
"Peace or War!" is the word we bear,
    Life and Death in the scale.

The leaves of October are dry on the ground,
The sheaves of Virginia are gathered and bound,
Her fallows are glad with the cry of the hound,
    The partridges whirr in the fern;
But deep are the forests and keen are the foes
Where Monongahela in wilderness flows;
We've labors and perils and torrents and snows
    To conquer before we return.

Hall and council-room, farm and chase,
Coat of scarlet and frill of lace
All are excellent things in place;
    Joy in these if ye can.
Mine be hunting-shirt, knife and gun,
Camp aglow on the sheltered run,
Friend and foe in the checkered sun;
    That's the life for a man!

War and Washington

Jonathan Mitchell Sewall

*This was one of the most popular metrical productions
and was sung by soldiers and civilians throughout
the Revolution.*

Vain Britons, boast no longer with proud indignity,
By land your conquering legions, your matchless
    strength at sea,
Since we, your braver sons incensed, our swords have
    girded on,
Huzza, huzza, huzza, huzza, for war and Washing-
    ton.

Urged on by North and vengeance those valiant
    champions came,
Loud bellowing Tea and Treason, and George was all
    on flame,

Yet sacrilegious as it seems, we rebels still live on,
And laugh at all their empty puffs, huzza for Wash-
    ington!

Still deaf to mild entreaties, still blind to England's
    good,
You have for thirty pieces betrayed your country's
    blood.
Like Esop's greedy cur you'll gain a shadow for your
    bone,
Yet find us fearful shades indeed inspired by Wash-
    ington.

.   .   .   .

Proud France should view with terror, and haughty
    Spain revere,
While every warlike nation would court alliance
    here;
And George, his minions trembling round, dismount-
    ing from his throne
Pay homage to America and glorious Washington!

George Washington

Mrs. Elsie J. Cosler Campbell

Upon Mount Vernon's fertile soil
A ruler's body lies, no spoil
Of triumph turned this man of toil
From those steadfast ways of his,
From love of home and family,
From faith and hope and charity,
From his dear country's destiny,
Nor from a guiding God that is.

From Washington's uncrowned, noble head,
And gentle heart that often bled,
The words of courage that he said,
America's golden crown was made—
A crown of the ideals true—
Ours! held by he and I and you,
To pass on, future ages through,
In glory that shall never fade.

At the Tomb of Washington

Clinton Scollard

Here let the brows be bared
    Before the land's great son,
He who undaunted dared,
    Our Washington!

From dole, despair and doubt,
    Deceit and enmity,
He led us up and out
    To Victory.

A Pharos in the night,
    A pillar in the dawn,
By his inspiring light
    May we fare on!
Day upon hastening day
    Still let us reverence him;
Fame, never, never may
    His laurels dim!

Our Cincinnatus

James Gabelle

They found the Roman leader at the plow
    And bade him sit in solemn state.
The crisis past, he put all gauds away—
    Such men as he are truly great.

So Washington: his homeland freed from chains,
    Retired to Sunny Potomac's shore.
He sleeps in peace on old Virginia's soil
    His fame secure forevermore.

George Washington

Harry Elmore Hurd

There have been giants on this ancient earth
Before whose strength no obstacle could stand,
And we dare hope that our beloved land
Shall fructify and once again give birth
To stalwart statesmen who will force events
To serve the highest purposes of men.
Humble and high was our first citizen—
He dealt with earthy facts like sacraments—
Once he knelt in his Gethsemane
And yielded up his might to the Divine,
But, in giving, gained a mightiness
That is most like a deeply rooted tree.
George Washington was like a wind-tossed pine
Whose lofty crown the white storms only bless.

The Cherry Tree

Lydia Chatton

Let others echo Rupert Hughes
    And mix up motes and beams . . .

The anecdotes that I peruse
    Were told by Parson Weems.

Some minds affect the Freudian styles,
    Or Cherry-Orchard themes;
The Cherry-Tree that still beguiles
    Is found in good old Weems.

Above iconoclastic views
    That little hatchet gleams!
"I cannot tell a lie," I choose
    The Washington of Weems.

Washington

William Cullen Bryant

Great were the hearts, and strong the minds,
Of those who framed in high debate,
The immortal league of love that binds
Our fair broad empire, state by state.

And deep the gladness of the hour,
When, as the auspicious task was done,
In solemn trust, the sword of power
Was given to GLORY'S UNSPOILED SON.

That noble race is gone; the suns
Of fifty years have risen and set;
But the bright links those chosen ones
So strongly forged, are brighter yet.

Wide—as our own free race increase—
Wide shall extend the elastic chain,
And bind in everlasting peace,
State after state, a mighty train.

Washington at Trenton

The Battle Monument, Oct. 19, 1893

Edmund Clarence Stedman

Since ancient time began
    Ever on some great soul God laid an infinite bur-
        den—
The weight of all this world, the hopes of man.
    Conflict and pain, and fame immortal are his
        guerdon!

And this the unfaltering token
    Of him the Deliverer—what tho tempests beat,
Though all else fail, tho bravest ranks be broken,
    He stands unseared, alone, nor ever knows defeat.

Know by the pillared sign
 For what brief while the powers of earth and hell
Can war against the spirit of truth divine,
 Or can against the heroic heart of man prevail.

Washington's Tomb

Ruth Lawrence

Would we could coin for thee new words of praise;
To call thee only great, is meaningless;
Thou didst the woes of humankind redress,
And the blest standard of our freedom raise;
Didst lead us safe o'er strange, untrodden ways,
And in thy life—that did all truth express—
Teach us thy cherished creed which we confess,
The equal rights of men to crown their days.
Thou didst not sleep in sound of city's toil;
The din of traffic, murmur of the mart,
Are far away; within thy native soil
We leave thee, heart of honor, Honor's heart;
Not in cathedral's gorgeous sculptured gloom,
But 'neath thy much loved stars, a fitter tomb.

Acrostic

Mabel Adams Ayer

When we hear the name of "Father,"
At once we know there is command,
Source of power and strength and goodness,
Heart beats for home and native land.
In such esteem we hold this "Father"
Numbered with the great of God—
George Washington, our country's savior,
The first in war—in peace—and love
Oh, may we emulate his virtues
'Neath "Stars and Stripes"—his life's reward.

An Episode in the Life of Washington

Virginia Wainwright

One time a British prisoner of war
Lay closely guarded, fettered hands and feet,
In squalid cell, where he had little food,
His cell was damp and lacking in all heat.

This brought to notice then of Washington
Right soon he visited this prisoner,
"You said you'd like to see all rebels hung,
All of us dead, you surely did infer."

"I say it still," the stalwart man replied,
"I'm loyal to our ever gracious king."
"Remove handcuffs forthwith," said Washington,
"This Moody now to better quarters bring."

"Such loyalty and Zeal are rare indeed,"
To moody prisoner of war he said,
"I wish that you *my soldier* could have been
In my own Continental force instead."

Washington

Francis Arden

Written in 1812 and sung before the Washington Benevolent Society in Washington Hall, New York in that year.

Since first its course around the sun
This Heaven supported ball has run,
Of all who live in deathless fame,
No earth-sprung child can boast a name
Like that lov'd Chief, enthron'd in light
Beyond the reach of mortal sight
Whose glory gilds this signal day,
With beams that mock the orient ray.
Then pour the graceful notes along,
'Tis WASHINGTON, that claims the song!

"Though born a victor-crown to wear,
He deemed the olive branch more fair,
His sword, the foremost in the fight,
Ne'er wav'd but for some sacred right;
Ev'n while the deadly conflict rag'd
Fond thoughts of peace his mind engag'd
And the first wish that warm'd his breast,
Was but to see his country blest!
Alas! That she should ever prove,
Unmindful of the Hero's love.

Washington

Mary Wingate

O noble brow, so wise in thought!
O heart, so true! O soul unbound!
O eye, so keen to pierce the night
And guide the "ship of state" aright!
O life so simple, grand and free,
The humblest still may turn to thee.
O king, uncrowned! O prince of men!
When shall we see thy like again?

The century, just passed away,
Has felt the impress of thy sway,
While youthful hearts have stronger grown
And made thy patriot zeal their own.
In marble hall or lowly cot,
Thy name hath never been forgot.
The world itself is richer, far,
For the clear shining of a star.
And loyal hearts in years to run
Shall turn to thee, O Washington.

Washington

Lord Byron

Where may the wearied eye repose
    When gazing on the great;
Where neither guilty glory glows,
    Nor despicable state?
Yes—one—the first—the last—the best—
The Cincinnatus of the West,
    Whom envy dared not hate,
Bequeath the name of Washington,
To make men blush there was but one!

Washington

G. B. Smith

His spirit lives in every noble deed
In love of country and of fellowmen
In reverence for ours and others' creed
In great words uttered or sent forth by pen.

His life calls forth the good in every soul
The longing that war in all lands shall cease
His high ideals shall ever be our goal
He lives in brotherhood, in love, in peace.

Washington

Elizabeth Toldridge

Some men are born to glory, as the day
    Awakes to travail and the night, to stars!
And he, the predestined, was of such fine clay
    It fit his spirit as white sails their spars.

Travail and star were ever rim to rim—
    His very toil was dream and prophecy.
Within, without—his life, the battle-hymn
    Of a Land of lands whose sons shall dare be free!

Some men are born to greatness upon earth—
    But they must rise to it, in utter stress. . . .
And he, the epitome of human worth,
    Is symbol of our everlastingness!

Washington Relics

William H. Rauchfuss

My heart is stirred within me
As I gaze on relics won
From predatory Time
That concerned our Washington.
May Guardian Angels keep them
In sight, so they may be
The heritage of all
Throughout eternity.

George Washington

Gertrude Perry West

George Washington, immortal son
Of Old Virginia; one by one,
    We come today to you who still
    Remain the idol by the will
Of your country: You, who won
For us the battle that begun
When Tyranny forced rebellion,
    By your courage and undaunted skill, George
        Washington.

To pay the homage you instil
In every bosom though peril
    Was yours, and in comparison,
    Pigmatic seems each skeleton
Who fought with you through Winter's chill, George
    Washington.

Washington Monument by Night

Carl Sandburg

1

The stone goes straight.
A lean swimmer dives into night sky,
Into half-moon mist.

2

Two trees are coal black.
This is a great white ghost between.
It is cool to look at.
Strong men, strong women, come here.

3

Eight years is a long time
To be fighting all the time.

4

The republic is a dream.
Nothing happens unless first a dream.

5

The wind bit hard at Valley Forge one Christmas.
Soldiers tied rags to their feet.
Red footprints wrote in the snow . . .
. . . and stone shoots into stars here
        into half-moon mist tonight.

6

Tongues wrangled dark at a man.
He buttoned his overcoat and stood alone.
In a snowstorm, red hollyberries, thoughts,
        he stood alone.

7

Women said: He is lonely
. . . fighting . . . fighting . . . eight years . . .

8

The name of an iron man goes over the world.
It takes a long time to forget an iron man.

9

.   .   .   .
.   .   .   .

Nor Shame His Dream

Virginia Spates

Impossible for us to understand:
Why elements which, by chance, make dull the fool
Had been so exquisitely blent to rule
In him that life expanded in his hand.
Call up great Alexander; and that one
Beloved of Rome; and him, the searing flame
That lighted France; all those who tasted fame;
And measure them against our Washington.
There was a dream no self-blind eye might see:
A man could rise above his baser part,
And lift the poorest to such destiny
That kings are made by nature, not by art.
His vision is a trust to you and me;
His love, a seal upon the Nation's heart.

A Paean to Washington

E. Dorcas Palmer

A poem to Washington—Shall we not give it,
Bright-winged from the fount of our soul's sincerity?
A poem, aye! But rather let us live it—
A nation's song he wrought in verity!

From an Ode on the Death of George Washington

Samuel Low

Recited by Mr. Hodgkinson, in the New York Theatre on the 8th of January, 1800.

From dread Jehovah's everlasting throne,
Celestial WISDOM on my numbers beam;
With thy inspiring gifts come down,
And let thy sacred light my off'ring crown,
For vast, sublime, and arduous is my theme.
Erewhile I vow'd fictitious aid,
And on young Fancy's pinions soar'd;
Or with the tuneful sisters stray'd,
And all their flow'ry paths explored;—
But now I hail bright TRUTH, whose varied ray
Illumines man's benighted way:

Oh; from thine altar let the fire
My elegiac verse inspire,
But ah! can even TRUTH or WISDOM tell
What speechless feelings ev'ry bosom swell,
How mighty is the loss we all endure;—
Our Washington, in glory grown mature,
COLUMBIA'S father, patriot, sage,
The pride, the glory of the age,
Now sleeps in dust; our eyes no more
Shall view the matchless hero we deplore.

Stuart's Washington

Irene Shirley Moran

Honors
To him were not
For proud display; he knew
The cost to those to whom there never came
Reward.

George Washington

Bessie Price Owen

A thrill goes through our being now
    As we think of that great day
That gave to us George Washington
    Who paved our nation's way;

His noble courage spurred men on,—
    His faith, in God was true,
With soleless, bleeding soldiers, firm,
    He won; he carried through;

And when the drums of battle ceased
    And the smoke had cleared away,
A Joyous, thankful people then
    Proclaimed a holiday;

His soothing hand bound up the wounds,
    His mighty guidance blest,
And brought forth peaceful plenitude
    To the North, South, East, and West.

And through the mists of centuries
    He lives today a part
Of world-wide progress toward the stars
    With his own gift the heart.

O Washington!, O Washington!,
    We bow before thy shrine!
A nation born, its flag unfurled,
    We hail this gift of thine!

A Day at Mt. Vernon, 1788

Beulah May

How the rain fell. All the morning, Martha busy at
    preserving,
Chid the servants, weighed and tasted, tied down pots
    of berry jam,
Till the house was sweet with spices.
    Nellie Custis played her spinet,
Filled the River Room with roses, worked a cross-
    stitch monogram.

While the General since breakfast, kersey coated, up
    on Blueskin,
Splashed about the wet plantation, watched the prime
    tobacco dried,
Helped the blacksmith mould a plowshare, tallied
    sacks of wheat and barley,
Then tramped stoutly home to dinner, Vulcan growl-
    ing at his side.

Gave a rousing shout of welcome as a rig whirled up
    the driveway,
And two muddy army cronies tumbled stiffly from the
    chaise,
On the porch they fought each battle, Yorktown,
    Monmouth, Saratoga.
Martha, smiling at their laughter, sent out flip on sil-
    ver trays.

Evening found the cozy parlors gay with candle-light
    and fire-light,
Neighbors proud in wigs and ruffles galloped swiftly
    up the hill.
Chairs were set for whist and ombre, Daddy Jack
    brought out his fiddle,
Youths and maidens bowed and curtsied in a stately
    old quadrille.

Musing, Washington ere bedtime took a turn along
    the river—
As a stripling toiled for Fairfax, stalked with Brad-
    dock through the snow,
Lived through Valley Forge's winter—So he dreamed
    in old Virginia,
Father of our young Republic, grave and fearless,
    long ago.

George Washington 1732-1932

Lillian M. Perkins

Said one,
"Achievement
Is the lengthened shadow
Of a man"
And well.

Today
Two Hundred
Years have not diminished
The shadow
He has made.

Upon
Not only
Our own lives, on children
Of the world
It falls.
And time
Has not yet
Thinned or shortened it, nor will.
We do him
Honor.

In memory
Of the man
We plant the sturdy oak, king
Of the forest,
His self.

Cause for Pride
Dr. Joseph H. Kenna

We are all proud to call ourselves children of
Washington.

Extract from the Portrait
John Pierpont, 1812

Thou spotless patriot! Thou illustrious man;
Methinks, that while yet on earth, thy heaven began;
For is there pleasure purer, more refin'd,
More worthy of thine own etherial mind,
Than thrilled, with lively transport, through thy
  frame,
And played around thy heart, with lambent flame,
To see Columbia, guided by thy hand,
Plant in the bosom of thy native land;
That tree that flourished so divinely fair,
And took such root, beneath thy fostering care,
As soon, o'er half a continent, to spread
Its fragrant leaves, and give a nation shade;—
That tree, whose root descended from the skies,
That grows by culture but neglected dies,
That tree, beneath whose boughs thy spirit fled,
That tree, whose fading leaves deplore the dead?—
And now, great father of thy country, say,
Ere angels bore thee to the fields of day,
Did not thine eye, with holy rapture, view
That Tree of Liberty, while yet it grew
Vig'rous and green?—And did it not impart,
To ev'ry fibre of thy godlike heart,
A joy, while waving o'er thy mortal brow,
Next to the Amaranth, that shields thee now?—

Washington
Marguerite MacAlman

The years
Have burdened him
With traits less human than
Divine. Leave him some common bond
With man!

Washington
Phronsie Irene Marsh

Washington lives again—
I saw him kneel to pray
Kneel to pray in the twilight
Within the shadow of a great oak
On Mount Vernon Hill.

He prayed most earnestly—most reverently
For the destiny of a great Nation
The future of the youth of America,
Generations yet unborn
And yea, for those whose hair is silver.

His voice faltered not a little
As he bowed his head and closed his prayer—
"God, grant that there be no more war dead
As long as there is life and hope
And, Oh, God! give the world men who dare
To believe in peace—
Men who have the courage to say,
'Always war will cease.' "

When I raised my head again
He was standing tall and straight
His figure full against the silent starlit sky.
I thought I saw a gleam—a gleam of hope
In his stern courageous gray eye.

Then, suddenly as he stood still
There came from afar
"I am the way the truth and the light."
And he followed as if there had been no night,
    No stars, no America.

Washington
James Jeffrey Roche

God wills no man a slave. The man most meek,
Who saw him face to face on Horeb's peak,
Had slain a tyrant for a bondsman's wrong,
And met his Lord with sinless soul and strong.
But when, years after, overfraught with care,
His feet once trod doubt's pathway to despair,
For that one treason lapse, the guiding hand
That led so far nor bared the promised land.
God makes no man a slave, no doubter free;
Abiding faith alone wins liberty.

No angel led our Chieftain's steps aright;
No pilot cloud by day, no flame by night;
No plague nor potent spake to foe or friend;
No doubt assailed him, faithful to the end.
Weaklings there were, as in the tribes of old,
Who craved for fleshpots, worshipped calves of gold,
Murmured that right would harder be than wrong,
And freedom's narrow road so steep and long;
But he who ne'er on Sinai's summit trod,
Still walked the highest heights and spake with God;
Saw with anointed eyes no promised land
By petty bounds or pettier cycles spanned,

Its people curbed and broken to the ring,
Packed with a caste and saddled with a King,—
But freedom's heritage and training school,
King's heads in dust and freemen's feet thereon.
His work well done, the leader stepped aside,
Spurning a crown with more than kingly pride,
Content to wear the higher crown of worth,
While time endures, First of earth.
Where men unruled should learn to wisely rule,
Till sun and moon should see at Ajalon
Kings heads in dust and freemen's feet thereon.

Washington

Elijah Parish, 1800

This serious air, this filent gloom around,
The mourning tokens, and the figh profound,
Proclaim the ruin Terror's king has made—
In Death's cold vault is Vernon's Hero laid.

When lofty hills shall sparkling volume raise.
With all his streams the SIRE of rivers blaze,
The Ades vanish, as a cloud of dust,
And stars and funs, their glorious orbits burst,
The fame of Vernon's honored CHIEF shall rise,
Survive the wreck of worlds, and triumph in the skies.

George Washington

Ramona Moore

We pay most loyal tribute and a nation's ardent love,
To the Hero of those battles that set our colonies free,
To th' Father of our emblems that so proudly wave
        above
And that led us ever Westward to th' splendor of
        the sea.
As a statesman and a warrior, we long have loved
        him well,
As pioneer of finance we have newer still a theme
And through the depths of this vast love,
        numerous great deeds dwell
While his greatest vision ever . . . was America's
        dream.

He fought that final battle just as nobly as the rest,
With the faith and with th' courage of a nation's
        fervent prayer,
While the angels planted peace upon that weary
        breast,
As they at last released him from the throes of mortal
        care.
"I am dying, Sir," so said he, "but not afraid to die."
As his spirit rose in triumph to those realms beyond
        the sky.

George Washington

Alice Wescott Marks

His picture hangs upon the wall
Within each public place;
There is a silent, ageless call
To look up to his face . . .
To look upon that brow so broad—
Those eyes—so fearless—keen—
The face of one who talked with God—
A man whose soul was clean.
What better pattern could we crave—
To whom, more homage pay,—
Than to the man who fought to save
Ideals for us to-day?

.   .   .   .

His picture hangs upon the wall,
Or should hang, in each place
Where we can look up, one and all,
And take courage from his face.

Washington

Geraldine Meyrich

It seems so simple now, that life of thine,
To us who from these turgid days look back,
As mariners from 'neath a stormy wrack
Peer out and see a verdant island shine
Behind them, where the storm has left no sign
Save freshness and new glory in its track;
To us, who midst sunk rocks still turn and tack,
So seem thy days all happy, free and fine.

Yet, wert thou here, wouldst not thy piercing gaze,
Thy steady hand and strong, compelling will,
Unravel the mixt strands of good and ill
That so perplex- In youth through wildwood maze
Thy skill surveyed clear paths; and later, lo!
The way was straight because thou mad'st it so.

George Washington

Florence Riley Radcliffe

He sought the solitude of wood and stream
And found beyond the sunset-bars, a dream.
He spent long hours in peril of his life,
And saw a land of peace beyond the strife.
Decreed by a determined destiny
The father of a nation yet to be,
He followed in the footsteps of his star;
The way was often rugged, lonely, far.
Doubts and disasters cast a sombre pall,
The greatness of his spirit pierced through all.

By faith, he saw beyond the darkest night
And waited for the dawning and the light.
At last it came—bright hour of victory—
Fulfillment of the sachem's prophecy.
From Valley Forge, its darkness and its toil,
To liberty on Yorktown's sacred soil.

Washington
S. Louise Marsh

He held the torch of patriotism high
To point our pathway ever toward the sky,
He wrote those deathless words upon the scroll
That keep our country's records clean and whole.
He kept the faith with God in heart and soul
And led his country on to freedom's goal.

He made this nation such an honored name,
It still gleams high from all the hills of fame.
He earned the name, "Humanity's dear friend,"
Because on him all people could depend.
To lend, to aid, that was his life-long task;
Without return he gave what men would ask.

Washington
Sylvia B. Malagisi

First Father of our Country,
Who took the oath to serve and honor,
To sacrifice his happiness.
To stand shoulder to shoulder,
For his country.
For he loved his fellow men,
To suffer and endure,
Fight and pray for right, for peace,
First in battle.
Never dreampt of losing,
Looked forward to a mighty nation,
Accepted no praise for his bravery,
But bowed in thanks before his maker.

Washington's Tomb at Mt. Vernon
Anna Lloyd

Lilacs were scenting all the April air
  As we drew near with slow and reverent feet;
And hidden mocking-birds were trilling their
  Melodious pleadings from some high retreat;
A gentle calm seemed brooding everywhere—
  Calm from a heart that long had ceased to beat.
And a great peace enfolded us, as light
  As gossamer—perennial as spring—
Yet sturdy as traditions burnished bright
  By the long line of pilgrims journeying
To that still place, where lilacs, mauve and white,
  Guarded a leader dearer than a king.

In Washington's Death Chamber
Kate Randle Menefee

From this small room, a spirit took its flight
To lands the eyes of men have never seen.
Yet something lingers, time may never glean—
A heart has left the halo of its light.
Against the shadows, falling with the night,
A form comes back, and smiling with serene
And loyal faith, a ghost of kindly mien
Still leads us onward to a loftier height.

Ideal statesman! In this quiet room
Your dreams take hold of men. The hour-glass turns,
And youth steps forward, calling out your name.
The room is empty, and they locked your tomb,
Yet down the years victorious memory burns
In starry white and red and azure flame.

Nor thoughtless was the choice; no love or hate
Could from its poise move that deliberate mind,
Weighing between too early and too late
Those pitfalls of the man refused by Fate:
His was the impartial vision of the great
Who seem not as they wish, but as they find.
He saw the dangers of defeat, nor less
The incomputable perils of success;
The sacred past thrown by, an empty rind;
The future, cloud-land, snare of prophets blind;
The waste of war, the ignominy of peace;
On either hand a sullen rear of woes,
Whose garnered lightning none could guess,
Piling its thunder-heads and muttering "Cease!"
Yet drew not back his hand, but gravely chose
The seeming desperate task whence our new nation
    rose.

George Washington
John Hall Ingham

This was the man God gave us when the hour
Proclaimed the dawn of Liberty begun;
Who dared a deed and died when it was done
Patient in triumph, temperate in power,—
Not striving like the Corsican to tower
To heaven, nor like great Phillip's greater son
To win the world and weep for worlds unwon,
Or lose the star to revel in the flower.
The lives that serve the eternal verities
Alone do mould mankind. Pleasure and pride
Sparkle awhile and perish, as the spray
Smoking across the crests of cavernous seas
Is impotent to hasten or delay
The everlasting surges of the tide.

The New-Come Chief

From "Under the Elm" July 3, 1775

James Russell Lowell

*Washington arrived at Cambridge, and on the following day,
(under the shade of the great elm on Cambridge Common,
now unfortunately blown down,) he took command of
the 16,000 men composing the American forces.*

Beneath our consecrated elm
A century ago he stood,
Famed vaguely for that old fight in the wood
Whose red surge sought, but could not overwhelm
The life foredoomed to wield our rough-hewn helm:—
From colleges, where now the gown
To arms had yielded, from the town,
Our rude self-summoned levies flocked to see
The new-come chief and wonder which was he.
No need to question long; close lipped and tall,
Long trained in murder-brooding forests lone
To bridle others' clamors and his own,
Firmly erect, he towered above them all,
The incarnate discipline that was to free
With iron curb that armed democracy.

Never to see a nation born
Hath been given to mortal man,
Unless to those who, on that summer morn,
Gazed silent when the great Virginian
Unsheathed the sword whose fatal flash
Shot union through the incoherent clash
Of our loose atoms, crystallizing them
Around a single will's unpliant stem,
And making purpose of emotion rash.
Out of that scabbard sprang, as from its womb,
Nebulous at first but hardening to a star,
Through mutual share of sunburst and of gloom,
The common faith that made us what we are.

That lifted blade transformed our jangling clans,
Till then provincial, to Americans,
And made a unity of wildering plans;
Here was the doom fixed; here is marked the date
When this New World awoke to man's estate,
Burnt its last ship and ceased to look behind:
Ye who with him for independence fought,
And the rough work of independence wrought;
Ye brave companions of his martial cares,
Inur'd to hardships, in his fame co-heirs;
Though in your eye the big tear stand represt,
Let sharper sorrow sting your manly breast;
To worlds unknown what friends have gone before!

The place that knew them, knows them now no more;
Your seats at annual feasts must be more bare,
Ev'n ye must be the wrecks of what ye were!
Till late, supported by his staff, appears
(Like some lone arch that braves the wrath of years)
One HOARY MAN, all helpless, pale unnerved,
The last alive with Washington who served!
And ye, who oft his public counsels heard,
Admir'd his wisdom and his words revered;
Ye senators! let mourning's voice succeed,
And join the cry, "The mighty's fallen, indeed!"

Mount Vernon Bells

M. B. C. Slade

Where Potomac streams are flowing,
Virginia borders through,
Where the white sailed ships are going,
Sailing to the ocean blue.

Sail O, Ships across the billows,
And bear the story far,
How he sleeps beneath the willows,
First in Peace and first in War.

Hush the sound of mirth and singing,
Silent every one,
Where the solemn bells are ringing,
By the tomb of Washington.

Tolling and knelling,
With a sad sweet sound,
O'er the waves the tones are swelling,
By Mount Vernon's sacred ground,

Sons of Washington

Maude Frazer Jackson

The Father of his Country had no son
Of his own blood; and yet, his sons now stand
A mighty host, the guardians of our land,
Who hold inviolate the freedom won.
The traitorous sons of Selfishness we find,
Tares with the wheat; but we are glad today
For sons of Washington, men of his kind,
God's workmen true in high or humble way.

Great patriot, who turned from dazzling crown
For Freedom's sake,—thy soul of honor bright
Lives on in these thy sons who love the right
And, worthy, wear thy mantle handed down.
To buy such men the world has not the price;
These, Washington, thy crown for sacrifice.

George Washington Activities

for

4-H Clubs

By
BELVA CUZZORT

WASHINGTON AS A FARMER AT MOUNT VERNON · · *Painted by THOMAS P. ROSSITER*

First in better farming, first in love of farm life, and first to vision a nation grown from the soil.

INTRODUCTION

THE United States George Washington Bicentennial Commission, recognizing the importance of the great national young people's organizations of the country, and appreciating the part these groups would take in the observance of the Two Hundredth Anniversary of the Birth of George Washington, prepared special programs for use of the 4-H Clubs through the United States.

In the Concurrent Resolution of the United States Congress respecting the Two Hundredth Anniversary of the Birth of George Washington, the nation was asked to commemorate this occasion "in such a manner that future generations of American citizens may live according to the example and precepts of his exalted life and character, and thus perpetuate the American Republic."

None better than the youth of our country can translate into practical living the inspiration of the Nation's First Citizen—one whose character, personality, and accomplishments fire the imagination and enkindle a desire to noble adventure.

George Washington Activities for 4-H Clubs

I. FOREWORD

You are a busy 900,000 young people of the farm—achieving a bigger and better agriculture and farm life. As such achievers, this George Washington program has been prepared for you. It is fittingly a program of achieving, for the Virginia boy, born two hundred years ago, did things. In his youth he accomplished what came in his way to do. He trained himself on the farm. In many respects, his problems and interests were like your own. Indeed, no group in the Nation is closer to the boyhood and youth of George Washington than the 4-H Clubs. Throughout his life he had a great zeal to improve his farms and farming. Thus there is no better way to celebrate this Two Hundredth Anniversary of his birth than *to follow his example in doing and in improving upon what has been done.*

Get acquainted with the experiences of Washington and the principles he lived by, and see what the inspiration lets you accomplish in your 4-H projects. You may thereby acquire better methods of work, greater self-confidence, improved skill, or in other ways add to your power to accomplish and your enjoyment of the farm. *What you achieve in your project and in yourself through the lift of Washington's life and personality will be your celebration of this great anniversary.*

Think of 900,000 of you in 1932, on your widely scattered farms, carrying on under the slogan: "Achieve as Washington Would!" Then, on 4-H Achievement Day in October, you come with your exhibits, and better still, *with the spirit of Washington,—the doer, the achiever, the leader,—within you, a living tribute to his memory.* This is the celebration supreme.

4-H Club Member! The challenge is yours; and when you have met it, you will possess, as though it were a smooth round charm—4-H Magic—the secret of achieving as Washington did.

II. GEORGE WASHINGTON ACQUAINTANCE DAY PROGRAM

You will probably both add to and take from the program here suggested to make it your own program—and it must be that. The time you give it does not take you from your 4-H interests, but the contrary. You come closer to them, for the purposes you have in your farm projects were often dreams of the man whose memory you honor.

The Acquaintance Program may be distributed over several 4-H Club meetings, one or two features being selected for each occasion.

FIRST NUMBER OF THE GEORGE WASHINGTON ACQUAINTANCE DAY PROGRAM
THE MAGIC SQUARE

The familiar subject-matter and scenes of the Magic Square call for little preparation. Each character may have his own lines copied, together with the speech preceding. Read or listen to the reading of the entire playlet. When your part has been assigned think of it in relation to the whole, enter into the part, speak naturally and distinctly, facing toward the audience that you will be heard. To do this, to feel natural and to be at ease will help your performance succeed. There will, of course, be a director and assistants who will prepare the squares and have ready the necessary stage furnishings. The play is divided into three parts allowing for intermissions and music.

The 4-H exhibit can be largely imagined, the animals viewed through a feigned window or door leading off stage. A jar of jelly, a few potatoes, and a placard with a small table or two supply the makings of the stage exhibit. But the Magic Number Square and the 4-H Achievement Square must be carefully made. There should be a rehearsal just before the program is put on.

TIME: Near Close of 4-H Exhibit Day.
PLACE: Porch outside Exhibit room.
CHARACTERS: May be 16 or 29.

PART I
PERSONS IN ORDER OF THEIR APPEARANCE

BLUE-RIBBON WINNERS:

Exhibitor of Sheep	Boy
Exhibitor of Home-Painted Furniture	Girl
Exhibitor of Potatoes	Boy

PINK-RIBBON WINNERS:

John	Boy
Mary	Girl

BLUE-RIBBON WINNERS:

Owner of Calf	Girl
Exhibitor of Jelly	Girl
Exhibitor of Pig	Boy

PINK-RIBBON WINNER:

Alice	Girl

OTHER MEMBERS OF 4-H CLUBS:

Member of Pig Club	Boy
Clothing Club Girl	Girl
Exhibitor of Pink-Ribbon Jelly	Girl
Judge of Calf	Boy

BOY—WHO HAD NO EXHIBIT ... Boy

As scene opens, three Blue-Ribbon winners stand toward the front on left side of stage; some are holding up their blue ribbons and others pinning them on their dress front. To the right, and even a little more to the front, stand Mary and John, of the same 4-H Club, facing sidewise toward the Blue-Ribbon group and the audience. These two are holders of Pink Ribbons. Mary holds hers partly behind her away from the view of the Blue-Ribbon winners and toward the audience. John holds his in his two hands and tries to appear indifferent.

Exhibitor of Sheep—Hurrah! Ours the Blue-Ribbon Club!

Exhibitor of Home-Painted Furniture—Blue ribbons for all except—— (*She looks across to Mary and John.*)

Exhibitor of Sheep—Oh, come over here, you two, and help us cheer. Three cheers for our Club! (*Mary and John come closer and cheer with the others.*)

Exhibitor of Potatoes—One of us will go to the National 4-H Camp in Washington, D. C.

Exhibitor of Sheep—That's right, I'd forgotten.

Exhibitor of Home-Painted Furniture—How will they choose the one to go?

Exhibitor of Potatoes—It will be hard, when so many made blue ribbons.

Exhibitor of Sheep—They might choose us by lot, this once.

Exhibitor of Home-Painted Furniture—Oh! Let's put our names in a box and see who gets to go.

Exhibitor of Sheep—I'll get the names ready. (*Goes to one side and soon returns with a box.*)

Exhibitor of Home-Painted Furniture—I'll go get Boy to draw a name (*exits*).

[*Enter other blue-ribbon winners—Owner of Calf, Exhibitor of Jelly, Exhibitor of Pig. They pin on one another's blue ribbons.*]

Exhibitor of Pig—Who do you guess will get to go to the National 4-H Camp? I say it's you. (*Points to a blue-ribbon winner. All the blue-ribbon group, as they fasten the ribbons point to one or another, breathing out—"I guess you." Mary and John stand aside.*)

Mary—I'm one who won't get to go. (*Crumpling her 4-H pink ribbon and flinging it to the floor.*)

John—Are pink ribbons so bad?

Mary—I'm just two from the bottom.

Alice—(*Enters wearing her pink ribbon.*)

John—Paul's calf got a blue ribbon. I thought mine looked about as good.

Alice—I heard the judges say——

John (*disappointed*)—What did the judges say?

Alice—They said it had a dull coat, listless eye, no calf spirit.

John—Pouf, those little things.

Mary—Well, if they are little things, they get us pink ribbons.

Alice—Who could make a calf have spirit, huh?

John—I've had four pink-ribbon calves. Guess it's my level.

Alice—I wear my ribbon. Thought I'd done pretty well.

Exhibitor of Sheep—Maybe they are all right for girls.

Mary—Alice almost failed. She's made good. A pink ribbon means a lot to her.

John—All I can say is that it would be fine to go to National Camp this year, it's the George Washington Bicentennial.

Exhibitor of Sheep and Exhibitor of Pig Together—That's right, it's the 200th anniversary of his birth.

Mary—Think of getting to go to our National Capital during 1932! [*Exhibitor of Home-Painted Furniture returns with Boy.*]

Boy—Where's the box of names? (*Draws one out.*)

Exhibitor of Home-Painted Furniture—Who is it?

Boy (*looking at name*)—It's not a blue-ribbon winner.

Several (*gasping*)—Not a blue-ribbon winner?

Exhibitor of Pig—Why, a blue-ribboner would have to go.

Boy—Not this time.

Exhibitor of Jelly—Why not?

Boy—You chose by lots.

Exhibitor of Potatoes—So we did.

Boy—Then it is done, and we should send the name to the State Club Leader, who'll decide.

Exhibitor of Sheep—Who is it? Hurry up and tell us.

Boy—It's Mary.

[*There are half-suppressed "Oh's!" from group.*]

Mary (*who has stood as one turned to stone while John leans limply against a support and Alice dances about at the glad news*)—Me? It can't be!

Boy—Three cheers for Mary!

Others (*Weakly*)—Three cheers for Mary!

Mary—Poor me! Poor me!

Alice—I thought you wanted to go?

Mary—Not as a pink-ribboner.

Boy (*Motions for others to exit*)—Don't take it so! You'll be a blue-ribboner before then.

Mary—You know I won't do. I just can't.

Boy—You just have to. You saw the exhibits on Achievement Day.

Mary (*In woebegone spirit*)—I can't achieve anything.

Boy—It's your chance and through you the chance of hundreds of thousands of 4-H boys and girls.

Mary—I'm afraid when I think you're going to recommend me to the State Club Leader to go to National Camp.

Boy—We're going to help you make good for us.

Mary—It's more than I can do.

Boy—Better just get busy.

Mary (*Appealingly and speaking as one making a startling confession*)—I don't know how to *try*.

Boy—Is that all?

Mary (*Bowing her head*)—I never get anything but pink ribbons.

Boy—Mary, try to do something you like. You'd make a blue ribbon.

Mary—I like to raise goats.

Boy—All right.

Mary—But if I raised one, it'ud be a pink-ribbon goat.

Boy—How d'ye know?

Mary—My hens were—my garden, sewing,—everything.

Boy—Say, Mary, I've something that'll help. It's as old as George Washington.

Mary (*showing some interest*)—Boy, what have you?

Boy—Maybe it helped George Washington.

Mary—Would it be good now?

Boy—As good as it ever was.

Mary—You're sure.

Boy—Why, it's magic. Here, I always keep one with me. (*Hands her piece of paper—a square.*)

Mary (*looking at it*)—It's only figures in squares.

Boy—All right! but if you knew how to use it——

Mary—What does it do?

Boy—It's a MAGIC SQUARE.

Mary—What good does that do me?

Boy—You look at it. You'll see. Keep it. (*Exit.*)

Mary—How can it help me? A lot of figures, and a lot of little squares. (*Looks at it, turns it about, yawns, and goes to sleep in chair.*)

PART II

Persons including any of the above except Mary and Boy help make the "living Magic Square." Others join to make the twenty-five needed to form the square. As later described five persons may form this square. Mary, Boy, George and Martha Washington, are the first speakers; others having parts later.

A large Magic Square as shown here hangs on the wall.

THE MAGIC SQUARE*

10	18	1	14	22
11	24	7	20	3
17	5	13	21	9
23	6	19	2	15
4	12	25	8	16

* From Claude Bragdon's, "The New Image."

Persons enter to form "living Magic Square." They march in files of five to the tune of "Hail Columbia." They wear placards on their chest hung on a string about the neck. On each of the paper on cardboard placards is a number of the Magic Square in large figures. The first file of five march in and sit on floor in a row facing the audience, the next file stand on knees behind first row, the third row sit in chairs, the fourth stand, the fifth stand on low bench. Thus all placards show. (The opposite side of the placards make the 4-H Square of Achievement.)

If there are not enough persons for this square, use only five persons, each of these entering stage alone to the tune of "Hail

Columbia" and bearing a strip of cardboard representing one vertical column of the Magic Square. They stand in a row facing audience and holding the cardboards before them so as to form the square. The cardboard strips must be in the right order. On the other side of these cardboards the figures of the horizontal rows of the Square are written. At the proper time the strips are turned and held to show the horizontal rows of the Square.

The dialogue is the same whether the Magic Square is represented with twenty-five persons or only five. The stage directions will refer to these groups as the twenty-five-group and the five-group respectively.

[*When living Magic Square is formed, music ends and George Washington, dressed in Colonial costume, enters from side facing Mary, who still sleeps.*]

George—Mary, it is no time to sleep.

Mary (*Trying to wake*)—Sir?

George—You were trying to get help for Achievement Day.

Mary—I remember. There was a Magic Square.

George—It will help you.

Mary—Yes, you know about the Magic Square?

George—I do, indeed!

Mary—I can't make anything of it.

George—Let me explain.

Mary—What do the numbers mean?

George—If you add the numbers of the vertical column on the left——

[*As he speaks, those forming this column lift the placard outward from their chest, or if it is the five-group, the person holding this column extends his arms full length so that the column stands out distinct from the other four vertical columns of the square.*]

Mary (*adding, looking at George*)—10, 21, 38, 61, 65. It's 65.

George (*This column is made to stand out separately from the other columns. George points to it.*)—Try the next column.

Mary—18, 42, 47, 53, 65. Why, that's 65!

George—And the next! (*stepping toward the column as it is held forward.*)

Mary—1, 8, 21, 40, 65. 65! (*Her face showing that she is puzzled and interested.*)

George—Now the fourth vertical column. (*Arranged as before.*)

Mary—14, 34, 55, 65 (*Adding quickly*), Of course, 65; but I don't see—(*to George*)

George (*Interrupting promptly*)—The last one——

Mary (*Adding*)—22, 25, 34, 49, 65. But why——?

George—Now, add the horizontal columns—one at a time.

[*The top horizontal is extended, or in case of the five-group, the cardboards are turned over and held in a horizontal position. In this manner, Mary proceeds adding the five columns.*]

Mary—They go the same; each one adds to 65.

GEORGE (*Tracing along it with sweeping gesture*)—Try this diagonal.

MARY (*Having added as he pointed*)—I'll declare—it's 65!

GEORGE (*Again tracing the diagonal with arm gesture*)—Now the *other* diagonal.

MARY—Sixty-five! Why! they must mean something!

MARTHA WASHINGTON (*Enters in Colonial dress and passes by George and takes seat near front across from Mary. She carries a paper cylinder formed by joining two sides of a paper Magic Square. Speaks in matter-of-fact tone*)—George, I discovered something.

GEORGE WASHINGTON (*In surprised, interested tone, moving toward her*)—What is it?

MARTHA WASHINGTON—I've made a cylinder of the Magic Square.

MARY—Can you add figures on it?

MARTHA—Come, see!

[*Boy enters.*]

MARY—The columns run in spirals. Why, you can add them!

BOY—Yes, the spirals, like the other columns, add to sixty-five. In all, twenty-eight columns of the Magic Square add to the same sum.

MARY—It's the strangest Square I ever saw.

MARTHA—It's more than a puzzle.

BOY—It's what I said—it's magic.

MARY—How does magic help one?

BOY—4-H Magic lets you achieve.

MARY—I don't see how.

GEORGE—Let me show you. These figures are put in perfect order.

MARY—I see that.

GEORGE—They have all the order and balance possible for mere numbers to have.

BOY—That's right, they have.

GEORGE—That's their magic. Grass grows by the same magic. Nature's laws join at the right time and a blade of grass springs from the ground.

MARY—I see that.

GEORGE—The Magic Square, Mary, is a symbol of what you may do with your own capabilities.

MARY—My capabilities? I had never thought of it.

MARTHA—He means for you to put your capabilities in order.

GEORGE—Yes, it is through order and balance that your capacities give you practical power.

MARY—Then it is by putting my abilities in order that I can raise blue-ribbon chickens and make blue-ribbon bread?

GEORGE—It is for you to make the test.

[*Boy gives signal to Magic Square group, who turn over their placards and instead of the numbers there appears this square:*]

4-H SQUARE OF ACHIEVEMENT

Judgment	Cooperation	Leadership	Sympathy and Patience	Self-Control
Technical Knowledge	Honesty	Foresight	Resource-fulness	Persever-ance
Order and System	Health	Industry	Skill	Faith and Self-Confidence
Initiative	Enjoyment and Enthusiasm	Aptitude	Sportsman-ship	Vision
Courage	Sense of Humor	Tact	Tolerance	Accuracy

[*If it is the five-group, they exeunt with the long cardboard slips and return with other strips forming the Square as above. Also Boy turns over the Magic Square hanging on the wall, showing on the other side the 4-H Achievement Square.*]

BOY—The 4-H Square of Achievement!

MARY—Another Magic Square?

BOY—4-H abilities put in order.

MARY—Oh!

GEORGE—Look, *industry* is in the center, surrounded by *foresight, resourcefulness, honesty, health, skill, enjoyment, aptitude* and *sportsmanship*. Look, too, *judgment* is matched by *accuracy; courage* by *self-control; leadership* holds hands with *sympathy* and *cooperation; tact* holds place between *sense of humor* and *tolerance*.

BOY—That's 4-H experience. I know it.

MARY—What's the magic?

GEORGE—There is magic in achieving!

MARY (*As if repeating*)—The magic of blue ribbons.

MARTHA—Yes, it is that.

MARY—But I don't have the 4-H Magic.

BOY—Mary, you can get it.

MARTHA—George, let's show her.

[*The Achievement Square group breaks up to take their places about their respective exhibits. Small tables with canned fruit, jelly, potatoes and other articles of the exhibit, are placed about. There are placards giving the acreage yield of corn, potatoes and other crops; and the cost and profit record of a pig.*]

BOY—Why you can see it in the 4-H Exhibit.

MARTHA—Come, let's look at the 4-H Exhibit.

GEORGE—Yes, let's see if there's magic in jelly, chickens, and calves.

MARY—Oh, can we see magic in jelly, chickens and calves?

EXHIBITOR OF HOME-PAINTED FURNITURE—What's he saying? (*Pointing towards George*).

GEORGE (*To Martha, as they stand before this placard*)

POTATOES
Yield per Acre, 300 Bushels.

Martha, look! 300 bushels to the acre! I was pleased with a yield of 40 bushels.

MARTHA—What fine potatoes—large and smooth.

GEORGE—Do they taste like the potatoes we grew?

EXHIBITOR OF POTATOES—Don't they look the same, Sir? (*Cuts open a potato.*)

GEORGE—They do indeed! How do you grow them?

EXHIBITOR OF POTATOES—Now we know how to grow potatoes.

GEORGE—It seems you do.

EXHIBITOR OF POTATOES—In 4-H Clubs, thousands of boys and girls profit by this knowledge. One grows a fine yield of potatoes, another a still better yield, and so on.

GEORGE—Oh! You have set one another good examples—and now have a yield of 300 bushels.

EXHIBITOR OF POTATOES—That's it. Our motto is "To make the best better."

GEORGE— Mary, this boy's powers were put in order.

MARY—How did he do it?

EXHIBITOR OF POTATOES—I took special care of every potato hill. I planted potatoes that would grow best in that soil.

GEORGE—You'll soon know, Mary. The magic of achieving is for everyone.

MARY—If others achieve, I will also.

MARTHA—I like your spirit. It will carry you to success.

GEORGE (*Moving along the exhibit line*)—Look, Martha, at this careful record! (*They read silently from placard held by Member of Pig Club.*)

MEMBER OF PIG CLUB—Twenty-two thousand boys and girls in the United States raised, one year, above sixty-five thousand pigs and a large number made the blue-ribbon grade.

GEORGE—How did they happen to grow such high-grade pigs?

MEMBER OF PIG CLUB—Club boys and girls who have for years been growing better and better pigs helped one another.

GEORGE—Oh, again the same secret. You learn from each other.

MEMBER OF PIG CLUB—Yes, Sir, and it is strange. There's a boy who had never met another pig club member, yet the first year he raised a blue-ribbon pig.

EXHIBITOR OF PIG—I felt I knew them.

GEORGE—Martha, these 20th century American boys and girls by inspiring one another, inspire me.

MARTHA—Look, George, at this jelly!

EXHIBITOR OF JELLY (*Taking lid from several of the glasses*)—Turn it out, Madam, on this platter.

MARTHA (*Taking up a glass and turning it on the large plate*)—See, it keeps its shape. (*Lifts plate.*) Look, it quivers yet does not fall. Let me try another. (*Has same result.*)

EXHIBITOR OF BLUE-RIBBON JELLY—Won't you dip a spoon into it?

MARTHA (*Taking spoon of jelly*)—Here, George, try it.

GEORGE—It's as good as the blackberry jelly down in Virginia.

EXHIBITOR OF JELLY (*Handing Martha a knife*)—You can cut it like bread.

MARTHA (*Sliding blade down through center of mold, and then laying each half upon its side*)—What jelly! It has not stuck to the knife. Look how the cut-surface sparkles; it's smooth as glass.

EXHIBITOR OF PINK-RIBBON JELLY—I can't make it like that; I have tried for four years, and it isn't that I don't know how.

MARY—Is it pink-ribbon jelly?

EXHIBITOR OF PINK-RIBBON JELLY—I can't make anything else.

GEORGE—Look, Mary. Do you not see magic and achievement in this beautiful calf?

4-H JUDGE OF CALVES—Sir, it is nearly perfect.

GEORGE—It's how the boy cared for it. Whose calf is it?

OWNER OF CALF—It's not a boy's. It's mine, Sir.

GEORGE—Why, good! Can you tell us how you cared for it?

OWNER OF CALF—I watched its pasture, and when it had more grass, I fed it less.

GEORGE—Ah! I knew it. You put your own powers in order. The calf shows it.

MARTHA (*Taking up cotton school dress, large size. Girl who made it is standing by*)—It's a nice material, and well made, but I don't like it, somehow.

MARY—She hadn't the magic. It looks like a dress for her mother.

CLOTHING CLUB GIRL—I know it's too old for me. It's not what you call smart. But I haven't the touch for it.

MARY—After a while I'll tell you how to do it. Study styles until you find what suits you. When you have that, you will make a dress you like.

MARTHA—Mary knows better what magic is now.

GEORGE—Unless your capabilities are put in order, you lack power.

4-H EXHIBITOR OF POULTRY—I lack something. Look at my flock.

MARTHA—Such sleepy looking hens I never saw.

EXHIBITOR OF POULTRY—Somebody said I kept them in the pen too much.

BOY—It was bad judgment and your flock shows it.

MARY—Magic is not easy.

GEORGE—When you order all your capabilities about something you wish to achieve, you make each stronger.

BOY—Each takes on magic.

EXHIBITOR OF HOME-PAINTED FURNITURE—I know, it is the "added something"; more industry, you say, than you thought you had.

JOHN—Yes, I see what you mean, it's having more patience to stay by to the end than you knew you had.

ALICE—When Jane sang at the convention without knowing the words to the song and with a hoarse voice, and Nancy played the accompaniment without any music, and both got through well, it was the "added something" in being willing, wasn't it?

BOY—Why not call it willingness *plus*?

JUDGE OF CALVES—I know a girl who has cheerfulness *plus*.

EXHIBITOR OF JELLY—And I know another who has foresight *plus*.

OWNER OF CALF—When I was a leader, one of the club members kept on with his project after the family had moved to another farm, four miles away; he walked back and forth so he could complete his work and also help along the club record. That was persistency *plus* and cooperation *plus*.

MARY—Ah! the magic! it's getting clearer all the time.

MARTHA—It was a whole set of *plus* qualities that made perfect each one of those fine glasses of jelly.

GEORGE—I'm stirred by all this, Martha. I too was a farm boy and my lands grew to thousands of acres, but these boys and girls are making true my dream of the farm.

BOY—You, Sir, made good surveys of wilderness land. That's magic.

[*Different 4-H Boys and Girls speak up about Washington's surveying as follows, while he turns away.*]

EXHIBITOR OF POTATOES—He swam his horses across swift rivers and creeks when his life was many times in danger.

EXHIBITOR OF JELLY—He was all the time looking for land of rich soil for his own. His surveying helped to know lands and to buy and pay for them. He had vision.

EXHIBITOR OF PIG—He enjoyed the outdoors. Trees and water were things of beauty to him. The other day I read in his diary about this surveying trip, he said:—

"We went through most beautiful groves of sugar Trees, and spent ye* best part of ye day in admiring ye trees and richness of ye land."

JUDGE OF CALVES—When the Indians came by with a scalp, for the tribes of the North and South were at war and the valley their war-path, Washington was friendly and courteous.

CLOTHING-CLUB GIRL—The Indians danced to amuse the young surveyors and parted from them with the friendliest feeling.

ALICE—Had he shown fear or been unfriendly, he would not later have won the confidence of the Red Men.

BOY—My! Everything had to be a *plus* in that experience, didn't it?

MARTHA—See, George is looking at the exhibit of the livestock and does not hear what you say; but well do I remember, when he came courting me, the experiences he told of, and without knowing he was braver or of more courage than others.

GEORGE (*Turning toward Boy*)—Where, my young man, is your exhibit?

BOY—I didn't have anything to exhibit.

GEORGE—How's that? You don't look like a failure.

BOY—I'm not. I do the best I can. (*He turns away.*)

EXHIBITOR OF POTATOES—Oh, he's our Club Leader. He always came around just as I was in trouble and needed help.

EXHIBITOR OF SHEEP—I could not have exhibited my products without him.

EXHIBITOR OF HOME-PAINTED FURNITURE—He's off now to help with the livestock and to keep from hearing us tell about him.

MEMBER OF PIG CLUB—He'd never let me tell how he took what he earned two years ago to buy me a calf.

CLOTHING-CLUB GIRL—He bought his mother a sewing machine instead of buying a calf for himself.

GEORGE (*To Boy as he returns*)—A boy who keeps confidence in himself and helps others has indeed put his capacities in good order.

BOY—I remember that you never lost your self-confidence.

GEORGE—I did my best.

BOY—Though losing battles you always saved your army and didn't let the enemy take you.

GEORGE—You're a boy after my own heart. Let's have a blue ribbon. (*He is handed a ribbon and pins it on Boy*) I hail you a Blue-Ribbon Boy!

ALL—Hurrah for our Club Leader! Hurrah for the Blue-Ribbon Boy!

BOY—I cheer for Mary and the National 4-H Camp.

MARTHA—Mary has the Magic. I see it in the look of her eye.

[*Exeunt all except Mary.*]

MARY (*waking, Paper Magic Square still in her hand*)—Oh! What happened? I remember. It was a perfect loaf of bread —my abilities put in order. Bread gone! But I can make another. I have new power. I know, 'twas this square. It's magic. George Washington had that magic. On Achievement Day I can win! Win as Washington did! (*Then another memory comes and her face gladdens.*) Where's Boy? I must tell him!

PART III

(*Use as a new dialogue.*)

Mary and Boy are on the stage alone at first. Wearers of the following placards enter when called later.

Faith and Self-Confidence.	Judgment.
Foresight.	Resourcefulness.
Vision.	Enthusiasm.
Accuracy.	Industry.
Technical Knowledge.	Perseverance.
Order and System.	Initiative.
Skill.	Self-Control.

Also George and Martha Washington.

* "Ye"—old English form pronounced as "the."

MARY—I've been reading how George Washington put his powers in order on that surveying trip.

BOY—Has it helped you?

MARY—Yes, I really know the secret of the Magic Square now.

BOY—Your Club record is good, Mary, if you can win a Blue Ribbon on your exhibit.

MARY—You mean I might really be good enough for National 4-H Camp.

BOY—That's it, and (shyly), too good, for me, Mary.

MARY (surprised)—Boy, I want to make good.

BOY—Make good now, Mary.

MARY—What shall I do?

BOY—Make blue-ribbon bread.

MARY—Shut your eyes and I'll call in my helpers.

[Boy shuts his eyes.]

MARY—Come, Helpers! (Enter persons wearing placards.)

MARY (Looking around)—I feel fussed. I wish I could call in George and Martha Washington, too.

BOY—Why?

MARY—For inspiration.

[Enter George and Martha Washington.]

WEARER OF PLACARD, FAITH AND SELF-CONFIDENCE—Wear this, Mary. (Takes off the placard and throws string over Mary's head resting placard on her chest.)

MARTHA—It is becoming to you, Mary.

MARY—I like it, too.

MARTHA—We want to see you win.

WEARER OF FORESIGHT-PLACARD (Arranges a table and makes believe to provide a kitchen and equipment for Mary)—All is ready.

MARY—My powers help put themselves in order.

VISION (Holding out placard that audience may see who speaks) Do you want me?

MARY—Vision, stay close by that I may have before me a picture of the perfect loaf of bread.

ACCURACY (Holding out placard)—It is, remember, white yeast bread.

VISION—Yes, Technical Knowledge has told me what such bread should be like.

TECHNICAL KNOWLEDGE—Smooth, crisp, golden-brown crust; crumbs elastic; creamy white texture and even cells.

FORESIGHT (Still arranging for making of bread)—There must be flour, bread board, and all the ingredients and equipment.

ORDER AND SYSTEM—These must in order. (Aiding in placing things on table.)

SKILL—It helps me along to have order.

MARY AS FAITH AND SELF-CONFIDENCE—Technical Knowledge will guide skill.

SKILL (Busy at table)—The ingredients are mixed—where can this liquid cool?

FORESIGHT—There was no place, but Resourcefulness has poured water into this pan. Set the bowl in it.

TECHNICAL KNOWLEDGE (moving toward bowl)—If too hot, it would kill the yeast; too cold, stop its growth.

ACCURACY—The test is that the outside of the bowl should be neither warm nor cool. (Mixes the dough.)

JUDGMENT—It is just right now.

SKILL (kneading the bread)—I must knead lightly.

TECHNICAL KNOWLEDGE—That will tell in the texture of the crumb.

JUDGMENT—It looks like the proper kneading. I would stop now.

ACCURACY—Too much kneading spoils the bread.

FORESIGHT—The warm place I had for the dough to rise is now too warm.

RESOURCEFULNESS (Opens up the door)—Soon the other room will be the right temperature.

JUDGMENT (going to door and standing a moment)—It is so now.

MARY—How promptly each ability does its part.

SKILL (Taking bowl brought by Industry)—I must first punch it.

TECHNICAL KNOWLEDGE—To punch it or to knead very lightly prevents the cells from being over large.

MARY—I know the flavor will be good.

JUDGMENT—It's ready for the second kneading.

SKILL—I must get a very light touch, now.

TECHNICAL KNOWLEDGE—Your skill is just right.

ENTHUSIASM—It is skill plus.

MARTHA—It's the magic.

TECHNICAL KNOWLEDGE (Speaking to Judgment)—In the baking, you must use Judgment plus.

JUDGMENT—The loaf is now risen to double its size.

MARTHA—What a nice-shaped loaf it is.

JUDGMENT—The oven is too hot.

FORESIGHT—Hurry, place the pan in a cooler place before the dough rises too high.

RESOURCEFULNESS—Shut down the heat, open the oven door, for a minute or two.

ORDER AND SYSTEM—The ingredients and mixing things can be cleared away.

JUDGMENT—The oven is just right now.

VISION—I yet see the perfect loaf—springy, soft crumb.

INDUSTRY—Let's get the loaf in the oven.

ENTHUSIASM—How well it goes!

MARY—I feel yet other powers wanting to help.

ORDER AND SYSTEM—They must wait their turn.

PERSEVERANCE—I helped Skill knead.

INIATIVE—I called in Concentration and Ambition.

SELF-CONTROL—I keep close to Enthusiasm so that it does not interfere with Industry.

GEORGE—Once your capacities are put in order, each one is stronger.

MARY—I never could do this before.

JUDGMENT—The oven has an even heat.

TECHNICAL KNOWLEDGE—Then the loaf will be right.

MARY (*To all*)—Come, see my bread.

[*All gather around her.*]

MARTHA—I can tell by the smell, it is thoroughly cooked.

GEORGE—I long for a taste.

BOY—Hurrah, Mary has the magic!

TECHNICAL KNOWLEDGE—The crust is a bit dry.

RESOURCEFULNESS—Butter it.

MARY (*To all*)—Wait a moment and you can see.

MARTHA (*Holding up the bread*)—A perfect loaf.

MARY—My own bread—perfect!

BOY—It's blue-ribbon bread.

ALL—Hurrah for Mary!

SECOND NUMBER OF THE GEORGE WASHINGTON ACQUAINTANCE DAY PROGRAM

GEORGE WASHINGTON
COUNTRY BOY AND MAN

Here follow twelve paragraphs revealing George Washington as farm boy and farmer. Assign a paragraph to each of twelve 4-H Club Members, who in turn read or tell its substance to the audience.

Born on a Farm that His Grandfather Had Owned

1. How many of our club members can say they belong to the country and to the farm as did young George Washington? He was the fourth generation of the Washington family to live on the farm where he was born. His birthplace was later called "Wakefield." George never saw a town of 5,000 population until he was a grown man.

George Had a Home at Three Farms

2. George Washington's father had three farms. When George was three years old, the family moved from Wakefield to a farm lying along the Potomac. Years later, his half-brother, Lawrence, named this farm Mount Vernon. When George was about seven years old, they moved to the third farm. This lay along the Rappahannock near the present town of Fredericksburg. When George was eleven his father died. There were still the three farms, and George had a home on each of them for his half-brothers, Lawrence and Augustine, had married and lived respectively at Mount Vernon and Wakefield, and his mother stayed on at the Rappahannock place. It was fifty miles up the Potomac from the farm where Washington was born to Mount Vernon, and his mother's farm lay approximately forty-five miles from either of the farms of her step-sons. In the journeys by water or land made between these farm homes, George became familiar with great stretches of country. This made him still more a country boy.

George's Ancestors in England were Landowners

3. George was not only born and brought up in the country but by family tradition he belong to the land. For six centuries back, the forebears of young George had possessed land. Their social standing and position in the world came from their titles to estates and country property. Washington could not get away from being a country boy. It was in his blood.

His Vision of Land Grows

4. Both of Washington's parents were landowners in the Virginia Colony. His mother had been left a farm of 400 acres by her father, who died when she was a little girl; and later, from her step-brother, several hundred acres lying in Stratford county. As if the three farms his father had owned, which ranged in size from 260 to 2,500 acres, did not give him enough of the country, he had the privilege of roaming over Belvoir—the large estate of Col. William Fairfax—where Lord Fairfax was staying. His friendship with the elder English nobleman brought yet more land into his life; for Lord Fairfax had enormous Crown grants of land in the Colony. Hired by Lord Fairfax to help survey it when he was sixteen years old, Washington came to know other great stretches of wild land. His interest in land became a part of his life and had to do with everything he did.

Landowners Looked Up To

5. In the Virginia Colony one had to be a landowner to wield power or influence—an idea brought from the Mother Country. In England, no man could vote unless he had title to land worth 40 shillings a year; in Virginia, it was the landowner who was sent to the House of Burgesses, it was the title-holder to acres of land who received the homage of his fellows as his big coach bumped over the roads. Whether the land had good soil or poor did not matter. When the land grants were made nobody cared anything about the condition of the soil. They gave no thought about the crops they could raise. It was land! Acres upon acres of land! Like many others of his day, George Washington's respect for large holdings of land was as much a part of his character as his hands and feet were part of his body; but in addition he believed in the land itself.

George Buys Land

6. George Washington bought land with his earnings at surveying. When he was seventeen years old he bought a tract of 550 acres called "My Bullskin Plantation." From this start he continued to buy land all his life. He had acquired in two tracts above a thousand acres when through the death of his half-brother, Lawrence Washington, Mount Vernon, an estate of 2,700 acres came into his control. He added to these holdings until at the age of twenty-five years he had 4,558 acres. Two years later he married the widow, Martha Custis, and thus her lands and those belonging to her two children were placed in his hands. Besides holdings in Virginia, he had land in the unsettled West. For his services in the French and Indian War he received 15,000 acres of wild lands beyond the Allegheny Mountains. He bought shares allotted to fellow soldiers who cared as little for the plots of ground in the unsettled Ohio region as most of us

would care for a few acres off in Siberia. It was his faith in the land that made him think it worthwhile to fight to keep the West for the English. At his death he had 63,000 acres, lying in what is now seven states and the District of Columbia.

Fought in Defense of Land

7. George Washington's allegiance to his lands and the principles by which free-born Englishmen held their rights made him willing to fight for that land to free it from control by any but himself. Most of his neighbors were born to a like tradition and felt much the same way. They became aroused to protect their farms, their homes, their stock and their crops, from unjust taxation; and to avoid the punishment that the home government threatened, these colonial farmers were ready to defend their rights even at the cost of life. So in every settlement they left their plows, hoes and fields, and grabbed their guns to do their part in the Revolution. Liberty, independence and land, were held together in Washington's mind. He was ready to give his life for all three and to scarifice his own wealth that through freedom there might be a nation built from the soil.

Loyal to the Old Homestead

8. The Mount Vernon estate, which by the addition of neighboring fields came to include 8,000 acres, was not very productive. Certainly few 4-H Club boys would care to struggle with some of the worn-out gullied fields of Mount Vernon. Washington tried in every possible way to build it up. There was not an agricultural college nor any authority on farming in the country for him to call upon for help. During his military travels he had learned much from observing other farms and had talked with many farmers and large plantation owners. He wrote long letters to the superintendents and overseers of his farms while he was away during the long war, telling and advising them what to do. But his place was run down when he returned and he renewed his efforts to build up the soil and to work out a system of planting, cultivating and harvesting. He tested soils and seeds. He marked off experimental plots of ground and watched carefully the results of his experiments. He even sowed salt to see the effect on the production of the soil. He tried to take the rich mud from the bed of the Potomac and put it on his land, but the undertaking was too difficult and costly. He rotated crops and pastured the meadows. In the end, the poverty of the soil discouraged him though he kept on farming it. But he treasured this family farm, praised its location and by his tree-planting and other careful improvements, helped to make it a place of unusual beauty and charm. To this day Mount Vernon carries much of the same atmosphere it had when George and Martha Washington lived there. It is by its beauty as well as its historical association an American shrine—thanks to the loyalty of Washington to the old farm home.

First Farmer of His Day

9. Concentration, spirit of adventure and experimentation, added to order and system governed his farm management. At 7 a. m. in summer and 8 a. m. in winter he got on his horse to make his morning rounds over his several farms, for 4,000 acres of the Mt. Vernon estate were tilled. Each of the separate farms into which the estate was divided had its own overseer, dwellings,

store-houses, and workshops for the making of things needed for the laborers, the stock, and the work. He saw for himself how his overseers were looking after his crops and how the laborers carried on their work. His records of the yield of the various farm products can be read in his diaries. He used business methods and was exact in his accounts. When he hired an overseer for a farm, the agreement was frequently put in writing telling the exact duties of both parties. He built a twelve-sided barn, first figuring out the number of brick needed and burning these on his own place. Often the new devices he tried did not work. He had an inventor come to Mt. Vernon to construct a threshing machine from the inventor's own plans. It threshed at first fifty bushels a day, then it fell to twenty-five, and finally failed completely before five hundred bushels had been threshed. But disappointments did not stop his efforts to progress. Jacks and jennies were sent to him by the King of Spain and by the Marquis de Lafayette. From these animals Washington bred mules which he found useful on the farm. He graded his flour and put it into barrels made by his own plantation coopers. In the West Indies, where quantities of flour bearing the name *George Washington,* were shipped, the islanders are said to have taken it without inspection. He had his own flour mills and gave careful attention to every process from selecting and testing the wheat seed to the grading and shipping of flour. His field crops did not cause him to neglect the common vegetables. He used for seed-potatoes his largest and finest, instead of small ones as many made the mistake of planting. He liked the carrot. It was his aim to make his farms supply most of the needs of his own family and the families of his farm help. By his own efforts he became the leading farmer of his day.

Forerunner of Modern Agriculture

10. Washington's faith in land and his vision made him a farmer well in advance of his time. He was among the first to follow a method of farming aimed to save and restore the soil. He believed that farmers owed a duty to the future of the ground they tilled. He wrote of the farming of his time, saying that "much ground had been *scratched* over, and none cultivated or improved as it ought to have been." In later years, he corresponded with leading agriculturists of Europe, among these Arthur Young of England, who gave Washington much help and information. Washington's library had many volumes on farming and related subjects. There were titles on gardening, husbandry, natural history, bees, horses and horsemen, and several volumes of *Young's Travels.* He wrote letters to Mr. Young of his delight in growing things. In one, he told how a contemplative mind was filled with more ideas than it were easy to express at seeing plants rise and flourish by the superior skill and bounty of the laborer.

Beauty in Farm Surroundings

11. As a boy, George roamed over hills and through valleys, crossing streams and wandering through deep woods. He saw white clouds play against the blue sky and he watched the seasons change the garb of the earth from green to somber brown, white,

and then to green again. Beauty of the open spaces—land, streams, sky—caught his eye. He wrote of it when he visited the Barbadoes Islands with his brother. He took pride in planting and improving upon the landscape of Mount Vernon. He laid out serpentine roads and designed gardens and grouped the plants with such a sense of balance and taste that Mount Vernon gardens, with their boxwood hedges and famous flower pots, are an inspiration to this day. He knew how to mass certain plants and to scatter others for the best effect. He planted trees of all kinds—those native to that locality, those brought from his travels, those sent from other places. His taste, in choosing and arranging trees and shrubs and in designing his garden, reveals the man. He made his country home a place of beauty because he had himself found the beauty of nature.

The Old Washington Plantation Today

12. George and Martha Washington went to live at Mount Vernon in 1759. He had retired from an active military service that had lasted over five years. It was now his purpose to live in quiet on his plantation for the rest of his life, but after sixteen years their home life was interrupted by the call of the Revolution and George Washington was away with the army for eight years. But during those early years, when he and Martha first lived at Mount Vernon, he laid the foundation for the Mount Vernon that we know today. Gradually and constantly he improved the old farm so that there was no more home-like place in all Virginia. There were old-fashioned gardens reached by well-trimmed paths. The fields were fenced, roads had been carefully made and the buildings were in good repair. Always it was the simple that accomplished his purpose—planting trees and shrubs, laying walks, improving garden plots, and looking to the upkeep of the buildings. Mount Vernon may well be called America's First Farm Home.

THIRD NUMBER ON GEORGE WASHINGTON ACQUAINTANCE DAY PROGRAM

MUSIC—The Battle of Trenton.....By James Hewitt (1770-1827)

This popular military sonata, dedicated to General Washington in 1797 is included in a publication of the United States George Washington Bicentennial Commission entitled "Music from the Days of George Washington." This collection was made and provided with an introduction by Carl Engel, Chief of Division of Music, Library of Congress, the music edited by W. Oliver Strunk, Assistant, Division of Music, Library of Congress.

During the Bicentennial year a copy of "Music from the Days of George Washington" may be obtained by addressing your request to the United States George Washington Bicentennial Commission, Washington Building, Washington, D. C.

FOURTH NUMBER OF THE GEORGE WASHINGTON ACQUAINTANCE DAY PROGRAM

GEORGE WASHINGTON HURDLES

Place on the stage or platform hurdles of different kinds and heights, as a rope hurdle, the ends laying across two chairs or held by two players; a coat or hat stand; two chairs placed side by side (for a long jump across the two seats); a box (hurdle for boy of ten or twelve). Each hurdle has fastened on it an appropriate label naming the quality which let George clear it. To make the hurdle more interesting one of those speaking the dialogue or some other person, jumps it. If it is desired, one of the hurdles may be higher than any can clear. The attire for George Washington may be merely a suggestion of the Colonial costume, as a white wig and three-cornered Colonial-style hat.

HURDLE NUMBER ONE

[A high rope hurdle. It is marked "Faith." Let this hurdle be high enough to call for the best hurdler of the 4-H Club, who clears it just before the following dialogue begins.]

FIRST SPEAKER—What do you think of that hurdle (pointing to the rope) for a growing boy?

SECOND SPEAKER—Why is it called "Faith?"

FIRST SPEAKER—That was how George Washington cleared it. The hurdle wasn't really a rope. It had to do with George's life.

SECOND SPEAKER—Tell me.

FIRST SPEAKER—It was this. His father dies leaving the two big farms for his half-brothers. George can look on at the advantages of his half-brothers (who were sent to England to school and who now have the best farms) without jealousy.

SECOND SPEAKER—Indeed that was not easy, and when he grew to be a 14-year-old boy and was wanting to do things, he must have felt out of sorts about it.

GEORGE WASHINGTON (as a boy of thirteen or fourteen years, coming from side stage)—You do not know my faith in my father. He only followed the customs of his time in leaving the large farms to my brothers.

FIRST SPEAKER—But many a boy would have sulked and balked.

GEORGE WASHINGTON—That would have invited the ill-will of my half-brothers, who did many kind things for me.

[George Exits]

HURDLE NUMBER TWO

[A coat-stand placed on chair, or some other hurdle no one can jump. A girl, holding a rope, flings the free end over the top of the hurdle to bring home the idea that it would take an unusual hurdler to jump it. The label on the hurdle is "Generosity." There follows this dialogue by the same or two other speakers.]

FIRST SPEAKER—But here's the highest hurdle George Washington may have jumped.

SECOND SPEAKER—Do you mean his braving bullets without caring?

FIRST SPEAKER—Not that, a soldier has to do such things.

SECOND SPEAKER—Was it that he kept silence when his own Generals tried to have his command taken away?

FIRST SPEAKER—You are getting nearer, for that too was generosity.

SECOND SPEAKER—What generosity of the man are you thinking of?

FIRST SPEAKER—You know that he was a rich man.

SECOND SPEAKER—He was a practical business man, too. Lots of hard common sense.

FIRST SPEAKER—Looked after the needs of his brothers' families, his sister's and even the children of his friends, making it necessary to borrow money for himself.

SECOND SPEAKER—Yes, he borrowed money when he was inaugurated President.

FIRST SPEAKER—It's funny how he stuck by his nephews and all his relatives and sent the children of his friends to school. Once when a man he had long known wanted a loan of money and the General didn't have any to lend, he was not satisfied until he set down all the facts so his friend could see for himself his lack of funds.

GEORGE WASHINGTON (*as a man*)—It would have been a comfort always to have had ready money. I did not like to borrow when I was inaugurated President. But the care of one's family and the urgent needs of relatives and friends cannot wait. It is practical sense to put first things first.

[*George Exits*]

HURDLE NUMBER THREE

[*A boy takes a long leap over the seats of the two chairs. This hurdle is labelled "Forgets Difficulties."*]

FIRST SPEAKER—You know about the wilderness trip?

SECOND SPEAKER—I surely do. He was shot at by an Indian, and came near being drowned and frozen. He had to manage to keep friendly with Indians ready to play him treachery and keep clear of schemes that might have brought disaster.

FIRST SPEAKER—Yet he wrote in his diary, at a stopping place on his way to the French, after the hardest and most difficult travel, "we arrived the 4th of *December* without any thing remarkable happening but a continued Series of bad Weather."

GEORGE WASHINGTON (*As a young man comes from side stage to center*)—A man wastes time talking or thinking about the difficulties he has already passed.

[*George Exits*]

HURDLE NUMBER FOUR

[*A boy of ten or twelve, jumps the box hurdle which calls for as high a jump as he can well make. The hurdle is labelled "Manliness."*]

FIRST SPEAKER—George lived in a raw, new country, but an English Nobleman was his neighbor and friend.

SECOND SPEAKER—My! That was good luck for him. How did that English Lord come to like George so well?

FIRST SPEAKER—They rode together fox-hunting and Lord Fairfax found what the boy was like. He said that he didn't talk much and that he tried to think things out and to reach just conclusions.

SECOND SPEAKER—A fellow would have to be a pretty fine sort, I'm thinking, to please an educated English nobleman.

FIRST SPEAKER—It was where being manly brought good luck. George got a good paying job surveying the Fairfax lands.

GEORGE WASHINGTON (*as a youth*)—I didn't know I was gaining Lord Fairfax's good will. I was having a fine time on the fox-hunt. He found out about me without my knowing it.

[*George Exits*]

FIRST SPEAKER—Let's see more about this boy, George Washington.

SECOND SPEAKER—I am with you, come along.

[*They Exeunt*]

FIFTH NUMBER OF THE GEORGE WASHINGTON ACQUAINTANCE DAY PROGRAM

[*A DANCE—Minuet and Gavotte.......By Alexander Reinagle (1756-1809)*]

The music for this dance, popular in Colonial Virginia, is found in the publication of the United States George Washington Bicentennial Commission referred to on page 563. Boccherini's minuet is obtainable for the victrola.

SIXTH NUMBER ON GEORGE WASHINGTON ACQUAINTANCE DAY PROGRAM

A 4-H-er's Biography of Young Washington in One Sentence.

(*To be memorized and spoken by a good 4-H Club speaker.*)

In the surroundings and under the conditions of his farm home, young George acquired habits of thrift and industry, learned secrets of the soil as it yielded crops years by year, took responsibility for younger brothers and sister, surveyed wilderness land for ordered cultivation and settlement, and became through his physical strength, practiced skill, knowledge, proven capacity and force of heart, a young man looked to for service and leadership.

SEVENTH NUMBER GEORGE WASHINGTON ACQUAINTANCE DAY PROGRAM

The Next Step in the 4-H Memorial to Washington

That 4-H Club Members may make their celebration a fitting one, they should follow the experiences of Washington as he achieves. No episode in his life serves better than his first job that took him for six weeks into wild country and demanded of him, under the leadership of a public surveyor, a definite accomplishment. This experience is described in an achievement square of twenty-five units which have to do with young George and the accomplishment of his task. Read at your Club meeting or at home. See how this youth put his powers in order and what it gained for him. The achievement square of his surveying trip does not recall the whole experience, for like your own achievement square, much is left out. Yet it shows how he brought his capacities together and used them for his purpose. During the Spring and Summer find all you can of the way the Founder of this Nation did things, how he thought, and how he made his dreams come true. When you feel a lift, a desire to be like him, put that inspiration into your your 4-H work. On Achievement Day in the Fall you can estimate *by your products and by yourselves what your Celebration of the Two Hundredth Anniversary of the Birth of George Washington has been.*

III. GEORGE WASHINGTON'S EXPERIENCES

Your 1932 4-H slogan—"Win as Washington Would!"

How Youthful George Washington Achieved in the Shenandoah Valley

George, at sixteen, was given work surveying wilderness land belonging to Lord Fairfax. This took him into the Shenandoah Valley for several weeks during a season of unsettled weather. Twenty-three-year-old George William Fairfax, Lord Fairfax's cousin, also took part in the work. The experience turned out well for George, since the next year his friend, Lord Fairfax, helped him to be appointed county surveyor. His own records of the surveying trip tell what he had to meet and to overcome and how he did his work. This wilderness adventure seems to have prepared him for many things—later adventures in wild unknown country, contacts with the Indians, unusual responsibilities. But look at it first as a specific piece of work—the laying out of wild, unsettled, rough country.

SPIRIT OF ADVENTURE

When George Washington was going to school he was quick in arithmetic. His teacher suggested that he learn surveying. This idea met finally with the approval of his mother, and the boy's probable dream of the sea with its thrills and adventure was turned to visions of land and the adventures to be found in tramping forests unknown to anybody but the Indians and wild beasts; in going over rivers and creeks, swimming and wading streams; scaling mountains; picking his way over swamps and meeting all the dangers and thrills that the unbroken wilderness can give. The spirit of adventure was strong in him.

How free he was! In the surveying of wild land he found the thrills a boy or girl longs for. Indian tribes were at war among themselves. Storms and other dangers had to be faced, and in all he must, by hook or crook, get his work done. It was adventure and yet with it was the necessity to be patient and to meet responsibility. It steadied him, balanced and strengthened his zeal, so that afterwards on his long wilderness trip to the Ohio region, through the French and Indian Wars and in the Revolution—under trying conditions—he kept his head. In the face of bullets he was calm. On the quiet of his farm he found adventure. Each experience left him more ready for the next.

AN ACHIEVEMENT SQUARE OF GEORGE WASHINGTON'S SURVEYING OF SHENANDOAH LAND

Spirit of Adventure Conquest of Fear	Patience	Cooperation	Industry	Interest in Land
Power of Observation	Aptitude and Liking for Surveying	Order and System	Tact and Friendliness with Indians	Ambition
Enthusiasm	Judgment in Using Knowledge	Accuracy and Painstaking Work	Self-Confidence	Skill
Power of Concentration	Enjoyment of Outdoors	Purpose and Goal	Spirit of Pioneering	Perseverance
Trust in Providence	Physical Sturdiness and Endurance	Instant Decision to Act	Resourcefulness and Planning	Adaptability & Readiness to Meet Hardships

CONQUEST OF FEAR

George's father had kept him from thinking of fear by teaching him to ride and he had become a good swimmer and fast runner. He could climb, wrestle, throw, and take care of himself in the ventures that came his way. He seemed to use every such experience to conquer fear—after he had seen Indians with scalps, this could not in the future frighten him. Thus, step by step, he ousted any fear he might have had. It is hard to realize how completely he was without it. Later on in battles, when bullets went through his clothes and horses fell wounded under him, he appeared braver than it seemed possible for a man to be. This was in part because he had early met most of the fears there were and conquered them.

PATIENCE

Although the wilderness land was not settled, there was an occasional cleared spot on which a house had been built with a family living in it. Youthful George did not take to these strange people. In fact, in a letter to a friend, he called them barbarians and said they were uncouth. To make the best of all such circumstances went into the day's work. Likewise, hardships brought by their pioneer way of life, which of course was in contrast to the comforts and interests of his home, were not the kind of adventure George liked best. He was forced to be patient. It was one of the traits of achieving.

Cooperation

When George wrote in his diary of the surveying experiences he used very often the word "we." He said, "We set out early;" "We swam our horses over;" "We breakfasted;" "We ran off four lots,"—and so on. He did things with others—cooperated. When the Indians came by he was friendly with them. Meeting all the changes of weather and circumstances of the outdoors was a kind of cooperation, too. The skill of surveying and following the directions of the leader called for team play. How the capacity to do things with others grew! In the trying time in the Revolution, when some of his own officers had plotted against him and their schemes were exposed, he let the slight pass and worked on with them for a common victory.

Industry

According to his diary, when the weather was good, he was out at work. He and his companion traveled in the rain, or otherwise made preparations to make the most of their time. He wrote, "finding y. River [Potomac] not much abated we in y. Evening Swam our horses over and carried them to Charles Polks in Maryland for Pasturage till y. next Morning.

"Monday 21st. We went over in a Canoe and travell'd . . . all y. Day in a Continued Rain to Collo Cresaps [a famous frontiersman who settled at 'Old Town' on the Maryland side of Potomac] right against y. Mouth of y. South Branch about 40 miles from Polks I believe y. worst Road that ever was trod by Man or Beast."

On another day he made this entry:

"We went and Survey'd 15 Hundred Acres of Land and Return'd . . . about 1 oClock about two I heard that Mr. Fairfax was come up and at 1 Peter Casseys about 2 Miles of in ye. same Old Field I then took my Horse and went up to see him we eat our Dinners and Walked down to Vammetris's we stayed about two Hours and Walked back again and slept at Casseys House which was ye first Night I had slept in a House since I came to ye Branch."

A biographer has called Washington "The first 'Do it now' man." His planning and his doing went hand-in-hand and so he accomplished much while he was yet a young man, and this industry followed him through life. There are more of his writings in the Library of Congress than those of any other person. Yet he was a man of action rather than a writer. The habit of industry practiced while he was young gave him power as a man.

Interest in Land

George liked land as an aviator likes airplanes, as a sea captain likes a ship. A year after this surveying trip he bought a tract of 550 acres. He watched out for fertile soil. Wandering over millions of acres and laying out boundaries, his vision of land widened. Without this joy in land, he would doubtless have cared less for surveying and would not have succeeded so well. Coming from a family of landholders, the tradition dating back several centuries. What was more natural than that he in a new country should become interested in land? He had a different sense of farm ground than most of the landowners of his time for he wanted to save the soil. How fitting it was that his first occupation was surveying land. To his last years he worked to improve his fields. His interest had not changed. In soil he saw a whole new system of agriculture. He may have dreamed of it as he surveyed in the wild Shenandoah Valley.

Power of Observation

It came natural for George to observe the outdoor scenes about him. He quickly saw the lay-out of the surrouding country. As he rode along his eye took in the change of scene and he was able to describe the landscape in few words. Of one observation he wrote: "The Trough is [a] couple of Ledges of Mountain Impassable running side and side together for above 7 or 8 Miles and ye River down between them." Memory of the lay of land, rivers, mountains, stayed with him. His quickness to get the topography of the surrouding country came to be useful in military exploits. When he came to a site that commanded both the Allegheny and Monongahela Rivers he put down that it was "extremely well situated for a Fort." Measuring unsettled country trained his powers to observe.

Aptitude and Liking for Surveying

His liking for land, his industry, his skill in measuring, the friendly interest of Lord Fairfax in his success, the good pay and the adventure afforded, all helped to turn his aptitude for surveying into an ambition to be a successful surveyor. Perhaps few who lay out land have the liking for the job as had Washington. He surveyed and resurveyed his home lands in the late years of his life.

Order and System

His diaries start with this surveying trip. He had evidently already learned to apply order and system. Lord Fairfax wrote George's mother who had asked the nobleman's advice about sending her son to England to school, that "method and exactness seem to be natural to George." No detail was too small for him to consider. Yet he was brief in what he wrote down. Later the methodical journal of his journey to Fort LeBeouf and return provided the information that is said to have started the French and Indian War. When his half-brother, Lawrence, went to Barbadoes for his health, George accompanied him. On the way over and also on the return trip, he amused himself by making and keeping a ship's log. His methodical habit helped him to become a well-informed man for he took care of the knowledge he gained.

Tact and Friendliness with the Indians

The surveying took him along the warpaths of the Northern and Southern tribes of Indians. From his parents and from neighborhood legends he must have learned much of the nature of the Redmen. At any rate, he showed a natural tact and understanding in dealing with the band of wandering Indians which they met while surveying. He was friendly and they were good humored, even dancing for the white men to see. George described this visit and the Indian dance in his diary:

"Wednesday 23d Rain'd till about two oClock and Clear'd when we were agreably surpris'd at y. sight of thirty odd Indians coming from War with only one Scalp . . . of whom we had a War Daunce there manner of Dauncing is as follows Viz They clear a Large Circle and make a Great Fire in y. middle then seats themselves around it y. Speaker makes a grand speech telling them in what Manner they are to Daunce after he has finished y. Best Dauncer jumps up as one awaked out of a Sleep and runs and jumps about y. Ring in a most comical Manner he is followed by y. Rest then begins there Musicians to Play ye. Musick is a Pot half [full] of Water with a Deerskin Streched over it as tight as it can and a goard with some Shott in it to Rattle and a Piece of an horses Tail tied to it to make it look fine y. one keeps Rattling and y. other Drumming all y. while y. others is Dauncing."

AMBITION

George desired to get a start in life, and, in keeping with the family tradition, he wanted to be a landowner. The way was offered through surveying. Besides he had pride in the occupation. The skill it called for and the life in the open appealed to him. All of these things had to do with his ambition to be a good surveyor, and his ambition to get on in the world made him the more eager to do well in the work he was starting. His earnings were a further satisfaction. He had to make his way. This work meant to him all that a first job and a chance mean to most American boys and girls ambitious to get on.

ENTHUSIASM

A 4-H boy or girl would soon have caught George's enthusiasm. It showed in his way of doing things. His was a quiet, lasting enthusiasm, as that of the modern young people who follow science and other interests in which their head, hands and heart join. He might have had the same capacities, yet without enthusiasm have done little with them. We are likely to undervalue this quality because some use enthusiasm merely in talk, but great accomplishment usually has strong emotion behind it. Enthusiasm brightens personality. It whets action and pushes energy out.

JUDGMENT IN USING KNOWLEDGE

George did not have schooling enough to give him the knowledge he needed. He learned most of what he knew as most boys and girls in 4-H clubs do—by finding something he wished to do or accomplish, and then discovering, as best he could, the right way to do it. He did not have such books and bulletins as boys and girls have today. By the time of the Revolution his practical sense was widely known. Patrick Henry said of him with respect to the men of the Continental Congress that for solid information and sound judgment he was unquestionably the greatest man on the floor.

ACCURACY AND PAINSTAKING WORK

The aid of Lord Fairfax in securing for George the position of county surveyor is evidence of how well he came through in the surveying trip. In this his most important accomplishment was his accurate and careful surveys. He was, it seems, too practiced in the habit of painstaking work for the difficulties of the wilderness to make him slip-shod. Like an airplane pilot flying in rough weather, his movements were at their best. The quality of his work showed up in practically everything he did. Later, when he moved his army across the Delaware, he did not leave a boat up or down the river for a distance of seventy-five miles. It was the same when he returned from war to manage Mount Vernon. In experimenting with seeds he measured his ground and laboriously calculated the number of seeds in a pound. He estimated that a pound of red clover contained 71,000 seeds, timothy 298,000, New River grass 44,000 and barley 8,925. With this information he could judge how much seed of each kind ought to be sown to an acre. It is not surprising that so painstaking a man was as a youth accurate on his first job. Lord Fairfax wrote George's mother that he presumed the boy to be "truthful because he is exact."

SELF-CONFIDENCE

George Washington had the habit of getting hold of all possible information beforehand for a task that he had to do. This gave him a quiet self-confidence that was very appealing to older people in their dealings with him. Lord Fairfax called it manliness, courage, and ability.

SKILL

His skill in his work is proven by the fact that the surveys that he made in 1748 and in the following three years have stood the tests of time and progress and are regarded with the highest respect by the surveyors of the present day. He acquired such skill as comes in partnership with industry. His was a high standard of workmanship. When he came to be the master of farm plantations, there were skilled craftsmen of various kinds—tailors, carpenters, shoemakers, smiths, employed on his plantations. The master instilled his ideals of good work in his help.

POWER OF CONCENTRATION

His work was never routine though by system, order and method, he put routine into it. His trip through the woods and across streams with his surveying equipment brought something new into his task all along. He had to think and to do at the same time. That he could keep up this kind of industry for so many hours tells what his power of concentration was. Surveying this land he trained a quality that grew into a powerful force for achieving and doing.

ENJOYMENT OF OUTDOORS

Was ever a boy's first job so close to what he liked? He did not mind taking great pains to make a straight, an honest line, because it was in the open. It was measuring land, and in its midst he was at home. Like a girl making a dress from material she likes, careful of her stitch and seam, George was the more accurate because the outdoors was agreeable to him. His enjoyment of the beauty of landscape and sky increased with the years. His eye caught at the same moment the outlay of the landscape, its plant growth and the richness of the soil. He was intimate with open spaces and when the chance came he planted trees, arranged gardens, marked out paths and walks so as to add to the beauty of nature. His diary shows that in May, 1786, he planted two rows of acorns of live and water oak, also pictachio nut, and in the shrubberies replaced dead cedars. He even laid out small wildernesses bringing young pines and other trees to replant. A record is left that these trees died and his would-be wildernesses did not thrive. As a boy he should have enjoyed a Forestry Club and the young wildernesses that modern boys and girls in these forestry ventures grow. You can not picture George Washington shut in from the outdoors.

PURPOSE AND GOAL

If you read his diary of this trip, dating from March 11 to April 13, 1748, you will discover many of Washington's traits. Sometimes the pay he received appeared very important to him. It ranged from around eight to as high as twenty dollars a day. In his letter to a young friend—in which he said he was in a place where no real satisfaction was to be had—he added that "there's nothing would make it pass of tolerably but a good Reward." The pay pleased him as it would anyone. Another interest that kept him alert to do his best and think of the immediate demands of the job was his aim to please Lord Fairfax with the work. This experience would help to qualify him for a position as public surveyor. His appointment as surveyor of Culpeper County reads:

"George Washington, Gent. produced a Commission from the President and Masters of William and Mary College, appointing him to be surveyor of this county, which was read and thereupon he took the usual oaths to his majesty's person and government." The goal and purpose closest to him spurred him on, and like most young people he was more conscious of these immediate desires than of ambitions to be realized in the remote future.

SPIRIT OF PIONEERING

When Washington was born, the Virginia Colony, dating from the Jamestown settlement, was a century and a quarter old. The landed class, despite the nearness to unsettled parts, had their established ways of living. The spirit of the pioneer was no more common to all then than now. Although George came from a land-holding family and was of the gentry, he had the make-up to meet new conditions and old conditions in new ways. All his life he remained the pioneer farmer, and his ways with his army told of the spirit of the pioneer in the Commander-in-Chief. This is found in his diary of 1748:

"Travell'd up ye Creek to Solomon Hedges Esq. one of his Majestys Justices of ye. Peace for ye County of Frederick where we camped when we came to Supper there was neither a Cloth upon ye. Table nor a knife to eat with but as good luck would have it we had knives of [our] own. . . . Last Night was a blowing and Rainy night Our Straw catch'd a Fire yt. we were laying upon and was luckily Preserv'd by one of our Mens awaking when in was in a [blaze] we run of four Lots this Day which Reached below Stumps. . . . Last Night was a much more blostering night than ye. former we had our Tent Carried Quite of with ye. Wind and was obliged to Lie ye. Latter part of

ye. night without covering. . . . one of our Men Shot a Wild Turkie."

PERSEVERANCE

Did George have so much persevering force that pushing through driving rain and terrible storms and keeping right on for weeks was only play? Perhaps these things took all the staying powers he had and made ready for the man's perseverance that in him was seemingly without measure. You know many of his exploits. When thrown into an icy river in water ten feet deep, he persevered and saved himself. It was a perseverance of a different order when he held out against the regulation of the Virginia Governor to let no Colonial in the Army have a higher rank than Captain. Washington had already made a strong fight against the practice of paying the Colonial less than the Royal officers and had declared that rather than waive his point of honor—since his services would equal those of the British— he would take no pay. At the second humiliation which put the Virginia officers in a lower rank than one with a Royal commission, he made a long journey to Boston to get the commander in chief to rectify it. A like persistency went into his efforts for justice and fairness to his soldiers throughout the Revolution. It was this trait in him which let Washington meet defeat yet keep himself separate from it—this power of a widely-used perseverance.

TRUST IN PROVIDENCE

George accepted the acts of Providence—storms, floods, and the forces of the elements beyond his control, as part of the experience. He was just a youth, taking in all that came his way and pioneering as would a boy camping out. Yet all unconsciously to himself he acted as one who believes his life has a purpose to serve and himself a destiny to fulfill. It was as important to him to make accurate measures of land and later grow plants well, to restore worn soil as to build a nation. He did things as one who has faith and trust.

PHYSICAL STURDINESS AND ENDURANCE

George, like all boys, tried his power at athletic games. Under his father's and then his half-brother's careful guidance, he was encouraged in all the sports and soon became known for his skill in wrestling, running, swimming, throwing, and such. Thus, without thinking about it at all, he prepared himself for hardships and hazards of outdoor life and this in turn hardened and developed his muscle and gave him new endurance. When growing up he was, for a time, round-shouldered and awkward. Not so, the man who took command of the Revolutionary forces.

"At that time he weighed 200 pounds and there was no surplus flesh about him. He was tremendously muscled, and the fame of his great strength was everywhere. His large tent, when wrapped up with poles, was so heavy that it required two men to place it in the camp wagon. Washington would lift it with one hand and throw it into the wagon as easily as if it were a pair of saddle-bags. He could hold a musket with one hand and shoot with precision as easily as did other men with a horse pistol."

He was at this time nearing forty-three and had spent many years on the farm. It would have been easy for him to have lost much of his physical perfection during this time. That he did not, tells something of the make-up of the man. Most certainly his regular horseback riding across long stretches of country, for he was a constant rider, had helped to keep him fit. There came occasions when his endurance, aided by a will of iron, seemed superhuman. At the time of General Braddock's final march against the French, Captain Washington, who was his volunteer aide-de-camp, had been left behind sick with a fever. On the evening before the battle that ended in the famous defeat of Braddock's army, Washington, too weak to ride, had been hauled to the front in a wagon. He went into the fray the next day, was under fierce fire for four hours, not out of the saddle until dark of the following day, and for a week after never had his clothes off. During the Revolution he met emergencies by reason of his ability to keep going without either food or sleep. He had built this force in him as he grew up, riding, living in the open, doing things.

INSTANT DECISION TO ACT

Roughing it in the woods and learning to be at home with the elements added to this young surveyor's experience. As he was a doer, it was often necessary for him to make quick decisions. He was not one who did things by guess. It was hard experience that whetted his power of quick decision and action. His accomplishments as a doer were increased by his care to make the right judgment. If, at critical times, he could not have seen what to do quickly his career would most probably have been short.

RESOURCEFULNESS AND PLANNING

Washington pulled through hard conditions because he was resourceful in unexepected ways. It became almost a recreation for him, keeping him from despair when tragedy and disaster were pending. When the army at Long Island seemed certain of capture, he took it to safety—men, baggage, and ammunition—without the loss of a man or the enemy discovering their departure until it was accomplished.

ADAPTABILITY AND READINESS TO ACCEPT HARDSHIP

George had on his surveying job a full taste of physical hardships—perhaps as much as his vigor could withstand. In his journal he gives a glimpse of the difficulties met:—

"Rain'd Successively all Last night this Morning one of our men Killed a Wild Turkie that weight 20 pounds."

"Our Provisions being all exhausted and ye Person who was to bring us a Recruit disappointing us we were oblige to go without untill we could get some at ye Neighbours which was not till about 4 or 5 oClock in ye Evening."

Doubtless many of his troubles on the trip were short-lived as described here, yet they let him try his metal and helped him to see the stuff he was made of—how adaptable he was. As one would guess of him, when hardships piled up later, he mentioned them scarcely at all. You know many such among your friends for Americans have their likeness to Washington; and being a good sport, meeting difficulties, is an American trait. Washing-ton is called, "The First American," and the proof of it two hundred years after his birth is that this likeness is seen in the people of the country he started on its way.

GEORGE WASHINGTON—THE ACHIEVER

You recall that in the dialogue of the "Magic Square" something was said about foresight *plus*, willingness *plus*, etc. In this connection *"plus"* names the "added something" of a capacity that gives one power beyond the average. A great actor has the *plus*. It marks off an individual from the common lot. George Washington attained the *"plus"* in many capacities. He was not a born genius but his capabilities, by use, gathered force and their combined power often let him accomplish the impossible. As a doer, as an achiever, his highest accomplishment was not a victory in battle, nor escaping with his army from capture by the British. It was no outstanding feat though he did the unusual time and time again. The biographer who said that Washington accumulated many defeats but was never himself defeated, named his star achievement. *He was himself never defeated*. A boy or girl likes to think and reflect on this fact.

JUDGMENT PLUS

Young George Washington's capabilities took on power as he trained them. Of these none were more outstanding that his judgment. A republic like the United States has much need of this quality in its citizens. See how it appeared in incidents of George Washington's life.

His determination, while yet a little lad, to acquire information of all kinds was a sign of his judgment.

His eagerness to learn woodcraft and Indian lore reached past the point of getting a thrill of adventure from the savages. He wanted to be on friendly terms with them and he was. It was good sense.

In surveying he learned land—timber, swamp and mountain—bers he managed to surrender so as to leave the scene with the full learned.

When he was at Fort Necessity fighting against superior numbers he managed to surrender so as to leave the scene with the full honors of war.

He was well acquainted with the leading men of his day from the Boston Port Bill and similar demands made by England upon Massachusetts. When the question of what Virginia should do to help Boston came before the Virginia convention, he is reported to have said, "I will raise 1,000 men, subsist them at my own expense, and march myself at their head for the relief of Boston." Trust in his judgment had much to do with the decision of his Colony to aid New England.

It was in part his practical sense that kept him from showing animosity toward opponents.

He was well acquainted with the leading men of his day from among whom he chose his Cabinet, selecting strong men regardless of political considerations. This reflects again to the credit of his judgment.

The layout of the Capital City is a present-day evidence of the practical judgment of Washington, who gave constant attention to the plans for the city that bears his name. His term of office expired before the removal of the seat of Government from Philadelphia so that he was never resident in the present Capital.

As President he set precedents in both foreign and domestic affairs that guide the Nation today. He had vision as to business affairs, education, politics based on practical insight. There are leaders who have courage, but those who have both courage and good judgment are rare. Washington's power of judgment came to a large degree from his early habit of seeking out knowledge and using it to achieve a desirable and a just purpose.

IV. GEORGE WASHINGTON ACHIEVEMENT DAY FOR 4-H CLUBS

Make this Day an Occasion of Memorial to George Washington. Let your tribute show:—

Unusual order and system in arranging your exhibit
Taste in the exhibit arrangement
Accuracy and clearness in reports
Previous preparation in matters of detail
Cooperation with other exhibitors

But the heart of your living tribute to this First American will be yourself, the things you have built up in your personality and character, made into habits of your daily living. Such self-improvements exhibit themselves not only on your exhibit day by your calm, poise, readiness to do, and in other ways; but at other times throughout your life, so that the generation of Americans who come after you, will see in you very definitely the resemblance to this man.

A SPECIAL GEORGE WASHINGTON PROGRAM FOR ACHIEVEMENT DAY

Achievement Day schedules were planned to include an hour's program in memory of Washington. Copies of publications may be secured from which to select appropriate music, pageant or play, together with colonial costumes.

A program similar to the following may be made from printed matter provided by the United States George Washington Bicentennial Commission:

MUSIC—Father of the Land We Love

(Words and Music by George M. Cohan)

PLEDGE TO THE FLAG ⎫
                   ⎬ Recited in Unison.
AMERICAN'S CREED   ⎭

PAGEANT—"Courier"—Scene 2 in the Pageant "Washington Returns."

or

PLAY—"A Youth of the Frontier."

MUSIC—"President's March."

(Arranged by James Hewitt)

V. A SELECTED LIST OF PUBLICATIONS
of the
UNITED STATES GEORGE WASHINGTON BICENTENNIAL COMMISSION

HONOR TO GEORGE WASHINGTON SERIES:

Pamphlet Number 1. Frontier Background of Washington's Career.

Pamphlet Number 4. Washington the Farmer.

Pamphlet Number 6. Washington the Colonial and National Statesman.

Pamphlet Number 9. Washington Proprietor of Mount Vernon.

Pamphlet Number 12. Washington the Business Man.

PAPERS FOR PROGRAMS NUMBERS:

1. Family Relationships of George Washington.

2. Homes of George Washington.

4. The Mother of George Washington.

6. George Washington the Man of Action in Military and Civil Life.

9. The Social Life of George Washington.

12. The Home Making of George and Martha Washington.

PROGRAM OF WAKEFIELD

A FOLK-MASQUE OF AMERICA

Being a Midwinter Night's Dream of the Birth of

WASHINGTON

BY

PERCY MACKAYE

with

MUSIC SELECTED, ADAPTED AND COMPOSED BY JOHN TASKER HOWARD

DIRECTED BY PERCY JEWETT BURRELL AND MARIE MOORE FORREST

PRESENTED AT CONSTITUTION HALL, WASHINGTON, D. C.

FEBRUARY 21, 25, 26, 1932

under the auspices of

UNITED STATES GEORGE WASHINGTON BICENTENNIAL COMMISSION

DISTRICT OF COLUMBIA GEORGE WASHINGTON BICENTENNIAL COMMISSION

I

PRODUCTION STAFF

Directors of Personnel

Bess Davis Schreiner   Maud Howell Smith

Helen Burton (Assistant)

Choral Director

Dr. Albert W. Harned   Jessie Masters (Assistant)

Dance Director

Caroline McKinley

Accompanists

Malton Boyce   Edith H. Hunter

Costume Director

Elizabeth Higgins Sullivan   Joy Higgins (Assistant)

Make-up Director

Denis E. Connell   Bernard J. McConnell (Assistant)

Scenic Director and Designer of Masks

Henry Wadsworth Moore   Dorothy Croissant (Assistant)

Construction Division Scenic Department

Oncken Owens

Technical Director and Stage Manager

Lewis Barrington

Lighting Director

Harold Snyder

Properties

Ethel Jones

Costume Room Personnel

Louise Wynne		Rose Bear
Mabel Wynne	Mabel Ridgeley	Elizabeth Harmon

Marshals for Personnel

Ruth Chindblom	Mary Gantley O'Hara	Alice Coyle Torbert
Helen Gardner	Elizabeth Pritchard	Katharine Wilfley
Janet Jackson	Dorothy Riess	Mabel VanDyke

Director Foreign Groups

Helen C. Kiernan-Vasa

Directors' Aids, Members of Troop 21, D. C. Boy Scouts

Edward Doolan	Theodore Mauck	Watson Fisher
John Kimball	R. Hyde	William Torney
Milton Crump	Charles Smith	

The Program

Illustrator—Arvia MacKaye

Organizer—James K. Knudson

CO-OPERATING ORGANIZATIONS

Music by

THE UNITED STATES MARINE BAND ORCHESTRA
Captain Taylor Branson, Leader, Conducting

ASSISTING GROUPS

Americanization School Association, American Legion, Henry D. Spengler Post and Unit American Legion Auxiliary, Arts Club, Avondale Country School, Community Center Department D. C. Public Schools, Caroline McKinley Studio, Committee on Religious Drama and Pageantry, Washington Federation of Churches, D. C. Boy Scouts, Drama Guild, Friendship House, Helen Griffith Studio, Howard University, Indian Bureau, Department of Interior, Jewish Community Center, Knights of Columbus, National Capital Choir, Neighborhood House, Shakespeare Society, Southern Society, Virginia State Society, Washington Club, Marie Zalipsky Vocal Studio, Scottish Clan McClellan, Alliance Francaise, St. Sophia's Greek School, Polish National Alliance, Danish Society, Swedish Lutheran Church, Russian Orthodox St. Nicholas Church, Ladies' Auxiliary to the Hiberians, St. David's Society.

GROUP LEADERS

Mrs. J. Jerome Lightfoote, Guy Guthridge, Col. Bruce Bentley, Col. E. R. Mattice, Maud Howell Smith, Jessie May Olin, Mrs. Margaret H. Worrell, M. S. Sachs, W. A. Mulligan, Capt. Chester M. Reich, Clara D. Neligh, Mabel Owens Wilcox, Dr. Thomas J. Gates, Miss Etta Toggart, Mrs. R. A. Allen, Mrs. Fulton Lewis, Prof. R. L. Tibbs, Sergt. John B. DeSpears.

COLONIAL PROGRAM GIRLS

Members of Manor House Chapter D. A. R.

Lillian Chenoweth, Regent

May Beall, Nell C. Embrey, Annie Hassell, Laura C. Hooff, Helen Montgomery, Adine Mudd, Anna J. Porter.

Arts Club

Edna Ellis Hilton, Elizabeth Schaublin.

THE OUTLINE OF "WAKEFIELD"

THE MASQUE: SYNOPSIS

In the Preface and the Appendix to the book of the Masque, *Wakefield*, by Percy MacKaye (published, as well as the Choruses and the Music, by the United States George Washington Bicentennial Commission) the Author states:

"*Wakefield* is a poem: a symbolic folk-poem, designed to be spoken, acted, danced and sung. Interpreting aspects of the American Folk Movement through the art of the theatre, it approaches history not from the concept of realism but of symbolism. It aims to express its vast theme in a new form of festival drama, wherein the motives of human psychology are based in symbols of folk-legendry and lore peculiarly the world-heritage of America.

"The Masque is a tribute of folk-spirits to our greatest of folk-heroes, Washington.

"Choosing for its central character the designation, *Wakefield* (after the birth-place of Washington), the author has sought to give to *the Folk-Spirit of America* (that 'airy nothing which is our very essence') 'a local habitation and a name'."

The following is a *Synopsis of the Masque*, in sequence of its Thirty-three Actions:

PROLOGUE (BIRTH)

1. The Chorus of the Ages voices the dramatic theme of the Masque: the conflict between the WILL of Freedom, symbolized by the brave, self-mastering Spirit of Washington, and DRIFT, symbolized by the muddle, self-enslaved "Fog-Spirits."

2. To pealing of Chimes and to Drums, the Spirit of Washington, the "Imbuing Presence" of the Masque, emerges from the dimness of Folk-Memory, casting his mystic shadow upon the Rock, and passes into the Rock itself, where later the historic tableaux-visions of his Will to Freedom are revealed.

3. The Angels of the Four Winds, with their trumpets, announce the Spirit of the North Star, *Polaris*, who appears in the high cleft of the Rock.

PART ONE

(GROWTH AND DRIFT)

4. *Polaris* proclaims the meanings of the starlit midnight—
"Star and Rock and Cedar, forged in one
Element—the Will of Washington—"

and greets the Constellations, *Orion* and *Cassiopeia*, who come to create the first "Star Spangled Banner" of America. Weaving in dance a fairy-ring, their Thirteen Stars create the Folk-Circle of the New World. Interrupted by the far voices of *Free* and *Brave*, calling each other, lost in the wilderness, they are bidden

by *Polaris* to go and fetch from beyond the "azure night" the dawn's "rays of red and rays of white," to "curtain the birth-bed" of Washington's nativity. They go.

6. Hearing the lost calls of *Free* and *Brave*, the maternal Folk-Spirit, *Wakefield*—Sibyl of the fairy-ring, emerges from the hollow of the great Cedar and speaks to the North Star:

"Now is the timeless night
When yesterday and dim tomorrow meet
To cradle a new day. O lonely star,
You only watch—and I. The mortal world
Sleeps, and no sleeper dreams what masterful
Scion the midwife Wilderness brings forth
Under a planet's knees. The mortal world
Sleeps, but the immortal wakes, and with it all
My boon folk-spirits wink their crocus eyes
Of childhood wonder, cupping the young dew
Of olden dawn, and sharp their prickling ears
To catch my clear call to their fairy-ring
And fetch their antic gifts and homeland songs
In homage to this birth-night."

While she listens, strains of folk-music—Indian Cradle-Song, Negro Spiritual and Appalachian Ballad—rise out of the night.

7. *Folk-Say*, the ballad-singing Woodsman, enters, bearing the firelog of the fairy-ring. The Spirit of Indigenous America, he announces—in his ancient folk-speech—the twenty-second of February.

8. Summoned by *Wakefield*, *Wappocomo*—spirit of the Indian folk-background—lights the logs, with sparks from two dry sticks. In the fire-glow appears old *Uncle Remus*, who sweeps the hoar-frost with a wild turkey's wing, and fiddles while *Brer'n Fox, Possum, Rabbit* and *Bear* dance the primitive running-set, *Zip-Coon*. *Wakefield* tells the three how their hearth-circle is menaced by the fog-spirit,

"that dims the eye
Of faith with its pollution,
Clouding the will and darkening resolution,
Till all is only drift on ground grown rotten
And Rock and Star and Cedar are forgotten."

The cries of *Free* and *Brave* recur. *Folk-say* goes to find them. *Uncle Remus* follows. *Wakefield* and *Wappocomo* enter the hollow Cedar.

9. *Free*, a Shepherd lad, with pipe and crook, comes in, singing, and cuddles down by the log-fire.

10. *Drift*, the Fog-Spirit enters. In a chant of vascillating rhythm, he lulls *Free* asleep. A Group-Person, he is composed of *Fear, Muddle, Cabal, Persecution, War, Gold, Greed, Hate* and others, who are about to capture *Free* in their murky Net, when they are dispersed by the call of *Brave*, which awakens *Free*.

11. Singing an old Carol, *Brave* enters with *Folk-Say* and is welcomed by his brother, *Free*. They recount how—driven from the Old World by *Poverty* and *Persecution*, they had lost each other in the wilderness. *Folk-Say* bids them beware of the Fog-Spirit, "Captain Drift o' the Bog Marines," who would lead them

a dance, "from Nowhar-town to Nix and back again."—"Let me fight this Drift," cries *Brave*. But *Folk-Say* answers:

"Who that grapples mist
Bloodies his own fist—
Nay, boy! Nary thing
Kin fight the drift o' fog
But this-here fire-log
That holds the folk-spell of our fairy-ring."

12. *Wakefield* re-enters with Wappacomo, who brings a tripod, on which he swings a Great Black Pot over the fire. There *Wakefield* receives from them their "Birth-Night" tokens: "Shepherd's Staff, Sling, Peace-Pipe, Rabbit's Foot, Cherry Sprig." She bids *Brave* blow his "Crumpled Horn":

"Now lift it to America, listening,
And wind a call to wake the secret caves
Of legendry and fetch my Folk-Spirits home.—
And first, my brave Explorers: call them here!"

13. The *Heroes of Venture* enter, in pageant: New-World Explorers: *Columbus, Amerigo Vespucci; Ponce De Leon; La Salle; John* and *Sebastian Cabot; Captain John Smith* with *Pocahontas; Hendrick Hudson, Sir Walter Raleigh;* with their attendants. *Wakefield* greets them, and bids *Free* summon more.

"Pipe now, anew,
Amerikee! to all the templed hills,
And fetch my native sprites and mountain fauns
To join our fairy-ring."

14. *Free's* pipe summons a Pageant of Log Fire Wonder: *Folk Sprites of Amerikee* (gathering for the first time, to the Art of the Theatre, a nucleus of our ancient, native American mythology): *Paul Bunyan,* the Giant Logger, toting his Blue Calf; *Complair Taureau,* the Bull-headed Lover of French New Orleans; *Solomon Shell,* of the Kentucky Mountains, with Chinkapin, his Sow; old *Rip Van Winkle,* of the Dutch Catskills, with Schneider, his hunting-dog; *Ghost-Gnome,* of Hendrik Hudson's crew, carrying his Ale Keg; gaunt *Ichabod Crane* and the *Headless Horseman,* of Sleepy Holler; *Hawk-Eye,* from the Mohican Trails; *Tony Beaver,* of Eel River, West Virginia; *Boonastiel,* wise simpleton, of the Pennsylvania Dutch; *Kemp Morgan,* striding from Texas; *Pecos Bill,* the Cow Boy; *John Henry,* from the Black River country; *Strap Buckner,* the Devil Fighter; *Old Stormalong,* Deep-Water-Man of the Atlantic Shoreline.

Following these come the *Pioneers,* including *Davy Crockett,* of Tennessee; *Daniel Boone,* of Kentucky; *Brigham Young,* of Utah; *Ethan Allen,* of the Green Mountains; *Zephaniah Kingsley,* with his Arab-Ethiopian wife, *Madegigine Jai,* of Florida.

The *Log-Fire Wonder* group dance the noisy, rollicking Folk-dance, *Gathering Peascods,* with *Folk-Say* as caller-off.

15. Now, in contrasted quiet, *Wakefield* turns to the Log-fire and the Old Black Pot of Folk-Life, into which she pours from a clay-bottle the first element of the birth-night charm: "Ponce de Leon's quest—water of the Fountain of Youth." Then, to the faint tom-tom beat of *Wappocomo,* and the mouth-harp thrumming of *Uncle Remus, Folk-Say* drops into the pot various root charms:

"hardy offerings of herbs and simples—broken roots of truth with sap of wonder, stubborned by shrewd test of bitter trial."

Again, in contrast, three different expressions of Folk-Life (*Shakespeare, Magna Charta, The Bible*) bring—in processionals, from the auditorium—their tokens of *Art, Justice, Religion,* welcomed by *Wakefield.*

16. Led by *Sylvia,* bearing the Mask of Shakespeare, to Schubert's music of *"Who Is Sylvia?"* now come in processional Hamlet and Ophelia, etc.

These dance a stately Minuet.

17. Led by *Magna Charta,* with scroll, come in processional King John, etc.

18. Led by *Revelation,* attended by *The Two Testaments,* come, in processional, the *Psalmists, Prophets and Apostles. Wakefield* again voices her dread of *Drift,*

"for only he
Can steal upon us, like a sudden sleep,
And rob us of our wills, before we know
That we are robbed. . . .
Round him, there flows a murky fowler's net,
Wherein himself and all his followers
Are snared; yet he is skilled to cast its skein
So blinding swift, that in its meshes all
This glowing circle of friends, this sacred fire,
And happy tryst might with a moment be
Blotted in warring chaos."

19. Even as she speaks, the gathered Folk-Circle is surrounded by *Drift* and his Fog-Spirits—while *Wakefield* begins her tale of Washington's birth-night:

"On a midwinter's night, when the North Star
Dreamed on the wilderness of a new world,
Deep in the tingling silence of a wood
A Spirit was born—a child of loneliness,
For he was sinewed out of Rock and Star
And Cedar Tree. So solemn was the hour
That great Orion swerved his starry trail
And Cassiopeia left her shining chair
To watch in wonder. For this Lonely One,
Who soon should make the Rappahannock lie
Under his arm, and curb the Alleghenies
With his divining-rod, would move through war
Tumult and peace to endless aftermaths
Where numberless unborn shall name him 'father.'

"Now, in that lonely wood, on this same night,
Two brother spirits, *Free* and *Brave,* were lost,
Calling each other, till they heard a carol
And found a fire-log and a fairy-ring
And glad folk-neighbors, all with friendly eyes
Of welcome. Round their circle music went
With feet of revel and with heart of song,
In charmed . . . forgetfulness . . . of all . . . which might . . ."

Suddenly *Drift* flings his loop. Pealing Fog-Cries, burst. Caught in the Net, *Free* is whirled outward in coiling darkness— black, terrible with Cries of Warring Chaos—above which the piercing cry of *Free* calls to his brother: "Brave, ho! SAVE!"

INTERLUDE (*RE-BIRTH*)

In darkness, to music by Bach, the Chorus of the Ages lulls the conflict, in song to the Imbuing Presence of the Masque:

"Thou art the Will who dost reveal
Whereby of wan delusion,
Of fear and blind confusion,
The Soul alone itself can heal."

PART TWO (*SELF-HEAL*)

21. A blood-dim light shows the Folk-Circle wrecked and dispersed. To save *Free* from the bondage of *Drift, Brave* appeals

to *Polaris*, the North Star, who bids *Wakefield* restore the fairy-ring by finding the herb, Self-Heal.—"Where does it grow," asks *Brave*, and *Wakefield* answers:

> "Over a grave, where Three lie low."
> "What three?"—"Self-pity, Anger and Pride
>   Lie there, side by side."

Folk-Say leads *Brave* away to the dark, lonely spot where Self-Heal grows.

22. *Polaris* tells *Wakefield* that the Fountain of Youth is not lost, but wells immortal from the childhood of the world—"Ah—Childhood! Where, then, may they be, my scattered children?" *Wakefield* asks, and *Polaris* answers:

> "They wander many paths of flint and flowers.
> They cry in alien wastes and Babel towers
> For sustenance and balm for ancient wrongs.
> They bear no mortal gifts: they bring their songs
> Here to their New-World home.
> So kindle again your hallowed fire
> From ashes. Burn the home-log higher,
> For lo, now, where they come
> Bearing the melody
> Of childhood dreams to this nativity."

23. Led by *Childhood*, the *English Processional* comes singing the oldest English Folk-song *Sumer Is Y-Cumen in*. *Brave* returns with *Folk-Say*, bringing roots of the herb, *Self-Heal*, as a charm against the power of *Drift*. Bidding good-bye to *Wakefield*, he goes to save his brother *Free*, and bring him back to the Folk-Circle.—*Wakefield* dedicates the Circle anew, as *Polaris* announces the coming of the Folk-Children of the World, to music "borne on the mingling bells of Babel tongues."

24. Through all aisles of the Auditorium enter *Thirteen Processionals* singing their own folk and cradle songs, in their several languages, as follows:

Scotch—*Auld Lang Syne*; Welsh—*Ar Hyd y Nos*; Irish—*Killarney*; German—*Wanderschaft*; Norwegian—*Nordmannen*; French—*Avec Mes Sabots*; Danish—*Herligt en Sommernat*; Italian—*Santa Lucia*; Greek—*The Dark Hills*; Swedish—*Vigar over daggstankta, berg, berg, berg*; Czechoslovakian—*Slovan jsen a Slovan budu*; Polish—*My Polska Brygada*; Russian—*The Volga Boatman*.

25. All of these join in the Folk-Song of America: *Old Folks At Home*.

26. *Wakefield* welcomes them all home to their "hearth of Cedar, Rock, and Star," as the Horn of *Brave* resounds eerily from within the Rock, where now *Brave* is revealed in an inner vision (Tableau I:1776) as *Washington Crossing the Delaware*.

27. *Polaris* announces a second vision in the Rock, where

> "Free has fallen, sore
> Wounded in bitter war,
> Where Powers of Drift beset
> Brother and brother;
> But Brave has snatched Free from their net
> And borne him through the smother
> Of blinding storm into the snowy gorge
> of *Valley Forge*." (Tableau II:1778)

28. In a third Vision—*Kingship Refused*—*Brave*, as *Washington*, is revealed, refusing the crown, offered him by officers of the Kingship Cabal (Tableau III: 1782).

29. *Polaris* announces the fourth Vision—*Washington*, at the *Framing of the Constitution* (Tableau IV: 1787).

30. *Polaris* interprets the fifth Vision, wherein *Washington*, turns from war and ambition and the world's gaze—

> "and takes his crumpled horn
> Of battle, back to the green pasture's byre,
> And plants his bitter root
> Of victory in the brown soil
> Of his own farm, where first his dreams were born.
>
> So the last vision lights our midnight masque
> Where Brave turns homeward to his noblest task—"

revealing *Washington, on his Farm at Mt. Vernon* (Tableau V: 1788).

31. At the close of this last Inner Vision, *Brave* rushes into the fireglow, bringing with him *Free*, whom he restores to the Folk-Circle. Showing his charmed root, *Self-Heal*, he cries to *Wakefield*: "Mother—it won! Self-Heal!—Drift hunts his grave."

Wakefield takes them to her arms, as the majestic cloaked figure of Washington appears, high above in the Cleft of the Rock, silhouetted against the Dawn.

32. *Orion* and *Cassiopeia* reappear, bringing

> "Rays of red and rays of white
> In the bannered blue of light"

as the first flag of America, with its Circle of Thirteen Stars, glows in the dawn.

33. Here, shadowed against the dawn, Washington speaks to the Folk-Circle of the World, in his own historic words:

> "Reflect—
> How much more delightful
> to an undebauched mind
> is the task of making improvements on the earth
> than all the vainglory which can be acquired
> from ravaging it
> by conquest."

The *Four Winds* peal their trumpets, as the *Entire Assembly* sing a new stanza (by Percy MacKaye) to the *Star Spangled Banner*.

THE MUSIC: SYNOPSIS

In his monograph on the music for *Wakefield* (in the appendix to the book of the Masque), John Tasker Howard, adapter and composer of the music, explains that the score has been drawn from folk-music, from classic sources, from the work of American composers, and from music especially composed for the Masque. The songs and instrumental works are incidental to the speech and action, yet the significance of the music is such that it forms an integral and essential part of the Masque, inseparable from these other elements of its structure.

The *Masque Theme*, "The Will of Washington," is taken from the opening theme of the fourth movement of Dvořák's *New World Symphony*. Dvořák composed this symphony as a tribute to America, commissioned originally by Percy MacKaye's father, Steele MacKaye, for performance in the *Spectatorium* which he erected for the World's Fair in Chicago (1893).

The introductory chorus is a choral adaptation of this movement from the Dvořák symphony. This is followed by Chimes, sounding the *Masque Theme*. This motif recurs at intervals throughout the Masque, sounded by the chimes or by the trumpets (the *Four Winds*), stationed in the four corners of the auditorium.

Folk-music must play a vital part in a folk-masque, and folk-songs and dances of America and the ancestral nations of its people are introduced throughout the action of *Wakefield*. An Indian Lullaby, a Negro Spiritual, an Appalachian Ballad, establishes the folk element of the music early in the Masque, while the folk-dances and running sets are accompanied by *Turkey in the Straw, Gathering Peascods,* and Stephen Foster's *Oh, Susannah.* In Part Two, when Wakefield summons the children, following the English Processional, *Sumer is Y-cumen In,* racial groups of thirteen nationalities, each entering in processional, sing in the tongues of their mother lands the folk-songs of their races. Here is symbolism showing the mixture of bloods and races that is America. When the children have gathered, and join together in singing one of America's own folk-song, Foster's *Old Folks at Home,* the symbol is complete; they are all Americans.

The music, other than folk-songs, is as follows:

FIRST ACTION

New World
    Choral Adaptation of fourth
    Movement, *New World Symphony*   Dvorák-Howard

FIFTH ACTION

Dance of the Thirteen Stars
    Farndole, L'Arlesienne Suite No. 2   Bizet

NINTH ACTION

Song of Free
    Shepherd's Song   Laura Barker Taylor

TENTH ACTION

Drift   John Tasker Howard

THIRTEENTH ACTION

Entrance of Heroes of Venture
    Amaryllis   Louis XIII-Ghys

SIXTEENTH ACTION

Processional of the Mask of Shakespeare
    Who Is Sylvia? (Shakespeare)   Schubert
Dance of the Mask of Shakespeare
    Minuet in A   Boccherini

SEVENTEENTH ACTION

Processional of Magna Charta
    Hymn   Thomas Tallis

EIGHTEENTH ACTION

Processional of Worship
    Twenty-Third Psalm (Adapted
    from a Hebrew Melody)   Albert W. Harned
    Coronation   Oliver Holden

TWENTIETH ACTION

Chaos   John Tasker Howard
Re-birth
    Two Chorales (Words by Percy MacKaye)

TWENTY-SIXTH ACTION

The Delaware
    Introduction to
    Land of Our Hearts   George W. Chadwick

TWENTY-SEVENTH ACTION

Valley Forge
    Largo, from *Sonata Tragica*   Edward MacDowell

TWENTY-EIGHTH ACTION

Kingship Refused
    Introduction to
    New England Symphony   Edgar Stillman-Kelley

TWENTY-NINTH ACTION

The Constitution
    Federal March   Alexander Reinagle

THIRTIETH ACTION

Mt. Vernon
    Élègie   Frederick S. Converse

THIRTY-THIRD ACTION

The Star Spangled Banner
    New Stanza by Percy MacKaye   John Stafford Smith
    The Music for "Wakefield" is published by the United States George Washington Bicentennial Commission.

PROGRAM

PERSONS AND GROUPS
OF THE ACTIONS AND TABLEAUX
In the Order of Their Appearance
NOTE: The Arabic Numerals indicate the
action in which the characters first appear.

PERSONS

2. THE IMBUING PRESENCE
    (Washington) ....Rev. Earle Wilfley, D.D.
4. THE NORTH STAR (Polaris) Arthur White
4. ORION ....Maurice Jarvis
4. CASSIOPEIA ....Grace Peters Johnson
6. WAKEFIELD ....MARGARET ANGLIN
7. FOLK-SAY ....Robert Chase
8. WAPPOCOMO ....Black Bird (*Shan-tungha-ba-hay,* of the Omaha tribe)
8. REMUS ....Edward Muth
9. FREE ....Hugo Schulze
10. DRIFT ....Caroline McKinley

10. Cabal ....Wallace Wright
10. Fear ....Ruth Harsha McKenzie
10. Muddle ....Thomas Cahill
10. Poverty ....Anne Ives
10. Persecution ....Eldred Wilson
11. BRAVE ....Harry Schonrank

GROUPS

1. THE AGES (Community Chorus) by NATIONAL CAPITAL CHOIR AUGMENTED TO 140 SINGERS.
Mrs. Margaret Anthony, Mrs. Joseph W. Aman, Mrs. Alma Allen, Mrs. Walter Adams, Charlotte Adams, Isabella Ager, Lil-

lian Aunger, Mrs. Phillip Addison, Mrs. R. M. Balliette, Mrs. Frances Berrett, Mrs. Harriet Blase, M. J. Beers, Helen Beach, Frances Brady, Mabel Byler, Agnes Cruickshank, Mrs. Almeda Croft, Mrs. E. M. Cooper, Mrs. Brenda Clark, Mrs. Charles H. Cecil, Mrs. H. C. Chilson, Mrs. Ada Compton, Mrs. Elsie Duck, Mrs. Dorothy W. Dickinson, Cora E. Donneberg, Ada Fowler, Mrs. Anna Fisher, Mrs. H. C. Causs, Mrs. Hilda Galliagher, Hrs. H. C. Glading, Mrs. W. H. Giesey, Mrs. Grace W. Groves, Lillian Graves, Ada Green, Lissetta Gasch, Louise Hohmann, Ernestine Hicks, Mrs. Florence Harned, Mrs. Paul Heyl, Mrs. Anna Huck, Hazel Johnson, Regina L. Kimmell, Irene Koehl, Nell Kuska, Mrs. Agnes Kohlman, Mrs. Ida Kimmerling, Katherine Lee, Rhoda Lewton, M. Pearl Lutz, Sara Lytte, Jessie Masters, Gertrude F. Menk, Eliza W. Merrill, Mavel Murray, Mrs. Lillian Miner, Mrs. H. H. Mitchell, Mrs. L. H. Marks, Mrs. Marie Muse, Cora Oliver, Anna L. O'Connell, Gertrude O'Connell, Clare Penn, Lucy Powell, Adelaide Philips, Mrs. Yolanda Pilgren, Mrs. Mary Carter Posnyjak, Mrs. H. B. Reese, Mrs. Albert T. Reed, Mrs. Etta Rauch, Mrs. Edna Rawlins, Mrs. James W. Robb, Mrs. Luella Robert, Hallie M. Reed, Monica Redel, Josephine Ryder, Clara Stewart, Mrs. Margaret Snyder, Mrs. Bledsoe C. Salle, Mrs. Marjorie Soper, Mrs. Charles I. Stanton, Mrs. Rebecca Torreson, Mrs. Dorath M. Tanty, Mrs. Mary Torrey, Mrs. Leon Truesdell, Mabel F. Thompson, Mrs. W. H. Vampett, Marie Whaley, Grace Wilson, Eunice Whitney, Mrs. W. H. Zeigel, Mrs. Clarence Zimmer, Warren Adams, Ralph Balliette, S. O. Burhall, Ray Berrett, William A. Blair, Albert P. Childes, H. C. Chilson, L. R. Conley, Eugene Dahl, R. Lovell Duck, Charles W. Dwiggins, Frank Finlay, James Garland, H. C. Gauss, Lynn Gillchrest, H. C. Glading, Ray Gustin, Jr., Claude R. Hanan, Ralph M. Harris, Dr. Paul R. Heyl, H. W. Jenks, A. E. Jones, A. B. Keefer, A. F. Kohlman, L. M. Kurkoski, George Leonard, Dr. F. L. Lewton, William H. Mahoney, Philip Ordwine, J. H. Randall, J. B. Rauch, Albert T. Reed, John J. Richardson, William A. Richan, Albert Rohrer, Dean H. Rose, Rial Rose, Victor Russell, Edwin Singer, L. E. Skeen, P. M. Smith, Samuel T. Smith, G. W. Terborgh, J. Day Torrey, W. H. Vampett, T. L. Well, J. F. Winter.

3. THE FOUR WINDS: Alva Beavers, Anita Callahan, Emily Miller, Adele Whiteside.

5. THE THIRTEEN STARS: By the Caroline McKinley Dancers.
   ORION GROUP: Judy Lyeth, Betty Sleeper, Helen Foley, Virginia Alexander, Sandy Alexander, Jean Craighead, Ellen Zirkle.
   CASSIOPEIA GROUP: Jessie Chase, Ruth Shoemaker, Rebecca Tarwater, Penelope Tarwater, Ruth Critchfield, Lilla La Garde, Martha Fisher.

6. VOICE OF AN INDIAN: Irene Koehl.

7. SINGERS OF SPIRITUAL: By Howard University: Clarence Jacobs, Livingston Smith, Ethel Wise, Louise Burge.

8. CREATURES OF UNCLE REMUS: By Avondale Country School.
   RABBIT .... Reed Smoot Nibley
   FOX .... Wesley Eddy
   POSSUM .... Claude Clements
   BEAR .... Preston Johnston

10. VASSALS OF DRIFT: By The Caroline McKinley Dancers including: Misses Fisher, Lyeth, R. Tarwater, P. Tarwater, Shoemaker, Sleeper, LaGarde, V. Alexander, S. Alexander, Foley, Critchfield, Chase;
also CABAL, FEAR, MUDDLE, POVERTY, PERSECUTION, as above,
and WAR .... Robert Claflin
    GOLD .... Helen Griffith
    GREED .... William Hespe
    HATE .... Alberta Smith
    JEALOUSY .... Gwendolin Tonahill

13. HEROES OF NEW WORLD VENTURE: By The Knights of Columbus.
    COLUMBUS .... W. A. Mulligan
    AMERIGO VESPUCCI ...... Fred J. Crovato
    PONCE DE LEON .... James J. Dugan
    LA SALLE .... James P. McKeon
    JOHN CABOT .... Charles D. Boone
    SEBASTIAN CABOT .... Joseph A. Fallon
    HENDRIK HUDSON .... Charles F. Dean
    SIR WALTER RALEIGH .... Charles W. Jefferies
    CAPTAIN JOHN SMITH .... Bernard Barton
    POCAHONTAS .... Helen Andrews

Followers: C. G. Hardy, R. F. Krogman, L. T. Kaster, J. B. Coyle, R. L. Mayhew, Raymond Robertson.
Indians by the Indian Bureau, Department of the Interior: Abde Saloli, Wanbli Kte (Kill Eagle), descendant of Chief Gall and Chief John Grass; Wanbli Chincha (Young Eagle), descendant of Chief Sitting Bull and Chief John Grass; Wanbli Wankatuya (High Eagle), descendant of Chief Rain in the Face and Chief Crazy Horse. All of these are Hunkpapa Sioux. The Chiefs tooks a very active part in the Custer Fight.

14. SHADOWS OF LOG-FIRE WONDER:
    PAUL BUNYAN .... Russel H. Clarvoe
    His Blue Calf .... Alexander Montgomery
    COMPLAIR TAUREAU .... Gifford Kirk
    SOLOMON SHELL .... Freeton Johnston
    Chinkapin, His Sow .... John Gilbert McIlwee
    RIP VAN WINKLE .... William J. Peters
    Schneider, His Dog .... Robert Walsh
    GHOST-GNOME .... M. S. Sachs
    ICHABOD CRANE .... Bernard J. Folliard
    HAWK-EYE .... T. W. Freedman
    TONY BEAVER .... Clifton Clark
    BOONASTIEL .... Herman Riess
    KEMP MORGAN .... Howard Whifield
    PECOS BILL .... Ray Montgomery
    JOHN HENRY .... Edward Eberly
    STRAP BUCKNER .... Newell Atkinson
    OLD STORMALONG .... Martin Scranage

MUSICIANS ("Uncle Tom and His Hired Help"):
    Dr. Thomas J. Gates (1st Violin).
    J. W. Simpson (2nd Violin).
    W. E. Simpson (Bass Violin).
    Harry Boroleo (Banjo).
    Charles P. Bailey (Guitar).
    J. E. Edwards (Guitar).
    Dr. T. David Gates (Accompanist and Soloist).

and Jilson Setters (Kentucky Mountain Fiddler), *guest.*

14. PIONEERS:

DAVY CROCKETT
  (Of Tennessee) . . . . Henry J. Staley
DANIEL BOONE
  (Of Kentucky) . . . . Clifford Berryman
ETHAN ALLEN
  (Of the Green Mountains) . . . Fulton Lewis
BRIGHAM YOUNG (Of Utah) . . . Frank B. Steele
ZEPHANIAH KINGSLEY . . . . Glen Brown
  with his Arab-Ethiopian wife
MADEGIGINE JAI (Of Florida)   Katherine Melton

16. PROCESSIONAL OF SHAKESPEARE: By The Shakespeare Society of Washington.

PRELUSIVE TRIO . . . . Irene Koehl, Marjorie
                                          Soper, Jessie Masters
SYLVIA . . . . Kate Tomlinson
HOLY ⎱
FAIR ⎰ By the Helen Griffith   Phyllis Armentrout
WISE ⎰   Studio   Nancy Lee Wright
                               Helen Matteson
HAMLET . . . . Clark Beach
OPHELIA . . . . Rosemary Arnold
ROMEO . . . . Kent Dyer
JULIET . . . . Olyve Barbee Hancock
PETRUCHIO . . . . Walter E. Thorne
KATHERINA . . . . Mabel Owens Wilcox
CALIBAN . . . . M. F. Reese
MIRANDA . . . . Lulu Adams
BOTTOM . . . . Eldridge Monroe
TITANIA . . . . Irma Vaughan
FAERIES . . . . Carola Belle Giovanoni
                                          Eloise Vanstory
VIOLA . . . . Dorothy A. Lawrence
MALVOLIO . . . . Orrin Elliott
FALSTAFF . . . . Leslie Waudby
TWO MERRY WIVES . . . . Helen Colhoun
                                          Alice W. Robinson
ROSALIND . . . . Esther Marshman
MACBETH . . . . E. V. Wilcox
WITCHES . . . . Anthony Thorne
                                          Frank Magill
                                          William Hall

17. PROCESSIONAL OF MAGNA CHARTA: By The Henry C. Spengler Post and Unit American Legion Auxiliary and The American Legion.

KING JOHN . . . . Dr. Douglas A. White
ARCHBISHOP . . . . Thomas P. Jordon
CHANCELLOR . . . . . . Charles H. Knight
MONKS . . . . Major Will Chase, Eli Bamford
                              Smith
CHIEF BARON . . . . . . Captain Chester M. Reich
SQUIRES . . . . Lt. John W. Kimes, Walter Hidde
PAGES . . . . Betty Chamberlin, Catherine L.
                              Dent, Carol Eiker, Loys Eaton,
                              Louise Teller, Margaret Kennedy

BARONESSES . . . . Jennie F. Knight, Louise White,
                              Eva A. Chase, Lillian Reagon,
                              Betty Chamberlin, Ruth Pritch-
                              ard, May D. Lightfoot, Rose L.
                              Hidde
BARONS . . . . J. Jerome Lightfoot, Victor H.
                              Deirk, James B. Jones, Henry L.
                              Cook, Robert L. Anderson, M. B.
                              Shaffer, Willis J. Nolan, Maj. J.
                              C. Fawcett.

18. PROCESSIONAL OF THE BIBLE: By the Committee on Religious Drama and Pageantry of the Washington Federation of Churches, and the Jewish Community Chorus.

REVELATION . . . . Rebecca Radford
THE TWO
  TESTAMENTS . . . . . Elsie Schulze, Caroline Brosius
DAVID THE SHEP-
  HERD BOY . . . . Leon Davis
THE PALMISTS . . . . . Ernest L. Ropes, A. W. Wilson,
                              E. W. Chapin, Eugene Kressin,
                              F. O. Hinz, Horace Gingell,
                              Roger Hequembourg, Robert
                              Lavender, Harry McKnee, Alan
                              Warfield, Mitchel David, Hugh
                              Brooks, David Leonard, George
                              Croft, Willard A. Buree
CYMBAL BEARERS . . Jane Hanna, Devereaux Green, Eula
                              May Emick, Mabel O. Rhine,
                              Mrs. Bernard Hearn, Edith
                              Weber, Rosalie Melton
PROPHETS . . . . Leon Steck, Louis Dreeben, Morris
                              Weingarten, Marvin Marx, David
                              Wallace, Irving Day, Bernard
                              Hearn, George Towberman, W.
                              H. Towberman, Jack Littman,
                              Albert Hall, George Hardy,
                              John J. Edson, Gus Nordstrom,
                              Charles Kretchman, C h e s t e r
                              Pask, N. K. Gardner
PROPHETESSES . . . . . Natalie Ropes, Mary Trenwith
                              Duffy
APOSTLES . . . . Elroy La Cross, William R. Russell,
                              William Powell, William Kilgore,
                              Jack Perry, Fred Vechery, Huber
                              Nash, Harold Toynton, Donald
                              E. Murch, Casson Crittenden,
                              Philip Irey, Ben Catchings

ENGLISH PROCESSIONAL AND FOLK SONG

23. ENGLISH GROUP LED BY CHILDHOOD: By Neighborhood House: Joe Walters, Bernard Tomardy, Paul Wilson, Milton Lee, Claude Hodgkins, George Keese, Charles Curtis, Grover Owen, Virginia Hughes, Catherine Frye, Rosemary Tomardy, Margaret Barghausen, Thelma Hopkins, Marie Hinson, Ethel Jones, Eloise Reid, Charlotte O. Heim, Dorothy Huth, Lillian Kendricks, Rose Jones, Hazel Johnson, Margaret Jasper, Lillian Hinson, Erna Jasper, Katherine Tinford, Margaret Koehler, Katherine

Poore, Helen Schwaner, Alice Hennessy, Virginia Hinson, Katherine Hart. Leader: Daniel Duff. *Childhood:* Virginia Hughes.

24. THE THIRTEEN PROCESSIONALS AND FOLK-SONGS: By Americanization School Association and Cooperating Groups.

24. SCOTCH: Mary Anderson, Ruby Borden, Mary Granger, Anna Parks, Mary Paterson, Anna Reid, Mary Reid, Peter Anderson, Daniel Duff, William Guthrie, William Hutcheson, Andrew Meldrum, George Park, Albert Paterson, John Davis.

24. WELSH: Alice Bowen, Mary Bowen, Mary Decker, Margaret Eckloff, Anna Edwards, Mary Evans, Margaret Fawcett, Pearl Griffith, May Hughes, Ann Jenkins, Mary Lewis, Margaret Thomas, Edith Williams, M. C. Bowen, J. W. Brush, T. W. Brush, Dr. Thomas Elias, Griffith Evans, T. W. Hughes, W. J. Hughes, C. M. Jones, Dr. T. Breese Jones, Marguerita Keat. Leader: Griffith Evans.

24. IRISH: Evelyn Collins, Teresa Collins, Margaret Daly, Rena Downing, Lillian Fay, Anna Grady, Eileen Haltigan, Helen Haltigan, Marie McGrath, Peggy Ryan, Genevieve Shanley, Mary Wood, Michael Buckley, Joseph Daly, Patrick Murphy, William O'Connor, Daniel Stanton. Leader: Lillian Fay.

24. GERMAN: Martha Bankmann, Martha Diehl, Anna Graff, Gusta Neuland, Magda Reimers, Hilda Weingart, Ewald Bankmann, Bernard Fuhler, Franz Greomping, Wilhelm Grun, Donald Helm, John Kiernan, Paul Lubkert, Adolf Miller, William Moeller, Anthony Narr, Gottlieb Narr, Kurt Ritter, Ferdinand Vogle, William Ziegler. Leader. Anna Graff.

24. NORWEGIAN: Gudrun Anderson, Elsa Bettum, Hildur Bettum, Ida Frohlin, Martha Goode, Ingeborg Growold, Anna Johnson, Hildur Kamm, Anna Monson, Hildur Nordberg, Marie Svendsen, Carl Andersson, Leif Bettum, William Bettum, Hjordis Jansson, John Nordberg, Jons Otterness, Arnold Qualley. Leader: Mrs. Hildur Bettum.

24. FRENCH: Marie Barbot, Germaine Companion Casson, Lucie Hauchart Chaconas, Marie de Chauny, Jean Dagenais Davis, Jeanne Faugere, Patricia Hunt, Germaine Goineau Johnson, Marie Livandais, Maria Peverini, Aimee Chamony Shepard, Anna Van Ingelgen, Pauline Perreu Whitsey, George de Chauny, George Chivard, Albert Hautenne. Leader: Madame Lucia Hauchart Chaconas.

24. DANISH: Agnes Anderson, Ingrid Buch, Marie Buch, Ingeborg Farstrup, Anna Harton, Ida Langmach, Ingrid Langmach, Gudrun Langmach, Otilia Nielsen, Sophie Sirola, Rev. P. L. Bjerre, Folmer Bodjerg, Laurito Christensen, Mikkel Frandsen, Frederik Hansen, Skat Hanson, Hans Jorgensen, Holger Langmach, Svend Langmach, Julius Nielsen. Leader: Rev. P. L. Bjerre.

24. ITALIAN: Elena Christando, Carmen Jaccarino, Evelyn Jaccarino, Carmel Ragusa, Phyllis Ragusa, Teresa Segretti, Mary Todaro, Dante Avon, Denio Basile, Giuseppi Bruno, Louis Galli, Romeo Guaraldi, Louis Martinelli, Guy Puglisi, Leo Puglisi, Louis Rosa, Frank Segreti, Gregorio Segreti, Louis Vasco, Falcone Vito. Leader: Carmel Ragusa.

24. GREEK: Catherine Chaconas, Lula Chaconas, Mary Chaconas, Mary Chacos, Erasmia Chantilles, Tasia Chantilles, Toula Comert, Tasia Dounis, Demetra Panagos, Vasha Panagos, Helen Peratino, Irene Peratino, Catherine Petrakis, Bessie Stathes, Helen Stathes. Leader: Mrs. Tasia Dounis.

24. SWEDISH: Nina Anderson, Vivan Anderson, Florence Bergstrom, Phebe Foberg, Ida Johnson, Nina Jones, Agnes Kelly, Gunvor Larsson, Tyra Liberg, Emma Marshall, Linea Monel, Ruth Nordberg, Alma Peterson, Karin Peterson, Caterin Sandberg, Darline Swanson, Dr. Harold Giese, Carl Johnson, Burton Tatterson, Arthur Wiberg. Leader: Carl Johnson.

24. CZECHOSLOVAKIAN: Julie Florianova, Marie Grubova, Rose Grubova, Zdenka, Grubrova, Karla Prokesova, May Salda, Sophie Slovak, Anna Sticova, Anna Vojtechova, Jan Pazourek, Vladmir Vasa, Frantisek Rosmer, Jindra Mala-Nolan, Dr. Schaeur. Leader: Karlo Prokesoua.

24. RUSSIAN: Mme. V. P. Ayvazaglou, Miss Lila Colonel, Mme. O. Colonel, Mme. O. V. Grinoff, Marjorie Isaacs, Luba Kaplan, Mme. H. Krynitsky, Mme. Luzanov, Mme. Maria Mertvago, Mary Paull, Mme. Clara Schinskaya, Mrs. Semin Christine, Fannie Spigel, Helen Steiner, Miss Mary Vasilieff, Mrs. N. A. Warner, Mme. Marie Zalipsky, Domenico Baiardo, Rev. John T. Dorosh, Rev. Illia Gavriliiak, V. V. Gzovsky, Mrs. Luzanov, Gregory Shlapak, Eugene Stepanoff, Mr. Taranim, General Uzefovick, Nate Wolin. Leader: Mme. Marie Zalipsky.

24. POLISH: Sophie Baran, Adolf Biniek, Dolores Biniek, Eugenia Biniek, Richard Biniek, Edward Blazucki, J. Blazucki, L. Broczkowska, Theresa Brockowska, Veronica Budacz, A. Bunkowska, Frances Dabrowska, E. Drozdowska, John Gracki, Marie Gracka, Magdalene Kielek, Marie Kielek, Helen Misiora, Anna Magowska, F. Mogowska, Joseph Mrok, Edward Podles, Emilia Rieselman, Cecilia Rybak, Anna Zniezko, A. Sobotka, Helen Szcybor, Eva Szymanska, Henrietta Warminska, A. Zukowski. Leader: Mrs. Bronislawa Bartosz.

AMERICAN PROCESSIONAL AND FOLK-SONG

25. AMERICAN: By Friendship House: Dorothy Deitz, Rose Biggs, Muriel Farrington, Mildred Rosenberger, Theresa Rooney, Elizabeth O'Brien, Catherine Evans, Cleo Lewis, Mary Frances Everett, Margaret Kirkwood, Virginia Rollins, Michael Basile, Ralph White, James Robb, Bernard O'Brien, James O'Brien, Mary Keene, Marion Lipscomb, Norma White, Theresa O'Brien, Jeanette Birch.

PERSONS AND GROUPS OF THE FIVE TABLEAUX
In the Order of Their Appearance

THE PRESENCE
(In Each of the Five Tableaux)

WASHINGTON, James Otis Porter, *"Crossing the Delaware"* and *"Valley Forge,"* Capt. C. C. Calhoun, *"Kingship Refused"* and *"The Constitution;"* Carlton Van Valkenberg, *"Washington at Mount Vernon."*

THE GROUPS

TABLEAU I   CROSSING THE DELAWARE: By Battery B, 260
Coast Artillery, Washington, D. C., National
Guards.

Boatmen-Soldiers ... Serg. John B. De'Spears
Corp. Walker A. Shea
Private Harry F. Rohrkemper
Private Geo. E. Herron

TABLEAU II   VALLEY FORGE: By Battery B, 260 Coast Artillery, Washington, D. C., National Guards.

Campfire Soldiers ⎫
A Comrade   ⎬ Same as Tableau I

TABLEAU III   KINGSHIP REFUSED: By Southern Society.
Officers .... Robert McNeil
Major Walter Burns
John Little

TABLEAU IV   THE CONSTITUTION: By Virginia State Society.
Ratifiers .... Lodge Hill
R. S. Tucker
Shirley D. Mayers
F. C. Baggarly

TABLEAU V   WASHINGTON AT MOUNT VERNON: By the
Washington Club.
Martha Washington ..... Mrs. Fulton Lewis
Gardener .... Charles Bittinger
Children .... Elizabeth Ann Hulburt
Bruce Burnside

At the close of "Wakefield," the audience is invited to join
with the Community Chorus in singing the following

NEW STANZA FOR

THE STAR SPANGLED BANNER

written by Percy MacKaye, to conclude the last action
of the Masque:

O say, can you see in the dawn's early light
Where the rays of our flag like the morning are stealing,
The strong Rock of our Faith, whose far peak through the night
Rose calm where the Chariots of Chaos were wheeling
While, beyond, the bright pole
Of a planet's strong soul
Shone steadfast to guide toward our victory's goal:
O say, does our star-spangled banner yet wave
O'er the land of the Free and the home of the Brave?

BOX-HOLDERS FOR THE PREMIERE

Box of The President and Mrs. Hoover
The Vice-President
His Excellency The Ambassador of Italy and Nobil Donna An-
tonietta de Martino
His Excellency The Ambassador of Cuba and Senora de Ferrara
His Excellency The Ambassador of France and Madame Claudel
His Excellency The Ambassador of Turkey
His Excellency The Ambassador of Japan and Madame Debuchi
His Excellency The Ambassador of Poland
His Excellency The Ambassador of Belgium and Madame May
His Excellency The Ambassador of Argentina
His Excellency The Ambassador of Mexico and Senora de Puig
Casauranc
Mrs. Woodrow Wilson
The Chief Justice and Mrs. Charles Evans Hughes
Mr. Justice and Mrs. Owen J. Roberts
The Attorney General and Mrs. William D. Mitchell
The Secretary of Agriculture and Mrs. Arthur M. Hyde
The Secretary of Commerce and Mrs. Robert P. Lamont
The Secretary of Labor and Mrs. William N. Doak
The President Pro Tempore of the Senate and Mrs. George H.
Moses
Senator and Mrs. James E. Watson
Senator and Mrs. Arthur R. Robinson
The Chief of Operations of the Navy and Mrs. W. V. Pratt
Representative and Mrs. Bertrand H. Snell
The Undersecretary of the Treasury and Mrs. Arthur A. Bal-
lantine
The Assistant Secretary of War and Mrs. Frederick H. Payne
Mrs. Nicholas Longworth
The United States George Washington Bicentennial Commission
The District of Columbia George Washington Bicentennial Com-
mission
The Daughters of the American Revolution

Descendants of the Washington Family
Sons of the American Revolution
The Order of the Cincinnati
Huguenot Society
The Society of Colonial Dames
Mrs. Walter R. Tuckerman, Chairman, Committee for George
Washington Bicentennial Ball
Mrs. McCook Knox, Chairman, Portrait Committee, George
Washington Bicentennial Historical Loan Collection
Mrs. James Carroll Frazer
Mrs. J. Borden Harriman
Mrs. Rose Gouverneur Hoes
Mrs. Leander Loose
Mrs. Marie Moore Forrest
Mr. and Mrs. Percy MacKaye
Mr. and Mrs. John Tasker Howard

OTHER MEMBERS OF THE DIPLOMATIC CORPS ATTENDING

The Minister of Switzerland and Madame Peter
The Minister of Greece and Madame Simopoulos
The Minister of Sweden
The Minister of Norway and Madame Bachke
The Minister of Guatemala and Senora de Recinos
The Minister of Lithuania
The Minister of Czechoslovakia and Madame Veverka
The Minister of the Irish Free State and Mrs. McWhite
The Minister of Nicaragua and Senora de Sacasa
The Minister of Yugoslavia
The Minister of Roumania
The Minister of Ecuador
The Minister of the Dominican Republic
The Minister of Venezuela and Senora de Arcaya
The Minister of Denmark and Madame Wadsted
The Minister of Panama and Senora de Alfaro

WAKEFIELD

A FOLK-MASQUE OF AMERICA

Being a Midwinter Night's Dream of the Birth of

WASHINGTON

BY

PERCY MACKAYE

With Illustration-Designs by
ARVIA MACKAYE

Together with
Three Monographs on the Masque
Written by the Author, the Illustration-Designer, and
JOHN TASKER HOWARD
Adapter and Composer of the Music

Designed and Written for the

UNITED STATES COMMISSION FOR THE CELEBRATION OF THE TWO-HUNDREDTH ANNIVERSARY OF THE BIRTH OF GEORGE WASHINGTON

WASHINGTON
(The Imbuing Presence)

PREFACE

In a quiet hallway of an old house on Nantucket Island, there stands a tall clock that has struck-in the birth of two centuries. Hand-wrought by its inventor, a first cousin of Benjamin Franklin, its works are wholly of seasoned wood, hand-hewn from soil of the Atlantic shore. It tells the seconds, the minutes, the hours, the days of the week, the months, the years, the centuries, the light and dark of the moon, the tides, the motion of the planets and of the constellations.

On February 22, 1832, it struck-in the One Hundredth Anniversary of the birth of George Washington. On February 22, 1932, it strikes-in the Two Hundredth Anniversary of his birth.

A contemporal historian of that vast occasion, it is also a timeless symbol of this folk-masque.

For it is concerned no longer with the ticking-off of minutes, months and years, in minutiae of transient biography. It is concerned instead with the centuries, the wane and flow of world-tides, the lyric and choral dance of planets and constellations: all these in relation to the home-bred bewildered Folk-Spirits of our land of "Free and Brave", who pay their naive tribute of wonder to the birth of a New World in the ever-renascent spirit of Washington.

His spirit is renascent because Washington belongs forever to a creative age of history which, in moulding the destiny of our country and, with that, the destiny of our planet, poured into the fabric of a new world order the quickening fecundity of an older age at high tide of its vitality.

That older age is the Folk-Age, whose continuity stretches into the mists of archeology. That other new world order, still in pangs of birth, is the Machine-Age, whose shadow is thrown on the mists of prophecy.

Who shall inherit that newest "new world"—the Folk, or the Robots? What shall be the dominant themes of its "New World Symphony"?

That must depend on which of two forces shall dominate the American Folk-Mind—*Will*, or *Drift*?

The opposition of those forces is the dramatic theme of this Folk-Masque.

---

* Washington, the Man Who Made Us, a Ballad-play by Percy MacKaye (published by Alfred A. Knopf, New York, 1919) was first produced by Walter Hampden, under auspices of the George Washington Memorial Association, Congress, and the Cabinet, at the Belasco Theatre, Washington, D. C., Feb. 21, 1920. Its Valley Forge Action, translated into French, by Pierre de Lanux (Brentano's, 1919), was produced by Jacques Copeau, under auspices of the American Academy and National Institute of Arts and Letters, at the Theatre du Vieux Colombier, New York, February 17-22, 1919. Other separate Actions, Young Washington at Mt. Vernon, Washington and Betsy Ross, George Washington at the Delaware, are published by Samuel French, New York. The play, with woodcut illustrations by Arvia MacKaye, has been serialized by The Scholastic magazine, November, 1931—February, 1932.

George Washington, the man, lived to see his friend, Franklin, fly a kite of coiled wire into a thunder cloud, to enslave the lightning of the Folk-Age. He died before he could watch the lightning tighten its coppery coil to enslave its enslavers.

But Washington, "the Presence" of this folk-masque lives on to imbue the metal of our new age—and of ever newer ages to come—with the elemental fire of his self-mastering spirit—a spirit nurtured by the ancient folk-charm, "self-heal", beside the "fire-log" of Wakefield.

This much perhaps is enough of hint concerning the content of this poem, which approaches history not from the concept of naturalism but of symbolism. In an earlier work,* on the theme of Washington, the writer has dealt with the subject in large measure naturalistically. There the events of "war" and of "peace" are focused upon Washington, the man, in their historical sequence.

But as *War* and *Peace* have taken on, in our time, changing connotations far different from those of the past, so the writer has conceived them, in this masque, not as separate allegorical entities clearly defined, but rather as coalescent creatures of a common "Group-Person"—the fog-spirit, *Drift*,—a psychic being that menaces all periods of history. Hence the "timeless" approach to this "Midwinter Night's Dream" of Washington's birth.

The historic birthplace of George Washington hitherto has been recorded in school books and biographies nearly always by a rather vague reference to "Westmoreland County in Virginia." Not till very recently, during preparations for the Bicentennial year, has the place of his birth begun to be associated more precisely in the public mind with the charming name of Wakefield—a name which perhaps in the future may as instantly conjure to all Americans the image of Washington, as the mere sound of Stratford-on-Avon conjures to all Englishmen the image of Shakespeare. To emphasize that American connotation has been one motive in the naming of this masque.

But the "timeless approach" to its theme, above referred to, implies the finding of a deeper significance in the soil of the Indigenous than merely the outward marking of historic facts of person, place and date. It implies an inward harmony of those elements which discovers in the local a planetary meaning, and in the universal a savor of personality. So, in choosing for the central character of this masque the designation, *Wakefield*, the author has sought to give to *the Folk-Spirit of America* (that "airy nothing" which is our very essence) "a local habitation and a name."

For the unprecedented opportunity of expressing the substance of this work to the American people, the author wishes to express his earnest appreciation. Early in 1931, he was privileged to receive, from the United States Government, a commission—the first of its kind accorded by the Federal Government—to create for this Bicentennial occasion a dramatic festival, expressing the spiritual leadership of Washington in forms of poetry and music adapted to the participation of large numbers of men, women and children.

The invitation was perhaps prompted by the fact of some twenty years' experience on the writer's part in the field involved. That experience has dealt with the vast potentiality and promise of an art of festival expression, essentially religious in nature, comparable to the communal dramas of ancient Athens and to the mediavel miracle plays, but designed quite as sacredly to express a different concept of the poet's function in the modern world: his function as creative craftsman of a Drama of Democracy, dedicated to the people themselves as artists of their own destiny. So, in his *Masque of Saint Louis* (bodied forth by 10,000 enactors), and in his Shakespeare Tercentenary Masque, *Caliban* (enacted, at the Harvard Stadium, by 5,000 citizens), the writer was concerned with racial memories and aspirations heroic in their proportions. So, too, in the present work, he deals with a theme of like magnitude, which he has sought to express in a new form of festival drama, wherein the motives of human psychology are based in symbols of folk legendry and lore which are peculiarly the world-heritage of America.

This masque, then, is a tribute of folk-spirits to our greatest of folk-heroes, Washington.

For comments and suggestions concerning the form and spirit of the masque in its relation to the growing Folk Movement in America, and for details in regard to its production, its illustration-designs and its music, the reader is referred to the three Monographs of this volume.

The old wooden clock in Nantucket, after all, is but a very recent antique in the quiet hall of Folk-Memory, where its cumulative tickings shall strike-in a Tricentennial as tranquilly as they now record the anniversary of this year. In that quiet of the centuries, one echo from the close of this masque (the author believes) shall still ring clear, in gracious admonition to a surviving Folk-World: the echo of Washington's own words of serene will—"Reflect!"

P. M.-K.

Washington, D. C.—January, 1932.

TEXT OF THE MASQUE

In Thirty-Three Actions and Five Tableaux

PERSONS AND GROUPS OF THE THIRTY-THREE ACTIONS

In the Order of Their Appearance

NOTE—Those marked with an asterisk (*), are mute. Before each, in Roman Numerals, is printed the number of the Action in which each first appears.

PERSONS

II.   THE IMBUING PRESENCE (*Washington*)
IV.   THE NORTH STAR (*Polaris*)
IV.   ORION
IV.   CASSIOPEIA
VI.   WAKEFIELD
VII. FOLK-SAY
VIII. WAPPOCOMO *
VIII. UNCLE REMUS *
IX.   FREE.
X.   DRIFT
X.   Cabal
X.   Fear
X.   Muddle
X.   Poverty
X.   Persecution
XI.   BRAVE

GROUPS

I.   THE AGES (Community Chorus: Men, Women, Choir-Boys)

III. THE FOUR WINDS (Women)

V.   THE THIRTEEN STARS (Children: Girls)
     Orion Group: 7
     Cassiopeia Group: 6

VIII. CREATURES OF *UNCLE REMUS* (Children)
      Br'er Fox, Br'er Possum, Br'er Rabbit

X.   VASSALS OF *DRIFT* (Men and Women: The first five speak)
     CABAL; FEAR; MUDDLE; POVERTY; PERSECUTION; *War; Gold; Pestilence; Greed; Hate; Jealousy;* Others Unnamed

XIII. HEROES OF NEW WORLD VENTURE
      Columbus, with Spaniards and Indians; *Amerigo Vespucci; Ponce de Leon; La Salle; John and Sebastian Cabot; Captain John Smith,* with *Pocahontas; Hendrik Hudson; Sir Walter Raleigh,* Other Early Explorers, with Followers

XIV. SHADOWS OF LOG-FIRE WONDER
     Paul Bunyan, with his Blue Calf; *Complair Taureau* (The Bull-Headed); *Solomon Shell,* with Chinkapin, his Sow; *Rip Van Winkle,* with Schneider, his Dog; *Ghost-Gnome,* with his Ale-Keg; *Ichabod Crane* and the Headless Horseman; *Hawk-Eye,* with his "Longue Carabine"; *Tony Beaver* (of West Virginia); *Boonastiel* (of the Pennsylvania Dutch); *Kemp Morgan* (of Texas); *Pecos Bill* (Cow Boy); *John Henry* (of Black River); *Strap Buckner* (Devil Fighter); *Old Stormalong* (Deep-Water Sailor)

XIV. PIONEERS
     Davy Crockett, (of Tennessee); *Daniel Boone* (of Kentucky); *Ethan Allen* (of the Green Mountains); *Brigham Young* (of Utah); *Zephaniah Kingsley,* with his Arab-Ethiopian wife, *Madegigine Jai,* (of Florida)

XVI. PROCESSIONAL OF *SHAKESPEARE*
     Sylvia, with *Holy, Fair and Wise* (3 Young Girls); *Florizel and Perdita; Romeo and Juliet; Orlando and Rosalind; Hamlet and Ophelia; Miranda, Caliban and Prospero; Falstaff and Anne Page; Oberon, Titania and Bottom* (the Ass-Headed); *Moth, and Peascod;* the *Three Witches* (of "Macbeth"); Other Characters of Shakespeare's Plays

XVII. PROCESSIONAL OF *MAGNA CHARTA*
      THE LAWS, THE SCIENCES

XVIII. PROCESSIONAL OF *THE BIBLE*
       Revelation, THE TWO TESTAMENTS, PSALMISTS, PROPHETS, APOSTLES

PROCESSIONALS OF *FOLK-SONG:*

XXIII. ENGLISH—*Led by Childhood*
XXIV. SCOTCH
  "   WELSH
  "   IRISH
  "   GERMAN
  "   NORWEGIAN
  "   FRENCH
  "   DUTCH
  "   ITALIAN
  "   GREEK
  "   HEBREW
  "   BOHEMIAN
  "   POLISH
  "   RUSSIAN
XXV.   AMERICAN

PERSONS AND GROUPS OF THE FIVE TABLEAUX

In the Order of Their Appearance

NOTE—All of these are Mute. By the lighting (which is imaginative, not naturalistic) the one PRESENCE distinctly individualized is that of WASHINGTON; the others are suggested only as component parts of the Groups revealed in the motionless pictures, whose dominant moods are intensified by their accompanying Music.

THE PRESENCE
(In each of the 5 Tableaux)

WASHINGTON

THE GROUPS

I.   BOATMEN-SOLDIERS
II. CAMPFIRE SOLDIERS and A COMRADE, lifted near
III. OFFICERS of the Kingship Cabal with their LEADER
IV. RATIFIERS of the Constitution
V.   MT. VERNON GROUP: Farm Overseers, Family, Neighbors

CHORUSES

(Sung by the Community Chorus, in Auditorium)

I. *NEW WORLD.* By Percy MacKaye. To Music of Dvořák's *New World Symphony*

XVI. *WHO IS SYLVIA?* By Shakespeare. To Music by Schubert

XVIII. *CORONATION.* Hymn, composed by Oliver Holden

Interl. *REBIRTH.* By Percy Mackaye. To Music by Bach.

XXIII. *SUMER IS Y-CUMEN IN.* Earliest English Folk-Song

XXV. *OLD FOLKS AT HOME.* Words and Music by Stephen C. Foster

XXXIII. *THE STAR-SPANGLED BANNER.* A New Stanza, by Percy MacKaye

SONGS, CAROLS AND CHANTS

NOTE—This list does not include Snatches of Song and Musical effects (vocal and instrumental), which are printed under *Synopsis of the Music.* There, also, are printed the Complete Words, with Translations, of the Songs under *Words of Folk-Songs.* The Titles of the Folk-Songs are here listed in English, but each is sung in its own folk-tongue.

VI. *The Mother's Vow.* Indian Cradle Song

VI. *O, Eb'ry Time I Feels de Spirit.* Negro Spiritual

VI. *The Cherry-Tree Carol.* Appalachian Ballad.

IX. *Shepherd's Song.* By William Blake. Music by Laura Barker Taylor

XI. *Good King Wenceslas.* Old English Carol

XXIII. *Sumer is Y-Cumen In.* Earliest English Folk-Song

XXIV. *O, Can Ye Sew Cushions?* Scotch Folk-Song

" *All Through the Night.* Welsh Folk-Song

" *Bendemeer's Stream.* Irish Folk-Song

" *The Sandman.* German Folk-Song

" *Paul on the Hill.* Norwegian Folk-Song

" *Brother John.* French Folk-Song

" *In Winter When It's Raining.* Dutch Folk-Song

" *The Wheelbarrow-Loaders.* Italian Folk-Song

" *Saint Basil.* Greek Folk-Song

" *Elijah, the Prophet.* Hebrew Chant

" *Hush-a-Bye, Baby Mine.* Bohemian Folk Cradle Song

" *Father Dear, Mother Dear.* Polish Folk-Song

" *Mother Volga.* Russian Folk-Song

XXV. *Old Folks at Home.* American Folk-Song. By Stephen C. Foster

DANCES

V. *THE THIRTEEN STARS. Rhythmic Dance.* To Music by Bizet

VI. *TURKEY IN THE STRAW. Running-Set.* To Old Appalachian Folk-Tune

X. *DRIFT. Rhythmic Movement.* To Music by John Tasker Howard

XIV. *GATHERING PEASCODS. Folk-Dance.* To Old English Folk-Tune

XVI. *"MASK" OF SHAKESPEARE. Minuet.* To Music by Boccherini

ORCHESTRAL COMPOSITIONS

NOTE—Besides the Composers already listed—Dvorak, Bizet, Taylor, Schubert, Howard, Boccherini, Holden, Foster—the following AMERICAN COMPOSERS are represented in this Masque, by their compositions which accompany the *Tableaux Visions,* in Part Two.

I. *CROSSING THE DELAWARE. Prelude to Cantata.* By George W. Chadwick

II. *VALLEY FORGE. Sonata Tragica.* By Edward MacDowell

III. *KINGSHIP REFUSED. New England Symphony. First Movement.* By Edgar Stillman-Kelley.

IV. *THE CONSTITUTION. Federal March.* By Alexander Reinagle

V. *"IMPROVEMENTS ON THE EARTH." Elegie.* By Frederick S. Converse

THE MASQUE STRUCTURE

The Structure of the Masque is conceived primarily for indoor production, within architecture of church or cathedral type, but is adaptable also to types of level-floored auditorium, provided with stage (and desirably, with balconies), as well as to outdoor production.

It is not technically planned for the commercial theatre, in which the audience is a non-participating factor. It is designed for a place of assembly, convocation or worship, in which the audience is a congregation definitely related to participants in the action. Of these participants, fourteen are persons who speak; the others—comprising groups of pantomime, dance (folk, rhythmic and classic), song (balladic and choral) and processional movement—may number from a hundred to a thousand.

Its form, in brief, is that of an actable Folk-Poem, designed for the expression of communal aspiration in dramatic forms of cadenced speech and music.

THE SETTING

THE SETTING

The Setting of the Masque is revealed out of darkness by starlight and the glow of a log-fire. It discloses the weathered contours of a vast cliff-like ROCK, disappearing upward into the screening foliage of a giant CEDAR TREE, the immense circle of whose ascending trunk is visible only in an arc one-eighth of its circumference.

The summits of Rock and Cedar are invisible in the upper night.

In the Cedar is a cave-like hollow, from which a path leads behind a cedar Sapling, some fifteen feet in height, which springs from a gnarled root of the great tree. Root and Sapling screen the dim passage that lies between the Cedar's trunk and the rising Rock wall leading backward into a forest wilderness suggested only by sounds of echo and song.

The half ellipse formed by the walls of Cedar (at left of the audience) and of Rock (at back and right) comprises the Stage, whose center is the "Fairy Ring."

High in the Rock wall is a central Cleft through which—from the winter sky of midnight—the North Star shines.

The Rock itself (simulated by the heavy folds of hanging curtains) contains two *Planes of Action*: The first (*Plane III*), elevated some five or six feet above the stage level, comprises the place of the Tableaux visions, and the stations of Orion and Cassiopeia. The Second (*Plane IV*), elevated some twelve or fifteen feet higher, is the Station of Polaris (The North Star).

In the ascending order of their several heights, *the Five Planes of Action* are as follows:

THE PLANES OF ACTION

Plane I comprises the level of the AUDITORIUM: Aisles and Arena. Three AISLES, leading toward the Stage, are crossed by the Chancel Aisle (nearest the Stage) and by another. Between these two aisles is the ARENA, an assembling space (enlarging the "Folk-Circle" of the Stage), apportioned in the Audience to the costumed Chorus and Processional Participants, as they gradually convene during the action.

Plane II comprises the level of the STAGE, which is connected, at center, with the lower of level of Plane I, by a ramp or stairway.

Plane III comprises the level of the Masque TABLEAUX, (behind the scene) and of the two visible ABUTMENTS, where *Orion* and *Cassiopeia* appear.

Plane IV comprises the level of the base of the Cleft, where *Polaris* stands, and just above which the point of the North Star appears.

Plane V comprises the level of the FOUR STATIONS—high in the four corners of the AUDITORIUM—where the *Four Winds* appear.

WAKEFIELD

A FOLK-MASQUE OF AMERICA
Being a Midwinter Night's Dream of the Birth of
WASHINGTON

PROLOGUE

(BIRTH)

FIRST ACTION

(New World)

Plane I. Prelude. Choral Procession. Music 1*

Darkness and silence.

Out of the silence, deep CHORAL VOICES are heard in momentary song, that dies away.

Then out of the dark, at right, along the Chancel Aisle, glimmering in candle-lighted vestments of deep blue, the CHORUS OF THE AGES crosses in procession to the Masque Arena and, dividing, assembles on either side of the Central Aisle.

There, having begun in deep unison, their voices mount in harmonies of mingled chorus (men, women and choir-boys), cadenced to the Fourth Movement of Dvorak's *Symphony of the New World*, the opening motive of which announces the theme of the Masque:

CHORUS OF THE AGES

Calm, 'mid the storms of time,
Truth wills to be free.
Brave, through all mortal drift,
Still radiant glows his Star.†

(During the music of these Choral Voices, a dim gray light, stealing over the Stage, vaguely reveals there the weathered contours of a vast cliff-like ROCK, disappearing into upper darkness, where, far up, through a central cleft in the Rock, the point of a single STAR glows gradually to a frosty keenness.)

---

* The Music numeral, printed in italics at the head of each Action, refers to **its** corresponding number in *The Music for "Wakefield,"* separately published **by** The United States George Washington Bicentennial Commission, Washing-**ton**, D. C.

† The words of this Chorus, in its varying Themes, are printed on page 634.

SECOND ACTION

(The Imbuing Presence)

Planes I & II. Induction. Single Movement. Music 2, a & b

With the final strains of the Chorus, a sudden pealing of CHIMES mingles silverly for a moment with the beginning of a deep rhythmic reverberation of DRUMS.

DRUMS—rolling, far off—ceaselessly rolling.

Plate 1.   POLARIS

591

DRUMS—completely encircling Auditorium and Audience—pulsing from the dark.

DRUMS—rolling and ebbing, like muffled roar of surf, quivering inward from a tidal circumference of rhythm.

And now, to that rolling surge, a SHADOWY FIGURE looms on the central Aisle—lit from behind by a single, level ray of misty light.

Tall, commanding, with Great Cloak thrown about him by one half-raised arm, shading the strong-featured face under Three-Cornered Hat, the Figure moves silently toward the Star—a lonely Presence, pacing to spirit drum-beats.

Passing amid the dusk Assemblage and the Chorus of the Ages, the majestic Form mounts the ramp to the Stage, pausing on its verge, as the Drums diminish and cease.

Facing the star-lit Rock, his SHADOW is cast there—immense: a mystic contour, dominating the Scene.

In silence, the PRESENCE passes onward—into the ROCK.

THIRD ACTION
(The Four Winds)

Plane V.   Proclamation.   Quadruple Appearance.   Music 3

As the Mystic Figure vanishes, FOUR TRUMPET-PEALS resound, in strong, austere tones of the Masque-Theme.

Simultaneously, from the four corners of the Auditorium, high up, FOUR WINGED-ANGELS, in colors of varied Elements, burst into vision, blowing their slender Trumpets of gold.

At their pealing call, in the cleft of the Rock where the point of the stellar light had shone, now appears its Spirit, THE NORTH STAR, (*Polaris*)—a Blake-like figure of youth, noble in stature.

With his radiant appearance, the Scene below him is revealed in mellower tints of winter starlight, disclosing a bough-shadowed Dell, nestled by the ROCK's sheer wall and the trunk of a vast CEDAR TREE, ascending beyond sight.   In the curving arc of its trunk—only one-tenth of whose circumference is visible—a cave-like HOLLOW leads inward.

PART ONE
GROWTH & DRIFT
FOURTH ACTION
(Cedar Rock, and Star)

Planes IV, III, II.   Speech (soliloquy & dialogue).   Transformations.   Music a & b

Now, as the FOUR ANGELS pale and disappear, THE SPIRIT speaks in deep, clear tones of soliloquy.

POLARIS

Cedar, rock and polar star
Now in hoary darkness are
Wrought to sculptured trinity;
And I, Polaris, of the three
Voice and beacon, answer here
The golden-throated Cherubim
Where, from the four-winded rim
Of night, they cry across the winter sphere
A new-world birth.

For now the lonely wild
Bears one who never shall be child
To immortal memory,
But to all time's children be
Cedar, grown in Lebanon;
Rock, to build a world upon;
Star, by whose unswerving pole
Wavering peoples chart their goal
Till freedom climbs to self-control:
Star and Rock and Cedar, forged in one
Element—the will of Washington.

(*The* TRUMPET-CALL *recurs, while the* NORTH STAR SPIRIT *listens.*)

Again—the four Wind Angels cry
Nativity!
Far as wonder can be felt,
And Orion girds his glowing belt
And down the laddered heaven
Brings here his starry Seven.

(Below him, on his right, out of the dark, appear the luminous outlines of a CONSTELLATION, with SEVEN STARS:

In a moment these vanish, transformed to the mythical Hunter of ancient legend: ORION.   An athlete Form, his azure tunic, belted with gold, is starred with his CONSTELLATION.

Simultaneously—on the earth below the abutment where he stands—appear his SEVEN STAR-CHILDREN, while POLARIS calls.)

Orion!

ORION

Hail, Polaris!   What

Far call compels me to this earthly spot?

(Again the far TRUMPETS peal forth, in Three Lessening Calls, as the Angels vanish.)

POLARIS

Hark! A triple knock—
Thrice, for Cedar, Star and Rock—
Dies on the unclosing doors of air,
And Cassiopeia leaves her silver chair
Guiding here her stellar band,
Three and three, on either hand.

(Below him, on his left, appears a CONSTELLATION of SIX STARS—five, clearly luminous, and one of fainter light—forming, in their outline, the Letter W, with starry points spread wide.

.   .

.   .

.   .

Dawning briefly, this gleaming rubric transforms to the silvery Queen of mythology, CASSIOPEIA. Majestic, her purple robe is jeweled by her CONSTELLATION.

On the earth, below her abutment, appear her SIX STAR-CHILDREN, as POLARIS calls from the Cleft.)

Cassiopeia!

CASSIOPEIA

Hail, Polaris! Why

Now are we summoned here to leave the sky?

POLARIS

One tonight is born, and slumbers
Still, who shall not cease to be.
You are keepers of the numbers
That inweave his destiny:
Seven—*Three* and *Three*.

For his cradle-cloth, *Thirteen*
Stars shall fleck the blue with sheen:
Thine, Orion, *Seven*.—Thine,
Cassiopeia, intertwine
Three with *Three* in mystic flame
To blazon the bright Initial of his Name.

So, to charm his February
Natal night of spirits, now
Underneath this ancient bough
In the hoar-frost, weave your Fairy-
Ring, for his nativity,
And let its widening circle be
For all mortal sadness—sanctuary.

FIFTH ACTION
(The Thirteen Stars)

Plane II. Rhythmic Dance. Pantomime. Echoed Song-Call.
Music 5, a, b, c

At Polaris' gesture toward the Dell below him, the STAR CHILDREN of ORION and CASSIOPEIA step forward there and conjoin their Groups, clasping hands in a circle of THIRTEEN STARS.

Then, moving outward to wider intervals that enlarge the Circle, they dance to mysterious music* a rhythmic Design of Motion.

In this DANCE, their luminous forms and patterned steps counterpart the sky-paths of their Constella-

* Wind and string instruments: *Farandole*, from Bizet's *L'Arlesienne;* Suite No. 2.

Plate 2a.   ORION

Plate 2b.   WIND-ANGEL

Plate 2c.   CASSIOPEIA

tions as they weave their fairy FOLK-CIRCLE on the earth.

Suddenly, in their dance, they pause with startled pantomime, as a FAR ECHOING CALL—mellow-clear as a Choir-Boy's Voice—lifts out of the dark beyond the Cedar Tree.

THE VOICE

Free—O Free! . . . Where? . . . Where?

POLARIS

Echoes . . . hark!—The azure night
Holds your woof and warp of light;
But to curtain his birth-bed
Rays of white and rays of red
Must still bestead.
Go, and fetch them from the dawn
To bind your starry token on!

(With ORION and CASSIOPEIA, the STAR-CHILDREN vanish in darkness.

POLARIS, himself disappearing, is replaced by the glowing point of the NORTH STAR, while the Echoing Voice, far off, is answered by Another.)

THE VOICES

Free—O Free! . . . Where? . . . Where?
Brave, ho!—Here!

SIXTH ACTION

(Wakefield)

Plane II. Speech (soliloquy) & Song. Music, 6, a, b, c, d, e, f

From the Hollow of the Cedar, A SOLITARY FORM emerges, listening. Garbed in color-tones of Cedar and weathered Rock, the form of WAKEFIELD seems almost to have risen from the dusky soil with which it blends.

Maternal, vital of earth, her figure is sibylline and calm, mysteriously blending aspects Classic and Amerind.

Over her head, a coif of rusty hue hangs downward, twined with heavy locks of braided black.

When she speaks, her voice is modulated with deeply varying moods of tenderness.

WAKEFIELD

What questing voices answer in the dark
Lost unto lost?—Now is the timeless night

When yesterday and dim tomorrow meet
To cradle a new day. O lonely star,
You only watch—and I. The mortal world
Sleeps, and no sleeper dreams what masterful
Scion the midwife Wilderness brings forth
Under a planet's knees. The mortal world
Sleeps, but the immortal wakes, and with it all
My boon folk-spirits wink their crocus eyes
Of childhood wonder, cupping the young dew
Of olden dawn, and sharp their prickling ears
To catch my clear call to their fairy-ring
And fetch ther antic gifts and homeland songs
In homage to this birth-night.

(Out of the dark, a far TOM-TOM sounds with fluttering beat.)

Plate 3.   WAKEFIELD

> Hark! I hear
The earliest partridge drum of dreamy April
Reddening the frozen sleep of February—
The drum of Wappocomo through the night
Pulsing of primal spring.

(To the lulling beat of the Tom-Tom, there rises now an INDIAN CRADLE-SONG, quavering the strangely mournful cadence of its *E dho he!* across the midnight.*

As this chanting ceases, the mellow VOICE OF A NEGRO WOMAN drifts upward in melody.)

> Now sweet and far
Another wakes, and the Black Mammy croons
In shadow song, by cabin tallow-light,
Her ancient psalm of birth to a new world.

(Led by the Afric fervor of the Woman's voice, the deeper Voices of Men lift their NEGRO SPIRITUAL † in choral rapture:

> O, *ebry time I feels de Spirit movin' in mah heart—*
> *I prays!*

As the Refrain dies to stillness, WAKEFIELD speaks again.)

> The night is big with song. Dear fairy-ring,
Your pool of quiet, stirred by the quick stars,
Shall widen in music to enripple the world
With their first rhythm. My folk-spirits shall keep
Your secret spell. The Red Partridge has rolled
His feathered drum. The Black Mammy has crooned
Her firelog psalm; and yonder
Now the White Woodman thuds his briskened ax
To wake the high-hole in his hollow bough
And rap an undersong.

(The STROKE OF AN AX sounds with rhythmic fall.)

> His frosty blade
Has made the cedared dark his dulcimore
To dingle his lone ballet.

(From nearby, the VOICE OF A MAN, keyed in mountainy pitch, sings with rich acrid savor, to strokes of his swung ax, punctuating the old Appalachian folk-tune.)

THE MAN'S VOICE

> *Joseph were a young man,*
> *A young man were he,*
> *And he courted Virgin Mary,*
> *The queen of Gallilee.*

---

* Cf., on page 628, the Indian Words of this song, *The Mother's Vow,* and the Music and Words in *The Music for "Wakefield"* (6, b).

† Cf., on page 628, the Words of this Negro Spiritual, and the Words and Music in *The Music of "Wakefield"* (6, d).

‡ Cf., in *The Music for "Wakefield"* (6, f), the music of this Appalachian ballet, *The Cherry Tree Carol.*

> *Mary and Joseph*
> *Were a-walkin' one day:*
> *"Here is apples and cherries*
> *A-plenty to behold."*

> *The Lord spoke down from heaven,*
> *These words he did say:*
> *"Bow you low down, you cherry tree,*
> *While Mary gathers some."*

> *The cherry tree bowed down,*
> *It was low on the ground*
> *And Mary gathered cherries*
> *While Joseph stood around.‡*

(As the Man's Voice ceases, an eerie COCK CROW sounds from the dark.)

WAKEFIELD

> Now
His dawny snatch has stirred the drowsing cock
To cry the day too soon.

SEVENTH ACTION
(Folk-Say)
Plane II. Dialogue

From the dim Cedar Path, the ballad-singing WOODSMAN enters.

His tawny garb is of deer's hide. In his coonskin cap is stuck a Sprig of Cherry. On his left shoulder he bears a Firelog; in his right hand an Ax. His features and skin, like his garb, are leathery, and his weathered smile slowly crinkles as WAKEFIELD greets him.

WAKEFIELD

> Good morrow, Folk-Say,
And welcome home to Wakefield.—What's o'clock?

FOLK-SAY

> Dark o' the Moon, lady. The tide tips
Nary way:
Nuther towards night nor day,
Winter nor Spring—nary.

> Old February
He's puckered his blue lips
And whistled Two and Twenty,
And the wild turkey-birds is here aplenty,
But the woods is lonesome still. They listens and
> waits.

WAKEFIELD

Yes, and the fates
Listen; for this is the eve of expectation
And more than mortal is born tonight. A nation
Of nations draws its breath
In incorruption, as the Apostle saith.
And what of my folk-spirits—have you blazed
Their homing trail?

FOLK-SAY

(Showing his ax)

This-here has grazed
The hick'ry bark, and fetched their firelog home.

WAKEFIELD

(Calling toward the Cedar-Path)

Ho, Wappocomo!—Come!

Plate 4.   FOLK-SAY

EIGHTH ACTION
(The Fairy-Ring)

*Plane II. Tinkling Rustle. Dialogue and Folk-Dance.
Echoed Song-Calls. Music, a, b, c, d, e*

From the dimness, there sounds a FAINTLY TINK-LING RUSTLE, as of wind-blown hail on frozen sedge-grass. This eerie sound pervades the dimness, as with the presence of TRIBAL SPIRITS. Then in silence,—save for this faint music of his own motion—WAP-POCOMO enters.

Under his heavy blanket of clay-red and black, his Indian garb is edged with metal Danglers—tiny tongueless bells of tin, that tinkle as he moves.

He wears no headdress. Instead, a single EAGLE'S FEATHER slopes backward above his immobile face, columned by the straight-hanging braids of his black hair.

In his hand are two dry sticks, to which WAKEFIELD points, as she greets him.

WAKEFIELD

Bring here your secret fire, and strike its spark
Out of the pithy wood, to glow the dark
And build a beacon-light to the world's end
Which shall befriend
All lost and lanternless, that grope
The jungled night for liberty and hope

(WAPPOCOMO moves to the Firelog, which FOLK-SAY has prepared with cones of pitchpine. There he rubs his sticks together, till their spark leaps in flame.)

Well struck! It kindles. Blow the ember
Till Rock and Cedar shall remember
The burning bush of old.

(From either side, WAPPOCOMO and FOLK-SAY blow the flame with their puffed cheeks for bellows till the Firelog irradiates a bright glow that ruddies the encircling Rock and Cedar's trunk.

This growing light reveals a Group of four quaint Figures, peering from the darkness: AN ANCIENT DARKY, with head of misty wool, around and between whose stooped legs three small Forest-Creatures spy at the Firelog; Brer'n Fox, POSSUM and RABBIT, snuggling the coat-tails of UNCLE REMUS, whom WAKEFIELD summons.)

Come, Uncle Remus! Bring
Your little furry brethren here!
Take a gobbler-turkey's wing
For broom, and sweep our frosty ring
Till it be clear
And dry, to let their fairy reel go round.

(Followed by the Creatures, UNCLE REMUS stubs forward and bushes the circle of earth with a turkey's wing.)

Now, Uncle, make your burring mouth-harp sound
Fine as a fiddle-saw
And let *Zip-Coon* chase *Turkey-in-the-Straw!*

(From his coat-tail pocket, UNCLE REMUS jerks forth a Jew's harp, which he twangs, seated in the firelight, while Fox, POSSUM and RABBIT dance *ZIP-COON* wildly in the Fairy-Ring, till their revel is interrupted by the far-calling CHOIR-VOICE, echoing as before.)

THE VOICE

Free!—O Free! . . . Where? . . . Where?

WAKEFIELD

Enough! Again I hear that losty cry
Hunting its home. More nigh
It echoes now.

(Turning to WAPPOCOMO, REMUS and FOLK-SAY.)

Keepers of my firelog—
Red, black and white—you three and I
Have laid this hearth on rock, but round us, bog
And feverous mire beget an enemy
Subtle to overwhelm us—the blind Fog.
I fear the drifting Fog, that dims the eye
Of faith with its pollution,
Clouding the will and darkening resolution,
Till all is only drift on ground grown rotten
And Rock and Star and Cedar are forgotten.

(Again the CALLING VOICES answer each other, echoing.)

THE VOICES

Free, O Free! . . . Brave, ho! Here!

WAKEFIELD

Those cries, still! 'Tis some wandering spirits need
Our hospitality. Folk-Say, take heed.
Go find them in the dark and guide them here.

(FOLK-SAY departs.)

Follow him, Remus! Fox and Possum, peer
In bog and bramble, and Br'er Rabbit light
His cotton-tail lamp to lure them through the night.

(REMUS and the CREATURES follow FOLK-SAY.)

Meantime, come, Wappocomo! Help me bring
The swinging black pot, to be simmering
Its birth-spell for tonight's folk-offering.

(WAKEFIELD and WAPPOCOMO disappear in the Cedar's hollow.)

NINTH ACTION

(Free)

Plane II. Song. Pantomime. Music 9, a & b

Clear, through the shadowy starlight, now rises the VOICE OF A BOY, singing, and soon FREE enters along the Cedar Path. Clad as a shepherd, with PIPE and CROOK, he strays into the Fairy-Ring. There, in the fireglow, he looks about him with a happy wonder, as he lifts his song artlessly.*

FREE

How sweet is the shepherd's sweet lot!
  From the morn to the evening he strays;
  He shall follow his sheep all the day,
    And his tongue shall be filled with praise.

---

*Cf., in *The Music for "Wakefield"* (9, a: "Song of Free"), the music, by Laura Barker Taylor, to these words of "Shepherd's Song," by William Blake, from his *Songs of Innocence*.

Plate 5   WAPPOCOMO

For he hears the lamb's innocent call,
And he hears the ewe's tender reply;
He is watchful while they are in peace,
For they know when their shepherd is nigh.

(Concluding his song, FREE plays a theme of its melody on his pipe, while he draws closer to the firelog. Then cuddling down on its hearth of rock, he peers into the flames.)

TENTH ACTION
(The Ambush of Drift)

Plane II. Rhythmic Movement. Faint Laughter (choral); Chanted Speech. (Single) Pantomime. Dialogue. Music 10, a, b, c

While FREE continues to pipe dreamy snatches of his song's melody, a faint FOGGY LAUGHTER drifts from beyond the Fairy Ring, where a strange many-limbed CREATURE OF FOG gropes inward, with rhythmic undulations, pausing hesitant on the verge of the fireglow. Around it, from the shadows, winking lights of opal and bluish-green flicker and vanish.

This composite Creature, DRIFT, is vaguely headed by a MISTY CROWN, from under which a murky NET,

† Cf., on pages 597, 602, 608, the descriptions of Drift.
‡ Cf., in *The Music for "Wakefield"* (10, a "Drift"), the music for this Action, composed by John Tasker Howard.

coiling and spreading backwards, almost conceals the form of its bearer and the lower-statured forms of his FOLLOWERS.†

Slowly elongating his netted arms, like the out-reached feelers of a vast silkworm, DRIFT sways toward FREE, in vacillating rhythm, while he chants.‡

DRIFT

Stray—stray—
Shepherd-boy, Free!
Follow Drift
Aimlessly.

Lay your crook
Under your head.
Fox-fire creep
On the firelog dead.

Forget your sheep,
Shepherd-boy, Free.
Driftingly
Sleep . . . drift . . . sleep . . .

During this Chant, FREE has drooped his head on his Shepherd's Crook, and fallen asleep.

Watching him, HALF VISIBLE FACES peer through the dusky Net.

Plate 6.   UNCLE REMUS, FOX, POSSUM, RABBIT   (See Plate 9)

Among these, two thin Shapes—CABAL and FEAR—emerge more distinct, on either side of a squat, corpulent Form—MUDDLE—that stands next to the Crowned Figure.

And now, pointing at FREE, the FIRST SHAPE touches the THIRD, with a rasping whisper.

CABAL

Now is the minute! Take him while he naps.
Quick, Muddle,—the hand-snare! I'll be the caster.

FEAR

Keep from the ring! Beware of fairy traps.

MUDDLE

Hold off, Cabal! Am I not master
And captain here
Of you underlings? Be silent, Fear,
Of our numbers! Answer, to the roll:—
Poverty.

POVERTY

Here.—I made him flee
From the Old World—yonder shepherd-boy, Free.

PERSECUTION

Nay, 'twas *I* drove him.

MUDDLE

       Hold your peace,
Persecution! Cease
Your voices, lest we give alarm.
Now answer, each by lifted arm:
Persecution . . . War . . . Gold . . .
Greed . . Cabal . . Hate . . Fear . . Jealousy . . hold!
  (As the last lifts a foggy arm from the Net, from near-by comes the singing cry of a BOY'S VOICE, calling.)

THE VOICE

Free!—O Free! . . . Where? . . . Where?

(At the cry, FREE starts from his trance.
Leaping to his feet in the firelight, he sings in answer.)

FREE

Brave—ho! Here!

MUDDLE

Whist!—'Tis Brave—his brother's call.
We'll take them both.—Lie near! . . . To ambush, all

(They disappear.)

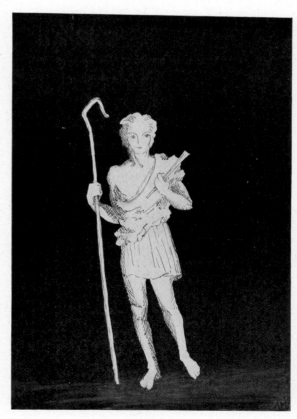

Plate 7a.   FREE

Plate 7b.   BRAVE

Plate 8.   DRIFT   (See Plate 9)

ELEVENTH ACTION

Plane II. Carol (of Two & Three). Dialogue. Music 11.

Outside, from close by, the choir-clear VOICE OF BRAVE is joined by the deeper TONES OF FOLK-SAY, as each takes his answering part in the old CAROL.*

BRAVE AND FOLK-SAY

Good King Wenceslas look'd out
On the Feast of Stephen,
When the snow lay round about,
Deep, and crisp, and even.
Brightly shone the moon that night
Though the frost was cruel,
When a poor man came in sight,
Gath'ring winter fuel.

(Folk-Say)

"Hither, page, and stand by me,
If thou know'st it, telling,
Yonder woodman, who is he?
Where and what his dwelling?"

(Brave)

"Sire, he lives a good league hence,
Underneath the mountain;

---

* Cf., in The Music for "Wakefield" (10); the Music of this Carol, Good King Wenceslas.

Right against the forest fence,
By Saint Agnes' fountain."

(Folk-Say)

"Bring me flesh, and bring me wine,
Bring me pine logs hither;
Thou and I will see him dine,
When we bear them thither."

(Both)

Page and monarch forth they went,
Forth they went together,
Through the rude wind's wild lament,
And the bitter weather.

(From the dim Cedar Path, FOLK-SAY and BRAVE come in. BRAVE, pausing wearily, with searching gaze, sings from the shadow.)

BRAVE

"Sire, the night is darker now,
And the wind blows stronger;
Fails my heart, I know not how,
I can go no longer."

FOLK-SAY

"Mark my footsteps, good my page,
Tread thou in them boldly:
Thou shalt find the winter's rage
Freeze thy blood less coldly."

(BRAVE steps into the fireglow. Springing forward, FREE takes his brother's hand in eagerly returned gladness, as ALL THREE carol together.)

FREE & BRAVE & FOLK-SAY

In his master's steps he trod
Where the snow lay dinted;
Heat was in the very sod
Which the saint had printed.
Therefore, Christian men, be sure,
Wealth or rank possessing,
Ye who now will bless the poor
Shall yourselves find blessing.

BRAVE

O Free, my brother, I have hunted long
To find you!

FREE

'Tis a happy carol-song
That brings you back, dear Brave.

BRAVE

And a glad fire
In the lonely dark. He fetched me here, through mire
And frost—our good friend, Folk-Say.

FREE

Who is he?

FOLK-SAY

Eh, lad, it's world o' mixin's what makes *me*:—
An old saw, with a sharpish tongue o' truth
To keep it filed, and ary wisdom tooth
Is sound yit: a hard nut fer fools to crack,
But meller meat fer chipmunks, gin they pack
Their winter storage in old Nature's bin:
A slick roof, to keep rain out and rhyme in:
A witchin'-stick, what finds a Bible-well
Under the rind of ary antic shell:
They-all is Folk-Say.

But enough o' that.
They's more in me than time kin listen at
From now to never. Uncle Noah's flood-bust
Warn't but a spoonful to my thundergust
Ef' be I'd cut the splashdam and spill over.—
But how come *you*, afoot, crosslots from Dover,
On sech a squander?

FREE

They drove us forth from yonder.

FOLK-SAY

Who druv ye forth?

BRAVE

Old Poverty

And Persecution. They would make us creep
Under their net, and be
Bound as their truckle-slaves, but Free
And I escaped over the awful deep,
By wrack and bitter weather,
Happy to make our home together
In this great wildness. So we wandered far,
Till in the dark, alone, each lost his way.
At last, I heard an ax and spied a star
Holding its quiet ray
High over this silent rock and cedar tree;
And then your carol sang—

FREE

And so you came to me,
And we have found each other.

BRAVE

But where were *you* straying, brother,
In this strange dark of the moon?

FREE

Following my willow pipe to the turn of a tun
Around the bend of rhythm.

Plate 9.   VASSALS OF DRIFT
(From left to right) *Cabal, Pestilence, Muddle, Poverty, War, Fear, Jealousy,
Persecution* (see Plate 8)

FOLK-SAY

                              And who might be
Around that bend?

FREE

            Myself and Liberty,

FOLK-SAY

Aye, willer is slick for whistles; but hickery
Is clever to heft an ax and build a home
For Liberty to raise a neighborly
House-warmin' with his folks, let snow-fly come.
And here, I reckon, your land and home's to be,
Young Brave and Free,
My lads.

BRAVE

            Lend me your ax to swing,
Folk-Say,
And let my brother keep his pipe to play,
And we will learn to build and sing
Together.

FREE

            Yea,
For I can tell you how
My pipe and I we met a wondrous thing
That rose up from a slough
Misty and blue and blindly shimmering
And drifted off like petals from a bough
Of shadbush in the spring,
Or like a swirl of snow-flowers. And now
It dipped and slanted like a swallow's wing,
And still it floated cloudy as a dream
In Indian summer, all as there did seem
To rise a foggish laughter
Around its drifting. So we followed after,
My pipe and I; till soon a dim bee-swarm
Of greenish glow-lamps winked about its form,
And droning lullabies began to sift
Out of darkness, humming—"Drift—sleep—drift!"

FOLK-SAY

So—Captain Drift o' the Bog-Marines!
I knows the Will o' wisp that flags his puddle
With fox-fire blues and greens
And goldy epaulets for his Major Muddle
To boss his fog-horned sperrets. *He'll* lead ye a
    dance,
Hill-up, dale-down, same as the King o' France
With his forty-thousand men,
From Nowhar-town to Nix and back again.

FREE

If he were Drift I saw, he murmured his name
Softly, and moved like wonder.

FOLK-SAY

                              All the same
Keep outen his clutch, lad; elsewise yet
Ye're like to find
Them in his crew ye thought were left behind
Back in the Old World; and they spreads a net
That bags more game than geese. A bird in the bush
Pipes merrier than four-and-twenty in the mush.

BRAVE

Nay, let me fight this Drift. Why should I dread
    him?
I'll come to grips with him, and overhead him.

FOLK-SAY

Who that grapples mist
Bloodies his own fist.—
Nay, boy! Nary thing
Kin fight the drift o' fog
But this-here fire-log
That holds the folk-spell of our fairy ring.

(FOLK-SAY glances near at WAKEFIELD, who has entered from
the Cedar Hollow and listened.)

TWELFTH ACTION
(The Crumpled Horn)

Plane II. Dialogue. Horn (blown thrice). Music 12

Accompanying WAKEFIELD from the Cedar, WAP-
POCOMO brings with him a rustic TRIPOD of three
charred Logs, grappled near the top by a heavy chain,
swinging a GREAT BLACK POT of smoky iron, which
he places above the burning Fire-log.

WAKEFIELD

And here's our old black pot to brew the spell
Where many a wind has swung it to the flames.—
Welcome, dear Free and Brave, for I have listened
Yonder, and love you well; and to your eyes
That ask me, I will answer: I am Wakefield,
Your New-World Mother. This fairy-ring is mine
Where you shall make your home with me, and
    these—
Folk-Say, and Wappocomo, and old Remus—
Who keep this fort of refuge without wall
For my folk-spirits, wandering the world,
Like you, for sanctuary.

FREE

Where are they
All, lady?

WAKEFIELD

Some are lost in yesterday,
Some in tomorrow, but from near and far
Tonight they meet to mingle here beneath
This Rock and Star and Cedar Tree.

BRAVE

Why, lady?

WAKEFIELD

Because, tonight, is born—but I will tell
That story when we sit together, all,
Around the firelog. Here you both shall help me
Prepare the hearthstone for their coming home.
And now, each one, hand me your birth-night tokens
To bind our charm of memory and morrow.

(She speaks, in turn, to FREE, BRAVE, WAPPOCOMO, REMUS, FOLK-SAY, who give her their several TOKENS.)

Your Shepherd's Staff—for Succour: armed with only
This, once a King reigned in an ox's stall.
Your Sling—for Courage: with that slender token
Young David faced the giant Philistine.
Your Pipe—for Peace. And what have *you* fetched,
    Uncle?
A Rabbit's Foot—for Luck! And you, good Folk-
    Say?

FOLK-SAY

A Cherry Sprig, to match it,
Lady. Not for to tell a lie,
I cut it with my little hatchet,
Aimin' to hand it down—for History.

WAKEFIELD

To every gift its humor, and with all—
Our love. So Wappocomo, lay them yonder
Beside the log-fire, till our rites begin.
Now, Brave—your bugle-horn! How quiet it lies
There in your hand! Yet yonder crumpled horn
Once tossed on the mad cow that jumped the moon,
And many a high and perilous venture, wild
With eerie legend, haunts its hollow shell:
Echoes of golden Troy falling in ashes—
The blast that toppled the walls of Jericho—
The faerie horn of Roland—the far bleating

Of sheep in the meadow of dreams, where lost Boy
    Blue
Lies under the haystack. All are slumbering there.
Now lift it to America, listening,
And wind a call to wake the secret caves
Of legendry and fetch my Folk-Spirits home.—
And first, my brave Explorers: call them here!

(Raising "the Crumpled Horn" to his lips, BRAVE blows upon it a TRIPLE BLAST, whose tones re-echo the *Theme of the New World*.)

THIRTEENTH ACTION
(New World Venture)

Plane II. Pantomime (group). Speech (single). Music 13, a & b

At this summons by the HORN OF BRAVE, there enters, left,* into the fireglow, a romantic PAGEANT of sombre color, touched with lights of rich splendor, in Groups of the HEROES OF VENTURE—NEW WORLD EXPLORERS of Spain, France, Holland, and Elizabethan England.

The Groups come, in non-processional order, with stately movement, cadenced to the music† of mediaeval instruments.

Among the LEADERS, accompanied by their legendary FOLLOWERS, with Insignia—are COLUMBUS, with his Spaniards and Indians; AMERIGO VESPUCCI; PONCE DE LEON; LA SALLE; JOHN SMITH, with POCAHONTAS; HENDRIK HUDSON, SIR WALTER RALEIGH.

As these arrive and form, in half-crescent, round the Fairy-Ring, they greet in pantomime WAKEFIELD, who now greets them, assembled.

WAKEFIELD

Heroes of Venture!
You that have wandered where the Four Winds cry
From lost Atlantis to the Fountain of Youth,
Questing San Salvador, Virginia,
Massachusetts and the chartless Mississippi
For new life—Seekers and Discoverers,
Welcome to Wakefield at this ageless hour.
More shall attend you. Free, show me your pipe!
Here once young Pan pouted his lips to lead
All Arcady in dance. Pipe now, anew,
Amerikee! to all the templed hills,
And fetch my native sprites and mountain fauns
To join our fairy-ring.

(Fingering his pipe, FREE blows his LOGFIRE CALL ‡—an up-leaping shower of fluted notes, that re-echo out of the night.)

FOURTEENTH ACTION

(Logfire Wonder)

Plane II. Pantomime (group). Speech (single). Folk Dance. Music 14, a & b

Called from the dark by this Pan-call of Free, there enters a pied Medley of amazing Forms: a PAGEANT OF LOGFIRE WONDER, composed not of Groups, but of Individuals—prodigious and gnomic, humoresque and weird, bombastic and secretive—each striding or straggling separately, to an elvish Music of DULCIMORES, FIDDLES and MOUTH-HARPS.

Among these FOLK SPIRITS OF *AMERIKEE*, —passing, or indifferently jostling one another, in trances of their own egos—come PAUL BUNYAN, the Giant Logger, toting his BLUE CALF; COMPLAIR TAUREAU, the BULL-HEADED Lover of French New Orleans, looping his great Horns with a Love-knot; SOLOMON SHELL, of the Kentucky Mountains, with CHINKAPIN, his Sow; old RIP VAN WINKLE, of the Dutch Catskills, with SCHNEIDER, his hunting Dog; GHOST-GNOME, of Hendrik Hudson's Crew, carrying his ALE-KEG; gaunt ICHABOD CRANE and THE HEADLESS HORSEMAN, of Sleepy Holler; HAWK-EYE, bearing his "LONGUE CARABINE" from the Mohican Trails; TONY BEAVER, of Eel River, West Virginia; BOONASTIEL, wise Simpleton of the Pennsylvania Dutch; KEMP MORGAN, striding from Texas; PECOS BILL, the Cow Boy; JOHN HENRY, from the Black River Country; STRAP BUCKNER, the Devil Fighter; OLD STORMALONG, Deep-Water Man of the Atlantic Shoreline.

Accompanying these, but separately gathered half way between them and the Heroes of New World Ventuure, is another varied Group: PIONEERS, including DAVY CROCKETT, of Tennessee; DANIEL BOONE, of Kentucky; BRIGHAM YOUNG, of Utah; ETHAN ALLEN, of the Green Mountains; ZEPHANIAH KINGSLEY, with his Arab-Ethiopian wife, MADEGIGINE JAI, of Florida.

Forming the other half-crescent of the Fairy Ring, these are greeted by WAKEFIELD.

WAKEFIELD

Changelings of Wonder!
You that have burst the bubbles of our clay
Like iris-horned moths from murk cocoons,
To hover on the twilight bourne of Nature
Talf elfin and half human, welcome here

Plate 10.   SHADOWS OF LOGFIRE WONDER

(From left to right) *Kemp Morgan, Complair Taureau, Solomon Shell, Paul Bunyan, Rip Van Winkle*

Out of the haunted peaks and hollow timber
Of Appalachia, and the falling waters
Of Kaaterskill, the ocean-rolling-earth
Of Oklahoma, Arkansas, Nebraska,
And the far beyond. Here you shall mingle now
With sea-born spirits, and swap your gnomish lore
And mountain laughter for running-sets of music,
Till I shall hush you to my firelog tale
Of this night's meaning. So, Folk-Say, lead on,
And set your fiddle-bow to *Gathering Peascods!*

(As FOLK-SAY takes his stand for "Caller-Off", and strikes the first chord for the FOLK-DANCE, these Strange Beings—forgetting their separate entities—join hands and Partners in the Fairy-Ring, where they dance *GATHERING PEASCODS* to the old rollicking Folk-Tune of its Running-Set, stressed by loud, staccato CLAPPING OF HANDS.

As the Dance reaches an apex of hilarity, WAKEFIELD makes a quieting signal to FOLK-SAY, who instantly stops his fiddle and calls to the Dancers.)

FOLK-SAY

High-Low! Jack
Your paces!
Shuffle pack
And count your aces:
Our Lady quiet of your Graces.

FIFTEENTH ACTION

(The Black Pot)

Plane II. Speech. Rhythmic Chant. Music 15, a & b

With strange suddenness, the FAIRY-RING has become silent, and the DANCERS dumb.

WAKEFIELD

Spirits, the black pot swings!
The winter cricket sings
By the ember:
Remember!
And now old Remus brings
Your hardy offerings
Of herbs and simples—broken roots of truth,
With sap of wonder, stubborned by shrewd test
Of bitter trial;
And Wappocomo, in this clay-shard vial—
Ponce de Leon's quest:
Water of the Fountain of Youth.

(Moving to the Tripod, WAKEFIELD stands in the ruddy glow and pours from the vial a slender shining stream into the shadowed Pot, while she speaks again, chantingly:)

Sung by Female Voices to Words of Shakespeare and Music by Schubert. See The Music for "Wakefield" *(16, a, b).*

Spirits, the black pot swings,
And winter sings
From the ember:
Remember!

Now, Folk-Say, while the grouse-drums tap,
Mingle fountain, root and sap.
Remus, thrum! Red, Black and White
Charm this night!

(Silhouetted at the center, facing the Tripod, FOLK-SAY takes from UNCLE REMUS a Rush-Basket, which he holds in his left arm, while he lifts out of it the ROOTS and DRIED HERBS that he names, and drops them in the Black Pot.

Squatted on FOLK-SAY's left, WAPPOCOMO taps rhythmically a deerskin Drum. On the right, UNCLE DEMUS thrums his Mouth Harp, while FOLK-SAY speaks, slowly and variedly, to his own pantomime.)

FOLK-SAY

High-John-the-Conqueror
touch-me-not

prince's feather
Samson root
ghost flower
Judas tree
Devil's shoestring
Snake root . . .
Jack in the pulpit
palma-Christian
rattlesnake-master
blood o' Jesus
herb of the cross
angel's root

plant of peace
Sky-after-rain . . .

SIXTEENTH ACTION

(The Mask of Shakespeare)

Planes I & II. Choral Song. Speech. Processional. Pantomime. Dance (minuet). Music 16, a, b, c

Far, on clear tones across the dim Auditorium, rises a SNATCH OF SONG,* on clear Choral tones.

THE VOICES

Who is Sylvia? What is she?

WAKEFIELD

Hark yonder, Spirits! Down the aisles of song
I hear new voices. Other pilgrims come
To join us, bringing with processional

Imagery, Order, Worship to our rites:
Three Destinies—of *Art, Justice, Religion*—
To sponsor what is born and shall enlarge
This little ring to measure the sky's arc.
But look—who *is* this, bearing in her hand
Our Shakespeare's Image, and within her train
His pied Imaginings?—Hearken! His song
Has named her—"Sylvia: holy, fair and wise."

(Again the Voices lift the song as a candle-lighted PROCES-
SIONAL OF "SHAKESPEARE" enters an Aisle of the Auditorium and moves, to its own music, joined by the Chorus,
toward the Chancel.)

VOICES OF PROCESSIONAL

Who is Sylvia? What is she
   That all her swains commend her?
Holy, fair and wise is she:
   The heaven such grace did lend her
That admired she might be.

This Moving Pageant is led by SYLVIA, who bears a
light Banner, blazoned with the MASK OF SHAKE-
SPEARE, designed after his image at Stratford-on-
Avon. A Maiden Figure, garlanded and clad in
Botticellian raiment of April green, SYLVIA is accompanied by three young girls, HOLY, FAIR and WISE,
clad in Blossomy White, Moss Rose, and Azure.

They are followed by a Pied Procession of SHAKE-
SPEAREAN CHARACTERS, in contrasted couples and

---

* A portion of this Processional, like those that follow later, if large in
numbers, may remain on Plane I, assembled between the costumed Chorus and
the Stage.

trios: FLORIZEL and PERDITA; ROMEO and JULIET;
ORLANDO and ROSALIND; HAMLET and OPHELIA;
MIRANDA between CALIBAN and PROSPERO; FALSTAFF
and ANNE PAGE; OBERON and TITANIA, with ASS-
HEADED BOTTOM; followed by MOTH and PEASCOD
and THE THREE WITCHES of "Macbeth."

These, with Others, proceed along the Aisle, and
mount the Stage,* to music of their continued song
to Sylvia.

   Is she kind as she is fair,
      For Beauty lives with Kindness?
   To her eyes Love doth repair
      To help him of his blindness,
   And being helped, inhabits there.

   Then to Sylvia let us Sing,
      That Sylvia is excelling.
   She excels each mortal thing
      Upon the dull earth dwelling.—
   To her garlands let us bring!

(Joining the circle of the Fairy-Ring, they greet WAKEFIELD
in pantomime, as SYLVIA hands the Banner to FAIR, who holds it
beside WAKEFIELD, revealing to her its MASK OF SHAKESPEARE.)

WAKEFIELD

Sylvia, this deathless mask, if it could speak,
Might only find true words to fit your welcome.
Let music speak instead, and your own feet
Print measures on the earth, for you—and these
Bright Creatures of this Mask—to sing with motion

Plate 11a.   SYLVIA, HOLY, FAIR & WISE   Plate 11b.   REVELATION   Plate 11c.   CHILDHOOD

(Forming their couples for a *MINUET*, these "Pied Imaginings" of Shakespeare—led by SYLVIA, partnered with OBERON—dance, with stately charm, a design of steps rhythmed to the touch of harpsichord.) *

At their conclusion, they are greeted again—with the Others—by WAKEFIELD.

WAKEFIELD

Dear Spirits, Beauty is a pollened flower
Whose stem is Freedom, and whose stamened heart
Is Order. Liberty is Law embattled,
And through the tempests of all Saxon change
Resounds the chant of Law—and Magna Charta.
Listen!

SEVENTEENTH ACTION

(Magna Charta)

Planes I & II. Processional Speech. Music 17

By another Aisle of the Auditorium, the PROCESSIONAL OF MAGNA CHARTA enters, to Music of sonorous dignity:† Groups of THE LAWS AND THE SCIENCES, who move toward the Stage, which the LEADERS mount, and join the Circle of Spirits.

There, MAGNA CHARTA hands his Scroll to Sylvia's second Child-Attendant, WISE, who holds it in the presence of WAKEFIELD, as she makes her greeting.

WAKEFIELD

Have welcome here, Masters of Law!
The Word Enscrolled has majesty, but mightier
The Word Unwrit which in the beginning was
With God. Of that begetting Word was spoken
Of old, by the Apostle:

*Though I speak with the tongues of men and of angels
and have not Love,
I am become as sounding brass
or a tinkling cymbal.*

*And though I have the gift of prophecy
and understand all mysteries and all knowledge
and though I have all faith so that I could remove
    mountains,
and have not Love—
I am nothing . . .
And now abideth Faith, Hope, Love,
these three;*

* Minuet in A, by Boccherini. See, *The Music for "Wakefield"* (16, c).
† Hymn, by Tallis. See *The Music for "Wakefield"* (17).
‡ The Music by Oliver Holden. Cf., the full words of this Hymn, on page 168. See, also, *The Music for "Wakefield"* (18).

*but the greatest of these
is Love.*

Hearken, spirits,
Yonder—to them who come hymning
The Lord of the Greatest of These!

EIGHTEENTH ACTION

(Revelation)

Planes I & II. Processional. Speech. Music 18

By a third Aisle of the Auditorium, to Organ Music, there enters now the PROCESSIONAL OF WORSHIP, led by REVELATION, a radiant Figure, bearing THE BIBLE, attended by two Child-Acolytes, THE TWO TESTAMENTS, followed by the PSALMISTS, PROPHETS and APOSTLES.

All these, joined by the Chorus, come singing the Hymn *Coronation*.‡

Mounting to the Folk-Circle, REVELATION—with her attendant TESTAMENTS—approaches WAKEFIELD, in whose presence THE NEW TESTAMENT steps forward, with the Child, HOLY, together holding the tokened Volume.

WAKEFIELD

Revelation, your Testament of Love

*beareth all things,
hopeth all things,
endureth all things.*

Now here abideth *Holy*, *Fair* and *Wise*,
That hold in token *Love* and *Hope* and *Faith*.

Folk-Spirits—you, my family, far-wandered
Out of the night into our family circle,
With guardians such as these, what oaf of evil
Shall sunder us, or mar our sanctuary?

FREE

I fear no evil in this fairy-ring.

BRAVE

What spirit would dare to harm its holy spell?

WAKEFIELD

One only do I dread, for only he
Can steal upon us, like a sudden sleep,
And rob us of our wills, before we know
That we are robbed. (Gazing intent)—Even now
I see him . . .

FREE

(Starting up)

Where?

WAKEFIELD

Here—in my second sight.

BRAVE

Who is he?

WAKEFIELD

Drift.

BRAVE

Ha, that same Drift whom Folk-Say told us of!
But what, then, *is* this Drift that we should fear him?

NINETEENTH ACTION

(The Net of Drift)

Plane I. Speech. Dialogue. Music 19.

As WAKEFIELD begins to answer, the shadowy
gleaming Form of DRIFT is seen to emerge from behind, trailing his undulating NET OF FOG, upborne
by his hidden FOLLOWERS.

While WAKEFIELD continues to speak to her intent
listeners of the Circle, DRIFT—in rhythmic motion,
to a faintly horning music—draws ever closer,
spreading his elongated mesh in a semi-arc around
the Folk-Spirits. Meantime, the ruddy glow of the
Firelog pales slowly to a sallow dimness, sprinkled with
purple Fox-Fires.

WAKEFIELD

Drift is the death-in-life that blurs the orb
Of reason to oblique its image, till
Ourselves become the phantoms that we fear—
Phantoms of War and Hate, Envy and Greed.
Drift is the fungus-gleam whose phosphor ray
Glamors the ruin it obliterates.
His mildew hand shadows a faceless clock
Whose ticking pendulum may tell no hour,
Forever moving between Now and Never
In vacillation towards oblivion.
Fog is his empire, and his misty crown
Glisters with marsh-fire. Through his rhythmic fingers
Round him, there flows a murky fowler's net,
Wherein himself and his followers
Are snared; yet he is skilled to cast its skein
So blinding swift, that in its meshes all
This glowing circle of friends, this sacred fire,
And happy tryst, might with a moment be
Blotted in warring chaos.

BRAVE

Nay, but that
Could *never* come to pass!

FREE

Are we not all
Too happy with goodwill ever to be
Other than now?

WAKEFIELD

Dear ones, we will indeed
Pray to be ever happy with goodwill
Even as now. So gather our fairy-ring
And, as I promised, I will tell you all
My timeless tale of Once-upon-a-time.

TWENTIETH ACTION

(Midwinter's Night)

*Plane I. Speech. Pantomime. Rhythmic Movement. Horn.
Cries in Darkness. Music 20, a, b, c, d*

WAKEFIELD sits on the gnarled Cedar-Root.
Crouching more close, on the earth, the FOLK-
SPIRITS gather their rapt Circle, near the open center
of which FREE and BRAVE lean forward, peering up in
the face of the Speaker—BRAVE lying on one arm, a
little apart from his Brother.

Unobserved in the dimming circumference, DRIFT
looms and sways, coiling a loop of his Net, while
MISTY HEADS AND ARMS of his FOLLOWERS—trickling pale-gold and black and rust-red—leer and point
at FREE, emitting at feeblest pitch their inarticulate
lulling of FOGGY LAUGHTER, which slowly loudens as
the voice of WAKEFIELD dwindles with poignant tones.

WAKEFIELD

On a midwinter's night, when the North Star
Dreamed on the wilderness of a new world,
Deep in the tingling silence of a wood
A Spirit was born—a child of loneliness,
For he was sinewed out of Rock and Star
And Cedar Tree. So solemn was the hour
That great Orion swerved his starry trail
And Cassiopeia left her shining chair
To watch in wonder. For this Lonely One,
Who soon should make the Rappahannock lie
Under his arm, and curb the Alleghenies
With his divining-rod, would move through war
Tumult and peace to endless aftermaths
Where numberless unborn shall name him "father."

Now, in that lonely wood, on this same night,
Two brother spirits, *Free* and *Brave,* were lost,
Calling each other, till they heard a carol
And found a firelog and a fairy-ring
And glad folk-neighbors, all with friendly eyes
Of welcome.   Round their circle music went
With feet of revel and with heart of song,
In charmed . . . forgetfulness . . . of all . . . which
    might . . .

    (DRIFT flings his loop.
    Pealing FOG-CRIES burst.
    Caught in the Net, FREE is whirled outward in coiling darkness . . .

    Then utter NIGHT—black, terrible with CRIES OF WARRING CHAOS.

    Only the discord of the Combatants * gives the clue to their blind struggle: FOG-SCREAMS of *War!—Cabal!—Gold!* clashing with FOLK-CRIES of *Rock!—Cedar!—Star!*

    Piercing them all, a WINDING HORN blasts a sudden STILLNESS, out of which floats a choir-shrill Call . . . *Free!—Free! . . . Where? . . . Where? . . .* answered by the far cry of *Brave, ho!—SAVE!*)

INTERLUDE
RE-BIRTH

Plane I.   Choral Song.   Music 20, a

Out of Darkness, lulling the Conflict with subduing harmonies, the CHORUS OF THE AGES sings.

CHORUS OF THE AGES†

    O Thou which art the thunder
        And tempest of the Soul,
    Thou are also the wonder
        And solace of the goal.

    Thyself the lure immortal
        To meet Thine own behest,
    Thou art the path and portal,
        The quester and the quest.

    The radiance to show Thee,
    The mastery to know Thee,
    Thou art the Will who dost reveal
    Whereby of wan delusion,
    Of fear and blind confusion,
    The Soul alone itself can heal.

---

    * To Music, composed, by John Tasker Howard. See *The Music for "Wakefield"* (20, a).
    † To Music by Bach. *Chorales, Numbers One and Two. Cf., The Music for "Wakefield"* (20, e).

PART TWO

SELF-HEAL

TWENTY-FIRST ACTION

(The Wrecked Circle)

Plane II & IV.   Dialogue

Gradual and serene, through the black obscurity, the unswerving ray of the NORTH STAR glows again above, while, below, a blood-dim pallor reveals the FOLK-CIRCLE wrecked and dispersed.

The Tripod is overturned; the Fire is scattered in smoking embers.

The place of the Fairy-Ring is strewn with shattered Symbols and Insignia of the routed Folk-Spirits.

The last of these are dimly visible, lifting to a black litter the child bodies of HOLY, FAIR and WISE, which they bear into the Cedar's Hollow.

Alone at the center, distraught, kneels BRAVE, clutching the broken shepherd-staff of his Brother.

On the left, in the same posture in which she was overwhelmed, WAKEFIELD sits in stupor on the Gnarled Root—between the motionless Figure of WAPPOCOMO and the crouched form of REMUS.

In the background, FOLK-SAY stands dazed, beside the fallen Tripod.

Suddenly, BRAVE leaps to his feet.

BRAVE

My brother, Free—
They have torn him away to captivity—
My brother!—They flung a snare—I grappled mist.
I struck the blinding fog. Ha, look—
My bloodied fist—
His broken shepherd-crook! . . .
Is here our fairy-ring? What blighting spell
Has fouled it? Who shall heal this bleeding scar,
And bring him back—my brother—
Home to our hallowed fire? . . . Mother,
Will you not tell?
Why do you stare on me?

    (Awesomely, he turns to the Others—WAPPOCOMO, REMUS, FOLK-SAY—but all are dumb to him. Then he turns to the ROCK, lifting his arms toward the Cleft. There, while he speaks, the NORTH STAR transforms again to POLARIS, who looks down, with benignant smile.)

BRAVE

O patient Star,
So calm you shine there through eternal boughs—
So calm and kind and strong—
Star, *you* will answer! Who shall rouse
These stricken ones to rise again—and save?

POLARIS

Brave.

BRAVE

What charmed herb can heal this wrong?

POLARIS

Self-heal.

BRAVE

Who will reveal
The place it grows, that I may bring
Its healing home to our fairy-ring?

POLARIS

Wakefield, for she has heard us. Touch her hand
Gently, and she will understand.
    (Turning to WAKEFIELD, where she sits still rigid, BRAVE
touches her hand, with light caress.
    Shuddering to life, she clutches him to her breast, and holds
him with passionate tenderness.)

WAKEFIELD

Brave!

BRAVE

Mother?

WAKEFIELD

You shall bring back your bother.—
But ah! It grows in a dark spot
And lonely!

BRAVE

What?

WAKEFIELD

That little herb—Self-heal. And we forget
To put it in the old black pot
With all the others. Nay, I thought
'It has a root too bitter—I will not
Mingle it with our joys.' And so our spell
Was foiled—and all this woe befell.

BRAVE

What is it like—Self-heal?

WAKEFIELD

Its black root stems a small blue flower,
Whose seed has hallowed power
To work us weal.

BRAVE

Where does it grow?

WAKEFIELD

Over a grave, where Three lie low.

BRAVE

What Three?

WAKEFIELD

Self-pity, Anger and Pride
Lie there, side by side.

BRAVE

Where shall I find the grave,
So I may fetch that bitter root, to save
My brother and restore our fairy-ring?

WAKEFIELD

Folk-Say, lead Brave
To where 'tis dug, and show it.

FOLK-SAY

Yea, lad, I know it
Right smart—Self-heal. It makes a prime ginseng
To steep a poultice when ye're stung with adder-
Pizen. Come Spring, it craps a gang
O' purty blooms in this-yer cedar shadder.
I's show ye the dark holler whar it banks
Yander. Come, lad!

BRAVE

(To Polaris)

O Star, I give you thanks!

———————

TWENTY-SECOND ACTION

(The Fountain of Youth)

Planes II & IV. Dialogue

As BRAVE follows FOLK-SAY into the darkness,
WAKEFIELD also greets POLARIS in the Cleft, above.

WAKEFIELD

And I—dear Star of benediction! Deep,
Too deep was the pale stupor of my sleep
From which you roused me by Brave's touch of love.
But now—how shall this blight of stupor's sin
Be blessed away?

POLARIS

Not from above
But from within.

WAKEFIELD

What hidden well can hallow us with ruth
And peace again?

POLARIS

The Fountain of Youth.

WAKEFIELD

That Fountain is lost. Its waters are spilled.
(Lifting from the earth a Broken Vial.)
This clay
Once held its wonder. It was hurled
And shattered in the fray!

POLARIS

That wonder is not held in hollow shells.
It is not lost. It wells
Immortal from the Childhood of the world.

WAKEFIELD

Ah—Childhood! Where, then, may they be,
My scattered children?—Even as Brave and Free
Sundered or snared in slavery!

POLARIS

They wander many paths of flint and flowers.
They cry in alien wastes and Babel towers
For sustenance and balm for ancient wrongs.
They bear no mortal gifts: they bring their songs
Here to their New-World home.
So kindle again your hallowed fire
From ashes. Burn the home-log higher,
For lo, now, where they come
Bearing the melody
Of childhood dreams to this nativity.

WAKEFIELD

O Spirits, hasten! Quicken those pale coals! Pile
New logs against old Winter's wile!
For now I hear the first
Chant of that happy isle
Where Song is cradled in sea-winds, and buds burst
Crying—*Now Sumer is y-cumen in!*

POLARIS

The Four Winds call it where the seas begin!

TWENTY-THIRD ACTION

(Childhood)

Planes I & II. Speech (dialogue). Pantomime. Music 23

In warm rays of dewy light, a glad PROCESSION appears at the far end of the Central Aisle: CHILDREN AND YOUNG FOLK OF OLD "MERRY ENGLAND." Garbed in hues of daffodils and hawthorn hedges, they are led by CHILDHOOD, who wears a coronal of cowslips.

While they approach the Fairy Ring and pause to enlarge its Circle in the Auditorium, (where CHILDHOOD mounts to the Stage), their fresh treble Voices (joined by the Chorus) lift their ancient FOLK-SONG, with artless spontaneity.

ENGLISH PROCESSIONAL

SUMER IS Y-CUMEN IN.   (23)

> *Sumer is y-cumen in.*
>   *Hlude sing Cuccu!*
> *Groweth sed*
> *And bloweth med*
>   *And springth the wode nu.*
>   *Sing—Cuccu!*
> *Awe bleteth after lomb,*
>   *Hluth after calve cu.*
> *Bulluc sterteth,*
> *Bucke verteth,*
>   *Murie sing Cuccu!*
>   *Cuccu!*
>   *Cuccu!*
> *Well singes thu Cuccu!*
> *Ne swik thu naver nu!*

WAKEFIELD

Peace is the melody of ceasing pain.
Dear Childhood! You have brought our peace again.

(Into the Firelight BRAVE has returned with swift steps. In his hand are two small DARK ROOTS, which he takes to WAKEFIELD.)

BRAVE

I bring you—Self-Heal. I have digged these roots
In that dark place you said, to ripe their fruits.
Here, Mother!
This one is for you. This one shall speed my brother
Out of his bondage, back to you.—Goodbye!
I go to deal with Drift, and one shall die.
Never fear—not I!

(He rushes into the dark.)

WAKEFIELD

My heart shall follow nigh! . . .
Self-Heal, Childhood, Peace: These Three shall prove
Our lost-restored ones—*Faith* and *Hope* and *Love*—
Restored, together.
Bright Star, "within—not from above"
I dedicate once more
Our stricken Circle, stronger than before.

(To WAPPOCOMO)

Give me that eagle-feather.
Here needs no Fount of Youth
To dip its plume; but here with tears of Truth
From a secret spring
I sprinkle all who guard this fairy-ring.

(Raising the EAGLE-FEATHER, with a gesture of blessing):

Wonder eternal
Keep our spirits vernal!

(To POLARIS.)

But speak, O quiet Watchman! What of the night?

POLARIS

Brave goes to succour Free. I hear his horn
Calling on the dark trails—*Brother*—
I am near! . . . But now another
Music is borne
On the mingling bells
Of Babel tongues, where your Folk-Children come
In singing caravels.—
Make wide your Circle for their welcome home!

TWENTY-FOURTH ACTION

(The Thirteen Songs)

Planes I & II. 13 Processionals & Folk-Songs. Music 24,
a–m (incl.)

Now, from various Entrances, through all the
Aisles of the Auditorium, THIRTEEN PROCESSIONALS
OF FOLK-SONG approach the Firelog Circle, some in
sequence of Song and Movement, others crossing one
another, mingling their folk melodies in contrapuntal
harmony. Bringing the heritages of many lands and
races in varicolored garb and symbols, they mass (on
Plane I), in pied assembly, within the extended rondure of the hearthlight.

With their increasing numbers, the contrasted
moods of their FOLK TUNES, the different cadences
and rhythms of their steps and their bearing in procession, all create an ever-growing composite vitality,
vibrant with the mystic YOUTH OF AMERICA.

Those overtones of racial tongues, music and actual
human presence, which no printed page can emanate,
may only be hinted to listening imagination by these
FOLK-SONGS* sung by their THIRTEEN PROCES-
SIONALS.

SCOTCH
O, CAN YE SEW CUSHIONS? (24, a)

O, can ye sew cushions, and can ye sew sheets,
And can ye sing ballaloo when the bairnee greets?
And hie and baw birdie, and hie and baw lamb,
And hie and baw birdie, my bonnie wee lamb.

(Refrain)

Heigh O! Heugh O! What'll I do wi' ye?
  Black's the life that I lead wi' ye;
  Mony o' ye, little to gie ye,
Heigh O! Heugh O! What'll I do wi' ye?

WELSH
AR HYD Y NOS (24, b)
(All Through the Night)

Holl amrantau'r sêr ddywedant,
  Ar hyd y nos,
"Dyma'r ffordd i fro gogoniant",
  Ar hyd y nos.
Goleu arall yw tywyllwch,
I arddangos gwir brydferthwch,
Teulu'r nefoedd mewn tawelwch,
  Ar hyd y nos.

IRISH
BENDEMEER'S STREAM (24, c)

There's a bower of roses by Bendemeer's stream,
  And the nightingale sings 'round it all the day long;
In the time of my childhood 't was like a sweet dream
  To sit in the roses and hear the bird's song.
That bower and its music I never forget,
  But oft, when alone, in the bloom of the year,
I think: Is the nightingale singing there yet?
  Are the roses still bright by the calm Bendemeer?

GERMAN
SANDMANNCHEN (2d, 4)
(The Sandman)

Die Blümelein sie schlafen schon längst in Mondenshein,
Sie nikken mit den Köpfen auf ihren Stengelein.
Es r telt sich der Blüthenbaum, er säuselt wei im Traum:

(Refrain)

Schlafe, schlafe, schlaf' du, mein Kindelein.

NORWEGIAN
PAAL PAA HOUGJE (24, e)
(Paul on the Hill)

Paal sine høno paa haugen utslepte,
  Hønun saa lett over haugen sprang;
Paal kunne vœl paa hønun fornema
  Rœven va ute mœ rumpa saa lang.
Kluk, kluk, kluk, sa' høna paa haugom;
Paal han sprang og rengde mœ augom;
  "Naa tor' e inkje koma heim aat 'n mor!"

---

* Cf., in The Music for "Wakefield" (24, a–m), the Music and Words of
all the Songs were printed: See, also, in this volume, The Complete Texts of
all of these Songs, with their Translations.

FRENCH
FRERE JACQUES (24, f)
(Brother John) NN N

Frére Jacques,
Frére Jacques,
  Dormez-vous?
  Dormez-vous?
    Sonnez les matines:
    Sonnez les matines:
Din, din, don! Din, din, don!

DUTCH
DES WINTERS ALS HET REGHENT (24, g)
(In Winter When It's Raining)

Des winters als het reghent,
  Dan zijn de paetjes diep, ha diep,
Dan comt dat looze visschertjen
  Visschen al inne dat riet.
Met sine rifstoc, met sine strijcstoc,
Met sine lapsac, met sine cnapsac,
Met sine leere, van dirre dom deere,
Met sine lere leersjes aen.

ITALIAN
GLI SCARRIOLANTI (24, h)
(The Wheelbarrow Loaders)

A mezzanotte in punto
  Si sente un gran rumor,
Sono gli scarriolanti, le rà
Sono gli scarriolanti, le rè,
A mezzanotte in punto
  Si sente un gran rumor,
Sono gli scarriolanti, le ra,
  Che vanno a far l'amor.

GREEK
Ἄη Βασίλης (24, i)

Ἄη Βασίλης (24, m)
(Saint Basil)

Ἅγιος Βασίλης ἔρχεται
Καὶ δὲν μᾶς καταδέχεται
Ἀπὸ τὴν Καισαρεία
Σ' εἰσ' ἀρχόντισσα Κυρία.

HEBREW
אליהו הנביא (24, j)
(ניגון יהודי)

אליהו הנביא,
אליהו החשבי
אליהו אליהו,
אליהו הגלעדי
כמהרה בימינו,
כמהרה בימינו,
יבוא אלינו
עם משיח בן דוד.

BOHEMIAN
HAJEJ, MUJ, ANDILKU (24, k)
(Hush-a-Bye, Baby Mine)

Hajej, muj, andilku, hajeje, a spi,
Maticka, kolibá detátko svy.
Hajej, nynej, dadej, milej!
Maticka, kolibá detátko svy.

POLISH
TATULA, MATULA (24,1)
(Father Dear, Mother Dear)

Tatula, matula, tatula, matula,
Blogoslaw mnie koniu
Bo ja jade w zolnierska parade
Racz mi Boze szczescie dac.

RUSSIAN
Вниз по матушке по Волге

Вниз по матушке по Волге, ах!
По широкому раздолью!
Разыгралася погода, погода,
Погодушка верховая...

TWENTY-FIFTH ACTION
(Home)

Planes I & II. Processional. Folk-Song. Music 25

Rising from her seat on the gnarled Cedar Root, WAKEFIELD moves to the verge of the Fairy-Ring, at center, overlooking the massed FOLK-SONG GROUPS below, and speaks to them there.

WAKEFIELD

Song is the promised land of liberty
Which every kind heart holds in simple fee
Against all brute invasion. Mingle your songs,
Children, and they shall bless away the wrongs
Of ancient tyranny,
To guide all yearning
Steps that roam
On alien pastures to the heart's returning
Home.

(By her gesture, WAKEFIELD salutes the CHORUS OF THE AGES, who rise amid the BABEL-TONGUED PROCESSIONALS where they are gathered, and—joined by All—sing the familiar *Folk-song of America*:)

ALL

OLD FOLKS AT HOME (25)

Way down upon de Swanee ribber,
  Far, far away,
Dere's wha my heart is turning ebber,
  Dere's wha de old folks stay.
All up and down de whole creation,
  Sadly I roam,

Still longing for de old plantation,
And for de old folks at home.
(Refrain)
All de world am sad and dreary,
Ebrywhere I roam,
Oh! darkeys how my heart grows weary,
Far from de old folks at home.**

TWENTY-SIXTH ACTION

(Visions of Remembrance)

Planes II & IV.   Speech (dialogue).   Muted Horn.   Music 26, a

Wakefield has returned to her seat.   And now, where these FOLK-CHILDREN OF THE WORLD gather round her in the Circle's ruddy glow, she greets them again.

WAKEFIELD

Welcome home——Spirits of the logfire light,
Here to your hearth of Cedar, Rock and Star!
Home is a folding of the wings in flight,
The nesting of remembrance, the found sight
Of visions lost.—Children, all things that are
Live only in remembrance. Firelight and far,
We who commune on this midwinter's night,
Of dreamers yet unborn, whom these bright beams
Beget. There is no world but what we will,
No providence but what we dare, no ill
But our own dread. Spirits, we ourselves
Must charm our fairy-ring, and be its elves
Of Will and Bravery
To guard it from the snares of Drift, for he—
Drift—is our only mortal enemy.

(The HORN OF BRAVE resounds eerily, within.)

Listen!—A horn, under the North
Star!—Even now, one of our own goes forth
Himself to be
The Spirit of this night's nativity.
Brave succors Free.
Bright Star, tell us—what of the battle?

POLARIS

Now

Self-heal has touched his brow
With Resolution. Cloaked in starry dark
He stands, the silent captain of his barque,
And sees the ice-rays quiver
Where Drift has risen round him from the river
To choke the crossing of the Delaware . . .
Look in the Rock—and see him there!

* *Cf., on page 638, further stanzas of this song, by Stephen C. Foster.*

TABLEAU, I

(Will)

Plane III.   Vision & Music 26, b

Below the high Cleft, midway of the sheer Rock, shimmering from within the HEART OF THE ROCK itself, now—to mysterious music,† as of waters commingling—appears an INNER VISION: outlines of another Night of Starlit Winter, disclosing a dark BOAT, rowed and poled dumbly through ice-shackled currents by SHADOWY OARSMEN-SOLDIERS.

In the prow, with wind-swept cape—his gaze fixed upon unseen shores—stands their silent COMMANDER—

WASHINGTON
CROSSING THE DELAWARE

(1776)

Plate 12   CROSSING THE DELAWARE

---

† *Prelude to Cantata, by George W. Chadwick. Cf., The Music for "Wakefield" (26, b).*

TWENTY-SEVENTH ACTION

(Brother and Brother)

Planes II & IV. Music 26, b (continuing, concludes). 27 (begins). Speech (dialogue)

As the Shimmering Light slowly fades, and the Music becomes muted, WAKEFIELD speaks to the intent Listeners of the Folk-Circle.

WAKEFIELD

That sight has vanished, but the vision lingers,
Etching the mind with after-pain of hope
And dread—for still those drifting Powers grope
The dark, and clutch his prow with frozen fingers.
All that we love follows his guiding Will
Home to this warm and glowing hearth, where still—

> Children—the black pot swings,
> And winter sings
> From the ember:
> *Remember*!

Plate 13. VALLEY FORGE

POLARIS

(Gazing from the high Cleft)

Remember more!—The silent Rock
Has bleaker vision to unlock
Where Self-heal curds with potion crude
The freezing blood of Fortitude.—

Now Free has fallen, sore
Wounded in bitter war,
Where Powers of Drift beset
Brother and brother;
But Brave has snatched Free from their net
And borne him through the smother
Of blinding storm into the snowy gorge
Of Valley Forge.

TABLEAU, II

(Fortitude)

Plane III. Vision and Music. 27

The Music* has deepened to a poignant threnody, austerely infusing the bleak light of a second VISION IN THE ROCK—a huge SWIRL OF SNOWSTORM—the half-smothered GLOW OF A CAMPFIRE, beyond.

In the foreground, A GREAT FIGURE has lifted a fallen SOLDIER-LAD,† overcome by the Storm. The Frail Body is folded round by the Cloak of the tall, benignant FIGURE—

WASHINGTON, AT VALLEY FORGE
(1778)

TWENTY-EIGHTH ACTION

(Candle Flame)

Plane IV. Music 27 (continuing, concludes). 28 (begins). Speech (dialogue)

In Flickering Shadows cast by the dimmed Firelog, after the Vision of Valley Forge has disappeared, WAKEFIELD and the FOLK-SPIRITS remain in dumb revery. Then, while the unpausing Music alters its theme, POLARIS speaks again.

POLARIS

From Valley Forge to victory
Brave climbs to lift his brother, Free,
Out of the vale of bondage; yet
Drift hides, to cast his finest net
In the hour of triumph.

---

* *Sonata Tragica.* By Edward MacDowell. Excerpt from the Third Movement. Cf., *The Music for "Wakefield"* (27).
† In form and feature, the Soldier Lad is seen to resemble *Free*.

WAKEFIELD

Shall that subtle blow
Once more bring wreck and blind disaster?

POLARIS

No.

Self-heal can light the blackest hour
Like a clear-blue candle-flower.
Brave sits alone in a dark place.
Only his candle lights his face
And the pale paper in his hands.
Near him in the shadow stands
Cabal, with his seductive dower,
Holding a Misty Crown toward Brave;
But Drift's sly snare cannot deprave
The conscious power
Of calm Self-Conquering.
Brave holds the paper in the flame:
The candle lights a nobler fame
Than "King."

Plate 14.   KINGSHIP REFUSED

TABLEAU, III

(Self-Abnegation)

Plane III.   Vision & Music.   28

Within the dark of the ROCK, appears at first, only a Fleck of Blue Light—THE FLAME OF A CANDLE. Then, while the gleam is intensified by illuming Music*—its widening glow reveals the VISION foreseen by Polaris—WASHINGTON, seated by a light-stand, his face intent upon a document which he holds.

From the background emerge vague Forms—OFFICERS OF THE KINGSHIP CABAL, whose LEADER extends toward WASHINGTON a gesture of deference.†

Between them, out of the air, appears the Aura of a CROWN—which melts away, as WASHINGTON quietly lifts the Document into the Candle's Flame, holding it there while it burns to ashes and darkness of the

KINGSHIP REFUSED

(1782)

TWENTY-NINTH ACTION

(Federation)

*Planes II & IV.   Music 28 (continues, concludes).   29 (begins).
Speech (soliloquy)*

With this obscuration of the INNER PICTURE, the outer hearth light of the FOLK-CIRCLE *gradually* brightens in color, while POLARIS speaks again.

POLARIS

Rebuked, and put to sullen route,
The Lords of Drift have turned about
And scattered seeds of anarchy
Behind the ploughs of Liberty
To harvest discord, fear and hate;
But Brave has risen to federate
The ploughmen of the common weal.
A sword of Reason, not of steel,
He whets, and strikes at dissolution,
To ratify—the Constitution.

* *New England Symphony*, by Edgar Stillman-Kelley. Introduction to the First Movement. Cf. *The Music for "Wakefield"* (28).
† Cf., *Washington, the Man Who Made us*, by Percy MacKaye.

TABLEAU, IV

(Poise)

Plane III. Vision & Music. 29

In mood contrasted with the Visions that have preceded, Music* sprightly, yet sedate in movement, now preludes and accompanies a brighter PICTURE WITHIN, partly disclosing A GROUP OF AMERICAN STATESMEN, in Session, at a polished Table, lighted by Candelabra.

Presiding at the center, where a Document lies spread before him, stands a tall upright FIGURE, nobly dressed as a Civilian, in bearing of impartial poise:

WASHINGTON AT THE FRAMING OF THE CONSTITUTION

(1787)

---

* *Federal March*. Composed for the Ratification of the Constitution, 1789. By Alexander Reinagle (Music instructor of Nelly Custis). Cf., *The Music for "Wakefield"* (29).

Plate 15.   THE CONSTITUTION

THIRTIETH ACTION

(The Noblest Task)

Planes II & IV. Music 29 (continuing, concludes). 30 (begins). Speech (dialogue)

With the passing of this Vision in the Rock, WAKEFIELD looks upward to the Cleft, and—while the after-strains of Music still continue—speaks again to POLARIS.

WAKEFIELD

Star, you have shown us omen of vast hope,
For Brave has mastered the momentous hour
That curbs the muddled Lords of Drift with scope
Of federated power.
Yet now—O tell us, for our hearts are waiting—
When shall the tensened labors
Of thought find ease? When shall there be abating
Of lonely tasks, to enjoy the boon of neighbors
And Nature's ministry
And home's fond welcoming?—
When shall Brave bring Free
Home to our Fairy Ring?

POLARIS

The time is near. For now
Brave turns from durance of unflinching toil
In the world's gaze—the knuckled brow
Of weary hope; the mastering of Drift;
The praise of triumph, and the sudden shift
To blame that Envy tries, with mute
Gesture of worship, when the broil
Of war has ebbed in mire:
From all—he turns, and takes his crumpled horn
Of battle, back to the green pasture's byre,
And plants his bitter root
Of victory in the brown soil
Of his own farm, where first his dreams were born.

So the last vision lights our midnight masque—
Where Brave turns homeward to his noblest task.

TABLEAU, V

("Improvements on the Earth")

Plane III. Vision & Music 30

Preluded and accompanied by Music* of a pastoral tenderness, suggestive of the lyric vitality of Nature, A WARM LIGHT DAWNS IN THE ROCK, revealing there a Scene of rural Charm and Simplicity:

Here, garbed as a country landholder, WASH-INGTON stands intent upon his heart's desire—the improvement of the soil's productivity.

Grouped about him are a few Friends his VIRGINIAN NEIGHBORS, to whom he is pointing out a practical experiment in the mixture of soils, for the better raising of farm plants.

In his hand, he holds a SMALL DARK ROOT.

Strains of Muted Music close this quiet scene:

WASHINGTON, ON HIS FARM AT MOUNT VERNON (1788)

Plate 16.   WASHINGTON ON HIS FARM AT MOUNT VERNON

THIRTY-FIRST ACTION
(Morning Star)

Planes II & IV.   Music 30 (continuing, concludes).   Speech (dialogue).   Dawning Appearance.   Music 31

The Muted Music dwindles to a half-breathless Silence, moved only by rhythms like the first stirring of morning air through cedar boughs.

* *Elegie.* By Frederick S. Converse.

Meanwhile, A DAWNING GLOW begins to spread over the upper greyness of starlight and to flush the SKY-CLEFT OF THE ROCK, where the form of POLARIS has vanished and, in its place, a SHADOWY SILHOUETTE grows gradually visible.

Drawn by this sense of immanence in air and music, WAKEFIELD rises from the gnarled-root seat, and moves wonderingly to the center of the Fairy-Ring.

There, as she stands, the sudden winding of a HORN, from close by, causes her to turn toward the Cedar Path, where BRAVE and FREE come leaping, together, and rush into the Circle.

Waving in his hand a Small Dark Root, BRAVE reaches it toward WAKEFIELD, *with a joyous cry.*

BRAVE

Mother—it won!   Self-heal!—Drift hunts his grave.

WAKEFIELD

(Taking them to her arms)
Children!—Home!—My Free and Brave!

FREE

(Pointing toward the Cleft)

See!—See there!   *He* came—to save!

(High above them, in the Cleft of flushing sky, THE SHADOWY SILHOUETTE has deepened its wine-dark Outline to a silent SHAPE OF GRANDEUR.

Under the Cedar boughs, the poised flecture of the head, pronged with three Star-Points, slants to folds of a Great Cloak, that—partly hid by the Cleft's abutment—appears like a weathered contour of the ROCK itself.)

WAKEFIELD

(Gazing upward, with a cry)

Star!—O Morning Star!—'Tis done!
Cedar, Star and Rock are one.

THIRTY-SECOND ACTION
(New Day)

Planes II & III.   Speech.   Appearances.   Unfurling Movement. Chimes.   Music 32

The flush of DAWN quickens and the muted tones of its Music mellow and quiver.

On the Cliff, at left and right, another GLOWING trembles—a silvery light—where ORION and CASSIOPEIA suddenly appear on the Abutments.

ORION

Lo—the dawn! Our quest is sped:
We have brought them—white and red—

CASSIOPEIA

Rays of red and rays of white
In the bannered blue of light!

(To their calling Voices, the gaze of the Folk-Circle is lifted where the TWO CONSTELLATIONS unroll downward over the cliff, beneath the CLOAKED FORM above, a vast BANNER OF RED AND WHITE AND BLUE.

In its spangled azure, a CIRCLE OF THIRTEEN STARS forms a FAIRY RING above the one below.

Simultaneously, a melodious clashing of CHIMES peals forth, and lulls again.)

WAKEFIELD

(To THE CLOAKED FIGURE beyond)

Now the new day is begun,
Greet us from the risen sun,
Rock and Spirit—Washington!

THIRTY-THIRD ACTION

("Reflect")

Plane IV. Then, I, II, III, V. Speech (single). Radiance. Trumpets. Choral Song. Music, 33, a

Shadowed against the Dawn, to the Listeners below, rapt now in utter silence, THE LONELY FIGURE speaks to the Folk Circle of the World.*

------

* These, Washington's own words, were written by him, August 5, 1786, in a letter to the famous English agriculturist, Arthur Young.

WASHINGTON

Reflect—
how much more delightful
to an undebauched mind
is the task of making improvements on the earth
than all the vainglory which can be acquired
from ravaging it
by conquest.

(From the Four Corners of the Auditorium, appearing in their SKYEY STATIONS, the FOUR WIND ANGELS, with their trumpets, peal forth the *Theme of the New World.*

Simultaneously, below, the CHORUS OF THE AGES, joined by THE ENTIRE ASSEMBLY, risen to their feet, sing—while the shape of "THE MORNING STAR" melts into day.)

CHORUS OF ALL

O say, can you see in the dawn's early light
Where the rays of our flag like the morning are
stealing,
The strong Rock of our Faith, whose far peak
through the night
Rose calm where the chariots of Chaos were
wheeling,
While, beyond, the bright pole
Of a planet's strong soul
Shone steadfast to guide toward our victory's goal:
O say, does our star-spangled banner yet wave
O'er the land of the Free and the home of the Brave?

END OF THE MASQUE

COMMENTARIES

1. THE FOLK-MASQUE: "WAKEFIELD"

MONOGRAPH BY PERCY MACKAYE

Ways of Producing This Masque. This Masque may be produced on a comparatively small scale, and on a large scale. Its production may also be imaginatively suggested by an adequate public reading of its text as printed in this book, accompanied by selections of the songs and music, in churches, schools, universities and other places of assembly. In any of these ways of expressing it, successful results will wholly depend upon the spirit of its producers enactors and audience. In order to clarify its aims and meanings and to submit various interpretive suggestions to producers and readers, the following commentaries are included here with the text:

Wakefield": its Form and Spirit. "Wakefield" is a poem: a symbolic folk-poem—designed to be spoken, acted, danced and sung. Its spirit is the folk spirit: the spirit of wonder and of awe; the naive spirit of childhood, which in early youth is "such stuff as dreams are made on," and in maturity is the substance of organic art: the reverential sense of nature's sublimities and msteries.

Because of its spirit, and because it has a story to tell us, its form is a special kind of poem: *a parable-poem;* and because its story is dramatic and actable, it is a *poem-play;* and because it is also to be danced and sung, it is a *masque;* and because it is an instrument for communal festival-expression, it is a *folk-masque,* which (as said in the beginning) is a *folk-poem—designed to be spoken, acted, danced, and sung.*

Such, being what "Wakefield" *is,* and because, in both form and spirit, its festival expression includes and conditions the *participation* of an audience gathered in sympathetic communion, the following are some different kinds of dramatic works (all potentially admirable) which are what "Wakefield" *is not.*

Though music and song are of its very essence, "Wakefield" *is not* an opera. It *is not* a cantata, nor an oratorio. Though its dramatic action has dialogue and plot, "Wakefield" *is not* a theatre-play. Though it involves effects of lighting and pictorial tableaux, "Wakefield" *is not* a motion-picture continuity. And though its poem-structure *includes* pageants and processionals, "Wakefield" *is not* a pageant.

The Folk Movement in America. This Folk-Masque is the first of its kind wholly devoted in design and spirit to the expression of one of the most vitally significant movements of American thought, which recently, in time of great need, has taken fresh impetus from earlier pre-war pioneerings in related fields. In those pioneerings the writer has shared.

The Setting. The Planes of Action. Intrinsically related to the inner form of the masque itself, these outward aspects are described in the front portion of this volume. Of the setting it is sufficient to remind the producer that great folds of hanging curtains can readily be made to stimulate the contours of Rock and Cedar Tree, when properly lighted; and that proper lighting throughout the masque is a *sine qua non* of its successful production.

The Dances. Of the five Dances, the Rhythmic Dance *of* the Thirteen Stars is related to the classic aspects of the masque, which the music by Bizet is peculiarly fitted to interpret.

The *Rhythmic Movement* of Drift, in Action X, is related to the masque's dramatic plot of "Free and Brave," and so has required its own music, imaginatively composed by John Tasker Howard, with intentionally "modernistic" connotations.

The other three Dances hold a purposeful "folk" relationship to the development of GROWTH, in contrast to DRIFT the two opposed motives of PART ONE. Beginning with a primitive *Running Set,* danced by Creatures of wild Nature, wholly animal (Fox, Possum, Rabbit), *"Turkey in the Straw"* is next followed (after the "set-back" of Drift's dance) by the rollicking, sturdy *Log-fire Folk-Dance ("Gathering Peascods")* performed by Creations of the developing Folk-Mind, still half-animal in form. Lastly, this mid-way stage of GROWTH is followed and transfigured by the highest imagery of Folk-imagination in the Group of *"The Mask"* of Shakespeare, whose characters perform their gracious *Minuet,* to the aristocrats, structural music of Boccherini.

All of these musical significances are implicit in the masque-poem itself, and were so conceived by the author from the beginning. They are in no sense mere adjuncts, selected arbitrarily for the sake of extraneous "effects."

ACTIONS I—XXXIII

I. *Lighting and Music.* The opening words, "darkness and silence," emphasize negatively the two basic elements of the masque production: *Lighting* and *Music* (which includes the *Music of Speech.*)

It is not feasable to provide here a Light-Plot. Every competent producer will devise his own, from a study of the text and the italicized headings of each Action; and, since all harmonious production requires correlation and synchronism of the appeals to Eye and Ear, the Light Director should of course, work out his Light Plot in close touch with the Stage Director and the Music Director.

II. *Chimes and Drums.* These effects should come from places concealed from the audience: the Chimes from behind the Scene, or from outer corridors desirably surrounding the Audience; the Drums from the corridors.

III. *Wind-Angels.* Their appearances and disappearances, throughout the masque, with the degree and duration of their visibility, should be carefully timed and cued to the action, in relation both to their effect upon characters in the masque, and upon the "festival" Audience itself, whom they represent as spokesmen, through their trumpets, just as the Chorus of the Ages represents it chorally.

IV. *Polaris.* As spokesman of the Masque, he serves to interpret its symbolism, and represents vocally, more than any other of its (classic) elements, the imbuing Spirit of Washington. It is especially needful, therefore, that the enactor of Polaris possess both charm and dignity of presence, power to enunciate clearly, and with perfect naturalness (wholly devoid of sophistication), his rhymed speeches. As a "broadcaster" of ideas and ideals, his voice should be sonorous, but should have none of the "announcing" intonations which usually characterize broadcasters of radio.

Constellation Signs. Their appearances, before the entrances of Orion and Cassiopeia, are for the purpose of beauty and wonder. The effects (by electric light, controlled by dimmer) should be completely mastered, or else omitted. But in any case, the constellation designs should be inwrought into the costumes, or the insignia, of Orion and Cassiopeia.

V. *Choir-boy Calls.* These recur throughout the masque. The notes—as themes of music—do not vary, but their expression—as intimations of drama—should vary subtly with every recurrence, according to the dramatic situation, becoming climactic at the final of Action XX.

VI. *Wakefield.* The Masque is a folk song, in a classic setting. All that exists in it is primarily for the sake of poetry. Wakefield is the heart of it—the presence of the folk-poet speaking—and all else emanates from Wakefield—the folk spirits, directly; the classic indirectly. Folk-Sybil, she is the Universal Spirit of the Indigenous—which is the ultimate source of all poetry.

It is, then, essential that the one who enacts Wakefield be unusually proficient in rendering the vocal cadences of poetry with sincerity and subtlety—wholly devoid of self-consciousness or "professionalism;" in brief, with the art which has mastered artifice. Printed books are not sources of poetry. So it may well be that one who has read little poetry, but who speaks it naturally and vitally, will be best suited to the part of Wakefield.

Indian Cradle-Song: Negro Spiritual: Appalachian Folk-Song. These represent the foundations of Folk-America. They set the mood of the Masque. They should be rendered authentically.

VII. *Folk-Say.* His own words to Free and Brave, in Action XI, express the intrinsic quality of Folk-Say. In his opening speech, of this Seventh Action, his indigenous speech rhythms and dialect forms are fused with the rhyme and metre of classic verse in ebb and flow and ultimate tidal reach (the ninth line, like a long ninth wave running up beach sands), to intimate the timeless "o'clock" of Washington's birth night.

VIII. *Wappocomo.* Though mute, his presence pervades the masque in a way not indicated by the printed page. Symbolic of our whole American background, he resembles more the Pueblo type of Indian than that of any other tribe today. Nothing about him should suggest the Indian of commercialized Rodeo shows or of usual Indian outfitters for historical pageants. The accompanying illustration best suggests his essential spirit.

Danglers. Probably never before used for the purpose, these should be secured in sufficient quantity (for use behind the scene) to create a distinctive *musical effect,* very moving and beautiful, if properly developed. Information concerning them can be secured from any Indian Museum, or from the Smithsonian Institute, Washington, D. C.

Uncle Remus: Brer'n Fox, Possum, Rabbit. Though also mute, the presence of Uncle Remus is as important and pervasive as that of Wappocomo. Sufficient in reference to his spirit and appearance, are the books of Joel Chandler Harris concerning him. Fox, Possum, Rabbit, of course, are acted by children.

IX. *Free.* Both Free and Brave should be lads of about twelve or thirteen, before their "choir-boy" voices have "changed." They must be unselfconscious and entirely lack any premature traits of childhood sophistication, which in their important parts would injure the whole production. In type, Free is the dreamer, the artist; Brave—the doer, the executor. Sympathetic, each requires the other. Note their dialogue in Action XI.

Shepherd's Song. The naive wonder of childhood, essential to this masque, is nowhere better expressed than by William Blake, in his *Songs of Innocence.* Since his own childhood, the writer has sung this *Shepherd's Song* of Blake, to the felicitous music of Laura Barker Taylor (Mrs. Tom Taylor, wife of the famous English dramatist). Her composition is now first published in *The Music for "Wakefield."*

X. *Drift.* Lighting is all important to every appearance of Drift, who as a "Group-Person" (comprising Himself and his Followers, as one entity), cannot be rendered corporate and organic simply by his enveloping Net, but must also be "costumed" with light, whose fluctuating *chiaroscuro* should effectually suggest the Fog which is his spirit. By the lighting also are suggested his Will o' the Wisps and his "marsh-fire crown." For his varied espects, see the descriptions of Drift in Actions VIII (by Wakefield), XI (by Free and Folk-Say), XIX (by Wakefield).

XI. *Carol.* "*Good King Wenceslas.*" This should be acted out, as well as sung.

Brave. "I'll come to grips!" "Why should I dread?" The actor of Brave should be chosen for this positive initiative of his spirit and bearing. Yet Brave also says: "We will learn to build and sing together." So the actor must never be bumptious in expressing bravery, but tolerant and sympathetic; for Brave goes forth "himself to be the spirit of this night's nativity" (see Action XXVI)—that is, the Spirit of Washington himself, with whom Brave becomes symbolically fused in the five Tableaux Visions of "the Rock."

XII. *The Black Pot.* An authentic, old-time, outdoor great "Supper-pot." This is a visual token of the folk-lore and the nursery-lore which embody a many-thousand-years' heritage of rough wisdom, culled direct from nature, of which the "superstitious" aspects survive quite as much in the pseudoscientific "literacy" of our machine age, which has shorn them of their earlier "illiterate" charm and savor.

Like Wappocomo and Uncle Remus, the Black Pot, though mute, is none the less an eloquent *dramatis persona* of the masque. Thus the "Crumpled Horn" speech of Wakefield here interprets "to America listening", the child lore of the nursery in its relation to vast feats of human legend and history. It should not be rendered rhetorically by Wakefield, but simply and stirringly.

XIII. *The Explorers.* In these *"Heroes of Venture"*, history is already half legend. The real is becoming "imaginary". Therefore the acting and costuming of these should be as much symbolic as history.

XIV. *Shadows of Log-Fire Wonder.* In these, history has become myth, the "imaginary" has become "real", the human—

"half elfin": conceptions of the folk-poets of literacy and of illiteracy are fused.

Here, then, for the first time in the theatre's art, are brought organically together some outstanding demi-gods of our Modern American Mythology—a Group highly significant to our folk-life, yet till very recently almost wholly ignored by our writers and artists and by historians of our "national" culture.

Thus the *Paul Bunyan* of modern lumberjacks and of James Stevens, the *Rip Van Winkle* of old Catskill Mountaineers and of Washington Irving, the *Solomon Shell* of modern Kentucky Mountaineers and of P. MacKaye, the *Hawk-Eye* of old Mohican trail-dwellers and of Fenimore Cooper, consort with their elfin comrades, *Blue Calf, Schneider, Ghost-Gnome* (of Boucicault) and the Sow, *Chinkapin,* on a fellow footing.

To produce this Group in a spirit at once authentic and imaginative will require unusual care and research on the part of those unfamiliar with its backgrounds.

Pioneer Group.—Here the historic, becoming legendary, hovers between the Explorers and the Logfire Shadows. *Davy Crockett, Daniel Boone,* etc., deserting libraries, take again to the trails of the backwoods. And here, for the first time, the masque-maker introduces to the public stage the redoubtable Zephaniah Kingsley, with his Arab-Ethopian consort, Madegigine Jai, of Florida.*

XV. *Folk-lore symbols in the plot.*—In this Action, it is especially needful that the audience catch very clearly the words and meaning of the speeches of Wakefield and Folk-Say. For here is forecast the "plot" of the symbolic drama, which PART TWO develops. Here, into the charm of the old Black Pot of folk-like, go "broken roots of truth, with sap of wonder," leaving (as with Achilles' heel) one ingress for mortal danger—the lack of the root, Self-heal—which culminates in the wreckage wrought by *Drift* (Action XX) and in the need for "Rebirth" (Interlude).

XVI. *A Midwinter Night's Dream.* The previous two Actions having developed, by fantasy, dance and folk-charm, the logfire mood for "A Midwinter Night's Dream" of America, the present Action now welcomes to that mood, and blends with it, elements of "A Midsummer Night's Dream," emanating from the mind of Shakespeare, as folk-poet not only of America's origins in old English, but of all modern Anglo-Saxon civilization. Thus the Ass-head of Bottom, the Elizabethan Weaver, hobnobs now with the Bull-head of Complair Taureau, the Louisiana Lover, while Sylvia makes a third female figure among the Folk-Spirits, with Madegigine Jai and Pocahontas.

XVII. *Magna Charta.* Of the civilization that produced Washington—"Shakespeare", "Magna Charta", "The Bible", are triune basic influences: guardian presences, therefore, of Wakefield's fairy-ring.

———

* These Floridian characters have been newly introduced to the American reading public by Carita Doggett Corse in her admirably vivid history of Fort George, *The Key to the Golden Islands* (cover Design by Keith Mac-Kaye: University of North Carolina Press, Chapel Hill, N. C.).

"Madegigine Jai," Mrs. Corse writes, "was tall, slender, dark, with delicate features, white turban and diamond necklace. Jephaniah Kingsley was small, spare, profane—usually clad in a Mexican poncho and silver buckeled shoes."

XIX. *The Net of Drift.* For this second entrance of Drift, careful stage-management is important, to correlate Drift's rhythmic, encircling movement with the speech of Wakefield, which conveys simultaneously the significances of Drift's nature and action.

XX. *Climax of Part One. "Chaos."* Equally careful correlation is needed here, concerned with lighting, stage-management, speech and movement. Effects of the Cries in Darkness should be rehearsed thoroughly to the music. The Cries should be called, screamed or shouted—not sung. They should be enveloped by the chaotic music and should not overtop it.

INTERLUDE. *Bach.* There is no pause. The music of Bach tells the spiritual story. The lulling of action and the music continue in darkness, till the light of the North Star illumines the opening of Part Two.

XXI. *Plot and Meaning, through Speech.—Self-heal.* After the climactic music of "Chaos", and the Chorus of "Rebirth", this Action (and the next) is purposely contrasted and concentrated (without any other music) upon developing the plot and its significances *through Speech*—with the Music of *Speech*—alone. The spiritual drama—and its solution through Self-heal—must, therefore, be clearly understood by the Audience, through words spoken clearly, simply, sincerely, with varying tonality and cadence. This requires careful rehearsal by a director who understands such things.

XXII. *The Fountain of Youth.* "Rebirth", through the immortal Spirit of Youth—of childhood—is a basic principle of Christianity, as of all advanced religions. It is also, and consequently (though not so often realized) a basic principle of folk art and of folk life. Hence its central function in this folk-masque. But youth—childhood—is instinctively joyous. Hence the joyous mood of the first folk-song Processional from the Auditorium.

XXIV. *The Thirteen Folk-Songs.* In his Monograph, Mr. John Tasker Howard treats this Action from the standpoint of music. As an expression of folk-life, more needed in the future than in the past, its significance imply a reversal of our older educational attitude toward the wonderful wealth of folk-cultures, which are the heritage of our country. Their differentiations are precious assets to the common weal of our New World. "Babel" is only "babble" to the culturally ignorant. Each folk-language is an epitome of culture, accumulated for ages. In each inheres its indigenous art, genius, civilization. The ideal of "Indigenous America" must welcome—not deny or deprecate—the indigenous folk-cultures whose racial strains *are* the American people.

For that reason these folk-songs are sung in their native tongues, not in translations. In this book, a reader who knows only English, even by glancing at the varied scripts, may catch some faint inkling of our country's richly varied heritages. How much more may an audience glean from the outpoured music of those printed pages in the emotion of song!

XXV. *Old Folks at Home.* "Song is the promised land of liberty", Wakefield says to the gathered "Babel" of the world. And here, devoid of all sophistication, is a song of the soil, naive in simplicity, which comprises, more than any other, our most popular American folk-song, surviving with undiminished vigor all onslaughts of the Machine Age. Though written and composed by a white man (Stephen C. Foster), its appeal to all our racial stocks vindicates that mystic genius of folk-music inherent in the Negro, whose yearnings in bondage it was originally written to express.

XVI-XXXII. *Brave succours Free.* So even freedom suffers its enslavements—liberated only by the charm of Self-heal. The following five Tableaux (with their interlude Actions) set forth that symbolism, through "visions" of the spiritual will-power of Washington. For that reason the Tableaux select vistas not of Washington's outward triumphs (such as at Yorktown) but of his inward-self-mastering struggles, his poise and his foresight of mankind.

Necessarily, the details of these Tableaux must be devised, by each producer, out of his own resources, in the spirit indicated by the text.

That spirit of symbolism implies that none of these "visions" shall be treated as a detached literal historic picture, thus detracting from the dramatic interest of the Masque's spiritual plot. In that respect the noble works of American composers that interpret the "visions", if faithfully performed, are a strong guarantee of right results.

In all of the Tableaux, only the figure of Washington should be given emphasis. The other figures should simply be sketched in, for the purposes of symbolism not of literal historic accuracy. For these purposes their historic identities are unimportant.

In all, the correlation of lighting with music is vital to the desired results.

XXXIII. *"Reflect."* The effect of this, the only speech of Washington in the Masque, expressed in his own words, will depend wholly upon the way in which it is delivered. In absolute silence it should be spoken with quietness, sincerity, naturalness, yet with sufficient rhythmic resonance to reach the farthest seat of the Auditorium. For any adequite production, under no circumstances should a loud-speaker be utilized to transmit the actor's voice.

The enactor of Washington should not fail imaginatively to realize that the presence, the voice and the words which he has been chosen to express are not his own, but Washington's.

The Star-Spangled Banner. This song of the American people, only recently become officialized, is far older and more important than any transient officialdom. It is a true-folk-song, its words having sprung with spontaniety from an occasion deeply stirring to America, its music dating back into old popular tradition. That its use, like that of the flag it extols, has at times been preempted or stereotyped by formalities, need not impair its use in a folk-masque dedicated to the deeper realities of our folk life. And as poets, in all eras, have made bold to offer their own humble additions to the growth of folk-song, so the writer has felt imboldened (out of the inner needs of the work itself) to offer, in this finale of his Masque, an additional stanza to "The Star-Spangled Banner", which perhaps may be of service beyond the moment of its stage production.

To reveal in that song (and elsewhere in this work) fresh meanings for the "Free" and the "Brave" of our country, has been one of his sincere incentives in making the Masque. If

he shall have attained that aim to some true extent, then to that degree this masque itself may have fresh significance as a poet's commentary on a folk-song.

II. THE ILLUSTRATION-DESIGNS
Monograph by Arvia MacKaye

Comments on the chief characters of the Masque will be found in the preceding Monograph. The illustrations themselves are not costume designs, but are impressions in black and white intended to provide certain visual and imaginative suggestions both to the producer and to the reader of this Masque. For the most part, they explain themselves visually, but the following comments may be of service in relation to costume and lighting.

Polaris. Being Greek in spirit, his costume should be of a material which will hang in beautiful folds; being symbolic of a star, it should also convey radiance. Suitable to these purposes would be white silk, of heavy texture, or white satin-crepe. If any footgear is needful, use Greek sandals.

Orion. Gold sword, azure shield with gold stars. Costume similar to *Polaris,* but should be cut to give the feeling of the hunter.

Cassiopeia. Costume similar to *Polaris* and *Orion* but more and heavier folds. Azure shield and gold stars.

In the case of the foregoing three *dramatis personae,* in order to give in costume a spiritual and impersonal impression of their stellar natures, probably the whole form of each should be garbed in some close-fitting white material, radiant in texture.

Wind Angels. Similar costume, all of white, but lighted by varying colors to suggest the various elements of North, East, South and West. Wings made of wire frames covered with white silk cloth or white crepe paper. Gold trumpets.

Wakefield. Material of light-weight wool, with heavy folds of warm earthy colors, in tones of autumn oak leaves. Her hair black, braided like an Indian's. Primitive sandals or moccasins.

Folk-Say. Dressed in soft unfinished leather. Boots supple. Cap of coonskin. His whole appearance weathered and unobtrusive.

Wappacomo. Wool blankets of warm dull Indian red, with design of black. Moccasins. Indian undergarb. See remarks on Wappocomo under Monograph I.

Uncle Remus, Fox, Possum, Rabbit. Follow faithfully the illustrations, by Frost, of Joel Chandler Harris' works on Uncle Remus.

Free. Costume of sheepskin, natural color of wool; not bulky. Bare limbs. Greek peasant kilts of white woolen material.

Brave. Costume the same as *Free,* except that he wears a tawny lion's skin, with Greek peasant kilts of light woolen material, tawny in color, to match.

Drift. The producer must use his own creative imagination, doubtless making use profusely of gauze, netting and cocoon-like silk. The lighting is all-important. See Monograph I.

Vassals of Drift. The same use of imagination and expert craftsmanship is needed with respect to *Drift's* followers. Masks, or subtle executed mask-like make-ups are necessary. They should all be treated symbolically, under no circumstances realistically.

Logfire Shadows. The emphasis of the designs of these costumes should not be symbolic but should be characteristic of the personality of each of the individuals. For data concerning them see Monograph I.

Sylvia: Holy, Fair and Wise. For the color and spirit of this processional, see the stage directions in the text of Action XXIII, and comments on *Sumer is y-cumen in,* under Monograph I.

Revelation. Costume all of white (heavy silk material), with gold stole. Large, white, constructed wings.

Childhood. Tunic of silk, daffodil yellow. The procession of children clad in spring-like colors—peach-bloom, apricot, apple-green, etc.

The Five Tableaux. Though the costuming of these tableaux should, of course, be historical in character, the treatment in lighting and composition should be symbolic and dramatic.

III. THE MUSIC
MONOGRAPH BY JOHN TASKER HOWARD

NOTE. Detailed instructions regarding the music of this masque and its rendering are given in the separately published volumes, *The Music for "Wakefield"* and *The Choruses for "Wakefield"* (both published by the U. S. George Washington Bicentennial Commission) and *The Orchestral Music for "Wakefield"* (published by G. Schirmer, Inc., New York).

The music for *Wakefield* has been drawn from folk-music, from classical sources, from the work of American composers, and from music especially composed for the Masque. The songs and instrumental works are incidental to the speech and action, yet the significance of the music is such that it forms an integral and essential part of the Masque, inseparable from these other elements of its structure.

At the very beginning of the Masque, in the darkness and silence of the Prologue, choral voices are heard chanting the Masque-Theme, *The Will of Washington:*

This is the principal theme of Dvořák's *New World Symphony,* Fourth Movement, and the chorus of the Prologue, sung by the Community Chorus in processional, is a choral adaptation of the first and second themes from the finale of this great work, composed as a tribute to America during the Bohemian composer's visit to this country. The *New World Symphony* was composed by Dvořák for Steele MacKaye's Spectacle-Music Drama of Columbus, *The World Finder,* performed in the *Spectatorium,* built for the Chicago World's Fair by Percy MacKaye's father, Steele MacKaye. It was put in rehearsal, at Chicago, by Anton Seidl, the famous conductor, but the financial panic of 1893 prevented the opening of the *Spectatorium.*

As the chorus brings the introduction to a close, with the words "Hark where they peal—Chimes, O Chime! Chime!

Chime!," a sudden pealing of chimes again announces the *Masque-Theme,* betokening the Self-Mastery of Washington's Spirit. A drum-roll, pulsing from the dark, encircling auditorium and audience, is heard as the figure of Washington, the lonely presence, passes onward, into the rock, and four trumpets, the Four Winds, sound again the *Masque-Theme* from the four corners of the auditorium. This theme is of vital significance in the *Masque;* it represents the element of strength in the struggle with the fog of *Drift.*

When the Thirteen Star Children are summoned from the sky by *Polaris,* they dance to the lilting strains of a *Farandole* by Bizet, and then comes another important theme—the *Song-Call of Brave,* seeking his brother, *Free:*

Free, O Free, where, where?

Soon this is answered by the confident, reassuring *Song-Call of Free:*

Brave, ho, here!

Next comes the first introduction of the folk-element, representing the three principal sources of American folk-song—an Indian Chant, a Negro Spiritual, and a "Ballet" (ballad) from the Southern Appalachian mountains.

After the Fairy-Ring Running Set (*Turkey in the Straw*), we hear again the questioning and answering calls of *Brave* and *Free,* and *Free* enters with his Shepherd's Pipe, singing a tender *Shepherd's Song,* composed by Laura Barker Taylor, to verses of William Blake.

Then, *Drift* enters, insinuating, luring, with foggy laughter and to music that is vague and futile. The motif of *Drift* consists of a quasi-cadence which proceeds aimlessly, never developing to the ear's satisfaction:

In the course of this music, the *Masque-Theme* is suggested, inverted, distorted and lacking its well-defined, robust rhythm:

The *Song-Calls* of *Brave* and *Free* are subtly satirized:

The calls are heard again, in their proper form, and *Brave* finally enters with *Folk-Say*, singing *Good King Wenceslas*. *Brave* then summons the Explorers with his *Horn-Call*, the opening phrase from the second theme of the Dvořák *New World Symphony*, Fourth Movement:

The Explorers enter to the strains of *Amaryllis*, and then *Free* summons the Folk-spirits with his *Log-Fire Call*—Stephen Foster's *Oh! Susannah*. The *Log-Fire-Folk-Dance* is the old-English *Gathering Peascods*, played by four fiddlers.

The Processionals of *The Mask of Shakespeare*—*Magna Charta*, and *Worship*—are accompanied respectively by the singing of *Who Is Sylvia?* (Schubert), the playing of Tallis' *Hymn*, and the singing of *Coronation* (Oliver Holden). The *Dance of the Mask of Shakespeare* is Boccherini's tuneful *Minuet in A*.

Later, as *Wakefield* tells the Folk Circle of the menace of *Drift*, the foggy music which described him is heard once more, as *Drift* himself, hovering in the background, draws ever nearer. *Wakefield* begins her timeless tale of *Once-upon-a-time*, the story of a midwinter's night.

Suddenly, *Drift* flings his loop, catches *Drift* in his net, and utter night, black and terrible, brings the clashing sounds of warring *Chaos*. The music of the orchestra is crashing, disorganized, shrieking. The *Drift* motif becomes piercing and shrill:

The parody of the *Song-Calls* of *Brave* and *Free* is even more satiric:

The *Masque-Theme* is cruelly distorted into an ugly canon:

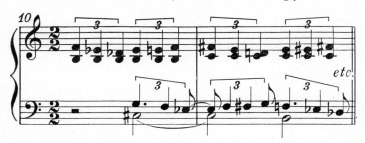

The music of the orchestra rises to a climax of noise and discord, with the fog-screams of "War! Cabal! Gold!" clashing with the folk-cries of "Rick! Cedar! Star!" Then a horn is heard sounding the *Masque-Theme*, *Brave* calls for *Free*, and the answer comes with a call to save!

Brave, ho, save!

In the darkness, the Community Chorus, the *Chorus of the Ages*, sings the promise of *Re-Birth*, a new poem, by Percy Mac-Kaye, to two Chorales of Bach. As the scene again appears, a blood-dim pallor reveals the Folk-Circle wrecked and dispersed. No music is heard until *Wakefield* calls for *Sumer Is Y-cumen In*, and the processional of English children enters, singing as a round, with the Community Chorus, one of the oldest folk-songs known to man.

Then, *Wakefield* summons the children, and music, "borne on the mingling bells of Babel tongues," fills the auditorium with childish voices. Children of thirteen nationalities, each entering in turn in processional, sing in the tongues of their motherlands the folk-songs of their races. Here is symbolism showing the mixture of bloods and races that is America, and when the children have gathered and joined together in the singing of America's loveliest folk-song, Stephen Foster's *Old Folks at Home*, the allegory is complete—they are all Americans.

While *Brave* is gone to rescue *Free* from the net of *Drift*, we hear his horn, this time sounding the *Masque-Theme*. The progress of his struggle, aided by *Self-Heal*, is depicted by the series of five tableaux, *Visions of Remembrance*, showing epic moments in the life of Washington.

For these visions, scenes and events, typically American, the music of American composers has been used for orchestral accompaniment. *The Delaware* is accompanied by the Introduction to George W. Chadwick's cantata, *Land of Our Hearts*; *Valley Forge* by part of the third movement of Edward MacDowell's *Sonata Tragica*; the *Kingship Refused* by the dignity of Edgar Stillman-Kelley's *New England Symphony* (Introduction to the First Movement); Washington presiding at the *Constitutional Convention* by the *Federal March*, which Alexander Reinagle (presumably music teacher to Nell Custis) composed to celebrate ratification of the Constitution by ten of the States; and the return to *Mt. Vernon*, symbolic of making improvements on the earth, by the restful, pastoral melody from the *Elegie* which Frederick Converse composed for the motion picture presentation of Percy MacKaye's *The Scarecrow*.

The *Masque-Theme* is heard again, as *Brave* achieves his victory, and finally once again in a new tonality, when Washington has uttered his few words of counsel—"Reflect!"

Then chorus, participants, audience, and orchestra, join their voices and their instruments in singing, to the music of *The Star Spangled Banner*, a new stanza, by Percy MacKaye—words of hope, of peace, and of strength.

DATA AND RECORDS

IV. SYNOPSIS OF THE MUSIC

PROLOGUE

BIRTH

FIRST ACTION

(New World)

Number	Title	By Whom Performed
1.	*New World,* (choral adaptation of Dvorak's *New World Symphony* (fourth movement) by John Tasker Howard).	Community Chorus of mixed voices, with boy sopranos, unaccompanied, in processional (Plane I).

SECOND ACTION

(The Imbuing Presence: Washington)

2, a.	*Masque-Theme* (The "Will of Washington")	Chimes, behind scene (Plane II).
2, b.	*Drum Roll*	Tympani and bass drums in corridors surrounding auditorium (Plane I).

THIRD ACTION

(The Four Winds)

3.	*Masque-Theme*	Four trumpets, one in each corner of auditorium (Plane V).

PART ONE

GROWTH AND DRIFT

FOURTH ACTION

(Cedar, Rock and Star)

4, a.	*Masque-Theme*	Four trumpets, one in each corner of auditorium (Plane V).
4, b.	*Masque-Theme* (Second phrase, three times)	Four trumpets, one in each corner of auditorium (Plane V).

FIFTH ACTION

(The Thirteen Stars)

5, a.	*Dance of Thirteen Stars* (From *Farandole, L'Arlesienne* Suite No. 2, by George Bizet)	Orchestra (Plane I).
5, b.	*Song-Call of Brave*	Boy soprano, behind scene (Plane II).
5, c.	*Song-Call of Free*	Boy soprano, behind scene, opposite side of stage from *Brave* (Plane II).

SIXTH ACTION

(Wakefield)

6, a.	*Tom-Tom*	Indian drum, behind scene, far back center (Plane II).
6, b.	*Indian Cradle Song* (The Mother's Vow)	Female Indian voice, unaccompanied, behind scene, far back center (Plane II).
6, c.	*Prelusive Strain of Spiritual*	Negro contralto voice behind scene (Plane II).
6, d.	*Negro Spiritual* (O, Eb'ry Time I Feels de Spirit, arranged by John Tasker Howard)	Mixed quartet of Negro singers, unaccompanied, behind scene, far back right (Plane II).
6, e.	*Rhythmic Ax-Stroke*	Off-stage effect, behind scene, middle left (Plane II.)
6, f.	*Appalachian Ballad* (The Cherry Tree Carol)	Male voice, (*Folk-Say*) accompanied by ax-stroke, behind scene, middle left (Plane II).

SEVENTH ACTION

(Folk-Say)

No music

EIGHTH ACTION

(The Fairy Ring)

Number	Title	By Whom Performed
8, a.	*Tinkling Rustle*	Off-stage effect of danglers, left in cedar hollow (Plane II).
8, b.	*Fairy Ring Running Set* (Turkey in the Straw)	Mouth-harp, played by *Uncle Remus,* on stage (Plane II).
8, c.	*Song-Call of Brave*	Boy soprano, behind scene (Plane II).
8, d.	*Song-Call of Brave* (First Phrase)	Boy soprano, behind scene (Plane II).
8, e.	*Song-Call of Free*	Boy soprano, behind scene, opposite side of stage from *Brave* Plane II).

NINTH ACTION

(Free)

9, a.	*Song of Free* (Shepherd's Song, by Laura Barker Taylor, words by William Blake)	Boy soprano (*Free*), on stage (Plane II), accompanied by orchestra (Plane I).
9, b.	*Song of Free*	*Free,* on Shepherd's Pipe, unaccompanied, on stage (Plane II). Or by flute or oboe, behind scene, as *Free* holds his pipe to his lips.

TENTH ACTION

(The Ambush of Drift)

10, a.	*Drift* (Composed by John Tasker Howard)	Orchestra (Plane I).
10, b.	*Song-Call of Brave*	Boy soprano, behind scene nearby (Plane II).
10, c.	*Song-Call of Free*	Boy soprano (*Free*), on stage (Plane II).

ELEVENTH ACTION

(Brave)

11.	*Good King Wenceslas*	Vocal Duet and Trio, unaccompanied, by *Folk-Say, Brave* and *Free,* behind scene and on stage (Plane II).

TWELFTH ACTION

(The Crumpled Horn)

12.	*Horn-Call of Brave*	French horn, behind scene (Plane II), as Brave holds his horn to his lips, on stage (Plane II).

THIRTEENTH ACTION

(New World Venture)

13, a.	*Entrance of Explorers* (From *Amaryllis,* air by Louis XIII, arranged by Henry Ghys.)	Orchestra (Plane I).
13, b.	*Free's Log-Fire Call* (Oh! Susannah, by Stephen C. Foster)	Shepherd's pipe played by *Free* on stage (Plane II), or by flute, or oboe behind scene as *Free* holds pipe to his lips.

FOURTEENTH ACTION

(Log-fire Wonder)

14, a.	*Entrance of Folk-Spirits of Amerikee* (Oh! Susannah, by Foster)	Dulcimores, fiddles, and mouth harps, played by musicians in costume, on stage (Plane II).
14, b.	*Log-Fire Folk-Dance* (Gathering Peascods)	Four Fiddles in unison, costumed, on stage (Plane II).

FIFTEENTH ACTION

(The Black Pot)

15.	*Night Charm* (Adapted from a Negro Spiritual and an Indian drum-beat, by J. T. Howard	Mouth harp, played by *Uncle Remus,* and Indian drum, played by *Wappocomo,* both on stage (Plane II).

Nos yw henaint pan ddaw cystudd,
Ond i harddu dŷn a'i hywrddydd,
Rho'wn ein goleu gwan i'n gilydd,
Ar hyd y nos.

ALL THROUGH THE NIGHT

(Ar Hyd y Nos)

Sleep, my love, and peace attend thee,
All through the night;
Guardian angels God will lend thee,
All through the night.
Soft the drowsy hours are creeping,
Hill and vale in slumber sleeping
Love alone his watch is keeping,
All through the night.

Though I roam a minstrel lonely,
All through the night;
My true harp shall praise thee only,
All through the night.
Love's young dream, alas, is over,
Yet my strains of love shall hover
Near the presence of my lover,
All through the night.

IRISH

BENDEMEER'S STREAM (24, c)*

There's a bower of roses by Bendemeer's stream,
And the nightingale sings round it all the day long;
In the time of my childhood 'twas like a sweet dream
To sit in the roses and hear the birds' song.
That bow'r and its music I never forget,
But oft, when alone, in the bloom of the year,
I think: Is the nightingale singing there yet?
Are the roses still bright by the calm Bendemeer?

No, the roses soon withered that hung o'er the wave,
But some blosssoms were gathered while freshly they shone,
And a dew was distilled from their flowers, that gave
All the fragrance of summer, when summer was gone.
Thus memory draws from delight, ere it dies,
An essence that breathes of it many a year;
Thus bright to my soul, as 'twas then to my eyes,
Is that bow'r on the banks of the calm Bendemeer.

——Words by Thomas Moore.

GERMAN

SANDMANNCHEN (24, d)

(The Sandman)

Die Blümenlein sie schlafen schon längst im Mondenshein,
Sie nikken mit den Köpfen auf ihren Stengelein.
Es rütelt sich der Blüthenbaum,
Er säuselt wei im Traum:

(Refrain)

Schlafe, schlafe, schlaf' du, mein Kindelein.
Die Vögelein sie sangen so süss im Sonnenschein,
Sie sind zur Ruh gegangen in ihre Nestchen klein.
Das Heimchen in dem Aehrengrund,
Es thut allein sich kund:

Sandmännchen kommt geschlichen und guckt durch's Fensterlein,
Ob irgend noch ein Liebchen nicht mag zu Bette sein.
Und wo er nur ein Kindchen fand,
Streut er ihm in die Augen Sand.

Sandmännchen aus dem Zimmer, es schläft mein Herzchen fein,
Es ist gar fest verschlossen schon sein Guckäugelein.
Es leuchtet morgen mir Willkomm
Das Augelein so fromm!

THE SANDMAN

(Sandmännchen)

The flow'rlets all sleep soundly
Beneath the moon's bright ray;
They nod their heads together
And dream the night away.
The budding trees wave to and fro,
And murmur soft and low.

(Refrain)

Sleep on! sleep on, sleep on, my little one!

The birds that sang so sweetly,
When noon-day sun rose high,
Within their nests are sleeping;
Now night is drawing nigh.
The cricket as it moves along
Alone gives forth its song.

Now, see, the little sandman
At the window shows his head,
And looks for all good children,
Who ought to be in bed.
And, as each weary pet he spies,
Throws sand into its eyes.

And ere the little sandman
Is many steps away,
Thy pretty eyes, my darling
Close fast until next day.
But they shall ope at morning's light
And greet the sunshine bright.

NORWEGIAN

PAAL PAA HOUGJE (24, e)
(Paul on the Hill)

Paal sine høno paa haugen utslepte,
Hønun saa lett over haugen sprang;
Paal kunne væl paa hønun fornema
Ræven va ute mæ rumpa saa lang.
Kluk, kluk, kluk, sa' høna paa haugom;
Paal han sprang og rengde mæ augom;
„Naa tor' e inkje koma heim aat 'n mor!"

---

* NOTE—The above song, by Thomas Moore, is provided for the use of communities in which there are no children who speak the Irish language; but for communities where it is practicable to gather a group of children who understand and speak the Gaelic, the following song is included and recommended:

AN MAIDRIN RUADH (The Little Red Dog). Page 28. *Songs of the Irish Gaels.* Seamus Clandillon. Oxford University Press.

Paal han gjekk se lit' lenger paa haugen,
   Fekk han saa ræven laag paa høna aa gnog;
Paal han tok se ein stein uti neve,
   Dugle han daa te ræven slog;
Ræven flaug, saa rumpa has riste;
Paal han gret for høna han miste;
   „Naa tor' e inkje koma heim aat 'n mor!"

„Hadd' e naa nebb aa hadd' e naa klo
   Aa vistee bare, kor ræven' laag,
Skuld' e dom baade rispe aa klore
   Framma te nakkjen aa bak over laar.
Skam faa alle rævann raue!
Gu' gjev at døm alle va daue!
   Saa skuld' e koma heim aat 'n mor!

„Inkje kan ho verpe aa inkje kan ho gala,
   Inkje kan ho krype aa inkje kan ho gaa!
E fæ gaa ner aat kvenne aa mala,
   Aa faa att mjøle, e miste igaar!
Men pyt!" a'n Paal, „e æ inkje bangen;
Kjeften aa mote ha hjelpt naa saa mangen,
   E tor' nok væl koma heim aat 'n mor!"

Paal han konne paa kvenne te aa sleppe,
   Saa at dæ ljoma i kor ein vegg,
Saa at agnan tok te aa flyge,
   Aa dei vart lange som geiteragg.
Paal han gav se te læ aa te knæggje:
   „ Naa fekk e like for høna aa for egge,
   Naa tor' e trygt koma heim aat 'n mor!"

PAUL ON THE HILL*
(Paal paa Hougje)

Paul in the farm-yard his chickens collected;
   There they could safely run over the ground.
Greatly he feared (for they seemed so dejected)
   Reynard, the fox, might be somewhere around.
"Cluck, cluck, cluck!" cried a hen on the hill-side;
Paul rushed to look for it, 'way past the mill-side,
   "Oh! to my mother can I never go home?"

Paul tried the harder his running to quicken,
   Soon came in sight of the wicked old fox,
Having a feast of the runaway chicken;
   Paul hit him hard with a handful of rocks.
Off ran Reynard, his long tail a-flying;
Paul for the chicken was bitterly crying,
   "Now to my mother I can never go home.

"Had I a beak and some claws made for scratching,
   If I but knew where the fox had his den,
Ah, what a punishment he would be catching,
   Ripping and tearing, again and again!
Shame upon foxes and other beasts like them,
May a kind Heaven with death quickly strike them!
   Then to my mother I could safely go home.

"Poor little chicken! No eggs she'll be laying,
   Nevermore cackle or wander at will.
Here on the hill it's no use in my staying;
   So I will go to my work at the mill.
Pooh, pooh, pooh! where's the need to be frightened?
Words, big and bold, many burdens have lightened,
   Maybe to mother I shall dare to go home."

Paul at the mill soon was busily plying,
   Grinding the grain he had brought with him there;
Loud was the racket and all around flying
   Chaff that was long as a nanny-goat's hair.
"Ha, ha, ha! I've a notion that's funny,
Pay for the hen with my flour for good money,—
   Now to my mother I can safely go home!"
                     —Translated by Anna Mathewson.

FRENCH
FRÉRE JACQUES (24, f)
(Brother John)

Frére Jacques,
Frére Jacques,
   Dormez-vous?
   Dormez-vous?
      Sonnez les matines,
      Sonnez les matines,
Din, din, don! Din, din, don!

BROTHER JOHN
(Frére Jacques)

Are you sleeping, are you sleeping,
   Brother John, Brother John?
      Morning bells are ringing:
      Morning bells are ringing:
Ding, ding, dong! Ding, ding, dong!

DUTCH
DES WINTERS ALS HET REGHENT (24, g)
(In Winter When It's Raining)

Des winters als het reghent,
   Dan zijn de paetjes diep, ja diep,
Dan comt dat looze visschertjen
   Visschen al inne dat riet.
Met sine rijfstoc, met sine strijcstoc,
Met sine lapsac, met sine cnapsac,
Men sine leere, van dirre dom deere,
Met sine leere leersjes aen.

Dat looze molenarinnetje
   Ghinc in haer deurtjen staen, ja staen,
Omdat dat aerdich visschertje
   Voor bi haer henen sou gaen.
Met sine rijfstoc, met sine strijcstoc,
Met sine lapsac, met sine cnapsac,
Met sine leere, van dirre dom deere,
Met sine leere leersjes aen.

"Wat heb ic jou misdreven,
   Wat heb ic jou misdaen, ja daen,
En dat ic niet met vreden
   Voor bi jouw deurtje mach gaen?

---

* From *Folk-Songs of Many Peoples.* Edited by Florence Hudson Botsford
G. Schirmer. New York. Reprinted by permission.

Met mine rijfstoc, met mine strijcstoc,
Met mine lapsac, met mine cnapsac,
Met mine leere, van dirre dom deere,
Met mine leere leersjes aen."

"Ghi hebt mi niet misdreven,
 Ghi hebt mi niet misdaen, ja daen.
Maer ghi moet mi driemael soenen.
 Eer ghi van hier meucht gaen.
Met uwe rijfstoc, met uwe strijcstoc,
Met uwe lapsac, met uwe cnapsac,
Met uwe leere, van dirre dom deere,
Met uwe leere leersjes aen."

IN WINTER WHEN IT'S RAINING *
(Des Winters Als Het Reghent)

In winter, when it's raining
 And all the pools o'erflow, o'erflow,
'Tis then the wily fisherman
 Down to the pond will go;
He with his net there, out in the wet there,
Casting a line, too, when he's a mind to,
All in the lathery wathery weather,
Down in his leather boots he goes!

The winsome, wily miller's wife
 Was waiting by her door, her door,
For there the goodly fisherman
 Needs must pass before;
He with his net there, out in the wet there,
Casting a line, too, when he's a mind to,
All in the lathery wathery weather,
Down in his leather boots he goes!

"What harm have I e'er done you,
 Or aught of ill also, also,
That I must fear some mischief here,
 When to the pond I go?
I with my net here, out in the wet here,
Casting a line, too, when I've a mind to,
All in the lathery wathery weather,
Down in my leather boots I go!"

"No harm have you e'er done me,
 Nor aught of ill I trow, I trow.
But kisses three you'll give to me.
 Ere to the pond you go!
You with your net there, out in the wet there,
Casting a line, too, when you've a mind to.
All in the lathery wathery weather,
Down in your leather boots you go!"
—English version by Dr. Th. Baker.

ITALIAN
GLI SCARRIOLANTI (24, h)
(The Wheelbarrow Loaders)

A mezzanotte in punto
Si sente un gran rumor,

Sono gli scarriolanti, le rà,
Sono gli scarriolanti, le rè,
 A mezzanotte in punto
 Si sente un gran rumor,
Sono gli scarriolanti, le rà,
 Che vanno a far l'amor.

 Alla mattina all 'alba
 Si sente scarriolar,
Sono gli scarriolanti, le rà,
Sono gli scarriolanti, le rè,
 Alla mattina all 'alba
 Si sente scarriolar,
Sono gli scarriolanti, le rà,
 Che vanno a lavorar.

THE WHEELBARROW LOADERS †
(Gli scarriolanti)

Just at the stroke of midnight
Joyous commotion we hear;
There go the scarriolanti, le rà!
There go the scarriolanti, le rè!
Just as the bells of midnight
Peal through the darkness above,
There go the scarriolanti, le rà!
Going forth gaily to love!

Just at the flush of daybreak
Rumble of noises we hear;
There go the scarriolanti, le rà!
There go the scarriolanti, le rè!
Just at the flush of daybreak,
Rolling their barrows along,
There go the scarriolanti, le rá!
Going to work with a song!
—English version by Angela Morgan.

GREEK.
"Αη Βασίλης (24, i)
(Saint Basil)

"Αγιος Βασίλης ἔρχεται
Καὶ δὲν μᾶς καταδέχεται
'Απὸ τὴν Καισαρεία
Σ' εἶσ' ἀρχόντισσα Κυρία.

Βαστάει πέννα καὶ χαρτὶ
Ζαχαροκάντιο ζυμωτὴ
Χαρτὶ καὶ καλαμάρι
Δὲς ἐμέ, τὸ παλληκάρι.

Τὸ καλαμάρι ἔγραφε,
Τὴν μοῖρά του τὴν ἔλεγε
Καὶ τὸ χαρτὶ ὡμίλει
Τὸ χρυσό μας καργυοφύλι.

'Αρχιμηνιὰ κι' ἀρχιχρονιὰ
Ψηλή μου δενδρολιβανιὰ
Καὶ ἀρχὴ καλός μας χρόνος
'Εκκλησιά, μὲ τ' ἅγιο θρόνος.

'Αρχὴ ποῦ βγῆκεν ὁ Χριστὸς
"Αγιος καὶ Πνευματικός,
Στὴ γῆ νὰ περπατήση
Καὶ νὰ μᾶς καλοκαρδίση.

* From Folk-Songs of Many Peoples. Edited by Florence Hudson Botsford.
G. Schirmer, New York. Reprinted by permission.
† From Folk-Songs of Many Peoples. Edited by Florence Hudson Botsford.
G. Schirmer, New York. Reprinted by permission.

SAINT BASIL *

Saint Basil comes and passes by,
And scorns us for no reason why;
He comes from Caesarea town.
Mistress, bring us something down.

He carries pen and paper white,
And sugar candies sweet and bright;
He brings his pen and ink for writing.
You should see me in the fighting!

The pen, it wrote and scribbled down;
He told our fortunes with a frown.
And then the paper spoke a trifle;
Yes, we swear by our gold rifle:

"A new month's eve, a New Year's Eve.
Sweet rosemary, I beg your leave;
Joy be your lot, the whole year round,
May your house be holy ground.

"The new year follows on Christ's birth:
So holy Christ who walks the earth
May bless you, every girl and boy,
And fill all good hearts with joy."
    —Translation by Aristides E. Phoutrides.

HEBREW.
(Elijah the Prophet)

אֵלִיָּהוּ הַנָּבִיא (24, j)
(נִגּוּן יְהוּדִי)

אֵלִיָּהוּ הַנָּבִיא,
אֵלִיָּהוּ הַתִּשְׁבִּי
אֵלִיָּהוּ אֵלִיָּהוּ,
אֵלִיָּהוּ הַגִּלְעָדִי
כִּמְהֵרָה בְיָמֵינוּ,
כִּמְהֵרָה בְיָמֵינוּ,
יָבוֹא אֵלֵינוּ
עִם מָשִׁיחַ בֶּן דָּוִד.

ELIJAH THE PROPHET *
(נִגּוּן יְהוּדִי)

O Elijah, the prophet!
O Elijah, the Tishbite!
O Elijah, O Elijah,
O Elijah, the Gileadite!

Speedily in our own day,
Speedily in our own day,
O may he come to us
With Messiah, David's son!
    —English version by B. H.

---

* From *Folk-Songs of Many Peoples*. Edited by Florence Hudson Botsford. G. Schirmer, New York. Reprinted by permission.

† Translation taken from *"Twenty Two Bohemian Folk-Songs."* Translated and compiled by Rev. Vincent Disek, D. D., Pastor of the Jan Haus Bohemian Presbyterian Church; 347 East 74th St., New York City. Copyright 1912 by Rev. Vincent Pisek. Reprinted by permission of the publishers.

BOHEMIAN
HAJEJ, MŮJ, ANDÍLKU (24, k)
(Hush-a-Bye, Baby Mine)

Hajej, můj andílku, hajej a spi,
Matička kolibá dětátko svy.
Hajej, nynej, dadej, milej!
Matička kolibá dětátko svy.

Hajej mi zlatoušku, hajej a spi,
Zambouři maličky očičky svy.
Hajej, dadej, dadej, milej!
Zambouři maličky očičky svy.

HUSH-A-BYE, BABY MINE †
(Hajej, Muj, Andilku)

Hush-a-bye, baby mine, peacefully rest;
Mother is rocking thee in thy soft nest.
Hush-a-bye, lullabye, hush-a-bye baby,
Mother is rocking thee in thy soft nest.

Hush-a-bye, baby mine, dim grows the light;
Close your eyes, go to sleep, darling good-night,
Hush-a-bye, lullabye, hush-a-bye baby,
Close your eyes, go to sleep, darling good-night.

POLISH
TATULU, MATULU (24, 1)
(Father Dear, Mother Dear)

Tatulu, matulu, tatulu, matulu,
Błogosław mnie koniu
Bo ja jadę w żołnierską paradę
Racz mi Boże szczęście dać.

Bądźcie zdrowi rodzice,
Co wciąż o mnie myślicie,
Bo ja jadę w tę drogę daleką
Już pod Boską opieką.

Bądź zdrowy miły bracie,
Co zostajesz w tej chacie,
Oj pono ja pono raz ostatni
Już się z tobą obaczę.

Bądźcie zdrowe me siostry,
Bo na wojnie miecz ostry,
Jak nie wrócę—za roczek, za drugi
Może wrócę, w rok szósty?

Jak wiatr wieje na polu,
Tak żołnierz zginie w boju,
Zasmuci się serce mej mateńki,
I całej mej rodziny.

FATHER DEAR, MOTHER DEAR
(Tautlu, Matulu)
(Free translation)

Father dear, mother dear, father dear, mother dear,
Bless me at parting, for I am going out to the army
for years, so may God be gracious to me.

Farewell, my dear ones, farewell my dear ones
Who stay at home, for I must go the long way under God's
protection.

Farewell, my little brothers, farewell, my little brothers,
Take good care of the hut where we see each othr for the last
time.

Farewell, my noble sisters, farewell, my noble sisters,
War is a sharp sword. Will it be one year or many that I must
wield before I can come home?

Now the storm breaks, now the storm breaks twice,
And if I should fall before the enemy, it will be sad for my
mother and all the little dear ones.

RUSSIAN (24, m)
(Mother Volga)

Вниз по матушке по Волге

Вниз по матушке по Волге,
По широкому раздолью,
Разыгралася погода,
Погода, погодушка верховая.

Верховая волновая.
Ничего в волнах не видно, —
Одна лодочка чернеет;
Никого в лодке не видно, —

Только парусы белеют,
На гребцах шляпы чернеют,
Кушаки на них алеют.
На корме сидит хозяин.

Сам хозяин в наряде!
В коричневом кафтане,
В перючневом камзоле,
В алом шелковом платочке,

В черном бархатном картузе;
На картузе козыречек;
Сам отецкой он сыночек.
Уж как взговорит хозяин:

"И мы грянемте, ребята,
Вниз по матушке по Волге,
Ко Аленину подворью,
Ко Ивановой здоровью!"

MOTHER VOLGA
ВНИЗ ПО МАТУШКЕ ПО ВОЛГЕ

Yonder, down on Mother Volga, Volga,
Where she rolleth free and boundless, Ah!

There the summer wind is playing, playing,
Leaping, mid the crested billows, Ah!

Naught appears upon the waters, waters,
Save a painted barque that heareth, Ah!

---

* Taken from *Sixty Russian Folk-Songs*, the English versions by Deems Taylor and Kurt Schindler. Copyright 1918, by G. Schirmer. Reprinted by permission of the publishers.

See its sails so white and shining, shining!
See its oarsmen strong and sturdy, Ah!

On their heads are caps of velvet, velvet;
Bright their belts of purple leather, Ah!

At the helm behold the master, master;
There he sits array'd in splendor, Ah!

His kaftan is brown and flowing, flowing;
Grey his jacket, laced with silver, Ah!

Round his neck a crimson kerchief, kerchief;
Black his visored cap of sable, Ah!

He, the image of his father, father,
With his bold and raskish bearing, Ah!

Now the bold young master, speaketh, speaketh,
To his young and brave companions, Ah! *

ACTION XXV

OLD FOLKS AT HOME (25)

Way down upon de Swanee ribber,
  Far, far away,
Dere's wha my heart is turning ebber,
  Dere's wha de old folks stay.
All up and down de whole creation,
  Sadly I roam,
Still longing for de old plantation,
  And for de old folks at home.

(Refrain)

All de world am sad and dreary,
  Ebrywhere I roam.
Oh! darkies how my heart grows weary,
  Far from de old folks at home.

All around de little farm I wander'd,
  When I was young,
Den many happy days I squander'd,
  Many de songs I sung.
When I was playing wid my brudder,
  Happy was I,
Oh! take me to my kind old mudder,
  Dere let me live and die.

One little hut among de bushes,
  One dat I love,
Still sadly to my mem'ry rushes,
  No matter where I rove.
When will I see de bees a hummin'
  All round de comb?
When will I hear de banjo tummin'
  Down in my good old home?

VI. WORDS OF CHORUSES

ACTION ONE

NEW WORLD

Chorus of the Ages *

I & II

Calm, mid the storms of time
Truth wills to be free.
Brave, through all mortal drift,
Still radiant glows his Star.

III

Yet from the womb of change
Man gropes into birth
And calls where far echo-songs
Call back through the dark!

IV

"Horn, wind a new World tune;
Pipe play me an Old
And both guide to where Truth dwells
Guide me, O guide me, there!"

V and VI, 1, 2

Now another echo calls:
"Nay, leave me where the drifting hours
Allure my dreams!
Leave me where the luring hours
Ensnare my dreams in will-less rhythm!"

VI, 3

Still an answering echo cries:
"Lead me far on a New World quest
Out of this mortal drift!
Lead me there far away
Let me forget the Old,
Let me forget!"

VII, 1

Yet, mid the storms of time
Truth wills to be free.
Calm, though all mortal drift
Still radiant glows his Star.

VII, 2

There, mid the winter night,
Chimes peal from afar:
"New World and Old are one
Where radiant glows his Star."

VIII

O, hark where the chimes are borne
Far through the winter night:
Hark where they peal
Chimes—chimes—chimes!

---

* Words by Percy MacKaye, written to the music by Antonin Dvorak (*New World Symphony*: Fourth Movement).
† Music by Oliver Holden.

ACTION XVIII

CORONATION †

All hail the power of Jesus' name!
Let angels prostrate fall;
Bring forth the royal diadem,
And crown him Lord of all!

Let every kindred, every tribe
On this terrestrial ball,
To him all majesty ascribe,
And crown him Lord of all!

Oh, that with yonder sacred throng
We at his feet may fall,
And join the everlasting song,
And crown him Lord of all!

VII. NOTE ON THE *THIRTEEN SONGS*
By John Tasker Howard

These folk-songs should be sung by children of the nationalities represented by the songs, in the original languages. Each is to be sung in unison (except for *Frére Jacques*, which may be used as a round), and may be taught to the children by rote.

The children are to enter in processional by nationality and to mass in pied assembly in the Arena on PLANE I, within the extended rondure of the hearthlight.

The various nationalities should enter from several parts of the auditorium, and proceed to the assembly by several routes. They should enter in order designated (i. e., Scotch, Welsh, Irish, German, Norwegian, French, Dutch, Italian, Greek, Hebrew, Bohemian, Polish, Russian). If time does not permit each nationality to sing its entire song before the next group commences, the second group may enter before the first has completed its song, from an opposite side of the auditorium, and sing the first half of its song while the first group completes the second half of its folk-song. Then, when the second group has proceeded half way through its song, the third group may enter, and so on through the entire thirteen. The resulting confusion of tongues will be symbolic, and yet will not destroy the individual character of each song to those of the audience seated near the singers of each group.

It has been impossible to obtain an equal number of stanzas for all of the songs, thus making the songs uniform. The director will therefore use his discretion in having the shorter songs repeated so that each will be of the proper length to occupy the time required for the processional of each group.

VIII. NOTE ON THE MUSIC FOR THE FIVE TABLEAUX
By John Tasker Howard

The compositions for the Tableaux have been selected and abridged with a view to their consuming the approximate time required for showing each Tableau, for change of setting and costume between Tableaux, and for the interpretative speeches of *Wakefield* and *Polaris*.

Local conditions may necessitate more or less music in some instances, but in every case each selection should commence according to its cue, and continue to its completion. If any selection should prove too short for its Tableau and the change of the scene, it may be repeated. If a number should prove longer than necessary it should continue during the next speech, subdued so that it forms a musical background.

IX. CONTENTS OF *THE CHORUSES FOR "WAKEFIELD"*

NOTE: This volume is published separately by the United States George Washington Bicentennial Commission.

1. *New World*, (choral adaptation of Dvořák's *New World Symphony,* Fourth Movement, by John Tasker Howard. Words by Percy MacKaye.

16, a. *Prelusive Strain of Shakespeare Processional.* (*Who is Sylvia?*)

16, b. *Processional of the Mask of Shakespeare* (*Who is Sylvia?*) by Schubert, arranged by Osbourne W. McConathy. Words by Shakespeare.

18. *Processional of Worship.* (*Coronation, by Oliver Holden.*)

20. *Re-birth* (*Chorus of the Ages,* words by Percy MacKaye, music by Bach).

23. *English Folk-Song* (*Sumer Is Y-cumen In*).

25. *American Folk-Song* (*Old Folks at Home,* by Stephen C. Foster, arranged by Osbourne W. McConathy).

33, b. *The Star Spangled Banner* (with new stanza, by Percy MacKaye).

X. CONTENTS OF *THE ORCHESTRAL MUSIC FOR "WAKEFIELD"*

Percy MacKaye's Folk-Masque of America

The Music Selected, Adapted and Arranged by John Tasker Howard

NOTE: This volume is separately published by G. Schirmer, New York.

5, a. *Dance of the Thirteen Stars* (from *Farandole, L'Arlesienne* Suite No. 2, by George Bizet).

9, a. Accompaniment to *Song of Free* (*Shepherd's Song,* by Laura Barker Taylor).

10, a. *Drift,* by John Tasker Howard.

13, a. *Entrance of Heroes of Venture* (from *Amaryllis,* air by Louis XIII, arranged by Henry Ghys).

16, b. *Processional of the Mask of Shakespeare.* (Accompaniment to *Who is Sylvia?*)

16, c. *Dance of the Mask of Shakespeare* (Minuet in A, by Boccherini).

17. *Processional of Magna Charta* (Hymn, by Thomas Tallis).

19. *Theme of Drift,* by John Tasker Howard.

20, a. *Chaos,* by John Tasker Howard.

26, b. *The Delaware* (Introduction to *Land of Our Hearts,* cantata by George W. Chadwick). (Copyright Boston Music Co.)

27. *Valley Forge* (From Third Movement, *Sonata Tragica,* by Edward MacDowell).

28. *Kingship Refused* (from Introduction to First Movement, *New England Symphony,* by Edgar Stillman-Kelley). (Copyright Edgar Stillman-Kelley.)

29. *The Constitution* (*Federal March,* by Alexander Reinagle).

30. *Mt. Vernon* (from *Elegie,* from *Scarecrow Sketches,* by Frederick S. Converse). (Copyright Oliver Ditson Co.)

33, b. *The Star-Spangled Banner.* (New stanza by Percy MacKaye.)

XI. LIST OF *PROPERTIES FOR USE IN "WAKEFIELD"*

NOTE.—The following Properties are listed in the order of the Actions in which they are first used. Directors of productions of the Masque may use their own discretion and invention in selecting or designing insignia for the Groups and Processionals and in providing properties for the Tableaux. For comments on some of these Properties, see Monograph I.

Candles
Golden Trumpets
Ax
Fire-log
Two Dry Sticks
Pitch-Pine Cones
Turkey's Wing
Jew's Harp or Mouth Harp
Pipe, or Lute
Shepherd's Crook
Net
Hand-snare (Same as coil of (Net)

Tripod (Comprising Three Charred Logs and Heavy Chain)
Large Black Pot
Sling
Rabbit's Foot
Cherry Sprig
Crumpled Cow's Horn
Insignia for :
  (a) *New World Explorers* Group
  (b) *Log-fire Shadows* Group
  (c) *Pioneers* Group

Vial (Containing Shiny Liquid)
Rush Basket
Deerskin Drum
16 Dried Herbs and Roots
Shakespeare Processional Candles (Optional)
Staff, With Mask of Shakespeare (or Banner, with painting of Mask)
Insignia for *Shakespeare* Group
Magna Charta Scroll
Insignia for *Magna Charta* Group
Coil, or Loop, of Net (Same as Hand-Snare)
Black Litter
Broken Shepherd's-Crook
Broken Symbols and Insignia
Broken Vial
2 Dark Self-Heal Roots
Symbols for 13 *Folk-Song Processionals*

Immense Banner of Red, White and Blue (First American Flag with Circle of 13 Stars)
Other Properties for the 5 Tableaux

SUGGESTED SCENES FOR PAGEANT EPISODES

The Boy Peacemaker

Washington Gives Up Sea Career

Washington and Fairfax, Sportsmen

Washington and Gist Crossing Allegheny

Washington Meets Martha Custis

Washington Reads Prayers in Camp

Winchester Citizens Appeal to Washington

Taking Command of Army at Cambridge

Crossing the Delaware

Washington and Lafayette at Valley Forge

Washington and Rochambeau at Mount Vernon

The Surrender at Yorktown

Mary Ball Washington's Reception

Washington's Farewell to His Officers

Resigning Commission at Annapolis

Washington the Farmer at Mount Vernon

Riding Through Trenton to Inauguration

The First Inauguration New York

GEORGE WASHINGTON

PAGEANTS

WRITTEN FOR THE

CELEBRATION OF THE TWO HUNDREDTH ANNIVERSARY

OF THE

BIRTH OF GEORGE WASHINGTON

INTRODUCTION

TO a greater extent than any other character in American history the life of George Washington lends itself to portrayal in pageantry. Through the medium of the pageant large numbers of citizens were made active participants in the dramatic phases of the Bicentennial celebration, re-learning and re-enacting the stirring events of Washington's day.

The force behind this far-reaching drama program was the United States George Washington Bicentennial Commission. Through its Pageant and Play Department, the Commission prepared the manuscripts of the official pageants, assisted hundreds of amateur writers who submitted their compositions for approval, and encouraged publishers to issue George Washington dramatic material. Through various other departments of the Commission, interest was aroused in the production of pageants and the result was the staging of George Washington pageants in many parts of the world.

Percy J. Burrell, of Watertown, Massachusetts, one of the recognized leaders in the field of pageantry, was placed in charge of the Pageant Department, with James K. Knudson as his assistant. Under their direction the pageants and other dramatic material included in this volume were published. Ethel Claire Randall gave valuable aid as dramatic editor.

Especial attention is called to the Masque *Wakefield*, by Percy Mac-Kaye. The premiere of this elaborate spectacle, directed by Mr. Burrell and Mrs. Marie Moore Forrest, was held in Washington on February 21, 1932, before a distinguished audience of Government officials, foreign diplomats, social and political leaders. The Masque and program thereof appear in full in this volume.

The United States George Washington Bicentennial Commission hereby expresses its appreciation to those authors who contributed freely several of the pageants in this book and likewise to all who participated in making the Bicentennial a success through the medium of the George Washington Pageant.

THE REDBUD TREE

A GEORGE WASHINGTON PAGEANT-PLAY FOR CHILDREN
By Olive M. Price

The Redbud Tree is especially designed to meet the dramatic needs of grammar grades and child groups in general for a simple, easy-to-stage performance featuring George Washington as a character.

CHARACTERS AND GROUPS

In the order that they appear

The Water Sprites
Two Baby Sprites
Mary Lou
Jackie
The Sandman
The Dryads
The Redbud Spirit
The Hours
The Spiders
The Great Great Grandfather Spider
The Lightning Bugs
The Very Old Lightning Bug
Martha Washington's Kittens
Vulcan—The French Hound
The Nellie Custis Rose
The Butterflies
The Soldiers
General George Washington
Lady Martha Washington

COSTUMES

The Water Sprites—*Filmy blue robes of gauze with transparent reflections. They flutter about like long scarfs when they dance.*

The Two Baby Sprites—*Little one-piece vests of green satin the color of water lily pads.*

Mary Lou—*A pretty frock after the manner of the modern school girl.*

Jackie—*The suit of a juvenile school-boy.*

The Sandman—*A golden brown cape and breeches with stockings and sandals to match. His knapsack is golden brown, too, and his hood, the traditional stocking cap.*

The Dryads—*Pale green costumes of gauze decorated with deeper green leaves of various trees.*

The Redbud Spirit—*A flowing white robe dotted here and there with the pink petals of the Redbud flowers. She wears blossoms in her hair and carries a willow wand.*

The Hours—*Knee breeches and waistcoats in various soft colors. The waistcoats are decorated with the faces of tiny black clocks.*

The Spiders—*Robes of silver gauze to represent cobwebs. They wear little collars of silver from which gray cords are suspended, spiral-like, for four pairs of legs.*

The Great Great Grandfather Spider—*He is dressed as all the other spiders with the exception of more silver gauze which makes him appear hoary with cobwebs.*

The Lightning Bugs—*One-piece costumes of shining black oilcloth. They carry tiny flashlights for "lightning."*

Martha Washington's Kittens—*The costume of Puss-In-Boots with powdered wigs and three-cornered hats.*

Vulcan—The French Hound—*A yellow waistcoat with breeches, top-boots, and high black hat.*

The Nellie Custis Rose—*A charming frock of pink satin fashioned like a rose in full bloom.*

The Butterflies—*Dresses of many colors, daffodil yellow, rose petal pink, larkspur blue, etc., with huge wings of paper or stiff gauze.*

The Soldiers—*Trim little Continental uniforms with three cornered hats.*

General George Washington—*Regulation uniform of the period with long cloak and three cornered hat.*

Martha Washington—*A colonial gown of blue satin and lace with brocaded slippers and fan.*

NOTE: *For design and description of costumes and uniforms of historical characters see "George Washington Play and Pageant Costume Book," issued by the United States George Washington Bicentennial Commission and sent on request.*

SCENE I

THE LAWN AT MOUNT VERNON

The Redbud Tree at Mount Vernon makes us think of the princess who never grows old. Why? Because it was planted nearly two hundred years ago and here it is today with its pink flowers (which look for all the world like dancing slippers for the fairies!) peeping out from its green, heart-shaped leaves . . .

The curtain rises disclosing the Redbud Tree on the lawn. It is elfin-like and beautiful—not quite so tall as more earthly trees—but this is the children's own—and never grows out of reach so they might even touch its branches. It stands in silhouette against the blue sky where a young moon hangs like a toy boat of silver. It is really not far from Mount Vernon Mansion but this is indicated only by the West Lodge Gate which one sees at the extreme left of the stage.

There are three entrances—left, right, and through the blue curtains which form a background in the rear.

TIME

It is dusk—and as every little girl and boy knows, this is a magic hour. The scene has all the charm and delicacy of those Japanese screens we see in the toy shops. Here in the twilight, something is certain to happen! Presently, there is the sound of fairy-like music . . . To the accompaniment of "Gavotte" from the opera "Mignon" by Thomas—THE WATER SPRITES enter left. They are the most enchanting sprites you ever saw! They wear fluttering robes of blue—a pale, mist-like blue—the color the Potomac River takes on by moonlight. They have really come to dance by the Redbud Tree which, as everybody in fairy-land knows, has the power of magic when the moon is quite young. Their dance expresses sheer joy. They are as gay as poppies asway on their stems until suddenly two Baby Sprites *enter right—bearing a lily-cup from the river. They approach the dancers quite gravely and pour the water upon the grass. The dancers at once become fearful because this really means that someone from Earth is near. The* Baby Sprites *hurry to the background and exit. There is a sound like a red-bird whistling . . . They appear almost in wrath for a moment—then, as though thinking better of it—they dance toward the back and vanish away.*

Now, it was not really a red-bird whistling at all—but a little boy, Jackie, *who enters right, followed by* Mary Lou. *They look around curiously. Suddenly,* Mary Lou *discovers the Redbud Tree. She claps her hands joyously and indicates it to* Jackie.

Mary Lou

Here it is! Look, Jackie, look!

Jackie

How do you know?

Mary Lou

[*Leaning against it lovingly*]—I can tell by the flowers. See how pink they are? How they dance on the bough?

Jackie

[*Scoffing*]—Flowers dancing! Ho! Ho!

Mary Lou

[*Warning him*]—Careful, Jackie. There is magic about when the little moon shines on a Redbud Tree.

Jackie

[*Looking up at the moon*]—The moon is only quick-silver.

Mary Lou

Listen!

[*From far-away comes the song—"I Am the Sleep Fairy" from "Hansel and Gretel."*]

Jackie

[*Surprised*]—There's someone singing!

Mary Lou

Come closer to the tree!

Jackie

[*Going to her reluctantly*]—There's nothing to be afraid of.

Mary Lou

Perhaps not. But the tree is kind. Remember that it lived here even when George Washington was a boy. Two hundred years ago! What stories it could tell!

Jackie

I wish that it could talk. I would like to know about his sword.

Mary Lou

[*Wistfully*]—I would like to hear about the ladies of Mount Vernon. What kind of slippers Martha wore to balls and parties . . . the flowers Nellie Custis tucked into her hair

. . . [*brightly*] Perhaps she wore some from this very tree!

[*The song comes clearer now. Suddenly, the* Sandman *appears in the background. He is a jolly little fellow who wears a brown cape and carries a golden knapsack. The children discover him.*]

Jackie

[*In fright*]—Look, Mary Lou! That queer little man! Come hide!

[*They endeavor to hide behind the tree. He laughs mockingly and approaches them. They huddle together as the song dies away.*]

The Sandman

[*Bowing and chanting*]—The little birds have said good-night,
    They sleep in their soft, downy beds,
But you, my dears, have taken flight,
    With a scheme in your pretty heads.
You thought to escape me tonight?
    Ha! Ha! What a rash thing to do!
Don't you know that at candle-light
    You must close your sweet eyes? Pray—do!
[*He opens his knapsack and tosses handfuls of sand at them. They begin to nod sleepily. Finally, they tumble to the foot of the tree, fast asleep. The* Sandman *looks down at them merrily and continues.*]

Goodnight little girl and boy! Adieu!
    Goodnight! Goodnight! Sweet dreams to you!

[*He picks up his knapsack and trudges off-stage right. Again there is charming music. It is "Melodie" from "Ballet Music" from Orpheus and Eurydice. To its lilting measures, a group of* Dryads *enter left. They are wearing green, the shade of young leaves in the springtime. They trip gaily to the music of the ballet unmindful of the children. Their dance personifies the rhythm and beauty of trees swaying with the wind. When it is over they drop in graceful attitudes on the grass. It is then that the* First Dryad *discovers the children. She hovers over them curiously.*]

The First Dryad

Look! Little people of the earth are sleeping here!

A Second Dryad

Tonight of all nights!

The First Dryad

Hush! She is coming!

[*The moon shines full on the Redbud Tree . . . There is the silvery tinkle of little bells which is the "Bell Song" from "Lakme." The trunk of the tree swings open and the* Redbud Spirit *steps out. She is the tallest of all the* Dryads *and the most beautiful. Golden hair hangs to her waist, she wears a crown of flowers and carries a willow wand. One knows at once that she is the queen of the* Dryads *because they all bow to her very prettily.*]

The Redbud Spirit

Greetings, Maidens.

The Dryads

Greetings, Queen Redbud.

THE REDBUD SPIRIT

Why do you look at me so strangely?

THE FIRST DRYAD

[*Indicating the children*]—Beware! They have fallen asleep under your branches!

THE REDBUD SPIRIT

[*Going to them*]—How charming they are! Two children! What do they seek?

THE DRYADS

We do not know. [*Fearfully*] Perhaps they would steal your flowers!

THE REDBUD SPIRIT

[*Distressed*]—Let us see.

[*She touches them lightly with her wand. The children sit up and rub their eyes.*]

MARY LOU

[*Drowsily*]—Where are we, Jackie?

THE REDBUD SPIRIT

You are in the land of the Redbud Tree . . .

JACKIE

[*Standing up*]—Is George Washington here?

THE REDBUD SPIRIT

[*Surprised*]—George Washington?

MARY LOU

[*Interrupting quickly*]—Hush, Jackie. George Washington died over a hundred years ago!

THE REDBUD SPIRIT

[*Gravely*]—No, he is not dead, Mary Lou. This is his home. His spirit will live here—forever . . .

JACKIE

[*Eagerly*]—Do you mean that we can see him?

THE REDBUD SPIRIT

I do not know. Perhaps. Perhaps not. People of the earth do not have the gift of *believing*. That is why the fairies are lost to them. When they grow up they laugh and think that we do not exist.

MARY LOU

[*Enchanted*]—Oh, but I believe in the fairies! There's a butterfly at home in my garden. I call her the Fairy Bright Wing. She is the color of yellow roses!

JACKIE

[*Irritated and boyish*]—What's that got to do with George Washington?

THE REDBUD SPIRIT

It has much to do with him, Jackie. If you visit Mount Vernon and really *believe* that his spirit lives on—you can actually see him walking down by the river he loved so well. You can hear him talking with Martha. You can see him as the young Colonel and the great General coming down the stairs . . .

JACKIE

[*Enthusiastically*]—That's what I want to see!

THE REDBUD SPIRIT

Come. It will be as you believe . . . [*She beckons to the* DRYADS] Arise! There is still hope that fairies are not lost to mortals . . .

[MARY LOU *and* JACKIE *follow* THE REDBUD SPIRIT *out. The* DRYADS *dance again exultantly, to the strains of "Melodie." The little moon dims its light as the curtains in the background part revealing—*]

SCENE II

THE CENTRAL HALL AT MOUNT VERNON

Everybody knows who has been to the mansion that the hall is lovely indeed. There is the wide stairway with the landing half-way up where the Grandfather Clock on the stairs ticks away the hours just as it did in George Washington's time.

The hall is bathed in a pale silver light with only the stairs and the clock completely discernible. There are other objects in the hall, too, such as the key of the Bastille presented to GEORGE WASHINGTON *by his friend, the Marquis de Lafayette, but these are not visible. Neither are his four swords, nor a marble top table, and two comfortable sofas.*

TIME

The clock strikes seven. A moment later, strains of "The Dance of the Hours" from "La Gioconda" are heard. From behind the clock come the gay little HOURS *tumbling over each other to begin their dance. They trip down the stairs and dance in the hall. Suddenly, there is a knock on the door. They listen. They scamper up the stairs. They disappear back in their hiding place . . . The door, center-back, opens. Enter* THE REDBUD SPIRIT *with* JACKIE *and* MARY LOU.

THE REDBUD SPIRIT

We are here. This is the hall at Mount Vernon.

JACKIE

[*Disappointed*]—It is quite empty. I can't see anything but the stairs.

THE REDBUD SPIRIT

[*Sadly*]—You are not looking.

MARY LOU

Listen! There's something buzzing!

THE REDBUD SPIRIT

Can you see anything, Mary Lou?

[MARY LOU *goes to the foot of the stairs. She looks up at the landing intently. Suddenly, she turns to them radiantly.*]

MARY LOU

They're coming! They're coming down here!

JACKIE and THE REDBUD SPIRIT

[*Simultaneously*]—Who?

MARY LOU

The Spiders!

JACKIE

[*Contemptuously*]—Spiders? Who wants to see spiders?

THE REDBUD SPIRIT

[*Harshly*]—Hush! You will frighten them away!

[*JACKIE is properly subdued and hangs his head. MARY LOU and the REDBUD SPIRIT wait eagerly. Presently a group of really glorified SPIDERS appear on the landing. They are dressed in the filmiest of cobwebs and each one, of course, has four pairs of legs. There are big spiders and little spiders. One seems particularly old and wears many more cobwebs than the others. He is the GREAT GREAT GRANDFATHER SPIDER who often hung his cobwebs in the West Parlor when GEORGE WASHINGTON was a boy. Certainly, that was wicked but he always managed to hide somewhere above the fireplace or under the tilt-top table. They pause for a moment at the top of the stairs—then to the accompaniment of "Harlequin's Serenade" from "Pagliacci" they come down to the hall where they go on with their dance. When it is over MARY LOU approaches the GREAT GREAT GRAND-FATHER SPIDER timidly. The other SPIDERS stand back, surprised.*]

THE GREAT GREAT GRANDFATHER SPIDER

Who is it?

MARY LOU

[*Bravely*]—It is Mary Lou.

THE GREAT GREAT GRANDFATHER SPIDER

What do you want?

MARY LOU

I am looking for George Washington.

THE GREAT GREAT GRANDFATHER SPIDER

Bless me! [*He nods comically to the others*] A child of the earth looking for George Washington! Come here.

[*MARY LOU approaches him a bit skirmishly.*]

MARY LOU

Do you know where he is?

THE GREAT GREAT GRANDFATHER SPIDER

I haven't seen him since he was a boy. [*He sits down on the bottom step and draws her into his arms.*]

MARY LOU

Tell me about it.

THE GREAT GREAT GRANDFATHER SPIDER

It was in the West Parlor. It was warm weather and I lived in my cobweb house in the fireplace. One day George Washington came into the room—

JACKIE

[*Approaching them*]—Really and truly George Washington?

THE GREAT GREAT GRANDFATHER SPIDER

Really and truly. He was a fine boy fourteen years old. He was very proud that day because he was dressed as a sailor.

JACKIE

A sailor? How jolly!

THE GREAT GREAT GRANDFATHER SPIDER

As everyone knows, George Washington wanted to go to sea. But his mother, Mary Ball Washington, didn't want him to. She wished him to stay on land.

MARY LOU

[*Dejectedly*]—Just like our mother, Jackie. Remember yesterday when we wanted cake we had to drink milk?

JACKIE

[*Nodding assent vigorously*]—Sure thing. Why are mothers that way?

THE GREAT GREAT GRANDFATHER SPIDER

[*Wisely*]—Mothers always know best, my dear. And George Washington's mother did too. Why, if she had allowed him to go to sea he would never have become the great man we know of today.

MARY LOU

She came to the West Parlor?

THE GREAT GREAT GRANDFATHER SPIDER

Yes, and I peeped out from my cobweb house. Do you know what I saw?

JACKIE

Tell us! Tell us!

THE GREAT GREAT GRANDFATHER SPIDER

I saw George Washington kneeling beside his mother—distressed at her tears.

MARY LOU

Why was she crying?

THE GREAT GREAT GRANDFATHER SPIDER

Because he was all ready to go to sea.

MARY LOU

What did he do when she cried?

THE GREAT GREAT GRANDFATHER SPIDER

He stayed at home to study more as she wished him to.

MARY LOU

What a good boy he was. You must remember that, Jackie.

JACKIE

[*Disdainfully*]—What happened then?

THE GREAT GREAT GRANDFATHER SPIDER

Somebody else must tell you that. [*He rises and shakes his cobwebs.*] We must get back to our spinning. We are making a web on the garden wall.

[*He stretches a bit lazily and saunters out of the hall. The others follow. MARY LOU is about to turn to THE RED-BUD SPIRIT when suddenly—all grows very dark.*]

JACKIE

Oh! Oh! What's happening? How very dark it is!

THE REDBUD SPIRIT

Wait!

MARY LOU

Here—give me your hand.

JACKIE

Look!

[*A tiny light flashes on and off in the darkness. A merry little group of* LIGHTNING BUGS *have invaded the hall. There is the lightsome music of the "Shadow Song," from Meyerbeer's "Dinorah."* MARY LOU *is so delighted that she dances along with them. Suddenly, the* VERY OLD LIGHTNING BUG *discovers her.*]

THE VERY OLD LIGHTNING BUG

Stop! [*The dancers stand quite still.*] There is a mortal among us. Who are you? Pray, speak.

MARY LOU

[*With a curtsy*]—I am Mary Lou. I am here in search of George Washington.

THE VERY OLD LIGHTNING BUG

George Washington! [*He chuckles in delight.*] Well, I never! Listen! [*He bends down to her comically.*] You will find him here before long. [*Confidentially.*] I used to light his way through the forest.

JACKIE

The forest? What was George Washington doing there?

THE VERY OLD LIGHTNING BUG

Ah, he was a great woodsman!

MARY LOU

[*Bewildered*]—A—a woodsman?

THE VERY OLD LIGHTNING BUG

Yes—yes, indeed. He surveyed land for Lord Fairfax. Hundreds of acres! He was a fine surveyor after he gave up going to sea.

JACKIE

Tell us more. More!

THE VERY OLD LIGHTNING BUG

While he surveyed all this land, Mother Nature brought him her gifts. You see, little friends, she was building his character so he could successfully meet experiences that were to come.

MARY LOU

[*Curiously*]—How?

THE VERY OLD LIGHTNING BUG

Well, he tramped over the Blue Ridge Mountains. That developed his muscles and gave him a strong, healthy body. I saw him lay out trails that are now wide roads through the forest. That gave him a keen and alert mind. He slept under the stars . . . That gave him calmness and vigor. You see, Mother Nature is wise.

MARY LOU

[*Pondering*]—I think she is good. George Washington—[*She stops speaking suddenly as the barking of a dog and the meowing of kittens are heard.*] Oh! Oh! what's that?

THE VERY OLD LIGHTNING BUG

Stand Back! Stand back! That must be Vulcan again!

JACKIE

Who is Vulcan?

THE VERY OLD LIGHTNING BUG

George Washington always loved dogs and horses. Vulcan is a fine French hound. He was a present from his friend, the Marquis de Lafayette.

MARY LOU

Fierce, is he?

THE VERY OLD LIGHTNING BUG

Yes. Yes, indeed. He likes nothing better than to chase Martha Washington's kittens! Stay close to me. I'll put out my light and he will not see you.

[*The* LIGHTNING BUGS *turn out their lights. There is only the glow of the moon. The meow of the kittens off-stage becomes whimpering and loud. Presently, "Waltz from the Kermess Scene" from Gounod's "Faust" is heard—and in dash a troupe of little black and white kittens. They hesitate a moment upon entering—look around cautiously—and then proceed with their half-scamper—half-dance. In a little while* VULCAN, *the big French Hound, enters slyly. He watches their pranks as though he is amused—then suddenly makes a mad dash to their midst. There is much plaintive meowing and scurrying as they run out of the hall in confusion.*]

MARY LOU

The—the beast! Why did George Washington like him?

THE VERY OLD LIGHTNING BUG

He won't really hurt the kittens. He just likes to frighten them. George Washington admired him because his strength was so great he could pull down a bear in the hunt.

JACKIE

Did George Washington like to hunt foxes?

THE VERY OLD LIGHTNING BUG

Yes. Yes. Very much. He always rode with the hounds. If it were daylight you could see his hunting horn here. It hangs in the hall.

MARY LOU

Tell us about George Washington's garden. It is said to be beautiful.

VERY OLD LIGHTNING BUG

[*Flashing on his light*]—I can't do that. I must be flying away. Perhaps somebody else will come.

MARY LOU

Goodbye! Goodbye!

[*The "Shadow Song" is heard once again as the* LIGHTNING BUGS *depart.*]

THE REDBUD SPIRIT

Are you enjoying your visit to Mount Vernon?

MARY LOU

It is—wonderful! I still believe I am going to see George Washington!

JACKIE

Hush!

[*There is exquisite music. It is the "Oberon Overture"—haunting, fairy-like, beautiful. Enter the* NELLIE CUSTIS ROSE—*its petals all prettily fluffed up as for a ball. It moves to the foreground, kneels, and stays quite still as though waiting to be awakened. A group of gaily hued* BUTTERFLIES *enter. They dance around the rose in a ring.*]

MARY LOU

[*Clapping her hands*]—Oh, how pretty! What is it? What is it?

THE REDBUD SPIRIT

[*Softly*]—It is the rose of Nellie Custis. It blooms in the flower garden and was named for her by George Washington.

JACKIE

Who was Nellie Custis?

THE REDBUD SPIRIT

She was Lady Washington's little granddaughter. He loved her very, very much.

MARY LOU

Look! Look!

[*A bright golden butterfly approaches the rose. She bends over it gracefully as though to give it a kiss. Suddenly its petals droop downward and the little girl,* NELLIE CUSTIS, *appears. The* BUTTERFLIES *are entranced by her. They dance about her ever so merrily. At last she moves toward the outer door, looking this way and that, as though expecting someone. She vanishes into the darkness, the* BUTTERFLIES *following.*]

JACKIE

Where is she going?

THE REDBUD SPIRIT

Back to the flower garden. She will wait there for George Washington and his Lady to come . . .

MARY LOU

Will they? Will they? Tonight?

THE REDBUD SPIRIT

You have seen all these things tonight because you believe that the spirit of George Washington will never die as long as Mount Vernon stands . . . Listen! Do you hear anything now?

[*There is a sound as of the beating of drums in the distance.*]

JACKIE

Someone's beating a drum!

THE REDBUD SPIRIT

[*Smiling*]—To be sure.

[*A trumpet is blown.*]

MARY LOU

I hear a trumpet!

THE REDBUD SPIRIT

Of course.

JACKIE

Is he coming? Is he?

THE REDBUD SPIRIT

Wait?

[*There is the spirited music of "The Parade of the Wooden Soldiers." A whole regiment of Continental Soldiers come marching in perfect military order down the stairs.* MARY LOU *and* JACKIE *stand spellbound. When their march is over the first soldier blows a trumpet. Everything grows very dim except for a path of light on the stairs.* GENERAL WASHINGTON *appears on the landing. He is in military attire.* LADY MARTHA WASHINGTON *also appears. She makes a graceful curtsy. He offers her his arm. They come down the stairs as the soldiers stand at attention. Now there is heard "The Star Spangled Banner." General and Martha Washington pass out through the same door as* NELLIE CUSTIS—*the soldiers follow at a respectful distance. As the last glorious strains of the music sounds—the curtains are drawn—and only the little moon shines on the Redbud Tree at Mount Vernon.*]

[CURTAIN]

FROM PICTURE BOOK TOWNE

A GEORGE WASHINGTON PAGEANT-PLAY FOR CHILDREN

By OLIVE M. PRICE

CHARACTERS

MAMMY—*an old family servant.*

ANNE FAIRWAY—*her mistress.*

DAVID FAIRWAY—*Anne's husband.*

KATHRYN—*their small daughter.*

THE PICTURE BOOK MAN—*from Picture Book Towne.*

GENERAL GEORGE WASHINGTON—*Master of Mount Vernon.*

LADY MARTHA WASHINGTON—*his wife.*

NELLIE CUSTIS—*his little adopted daughter.*

MARQUIS DE LAFAYETTE—*a visitor at Mount Vernon.*

MARY BALL WASHINGTON—*George Washington's Mother.*

GEORGE WASHINGTON'S SLAVES.

GUESTS AT MOUNT VERNON.

THE DANCERS.

TWO PAGES.

> Place: *An old house near Mount Vernon.*
> Time: *The present.*

COSTUMES

MAMMY: *a printed cotton dress and a red bandanna.*

ANNE FAIRWAY: *a colonial gown of satin and lace with brocaded slippers.*

DAVID FAIRWAY: *satin knee-breeches and waistcoat. White silk hose and black slippers.*

KATHRYN: *a pretty little frock of the present day.*

THE PICTURE BOOK MAN: *the costume of a page like those seen in fairy books. The color is scarlet.*

GENERAL GEORGE WASHINGTON: *First appearance: a military costume with long cloak and three-cornered hat. Second appearance: a colonial costume with waistcoat and knee breeches.*

LADY MARTHA WASHINGTON: *a quaint colonial gown of satin.*

NELLIE CUSTIS: *a colonial gown of satin and ribbons.*

MARQUIS DE LAFAYETTE: *the elaborate costume of a French gentleman about the time of Louis XVI.*

MARY BALL WASHINGTON: *a black satin gown with a fichu of white lace.*

SLAVES: *Women: faded cotton dresses and colorful bandannas. Men: Soft shirts and blue homespun trousers.*

GUESTS OF MOUNT VERNON: *elaborate colorful costumes.*

THE DANCERS: *Women: Colonial dresses of satin and lace, brocaded slippers, etc. Men: waistcoats and knee breeches of satin and velvet.*

NOTE: *for design and description of costumes and information of historical characters see:*

> *"George Washington Play and Pageant Costume Book," issued by the United States George Washington Bicentennial Commission and sent on request.*

SCENE

A parlor in an old Revolutionary mansion near Mount Vernon, Virginia. There is a fireplace down left. In the center rear is what appears to be a large bay window with the curtains drawn as for the night. The room is furnished after the colonial manner and the only modern piece is a radio in a far corner. A little fire burns brightly upon the hearth and two lighted candles illuminate the room. The corners are dim and shadowy.

The "Huge Picture Book" mentioned may well be made of painted cardboard with the page in which the successive pictures appear cut-out like a picture frame. The wharf at Mount Vernon may be accomplished by suggestion only—with screens or hangings to represent a river with a tree bordering the far shore. The portico may be indicated by not more than two columns and a whole garden scene contrived by a single stalk of paper hollyhocks. The door at the West Front may also be made of cardboard.

> [*An old Negro* MAMMY *sits in a big chair near the fireplace. She wears a red bandanna.* ANNE FAIRWAY, *a lovely young matron, enters right. She is dressed in satin and lace after the manner of ladies in George Washington's time.*]

ANNE [*calling*]—MAMMY! MAMMY! Where are you?

MAMMY [*starting up*]—Here I is, Missie.

ANNE—Come, button me up. I am not accustomed to dressing for masquerade balls.

MAMMY [*clasping her hands*]—Yo' do look too sweet, Missie. Jus' lak a flower in de spring! [*She rises and adjusts a little ruffle here—a flounce there on Anne's gown.*] I bet yo' will be the prettiest lady at de George Washington Ball!

ANNE [*laughing*]—You are flattering me, Mammy. Where's Kathryn?

MAMMY—She am studyin' her lessons, Missie. Tomorrow bein' George Washington's burfday, she must know all about him.

ANNE—Let her listen to the George Washington program on the radio, Mammy. The Picture Book Man goes on the air at nine.

MAMMY—Yas'm, Missie. She sho will lak dat.

> [*Enter* DAVID FAIRWAY. *He is wearing the knee-breeches, long coat, and waistcoat of colonial times and carries a lady's cloak.*]

DAVID—Ready, dear?

ANNE—In a moment. [*She goes to him coquettishly.*] My, what a handsome gallant *you* are!

DAVID [*Bowing with ceremony*]—Thank you, Beautiful Lady. May I assist you with your cloak?

> [*He wraps the cloak about her. They go out together, pausing in the doorway as* KATHRYN, *a little girl six years old enters. She stares up at them delightedly.*]

KATHRYN—Mamma! Papa! Why, how pretty you look! Just like the people in my picture books!

Anne [*Bending down to kiss her*]—Thank you, darling. Are you going to be a good girl?

Kathryn [*demurely*]—Very good.

David [*Playfully*]—Then I'll bring you George Washington's hatchet home from the ball. Good-night.

Kathryn [*Looking after them admiringly*]—Good-night! Good-night!

[Mammy *sits down again in her chair. She dozes a little.* Kathryn *approaches her mischievously from in back of the chair.*]

Kathryn [*Loudly, in* Mammy's *ear*]—Boo!

Mammy [*Terrified*]—Gracious, child! What yo' do that for? Yo' sho frightened yo' pore Mammy!

Kathryn—I'm sorry. [*She perches herself on the arm of the chair.*] Tell me more about George Washington.

Mammy [*Reminiscently*]—Now, let me rekolect. I've done tole yo' how dis house is built on his ole carriage road. Why, chile, he used to ride past our very door on his way down to Pohick Church. He done got caught in a big storm one night and slept in dis house.

Kathryn—Upstairs?

Mammy—No, honey. Right here in dis room.

Kathryn [*Awed*]—In this room, Mammy [*Skeptically*] Who told you?

Mammy—My great-great-grandfather told me all about it.

[*A clock strikes nine.* Mammy *rises and goes to the radio.*]

Kathryn—What are you going to do?

Mammy—Turn on de radio, Honey. De Picture Book Man is on. You and I will jus' sit in dis big chair and listen—an' maybe while he's talkin' George Washington will look in at de window. [*Solemnly*] Dey always say, chile, dat our ghosts come back again to places dat we used to know.

Kathryn—Ghosts? Ooh! I'm—I'm afraid of ghosts, Mammy.

Mammy—Hush, darlin'! [*She turns on the radio*] Listen! Here's de station.

[*There is soft music.* Mammy *and* Kathryn *who sit in the big chair are lost in the shadows. The curtains on the bay window part revealing in the enclosure a huge illustrated Picture Book.* The Picture Book Man—*dressed in scarlet like a little page—stands there, as on the front page, immovable. As the music ends, he steps forward as a figure in a portrait might step daintily out from its frame.*]

The Picture Book Man [*Bowing*]—

Come one, come all! Children, gather around,
The Picture Book Man from Picture Book Towne,
Hark ye! Tonight we will tell of great fame—
To honor again George Washington's name!

[*He blows a trumpet . . . The Picture Book is lost in shadow as the lights go dim. A moment later, a picturesque tableau group of slaves is revealed as though on the next page. They are singing a spiritual, "Oh, Rise and Shine." When the song is ended, one* Old Darkey *rises and stands as though looking for someone. There is the sound of a bell tolling. The slaves pantomime delight.*]

The Picture Book Man—

Hark ye, again! On this day long ago—
Mount Vernon a-waited all in a glow,
Its Master's return from battles a-far,
He had bidden farewell to drums and to war.

[*The slaves step out of the book and stand clustered eagerly around the* Picture Book Man. *He turns to the next picture . . .* George Washington, *in military garb, is seen arriving at the Entrance Gateway to Mount Vernon.* Martha Washington *and* Nellie Custis, *almost five years old, and gowned in the quaint colonial fashion, are with him. He bows to the assembled company as the* Picture Book Man *speaks again.*]

The Picture Book Man—

See, he has come! Oh, so gallant and true,
To his dear home by the river so blue,
Oh, flow on, Potomac! Gently, we pray,
You sing once again of Washington's day.

[General Washington *steps from the picture accompanied by* Martha *and* Nellie *who lean upon his arm. They go off stage, right, followed by the servants who trudge after them, elated. A moment later there is a sound of a hunting horn echoing through the forest . . .*]

Oh, days at Mount Vernon, festive and fair!
Up with the dawn! Look! The fox in his lair!
Blow on the horn! The hounds hot in the chase—
Come on anon with the hunters apace!

[*The next picture reveals* General Washington *and the* Marquis de Lafayette *on the portico at Mount Vernon after a morning hunt. They wear scarlet hunting coats.* Martha *and* Nellie *greet them as a servant passes mint juleps on a tray.*]

The Picture Book Man—

Here is a guest at the mansion, you see,
The great Lafayette from a far country,
Who took up arms to defend us from foes,
And sought to revenge the colonists' woes.

[*The* Marquis *bows playfully to* Nellie *and offers her his hand. She skips along beside him. They go out followed by* General *and* Martha Washington. *There is the sound of female slaves singing another spiritual—"Hallelujah!"*]

The Picture Book Man—

The spinning wheels hummed at Mount Vernon fair,
Of all the many things that were made there!
There were rag carpets—and silk? Oh, indeed!
And just everything the household could need!

[*The next picture reveals a group of slave girls sitting at spinning wheels.* Martha Washington *walks back and forth superintending their work.*]

The Picture Book Man—

See how they spin? Just as busy as bees,
There's much to be done and how the time flees!
Merrily, merrily, the spinners sing,
So they need not import goods from a king!

[*The slaves depart singing.* Martha *follows them.*]

THE PICTURE BOOK MAN—

There's a spot at Mount Vernon—fair to see—
You guess it? The garden! How charmed you'll be!
Here stately flower beds laugh in the sun,
Here the guests mingle when the day is done.

[*The picture book reveals a corner of the flower garden. The* MARQUIS DE LAFAYETTE *is planting a tree.* GEORGE WASHINGTON, NELLIE, *and* MARTHA *are watching gaily and intently. Several guests look on also.*]

THE PICTURE BOOK MAN—

Another quaint custom! Lovely, you'll grant,
Distinguished guests were invited to plant
A tree or a shrub or only a rose,
Oh, that is the way a great garden grows!

[*The* MARQUIS *rises.* NELLIE *and* MARTHA *make pretty curtsies to him. He bows and they go out merrily followed by the others.*]

THE PICTURE BOOK MAN—

Sweet NELLIE sang in George Washington's day,
Songs that he loved best of all, so they say,
Often, at evening, by candle-light's glow—
She held him enchanted singing quite low.

[*There is a piano prelude. Presently;* NELLIE *appears and sings old songs.* GENERAL WASHINGTON *sits listening near by. When the songs are ended she goes to him—looks down at him teasingly. He rises and takes her hand. She stands on tip-toe and whispers something in his ear. He nods acquiescence and they go out together.*]

THE PICTURE BOOK MAN—

Such were Mount Vernon days after the war,
The glory of peace as never before
Cast its warm glow on the country around
Until—Hark! Someone comes! What is that sound?

[*There is the clatter of horses feet racing over the cobble-stones in the Entrance Gateway . . . The next picture reveals the West Front at Mt. Vernon. A slave is conducting one who is evidently a person of importance toward the door.*]

THE PICTURE BOOK MAN—

Impressive, he comes with a note of state,
The country is calling! It is the fate
Of the master here to serve once again
America's flag—as a leader of men!

[*The door opens and the messenger goes in. It is closed again at once.*]

THE PICTURE BOOK MAN—

He answered the call as good soldiers do,
And bid fond farewell to someone most true,

Look! Here he kneels as when he was a youth,
Seeking a blessing of beauty and truth.

[*The picture reveals* GEORGE WASHINGTON *kneeling beside his* MOTHER. *She places her hand on his shoulder in a gesture of pride and trust.*]

THE PICTURE BOOK MAN—

Of all the blessings there is none so fair,
As that of a mother—beyond compare,
First in her heart is the son of her pride—
The man so beloved by all far and wide.

[GEORGE WASHINGTON *rises and gives his hand to his* MOTHER. *They go out together. There is darkness again and with it the sound of exquisite music. It is a minuet . . . Suddenly, a flash of golden light suffuses the Picture Book and a host of gay little dancers trip out from its page. They assume their positions in the foreground as* THE PICTURE BOOK MAN *speaks.*]

THE PICTURE BOOK MAN—

Such beauty! Such charm! It is the grand ball,
Of our first President, honored by all—
He who was foremost in peace and war,
Let us all proclaim him near and a-far!

[*The "Minuet," by Mozart, is danced gracefully. When it is over two pages appear blowing trumpets. The last page of the Picture Book shows* PRESIDENT GEORGE WASHINGTON *standing alone. The entire company bows and curtsies to him. At last, with a final gesture of farewell, he departs,—and the little dancers scamper after him into the book.*]

THE PICTURE BOOK MAN—

That's all for tonight. The story is told,
The glory of it will never grow old,
Hail to GEORGE WASHINGTON, great and far-famed!
All honor we pay to his splendid name!

[*He bows with ceremony.*]

Now, goodnight, little guests, may you dream of renown,
Brought back once again from Picture Book Towne.

[*He, too, hastens into the book and draws the curtains after him. There is silence for a moment . . . Presently,* KATHRYN *arouses herself as from a dream and speaks softly.*]

KATHRYN—Oh, I like that, Mammy. [*Eagerly*] Did it seem to you that the Picture Book Man and George Washington and everyone he told us about was here?

MAMMY [*Chuckling*]—Bless yo', darlin'. I tole yo' George Washington slept in dis very room. And dat he might peek in at de window!

[*She rises and blows out the candles. Only the glow of the fire is seen.*]

[CURTAIN]

THROUGH THE CALENDAR TO MOUNT VERNON

A GEORGE WASHINGTON PAGEANT-PLAY FOR CHILDREN

By EDNA M. DUBOIS

CHARACTERS

[In order of their appearance]

MODERN:

 ROGER BLAND
 ELSIE BLAND
 JIMMIE BLAND
 TOMMIE BLAND

HISTORICAL:

 REVELATION, *a little colored boy*
 ELEANOR PARKE CUSTIS, GEN. WASHINGTON'S *stepgrandchild*
 GEORGE WASHINGTON PARKE CUSTIS (*called* "WASHINGTON"), ELEANOR'S *brother*
 GEN. GEORGE WASHINGTON
 MARTHA WASHINGTON
 MR. WINSTON
 MRS. WINSTON
 A GROUP OF COLORED CHILDREN

TIME: *February twenty-second of the present year.*

PLACE: *The living room in a well-to-do American home.*

DESCRIPTION OF CHARACTERS:

ROGER, *age 12*
ELSIE, *age 11* } *Dressed in garb of modern school children.*
JIMMIE, *age 10* { *Of different heights and temperament.*
TOMMIE, *age 8*

ELEANOR PARKE CUSTIS: *Delicate but lively. Dark hair; dressed as Colonial child in a frock with full skirt, full low-necked bodice with puffed sleeves, broad belt or sash both back and front.*

GEORGE WASHINGTON PARKE CUSTIS: *Small; expressive face, dark eyes. Dressed in smallclothes of blue velvet similar to adults.*

GENERAL GEORGE WASHINGTON: *Six feet two inches tall, in weight about two hundred pounds; rather large boned, but well proportioned, graceful, dignified and commanding, though modest in deportment. Complexion rather sallow; his hair light brown in color, worn in a queue, powdered. Dressed in military uniform of General.*

REVELATION: *A small darkey, about ten years old, dressed in torn white linen garments reaching to his knees.*

MARTHA WASHINGTON: *Short, inclined to plumpness, with a round placid face; direct, understanding eyes. She is calm, collected, witty; a splendid hostess; she speaks in soft, well-modulated tones. Her powdered hair is worn high on her head, in the mode of Colonial days, embellished by a small lace cap. Her silk gown is of the flowered polonaise type with a petticoat of frilled white silk; about her shoulders a dainty lace 'kerchief.*

MRS. WINSTON: *Middle age. Dressed in brightly colored polonaise gown and dark cape.*

MR. WINSTON: *Middle age; dressed in rich dark smallclothes, carries tricorne hat and greatcoat.*

SET: *Divide the stage from right to left into two portions by means of a light cloth curtain, on which a large calendar for the month of February, 1784, is painted or sewed. This curtain is split in the center so that it can be parted and drawn back. The narrower portion of the stage in front of this curtain is set for a modern living room, in which the children are discovered at play. When the children pass through the center [calendar] the curtains are drawn to reveal the deeper portion of the stage set for the Mount Vernon scene.*

 [ROGER *and* ELSIE *seated on couch, right, are looking at a book.* JIMMIE, *at window, left, is gazing disgustedly at a snowstorm outside.* TOMMIE, *seated on floor, center, is working a puzzle.*]

JIMMIE [*Crossly*]—Why can't we go out to play, I'd like to know! What if it is snowing? Snowflakes aren't bullets, are they? They can't hurt anyone.

ELSIE [*Glancing up from the book*]—Mother said it was too frosty for us to go out. She's afraid we might catch cold.

ROGER [*Turning page*]—She said, since it is Washington's Birthday, we might take this book, which tells all about the things Washington wrote, and see what lessons we could learn from it.

JIMMIE [*Sulkily*]—This is a holiday. I don't want to learn lessons. I want to go out and make a snow fort.

TOMMIE [*Eagerly*]—Oh, I know a lesson we can learn from George Washington. My teacher told us about it. When he was a little boy, George had a hatchet, and——

JIMMIE—That old cherry-tree story again! I'm sick of it! Well, I'm going to tell you something—[*Looks cautiously about, then continues*] I don't believe a word of that story!

TOMMIE [*Almost in tears*]—O-o-o-h! It must be true, for my teacher told us that story. And we made hatchets and cherries 'n everything. Isn't it true, Roger?

ROGER—Don't mind what Jimmie says, Tommie. He doesn't know everything.

ELSIE—Jimmie is cross because he can't go out-doors. At any rate, George Washington hated falsehood.

TOMMIE—Oh, I'm so glad! I'm sure he cut down a tree with his hatchet, too!

JIMMIE [*Comes over to couch where* ROGER *and* ELSIE *are sitting*]—Well, what lessons have you learned? How to fight Indians, I suppose! What good will that do us? We don't have to fight Indians. I just wish we did! It would be something to do.

ELSIE [*Excitedly*]—Oh, Boys! Listen to this! "Rules Written for His Own Guidance in His Fourteenth Year." Just think! George Washington was only a little older than we are now, when he copied these rules. What do they say? You read them, Roger.

ROGER [*Reads*]—"Every Action done in Company ought to be with Some Sign of Respect, to those that are present."

ELSIE [*To* JIMMIE, *who has been whistling*]—Hear that, Jimmie. It's not respectful to whistle.

JIMMIE—Oh, that means to older people. [*Seats himself at table, hums and taps on table with fingers.*]

ELSIE—But it doesn't say "older people." Go on, Roger.

ROGER [*Reads*]—"In the Presence of Others, sing not to yourself with a humming Noise, nor Drum your Fingers or Feet."
[ELSIE, ROGER *and* TOMMIE *look at* JIMMIE.]

JIMMIE [*Rising angrily to come and look at the book over* ROGER'S *shoulder*]—That's not in the book, Roger. You know you are just making that up as you go along.

ROGER—It is—every word of it! And here is something else [*Goes on reading*]—"Come not near the Books or Writings of Another so as to read them" [JIMMIE, *who has been looking at the book over* ROGER'S *shoulder, walks softly back to the table and sits down*] "unless desired or give your opinion of them unask'd also look not nigh when another is writing a Letter."

ELSIE—That's a good rule. I hate to have any one see a letter I am writing. Read some more.

ROGER [*Reads*]—"Shew not yourself glad at the Misfortune of another though he be your enemy."

JIMMIE [*Delightedly*]—Hear that, Elsie? You laughed yesterday when I fell down and got myself all muddy.

ELSIE—I know, I shouldn't have laughed! It was rude of me. I'm ever so sorry, Jimmie.

JIMMIE—Oh, it's all right.

ROGER [*Reads*]—"When a man does all he can, though it succeeds not well, blame not him that did it." That's like Tommie with his puzzle. He hasn't put it together yet, but he's done his best, so we shouldn't blame him.

TOMMIE—I will put it together. You wait and see if I don't!

ELSIE—Of course you will, Tommie.

ROGER [*Reads*]—"Wherein you reprove Another, be unblameable yourself; for example is more prevalent than Precepts."

JIMMIE [*Interested*]—That's a hard one. What does it mean?

ROGER—It means if I tell you not to get angry and lose your temper, I must make sure not to get angry and lose my own temper.

JIMMIE—That's fair enough. Are there any more?

ROGER—Three or four. Here is the next one: [*reads*] "Play not the Peacock, looking everywhere about you to See if you be well Deck't."
[*The boys all look at* ELSIE.]

ELSIE [*Laughing*]—I suppose you think I'm vain, don't you, Boys? Well, perhaps I do think too much of pretty clothes, but I do like to look nice.

TOMMIE [*Indignantly*]—Elsie isn't a peacock!

JIMMIE—Well, I've heard George Washington was very particular about the way he dressed.

ROGER [*Reads*]—"Be not immodest in urging your Friends to Discover a Secret." That's a rule for me to remember. Remember how I tried and tried last week to make Jimmie tell me the reason he had to stay after school?

TOMMIE [*Nods his head*]—I remember!

JIMMIE—You didn't find out!

ROGER [*Reads*]—"Be not Angry at the Table, whatever happens and if you have reason to be, Shew it not but on a Chearfull Countenance especially if there be Strangers for good Humour makes one Dish of Meat a Feast."
[*The rest look at* TOMMIE, *who hangs his head.*]

JIMMIE—Here's Tommie! [*Banging his fist on table*]—"I won't eat my oatmeal! I won't, I won't! Boo-hoo! Boo-hoo!"

TOMMIE—I didn't cry—much.

ELSIE—Well tomorrow morning, when you're eating your oatmeal, you think of George Washington—and smile.

TOMMIE—Will it make oatmeal a feast?

JIMMIE—Washington says so.

ROGER [*Reads*]—"Labor to keep alive in your Breast that Little Spark of Celestial fire called Conscience."

TOMMIE—I don't see what that means!

ELSIE—Didn't you ever want to do something very much, Tommie, and a little voice inside you kept saying, "No!" and "You shouldn't do that!"?

TOMMIE—Ye-es!

ELSIE—Well, that little voice that helps you know what is right and what is wrong is your conscience.

JIMMIE—Did Washington really and truly write all those?

ELSIE—Really and truly! They are good rules and helped George Washington to become a real gentleman and a great man. [*Jumping up and clapping her hands*]—What do you say to our adopting them and making them our rules, too?

ALL—Fine! George Washington's rules shall be our rules!

ROGER—I shall try never, never, to pry into other folks' secrets again!

TOMMIE—I like the one about conscience—the little voice that goes about with you always and tells you what is the right thing to do.

JIMMIE—The one that says we should be respectful to everyone present is a good one—I'm sure George Washington was just as polite to his own friends as he was to grownup people.

ELSIE—"Show not yourself glad at the misfortune of another." That is the best rule George Washington wrote, for it means we must all be good and kind to one another, especially when trouble comes.

JIMMIE—That's right.

ELSIE—We are having the best time reading the rules George Washington made when he was our age, aren't we? We are going to use them, too!

JIMMIE—Don't I wish I could have lived when George Washington did! Everything nowadays is just as stupid as it can be!

ELSIE—I'm afraid I'd rather see the things *Alice-in-Wonderland* saw than have lived a long time ago. It'd be just as much fun.

JIMMIE—Say, how do you make that out? Why George could fish and everything, and now when you fish you never catch anything, and when you hunt or trap you never yet anything except rabbits!

ROGER—Wouldn't it be fine to shoot deer and bears and big game!

ELSIE—Wouldn't it be fine to go through the looking-glass, as *Alice* did, and see things backward!

JIMMIE [*Decidedly*]—No going through the looking-glass for me! Though I wouldn't mind going through the calendar and turning it back a couple of hundred years.

ELSIE [*Jumping up excitedly*]—Let's see if we can turn the calendar back!

Tommie—Let's!

Elsie—Where shall we turn it to?

Jimmie [*Interrupting*]—Let's make it 1784—then the Revolutionary War'll be over and they can tell us all about it.

Tommie—I wish I could see George Washington.

Roger—Huh! You can't turn back the calendar and have those old days back again.

Elsie [*Sarcastically to* Roger]—Oh, we can't, can't we! Well, I'm going to try anyway. *Alice* went through the looking-glass, so why can't we go through the calendar?

Roger—Aw, it's too silly!

Elsie [*Goes nearer the calendar, which is large enough for the children to pass through. She lifts the leaf for February, 1932, then turns the leaf for 1784*]—Come on, I'm going through!

Roger—Ah, that's too silly a thing to do, Elsie. Going through a calendar! Perhaps some folks would like to do it, but not I. Come on, boys, it's stopped snowing. Now for some real fun!

Elsie—Aren't you coming, Tommie?

Tommie—I guess not!

Jimmie—Well, go on, Elsie, I'll go with you.

[Roger *and* Tommie *go out.* Elsie *and* Jimmie *go through the calendar. They walk up and down as if in search of something.*]

Jimmie—We've come through the calendar to 1784, but do you suppose we can find George Washington at home?

Elsie—I know George Washington's house was called Mount Vernon and that it was built on a hill overlooking the Potomac River.

[*A group of colored children run past them, singing and dancing as they go.*]

Jimmie—Hello there! We are looking for Mount Vernon, the home of George Washington. Can you tell us where it is?

Revelation—Yas'm. I helps about dis hyar place. Mah brudders an' sisters do too. Massa George done got a right smart piece ob land hyar an' it done take a passel ob niggers to 'tend it. We's plum glad hyar wid our Massa. Come on out hyar, yo niggers—us is g'wine sing a song 'fore Massa George gits hyar.

Elsie—Oh yes, please!

Revelation—Come on hyar, yo niggers!

[*The children come back, sing a song and dance a hoedown. While they are dancing,* Eleanor *and her brother* "Washington" *enter, without seeing* Elsie *and* Jimmie. "Washington" *waves the pickaninnies away. They all go except* Revelation.]

"Washington"—Why, Grandpapa Washington isn't here!

Eleanor [*In a disappointed tone*]—Where do you suppose he is, "Washington"? I do long to see him!

"Washington" [*As he looks around*]—And so did I. He's expecting the boat today, and I want to ask him to send over sea for some things for me.

Eleanor—He's going to send for some new ribbons for me—and perhaps—a doll.

"Washington"—A year is a long time to wait, so I hope that he doesn't forget me when he orders the things.

[Jimmie *and* Elsie *step forward.*]

"Washington"—Why! Who are you? And where do you come from?

Jimmie—Well, we're Elsie and Jimmie Bland, and we just came from home. Who are you?

Eleanor—We are General Washington's grandchildren. I am Eleanor.

"Washington"—I am George Washington Parke Custis, only Grandpapa calls me "Washington."

Elsie—Then you're the people we came through the calendar to see.

Eleanor [*Surprised*]—Through the calendar!

Jimmie [*Nods his head*]—Yes, it was 1932* when we came through.

Eleanor [*Shakes head*]—But it's only 1784!

"Washington"—I don't see how that could be!

Elsie—Neither do I, but here we are.

Jimmie [*Shivers with cold*]—Whew! But it's cold in this house.

Revelation—Yas, suh, tis fah sho' am wa'm. Ah ain't nebber seed no place dis wa'm in all mah life.

Elsie—It was nice and warm in our house when we left home.

Jimmie [*Looking around*]—The furnace must be low. I'm nearly frozen.

"Washington"—What's a furnace?

Elsie—My! [*Looks at* Eleanor *and* "Washington" *in astonishment*]—Haven't you a furnace to heat your house? I always thought George Washington was wealthy and had everything.

Eleanor—I never heard of a furnace. We keep our house warm with fireplaces.

Elsie—Oh, we have a fireplace too, but we have a furnace that we keep going when the weather is cold!

Jimmie—Nothing but a fireplace! ["Washington" *shakes his head.*] My! but it must be cold in the winter time.

Elsie [*Sighs*]—I never could get used to being way back in 1784 and have no furnace.

Revelation [*Enters with a lighted candle*]—Massa George, he done saint yo-all dis candle. [*Puts it on the mantel and goes.*]

Elsie—And you use candles? They don't give much light.

Jimmie—If you tell me where the button is, [*Looks around*] I'll switch on the electric lights for you.

"Washington" [*Shakes his head*]—Electric lights! You must have many strange things where you came from.

Eleanor [*To* Elsie]—Tell me about your playthings—have you a doll?

"Washington"—I can't see why you wanted to come way back here.

Jimmie—Oh, I like to hunt and trap, so I thought it would be fun.

"Washington" [*Looks at him and laughs*]—Why, you couldn't begin to carry a musket. They're too heavy for a boy as small as you are.

George Washington [*Enters, followed by Martha Washington*]—At last I have the order for our yearly supply of goods from over the sea made up and sent.

Martha Washington—And did you remember the things for "Washington" and Eleanor?

[George Washington *nods.*]

George Washington [*To* Eleanor]—And who are your new little friends, Eleanor?

Eleanor [*Curtsies.* George *and* Martha *sit down*]—They told

---

* Change this date to present year for production purposes.

us, General Washington, that they came in through the calendar.

GEORGE WASHINGTON [*Surprised*]—Through the calendar?

ELSIE—Yes, it was 1932, when we left.

MARTHA WASHINGTON—Why, it's only 1784.

GEORGE WASHINGTON [*Laughs*]—Don't forget, and it is my birthday, Patsy, dear.

JIMMIE—Why! it was your birthday when we left to come through the calendar! [*Turns to* ELSIE]—Wasn't it, Elsie?

ELSIE—Oh, General Washington, it's just like a fairy story coming through the calendar and seeing you and Mrs. Washington at home in Mount Vernon!

JIMMIE—Yes, Sirree, I'd rather be here than listening to the best radio entertainment in the world!

GEORGE WASHINGTON—Radio? And what is that?

ELSIE—Why, you get Chicago and San Francisco and most any place and hear the nicest music. Where's your radio? [*In confusion*] Oh, I forgot! There aren't any radios here, are there? I—that is, there are radios on the other side of the calendar, but there aren't any on this side. [*Pauses confused.*] Now, how can there be radios on the other side and none here?

GEORGE WASHINGTON—Chicago? San Francisco? What year did you say it was when you came through the calendar?

JIMMIE [*Excitedly*]—Nineteen hundred and thirty-two. There was a Chicago and San Francisco in 1932, but now it's 1784 and that's before there was a Chicago or a San Francisco, and so there isn't a Chicago or San Francisco any more. [*Looks puzzled.*] But there must be a Chicago and a San Francisco, or how could we get them on the radio?

ELSIE [*Nods her head emphatically*]—Yes, that is so, but they're on the other side of the calendar.

GEORGE WASHINGTON—Please tell me what you mean. Chicago? San Francisco? The other side of the calendar?

ELSIE [*Timidly*]—General Washington, we have read a lot in our history books—that you were our Commander-in-Chief and that there were only thirteen States along the eastern coast then——

JIMMIE [*Interrupting, to* ELSIE]—Let me tell General Washington some of the wonderful things that have happened in our country.

ELSIE [*To* JIMMIE]—It was only because I am so proud of our country that I wanted to tell General Washington all about it.

JIMMIE—You see, General Washington, since your day our country has spread westward and there are forty-eight States now, where you had thirteen. Chicago is a city on Lake Michigan and it is the largest lake port in the world. San Francisco is a great seaport on the Pacific Ocean. Through it we trade with China and Japan.

GEORGE WASHINGTON—But China is to the Eastward.

ELSIE—No, to the West. Ships can take us across the Pacific Ocean.

WASHINGTON—Wonderful—wonderful!

REVELATION [*Enters and bows awkwardly*]—Mis' Washington, des some fine white fo'ks what wants to see yo'.

MARTHA WASHINGTON—Show them in, Revelation. [REVELATION *goes out.*]

GEORGE WASHINGTON—It is a friend indeed who will drive twenty miles to help celebrate one's birthday.

[REVELATION *returns with* MR. *and* MRS. WINSTON. *The ladies curtsy, men bow.*]

MARTHA WASHINGTON—Welcome to Mount Vernon, MR. and MISTRESS WINSTON.

MR. WINSTON—Knowing it was your birthday, General Washington, we drove over to help you celebrate it.

MARTHA WASHINGTON [*Solicitously*]—You must have started hours ago.

MRS. WINSTON—The roads were very good. It took us but three hours to make the journey.

JIMMIE—Why our car would make it in less than an hour! [*Stops*] Oh, I forgot all they have are coaches and horses, and it isn't nineteen hundred thirty-two; it's just seventeen hundred eighty-four.

MARTHA WASHINGTON—You must, indeed, be quite worn out with such a long journey.

GEORGE WASHINGTON—It seems to me it is time for the others to have arrived.

ELSIE [*To* ELEANOR. *The children stand apart while the elders are engaged in conversion among themselves.*] Are you going to have a party?

ELEANOR—We always have one when Mr. Washington has a birthday.

"WASHINGTON"—All the neighbors come in and we have all kinds of good things to eat.

JIMMIE—Ice cream?

"WASHINGTON"—[*Shakes his head*]—Ice cream? You mean cream-ice? Yes, we'll have some.

JIMMIE—We call it ice-cream on the other side of the calendar.— Umm—it's good!

MARTHA WASHINGTON—"Washington" and Eleanor, bid your little friends goodnight. Perchance they may come through the calendar to visit you another time.

[ELEANOR *curtsies,* "WASHINGTON" *bows low—to* ELSIE *and* JIMME—*to* MR. *and* MRS. WINSTON *and back out.*]

ELSIE and JIMMIE—Good-night! Goodnight!

GEORGE WASHINGTON—There are the others now!

[REVELATION *shows in the other guests*]

GEORGE WASHINGTON—Good evening. Good evening. I was but now saying to the Winstons it was time for you to be here.

ALL [*Enter, shake hands*]—Good evening, General Washington, Mr. Winston. Good evening, Mistress Washington, Mistress Winston.

GENERAL and MRS. WASHINGTON-MR. and MRS. WINSTON—Good evening. Good evening.

ELSIE—Oh, if they would only dance the minuet.

GEORGE WASHINGTON—Then you do know about the minuet?

ELSIE—Yes, we dance it at costume balls.

JIMMIE—But I'll bet you can do it better.

ELSIE—Will you show us?

WASHINGTON—If the ladies will do us the honor?

LADIES—We shall be most happy.

[GENERAL WASHINGTON *and* MRS. WINSTON, MR. WINSTON *and* MARTHA, *pair off—as do the others and dance the minuet. While they dance, the scene dims. When it is light again,* ELSIE *and* JIMMIE *are in their own home.*]

ELSIE [*Clasping her hands*]—Hasn't it been wonderful to see the beautiful, beautiful ladies and stately gentlemen?

JIMMIE––It was fine to know about General Washington and we'll love him all the more, but I'm happy to be back through the calendar all the way to 1932.

ELSIE—So am I, but let us salute the Stars and Stripes, and sing a tribute to our wonderful "America."

[*All the class enter, salute flag and sing* "America."]

[*Curtain*]

CHILDHOOD DAYS IN WASHINGTON'S TIME

A PAGEANT FOR ELEMENTARY SCHOOLS

By FLORENCE C. FOX

Associate Specialist in Elementary Education, U. S. Office of Education

Published under the direction of the UNITED STATES GEORGE WASHINGTON BICENTENNIAL COMMISSION

INTRODUCTION

By WILLIAM JOHN COOPER, *United States Commissioner of Education*

TO TEACHERS, PRINCIPALS, AND SUPERINTENDENTS:

The episodes herewith presented were intended primarily to suggest possible interesting devices for celebrating the two hundredth anniversary of the birth of George Washington. But if they served also to suggest to pupils the preparation of pageants and plays of their own composition during the bicentennial year and afforded teachers an insight into a most promising teaching device, they will have served to hasten the arrival of a much desired era in American education.

For when an American philosophy of education has been developed, and teachers are steeped in it, doubtless the pageant, written by pupils, will find large part in the curricular activities, especially in the elementary grades. For the writing and presentation of a pageant require pupils to use in one purposeful social activity, three of the four essential tools which should be mastered in the elementary school—the mother tongue (reading to secure facts and written English to prepare the script), music (for the singing parts and dances), and art (for the costumes, scenery, etc.). In addition, physical activity and the desirable social habit of cooperation are involved.

TO BOYS AND GIRLS IN AMERICA'S SCHOOLS:

When your teacher reads to you the manuscripts prepared for these pageants, or loans the pamphlet to you to read, I suppose that you will want to do one of two things—first, reproduce this little play itself, or second, write one of your own for production in your school. I myself hope that you use this manuscript as a model and prepare one which will exactly suit the individualities of the boys and girls in your school or in your class.

When you are writing a text for George Washington, the boy, do not let yourself be overcome by the preeminence of George Washington, the great general, or George Washington, the first President. Remember that George Washington was a boy of your age at the period you are attempting to reproduce on the stage. He did his school work as an intelligent lad who wanted to make the most of the abilities which the Creator had given him. He made

mistakes just as you make mistakes. If you have a chance to read some of his early letters, you will discover that he did not always spell correctly; if you could see the originals of some of his later letters, you will discover that he had his "spelling demons."

He was fond of fishing, hunting, and horseback riding. The ease and grace shown in the pictures which portray him on horseback were acquired by long practice, just as any intelligent American boy who has the opportunity can acquire them. The games which he played were the games commonly played by the boys of his day in Virginia and grew out of the fact that there was much talk about Indian raids and always danger of foreign wars between the mother country and her enemies.

He had a longing for the sea, but his Uncle Joseph Ball in England advised George's mother against it, informing her that there was little chance for a Colonial in the navy and that a sailor had practically no opportunity to work his way up in the merchant marine. Although this decision was disappointing to the boy, respect for his mother's wishes was uppermost in his mind.

If you have opportunity to read the rules of conduct which George took the trouble to write out in his own copybook, you will discover that he earnestly endeavored to behave as the best-bred people of his day behaved. These rules of conduct, in company, toward superiors, toward inferiors, and even toward enemies constitute an interesting key to a chief reason why George Washington became a leader of men.

If you are by any chance privileged to act the part of George Washington, merely attempt to represent the noblest person you yourself are capable of being rather than to make any effort to imitate what you think the great man was when a boy.

FOREWORD

It is the purpose of *Childhood Days in Washington's Time* to place in the hands of the elementary school teachers a short and simple exercise, in pageant form, that depicts the boy Washington in his relation to the children with whom he associated.

Many sources have been drawn upon for the material used in these episodes. Authentic data in regard to George Washington's boyhood is almost entirely lacking in colonial archives and only a few isolated stories have been preserved. Hence, if one should ask for proof concerning the various episodes recorded here we would reply that a pageant is a picture, "a theatrical spectacle," and is not necessarily dependent upon factual material for its construction.

It has been thought wise, however, to gather these scattered threads and to weave them together into a series of incidents which may reveal to the children of today some of the influences that helped to shape the noble proportions of this great character.

Five types of children have been selected as representing the social life of that time, each type being presented in an episode or dramatic incident peculiar to that period of American history: Episode I, The Farmer Boy; II, The Bond Child; III, The Slave Boy; IV, The Planter's Sons and Daughters; V, The Young Indian Prince; VI, An Epilogue, Under the American Flag.

The pageant may be given in its entirety by groups of children in any grade from 5 to 8, inclusive, or certain episodes may be selected and given as units without reference to the others. It may also be worked out in a single school building as a community project by assigning one episode to each room in the school.

The songs and dances are simple, and the directions for drills are so definite and clear that they may be taught by the special teachers in those subjects or by the home teacher during opening exercises and music periods.

Ample time should be allowed for the preparation of the pageant to avoid undue haste just before the date of presentation. If it is to be given during the week of George Washington's birthday, the drills on songs and dances should begin in the preceding fall.

The beauty and effectiveness of each exercise will depend on the precision and accuracy with which it is rendered.

The costumes are simple and inexpensive and may be made in the home without difficulty. The standard fashion magazines contain patterns for fancy-dress costumes that are required.

THE PAGEANT

PART I

PROLOGUE

(To be recited by one of the pupils)

Come, let us work and play with young Washington in the days of his boyhood before he became the commanding figure of the history books. Let us go with him to the old field school; visit with him the court room in old Alexandria; steal away with him at night to a possum hunt and follow him through the Maypole dance with little Sally Fairfax; let us tramp with him through the forest as he surveys the trackless wastes of the wilderness. Come, let us know George Washington in all his vigorous youth and young manhood.

In these episodes we shall see him win his battles in defense of the unfortunate schoolmaster; we shall see him as he rescues the little bond girl from her cruel master; as he repents of his own unjust treatment of the humble plantation pickaninny; as he begs for clemency toward a culprit sentenced to the pillory for cheating. We shall admire his tact and skill in dealing with the Indians, always endeavoring to placate and never to antagonize the people who afterward became the deciding force in the struggle between the French and the English.

NOTE.—The chief characters in the Episodes should stand in line behind the speaker, with George Washington at right.

As we follow him through this pageant we shall understand more clearly the influences that shaped his character. We shall appreciate the lessons he learned of courage, forbearance, and fortitude, which prepared him to become at a later time a great leader in a great crisis.

And finally we shall see his flag, the flag of the Nation he founded, floating over the boys and girls of today, his flag—a fitting emblem of this great character, who one hundred and fifty years ago laid the foundation stone of our Republic.

EPISODE I: HOBBY'S SCHOOL

George Washington and William Bustle, The Farmer Boy

CHARACTERS

GEORGE WASHINGTON.

WILLIAM BUSTLE.

LAWRENCE WASHINGTON, brother of George.

MARY BALL WASHINGTON, mother of George and the stepmother of Lawrence.

HOBBY, the schoolmaster.

Farmer boys.

Stage setting: School room. Door at right leads to playground. Door at left opens on path that leads up from the road. Bench along the wall at back. Hobby's table and chair at right, sidewise to audience. Door at right directly behind Hobby's chair. Water pail and dipper in right back corner.

Costumes: George and Dicky Lee in planter's costume, short, cutaway coats, three-cornered hats. Farmer boys in brown smocks fringed on lower edge and on the collar and cuffs. Hobby, patch over one eye, in a dilapidated planter's costume. Lawrence in military costume, if possible, otherwise in planter's dress. Mother in planter's wife costume, hood, cape, long full dress.

PROCEDURE

SCENE I: *School room.*

Group of boys at right front talking together. Dicky Lee enters at left. They tell him they are planning to scare old Hobby, the teacher, into a fit so he will close the school and they can go fishing. George enters left and Dick refers it to him.

George grins but shakes his head. Explains that Hobby is a poor old bond servant brought from England by his father, etc., that they better take some one their size. Says his brother Lawrence thinks a man's a coward who picks on some one weaker than oneself.

Dicky Lee tells the boys that George is against it, wants to study, etc.; William, angry, calls George a spoil sport. George tells him to go ahead but that he thinks it poor sport. Dicky Lee hesitates. William tells boys he'll fix George, he's so high and mighty.

Hobby enters left, as William exits right. First class in spelling called. Hobby counts the members by tapping each with his cane. Asks for William. Joe Hooper says he went back into the woods. William appears behind Hobby and throws a little snake over the cane. Hobby falls in a fit. George on his knees beside him trying to quiet him. Dicky Lee fetches a dipper of water. Hobby revives, gets on his feet, sinks in a chair. Pupils start to laugh and then are frightened. Hobby drinks water and dismisses class for recess. As they go out George says to get ready for drill in Spanish war. William wants to play Indian warfare. All agree, troop out.

Joe Hopper enters left and tells Hobby that Mrs. Washington and Lawrence are coming up the path. Enter Mrs. Washington and Lawrence. Hobby stands, shakes hands with Lawrence. Mrs. Washington cries, says Lawrence wants to take George away from her. Lawrence explains he wants George to go to a better school. That he is running wild, wants him at Mount Vernon. Hobby agrees.

George comes in holding his hand over his eye, with a group of indignant schoolmates, who tell that William Bustle has thrown a stone and hit George in the eye. Mrs. Washington alarmed. Lawrence tells George to trounch William. Mrs. Washington demurs. They go out on playground.

SCENE II: *Playground.*

William defies George, who knocks William down and pounds him until he cries "enough"! and walks away muttering threats. Hobby, George, Mrs. Washington, and Lawrence stand in front. Lawrence tells George he wants him to come to Mount Vernon for a while and go to Mr. Williams's school. Mrs. Washington weeps. George is sorry for his mother but wants to go. Lawrence offers George a horse and red coat. Mrs. Washington protests, but George finally decides to go with Lawrence and mother goes off left, alone, calling good-by to George, who stays to say good-by to his schoolmates. He joins the farmer boys, who form in line at the back of stage. They march forward and back singing a school song—*School Days.*

SCENE I: *The* SCHOOLROOM

DIALOGUE (*See Procedure*)

(*William Bustle, Joe Hopper, and a group of farmer boys at right front talking*)

FIRST FARMER BOY (*to William Bustle, the biggest boy in the group*).—You do it, William.

WILLIAM BUSTLE (*as Dicky Lee comes in from left*).—Here comes Dick Lee. See what he says.

SECOND FARMER BOY (*as Dicky Lee crosses to right front and joins the group*).—We're planning to scare old Hobby, the teacher.

WILLIAM BUSTLE.—You see, Dick, we want to go fishin'. I'm going to get a snake—a garter—and steal in behind Hobby and throw it over his cane.

THIRD FARMER BOY.—That'll scare him proper.

FOURTH FARMER BOY.—He's powerful afraid of snakes.

FIFTH FARMER BOY.—He's afraid of black magic, too.

SIXTH FARMER BOY.—He won't go near a black if he can help it.

DICKY LEE.—Well, first, you better guard that door. He'll be coming in any time now. You stand by the door, Joe Hopper.

JOE HOPPER (*a little boy, crosses to door and looks out*).—Hobby ain't in sight, but George Washington is coming.

DICKY LEE.—Let's hear what George thinks.

WILLIAM BUSTLE.—Oh, shucks, I know what George'll think. He's all for study and mindin' the teacher. (*George enters at left door.*)

DICKY LEE (*leaves the boys and crosses to meet George*).—Halloo, George, I'm glad you've come. We're planning to scare Hobby into a fit, and then we'll get a holiday. We can set our traps in the woods.

GEORGE (*grins and shakes his head*).—Plenty of time to set traps after school.

DICKY LEE.—Oh, George, what a stick you are. Never want any fun.

GEORGE.—I like fun as well as you do, but I like school, too. I want to get on with my studies. (*Walks to bench and sits down.*)

DICKY LEE.—Still planning that surveying stuff? I won't go out with you again and hold your old tape lines.

GEORGE.—I don't want you to go. All you do is steal birds' nests and plug up badger holes. Besides, mother wouldn't like it if I teased Hobby. You know father brought him over from England as a bond servant to be sexton of our chapel and teach our school. He's a poor old one-eyed man, and kind to all of us.

DICKY LEE (*scornfully to boys*).—Hey, boys, George is against it. He loves his school and he loves his teacher.

WILLIAM (*angrily*).—Oh, go to pot! George, I knew you'd try to spoil our sport.

GEORGE.—My brother Lawrence says it's no sport to take advantage of any one weaker than you are. (*Takes out an arithmetic and becomes absorbed in it.*)

WILLIAM (*to the boys*).—I'll fix him for that. He's so high and mighty!

DICKY LEE (*looks at George, seems undecided, says to William*).—Well, William, you know Hobby is a poor old codger.

WILLIAM.—What's he teachin' school for then, afraid of snakes and black magic and everything.

JOE HOPPER (*looking out the door*).—Teacher's comin'. (*William Bustle disappears through the door at right. Hobby enters at left. All boys in seats on bench.*)

HOBBY (*walks to his chair at right near the door behind a rude table. He sits a minute until all is quiet*).—Spelling class comes up. (*Boys stand in row in front of table while Hobby counts them, tapping each with his cane.*) Where's William Bustle?

LITTLE JOE HOPPER.—He went back into the woods.

HOBBY (*with his back to the door*).—Confound the boy. Always up to some mischief. (*William creeps in and throws a little garter snake over his cane. Hobby drops the cane and starts back in horror, trembles and shakes in a sort of fit, and falls to the floor.*)

CHILDREN (*starting to laugh and then are frightened*).—Oh! Oh! My! Oh! Oh!

GEORGE (*kneeling beside him and trying to pacify him*).—It's nothing, sir; the snake is harmless.

DICKY LEE (*as though to make amends, runs to the water pail and fetches a dipper of water*).—Geminie, George, who'd ever thought a little snake would scare him so.

GEORGE.—William did. I warned him.

DICKY LEE (*as Hobby opens his eyes*).—Have a drink of water, sir.

HOBBY.—Help me up, boys; I'm all right. (*George and Dicky Lee help him into a chair. He rests his head on his hands and seems a little dazed.*)

DICKY LEE (*who is very much frightened*).—Have a drink of water, sir.

HOBBY (*drinking from the dipper*).—You may have recess. (*Joe Hopper is the first to leave the room at right door.*)

GEORGE (*trying to ignore the fright as they move toward the door at right*).—I vote for Spanish war drill. Get your cornstalks, boys.

WILLIAM (*who has stood with a sneer on his face*).—No, sir; Indian battle, and I'm the leader.

GEORGE (*to William*).—William, Hobby will die in one of those fits some day.

WILLIAM.—Oh, Foo! that was half put on.

GEORGE.—And whoever brings it on will be guilty of murder.

WILLIAM.—I don't believe ye.

GEORGE.—Well, I've warned you. (*As they pass out on the playground right, back, Joe Hopper enters left and hurries up to Hobby's desk.*)

JOE HOPPER (*to Hobby who sits with his head in his hands*). Oh, sir, Mrs. Washington and Lawrence Washington, George's mother and brother, are coming up the path.) (*Exits at right door.*)

HOBBY (*sitting up and trying to compose his shaken nerves*). —Now, I wonder what they want to see me about.

(*Lawrence and his mother come on through left door into the school room. Hobby brings his chair around to front of table and Mrs. Washington is seated. Hobby shakes hands with Lawrence who stands beside his mother, facing Hobby, his table behind him. This brings the group into center of the stage.*)

LAWRENCE (*to Hobby*).—I've come to take George to Mount Vernon with me, Hobby.

MRS. WASHINGTON (*beginning to cry*).—Lawrence wants to take George away from me.

LAWRENCE (*to Hobby.*)—I want him to go to a better school than this, with all due respect to you. He's running wild here. I want him at Mount Vernon, and Anne, my wife, wants him, too.

MRS. WASHINGTON (*to Hobby*).—But what shall I do without him?

HOBBY (*to Mrs. Washington*).—You're too busy with your farm, Madam, to look out for George. He ought to go to Mr. Williams's school near Mount Vernon where he can study map drawing and land measurement.

MRS. WASHINGTON.—I don't want him to be a surveyor.

LAWRENCE (*to Mrs. Washington*).—Well, Lord Fairfax will want some one to survey his land when he comes over from England. George might do that. (*Commotion on the school grounds.*)

BOYS (*yelling in right wing*).—Now, see what you've done, William Bustle!

DICKY LEE (*right wing*).—You've hurt George's eye.

JOE HOPPER.—I'm going to tell teacher.

MRS. WASHINGTON (*listening and rising from her chair*).—What has happened, Hobby?

DICKY LEE (*entering right*).—George's eye is hurt.

JOE HOPPER (*to Hobby*).—William Bustle did it.

DICKY LEE (*to Mrs. Washington*).—William Bustle hit him in the eye with a stone, the big blunderbuss!

JOE HOPPER (*to Mrs. Washington*).—Blunderbuss! He did it a-purpose, I see him. I see him.

(*Lawrence goes out right and brings George into the school room. George holds his hand over his eye. Lawrence and mother center, facing George, Hobby behind, Joe and Dick behind Hobby.*)

LAWRENCE.—Let's see your eye, George. Take your hand down. (*Lawrence and Mrs. Washington look anxiously at George's eye. George's eye black and swollen. Mrs. Washington sinks into the chair and covers her face with her hands.*)

LAWRENCE (*to his mother*).—Now you see, mother, that shows George needs to get away from here. (*To George*) Where is this William Bustle, George?

GEORGE.—He's out on the playground.

LAWRENCE.—Let's go out and see him.

MRS. WASHINGTON (*to Lawrence*).—I don't want him to fight.

LAWRENCE.—No one else will fight his battles for him.

(*Mrs. Washington, Lawrence, Hobby, George, Dicky Lee, and Joe Hopper all pass through the door at right as a drop curtain falls in front of this scene. In lieu of a drop, screens may be placed in front of the school room scene, or the bench and table may be removed without a curtain being used. Trees set in standards may be placed at back of stage.*)

SCENE II: *The PLAYGROUND*

(*A group of boys at right stand waiting as the others enter from left, Lawrence leading with George, Mrs. Washington, and Hobby following and Dicky Lee and Joe Hopper behind.*)

LAWRENCE.—Which is William Bustle?

DICKY LEE (*to Lawrence*).—There he is, sir, the biggest one.

LAWRENCE.—What are you going to do, George, trounce him?

GEORGE.—I'd like to give him a good beating.

WILLIAM BUSTLE (*comes up to George and shows his fists*).—You would, would you? Well, come on. (*George knocks him down, sits on him, and pummels him. Boys make a ring and clap their hands.*)

DICKY LEE.—Pound him, George.

LITTLE JOE HOPPER.—Give it to him.

FIRST BOY.—Beat him! Beat him!

SECOND BOY.—Knock the stuffin' out of 'im.

WILLIAM (*howls*).—Let me up.

GEORGE.—Had enough?

WILLIAM.—Let me up.

GEORGE.—Had enough?

WILLIAM.—Yes. (*George lets him up and he walks away muttering threats.*) You just wait! I'll fix you! You're so all-fired smart!

BOYS.—Oh, come on! Fight's over. Let's play Hop Scotch. (*Boys go on with their games.*)

(*Mrs. Washington, Lawrence, George, and Hobby move over to left front and Lawrence facing George places his hand on George's shoulder. Mrs. Washington on the far side of George and Hobby behind him.*)

LAWRENCE (*to George*).—I want you to go home with me, George, and stay a while at Mount Vernon. Anne wants you, too.

MRS. WASHINGTON (*beginning to cry*).—George, I don't want you to leave me.

LAWRENCE (*to George*).—I want to send you to Mr. Williams's school. Some of your best friends go there—Langy Dade and the Willis boys.

GEORGE (*to his mother*).—Will you let me go, mother?

LAWRENCE (*to George*).—I'll give you a horse of your own and a red coat.

GEORGE (*to Lawrence*).—I'd like to go. (*Looks at his mother.*)

LAWRENCE (*to Mrs. Washington*).—He can come to see you often.

GEORGE (*hesitating and then walking away to right with Lawrence, Mrs. Washington walks away to left weeping*).—Good-by, mother. Say good-by to Betty for me. (*To Lawrence*) I'll say good-by to the boys first. (*He joins the boys who form in line at back of stairs, George and Dicky Lee in middle. They march back and forth singing "School Days."*)

SONG—SCHOOL DAYS

(*Adapted from a popular song*)

School days! school days! dear old golden rule days,
Readin' and 'ritin' and 'rithmetic
Taught to the tune of a hickory stick,
Playing at war when our work was done,
With a stick and a stone and a cornstalk gun
Bravely we fought and proudly we won,
In the days of the old Hobby school.

[*Curtain*]

School Days
(When We Were A Couple Of Kids)

Valse moderato   By COBB and EDWARDS

School days, school days, dear old gol-den rule days, Read-in' and rit-in' and 'rith-me-tic, Taught to the tune of a hick-'ry stick, You were my queen in cal-i-co, I was your bare-foot bash-ful beau, And you wrote on my slate, "I love you, Joe," When we were a cou-ple of kids. (just two kids.)

Copyright MCMVII by Gus. Edwards Co., 1531 Broadway, New York City
Copyright assigned MCMXXV to Mills Music, Inc., 148-150 W. 46th St., New York

EPISODE II: THE RUNAWAY BOND GIRL

George Washington and Margaret Anderson, the Little Bond Girl

CHARACTERS

GEORGE WASHINGTON.

MARGARET ANDERSON, bond girl.

DICKY LEE.

MASTER.

JUDGE.

CLERK OF COURT.

CONSTABLE.

BAKER.

BLACKSMITH.

INNKEEPER.

TAVERN GUEST.

Bond boys and girls, bystanders.

Stage setting: Court room in justice's office; judge's desk and chair, raised, center back; clerk's table and chair at left of judge. Two or three chairs at right and left against the wall. Constable seated at right of judge's desk.

Costumes: George and Dicky Lee in planter's costumes. Bond girls in white cap, kerchief and apron, long dresses. Bond boys in brown smocks. Master in merchant's dress, shorts, cutaway coat, very plain, with whip in his hand. Judge in white wig and gown. Clerk in black cap and gown. Baker, white cap and apron, carries tray in front of him suspended by a cord around his neck with cakes for sale. Blacksmith, brown apron and hammer. Innkeeper, shabby planter's costume, specs up on forehead, pen behind ear. Guest, well dressed, in colonial costume.

PROCEDURE

SCENE I: *The court room.*

Enter George and Dicky Lee with bond girl from left followed by master with whip and bystanders. George and Dicky Lee and bond girl stand at left, master in front at right, with bystanders behind him. One of the bystanders may be the baker with his tray of cakes, the blacksmith with hammer and leather apron, innkeeper with specs on forehead and pen behind his ear, and guest, a well-dressed citizen.

Master flourishes his whip and explains that the child is his bond servant, that he bought and paid for her, etc.

The bond girl begs George to protect her, and Dicky Lee calls attention to the marks of the whip on her neck and arms. The bystanders threaten the master with stocks and pillory, and the master retorts that the judge will decide the case.

Judge enters at back in wig and gown and sits at desk. The trial proceeds. Master is sworn and testifies. Judge reprimands Margaret for running away. Then George testifies and calls attention to the marks on Margaret's neck and arms. The judge is shocked and reprimands the master. George proposes to ask his brother Lawrence to pay the child's indenture and free her. The bystanders propose to raise a dowry to provide for her until she finds another place. This is done and a record made of the donations by the clerk of the court.

SCENE II: *The street in front of the justice's office.*

A crowd has gathered outside the office to see the master and bond girl. Bond children are there who greet Margaret and the judge proposes a song and dance. Simple songs may be sung—"This is the way we wash our clothes" by the girls and "Farmer in the Dell" by the boys, ending in the "Virginia Reel."

SCENE I: *The* COURT ROOM

DIALOGUE. *(See Procedure)*

(*Clerk is busy at his table with papers. Judge's seat vacant. Enter George and Dicky Lee with little bond girl. Following them enter master with whip, the innkeeper, guest at tavern, baker, blacksmith, and two or three bystanders. George, Dicky Lee, and bond girl stand at left, master in front at right, others behind him.*)

MASTER (*to George, and flourishing his whip*).—I tell you she's my bond child. I'm her master. She's run away.

MARGARET ANDERSON (*to George, crying*).—Oh, please save me, sir. I only broke a dish, and he beats me for everything I do.

DICKY LEE (*to George*).—Oh, George, don't let her go with that man. Look at the marks on her arms and neck.

MASTER (*to George*).—She's mine, I tell you. I've bought her and paid for her. I can prove it.

INNKEEPER (*peering over his glasses at the little girl who stands before George with her face in her hands crying bitterly*).—Poor child. Look at the marks of the whip on her arms.

BAKER (*shaking his fist at the master*).—He ought to be whipped hisself.

GUEST.—I'd put him in the stocks.

BLACKSMITH.—Put 'im in the pillory.

MASTER (*glaring at the bystanders*).—You can't do nothin'. The judge has the say of that.

JUDGE (*entering from the back in wig and gown*).—What's this you say? State it to the court. I'll have my clerk make a record of it. (*To clerk.*) Swear this witness.

CLERK (*stepping forward with a Bible, and holds up his right hand; to Master*).—Do you solemnly swear to tell the truth, the whole truth, and nothing but the truth?

MASTER (*with right hand raised and left hand on the Bible*).—I do, so help me God.

MASTER (*to Judge*).—Please, your honor, I bought this girl in the market in Alexandria. I paid 500 pounds of tobacco for her passage. But she runs away, your honor, and tells in the streets that I abuse her.

JUDGE (*to Master*).—How much longer has she to serve?

MASTER (*to Judge*).—Her term is nearly up. She has one more year to serve. She's 10 now, your honor.

JUDGE (*to Master*).—Well, what's the trouble? Keep her another year and let her go. (*To Margaret.*) No more running away, young lady, or you'll have to serve your master still another year. (*The Master steps forward to lead Margaret away. She cowers down behind George and Dicky Lee, sobbing.*)

BYSTANDERS (*muttering and moving about in groups, whispering together*).—It's a shame. That master's a beast. The court ought to free her.

JUDGE (*pounding on his desk*).—What's this commotion? Silence in the court. Constable, clear the room.

GEORGE (*to Judge*).—Please, your honor, may I speak?

JUDGE.—Order in the court! (*To clerk.*) Swear this witness.

GEORGE (*to Judge, after being sworn*).—Please, your honor, this girl has been beaten. She shows the marks of the whip. She can tell a sorry tale of her bondage, I make no doubt.

JUDGE (*to Clerk*).—Bring her forward. (*Clerk uncovers her arms and neck by taking off her kerchief and discloses the raw, red marks of the whip.*)

JUDGE (*to Master*).—You did this thing to this young girl? But why?

MASTER (*to Judge, sullenly*).—She's lazy, your honor, and careless; I have to whip her to make her work.

BYSTANDERS (*muttering together*).—He's a beast. He ought to be punished. He ought to be put in the stocks.

JUDGE.—Order in the court.

GEORGE (*to Judge*).—Your honor, I think my brother Lawrence could free this bond slave. I'm sure he'll go security for 500 pounds of tobacco if you'll let her go.

FIRST BYSTANDER.—Praises be, he's going to free her. Let's give her a dowry. She's a poor lass. She'll need something to live on till she finds a place. I'll give 10 pounds of tobacco.

SECOND BYSTANDER.—I'll give 10 pounds.

THIRD BYSTANDER.—I'll give 10.

FOURTH BYSTANDER.—I'll give 20.

FIFTH BYSTANDER.—I'll give 20.

DICKY LEE.—I'll give 30 pounds; at least I know my father will.

JUDGE (*to clerk who has been writing in a book*).—What have you now?

CLERK (*to Judge*).—Your honor, I have 100 pounds.

JUDGE (*to Margaret*).—Dry your eyes, young maiden. You are free if Mr. Lawrence Washington will pledge the 500 pounds of tobacco, and have 100 pounds of tobacco for capital. Seek a good home and do not shirk your work. Be diligent and industrious and you will find happiness. (*To the Master.*) I have been shocked many times of late at the cruelty of masters toward their bond servants. I will make an example of the next master who takes advantage of these helpless children. I shall order him to stand in the pillory from noon to sundown. There he may think on his evil ways and repent of the wrong he has done to a little child. Court is dismissed. (*The Master slinks out of the court room and the bystanders crowd around George and Dicky Lee shaking hands and patting Margaret on the back. They exit slowly from the court room. Judge leads the way.*)

JUDGE (*leading out*).—We'll dance and sing on the village green. Come one, come all (*to the children gathered there*).

SCENE II: *The* VILLAGE COMMONS

(*A crowd of bond children in caps, kerchiefs, and aprons, boys in smocks, greet Margaret. They form in line, choose their part-ners, and dance the Virginia Reel. II. Bystanders watch at back of stage.*)

NOTE.—Some simple little songs may be introduced here. "This is the way we wash our clothes" for the girls, and "Farmer in the Dell" for the boys. The previous dialogue is short and there will be a longer time for the songs and dance.

[*Curtain*]

VIRGINIA REEL

Formation.—Sets of eight in two lines about 4 feet apart; partners opposite, all facing center. (No. 1 in one line, No. 2 in other line.)

Step.—Skip step or walking step. No. 1 of head couple and No. 2 of foot couple lead in each figure. No. 2 of head couple and No. 1 of foot couple repeat the figure.

FIGURE 1.—Balance corners. Forward to center, bow to partner and backward to position. (Head lady and foot gentleman, and vice versa.)

FIGURE 2.—Forward to center, join right hands and turn. Backward to position.

FIGURE 3.—Repeat figure, joining left hands.

FIGURE 4.—Repeat figure, joining both hands.

FIGURE 5.—Forward to center, pass back to back, right shoulders first, backward to position.

FIGURE 6.—Repeat figure, passing with left shoulder first.

FIGURE 7.—Head couple join both hands, arms extended, slide step (side, close) to foot and back to head of set.

FIGURE 8.—Head couple hook right arms (or join right hands) and turn one and one-half times to place. Give left hand to neighbor on opposite side and turn around. Right arm to partner and turn once around. Continue down the lines, turning partner and neighbor alternately to the foot of set. Turn partner one and one-half times around and take position for slide step.

FIGURE 9.—Slide step to head of set, to foot of set, and back to head.

FIGURE 10.—Head couple drop hands and all face forward. Head couple lead off turning toward foot of set on outside of set. Others follow, all clapping. At foot, head couple join hands and continue to position at head of line. Face each other, join both hands and form arch by raising both arms. Other couples follow, taking their own places in line and forming arch. Last couple pass through arch to head of set. All drop hands and take proper distance. Repeat the dance till all couples are in their original position.

In *Detroit Course of Study in Rhythms and Dances*, p. 140.

EPISODE III: THE POSSUM HUNT

George Washington and Little Peter, the Slave Boy

CHARACTERS

GEORGE WASHINGTON.

LITTLE PETER, slave boy.

DICKY LEE.

BIG JIM (with his dog on leash).

Pickaninnies.

Stage Setting: Woods.

Costumes: The Negro costumes are made of bright-colored cotton cloth in two pieces like a track suit. A black stocking pulled over the head like a cap and covered with tufts of black curled hair makes the wig. The face, next, arms, hands, legs, and feet should be blackened with theatrical paste made for this purpose.

PROCEDURE

SCENE I: *The forest at evening.*

Dicky Lee at right front with a lantern looking into right wing for George. George comes running, grabs Dicky, and they run across to left front.

Dicky asks what happened to keep George so long. Talks about the possum hunt, thinks it time they were coming. George explains that it was hard to get away. Big Peter was sound asleep but Little Peter was skulking around watching his window. George tells what he intends to do to Little Peter to cure him of skulking and watching, and running and telling on him.

Dicky Lee sets down the lantern. It tips over and goes out. They sit in the dark on a log. Little Peter runs on the stage from the right, sees George and starts back. George calls him, Little Peter comes slowly forward. George scolds him and slaps him. Little Peter falls down and plays possum. George is scared and bends over Peter and lifts him up. He asks him if he is badly hurt. Little Peter laughs and says, "You hits mighty hard, Marse George."

George tells Little Peter to help him catch the possum alive. When Big Jim comes with his dog Peter is to tell Jim to hold his dog in leash and not let him get the possum. Then Peter is to hold a bag and George will throw the possum into it and Little Peter must hand the bag to George. Little Peter promises. Dicky Lee asks why he wants a live possum. George says he'll tell him later. Noise of possum hunt comes from right wing. Dogs barking, pickaninnies laughing and shouting. Then a crowd comes from right with lanterns, a dog on leash, pine torches, etc. George and Dicky Lee and Little Peter go to right to join them. The possum comes out of bushes at back center, turns and scurries out left wing. George sees him, shouts "Possum, possum," and all except Jim and Little Peter run off left. Little Peter tells Jim not to let his dog get the possum. Dogs bark, darkies shout and yell snatches of song. Commotion in left wing.

Shouting at left. Crowd comes back, George leading, carrying possum by the tail. He holds up the possum and the pickaninnies crowd around. George asks who wants it, and of course every pickaninny cries "I." George tells them to "Kotch it in de bag." Peter stands in front of him with his open bag. George tosses Peter the possum, who catches it in his bag and hands it to George. Pickaninnies with bags over shoulder laugh boisterously at the trick.

Dicky Lee looks at George's bag and finds it empty. He tells George, who seems surprised, and says that the little varmint must have got away. They all form in line at the back, march back and forth chanting "Kotch dat possum"; at each refrain, "Kotch him in de bag," they swing the bag around and bend down to touch the floor with it.

DIALOGUE.   (See Procedure)

(*Dicky Lee at right front with a lantern looking into right wing for George. George comes running, grabs Dicky, and they run across to left front.*)

GEORGE (*breathlessly*).—Have I missed the possum hunt?

DICKY LEE.—No; they haven't started yet. They're bound to come this way, and I've been here since dark.

GEORGE.—You sure you haven't missed 'em?

DICKY LEE.—Sure, I heard a dog bark down by the river, but that's all. What made you so late? Couldn't you get away?

GEORGE.—No, I couldn't. (*Angrily.*) Little Peter smelled a mouse and hid in the bushes just outside my window. If he follows me out here and I catch him, there'll be one black boy gets a good beating.

DICKY LEE.—Never mind, George; better think a minute before you lick him. Remember your hot temper.

GEORGE.—You know, Dick, Lawrence doesn't like to have me go out with these rough river darkies, and the only way I can get to go is by stealing away at night. If young Peter finds out I've gone to a possum hunt and tells, Lawrence will be awfully disappointed in me.

DICK LEE.—Maybe Peter is just curious, wants to know where you go and what you do. You know, George, some way or other you've made those darkies think you're a god, or something.

GEORGE.—Well, Peter'll think I'm the Day of Judgment if I catch him spying on me.

DICKY LEE.—Well, let's sit here on this log and wait for the boys. (*Sets down his lantern; it tips over and goes out.*) Oh! this lantern's out. Now we'll have to sit in the dark.

GEORGE.—Never mind, Dick; the boys'll have torches.

DICKY LEE (*in a frightened voice*).—What's that over in that shadow? I saw some one moving.

GEORGE (*to the shadow*).—Here you, come here. (*Peter comes toward them.*) What you mean spying on me and tagging after me this time o'night? Take that. (*He gives the little darkey a slap across the face, who falls down and lies motionless at his feet.*)

DICKY LEE.—George, what have you done? You're so strong.

GEORGE.—If we only could see. (*Frightened and bends over Peter.*) Hey, Peter, come to life; quit your fooling. (*Lifts up the boy, shakes him gently, and stands him on his feet.*)

DICKY LEE.—He's playing possum, I do believe. Let's shake him good.

PETER (*opening his eyes and grinning*).—You hits mighty hard, Marse George.

GEORGE (*much relieved*).—Here, Peter, I want to talk to you about the possum hunt. I want you to get me that possum. I want him alive.

DICKY LEE.—What in the world do you want with a live possum?

GEORGE.—Never mind, Dick; I'll tell you later. (*To Peter.*) Now, Peter, listen carefully. This is what I want you to do. You tell Jim, who is bringing his dog, to keep the dog in leash and not let him get at the possum. Will you do that?

PETER.—Shore, Marse George; I'se tell him you say so.

GEORGE.—All right. Now there's something more I want you to do. I want you to catch the possum for me.

PETER.—How'll I kotch dat possum, Marse George?

GEORGE.—That's easy. You get a bag and hold it open, and I'll throw the possum into it.

PETER (*grinning and delighted with the plan*).—Yas, sah, Marse George; I'll kotch dat possum dat-a-way.

(*At left a dog barks, shouts and laughter. Boys enter with Big Jim holding dog. Torches flare and much excitement prevails. Crowd walks about looking up trees and beating bushes.*)

GEORGE.—Hey, there goes a possum. (*Starts toward the left wing. All of the crowd follows except Jim and his dog and little Peter. The dog is nosing in the bushes and Jim is pulling on the leash. Peter takes hold of the leash. Noise in left wing.*)

PETER (*to Jim with dog*).—Hey, Jim, Marse George he say he want to kotch dat possum hisself.

JIM.—What fer?

PETER.—He jes want him, dat's all.

JIM.—Mighty queer. Dis here dog's the most bloodthirsty of my whole pack. He'd chaw up a brass possum.

PETER (*emphatically*).—Marse George, he done say not to let dat dog kotch dat possum.

JIM.—Well, whatever Marse George say, I does.

GEORGE (*coming back from left wing holding possum up by the tail. Laughs and swings the possum back and forth while the crowd grin and watch him, wondering what he is going to do*).—Who wants this possum?

CROWD (*shouting and laughing*).—Here! Here! Give him here! (*The dog lunges toward him but Jim holds him back.*) Let the dog have him!

GEORGE.—Hold your bags! (*Swings the possum and chants the refrain.*) "Kotch dat possum." (*He throws it in Peter's bag, who closes it and hands it to George.*)

GEORGE.—A song, boys, let's have a song.

DICKY LEE (*looking at the bag and saying in an aside to George*).—Why, George, where's the possum? He isn't in the bag.

GEORGE (*laying the bag down and looking at it*).—That's so. The little varmint must have got away.

(*Crowd with George and Dick form in line at back of stage, march back and forth and sing, "Kotch dat possum."*)

SONG—KOTCH DAT POSSUM

TUNE: *Carve dat Possum*

De possum meat am good to eat,
    Kotch him in de bag;
You'll always find him good and sweet,
    Kotch him in de bag;
My dog did bark and I went to see,
    Kotch him in de bag;
And dar was a possum up dat tree,
    Kotch him in de bag.

Chorus: Kotch dat possum, kotch dat possum, children,
    Kotch dat possum, kotch him in de bag;
Oh, kotch dat possum, kotch dat possum, children,
    Kotch dat possum, kotch him in de bag.

I reach up for to pull him in,
    Kotch him in de bag;
De possum he begin to grin,
    Kotch him in de bag.
I carried him home and dress him off,
    Kotch him in de bag,
I hung him dat night in de frost,
    Kotch him in de bag.

Chorus: Kotch dat possum, kotch dat possum, children,
    Kotch dat possum, kotch him in de bag;
Oh, kotch dat possum, kotch dat possum, children,
    Kotch dat possum, kotch him in de bag.

[*Curtain*]

EPISODE IV: THE MAYFAIR

George Washington and Sally Fairfax, the Planter's Daughter

CHARACTERS

GEORGE WASHINGTON.
SALLY FAIRFAX.
GEORGE MASON.
MARY CARY.
ROBIN WASHINGTON.
BETTY WASHINGTON.
DICKY LEE.
FRANCES MASON.
LANGY DADE.
JANE CARLYLE.
LEWIS WILLIS.
MARTHA CARTER.
JACK WASHINGTON.
NELLY THORNTON.
GEORGE LEWIS.
MILDRED WASHINGTON.
FIELDING LAWRENCE.
SALLY FITZHUGH.
WILLIAM BUSTLE.
BIG BEAR, Indian Prince.
MARGARET ANDERSON.
LITTLE PETER, Slave Boy.
CONSTABLE.
BAKER.
Farmer boys, Indians, bond children, pickanninnies, etc.

Stage setting: Corner of the fair grounds. Stalls at back with articles for sale, guns, ammunition, many-colored blankets, Indian baskets and pottery, knives, chains, bells, combs, and tin mirrors.

Foodstuffs at one stall, front right. William Bustle selling bread, little cakes, and fish.

Pillory stands at left back; Maypole center. Drop curtain across center of stage which may be lowered to shut out the stalls.

Game of quoits front left.

Costumes: For Indian costumes see Episode V; for bond children, Episode II; for farmer boys, Episode I; for pickaninnies, Episode III.

Colonial costumes (Chubb), GENTLEMEN: Lavender sateen coat and trousers of the Revolutionary period style, with curled powdered wig and tricornered hat; white stockings, and low black shoes. The wig can be made of cotton batting and the hat of black buckram, finished with gold or lavender cockade.

Colonial costumes (Chubb), LADIES: A full skirt of green voile with overskirt and bodice of white and red figured silkoline; white guimpe; white stockings and low black shoes; straw bonnet-shaped hat, trimmed with red flowers and streamers. The skirt is made full and round; the overskirt, a straight, scant strip gathered into skirt band and caught up at sides. An ordinary short-waisted bodice over a white guimpe laced in front with black ribbons. The hat is trimmed with tissue-paper flowers.

PROCEDURE

Group of boys and girls buying at stalls, bond children and pickaninnies, Big Bear, the young Indian prince, and other Indian boys trading pelts for tin mirrors. The Indians look at themselves in the mirrors with grave satisfaction. George and Dicky Lee look at stalls. See William Bustle. Get up a game of quoits.

Boys playing quoits. George and his boy friends at one peg, a group of farmer boys at other.

Betty Washington and Sally Fairfax and her girl friends go to William's stall to buy some cakes with money George has given Betty. William weighs the cakes, keeps his finger on the scale. Girls nudge each other. They walk away (left center) talking about William and his cheating. Some think they ought to tell on him. Others not. They watch the game of quoits. Cheer George when he beats.

Sudden commotion. Constable leading William to the pillory. Girls surround them, ask what he has done. Accused of short weight by the baker. Girls call George, tell him of William's cheating. Ask him to help free William. George asks the constable to let him go. William wrings his hands and promises to be good. Begs George to save him. George thinks Lawrence will go security for him. William is released. Girls and boys in Maypole dance exeunt.

A curtain may be drawn to shut off the back of the stage leaving the Maypole alone in center.

Reference: CHUBB, PERCIVAL. Festivals and plays. New York, Harper Bros. Planters' children troop onto the stage, form a circle around the pole, and sing the Maypole song. They step forward toward the pole and each takes a streamer in his hand—boys red, girls white, alternately. Then the winding begins. Boys bow to partners, girls curtsy, boys stand still and girls move out and in between them with a skipping step. At certain notes in the music a stop is made in front of partners. Boys bow and girls drop a deep curtsy. When the first round has been made, girls unweave in and out. The air of Robin Adair can be used for the Maypole dance with good effect, salute to partner occurring on long accented notes.

DIALOGUE (See Procedure)

(*George and Dicky Lee are walking about.*)

DICK (*to George*).—Well, look there, George, if there isn't William Bustle selling cakes at one of those stalls.

GEORGE (*to Dick*).—Yes; he sells them for his mother. (*Joe Hopper passes.*)

DICKEY LEE (*to Joe Hopper*).—Hi there, Joe, who you with?

JOE HOPPER.—Some of us farmer boys. Want a game of quoits?

DICKY LEE.—All right. Where are the pegs set?

JOE HOPPER.—Down by the pillory.

GEORGE.—We'll get some of our crowd and meet you there. (*They walk over to the game of quoits.*)

DICK (*pointing to the pillory*).—What's the pillory doing here on the fair grounds?

GEORGE.—They've had so much cheating they're bound to stop it. Anyone who underweighs his bread or cake or fish goes into the pillory. They've tested every weight on the grounds to be sure they're right.

DICKY LEE (*meeting Langy Dade and Fielding Lewis*).—Come on, boys, let's have a game of quoits. Joe Hopper and his crowd are joining us. (*They are joined by the farmer boys and the game begins. For a description of this game, see Appendix.*)

BETTY WASHINGTON (*with Sally Fairfax and a crowd of planters' daughters coming up to the game. Aside to George as the others watch*).—George, did you know William Bustle was here selling cakes?

GEORGE.—Yes; they're poor and he's trying to help by selling his mother's cakes. Why don't you buy some, Betty? Here's some money. Lawrence says his father's laid up with the rheumatism and can't work, so his mother makes cakes and William sells them.

BETTY.—Oh, George, you're the kindest and best of any of us Washingtons, not even excepting your beloved Lawrence. I should think you'd hate William Bustle.

DICKY LEE (*coming up in time to hear the last remark*).—Oh, you needn't worry about George, Betty; he always comes out on top. You should have seen him sitting on top of William in their famous fight. (*All laugh.*)

BETTY WASHINGTON (*to Sally Fairfax*).—Come on, Sally, let's buy some cakes of William.

SALLY FAIRFAX.—Oh, let's; I'm so hungry.

JANE CARLYLE (*who is behind, and has been talking to Langy Dade*).—Wait a minute, girls, come back here; I want to tell you something. (*Girls turn back, put heads together.*) Langy says that William Bustle is cheating.

MARY CARY.—George Mason says he sells everything under weight.

MOLLY THORNTON.—The baker is watching him and trying to catch him.

BETTY WASHINGTON.—I wouldn't wonder a bit. It would be just like him. You know how he hurt George. Nearly put out his eye. I wish I could catch him cheating.

FRANCES MASON.—Dicky Lee says that sometimes a baker is dragged on a hurdle through the town with the loaf of bread he has sold under weight tied around his neck. (*Nods her head solemnly.*)

BETTY WASHINGTON.—Let's try William and see; maybe we can catch him at it. (*They go up to William's stall. To William.*) Halloo, William.

ALL THE GIRLS—Hallo, William; how you getting along?

WILLIAM (*sheepishly grinning*).—Good day, ladies; want to buy something?

BETTY WASHINGTON.—Yes; we want some of your mother's cakes.

WILLIAM—How many do you want?

JANE CARLYLE.—How much are they?

WILLIAM.—They're 2 shillings a pound.

SALLY FAIRFAX.—How much are they apiece?

WILLIAM.—I don't sell 'em by the piece. I only sell 'em by weight.

BETTY (*to the girls*).—Let's buy a pound and divide 'em between us. I'll pay for 'em. It's my treat. That is, George gave me the money.

ALL THE GIRLS.—Oh, thank you, Betty, that is nice. Thank George, too. (*William weighs out the cakes and the girls watch him. Betty pays the money and takes the cakes. They turn away. Cross to right front.*)

JANE.—Oh, girls, did you see William Bustle cheating?

BETTY.—Did you see it, Jane?

JANE.—I did. He held his finger on the pan.

SALLY.—I saw it, too. I've heard he cheated, but no one has caught him.

BETTY.—Let's tell the constable.

JANE.—If we do, he'll be punished.

MARY CARY.—He'll be put in the pillory.

BETTY.—Serve him right!

SALLY.—Oh, not that. It'll spoil our Maypole dance.

JANE.—I couldn't dance with a boy we knew standing in the pillory.

BETTY.—But think what he did to George.

JANE.—He'll be caught, anyway, if he goes on cheating. Let's not tell till after the fair is over.

BETTY.—It's too late, then.

SALLY.—How'll we prove it? We'll have to prove it.

JANE.—Let's watch the game and forget it.

BETTY.—Oh, George is winning; come on. (*They stand and watch the game of quoits and clap their hands when George's side wins.*)

SALLY (*to Betty as a sudden commotion occurs in William bustle's stall*).—Oh, look, Betty; the constable is talking to William Bustle. (*All the girls and boys turn toward William's stall.*)

BETTY.—They're arresting him! (*Constable leads William across the stage toward the pillory. He comes near the group of boys and girls, followed by the baker with his tray and a group of people of all sorts who are attending the fair.*)

SALLY (*to the constable*).—What has William done, Constable?

OFFICER.—Done, Miss. He's been short weighin'. He's had the name, and now we've caught him, red handed.

BAKER (*with tray of food, cakes, etc.*).—I been a-watchin' him. I seen him. He puts his finger on the pan and pulls it down.

GEORGE.—Oh, are you sure?

BAKER.—Sure? Didn't I say I seen him, plain as day?

BETTY (*to George*).—We saw him, too, George, but the girls didn't want to tell on him.

GEORGE (*to William*).—Is that true, William?

WILLIAM (*blubbering*).—I only did it once.

GEORGE.—Once? The girls saw you, the baker saw you; that's twice at least.

WILLIAM (*to George*).—Oh, George, if you'll only get me off this time, I'll never do it again.

SALLY (*to William*).—What made you do such a thing, William?

WILLIAM (*to Sally*).—Oh, Miss Sally, please help me. My mother works so hard, we're so poor, I wanted to make more money.

SALLY (*to George*).—Couldn't you ask the constable to let him off this time, George?

GEORGE (*to officer*).—I think William will never cheat again, Constable, if you'll let him go.

OFFICER (*to Baker*).—How about you, Baker, you willin' to let him go?

BAKER.—If he don't sell any more cakes and bread on this fair ground.

WILLIAM.—I promise. (*Officer releases him, he turns to George.*) George, you are a proper lad, after what I did to you. I won't forget the lesson I've learned. (*Goes to his stall, puts food in basket, and leaves at right front. Girls and boys exit right, talking excitedly.*)

DICKY LEE (*to George*).—Well, George, you are a simpleton letting him go, after all he did to you.

SALLY (*to Dicky Lee*).—He did just right.

JANE.—I felt sorry for him.

MARY.—I didn't want him to spoil our dance.

GEORGE.—What he said is true. They are dreadfully poor, and I believe he has learned his lesson.

BETTY (*taking hold of George's arm*).—What a dear you are, George. Always on the side of the under dog. Oh, George, I'm so glad you're my brother.

(*Curtain falls and shuts off the back of the stage, leaving the Maypole in the center. Planters' children troop onto the stage, form a circle around the pole, and sing the Maypole song. They step forward toward the pole and each takes a streamer in his hand—boys red, girls white, alternately. Then the winding begins. Boys bow to partners, girls curtsy, boys stand still and girls move out and in between them with a skipping step. At certain notes in the music a stop is made in front of partners. Boys bow and girls drop a deep curtsy. When the first round has been made, girls unweave in opposite direction. When this round is over girls stand and boys weave in and out. The air of "Robin Adair" can be used for the Maypole dance with good effect, salute to partner occurring on long accented notes.*)

[*Curtain*]

MAYPOLE DANCE

Come, lassie and lad, be blithe and glad, and away to the Maypole hie,
For every fair has a partner there, and the fiddler's standing by.
For Willy shall dance with Jane, and Johnny shall dance with Joan,
    And trip it, trip it, trip it, trip it, trip it up and down,
    And trip it, trip it, trip it, trip it, trip it up and down.

"You're out" says Dick, "Not I" says Nick, "'Twas the fiddler play'd it wrong,"
"'Tis true" says Hugh, and so says Sue, and so says every one;
The fiddler then began, to play the tune again,
    And every girl did trip it, trip it, trip it to the men,
    And every girl did trip it, trip it, trip it to the men.

"Good night" says Harry, "Good night" says Mary, "Good night" says Poll to John,
"Good night" says Sue to stalwart Hugh, "Good night" says every one.
Some walk'd and some did run; some loiter'd on the way,
    And bound themselves by promises twelve, to meet the next holiday,
    And bound themselves by promises twelve, to meet the next holiday.

In *High school songbooks*. By Gertrude B. Parsons. New York, Silver, Burdette & Co., pp. 98-99.)

THE MAYPOLE

From "The Westminster Drollery,"   Old English Melody

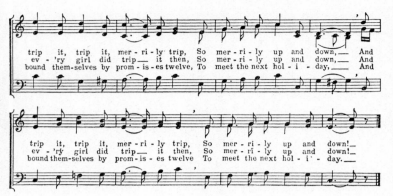

trip it, trip it, mer-ri-ly trip, So mer-ri-ly up and down,__ And
ev-'ry girl did trip__ it then, So mer-ri-ly up and down,__ And
bound them-selves by prom-is-es twelve, To meet the next hol-i-day, And

trip it, trip it, mer-ri-ly trip, So mer-ri-ly up and down!__
ev-'ry girl did trip__ it then, So mer-ri-ly up and down!__
bound them-selves by prom-is-es twelve To meet the next hol-i-day.__

ROBIN ADAIR

C. KEPPEL　　　　　　　　　　　　　　　　　　　　　Celtic Air

1. What's this dull town to me? Rob-in's not near. What was't I wished to see,
2. What made th'as-sem-bly shine? Rob-in A-dair. What made the ball so fine?
3. But now thou'rt cold to me, Rob-in A-dair. But now thou'rt cold to me,

What wish'd to hear? Where's all the joy and mirth, That made this town a
Rob-in__ was there; What, when the play was o'er, What made__ my
Rob-in A-dair; Yet him I loved so well, Still in__ my

heav'n on earth? Oh! they're all fled with thee, Rob-in A-dair.
heart so sore? Oh! it was part-ing with Rob-in A-dair.
heart shall dwell; Oh! I can ne'er for-get Rob-in A-dair.

EPISODE V: SURVEYING

George Washington and Big Bear, the Young Indian Prince

CHARACTERS

GEORGE WASHINGTON.

BIG BEAR, Indian Prince.

GEORGE WILLIAM FAIRFAX.

HENRY ⎱
BILL　⎰ Rangers.

Two German boys, aged 10 and 8; one little German boy, aged 5; Indians.

Stage setting: The forest at evening. A German's cabin at left back. A large screen with triangle at top to represent the gable end of a cabin, covered with unbleached cotton, painted to represent logs, window on left side and door on right. Door should be set in a frame so it will open and shut. Screen may be set across the left back corner of the stage. Background of trees, same as used in Episodes I and III.

Costumes: George and Fairfax in ranger costumes with cocked hats. Rangers in ranger costumes with homespun caps. Children in ragged homespun, bare-footed and dirty.

Properties: A sextant and large scale.

PROCEDURE

Big Bear enters left and prowls around the cabin. Other young Indians join him. Make signs of being hungry. Big Bear pushes open the door of cabin and creeps in. Comes out with a kettle of soup and a loaf of bread. Dog follows to door barking. Children pull him back and shut the door. Indians squat on the ground around the kettle, fishing out bits of meat and soaking bread in the soup. Children watch from the window. Indians start away. Children open door, dog rushes out at Big Bear, who hits the dog on the head and kicks him into the bushes. Indians exeunt. Children run out, look at dog, cry, run into the house and reappear at door, oldest boy in front with gun, other children behind him.

Enter George with surveying party. Sees children, finds out their trouble. The party make camp, feed the children, and George resuscitates the dog. They are on the lookout for the Indians. Decide to feed them if they return. They come, are fed, and then they dance. All join in at the close of the dance.

DIALOGUE. (*After pantomime of Big Bear and Dog.*) (*See Procedure*)

OLDEST BOY. (*Looking in the bushes at the dog.*)—They've killed our dog. (*Howls.*)

SECOND BOY (*crying*).—I'd like to kill them.

THIRD BOY (*crying*).—Let's kill 'em.

OLDEST BOY.—I'll get the gun, and if they come back I'll shoot 'em.

THIRD BOY.—I'm hungry.

OLDEST BOY.—They et up all our soup.

SECOND BOY.—And took our bread.

(*They go into the cabin. Oldest boy comes to the door with a gun, the other children behind him. Enter George and Fairfax, from left, with old Peter carrying surveying instruments, followed by two rangers, Henry and Bill.*)

GEORGE (*walking on to center*).—Here's the place. (*Looks around at the cabin. Sees small boy with gun in open door of cabin. Two smaller boys behind.*) What the devil does this mean?

OLDEST BOY.—If you touch my brothers, I'll shoot you.

GEORGE.—Here, here, put up that gun. What ails you, any-way?

OLDEST BOY.—An Injun killed our dog.

SECOND BOY (*crying*).—They ate up all our soup.

GEORGE.—Where's your folks; gone after the Indian?

OLDEST BOY.—No, sir; our folks has gone to town to settle our claim. (*Children all begin to cry. The others stand looking on and then begin to laugh.*)

FAIRFAX (*to George*).—Ho, ho, they're afraid we surveyors will drive 'em off. They must have been in a hurry to go and leave these children all alone.

GEORGE (*to children*).—Here, stop your snivellin'; crying won't bring your folks back.

OLDEST BOY.—Our food's all et up.

GEORGE (*to children*).—Oh, well, we've got food. You can have some of ours.

SECOND BOY.—Our dog's dead.

GEORGE (*to rangers*).—Let's get camp started. Get the children to help you.

HENRY (*to the children, as they all move to the center of stage*).—Do you know how to build a fire? You want to get me some dry sticks? I'll get some water from the brook. (*Little boys gather firewood.*)

GEORGE (*to Fairfax*).—I'm going to get that dog. He may not be dead. (*Goes into bushes and drags out the dog, which may be trussed with light cords so he won't move. Calls to children.*) Here, get me some water. Your dog isn't dead. (*Children run with water. They douse the dog, who revives slowly. Cuts the cords. They carry him into the cabin. Children come out and all gather* around the camp fire. Surveyors take food out of knapsacks and share with children. Be careful here to speak first and eat afterward.)

FAIRFAX (to George).—You're quite a hero, George. Sonny here can't take his eyes off you.

GEORGE (to children).—Here's another cookie for you children. You must go into the house and get to bed, now (children go into cabin and shut the door); and you too, Peter. (Peter rolls in his blanket and sleeps by the fire. George lowers his voice.) You know, boys, I think that was Big Bear, the old chief's son, who was here to-night. He's always up to some mischief, but I don't think he's vicious. He's out to-night with some of his chronies foraging, and they're the biggest thieves in the country. I believe he'll come back here to-night after food, and if we feed him well, he'll go off. There's one thing I must warn you about. One of his favorite tricks. He'll want to shake hands with you. And when he has your hand in his he'll squeeze it so hard you'll yell. All the young bucks like to see white men cringe. If he tries it on me I mean to grapple with him because I'm stronger than he is, but unless you have cultivated a specially strong grip, refuse his hand.

(The door of the cabin opens and the three little boys come up to the fire.)

OLDEST BOY (to George).—We-all wants you to have our bed. We air sleepin' by the fireplace. (The others begin to laugh, but George gets up quickly and goes with the children into the cabin.)

FAIRFAX.—Well, what had we better do about the Indians? To tell the truth, I don't think the young savages are quite as peaceful as George does. Nevertheless he knows more about the Indians in these woods than I do. I'm willing to take his word on it.

GEORGE (coming out almost at once).—Any of you want a bed? (All begin to laugh.) The bed is a little straw on the floor with a dirty blanket over it. They're afraid the Indians will come back, but I told them we'd be right here till morning.

HENRY.—I think we'd better lie here in our blankets and keep our ears open.

BILL.—All right. I'm willing.

GEORGE.—You boys go to sleep and I'll keep the first watch. When an hour is up I'll call you. (All roll in blankets and sleep by fire. George walks back and forth in front of the fire. Big Bear watches and peers out from behind a tree. Finally George rouses the others, and they hide behind the cabin. In a moment Big Bear crosses the clearing and comes up to the fire alone.)

GEORGE (to Fairfax).—That is Big Bear. You see he's quite friendly. (George and Fairfax step out of hiding and boldly walk to the fire, rangers and Peter following.)

GEORGE (to Big Bear).—How, Big Bear. (Big Bear grins and holds out his hand. George grips his hand and Big Bear grunts, pulls away his hand, and shakes it up and down. His friends come up to the fire and all sit in a circle, surveyors in center. Big Bear makes motions for something to eat. Rangers take out food from knapsacks and pass it. All the Indians eat. White men eat with them. Big Bear gets up and motions to George that they will dance. George grins, nods his head, and claps his hands. Indian dance follows.)

BIG BEAR (stands and motions to braves).—Ha! ha! ho-e-oh! (Indians rise one after another and begin to chant and circle round the fire, keeping time to the music. George and George Fairfax

stand in center watching. Indians swing out in line at the back of stage. George and George Fairfax in the middle. Rangers at each end. They march back and forth across the stage chanting and making appropriate gestures. See directions for Indian dance.)

[Curtain]

INDIAN WAR DANCE

Directions

A scout appears crouching and looking for footprints. Another follows him. Both show great caution. Scout 1 finds a footprint in center of room, carefully brushes loose dirt from it, beckons the other. Both examine it closely, listen at the ground, seem to discuss its direction. Scout 1 rises, unfastens his blanket which has been tied around his body, swings it and throws it in the direction the footprint is pointing (i. e., the direction of the final exit). This is a signal to his comrades in ambush. They rush in to drumbeats with the step used frequently at the opening of war dances. Knees are slightly bent, the body is carried forward and the heels are raised slightly. The step is short, quick and shuffling, and the feet never leave the ground. They form a large circle around the footprint.

Dance

Have children count off in twos.

Measures 1-2.—Touch right toe forward, knee slightly bent (count 1), lower heel (count 2). Same, left (counts 3-4).
Repeat same.

Measures 3-4.—Repeat, moving backward.

Measures 1-4.—Repeat all.
Repeated.

Measures 1-10.—Step sideward right, bend body slightly to the right (counts 1-2).
Bring left foot to right with a stamp, straightening body, (counts 3-4).
Repeat nine times.

Measures 11-12.—No. 1's move to center, examine footprint, striking the ground with tomahawks and yelling sharply "hi-a!" on the fourth beat of the twelfth measure.
At the same time No. 2's fall back to large circle.

Measures 13-14.—No. 2's go into center with striking and yelling while No. 1's go out.

Measures 15-18.—Repeat last four measures.

Measures 19-24.—Indian step; similar to skipping step (hippity-hop) but with high knee action and a very short step covering little ground.
With this step, the large circle is formed and moves to the right with occasional leaps while yelling and brandishing tomahawks, increasing in speed and excitement. As the first scout comes a second time to point in the circle nearest the direction of the footprint, he breaks away and followed by all the braves, single file, takes to the "trail" on a run. The last four measures should be repeated as often as is necessary to get all the warriors off the floor.
The effect of drumbeats may be given by a low A on the piano with four regular beats to a measure, the first of each being sharply accented.

PART II

PROLOGUE

(To be recited by one of the pupils)

And now, after 200 years have rolled away since the birth of George Washington, we meet under the Stars and Stripes which symbolize the great Republic which he founded. We have brought with us the children who knew him in his boyhood to join us in this celebration, under the American flag. (Address to the Flag, suspended over the front of the platform.)

OLD FLAG

By HUBBARD PARKER

What shall I say to you, Old Flag?
You are so grand in every fold,
So linked with mighty deeds of old,
So calm, so still, so firm, so true,
My throat swells at the sight of you, Old Flag.

What of the men who lifted you, Old Flag,
Upon the top of Bunker Hill?
'Mid shock and roar and crash and scream,
Who crossed the Delaware's frozen stream,
Who starved, who fought, who bled, who died,
That you might float in glorious pride, Old Flag.

What is your mission now, Old Flag?
What but to set all people free,
To rid the world of misery,
To guard the right, avenge the wrong,
And gather in one joyful throng
Beneath your folds in close embrace
All burdened ones of every race, Old Flag.

NOTE.—The chief actors in the episodes, dressed in character costumes, take the same positions as in the first prologue. Each holding an American flag. At the first note of the march, the girls step into the girl's line of march, Sally Fairfax leading, and the boys into the boy's line, George Washington leading. The time of this episode is the present.

EPISODE VI: UNDER THE AMERICAN FLAG

THE FLAG MARCH

Characters.—Children from different rooms may participate in this exercise, with each room responsible for one of the movements, if the stage is large and can accommodate a large number of children. The march may also be given with the members of one class or a single room with pleasing effect.

Stage setting.—The stage is draped with flags. Either a bust of Washington on a high pedestal should be placed in the center of the stage or a large picture of Washington should be hung at the back and draped with flags.

Arrangement of pupils.—Pupils are arranged in two groups, boys on right side, girls on left, lined up according to height, the tallest first.

Holding the flag.—Flags are carried in the right hand, the staff resting against the right shoulder at an angle of 45°, with the banner unfurled over the right shoulder.

Music.—The words to the choruses of the songs are given on pages 664-5. The children sing the songs indicated in each movement, usually the chorus only. Victrola records may be substituted or used as accompaniment to the children's voices. See lists of Victor records in references.

Drills and rehearsals.—Plenty of time should be given to the preparation of this episode. The beauty of the exercise depends upon the precision and accuracy of movement in marching as well as upon the rendition of the songs.

PROCEDURE

FIRST MOVEMENT, SONG NO. 1 AND SONG NO. 14

Line enters at back of stage, boys right, girls left. They march across the back of stage to opposite corners, girls' line passing in front of boys' line. Leaders at back corners turn toward front, march to front corners, turn toward middle, meet, and stop, forming a line across the front of stage. They stand and sing song No. 14 with appropriate gestures. The verses may be omitted and only the last chorus sung. The audience may be asked to join in this chorus.

SECOND MOVEMENT, SONG NO. 3 AND SONG NO. 5

At the first note of *Yankee Doodle* the lines turn, boys toward right, girls toward left, and follow leaders to front corners, girls' line passing in front of boys' line. Turn at corners and march to back corners, turn toward middle back, meet at middle, forming couples as they march down center of stage, two by two, to middle front. Here they separate, turning, boys to right, girls to left, forming wide circles gradually winding up into a spiral with leaders in center and smaller children on the outside. They keep moving round and round in this formation singing song No. 5, holding the last note, full and strong, and raising the flags high above their heads.

THIRD MOVEMENT, SONG NO. 11 AND SONG NO. 2

At the first note of Dixie the children in the spiral turn about face, and reverse the direction of marching. This leaves the smallest children on the outside as leaders. Boys swing across to opposite side, forming large open circle, girls to opposite side in large open circle. Repeat the Dixie chorus. At the first note of the repeat the children in the large circles right-about face, circle once in opposite direction, and the leaders swing to back corners of stage, move toward middle back, and meet there. The leaders hold up their flags tip to tip, forming an arch. The next couple just behind step through the arch, stop in front of leaders, and raise their flags tip to tip. Third couple follows, then fourth and fifth, until all have passed under the arch. This leaves the smallest couple in front. Children resume position of flags and couples separate, boys marching to right front corner, girls to left front corner, forming a line across the front of the stage. Here they stand and sing song No. 2, Washington and the Flag, with appropriate gestures, turning toward the back and marching off the stage on either side singing the last two lines of the chorus.

[*Finale*]

MUSIC SUGGESTED FOR THE FLAG MARCH
FATHER OF THE LAND WE LOVE

By GEORGE M. COHAN

Every little lad and lass,
Boys and girls of every class,
Here beneath the flag of stripe and star.
From the time they start to school,
When they learn the golden rule,
Always have been proud of what they are.
And every day with lessons done,
They sing their song of Washington,
A song of love that reaches near and far.

Chorus

First in war,
First in peace,
First in the hearts of his countrymen.
That is the story of Washington,
That is the glory of Washington,
His spirit is here.
His spirit is here.
He's standing, commanding above.
In word and deed we follow the lead
Of the Father of the land we love.

When to manhood comes the youth
With the knowledge and the truth,
Of the Revolutionary fray.
Proud he is to be a son
Of Immortal Washington,
Sacred is the memory of his day.
Whenever drums begin to roll,
Within the Nation's heart and soul,
A patriotic something seems to say:

1. FLAG DAY

Sing a song about our flag,
See the colors waving high.
All salute, all salute,
When the flag passes by.

2. WASHINGTON AND THE FLAG

George Washington, George Washington,
We sing to-day of you;
You fought to make our country free;
You were our leader true.
George Washington, George Washington,
We sing to-day of you;
And wave on high our starry flag;
Our own red, white and blue.

3. YANKEE DOODLE

Yankee Doodle went to town,
Upon a little pony;
He stuck a feather in his cap
And called it Macaroni.
Tra la la la la la la;
Tra la la la la la
Tra la la la la la la,
He called it Macaroni.

4. HAIL, COLUMBIA

Chorus: Firm, united, let us be,
Rallying round our liberty;
As a band of brothers joined,
Peace and safety we shall find.

5. THE STAR-SPANGLED BANNER

Chorus: Oh, say, does that Star-Spangled Banner
yet wave
O'er the land of the free, and the home
of the brave.

6. YANKEE DOODLE

Chorus: Yankee Doodle keep it up,
Yankee Doodle dandy,
Mind the music and the step,
And with the girls be handy.

7. BATTLE HYMN OF THE REPUBLIC

Chorus: Glory! glory! Hallelujah!
Glory, glory! Hallelujah!
Glory, glory! Hallelujah!
His truth is marching on.

8. THE FLAG

Chorus: The love of the flag with its crimson bars,
And its field of blue with the spangled stars;
The love of the flag with its crimson bars
And its field of blue with the spangled stars.

9. TO THEE MY OWN AMERICA

Chorus: America! America!
Beloved home to me,
May God who led thy patriots
Forever keep thee free.

10. OUR COUNTRY'S FLAG

Chorus: Then, hurrah for the flag, our country's flag.
Its stripes and white stars too,
There is no flag in any land
Like our own red, white, and blue.

11. DIXIE LAND

Chorus: Den I wish I was in Dixie,
Hooray! Hooray!
In Dixie Land I'll take my stand
To lib and die in Dixie.
Away! Away!
Away down south in Dixie,
Away! Away!
Away down south in Dixie.

12. AMERICA THE BEAUTIFUL

Chorus: America! America! God shed his grace on thee
And crown thy good with brotherhood
From sea to shining sea.

13. TENTING ON THE OLD CAMP GROUND

Chorus: Many are the hearts that are weary to-night,
Wishing for the war to cease,
Many are the hearts looking for the right
To see the dawn of peace.
Tenting to-night,
Tenting to-night,
Tenting on the old camp ground.

14. COLUMBIA, THE GEM OF THE OCEAN

Chorus: When borne by the red, white, and blue,
When borne by the red, white, and blue,
Thy banners make tyranny tremble,
When borne by the red, white, and blue.
Chorus: The boast of the red, white, and blue,
The boast of the red, white, and blue,
With her flag proudly floating before her,
The boast of the red, white and blue.
Chorus: Three cheers for the red, white, and blue,
Three cheers for the red, white, and blue,
The Army and Navy forever,
Three cheers for the red, white, and blue.

SUGGESTIONS FOR PRODUCTION

The pupils may assist greatly in the preparation for the pageant by preparing scenery and drop curtains and by helping make the costumes and furniture used in the different scenes.

In Hobby's School, Episode I, the rough benches and teacher's table used in the schoolroom scene may be made in the school workshop.

In the bond girl episode the furniture used in the lawyer's office may be made in manual-training periods. The making of the old-fashioned lantern used in Episode III during the possum hunt, the making of the pillory, Maypole, and stalls at the Mayfair will give the boys in manual training some interesting projects to work out, as will the representation of the German cottage in the surveying episode. This may be made like a screen, covered over with cotton cloth, and paintd to represent a log cabin. A door hung within a frame should be included. In this way the expense of providing the costumes and stage settings will be minimized, and valuable lessons in construction work will be taught.

The trees that are used in each episode may be secured by the pupils in the woods and mounted on standards with pans of water in each standard. In this way the trees will keep fresh and green for a considerable time.

The shifting of scenery may be done by the pupils behind the front curtain or in view of the audience and will require but a moment of time between each scene.

MUSIC REFERENCES

The following music is available on phonograph records:

AMERICA THE BEAUTIFUL (*Ward*)
BATTLE HYMN OF THE REPUBLIC (*Howe*)
COLUMBIA, THE GEM OF THE OCEAN (*à Becket*)
DIXIE (*Emmett*)
HAIL, COLUMBIA (*Phile*)
MAYPOLE DANCE
STAR-SPANGLED BANNER (*Key-Smith*)
TENTING ON THE OLD CAMP GROUND (*Kittredge*)
TRAMP, TRAMP, TRAMP (*Root*)
VIRGINIA REELS (*American*)
WAR DANCE (*Cheyenne*)
YANKEE DOODLE

SONGS

12. AMERICA THE BEAUTIFUL. *In* The Music Hour, vol. 5. By Osbourne McConathy, W. Otto Miessner, and others. Boston, Silver, Burdette & Co., 1928, p. 162.

7. BATTLE HYMN OF THE REPUBLIC. *In* The Music Hour, vol. 5. By Osbourne McConathy, W. Otto Miessner, and others. Boston, Silver, Burdette & Co., 1928, p. 160.

14. COLUMBIA, THE GEM OF THE OCEAN. *In* The Music Hour, vol. 4. By Osbourne McConathy, W. Otto Miessner, and others. Boston, Silver, Burdette & Co., 1928, p. 144.

9. DIXIE LAND. *In* The Music Hour, vol. 4. By Osbourne McConathy, W.

Otto Miessner, and others. Boston, Silver, Burdette & Co., 1928. p. 148.

8. (THE) FLAG. *In* Wooster Patriotic Guide and Speaker, Chicago, Ill. p. 288.

1. FLAG DAY. *In* The Music Hour in the Kindergarten and First Grade. Boston, Silver, Burdette & Co., 1928. p. 153.

FLORA. *In* Festivals and plays. By Percival Chubb. New York, Harper Bros., 1912. p. 190.

4. HAIL, COLUMBIA. *In* The Music Hour, vol. 4. By Osbourne McConathy, W. Otto Miessner, and others. Boston, Silver, Burdette & Co., 1928. p. 78.

MOUNT VERNON BELLS. *In* New common-school songbook. By Laura Rountree Smith, Arthur Schuckai, and others. Chicago, Beckley-Cardy Co., 1917. p. 89-90.

10. OUR COUNTRY'S FLAG. *In* Wooster Patriotic Guide and Speaker, Chicago, Ill., p. 297.

5-6. STAR-SPANGLED BANNER. *In* The Music Hour, vol. 4. By Osbourne McConathy, W. Otto Miessner, and others. Boston, Silver, Burdette & Co., 1928. p. 150.

13. TENTING ON THE OLD CAMP GROUND. *In* New common-school songbook. By Laura Rountree Smith, Arthur Schuckai, and others. Chicago, Beckley-Cardy Co., 1917. p. 139-140.

11. TO THEE, MY OWN AMERICA. *In* Wooster Patriotic Guide and Speaker, Wooster & Co., Publishers, Chicago, Ill. p. 294.

2. WASHINGTON AND THE FLAG. *In* The Music Hour in the Kindergarten and First Grade. Boston, Silver, Burdette & Co., 1928. p. 151.

3. YANKEE DOODLE. *In* The Music Hour, vol. 4. By Osbourne McConathy, W. Otto Miessner, and others. Boston, Silver, Burdette & Co., 1928. p. 123.

WASHINGTON RETURNS

A Pageant in Four Episodes and Eight Scenes Adaptable to a Cast of 100 to 500 Students of Primary and Grammar Grades and High School

By KATHLEEN READ COONTZ

An historical pageant is a manifestation of national consciousness. While the author may prepare the text, the dignity and beauty of the pageant depends upon the presentation. In pageantry less is said than done; and in the doing even the smallest part contributes to the whole. If every participant in WASHINGTON RETURNS *will feel himself a character of the times and reveal through his pantomime the spirit of the times, then indeed will the presentation of the pageant be an expression of the community's soul.*

If the enactment of WASHINGTON RETURNS *stimulates more genuine interest in, and deeper devotion to, the life and character of the great statesman it will have achieved a worthy mission. If, in addition, the pageant is instrumental in lighting new fires of patriotism in youthful—and older—bosoms it will have fulfilled the author's highest purpose.*

The asterisk in the text is used to denote authentic utterances, although not spoken necessarily under the circumstances enacted.

SYNOPSIS OF PAGEANT

PRELUDE SCENE

School children of Today are studying about Washington in their History lesson. A small visitor (who later becomes POSTERITY) falls asleep and WASHINGTON appears to her from behind the flag. HISTORY gives her Prologue and taking the child by the hand leads her, and the audience, through the scenes of Washington's life.

———

FIRST EPISODE—*THE YOUTH AND ADVENTURE*

This Episode with a Prologue by ADVENTURE is founded on WASHINGTON's love of Adventure.

SCENE 1—SEA DREAMS

Deals with his boyhood ambition for a sea life and his mother's final denial of plans.

SCENE 2—THE COURIER

Pictures his early adventures among Indians.

———

SECOND EPISODE—*THE MAN AND HOME*

This Episode, with a Prologue by HOME, reveals the romantic and home loving side of WASHINGTON's nature.

SCENE 1—COURTSHIP

The incident of his meeting with WIDOW CUSTIS.

SCENE 2—MT. VERNON

At home with his family.

THIRD EPISODE—*THE GENERAL AND FAME*

This Episode, with a Prologue by FAME, is founded on the period in history that brought fame to our hero.

SCENE 1—THE GLORY OF THE REVOLUTION

Pictures WASHINGTON in his elevation to Commander-in-Chief of the Continental Army.

SCENE 2—THE GLOOM OF THE REVOLUTION

Shows him in the "darkest days of the War." *Valley Forge.*

———

FOURTH EPISODE—*THE STATESMAN AND IMMORTALITY*

SCENE 1—A NATION'S HOMAGE

His triumphal journey to the Presidency.

SCENE 2—FRIENDSHIP'S TRIBUTE

One of the closing scenes of the great life, depicting his last birthday, when friends gathered to voice his immortality.

POSTLUDE SCENE

Before the final curtain this scene gathers together the entire cast in groups representing ADVENTURE, HOME, and FAME and a pantomime is enacted by the Symbolic characters revealing the deeper meaning of the pageant. WASHINGTON RETURNS *to us through the centuries bearing* POSTERITY *in his arms.* FAME crowns him, HISTORY places MARTHA WASHINGTON by his side and POSTERITY caresses her. HOME keeps a tender guardianship over all, and ADVENTURE dances in and out among Indians and Sailors, imparting dash and thrill to the picture.

SYMBOLIC CHARACTERS
POSTERITY

| HISTORY | HOME |
| ADVENTURE | FAME |

THE PAGEANT
———

PRELUDE

Time—The Present

Place—Any American schoolroom

———

Speaking Characters

GEORGE WASHINGTON
THE TEACHER
CHILD [who later becomes Posterity.]
GROUPS
Ten or more pupils of today with good singing voices.

———

[*The stage is set to indicate a modern schoolroom. Blackboard at rear of stage contains the words:*

GEORGE WASHINGTON
FATHER OF OUR COUNTRY

The teacher's desk at center of stage. On the left is a recitation bench. On the right wall, a little to the rear of the stage, *hangs a large American flag. The curtain rises on the recitation of the history lesson. Teacher sits at her desk, pupils on the bench. On the end of the bench nearest the audience the* CHILD *is seen, sitting, apparently, with an older sister, who has her arm around the little one.*]

TEACHER [*rising*]—The Principal has called for your history reports. Please continue your study, children, while I am absent from the room. [*She turns to the* CHILD *and addresses her.*] Would you like to sit at my desk while I am gone, little visitor? [*The* CHILD *nods shyly and takes Teacher's place as she leaves the room.*]

FIRST PUPIL [*reading aloud*]—George Washington was a high-spirited youth and sought adventure.

SECOND PUPIL [*reading aloud in a sing-song way*]—He loved his home and was a devoted husband and father.

CHILD [*interestedly*]—Who was George Washington, Sister?

THIRD PUPIL [*from book*]—He was a great soldier and a wise statesman.

CHILD [*persistently*]—Where is he now?

PUPILS [*in unison*]—DEAD!

[*Pupils go back to their studying. The* CHILD *slumps down sleepily on the desk. Silence. The great flag stirs and is drawn back disclosing* WASHINGTON *clad in his General's uniform of buff and blue. He holds the flag back with one hand, the other rests on his sword. The* CHILD *sits up and rubs her eyes. The pupils are bent on their lessons and do not look up.*]

CHILD [*pointing to the flag*]—Why, there he is now!

[WASHINGTON *releases the flag and it falls, again concealing him.*]

PUPILS [*looking up*]—Who?

CHILD [*excitedly*]—GEORGE WASHINGTON! I saw him. [*Pupils laugh.*]

FIRST PUPIL—That is only the flag, Betty.

[*The pupils again go back to their studying. The* CHILD *lays her head on the desk. Again, the flag stirs and* WASHINGTON *steps out in front of it. The* CHILD *sits up, looks at him and rubs her eyes. He smiles and crossing over to the* CHILD *holds out his hand. Hesitatingly, she takes it and rises from her seat. Together, they walk slowly across the stage to center front. The stage curtain falls behind them and the remainder of the Prelude is given before the curtain, which provides the necessary time for arranging stage for Scene 1. The simple sets should be shifted without talking and with the smallest possible amount of noise.*]

CHILD [*still looking up into* WASHINGTON'S *face*]—W-h-y [*drawn out*] they said you were dead!

[WASHINGTON *smiles and shakes his head as he looks down into the little face.* HISTORY *strides out with dignity from stage left. The* CHILD *drops* WASHINGTON'S *hand and stands before her, viewing her with awe.*]

CHILD—Who are you?

[HISTORY *unrolls the long scroll, views it with a solemn eye, lifts it towards the audience and delivers the* PROLOGUE *in the Prelude scene.*]

I AM HISTORY!

What I inscribe herein will never fade,
But glow in solemn truth
For children yet unborn!
I write of Wars where fields run red with blood.
Of Peace, which triumphs still.
I write Adventure with a flourish bold,
The march of Progress note.
I write of Life and Death and Deeds—
I transfix Time and Tide!
Accept me, CHILD with eager mind!
Behind your youth I stretch
A tapestry of years—
TURN BACK . . .

[HISTORY *moves over to the* CHILD *and traces her finger along the writing on the scroll.*]

HISTORY [*with a stately gesture towards* WASHINGTON]—
I have writ his name many times, little Child.

CHILD—Do you ever write my name down there?

HISTORY [*nodding gravely*]—My book is writ for you.

CHILD [*looking from* HISTORY *to* WASHINGTON]—But, *you don't* know *my* name, do you?

HISTORY [*with a gesture towards the audience*]—*They* call you by one name, *I* call you by another.

[HISTORY *lays one hand on* WASHINGTON'S *arm and takes the* CHILD'S *hand with the other. They begin to walk slowly towards stage left. Just before they reach the exit they pause and the* CHILD *tugs at* HISTORY'S *hand and looks up into her face.*]

CHILD—What name do you call me by?

HISTORY—I call you POSTERITY, my dear. You are the golden link in the chain of Life.

[*The Group passes off the stage.*
HISTORY *holding* POSTERITY *by the hand appears from stage left and stations herself at the left of curtain.* ADVENTURE *whirls out from stage right and rushes across the stage once or twice, lifting Neptune's trident high above his head.*]

POSTERITY [*tugging at* HISTORY'S *hand*]—Who is that bold boy?

HISTORY—He writes magic happenings on my scroll for you.

[ADVENTURE *darts to the front of the stage and speaks her Prologue.*]

I AM Adventure!
My ancient call is known to many men,
A wild persistent urge.
It breaks into the peaceful hours of night
And scatters plans by day.
It lures feet on and on the magic road,
Through desert wastes, on peak and by the silent sea.
Comfort and ease I scorn and hardships woo!
I laugh into the solemn face of Death,
And court new thrills.
Child, of a country carved from Wilderness,
Dost know that I have walked besides
The Heroes of your mighty land?
GEORGE knows me well!

[ADVENTURE *darts to curtain right and with* HISTORY *waves it up.*]

HISTORY [*waving her scroll towards the curtain*]—THE YOUTH AND ADVENTURE!

ADVENTURE [*flourishing the trident towards the curtain, as he announces the scene*]—SEA DREAMS!

CURTAIN RISES

FIRST EPISODE

THE YOUTH AND ADVENTURE

SCENE 1

SEA DREAMS

Place—The docks on the river front,

Alexandria, Virginia.

Time—About 1746.

Speaking Characters

GEORGE WASHINGTON

CAPTAIN TUCK

LAWRENCE WASHINGTON

ROBIN WASHINGTON

THREE SAILORS.

GROUPS

Fifteen to thirty sailors.

Two or three fishermen.

[*The setting of a water front may be suggested by a simple drop curtain at the rear showing a street leading off and a few hogsheads and barrels on the stage. At stage left protrudes the jib boom of the Antelope. The fishermen are mending their nets at stage right. As the curtain rises we see young* GEORGE WASHINGTON *seated on one of the barrels, his face turned, interestedly, to stage left from which comes the creaking of windlasses and sailors' voices singing the old English sea chantey, "BLOW THE MAN DOWN." Immediately they come on stage, swaggering on sea legs, caps on the side of their heads, arms thrown around each other—a carefree, rollicking bunch, singing boisterously.*]

FIRST SAILOR [*stepping forward and dancing a few steps*] sings:
I'm a deep water sailor just come from Hong Kong,
To me, way-eye, blow the man down.

SECOND SAILOR [*pushing him over and taking his place*] sings:
If you'll give me your notice I'll sing you a song,
Oh, give me some time to blow the man down.

[SAILORS *join in last line and suit the action to the word by a lively endeavor to knock each other down.*

The sailors group themselves around the fishermen, bending over to display their tatooed arms, etc.]

CAPTAIN TUCK [*approaching stage left*]—Well, if it tain't young MISTER WASHINGTON, here, dock walloping again. I've heard you are hankerin' after the sea yourself, sir?

GEORGE WASHINGTON—Yes, CAPTAIN TUCK, I am. I've always wanted to go to sea. Ever since my brother LAWRENCE came home from fighting with Admiral Vernon. *Now,* I am about to have my wish!

CAPTAIN TUCK—A commission in the Royal Navy?

GEORGE WASHINGTON [*shaking his head*]—My brother failed to get me the commission. I am going as a common sailor.

CAPTAIN TUCK [*drawing closer*]—A common sailor—before the mast, young sir?

GEORGE WASHINGTON [*nodding his head*]—My mother has at last agreed. I am to ship as a common sailor.

CAPTAIN TUCK—The life's a rough one, young sir, for one well raised.

GEORGE WASHINGTON [*rising*]—But it will bring adventure and thrills—strange lands—new faces—danger—peril——

CAPTAIN TUCK—That it will, young sir, if it's adventure you're after. This trip the Antelope ran into more thrills than she was looking for, eh lads? [*turns to sailors.*]

SAILORS—Aye, aye, Sir!

FIRST SAILOR—A bally chase!

SECOND SAILOR—Top jib cut away!

THIRD SAILOR—Jolly Roger flapping in the wind!
　　[*In rapid succession.*]

GEORGE WASHINGTON [*excitedly*]—Pirates?

　　[CAPTAIN TUCK *nods smilingly. From offstage comes the sound of voices and* LAWRENCE WASHINGTON *and* ROBIN *enter on stage right.*]

CAPTAIN TUCK [*to George*]—Your brother, SQUIRE WASHINGTON, and your young cousin! [CAPTAIN TUCK *greets the two and speaks to* LAWRENCE.] Fine lad is your young brother, Sir. He may even be a Captain some day! [*Winks at the sailors and leaves stage by left.*]

LAWRENCE WASHINGTON [*going over to* GEORGE]—I thought you were in the pasture breaking the filly, GEORGE.

GEORGE WASHINGTON—I was, all morning. Then I rode her to Alexandria to see how she takes to town.

LAWRENCE WASHINGTON [*kindly*]—And to be here when the Antelope came in?

　　[GEORGE *nods and turns to* ROBIN.]

GEORGE WASHINGTON—ROBIN, you should have heard the tales the sailors brought back. The *Antelope* was chased by pirates!

ROBIN—PIRATES!

　　[GEORGE *nods and looks over at the sailors for confirmation.*]

LAWRENCE WASHINGTON [*laying his arm around* GEORGE's *shoulder*]—ROBIN has just come from your mother. He bears disappointing news, little brother.

GEORGE WASHINGTON [*grasping* ROBIN's *arm*]—She hasn't changed her mind about my enlistment, ROBIN? Don't tell me that!

　　[ROBIN *appeals to Lawrence, the while he registers sympathy for* GEORGE.]

LAWRENCE WASHINGTON—Your disappointment is mine, GEORGE. Yes, your mother has withdrawn her consent to your plans. She has just received a letter from your Uncle Joseph Ball in which he advises her that a common sailor before the mast has little liberty and small chance for promotion and he thinks she had far better apprentice you to a tinker than to allow you to follow your inclinations.

GEORGE WASHINGTON [*speaking hotly*]—I won't take up a stupid tinker's trade. I will run away first. I want to see the world and have adventure!

LAWRENCE WASHINGTON—There may be some other way; let me think. Hold on to your temper, GEORGE.

　　[SAILORS *sing another verse of* BLOW THE MAN DOWN, *during which* GEORGE *lays his head disconsolately on his arms in boy fashion.*]
　　[*Enters* LORD FAIRFAX *from stage right.*]

LAWRENCE WASHINGTON—Good morning, LORD FAIRFAX!

LORD FAIRFAX—Heigh-ho, my young neighbors! Why this serious conference, when Mt. Vernon guests are riding to the hounds?

LAWRENCE WASHINGTON—Your Lordship, my young brother is much upset over his mother's final decision against a sea-faring life. He is a high-spirited lad and longs for Adventure.

LORD FAIRFAX [*putting both hands on the boy's shoulders and looking in his face*]—So it is Adventure you are wanting, my boy?
　　[GEORGE *swallows hard.*]

GEORGE WASHINGTON—Yes, your Lordship!

LORD FAIRFAX [*seriously*]—Adventure is one of the oldest cravings of mankind, GEORGE. It has made wanderers of many feet. But you do not have to leave America to find Adventure. Adventure lurks around every corner in this great wilderness!

LAWRENCE WASHINGTON—Your surveyors encounter a bit of it, Sir? [LORD FAIRFAX *nods and addresses himself still to the disconsolate boy.*]

　　You have a good head for mathematics and a fair hand at drawing. I've seen the map you made of your brother's turnip field. Why not turn your talents to surveying? I can give you employment on my estates. Surveying means exploring! It means encounters with the Indians!

GEORGE *and* ROBIN [*together*]—Exploring! Indians!

LORD FAIRFAX—When you have learned what my cousin, George William Fairfax, can teach you your work will command a doubloon a day!

BOTH BOYS [*together*]—A doubloon a day!

LAWRENCE WASHINGTON—'Tis a fine offer you are making my brother, your Lordship.

LORD FAIRFAX—I have watched him since he came to live with you, in his detailings with his young friends. He will make his mark in life because he possesses the qualifications for leadership. [*Turning to* GEORGE, *who has been conferring with* ROBIN.] Then, my boy, will you cast your lot as a surveyor?

GEORGE WASHINGTON—How can I ever repay you for your kindness, Sir?

LORD FAIRFAX—There will be hardships, young squire—sometimes a hint of danger. [*He turns to* LAWRENCE *and smiles knowingly.*]

GEORGE WASHINGTON—I will not shirk, Sir. [*Turns and addresses*

LAWRENCE]—May I ride to Fredericksburg with ROBIN and lay the new plans before my mother?

LAWRENCE WASHINGTON—Yes. It may all be for the best after all.

[*The four start off stage right,* LORD FAIRFAX *and* LAW-RENCE WASHINGTON *leading and the two boys with locked arms behind. As they do so the sailors begin singing again and walk across the stage in the direction of the Antelope.*]

" 'Lay aft' is the cry to the break of the poop,"
To me, way-aye, blow the man down!
"Or I'll help you along with the toe of my boot!"
Oh! Give me some time to blow the man down!

[GEORGE WASHINGTON *drops* ROBIN's *arm and turning, follows the sailors a few steps, then stands still and gazes longingly after them. This bit of silent acting should portray* GEORGE's *deep yearning for a sea life and the final pang of renunciation.*]

SLOW CURTAIN

[*As the curtain begins to lower on the sailors singing,* ADVENTURE *moves swiftly from his place at curtain right and catching* GEORGE *by the hand pulls him before the falling curtain. They may even squeeze under it, boy-like, when it is nearly down.* HISTORY, *stepping back a bit motions* POSTERITY, *from left wing, to her side and they join the other two at stage front.* POSTERITY *drops* HISTORY's *hand and skipping over, sidles between the two boys and the three swing hands.*]

POSTERITY [*looking up at* GEORGE WASHINGTON]—Suppose you had gone to sea?

HISTORY [*solemnly, consulting her scroll*]—The rest might never have been written!

[ADVENTURE *hands the trident to* HISTORY, *who gives it to* POSTERITY *to hold.* ADVENTURE *darts to stage right and appears with a quivver of arrows and a bow. He runs to* GEORGE, *and throws his arm companionably over his shoulder. They leave the stage together on the right.* HISTORY *and* POSTERITY *walking off on stage left.*]

SCENE 2

[HISTORY *takes her place at curtain left,* ADVENTURE *at curtain right.*]

HISTORY [*announcing the Episode*]—THE YOUTH AND ADVENTURE!

ADVENTURE [*announcing the scene*]—WASHINGTON, the Courier!

CURTAIN RISES

SCENE 2

THE COURIER

Place—Junction of the Allegheny and Monongahela rivers.

Time—The Fall of 1753.

Speaking Characters

GEORGE WASHINGTON

CHRISTOPHER GIST

VAN BRAMM

COMMANDANT ST. PIERRE

INTERPRETER

Pantomime Characters

HALF KING

BLACK FEATHER

MESSENGER

GROUPS

Indians

Ten to fifteen boys

French Soldiers

Frontiersmen

[*The setting of this scene is an exterior. A wigwam or so at rear of stage may be used to suggest the Indian camp, or a backdrop of some woodland scene.*

As the curtain rises we see the assembled Indians preparing for the False Face Dance. They are seated in a circle around the camp fire intoning the music of the False Face Dance and shaking large, brightly colored rattles. HALF KING, *the chief, stands a bit apart viewing the ceremony with folded arms.* BLACK FEATHER, *the leader, springs to his feet with a slow toe-heel step, described in dance directions given elsewhere, with body bent. He passes from member to member searching each face for signs of disease. He carries a bright bag from which he scatters wood ashes on the heads of some of the Indians and signals for them to arise. The Indians spring to their feet fastening on the grotesque false faces, which they have kept concealed, and begin the dance.*]

FALSE FACE DANCE

[*As the dance draws to a close an Indian runner dashes on the stage and in pantomime gives a message to* HALF KING *who signals his people to silence and they draw aside in groups as* WASHINGTON *and his party enter from stage left.* HALF KING *steps forward with majestic movement and stands before the visitors.*]

GEORGE WASHINGTON [*turning to* GIST]—Interpret. Brother, I come from the Great Governor of Virginia. I am on my way to the French fort, two suns off, with a demand to the French

Commander that he vacate the territory belonging to the English. The great White Father in Virginia sends you greetings and gifts and trusts that your people will continue in the friendship they have always shown their English brethren.

Music—"From an Indian Lodge"—Cadman.

[GIST *turns to* HALF KING *and translates, in pantomime,* WASHINGTON'S *speech.* HALF KING *gives his answer in pantomime and Interpreter again turns to* WASHINGTON. *Music softens as he speaks.*]

GIST [*interpreting to* WASHINGTON]—HALF KING says that the French have not treated his people right. The French Commandant, St. Pierre, told him that the Red Men owned not so much as the black of his fingernails of this land. HALF KING will go with you to deliver the message to the French. He is your friend and will stand with you against French invasion.

HALF KING [*raising his arm*]—E-hun-ga.

[*The Indians circle around singing the Peace Pact song.*]

PEACE PACT SONG

[*Indians then seat themselves in a semi-circle with* HALF KING *near the camp fire,* WASHINGTON *on his right and* BLACK FEATHER *on his left.* BLACK FEATHER *lights the Peace Pipe at the fire and hands it to* HALF KING *who blows a puff towards the sky. The Pipe stem is then pointed to the sky and then to the earth after which it is passed to* WASHINGTON *and so on down the line. It is then returned to* HALF KING *and passed the other way around.*]

WASHINGTON [*to* GIST *on other side*]—Lord Fairfax, in whose service I first became acquainted with Indian customs, has often blessed the Indian who invented the pipe. For while a man smokes he cannot discourse and must needs obtain time for sober reflection.

GIST—Let us hope this expression of friendship is sincere on the part of HALF KING. With these Indians as allies the English may be better able to press their demands against the French.

WASHINGTON—I believe HALF KING to be sincere.

[*At this point the stage is darkened or curtain is lowered a moment to denote the passage of time. This permits of the removal of Indian lodge and replacing of outdoor back drop with one showing a frontier post. In the absence of this a plain drop may be used, the picturesque groups of French soldiers providing the suggestion of a post. As the curtain rises the soldiers are seen exchanging the time of day with one another. The French Commandant,* ST. PIERRE, *is seen on stage right strutting down the street in lordly style. As he passes he receives the homage of the various groups. Two soldiers come to a standstill and salute. The men bow elaborately and call out "Bon jour! Commandant . . . Bon jour!" The women curtsy low.*]

SOLDIERS—*Le bon Commandant!*

[*While this pantomime takes place any old French air may be played very softly, off stage, to accent the French setting.*

WASHINGTON *and his party now appear on stage left.* WASHINGTON *identifies the commander of the Post and,*

going forward, salutes him. The Indians go off in a group and view the settlers with scowling faces.]

ST. PIERRE—*N'est ce qui me procure l'honneur de votre visite?*

WASHINGTON [*turning to* VAN BRAAM]—Sir, will you translate? Between my two worst enemies, my temper and my French, the *latter* has best worsted me.

[ST. PIERRE *repeats his question in French.* VAN BRAAM *struggles to translate.*]

WASHINGTON [*impatiently*]—I brought you as an interpreter and you seem ignorant of the language.

VAN BRAAM [*shaking his head*]—It has a different sound here, Sir.

ST. PIERRE [*signalling to an officer*]—*Interprete, si vous plais.*

[WASHINGTON *hands* COMMANDANT PIERRE *the letter. The Commandant proceeds to read and, turning to his interpreter speaks in pantomime. The interpreter translates for* WASHINGTON, ST. PIERRE'S *words.*]

INTERPRETER [*to* WASHINGTON]—The Commandant must have time to consider the demand of the honorable English governor that the French vacate the post. He begs that you will make yourself at home. His aide will show you your quarters.

[*Aide salutes and leads way off stage by left followed by* WASHINGTON, GIST *and* HALF KING. *The Indians remain on the stage.*]

The French Commandant is seen leaving on stage right, so indicating that he had no part in the action that follows. The settlers group together and begin to discuss the situation excitedly in pantomime. Several of the men withdraw to one side and begin to plot how the Indians might be won over to their side. Their frequent gestures towards the Indians indicate to the audience the nature of the discussion. Now the men produce liquor and pockets and trading bags are emptied for trinkets with which to curry the Red Man's favor. BLACK FEATHER, *the leader of the Indian group, is the first to show interest. The others follow his example and are soon clusters around the settlers receiving gifts and listening to plans.* WASHINGTON *and* GIST *enter from stage right. The plotters separate to allow them to pass and their eyes follow the Courier. Out of sight of the gathering, the two men wheel and remain stock-still at stage left to overhear the plot.*]

WASHINGTON [*to* GIST]—See, they are giving the Indians rum!

GIST—Already they seem to be won over.

[*Indians begin to hop up in the air and utter whoops.* BLACK FEATHER *is singled out by the soldiers for much attention and seems to have been chosen for some task. The Indians point to him repeating his name again and again. "Sha-ha-whe . . . Sha-ha-whe . . . Sha-ha-whe." The soldiers gradually drop away on stage right leaving only the Indians who are in high spirits. They circle around* BLACK FEATHER *sing-songing his name together.* SHA-HA-WHE. *He leads them off stage in the toe-heel step.*]

WASHINGTON—We must obtain ST. PIERRE'S answer and leave at once. [*Drops a sheet of paper.*]

Gist [*picking it up*]—*The Commandant's reply?*

Washington [*shaking his head*]—No, merely plans of the fort I sketched for the Governor while we waited.

Gist—A long head you have on your young shoulders, Sir!

Washington—Years of surveying sharpen one's powers of observation.

> [*The two men, backs to stage left, study the plans. BLACK FEATHER is seen stealthily creeping up behind them. He kneels, draws his bow and directs an arrow towards WASHINGTON. The men turn in time to avoid it. GIST springs across the stage and seizing BLACK FEATHER drags him out.*]

Gist [*raising his gun above the Indian*]—You red dog, you will die for this!

Washington [*interposing*]—Let HALF KING deal with the offender. We must be on our way.

> [*Music "From an Indian Lodge," or other Indian theme. HALF KING and Indians approach on stage left. ST. PIERRE and French settlers on right. ST. PIERRE steps forward and begins to protest his innocence of the soldiers' actions. Soldiers are apologetic. HALF KING faces WASHINGTON, after bidding two of his people to seize BLACK FEATHER. He raises his hands majestically absolving himself from intrigue as he delivers his speech. In pantomime, later to be spoken by the interpreter.*]

Gist [*interpreting, turns to WASHINGTON*]—HALF KING says to you: BLACK FEATHER will be punished for his guilt. HALF KING will keep faith with the great father in Virginia. He sends him a wampum belt as a token of his everlasting friendship.

> [HALF KING *steps forward and hands* WASHINGTON *the wampum belt.*
> HALF KING *then delivers himself of another speech in pantomime which* GIST *interprets.*
> *Music softens during following speech.*]

Gist [*interpreting*]—The rain comes and the snow flies and flowers spring up in their wake. But where the white man passes only sorrow and trouble spring up for the red man! More and more will the pale face war over the Indians' hunting ground until some day they will hunt no more.

CURTAIN

> [*Again* ADVENTURE *leaves his post on curtain right, as it is about to be lowered, and leads* GEORGE WASHINGTON, *the Courier, to the stage front. Again* HISTORY *motions* POSTERITY *from left exit.*
>
> *In front of curtain Music, Cadman's "Indian Melodies."*
>
> HISTORY *moves to* WASHINGTON's *side, and looses* ADVENTURE's *hold on him.*]

History [*to ADVENTURE*]—He must leave you now, my roving lad.

> [WASHINGTON *nods.*]
>
> [*Walking between* HISTORY *and* POSTERITY *with* POSTERITY *on outside, he leaves the stage on the left. ADVENTURE, casting longing eyes backward, a bit disheartened, leaves on right. Just as* WASHINGTON *reaches the*

exit, *he turns and salutes* ADVENTURE, *who blithely, now, waves his hand in farewell.*]

SECOND EPISODE

THE MAN AND HOME

> [*Music off stage—"Home Sweet Home."*
> *When it is time for the curtain to rise on Episode Two the Washington of this Episode, with* HISTORY *and* POSTERITY *on either side, comes on the stage from right. Behind them prances* ADVENTURE. *He is juggling a globe of the world in his hands and seeks at every opportunity to gain* WASHINGTON's *favor. Each time he steps up beside* WASHINGTON, HISTORY *waves him back. As they near the center of the stage,* HOME, *in her white robes, appears from stage left and moves softly and gracefully to* WASHINGTON's *side. She wears a rose on her breast, which she unfastens and lays in his hand.*]

Posterity [*running to* HOME]—I have seen your lovely face many times, who are you?

History—You have, my child. This is HOME, your tenderest guardian.

> [HOME *lifts her arms in a sort of gesture of benediction above* WASHINGTON *and then extends them lovingly to the audience. The others group around her and* HOME *moving a step forward recites the Prologue to Episode Two—The Man and Home.*]

――――

PROLOGUE

[HOME *speaks*]

I am HOME.
I croon a tender song and mild
Unto the heart of man.
I sing of hearth-fire's glow and garden borders bright,
Of Love that outlives Death.
I sing of Friendship's ties and children's voices clear;
My white wings shed content.
Honored by humble and renowned
By rich and poor—[*turns to* POSTERITY].
Dear CHILD, together, we must walk by HISTORY's side.
For when at last Life's heroes turn
Back from the World's acclaim,
Their weary heads they cradle on my breast
And fall asleep.

――――

> [WASHINGTON, *and* POSTERITY, *hand in hand, walk off stage left.* ADVENTURE *shows his globe to* WASHINGTON *and then to* HOME. *He beckons them, and receiving no attention, rushes off stage at right.* HISTORY *moves back to her place by the curtain on the left and* HOME *takes up her post on the right.*]

History [*introducing* HOME *and Episode Two.*]—THE MAN AND HOME!

Home [*announcing the scene.*]—Courtship.

CURTAIN RISES

SCENE 1

COURTSHIP

Place—On the porch or lawn of Major Chamberlyne's home at William's Ferry, Virginia.

Time—The Spring of 1758.

Speaking Characters

COLONEL WASHINGTON

MAJOR CHAMBERLYNE

MRS. MARTHA CUSTIS

JACKIE CUSTIS

MARY CHAMBERLYNE

LOU DANDRIDGE

CYNTHIA GREEN

SALLY PARHAM

PATSY CUSTIS

BILLY [Negro body guard].

RENE [Negro maid].

GROUPS

Young lady guests.

Partners for the Roger de Coverly.

[*Any number may dance.*]

[*The setting is an exterior. A back drop showing an old southern home may be used; or the home may be merely indicated by a door with windows on either side at the rear of the stage. The door should be wide enough to permit the dancers to throng through. Old-fashioned chairs and settles, a few blooming plants, etc., will add to the scene. As the curtain rises we see the five pretty colonial belles seated around the stage. Two occupy a low settle. Martha Custis sits in a low settle, with her two children, Jacky and Patsy, hanging over her. They are all embroidering.*]

MARY CHAMBERLYNE—My father thinks COLONEL WASHINGTON combines all the traits of leadership.

LOU DANDRIDGE—And yet there are many who find fault with him!

CYNTHIA GREEN—A bit of jealousy, thinks I. Truly he has served the Colony well.

SALLY PARHAM [*putting down her sewing*]—La, la, truly he has been more wined and dined than anyone. Wherever he goes, north or south, doors fly open to him. Such a hero!

LOU DANDRIDGE—They say he dresses in the height of style!

CYNTHIA GREEN—And that he can dance hour upon hour without tiring!

JACKIE CUSTIS [*leaning over his mother*]—What's a hero, Ma?

MARTHA CUSTIS—A man who does great deeds, JACKIE.

JACKIE CUSTIS—What's *he* done, Ma?

MARTHA CUSTIS [*to* MARY CHAMBERLYNE]—You'll have to tell him about the hero, MARY. [*Laughs*]

MARY [*holds out her hand*]—Come over here, children. [*They go to her side.*]

MARY—Colonel Washington is a hero, JACKIE, because he is fearless and brave and honest. He has fought many battles, but he hasn't won all of them. Sometimes he thought it best to retreat when he saw the enemy was too strong. *But he never acted cowardly.* When General Braddock came over from England to lead the Virginia forces against the French he chose WASHINGTON for his aide. They were in a terrible battle and General Braddock was mortally wounded. WASHINGTON rallied the Virginia forces and saved the British army from being wiped out.

JACKIE—He wasn't afraid! [MARY *shakes her head.*]

MARY [*continuing*]—Then our Governor saw that WASHINGTON was better fitted to lead Virginia forces than any other soldier, and he made him Commander-in-Chief of all Virginia forces. . . . Oh, yes, JACKIE, he is a great hero!

BOTH CHILDREN [*unison*]—Yes, he is! [*They go over to their mother.*]

SALLY PARHAM—A great hero he is, but one who has failed to vanquish Dan Cupid.

LOU DANDRIDGE—He has had many affairs of the heart, they say. Betty Fauntelroy of Richmond, Mary Phillipse of New York—

MRS. MARTHA CUSTIS [*laying down her sewing and looking around at the girls*]—Methinks these ladies must have lost their minds if this young man is all that people are claiming for him!

[*The others laugh. Voices are heard off stage. The girls start up.*]

MARY—Sh—h!—Father is bringing some one up from the landing.

[*The girls put their hands to their hair, jump up, view their frocks and with Oh's! and Ah's! all fly off stage through center doorway.*
COLONEL WASHINGTON *and* MAJOR CHAMBERLYNE, *followed by* BILLY, *the Negro body guard, appear from stage right.*]

MAJOR CHAMBERLYNE—I shall not hear of your leaving, COLONEL, until you have dined and met my daughter and her guests.

COLONEL WASHINGTON—Most kind of you, MAJOR, but my business at Williamsburg is important and I should not tarry long, even in the presence of such a fair gathering.

MAJOR CHAMBERLYNE—Ah, COLONEL, if I hear aright, you are not indifferent to feminine wiles. Wait until you meet the young and charming and wealthy widow who is visiting here. She may serve to pluck stern Duty from your mind! [*They both laugh.*]

COLONEL WASHINGTON [*turning to* BILLY]—Bring up my horse in an hour, BILLY. We must be on our way.

BILLY [*bowing respectfully*]—Yes suh, yes, MARSE GEORGE. [*He leaves by stage right.*]

Colonel Washington—I am only fair presentable to meet the ladies.

Major Chamberlyne—Sir, you always maintain an appearance suitable for a Virginia gentleman of fortune, possessing an eminent position in society.* [*They pass off stage through center doorway.*]

[*Other guests begin to arrive. Fair ladies and gallant swain, wearing the charming costumes of the period and representing the beauty and chivalry of Colonial society. They are laughing and chatting as they cross the stage and enter the front door of the mansion at stage center. The shades on the two windows should be arranged to permit of a silhouette of the guests within as they meet one another with bows and curtsies. Off stage. Music. "Drink to Me Only With Thine Eyes." Soon the guests within the mansion off stage raise their voices in the song "Drink to Me Only With Thine Eyes, And I Will Toast With mine," etc. Billy enters stage on the right as Colonel Washington comes out from the mansion through center door.*]

Billy [*bowing low*]—Old Silversides am ready at de block, Marse George.

Colonel Washington—Have him up again in two hours, Billy!

[*The Negro bows and leaves stage on right. The Colonel goes within. The singing continues. Upon one of the window shades appear the silhouettes of Colonel Washington and the Widow Custis; he, tall and gallantly bending low to catch each word; she, petite and coy, fluttering her fan as she talks. Billy again makes his appearance from stage right and is met at the door of the mansion by the maid.*]

Rene—Here you is again, Mister Billy, and de Cun'el ain't studyin' 'bout goin'.

Billy—De sun am gone down and I is been up with de hoss fo times. What's ailin' Marse George, gal? Ain't never seen him act like dis befo [*Scratches his head*].

Rene—Laws a mercy, Mister Billy, maybe it's de spring sun on his haid, but me, I thinks it's Mrs. Martha Custis on his heart. He ain't done nothin' but hang over her all evenin'.

Billy—Go long, gal. Tell Marse George his man and hoss is waitin'.

[*Singing continues.*]

Rene [*disappearing and coming back almost immediately*]—De Cun'el say to put up his hoss fer de night. He won't leave fer Williamsburg till morning.

Billy [*shaking his head*]—Tain't like Marse George. Jes ain't like him!

[*Rene goes over to the window and peeps in. She then turns and beckons to Billy.*]

Rene—Cum see fer yerself, Mister Billy. [*Billy cautiously, and guiltily, crosses over to the window and they both peek in. From within come the singing voices in the old song. "Believe Me If All Those Endearing Young Charms."*]

[*Billy turns from the window and walks towards stage right, waving his hand to left.*]

Billy—Goodbye, Sis Williamsburg, Marse George's in love again. [*Leaves.*]

[*Music of Reel is heard off stage and through center door flock the dancers onto the stage. Colonel Washington and the Widow Custis are the last to appear. They are all laughing and chatting. They form in line to dance the Reel, with Lou Dandridge and her partner nearest to the audience.*]

Lou Dandridge [*from behind her fan*]—Cupid's dart has done what bullets have failed to accomplish. See how the Colonel has succumbed!

Partner—And the lady herself seems not indifferent!

THE ROGER DE COVERLY DANCE

[*At the last figure of the dance Washington and Martha Custis dance to the front of the stage.*]

Colonel Washington—Then, Madam, when I return from Williamsburg, you will be at your home?

Martha Custis [*looking up into his face*]—Yes, waiting to welcome you, Colonel.

[*Dance is continued and curtain falls on dancing.*]

CURTAIN

————

[*Immediately after curtain is lowered Music of Reel continues.*

Home *leaves her place at the right of curtain and stepping back in the right wing, returnrs leading Washington and the Widow Custis by the hands. History beckons Posterity from the left wing, and the child runs forward to Mrs. Custis, admiring her dainty apparel, examining her fan, etc. Home moves up with the group at the center front of stage and joins the hands of Martha Custis and George Washington. The bold face of Adventure is seen peering out from stage left, but he is quickly waved back by History, who begins to write on her scroll. The group move toward the left exit, to the music of the minuet. Home leads the way swaying softly to the music. In front of curtain. Behind Home come Washington and Mrs. Custis, hand in hand, and treading the Minuet. History follows them, writing on her scroll. Little Posterity breaks away from the group and disappears on the right. She comes back immediately bringing Jackie and Patsy Custis by the hand. The three children run across the stage to catch up the others. As they reach the left exit, Jackie and Patsy curtsy and bow, and Posterity kisses her hand to the audience.*

When it is time for the curtain to rise on Scene 2, in the Home Episode, the music of "Home, Sweet Home" is again played, and History and Home take their places at the curtain. History on left, Home on right.]

History [*announcing the Episode*]—The Man and Home!

Home [*announcing the scene*]—May Day at Mount Vernon! [*Together they wave up the curtain. History has her scroll; Home, a bouquet of roses.*]

CURTAIN RISES

———

SCENE 2

MOUNT VERNON

Place—The lawn at Mount Vernon.

Time—May Day about 1763.

———

Speaking Characters

COLONEL WASHINGTON

MRS. WASHINGTON

COLONEL GEORGE WILLIAM FAIRFAX

MRS. FAIRFAX

COLONEL GEORGE MASON

MRS. MASON

LITTLE JACKIE CUSTIS

PATSY CUSTIS

LITTLE SALLY FAIRFAX

JOHNNY CARLYLE

MAMMY LOU [Negro mammy].

———

GROUPS

Fifteen to thirty small children.

[*The setting of this scene is an exterior. It requires little change from the one previously used. If possible, a fac-simile of the original Mount Vernon shown on a drop would be effective, but it is not necessary. Lanterns strung around the stage give it the festive appearance of a party. As the curtain rises we see* COLONEL *and* MRS. WASHINGTON *sitting on a bench at stage right conversing happily.* BILLY *and* MAMMY LOU *are bustling around making last-minute party preparations. They place chil-dren's chairs around the stage.* MAMMY LOU *gives a last-minute brush with her broom while she hums "Swing Low, Sweet Chariot." The center stage door opens and little* JACKIE *and* PATSY *come out dressed in their best and walking primly.* MAMMY LOU *runs to meet them.*]

MAMMY LOU [*taking their hands*]—Ain't my chillun likely, all drest up in their fine clothes jes come from Lun'on? [*She leads them over to their parents.*] PATSY *curtsies.* JACKIE *bows, hands behind his back.*

COLONEL WASHINGTON—A fine little lady and gentleman!

MRS. WASHINGTON [*looking towards stage left*]—See your little guests are already arriving! Go and meet them, children.

[*Small guests begin to arrive on stage left. Some are ac-companied by colored mammies wearing bright bandannas.* JACKIE *and* PATSY *curtsy and bow to each little guest who return the greeting in the same manner. The children then cross the stage and curtsy and bow to the Washing-*

tons. BILLY, *at stage left, announces the guests as they arrive and* MAMMY LOU *makes them comfortable. During this pretty pantomime any English May Day music may be played.*]

MRS. WASHINGTON [*surrounded by a bevy of children*]—A happy May Day to you, children.

COLONEL WASHINGTON—And a warm welcome to Mt. Vernon!

[*There are cries of "Thank you,* MISTRESS WASHINGTON!" "Thank you, COLONEL WASHINGTON!" *They sing "Happy May Day to You."*]

PATSY—We are going to play singing games, if it pleases you.

[*Children clap their hands and scamper over to form a circle.*]

BILLY [*announcing*]—COLONEL *and* MRS. FAIRFAX, *and* MISS SALLY!

[*They enter stage on left. Little* SALLY *carries a beautiful May basket which she gravely presents to the* COLONEL. *He bows low to thank her and take her little hand.*]

MRS. FAIRFAX—Flowers always for the COLONEL, everywhere he goes.

BILLY [*announcing*]—COLONEL *and* MRS. MASON!

[*They cross the stage and greet the hosts, patting the chil-dren on the head. The small guests stand in a circle, hold-ing hands. They have chosen* JACKIE *and* PATSY *for the center, and begin to skip around singing. King William was King James' Son, By the royal race he won, He wore a crown upon his breast, pointing to the east and west— Go choose your east, etc., etc. Suggested songs of English origin given elsewhere. After one or two singing games,* JACKIE CUSTIS *and* SALLY FAIRFAX, JOHNNY CARLYLE *and* PATSY CUSTIS *dance a little polka or folk dance. The chil-dren clap their hands. The older onlookers also applaud.* MAMMY LOU *and* BILLY *appear in the doorway with great silver waiters laden with fruit and cakes. The children scamper for seats and are served.* JACKIE *and* PATSY *show themselves the mannerly children of the time,—solicitous for the welfare of the guests. Music continues.*]

MRS. MASON [*to* MRS. WASHINGTON]—I trust country life will not seem dull to you after your gay season at Williamsburg as the wife of a Burgess?

MRS. WASHINGTON—Home is never dull to those who love it.

COLONEL WASHINGTON—And one's own vine and fig tree furnish greatest happiness after the clangor of arms and bustle of camp.*

COLONEL GEORGE MASON—Something tells me that the country will not permit you to enjoy home long, my friend.

COLONEL WASHINGTON—Let us hope so. The longer I am ac-quainted with farming affairs the more they engross me. And the mistress of Mt. Vernon is a famous home-maker. [*He bows to her, and she acknowledges the compliment with a curtsy and a "Thank you,* COLONEL".]

MRS. WASHINGTON [*with a gesture towards the children*]—How happy they are today.

COLONEL WASHINGTON—Their welfare is our responsibility.

GEORGE MASON [*vehemently*]—And *anything* that threatens their rights and liberties must be struck down!

FAIRFAX—You speak ominously, neighbor!

George Mason—Trouble is brewing for the colonies!

Fairfax—Ah, my friend, I pray the colonial sky will always be as blue as the one that bends over Mt. Vernon today.

George Mason—A vain wish, Fairfax, the storm is gathering.

Women [*All together looking at the sky*]—Storm!

Mason—News has reached me but lately of new taxes to be placed on the Colonies to raise revenue for England.

Fairfax—England knows best.

Mason [*stepping forward and speaking warmly*]—*Taxation without representation is the canker that eats into Peace and Prosperity!*

Fairfax [*turning to* Washington]—Our illustrious neighbor is silent!

George Mason—His words are writ in action. His arm will be ready to strike when it is needed.

Colonel Washington—You have spoken with truth, old friend.

Mrs. Washington—Come, let us put such gloomy talk aside and remember only that it is May Day at Mt. Vernon! [*There is a murmur of assent from the ladies.*]

> [*The children again form a ring, this time with little* Sally Fairfax *and* Johnny Carlyle *in the center. They sing* "Come, Take a Little Partner".]

Sally [*darting out from the circle and catching* Washington *by the hand*]—I choose you, Colonel.

Johnny Carlyle [*following her example with* Mrs. Washington]—And I choose you, Mistress Washington!

> [*The Washingtons allow themselves to be drawn in the ring, and the children circle around, singing.*]

CURTAIN.

> [*The children's voices continue singing behind curtain, as* Posterity *and* Jack *and* Patsy *run on stage from left in front of curtain.* Washington *and* Mrs. Washington *approach from stage right.* History *and* Home *join them at center front. The form of* Fame *is seen at left but he does not join the group.*]

History [*to* Home, *gesturing to* Fame]—Another has come to claim him, Home. [*They move off stage.*]

THIRD EPISODE

THE GENERAL AND FAME

> [*Music off stage,* "America, the Beautiful."
> *When it is time for the curtain to rise on Episode Three,* Washington, *attired in General's uniform, as in the Prelude, walks thoughtfully onto the stage from the right.* Home *follows close behind, seeking to gain a place by his side, but is brushed gently aside each time by* History, *who holds* Posterity's *hand. From the left approaches the golden figure of* Fame, *who sounds a call on his golden bugle as he enters.* Home *retreats a few steps to the right and holds out her arms to* Washington.]

Posterity [*tugging at* Washington's *hand*]—"See, dear sweet Home is calling you!" Washington *shakes his head as* History *moves to his side, and* Fame *touches him on the shoulder.*

Fame [*in loud tones*]—I claim him now, Posterity.

Posterity [*to* History]—Tell me, who is it, History?

History—Listen, my child, all are silent when he speaks!

> [Home *creeps silently away on stage right, as* Fame *strides to the front and gives the* PROLOGUE *to Episode Three.*]

PROLOGUE

I am FAME!
Whom I emblazon on that honored scroll,
Is deathless!
I write of men whose dreams were for mankind!
Whose hopes refused to die.
Whose vision swept a troubled sky of cloud.
I write of men who counted pain a trifling thing,
And honor *all!*
Of men who wore their valor like a crimson rose,
Their wisdom like a cloak.
Oh, Child, with soul wide open to the sun [*turns to* Posterity]
Reach high to touch my hand!
Stand here within the halo of those names [*points to* History's *scroll*]
And learn of one.

> [Adventure *appears from stage left carrying a sword which he extends to* Washington. Fame *takes the sword from* Adventure *and fastens it at* Washington's *side, saluting him as he does so.* Fame *escorts* Washington *off the stage on the right.* History *and* Posterity *leave on the left.* History *and* Fame *reappear immediately and take their places at the curtain.* History *at left,* Fame *at right.*]

History [*introducing* Fame *and the episode*]—The General and Fame!

Fame [*announcing the scene*]—The Glory of the Revolution! [*Together they wave wave up the curtain on Episode Three.*]

———

CURTAIN RISES

Scene 1

THE GLORY OF THE REVOLUTION

———

Place—The Cambridge Common near Boston.

Time—July, 1775.

———

Speaking Characters

General Washington

Captain Quincy

Lieutenant Clark

Young Corporal

First, Second, Third, Fourth and Fifth Soldier

Messenger

Groups

Thirty to one hundred soldiers. Band and riflemen.

[*The setting is an exterior. If staged out of doors an elm tree may be featured in the background. Otherwise, the suggestion of a tree and a few soldiers' tents at rear of stage will be sufficient.*

As the curtain rises we see a contingent of the Massachusetts troops encamped under the elm. They show signs of their recent hard fighting at Bunker Hill. Several wear bandages on their heads and around arms and legs. They are weary but not discouraged. One is writing home, another reading. The two officers are playing chess. A group of soldiers are rehearsing recent events.]

FIRST SOLDIER—We'd be sitting on top of old Bunker Hill now if something hadn't happened.

SECOND SOLDIER—You mean, if a few things hadn't happened.

THIRD SOLDIER—Powder gave out!

FOURTH SOLDIER—Orders misunderstood!

FIFTH SOLDIER—General Warren killed!

SIXTH SOLDIER—Rear rank opened to attack!

FIRST SOLDIER—We had them on the run at Lexington and we can do it again. It might mean a right smart fighting and maybe dying. . .

YOUNG CORPORAL—*Dying!* Isn't Death a small price to pay for Liberty?

[*The group burst into cheers and toss up their caps. The two officers stop playing chess and turn to watch them.*]

LIEUT. CLARKE [*to* CAPTAIN QUINCY]—The lads have the spirit, Captain, and they put up a splendid fight on the Hill. But we haven't troops enough to push the Red coats into the sea alone.

CAPTAIN QUINCY—You're right about that. We need the Virginia troops to take up arms with us.

LIEUT. CLARKE—And we need a Commander-in-Chief that knows soldiering!

CAPTAIN QUINCY—Congress has, no doubt, already made this selection. We should receive the information shortly.

LIEUT. CLARKE—The honor may go to General Ward?

CAPTAIN QUINCY—Or General Putnam.

[*Messenger approaches on stage left and saluting* CAPTAIN QUINCY, *hands him a document. Captain breaks the seal and reads. Then gives a command.*]

CAPTAIN QUINCY—Attention, soldiers! [*Soldiers rise and come to attention.*]

CAPTAIN QUINCY—Congress has appointed COLONEL GEORGE WASHINGTON of Virginia as Commander-in-Chief of the Continental Army.

SOLDIERS [*together*]—GENERAL WASHINGTON OF VIRGINIA!

CAPTAIN QUINCY [*sternly*]—Attention! The information has been delayed in reaching this camp, and GENERAL WASHINGTON is due to arrive at any time. At ease, but stand ready to come to attention.

FIRST SOLDIER—They say he is a great soldier.

SECOND SOLDIER—We had great soldiers from around these parts, didn't we?

YOUNG CORPORAL—We're all fighting for the same cause, ain't we?

LIEUT. CLARKE—The Virginia Colonists will stand behind GENERAL WASHINGTON. They trust his judgment.

CAPTAIN QUINCY—The Commander-in-Chief has the undying support of us all!

YOUNG CORPORAL—Pledge it, boys. Cheers for our Commander-in-Chief!

[*Soldiers cheer*—WASHINGTON! WASHINGTON! WASHINGTON!

Off stage is heard the tramping of feet.]

MESSENGER [*facing stage left*]—Our comrades of the Massachusetts Bay Colony are here. [*Soldiers cheer.*]

[*A sharp order—"Halt!"—is given off stage and is heard repeated down the line. Then "At Ease!"*

Cheering off stage.]

MESSENGER [*announcing*]—GENERAL WARD has dismounted and is being greeted by his men.

[*Soldiers on stage cheer.*

Tramping off stage and Fife and Drum music.]

MESSENGER [*announcing*]—GENERAL WARD'S Band are wearing their new uniforms!

[*The Band marches on the stage playing "Yankee Doodle." The soldiers cheer and burst into singing "Yankee Doodle," Orders Halt and At Ease are given the Band.*

Tramping off stage.]

MESSENGER [*announcing*]—The Connecticut and New Hampshire regiments are arriving.

YOUNG CORPORAL [*excitedly*]—Comrades, look. A glorious sight. The assembling of the Continental Army of America!

[*Soldiers cheer.*

Tramping off stage continues.]

FIRST SOLDIER [*facing stage left*]—Say, who *are* those huntsmen with the long rifles?

SECOND SOLDIER—Blow me down! *If it ain't* GENERAL WASHINGTON'S *Virginia Riflemen!*

YOUNG CORPORAL [*fervently*]—The Virginia Colony has taken up arms! Comrades, in Union there is strength.

[*Soldiers cheer as Riflemen march on and off the stage.*]

LIEUT. CLARKE—These riflemen have had a famous fighting record.

CAPTAIN QUINCY—Thank God for that!

MESSENGER—The Commander-in-Chief of the Army has arrived!

[*A bugle sounds off stage, followed by the command "Present Arms."*

The order is repeated down the line until it reaches the troops on the stage.

GENERAL WASHINGTON *advances. He is accompanied by* GENERAL CHARLES LEE, GENERALS WARD *and* PUTNAM.]

GENERAL WASHINGTON [*addressing the soldiers*]—Soldiers of the United Colonies of America! In tendering their troops to me, GENERAL WARD *and* GENERAL PUTNAM have told me how well you served them in the recent engagements. Congress has seen fit to appoint me Commander-in-Chief of the United Army. Together we must make safe the liberties of our Country—United we stand, divided we fall!

[*Orders are given to "Pass in Review." The Band starts up; the soldiers fall in line and begin the march. They* march four abreast or eight abreast as the size of the stage permits. A splendid effect of a large army may be gained by marching the same soldiers on and off the stage in an unbroken line.

Curtain falls on marching soldiers.]

CURTAIN

———

[*When it is time for the curtain to rise on Scene 2 of this episode, Posterity comes on the stage from the right leading the School Chorus (Prelude Group), who pass across the stage singing* The Star-Spangled Banner. *Posterity wears a little cocked hat and carries a flag. History and Fame take their places by the curtain, and as soon as the children have made their exit on left, wave up the curtain on Scene 2.*]

History [*announcing the Episode*]—The General and Fame!

Fame [*announcing the Scene*]—The Gloom of the Revolution!

[*Together they wave up the curtain.*]

CURTAIN RISES

———

Scene 2

THE GLOOM OF THE REVOLUTION

Place—Washington's Winter Quarters

at Valley Forge.

Time—February, 1778.

Speaking Characters

General Washington

Governor Patrick Henry

Secretary to Washington

James Bixby

Lady Washington

Mrs. Thomson

Hans Wetzel

———

Groups

Pennsylvania German farm folk. Any number of men, women and children of all ages.

Chorus of Soldiers [*off stage*].

———

[*The setting is an interior. Door on right at back of stage. A small tattered flag hangs on the wall. There is a table on the right side of the room heaped with soldiers' garments. On the left side a desk bears many letters and writing paraphernalia.*

As the curtain rises we see Mrs. Washington *and* Mrs.

Thomson *sorting garments on the table at the right of the stage. At the desk on the left sits the secretary writing.* General Washington *and* Governor Henry *stand nearby in deep conversation.*]

Mrs. Thomson—Things have seemed a lot brighter since you came, Lady Washington.

Mrs. Washington—There is little that I can do to help, my good woman.

Mrs. Thomson—You've got all the women a-working. [*Pauses and gathers up some of the garments.*] I'll take some of these things down to Mrs. Pott's now. [*Picks up a sock.*] Socks ain't much but holes these days!

Mrs. Washington—Those German farmers down in the valley seem to have abundance. If only they would help out our soldiers!

Mrs. Thomson—Sure, and a little would go a long ways now, while we are a-waiting for the army supplies. What could have happened to them, Ma'am?

Mrs. Washington [*sighing*]—Something seems to have gone wrong, somewhere!

Mrs. Thomson—And the poor soldiers' feet almost on the ground!

Mrs. Washington [*sits down and starts to darn*]—We can only work and pray, Mrs. Thomson. Women's prayers may avail as much as men's arms.

Mrs. Thomson [*glancing towards* Washington]—Poor General, he's carrying a heavy load! I see his light far into the night, as he sits at his desk writing.

Mrs. Washington [*again sighs*]—And the letters bring so little response!

[Mrs. Thomson *crosses the room and addresses* Washington.]

Mrs. Thomson—'Scuse me, General, but the quartermaster came over this afternoon and borrowed our last sack of salt.

[Washington *shakes his head and stifles a sigh.*]

General Washington—Share with the men what we have, at headquarters, Mrs. Thomson.

[Mrs. Thomson *curtsies and leaves the room.*]

Governor Henry [*with feeling*]—Ah, General, in this dark hour when the fate of the nation is at stake we find ourselves without sufficient powder, cannon, musket, clothing or food, because of a fatuous policy of Congress in changing the commissariat organization. Your men are hungry and cold. Unfit for any sort of duty!

General Washington—Divine Providence to whom we have appealed for the rectitude of our actions will succor us in this trying hour, I feel sure, my friend. We should not be too harsh on Congress nor expect it to move with the alacrity of armies in the field. We should remember that the process by which it arrives at national action is one of fusing. Let us not despair.* The accomplishment of the great design which I firmly believe the Dispenser of all good had ordained for us, is within our own hands. To play the game well is our part.*

Secretary [*addressing* Gov. Henry]—Sir, in addition to these hardships, the General must face the bickerings and jealousies among officers, and criticism from higher sources.

Washington [*holds up his hand*]—If nothing impeaching my honor or honesty is said, I care little for the rest. Truth will ultimately prevail, where there are pains taken to bring it to light.*

GOVERNOR HENRY—You have already won undying fame by your impartial and wise leadership, GENERAL.

GENERAL WASHINGTON—Fame. An empty word!

GOVERNOR HENRY—But a glorious one when coupled with that of LIBERTY!

[WASHINGTON *rises and going to the window stands looking out. The scratching of the Secretary's quill is the only sound.*]

GENERAL WASHINGTON [*softly*]—Liberty! Out there two thousand men are warming themselves by that word!

[*A knock is heard at the door. BIXBY answers it, and addresses WASHINGTON.*]

BIXBY—GENERAL, Mr. Hans Wetzel from the German colony, nearby, wishes an audience.

GENERAL WASHINGTON [*coming to center of stage*]—Admit MR. WETZEL.

[WETZEL *enters carrying his large hat. He approaches WASHINGTON and makes a respectful bow.*]

HANS WETZEL—Herr General. News haf reached us dat your supplies vas delayed and your sojers starve. Ve half brought help!

[*Without waiting for WASHINGTON to reply, he signals BIXBY to open the door. The German farm folk come crowding in. Men and women and little children in the quaint, picturesque costume of the elders. In their arms they bear supplies of every description. Little boys carry big cheeses, some have hams in their arms, some home-spun sacks of potatoes and apples. MRS. THOMSON bustles in and moves around excitedly finding places on the table and floor for the gifts. Apples and potatoes roll out of the sacks and are picked up by the children and presented to her. They are all beaming and kindly. MRS. WASHINGTON moves around among the guests patting the little children on the head and praising them by appropriate gestures to their mothers. The mothers beam and smooth their aprons. One small girl marches up with a string of sausages in her hand and solemnly presents them to MRS. WASHINGTON. WASHINGTON clasps the hands of the men who cluster around him.*

Music may accompany pantomime.]

GENERAL WASHINGTON—Thank you, thank you, and again thank you, my kind neighbors!

GERMAN FARM FOLK [*calling out*]—Der grosse General . . . Der grosse General . . . . Der grosse General.

[*The woman standing nearest to MRS. WASHINGTON catches her by the hand and draws her to the GENERAL's side.*]

WOMAN—De gute Frau . . . de gute Frau.

GERMAN FARM FOLK [*in unison*]—Der gute Frau!

HANS WETZEL [*to WASHINGTON*]—Dey call you der gre-et General and her [*motioning towards* MRS. WASHINGTON] de gute vife!

[*The GENERAL and* MRS. WASHINGTON *smile and bow.*]

GENERAL WASHINGTON [*to Gov. HENRY*]—And so, my friend, will the rest of our countrymen respond when they know our great needs.

GOVERNOR HENRY—Verily, sir, the fires of Liberty are being lighted upon new hearthstones every day!

[*From off stage come the soldiers' voices singing. Any song of the Revolutionary Period.*]

WASHINGTON [*goes to the window and draws back the curtain.*] The cast should separate to allow of an unobstructed view of the GENERAL as he looks out the window.

[*Singing continues.*

WETZEL *has followed him across the room and now stands near.*

Singing softens.]

GENERAL WASHINGTON [*to* WETZEL]—Hear! Your kind gifts have put new heart in my men!

HANS WETZEL—Ve vill bring more, GENERAL!

GENERAL WASHINGTON [*with feeling*]—My good neighbor. Deeds such as yours will one day bring this great country into such unity that all will call our commonwealth "The United States of America!" Let us teach that name to our people.

FOURTH EPISODE

THE STATESMAN AND IMMORTALITY

[*Music, off stage, "President's March."*

When the curtain is ready to rise on Episode Four, HISTORY comes on the stage from the left chanting "First in War, First in Peace and First in the hearts of his Country-men." POSTERITY follows repeating the words. FAME and WASHINGTON walk on stage from right, arm in arm. As they approach the center of the stage, WASHINGTON unbuckles his sword; FAME takes it and passes it to HISTORY, who lays it across POSTERITY's arms. HOME appears at stage left and holds out imploring arms to WASHINGTON. HISTORY waves her off the stage. FAME takes the laurel wreath from his own head and holds it high as though to crown WASHINGTON.]

FAME [*in impressive voice*]—I measure him by the shadow he has cast across the centuries.

[HISTORY *puts out her hand and stays* FAME's *arm.*]

HISTORY—Tarry a bit. His star is yet ascending!

[HISTORY *moves back to her place at the curtain left and* FAME *to the curtain right.* WASHINGTON *and* POSTERITY *go off on left.*]

HISTORY [*announcing the Episode*]—THE STATESMAN AND IMMORTALITY!

FAME [*announcing the Scene*]—A NATION'S HOMAGE!

[*Together they wave up the curtain.*]

CURTAIN RISES

SCENE 1

A NATION'S HOMAGE

Place—Bridge just south of Trenton, New Jersey.

Time—April, 1789.

Speaking Characters

PRESIDENT-ELECT WASHINGTON

TWO ESCORTS OF GENERAL WASHINGTON

DEBORAH BROWN

ANNIS STOCKTON

PARSON

BEREFT MOTHER

CRIPPLED SOLDIER

ANGELINA

GROUPS

Chorus of thirteen young girls.

Thirteen flower girls.

Committee of townspeople [*five or more with Governor at head*]

Populace

———

[*The setting of this scene is an exterior. A simple framework showing the hand rail of a bridge occupies the center of the stage, running from left to right. Across the bridge extends an arch fashioned of evergreens and bearing the words,* THE DEFENDER OF THE MOTHERS WILL BE THE PROTECTOR OF THE DAUGHTERS. *As the curtain rises we see the Trenton assemblage awaiting the arrival of the President-Elect. The townspeople line the stage back waving small flags. The Welcoming Committee stands headed by the Governor at stage right. The thirteen young girls in the chorus are lined up along the bridge. The little children carrying flower baskets are grouped at the left of the bridge.*]

DEBORAH BROWN [*turning to* ANNIS]—You have designed a wonderful arch, ANNIS.

ANNIS—But see who is our inspiration. Surely no king has ever been so royally feted as is the man chosen to be our first President. I wonder if he will be thinking of that dreadful day twelve years ago when he held this bridge with Cornwallis at his heels?

DEBORAH BROWN—They say he looks ahead, never behind. No doubt he is pondering now on the problems of the new government.

[*Cries from the people. "Here Comes* WASHINGTON! *Here Comes* WASHINGTON!" *As he enters stage on left there is loud cheering and cries of "Long Live Our First President! Long Live* WASHINGTON!" *The flower children step forward and begin to strew his way with flowers; the committee of townspeople headed by Richard Howell greet him. The chorus sings.*]

Welcome mighty chief once more
Welcome to this grateful shore,
Now no mercenary foe,
Aims again the fatal blow,
Aims at thee the fatal blow.
Virgins fair and matrons grave,
Those thy conquering arms did save,
Build for thee triumphal bowers

Strew, ye fair his way with flowers
Strew your hero's way with flowers.

[*Band off stage plays*]

ANGELINA [*stepping forward and handing* WASHINGTON *a huge bouquet of flowers.*]—From the children of your country, Sir. [*There are cries of "Speech! Speech!"* WASHINGTON, *visibly moved holds up his hand and shakes his head. The cries continue.*]

WASHINGTON [*taking a step forward and drawing himself up*]—Fellow Countrymen: The love of my country will be the ruling influence of my conduct.

[*Cheers from the people.*]

PARSON [*advancing and humbly removing his hat.*]

WASHINGTON—Put on your hat, parson, and I will shake hands with you.

PARSON—I cannot wear my hat, General, when I think of what you have done for our country.

WASHINGTON—You did as much as I.

PARSON—No! No!

WASHINGTON—You did as much as you could. I've done no more. [*They shake hands.*]

PARSON—The blessings of the Church on you in your great office.

WASHINGTON—I shall always strive to prove a faithful and impartial patron of genuine, vital religion.

[*A woman runs forward and kneeling attempts to kiss his hand.* WASHINGTON *raises her and takes her hand.*]

BEREFT MOTHER—My son fell at Yorktown.

WASHINGTON—Who does not rather envy than regret a death that gives birth to honor and a glorious memory.

[*Music—band or victrola—starts up and the crowd presses forward, registering a scene of American hero-worship. Men clasp* WASHINGTON'S *hand and children run forward to touch his coat. One crippled soldier tenders him a battered flag. Women raise little children in their arms to see him; some weep, all cheer. Good silent acting will lend realism and impressiveness to this scene. The thirteen girls representing the colonies draw to one side and, close together in a single column, raise a sword in their uplifted hands while they sing the song: "Welcome Mighty Chief Once More."*]

CURTAIN

[*Music. Any appropriate strain.*
When it is time for the curtain to rise on the last scene HOME *comes on the stage, from left, holding* POSTERITY *by the hand.* FAME *approaches with* HISTORY *from right.*]

HISTORY [*repeating a few lines of her Prologue as she hands her scroll to* POSTERITY.]

Accept this, Child of eager mind!
Behind your Youth I stretch
A tapestry of years!

[HOME *holds out her hand and* FAME *places his trumpet in it.*]

HOME [*repeating the last lines of her Prologue.*]

And when at last Life's heroes turn
Back from the world's acclaim,

Their weary heads they cradle on my breast,
And fall asleep.

[HISTORY *moves to her place at curtain left.* FAME *to curtain right.* POSTERITY *skips off stage on left.*]

HISTORY [*announcing the Episode*]—THE STATESMAN AND IMMORTALITY!

FAME [*announcing the Scene*]—FRIENDSHIP'S TRIBUTE!

[*Together they wave up the curtain.*]

CURTAIN RISES

SCENE 2

FRIENDSHIP'S TRIBUTE

Place—The drawing-room at Mount Vernon.

Time—February 22, 1799—The Last Birthday.

Speaking Characters

EX-PRESIDENT WASHINGTON

MRS. WASHINGTON

NELLIE CUSTIS, the Mount Vernon Bride

LAWRENCE LEWIS, the Bridegroom

DR. CRAIK

THE RECTOR

GENERAL HARRY LEE

GEORGE CALVERT

BILLY [Negro servant to Washington]

GROUPS

Wedding Guests—any number

Eight Couples—minuet dance

[*The setting of the scene is an interior. The drawing-room at Mount Vernon should be ablaze with candle light from myriads of silver candlesticks and candelabra. Evergreens are festooned over the doors and windows. An old-fashioned grandfather's clock in the corner will give a suggestion of changing time and customs. Little other furniture should be used, as the guests and minuet dancers provide the main setting for the scene.*

As the curtain goes up we find ourselves in the midst of a wedding celebration. The ceremony is over and the guests are congratulating the Bride and Bridegroom, with kisses and handshakes. GENERAL and MRS. WASHINGTON and young WASHINGTON CUSTIS, the brother of the bride, stand nearby sharing in the attention of the hour. The RECTOR is talking with MRS. WASHINGTON. This pantomime is accompanied by music.]

RECTOR [*lifting up his hands for silence*]—Dearly beloved Friends. You have just witnessed the marriage of MISS NELLIE CUSTIS

and MR. LAWRENCE LEWIS, without, perhaps, knowing that this is an occasion for *double rejoicing.* For this happy day that joined the lives of these two young people who have called Mt. Vernon, home, is, also the birthday anniversary of our illustrious friend and neighbor, in whose home we are now gathered. My friends, I firmly believe that the boy born sixty-seven years ago today was sent by a Divine Providence to fulfill the high destiny to which his country called him. To GENERAL WASHINGTON was given the singular destiny and merit of leading the armies of his country successfully through an arduous war, establishing its independence; conducting its councils through the birth of a government, new in form and principle, and of scrupulously obeying its laws through the whole of his career, civil and military. Few men receive the *kiss of Immortality* before they have laid aside this earthly flesh. GENERAL WASHINGTON is the exception. In the name of those of us who have known him, not only in his exalted rank but in an intimate capacity, I extend to him on this birthday our love, friendship and congratulations.

[*There is a cordial clapping of hands and the guests press around the General.*]

WASHINGTON [*turning to the* RECTOR]—You are too kind, Sir. I feel now as I conceive a wearied traveller must do, who after treading many a painful step with a heavy burden on his shoulders is eased. I wish, only, to move gently down the stream of life until I sleep with my Fathers.*

DR. CRAIK [*approaching and takes his hand*]—Speak not of death, dear Friend.

WASHINGTON—I am not afraid to die*. Doctor.

WOMAN GUEST [*clasping his hand*]—A very happy occasion, GENERAL.

WASHINGTON [*looking at* LAWRENCE, *who stands near with a twinkle in his eye*]—Very happy indeed Madam! I have always considered marriage the most interesting event in a man's life.*

GENERAL "LIGHT HORSE" HARRY LEE [*grasping* WASHINGTON'S *hand*]—It has been many a day since the spin-top days of your boyhood, Sir.

WASHINGTON [*looking into his face*]—And we have travelled many roads together since, GENERAL.

CALVERT [*taking* WASHINGTON'S *hand*]—May all the birthdays be spent, now, at Mount Vernon!

WASHINGTON—And here I shall continue, I hope, to the end of my days.

CALVERT—But you will not withdraw your council when needed *There are great questions before us still.*

WASHINGTON—The mass of our citizens require no more than to understand a question to decide it properly themselves.*

[*The music for the minuet begins and the dancers clear the floor for the dance. The Bride throws her veil over her arm and leads the figures with the Groom.*

As many measures of the minuet as desirable may be danced. At the last measure NELLIE LEWIS, *the Bride, runs over to* WASHINGTON, *and holds out her hands. He shakes his head and smiles. She insists and seizes him by the arm. He yields and stepping into the center of the room, treads a few stately measures with the Bride. The Guests applaud and the dancers scatter as* BILLY *brings in beverage glasses on a large silver waiter. Red cardboard glasses, now obtainable, would add a colorful note to the picture.*

As BILLY serves a guest near the front of the stage, he nods his head and chuckles.]

LAWRENCE LEWIS [*Stepping into the center of the room, and lifting his glass*]—To the BRIDE OF MT. VERNON.

[*They all drink.*]

GENERAL LEE [*raising high his glass*]—*To the Father of His Country. First in war, First in peace, and First in the hearts of his countrymen.

CURTAIN

NOTE—*If preferred the scene may end when* WASHINGTON *is treading a measure of the minuet with the Mt. Vernon Bride.*

POSTLUDE

As soon as the curtain falls, the PUPILS of the Prelude come on the stage singing FATHER OF OUR COUNTRY. Behind them walk WASHINGTON and POSTERITY, with FAME, HOME and HISTORY following. Chorus walks off and is heard singing softly behind.

POSTERITY [*looking up in* WASHINGTON'S *face and pointing to the* PUPILS]—And they said you were dead! [*He smiles and shakes his head.*] HISTORY advances and giving WASHINGTON the quill kneels down and supports the scroll on a tablet that he may write. He leans over and FAME stealing up behind him crowns him with the laurel wreath. As he finishes writing POSTERITY throws her arms around him. He rises with the child in his arms, just as the curtain rises on the entire cast, grouped according to suggestion on chart. ADVENTURE skips over to the Indian and Sailor group, HOME seeks out the Mt. Vernon group. POSTERITY from WASHINGTON'S arms holds out her hand to MRS. WASHINGTON. She hesitates. HISTORY crosses the stage and escorts her to WASHINGTON'S side and FAME places her hand in his arm.

All Sing

FATHER OF OUR COUNTRY
(M. McClelland Stevens)

Father of our country,
Great thy name and fair,
Loyal sons and daughters,
Praise thee everywhere.
George Washington, George Washington,
Thy spirit stands apart,
With vigilance and goodness
Enshrined in each one's heart.

Curtain

SUGGESTIONS FOR PRODUCTION

I. Time and Place

If there is reasonable promptness in arranging sets between Episodes this Pageant may be presented in two hours. If a shorter Pageant is desired one scene, instead of two, may be given in each Episode.

The Pageant may be prolonged over four days, or as many weeks, presenting one Episode at a time with the Prologues arranged in their proper places.

The Pageant may be presented as an inter-school or inter-community celebration, staged by four different organizations on four different sites, the audience moving from one to the other. It is entirely available for use in *one school* where the cast is drawn from every grade. It may be staged entirely outdoors, using a larger number in the Populace Groups and more elaborate exits and entrances, or it may be staged on an indoor stage with a limited cast.

II. Presentation

The Pageant Director who assumes charge of the presentation, will do well to appoint a conductor for each Episode, who will be responsible for the promptness of the cast and help to stimulate the silent acting of the groups in his Episode. When the casts of the four Episodes vie with one another for an artistic performance, the success of the Pageant is assured. Too much rehearsing of the entire Pageant tends to rob the performance of its spontaneity. *Speaking* groups should be well drilled, with a few rehearsals by the entire cast.

III. Costume

A general Wardrobe Mistress to plan the costumes and one for each Episode to superintend the making simplifies this important feature. Through the costuming the pageant is given its color and splendor and the Wardrobe Mistress should be chosen with care. The older members of the cast will enjoy making their own costumes, while sewing circles and groups in the community may be organized to sew for the tots. Material bought in large quantities is a great saving and may be shaded by a dye dip, so that the colors will not be uniform.

Further suggestions for the costumes required for each Episode are given under direction for the scenes.

IV. Casting

There are many boys and girls in the High Schools who possess real dramatic ability. These should be chosen to carry on the principal parts. Students from the public speaking classes should be assigned the roles of HISTORY, ADVENTURE, HOME and FAME. The role of WASHINGTON may be played by four boys or one, of good voice and personality.

WASHINGTON as he appears in the Prelude is the WASHINGTON of *Episode Three*. The WASHINGTON of *Episode One* is a youth of fifteen; of *Episode Two,* a young man of twenty-six, and of *Episode Four,* of mature years.

In the Prelude WASHINGTON wears his general's uniform of buff and blue, with a scarlet lined cloak thrown over his shoulders and a sword knot of red and gold at his side.

V. Music

Local conditions must determine whether a band, orchestra, piano or victrola music is used for the accompaniment off stage. This music should cease during realistic scenes carrying dialogue and begin again softly to accentuate the impressiveness of a certain speech. It ties together those bits of pantomine when there is no spoken word to serve this purpose. Appropriate music for Pageantry may be found in ROLAND HOLT'S, *Music for Plays and Pageants*.

VI. *Symbolic Characters*

POSTERITY—A small girl wearing modern dress. She must have acting ability and speak in a clear carrying voice.

HISTORY—A High School girl clad in purple Grecian dress and carrying a scroll and quill. This character speaks and moves with deliberation. When she writes the quill is poised a moment above the scroll before inscribing; her gestures are all important ones.

ADVENTURE—A boy [*High School or upper grade*] wearing a scarlet costume of doublet and hose. ADVENTURE appears each time with a different object; Neptune's trident, bow and arrow, globe of the world. ADVENTURE speaks in a ringing voice, with a hint of breathless excitement. He moves swiftly—surely on the balls of his feet. *He is the life of the Symbolic Group.*

HOME—A High School girl clad in a creamy-white Grecian robe and wearing her long hair unbound. She speaks in a gentle, but clear, voice. She moves softly and gracefully, frequently lifting her long, white sleeved arms in a gesture of protection.

FAME—A High School boy. FAME is arrayed in a gorgeous costume of gold cloth, cut in the fashion of a medieval knight. The cape hanging from the shoulders is lined with crimson. FAME carries a trumpet and a wreath at different times. FAME speaks in a dramatic voice, and moves in an inspiring and majestic manner.

SUGGESTIONS FOR THE GROUPING OF CAST FOR THE FINAL CURTAIN

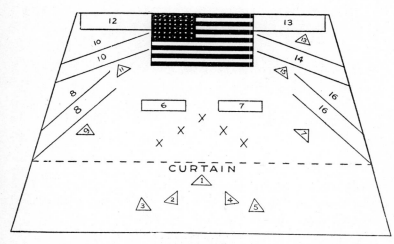

Two platforms placed at the rear of the stage will serve to elevate Group 12 and 13.

When the curtain rises the group in front moves back to positions indicated by crosses.

1. Washington and Posterity
2. Fame
3. Adventure
4. History
5. Home
6. History pupils
7. History pupils
8. Indian Group
   (First row squat on one knee)
9. Half King and Black Feathers.
10. Sailor Group
11. Captain Tuck
12. Dutch Villagers
13. Jersey populace
14. Soldier Group
15. Generals Lee, Putnam, Ward
16. Reel, Minuet dancers and May Day tots

17. The Mt. Vernon Family

The shortest members of each group should, of course, stand in front.

Care should be taken to keep a passage clear from Washington to flag.

* NOTE ON HISTORICAL BACKGROUND

While the scenes of the pageant are founded on historical data, it is not possible always to adhere to it in small details. Certain happenings are frequently telescoped for dramatic effect. An asterisk denotes authentic utterances, although not spoken necessarily under the circumstances enacted.

HISTORICAL BACKGROUND—EPISODE ONE THE YOUTH AND ADVENTURE

SCENE 1—SEA DREAMS

1746

This scene is founded on the tradition that George Washington, the youth, yearned for a seafaring life: a tradition confirmed by a letter from Joseph Ball to his sister, Mrs. Mary Washington, dated May 19, 1747. The surveys and maps made while in the employ of Lord Fairfax and still preserved testify to this association.

"Washington was a bold and adventurous boy eager to see the world. To the youth the romance of the sea was represented by the tobacco ships creeping up from the river and bringing luxuries and necessities from vaguely distant countries."—*Lossing*.

COSTUMES

Sailor costumes of white middy and blue sailor trousers, much the same as those worn today.

Colonial costume of *this period* (1747). Hair powdered and tied back with black bow or encased in wig case. Coat cut squarely to knees and slightly flaring, with long waistcoat, knee breeches, buckled shoes, and carrying, under arm, a three-cornered hat. *The Revolutionary period [later] saw the waistcoat shorter, the coats cut away in front.*

CAST—15-30 Boys of High School Age.

GEORGE WASHINGTON—A youth of fourteen, tall, well built and spirited.

His Brother, LAWRENCE WASHINGTON—Fourteen years older than George.

ROBIN WASHINGTON—George's favorite cousin of about his own age.

LORD FAIRFAX—Of vast estates and a lifelong friend of WASHINGTON. He is dressed in the style of the day in rich material and wears a mustache and goatee.

CAPTAIN TUCK—Tanned and weather-beaten and wearing a merchant captain's cap and uniform.

SAILORS—Just in from far ports and full of spirits.

SET, *Scene 1*—The docks at Alexandria. A large round beam to represent the jib boom of the Antelope. It should be supported off stage and protrude as pictured in opening of scene. Boxes and barrels. A fishing net, which fishermen are mending.

FEATURES

SAILORS' CHORUS—The English sea chantey, BLOW THE MAN DOWN. (Words and music given.)

A Sailor's Hornpipe dance, if desired.

HISTORICAL BACKGROUND
Scene II—THE COURIER
1753

For years the rival nations, France and England, had been claiming possession of the Ohio country and seeing each in its way, to win the Indians over. Governor Dinwiddie of Virginia, hearing that the French had built a fort on territory claimed by the English, sent GEORGE WASHINGTON, whom LORD FAIRFAX had described as "young and daring yet sober minded and responsible," to take a message to the French commander and bring back a report of activities in that region. WASHINGTON, accompanied by CHRISTOPHER GIST, guide, the boldest of Virginia frontiermen, and his fencing master, VAN BRAAM, who purported to know French, and servitors, set forth. On this trip WASHINGTON's life was threatened by an Indian. The French employed wiles to win over members of the Six Nations, but HALF KING, the Indian Chief, remained loyal to the English. WASHINGTON's diary and GIST's narrative of the expedition fix this trip, historically.

COSTUMES

The Indians wore headdresses of animal skins and cap turbans of soft buckskin ornamented with feathers. The favorite head gear was a *gus-to-weh*, or real hat, a small, round, close-fitting cap over which gayly hued feathers were sewed in a fringe. Their bodies naked from the waist up were decorated with paint and strung with feathers and wampum.—*From Salomon's Book of Indian Craft.*

Costume worn by the American party was that of the Virginia frontiersman and was adopted by WASHINGTON both in his activities as a surveyor and later by the men of his Virginia regiment, Coon skin cap, fringed buckskin coat, leggins and long hunting rifle.

FRENCH COMMANDER—Uniform of French blue cut in the style of the time. Long coat to knees square cut and slightly flaring, elaborately braided with many gold buttons. Large cuffs braided, close

fitting boots, military insignia and rolled hats. French soldiers similarly clad with less trimmings.

FRENCH SOLDIERS AND FRONTIERSMEN—The soldiers are dressed similarly to the French Commander. The Frontiersmen wear buckskin leggings, hunting coats, and fur caps.

(Women)—Gowns of homespun cut full and long with tight bodices and bright kerchiefs around the head. *Children dress like their elders.*

CAST—30 or more—*High School and Eighth Grade*

GEORGE WASHINGTON—Courier from Gov. Dinwiddie (21 yrs. old).

CHRISTOPHER GIST—Guide and interpreter.

JACOB VAN BRAAM—Fencing Master and French interpreter.

TWO SERVITORS in WASHINGTON's party.

HALF KING—Chief of the Six Nations' Tribes.

IROQUOIS INDIANS—(Ten or more).

COMMANDER ST. PIERRE—A dapper little French Commander.

TWO OR MORE FRENCH SOLDIERS.

FRENCH SETTLERS—(Ten or 20 from *all* grades), Men, women and children.

BLACK FEATHER—The traitor Indian.

SUGGESTION FOR ACCOMPANYING MUSIC FOR PANTOMIME
INSTRUMENTAL

American Indian Melodies . . . . *Farwell, Schirmer & Co.*
To A Vanishing Race . . . .*Cadman*
From An Indian Lodge . . . .*McDowell*
The Red Man (for band) . . . .*Sousa*

DIRECTIONS FOR FALSE FACE DANCE

NOTE—The following dance of the Iroquois Indians is given as recorded by the Bureau of American Ethnology. According to Iroquois belief, the evil spirits, which bring disease and disaster to the tribe may be frightened away by the false faces employed in the dance.

The steps employed in the False Face Dance are the TOE-HEEL step and the HOP-STEP, the commonest of Indian dance steps.

TOE-HEEL STEP

The weight of the body is shifted to one foot and the other, is advanced so that the heel is lifted and toe touches the ground. The heel is then brought down sharply with force. The movement is repeated with the other foot, the toe being brought down on the loud beat, the heel on the soft beat. This step may be done fast or slow.

HOP-STEP

The hop-step is a skipping step with a double hop on each foot. The movement is on the ball of the foot with knees flexed and lifted high. The heel does not touch the ground.

THE DANCE

First Round—Following the leader who holds high the bag, the dancers using the *toe-heel step*, dance slowly and solemnly around the circle, their bodies bent low (raised knee flexed).

Second Round—*Hop-Step* slowly.

Third Round (Quickened Time)—Dancers raise their rattles, fighting imaginary battles with evil spirits and beating them off. They lay low the enemy, beating the ground with rattles.

Fourth Round (Slow)—Using the toe-heel step, dancers circle around in a slow spiral that winds and unwinds itself and ends with a wild raising of the rattles, a leap in the air and the call of "ZHA-WHA" (Rejoice). This climax brings the sitters springing to their feet, with a vehement shout, "ZHA-WA" . . .

3

Iroquois False-Face
Dance

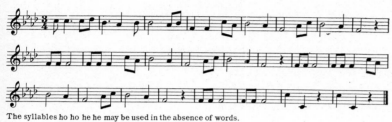

The syllables ho ho he he may be used in the absence of words.

WORDS TO THE SAILOR SONG—BLOW THE MAN DOWN

Come all ye young fellows that follow the sea
  To me way-eye, blow the man down!
And pray pay attention and listen to me,
  Oh! Give me some time to blow the man down!

I'm a deep water sailor just come from Hong Kong
  To me way-aye, blow the man down!
If you'll give me some whisky I'll sing you a song
  Oh! Give me some time to blow the man down!

'Twas on a Black Baller I first served my time—
  To me way-aye, blow the man down!
And in the Black Baller I wasted my prime,
  Oh! Give me some time to blow the man down!

'Tis when the Black Baller is clear of the land—
  To me way-aye, blow the man down!
The crew musters aft at the word of command
  Oh! Give me some time to blow the man down!

"Lay aft," is the cry, "to the break of the poop!"
  To me way-aye, blow the man down!
"Or I'll help you along with the toe of my boot!"
  Oh! Give me some time to blow the man down!

Aye first it's a fist and then it's a fall—
  To me way-aye, blow the man down!
When you ship as a sailor aboard the Black Ball—
  Oh! Give me some time to blow the man down!

One of the oldest and most popular of the English sea chanties.

The Black Ball Line was famous line of packets between New York and Liverpool.

2

Blow The Man Down

DIRECTIONS FOR DANCING ROGER DE COVERLY
(OR VIRGINIA REEL)

Form two long lines facing partners, girls on right, boys on left.

Front girl and back boy (Corners) advance to centre, take right hands and turn, return to places. (Repeat).

Front boy and back girl repeat.

Front girl and back boy advance, take both hands, turn and retire.

Front boy and back girl repeat.

Front girl and back boy advance, curtsy, bow and retire.

Front boy and back girl repeat.

Lines divide to right and left, lead round meet at back; leading couple join hands held high, while those following pass underneath and come down centre.

Thus the front couple becomes the back couplee.

The Step—One step forward on left foot and hop. Same with right foot.

1

Sir Roger de Coverley

4

Song of the Peace Pact

Indians circle round and round while singing. At the last e huñ-ga they raise their arms to heaven, sit down and draw out the peace pipe which they pass from member to member.

HISTORICAL BACKGROUND—EPISODE TWO

THE MAN AND HOME

1758-1773

Scene 1—Courtship

WASHINGTON was a popular hero following his services with Braddock in the French and English engagements and his appointment as Colonel of the Virginia Regiment and Commander-in-Chief of Virginia forces. The incident upon which Scene 1 is based is traditional.

"One loves to picture that gallant, generous, youthful figure, brilliant in color and manly in form, riding gayly on from one little colonial town to another, feasting, dancing, courting and making merry. For him the myrtle and ivy were entwined with the laurel and fame was sweetened with youth."—*Lodge.*

WASHINGTON resigned his commission, was married shortly afterward and settled down to the life of a country gentleman at Mt. Vernon—the longest and most unbroken period of the home life he so loved that he was ever again to experience.

———

COSTUMES—*The same in Scene 1 and 2*

The gala attire of the Colonial gentleman of this period consisted in *square cut coats* of satin or velvet, reaching to the knees and standing out from the figure to show the elaborate long waistcoats. Stockings were scarlet, blue or white with embroidered clocks, knee breeches buckled and tight fitting and of a different color from the coat. The neck and front of the shirt, finely ruffled or lace.

The ladies wore full overdresses with tight bodices, low square cut necks, falling away (but not *looped at this period*) from elaborately trimmed petticoats. Patches and fans. Children's costumes were duplicates of their elders in every detail.

—*From "Costume of the American Colonist."*

CAST IN EPISODE TWO—HOME

Twenty or more. High School. Two First Grade Children.

COLONEL WASHINGTON—The Virginia Hero.

SCENE 1

MARTHA CUSTIS—A Young Widow.

JACKIE AND PATSY CUSTIS—Her Children (4 and 2).

MAJOR CHAMBERLYNE—Host.

MARY—His Daughter.

ANN PARHAM, CYNTHIA GREEN, LOU DANDRIDGE and three other girls—Guests and Reel Dancers.

BILLY—WASHINGTON's body guard.

RENE—Colored Maid.

Eight or Twelve Tall Boys for Partners in the Virginia Reel.

The cast uses 20 or more High School Students, with *two small* children of *kindergarten* age.

Ten SPEAKING PARTS.

———

FEATURES

Dance. The ROGER DE COVERLY (Virginia Reel). One of the most popular dances with the younger set.

SET

The lawn or porch of Major Chamberlyne's home.

A back drop showing the front of an old southern home may be used. Or the front of the house may be indicated by a wide central doorway with windows on either side. A very pretty lawn, which adds a colorful and realistic touch to the setting, may be obtained by the use of the artificial turf employed for miniature golf courses.

———

MUSIC

Drink to Me Only With Thine Eyes.
Believe Me If All Those Endearing Young Charms.

FEATURES

The singing games and little folk dances by the children.
Choice of—
King William Was King James' Son.
Come Take A Little Partner.
A-Hunting We Will Go or others of English origin.

———

MUSIC

Any May Day music may be used to accompany the parts of the scene which are pantomime.

Kimmins G. T. Guild of Play Books—J. Curwen & Sons.
Burchenal, Elizabeth—Folk Dances and Singing Games.

HISTORICAL BACKGROUND

Scene 2—May Day at Mt. Vernon.

While there is no historical basis for this particular scene, it is written around the traditional Mt. Vernon hospitality. It *might* have happened any May Day during that happy period when WASHINGTON was a private citizen, engrossed in the interests of the farm and household. In his "Reminiscences," George Washington Parke Custis, grandson and adopted son, writes:

"The General was very fond of children, and although not particularly at ease with them, delighted in watching them at play. There were many young guests at Mt. Vernon when the Custis children were growing up."

———

CAST

(15-30 kindergarten, first, second grade children.
7 high school and eighth grade roles.)

COLONEL WASHINGTON.

MRS. WASHINGTON, her children, JACKIE and PATSY CUSTIS (9 & 7.)

COL. AND MRS. FAIRFAX, friends and neighbors.

COLONEL MASON, friend and neighbor.

LITTLE SALLY FAIRFAX, niece of Col. Fairfax.

LITTLE JOHNNY CARLISLE, son of Alexandria friends.

MAMMY LOU, Colored Mammy.

BILLY, Colored Body Guard.

Child Guests—Any number.

SET

The Lawn at Mt. Vernon. The same set as used in Scene 1 of this episode may be used, with small changes. Lanterns should be strung around the stage. Real food served to the small guests in the party scene will enhance the action and render natural the pantomime for the small actors.

HISTORICAL BACKGROUND—EPISODE THREE

THE GENERAL AND FAME

Scene 1—The Glory of the Revolution.

A few days after the Battle of Bunker Hill. July, 1775.

This scene is founded on the tradition that WASHINGTON assumed command of the Continental Army under the Cambridge elm on the outskirts of Boston, where a regiment of New England soldiers were encamped. The city was held by the British.

One of WASHINGTON's aides writes:

"The entire army if it deserved the name was but an assemblage of brave, enthusiastic, undisciplined country lads; the officers in general, with the exception of a few elderly men, as ignorant of military life as the troops." A little later the same writer records: "There is a great overturning in the camp since GENERAL WASHINGTON took command. A sharp distinction between officers and soldiers, order, regularity, laws and punishments."

Henry Cabot Lodge writes:

"A slave owner, an aristocrat and a churchman, WASHINGTON came to Cambridge to pass over the heads of native generals to the command of the New England Army, among democratic people. Yet he never lost the allegiance he won for himself when he first took command."

COSTUMES

GENERAL WASHINGTON uniform, the well known buff and blue, and wearing across his breast the blue ribbon of supreme command.

SOLDIERS. The more varied the costume of the assemblage of *soldiers* the better. Their costumes were mainly improvised. Fisher lads, farmer boys, etc. OFFICERS wear nondescript uniforms.

THE DRUM AND FIFE BAND. Attired (by General Ward) in blue coats and red breeches.

VIRGINIA RIFLEMEN. Coon skin cap, fringed buckskin coat, leggins and hunting jacket. Same worn by WASHINGTON in Episode One, Scene 2.

CAST

30-100 Seventh, Eighth and High School.
Ten Speaking Parts. High School.

GENERAL WASHINGTON, Commander-in-Chief of the Army.
GENERAL WARD, Commanding Troops of Massachusetts Bay Colony.
GENERAL PUTNAM, Commanding Connecticut Troops.
GENERAL LEE.
TWO AIDES TO WASHINGTON.
CAPTAIN QUINCY.
LIEUT. CLARKE.

YOUNG CORPORAL, a Burning Young Patriot.
FIVE SPEAKING SOLDIERS.
MESSENGER.
FIFE AND DRUM BAND BOYS (They were mere lads), 7th Grade.
OTHER SOLDIERS.

SET

Staged outdoors with a large cast, the scene may be made most impressive, but a good effect may be gained on an indoor stage with a smaller cast. Little scenery is needed. The Cambridge elm tree should be featured wherever staged. GENERAL WASHINGTON and his aids may arrive on horseback, in an outdoor performance.

FEATURES

The Fife and Drum Band. In the absence of musicians for a real band, the Victrola, for which good records of Fife and Drum music have been made, may be used off stage.

MUSIC

Yankee Doodle, and other songs characteristic of the period.

HISTORICAL BACKGROUND

Scene 1—The Gloom of the Revolution

This scene is based upon the historical record of GENERAL WASHINGTON's "darkest days" of the Revolution. Supplies for his ill-clad, ill-fed soldiers failed to reach their destination, owing to the unfortunate policy of Congress. Criticism and jealousy ran riot among the officers and desertions and discontent among the men.

"The tradition of WASHINGTON's prayer of sorrowful supplication has found an imperishable place in American thought."

MRS. WASHINGTON brightened the winter quarters with her kindness and constantly employed her needle in mending and making soldier garments. While there is no record of Gov. Henry's visit, it might have taken place. The German farm folks from the settlement above Valley Forge brought temporary relief to the hungry soldiers with their *dole.*

COSTUMES

The soldiers wear uniforms of buff and blue, as does the Commander-in-Chief. The coat shows a slight change from the earlier period, in that it slopes away from the front with shorter waistcoat. (See pictures of that period.)

THE GERMAN FARM FOLK are dressed in the peasant costume of their native land. The men wear full long trousers, colored shirts and high caps or broad hats. The women wear bright colored, full skirts, white blouses and cap of muslin.

THE CHILDREN dress like elders.

MRS. WASHINGTON and MRS. THOMSON are dressed in the style of that period, which varies from that described in Episode Two, in that the overdress is looped back in panniers, instead of falling straight.

CAST

(25-50 from *All Grades*—7 *High School* roles.)

GENERAL WASHINGTON.

MRS. WASHINGTON.

PATRICK HENRY, Governor of Virginia.

SECRETARY TO THE GENERAL.

MRS. THOMSON, Housekeeper at Headquarters.

HANS WETZEL, Spokesman for the German Farm Folk.

THOMAS BIXBY, Guard.

BILLY, GENERAL WASHINGTON'S Negro Body Guard.

GERMAN FARM FOLK—Any number, and all Grades.

SOLDIER CHORUS—(Off Stage).

———

SET

Room at Valley Forge Headquarters. Window at back. Door at right, back. Desk at stage left; table at right front. A small tattered flag hangs on the wall. Correspondence piled on desk. Soldiers' garments on table.

———

MUSIC

During the silent acting by the farm folk, any German folk music may be played.

Any Revolutionary soldier songs may be used for soldier chorus. *Yankee Doodle, Ballad of the Tea*, etc., etc.

HISTORICAL BACKGROUND—EPISODE FOUR

THE STATESMAN AND IMMORTALITY

Scene 1—A Nation's Homage

1789

"From Mt. Vernon to New York the President-elect's was a triumphal march. There was no imperial government to lend its powers and military pageantry. There were no armies with trophies to dazzle the eyes of the beholder, nor was there wealth and luxury to give pomp and splendor to the occasion. It was the simple out-pouring of popular feeling, untaught and true, but full of reverence and gratitude to a great man. It was the noble instinct of hero-worship, always keen in humanity when the real hero comes to awaken it to life."—*Lossing*.

This scene is founded upon a published description of the celebration which Trenton staged to the President-elect on his way to take the oath of office. His route lay across the same bridge in the town, where, twelve years before, he had met Cornwallis on the evening previous to the battle of Princeton. Upon this bridge the celebration took place.

———

COSTUMES

Villagers and townspeople wear the style of the day. Men and boys in coats of the Revolutionary period cut, knee breeches, etc. Women and girls with full skirts and panniers.

THE PARSON wears a long black robe with flat hat.

SOLDIERS—Revolutionary uniforms.

WASHINGTON wears a "brown home-spun suit cut after the fashion of the day."

THIRTEEN GIRLS OF CHORUS. Dressed in white high-waisted full dresses and wearing flower wreaths on their heads.

FLOWER CHILDREN. In pastel colors, carrying baskets.

———

CAST

(40-150 *All Grades*.)

PRESIDENT-ELECT WASHINGTON.

HIS TWO ESCORTS.

DEBORAH BROWN.

ANNIS STOCKTON.

RICHARD HOWELL, Composer of Song of Welcome.

PARSON.

BEREFT MOTHER.

CRIPPLED SOLDIER.

ANGELINA, Small Girl.

THIRTEEN YOUNG GIRLS FOR CHORUS.

THIRTEEN CHILDREN (1st and 2nd grades) for Flower Bearers.

COMMITTEE OF TOWNSPEOPLE.

POPULACE.

———

SET

Simple framework of bridge showing handrail reaches across stage. Over the center of the bridge rises an arch. It is decorated with evergreen and bears the lettering, THE DEFENDER OF THE MOTHERS WILL BE THE PROTECTOR OF THE DAUGH-TERS. The arch may be used without the bridge framework, if desirable, information on the programs that the scene takes place on the bridge being all that is necessary.

———

MUSIC

Welcome Noble Chieftain.

WASHINGTON'S March, or other music.

———

HISTORICAL BACKGROUND

Scene II—Friendship's Tribute

1799

Eleanor Custis, affectionately known as "Nelly," was, undoubt-edly GENERAL WASHINGTON'S favorite of the many young people who called at Mt. Vernon during his time. Upon the death of John Parke Custis (JACKIE), MRS. WASHINGTON'S only son, GENERAL and MRS. WASHINGTON took charge of the two younger children, "Nelly" and Washington, and brought them up as their own. "Nelly" adored the General and stood in no awe of him. She lived to a great old age and recounted many charming experiences at Mt. Vernon, including her own wedding on the General's last birth-day. On Feb. 22, 1799, Eleanor Custis and Lawrence Lewis, son of GENERAL WASHINGTON'S only sister, Betty, were married in the drawing room at Mt. Vernon. There is no exact account of that wedding and the scene drawn here is merely one that might have taken place.

COSTUMES

The bride wears a gown of white satin, cut in the style of the day, with tight bodice, full petticoat and pannier. She wears a veil and carries a colonial bouquet. (Round and edged with lace.)

The minuet dancers and guests wear gala day attire of the period. Satins and velvets for the men, frills and laces for the ladies.

The bridegroom wears a wedding suit of blue satin.

GENERAL WASHINGTON wears his general's uniform of buff and blue, and General Lee is likewise attired.

———

CAST

(25-50 Eighth Grade and High School.)
Seven Speaking Parts—High School.

EX-PRESIDENT WASHINGTON.
MRS. WASHINGTON.
THE BRIDE, ELEANOR CUSTIS.
THE BRIDEGROOM, LAWRENCE LEWIS.
THE RECTOR (wearing a flowing black gown).
GENERAL "HARRY" LEE, Washington's life-long friend, and one of his ablest Generals in the Revolution.
DR. JAMES CRAIK, Intimate Friend.

GEORGE CALVERT, a member of the Maryland family of Nelly's mother.
BRIDAL ATTENDANTS and MINUET DANCERS. (The same or different groups.)
GUESTS—Any Number.
BILLY (in scarlet livery of the WASHINGTONS). Negro bodyguard.

———

SET

The drawing room at Mt. Vernon. Much furniture will be in the way, but the grandfather's clock in the corner or some other old piece may be used. The atmosphere of the festivities of the period may be obtained best through the use of many silver candlesticks and candelabra, lighted if possible.

———

MUSIC

Wedding March and Minuet.

———

FEATURES

Dancing of the Minuet.

THE BOYS' GEORGE WASHINGTON

By M. ELIZABETH SALOIS

A GEORGE WASHINGTON PAGEANT

Copyright, 1931, by M. Elizabeth Salois

CHARACTERS AND SCENES

BOYS OF TODAY

JACK, *a large boy.*

HANS, *a German schoolmate, much younger.*

Both boys appear in every scene.

HISTORICAL

SCENE 1: *GEORGE WASHINGTON, THE YOUTH.*

FIRST BOY.
SECOND BOY.
SANDY.
THIRTEEN BOYS.
GEORGE WASHINGTON, *the youth.*

SCENE 2: *COLONEL WASHINGTON AND GENERAL BRADDOCK.*

EIGHT COLONIAL SOLDIERS.
GENERAL BRADDOCK.
DANIEL MORGAN.
EIGHT BRITISH SOLDIERS.
COLONEL GEORGE WASHINGTON.

SCENE 3: *THE CONTINENTAL CONGRESS.*

JOHN HANCOCK.
CHARLES THOMSON, *secretary.*
JOHN ADAMS.
PATRICK HENRY.
JOHN JAY.
BENJAMIN FRANKLIN.
MEMBERS OF CONGRESS.
GEORGE WASHINGTON, Commander-in-Chief.

SCENE 4: *OVER THE DELAWARE TO TRENTON.*

GENERAL NATHANAEL GREENE.
GENERAL JOHN SULLIVAN.
TWO COMPANIES OF SOLDIERS.
GENERAL WASHINGTON.

SCENE 5: *THE FIRST INAUGURATION.*

CHANCELLOR LIVINGSTON.
JOHN ADAMS.
ALEXANDER HAMILTON.
ROGER SHERMAN.
HENRY KNOX.
BARON VON STEUBEN.

ARTHUR ST. CLAIR.

SENATORS.

REPRESENTATIVES.

A CROWD OF SPECTATORS.

PRESIDENT GEORGE WASHINGTON.

SCENE 6: *PRESIDENT WASHINGTON REFUSES A THIRD TERM.*

FIRST MAN.

SECOND MAN.

CROWD OF COLONIAL MEN AND WOMEN.

PRESIDENT GEORGE WASHINGTON.

TIME: The present.

SET: A shallow front stage with lounging chairs for JACK and HANS. Then, since four of the inserted scenes occur out of doors and but two indoors, it is suggested that the larger stage be curtained at back and sides and a few articles of furnishing appropriate to the individual locale be placed against the curtains, such as: a fence for the school yard; a tree or two for the forest; a balcony for the Inaugural; a desk and chair for the PRESIDENT's house in Philadelphia.

COSTUMES: The historical characters are to be dressed in costumes appropriate to the period: military uniforms, smallclothes, wigs, bright colored waistcoats, polonaise gowns, etc. (See the *George Washington Play and Pageant Costume Book* issued by the Commission for suggestions.)

[*At one side of the stage sit* JACK *and his little German friend,* HANS. JACK *is reading a large history book;* HANS, *mending a skate strap. It is the day before Washington's birthday.*]

JACK—What are you going to do tomorrow, Hans?

HANS—Tomorrow? Just go to school. For why do you ask?

JACK—Why, Hans! Going to school! Don't you know that tomorrow is a holiday?

HANS—Holiday! Holiday! We just celebrated Lincoln's birthday. What day is tomorrow, then?

JACK—Washington's birthday. I thought everybody knew that!

HANS—Washington?

JACK—George Washington, the Father of Our Country.

HANS—Who's he, Jack? Tell me of him.

JACK—Why everybody knows that! Every history book tells you about him. Don't you study history?

HANS—Please not to ask me any more questions, Jack, but tell me of the great man, please. Where did he live?

JACK—Why he lived away down in Virginia—near the Potomac River.

HANS—A long time ago, perhaps?

JACK—Yes, Hans, ages ago. It's two hundred years ago since he was born.

HANS—And he lived in a log cabin?

JACK—You are thinking of Lincoln. George Washington lived in a beautiful house—that is, most of his life he did. It is called Mount Vernon.

HANS—Well but what did he do that everybody calls him the Father of Our Country and that we have no school on his birthday?

JACK—I'm afraid he did so much that it's hard to begin to tell about him, Hans.

HANS—He was once a little boy like me?

JACK—Oh, yes, indeed, he was! You just stay here beside me and I'll tell you all about him. But first I'll show you just what George Washington did when he was a boy.

[*The curtains then part to disclose several groups of boys in a school yard. Some of the boys are spinning tops, others playing marbles, and the remainder of the boys are looking on. Time about 1742.*]

JACK—Listen, Hans. When George Washington was a boy his favorite game was playing soldiers. The other fellows always chose him for their leader. He was a good leader, too. You just watch this.

SCENE 1

GEORGE WASHINGTON, THE YOUTH

[*Enter a boy who takes the part of* WASHINGTON. *He watches the marble game unnoticed until one boy, looking up, sees him.*]

FIRST BOY—Oh, hello, George. Say, fellows, here is George and now we can have a real game.

[*The boys stop playing and crowd around* GEORGE.]

GEORGE—Well, boys, what do you want to play?

FIRST BOY—We want to play soldiers!

BOYS [*in chorus*]—Yes, yes! let's play soldiers!

FIRST BOY—Who'll we have for a leader? I choose George Washington.

SECOND BOY—I choose George Washington, too. You all choose George Washington for a leader, don't you, boys?

BOYS—We choose George Washington—George Washington for our leader!

FIRST BOY—George, you are leader again. Somehow, fellows, I feel that George will always be our leader.

GEORGE—All right. Fall in. [*Each boy takes a gun or a stick to represent a gun and falls into line.*] My men, I hear that Indians are on our trail. Sandy, I appoint you to be a scout. Find out where these redskins are and report to me. [*They salute and* SANDY *goes out.*] Left dress! [*Boys straighten line.*] Mark time! Left! Right! Left! Right! Forward march! [*Boys march to the front of the stage.*] Halt! One! Two! About face! One! Two! Forward march! Left! Right! Left! Right! [*Boys march to the rear of the stage.*] Halt! One! Two! About face! One! Two! Ready! Load! Aim! Fire!

[SANDY *the scout re-enters running, halts in front of* GEORGE *and salutes.* WASHINGTON *returns salute.*]

SANDY—Captain Washington, the redskins, in war paint, are in the woods at the rear. [*Salutes and gets into line.*]

GEORGE—The Indians are approaching for an attack. We must surprise them and drive them back before they can enter our fortress. Fight for your king, your country, and your home. We go to fight the redskins. Shoulder arms! Left face! Forward march!

[WASHINGTON *and the boys march out. Curtain.*]

HANS—*My!* but the boy George liked the game of war and soldiers, didn't he; and was he ever in a real war?

JACK—He often went into the deep, dark Virginia forests with only his dog and his gun. He would have been a good boy scout, the best ever.

HANS—To be a boy then was more fun than now.

JACK—I just wish that I'd been a boy then. I would have done things, too. He could build a shelter for the night, build a fire, cook what he had trapped or shot, and then lie down to sleep alone in the forest.

HANS—What a brave boy, that!

JACK—Wasn't he? There never was any braver, Hans.

HANS—Wasn't he a bit afraid?

JACK—Not a bit. He even lived alone in the forest for awhile.

HANS—For why did he do that, Jack?

JACK—You will have to study history! It's fine but I'll tell you now. He was a surveyor and he was only a little older than I am.

HANS—But the Indians when he was surveying in those woods?

JACK—Oh, he met lots of Indians. He learned to fight them, too.

HANS—And he was not killed?

JACK—Killed? Hans, you just listen to this.

SCENE 2

COLONEL WASHINGTON AND GENERAL BRADDOCK

[*The curtains at the back part—enter* WASHINGTON *as a Virginia Colonel. He is followed by the* VIRGINIA COLONIAL TROOPS *and by* BRADDOCK *and his* BRITISH SOLDIERS. *This scene takes place in the woods. Time, 1755.*]

GEN. BRADDOCK—I tell you, Colonel Washington, I intend to build a road through the forest and march in true military fashion.

COL. WASHINGTON—That, of course, would be the correct way in Europe, General Braddock, but here in America we have to proceed in a different fashion. A long train of heavily loaded wagons would move too slowly. The Indians will be sure to surprise you.

GEN. BRADDOCK—Indians? Colonel Washington, the Indians will run when they see the trained troops of the English king. They will be thoroughly frightened.

COL. WASHINGTON—General Braddock, I would advise you to move quickly and fight in the Indian fashion. Give each soldier instructions to hide behind a rock, a tree, or a bush, whenever they are fighting Indians.

GEN. BRADDOCK—My soldiers fight in such a cowardly way? Never! These savages may be dangerous to raw militia but it is impossible that they should make any impression on the King's troops. [*A savage war-whoop is heard in the near distance.*] What is that ungodly noise, Colonel Washington?

COL. WASHINGTON—That, General Braddock, is an Indian war-whoop.

GEN. BRADDOCK—God save the King! Stand your ground, **my** brave English men!

COL. WASHINGTON—There is no way to fight an Indian except in true Indian fashion. Take to the trees, my Colonials!

[WASHINGTON, BRADDOCK, *and the* SOLDIERS *go out. War-whoops are heard from the distance. Curtain.*]

HANS—That General Braddock! I do not think, Jack, I would have liked him!

JACK—Of course, Hans, Braddock thought that George Washington was a backwoodsman who knew nothing of war.

HANS—But, Jack, you do not tell me enough!

JACK—You'll soon hear more, Hans. I've told you about Daniel Morgan, haven't I?

HANS—Of a certainty, you have.

JACK—Well, Daniel Morgan was in this battle. He was a wagon driver. Now watch!

[*The curtain parts and* WASHINGTON *with his men re-enter accompanied by two* BRITISH SOLDIERS.]

COL. WASHINGTON—Alas, poor Braddock!

DANIEL MORGAN—Well, if General Braddock had taken your advice, Colonel Washington, all this need not have happened.

COL. WASHINGTON—Yes, poor Braddock thought it was cowardly to fight an Indian by hiding behind a tree; hence, some sixty-three of his officers and two-thirds of his brave soldiers were killed, and Braddock himself mortally wounded.

DANIEL MORGAN—You saved the day, Colonel Washington.

COL. WASHINGTON—Gather the men together, Morgan. We must all make a swift retreat into Virginia. It grieves me that we cannot return as a victorious army. Forward, men!

[WASHINGTON *and the* SOLDIERS *go out. Curtain.*]

HANS—That Washington was wise, Jack.

JACK—I tell you Washington was always right. It was mighty lucky for us he wasn't killed that day.

HANS—Killed, Jack!

JACK—Came near it! Hans! Four bullets went through his clothes and two horses were shot under him.

HANS—I just wish that I could have been there. I would have helped Washington shoot every Indian there!

JACK—Tush, Hans, Washington didn't need you or me.

HANS—But he fought more?

JACK—He certainly did. He was always first in war. Want to see him again, Hans?

HANS—You know I do, Jack.

SCENE 3

THE CONTINENTAL CONGRESS

[*This scene takes place in Independence Hall.* JOHN HANCOCK, *the President of the Continental Congress, is seated at a desk;* CHARLES THOMSON, *the secretary, at one side;* WASHINGTON *and the members of The Congress are in their places, talking quietly. Time, 1775.*]

JOHN HANCOCK [*pounding with a gavel*]—The members of this Congress will please come to order. [*Members become quiet and give attention*] Mr. Thomson, will you please give a short review of the work done by this Congress?

MR. THOMSON—Mr. President and honored members of the Continental Congress, in compliance with the request of President Hancock I beg to announce that a petition to the King has been prepared and forwarded by special messenger; addresses have been prepared to the people of Great Britain, Ireland, and Canada; the issue of bills of credit or paper money to the amount of two millions of dollars has been authorized; a day has been set apart for fasting and prayer; various Colonies have been authorized to form local governments; and a motion has been passed to raise an army of fifteen thousand men.

JOHN HANCOCK—Is there any other business to come before this meeting?

JOHN ADAMS—Mr. President.

JOHN HANCOCK—Mr. Adams.

JOHN ADAMS—The position of Commander-in-Chief of the Continental Army must be held by one whose patriotism and integrity can never be doubted, by one whose courage and bravery transcends that of the average man, whose patience is superior to that of the ordinary man, by one whose leadership is inborn, and by one whose courage and stamina on the battlefield have already been proven. These requirements are high but they are found in one of our members, and he is the man whom I suggest—George Washington of Virginia!

[WASHINGTON *shows surprise, springs to his feet, and hurries from the stage.*]

THOMAS JOHNSON—Mr. President.

JOHN HANCOCK—Mr. Johnson.

THOMAS JOHNSON—I concur in the timely remarks of Mr. Adams. I therefore nominate as Commander-in-Chief for the Continental Army Mr. George Washington. I consider this selection to be one of supreme importance to every inhabitant of these Thirteen Colonies.

[*There is a commotion of approval.*]

SAMUEL ADAMS—I second the nomination of George Washington.

JOHN HANCOCK—All those in favor of appointing George Washington to be Commander-in-Chief of the Continental Army signify by saying, "Aye."

MEMBERS OF THE SECOND CONTINENTAL CONGRESS—Aye! Aye!

JOHN HANCOCK—Opposed? [*No votes against* WASHINGTON.] George Washington is unanimously chosen Commander-in-Chief of the Continental Army.

JOHN HANCOCK—Mr. Henry, will you please ask our new Commander-in-Chief to return?

[PATRICK HENRY *leaves, using the same exit used by* WASHINGTON.]

JOHN JAY—Mr. President.

JOHN HANCOCK—Mr. Jay.

JOHN JAY—I move that we pay General Washington a salary of five hundred dollars per month during the time that he serves as Commander-in-Chief of the Continental Army.

BENJAMIN FRANKLIN—I second the motion.

JOHN HANCOCK—All those in favor of paying a salary of five hundred dollars to General Washington during the time that he is Commander-in-Chief signify by saying "Aye."

MEMBERS OF THE SECOND CONTINENTAL CONGRESS—Aye! Aye!

JOHN HANCOCK—Opposed? [*There are no votes against the motion.*] It is passed.

[WASHINGTON *returns with* HENRY.]

JOHN HANCOCK—Mr. Washington, I have the honor to announce to you that you have been chosen unanimously to the position of Commander-in-Chief of the Continental Army at a salary

of five hundred dollars a month. I congratulate you and wish you success.

GEN. WASHINGTON—Mr. President and members of the Second Continental Congress, I accept the position of Commander-in-Chief of the Continental Army and thank you for the honor that you have conferred upon me, but lest some unlucky event should happen unfavorable to my reputation, I beg it may be remembered by every gentleman in this room, that I this day declare, with the utmost sincerity, I do not think myself equal to the command I am honored with. As to pay, I beg leave to assure the Congress that, as no pecuniary consideration could have tempted me to accept this arduous employment, at the expense of my domestic ease and happiness, I do not wish to make any profit on it. I will keep an exact account of my expenses. Those I doubt not they will discharge, and that is all I desire.

[*Curtain*]

HANS—Jack, I will be a general like Washington!

JACK—Well, if I can't be a general, I'm going to be just as nearly like Washington as I can.

HANS—What war was this, Jack?

JACK—Hans, Hans! I thought everybody—even you—knew that!

HANS—And Washington won all the battles?

JACK—No, Hans, he didn't and at one time things looked very dark and dismal. Everyone thought the cause of liberty was lost, but Washington won a brilliant victory and then every one was cheerful and hopeful again.

HANS—And what battle was that, Jack?

JACK—Trenton. You'll learn a little about it now.

SCENE 4

OVER THE DELAWARE TO TRENTON

[*The curtains part. This scene takes place on the east bank of the Delaware River. GENERAL WASHINGTON with two of his generals, GREENE and SULLIVAN, stand with their men ready to march to Trenton. The men are dressed as for cold weather, although some of the men are barefooted. Early Morning, Dec. 26, 1776.*]

GEN. WASHINGTON—General Greene, has every soldier crossed safely?

GEN. GREENE—Yes, General Washington, the Delaware has claimed not one. Thanks to our Massachusetts fishermen who guided the boats with great skill, twenty-four hundred men crossed in safety.

GEN. SULLIVAN—I never thought this could be done, General!

GEN. WASHINGTON—It could not have been done without the skill and courage of my brave boatmen. [*To the* SOLDIERS] My gallant men, there are now nine miles to march to Trenton. In this rain and hail, the roads will be in dreadful condition. However, the Hessians will be so sure of not being attacked that we shall surprise them all after Christmas parties and games, surround them, and make a quick and sharp attack.

GEN. SULLIVAN—General, the muskets are so wet that we cannot fire them off. What shall we do?

GEN. WASHINGTON—Use the bayonet. My brave men, since all is ready, let us press forward.

GEN. GREENE—Forward march!

GEN. SULLIVAN—Forward march!

[*The* GENERALS *and the men march off. Curtain.*]

HANS—It was a great battle, Jack?

JACK—Yes, Washington was victorious. The battle only lasted three quarters of an hour. Washington captured nearly a thousand Hessians. The hearts and spirits of the Americans rose again. The cause of liberty was not lost.

HANS—Then Washington won the Revolutionary War, didn't he?

JACK—I'll say he did but he must have been glad to return to Mount Vernon.

HANS—He loved it, his home?

JACK—He had earned a long rest, Hans, but he couldn't remain there long.

HANS—Why not?

JACK—Because you see the people had made a new government and they needed a president.

HANS—Oh, then the General Washington was elected to President?

JACK—The First President of the United States!

SCENE 5

THE FIRST INAUGURATION

[*The curtains part. This scene depicts the Inauguration of* WASHINGTON *at Federal Hall in New York, April 30, 1789. Enter* WASHINGTON, *followed by* CHANCELLOR LIVINGSTON, JOHN ADAMS, HAMILTON, SHERMAN, KNOX, STEUBEN, ST. CLAIR, *and both Houses of Congress. A crowd of spectators cheers as* WASHINGTON *comes forward. He lays his hand on his heart and bows several times.*]

CHANCELLOR LIVINGSTON [*Giving oath of office*]—George Washington, do you solemnly swear that you will faithfully execute the office of President of the United States, and will to the best of your ability, preserve, protect, and defend the Constitution of the United States?

WASHINGTON—I swear, so help me God. [*Kisses the Bible.*]

[*The spectators cheer and bells ring.* WASHINGTON *bows.*]

HANS—Is that all a President must do?

JACK—All he has to do! Hans, Washington was President eight years and guided us through some of the hardest time in our history.

HANS—He had to do everything first, did he not, Jack?

JACK—Yes, no one had done this work before. There was no one for him to copy.

HANS—Eight years! And his beautiful plantation on the Potomac?

JACK—You'll find out in just a moment. One more little lesson, Hans, and you'll know much about him.

SCENE 6

PRESIDENT WASHINGTON REFUSES THIRD TERM

[*The curtains part. This scene takes place in the house that was occupied by* WASHINGTON *in Philadelphia. Enter* WASHINGTON *with a group of men and women about him.*]

FIRST MAN—PRESIDENT WASHINGTON, we have come to ask you to stand a third time for the Presidency.

PRESIDENT WASHINGTON—My friends, you no longer need me as President.

SECOND MAN—We cannot give to another the highest office in the country. We fear that no other can be safely entrusted with the great responsibilities which you have borne so nobly.

PRESIDENT WASHINGTON—The Government is now firmly established. There are others who can fill the position of President of the United States. I will not accept office again. I shall retire to my beloved plantation at Mount Vernon and I hope to spend a few years among the scenes that I love. In bidding you farewell I advise you: "Beware of attacks upon the Constitution. Beware of those who think more of their party than of their country. Promote education. Observe justice. Treat with good faith all nations. Adhere to the right. Be united! Love your country."

[*Curtain*]

JACK—Now, Hans, do you understand why George Washington is called the Father of Our Country?

HANS—Certainly, Jack, I know now and I shall not forget it. [*Rises and faces a picture or bust of* WASHINGTON.] Father of Our Country, I salute you! [*Salutes bust or picture of* WASHINGTON.] I hope then, Washington had a nice long vacation at the beautiful Mount Vernon.

JACK—Not for very long. He died a few years later and was mourned by everyone in the country. So, Hans, now you know why there is a holiday tomorrow.

HANS—I know what day tomorrow is. [*Jumps up and salutes bust or picture again.*] All honor to Washington!

JACK—And for a last thing, Hans: Let me tell you what Lincoln said about Washington: "To add brightness to the sun or glory to the name of Washington is alike impossible. Let none attempt it. In solemn awe pronounce his name, and in its naked, deathless splendor leave it shining on."

[*Curtain.*]

Living Pages From Washington's Diary

By Kathleen Read Coontz

A GEORGE WASHINGTON PAGEANT

FOREWORD

Living Pages From Washington's Diary has been written and arranged to meet the need for a simple and artistic production on the life of George Washington.

Women's Clubs, especially, composed largely of busy mothers and housewives, will welcome, no doubt, a George Washington Bicentennial celebration feature that may be given without too much time required for rehearsal and in which there are but few spoken parts.

From time immemorial the tableau has lent itself to this type of entertainment and rarely fails to call forth an appreciative audience.

George Washington's Diary has been carefully searched for entries characteristic of various phases in his illustrious life which best permit of artistic picturization. A note concerning the diary itself is given on page 702, with the hope that it may stimulate a greater interest in this remarkable record of the daily activities of a world-renowned character.

The prints are reproduced to serve as suggestions for costuming, grouping and setting for the tableaux and may, of course, be enlarged upon or simplified as the producer sees fit.

The charm of the *Candle-Time Reverie* will depend upon the ease and grace with which the music, dialogue, and tableaux are correlated.

SYNOPSIS

I: THE REVERIE.
II: THE TABLEAUX.

1. The Queen's Birthnight Ball
2. The Mother and Her Son
3. After the Hunt
4. Washington Accepts His Commission
5. The Soldier's Return
6. Christmas at Mount Vernon
7. The President's Levee
8. Thanksgiving Day
9. Music Hour at Mount Washington
10. Independence Day With Washington
11. The Portrait

THE REVERIE

PLACE—*Wherever books are treasured.*
TIME—*Any candletime.*

SPEAKING CHARACTERS

ARCHIVIST, *whose candlelight weaves the spell.*
SPIRIT OF BYGONE YEARS, *who lifts the Curtain of the Past.*
SINGERS OF OLDEN SONGS, *who bring "a starry crown of song."*

SYMBOLIC CHARACTERS

QUILLS, *custodians of the Diary.*
THE DAY
THE MONTH   } *the dates which "slip away in smiles and tears."*
THE YEAR

GROUPS

GEORGE WASHINGTON, *central figure in the eleven tableaux.*
MINUET DANCERS *and* PRESIDENT'S LEVEE GUESTS.
FOX HUNTERS.
CHRISTMAS GUESTS.
STATESMEN GROUP.
WORSHIPERS.
MT. VERNON FAMILY.
INDEPENDENCE DAY CELEBRATORS.

[*The stage curtain rises upon the* ARCHIVIST *standing before a shelf of musty looking old books on the stage left. He is reading from a queer looking little volume by the light of the candle which he holds. There he stands "the world forgetting by the world forgot," his candle making a nimbus of light in an otherwise darkened room. After a moment he moves slowly to the table nearby, places his candlestick on it and sinks down in the chair without removing his gaze from the pages of the book. He reads on a bit, then looks up.*]

ARCHIVIST [*speaking wonderingly as though to himself*]—Washington's diary! . . . . . George Washington's diary! [*Glances down and turns the pages. Then reads aloud the following entry:*] "Breakfasted at Queen Anne's. Dined in Annapolis and lodged at Rock Hall." [*Looks up, rises and walks to the center of the stage fondling the little volume meditatively*]— Time, Fate and Death, that trio old, hath long since closed the book I hold!

And yet the Life that plied that quill, has power e'en now to awe and thrill!

These yellowed names o'er which I pore . . . Ah! would they might in truth, tell more!

Today—mere shadows on a page—once . . . moved in grace across Life's stage! [*Turns the volume over reverently, then extends his hand in a gesture of invocation.*]

Out of the mists that round thee lie . . . Come forth, O Spirit of years gone by!

Thy magic wand wave o'er this page . . . Transport us to a bygone age.

Turn back the centuries for tonight. Recall the Ages from their flight.

This Diary that for long hath lain . . . make glow with Life and Love again!

[*Lights come up. The* SPIRIT OF BYGONE YEARS *in her gray and lavender Colonial dress, steps out from the Curtain of the Past. She carries a long-stemmed rose—the Rose of Art—which she uses as a wand. She makes a graceful curtsy before the Curtain of the Past then moves to the front of the stage and curtsies to the* ARCHIVIST. *He removes his glasses and starts to rise.*]

The lady bids him with gentle gesture to remain seated.]

SPIRIT OF BYGONE YEARS [*with finger raised*]—The dreary world is wrapped in sleep, whilst you, with candle tryst doth keep! [*Draws closer.*] Now, candlelight strange spells doth weave. . .

ARCHIVIST—Aye, even now my eyes deceive!

SPIRIT OF BYGONE YEARS [*taking the Diary from his hands*]—Wouldst animate and make *this* glow?

ARCHIVIST—Ah, lovely lady, even so!

SPIRIT OF BYGONE YEARS [*stepping back and extending the rose wand*]—As I came at your beckon call, I plucked this rose from a crumbling wall.

The Rose of Art—so might we say—to waft us back to yesterday,

To call back springtide's long forgot, and make them bloom like a garden plot. [*Turns and waves the Rose of Art toward the Curtain of the Past*] Sir Quills!

[*The two* QUILLS *dressed in black and white with headpieces patterned after the feather end of a quill, appear from the Curtain of the Past, move stiffly forward and bow before the* SPIRIT OF BYGONE YEARS *with a little click of the heels.*]

SPIRIT OF BYGONE YEARS—Sir Quills, bring forth the Diary rare, and we will paint the pictures fair!

[*The* QUILLS *bow again and leave right, whence they reappear immediately, pushing in the huge Diary. It is placed in the center of the stage, the* QUILLS *taking places on either side. The* SPIRIT OF BYGONE YEARS *takes the* ARCHIVIST'S *hand and draws him over to the diary. She turns a page.*]

SPIRIT OF BYGONE YEARS—Herein full many a date, for a century and more hath lain in wait!

But lo! they will e'en now appear . . . [*waving Rose of Art*] . . . The Day . . . The Month . . . The Year . . .

[*At the mention of their names the three Dates come forth from behind the Diary. The* DAY *is clad in red, and skips forth; The* MONTH *and* YEAR *in white and blue move with relative deliberation. They form themselves in a bright little red, white and blue line, bow primly in unison, and seat themselves on a footstool by the* ARCHIVIST'S *desk.*]

ARCHIVIST [*reading aloud the Diary entry*]—May 19, 1769, Williamsburg. "Went to the Queen's Birth Night at ye Palace."

[*The music of the minuet begins. The* QUILLS *push the Diary over to the right of the stage, where it is placed in such a position as will enable the audience to refer to the entry. They take up their stand at either side, arms folded. The* ARCHIVIST *goes to his chair by the desk. The* SPIRIT OF BYGONE YEARS, *moving backward in a series of curtsies, waves her Rose of Art, and draws aside the Curtain of the Past on the tableau—*

THE QUEEN'S BIRTHNIGHT BALL

[*After a count of about eight,* MARTHA *and* GEORGE WASHINGTON *step out of the picture, dance a measure or so to the stage front, and then step back again to their places, where they hold positions for a moment. Curtain of the Past closes.*]

SPIRIT OF BYGONE YEARS [*advancing and addressing the* ARCHIVIST] —And so . . . in chivalry and grace . . . full many an hour. . . Forsooth, their love and laughter long

Suggestion for first tableau: THE QUEEN'S BIRTHNIGHT BALL

Note: The tableau should contain more dancers, than the picture, grouped in minuet formation with George Washington **and** Martha in the foreground

Didst weave a starry crown of Song!
  [*Music of song begins!*]
Spirit of Bygone Years [*raising the Rose of Art*]—Come hither,
  ye Singers of Olden Songs!
  [*The* Two Singers of Olden Songs, *a Colonial Beau
  and Belle, step forth from the Curtain of the Past,
  curtsy and bow to each other. They walk to the
  front of the stage and the stage curtain is lowered behind them. Song, "With Pleasure Have I Passed My
  Days." During the singing the Diary is placed in the
  center of the stage, where it is discovered when the
  stage curtain rises at close of song with the* Archivist
  turning the pages. The Quills *stand on either side;*
  The Day, The Month *and* The Year *cling to the
  skirts of the* Spirit of Bygone Years.]
Archivist [*reading aloud*]—January 16, 1760. "Returned in the
  Evening to Mother's—all alone with her. . ."
  [*Music of song begins.* Quills *move the Diary to
  its place on stage right.* Spirit of Bygone Years
  *and the three dates take their stand by the Curtain of
  the Past. The* Archivist *goes to his desk as the*
  Singer of Olden Songs *slips out from the Curtain
  of the Past singing the words, "Backward, turn backward Oh Time in your flight . . . Make me a child
  again . . . just for tonight" . . . After the first verse
  of the song the Curtain of the Past is drawn apart
  on the tableau—*

The Mother and Her Son

The Singer [*continuing*]—

  "Over my heart in the years that have flown
  No love like a mother's love, ever was known,
  No other worship abides and endures,
  Patient, unselfish and loving as yours. . . ."

  [*The stage is darkened as the Curtain of the Past closes.
  The* Archivist *is seen reading by candlelight.*]
Archivist [*looking up and musingly*]—Today, she is remembered
  only as Mary, the mother of Washington.
Once—long ago, in the years that knew him not—she was known as
  the Rose of Epping Forest. . . . .
  [*Stage curtain closes; diary is placed stage center and stage
  curtain rises on the group of five before the Diary.*]
Archivist [*reading the Diary*]—November 25, 1771. "Went a
  hunting with Jacky Custis. Returned about 12 oclock and
  found Colo. Fairfax and Lady here, Mrs. Fanny Ballendine and
  her nieces, Miss Sally Fairfax and Mr. R. Adam, Mrs. Jas.
  Adam and Mr. Anthy. Ramsay. . . . ."

  [*The Diary is pushed aside by the* Quills. Spirit of
  Bygone Years *and the* Dates *move back to guard
  the Curtain of the Past.*]
Archivist [*turning to audience*]—Fair ran the peaceful river to
  the East,
Far spread the grander forest to the west;
And baying hounds and call of hunter's horns,
Didst offtime greet the proud Mt. Vernon guest!

  [*Music begins.*]

Suggestion for second tableau: The Mother and Her Son

Archivist [*meditatively walking back to his chair*]—How oft do
  we find him riding to the hounds with Jack, his son by marriage! How oft the noble name of Fairfax, friend and neighbor, doth grace these pages!
  [Spirit of Bygone Years *and the* Dates *draw the
  Curtain of the Past revealing the tableau—*

After the Hunt

  [*Just before the Curtain of the Past closes on the picture, the* Singers of Olden Songs *enter, and standing, unseen, in the right wing, sing the first verse of
  the hunting song, "O'er the Hills." They then stroll
  to the front of the stage and sing the remaining
  verses before the stage curtain.*]
  [*Stage curtain rises on the group before the Diary.*]
Archivist [*reading aloud*]—June 15, 1775. "Spent the Evening
  on a Committee."
  [*The* Archivist *turns to the audience as* Quills
  push the Diary to its place on stage right.]
Archivist [*slowly and solemnly*]—So *little* doth this sentence tell,
  so *much* it doth conceal! . . [*Pauses and moves forward a few
  steps.*] On that same day, George Washington, Esquire, was
  unanimously elected General and Commander-in-Chief of all
  forces raised or to be raised by the United Colonies. Yet no

Suggestion for third tableau: AFTER THE HUNT
Note: Consult the diary entry for change in setting and characters

word of the exaltation appears in this Diary. Merely the mention of the Committee Meeting which drafted the rules and regulations for the government of the army! What mingled emotions must have stirred the heart of the Master of Mt. Vernon as he stood before Congress on that memorable day in 1775 and accepted his new task—Commander-in-Chief of an army to fight against the King and the Motherland! [*Goes to his desk. Curtain of the Past parts on the tableau—*

Suggestion for fourth tableau: WASHINGTON ACCEPTS HIS COMMISSION
Note: No women should be shown in the background

WASHINGTON ACCEPTS HIS COMMISSION

ARCHIVIST [*pausing a few moments before speaking*]—Thine is the honor, O my country! thine,

To be the battleground of Liberty;—
Strong be thy arm; may Providence benign
With love sustain, with light encompass thee!

[*The Curtain of the Past closes and the stage curtain is lowered immediately afterwards. THE SINGERS OF OLDEN SONGS, wearing the uniforms of the Continental Army, come on the stage in front of the stage curtain and sing "Follow Washington." During the song the Diary is moved to the center of the stage where it is discovered at rise of the stage curtain with the QUILLS standing guard on either side, the ARCHIVIST turning pages. SPIRIT OF BYGONE YEARS and DATES stand by the Curtain of the Past.*]

ARCHIVIST [*reading aloud*]—September 9th, 1781. "I reached my own Seat at Mt. Vernon where I staid till the 12th. . . . "

[*Music of "Soldier's Return" begins.*]

ARCHIVIST [*slowly, as QUILLS push aside the Diary*]—A battlefield for six long years . . . and then . . . Mt. Vernon! Behind him stretched defeat and victory . . . treason and trust . . . humiliation . . . sacrifice . . . Before him loomed . . . Yorktown . . . and triumph!

[*ARCHIVIST takes his place at his desk as the Curtain of the Past parts on the tableau—*

THE SOLDIERS' RETURN

[*Stage curtain lowers.*]

INTERMISSION

[*This intermission will provide the extra time needed for the arrangement of the tableau—CHRISTMAS AT MT. VERNON. The stage curtain rises on the group before the Diary. THE DAY wears a holly wreath and is jumping up and down clapping his hands.*]

ARCHIVIST [*reading from the Diary*]—December 25, 1785. "Count Castiglioni, Colo. Ball, and Mr. Willm. Hunter came here to dinner. . . . "

[*QUILLS push the Diary to its place on stage right, as the ARCHIVIST turns to the audience.*]

ARCHIVIST [*slowly*]—1785! Once again hath the White Dove of Peace spread its wings above the old home on the Potomac.

[*Curtain of the Past is drawn revealing the tableau—*

CHRISTMAS AT MT. VERNON

ARCHIVIST [*continuing slowly after the tableau has been shown a few seconds*]—And once again, looking into candle-lit faces, does Washington give his immortal toast!

[*Music of song begins softly. WASHINGTON, from the tableau, lifts his glass a trifle higher. "To all our friends!"*]

[*As the Curtain of the Past closes on the tableau, several SINGERS OF OLDEN SONGS come upon the stage from either wing singing "Drink to me Only with Thine Eyes." They stroll to the front of the stage,*

Suggestion for fifth tableau: THE SOLDIER'S RETURN

Note: If it is unpracticable to use the horses in the tableaux, the arrival can be pictured as being afoot.

Suggestion for sixth tableau: CHRISTMAS AT MT. VERNON

the stage curtain is lowered, and the other verses are
sung in front of it.]
[*Curtain rises on Group around the Diary.*]

ARCHIVIST [*reading aloud*]—1790. Friday, January 1. "The Vice
President, the Governor . . . and all the respectable citizens,
came . . . to pay the compliments of the season to me—and in
the afternoon a great number of gentlemen and ladies visited
Mrs. Washington on the same occasion."

[*The* SPIRIT OF BYGONE YEARS *motions the* QUILLS
*to move the Diary to its place on stage right, and
moves back with the* DATES *to take her post by the
Curtain of the Past. The* ARCHIVIST *goes over to his
desk. The Curtain of the Past is drawn to reveal the
tableau—*]

MRS. WASHINGTON'S RECEPTION

[*Music "The President's March" is played during the
tableau, and continues as Curtain of the Past closes.*]
[*The stage curtain remains up and the two* QUILLS
*come forward and give a stiff, marionette-like march,
after which they seize the Diary and turn it so that
the* ARCHIVIST *may read.*]

ARCHIVIST [*reading the entry from his desk*]—November 26, 1789.
"Being the day appointed for a thanksgiving I went to St.
Paul's Chapel though it was most inclement and stormy—but
few people at Church. . ."
[*Music "Old Hundred" begins. Curtain of the Past
is drawn aside revealing the tableau—*]

THANKSGIVING DAY

[*After the tableau is held a moment, the worshippers,
with the exception of the* WASHINGTON FAMILY, *step
out of the frame, and grouping themselves on either
side, sing the words of the old hymn. At the close
of the song the Curtain of the Past is partly drawn to
enable the singers to again take their places in the
tableau. After which it is parted, for a moment, on
the completed tableau. Curtain of the Past closes.*]
[*The* SPIRIT OF BYGONE YEARS, *holding the hand of
the* YEAR *comes forward. The* YEAR *is tagged 1747
They curtsy and bow before the* ARCHIVIST.]

SPIRIT OF BYGONE YEARS—See, I bring you a year from out his
Youth. . .

ARCHIVIST [*taking* THE YEAR'S *hand*]—One of the earliest speci-
mens of GEORGE WASHINGTON's handwriting has come down
to us from this year. It is in his copy of "The Rules of
Civility" which guided him throughout his life. [*To*
THE YEAR]—Canst tell us some?
[THE YEAR *steps forward, and recites the following
maxims from the "Rules of Civility:"*]
"Labour to keep alive in your Breast that Little Spark
of Celestial fire called Conscience.
"Be not Tedius in Discourse or in reading unless you
find the Company pleased therewith.
"Let your Countenance be pleasant but in Serious
Matters Somewhat grave.
"Shew Nothing to your Friend that may affright
him."
THE YEAR *then goes over to the Diary and taking off
the 1741 placard receives from the* QUILLS *a 1798
placard—the date of the next entry to be read. The*
ARCHIVIST *approaches the Diary and standing before
it points out the entry.*]

ARCHIVIST [*reading*]—January 8, 1798. "A Mr. Marshall, Music
Master, came here, tuned Nelly Custis's harpsichord and returned after dinner."

[*Music of "Wayworn Traveller" begins. Curtain of
Past parts on the tableau—*]

MUSIC HOUR AT MT. VERNON

ARCHIVIST [*speaking slowly, affectionately*]—Nelly Custis . . . her
winsome youth . . . her filial love . . . how brightened they his
later years. His letters . . . his gifts to her . . . of these we
have a few today . . . mute witnesses of that rare companionship. The harpsichord, a pair of foolish, golden earrings . . . a
yellowed sheet of music . . .

SPIRIT OF BYGONE YEARS—And so . . .ofttimes, when shadows wrap
that mansion old . . .
Her voice, mayhap, comes clear and sweet the years along,
Singing to him this favorite song . . .

Suggestion for seventh tableau: MRS. WASHINGTON'S RECEPTION

Note: The President while present at the reception did not receive with Mrs. Washington

Suggestion for eighth tableau: THANKSGIVING DAY

Note: This picture was posed for the George Washington Bicentennial Commission in the Washington pew in Christ Church, Alexandria, Va. The tableau should include the two Custis grandchildren who lived with Washington; Nelly, ten, George Washington Parke, eight, and an additional pew of other worshippers.

[NELLY *sings one verse of "The Wayworn Traveller",
after which the* SPIRIT OF BYGONE YEARS *holds out
her arms to her. * NELLY *steps from the picture, takes
her hand, and is escorted to the front of the stage
where she sings the other verses. The picture is held.
Stage curtain.*]

[*Curtain rises on Diary in place, center stage, with*
QUILLS *on either side. The* ARCHIVIST *turns one or
two of the big leaves as though searching for some
item.*]

ARCHIVIST [*eagerly*]—I must find it . . . I must find it . . . That,
entry which marks his last public appearance . . . [*Pauses*]
Ah . . . here it is . . . [*Reading aloud*]—July 4, 1799. "Went
up to Alexan. and dined with a number of the citizens there in
celebration of the Anniversary of the Declaration of American
Independe. at Kemps Tavern."

[*Music of "Hail Columbia" begins. The Diary is
pushed to its place on stage right. Curtain of the Past
parts revealing the tableau—*

INDEPENDENCE DAY WITH WASHINGTON

[SINGERS OF OLDEN SONGS, *unseen in the wings, sing
a verse or so of the song during the tableau. Curtain
of the Past closes.*]

[*The* SPIRIT OF BYGONE YEARS *motions to the* DATES
*and holds back the Curtain of the Past a bit through
which they vanish. The* QUILLS *lay hold of the
Diary as though to take it away. The* ARCHIVIST
leans forward and snuffs his candle.]

SPIRIT OF BYGONE YEARS [*addressing the* ARCHIVIST]—My Rose of
Art, with petals bright, hath brought them back to you,
tonight . . . And now . . .
Sir Quills are bearing off the book, to place it in its treasured nook!
The little Day, The Month, The Year . . . have slipped away with
smile and tear . . .
Yon candle in its sconce burns low . . . I kiss my hand to you . . .
And [*curtsying backward*] . . . go . . .

[SPIRIT OF BYGONE YEARS *kisses her hand and disappears into the Curtain of the Past. The* ARCHIVIST
*rises and takes a few steps in that direction holding
out his hand as though to call her back. Then, observing the* QUILLS *making off with the Diary he
addresses them.*]

ARCHIVIST—A century long your ink hath dried, no longer need
you here abide . . . The guardianship of this book *is mine* . . .
Avaunt!

[*The* QUILLS *draw up with a click of the heels, and
arm-in-arm, solemnly leave the stage. The* ARCHIVIST
*picks up his candlestick. As he moves toward the
Diary he pauses and speaks as though to himself.*]

ARCHIVIST—And now . . . the dark dawn hints the coming day . . .
the spell of candle-light will soon be o'er . . .

[*The stage is darkened, as the* ARCHIVIST *stands before the Diary, which his candle raised high above his
head, illumining this entry . .*] *Feb. 20, 1790. "Sat
from 9 until 11 for Mr. Trumbull."

---

* This entry shows that Washington sat for the artist Trumbull rather than
Stuart, but the Stuart portrait is used for effectiveness.

Suggestion for ninth tableau: MUSIC HOUR WITH NELLY CUSTIS

Note: The harpsichord (or small grand piano) may be out of the tableau with only the keyboard indicated. Washington seated in an
easy chair, listening to Nellie sing his favorite song, completes the tableau.

Suggestion for eleventh tableau: The Portrait

The Portrait

[*Slowly, the Curtain of the Past parts, disclosing*
Washington *in the Stuart pose. The picture is held
for a short count before the candle flares up and goes
out. The stage curtain falls on the darkened stage.*]

Final Curtain

APPENDIX
The Diaries

The following information about the George Washington
diaries may be read before the Reverie, or printed on the programs.

At present forty original diaries written by George Washington
and a few pages of another are known to be in existence. Thirty-
six of these are in possession of the United States Government and
now repose in the Library of Congress at Washington.

The history of Uncle Sam's collection of these diaries is in itself
a romance. Bushrod Washington, who inherited most of his uncle's

important papers along with the Mount Vernon estate, gave away a
number of the diaries in his lifetime. Most of these have been re-
covered by the Government although several are still privately
owned. One or two disappeared in ways decidedly questionable.

George Washington kept a diary for many years. The earlier
diaries begun in 1748, tell of boyish experiences in surveying and his
trip to the Barbados with his brother Lawrence. From 1767 the
record was faithfully kept until Washington's election as Commander-in-Chief of the Continental Army in June, 1775. War
activities compelled him to discontinue the diaries until after he
returned home to Mount Vernon, Christmas, 1783.

As a whole, the diaries constitute the record of a remarkable
man. The homely record of day after day at Mount Vernon gives
us a clearer conception of the real George Washington than can be
obtained through reading the numerous biographies of his life. The
matter-of-fact, unemotional recital of daily happenings carries with
it a personal flavor impossible to resist and its biographical value is
inestimable.

The Mount Vernon Ladies' Association of the Union, to whom
the Nation is indebted for the restoration and care of Mount
Vernon, is responsible for the complete publication of the diaries
and Dr. John C. Fitzpatrick, Manuscript Division of the Library of
Congress, for the editing of them. Four large volumes, bearing
Washington's coat-of-arms on the cover, today repose on library
shelves throughout the country and are available to readers who
enjoy the character analysis of the "Father of His Country" from
first-hand sources.

NOTES ON PRODUCTION
The Curtain

This production calls for two curtains, the regular Stage Curtain and the *Curtain of the Past*.

The Curtain of the Past is hung about six feet behind the stage
curtain. It should extend across the stage so that the tableaux may
be readily grouped behind it while action is taking place before it.
A smaller curtain may be used augmented on the sides with screens.
The Curtain of the Past is effective of dull fabric in a deep purple
shade. It should be in two sections to allow of a center parting, and
hung from a rod on which it may be easily drawn. A straight
valance across the top with a shield bearing the Washington Coat of
Arms in the middle, is effective, though not necessary.

The Picture Frame

Directly behind the *Curtain of the Past* stands the frame for
the living pictures. The dimensions of the frame are seven feet
high by twelve feet long, with an eighteen inch golden border. If
the production is given on a stage with limited stage sets, it might
be well to build a box-like extension behind the frame, for the purpose of cutting off undesirable glimpses of the wings. Ordinarily,
stage backing placed around the group answers this purpose. While
the picture frame will add to the artistry of the production, it is not
absolutely necessary, as the tableaux may be grouped directly behind the *Curtain of the Past*.

The Diary

Any good carpenter should be able to design the *Diary* which
is a major feature of this production.

The *Diary* should be, at least six by eight feet with a thickness
of two feet. It may be fashioned of beaver board or other light ma-

terial, in book shape. The front cover and at least five pages in the book must be hinged or fastened in to permit of easy turning. The rest of the pages may be indicated by painted lines.

If but five pages are hinged, the entries must be written on both sides of the page; if ten hinged pages can be provided, the effect will be better. Large, loose writing, somewhat after the manner of Washington's signature, or printed letters, may be used to inscribe the entries. The volume should be securely fastened on an easel equipped with noiseless, ball-bearing rollers.

STAGE SETTING

The stage setting remains the same throughout the Reverie and is very simple.

At the extreme left of the stage, about half way between the *Curtain of the Past* and the Stage Curtain, a shelf of books is placed. Nearby is the ARCHIVIST's desk, chair and footstool.

This grouping is balanced on the right side of the stage by the *Diary*, which is pushed into place after the readings. It should be so turned as to enable the audience to consult the entry being depicted.

The candle that "strange spells doth weave," can be best handled and is most effective in one of the old, ringed candle-sticks. Candle-snuffers are on the desk.

COSTUMES

With the exception of the ARCHIVIST, the QUILLS and DATES, all of the costumes are of the late Colonial period.

ARCHIVIST: Wears a knee-length smock of black. He is made up to look like an old man, with flowing beard, wearing glasses and a skull cap. He sits humped up over his desk and moves with the slow, uncertain steps of one who has lost contact with the world save through his books.

THE QUILLS: Should be the same height. They move stiffly and in unison. They are dressed in white one-piece pajama-like costumes with a tall headgear fashioned to represent the feather-end of a quill. The head pieces are black and white and rise to a peak. They may be made of stiff white paper or buckram, cut extremely high to give an elongated effect to the figures which guard the big *Diary*.

THE DATES: THE DAY, THE MONTH, and THE YEAR will be attractively dressed in doublet and hose, page-wise. THE DAY, in bright red, THE MONTH in white and THE YEAR in blue. As the mission of the DATES is, mainly, to inject an ornamental touch of the national colors in the black and white stage-setting, their placement, at various times during the Reverie, is unimportant and subject to change.

SINGERS OF OLDEN SONGS: Any number of SINGERS OF OLDEN SONGS may carry on the musical program which accompanies the Candle-time Reverie. The BEAU and BELLE who sing two duets are the main singers. THE SINGERS OF OLDEN SONGS wear the costumes of the period.

SONG SUGGESTIONS

FIRST TABLEAU—*The Queen's Birthnight Ball*.
    Music: (a) *The Minuet*—Boccherini.
    Song: (b) *With Pleasure Have I Passed My Days*—Francis Hopkinson.

SECOND TABLEAU—*The Mother and Her Son*.
    Song: *Backward, Turn Backward*.

THIRD TABLEAU—*After the Hunt*.
    Song: *O'er the Hills*—Francis Hopkinson.

FOURTH TABLEAU—*Washington Accepts His Commission*.
    Song: *Follow Washington*.

FIFTH TABLEAU—*The Soldier's Return*.
    Song: *Soldier's Return or The Toast* by Francis Hopkinson.

SIXTH TABLEAU—*Christmas at Mt. Vernon*.
    Song: *Drink to Me Only with Thine Eyes*—Poem, Ben Jonson.

SEVENTH TABLEAU—*Martha Washington's Reception*
    Music: *The President's March*—Philip Phile.

EIGHTH TABLEAU—*Thanksgiving Day*.
    Song: *Old Hundred*—Any standard hymn.

NINTH TABLEAU—*Music hour with Nellie Custis*.
    Song: (a) *The Wayworn Traveller* (Washington's favorite Song)—Francis Hopkinson.
        (b) *My Days have been so Wondrous Free*—Francis Hopkinson.

TENTH TABLEAU—*Independence Day with Washington*.
    Song: (a) *Liberty Song* (Hearts of Oak)—Dr. William Boyce.
        (b) *Hail Columbia*—Joseph Hopkinson.

THE FATHER OF HIS COUNTRY

By ESTHER C. *and* LAWRENCE A. AVERILL

A GEORGE WASHINGTON PAGEANT

Copyright, 1931, by Esther C. Averill and Lawrence A. Averill

SCENES AND CHARACTERS

PROLOGUE—CLIO, THE MUSE OF HISTORY

EPISODE 1

Scene 1: WASHINGTON IN THE WILDERNESS
    NARRATOR
    WASHINGTON
    GIST
    HALF-KING
    OTHER CHIEFTAINS

Scene 2: WASHINGTON'S FIRST TASTE OF BRITISH GENERALSHIP
    NARRATOR
    WASHINGTON
    FRANKLIN
    BRADDOCK

Scene 3: ROMANCE COMES TO THE VIRGINIA COLONEL
    NARRATOR
    WASHINGTON

Mistress Custis
Chamberlayne
Bishop

INTERLUDE I
THE SPIRIT OF FREEDOM: Dancer

EPISODE 2

Scene 1: WASHINGTON TAKES COMMAND OF THE ARMY
Narrator
Washington
Ward
Fifers
Soldiers
Men, Women, Children

Scene 2: THE DECLARATION OF INDEPENDENCE

Narrator
Washington
Soldier
Aide
Officers

INTERLUDE II
THE SPIRIT OF '76: Three Characters

EPISODE 3

Scene 1: WASHINGTON AT THE DELAWARE
Narrator
Washington
Ewing
Cadwalader

Scene 2: THE WINTER AT VALLEY FORGE
Narrator
Washington
Three Soldiers

Scene 3: NOTED HELPERS FROM BEYOND THE SEA
Narrator
Washington
Mistress Washington
DeKalb
Von Steuben
Knox
Mistress Knox
Greene
Mistress Greene
Lord Stirling
Lady Stirling
Wayne
Lee
Hamilton
Lafayette
Pulaski
Kosciuszko
Aide

Scene 4: SURRENDER OF CORNWALLIS AT YORKTOWN
Narrator
Washington
Hamilton
Knox
Von Steuben
Lafayette
Rochambeau
Lincoln
O'Hara
Other Officers

INTERLUDE III
MINUET—Dancers

EPISODE 4

Scene 1: THE GENERAL REFUSES A CROWN
Narrator
Washington
Officer
Soldier
Symbolic Figure

Scene 2: AT BELOVED MOUNT VERNON
Narrator
Washington
Mistress Washington
Child

Scene 3: THE IMMORTAL FOUNDER BECOMES THE FIRST PRESIDENT
Narrator
Washington
Livingston
John Adams
Otis
Sherman
Hamilton
Knox
St. Clair
Von Steuben
Men, Women, Children

Scene 4: WASHINGTON, FOUNDER OF THE FEDERAL CITY
Narrator
Washington
Grand Master
Military Men
Masons
Civilians
Children

INTERLUDE IV
THE WELDING OF THE NATION
Washington
Thirteen Young Women
Columbia

EPISODE 5

MEMORIALS OF WASHINGTON

NARRATOR
TEN YOUNG WOMEN

FINALE

ENTIRE CAST

EPILOGUE

CLIO, THE MUSE OF HISTORY

PROLOGUE

CLIO, THE MUSE OF HISTORY [*in symbolic costume, enters the amphitheatre and approaches the middle of the green. She speaks the Prologue*]—

What memories yet cluster 'round his name—
Immortal Founder of a commonwealth—
Great Washington! Surviving the oblivion of Time,
That sepulchres in pale, corroding dust
The fame of humbler men, his lustrous fame
More radiant scintillates across the years
That separate from these those ancient days.
Wherein were forged upon the anvil of his breast
The first stout girders of a Nation's strength!
Immortal Founder! His perceiving ear
Detected in the sundering dissonance
And jealousies of men an overtone
Of blending harmonies that by the touch
Of master hand upon the strings might grow
In swelling diapason till it filled.
The earth with tuneful melody, and stirred
The souls of mortal races 'neath the sun
To hoist the pennons of democracy!

Immortal Founder! His the faith to glimpse
In vision what a commonwealth might be,
Whose builders, lured by higher concept, dared
To set in Freedom's masonry the corner-stone,
And bond in close confederation men
Of diverse clan and caste. His, too, the fostering hand
To guide the builders in their enterprise,
And point the way to that concordant mind
Imperative to Statehood's lasting course!

EPISODE I

THE NARRATOR [*a maid clad in early colonial costume, advancing to the center of the green*]—The young Virginian, George Washington, ran the full gamut of affliction, adventure, peril, and romance. Bold, dashing, and fearless, his was a nature to challenge the respect of man and intrigue the heart of woman. During the eventful years of his youth, those virtues were shaping which were destined in later years to come to full fruition in the Immortal Founder! At the early age of 16, young Washington was appointed surveyor of the vast Fairfax property, and for three years most of his time was spent on the frontier. At 19, he accompanied his half-brother, Lawrence, to the Barbados, where he fell ill of smallpox, which left him marked for life. Returning to Virginia, he was appointed by Governor Dinwiddie to make the pilgrimage to the French fortified post in western Pennsylvania. The name and fame of the brave young frontiersman preceded Washington through the forests.

SCENE 1

1753. WASHINGTON IN THE WILDERNESS

[*Several INDIAN CHIEFTAINS approach the center of the green, shaking their heads ominously. They seat themselves in a half-circle. HALF-KING, the leader, smokes silently from a long pipe. From the opposite side WASHINGTON enters, accompanied by GIST, the latter bearing belts of wampum. WASHINGTON wears a woodsman's costume.*]

WASHINGTON [*addressing himself to the chieftains*]—Chieftains, two great tribes of the white men have for many moons laid claim to the great Ohio valley. They are the Englishmen and the Frenchmen. By prior right, this wide wilderness is ours, and we shall keep it. The English are friends of the red man, and will protect him. I am charged by the Governor of Virginia to seek out the fort which the French have built far up on a branch of the Allegheny River, and command them to leave. But the forest is large and it is hard to find the way. The red man knows the woods. I have brought wampum for my friends, the red men. They shall have it, if they will but guide me.

[*CHRISTOPHER GIST advances and hands the belts of wampum to WASHINGTON.*]

GIST—Here is the wampum, Major Washington.

WASHINGTON—Give it all to the brave chieftain, Half-King.

[*GIST hands the wampum belts to HALF-KING, who takes them and examines them greedily. The other chieftains gather about, eyeing the belts covetously.*]

HALF-KING [*to the other CHIEFTAINS*]—The white man is free with his wampum!

WASHINGTON—And so will the Englishman ever be toward his brave Indian brothers if they will unite with him against the French intruders.

HALF-KING—The Frenchman, also, has given us wampum.

WASHINGTON—With his wampum, the Englishman gives also his friendship! Will not you, Half-King, accept his friendship with his wampum, and guide him through the forest to the great river?

[*The CHIEFTAINS confer among themselves. Finally, HALF-KING rises to his feet, and speaks to WASHINGTON.*]

HALF-KING—Conotocarius! Devourer of Villages! This is a serious matter. But Conotocarius is brave and daring. The red man knows his courage. The red man welcomes the friendship of the bold pale-face. My chieftains will take the side of the English. They will lead him to the Frenchman's fort.

WASHINGTON—Conotocarius is happy at these words, Chief Half-King!

HALF-KING—I, Half-King, will myself go with the pale-face brave! I will show him the way.

WASHINGTON—You have chosen well, Half-King! Chieftain of the Senecas! I am grateful to you! Be assured the English will always be your friends!

[*WASHINGTON marches off, with HALF-KING. GIST follows. The other INDIANS disappear in the opposite direction into the forest, while the band plays the "Shawnee Indian Hunting Dance."*]

THE NARRATOR—The youthful ambassador, having successfully concluded his mission to the French commander, was, upon his return, appointed

Lieutenant-Colonel of a Virginia regiment. For the service he subsequently rendered in several forays against the French and Indians, he received the formal thanks of the Virginia House of Burgesses. Upon General Braddock's arrival in the Colony to assume active offense against the French, Washington was made a volunteer aide on his staff.

SCENE 2

1755. WASHINGTON'S FIRST TASTE OF BRITISH GENERALSHIP

[GEORGE WASHINGTON *and* BENJAMIN FRANKLIN *enter the green. Their conversation becomes audible as they approach the center.*]

FRANKLIN—You, no doubt, can tell me, Colonel Washington, what progress General Braddock is making in his plans to drive the French out of the Ohio valley.

WASHINGTON—Slow, Mr. Franklin, I very much regret to say! The General seems to be quite lacking in ability to adjust himself to our lack of those facilities to which he has always been accustomed heretofore in warfare.

FRANKLIN—That is decidedly unfortunate! Something should be done immediately to hasten matters along!

[GENERAL BRADDOCK, *in Red-coat uniform, enters.*]

BRADDOCK—Good day, gentlemen.

FRANKLIN—Good day, General Braddock. I am informed from diverse sources that you are progressing but slowly in your preparations for the campaign. We in Pennsylvania are becoming uneasy. We had hoped that the French might be soon dislodged from the Ohio country.

BRADDOCK [*hotly*]—It's the abominable roads, sir. They must be improved before we can even consider passing over them with an army. And worse than that, is the disgusting lack of support from these wretched countrymen of yours!

FRANKLIN [*placatingly*]—Wherein lies this neglect, sir?

BRADDOCK—The knaves! These Virginia contractors of yours have failed to fulfill their engagements. They promise me abundant means of transportation; and what do they do, sir? They send me a few wretched wagons, and no more than a hundred draft horses! And, gad, sir! There are no prospects of more to come! You colonists know nothing of military tactics!

WASHINGTON [*quickly*]—Perhaps not, General. But we know how to fight Indians, I dare say, better than you! The savage shoots from behind trees and ledges. I fear, sir, that they will mow down your cumbersome line of soldiers faster than they can advance!

BRADDOCK—These savages may indeed be a formidable enemy, Colonel Washington, to raw American militia! But upon regularly trained and disciplined troops it is ludicrous to suppose that they can make any impression!

FRANKLIN—Colonel Washington is right! You would best adopt the Indian tactics for yourself.

BRADDOCK [*testily*]—This is insufferable, gentlemen! I have campaigned all over the continent of Europe, and I do not wish any advice from you Americans, who have never even seen a real battle! [*He strides angrily off.*]

FRANKLIN—Braddock's attitude makes me fearful for the outcome of the campaign! What think you, Colonel?

WASHINGTON—In such obstinate circumstances as these, I greatly fear that disaster to our cause is inevitable! [*They walk away opposite.*]

THE NARRATOR—Franklin and Washington were right. Braddock was defeated. But the youthful Colonel Washington acquitted himself so conspicuously in the field that, at the age of twenty-three, he found himself commissioned as Commander of the Virginia forces. As such, for the next two years his chief responsibility lay in defending a frontier of more than three hundred and fifty miles in extent. While making preparations for the expedition against Fort Duquesne, Washington chanced to meet the charming young widow, Martha Custis.

SCENE 3

1758. ROMANCE COMES TO THE VIRGINIA COLONEL

[*While an unseen voice sings, "Come Live With Me and Be My Love,"* BISHOP, *a servant, leads two saddled horses on to the background of the green.* COLONEL WASHINGTON *and* MRS. MARTHA CUSTIS *stroll to and fro in the foreground.*]

WASHINGTON—I am thankful to Major Chamberlayne for bringing me to his home today, since it gave me the good fortune of meeting you, Mistress Custis!

MISTRESS CUSTIS—I am honored that a gentleman so busy with the affairs of the Colony is minded to tarry for awhile in my poor company.

WASHINGTON—How swiftly the hours have sped, Mistress Custis! I had contemplated merely making a hurried call upon my good friend, Major Chamberlayne, and then off in haste to Williamsburg within the hour. But you have beguiled me into extending the visit until nightfall.

MISTRESS CUSTIS—You flatter me, Colonel! For me, also, the hours of your visit have passed all too swiftly.

[MAJOR CHAMBERLAYNE *makes his appearance in the rear. He hurries to* WASHINGTON'S *side.*]

WASHINGTON—Ah, here is your host, Major Chamberlayne, come to bid me farewell.

CHAMBERLAYNE [*smiling comprehendingly at the pair*]—Well, well, Colonel Washington, I perceive you are still here!

WASHINGTON [*embarrassed*]—I must not tarry another moment! [*Calls to* BISHOP]—Bishop! My horse!

BISHOP [*advancing with the mount. Tartly*]—I hardly know whether this long day's waiting has been worse on the horse or on me!

MAJOR CHAMBERLAYNE—My dear Colonel Washington! Night is already upon us. I never allow guests of mine to journey away from my doors after sunset!

WASHINGTON [*resolutely, but glancing at* MISTRESS CUSTIS]—I must go, Major! I assure you, my business is imperative!

MISTRESS CUSTIS [*coyly*]—Is the business so imperative, Colonel Washington, that you cannot postpone it until the morrow—if *I* ask it?

WASHINGTON [*yielding*]—Fair enchantress! If you were to ask it, I could not find it in my mind to refuse!

MAJOR CHAMBERLAYNE [*to* BISHOP]—To the stable with Colonel Washington's horse! He will not be leaving until the morning!

BISHOP [*dragging the horses off*]—Nor probably then, either!

[MAJOR CHAMBERLAYNE, *chuckling, goes off on one side.* WASHINGTON *and* MISTRESS CUSTIS *stroll off, opposite, each deeply engrossed in the other.*]

INTERLUDE I

THE SPIRIT OF FREEDOM

An Interpretive Dance Depicting the Struggle for Freedom

EPISODE 2

THE NARRATOR—The acquaintanceship of Colonel Washington and Mistress Custis ripened soon into love, culminating some months later in a happy marriage. Meantime, the Virginia Commander assisted in the reduction of Fort Duquesne, which effectually terminated the troubles of the southern frontier. Upon ceasing active participation in frontier affairs, Washington retired to his Virginia estate, where for a season he was privileged to enjoy the felicities of home life. He was appointed by the Governor to the bench of the county court, and was repeatedly elected to the Virginia House of Burgesses. But these homely pleasures and civic responsibilities were soon rudely disturbed by the growing certainty of war with the mother country. In this exigency, the Second Continental Congress, casting about for a leader, turned at length to George Washington as the Commander-in-Chief of the Continental Army.

SCENE 1

1775. WASHINGTON TAKES COMMAND OF THE ARMY

[*A group of colonial men, women, and children enter the green. They stand at one side, waiting expectantly. As fifers play the tune: "Chester,"* GENERAL WASHINGTON, *preceded by the players and followed by several soldiers and officers, enters on horseback. The colonists cheer enthusiastically.* GENERAL ARTEMAS WARD *steps forward to greet the new Commander. The soldiers salute.* WASHINGTON *dismounts, turning his horse over to an aide.*]

GENERAL WARD—It is a signal honor, General Washington, which this day confers upon me. In the name of the people of Massachusetts Bay, and in accord with the action of the Continental Congress, I now entrust into your capable hands and genius the leadership of the Colonial armies!

GENERAL WASHINGTON—Gentlemen, your kind congratulations upon my appointment and arrival demand my warmest acknowledgment and will ever be retained in grateful remembrance. In exchanging the enjoyments of domestic life for the duties of my present honorable but arduous station, I only emulate the virtue and public spirit of the whole province of Massachusetts, which with a firmness and patriotism unstinted has sacrificed all the comforts of social and political life in support of the right of mankind and of our common country. My highest ambition is to be the happy instrument of vindicating these rights and to see this devoted Province again restored to peace, liberty and safety!

GENERAL WARD—In you, General Washington, we repose all our hopes for the successful culmination of the joint task upon which we are entered. The events of this day will be remembered as long as the Colonies of America shall endure!

[*Preceded by the players,* GENERAL WASHINGTON *and* GENERAL WARD *leave the green. The* SPECTATORS *follow, well-pleased with the new Commander-in Chief.*]

THE NARRATOR—From a band of raw men, undisciplined and poorly equipped, Washington builded the army of the Revolution. Within a few short weeks, he had it in surprisingly good form. During the Siege of Boston, in order effectively to harrass the British supply ships, he proceeded on his own initiative to fit out and man a fleet of armed ships, thus laying the foundations for the subsequent development of the American navy. By a brilliant manoeuver, Washington occupied a strategic position on Dorchester Heights, from which he was able to command the entire town and harbor of Boston. On the 17th of March, 1776, the British forces were compelled to evacuate. Thenceforth the scene of the struggle of the Colonists was transferred to points outside New England. Less than four months after the capture of Boston, the Declaration of Independence was adopted by Congress.

SCENE 2

1776. THE DECLARATION OF INDEPENDENCE

[*At the conclusion of "The Liberty Song," sung by an unseen voice,* A COLONIAL SOLDIER *proceeds to the middle of the amphitheatre, and speaks to the audience as if to the Army.*]

SOLDIER—General Washington is about to communicate to his Army the contents of a document, called the Declaration of Independence, which he has but now received.

[GENERAL WASHINGTON *enters, accompanied by an* AIDE *and several officers. They proceed to the foreground.*]

GENERAL WASHINGTON—Men of the Armies of America, the words that are shortly to be read to you are destined, under providence of God, to become an immortal document to all future generations.

[*He hands the document to an* AIDE, *who reads while the others stand at attention.*]

AIDE—When in the course of human events, it becomes necessary for one people to dissolve the political bands which have connected them with another and to assume among the Powers of the earth the separate and equal station to which the Laws of Nature and Nature's God entitle them, a decent respect to the opinions of mankind requires that they should declare the causes which impel them to the separation. . . . We therefore, the representatives of the United States of America, in General Congress assembled, appealing to the Supreme Judge of the world for the rectitude of our intentions, do, in the name, and by the Authority of the good People of these colonies, solemnly publish and declare, That these United Colonies are, and of Right ought to be Free and Independent States; that they are absolved from all Allegiance to the British Crown, and that all political connection between them and the State of Great Britain is and ought to be totally dissolved; and that as Free and Independent States, they have full Power to levy War, conclude Peace, contract Alliances, establish Commerce, and do all other acts and Things which Independent States may of right do. And for the support of this Declaration, with a firm reliance on the Protection of Divine Providence, we mutually pledge to each other our Lives, our Fortunes, and our sacred Honor.

[*As the band plays "General Washington's March,"* the COMMANDER-IN-CHIEF, *followed by his officers, the* AIDE, *and soldiers, proceeds ceremoniously from the green.*]

INTERLUDE II

THE SPIRIT OF '76

A Picturization of the Famous Painting, with Action and Music

Episode 3

THE NARRATOR—The darkest hours of the Revolution were at hand. Driven out of Boston, the British concentrated their efforts upon capturing New York. They succeeded so well in their plans that Washington was compelled, following the defeat of his forces at the battle of Long Island, to withdraw from Brooklyn Heights, where he occupied a strategic position, across the Hudson to New York. This catastrophe was followed by the evacuation of the city; and though Washington eluded Howe's attempt at White Plains to destroy his force, the fall of Fort Washington and the evacuation of Fort Lee, on opposite banks of the Hudson, gave the British full possession of the region. Washington retreated across New Jersey, hoping at least to save Philadelphia. But the enemy followed closely, and occupied Trenton. The discouraged American soldiers were leaving the army in great numbers. Winter was upon them. The capture of Philadelphia seemed inevitable. It was in this serious situation that the Commander-in-Chief displayed his highest generalship.

Scene 1

1776. Washington at the Delaware

[WASHINGTON *and* EWING *enter the green. They are muffled as against great cold.* CADWALADER *follows, muffled also. The three officers are talking heatedly.*]

EWING—General Washington, I must insist that this is not the time of year for armies to be in action!

WASHINGTON—That is the very reason for the undertaking! The enemy will not expect an attack and will therefore be unprepared.

CADWALADER—But, General! You expect us to move on this of all nights? Christmas night!

WASHINGTON—So much the better for a surprise attack upon the enemy!

EWING—Impossible, sir! The night is too severe for such an undertaking as you propose!

CADWALADER—Our forces are hopelessly outnumbered by the enemy's!

WASHINGTON—Sirs, "necessity, dire necessity, will, nay must, justify an attack!"

EWING—I, for one, will not lend myself to anything so fool-hardy!
[*He strides away.*]

WASHINGTON—Where is General Putnam? Has he not arrived from Philadelphia, to aid us?

CADWALADER—No, sir!

WASHINGTON—I trust, Cadwalader, that to this seeming general lack of confidence in my plans, you will not yourself be a party?

CADWALADER—For the army to attempt to cross with the river running as it is seems almost suicidal.

WASHINGTON—A victory now will raise the morale of the army.

CADWALADER—But have you considered, sir, what a defeat would mean? It would be the final blow to the hopes of the colonists!

WASHINGTON—Victory will prevent Philadelphia from falling into the hands of the British! It will dislocate their whole system of posts guarding New Jersey!
[CADWALADER *turns away.*]

WASHINGTON—Alone, if necessary with my own men, I will cross the Delaware this night, and drive the enemy from Trenton!
[WASHINGTON *strides off right,* CADWALADER *left.*]

THE NARRATOR—Notwithstanding the lack of confidence in his plan, General Washington ferried his twenty-four hundred men safely over the swollen Delaware on Christmas night. Next morning, with the loss of but two men, he captured Trenton and nearly a thousand prisoners. The effect of this brilliant strategy upon the colonists was most salutary. It was followed within ten days by a second victory at Princeton. But the cause of America was not yet assured. In the months that followed, the enemy kept the American forces hard pressed, inflicting defeat upon them at Brandywine and Germantown. The little army passed the following winter in camp at Valley Forge. It was here that the suffering and hardship of the soldiers reached their climax. Only personal loyalty to Washington kept the army together.

Scene 2

1778. The Winter at Valley Forge

[*Two soldiers, in earnest conversation, enter. They are barefoot, with blood marks on their feet. Their clothes are in tatters.*]

FIRST SOLDIER—This everlasting, gnawing hunger is unbearable!

SECOND SOLDIER—The hunger is bad enough, I grant, Comrade. But the cold! It bites into one's very heart!

THIRD SOLDIER—Aye! At night when I lie down on the frozen ground, I expect to freeze before morning. And we have not tasted meat for more than a month. They feed us nothing but baked flour and water!

FIRST SOLDIER—I cannot stand this any longer!

THIRD SOLDIER—If the people care so little about our welfare, we should give up fighting their battles and go home!

SECOND SOLDIER—Home! Heaven itself would seem no sweeter to me just now!

FIRST SOLDIER—Let us go!

THIRD SOLDIER—Yes! Away from this miserable place! What have we known here but famine, death, untold plagues!

SECOND SOLDIER—Yes, home to peace—warmth—comfort!
[GENERAL WASHINGTON *enters.*]

WASHINGTON [*heartily*]—Good morning, my men!

FIRST SOLDIER—Good morning, General Washington!

WASHINGTON—Poor fellows! You seem to be in a pitiable condition!

SECOND SOLDIER—We most truthfully are, Sir!

FIRST SOLDIER—We are going home!

THIRD SOLDIER—We are resolved on it!

WASHINGTON [*sadly*]—I am grieved to hear this.

FIRST SOLDIER—We cannot bear this suffering longer!

THIRD SOLDIER—Our time in the army has expired.

WASHINGTON—All too true, but——

SECOND SOLDIER—We are both freezing and starving!

WASHINGTON—This tears at my heart! If only I could make Congress understand our plight!

FIRST SOLDIER—You know well, General Washington, we are loath to leave you.

THIRD SOLDIER—We can't stand it longer!

WASHINGTON [*to* FIRST SOLDIER]—My man, if your commander had food, he would gladly share it with you; that you know.

FIRST SOLDIER [*saluting*]—And starve yourself, we have heard.

WASHINGTON [*to* SECOND SOLDIER]—And you!

SECOND SOLDIER—I am freezing! [*He shivers.*]

WASHINGTON [*removing his great-coat*]—Will you put this on? You need it more than I!
[*The Second Soldier puts on the coat.*]

WASHINGTON [*regretfully*]—And so, you are giving up the Cause?

FIRST SOLDIER—No, General Washington! I for one shall stay on with you to the end!

THIRD SOLDIER—And I, sir!

SECOND SOLDIER—And I! I will give my life, if need be, for such a great and kindly leader as you!

WASHINGTON [*turning away*]—Men, your loyalty moves me more than I can express! I thank you for your brave decision!

[*The* SOLDIERS *leave the green.* WASHINGTON *follows slowly, his head bent, as though in deep suffering for his men.*]

THE NARRATOR—The final consummation of the alliance with France was a great boon to the Americans and did much to raise the morale of the army. Adventurous officers from several countries of Europe gave their support to the cause of independence, and promoted the final victory of the United States.

SCENE 3

1778. NOTED HELPERS FROM BEYOND THE SEA

[*Six* OFFICERS *and three* LADIES *enter the amphitheatre.* GENERAL WASHINGTON *and* MISTRESS WASHINGTON *advance to meet them. Handshaking and greetings follow.*]

WASHINGTON—Good-day to you, General Greene, and you, Mistress Greene! Ah, General Knox, and Mistress Knox! Welcome, My Lord and Lady Stirling! Good-day, General Wayne and General Lee! And Colonel Hamilton, my boy!

MISTRESS WASHINGTON—'Tis heartening news, indeed, that we celebrate!

GENERAL KNOX—Thank God that France at last recognizes the United States!

GENERAL GREENE—And allies herself with us definitely against King George!

[*An* AIDE *enters.*]

AIDE—The Marquis de Lafayette!

[*As* LAFAYETTE *approaches and greets* WASHINGTON, *the bands plays strains from* "La Marseillaise".]

AIDE—Baron DeKalb and Baron von Steuben!

[*Strains from* "Die Wacht am Rhein".]

AIDE—Count Casimir Pulaski, and Captain Tadeusz Kosciuszko!

[*Strains from* "Jeszcze Polska".]

WASHINGTON—My Country is deeply honored by your proffered help, gentlemen, in this our dire hour of need, and in gratitude do we accept it. And now, my friends, pray join us in our humble feast of thanksgiving for the welcome news that the great country of France, fatherland of the Marquis de Lafayette, has championed our lofty cause! [*Exeunt.*]

THE NARRATOR—With the winning of the battle of Monmouth, the last encounter of importance on Northern soil, the scene of the struggle for independence shifted to the South. The winter spent by Washington's army in quarters at Morristown was even worse than the winter at Valley Forge had been. Late in the summer of 1781, Clinton's army, occupying New York, was thoroughly expecting an attack by the Americans. Even the men of Washington's army anticipated that an attempt would shortly be made upon Clinton. Instead, Washington marched his army straight to Chesapeake Bay, embarking it thence for Yorktown, the fortified headquarters of Lord Cornwallis. The British commander, gazing over his walls to see the French fleet on one hand and the combined forces of Washington and Rochambeau on the other, realized that his position was a hopeless one. Within the month, he surrendered.

SCENE 4

1781. PANTOMIME. THE SURRENDER OF CORNWALLIS

[GENERAL WASHINGTON, *on horseback, enters. He is accompanied by* ROCHAMBEAU, *and followed by* HAMILTON, KNOX, STEUBEN, LAFAYETTE, LINCOLN, *and other officers. The band plays* "The World Turned Upside Down." GENERAL O'HARA, *representing Lord Cornwallis, and accompanied by a guard of* REDCOATS, *advances to* GENERAL WASHINGTON, *tendering to him Cornwallis' sword.* WASHINGTON *indicates that* GENERAL LINCOLN *is to receive the sword.* LINCOLN *takes it, holds it for a moment, and at a sign from* GENERAL WASHINGTON *returns it to* GENERAL O'HARA. *The British march off, the band still playing the same air. They are followed by the* AMERICANS, GENERAL WASHINGTON *in the lead.*]

INTERLUDE III

A Minuet

Music: "Minuet," *by Mozart.*

EPISODE 4

THE NARRATOR—The great war of the Revolution was ended. But the new nation was still in the throes of being born. The army was embittered because Congress had devised no means or plan to satisfy the soldiers for their eight years of arduous service in the field. During the closing years of the war, it had been largely the patriotic exhortations of the Commander-in-Chief that had kept them loyal to the cause. To protect themselves and their soldiers, some of the officers now conceived the plan to overthrow the flimsy federation of the thirteen States, and to set up in its stead a monarchy, with Washington at its head. Washington sternly rebuked them, however, and pointed them to a higher loyalty.

SCENE 1

1782. THE GENERAL REFUSES A CROWN

[GENERAL WASHINGTON *paces to and fro across the green, in meditation. An* OFFICER, *accompanied by a* SOLDIER, *approaches the Commander-in-Chief, and salutes.*]

OFFICER—I have the honor, General Washington, to present to you a letter sent by Colonel Lewis Nicola. I beg of you to give it most serious consideration.

WASHINGTON [*taking the letter*]—My thanks to you Lieutenant!

[*In growing surprise,* WASHINGTON *peruses the letter. Then he gazes soberly out over the green.*]

OFFICER—I trust, General, that you will subscribe to our plans of doing away with the present republican form of government, and that you will concur in the proposal of the officers of the army to establish a monarchy similar to that of England, with yourself, sir, our ruler and king!

[*As the* OFFICER *speaks, a symbolic figure, wearing a flowing white robe draws near. She holds aloft a gleaming crown of gold.* WASHINGTON'S *gaze falls upon her in astonishment. Suddenly he starts, turns angrily, upon the* LIEUTENANT, *and addresses him spiritedly.*]

WASHINGTON—I am much at loss to conceive what part of my conduct could have given encouragement to an address which to me seems big with the greatest mischief that can befall my country. If I am not deceived in the knowledge of myself, you could not have found a person to whom your schemes are more disagreeable. I must add that no man possesses a more sincere wish to see ample justice done to the army than I do; and as far as my powers and influence, in a constitutional way, extend, they shall be employed to the extent of my abilities to effect it, should there be any occasion. Let me conjure you, then, if you have any regard for your country, concern for yourself or posterity, or respect for me, to banish these thoughts from your mind, and never communicate, as from yourself to any one else, a sentiment of the like nature.

[*During* WASHINGTON'S *rejoinder, the symbolic figure lowers the crown, turns about, and sorrowfully disappears.* WASHINGTON *strides angrily from the green. The* LIEUTENANT *and the* SOLDIER *go off opposite, deeply chagrined.*]

THE NARRATOR—On the 4th of December, 1783, General Washington bade farewell to the officers of his army. All present were deeply moved at the leave-taking. A few days later, he returned to Congress his commission as Commander-in-Chief of the army. Once more a private citizen, he hastened to his beloved Mount Vernon.

SCENE 2
1786. AT BELOVED MOUNT VERNON

[*The band plays softly "The Mansion of Peace".* GENERAL WASHINGTON *and* MARTHA *stroll slowly across the green.* GEORGE WASHINGTON PARKE CUSTIS, *their grandchild, now five years of age, romps about with a dog.*]

WASHINGTON—Yonder, by the ridge, Martha, I mean to set the strawberry shrubs from Monticello. And here will be an excellent place for the new rose that I have named Mary Washington, after my mother.

MARTHA—How rejoiced I have been during these months, my husband, to have you again at home! How dear Mount Vernon seems, after the many years that we were unable to enjoy it together!

WASHINGTON—This has ever been the dearest spot on earth to me!

MARTHA—With war a fading memory, we are now happy again!

WASHINGTON—At home, once more, with you! I can think of no happiness greater than that!

MARTHA—Nothing could give me deeper joy, my husband, than having you with me here!

WASHINGTON [*calls*]—Come, my boy! Leave Sweetlips! Tell me how much you love me!

CHILD—Everybody loves you, sir!

[*The* CHILD *runs to* WASHINGTON, *who swings him up on to his shoulder. He twines his arms lovingly about* WASHINGTON'S *neck. Passing an arm about* MARTHA, WASHINGTON *leads her slowly from the green.*]

THE NARRATOR—During the interim between his relinquishment of the life of a soldier and his resumption of public office, Washington's dominant ambition was to see established a strong union of the thirteen States. When the Constitutional Convention finally convened to effect this more powerful federation, it turned to Washington to preside over its deliberations. Thus it was that the Immortal Founder, who had served his country on the battlefields, led the delegates to the Convention in the drafting and subsequent adoption of the Constitution of the new Republic. In 1789, he was chosen the first President of the United States of America.

SCENE 3
1789. THE IMMORTAL FOUNDER BECOMES THE FIRST PRESIDENT

[ATTENDANTS *carry on to the green a flower-decked arch, and retire. A throng of men, women, and children surges into the amphitheatre, shouting "Washington! Washington!" As* WASHINGTON *enters from the rear, a group of young girls, dressed in white, approaches him from the left, strewing flowers in his path. The band strikes up "The President's March," and* WASHINGTON *proceeds under the arch to the extreme right of the green. Here, is is joined by* JOHN ADAMS, *who stands at his right;* ROBERT LIVINGSTON, *Chancellor of New York, and* MR. OTIS, *Secretary of the Senate, who stand at his left.* OTIS *bears a Bible on a crimson cushion.* ROGER SHERMAN, ALEXANDER HAMILTON, *and* GENERALS KNOX, ST. CLAIR, *and* BARON STEUBEN *take places in the rear. The throng is silenced shortly by the Chancellor's upraised hand.* WASHINGTON *places his right hand on the Bible as* LIVINGSTON *gives him the oath.*]

LIVINGSTON—Do you solemnly swear that you will faithfully execute the office of President of the United States, and will, to the best of your ability, preserve, protect, and defend the Constitution of the United States.

WASHINGTON [*bending over and kissing the Bible*]—I swear, so help me, God!

[*The* CHANCELLOR *steps a few paces forward.*]

LIVINGSTON—Long live George Washington, the President of the United States!

[*A soldier runs up the flag. The crowd bursts into cheering.* WASHINGTON *leads the procession back under the arch and off the green. Attendants remove the arch.*]

THE NARRATOR—Convinced that the new Nation was destined to enjoy a lasting and brilliant future, the President applied himself to the task of establishing its foundations in accordance with the wisdom of enlightened and far-seeing statesmanship. It was one of his strongest convictions that a potent factor in arousing universal respect at home and abroad for the young Republic would be the erection of a seat of government that should be in all respects worthy of a great Nation. He was warmly in favor of the choice of a site on the banks of the Potomac. He took great interest in the preparation of the plans for the city, and actually supervised the undertaking personally. It was he who selected the site for the "Federal House for Congress," and approved the name "The Capitol" for this edifice, himself laying the corner stone of it in 1793.

SCENE 4
1793. WASHINGTON, FOUNDER OF THE FEDERAL CITY

[*Several large attendants bring in a cubical block of stone, which they deposit in the center of the green. They retire. As the band plays Mozart's "Turkish March," a procession, headed by* PRESIDENT WASHINGTON, *enters. The* GRAND MASTER,

MASONS, MILITARY MEN, *and* CIVILIANS *are in line.* SOLDIERS *carry flags,* MASONS *bear Masonic emblems. The company gathers near the corner-stone. The* GRAND MASTER *of the* MARYLAND MASONS, *bearing in his hands a silver plate, approaches the President, and speaks.*]

GRAND MASTER—I have the honor, your Excellency, to acquaint you with the inscription which the corner-stone of the Capitol building is to bear. [*Reading from the plate.*] "This south-east corner of the Capitol of the United States of America, in the City of Washington, was laid on the 18th day of September, 1793, in the thirteenth year of American independence, in the first year of the second term of the Presidency of George Washington, whose virtues in the civil administration of his country have been as conspicuous and beneficial as his military valor and prudence have been useful in establishing her liberties, and in the year of Masonry 5793, by the President of the United States in concert with the Grand Lodge of Maryland, several lodges under its jurisdiction, and Lodge No. 22 from Alexandria, Va."

[*The* GRAND MASTER *deposits the plate on the stone, and steps back.* WASHINGTON *advances, and draws a trowel across the stone.*]

WASHINGTON—By this act, gentlemen and friends, it is my privilege to place in position the corner-stone of our national Capitol building. I have taken the greatest pains to insure that this house of government shall be in its conception and in its architecture in every way worthy of the future Federal City. Yonder to the westward, you may see already rising the walls of the Presidential Palace, where those who shall come after me in this exalted office will dwell. As we build today, let it be in the full expectation and confidence that Federal City shall one day be counted among the most beautiful seats of government in the world!

[*At the conclusion of the President's remarks, several children, in costume, bank the stone with flowers. The band resumes the "Turkish March" as the procession leaves the green.*]

INTERLUDE IV

Allegory: The Welding of the Nation
[*To the music of "America," thirteen young women enter the green. Each is clad in white symbolic costume, and wears a sash over her shoulder bearing the name of one of the thirteen States. They advance into the center of the amphitheatre, and assume the position of a huge heart. From the rear,* WASHINGTON *escorts* COLUMBIA, *a symbolic figure, straight into the center of the heart. At this juncture, the young women sing the first and fourth stanzas of "America," while Columbia stands silent.* WASHINGTON *moves along the line of the young women, joining their hands as he passes. At the conclusion of the singing, while the band continues playing "America,"* WASHINGTON *escorts* COLUMBIA *off through the rear, passing directly through the apex of the heart. The symbolic figures follow.*]

EPISODE 5

THE NARRATOR—Less than three years of life remained for the Immortal Founder after he laid down the cares of the Presidency. Those years were passed busily and happily at beloved Mount Vernon. To his hospitable doorway, his friends and admirers beat a well-worn path. Beloved and respected by his countrymen, and sought out by both the curious and the grateful, he was made to feel continually the esteem in which all people held him. When he died, just at the close of the century, these sentiments were most happily expressed by John Marshall, quoting Harry Lee, when news of Washington's death reached Congress: "First in war, first in peace, and first in the hearts of his countrymen!" The innumerable memorials which have been graced with the glorious name of Washington, in the decades since, testify eloquently to the aptness of this expression.

SCENE 1

1932. PANTOMIME: MEMORIALS OF WASHINGTON

[*Ten young women, in white Hoover aprons, enter from the rear, in single file. The band plays Sousa's "Washington Post March." Each character wears across her breast a large black letter which, when all ten have spread out across the center of the green, helps to spell the name W-A-S-H-I-N-G-T-O-N. Each bears a banner, in the following order: CAPITAL, STATE, MONUMENT, MOUNTAIN, SCHOOLS, C O U N T I E S, TOWNS, PARKS, STREETS, BRIDGE. The formation then goes through a drill, in which the appropriate characters are brought into the foreground so that the letters they wear spell, one word at a time: W-A-S-H-I-N-G-T-O-N H-A-S W-O-N A N-A-T-I-O-N. At the conclusion of the drill, the characters proceed to the rear of the green, in their original order.*]

FINALE

CLIO—MUSE OF HISTORY[*proceeds to the middle of the green, and speaks the* EPILOGUE:]

Immortal Founder! Lo, a Nation rears
Her noble temples on the constant base
His genius laid. A grateful people lauds
And venerates his name who visioned first
The glory of America, and saw,
Beyond the shaping years, what was to be
When our loved Republic, under God,
Should win her place of lofty eminence
Among the mighty nations of the earth!

Immortal Founder! Crumpled long to dust
The hand that laid the sure foundation stones
Of our Democracy! In bowered tomb
On green Virginia slope his mortal part
Awaits the dawn, beneath the clinging vines
That ramble lovingly above the sepulchre.
Yet not in dim sarcophagus his spirit sleeps,
Nor mausoleums building to his fame:
Behold! For aye, throughout this land and those
Beyond the seas, his spirit lives, still fresh and fair!

THE END

Appendix

Costumes

Special costumes, when needed, are indicated in the script. Otherwise, regular costuming suited to the characters and the period should be followed. For full information as to civilian costumes and military uniforms of the Revolutionary period consult the *George Washington Play and Pageant Costume Book* issued by the United States George Washington Bicentennial Commission.

Properties

The following properties are essential: Indian pipe for the Half King; belts of Wampum for Gist; saddle horses for Bishop and Washington; fifes; military accoutrements; copy of Declaration of Independence; drums, letter for Washington; crown; arch; flag-pole; flowers, pillow and Bible for Otis; corner-stone; flags; Masonic emblems; trowel; sashes for girls bearing names of thirteen states; ten large black letters on pasteboard spelling W-A-S-H-I-N-G-T-O-N.

Notes on Production

The Commission published a booklet, *"How to Produce a Pageant in Honor of George Washington,"* especially prepared by a well-known authority on the subject of pageantry. See page 724.

The subjects treated are: Sources of Material, Writing the Pageant Text, Outdoor Sites, Indoor Settings and Decorations, Costumes, Music and Dances, Lighting, Organization, Rehearsings Advertising and Financing, and a Bibliography.

Directors will find this booklet a handy reference.

Music Plot

Episode and Scene	Title	Composer	Rendition
Episode 1			
Scene 1......Shawnee Indian Hunting Dance..Skilton			Band
Scene 3......Come Live With Me and Be My Love ....Marlowe			Vocal
(See Hatton's Collection of Old English Ballads)			
Episode 2			
Scene 1......Chester ....Billings			Fifers
(Music may be found in Elson's *History of American Music*)			
Scene 2......Liberty Song			
Scene 3......Star Spangled Banner...........F. Scott Key			Band, Vocal
Interlude II...Yankee Doodle			Fife & Drum
Episode 3			
Scene 3......La Marseillaise			Band
Die Wacht Am Rhein...........			Band
Jeszcze Polska			Band
Scene 4......The World Turned Upside down..			Band
Interlude III..Minuet ....Mozart			Instrumental
Episode 4			
Scene 2......The Mansion of Peace..........Webbe			Band
Scene 3......President's March (Hail Columbia) Phile?			Band
Scene 4......Turkish March ....Mozart			Band
Interlude IV..America (Verses 1-4)...........			Band, Vocal
(1932 is the 100th anniversary of the composition of this song....			
Episode 5			
Scene 1......Washington Post March..........Sousa			Band
Finale ....America, the Beautiful.........Peabody			Band & Cast

Note: The following music listed above was used in the period portrayed: "Shawnee Indian Hunting Dance"; "Come Live With Me and Be My Love"; "Chester"; "Liberty Song"; "General Washington's March"; "Yankee Doodle"; "The World Turned Upside Down"; "Minuet"; "The President's March"; "Turkish March."

The other musical renditions are incidental, not historical.

For further information as to music appropriate for George Washington occasions see the music booklet issued by the Music Department of the United States George Washington Bicentennial Commission.

Many Waters

A GEORGE WASHINGTON PAGEANT

By Marietta Minnigerode Andrews

With Music Arrangement by Lyman McCrary

FOREWORD

This pageant is arranged in thirteen scenes; thirteen sponsors will develop it for the thirteen original colonies. Each director will expand or simplify the pageant according to the conditions under which it is produced. The experienced director will need no suggestions as to the action. For those less experienced each scene is introduced with a few recommendations.

Contrary to the usual technique of this form, it alternates its action from recitation and pantomime to dialogue, that the medium of expression may suit the varying themes, the more intimate groups being in dialogue, the spectacular events in pantomime with music.

The pageant begins and ends as the life of George Washington began and ended—to the sound of great waters. This water motif is the musical accompaniment, typifying the gathering forces and potentialities of the human life it portrays.

The scene shifts north, south, east and as far west as was known to George Washington along the streams which were the thoroughfares of traffic and travel; along those waterways which, in his plans for further facilitation of commerce, were to connect the east and west by additional canals and along which the early towns were built, and in sight of which the great campaigns were made; rivers upon which the manufactories of the north and the agriculture of the south were equally dependent for watering the acres and turning the wheels and conveying necessary commodities, both exports and imports.

The pageant closes in hearing of the Potomac, when the last sound about the Mount Vernon estate stilled in the gathering darkness, the Potomac rippling about the piers of the little home-made boat-landing at the foot of the hill, murmurs flowing on its way to the sea. The last scene completes the cycle: the elderly couple in the warmth of Mount Vernon, little Nellie Custis tracing their shadows cast on the wall by the candle light.

SCENES AND CHARACTERS

(In the order of their appearance)

Prolocutor—Spirit of the Rivers

Scene I: THE BOY WASHINGTON PLANTS TREES IN FREDERICKSBURG

George Washington
Mary Ball Washington
Royston
Thornton
Allen
Jackson
Taylor
Taliaferro
Braxton
Lewis
Berkley
Clowder
Mrs. Fauntleroy
Willis
Walle
Ladies and Gentlemen
Negroes
A Frontiersman

Scene II: THE BURIAL OF GENERAL BRADDOCK

Indian Warriors
General Braddock
Colonel George Washington
Soldiers at Burial of Braddock
Hugh Mercer
Dunbar
Dr. Craik
Peter Wagener

SCENE III: WASHINGTON VISITS MARTHA CUSTIS AT HER HOME

Mrs. Martha Dandridge Custis
Old Negro Butler
Colonel George Washington

Scene IV: WASHINGTON TAKES COMMAND OF THE CONTINENTAL ARMY

General George Washington
Group of Statesmen and Officers
Populace
Children

Scene V: GENERAL AND MARTHA WASHINGTON AT VALLEY FORGE

Martha Washington
Soldier
General Washington
Major General Lafayette
General Von Steuben
Ragged Man

Scene VI: THE SURRENDER OF CORNWALLIS AT YORK-TOWN

Officers at Surrender of Yorktown
The French under Rochambeau

Scene VII: CHRISTMAS FESTIVITIES AT MOUNT VERNON

Negroes
An Old Mammy
Butler
A Parlor Maid
General Washington
Lady Washington
Guests

Scene VIII: SUNDAY MORNING AT POHICK CHURCH

The Notables who Assemble at Pohick Church
Children with their Black Mammies
The Reverend Lee Massey

Scene IX: THE FIRST INAUGURAL

A Group of Children
A Group of Revolutionary Veterans
General Washington
Governor Clinton
General Knox
Alexander Hamilton
Baron Von Steuben
General St. Clair
Vice-President John Adams
Signers of the Declaration of Independence
The Chancellor of New York, Robert Livingston
Mr. James Otis

Scene X: PRESIDENT WASHINGTON INTERVIEWS A SCOTCH LAND OWNER

President Washington
Three Commissioners
Marcia Burns
David Burns

Scene XI: L'ENFANT SHOWS THE PRESIDENT PLANS FOR THE FEDERAL CITY

Major L'Enfant
Thomas Jefferson
President Washington
A Servant

Scene XII: THE PRESIDENT SITS BEFORE GILBERT STUART

Gilbert Stuart
President Washington
Joseph, a Footman
Martha Washington
Nelly Custis
Mr. and Mrs. Robert Moore
Mr. Lawrence Lewis
Miss Rebecca Gratz
The Secretary of State
Major L'Enfant
The Secretary of the Treasury
Mr. and Mrs. Wharton
The Attorney General and Mrs. Lee
Mrs. Bordley
Miss Elizabeth Bordley
The Vice-President
Colonel Carter of Virginia
Mrs Carter

Scene XIII: TRACING SILHOUETTES
PRESIDENT WASHINGTON
MARTHA WASHINGTON
NELLY CUSTIS
LAWRENCE LEWIS
HOUSEHOLD SERVANTS
Overture—Handel's "WATER MUSIC" (Orchestra)

PROLOGUE

Music: obligato, "Allemande," from "WATER MUSIC"

THE SPIRIT OF THE RIVERS [*appearing on the apron stage. She is clad in clinging silken garments, shading from deep to light shades through bronze-green, olive-green, golden-green, topaz and amber, to blue green.*]—
George Washington! What mighty waters sang
Through thy momentous life in varying tone!
In babyhood, the pleasant, lapping sound
Of Pope's Creek, as its silver tide curled 'round
Wakefield, the homestead that thy fathers built.

A boy, the Rappahannock sang for thee
In more adventurous theme, around the rocks
At Fredericksburg; thou knewest its fierce, swift ways
And all the moods it voiced, grave or gay.

A youth, thou stoodst beside a broader stream,
And watched the blue Potomac flowing on;
Dreaming fair dreams of cities to appear
In later years along those wooded shores.
The rhythm of the rivers stirred thy blood,
As Shenandoah, from its mountain source
Met the Potomac.——
                As the Alleghany
Met the Monongahela at Duquesne.
The glistening Rivanna, as it cleft
The Blue Ridge, through the hills of Albemarle
And the reflection of an old White House,
Near the Pamunkey, where thy Martha lived.

The Severn and the Susquehanna shone
Before thine eyes; Hudson and Delaware;
And York and Charles; great dangers and great triumphs
Along the rivers of thy native land,
As life ran on from infancy to age.
A net-work of proud rivers and a glimpse
Of a vast ocean far beyond the bays,
Drawing the rivers surely to itself.

Then, as thy life, lived so abundantly,
Drew to its close like river drawn to sea,
Walking with Martha in the sunset hours,
Thy vision swept across a placid stream;
Mount Vernon's green hills sloping to the river,
Potomac's rippling music in thine ears,
Even as thine eyes closed on this earthly scene.
        [*The* PROLOCUTOR *steps through curtains behind her, There is a brief interlude of music from the Handel suite.*]

SCENE I

THE BOY WASHINGTON PLANTS TREES IN FREDERICKSBURG

SPIRIT OF THE RIVERS [*appearing before curtain and speaking in a phrase of the "Water Music"*]—1744. In hearing of the Rappahannock River, on the outskirts of Fredericksburg.

[*The curtains part to show the action taking place on the main stage. School children are playing a game of "London Bridge is Falling Down." (Music: "London Bridge" called "Fallen Bridge"); others loiter along from school; two lads are wrestling good-naturedly; ladies and gentlemen; Negroes; a frontiersman in buckskins.*]

ROYSTON—Here comes George now with his mother.

GEORGE [*to his* MOTHER]—If I see you to your gig, mother, may I be excused to play with the boys

MARY BALL WASHINGTON—The horse is hitched not far from the bridge—'tis but a step—then you may go. I must haste to plant these Sweet William roots.

GEORGE—And for me, I shall plant my chestnut burrs here on the green!
        [GEORGE *accompanies his mother off stage.*]

THORNTON—George has been in town. His mother allows him to deal for her.

ROYSTON—He thinks he's a man.

THORNTON—And he is nigh to being a man. When a boy's father is dead, and his mother is a widow-woman, then a boy is nigh to being a man.

ROYSTON [*as* GEORGE *returns*]—Good day, Master George Washington.

GEORGE—What do you think? I have horse chestnuts in my pouch! We do not see this tree in our parts, it has a rare brave blossom. Methinks it would be fine to plant these seeds.
        [*The boys stand close beside him in admiration.*]

THORNTON—How many have you?

ROYSTON—Count them, George.

GEORGE [*counting*]—1, 2, 3, 4, 5, 6, 7, 8, 9, 10, 11, 12, 13. Thirteen—that's odd!

THORNTON—I see no oddity to it, thirteen is bad luck.

GEORGE—Old conjure tales from your mammy! Thirteen is the number of our colonies—that turns the luck!
        [*Other boys join the group.*]

ALLEN—What are you doing?

ROYSTON—George has thirteen chestnut burrs.

JACKSON—Going to plant them?

GEORGE—Yes.

CLOWDER—All those?

GEORGE—What now, boys, shall we name these nuts for our thirteen colonies and plant in Fredericksburg a tree for every one?

[*Cries of "Yes!"* GEORGE WASHINGTON *distributes the nuts, naming the lads as he deals them out—* ROYSTON, THORNTON, TALIAFERRO, TAYLOR, JACKSON, ALLEN, CLOWDER, BRAXTON, LEWIS, BERKLEY. *The boys scratch in the ground.*]

GEORGE—Proper planting is with a spade and deeper. Scoop you a good hole, Lewis, and trample it down firm.
    [MRS. FAUNTLEROY *passes*.]

MRS. FAUNTLEROY—What are you doing, George?

GEORGE—Planting some trees and naming them for the thirteen colonies. They come from afar. Their blooms are upstanding like candles.

MRS. FAUNTLEROY—Horse chestnuts! May I plant one?
    [*Two other boys*, WILLIS *and* WALLE *join the group*.]

GEORGE—Gladly, Madam. [*Handing her one of the remaining three*. WILLIS *and* WALLE *step forward and say simultaneously*]——

WILLIS AND WALLE—May I dig the hole for you, Mrs. Fauntleroy?

MRS. FAUNTLEROY—Thank you. [GEORGE *watches the digging and planting*.]

GEORGE [*to* WILLIS *and* WALLE]—Here are my two last nuts. Will you each plant one? And I have one for myself.

MRS. FAUNTLEROY—Mine is for South Carolina.

BOYS [*in turn*]—
    Massachusetts,
    Pennsylvania,
    New York,
    New Jersey,
    Georgia,
    Rhode Island,
    North Carolina,
    Delaware,
    Maryland,
    Connecticut,
    New Hampshire.

GEORGE—Mine is for Virginia!

Curtain

[*Entr'act—Music:* "Greensleeves."]

SCENE II

THE BURIAL OF GENERAL BRADDOCK

SPIRIT OF THE RIVERS [*appearing:* "Water Music"]—1755. In hearing of the Allegheny and Monongahela—the Western Frontier.
    [*Military music:* "British Grenadiers".]

SPIRIT OF THE RIVERS—

From Alexandria bravely starting out
Went Braddock's Expedition toward the West—
The French and Indians harrying the land—
The British and Colonial forces marched
To fight, their destination Fort Duquesne,
(Now known as Pittsburgh), where the Allegheny
Meets the Monongahela, joining there
To form the great Ohio's mighty stream.
    [*The curtains part, revealing several Indians,—listening, crouching, drawing the bow; one Indian to stand off to one side, immovable throughout the scenes that follow, as spectator of the burial. Music:* "Alkonook."]

SPIRIT OF THE RIVERS—

With General Braddock was his youthful aide,
George Washington, whose youth spent in the wilds—

Had well acquainted him with savage wars
And treacherous methods of red warriors;
Well known to him, the secret Indian trails.
He marked the wild geese flying overhead,
Knew sultry summer suns and wintry gales,
Knew the migrations of the cedar birds
And marked the poisoned arrows whistling flight
    And stratagems of the untutored foe.

Curtains

[*To the military music:* "British Grenadiers", *loud and aggressive, two figures cross the apron stage in earnest conversation*.]

SPIRIT OF THE RIVERS—

He warned the gallant Braddock of these things,
Respectful as a junior officer,
Yet earnest, since he knew whereof he spake;
But rank and military training gave
The General confidence in old world ways—
For Braddock also knew whereof he spake—
He was a seasoned and intrepid soldier—
Deaf ears were his. In gallant uniforms
Of red and white, to martial music, on
The British marched with much of lordly pomp
(Their lurking enemy were vast amazed)
And such parade as Washington deplored.

    [*The battle orchestration dies out and a ringing shot is heard. Silence—followed by the dirge. Music:* "The Dead March". *The curtains part on the burial scene. It takes place in the middle of the road which* GENERAL BRADDOCK'S *soldiers had so laboriously builded. When the service has ended, Trumpet calls* "Last Post."]

SPIRIT OF THE RIVERS—

The General met his death at the Great Meadows.
There was he buried, mourned and honored; there,
On the Frontier, the forest's groined arch
Was his cathedral, and the whispering winds
His Requiem. The Chaplain, Hamilton,
Was sorely wounded, so it happened that
No consecrated priest was present. Then
The General's youthful Aide, George Washington,
Schooled in the ritual of the English church,
Himself performed the priestly office.
    [*The solitary* INDIAN *remains as he stood, arms folded. Indian music*.]

SPIRIT OF THE RIVERS—

His towering figure and his boyish face
Presided o'er the solemn scene, the Book
Held open in his hand. With bare heads bowed
Gage, Morgan, Dunbar, Craik and Peter Wagener,
Made the responses, murmured the "Amen."
Mayhap stealthy Indians, lurking in the shadow
Immovable, watched the tall, pale-faced youth

Scatter a little dust into the grave—
"Ashes to ashes," said he, "dust to dust."

Curtains

[*Entr'act music: Funeral Hymn, "O God Our Help"
—St. Anne—by quartet of male voices.*]

Scene III

Washington Visits Martha Custis at Her Home

Spirit of the Rivers [*appearing: "Water Music"*]—in 1758. In the sound of the Pamunkey River—at the White House, the home of the Widow Custis in Kent County.

[*The curtain rises. On the main stage the drawing room at White House. It is late afternoon. The Dame Custis sits at the window looking out upon the Pamunkey. The sounds of Negroes coming in from the fields reach her; they are singing. (Music: "Dundee"); she has been occupying herself rolling tapers for the lighting of the candles and whale oil lamps but her work falls to her lap as she listens. An old Negro butler enters, announcing Colonel Washington, who strides into the room. At sight of the lady he bows low and kisses the fingers she extends to him. They do not speak. He stands gazing out of the window.*]

Martha—Dear Sir, you are so serious. Could you not lay aside these burdens when in my company? I fain would lighten your mood with a little laughter.

Washington [*tenderly*]—It is your understanding which doth always ease me. The thought of you lightens my heart and brings nearer all that I desire for our beloved Colony.

Martha [*looking up inquiringly*]—You have much in mind for Virginia?

Washington [*hesitates, listening absent-mindedly to the strains of melody floating in from the slave quarters*]—I dream—the great projects that lie ahead. Schools to be built, teachers to be trained—that our colonists may meet the world on a fairer basis—universities; science runs on apace in this progressive age, we must have institutions equal to any in the world, for we cannot today calculate upon the future. The Crown——

Martha—Think you the Crown will ever acquire territories beyond our present boundaries?

Washington—Aye, vast lands, areas of which as yet we know nothing. And with the influx of foreign born into these colonies——

Martha—You seem not to have thought of the poverty now existent among us; except for such as live in Manor houses, and they, often, fare too luxuriously. How would we feed this increasing population?

[*The daylight has faded; the old Butler enters with silver candlesticks, lighting them with a taper; he draws the window curtain and bows himself out.*]

Martha—I must own to a sincere affection for my Negroes.

Washington—I, likewise, for mine—and a greater need. I must wonder at the dispensations of Providence, which, by means of a traffic obviously iniquitous, provides our agricultural districts with labor essential to success.

[*The couple remain silent while a new Negro melody (Music: "Arlington" called "Ataxerxes") comes from without.*]

Martha—How melodiously these serenades fall upon the ear! There is in them an aspiration for which I cannot account—always the undertone of tears.

Washington—It moves me that in so many things we think alike. Since that happy hour when we made our pledge to one another, my dear, my thoughts go out to you as to another self.

Martha—It pleasures me truly to hear your sentiments.

Washington—Would you sing for me my favorite—"Give Me Thy Heart"?

Martha [*before seating herself at the harpsichord*]—I trust this day has been to your contentment?

Washington—No day, dear Madame, is long enough for the accomplishment of all I have in mind.

[*Martha's fingers stray over the opening chords of the song, "Give Me Thy Heart" by Francis Hopkinson.*]

Curtains

[*Entr'act Music: "Robin Adair".*]

Scene IV

Washington Takes Command of the Continental Army

Spirit of the Rivers [*appearing: "Water Music"*]—1775. In the sound of the Charles River, Cambridge, Massachusetts.

[*The curtains part. This tableau should be enacted from a balcony; a group of statesmen on the main stage facing the audience; the populace with their backs to the officers and audience. Children will figure well in this, babies lifted upon their fathers' shoulders.*]

Spirit of the Rivers—

On July third, seventeen seventy-five,
George Washington took full command at Cambridge
Of Continental armies all. And thus
Virginia, to her sister colony
Massachusetts, sent her best loved son;
Forming a bond in friendship, as in blood,
Between these two first English colonies.
John Adams, wise New Englander, devised
This policy, and down to our own day
Is felt the sympathy the act engendered.

[*Interlude of martial music: "The Girl I Left Behind Me".*]

Spirit of the Rivers—

Six months had passed since that heroic moment
The temper somewhat altered, sterner grown,
Anxiety pressed hard on every heart.
Some symbol was required to represent
Those holy rights for which the patriots fought.

[*Interlude: A chorus of children singing, "See the Conquering Hero Comes"—Handel, with words of the chorus sung at Yorktown.*]

Spirit of the Rivers—

Then, from the balcony of Craigie house,
A banner flung its folds out to the breeze.
The General in command raises his flag:
Distinguished patriots stand beside him as
He spreads the sacred folds before their eyes.
Long years ago, in childhood, he had planted
Thirteen brown nuts and named them, one by one,
For thirteen colonies; today, he shows
In thirteen stripes of red and white, the same
Bound closer now and indivisible.
Yet still the left-hand upper corner bears
An old device inherited from England,
Ours, as our English blood—the crimson cross
On field of blue, Saint Andrews' cross of Scotland.
This, known as "The Grand Union", soon gave place
To the blue field with silver stars; a star,
At first, for every colony; today,
For every State—a galaxy of stars.

Curtains

[*Entr'act music: "Song of Faith"—John Alden Car-penter.*]

Scene V

General and Martha Washington at Valley Forge

Spirit of the Rivers [*appearing: "Water Music"*]—1778. In the sound of the Schuylkill River—Valley Forge.

[*The curtains part. The scene occupies the main stage and shows the interior of the living room in the stone house at Valley Forge. Martha is engaged in overseeing the preparations for supper.*]

Martha [*to the soldier acting as servant*]—John, it is time for the General's return. Major-General Lafayette will accompany him. Ah, here they are! Put on another log.

[*Shuffling sound at the door. It opens with a gust of wind and snow. Two men enter. Martha brushes the snow from her husband's cloak, the Soldier performs the same office for Lafayette. Lafayette kisses Mrs. Washington's hand.*]

Washington—My dear Patsy, Von Steuben will be here in a moment. It will not incommode you?

Martha—Assuredly not. He is most welcome. John, another place at table. Perhaps Major-General Lafayette will sing for us one of his gay national songs while we wait for Baron von Steuben? A song will seem of good cheer, methinks.

Lafayette—With the utmost of pleasure, Madame.

[*Lafayette sings "Marlbrook s'en va t'en guerre." A loud rap on the door interrupts. Baron von Steuben enters. General Washington relieves him of his dripping cloak and leads him to the fire.*]

Washington—Welcome, most welcome, Baron.

Von Steuben—Ach, Herrschaften, but it makes bad weather yet—Donnerwetter!

Martha—We are happy to see you, sir. [*he kisses her hand.*] Your old world courtesy is most charming. This young man

has already spoiled me. In so rough a world as our winter camp, we hardly look for knightly bearing. The supper is ready. Will the General ask the blessing?

Washington—For these, Thy blessings we are about to receive, we thank Thee, Lord.

Von Steuben [*when they are seated*]—Was fur ein Essen! sacra bleu! Im Lager ein Gottesgaben.

Martha—You speak German to puzzle me. I learned some French but we were not taught by our tutors your guttural speech.

Lafayette [*laughing*]—He would only say, fair Madame, that this is a rare repast, a gift of the gods found here in a military camp. The Baron can swear in several tongues besides the King's English.

Von Steuben—Der King's English! But dat is droll! We of three nations are in arms against him. Yet already now him I can curse, gnadigste in all languages.

[*A knock at the door.*]

The Servant—Dispatches for the General.

[*A Man enters, emaciated and ragged, with a letter. He pictures the misery of all.*]

Martha—Here, my good man, draw up to the fire.

Lafayette—What may the tidings be, my General?

Washington—Of great distress. I must go hence and see what can be done for these poor fellows. For myself, I fare not badly, but oh, the men! I have a constitution equal to the strain—but they—it is a bitter thing to behold suffering beyond one's power to alleviate. How I long for Spring—the blue-birds are already at Mt. Vernon——

Lafayette—Mon General, so long as you are spared to lead us, we shall endure.

Curtains

[*Entr'act Music: "Blow, Blow Thou Winter Wind".*]

Scene VI

The Surrender of Cornwallis at Yorktown

Spirit of the Rivers [*appearing: "Water Music"*]—1781. In the sound of the York River—Yorktown.

[*The curtains part. The surrender of Cornwallis, shown in tableau on the main stage and apron, composed after the painting, in the Rotunda of the Capitol, by John Trumbull—the key to which lists all the officers present. This ballad is recited in a spirited manner.*]

Spirit of the Rivers—

Here on the coast of Virginia it ended—
Cornwallis ensnared in the trap he had set!
None guessed George Washington boldly intended
To sweep from the north and to join Lafayette.
Like Jove he bore down, and a great combination
Of forces took place he, assuming command,
With relentless, immediate, and sure concentration,
Then bottled them up both by sea and by land.

[*Music: "Ode to Columbia's Favorite Son".*]

Spirit of the Rivers—

So what could the enemy do but surrender?
The flag of truce hoisted, their own flag was furled.
Eight thousand strong, their arms they delivered,
While their bands played a tune of an "Upside-down-world."
[*Music: "The World Turned Upside Down".*]

Spirit of the Rivers—

The French under Rochambeau stood in formation.
They who, when hard fortune drove us to the wall,
Stood sponsors and fighters for our young nation.
General Washington rode in command of them all.
[*Music: "Marlbrook s'en va t'en guerre".*]

Spirit of the Rivers—

Cornwallis plead illness, so General O'Hara
Proffered in name of Cornwallis his sword;
General Lincoln, at gesture from Washington, took it,
Bowed low, and returned it with never a word.
"They are gone," said George Washington, "soldiers and sailors,
The invaders already are sailing the sea!
He thought of his Martha—he thought of his mother,
"Mount Vernon and Fredericksburg—waiting for me."

Curtains

[*Entr'act Music: "Yankee Doodle".*]

Scene VII

Christmas Festivities at Mount Vernon

Spirit of the Rivers [*appearing: "Water Music"*]—1783. In the sound of the Potomac with a memory of the Severn and Chesapeake Bay—Mount Vernon.

[*Before the curtains part, there is a sketch by the Negroes, "a break-down dance" with music ("Possum up a Gum-Tree") of banjos and bones, which ends with a cake-walk across the stage, an* Old Mammy *leading it with the prize cake held proudly above her head. Then the curtains part. The drawing room at Mt. Vernon is disclosed, gay with evergreen and holly. There is a big bowl of punch surrounded with many glasses;* Two Old Servants, Parlor Maid *and a* Butler, *are busy with finishing touches.*]

Butler—Billy Lee, he done got so uppity after he done bin to 'Napolis, he ain't gwine fotch in no mo' wood. He say, what Massa got us niggahs fo' but fo' to fotch in wood an' draw watah? Dat niggah done think hisself white, sense de Gen'al done tuk him to 'Napolis an' he done seen de Gen'al 'sign his 'mission.

Maid—'Tain't no class to go to 'Napolis. Ma ole man's up to 'Napolis. That no-count Niggah gits sold every Monday mawnin' reg'lar as de wash done sot on de line. He be's up fo' sale ebery day. What done happen at 'Napolis when de Gen'al he 'signs?

Butler—Ma! but dey speeched an' dey shouted an' dey et all day! Ay ain't neber seed sech a batch o' chickens in ma' life. Dey done got some highfalutin' biscuit—hops in 'em lak yo' puts in ma' brew—looks lak it sho' would mak 'em sick. When Ah eats biscuit, Ah wants biscuit. 'Napolis sho' done turn out to see our Massa 'sign.

Maid—'Sign? He ain't done sign nuthin', Niggah! When yo' sign, yo' writes down yo' name an' c'ain't get outten it. Ah done it onct when Ah ma'hied ma' Sam'l. Fo Gawd, dat's de las' time dis niggah eber goin' *X!* Boy, yo' bin talkin' 'bout resign. What Massa George he done got hisself inter som'pin an' him fix jest lak Ah did with ma' Sam'l for to get rid of it.

Butler—Gal, yo' talk lak yo' ben lookin' in de Massa's books.

Maid—Misses say, he ain't agwine to be Gen'al no mo'—jest gwine stay put, amindin' us niggahs an' aworkin' wid flowers an' watchin' de fa'ms.

Butler—Get outten heah! Heah dey come!

Maid—Ah tell yo', Niggah——! [*They hurry out.*]

[General *and* Lady Washington *enter, surrounded by a gay group.* Washington *dispenses hospitality while some one sits at the harpsichord and a group gathers around her to sing a Christmas carol ("I Saw Three Ships Come Sailing".) Negro musicians enter with fiddles, banjos and bones, and approach* Martha *with bows.* Martha *assigns them places and an old-fashioned reel is danced. (Music: "Lillibulero".) The guests form for the minuet (Music: "Minuet Danced before George Washington" —"Minuet Danced before Martha Washington".)* General Washington *leading it with his wife. The scene concludes with a grand march, in which additional characters may be brought on to advantage. Informal freedom marks the occasion and the real spirit of Christmas in the country is evident throughout.*]

Curtains

[*Entr'act Music: "The Toast to Washington"—Hopkinson, mixed voices.*]

Scene VIII

Sunday Morning at Pohick Church

Spirit of the Rivers [*appearing: "Water Music"*]—1786. In the sound of the Potomac River—Pohick.

[*The curtains part. Sunday morning at Pohick Church, equi-distant from Mt. Vernon and Gunston Hall, home of George Mason. The notables assemble before the service and discuss the news of the day.* Children *with their black* Mammies. *If desired, the scene can be played in two parts: the alcove serving as the entry to the church in one part; and the balcony above for the pulpit of the* Reverend Lee Massey, *in the second part. In both instances, the arrivals assemble on the main stage. Music: "The Pastorale" from the "Messiah" of Handel.*]

Spirit of the Rivers—

In coaches they come by the highway: their liveried outriders advance,

Postillions erect on the leaders, right proudly the four horses prance.

Lovely ladies are smiling "Good morning" to gentlemen mounted and brave,

Who spring from the saddle to greet them, tossing lightly the reins to the slave.

In the shade of Pohick they assemble, exchanging the news of the day,

While the snuff boxes pass 'round politely till the bells call to praise and to pray.

The Coffers, the Pollards, Ellzeys, the Hendersons, Washingtons, Moores,

The Gibson's, McCartys, Deneales, are kneeling. This house is the Lord's.

The parents have entered the church door, the sound of the hymn fills the air,

Reverend Massey stands robed in the pulpit and summons his people to prayer.

Curtains

[*Entr'act Music:* "Old Hundred" *or* "Coronation"—*Choir.*]

SCENE IX
THE FIRST INAUGURAL

SPIRIT OF THE RIVERS [*appearing:* "*Water Music*"]—1789. In the sound of the North (or Hudson) River and the East River, with breezes from the Atlantic Ocean—New York.

[*The curtains part. Use main stage, fore-stage and balcony. Handel's river music, "Maestoso Triumphant", as prelude to bands playing, bells ringing, cannons roaring. A* GROUP OF CHILDREN *scatter flowers; much noise and demonstration, words cannot be heard. At Federal Hall,* GENERAL WASHINGTON *is met by a group of* REVOLUTIONARY VETERANS. *Music: "Rinaldo March" from the "Beggars' Opera."*]

WASHINGTON—My old friends!

VETERANS [*crowding around him*]—Long live our leader! Welcome, General!—Do you remember Princeton?—Hurrah to the memory of Hugh Mercer!—Monmouth!—Damn Charles Lee!—Damn Benedict Arnold—Trenton!—huzzah, huzzah!

[*Shaking hands with as many as can reach him,* GENERAL WASHINGTON, *escorted by* GOVERNOR CLINTON *and* GENERAL KNOX, *makes his way between the cordon of* SOLDIERS *and* SAILORS *to his place on the balcony. Recognizable in the company are some who were at Valley Forge, Yorktown, and in other campaigns;* ALEXANDER HAMILTON, BARON VON STEUBEN, GENERAL ST. CLAIR, *the* VICE-PRESIDENT JOHN ADAMS, *some who drew up the Declaration of Independence, and* ROBERT LIVINGSTON, *Chancellor of New York, who administers the oath of office.*]

WASHINGTON [*repeating after* MR. LIVINGSTON]—I do solemnly swear that I will faithfully execute the office of President of the United States; and will, to the best of my ability, preserve, protect, and defend the Constitution of the United States.

[SECRETARY OTIS *presents the Bible. The* PRESIDENT *kisses it.*]

ROBERT LIVINGSTON—Long live the President of the United States!

THE ASSEMBLY—Long live the President of the United States!

[*The flag is unfurled, a salute of thirteen guns is fired, the bells ring tumultuously, the* REVOLUTION-ARY VETERANS—*an excited group of men in shabby uniforms—wave flags; and above the din, the voice of the populace rings cheeringly,* "Long live the President of the United States".]

[*Entr'act Music:* "The President's March".]

Curtains

SCENE X
PRESIDENT WASHINGTON INTERVIEWS A SCOTCH LAND-OWNER

SPIRIT OF THE RIVERS [*appearing:* "*Water Music*"]—1791. In the sound of the Potomac.—The site of the Federal City.

[*The curtains part to reveal the farm and orchard of the Scotch farmer,* DAVID BURNS (*main stage*). WASHINGTON *appears with* DR. DAVIS STUART, DANIEL CARROLL *and* THOMAS JOHNSON, *in animated discussion over a map which they are consulting. Arriving at the door of the Burns' log cabin (the alcove), they roll the map and knock on the door. Their summons is answered by* MARCIA BURNS, *the little daughter of* DAVID BURNS.]

COMMISSIONER—Is Mr. David Burns at home?

MARCIA [*curtsying*]—Aye, ye Honors, an' who may ye be?

COMMISSIONER—General Washington and friends.

MARCIA—Me faither is in the hoos; he will be verra pleased. Faither, faither! here be bonny gentlemen!

[*Heavy step with thump of a stick. The old Scotchman comes to the door. He is sturdily built, florid, with grizzled hair. His manner is not gracious.*]

BURNS—Ye be come again? An' for what comes so great a General to see a puir body?

[DR. DAVIS STUART, MR. DANIEL CARROLL, MR. THOMAS JOHNSON, *are surprised.*]

WASHINGTON—Not so poor, not so poor, my friend—with all the land along the river——

BURNS—Wad the prospect of sa bonny a stream entice the gentlemen tae a stroll along its banks——?

[THE COMMISSIONERS *walk toward the river (forestage).* BURNS *motions* GEORGE WASHINGTON *to seat upon a bench at the door and seats himself beside him clumsily. Little* MARCIA *lingers near her father but he turns upon her.*]

BURNS—Tae yer dollies, lassie, tae yer dollies. I ken Mr. Washington, hoo ye, hae yer e'e upon m' acres—yon French jackanapes L'Enfant I wad hae it for his toon. Weel, maland is ma ain.

WASHINGTON—This tract would be highly desirable, Mr. Burns. Other landsmen have acceded to the request of the government. And you know the proximity of the Federal City has made you a rich man. Miss Marcia will be a great heiress.

BURNS—The Wee-un'll be a great heiress?

WASHINGTON—And I would remind you, sir, that it lies within the power of the government to confiscate for the public good, I think——

[BURNS *rises angrily to his feet.*]

BURNS—Ye think—an' I ken, too, an' ma thoughts wadna be tae the liking o' yer Generalship. [*shaking his head angrily*] Ye wad threaten me, wad ye? Ye wad confiscate ma land and appre-hend ma person, very like! An' marry ma lassie tae some young whippersnapper! An' where wad you hae been yersel, for all ye think yer words pure gold, had ye nae married the rich widow Custis wi' her naygurs an' her lands?

WASHINGTON—Enough! Child, call my friends.

> [*He stands examining the apple trees until they re-appear. DAVID BURNS walks angrily back and forth. As his friends join him, WASHINGTON bows ceremoni-ously to MR. BURNS. The COMMISSIONERS do the same as they depart. MARCIA trips beside her father, trying to pacify him.*]

BURNS—An' Mr. George Washington wi' the Widow's mickle siller —auld Davy Burns gie's nay a whistle for sic talk. Nae non shall tak ma' ain land frae the lassie an' me——!

MARCIA—Na, na faither, the gentlemen meant ye na harm——

BURNS—Ye tell me that? tae ma face! Hae ye nae tasks? Hae ye nae dollies, that ye wad harry ye puir faither? Come noo——!

MARCIA—Noo, faither, ye ken ye will yield right enough, gie ye time.

BURNS—Time? time!——

Curtains

> [*Entr'act Music: "Ombra mai fu" from the Handel Opera "Xerxes". Recitative and Aria, male solos.*]

SCENE XI

L'ENFANT SHOWS THE PRESIDENT PLANS FOR THE FEDERAL CITY

SPIRIT OF THE RIVERS [*appearing: "Water Music"*]—1791. In the hearing of the Potomac.—Georgetown.

> [*The curtains part. Main stage. Without, a splash of the water, voices of workmen and boatmen. THOMAS JEFFERSON and MAJOR L'ENFANT at a table littered with papers in L'ENFANT's headquar-ters; maps on the walls; surveyors' implements in sight. MAJOR L'ENFANT is restless; looks constantly toward the street entrance; listens.*]

L'ENFANT—It is not his practice to be late! Military precision is a leading quality of the President.

JEFFERSON—Yes. An orderly brain. A life of discipline. George Washington knows the value of method and routine.

> [*L'ENFANT paces the room, stands looking out of the window. MR. JEFFERSON rises and joins him at the window.*]

JEFFERSON—Ugh!—see that mother on the deck—she has stopped her preparations for dinner to chastise her baby!

L'ENFANT—Do you recall the view from the chateau at Ecouen, near St. Denis, outside of Paris? The castle of the Mont-morency, overlooking the city and the fertile, intervening val-ley? So will be the environs of our Capitol. Its dome against the sky, avenues running like the rays of a star from a central focus——

JEFFERSON—We can hardly project our imaginations to the vision

of what one day will be seen from these heights. Colleges and factories will rise above the river, beautiful mansions along the crest of the Virginia hills, bridges spanning the river with highways into the whole south through Virginia——

L'ENFANT—Oh, that I might live to see this dream come true! to view from such a vantage ground the shining walls of our Federal capitol!—the great vessels, the commerce of the world, the coming and going of diplomats of all countries——!

JEFFERSON—Navigation will never get beyond this point. Yet is it no hardship to believe that the wild beauty of this rocky bottom may be preserved as a spot of untrammeled nature in the midst of a world of brick and mortar, a refuge for birds, perhaps.

> [*WASHINGTON enters.*]

WASHINGTON—Pardon my tardiness, gentlemen. [*greets JEFFER-SON courteously and L'ENFANT affectionately*] Mr. Secretary, our young friend informs me that within twenty-four hours you have furnished him with plans of a dozen European cities. Your learning and versatility, sir, amaze me.

L'ENFANT—Mon General, it is ever so. Monsieur Jefferson knows Europe. It is interesting and valuable that we compare our own plans with older places which have stood the test of time. Mr. Jefferson, of all Americans, comprehends the classical and aca-demic in art, and it will be his taste which will be the basis of American taste in art and architecture. Myself, pour moi, J'aime beaucoup le style de le Notre, and it would be the plans of Versailles to which I cling, the vision de Notre modified to the topography of this district and adapted to the sentiment of a republican people. Will you Excellency inspect my draw-ings?

> [*The three seat themselves at the table. L'ENFANT displays his drawings, leaning earnestly over the table to point with his finger to certain spots.*]

L'ENFANT—Here is the Potomac River, here the Eastern Branch, Georgetown, where we stand, is in this direction. The streets run north, south, east, and west. The city will have every requisite for beauty, health, and every reason to expand.

WASHINGTON [*rising and extending his hand to L'ENFANT*]—Con-gratulations, Major L'Enfant! I felt I had not miscalculated. I confess I have pondered with some concern over this matter— a matter of utmost moment—but all that you have done is agreeable to me, as I see it is to Mr. Jefferson, [*extends hand to JEFFERSON*] and will be to the pride and satisfaction of the American people.

> [*L'ENFANT rings and a servant appears with wine and glasses on a tray. L'ENFANT, with much emotion, embraces the PRESIDENT, exclaiming: "Mon General! mon President!" He then embraces MR. JEFFERSON. "A toast to the glory and prosperity of the United States of America!" Music: "Fill Every Glass" from "The Beggars' Opera".*]

Curtains

> [*Entr'act Music: "The Johann Stamitz Trio, No. 5" instrumental.*]

SCENE XII

THE PRESIDENT SITS BEFORE GILBERT STUART

SPIRIT OF THE RIVERS [*appearing*: *"Water Music"*]—1796. In the sound of the Delaware and Schuylkill Rivers—Philadelphia.

[*The curtains part, revealing the interior of* GILBERT STUART'S *studio. Portraits of* WASHINGTON *and other notables around the walls and on the floor. The* PRESIDENT *sits at ease in an arm chair. The painter, palette and brushes in hand, walks back and forth before his sitter and the nearly finished canvas. The studio opens into a large room, dining-salon or hall (the alcove).*]

STUART—The light has changed, your Excellency, and by the time [*the clock strikes four*] your Excellency has stretched his legs and I have put my tools in order, our friends may be arriving.

[*The* PRESIDENT *walks about.*]

STUART—The Secretary of State has signified his intention to call and I trust this very evening he may bring Major L'Enfant with him. L'Enfant is no mean artist himself—his father is a court painter of much merit and a designer of the Gobelin tapestries.

[*The painter meticulously puts his box in order—the* PRESIDENT *inspects his portrait.*]

WASHINGTON—Lifelike but severe, rather severe.

STUART—Grave, your Excellency, as one who has borne grave responsibilities. Of all the portraits I have humbly essayed to do of your Excellency, this promises to be the best, sir.

WASHINGTON—That is well. To a farmer and a soldier, it is miraculous that upon a flat surface you can create the impression of projection and that mere pigment can so reproduce flesh and blood.

STUART—And to a mere painter, your Excellency, such achievements as your own in field and council chamber are especially amazing.

[*Enter* JOSEPH, *a footman.*]

STUART—Are preparations complete in the dining room?

JOSEPH—Yes, sir.

STUART—Your Excellency, shall we refresh ourselves?

[JOSEPH, *after the exist of* WASHINGTON *and* STUART, *goes through a pantomime mimicing first the* PRESIDENT *and then the painter; struts the room, pulls an imaginary queue, then makes a feint of painting in most exaggerated burlesque of his master. The* PRESIDENT *and* STUART *return. A knocking at the door saves the situation.*]

STUART [*to* WASHINGTON]—L'Enfant is a friend of John Trumbull and barring some differences of opinion upon theory and technique, Trumbull and I are—umph——

WASHINGTON—L'Enfant—a gifted Frenchman, wounded and imprisoned in our cause.

[*Enter* MARTHA WASHINGTON *and* NELLIE CUSTIS.]

WASHINGTON—And how is my dear Patsy?

MARTHA—And how is my dear President?

STUART [*bowing low*]—What think you of the picture?

JOSEPH—Mr. and Mrs. Robert Moore; Mr. Lawrence Lewis; Miss Rebecca Gratz.

[*There is a general interest manifest. Murmurs of "The beautiful* REBECCA," *"The lovely Jewess." All are desirous of paying her honor.*]

JOSEPH—The Secretary of State! Major L'Enfant.

[*A continual exchange of bows and curtsies.*]

JOSEPH—The Secretary of the Treasury, Mr. Walcott; Mr. and Mrs. Wharton; the Attorney General and Mrs. Lee; Mistress Bordley! Miss Elizabeth Bordley!

[*Groups stand about in conversation or move to the adjoining room.*]

JOSEPH—The Vice-President! Colonel and Mrs. Carter of Virginia!

[MAJOR L'ENFANT *comes to contemplate the portrait;* STUART *joins him. Obligato from "Water Music" (Maestoso), heavy and ominous toward end.*]

L'ENFANT—C'est une technique encroyable, M'sieur; mais vous ete hereux d'avoir cette facilite d'exprimer la carataire si' parfaitment.

STUART—From Major L'Enfant this is praise. But, sir [*he speaks excitedly*] there are stirring scenes I would fain reproduce—the General crossing the Delaware——!

L'ENFANT—Vraiment! Vraiment! [*equally agitated, gesticulating both of them before the easel.*]

STUART—Dark—winter—depression—heavy gray skies—a gray fog—ice—in the foreground a fire—they are cold—yellow, red, white the light—figures move——

L'ENFANT—Oui, oui, M'sieur! The people in silhouette against de—de——

STUART—Lurid, livid light—some have burning torches.

L'ENFANT—Illumination—infernal—hellfire, you say. C'est aussi dramatique. C'est pour la musique quelquechose charmant, tetriste, tragique—Moins pour la vision—a thing of sound not of sight—for the ear, not the eye——

STUART—Yes, I grasp your thought! Listen, the howling of the wind, battering of boats against the ice! the threatening voice of the river, angry in flood!

L'ENFANT—The voices of men—they exclaim: "They dare not! It is murdair, General! General, what would the country do without you?" Over all, the voice of mon General, "I go!"

STUART—"Have you looked to the boat? Is she sea worthy?"

L'ENFANT—"She is, she is!" They shout us, she is safe!

STUART—"Man the oars! the locks. Hold a torch! make sure of the locks."

L'ENFANT—"Have you ropes? Hold fast to your cloaks! 'Tis a ripping wind!" They are off—the boat scrapes, you say, scrapes? "Hark, hark! Halt! On the other shore make a fire"—Eh, bien, then respond, they will light a signal fire—the sound of oars against the ice——

STUART—The fire this side dies down—the throng have massed into one vast shadow—groans!

L'ENFANT—Weeps——!

STUART—Prayers——!

L'ENFANT—Mon Dieu!　They arrive!　the fire burns on the far bank! they are across!　You will one day paint it.　Magnifique, M'sieur, un courage magnifique!

Curtains

[*Entr'act Music: "Mansion of Peace," by Samuel Webbe.*]

SCENE XIII

TRACING SILHOUETTES

SPIRIT OF THE RIVERS [*appearing: "Water Music"*]—1799.　In the sound of the Potomac with a memory of the Severn and Chesapeake Bay—Mt. Vernon.

[*The curtains part to show the main stage.　GENERAL and MRS. WASHINGTON are in the library.　WASHINGTON sits near the table, the candle light falling on the "Alexandria Gazette" in his hand.　MARTHA is making lace.　The windows are open and from the slave quarters come the sound of fiddling and dancing.　(Music: "Zip Coon" or "Turkey in the Straw.")　The music drifts into crooning and songs as the evening wears on.　NELLIE CUSTIS stands near her grandparents.*]

NELLIE—I have a fancy to do your portrait, Grandfather.　The shadow falls so clear upon the wall.　Have I your permission to trace it in lampblack on a bit of paper?　[*The GENERAL nods and takes the chair she indicates.　She prepares the materials, makes the tracing, her grandmother rising to watch her.*]　And Grandmother, you also—your filly cap and kerchief will be fair.

[*WASHINGTON gives his chair to MARTHA, who sits straight and prime while NELLIE replaces the paper on the wall and traces her profile also.*]

NELLIE—These portraits will be a joy to me, as the harpsichord has been to all of us.　They are very like.　I shall treasure them dearly and the memory of this evening.

WASHINGTON—My child, sing "The Wayworn Traveller."　It is a song for which I have an affection.

[*NELLIE seats herself dutifully at the harpsichord and sings.*]

WASHINGTON—We little thought when we ordered the harpsichord for you from London the pleasure we should derive from it in our later days.

[*NELLIE's fingers stray idly over the keys in a bar of "Annie Laurie."*]

WASHINGTON [*to MARTHA*]—Well, Patsy, shall we have prayers and retire?

MARTHA—Yes, George, I am tired.

[*LAWRENCE LEWIS enters, announced by a servant.*]

WASHINGTON—Well, Nephew, just in time for prayers.　[*LAWRENCE bows.*]

MARTHA—Nellie, will you ring for the servants?

WASHINGTON [*to LAWRENCE*]—You will join us?

LAWRENCE—If I may be permitted.

[*NELLIE rings the bell and hands a prayer book to her grandmother.　The HOUSEHOLD SERVANTS enter modestly six or seven and MARTHA WASHINGTON motions them to be seated, reads Psalm 39, after which they bow themselves out, with "Good night,*

Massa" and "Goodnight Missus" and "Good-night Missie Nellie and Marse Lawrence."]

WASHINGTON [*to LAWRENCE*]—You will not think us uncivil if Patsy and I excuse ourselves?

LAWRENCE—Not at all.

[*NELLIE kisses her Grandmother's cheek and holds open the door, kissing the GENERAL's hand as he passes out.　A maid with a candle is waiting outside.*]

LAWRENCE [*embracing NELLIE*]—Nellie, my love, it is friendly of them to grant me a few moments alone with you.　How I long for such moments.

NELLIE—Yet—Grandmother disapproves of young men and maidens sitting too long and too late together, and I always visit her room before retiring.　Will you say goodnight?　I am sure they expect you to stay here, rather than ride home this late.　We shall meet in the morning.　[*Wistfully*] Lawrence, they are always wonderful.　Do you think when we have been married as long we shall be as they?

LAWRENCE—I am of his blood, you are of hers; and we have had their example.

[*NELLIE extends her hand, dismissing him.　He kisses it tenderly.*]

LAWRENCE—Goodnight, my love; good angels guard you!　[*Exits.　Alone in the room NELLIE returns to the harpsichord and her fingers stray over the keys.　(Music: "Drink to Me Only with Thine Eyes".)　At the end of the song, the girl stands at the window listening to the sounds of the banjo, the singing and crooning, which still sound faintly from the slave quarters.　After a moment she snuffs out the remaining candles and in the darkness leaves the room.　The melodies from the quarters die out.　There is only the murmur of the River Potomac flowing, flowing past Mount Vernon on its way to the sea.　"Water Music" while the curtains close slowly.*]

Finis

APPENDIX

STAGE

The most practicable stage upon which to set "Many Waters" would undoubtedly be a curtained stage affording a fore-stage (apron) and a main stage with a large balcony or raised platform. If the balcony is used and can be above an alcove, the set can be enriched by the use of appropriate back-drops, French doors, and the like.　The furnishings necessary for the various scenes, especially the outdoor scenes, might be by suggestion only.

COSTUMES

All historical characters are to be dressed in costumes and uniforms of the period.　For full information regarding costumes consult the "George Washington Play and Pageant Costume Book" issued by the United States George Washington Bicentennial Commission and sent upon request.

MUSIC

The musical motif of "Many Waters" is agreeably suggested by the orchestral "Water Music Suite" of Handel.　It is intended that the various movements of the Suite, performed as an obligato whenever the SPIRIT OF THE RIVERS speaks and to begin and end the piece, should form the musical continuity of the Pageant. The various folk tunes and songs are historically accurate for the period which they serve to embellish. Those of the Indians are open to debate, as we have no record of their own productions; of the Negroes likewise, although we know that the slaves did learn to fiddle for the dances and to imitate their masters in songs and hymns. Orchestral and band music is used to suggest the martial and ceremonial actions of the drama and chamber music for the more intimate domestic scenes. Our musical heritage at the time of the Revolution was as English as our speech and customs, and it was not until the founding of the Republic that our native genius began to flower.

MUSIC PLOT

OVERTURE: "Water Music" Handel (Orchestration).

PROLOGUE: Obligato "Allemande" from "Water Music."

SCENE I: "London Bridge"; "Greensleeves" (Song—children's voices).

SCENE II: "British Grenadiers"; Indian Music—"Alknomook"; "Dead March"—Handel; "Last Post" (Trumpet Call); "O God Our Help"—St. Anne (Funeral hymn sung by quartet male voices).

SCENE III: "Dundee", "Arlington" (Negro music); "Give me Thy Heart"—Hopkinson; "Robin Adair" (curtain music).

SCENE IV: "The Girl I left Behind Me," "See the Conquering Hero Comes" (Unison chorus); "Song of Faith" (curtain music).

SCENE V: "Marlbrook S'en ra t'en guerre," "Blow Blow Thou Winter Wind" (curtain music, men's voices).

SCENE VI: "Ode to Columbia's Favorite Son"; "The World Turned Upside Down"; "Marlbrook s'en ra t'en guerre"; "Cornwallis Burgoyned" to the tune of "Chester" or "Maggie Lauder," "Yankee Doodle" (curtain music, band).

SCENE VII: "Possum Up a Gum Tree"; "I Saw Three Ships Come Sailing"—Carol; "Lillibulero" from "The Beggars' Opera" (Reel); Minuet; "The Toast to Washington"—Hopkinson (curtain music, mixed voices).

SCENE VIII: "Pastorale" from Handel's "Messiah"; "Old Hundred" or "Coronation" (curtain music, by choir).

SCENE IX: "Rinaldo March" from "The Beggars' Opera"; "The President's March" (curtain music, band).

SCENE X: "Ombra mai fu" from the opera "Xerxes" by Handel; "Recitative and Aria" (male solo, curtain music).

SCENE XI: "Fill Every Glass" from "The Beggars' Opera"; "The Johann Stamitz Trio, No. 5" (curtain music, instrumental).

SCENE XII: "Mansion of Peace" by Samuel Webbe (curtain music, solo).

SCENE XIII: "Zip Coon"; or "Turkey in the Straw"; "The Wayworn Traveller"; "Annie Laurie"; "Drink to Me Only With Thine Eyes"; "Water Music"; "Washington's March" (curtain music, band).

(For references to above music consult the historical pamphlet "The Music of George Washington's Time" and the music booklet, "Music From the Days of George Washington," issued by the United States George Washington Bicentennial Commission.)

How to Produce a Pageant

In honor of

GEORGE WASHINGTON

By

Esther Willard Bates

Written Especially for

The George Washington Bicentennial

No type of commemoration comes nearer to the heart than one in which the individual takes part and expresses himself while he is expressing a great theme. A pageant in honor of the Two Hundredth Anniversary of the Birth of George Washington is such a commemoration.

A participant not only has the opportunity of contemplating the greatness of George Washington but of actually living, for the time being, in that greatness of spirit. He experiences the patience of waiting, the wise recognition of human shortcomings, the unselfish abnegation of personal longings, the thrill of courage and the high dedication which characterized not only Washington but the men of Washington's time. He enters also upon a community undertaking in which cooperative endeavor is at a maximum. In circumstances the like of this, members of a community grow in citizenship. Thus, the pageantic opportunity of the Bicentennial is to be joyfully acclaimed.

The aim of this pamphlet is to aid, in so far as possible within the limits of a few pages, such communities as wish by their own efforts to honor the Father of Our Country in pageantry, and while the full possibilities of beauty and perfection march far ahead of many amateur undertakings, painstaking and enthusiastic production offers rewards well worth while.

WRITING A PAGEANT

First, the text of a pageant should not be too long. Its episodes should be written dramatically; employing suspense, surprise, characterization, and climax. These episodes are usually connected by prologues or by allegorical interludes which convey the deeper meaning of the entire pageant. Action is desirable throughout. Dialogue should be brief, pointed, and euphonious. The finale, providing as it does for the massing of the entire cast, should be the most impressive scene of all. A pageant must employ, whenever suitable, colorful costumes and setting; music, both vocal and instrumental; pantomime; and dancing.

Material

With these requisites in mind, the author will begin his work of gathering material. Research should be confined to the subject immediately in hand. From the more brief accounts of the life and times of George Washington, choose such episodes as do not require more players than the selected stage can accommodate. Scenes in which there is an element of conflict are especially desirable. Enrich these episodes with details of daily living. Enliven the scenes with picturesque characters out of the imagination. Finally, do not lose sight of the effect which contemporary European events had upon the American struggle.

Length

The length of the pageant must be determined. If it is planned for out-of-doors, it may last as long as three hours, since novelty of surroundings prevents boredom on the part of the audience. Two hours and a half is ideal. For indoors, unless the pageant is exceptionally colorful and exciting, one and one-half to two hours is long enough. The playing length of a manuscript may be estimated by allowing a page (double-spaced and typewritten) a minute to the dialogue; pantomime, unless described in great detail, plays four or five pages to the minute. A pageant of eight episodes will probably average ten minutes to an episode—that is, ten pages of dialogue. The remaining time will be given over to the link passages between episodes. Inasmuch as these link passages may take the form of a poetic "chorus," a poem preceding each episode like a prologue but set to music and sung; or a series of symbolic tableaux interspersed throughout the action; or pantomimic allegories; or even interpretive dances, telling the story of the natural background of field, wood and the spirits that dwell therein,—the variation in playing time is necessarily so great that the only sure test is actual rehearsal.

OUTDOOR SITES

A natural amphitheatre is greatly to be desired, but in any case the site should be chosen for beauty, for space and for the excellence of its acoustics. A lake or stream adds to the acoustic advantages, as well as to the beauty of scene. The ground must be firm and level for the dances and dramatic action. If possible, the prevailing breeze should blow from players to spectators. Temporary seats may be used, a grandstand erected, or the audience may sit on the grassy hillside. Unstable weather conditions can be met either by providing an alternate date or an alternate place within doors.

Historic Sites

It is a popular and worthy custom to stage an historic pageant on the very site where the major event of the pageant occurred. If possible, this is a wise precedent to follow. General Washington travelled up and down the entire Atlantic seaboard during his years as Commander-in-Chief of the Continental Army. There were battles fought where the lay of the land is still somewhat open. There are standing edifices in which he spoke, churches where he worshiped, and houses where he slept. It will be more than fitting that such places serve as the background of pageants in his honor. So great an occasion as the Two Hundredth Anniversary of the Birth of George Washington, however, should arouse every community and every organization to universal mustering of service, whether or not a site has been hallowed by memories of Washington's presence.

Size

A pageant with a cast of not more than forty people may be staged on a grass plot as small as fifteen by thirty feet. Such a pageant should play to an audience of only three or four hundred. The stage must be increased steadily in size as the number of actors is increased. The proportions of the cast of the pageant are curiously relative to the size of the audience, a pageant of three hundred actors playing suitably to an audience of two to three thousand. This, however, is no arbitrary rule and if the number of spectators is diminished, the number of performances may be increased. A small pageant, presented on a series of afternoons and evenings, may be produced before as large a number of spectators in the aggregate as the large pageant played but once or twice. But the great outdoor spaces seem to call for a multitude. A playing space nine hundred feet long by six thousand feet deep is not too large for a community to prepare and then to fill with inspiring pageantry.

Essentials

Much is essential in an outdoor site beside the size. Unless the pageant is played upon land which has been rolled and cut regularly for at least a year, the uneven conditon presents a serious problem. The best thing to do is to roll the ground site heavily again and again and cover it with sand, pine needles, or other material to bring it to a level. A stage may be built, having a sort of inner stage for episodes requiring a small cast and for dances. This outdoor stage should be painted to approximate the shade of the surroundings. But such a stage is artificial and should only be used where time is short and every other device seemingly impracticable.

Center for Stage

A focus for the audience, which shall mark the center of the playing space and help the director arrange his groups properly, may be a natural object such as an unusually large tree or rock, or may be built artificially. Sometimes an arch spans the playing place, back center; sometimes an altar marks a middle point. Pylons or columns may be placed in a design to serve as background or to afford entrances. Pedestals, thrones, platforms, raised dais or other details, if the action permits, are all suitable for out-of-doors. A rustic air may be given them with vines and evergreens. For historic purposes, Indian tepees, forts, blockhouses, or cabins are often necessary. The important thing to remember is that all stage furnishings should be related to as much of the action as possible. If they play but a minor part, they should be placed unobstrusively at one side of the pageant stage or be blocked out by portable screens of foliage when not required. It is permissible to have a series of centers for a pageant stage and place one action about a fort or other device, which for the time is the focal point in the arena; then center later episodes, as expedient, to left or right of the fort, only taking care not to move the center of interest too far from any portion of the spectators nor to place the scene of the climax too far from the stage center.

Background

No art can exceed nature's own background; the sky-line, the rocks, the forests, the waters all contribute. When there are no trees, trees can be potted temporarily on location or planted for permanent beautifying of the pageant site. For the aspect of spring, small bare trees, pink with blossoms made of bits of cloth or crepe paper twisted profusely upon them, serve nicely. Meshed wire, interwoven with evergreen boughs, is always a practical scenic aid. Rows of trees or evergreens will be found a great convenience where screened entrances are needed. Banks of trees at the back and sides of a pageant stage help to conserve and direct the sound effects.

Properties

For properties: settees, tables, stools, spinning-wheels, hand-looms and the small household accessories (such as kettles, pails, chopping trays and outdoor cooking and washing utensils) are permissible and add not only to the action but to the realism of the pageant.

Orchestra or Band

The musicians must be near enough the stage, whether directly in front or to the side, to make it possible for them to give the pitch to the singers easily and to send and receive cues to and from the players in the scenes that require music.

Grandstand

For the audience, wide aisles are requisite and many exits. In the simpler outdoor pageant, the audience may sit on the grass of the slopes. Mats and cushions can of course be offered for rent. If there is a level spot on the site, chairs should be provided. With pageants that are thrown open to a community free of charge, this is often the best way inasmuch as grandstands materially increase the cost of a production. A grandstand may be built for the occasion that will serve as a permanent addition to the civic life of the community. Where such is not desirable or possible, stands can be hired from firms in the larger cities. Funeral directors rent chairs in varying numbers and seats may be borrowed from schools and churches. When the spectators are to be seated on planks, fifteen to eighteen inches—marked off by heavy lines stenciled in black—should be allowed to each spectator and plainly numbered to make clear the rights of each ticket holder. The greatest care should be taken to meet the legal building requirements in order to insure safety for all.

Accommodations for Spectators

The following accommodations are usual back of the grandstand: parking space for cars; dressing rooms for ladies and gentlemen; make-up rooms; wardrobe rooms; rest rooms for both men and women; and a Red Cross room. These "rooms" are frequently tents. The space within the circle of these tents is assigned as a gathering place for the players who await their cues. This central space is overseen by marshals, or episode directors, and callboys. Settees should be provided, but not so many that the players are prevented from moving freely. Naturally the area is to be screened from passersby.

Traffic

Traffic of all kinds should be kept as far from the playing place as possible. Authorities may be prevailed upon to divert traffic during the hours of the pageant and thus an otherwise annoying obstacle is removed.

Weather

There being no way to insure good weather, pageant directors ought to arrange either for a postponement in case of rain, stating the second choice with time and place upon the ticket, or for indoor

performance, as an alternative. Always provide for indoor rehearsals in case the weather makes them necessary, and post the two
places of meeting long beforehand.

Insurance

Remember, even though the sky is clear, a wet pageant ground
ruins costumes, spoils dances and makes the next performance a
tawdry one. If heavy expense accompany the production, it is wise
to carry insurance against the financial loss from bad weather and
consequent postponement.

INDOOR SETTINGS

In a theatre, plan to use the entire floor space of the stage. In a
hall, build a platform that will accommodate the players of the
largest episode without crowding. Proportions of hall and platform
should be studied by an architect or an artist who can advise as to
the size of the platforms, the placing of entrances and stairways
and the adaptations necessary for any special grouping of symbolic
characters in balconies and niches. Churches which are suited to
community observances offer interesting possibilities in the proportion and design of the chancel, the location of pulpit and reading
desk, and oftentimes in lofty niches.

Levels

A use of different levels will make the plainest platform varied
and decorative. There may be a raised dais, a small platform, niche,
or arched pedestal in the center back, or at either side. Small platforms, approached by steps, are admirable for symbolic figures.
George Washington may be given the highest level to stand upon
whenever the action permits. Grouping is greatly enhanced by
such devices and more players can be utilized. Other units are
columns, altars and arches. An arch, center front in one episode,
if placed diagonally to one side and draped with vines can be made
to serve as an entrance in another episode. Platforms, pedestals
and the like are to be hired from firms dealing in scenery, with permission to paint them. Unsized water-soluble paint washes off.
Use exactly the right color needed for the general scheme of decoration. Metal also will take this kind of paint, and interesting
effects may be had by using such simple devices as metal waste-
baskets, colored and turned upside down for stools and pedestals.
By adding scrolled backs of beaverboard, the most commonplace
wooden chairs, when bronzed or tinted, are converted into splendid
thrones.

Screens also are very adaptable portable units and, painted
differently on front and back, when turned, give the impression of
a different set. By rolling on two screens, stenciled with pine
boughs against a sky, and adjusting the lights to the time of day
and to out-of-doors, the effect of woodland country may be given.
Little pines on standards draped with evergreens may be placed
about. Other outdoor backgrounds may be made of mesh wire
thickly woven with pine and hemlock boughs. Pine needles make
a realistic ground covering. Grass may be represented by grass mats
rented from funeral directors' establishments.

Stairways to the platform may be placed from either aisle, in
the center, or at both ends. Wherever placed, they make interesting
approaches and permit actors upon occasion to group themselves
and become a part of the setting. But stairs and platforms must
not squeak. The lumber must be well-seasoned and securely nailed.
A covering of heavy cloth or padding insures quiet at the same time
that it improves appearances. Usually this covering should be

brown or green. The neutral brown of the wrong side of old
Brussels carpet is an unobtrusive shade.

Changes in Setting

Changes in setting may be made behind a curtain while the
portions of the link plot are going on. They may be made openly,
the articles being brought on and off by property men, preferably
in costume. They may be made in darkness. Organization and
much rehearsing is essential to speed and quiet.

Curtains

A safe background for a pageant is a curtain, hung close to the
back wall to give all possible playing space and flanked with side
curtains, divided once or twice, to afford the requisite number of
entrances. Curtains may be made from canton flannel, denim,
monks-cloth, poplin, velveteen, if the purse permits, or from dyed,
lined or doubled, unbleached cotton cloth. Abundant fullness to
folds and an agreeable neutral color are the desiderata. A soft gray-
green may suggest an interior; with trees and screens of evergreens,
a forest background. Sky blue is a horizon-line color when judici-
ously lighted. Gray is also an adaptable atmosphere color, but
should not be too dark. Home-dyed fabrics have a slight uneven-
ness which gives the effect of varied texture, though careless dyeing
may result in streakiness. When curtains are introduced, a frame
to enclose the front of the stage, or some other device to take the
place of the proscenium arch, is needed. A simple way of meeting
the problem is to hang a valance overhead from a temporary rod,
for covering shifts in setting or changes in episodes. Shallow side
curtains, added to the valance and as screening to the entrances, are
necessities, as is a draw curtain.

Flats

It may be that canvas-made scenery is preferable to back the
stage. Such scenery is made by tacking unbleached domestic sheet-
ing upon wooden frames made of 1 x 3 inch lumber. The cloth
comes in seventy-two inch width. Size it with flake-white glue
dissolved in the proportions of one cup of glue to four quarts of
water; give twelve hours for drying; then paint with any dry color
paint mixed in water. These sets should be equipped with three
hinges to each unit and painted a different color on each side that
they may be reversed. To provide a different set of scenery for
each of the six to ten episodes necessitates too much time given to
scene shifting. Furthermore, as the episodes are brief compared
with the acts of a play, many changes will prove confusing, and
it is difficult to hold the spell over the imagination once it is broken.
Always in planning the stage design of a pageant, keep the settings
flexible so that they may be easily put up and taken down.

Decorative Devices

Decorations of national or historic insignia used freely in the
auditorium add much to the spirit of the occasion. Coats of arms
of city, state, or of George Washington and his associates, make
beautiful units, stenciled and colored and placed about the hall
over the sconces or doorways or on pillars. These may be done on
oiled paper or on tracing paper and illuminated. They may likewise
be stenciled on the stage curtains.

Civic and military designs, mottoes, crossed swords and muskets may equally well be used as units of decoration. Long panels,
in patriotic colors, with pictures or designs upon them, may be
painted on ordinary wrapping paper, weighted and hung from the

very top of the wall to reach nearly to the floor. Such decoration will do much to transform an interior.

Banners should be treated in the same way, hung flat to the wall, or, after the manner in European cathedrals, hung out at right angles. They may be carried in processional and recessional and always make an inspiring finale. They can hardly be too large or too broadly designed or brilliantly colored. Ushers should wear costumes of the period. Flowers, tree boughs, vines and evergreens add to the note of festivity. Nothing should be left undone to create an atmosphere of rejoicing in the great American traditions that General Washington helped so richly to bequeath to us.

COSTUMES

A person with dependable artistic feeling should be in charge, for, in addition to historical accuracy in designing pageant costumes, group effect must be studied and color schemes for each episode and for the finale arranged with a full knowledge that colors change under different lights. Color, like music and light, is important in arousing emotion and stimulating attention as well as in giving beauty. It should be used liberally, therefore, with all the richness and ingenuity possible. Pageantry demands it.

Color Combinations

The intermediate shades, mauves, apricots and blue greens, which are obtainable nowadays, were seldom seen in Washington's day. Soldiers' costumes are dictated by history as to color. Ordinary costumes will probably combine well, if the designer sticks to the usual shades of red, blue, green and the less frequent purples, thrown into relief by the more common browns, grays and blacks. When ladies are dressed in delicate hues, care must be taken not to destroy the values of the tones by vivid suitings for the men. Sunlight gives colors at their full values; artificial light, when gelatine screens of different shades are used, makes strange and unexpected changes. In consequence, all costumes must be donned at an early rehearsal, while there is still time to make sweeping alterations. Distance, out-of-doors, softens color and adds a faint atmospheric blue.

Dyeing

For fabrics, unbleached muslin, denim and canton flannel are the least expensive. These should be bought at wholesale and dyed to suit. Dyeing gives a wider choice of color and it can stimulate faded and worn effects. It also, at a distance, being slightly uneven, gives the impression of softer and more beautiful textures.

Blockprinting

Blockprinting and stenciling, to simulate embroidery, are easily done; hence should be used liberally. For economy stencils are made from brown paper, stiffened with shellac, the cutting out of the design done with small, sharp scissors. Any oil paint, dissolved in a small quantity of turpentine, will serve. Decorations may be put on free hand, if the worker be sufficiently skilful. For this the least expensive paint comes under the heading of "Show Card Colors." For blockprinting, the design is first drawn on a piece of wood or linoleum, then cut out, in order to leave the pattern elevated a little on the surface of the block. The cloth to be blockprinted is spread on a pad of blotting paper or old soft cloth. The design, after being painted in the color desired, is placed face down on the garment and pressed firmly upon the fabric. When stenciling is to be done in gold, the powdered gold is purchased in tins and mixed with what is known as "bronzing liquid." For blockprinting in gold or metallic colors, buy what is called "silver size" and print with it as if it were the colored paint, but while it is still moist sprinkle the powdered gold or silver on it, letting stand for twelve hours before brushing off. An inexpensive fabric, dyed a lovely color and decorated with gold or silver embroidery, gives the impression of a very rich and beautiful garment.

Period Properties

Special care must be taken to provide hats and shoes of the right period. Buckles can be fashioned of pasteboard, painted silver, and an elastic band run through the buckle over the shoe and under the instep, or buckles may be cut from tin. Hats are easily concocted of canton flannel over pasteboard foundations. High boots are cut from leatherette or enamel cloth after the fashion of leggings and are finished by an unobtrusive strap of black elastic passing under the foot. The cheapest of paper fans, gilded and painted, look decorative and furnish a brilliant note of color. The eighteenth century was a courtly period, and the value of its picturesque details of reticules, snuff boxes, canes, laces, rosettes, buckles and jewelry cannot be overlooked.

The Professional Costumer

Professional costumers give historical accuracy and save time and trouble. They will costume an entire pageant, down to the last items of hat, shoes, wig and such accessories as fan, snuff box, bow and arrows, gun and powder horn. This is, of course, the easiest way, and sometimes not much more expensive than buying the cloth and making the garments. Out of fairness to the costumer, however, pains should be taken to give him, as early as possible, a complete list of the characters with their approximate ages and sizes, and whether or not shoes, hats and wigs are to be added. Estimates from all available costumers should be secured. Before closing with the accepted firm, a representative committee should personally inspect the garments to be hired. If the costumers are contracted early, they have opportunity to get material and make costumes. It goes without saying that costumes should be well treated and returned promptly.

With an artist to make designs and a good corps of workers, it cannot be denied that a more distinctive group of costumes, more carefully copied from portraits, may be achieved by home talent. If, in addition, great economy is used in the purchase of material at wholesale, the costumes will usually cost a little less and may be rented later, or used again and again; while if they are good, sometimes the entire outfit can be sold to a firm of costumers. Certainly these garments have a better fit. Incidentally, individual players often take a keen interest in and make their own costumes or pay to have them made.

The United States George Washington Bicentennial Commission has issued a booklet on costumes of the time of George Washington, entitled "George Washington Play and Pageant Costume Book," which illustrates and describes the civilian costumes of the period for men, women and children, as well as military uniforms.

MAKE-UP

Theatrical make-up is essential to any pageant. It need not be as minutely done as on the professional stage, but it should be well done. Since the players are seen under brilliant lights, too great care cannot be taken with the detail of their appearance. Usually it is economical to have the firm of costumers furnish the make-up artists. Where there are few principal actors and many super-numeraries, one experienced make-up man to every twenty players will suffice. He may have as assistants volunteer helpers who know enough about the art of make-up to apply powder, rouge, lip salve and eyebrow pencil. If a professional make-up man cannot be provided, study any good book on make-up for explicit directions. Make-up should then be experimented with at the dress rehearsal, or before, and wigs tried on and fitted.

The simplest make-up for a hundred or more pageanteers consists of dry powder: flesh color for women; dark flesh, mixed with a little brown, for the men. Instead of buying a single kind for each sex, it is well to get several kinds; pale flesh for necks and arms, pink for faces, a deeper pink and also two or three of the sunburn colors or browns. Powder is easy to mix by spreading a sufficient quantity on a large piece of paper, and stirring it. Not only the face, but necks and ears, and, if they are uncovered, arms and legs as well, must be made up. The white skin of the body looks unnatural on the stage, and with men especially great pains should be taken to powder such portions of the skin as the character in the episode might leave exposed to weather.

For Indians, or characters which are required to be painted all over, use two cupfuls of unsized dry powder. (Even kalsomine has served the purpose.) Mix with water till creamy, add one cupful powdered zinc oxide and one-half cupful of glycerine, and apply with a sponge. A quart of this mixture suffices to paint twelve medium-sized people. The best color for Indians is known as "Dutch Pink." It gives a warm brown tint and washes off with plain water. A powder known as *bolominia* can be bought at drug stores specializing in make-up and is often used for Indians. Mixed in varying proportions with flesh powder it gives beautiful sun-tan values. Black and very dark brown powder can be purchased, also yellows and yellow browns, so that practically any shade of skin may be imitated.

Rouge and Lip-Stick

Dark rouge for men and light rouge for women is the rule; the color placed low on the face for age, high for youth, but always approximating the natural flush upon the individual face. Lipstick should be used sparingly, very little or none at the corners of the mouth.

For a more elaborate make-up with grease paint, such as should be given to prominent characters, be sure to have a drawing of the original for the make-up artist to copy. *Thespaint,* a substitute for the older grease paint, has a water-soluble foundation and is easier to remove than grease paint. It comes in all shades.

False Hair

Dark hair may be powdered gray or white. Moustaches and beards are made from "crepe hair." This comes in black, brown, white, auburn and blonde shades. A third of a yard may be purchased at any store which deals in theatrical make-up; unbraided, soaked until it is straight, and the beards or moustaches fashioned by twisting with the fingers. The strands are put in place with spirit gum. Beards should be put on lock by lock, beginning low on the chin and gradually rising higher, till the right line of growth along the cheek is reached. Moustaches are put first on one side of the upper lip, then on the other. The artists of the community usually prove more or less deft at this type of work, although a professional is always best.

LIGHTING

Candles

A pageant of colonial times needs to pay especial attention to the types of formal lighting then in use. Fortunately the candles of the period were reasonably similar to the cheapest white candles in use today. The candles were placed in candlesticks and candelabra of a variety of sizes and shapes. Holders called sconces, which were placed at either side the mantel or on either side of large mirrors, were frequent. Sometimes the candelabra were triple, five and even seven-branched. Occasionally rounded glass chimneys were placed over candles. At Mount Vernon a candle hung from the ceiling in a rectangular case of iron and crystal, approximately ten to twelve inches square and was called a lantern.

Lanterns and Torches

The oil lamps of the period had round, slender bases and round chimneys. Outdoor lanterns, such as those common among farmers, were ordinarily of iron, square or cylindrical in shape, with perforations for the light to come through and wire handles. Torches of resinous pine knots and home-made oil torches were both in use.

Fire-places and camp-fires were other means of lighting ordinarily employed. These are easily devised by wrapping small light bulbs in a two or three plug attachment and placing twigs over them. A piece of lighted punk provides the smoke. Pocket flashes may be substituted for bulbs when it is impossible to attach to an electric current.

Fire Precautions and Lighting

Electricity and fire are always attended by some risk. Therefore a licensed electrician should be in attendance. Town regulations must be carefully observed and all necessary permits obtained in good time. To provide against the blowing out of fuses, each ten ampere fuse should be replaced by a fifteen ampere fuse. Cables and cords should be kept dry. Powerful bulbs not protected by boxes or stands should be laid on a piece of asbestos. Camp-fires should be set over a piece of asbestos. If burning punk is used, the punk should be placed in a metal dish and safe-guarded from touching any cloth-sheathed cable. Open fires and blazing torches should never be allowed near players in flimsy garments. Curtains, hangings, and the wearing apparel of players close to unprotected fires should be treated with fire-proof solutions.

Lighting for a Hall

Assuming that the pageant is to be given in a hall and on a platform, the very minimum of equipment is a couple of spotlights, one on either side, slightly above the level of the faces of the players; lights and operators to be concealed from the spectators by screens. Other simple units are a set of footlights; borders, augmented by bunch lights and spotlights at either side, and a floodlight trained from the balcony, according to the resources and ingenuity of the electrician. A set of dimmers is a great addition to the outfit; so, too, is a set of colored gelatine slides. Footlights, border lights and bunch lights may be made by amateurs. Strap sockets are procurable at the five and ten cent stores. Bunch lights can be backed by a tin pan as a reflector. Overhead lights must be concealed by strips of cloth.

Spotlights

Spotlights are large, medium and small. They are most suited to a small stage or platform and should have ground glass lenses to give softness. If it is impossible to rent or purchase them, bridge lamps or reading lamps may be borrowed, metal reflectors contrived from dish pans, and bulbs of two hundred and fifty watts screwed in.

Floodlights

Floodlights cover the largest lighting area. Placed at the back of the hall on a sufficiently high pedestal, or trained from the back of the balcony or from either side of it, they may supplement the spotlights, help in the obliteration of shadows, and are useful near the end of a pageant for some allegorical group of great beauty and for the finale. They are most necessary for a large stage or out-of-doors.

Dimmers

A rheostat, more often called a dimmer, is an apparatus for controlling the volume of current—in other words, to increase or decrease the amount of light by imperceptible degrees. By means of it the dawn flushes into day, the dusk deepens into night. It reveals a scene little by little; it permits a scene to fade slowly from the eyes of the spectators like a dream. It is light, modulated as is music or the human voice. A series of dimmers, one to every circuit, is ideal. But the device is comparatively expensive and a minimum of two can be effective.

Renting Supplies

Lamps, dimmers, and sometimes cable can be rented from supply shops for about one-tenth of their retail price. Really good lamps are durable, easily adjusted to height or angle, have adjustable color plates and are light-tight, so they do not leak light. Plenty of cable is needed for the various outlets provided by the hall, since few halls are built with a view to elaborate pageant lighting. Cable should be strong enough to carry a far heavier current than the electrician plans to use. Sometimes much of the equipment may be borrowed from the theatre.

Placing the Lights

In placing the lights, the chief consideration is the avoidance of shadows. One shadow obliterates the opposite one, so opposite spots safeguard each other. A flood at the back helps to do away with shadows, although if it is over powerful compared to the spots, it spreads a shadow of its own. Foot and border lights, in turn, aid in dispelling the shadow thrown by the flood. Thus a complete lighting equipment is desirable. Then, too, the combination gives brilliancy and verve to the scene. A concealed spot may be focussed upon a group of candles so that one corner of the scene may have a special pool of light about the candelabra and the illusion be given that all the light proceeds from the gentle flicker of the tapers. The same can be done with a camp-fire or grate-fire. The scene, if at night, is probably a blue flood, dimmed slightly. The fire makes its own special glow, and a soft concealed light of amber brightens unobstrusively the group which sits about or before the embers.

Enough light should always be used to reveal changes of expression in the actors' faces. Brief intervals of darkness are excellent by way of contrast—a scene ending thus may be as beautiful as a dying strain of music—yet during the major portion of any scene, unless the audience sees the faces, it becomes inattentive.

Principles of Color Lighting

The next considerations are the atmospheric ones, due to the time of day and night, sun or shadow, and the changes which will naturally occur in any given scene. Gelatine slides should be chosen for the exact coloring. These are purchasable for about twenty cents apiece. Most shops offer a choice of forty colors. Remember, however, that they melt from too much heat and break from dryness. See that the spot or flood has air holes to prevent the colored slides from melting.

The principle of color lighting is to remember that in sunlight there are all the colors of the rainbow. Other light must have its color adjusted by combinations. Red, blue and yellow lights combine to give green, orange and violet values. If you desire a red light, you turn off the blue and green. The proportion in which the colors blend needs to be determined in rehearsal after the sets are painted and the costumes chosen. When in doubt, keep to amber. For night, blue is most often used. Backdrops of outdoor scenes should be flooded with a pale blue light. Be careful that every change of color means something. Too frequent changes of color within a scene make for artificiality, while changes of color for mere novelty, such as are sometimes thrown upon groups of dancers, are garish and tend to cheapen a production.

Special Lighting

The link plot of a pageant often calls for special lighting devices. A small elevation or niche on either side of the stage may be used for allegorical figures or for tableaux. Within these the speakers of the prologues may stand hidden behind gauze drops. At the base and above, border strips of light connect with a dimmer. When an episode ends and the hall is in darkness, the lights of these borders are brought on gradually, with the result that the characters back of the gauze emerge slowly from a mist, like a vision; for despite its apparent thinness, theatrical gauze is entirely opaque when no light is turned on behind it. If sized, it will take gold, silver and colors. These drops may carry a design of patriotic emblems, with buff and blue insignia, or with the Washington motto, "Exitus acta probat." So, when the shining spirits of Freedom and Liberty gleam softly through the rich and colorful screen and then speak nobly, the spectators are surprised and deeply moved. The same lighting devices may shine through stained glass windows, devised of oiled paper but decorated and painted as richly and imaginatively as the artist wishes. If there is no curtain for the stage and the hall is in darkness, the stage may be silently reset for the next scene during the speech of the characters in the link plot.

Outdoor Lighting

Outdoor lighting is more expensive than indoor, owing to the larger spaces to be lit. If the pageant is an afternoon one and out-of-doors, there will of course be no light except that of day. In those states which have daylight saving and evening does not really arrive till about nine o'clock, a late afternoon pageant is most charming. The declining sun turns browns and fawn colors to pure gold, and gives a flower-like vividness to blues and reds. As the sun sinks at last, the liquid blue of early evening deepens imperceptibly into a softer and softer beauty. The dusk comes, torches and red flares are brought on, and the shadowy players disappear into the dusk, their "insubstantial pageant" fading, their lights growing fainter and fainter, and the music dying away into silence.

For evening presentation, flambeaux, pine torches, lanterns—any type of lighting which gives an *al fresco* air to a festival—are in keeping for small pageants, provided sufficient visibility is afforded. Otherwise recourse must be had to electricity. Even stage furnishings can be suggested out-of-doors by this. For instance, a square of brilliant light upon a dark outdoor stage can give the impression of a room, a prisoner's cell, or an assembly hall. One or two cautions are necessary, however. A powerful current, such as is used out-of-doors, requires a heavy cable. Insect life needs to be taken into consideration, for light attracts mosquitoes and moths. On the other hand, a light wind will usually blow them away.

And last but not least, there should be plenty of light rehearsals, as well as a sufficient number of intelligent cooperative assistants. Few faults mar a pageant so much as careless and inadequate lighting, and conversely, no one adjunct can do more to give it beauty.

MUSIC

Historically a George Washington pageant will find itself rich in contemporary music. Musical instruments of the eighteenth century were sufficiently numerous to make up an orchestra. The music of Europe was popular, as was that of the American composer, Francis Hopkinson. Martial, Indian and Negro music were familiar. Where the text gives opportunity, sounds of bells, drums, gourds, tomtoms, or watchman's rattles may be used appropriately. Interpretive music, apart from music used in episodes, may very well be drawn freely from any periods; the songs, the dances used in episode and link plot will undoubtedly be both antique and interpretive. Finally, since no part of the pageant requires more careful attention than the music, early preparation, adequate rehearsing and the advice of a competent musician are imperative.

Musical Instruments

The guitar was a favorite with young ladies, who were taught at boarding school to play it, as well as the spinet, the harpsichord, the organ, and the "forte piano." Old spinets and harpsichords are still to be found treasured by private families and in public collections. Their delicate tinkle makes an appealing accompaniment to song or dance in a small indoor pageant, but out-of-doors, or in a really large hall, their music is too thin to have value. Other instruments in common use were the flute, the violin, viola, 'cello and bass viol. Trumpets, hautboys, French horns and kettledrums were in evidence at the time as were fife and drum for martial music.

For a very small indoor pageant, a three-piece orchestra of piano, violin and 'cello or flute, will serve very well. Five pieces are better, however; more, if the size of the hall or theatre demands it. When contracting with orchestra or band, plan for as many rehearsals as possible, in order that the conductor may become familiar with the mood and tempo of the scenes.

The tomtom was and is the instrument of the Indian. Such a drum may be imitated by stretching leather across the top of a wooden mixing bowl, drawing it as taut as possible and then tacking it closely about the rim just below the edge, and the bowl painted in an Indian design. A padded wooden stick serves for drumsticks. Dried gourds may be painted and used as rattles to accompany the tomtom. These Indian drums are sometimes as large as small tubs and sometimes no more than twelve inches in diameter. Two or three Indians can crouch about the larger ones,

all beating on the same instrument. The trumpet may be used by itself to announce or to close an episode.

DANCES

Dancing was done to the harpsichord, spinet, flute and violin. Two or four fiddles give a good accompaniment even out-of-doors. Costume the fiddlers and make them a part of the action of their episode. Many of the formal dances consisted largely of deep bows and curtsies. A swinging cape was worn by the gentlemen, the end of which could be held high in the lifted hand, while the lady balanced his gesture with her open fan held aloft.

Two dances were preeminently characteristic of the days of Washington: the formal minuet for the stately gathering; the Virginia Reel, or, as otherwise known, the Sir Roger de Coverley, for the more simple ones. The minuet has many steps and variations. Accounts of them are to be found in many books on dancing. Any of the typical minuet music written by a dozen and more contemporary composers can be used. The Virginia Reel is equally easy to teach. Both dances have the advantages of using practically any number of men and women.

Other dances of the time include jigs, reels, country dances—such as the "Successful Campaign," May Pole dances, the Highland Fling, the Hornpipe, the more formal Gavotte. It is possible that "Pop Goes the Weasel" and "Money Musk" were known. Both music and steps to many of these dances are given in *Old Familiar Dances with Figures,* by George C. Gott, published by the Oliver Ditson Company of Boston.

Dancing, especially Negro dancing, where clapping, stamping and "patting juba" were a part of the dance, was sometimes done to the words of a song. Negro dancing and singing is too well known not to have its values appreciated. Some of the spirituals may have been sung then as now, and the Negro shuffles and breakdowns danced.

The elemental qualities of the Indian dance is known to every one, as are the crouching, the leaping, the cry and the curious, rather intricate, shuffling step. Choosing music for the Indian dance, however, provides another problem, inasmuch as the music differed with the tribes, and the period is too distant for us to know how the dances of the Indian Nations resembled, in the eighteenth century, or differed from, the dances of the west and southwest Indians of today. The safest way is to choose music of a general Indian character, such as MacDowell's "From an Indian Lodge," Coleridge Taylor's "Hiawatha's Wedding Feast," Converse's "Pipe of Peace," Arthur Farwell's wide range of Indian music, and Frederick Burton's "American Primitive Music, with special reference to the songs of the Ojibways."

A collection of the dance music of the time of George Washington was issued by the United States George Washington Bicentennial Commission.

REHEARSALS

The first players to be enlisted must be sought out and encouraged to take part; others will follow voluntarily. Speaking parts may be assigned at a series of tryouts immediately before the beginning of rehearsals. The players temporarily assigned to each episode read and walk through their parts. Five to eight minutes may be spent with a group. The director makes notes copiously, jotting down name, address, height, approximate weight, coloring, voice, carriage and ability to characterize. He reserves the privilege of shifting the parts, even after the players have been cast, since subsequent rehearsing often enlightens him further as to the abilities of the individuals.

Work upon the pageant begins with a reading rehearsal. The director or author describes the pageant as a whole, gives the mood of the episode to be read and establishes the background. Discussion as to the characters, the emotional values, the placing of the climax, the rhythm and the tempo of the piece is encouraged, and the rehearsal schedule is mapped out, with day, hour and place. The episode director assumes responsibility for notifying the players and for following up absentees.

Each player has been sent a carbon copy of his episode. Then at the first rehearsal the distances and movements are made clear to him and entrances and exits designated. If the rehearsals are to be held out-of-doors, pains will have been taken to mark off boundaries with rope or lines of whitewash on the grass and routes through trees and shrubbery indicated by bright-colored tags tied to bush or tree, or the same type of numbering by which motor routes are indicated may be followed. As it is interesting to an outdoor audience to see players emerge from different places, a variety of entrances and exits should be devised.

After each player is letter perfect in his part, rehearsals may be devoted to particular aspects of acting and to special scenes. Important figures should be seen near the front of the stage more frequently than should the minor characters, unimportant figures remaining farther to one side or the other, or toward the rear. In so pictorial a production as a pageant, grouping is of great importance. Changes of position should follow one another as a series of pictures. Balance is a matter of feeling and appropriateness rather than of rule, yet the wise director is he who realizes the difficulties to be encountered and has the major actions and groupings planned before the cast assembles.

A director who is economical of his actors' time and strength finds the actors in turn increasingly conscientious. The evening may be divided up, the players notified which scenes will come at which periods, in order that they need only be present when required. Supernumeraries, once given written instructions, are summoned for a few general rehearsals toward the last. All singing is rehearsed separately, as is the dancing.

The dress rehearsal should be carefully organized beforehand: each episode leader being held responsible for his players and the prompt and effective rendering of the individual scene. A typed sheet of instructions, with placing of properties, music and light-cues, locations of costume and make-up tents, waiting places for players not on the stage, entrances and exits and final disposition of all players awaiting the finale, is handed to each episode director. The details are gone over with him from beginning to end and all obscure points made clear. Then when the actual complete rehearsal takes place, it should go with as much vim as if it were the premiere and the audience on hand to behold and applaud.

ORGANIZATION

Time for Preparation

A pageant needs organization as much as a city needs a system of government. The prime mover enlists enthusiasts who form an initial committee. This group, in turn, secures author and director and forms a general committee. The duties of casting, costuming, stage design, of selecting outdoor site or hall, superintending music, dancing, art, attending to the finance, publicity, and business—all require responsible committees, who not alone make plans but who see to the execution of them. Especially important is the choice of episode directors to serve as captains for the groups of players. The available time for preparation must be carefully allotted that specified progress will be made at specified times. The labor of organization is complete only after the production has been given for the last time, the costumes and properties duly returned, the bills paid, and the treasurer's report audited.

Publicity and Budget

Publicity is necessary, both to insure success and to make the pageant widely representative of every class and creed by an appeal for aid to all organizations in the community, social, racial, secular, religious. Attendance at the pageant depends upon the success of the publicity, as does its financial status.

At an early date a tentative budget should be made by a cautious reckoning of the gate receipts. In conference with the committee chairmen, allotments can then be made to each division of the work. Solicitation for contributions of costumes, properties, antiques, and of personal services of all kinds; wholesale buying, thrift in expenditure—these are wise economies. For early expenditures a guarantee fund must be arranged. Later bills are paid out of the gate receipts, concessions, and minor sources of income. Publicity should be cumulative and increase in size, in frequency, and in attractiveness, until the tickets are put on sale. Then it should be sustained at a high level up to the very day of performance. Definite information is the first essential; interesting data is the second. Consult a publicity expert.

After all is said and done, it is to be hoped that a surplus will remain as the nucleus for a permanent George Washington Memorial.

TYPES OF GEORGE WASHINGTON PAGEANTS

The material for a George Washington pageant is at once so varied in range, so rich in possibilities of reproduction, that the task is in limiting the selection rather than in having to piece it out. Almost any group can go to the events of Washington's life and find scenes to satisfy its peculiar needs. Roughly, the events of the Washingtonian era fall into scenes adaptable to schools, rural audiences, civic and community playing, the military, fraternal orders, the Church. The initial step is to determine the occasion for which it is to be used and the group, both for whom it is intended and who will be the actors in it. A pageant designed for performance before a school or college audience by players of school and college age would treat of scenes from one angle, while a pageant upon the same subject but designed for presentation before a military or civic group would treat of the scenes from quite another, supposing the same scenes to have been chosen.

School Pageant

For school, suitable scenes can readily be found in the home life of the boy Washington, first in his mother's home, then the homes of his half-brothers; in his associations with the neighboring families, especially in that delightful friendship between the sixteen-year-old boy and the elderly Lord Fairfax; in his forest experiences while on surveying trips; in his military training under his half-brother Lawrence, and his early military ventures with the British troops and later with the militia in the Colonies.

Rural Pageant

A rural pageant might include scenes of plantation and country life with varied activities appropriate to the seasons and to occupations connected with field, forest and river. Outdoor life at Mt. Vernon should be especially studied.

Civic Pageant

A civic pageant might very well deal with the public life of Washington, in which case it would draw upon Washington's associations with the House of Burgesses, the Continental Congresses, as President; not omitting pictorial mention of events from those years when Washington, though a private citizen, nevertheless kept in the closest touch with official affairs and gave his best advice to the guidance of the Nation.

Community Pageant

A community pageant that appeals to a mixed audience is the least restricted in its portrayal of episodes. Sentiment, picturesqueness, diversity—these are the first and foremost requisites. Mary Ball Washington, Martha Washington and Nellie Custis take a place in such a production by right; slaves, indentured servants, frontiersmen, settlers, Frenchmen, both religieux and soldiers, British regiments of the line and horse, Continental troops, foreign nobles—move across the stage with all their picturesque trappings and paraphernalia. It would seem every interest, every mood, must be satisfied.

Military Pageant

Washington's career as a soldier and as Commander-in-Chief affords a wide field for selection of significant scenes, some of which are noted below.

Fraternal Pageant

While the choice of material for the fraternal pageant is limited, the scenes can be wonderfully effective: scenes connected with Washington's initiation into Masonry; his decision to return the lost British charter, his attendance at a Masonic funeral; his laying the cornerstone of the Capitol with Masonic ceremonies.

Church Pageant

The Church pageant finds a narrow choice, perhaps, but one large in meaning. Commencing with scenes of family worship at Fredericksburg, and later, services at Pohick Church and in the midst of the desolation of Valley Forge, the theme widens to present the nobility of Washington's relationships with those from every walk in life, with whom he came into contact, until his own great last utterance, "I am not afraid to die."

Whether presented as tableaux or pantomime, accompanied or unaccompanied by appropriate vocal or instrumental music, and introduced by prolocutor or symbolic characters, or as brief dramas held in sequence by entr'acte music, dancing or narratives—the suggested scene, if infused with an earnest desire to pay homage to our first American, will meet with an eager enthusiasm in the audience and will circle the continent with praise of Washington.

The United States George Washington Bicentennial Commission issued a series of pageants and plays, centering around the theme of George Washington and suitable for various auspices.

SUGGESTIONS FOR PAGEANT EPISODES

1747—The frustration of Washington's boyish dream of going to sea.

1748—Washington begins his career as a surveyor, on the estate of Lord Fairfax.

1753—Washington's visit to Fort Le Boeuf to demand the withdrawal of the French from the Ohio Valley.

1753—Queen Aliquippa of the Delaware Indians receives Washington.

1755—Washington as aide to General Braddock.

1756—Washington presents a petition on military rank to Gov. Shirley, at Boston.

1759—Washington marries Mrs. Martha Dandridge Custis.

1760—Washington, the inventor, forging his plowshare at Mount Vernon.

1774—Washington, at the Virginia Convention, offers to lead troops to the relief of Boston.

1775—Washington is elected "General and Commander-in-Chief of the Army of the United Colonies."

1775—Washington takes command of the army besieging Boston.

1776—Washington causes the Declaration of Independence to be read before the troops on parade, in New York City.

1776—Washington crosses the Delaware on Christmas night and surprises the British.

1777—Washington receives the Marquis de Lafayette at Philadelphia.

1777—Washington takes his army into winter quarters at Valley Forge, where, with the assistance of Von Steuben, the straggling troops are disciplined into a real army.

1778—Washington makes known the French Alliance to his army at Valley Forge.

1778—Washington rallies the troops at Monmouth.

1780—The conference of General Washington and the Count de Rochambeau at Hartford, Conn.

1781—Washington's first visit to Mount Vernon since May, 1775.

1781—The surrender of Cornwallis at Yorktown.

1783—Washington replies to the Newburgh addresses on Army complaints.

1783—Washington dines on a British warship near West Point with General Carleton. Upon departure he is honored by a salute of seventeen guns to a new nation.

1783—Washington takes leave of his officers at Fraunces' Tavern.

1783—Washington resigns his commission as Commander-in-Chief of the Army, at Annapolis.

1783—Washington's first Christmas at home after his absence of eight years.

1787—Washington presides over the Constitutional Convention.

1789—Washington takes leave of his mother at Fredericksburg.

1789—Washington's triumphal journey to New York to take office.

1789—Washington's Inauguration as the first President.

1791—Washington and L'Enfant plan the Federal Capital.

1793—Washington witnesses a balloon ascension at Philadelphia.

1793—Washington discusses the Neutrality Proclamation with his Cabinet.

1793—Washington lays the cornerstone of the Capitol.

1798—Washington at Christ Church, Alexandria.

BIBLIOGRAPHY

1

SOURCES OF MATERIAL

AVERY, ELROY M.—*United States.* (*Vols. 4-7 of this General History are particularly valuable, not for Washington's life but for accurate illustrations, reproductions of contemporary objects, scenes, etc.*) The Burrows Co., Cleveland, Ohio.

BAKER, WILLIAM S.—*Itinerary of General Washington* (1775-1783). J. B. Lippincott Co., Philadelphia, Pa.

BAKER, WILLIAM S.—*Washington after the Revolution.* J. B. Lippincott Co., Philadelphia, Pa.

CORBIN, JOHN—*Unknown Washington.* Charles Scribners Company, New York.

CUSTIS, GEORGE WASHINGTON PARKE—*Recollections and Private Memoirs of Washington.* Derby & Jackson, New York.

FITZPATRICK, JOHN C.—*George Washington, Colonial Traveller.* The Bobbs-Merrill Co., Indianapolis, Ind.

FORD, PAUL LEICESTER—*The True George Washington.* J. B. Lippincott Co., Philadelphia, Pa.

FORD, WORTHINGTON CHAUNCY—*George Washington.* (2 vols.). Charles Scribners Company, New York.

FROTHINGHAM, THOMAS G.—*Washington, Commander-in-Chief.* Houghton Mifflin Co., Boston, Mass.

GABRIEL, RALPH H.—*Pageant of America.* (This general work is of the greatest value for pageant purposes; being made up of illustrations—mainly contemporary—that gives proper ideas of the appearance of objects, scenes, persons, etc. All the volumes, except 7 and 9, include the period of Washington's lifetime.) The Yale University Press, New Haven, Conn.

HAWORTH, PAUL L.—*George Washington, Country Gentleman.* The Bobbs-Merrill Co., Indianapolis, Ind.

HENDERSON, ARCHIBALD—*Washington's Southern Tour.* Houghton Mifflin Co., Boston.

HULBERT, ARCHER B.—*Washington and the West.* The Century Company, New York.

LODGE, HENRY CABOT—*George Washington* (2 vols., in The American Statesman Series). Houghton Mifflin Co., Boston.

MITCHELL, S. WEIR—*The Youth of George Washington.* The Century Co., New York.

MOORE, CHARLES—*The Family Life of George Washington.* Houghton Mifflin Co., Boston.

SAWYER, JOSEPH DILLAWAY—*Washington* (2 vols.). The Macmillan Company, N. Y.

THAYER, WILLIAM ROSCOE—*George Washington.* Houghton Mifflin Co., Boston.

TURNER, NANCY BYRD—*The Mother of Washington.* Dodd, Mead Company, N. Y.

WASHINGTON, GEORGE—*Diaries.* Houghton Mifflin Co., Boston.

WILSON, WOODROW—*George Washington.* Harper & Bros., N. Y.

WILSTACH, PAUL—*Barons of the Potomack and the Rappahannock.* The New York Grolier Club, New York City.

WILSTACH, PAUL—*Mount Vernon.* Doubleday, Page & Co., Garden City, N. Y.

WISTER, OWEN—*The Seven Ages of Washington.* The Macmillan Co., New York.

2

WRITING THE PAGEANT TEXT

BAKER, GEORGE PIERCE—*Dramatic Technique.* Houghton Mifflin Co., Boston.

CRAWFORD, JACK RANDALL and BEEGLE, MARY PORTER—*Community Drama and Pageantry.* The Yale Press (out of print but in most large libraries).

BATES, ESTHER WILLARD—*The Art of Producing Pageants.* The Walter H. Baker Co., Boston.

*To be secured without charge on application to the United States George Washington Bicentennial Commission, Washington Building, Washington, D. C.

DICKINSON, THOMAS WOOD—*The Case of American Drama (See chapter on Festivals and Pageantry).* Houghton Mifflin Co., Boston.

3

MUSIC AND DANCES
A—REFERENCE BOOKS

BROWNE, C. A.—*The Story of Our National Ballads.* Thomas Y. Crowell Co., New York.

BURTON, FREDERICK R.—*American Primitive Music.* Moffat, Yard & Co., New York.

ELSON, LOUIS C.—*The National Music of America.* The Page Co., Boston.

GOTT, GEORGE C.—*Old Familiar Dances with Music.* Oliver Ditson Company, Boston.

HOLT, ROLAND—*A List of Music for Plays and Pageants.* D. Appleton & Co., New York.

HOWARD, JOHN TASKER—*Our American Music.* Thomas Y. Crowell Co., New York.

HOWARD, JOHN TASKER—*The Music of George Washington's Time.* U. S. George Washington Bicentennial Commission, Washington, D. C.

SONNECK, OSCAR G. T.—*George Washington as a Friend and Patron of Music.* U. S. George Washington Bicentennial Commission, Washington, D. C.

SONNECK, OSCAR G. T.—*Report on "The Star Spangled Banner," "Hail Columbia," "America," "Yankee Doodle."* Government Printing Office, Washington.

SONNECK, OSCAR G. T.—*Early Concert Life in America.* Breitropf & Haertel, Leipsic.

SONNECK, OSCAR G. T.—*Early Opera in America.* G. Schirmer, Inc., New York.

B—COLLECTIONS OF MUSIC

ENGEL, CARL and STRUNK, W. OLIVER—*Music from the Days of George Washington.* U. S. George Washington Bicentennial Commission, Washington, D. C.

FISHER, WILLIAM AMES—*Ye Olde New England Psalm Tunes.* Oliver Ditson Company, Boston.

HOWARD, JOHN TASKER—*A Program of Early American Piano Pieces.* V. Fischer & Bros., New York.

MILLIGAN, HAROLD V.—*The First American Composer, Six Songs by Francis Hopkinson.* A. P. Schmidt Company, Boston.

MILLIGAN, HAROLD V.—*Colonial Love Lyrics, Six Songs by Francis Hopkinson.* A. P. Schmidt Company, Boston.

MILLIGAN, HAROLD V.—*Pioneer American Composers.* A. P. Schmidt Company, Boston.

VERNON, GRENVILLE—*Yankee Doodle-Doo; a Collection of Songs of the Early American Stage.* Payson & Clarke, New York.

4

COSTUME AND MAKE-UP

McCLELLAND, ELISABETH—*Historic Dress in America* (Vol. 1). G. W. Jacobs, Philadelphia, Pa.

EARLE, ALICE MORSE—*Two Centuries of Costume in America.* The Macmillan Co., New York.

GRIMBALL, ELIZABETH and WELLS, RHEA—*How to Costume a Play.* The Century Company, New York.

WHORF, RICHARD—*Time to Make Up.* Walter H. Baker Co., Boston.

Lapish, Edith Porter and Lawrence, R. B.—*George Washington Play and Pageant Costume Book*. United States George Washington Bicentennial Commission, Washington, D. C.

5

LIGHTING

Jacobs, Michell—*The Art of Color*. Doubleday, Page & Co., N. Y. (Now Doubleday, Doran & Co.)

Luckiesh, Matthew—*The Lighting Art*. McGraw-Hill Book Co., New York.

Fuchs, Theodore—*Stage Lighting*. Little, Brown & Co., Boston.

Sellman, Samuel and Sellman, Hunton D.—*Stage Scenery and Lighting*. F. S. Crofts, New York.

6

INDOOR SETTINGS AND DECORATIONS

Smith, Andre—*The Scenewright*. The Macmillan Company, N. Y.

Smith, Milton D.—*The Book of Play Production*. D. Appleton Co., New York.

Crafton, Allen and Royer, Jessica—*The Process of Play Production*. F. S. Crofts, New York.

Dolman, John—*The Art of Play Production*. (See chapter on Scenery.) Harper and Brothers, New York.

Sellman, Samuel and Sellman, Hunton D.—*Stage Scenery and Lighting*. F. S. Crofts, New York.

7

OUTDOOR SITES

Waugh, Frank—*Outdoor Theatres*. Richard G. Badger Co., Boston.

Crawford, Jack Randall and Beegle, Mary Porter—*Community Drama and Pageantry*. (See chapter on Costume and Setting.) The Yale Press, New Haven, Conn.

Horabin, T. L.—*Rejoice Greatly: How to Produce Public Ceremonies*. British Institute of Industrial Art. Sun Engraving Co., London.

8

ORGANIZATION

Bates, Esther Willard—*The Art of Producing Pageants*. (See chapter on Organization.) Walter H. Baker Co., Boston.

Dean, Alexander—*Little Theatre Organization and Management*. (Many fundamental suggestions apply also to pagentry.) D. Appleton & Co., New York.

9

REHEARSING

Crawford, Jack Randall and Beegle, Mary Porter—*Community Drama and Pageantry*. (See chapters on Acting and on Grouping.) The Yale Press, New Haven, Conn.

Dolman, John—*The Art of Play Production*. Harper and Brothers, New York.

Calvert, Louis—*The Problem of the Actor*. Henry Holt & Co., New York.

10

ADVERTISING AND FINANCE

Bates, Esther Willard—*The Art of Producing Pageants*. (See chapters on Finance and Publicity.) Walter H. Baker Co., Boston.

Crawford, Jack Randall and Beegle, Mary Porter—*Community Drama and Pageantry*. The Yale Press, New Haven, Conn.